Money, Banking, and Financial Markets:

An Economics Approach

Money, Banking, and Financial Markets:
An Economics Approach

MICHAEL R. BAYE

Pennsylvania State University

DENNIS W. JANSEN

Texas A & M University

Houghton Mifflin Company   Boston   Toronto

Geneva, Illinois   Palo Alto   Princeton, New Jersey

To my parents, Firmin and Jaynet Baye,
for their loving support over the past 36 years.
MRB

In memory of Elmer Jansen and William Hennessey.
DWJ

SPONSORING EDITOR:	Denise Clinton
BASIC BOOK EDITOR:	Karla Paschkis
SENIOR PROJECT EDITOR:	Susan Westendorf
ASSOCIATE PRODUCTION/DESIGN COORDINATOR:	Caroline Ryan-Morgan
SENIOR MANUFACTURING COORDINATOR:	Marie Barnes

Credits

Cover design: Judy Arisman
Cover image: William Whitehurst, NYC

Printed in the U.S.A.
Library of Congress Catalog Card Number: 94-76473
ISBN: 0-395-64395-3
ISBN EXAM: 0-395-71667-5

1 2 3 4 5 6 7 8 9-DH-98 97 96 95 94

Brief Contents

PART ONE   *INTRODUCTION TO MONEY AND BANKING*   1

     CHAPTER   1   *Money and Banks*   2
              2   *Financial Markets, Financial Institutions and Instruments, and Money*   31
              3   *Money, Inflation, and Interest*   61

PART TWO   *THE MICROECONOMICS OF BANKING AND FINANCIAL MARKETS*   91

     CHAPTER   4   *Supply and Demand in Financial Markets*   92
              5   *The Bank as a Firm: Loans*   130
              6   *The Bank as a Firm: Deposits*   166
              7   *The Banking Industry*   201

PART THREE   *THE VALUATION OF FINANCIAL ASSETS*   235

     CHAPTER   8   *The Time Value of Money and Asset Pricing*   236
              9   *Risk, Uncertainty, and Portfolio Choice*   269
            10   *The Term Structure of Interest Rates*   306
            11   *Foreign Exchange Markets*   330
            12   *Rational Expectations and Efficient Markets*   369

PART FOUR   *THE CREATION OF MONEY*   405

     CHAPTER 13   *The Federal Reserve System: History, Modern Structure, and Policy Tools*   406
            14   *The Money Supply Process*   446
            15   *The Demand for Money and Equilibrium in the Money Market*   489

PART FIVE   *MONEY AND THE MACRO ECONOMY*   525

     CHAPTER 16   *A Simple Macroeconomic Model*   526
            17   *Open Economy Macroeconomics*   586
            18   *Money and Economic Activity: A Look at the Evidence*   625

PART SIX   *SPECIAL ISSUES IN MONETARY ECONOMICS*   665

     CHAPTER 19   *An Introduction to Monetary Policy*   666
            20   *Monetary Policy: Rules, Discretion, and Games*   708
            21   *Government Spending and Finance: the Deficit Problem*   746

The Authors

Michael R. Baye (Penn State) received his B.S. in economics from Texas A&M University in 1980 and his Ph.D. from Purdue University in 1983. He has taught at Purdue University, where he received the Outstanding Graduate Instructor award, as well as the University of Kentucky, Texas A&M University, and The Pennsylvania State University. His primary research interests are game theory and industrial organization. He is the author of three books and 30 articles published in economics journals, including *American Economic Review, Journal of Political Economy, Econometrica,* and the *Review of Economic Studies.* He has been honored with a Fulbright Lecturer/Research Scholar Grant as well as a research grant from the National Science Foundation.

Dennis W. Jansen (Texas A&M) received his A.B. in economics and mathematics from St. Louis University in 1978 and his Ph.D. from the University of North Carolina at Chapel Hill in 1983. He has taught at the University of North Carolina, North Carolina State University, Indiana University, and Texas A&M University. His primary research interests are monetary and macro economics. He is the author of two books and over 30 articles published in economics journals, including *The Economic Journal, Review of Economics and Statistics, Journal of Money, Credit, and Banking,* and *Journal of Econometrics.* Since 1992, Jansen has been a Research Fellow at Texas A&M University's Center for Research in Free Enterprise; he has also been a Visiting Scholar at the Federal Reserve Bank of St. Louis, and on the visiting faculty at Catholic University of Leuven and Erasmus University of Rotterdam.

Contents

Preface   xxiii

PART ONE   *INTRODUCTION TO MONEY AND BANKING*   1

CHAPTER 1

Money and Banks   2

MONEY   3

Functions of Money   5
The Origin of Money   8
Types of Money   9
Physical Properties of Money   12

THE EVOLUTION OF BANKS   14

Banks as Depositories   15
Demand Deposits   15
Bank Notes   16
Fractional Reserve Banking   18
Banks as Financial Intermediaries   22

Conclusion   27

Box 1.1   THE DATA BANK   Components of the Money Supply   4

Box 1.2   INTERNATIONAL BANKING   Money on the Yap Island and Gold Transfers Among Nations   10

Box 1.3   INSIDE MONEY   Cigarettes as Money in a Prisoner of War Camp   14

Box 1.4   INSIDE MONEY   Where Are All the Dollars?   17

CHAPTER 2

Financial Markets, Financial Institutions and Instruments, and Money   31

FINANCIAL MARKETS   31

Debt Markets   33
Equity Markets   33
Financial Service Markets   33

FINANCIAL INSTITUTIONS   35

Depository Institutions   35
Nondepository Institutions   36

FINANCIAL INSTRUMENTS   41

Money Market Instruments   41
Capital Market Instruments   45
International Financial Instruments   52

OFFICIAL DEFINITIONS OF THE MONEY STOCK   54

M1   55
M2   55
M3   55
L   56
Conclusion   57

BOX 2.1   *THE DATA BANK*   *Changes in the Relative Size of Financial Institution Assets, 1976–1990*   38

BOX 2.2   *INSIDE MONEY*   *Money Market Rates from* The Wall Street Journal   46

BOX 2.3   *INSIDE MONEY*   *A Lexicography for Bonds*   48

BOX 2.4   *INSIDE MONEY*   *Are All Bonds Created Equal?*   53

CHAPTER 3

Money, Inflation, and Interest   61

DISTINGUISHING BETWEEN INFLATION AND ECONOMIC GROWTH   61

The Price Level and Real Output   62
Inflation and Economic Growth   64
The Relationship Between Inflation and Economic Growth   65
Causes of Inflation   67

INTEREST RATES   72

What is Interest?   73
The Time Value of Money   75

HOW INFLATION AND TAXES AFFECT INTEREST RATES   80

The Real Interest Rate   80
The Aftertax Interest Rate   85

HISTORICAL DATA ON INTEREST RATES   86

Conclusion   88

BOX 3.1   *INTERNATIONAL BANKING*   *Inflation Rates Around the World*   66

BOX 3.2   *INSIDE MONEY*   *Points and Mortgage Interest Rates*   74

BOX 3.3   *INSIDE MONEY*   *15-Year Versus 30-Year Mortgages*   76

BOX 3.4   *INTERNATIONAL BANKING*   *Real Interest Rates Around the World*   84

PART TWO   *THE MICROECONOMICS OF BANKING AND FINANCIAL MARKETS*   91

CHAPTER 4   *Supply and Demand in Financial Markets*   92

BASIC SUPPLY AND DEMAND ANALYIS: A BRIEF REVIEW WITH APPLICATIONS TO FEE-BASED FINANCIAL SERVICES   92

Demand for Fee-Based Financial Services   93
Supply of Fee-Based Financial Services   96
Equilibrium in the Market for Fee-Based Financial Services   98
Changes in Equilibrium: Applications to the Insurance Market   100

THE MARKET FOR LOANABLE FUNDS   104

The Demand for Loanable Funds   104
The Supply of Loanable Funds   110
Equilibrium in the Market for Loanable Funds   115

APPLICATIONS OF THE LOANABLE FUNDS MODEL   116

The Tax Reform Act of 1982 and Interest Rates on Consumer Credit   116
Inflationary Expectations and the Mortgage Interest Rate   117
Returns on Real Estate Investments and Corporate Interest Rates   118
Recessions and the Prime Interest Rate   120
The Federal Deficit and Interest Rates on Government Bonds   122
Tax Policy and Interest Rates on Municipal Bonds   123
Interest Rate Ceilings   123
Interest Rate Floors   124

Conclusion   127

BOX 4.1   THE DATA BANK   Actual and Expected Rates of Inflation   108

BOX 4.2   INSIDE MONEY   Tax Rates and the Aftertax Interest Rate in Two States   113

BOX 4.3   INSIDE MONEY   Nominal Interest Rates and Expected Inflation Rates   119

CHAPTER 5   *The Bank as a Firm: Loans*   130

PURELY COMPETITIVE BANKS   130

Market Demand and the Demand for an Individual Bank's Loans   132
The Purely Competitive Bank's Loan Decision   134

BANKS WITH MARKET POWER   139

Sources of Market Power for Banks   139
Profit-Maximizing Loan Decisions for Banks with Market Power   143

OLIGOPOLY BANKS 147

The Nature of Oligopoly Interdependence 148
Using Game Theory to Model Oligopolistic Interdependence 148
Repeated Interaction 151

BANKS WITH IMPERFECT INFORMATION 153

Symmetric Information 153
Asymmetric Information and Adverse Selection 154
Bank Strategies for Countering Asymmetric Information 158

Conclusion 163

BOX 5.1 **THE DATA BANK** *Economies of Scale in Banking* 142

BOX 5.2 **INTERNATIONAL BANKING** *Concentration Ratios in Banking* 149

BOX 5.3 **INSIDE MONEY** *Going for Broke in the Savings and Loan Industry* 162

CHAPTER 6

The Bank as a Firm: Deposits 166

DEPOSITS AS AN INPUT IN PRODUCING LOANS 166

Total and Marginal Product 167
A Simple Technology for Producing Loans 168

THE DEMAND FOR DEPOSITS BY PURELY COMPETITIVE BANKS 171

Market Supply and the Supply of Deposits to an Individual Bank 171
The Value Marginal Product of Deposits 173

THE DEMAND FOR DEPOSITS BY BANKS WITH MARKET POWER 176

Market Power in the Loan Market Only 177
Market Power in Both the Loan and Deposit Markets 181

UNCERTAINTY AND BANK DEPOSITS 185

Bank Withdrawals and the Law of Large Numbers 185
Bank Panics 190
Moral Hazard 193

Conclusion 197

BOX 6.1 **THE DATA BANK** *Loan and Deposit Interest Rates* 174

BOX 6.2 **INSIDE MONEY** *The Law of Large Numbers and Deposit Withdrawals* 188

BOX 6.3 **INTERNATIONAL BANKING** *The Bank Panic of 1907* 192

Box 6.4   INSIDE MONEY *Failures of Insured Thrifts and Banks, 1934–1989*   196

CHAPTER 7   ***The Banking Industry***   201

DUAL BANKING   201

ACQUIRING A BANK CHARTER   202

SUPERVISION AND EXAMINATION OF BANKS   202

Status of the Loan Portfolio   204
Bank Capitalization   204
Overlapping Responsibilities   205

THE FEDERAL RESERVE SYSTEM   206

THE FDIC   207

The S&L Crisis and Changes in the FDIC   209

AN OVERVIEW OF BANKING REGULATION   211

HOW BRANCHING RESTRICTIONS SHAPED THE BANKING INDUSTRY   212

Bank Holding Companies   212
Electronic Banking   214
Current Status   214

HOW GLASS-STEAGALL SHAPED THE BANKING INDUSTRY   214

Restrictions Against Investment Banking   215
Interest Rate Restrictions   216

THE ECONOMIC IMPACT OF BANKING REGULATIONS   220

Bank Charters   220
Branching Restrictions   222
Interest Rate Regulations   224
Uniform Reserve Requirements   226
Deposit Insurance   228
Bank Examination as a Solution to Moral Hazard and Adverse Selection   229

Conclusion   230

Box 7.1   INSIDE MONEY *Requirements for Obtaining a Bank Charter*   203

Box 7.2   INTERNATIONAL BANKING *Banking in the European Community and the Principle of Mutual Recognition*   213

Box 7.3   THE DATA BANK *Employment in Banking and ATM Machines*   215

Box 7.4   INSIDE MONEY *The Long Phaseout of Regulation Q*   217

PART THREE   *THE VALUATION OF FINANCIAL ASSETS*   235

CHAPTER 8   **The Time Value of Money and Asset Pricing**   236

THE TIME VALUE OF MONEY   236

THE VALUATION OF DEBT INSTRUMENTS   238

Treasury Bills and Other Debt Instruments Sold on a Discount Basis   239
Coupon Bonds and Other Interest-Bearing Debt Instruments   244

THE EQUILIBRIUM PRICE AND QUANTITY OF BONDS   251

Bond Prices: The Loanable Funds Approach   252
Bond Prices: The Supply and Demand of Bonds Approach   253

VALUING STOCK AND OTHER ASSETS   257

Income Stocks   259
Growth Stocks   260

EQUILIBRIUM PRICE AND VOLUME OF STOCK TRANSACTIONS   262

Conclusion   265

BOX 8.1   INSIDE MONEY   How to Read Information on Treasury Bills in the Wall Street Journal   241

BOX 8.2   INSIDE MONEY   How to Read Information on Treasury Bonds and Notes in the Wall Street Journal   246

BOX 8.3   INSIDE MONEY   How to Read Information on Corporate Bonds in the Wall Street Journal   250

BOX 8.4   THE DATA BANK   The Inverse Relationship Between Bond Prices and Interest Rates   254

BOX 8.5   INSIDE MONEY   How to Read Information on Stocks in the Wall Street Journal   258

CHAPTER 9   **Risk, Uncertainty, and Portfolio Choice**   269

UNCERTAINTY AND RISK   269

Expected Value   271
Variance   272
Risk Preference   273

VALUING RISKY FINANCIAL ASSETS   274

Default Risk   275
Liquidity Risk   282
Interest Rate Risk and Call Risk   285

The Inflation Premium and Inflation Risk 289

Tax Risk 291

MINIMIZING FINANCIAL RISK 294

Diversification 295

Future Markets 297

Options Markets 299

Conclusion 303

BOX 9.1 INSIDE MONEY *What Bond Ratings Mean* 277

BOX 9.2 THE DATA BANK *Interest Rates on Aaa, Baa, and U.S. Treasury Bills, 1971–1992* 283

BOX 9.3 INSIDE MONEY *What Are Junk Bonds and Convertible Bonds?* 284

BOX 9.4 INTERNATIONAL BANKING *The Beginning of World War II and Interest Rates* 293

BOX 9.5 INSIDE MONEY *How to Reach Information on Future Markets in the* Wall Street Journal 298

BOX 9.6 INSIDE MONEY *How to Read Information on Futures Options Markets in the* Wall Street Journal 301

CHAPTER 10

The Term Structure of Interest Rates 306

THE YIELD CURVE 306

EXPLANATION OF THE TERM STRUCTURE OF INTEREST RATES 309

The Expectations Hypothesis 311

The Segmented-Markets Hypothesis 319

The Preferred Habitat Hypothesis 322

Conclusion 327

BOX 10.1 INTERNATIONAL BANKING *Yield Curves for Different Countries* 310

BOX 10.2 INSIDE MONEY *How to Read Information on the Treasury Yield Curve in* The Wall Street Journal 312

BOX 10.3 THE DATA BANK *Calculating Expected Future Interest Rates* 318

CHAPTER 11

Foreign Exchange Markets 330

FUNDAMENTALS OF FOREIGN RATES 330

THE MARKET FOR FOREIGN EXCHANGE 335

Long-Run Exchange Rate Determination 336

Exchange Rates in the Short Run 344

SPOT AND FORWARD EXCHANGE RATES 351

    Participants in the Forward Market 352

FIXED AND FLEXIBLE EXCHANGE RATE SYSTEMS 357

    Flexible Exchange Rates 357
    Central Bank Intervention 357
    Fixed Exchange Rates 359

A BRIEF HISTORY OF THE FOREIGN EXCHANGE RATE SYSTEM 362

    The Classical Gold Standard 362
    Bretton Woods 363
    Post-Bretton Woods 364

Conclusion 366

BOX 11.1   INSIDE MONEY Exchange Rate Information in the Wall Street Journal 332

BOX 11.2   THE DATA BANK Exchange Rate Movements between the U.S. Dollar and Four Major Foreign Currencies 334

BOX 11.3   INTERNATIONAL BANKING Purchase Power Parity, the Big Mac Standard, and the Economist Standard 345

BOX 11.4   INTERNATIONAL BANKING The European Monetary System 365

CHAPTER 12   **Rational Expectations and Efficient Markets** 369

THE ROLE OF EXPECTATIONS IN FINANCIAL MARKETS 369

THREE THEORIES OF EXPECTATION FORMATION 370

    Markov Expectations 371
    Adaptive Expectations 372
    Rational Expectations 379

A CRITIQUE OF THE VIEWS OF EXPECTATIONS FORMATION 390

EFFICIENT MARKETS 393

    The Efficient Markets Hypothesis 393
    Rational Expectations and Efficient Markets 395
    Versions of the Efficient Markets Hypothesis 396
    Weak-Form Market Efficiency 396
    Efficient Markets and Expectations 399

Conclusion 400

BOX 12.1   INSIDE MONEY Error in the Inflationary Expectations of "Experts" 380

BOX 12.2   INSIDE MONEY The Importance of Using the Correct Model When Forming Rational Expectations 387

Box 12.3   *THE DATA BANK*   *The Random Nature of Stock Returns,*
Interest Rates, and Inflation   397

PART FOUR   *THE CREATION OF MONEY*   405

CHAPTER 13   **The Federal Reserve System: History, Modern Structure, and Policy Tools**   406

A BRIEF HISTORY OF CENTRAL BANKING IN THE UNITED STATES   407

Banking in the United States Before 1791   407
The First U.S. Central Bank: First Bank of the United States   408
The Second U.S. Central Bank: Second Bank of the United States   409
The Absence of a Central Bank: 1836–1913   409
The Third U.S. Central Bank: The Federal Reserve System   412

THE STRUCTURE AND ROLE OF THE MODERN FEDERAL RESERVE SYSTEM   417

The Institutional Structure   417
The Roles of the Fed   422

TOOLS OF MONETARY POLICYMAKERS   424

Open Market Operations   424
Reserve Requirements   428
Discount Window Policy   432
Other Monetary Policy Tools   434

THE DEBATE OVER FEDERAL RESERVE INDEPENDENCE   437

Conclusion   438

Box 13.1   *INSIDE MONEY*   *Declining Bond Prices and Bank Failures During the Free Banking Era*   411

Box 13.2   *INSIDE MONEY*   *Making the Fed More Responsive to the Electorate: The Rebirth of an Old Idea*   422

Box 13.3   *THE DATA BANK*   *Open Market Operations and Churning*   430

Box 13.4   *INTERNATIONAL BANKING*   *The Benefits of Central Bank Independence: A Look at Inflation Around the World*   439

CHAPTER 14   **The Money Supply Process**   446

THE BALANCE SHEET OF BANKS AND MULTIPLE DEPOSIT CREATION   447

How a Bank Responds to a Change in Reserves from Within the Banking System   448
How the Banking System Responds to Infusions and Contractions of Reserves   455

A GENERAL MODEL OF MONEY CREATION   465

The Monetary Base   466
The Complete Deposit Multiplier   467
The Complete Currency Multiplier   469
The Complete Money Multiplier   470

DETERMINANTS OF THE MONEY SUPPLY   474

Federal Reserve Determinants of the Money Supply   476
Banking System Determinants of the Money Supply   477
The Public's Determinants of the Money Supply   479

THE MONEY SUPPLY CURVE   482

Exogenous Money Supply Curve   483
Endogenous Money Supply Curve   484

Conclusion   486

BOX 14.1   THE DATA BANK   *The Balance Sheet of the Commercial Banking Sector*   449

BOX 14.2   INSIDE MONEY   *Reserve Requirements of the United States*   462

BOX 14.3   INSIDE MONEY   *The M2 Multiplier*   472

CHAPTER 15   **The Demand for Money and Equilibrium in the Money Market**   489

THE CLASSICAL VIEW OF MONEY DEMAND   490

The Simple Quantity Theory   490
The Cambridge Theory   493

KEYNES'S VIEW OF MONEY DEMAND   495

The Modified Cambridge Theory   496
The Inventory Approach to Money Demand   498
The Portfolio Approach to Money Demand   502

THE MODERN QUANTITY THEORY OF MONEY DEMAND   506

Factors that Influence the Opportunity Cost of Holding Money   508

MONEY DEMAND: AN HISTORICAL NOTE AND CURRENT THOUGHT   509

An Historical Note   509
Current Thought   510

EQUILIBRIUM IN THE MONEY MARKET   510

Equilibrium with an Exogenous Money Supply   512
Equilibrium with an Endogenous Money Supply   515

KEYNESIAN AND MONETARIST VIEW ON MONEY DEMAND   518

USING THE LOANABLE FUNDS MODEL TO ANALYZE MONETARY POLICY   520

Conclusion   522

BOX 15.1   *INTERNATIONAL BANKING*   **Money Demand in Mexico**   494

BOX 15.2   *THE DATA BANK*   **Velocity and Interest Rates**   497

BOX 15.3   *INSIDE MONEY*   **Currency Substitution**   505

BOX 15.4   *THE DATA BANK*   **Money Demand in the United States**   511

PART FIVE   *MONEY AND THE MACRO ECONOMY*   525

CHAPTER 16   **A Simple Macroeconomic Model**   526

AGGREGATE DEMAND   527

Why the Aggregate Demand Curve Slopes Downward   528
The Components of Aggregate Demand and Their Determinants   530
Determinants of Consumption Demand   530
Adding Up the Components to Obtain Aggregate Demand   540
Why Aggregate Demand Does Not Depend on Income   541
Changes in Aggregate Demand   543

SHORT RUN AGGREGATE SUPPLY   546

Why the Short-Run Aggregate Supply Curve Slopes Upward   546
Determinants of Short-Run Aggregate Supply   549

SHORT RUN MACROECONOMIC EQUILIBRIUM   550

Achieving Equilibrium   553
Changes in Equilibrium   553

VERTICAL LONG-RUN AGGREGATE SUPPLY AND LONG-RUN EQUILIBRIUM   556

FISCAL POLICY AND THE GOVERNMENT BUDGET RESTRAINT   561

What is the Government Budget Restraint   561
Government Purchases Financed by Taxes   562
Government Purchases Financed by Borrowing: Deficit Finance   567
Government Purchases Financed by Money Creation   570

MONETARY POLICY: OPEN MARKET OPERATIONS   573

Conclusion   576

BOX 16.1   *THE DATA BANK*   **Components of Aggregate Demand**   531

Box 16.2   THE DATA BANK   Components of Government Spending, 1962, 1977, and 1992   539

Box 16.3   INSIDE MONEY   Income Taxes, Indentation, and Inflation   564

Box 16.4   INSIDE MONEY   Did Indexation Cause the Budget Deficits of the 1980's?   571

CHAPTER 17

Open Economy Macroeconomics   586

THE BALANCE OF PAYMENTS   587

The Current Account   588
The Capital Account   590
Recent U.S. Balance of Payments Accounts   591

THE DEMAND FOR NET EXPORTS   593

OPEN ECONOMY MACROECONOMIC EQUILIBRIUM   601

Aggregate Demand in an Open Economy   601
Short-Run Aggregate Supply in an Open Economy   603
Long-Run Aggregate Supply in an Open Economy   604

FIXED EXCHANGE RATES, FLEXIBLE EXCHANGE RATES, AND POLICY EFFECTIVENESS   607

FISCAL POLICY IN AN OPEN ECONOMY   608

Tax and Tariff-Financed Increases in Government Purchases   608
Government Purchases Financed by Borrowing: Deficit Finance   611
Government Purchases Financed by Money Creation   614

THE TWIN DEFICITS: THE BUDGET AND CURRENT ACCOUNT DEFICITS   614

Investment, Saving, and the Budget Deficit   615
The Supply of Loanable Funds in an Open Economy   617

MONETARY POLICY: OPEN MARKET OPERATIONS   619

Conclusion   622

Box 17.1   THE DATA BANK   Net Exports and the Exchange Rate   598

Box 17.2   INSIDE MONEY   The Impact of NIFTIER on Output and Employment   600

Box 17.3   INTERNATIONAL BANKING   Fixed Versus Flexible Exchange Rates: The European Experience   609

CHAPTER 18

Money and Economic Activity: A Look at the Evidence   625

THE LONG-RUN RELATIONSHIP AMONG MONEY, PRICES, AND REAL OUTPUT   625

Theoretical Relationships Between Money and Economic Activity 625
U.S. Evidence on the Long-Run Relationships Between Money and Economic Activity 628
International Evidence on the Long-Run Relationships Between Money and Economic Activity 632

THE SHORT-RUN RELATIONSHIP AMONG MONEY, PRICES, AND REAL OUTPUT 638

Theoretical Relationships Between Money and Economic Activity 638
Empirical Evidence on the Short-Run Relationship Between Money and Economic Activity 639

RECONCILING THE LONG-RUN AND SHORT-RUN RESULTS 643

INFLATION, MONEY GROWTH, AND INTEREST RATES 650

REAL MONEY BALANCES, VELOCITY, AND INTEREST RATES 654

Real Money Balances, Real Income, and the Interest Rate 654
Inflation, Velocity, and Real Money Balances 657

Conclusion 660

BOX 18.1 INTERNATIONAL BANKING Money Growth, GDP Growth, and Inflation in the United Kingdom: 1 636

BOX 18.2 INSIDE MONEY Does Money Create Income, or Does Income Create Money? 644

BOX 18.3 INTERNATIONAL BANKING Money Growth, GDP Growth, and Inflation in the United Kingdom: 2 649

PART SIX **SPECIAL ISSUES IN MONETARY ECONOMICS** 665

CHAPTER 19 **An Introduction to Monetary Policy** 666

TARGETS AND INSTRUMENTS 666

Monetary Policy Goals or Targets 668
Monetary Policy Instruments 669
The Number of Independent Instruments and Targets 671

THE LINK BETWEEN MONEY AND POLICY TARGETS 674

INTERMEDIATE TARGETS 679

A Money Aggregate as an Intermediate Target 681
An Interest Rate as an Intermediate Target 682
The Choice Between Interest Rates and Money as an Intermediate Target 684
Other Suggested Intermediate Targets 686

FEDERAL RESERVE OPERATING PROCEDURES 692

Federal Funds Rate Targeting 694
Nonborrowed Reserves Targeting 695
Borrowed Reserves Targeting 696
The 1990's: A Return to Interest Rate Targeting 696

PROBLEMS IN MONETARY POLICYMAKING 697

Lags 700
Instrument Instability 703
Inaccurate Macroeconomics Models 704
Conflicting Goals 704
Conflict Among Policymakers 704

Conclusion 705

BOX 19.1 INTERNATIONAL BANKING Monetary Policy Gone Awry: Hyperinflation in Yugoslavia 677

BOX 19.2 THE DATA BANK Does the Fed Hit Its Money Targets? 683

BOX 19.3 INSIDE MONEY P-Star: A New Target for Monetary Policy? 698

CHAPTER 20

Monetary Policy: Rules, Discretion, and Games 708

SHOULD THE FED PURSUE AN ACTIVE OR PASSIVE MONETARY POLICY? 708

The Case for Active Monetary Policy 709
The Case for Passive Monetary Policy 717
So Who's Right? 721

SHOULD MONETARY POLICY BE GUIDED BY RULES OR BY DISCRETION? 723

The Case for Discretionary Monetary Policy 723
The Case for Monetary Policy Rules 724
Why Does the Fed Have Discretion? 729

PASSIVE VERSUS ACTIVE RULES 733

A Change in Aggregate Demand 733
A Change in Aggregate Supply 735
The Pros and Cons of Activist Rules 737

ANTICIPATED VERSUS UNANTICIPATED CHANGES IN THE MONEY SUPPLY 738

Unanticipated Changes in the Money Supply 739
Anticipated Changes in the Money Supply 740
Relevance for Monetary Policy 742

Conclusion 742

BOX *20.1*   *THE DATA BANK*   *The Path of the Price Level and Output Over Time*   710

BOX *20.2*   *INSIDE MONEY*   *Inflation and Politics*   718

BOX *20.3*   *INTERNATIONAL BANKING*   *International Policy Coordination*   203

CHAPTER 21

Government Spending and Finance: The Deficit Problem   746

AN HISTORICAL LOOK AT GOVERNMENT SPENDING AND ITS FINANCE   747

The Federal Government Budget   747
State and Local Budgets   750
The Aggregate Government Budget   751

THE FEDERAL DEBT   754

THE DEFICIT AND THE GROWING DEBT: ARE THEY BAD FOR THE ECONOMY?   756

Deficits Will Lead to Inflation   757
A Burden on Future Generations?   760
Crowding Out   763

RICARDIAN EQUIVALENCE AND FISCAL POLICY   765

Is the Ricardian Equivalence Idea Correct?   766
The Impact of the Ricardian Equivalence Idea on Our Macroeconomic Model   767

CAN THE FEDERAL DEFICIT CONTINUE TO GROW?   770

The Primary versus the Total Budget Deficit   770
The Impact of Growing Deficits: An Illustrative Example   771
The Bottom Line for the United States   773

Conclusion   777

BOX *21.1*   *INTERNATIONAL BANKING*   *The Government Budget Constraint in Action: The Case of Mexico*   758

BOX *21.2*   *THE DATA BANK*   *The Government Budget Constraint in Action: The United States*   761

BOX *21.3*   *INSIDE MONEY*   *Is Debt a Problem?*   774

Glossary   G-1
Solutions   S-1
Index   I-1

Preface

As a result of banking deregulation over the past decade, banks today are like most firms in the economy in that they must set their own interest rates and vigorously compete with one another for depositors and loan customers. These recent changes in the U.S. banking system led us to write a money and banking text with a firm foundation in basic economic theory. Our book uses economic tools like supply and demand analysis, the theory of the firm, the economics of information, game theory, rational expectations, and AD/AS to analyze the workings of the banking system and the effects of Fed policies on it.

When we were undergraduate students of money and banking in the late 1970s, the U.S. banking system was highly regulated and banks had little discretion in setting interest rates. Consequently, texts at the time were institutional in nature and T-accounts were the primary tool used to look at bank operations. We left wondering why our money and banking texts didn't reflect what we learned in our introductory economics courses about supply and demand and firm behavior. We also remember times when the facts in the text were no longer accurate, due to daily changes in the rules and regulations of the banking system. These changes made it extremely difficult for us to learn, and for our instructors to teach, a coherent framework for analyzing the banking industry. We believe the situation is much better today.

Our use of basic economic theory that is accessible to undergraduates means that instructors no longer need to center their lectures on institutional details of the banking system—details that change as frequently as the weather. Each chapter in this book develops timeless economic models—models we use to analyze the economic consequences of past and present regulations on the banking system and the overall economy. A quick glance through the book reveals that we rely heavily on simple graphs and economic models to analyze the real-world workings of the banking system, rather than using the accounting or institutional approach. We believe this makes using our money and banking text easier, more fun, and of more lasting value than memorizing what a competing institutional text says is the most recent piece of banking legislation. It is inevitable that some institutional changes will occur after this book is published, but the theoretical foundation and real-world focus of this book gives students the tools to analyze them too.

CONTENT AND ORGANIZATION

Since banks are firms, we believe a modern money and banking course should contain elements of both microeconomics and macroeconomics. Issues such as how banks set interest rates, attract deposits, or ration credit, and how the banking industry is subject to the pitfalls of adverse selection and moral hazard are all microeconomic in nature. Accordingly, Chapters 5 and 6 provide self-contained models of the microeconomic decisions of individual banks, while Chapter 7 looks at the implications of banking regulations for the entire banking industry. The remainder of the book presents models of the more traditional financial and macroeconomic issues. Those instructors who choose not to concentrate on the microeconomics of banking can skip Chapters 5, 6, and 7 without loss of continuity.

A noticeable feature of our book is that it contains 21 chapters instead of the 30 or so that many other money and banking texts include. Recognizing that few instructors actually have time to cover the 30 chapters and based on reviewer comments, we grouped related topics into fewer chapters. Our hope is that more complete, self-contained chapters will make it easier to use our book. Students gain a deeper, less fragmented sense of money, banking, and the economy overall. Each chapter includes extensive cross references to point readers to related topics elsewhere in the text.

We divide *Money and Banking* into six parts. **Part I Introduction to Money and Banking,** Chapters 1–3, provides a broad overview of money and banking and some of the key concepts and terms that underlie analyses throughout the book. These chapters explain the rudiments of money and various financial instruments, discuss how they evolved, and provide practical definitions of the money multipliers, M1, M2, M3, and L. They also provide an overview of money creation, present value analysis, and the relation between monetary growth and inflation.

Part II The Microeconomics of Banking and Financial Markets, Chapters 4–7, begins with a simple supply and demand framework for loanable funds that builds on what students learned in their introductory course. Chapters 5, 6, and 7 show how individual banks operate much like other firms in the economy, using the tools of microeconomics and industrial organization to look at banks and the banking industry. Again, Chapters 5, 6, and 7 are self-contained, giving instructors who stress macroeconomic issues the flexibility to omit them if desired.

Part III The Valuation of Financial Assets, Chapters 8–12, first studies the time value of money in Chapter 8. Chapters 9 and 10 examine the impact of risk on asset prices and explain the term structure of interest rates. Chapter 11 develops short and long-run models of foreign exchange rate determination setting the state for the open economy material in Part V. Chapter 12 presents basic models of expectation formation like rational expectations. These chapters, particularly Chapters 11 and 12, begin a shift toward the macroeconomic issues that are covered in Chapters 13–21 of the text.

Parts IV and V, The Creation of Money, Chapters 13–15, and **Money**

and the Macro Economy, Chapters 16–18, present the core material of money and the macroeconomy. While the introductory material in Part I acquaints students with basic macroeconomic terminology, these chapters develop simple macroeconomic models that help them to understand the macro economy more fully. Part IV begins with a brief overview of the Federal Reserve System in Chapter 13, then turns to a discussion of the money supply process (Chapter 14) and the demand for money (Chapter 15). Part V focuses on key macroeconomic models: Chapter 16 develops a closed economy macro model and discusses both the workings of the model and the impact of monetary and fiscal policy. Based on reviewer comments, the main text of Chapter 16 relies exclusively on an AD/AS model, while an Appendix includes the IS/LM framework for those instructors who choose to integrate it into their courses. Chapter 17 presents the open economy model as an extension of the closed economy model that allows an endogenous determination of the exchange rate and net exports. Chapter 18 closes this action with a presentation of some of the empirical evidence on macroeconomic propositions linking money to macroeconomic variables.

Part VI Special Issues in Monetary Economics, Chapters 19–21, provides more detailed, applied treatments of monetary issues for those instructors who have the time (or preference) to cover one or more of these chapters. Chapter 19 looks at the theory of monetary policy, including a discussion of targets and indicators, while Chapter 20 looks at monetary policy games and the rules versus discretion debate. The material is presented at a level accessible even to students who have not been previously exposed to game theory. Finally, Chapter 21 is devoted exclusively to the government budget constraint and provides an economic analysis of the dilemma facing Washington today regarding how to finance the growing federal budget deficit. While many of the issues covered in Part VI are treated elsewhere in the book, the comments of numerous reviewers suggest that many instructors want to cover some of these topics more deeply, as in these chapters.

SPECIAL FEATURES

This text has many features designed to enhance the learning and teaching experience.

Boxed Examples. Each chapter includes boxes that use real-world examples to show how the theory developed in the text relates to the actual workings of the economy. These boxes are organized into three broad categories. **The Data Bank** boxes examine published economic and financial data through the lens of the models used in the text (see The Data Bank 4.1: Actual and Expected Rates of Inflation). **Inside Money** boxes focus on special topics or issues related to money and banking that most students will find relevant (see Inside Money 3.3: 15-Year Versus 30-Year Mortgages). Finally, **International Banking** boxes acquaint students with money and banking around the world (see International Banking 5.2: Concentration Ratios in Banking).

Summary Exercises. Each chapter contains numerous summary exercises with answers immediately following. This lets students verify that they have mastered material in a section before reading on and, based on our own experience, considerably reduces the frequency with which students need to find the time for one-on-one consultation with their instructors.

End-of-Chapter Questions and Problems. The end of each chapter contains numerous questions and problems. Selected answers appear in the back of the book.

Key Terms. Each chapter includes an extensive list of key terms, all of which are defined in the end-of-text glossary.

Selections for Further Reading. Each chapter includes a list of articles accessible to students and instructors who desire further information about topics included in the chapter.

Glossary and Index. A glossary defines all key terms highlighted in the text, and an extensive index aids students and instructors in cross-referencing material in the book.

SUPPORT PACKAGE

To help both students and teachers using this textbook, Houghton Mifflin offers an accompanying support package. **The Study Guide** includes chapter synopses and a wide range of practice questions and exercises with answers and helpful hints. The **Instructor's Resource Manual/Test Bank** contains sample course outlines and, for each chapter, helpful classroom hints, a summary of key concepts, and solutions to text questions and problems. The Instructor's Resource Manual/Test Bank also contains over 800 test questions, including multiple choice, essay, and discussion questions, many of which have accompanying graphs. These test questions are also available in a **Computerized Test Bank** for IBM-PC and compatible microcomputers.

ACKNOWLEDGMENTS

Our product has been improved by the feedback and thoughtful comments of numerous students, colleagues, and professionals at Houghton Mifflin. Denise Clinton, the economics Sponsoring Editor of Houghton Mifflin, managed the project and was instrumental in molding our initial view of this text into what it is today. Her support and constructive criticism throughout the development process, but most importantly her vision and her patience with hardheaded authors, is deeply appreciated.

We owe a special debt to our two Basic Book editors at Houghton Mifflin—Tom Mancuso, who helped us during the early stages of the book, and Karla Paschkis, who helped us enliven the manuscript and forced us to better organize our thoughts. Our Senior Project Editor, Susan Westendorf, did a superb job managing production and those responsible for producing the final manuscript. Countless others at Houghton Mifflin—Greg Tobin, Sue Warne, and Mike Ginley, to name just a few—challenged and encouraged us during day long development meetings in Boston. Thanks, folks.

Numerous reviewers across the country provided feedback on our manuscript, not only correcting errors but helping us better see their own needs as well as the needs of the market.

These reviewers included:

Thomas Bonsor
Eastern Washington University

Kathleen Brook
New Mexico State University

Colleen Callahan
Lehigh University

Mitch Charkiewicz
Central Connecticut State University

David Craig
Westark Community College and Arkansas State University

Eleanor Craig
University of Delaware

Mario Crucini
Ohio State University

Al Culver
California State University at Chico

Andrew Dane
Angelo State University

Stan Eakins
East Caroline University

Peter J. Ferderer
Clark University

Dennis Fixler
George Washington University & Bureau of Labor Statistics

Peter Frevert
University of Kansas

Lance Girton
University of Utah

John Grobey
Humboldt State University

Nell Gullet
University of Tennessee at Martin

Scott D. Hakala
Southern Methodist University

Bassam E. Harik
Western Michigan University

Gay Hatfield
University of Mississippi

Thomas Havrilesky
Duke University

Emily Hoffnar
University of North Texas

Lora Holcombe
Florida State University

Randall G. Holcombe
Florida State University

Daniel Houser
University of Minnesota

Harry Huizinga
Stanford University

Charles W. Johnston
University of Michigan—Flint

Arthur E. Kartman
San Diego State University

Richard H. Keehn
University of Wisconsin— Parkside

James Kelley
Texas A&M University

Elizabeth Sawyer Kelly
University of Wisconsin— Madison

Jane Knodell
University of Vermont

James Lynch
Robert Morris College

Rich MacDonald
St. Cloud State University

David MacPherson
Florida State University

W. Douglas McMillan
Louisiana State University

Robert M. Mulligan
Providence College

Charles Murray
Northeast Missouri State University

Douglas K. Pearce
North Carolina State University

Malcolm Robinson
University of Cincinnati

Charles Sawyer
University of Southern Mississippi

Amin U. Sarkar
SUNY—Fredonia

Richard T. Selden
University of Virginia

Calvin Siebert
University of Iowa

Harinder Singh
San Diego State University

Neil Skaggs
Illinois State University

Paula Smith
University of Central Oklahoma

John Soper
John Carroll University

Robert Sorenson
University of Missouri—St. Louis

Frederick Thum
University of Texas

Thom Thurston
City University of New York

Anne P. Villamil
University of Ilinois at Urbana—Champaign

John C. Wassom
Western Kentucky State University

Eugene White
Rutgers University

James Wible
University of New Hampshire

Raymond Zelder
Western Michigan University

To all of you, thanks.

We owe our special thanks to the text's dedicated accuracy reviewers: Daniel Houser, University of Minnesota; James Kelley, Texas A&M University; and Thom Thurston, City University of New York.

We are also grateful to John Wells and Dennis Powers for the careful job they did checking problems, collecting data, and proofing our work at various stages of the project. Jim Kelley also assisted with the manuscript, and our assistants, Sue Bryant and Tamara Ariens helped make this project manageable. Finally, we thank our children and wives (actually, we have only one each) for putting up with busy fathers and husbands who have yet to learn how not to overcommit.

MRB University Park, Pennsylvania
DWJ College Station, Texas

Money, Banking, and Financial Markets:

An Economics Approach

PART ONE

Introduction to Money and Banking

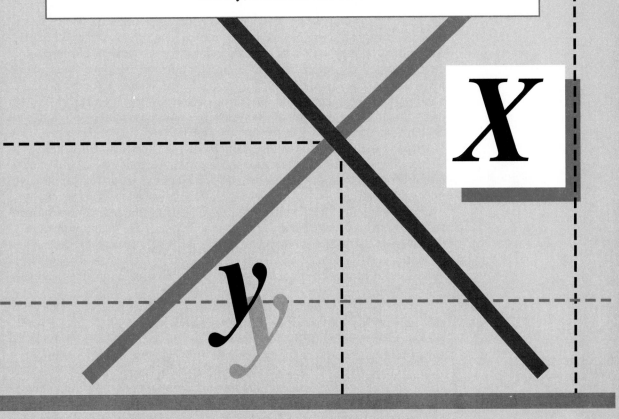

CHAPTERS

1

Money and Banks

2

Financial Markets, Financial Institutions and Instruments, and Money

3

Money, Inflation, and Interest

1

Money and Banks

his book is about money and banking, two subjects closely intertwined with our daily lives and with the everyday functioning of our economy. On a typical day, you encounter money and banks in many forms—from the obvious contact made when you use dollar bills to buy lunch or ''go to the bank'' to withdraw funds to the almost invisible contact via the investment of your school's endowment. When you write a check, withdraw funds at the corner ATM, or use a credit card to purchase this book, you interact with the banking system. If you work, you may be paid in the form of a check or a direct deposit into your bank account. If your parents send you money from home, it may arrive as cash delivered in person, as a check mailed directly to you, as a check deposited directly into your account, or as a wire transfer. If you have some savings, you may invest them in a savings account, a money market mutual fund, or various forms of bonds or stocks. All of these situations are interactions between you and the banking and financial system.

Taking the larger view, money and banks, and the financial system as a whole, play a vital role in the national economy. The total quantity of money in the economy and the rate at which that quantity grows over time have important implications for interest rates, inflation rates, and the economy's overall functioning. In later chapters, we will see how the federal government has appointed a central bank to regulate and control the quantity of money and oversee the health of the banking system and, to some extent, of the entire financial system. We will also see how the central bank accomplishes its tasks and how well it achieves its goals of low inflation rates and full employment.

At this point, you may have little knowledge of how banks work or what money really is. At the end of this course, however, you will have a much greater understanding of the roles money and banks play, both on the individual level and in the economy overall. This chapter begins with an overview of these roles and discusses the evolution of money and banks as we know them today. We will see that money is not simply bills and coins; it is anything widely used to pay for goods and services. Throughout the history of humankind, numerous things have served as money, including shells, stones, beads, sacks of grain, gold, cigarettes, paper bills, and checks. We will also see that money is not synonymous with ''wealth'' or ''income.''

An individual's *wealth* refers to the stock of assets the individual owns, less his or her debts. For example, your wealth includes the total value of your holdings of real estate, stocks and bonds, cash on hand, money deposited in banks or other financial institutions, cars, and even textbooks, minus the amount you owe to others. In contrast, *income* refers to a flow of earnings over some given time interval, say, a week, month, or year. Your wealth is like an ''inventory'' of everything you own minus debts owed to others, while your income represents the ''change'' in the inventory that occurs during a given time period.

With these concepts in mind, we will now look more closely at the nature and role of money in our economy and at the origin of money and banks.

MONEY

Money is anything generally accepted as a medium of exchange. A **medium of exchange** is virtually anything used to pay for goods and services or settle debts. Thus, the distinguishing feature of money is that society widely accepts it to settle transactions. In the United States, money takes many forms. Obviously you use the dollar bills (more technically, **Federal Reserve notes**) and coins in your pocket to pay for things like compact discs and restaurant meals. Thus, Federal Reserve notes and coins minted by the U.S. Treasury are money. In popular use, the term *money* is often a synonym for these two media of exchange. Coins and dollar bills, however, are called **currency** and comprise only part of the money supply. As Box 1.1 shows, traveler's checks and checks written against checking accounts at banks, savings and loans, and credit unions are also commonly accepted as payment and are therefore money.

Other financial assets, such as savings account balances, are sometimes considered money. However, savings account balances clearly are not a medium of exchange, since it is difficult to literally exchange your savings account balance for a meal at a restaurant. Instead, you must first convert your savings account into another asset, such as currency or a check, and then exchange the currency or check for a meal. Some assets—your house, for instance—cannot be quickly and easily converted into a medium of exchange. It often takes substantial real estate commissions and time to convert a house into currency or checkable deposits. Your automatic teller machine (ATM) card is not money either, since you cannot directly purchase a meal by handing over the card. You can, however, use your ATM card to obtain money from your checking or savings account. Thus, ATM cards are instruments that allow the user to convert checking or savings account balances into currency.

Liquidity is the term economists use to describe how cheaply and easily an asset may be converted into a medium of exchange. Savings account

The Data Bank

Box 1.1

Components of the Money Supply

If you wished for all the money in the U.S. economy and your wish came true, what would you get? The following chart, which is based on a definition of the money supply the Federal Reserve System calls *M1*, provides the answer: $1.04 trillion. As you can see, money consists of much more than the dollar bills and coins in your pocket. The M1 money supply includes currency in the hands of the public, demand deposits (checking account balances at commercial banks), other checkable deposits (money market deposit accounts and various checkable deposits at savings and loans, credit unions, and mutual savings banks), and traveler's checks. There are also other official Federal Reserve System definitions of the money supply, such as M2 and M3, which we discuss in more detail in Chapter 2.

Of the roughly $1 trillion of M1 money in the United States, only 28 percent is in the form of currency. Demand deposits and other checkable deposits together comprise the lion's share (71 percent).

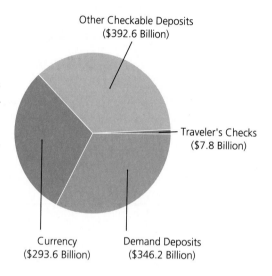

Total U.S. Money Supply (M1) in January 1993: $1.04 Trillion

Other Checkable Deposits ($392.6 Billion)

Traveler's Checks ($7.8 Billion)

Currency ($293.6 Billion)

Demand Deposits ($346.2 Billion)

Source for data: Board of Governors of the Federal Reserve System, *Federal Reserve Bulletin,* various issues, and Citibase electronic database.

balances are a liquid asset, since they can be quickly and easily converted into a medium of exchange. Real estate, on the other hand, is not quickly and easily convertible, and therefore is an illiquid asset. Dollars (i.e., currency) and checkable deposits, the primary media of exchange in the United States, are the most liquid of all assets.

Summary Exercise 1.1 Most dictionaries include variations of one or more of the following definitions of money: (1) portable pieces of metal used as a medium of exchange;

(2) currency and coins; (3) wealth. Comment on which, if any, of these definitions corresponds with an economist's definition of money.

Answer: These definitions are all deficient to an economist. The first definition identifies money as a medium of exchange but limits money to coins. This seems to exclude paper currency as well as checking accounts. The second definition mentions coins and currency but does not mention checkable deposits. The third definition treats money as being synonymous with wealth; for example, "He's got a lot of money" is a popular way of saying "He's wealthy." Economists, however, do not use *money* as a synonym for *wealth.*

Functions of Money

You now have an overview of what money is and recognize the distinctions among money, income, and wealth. We now examine four roles of money in an economy. As we will see, money serves as a medium of exchange, a unit of account, a store of value, and a standard of deferred payment.

Medium of Exchange.   As mentioned earlier, the primary function of money in an economy is to serve as a medium of exchange. This simply means that when you buy goods, services, or financial instruments (such as stocks or bonds), you pay with money. In the United States, people almost always use money in the form of currency or checks as the medium of exchange. *Barter*—the exchange of goods and services without the use of money—is a possible but rare method of making transactions.

It is hard to envision life without money as the medium of exchange. Imagine a barter economy—an economy that has no money in which goods are traded directly for other goods. If a baker wants shoes, it is not enough to find a shoemaker; the baker must find a shoemaker willing to trade shoes for bread. Barter transactions require a **double coincidence of wants**: Each individual must have something the other desires. If this happens, exchange will take place; the shoemaker will get bread, and the baker will get shoes. But if the baker does not want shoes, or vice versa, no exchange will take place. In this case, the two parties will have to continue to search for someone who wants what they have for trade.[1]

Thus, we see that barter is highly inefficient, since the baker would have to spend considerable time searching for someone willing to accept bread as payment for some other good. This search time is a **transactions cost**: a cost borne in making an exchange. When money is used as the medium of exchange, the baker can use money to buy shoes from the shoemaker even if the shoemaker does not want bread. The shoemaker, in turn, can use the

---

[1] Of course, intermediate exchanges might occur in which the baker first trades for apples and then trades for shoes. Indeed, when one good becomes an acceptable intermediate exchange in all transactions, that good has become money!

money received to buy whatever he or she desires from a third party. In effect, in a monetary economy all individuals find money useful (and thus want money); thus, money satisfies the double coincidence of wants. Therefore, one main advantage of a *monetary economy*—an economy that uses money as a medium of exchange—is that it eliminates the problem of finding a double coincidence of wants; that is, it reduces the transactions costs of exchange. As we will see, monetary economies have other advantages.

Unit of Account.   Money also serves as a **unit of account**: The values of goods and services are stated in units of money, just as time is measured in minutes and distance in feet. Accountants record the revenues and costs of companies like AT&T in terms of money. Similarly, individuals budget their expenditure and income flows in terms of money.

In a monetary economy, the medium of exchange nearly always also serves as the unit of account. Because the medium of exchange is common to virtually all transactions, it is convenient to state the prices of goods and services in terms of the medium of exchange. In the United States, the unit of account is the U.S. dollar, which is also the medium of exchange.

The use of money as the unit of account reduces the amount of information individuals need to make purchase decisions. In a monetary economy, prices are quoted in terms of the unit of account (be it dollars, yen, or shells). If there are 1,000 goods for sale, there are 1,000 prices—one for each good. Each price specifies how many units of money must be given up to receive one unit of each good. In a primitive monetary economy, one loaf of bread might cost 1 shell, one cow might cost 100 shells, and so on. In the modern U.S. economy, the U.S. dollar is the unit of account, and these prices are quoted in dollars: $1.59 for one loaf of bread, $1,250 for one cow.

In the absence of a common unit of account, there would be more prices than goods in the economy! To see this, imagine you live in a simple barter economy with only four goods: apples, oranges, shoes, and bread. Apple sellers would have to quote three different prices. One price tag would indicate how many oranges it takes to buy an apple, a second price tag would state how many pairs of shoes it takes to buy an apple, and a third price tag would reveal how many loaves of bread it takes to buy an apple. Similarly, orange sellers would have to specify how many apples, shoes, or loaves of bread it takes to receive an orange. Of course, if millions of goods were available, as in our economy, there would be millions of price tags to put on each item.[2] Imagine how costly it would be for you to figure out whether you could afford to buy an item when each item had millions of price tags!

---

[2] If there are n goods, the number of prices in a barter economy is given by the formula $n \times (n - 1)/2$. In our four-good economy, there are six prices. If $n = 1,000$, the number of prices is 499,500.

Fortunately, we live in a monetary economy, and we use money as a unit of account. All prices are stated in terms of dollars, and thus each good has a single price tag. The presence of money as a unit of account reduces the amount of price information you need to buy goods in the marketplace, and this too reduces the transaction's costs associated with exchange.

Store of Value.

Money also serves as a **store of value**: It is a means of storing today's purchasing power to purchase, say, a house or a car tomorrow. In the absence of money or other assets as a store of value, individuals and companies would have to maintain stocks of goods to use to trade in the future. This approach would be inefficient for two reasons. First, some commodities, like fruit and milk, are perishable and would be of little or no value if stored for future use. Second, even when a commodity is not perishable—a car, for instance—it can be very costly to use it to store value over time. General Motors would find it very costly to maintain inventories of extra cars to use to pay their workers. GM workers, in turn, would find it useless to be paid in engine parts or transmissions, for they would have a difficult time finding someone willing to accept an engine part or a transmission as payment for food or housing.

The absence of money as a store of value would also lead people to hoard a variety of goods—even goods they did not personally wish to consume (liver or licorice, perhaps?)—in the hope of locating another person who offered something they wanted and required one of those goods as payment. In contrast, in a monetary economy, people hold inventories of money—not transmissions, liver, or licorice—to use to pay for goods and labor services.

Of course, money is not the only store of value. Indeed, many other assets—savings accounts, stocks, and bonds, to name just a few—are often better stores of value than money. These assets pay interest or dividends, whereas currency and many checkable deposits do not. Thus, while money provides a convenient store of purchasing power, it is not wise to use money as a store of value over long periods of time. However, money is unmatched by other assets in its liquidity, which gives it an advantage over other assets as a temporary store of value.

Standard of Deferred Payment.

Finally, money serves as a **standard of deferred payment**; that is, a payment that is deferred to the future is usually stated as a sum of money. For example, if you owe money to a friend and plan to pay it back in a week, you usually state the amount you owe in money terms, such as $5. In the absence of money, you would have to plan on making payment in terms of some other good. Having a common standard for deferred payments, which is the same as the medium of exchange and the unit of account makes it relatively easy to determine exactly how much a deferred payment will be. There are efficiencies in thinking of payments today and payments tomorrow or next year in terms of a common item—money. However, we will see that just as money is a store of value, but not the best store of value, money is a standard of deferred payment, but not necessarily the best standard for all purposes.

The Origin of Money

The origins of money are little known. Historians believe money originated as religious objects of value, which ultimately evolved into a medium of exchange. By the ancient Babylonian, Greek, and Roman civilizations, monetary systems included coins.

After the fall of Rome, the medieval economies of Europe moved toward a barter system. The feudal system was built largely on barter, with debts between lord and vassal paid in terms of goods and/or services—most frequently labor services. Thus, a noble would owe military service to his lord, and a serf would owe labor to his lord. Taxes were often collected in the form of agricultural products or labor services.

However, barter was neither a permanent nor a worldwide phenomenon. Indeed, in Byzantium (now Constantinople) the Eastern Roman Empire survived until the eleventh century and with it the *nomisa* gold coin, which was the standard currency of the Mediterranean world. In Europe, the feudal system and the use of barter eventually diminished, and a monetary economy gradually reemerged. By the eleventh century, there was a revival of trade and a renewed growth of towns, and gold emerged as a medium of exchange. After William the Conqueror won the Battle of Hastings in 1066 and became ruler of England, he allowed only royal coinage to be used in his kingdom.

The presence of a monetary economy in Europe was not without controversy. Phillip IV allegedly debased the French currency during his rule (1285–1314) by minting coins that contained a lower amount of gold or silver than promised and substituting small amounts of lead to maintain the weight and feel of the declared quantity of precious metal.[3] Despite episodes such as this, however, Europe gradually moved closer to the monetary economy of today.

Summary Exercise 1.2

Credit cards are often used to pay for items purchased at retailing outlets. Are credit cards ''money''?

Answer: Believe it or not, this is a controversial question. To answer, note that a credit card is *not* money; you do not give someone your plastic card in exchange for a good. Instead, a credit card is a money substitute.

---

[3] Debasement of coinage meant that the monarch could issue more coins from a given supply of gold or silver and by so doing could buy more goods and services from the general public than would have been possible otherwise. Thus, debasement was an attempt by Phillip IV to tax the general public without their knowledge.

Using the card is taking out a loan from a preapproved line of credit. The merchant receives a signed voucher from the buyer that can be exchanged for money. If you paid the merchant with dollar bills or coins, the merchant would directly receive money and could instantly use the bills or coins as a medium of exchange in another transaction. In contrast, a credit card voucher gives the merchant the right to collect a specified amount of money from the credit card company at the end of the month. Thus, the credit card voucher the merchant receives is an IOU that cannot be quickly converted into a medium of exchange to use in another transaction. For this reason, economists typically do not consider credit cards to be money.

Types of Money

Historically two types of money have been used as a medium of exchange. The first type was commodity money—money backed by stores of a commodity such as religious relics. Much later, a second type of money emerged: fiat money. Marco Polo observed the Chinese using fiat money during his famous travels in the thirteenth century. Fiat money is money that is not ''backed'' by a commodity such as animal pelts or gold but is valuable as money because of government pronouncement or fiat. *Fiat* is a Latin word that means literally the pronouncement ''let it be done.''

Commodity Money. The first type of money used by civilization—religious relics—was a form of commodity money. **Commodity money** is a physical commodity that is used as money but also has alternative, non-monetary uses. More recent examples of commodity money are gold and silver coins. Gold and silver are used in jewelry and for other decorative purposes and thus have value independent of their use as money. But when they circulate as money, they are valuable as a medium of exchange, that is, to purchase other commodities.

In addition to religious relics, gold and silver, numerous other goods have served as commodity money in human history: live animals, sacks of corn, and even huge stone wheels (See Box 1.2). The common characteristic among all forms of commodity money is that something valuable to society for its physical properties is chosen to perform a second function as the medium of exchange.

A type of commodity money in which the commodity itself circulates as money is called **full-bodied money.** As the term implies, the monetary value of full-bodied money exactly equals its nonmonetary value. Animal pelts, for example, were full-bodied money.

The most recent example of full-bodied money is the gold coins that were minted by the U.S. Treasury until 1914. The value of the gold in each coin was equal to the value of the coin as money. For instance, if the price of gold was $1 per ounce, a $1 gold coin contained one ounce of gold. The coin could then be used to purchase $1 worth of candy, or it could be melted to extract one ounce of gold for use in jewelry.

International Banking

Box 1.2

*Money on the Yap Island
and Gold Transfers among Nations*

The ancient inhabitants of the Yap island in the Pacific Ocean had a most peculiar full-bodied medium of exchange: a large stone wheel called a *fei*. The fei was sculpted from limestone obtained on an island hundreds of miles from Yap. The value of a fei depended in part on its size; it had a diameter that often exceeded the height of an average man. Smaller fei were carried on wooden poles placed through the hole in the middle, but large fei were seldom actually moved. Instead, when an islander made a purchase that required the payment of a huge fei, the fei would remain in a fixed location and the new owner would merely accept the acknowledgment of ownership as payment for the goods.

You might find it odd that the fei served as a medium of exchange without physically changing hands. This peculiarity, however, is not limited to the Yap Island; even today most gold transfers among nations are conducted in underground vaults such as those at the Federal Reserve Bank of New York. When a transaction that requires the transfer of gold from, say, the Netherlands to Germany occurs, the gold is not actually shipped from one country to the other. Instead, it is merely moved from the vault that stores the Netherlands' gold to the vault that stores Germany's gold. This journey of a few meters helps keep the ownership record intact but is otherwise similar to the practice of the Yap islanders, who merely transferred the acknowledgment of ownership rather than the physical location of large fei.

Sources: Norman Angell, *The Story of Money* (New York: Garden City Publishing Company, 1929), 88–89; *Journal of Political Economy,* 90 (August 1982), back cover.

In contrast to full-bodied money, **representative full-bodied money** is paper money that represents a claim to a specific quantity of some commodity. The actual commodity is held as an inventory in a bank vault or other depository and does not circulate. During the early part of this century, the U.S. Treasury issued representative full-bodied money called *gold certificates.* **Gold certificates** were pieces of paper that could be redeemed for a specified amount of gold. For instance, if the price of gold was $35 per ounce, a $1 gold certificate represented a claim to 1/35 ounces of gold. Anyone holding such a gold certificate could convert it into 1/35 ounces of gold on demand.

The advantage of representative full-bodied money is that the commodity itself does not have to circulate; only the paper claim to the commodity does. The innovation of representative full-bodied money significantly reduced the need to carry around heavy bags of gold to use in exchange. Paper gold certificates were much lighter and more practical. An interesting feature of representative full-bodied money is that the actual item exchanged during purchases (paper in the case of gold certificates) has negligible value as a commodity.

Fiat Money. The use of representative full-bodied money accustomed people to using paper money. The next innovation was the issuance of unbacked money in the form of token coins and unbacked (fiat) paper money. **Fiat money** has no value as a commodity and does not represent a claim to any physical commodity. It is the type of money used in the United States today. The United States went off the gold standard during the Great Depression, and Federal Reserve notes (dollar bills) have been a fiat currency ever since.

Token coins—the pennies, nickels, dimes, and quarters in your pocket—resemble commodity money coins but contain less valuable metals such as copper, nickel, or zinc instead of gold or silver. The physical value of these coins as commodities is less than the value of what you can purchase with them. In other words, if you went into the business of melting down quarters and selling the resultant metal, you would end up in the poorhouse.

Fiat money also takes the form of unbacked paper money, usually fairly small, rectangular pieces of paper with fancy engraving. Unlike representative full-bodied money, however, fiat money is not backed by gold or silver held in a depository. As a commodity, fiat money is worth only the paper it is printed on. But fiat money is valuable as a medium of exchange, because it can be used to purchase compact discs and other items. U.S. Federal Reserve notes—the dollar bills in your pocket—are fiat money. Nothing is held in a depository to back these paper dollars.

A final category of unbacked money is unbacked money issued by banks and other financial institutions. The best-known example is checkable deposits such as your checking account at your bank. You write checks and businesses accept them as payment, even though the checks are backed by no commodity. Instead, they are backed either by paper money held in the bank vault or, more likely, by nothing tangible. We will say more about the development of checks as money later in this chapter. As you will see, banks can literally create money by creating checking account balances—balances that are not even fully backed by holdings of paper dollars.

Does anything back fiat money? To answer this, consider gold coins. You can always melt gold coins for their gold content. If the coins are full bodied, the gold will equal their value as money. Even representative full-bodied money, such as a gold certificate, is backed by the gold held in a depository—gold that the owner of a gold certificate can obtain in exchange for the certificate.

Fiat money, on the other hand, cannot be melted to yield an equivalent value of metal, nor can it be exchanged for a commodity held in a depository.

Instead, fiat money is backed only by its general acceptance by society as the medium of exchange. Without this acceptance, no one would value U.S. dollar bills or accept them in exchange for goods and services. You accept these Federal Reserve notes (or checks payable in Federal Reserve notes) as payment for your work only because you are confident that your landlord and your supermarket will accept these same notes in exchange for rent and groceries. If all other people in society decided that Federal Reserve notes were no longer acceptable as money, you would not accept them as payment for your labor services.

Summary
Exercise 1.3

Determine whether the following episodes involve full-bodied money, representative full-bodied money, or fiat money: (a) During World War II, prisoners of war used cigarettes as the medium of exchange and unit of account for chocolate candy, cookies, and other items. (b) Yap islanders, tired of hauling around stone wheels as the medium of exchange, decided to use verbal acknowledgments of the ownership of stone wheels as the medium of exchange. (c) The U.S. government decreed that its paper bills are legal tender for all debts, both public and private.

Answer: (a) In the POW camps, cigarettes were full-bodied commodity money. (b) Verbal acknowledgments of ownership of stone wheels are representative full-bodied money. (c) The paper bills are fiat money, since they are valuable as a medium of exchange only by government decree.

Physical Properties of Money

Our discussion of the roles of money provides numerous reasons money—be it animal pelts, gold coins, or paper—tends to emerge in even the most primitive societies. The numerous commodities that have served as money throughout history, as well as the fiat money currently used in the United States and other industrialized countries, all have certain desirable physical properties. What makes a commodity a good choice to serve as money? Ideally, money should be portable, divisible, durable, and of recognizable value.

Portability. For ease of use in transactions, money should be portable. The easier it is to carry around, the more effective it is as a medium of exchange. Thus, commodity money should generally be a substance that is valuable in small quantities. This explains why early humankind quickly turned to gold and silver as forms of money. Even small quantities of these rare metals are valuable enough to be used for large purchases. In contrast, lead makes a poor choice as a medium of exchange, since large purchases would require large amounts of lead.

Divisibility. To permit transactions of various sizes, money should be made of a commodity that is divisible into smaller units to facilitate making "change." Gold and silver also serve well in this respect, since small coins can be minted to facilitate small transactions. In contrast, diamonds, which are very portable (due to their high value per unit of weight) are not easily divisible, making them a poor choice for a medium of exchange.

Durability. Money should be durable; that is, it should not wear out in use and should not depreciate quickly when not in use. Gold and silver also meet this criterion. Eggs, obviously, would serve poorly as a medium of exchange.

Recognizable Value. Money should have easily recognizable value; that is, it should be easy for people engaged in exchange to agree to the value of the good used as money. Part of the motivation for coining gold was to provide this property. In the days of gold coins, the coins were stamped with a face value equal to the value in weight of the gold they contained. In addition, each coin was stamped with the seal of the government or the "face" of the king as a guarantee of the coin's authenticity and weight. This practice made it difficult for unscrupulous individuals to snip off portions of gold or manufacture "counterfeit" money. It also reduced the uncertainty regarding whether a particular coin was indeed worth the value stated by the individual wishing to exchange it, thus increasing the acceptability of gold coins as payment.

A desire for recognizable value is also behind efforts to foil counterfeiting of fiat currency. Modern paper currency has complicated engraving, rare papers and inks, and sometimes embedded metal strips. All of these attributes make it easier to recognize genuine currency and more difficult to produce counterfeit bills.

Box 1.3 describes a commodity that possessed all four physical properties of money: cigarettes in a World War II POW camp.

Summary Exercise 1.4

Do modern-day checks satisfy the desired properties of money?

Answer: Obviously checks are easy to carry around (portable), can be written in various amounts (divisible), and are reasonably durable. However, checks are not always of recognizable value. If a stranger offers you a $30,000 check for your car, chances are you will not hand over the keys. The problem is that you do not recognize the true value of the check—it may bounce, in which case you are out one car. Recent advances in electronic check verification, however, are making it easier for some check recipients (primarily businesses) to verify checks quickly.

Inside Money

Box 1.3

*Cigarettes as Money
in a Prisoner of War Camp*

During World War II, Allied prisoners in a German POW camp developed a monetary system in which cigarettes served as the medium of exchange. Cigarettes played a dual role in this POW camp: They could be used as a commodity (smoked) or to purchase other goods. The choice of cigarettes as the medium of exchange stemmed from their attributes. They were divisible, from carton to pack to individual cigarette. They were also durable, portable, and of easily recognizable value.

The prisoners received fixed weekly rations from the Red Cross, which included various foodstuffs in addition to cigarettes. They could trade the food among themselves to reallocate the rations according to their preferences for various items, but this practice required a double coincidence of wants. When cigarettes emerged as the medium of exchange, prices of chocolates and other goods began to be stated in terms of the number of cigarettes needed to buy the goods. Even nonsmoking prisoners were willing to sell chocolates in exchange for cigarettes, which they could then use to purchase items of value from a third party.

Because cigarettes were useful as money, few cigarettes were actually smoked. While the camp received a fairly steady supply of new cigarettes, a stock of unsmoked cigarettes circulated as money. Smokers would have enjoyed seeing all of the money go up in smoke, but they did not because cigarettes were valued as the medium of exchange. The use of a commodity money (like cigarettes) solves the double coincidence of wants problem, but it reduces the consumption of the good used as money.

Source: R. A. Radford, ''The Economic Organization of a P.O.W. Camp,'' *Economica* (November 1945), 189–201.

THE EVOLUTION OF BANKS

Soon after society recognized the benefits of using money as a medium of exchange, it recognized the need for a safe place to store it. This ''safe place'' ultimately evolved into the banks of today—financial institutions that accept deposits and make loans. The remaining chapters of this book will explain in more detail the operation of modern banks and other financial institutions such as savings and loan associations, credit unions, and mutual savings banks. For now, bear in mind that all of these institutions are similar in that they accept deposits and make loans. The remainder of this chapter offers some background on how these institutions originated and evolved into today's banking system.

Banks as Depositories

Banking existed in Babylonia and in ancient Greece and Rome. During the Middle Ages, gold and silver (known as **specie,** from the Latin for "in-kind") served as a full-bodied medium of exchange. People naturally wanted to store their specie in a location safe from theft, fire, and other hazards. Such a location required some sort of safe or strongbox, and the town goldsmith was one place that invariably offered such accommodations. Other wealthy individuals or businesses also had strongboxes for their own valuables and leased space in them to others, but goldsmiths of necessity had strongboxes to store the gold they used in their trade.

Demand Deposits

A convenient way to illustrate the operation of banks as depositories is depicted in Table 1.1, which is called a *T-account*. In a T-account, the bank's assets are listed on the left side and its liabilities are listed on the right side. In this T-account, individuals have deposited $75 in gold, which are held in reserve in the bank's vault. This represents the bank's assets. Notice that the gold on deposit is not a "gift" to the bank; the depositors are free to withdraw it whenever they choose. The obligation to give back $75 in gold to depositors at their demand represents a liability to the bank. For this reason, even today checkable deposits at banks are called **demand deposits.** Demand deposits account for the $75 in liabilities on the right-hand side of the T-account in Table 1.1.

At first, goldsmiths merely provided safekeeping for specie deposits and charged depositors a fee for this service. When depositors wanted the use of their gold or silver deposits, they went to the goldsmith's place of business and asked for their specie. However, it became apparent that it was not really necessary to make a trip to the goldsmith to obtain specie for purchasing goods. Instead, a depositor could use a *written order to pay* for goods. In effect, a person with deposits at a goldsmith would trade this written order for goods and services.

The written order to pay would state that the depositor was authorizing the goldsmith to pay a specified amount of specie to the person named on

Table 1.1	
A Bank Holding Demand Deposits	
Assets	**Liabilities**
Reserves (gold in vault) $75	Demand Deposits $75

the order. These orders to pay were the precursor of today's familiar checks. Consider the check you probably wrote to pay for your books at the beginning of the semester. On that check you indicated who was to be paid (XYZ Bookstore), the amount to be paid, and the date, and you signed the check to verify that it was you who wrote it. The bookstore was then free to present the check to your bank, and your bank gave the bookstore the indicated funds from your checking account. Except for the facts that goldsmiths held gold deposits and written orders to pay indicated that gold was to be paid, the early checking account arrangements worked just like today's checking accounts.

The innovation of the written order to pay made it easier to buy goods. A shopper no longer had to visit the goldsmith to obtain gold before shopping; she or he could write checks for purchases once inside a store. Shoppers were also less likely to be robbed, since they did not have to carry gold on shopping trips.

The original written orders to pay were along the lines of "I, Jane K. Depositor, order Gary Goldsmith to pay Sam J. Shoemaker X amount of gold." As we noted, these written orders to pay were very convenient, and Sam J. Shoemaker actually had several options when he received such a check. He could turn in the check to Gary Goldsmith and receive the indicated gold from Jane's account; he could turn in the check to Gary and ask him to take the gold out of Jane's account and put it in his own account; or he could endorse the back of the check and pass it on in a subsequent exchange, perhaps with Theresa Tanner. In the latter case, Theresa Tanner had the same options Sam did. Notice, however, that if Sam wanted to simply endorse the check and use it to pay Theresa, the value of the purchase had to be the same as the amount specified on the check from Jane to Sam. Otherwise, Sam or Theresa would have had to "make change" from the amount stated on the check. This inconvenience limited the number of times any check would change hands before being presented at the bank for redemption.

Box 1.4 shows the recent growth in currency and checking account balances in the United States.

Bank Notes

Another innovation was the **bank note,** a document written by the early banks (goldsmiths) promising to pay a sum of specie to the bearer on demand. A bank note stated something like "I, Gary Goldsmith, promise to pay the bearer X amount of gold upon demand." Bank notes were issued in convenient denominations and could be used to buy goods and services. Thus, when Jane K. Depositor deposited gold with the goldsmith, she could elect to exchange some of the gold for bank notes. She then used these bank notes as money, and anyone who received them could exchange them for gold at Gary Goldsmith's or use them to buy something.

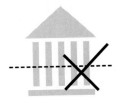

Inside Money

Where Are All the Dollars?

Box 1.4

The figure below plots currency and checking account balances per capita in the United States between 1980 and 1992. Notice that in 1992, the average checking account contained almost $3,000 per person and the average amount of currency held per person was nearly $1,000. The large amount of currency held per person is something of a puzzle: How many families of four do you know who keep $4,000 ($1,000 for each person) in their home or pockets?

Most households hold a minimal amount of currency, but businesses hold larger amounts to use in making change. However, businesses and households alone cannot account for the large amount of currency per person in the United States. One more likely group holding large cur-

rency balances is individuals who participate in the "underground economy," especially those who buy and sell illegal drugs. Currency, unlike checks, cannot be traced and is thus the preferred medium of exchange for people involved in illegal activities.

Another group holding U.S. currency is residents of foreign countries. The U.S. government does not keep records of its currency held outside the United States, but the Federal Reserve System estimates that as much as two-thirds of U.S. currency is held abroad.

Source for data: Board of Governors of the Federal Reserve System, *Federal Reserve Bulletin,* various issues and Citibase electronic database.

Dollar Value of Currency and Checkable Deposits per Capita in the United States, 1980 – 1992

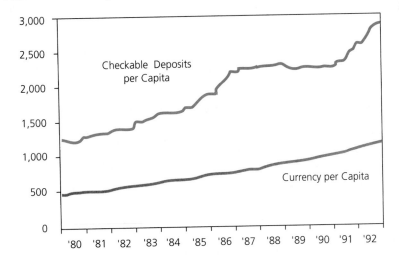

Notice that bank notes, like modern-day checks and currency, serve as money. The main difference is that bank notes and checks are supplied by banks rather than by the government. Moreover, bank notes have one big advantage over checks: They are issued in convenient denominations that facilitate their use in trade and thus stay in circulation for a longer time than checks do. A check written for a specific amount to a particular person is more difficult to use in a second transaction, and therefore the payee usually takes it to the bank for redemption.

Bank notes do have one disadvantage compared to checks. Since bank notes pay the bearer on demand instead of indicating payment to a particular person, they are much more prone to theft than checks are. Using stolen bank notes to make purchases is as easy as using gold, whereas it is difficult for Joe Thief to cash a check payable to Hank Tanner.

Today two types of bank notes are issued in the United States. The more prevalent type is the fiat currency issued by the Federal Reserve System, the central bank of the United States established by the U.S. government to manage the nation's money supply. In contrast to the early bank notes, which were issued by private banks and backed by gold, Federal Reserve notes are not backed by gold or any other commodity. The second type of bank note commonly used today, although comprising less than 1 percent of all money used, is traveler's checks. These bank notes are issued by major banks and are redeemable for Federal Reserve notes on demand.

The effect of issuing bank notes can be visualized using the bank's T-account. Suppose the bank we examined in Table 1.1 issues $25 in new bank notes in exchange for $25 in gold. This increases the reserves of the bank (gold in the vault) from $75 to $100, which is reflected on the asset side of the T-account in Table 1.2. Since the bank notes are redeemable for gold, they reflect a $25 liability for the bank. This accounts for the additional entry on the liability side of the T-account.

Table 1.2 A Bank Issuing Bank Notes			
Assets			**Liabilities**
Reserves (gold in vault)	$100	Bank Notes	$25
		Demand Deposits	$75

Fractional Reserve Banking

Initially goldsmiths functioned solely as depositories and issuers of bank notes in exchange for specie, honoring requests for redemption of both bank notes and demand deposits. In this function, the banks held specie in their vaults to cover all possible redemptions of bank notes and demand deposits. This practice is called *100 percent reserve banking,* since the bank holds reserves (in this case, specie in the vault) equal to the total value of outstanding bank notes and demand deposits. Reserves, being 100 percent of deposit and note liabilities, fully cover the hypothetical situation in which all deposits and bank notes are withdrawn on the same day.

Under 100 percent reserves, banks earn profits by charging a fee to store deposits and to trade specie for bank notes. However, banks soon realized that most of the specie in their vaults was never withdrawn; it sat idle while demand deposits and bank notes circulated as money. These early banks realized that they could in fact loan out some of their reserves and earn additional profits on loans. This approach led to **fractional reserve banking**, in which bank reserves equal only a fraction of outstanding demand deposits and bank notes. With fractional reserve banking, banks held some deposits as reserves in the vault but loaned out the remainder to people in need of funds. In fact, a bank would actually lend in the form of bank notes, issuing more such notes than there was gold in the vault. The bank would charge interest on this loan and hence had a second source of revenue in addition to the storage charges assessed on deposits.

To see the impact of fractional reserve banking, suppose the bank in Table 1.2 decides to keep only 20 percent of its bank note deposits in reserve instead of 100 percent. Thus, for every $100 in liabilities, the bank decides to keep $20 in reserve and loan out the remaining $80 in gold. The bank's rationale for doing this is simple. Since it is unlikely that all depositors will withdraw their gold on the same day, much of its previous reserves sat idle in the vault. By loaning out a fraction of these reserves—keeping enough to cover expected withdrawals but loaning out the rest at a profitable interest rate—the bank can profit. The bank in Table 1.2 had $100 in liabilities, so it keeps 20 percent ($20) in reserve and issues loans of $80. This leads to the T-account in Table 1.3, where the bank has assets consisting of $20 in reserves and $80 in loans. Its liabilities are still $25 in bank notes and $75 in demand deposits; the bank simply converted one form of an asset (reserves) into a different asset (loans).

Table 1.3
A Bank Issuing Loans

Assets		Liabilities	
Reserves (gold in vault)	$20	Bank Notes	$25
Loans	$80	Demand Deposits	$75

Note what happens to the available supply of money due to banking activities. Suppose the public has $100 of gold. With no banking, the money supply is $100 in the form of gold that circulates as the medium of exchange. When banks issue demand deposits and bank notes but keep 100 percent in reserves, as in Tables 1.1 and 1.2, the money supply in the hands of the public is still only $100. The only difference is that with demand deposits and bank notes, the gold that used to circulate as the medium of exchange is placed in a bank vault and paper circulates as the medium of exchange.

In contrast, consider what happens with fractional reserve banking, the situation in Table 1.3. Here the money supply in the hands of the public consists of $25 in bank notes, $75 in demand deposits, and $80 in gold that was placed back in the hands of the public when the bank issued the loan. The total money supply is now $180. Of this, $25 is in the form of bank notes, $75 is in the form of demand deposits, and $80 is in the form of gold. By engaging in fractional reserve banking, the bank has created $80 in additional money—seemingly out of nothing—by loaning out a fraction of deposits and bank notes!

The story does not end here, however. The borrower who has obtained $80 in gold from the local bank is not likely to have borrowed those funds just to keep them idle. Instead, she will probably spend them. Once she has, what will the new holder of the $80 in gold do with it? If he holds on to the gold, the money supply will stay at $180. However, if he deposits the $80 in the bank, the bank's gold reserves will increase by $80 to $100. Its demand deposits will also increase by $80 to $155, leading to the T-account in Table 1.4.

Table 1.4 A Bank Gets New Deposits			
Assets			**Liabilities**
Reserves (gold in vault)	$100	Bank Notes	$25
Loans	$80	Demand Deposits	$155

The bank is willing to lend out 80 percent of the value of its liabilities, keeping only 20 percent in reserve. The new demand deposits at the bank allow it to make additional loans. In particular, 80 percent of its current liabilities of $180 is $144, but the bank has issued only $80 in loans. Thus, the bank can increase its loans by $64 and still have reserves equal to 20 percent of its outstanding liabilities. Assuming the bank makes this loan, it ends up with the T-account in Table 1.5.

Table 1.5 A Bank Issues New Loans			
Assets			**Liabilities**
Reserves (gold in vault)	$36	Bank Notes	$25
Loans	$144	Demand Deposits	$155

Notice in Table 1.5 that the bank has gold reserves of $36 and loans of $144 for total assets of $180. What is the value of the money supply in the hands of the public? There are $25 in bank notes and $155 in demand deposits, and the bank just made a $64 loan of gold that some individual holds, making a $244 money supply. (Note that we do not count the original loan of $80, since that loan is now included in the demand deposits in Tables 1.4 and 1.5.) Thus, with just two loans, the bank has transformed a money supply consisting of $100 in gold into a $244 money supply!

This is still not the end of the story. The person who obtained the last loan for $64 in gold is almost sure to spend it, and the person receiving the $64 in payment for goods and services is likely to deposit it in the bank. Compared with Table 1.5, demand deposits would increase by $64 to $219, and reserves would likewise increase by $64 to $100 of gold. Then, of course, the bank would have $244 of liabilities and can loan out up to 80 percent of those liabilities, or $195.20. With $144 of loans already made, the bank can lend $51.20 while still meeting its self-imposed 20 percent reserve rule. In fact, the bank can keep making loans, as long as the gold eventually gets redeposited in the bank after the borrower spends it, until the T-account looks like Table 1.6.

In Table 1.6, the bank has $500 of liabilities and, under its 80 percent rule, has made loans of $400 while maintaining gold in the vault equal to 20 percent of liabilities, or $100. At this point, the bank is "fully loaned

Table1.6 A "Fully Loaned-Out" Bank			
Assets			**Liabilities**
Reserves (gold in vault)	$100	Bank Notes	$25
Loans	$400	Demand Deposits	$475

out''; it can no longer make a loan without violating its 20 percent reserve rule and thus can no longer create money. However, notice what the money supply has become under fractional reserve banking. Money in the hands of the public is $500 ($25 in bank notes and $475 in demand deposits). Notice that all of the original $100 of gold is again in the bank vault, just as it was under 100 percent reserves. However, with 20 percent fractional reserve banking, the $100 of gold in the vault ''creates'' a money supply of $500.

Under fractional reserve banking, if all deposits and bank notes were presented for redemption in a single day, the bank would be unable to honor its pledge of redemption. Indeed, the bank in Table 1.6 is obligated to redeem ''paper'' for $500 in gold but has only $100 in gold in the vault. If this happened, the bank would not be bankrupt in the sense that it had a negative net worth. Instead, it would be illiquid—unable to honor its obligations.

Note the difference between illiquidity and bankruptcy. Illiquidity is a situation in which a bank cannot redeem its deposits on demand. In bankruptcy, the bank's assets—the value of its reserves and the loans it has made—are less than its liabilities—the value of the deposits it has accepted. A bank can be illiquid but not bankrupt, and a bank can be bankrupt without being illiquid.

If the bank were unable to honor its obligation to redeem demand deposits and bank notes ''on demand,'' it would have to stop redeeming deposits and notes. When a bank faces a long line of depositors and note holders demanding redemption, we say that a ''run on the bank'' has occurred. Under a fractional reserve banking system, such an event is very dangerous even to otherwise healthy banks, because no bank in such a system can actually honor all its obligations to pay on demand if they are all redeemed at the same time.

The U.S. banking system today is in fact a variation of the fractional reserve banking system just described. Modern banks issue loans and hold checkable deposits (demand deposits) that far exceed their actual reserves. Figure 1.1 compares the level of reserves financial institutions hold and the level of checkable deposits depositors could withdraw on demand. The total reserves in January 1993 were $56.01 billion, which is considerably less than the $738.8 billion in checkable deposits.

In later chapters, we will say much more about fractional reserve banking, money creation by banks, and government regulation of fractional reserve banks. Now you should have a basic understanding of how banks evolved from depository institutions into fractional reserve banks and how fractional reserve banking increases the amount of money used as a medium of exchange.

Banks as Financial Intermediaries

Financial markets link savers and borrowers. This link is accomplished through either direct finance or indirect finance. **Direct finance** occurs when

As of January 1993, $738.8 billion in checkable deposits were on account at U.S. financial institutions. However, these banks and savings and loans kept only $56.01 billion of the deposits as reserves against withdrawals and loaned out the remainder. Of the $56.01 billion in total reserves, $54.75 billion was required by law.

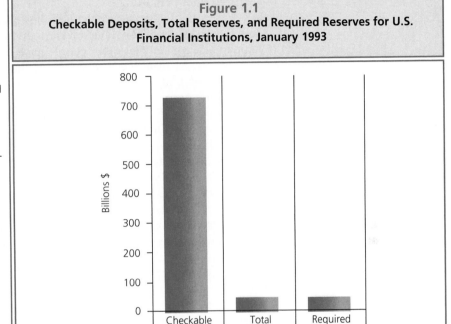

Figure 1.1
Checkable Deposits, Total Reserves, and Required Reserves for U.S. Financial Institutions, January 1993

SOURCE: Board of Governors of the Federal Reserve System, *Federal Reserve Bulletin,* various issues and Citibase electronic database.

savers lend funds directly to borrowers. For example, if you ask a classmate to loan you money to buy a new car and she agrees, you are engaging in direct finance. No third party matched you (the borrower) with your classmate (the lender). In fact, however, direct finance most often involves the assistance of a third party, such as a broker, who brings buyer and seller together. When IBM issues new bonds, it uses the services of various specialists in the financial markets. The exact procedure need not concern us here; simply note that the ultimate buyers of the IBM bonds will usually engage the services of a broker to arrange the sale. This is one way financial markets facilitate direct finance.

In contrast, **indirect finance** involves a particular type of middleman—a third party who stands between the borrower and the lender. This middleman is called a **financial intermediary,** and his or her role is to accumulate funds from various savers and lend those funds to borrowers. Banks are financial intermediaries because they accept deposits and lend those funds to borrowers. Credit unions and savings and loan associations also are financial intermediaries. Less obviously, life insurance companies and pensions accumulate savings and lend those funds to borrowers, thus performing the role of financial intermediaries.

In all these cases, the financial intermediary borrows funds from savers and lends them to borrowers. If you obtain a car loan from a bank, the bank is actually loaning you money that other people have on deposit there. The depositors receive interest from the bank; you pay the bank interest on the loan. The bank is in the middle, earning a profit on the difference (margin) between the rate you pay for the loan and the rate it pays depositors.

There is an important distinction between the function of a financial intermediary and that of a broker. A broker brings together a buyer and a seller of a financial instrument such as a bond, but does not personally issue a bond or otherwise lend to the borrower; instead, the broker facilitates the transaction without personally creating a financial instrument. In contrast, a financial intermediary accumulates savers' funds and lends them to borrowers by making a loan from itself. Thus, a bank makes a loan to a borrower instead of merely introducing the borrower to one or more depositors and brokering a loan between the two.

Thus, banks and other financial intermediaries are a special kind of middleman. They profit on the difference between the interest rate they pay on deposits and the interest rate they collect on loans. Their function is to repackage depositors' savings into loans to borrowers in the same way a retailer might purchase produce in bulk from produce dealers and repackage it for sale at the supermarket produce counter.

Figure 1.2 indicates the flow of funds between lenders and borrowers under direct and indirect finance. With direct finance, the final lender (here Ross Perot) provides funds directly to the borrower (AT&T). In this case, the role of financial markets is to facilitate the transaction, and Ross Perot will probably rely on a broker to carry it out. With indirect finance, Ross Perot would deposit money in a financial intermediary such as NationsBank, which in turn would make a loan to AT&T. Note that in this case, the financial intermediary is both a borrower (from depositors) and a lender.

Why don't depositors skip intermediaries and engage in direct finance? After all, since a bank charges a higher rate on a loan than it pays depositors, it would seem that a depositor could do better by making a direct loan to a borrower or a borrower could get a lower rate by borrowing directly from a saver. The answer to this question lies in the role intermediaries play in an economy. Notice that we could also ask this question about product markets: Why don't consumers buy directly from factories instead of from retailing outlets? The answer, of course, is that the benefits derived from using intermediaries exceed the extra cost of dealing with them.

What benefits do depositors (savers) and borrowers obtain from banks that make it worth the extra cost? First, banks match up savers who want to lend funds for short time periods with borrowers who want to borrow funds for long time periods. Another way to say this is that financial intermediaries are in a position to borrow short and lend long. Banks, for example, effec-

With direct finance, the final lender (Ross Perot) lends money directly to the final borrower (AT&T). Under indirect finance, the financial intermediary (NationsBank) borrows money from Ross Perot and then lends the funds to AT&T. The financial intermediary earns a profit on the difference between the rate at which it borrows and the rate at which it lends funds.

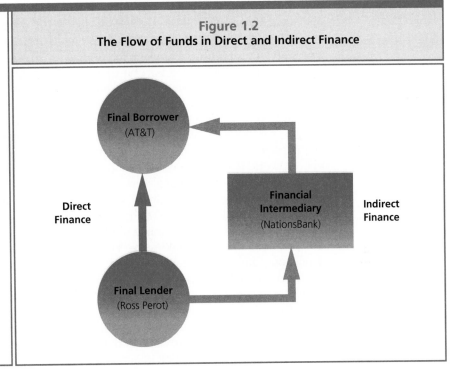

Figure 1.2
The Flow of Funds in Direct and Indirect Finance

tively borrow funds from savers when they accept savers' deposits. These deposits are often redeemable on demand, or at least on relatively short notice. Funds in checking accounts, for example, are redeemable on demand. In contrast, banks often loan funds for fixed terms, and these terms may vary from months (car loans) to years (home mortgages). The bank performs the valuable function of converting funds that savers are willing to lend for only short periods of time into funds that the bank itself is willing to lend to borrowers for longer periods. Of course, a bank could get in severe trouble if a depositor demanded redemption of her or his demand deposits while the deposited funds were loaned out in a 15-year loan. If unable to come up with the funds to redeem the demand deposits, the bank would be illiquid.

Banks are able to avoid illiquidity while borrowing short and lending long by using several business practices. First, a bank seeks a widely diversified set of depositors so that no one depositor is likely to cause a liquidity problem by withdrawing funds on short notice. Also, with a large number of depositors, the odds are that on most days the dollars added to some accounts and withdrawn from others will roughly cancel each other out, leaving total deposits fairly stable. Second, a bank keeps a small amount of deposits as reserves against sudden withdrawals and, more important, establishes several lines of credit with other banks and with government regulators (e.g., the Federal Reserve System). These lines of credit can be used to meet unexpectedly large withdrawals of deposits. Third, a bank makes long-term loans to only a small fraction of its loan clients. For example, banks make a very small proportion of housing loans relative to their total loan portfolios. Finally, a bank ''lends'' a portion of its funds by purchasing government bonds, which are relatively easy to convert into currency. In this way, a portion of the bank's loan portfolio is kept in highly liquid assets, which can be sold to obtain funds to meet unexpected withdrawals.

The second valuable function banks perform as intermediaries in financial markets is pooling many small deposits to make relatively large loans to borrowers. If you have only $1,000, you cannot make a $100,000 loan to someone seeking a mortgage. But with a bank serving as an intermediary, you and other individuals can deposit your small sums in a bank to earn interest. The bank, in turn, can pool the numerous small deposits into a sizable quantity of funds to make the $100,000 mortgage.

The third function banks serve is helping depositors reduce risk. Small depositors, and even relatively large depositors, often find it difficult to minimize the risk they face in lending funds directly to borrowers. If Natalie lends her entire life's savings to a single borrower who defaults, she loses everything. While this may be an unlikely occurrence, it is not impossible. An alternative for Natalie is to lend out her life savings in smaller amounts to a large number of borrowers so that if one borrower defaults, all is not lost. This alternative is called *diversifying:* The saver lends his or her funds to a diverse group of borrowers so that all is not lost if one or even several borrowers default. It is difficult to engage in diversification without a financial intermediary; borrowers typically want large sums of money, and small depositors usually cannot supply large sums to a diverse group of borrowers. Thus, banks provide a way for savers, especially small savers, to diversify. Each depositor bears only a small risk, since default by one or even several borrowers will have relatively little impact on the bank or its depositors.

Finally, financial intermediaries economize on transactions costs relative to those that would occur with direct finance. We have seen that transactions costs are the costs borne in making an exchange, such as the time and legal costs associated with a mortgage contract. One major transactions cost in making loans is the cost of checking the creditworthiness of a potential borrower. If individual savers attempt to diversify without using a financial intermediary such as a bank, each will make small-denomination loans to a number of borrowers. In so doing, each saver will want to personally verify the creditworthiness of the borrower, and a duplication of effort will result. For example, suppose a borrower wants to borrow $10,000 from each of 10 individual savers. Each saver will want to check the borrower's creditworthiness. Thus, 10 separate credit checks will be done before the borrower obtains $100,000 in loans. In contrast, a bank can borrow $10,000 from each of the 10 savers, pool their funds, and make a single $100,000 loan to the borrower. This will require only a single credit check, saving the time and effort involved in the nine extra credit checks that would be necessary under direct finance.

Another transactions cost associated with lending is the cost of monitoring the borrower. This involves ensuring that payments are current and, more important, that the borrower stays in relatively good financial health. Again, 10 savers engaged in direct finance would each have to bear these costs, while a bank that pooled these 10 savers' funds would have to bear these costs only once. Moreover, banks specialize in making loans, and this specialization leads to greater knowledge and efficiency in conducting credit checks and monitoring loans. Obviously the average individual saver cannot perform these tasks as efficiently as a bank can.

Summary
Exercise 1.5

How did bank loans evolve?

Answer: As society began using commodity money as a medium of exchange, a need for a safe place to deposit money developed. Early banks were depositories in which individuals paid a fee for the privilege of depositing commodity money such as gold. Due to the transactions costs associated with having to go to the bank to obtain gold to use in transactions, demand deposits (checking accounts) and bank notes emerged. As these forms of "paper money" became widely accepted as the medium of exchange, banks recognized they had much more gold in their vaults than they needed to honor demands for gold by depositors. Consequently, they began loaning out a fraction of their deposits to earn additional profits in the form of interest payments. Today, banks function as middlemen, or intermediaries, in financial markets by (1) borrowing short and lending long, (2) pooling small deposits into large loans, (3) diversifying risk, and (4) economizing on transactions costs relative to engaging in direct finance.

CONCLUSION

This chapter examined what money and banks are and the economic reasons for their existence. *Money* is not synonymous with *income* or *wealth;* rather, it is anything that is widely and generally accepted as the medium of exchange. Money is the most liquid of all types of assets; that is, it can easily be converted into other assets or commodities. In addition to serving as a medium of exchange, money serves as a unit of account, a store of value, and a standard of deferred payment.

While various types of money have been used as a medium of exchange in the history of humankind, societies learned very quickly that money should consist of something durable, divisible, portable, and easily recognizable in value. The first type of money civilization used was full bodied commodity money—a commodity with nonmonetary value that circulated as the medium of exchange. Representative full-bodied money (paper money that is "backed" by some commodity) was a predecessor to the current fiat money (unbacked paper money) used today. Individuals accept fiat money for payment only because they believe other individuals and businesses will in turn accept it from them as payment for goods and services.

The emergence of money as a medium of exchange led to the need for banks as depositories. Demand deposits (checks) and bank notes developed out of a need to reduce the transactions costs of having to be physically present to withdraw money from depositories before making purchases. This development led to fractional reserve banking, wherein banks hold a fraction of deposits in reserve and make loans to depositors in need of funds. Fractional reserve banking exists in the United States today and provides a means by which banks actually "create money" and function as financial intermediaries.

KEY TERMS

money

medium of exchange

Federal Reserve note

currency

liquidity

barter

double coincidence of wants

transactions cost

unit of account

store of value

standard of deferred payment

commodity money

full-bodied money

representative full-bodied money

gold certificate

fiat money

specie

demand deposit

bank note

fractional reserve banking

direct finance

indirect finance

financial intermediary

QUESTIONS AND PROBLEMS

1. Look up the definition of *money* in your dictionary. Does this definition agree with an economist's definition? Why or why not?

2. On the island of Maka, the government has been unable to control the counterfeiting of its bills. Consequently, individuals and merchants rely almost exclusively on barter as a means of exchange. Why do you think counterfeiting would lead individuals to shun money and turn to barter?

3. Discuss the advantages and disadvantages of using the following commodities as money.

   (a). Bricks
   (b). Wine
   (c). Corn
   (d). Pearls
   (e). Platinum
   (f). Uranium

4. Suppose you live in Llano, Texas, a small town with a population of 2,500. Rank the following assets from most liquid to least liquid, and explain why you ranked them as you did.

   (a). One hundred shares of IBM stock
   (b). A house in Llano, Texas
   (c). A used computer
   (d). A used car
   (e). One British pound (the medium of exchange in Britain)
   (f). A roll of quarters

5. How would your answers to Problem 4 change if you lived in London, England?

6. In the early days of banking, goldsmiths promised to pay a specified quantity of gold to anyone presenting a bank note or an endorsed check at their place of business. What does your bank promise to pay you if you present the following?

   (a). An endorsed check
   (b). A Federal Reserve note

7. What would happen to your bank if all depositors showed up at 9:00 A.M. next Thursday and demanded payment for their deposits?

8. Your brother-in-law wants to borrow $1,000. Relationship aside, why might you prefer to deposit the $1,000 in a savings and loan and have your brother-in-law borrow the funds there instead of loaning him the $1,000 directly?

9. In the example of fractional reserve banking presented in the chapter, the bank decided to keep only 20 percent of its liabilities in reserve. What would the final T-account look like if the bank decided to keep only 10 percent of its liabilities in reserve?

10. Explain why money reduces transactions costs. Are there any other advantages to a monetary economy? Are there any disadvantages?

11. Explain how the banking system reduces transactions costs. Are there any other advantages to the banking system? Are there any disadvantages?

12. What is the difference between full-bodied money and representative full-bodied money? Between representative full-bodied money and fiat money?

13. Is one dollar or one dollar's worth of gold more valuable? Explain carefully.

14. "U.S. dollars are backed by the gold in Fort Knox, Kentucky." Is this statement true or false? Explain.

15. Can something serve as money without serving as the unit of account? (Hint: How many checks does it take to buy a shirt? A suit? A house?)

SELECTIONS FOR FURTHER READING

Aschheim, J., and G. S. Tavlas. "Doctrinal Foundations of Monetary Economics: Review Essay." *Journal of Monetary Economics,* 28 (December 1991), 501–510.

Buehler, J. E. "The Specific Role of Interest in Financial and Economic Analysis under Inflation: Discussion." *American Journal of Agricultural Economics,* 67 (May 1985), 396–397.

Davis, S. I. *Managing Change in the Excellent Banks.* New York: St. Martin's Press, 1989, xi, 163.

Fenstermaker, J. V., and J. E. Filer. "The U.S. Embargo Act of 1807: Its Impact on New England Money, Banking, and Economic Activity." *Economic Inquiry,* 28 (January 1990), 163–184.

Ng, K. "Free Banking Laws and Barriers to Entry in Banking, 1838–60." *Journal of Economic History,* 48 (December 1988), 877–889.

Palasek, K. "The Case for a Laissez-Faire Monetary System." *Cato Journal,* 9 (Fall 1989), 399–403.

Rockoff, H. "The 'Wizard of Oz' as a Monetary Allegory." *Journal of Political Economy,* 98 (August 1990), 739–760.

Towey, R. E. "Money Creation and the Theory of the Banking Firm." *Journal of Finance,* 29 (March 1974), 57–72.

Webb, S. C. "The Deficient Treatment of Money in Basic Undergraduate Texts: A Comment." *Journal of Money, Credit, and Banking,* 4 (February 1972), 109–112.

Wells, D. R., and L. S. Scruggs. "Historical Insights into the Deregulation of Money and Banking." *Cato Journal,* 5 (Winter 1986), 899–910.

White, L. H., and G. A. Selgin. "The Evolution of a Free Banking System." *Competition and Currency: Essays on Free Banking and Money.* Cato Institute Book. New York and London: New York University Press, 1989, 218–242.

Wicker, E. "A Reconsideration of the Causes of the Banking Panic of 1930." *Journal of Economic History,* 40 (September 1980), 571–583.

Wulwick, N. "The Radcliffe Central Bankers." *Journal of Economic Studies,* 14 (1987), 36–50.

2

Financial Markets, Financial Institutions and Instruments, and Money

*I*n Chapter 1, we saw how and why money and banking evolved and looked briefly at the roles banks play as intermediaries in financial markets. In this chapter, we turn to the modern world of financial markets and institutions. Understanding this world helps on a practical level, such as when saving money for a new car, a house, or even retirement. More important, it is fundamental to understanding the workings of the economy and the concepts covered in the remainder of this book.

We distinguish among three basic types of markets: debt, equity, and financial service markets. We describe the financial institutions that participate in these markets and the different kinds of assets these institutions hold. We examine both commercial banks and nonbank depository institutions such as savings and loan associations, as well as nondepository institutions such as insurance companies and pension funds. As we will see, recent deregulation of the banking industry has blurred the distinction between banks and nonbank institutions. Finally, we look at the official definitions of the money supply used by the U.S. Federal Reserve System. As you read this chapter, keep in mind the functions and properties of money discussed in Chapter 1.

FINANCIAL MARKETS

Economists define a *market* as an institution or arrangement that facilitates the purchase and sale of goods, services, and other things. A **financial market** is an institution or arrangement that facilitates the exchange of financial assets, including deposits and loans, corporate stocks and bonds, government bonds, and more exotic instruments such as options and futures contracts. This market may or may not have a precise physical location. For instance, the New York Stock Exchange (NYSE) is physically located on

Wall Street in New York City, whereas the over-the-counter (OTC) market for stocks, called the National Association of Securities Dealers (NASD), consists of brokers disbursed throughout the country who track prices via computer and telecommunication lines. NASD is best known for the newspaper quotes of stock prices it generates, called NASDAQ (National Association of Securities Dealers Automatic Quotation System).

There are several ways to classify financial markets. One obvious method is to classify markets by the type of asset traded, for example, short-term or long-term assets. (We will discuss these two classifications when we look at financial instruments later in this chapter.) The broadest way to categorize markets is to distinguish between primary and secondary markets. In a **primary market,** new issues of financial assets are bought and sold. For instance, if AT&T issues a new share of stock, (stock that has never been owned by an investor before) the stock is sold in the primary market for new issues of corporate stock. In contrast, existing financial assets are bought and sold in a **secondary market.** You already know of a famous secondary market for stocks: the New York Stock Exchange. If you wish to sell a share of your AT&T stock, you sell it in the secondary market. The person who buys your share of stock will purchase it in the secondary market.

The primary market for U.S. savings bonds is very widespread. These instruments can be purchased from commercial banks nationwide, as well as through payroll deductions. There is no central clearinghouse for such purchases, nor is there a secondary market for U.S. savings bonds. You can redeem the bonds, but you cannot sell them to a third party.

In contrast, U.S. Treasury bonds, which the U.S. government issues to finance the federal debt, have active primary and secondary markets. The primary market for these bonds is an auction held by the U.S. Treasury at which banks, securities dealers, and other institutional investors bid for new issues. The secondary market for these bonds is an over-the-counter market, much like the NASD, that has no precise physical location.

The existence of a secondary market for a financial asset enhances the asset's liquidity. For example, suppose you purchase a share of IBM stock in the primary market but later decide to sell it for cash to use as a down payment on a house. Since IBM stock is actively traded in the secondary market, it is relatively easy to sell. You simply call a brokerage firm such as Merrill Lynch or Charles Schwab and tell the broker you wish to sell. The broker, in turn, locates a buyer and sells your stock for you. The entire process can be carried out in seconds.

Because a secondary market makes it easier for buyers and sellers to find each other, it lowers the transactions costs of buying or selling an asset. In the absence of a secondary market for a stock, you would have to personally locate someone willing to purchase the stock from you. Not only could this take considerable time; you would be unlikely to locate a buyer willing to pay the highest price for your stock. Moreover, if you thought it would be difficult to sell a financial asset such as IBM stock, you would be less likely to buy it in the first place; doing so would tie up your wealth in an illiquid asset that you could not easily convert into cash. A secondary market that allows trades between buyers and sellers of existing shares enhances the liquidity of corporate stock. This induces investors to own stock and makes it easier for firms to acquire funds in the primary stock market.

In addition to distinguishing between primary and secondary financial markets, we can classify financial markets according to the nature of the instruments traded. This classification consists of debt, equity, and financial service markets. A brief description of the nature and role of each type of financial market follows.

Debt Markets

The financial market most familiar to students and professors alike is the debt market. In the **debt market,** lenders provide funds to borrowers for some specified period of time. In return for the funds, the borrower agrees to pay the lender the original amount of the loan (called the *principal*), plus some specified amount of interest. (We will examine interest in more detail in Chapter 3.) Individuals use debt markets to borrow funds to finance purchases such as new cars and houses. Corporate borrowers use them to obtain working capital and new equipment. Federal, state, and local governments use debt markets to acquire funds to finance various public expenditures. New funds (the issue of a new bond or a new-car loan, for instance) occur in the primary debt market. When an individual or a financial institution buys or sells an existing loan—such as when Sallie Mae buys your student loan—the transaction takes place in the secondary debt market. Assets in the debt market are further classified as **short-term** if the underlying obligation when issued is one year or less, **intermediate-term** if the obligation when issued is between one and ten years, and **long-term** if the obligation is more than ten years in length.

Equity Markets

Ownership of tangible assets (such as houses or shares of stock) are bought and sold in an **equity market.** New houses and new issues of stock are sold in primary markets; existing houses and existing shares of stock are traded in secondary markets. An example of a secondary equity market for shares of stock is the American Stock Exchange.

Financial Service Markets

Individuals and firms use **financial service markets** to purchase services that enhance the workings of debt and equity markets. For instance, commercial banks provide depositors not only with interest on deposits but also with a host of services such as check processing, safety deposit boxes, or

ATM transactions. As we saw in Chapter 1, banks use funds on deposit to participate in the debt market (by issuing loans). But banks really do more than serve as an intermediary; they also provide "convenience," a valuable service that consumers are often willing to pay fees to enjoy. No secondary market exists for financial services, since people do not sell "used" financial services to third parties.

Another financial service is brokerage services. *Brokers* are intermediaries who compete for the right to help people buy or sell something of value. Real estate brokers help individuals buy or sell houses; stockbrokers help individuals buy or sell assets such as stocks and bonds. As intermediaries, brokers receive a fee for performing the service of matching buyers and sellers of assets. Dealers differ from brokers in that dealers actually buy and sell securities from their portfolio, and do not just match up buyers and sellers.

Finally, financial service markets provide individuals and firms with a means of insuring against various forms of loss, from loss of life to the loss of a valuable painting. These services too are performed for a fee; the proceeds are used not only to pay out insurance claims but also to purchase financial assets in debt and equity markets.

Summary
Exercise 2.1

Is the market for used cars a primary or a secondary market? How are financial brokers similar to car dealers? How do they differ?

Answer: The market for an existing or "used" asset is the secondary market. Thus, the used-car market is a secondary market. When cars are sold in the secondary market, General Motors, Ford, and Chrysler do not obtain funds. Of course, if you buy a used car from a dealer, the dealer will obtain funds. But a used-car dealer acts as an intermediary in the market, earning a profit on the margin between what the dealer paid an individual for the used car and what it sells the car for. Of course, the same is true when a financial asset such as a stock or bond sells on the secondary market. Note that if a used car is purchased by a car dealer, it is still a used car, and as such the car dealer provides a brokerage or intermediary service: buying the car from you to sell to another purchaser. The car itself is still a "used car," and the market for used cars remains a secondary market.

More generally, securities dealers and brokers, like car dealers, can deal in both primary and secondary markets at the same time. Thus, a stockbroker sometimes helps with the sale of a new issue of stock while also offering her or his services to investors wishing to buy or sell existing shares of stock in the secondary market. The main distinction between car dealers and securities brokers is that a car dealer actually purchases the used car and resells it later, whereas a broker never actually owns the stock but instead facilitates a trade between buyer and seller.

FINANCIAL INSTITUTIONS

Depository institutions (e.g., banks) and nondepository institutions (e.g., insurance companies) both serve financial markets. In this section, we look at the three basic markets in which these institutions participate, the services they offer and how they provide them, where they obtain funds, and the assets they hold.

Depository Institutions

Depository institutions accept deposits from individuals and firms and use these funds to participate in the debt market, making loans or purchasing other debt instruments such as Treasury bills. As we saw in Chapter 1, the deposit market is a special type of loan market in which depositors "loan" money to depository institutions, which in turn use the funds to purchase other financial assets. The major types of depository institution are commercial banks, savings and loan associations, mutual savings banks, and credit unions.

Commercial Banks.   **Commercial banks** are the largest and most important depository institutions. The roughly 12,000 commercial banks in the United States have the largest and most diverse collection of assets of all depository institutions. Their main source of funds is demand deposits (i.e., checking account deposits) and various types of savings deposits (including time deposits and certificates of deposit). As Figure 2.1 reveals, the major use of funds by commercial banks is making loans. In 1992, loans made up 61.5 percent of commercial banks' assets; of these, 24.7 percent were real estate loans and 36.8 percent were other loans such as loans to businesses and automobile loans. The remaining 38.5 percent of commercial banks' assets includes securities (primarily federal government bonds), vault cash, and deposits at Federal Reserve banks.

Savings and Loan Associations.   **Savings and loan associations (S&Ls)** were originally designed as mutual associations, (i.e., owned by depositors) to convert funds from savings accounts into mortgage loans. The purpose was to ensure a market for financing housing loans. Over the past 20 years a very active market for mortgages has developed, diminishing the need for regulations forcing S&Ls to concentrate on housing loans. Largely for this reason, during the 1980s government regulation of the types of assets savings and loans can hold was weakened, and today the distinction between S&Ls and commercial banks is minimal. However, Figure 2.2 reveals that as recently as 1992, nearly 74 percent of the assets held by S&Ls were mortgages. Thus, S&Ls continue to hold a less diversified set of assets than commercial banks do.

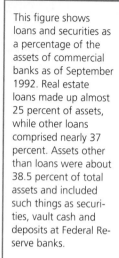

This figure shows loans and securities as a percentage of the assets of commercial banks as of September 1992. Real estate loans made up almost 25 percent of assets, while other loans comprised nearly 37 percent. Assets other than loans were about 38.5 percent of total assets and included such things as securities, vault cash and deposits at Federal Reserve banks.

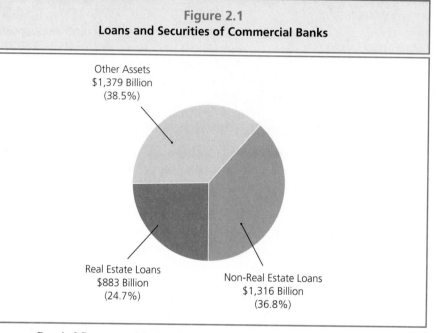

Figure 2.1
Loans and Securities of Commercial Banks

Other Assets
$1,379 Billion
(38.5%)

Real Estate Loans
$883 Billion
(24.7%)

Non-Real Estate Loans
$1,316 Billion
(36.8%)

SOURCE: Board of Governors of the Federal Reserve System, *Federal Reserve Bulletin,* January 1993, Table 1.25.

Mutual Savings Banks.   **Mutual savings banks** are much like savings and loans, but are owned cooperatively by members with a common interest, such as company employees, union members, or congregation members. Originally they accepted deposits and made mortgage loans. As with savings and loans, recent deregulation allows the approximately 500 mutual savings banks in the United States to issue checkable deposits and engage in financial activities roughly on par with other depository institutions.

Credit Unions.   **Credit unions** are organized as cooperative depository institutions, much like mutual savings banks. Depositors are credited with purchasing shares in the cooperative, which they own and operate. Like savings and loans, credit unions were originally restricted by law to accepting savings deposits and making consumer loans. Recent regulatory changes allow them to accept checkable deposits and make a broader array of loans.

Nondepository Institutions

In contrast to depository institutions, nondepository institutions do not accept checkable deposits. With one exception that will be noted shortly, you cannot simply write a ''check'' to withdraw funds from a nondepository institution.

Nondepository institutions serve various functions in financial markets, ranging from financial intermediation to selling insurance against risk. We discuss the principal types of nondepository institutions next.

Mutual Funds.   Mutual funds sell shares to investors, and invest the proceeds in a wide choice of assets. Owners of shares receive pro rata shares of the earnings from these assets, minus management and other fees assessed by the fund. Some mutual funds, called **money market mutual funds**, invest in short-term, safe assets such as U.S. Treasury bills and large bank certificates of deposit. Largely for historical reasons, money market mutual funds are not considered depository institutions even though shareholders are often allowed to write checks on their accounts. Unlike depository institutions, money market mutual funds do not promise that the price of a share will stay constant, but in fact, the price of each share tends not to fluctuate over time like prices of stock mutual funds do. Fund managers work to keep share prices constant, and owners of these "shares" receive a portion of the earnings derived from the assets bought with the money received for the shares. These funds enjoyed widespread popularity in the late 1970s and

This figure shows loans and securities of S&Ls insured by SAIF (Saving Association Insurance Fund) as of August 1992. Mortgage loans and mortgage-backed assets made up about 74 percent of assets, other loans about 6 percent, and other securities about 20 percent.

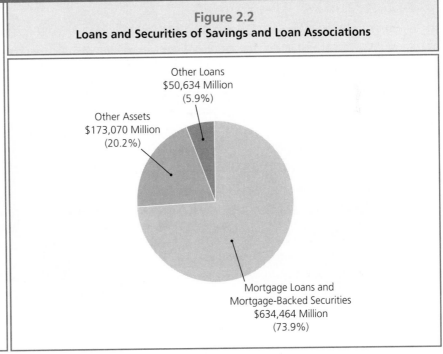

Figure 2.2
Loans and Securities of Savings and Loan Associations

Other Loans
$50,634 Million
(5.9%)

Other Assets
$173,070 Million
(20.2%)

Mortgage Loans and
Mortgage-Backed Securities
$634,464 Million
(73.9%)

SOURCE: Board of Governors of the Federal Reserve System, *Federal Reserve Bulletin,* January 1993, Table 1.37.

The Data Bank

Box 2.1

Changes in the Relative Size of Financial Institution Assets, 1976–1990

The accompanying figure shows the percentage of assets held by various classes of financial institutions in 1976 and 1990. In March 1976, total assets held by life insurance companies, money market mutual funds, commercial banks, and institutions insured by Federal Savings and Loan Insurance Corporation, or FSLIC (i.e., savings and loans), were $1,561 billion. Of this amount, commercial banks had the lion's share—almost 59 percent—while FSLIC-insured institutions and life insurance companies divided up most of the remainder—about 22 and 19

percent, respectively. Money market mutual funds had a paltry .2 percent of total assets.

Compare that to the situation in October 1990, not quite 15 years later. In that year total assets of these four types of institution totaled $4,281 billion, an increase of 174 percent. This translates into a yearly increase of 7.2 percent for 14½ years.

Note, however, that while total holdings grew, the distribution of these assets among the four types of institution also changed, some-

Continued on p. 39

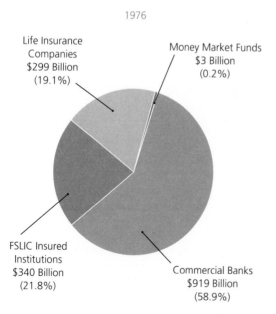

1976

Life Insurance Companies $299 Billion (19.1%)

Money Market Funds $3 Billion (0.2%)

FSLIC Insured Institutions $340 Billion (21.8%)

Commercial Banks $919 Billion (58.9%)

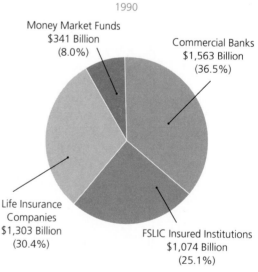

1990

Money Market Funds $341 Billion (8.0%)

Commercial Banks $1,563 Billion (36.5%)

Life Insurance Companies $1,303 Billion (30.4%)

FSLIC Insured Institutions $1,074 Billion (25.1%)

Continued from p. 38

times dramatically. For instance, by 1990 the share of assets held by commercial banks had fallen to 36.5 percent, while the share of assets held by the other three categories had expanded. FSLIC-insured institutions' share had expanded from 22 to 25 percent, life insurance companies' share from 19 to more than 30 percent, and money market mutual funds' share from 0.2 to 8 percent.

How can we explain these movements of funds among institutions? During the 1970s, two factors led depositors to seek alternatives to commercial banks. First, inflation rates were generally increasing. Second, checking accounts at commercial banks (demand deposit accounts) were prohibited from paying interest. The increased inflation rates were reflected in higher interest rates on financial instruments that were substitutes for deposits at banks. Depositors responded in two ways. First, money market mutual funds offered attractive interest rates and at least some checking privileges, and many depositors moved their deposits to these funds. Sec-

ond, savings and loan associations began offering *share draft accounts* (essentially interest-bearing checkable accounts), which attracted depositors away from commercial banks. It is interesting that even after the troubles the savings and loan industry experienced in the 1980s, the share of assets held by S&Ls increased relative to commercial banks.

Life insurance companies also gained market share due to the innovation of offering a broad range of alternative accounts that allowed savers to take advantage of high interest rates through life insurance policies. Another factor in the growth of life insurance assets was demographics. The baby boom generation was aging and entering the market for life insurance in large numbers. This change in demographic structure increased the market share of life insurance companies relative to other financial institutions.

Source: Board of Governors of the Federal Reserve System, *Federal Reserve Bulletin* and Citibase electronic database.

early 1980s, when they grew at a rate of 37 percent per year. Box 2.1 gives some reasons for this growth.

Insurance Companies. **Insurance companies** protect individuals against risk. Life insurance companies accept regular payments from individuals in exchange for contracted payments in the event of the insureds' death. By insuring a large pool of individuals, life insurance companies can consult actuarial tables and predict very accurately what percentage of the insured individuals will die each year. Because of this, life insurance companies hold long-term assets, including long-term bonds. They also hold substantial quantities of commercial real estate.

Figure 2.3 shows the disposition of assets of life insurance companies. Loans make up only about 24 percent of assets, and the majority, roughly 20 percent, are mortgage and other real estate loans. The bulk of life insurance company assets, around 76 percent, are not in loans. This is in sharp contrast to both commercial banks and savings and loans. Furthermore, the assets insurance companies hold are purchased with insurance premiums

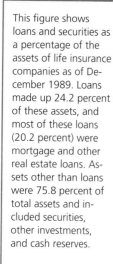

This figure shows loans and securities as a percentage of the assets of life insurance companies as of December 1989. Loans made up 24.2 percent of these assets, and most of these loans (20.2 percent) were mortgage and other real estate loans. Assets other than loans were 75.8 percent of total assets and included securities, other investments, and cash reserves.

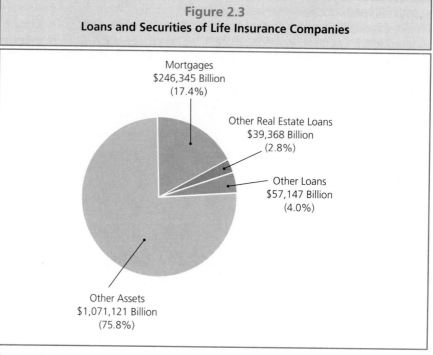

Figure 2.3
Loans and Securities of Life Insurance Companies

Mortgages
$246,345 Billion
(17.4%)

Other Real Estate Loans
$39,368 Billion
(2.8%)

Other Loans
$57,147 Billion
(4.0%)

Other Assets
$1,071,121 Billion
(75.8%)

SOURCE: Board of Governors of the Federal Reserve System, *Federal Reserve Bulletin,* various issues and Citibase electronic database.

rather than deposits. Thus, it is not possible to write a check against an insurance policy.

Other insurance companies, called *fire and casualty insurance companies,* insure against loss from fire, theft, and accident. If you own a car or a house, you probably have purchased this type of insurance. Insurance claims on these policies are somewhat less easy to predict. More important, the duration of the liability (e.g., the "life expectancy" of your car) is lower than for life insurance, so these companies usually invest in more liquid, shorter-term assets.

Pension Funds. Private and government (including federal, state, and local) **pension funds** provide retirement income to employees covered by the pension plan. Funds are collected by regular contributions from employees, usually via payroll deduction. Since the funds flowing in are not demand deposits, you cannot write a check against your balance in a pension fund. Like life insurance companies, these institutions can accurately predict payouts and hence can hold long-term assets. They hold portfolios consisting mostly of stocks and bonds. The returns on these assets are paid out to participating individuals when they reach retirement age.

Brokerage Firms.   As we already noted, **brokerage firms** serve the valuable function of linking buyers and sellers of financial assets. In this regard they function as intermediaries, earning a fee for each transaction they create. Unlike garden-variety nondepository institutions, however, modern brokerage firms such as Merrill Lynch and Charles Schwab also compete with depository institutions in the deposit market, where they attract depositors with money market mutual funds. Nonetheless, brokerage firms are not formally considered depository institutions because their main function is to serve as brokers in the secondary debt and equity markets.

Summary Exercise 2.2

Would you think commercial banks' or life insurance companies' assets are more liquid? Why?

Answer: Commercial banks are depository institutions, whereas life insurance companies are not. A depositor at a commercial bank can withdraw funds on demand by writing a check, whereas the owner of a life insurance policy cannot write a check against the policy. For this reason, banks tend to hold more liquid assets than life insurance companies do.

FINANCIAL INSTRUMENTS

If you follow the financial news, you have heard of T-bills, commercial paper, and federal funds. In this section, we will see what these and other types of financial instruments are and how they are used to link borrowers and savers in financial markets. Our discussion will use a classification scheme that distinguishes between the market in which short-term financial instruments are traded (the money market) and the market for longer-term instruments (the capital market). We begin by introducing money market instruments, which are used in the market for short-term funds. We then look at capital market instruments, which link long-term borrowers and lenders.

Money Market Instruments

The most liquid, short-term debt obligations are traded in the **money market.** As we will see at the end of this chapter, the instruments traded in this market are included in one or more official definitions of the money stock. Figure 2.4 indicates the size of various money market instruments in 1976 and 1992 and also shows the relative growth in the various instruments over this period. For example, money market mutual funds increased from $2.4 billion in 1976 to more than $360 billion in 1992. In this section, we examine each money market instrument shown in Figure 2.4 in detail.

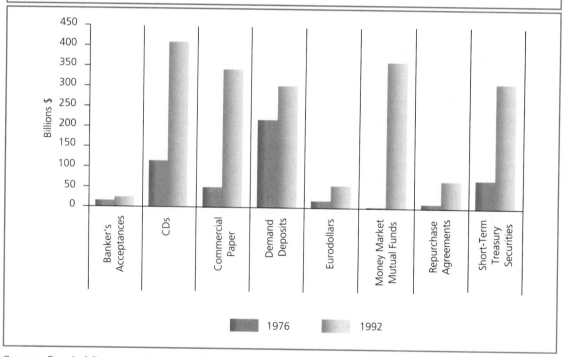

Figure 2.4
The Size of U.S. Liquid Asset Accounts

This figure shows the quantity of banker's acceptances, negotiable CDs, commercial paper, demand deposits, Eurodollar deposits, money market mutual funds, repurchase agreements, and short-term Treasury securities in 1976 and 1992. Notice that while these categories grew over that 16-year period, some categories grew slowly and others rapidly. Banker's acceptances grew modestly, from $11 billion to nearly $24 billion. In contrast, negotiable CDs grew from $119 billion to $416 billion, a 250 percent increase. Commercial paper showed even more rapid growth, from $50 billion to $339 billion—a 578 percent increase. Demand deposits increased at a snail's pace, from $220 billion to $300 billion, or 2 percent per year. The biggest gainer, however, was money market mutual funds, which increased from $2.4 billion to $360 billion, or 37 percent per year. This rapid increase in money market mutual funds was due to the movement of funds out of demand deposits and time deposits in the late 1970s and early 1980s, when these accounts paid no interest, and into the relatively high-interest-paying money market mutual funds.

SOURCE: Board of Governors of the Federal Reserve System, *Federal Reserve Bulletin,* various issues and Citibase electronic database.

Commercial Paper.   Commercial paper is a form of direct short-term finance by large, creditworthy companies. If a company such as AT&T needs immediate funds, it can sell commercial paper (a debt instrument) to another corporation or financial institution. **Commercial paper** is a promise to pay back a higher specified amount at a designated time in the immediate future—say, 30 days. By issuing commercial paper, a corporation avoids the process of applying for a loan and instead engages in direct finance. To engage in direct finance effectively, the issuing company must be large and creditworthy enough to find someone willing to accept its commercial paper, which is sold with the aid of brokers. As Figure 2.4 shows, the use of commercial paper grew from $50 billion in 1976 to $339 billion in 1992, an increase of about 12.7 percent per year. The growing use of commercial paper has increased the competitive pressure on banks, which are finding some of their potential loan customers turning to the commercial paper market.

Negotiable Bank Certificates of Deposit. **Certificates of deposit (CDs)** are debt instruments sold by banks and other depository institutions. A CD pays the depositor a specified amount of interest during the term of the certificate, plus the purchase price of the CD at maturity. For example, a $1,000, one-year CD paying 5 percent interest would pay $1,000 plus $50 interest at the end of one year (the term of the CD). Today negotiable CDs are sold in large denominations (over $100,000) and can be resold in the secondary market. This makes negotiable CDs highly liquid. The original purchaser need not hold the CD to maturity or pay "a substantial penalty for early withdrawal" if he or she needs to liquidate the CD. Instead, the person can sell the CD in the secondary market at a price that will depend on the market interest rate in effect when it is sold. As Figure 2.4 shows, the use of CDs grew from $119 billion in 1976 to $416 billion in 1992.

Treasury Bills. U.S. **Treasury bills,** or **T-bills,** are short-term debt instruments used by the federal government to obtain funds. They are issued in 3-, 6-, and 12-month maturities. These instruments do not pay regular interest payments, but instead are sold at a discount. This means they are sold for an amount that is less than what the government promises to pay at maturity, and the difference between the purchase price and the face value is the return from buying the T-bill. For instance, if you purchased a one-year Treasury bill in July 1994 for $9,766, in July 1995 (when it matures) the government would pay you $10,000.

There is a very active secondary market for U.S. Treasury bills. If you purchased the above Treasury bill but decided to liquidate it for cash before maturity, a simple phone call to a broker would allow you to sell it to another investor. Furthermore, the likelihood that the U.S. government will default on its obligation (not pay) is very low. These two factors make U.S. Treasury bills one of the most liquid of all financial instruments.

It is important to distinguish Treasury bills from other U.S. government securities such as Treasury bonds. T-bills mature in less than 1 year, T-notes mature in 1 to 10 years, and T-bonds mature in more than 10 years. One other practical difference exists among bills, notes, and bonds. U.S. Treasury bills, unlike T-notes and T-bonds, pay no explicit interest. Instead, interest is earned implicitly, that is, based on the difference between the purchase price and the face value. For example, some Treasury bills have a $10,000 face value, and this is the amount the U.S. government promises to pay you when the bill matures. You would pay less than the face value to purchase this T-bill, perhaps $9,500. The difference between the price you pay and the face value, $500, is the implicit interest you earn from lending the government your money. Unlike with other bonds, this interest is not paid monthly or quarterly but instead is received at maturity. Hence these Treasury bills are called *zero coupon instruments*. As Figure 2.4 indicates, Treasury bills and other short-term Treasury securities increased substantially in volume over the 1976–1992 period, from $73 billion to $317 billion.

Repurchase Agreements.   A **repurchase agreement** (or simply **repo**) is an agreement by two parties in which the borrower sells and agrees to buy back a financial instrument such as a government bond, note, or T-bill. Suppose a bank needs short-term cash today. The bank can sell some Treasury bills to a firm such as IBM with the agreement that the bank will repurchase the T-bills in 30 days at a higher price. In effect, this repurchase agreement is a short-term loan in which the Treasury bills serve as collateral. As Figure 2.4 shows, repurchase agreements accounted for $71 billion of liquid assets in the United States in 1992.

Eurodollars.   **Eurodollars** are U.S. dollars deposited in banks located in other countries. Foreign banks and offshore branches of U.S. banks hold dollar deposits to service firms engaged in international trade, as well as for other purposes. U.S. banks sometimes borrow Eurodollars when they need short-term funds. The growth of the Eurodollar market in the 1970s was spurred by the relative lack of regulations on these funds, including the absence of regulations requiring banks to hold reserves against Eurodollar loans. Figure 2.4 reveals that Eurodollars increased from $14 billion in 1976 to $56 billion in 1992.

Banker's Acceptances.   A **banker's acceptance** is a letter of credit (a bank's promise to pay on a specific date) that has been stamped as "accepted" (guaranteed) by another bank. You might think of a banker's acceptance as analogous to a post-dated "check" or bank draft. If the party issuing the check has insufficient funds in the account to cover the draft when it is payable, the bank that stamped the draft is obligated to pay the amount of the "check" to the party who holds it. Obviously a banker's acceptance is more valuable as a medium of exchange than a standard check, since a bank guarantees that the banker's acceptance will be honored. The party issuing a banker's acceptance pays a fee to the bank for its guarantee.

Banker's acceptances are particularly valuable in international transactions, since it is extremely costly for a firm located in, say, France to recover a bad check from a party located in Egypt. There is a relatively small secondary market for banker's acceptances, which essentially operates as a scaled-down version of the market for Treasury bills. Figure 2.4 shows that banker's acceptances accounted for only $23 billion of the outstanding money market instruments in 1992.

Federal Funds.   Suppose it is 2:50 P.M. and a bank needs $10 million by 3:00 P.M. to meet the reserve requirements set by the Federal Reserve. Obviously it is too late to attract additional deposits, and the bank must find a quick way to acquire the funds. One way the bank can obtain such funds on short notice is to acquire federal funds. **Federal funds** are simply short-term (usually overnight) loans between banks. The funds are loaned at an interest rate known as the *federal funds rate.* They are called *federal funds* because they are held in deposit at the Federal Reserve rather than because they are loaned by the federal government. In fact, the transfer of federal funds is merely a bookkeeping transfer from the ledger of a bank with an excess of reserves to the ledger of a bank with deficient reserves. Box 2.2 gives a sampling of money market interest rates as published in the *Wall Street Journal.*

Capital Market Instruments

In contrast to money market instruments, which have maturities of one year or less, **capital market instruments** have maturities of more than one year. The principal capital market instruments are described next.

Corporate Stock.   A share of **corporate stock** is an equity instrument that represents ownership of a share of the assets and earnings of a corporation. When a corporation like AT&T needs long-term funds, it can sell shares of stock to individuals or other investors. AT&T uses the funds received to purchase assets and run the company; in return, the shareholder owns a share of these assets and the earnings they generate for AT&T. The profits earned by a corporation and paid to shareholders are known as *dividends.* Unlike interest payments, dividends can vary with the health of the company.

It is important to emphasize that the only time a corporation receives money from stock is the time at which it issues the stock—the primary market transaction. When the company decides to issue stock, it offers the shares to underwriters, investment banks that guarantee the firm a certain price for the issue. Then the investment banker (or bankers, if the issue is large) sells the stock to individual investors, with the assistance of brokers, at what they hope is a higher price than the guaranteed price. Effectively the underwriters provide insurance to the company issuing the new stock and bear the risk associated with the low price investors pay for the stock.

Once a new issue is in the hands of individual investors, the stock can be sold and purchased by another investor (with the aid of a broker) in a

Inside Money

*Money Market Rates from
the* Wall Street Journal

Box 2.2

The *Wall Street Journal* publishes a variety of money market interest rates each day. The first item listed is usually the prime interest rate—the interest rate banks charge on loans to credit worthy corporate borrowers. Market analysts often use changes in the prime interest rate as a barometer of other interest rates.

Source: The *Wall Street Journal,* April 12, 1993. Reprinted by permission of the *Wall Street Journal,* © 1993 Dow Jones & Company, Inc. All Rights Reserved Worldwide.

MONEY RATES

Monday, April 12, 1993

The key U.S. and foreign annual interest rates below are a guide to general levels but don't always represent actual transactions.

PRIME RATE: 6%. The base rate on corporate loans posted by at least 75% of the nation's 30 largest banks.

FEDERAL FUNDS: 3⅛% high, 3% low, 3% near closing bid, 3 1/16% offered. Reserves traded among commercial banks for overnight use in amounts of $1 million or more. Source: Prebon Yamane (U.S.A.) Inc.

DISCOUNT RATE: 3%. The charge on loans to depository institutions by the Federal Reserve Banks.

CALL MONEY: 5%. The charge on loans to brokers on stock exchange collateral. Source: Telerate Systems Inc.

COMMERCIAL PAPER placed directly by General Electric Capital Corp.: 3.07% 30 to 119 days; 3.08% 120 to 149 days; 3.10% 150 to 179 days; 3.13% 180 to 239 days; 3.15% 240 to 270 days.

COMMERCIAL PAPER: High-grade unsecured notes sold through dealers by major corporations: 3.15% 30 days; 3.15% 60 days; 3.16% 90 days.

CERTIFICATES OF DEPOSIT: 2.61% one month; 2.64% two months; 2.68% three months; 2.78% six months; 2.94% one year. Average of top rates paid by major New York banks on primary new issues of negotiable C.D.s, usually on amounts of $1 million and more. The minimum unit is $100,000. Typical rates in the secondary market: 3.02% one month; 3.04% three months; 3.12% six months.

BANKERS ACCEPTANCES: 3% 30 days; 3% 60 days; 3% 90 days; 3.02% 120 days; 3.04% 150 days; 3.05% 180 days. Negotiable, bank-backed business credit instruments typically financing an import order.

FOREIGN PRIME RATES: Canada 6%; Germany 9%; Japan 4%; Switzerland 7.50%; Britain 6%. These rate indications aren't directly comparable; lending practices vary widely by location.

TREASURY BILLS: Results of the Monday, April 12, 1993, auction of short-term U.S. government bills, sold at a discount from face value in units of $10,000 to $1 million: 2.89%, 13 weeks; 3%, 26 weeks.

FEDERAL HOME LOAN MORTGAGE CORP. (Freddie Mac): Posted yields on 30-year mortgage commitments. Delivery within 30 days 7.07%, 60 days 7.18%, standard conventional fixed-rate mortgages; 4.125%, 2% rate capped one-year adjustable rate mortgages. Source: Telerate Systems Inc.

FEDERAL NATIONAL MORTGAGE ASSOCIATION (Fannie Mae): Posted yields on 30 year mortgage commitments (priced at par) for delivery within 30 days 7.16%, 60 days 7.26%, standard conventional fixed rate-mortgages; 4.95%, 6/2 rate capped one-year adjustable rate mortgages. Source: Telerate Systems Inc.

MERRILL LYNCH READY ASSETS TRUST: 2.76%. Annualized average rate of return after expenses for the past 30 days; not a forecast of future returns.

secondary stock market such as the New York Stock Exchange or the American Stock Exchange. Notice that the funds transferred in these secondary markets pass between individual buyers and sellers of the stock rather than to the corporation. Individuals own the majority of stock in the United States, and pension funds, insurance companies, and mutual funds own the remainder.

Corporate Bonds.

A **corporate bond** is a debt instrument issued by a corporation that states the firm will make specified interest payments (typically twice each year) and a principal amount or "face value" (usually $1,000) at maturity (say, 30 years). The original purchaser of a bond buys this promise from the firm for an up-front amount, known as the *price* of the bond. Unlike stockholders, bondholders own no share of the profits; rather, they are entitled only to the interest payments and the face value due on maturity. Obviously the firm's "promise" is valuable to the purchaser of the bond only if the firm does not go bankrupt. For this reason, only corporations with strong credit ratings tend to issue bonds. If a company fails to meet its payment obligations, it is said to be *in default*.

Corporate bonds, like corporate stock, provide funds to the issuing firm when sold in the primary market. Like stocks, new bond issues are underwritten by investment banks, which sell the bonds to individual investors. When bonds are bought and sold in the secondary bond market (for example, the New York Bond Exchange), money changes hands among individual investors, and no funds flow to the corporation that issued the bond. Box 2.3 describes the most common types of corporate bonds.

Mortgages.

A **mortgage** is a debt instrument used to finance the purchase of a home or other form of real estate when the underlying real estate serves as collateral for the loan. If the borrower defaults, the lender receives title to the real estate as payment of the debt. Several terms common to mortgage market transactions are useful not only to students of money and banking but to anyone who plans to use a mortgage to finance a house.

The two major types of mortgage instruments today are fixed-rate and adjustable-rate mortgages. Each type of mortgage specifies a term (the length of the mortgage), a down payment (usually expressed as the fraction of the house value the buyer must finance personally), and points (the fraction of the loan value that must be paid up front as prepaid interest). A *fixed-rate mortgage* specifies an interest rate that is fixed during the term of the loan, whereas the rate on an adjustable-rate mortgage (ARM) can change (usually every one or three years). An adjustable-rate mortgage also stipulates a *margin* that reflects the premium above some index of interest rates (usually one-year U.S. Treasury bills) that will be used to adjust the interest rate at specified times during the term. An adjustable-rate mortgage also stipulates a *cap*, which is the maximum amount by which the rate can change at any adjustment point, and a *ceiling* and *floor*, or the maximum and minimum interest rate that will be charged during the life of the mortgage.

To illustrate these two mortgage instruments, suppose you wish to finance a $100,000 house. A 30-year fixed-rate mortgage at an interest rate

Inside Money

Box 2.3

A Lexicography for Bonds

Bonds take many forms. Definitions for some of the most common bonds are provided below.

◆ A *debenture* is backed not by any specific collateral but by "the full faith and credit" of the selling firm or institution. For example, if you take out a mortgage loan, the property you purchase is the collateral; thus, this loan is not like a debenture. However, a signature loan—a loan that you promise to pay on your good word—is analogous to a debenture.

◆ A *subordinated bond* is a bond whose claim on the assets of the issuer—the borrower—is subordinate to a claim by another bond. The latter is called a *senior bond,* since its claim must be paid before the claim of the subordinated bond. If the issuing firm goes bankrupt, the senior claims are paid before the subordinated claims.

◆ A *junk bond* has a relatively high risk of default. Junk bonds are riskier than most other bonds and thus pay a higher interest rate.

◆ A *callable bond* can be called, or redeemed, by the issuer after a specified period. Borrowers prefer callable bonds if they are concerned that interest rates will fall in the future. If this occurs, the borrower can call the bond, paying off the principal early, and then issue new bonds at the lower interest rate. This allows the borrower to refinance his or her bond debt, just as a homeowner might refinance a mortgage when the interest rate falls.

◆ A *bearer bond* can be redeemed by whoever holds it. It is payable "to the bearer." Bearer bonds are similar to U.S. Federal Reserve notes—dollar bills—which are payable "to the bearer" on demand.

◆ A *registered bond* is registered to the owner; that is, the owner's name and address are known to the issuer, and the bond is redeemable by the owner.

of 9 percent, a 5 percent down payment, and 1 point works as follows. First, you are required to pay 5 percent of the purchase price of the house as a down payment, which amounts to $5,000. The rest, $95,000, is the amount to be financed at an interest rate of 9 percent, with monthly payments for 30 years (360 payments in all). In addition, you pay 1 point, or 1 percent of the loan amount, in the form of prepaid interest; in this case, 1 point amounts to $950. The bank loans you $95,000 in return for your promise to abide by the terms of the agreement.

In contrast, suppose you obtain a 30-year adjustable-rate mortgage for the $100,000 house. The down payment and points work just as in the case of a fixed-rate mortgage. However, the interest rate will vary during the course of the loan. Suppose the initial interest rate is 7 percent but varies each year, and the ARM stipulates a 3 percent margin, a 2-percent-per-year cap, a 13 percent lifetime ceiling, and a 0 percent floor. Next year, if the interest rate index is 4 percent, your interest rate for that year will remain at 7 percent (your interest rate next year is the index plus the margin, in this case 4% + 3% = 7%). But if the index increases to 5 percent, your interest rate next year will be 8 percent (the index plus the margin, in this case 5% + 3% = 8%). If the index drops to 3 percent, your interest rate will drop to 6 percent (3% + 3% = 6%). Notice, however, that if the index increases to 10 percent, your interest rate next year will increase to only 9 percent, since the cap on the amount by which your rate can change in any one year is 2 percent above the previous year's rate (which was 7 percent). Over the life of the mortgage, your rate will never rise above the ceiling rate of 13 percent or fall below 0 percent, regardless of how high or low the index is.

Various types of financial institutions issue mortgages, and there is an active secondary market in which mortgages are bought and sold. If you obtain a mortgage, it is unlikely that the original lender will hold the mortgage for the life of the loan; in fact, your mortgage can change hands numerous times during its life if the holders need to liquidate the loan for immediate cash.

Numerous government and private agencies participate in the mortgage market by insuring mortgages; that is, they guarantee that lenders will be paid back in the event borrowers default. The Federal Housing Administration (FHA) is a federal agency that insures mortgages for individuals, while the Veterans Administration (VA) insures mortgages for veterans. The Government National Mortgage Association (GNMA, or Ginnie Mae) is a government organization that buys mortgages issued to low-income borrowers and also guarantees mortgage-backed securities issued by private lenders. The two major private companies that buy mortgages are the Federal National Mortgage Association (FNMA, or Fannie Mae) and the Federal Home Loan Mortgage Corporation (FHLMC, or Freddie Mac). These two private companies operate with an implicit government guarantee and also guarantee mortgage-backed securities issued by private lenders.

Parts a and b of Figure 2.5 show the mortgage debt held by various institutions in 1971 and 1991, respectively. In 1971 the total mortgage debt held by these institutions was $524 billion, and of this amount the largest portion, 45 percent, was held by savings institutions. Commercial banks, life insurance companies, and other lenders each had about a 15 percent share of the mortgage market, and federal agencies held less than 9 percent of mortgage debt. The picture has changed dramatically in recent years. By 1991, the dollar value of mortgage debt held by all institutions had grown to $3,919.5 billion, an increase of 648 percent! This translates into a growth rate of about 10.6 percent per year for 21 years. In addition, notice the change in the distribution of mortgage debt holding. Savings institutions

Figure 2.5
Mortgage Debt Held by Institutions, 1971 and 1991

This figure shows the dollar value (in billions) of mortgage debt held by major financial institutions in 1971 and 1991. The institutions include savings institutions (savings and loan associations and mutual savings banks), commercial banks, life insurance companies, federal and related agencies (including the Government National Mortgage Association, the Federal Housing Administration, the Veterans Administration, the Farmers Home Administration, and U.S.-sponsored institutions such as the Federal National Mortgage Association, the Federal Home Loan Mortgage Corporation, Federal Land Banks, and mortgage pass-through securities issued or guaranteed by these agencies), and others (which includes individuals and private mortgage pools). In 1971 savings institutions were the major holders of mortgages, followed by commercial banks, life insurance companies, and other investors (including individuals). Federal agencies held less than 9 percent of this debt. By 1991 the largest holders of mortgages were federal agencies, which accounted for almost 37 percent of mortgage debt. Commercial banks were second with 22 percent, followed by savings institutions and other investors. Life insurance companies had slipped to less than 7 percent.

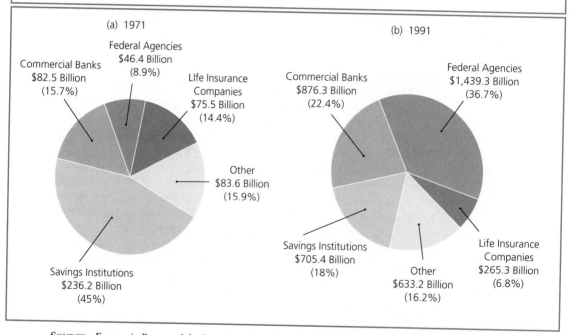

SOURCE: *Economic Report of the President*, (Washington D.C.: U.S. Government Printing Office, 1993).

held 45 percent of mortgage debt in 1971 but only 18 percent in 1991. The share held by life insurance companies fell from more than 14 percent to under 7 percent, while the share held by commercial banks increased from less than 16 percent to more than 22 percent. The big gainer was federal agencies, with an increase in share from less than 9 percent in 1971 to nearly

37 percent by 1991. Government or government-sponsored agencies now lend well over $1 of every $3 in mortgage loans, and the trend appears to be continuing.

Government Securities.

How does the federal government finance its debt, which is more than $3 trillion? To pay off the debt today, the government would have to send a bill to every adult and child in the United States for roughly $14,000. Since few families of four could afford to cough up the required $56,000, the government issues more government securities. **Government securities** are debt instruments issued by the U.S. Treasury and include such instruments as Treasury bonds. The funds obtained from the sale of these bonds are used to refinance the current federal debt as well as current federal deficits (the amount Congress spends this year in excess of tax revenues). We will look at government finance many times in this book, including Chapters 16 and 17, and Chapter 21 is devoted entirely to this topic. For now, we concentrate on the financial instruments. Because there is an active secondary market for government securities and the instruments are backed by the full faith and credit of the U.S. government, government securities are the most liquid of all capital market instruments.

Consumer and Commercial Loans.

Consumer loans are loans obtained by individuals for intermediate-term purchases such as car purchases, as well as merchandise bought with credit cards. **Commercial loans** are essentially credit lines issued to businesses. There is a less active secondary market for consumer and commercial loans, making them the least liquid of all capital market instruments. However, there has been a growing movement to securitize (convert to marketable securities) some consumer debt.

Figure 2.6 shows the major categories of consumer credit in 1992. Automobile loans constituted the largest component of consumer credit (about 35 percent), followed closely by revolving credit (about 33 percent), which includes personal bank lines of credit and credit issued by credit card companies.

Municipal Bonds.

State and local governments issue **municipal bonds** to obtain long-term funds for such things as highways and schools. The interest payments holders of these bonds receive are exempt from federal income tax (although some state and local governments do collect income tax on municipal bond interest earnings). This makes municipal bonds an attractive investment for lenders in high-income tax brackets. Box 2.4 compares municipals with other types of bonds.

For example, a person in a 36 percent tax bracket earning 10 percent taxable interest gets to keep only 6.4 percent after tax. A tax-free municipal bond paying 6.5 percent or more would be an attractive investment in this case. A secondary market exists for municipal bonds issued by large cities

This figure shows outstanding consumer credit in February 1992 broken down by various categories. These figures are for all nonmortgage loans to consumers from financial institutions. Automobile loans made up about 35 percent of consumer credit, followed by revolving credit (such as credit cards) with around 33 percent and other credit comprising about 30 percent. Mobile home credit lending made up less than 3 percent of consumer credit outstanding.

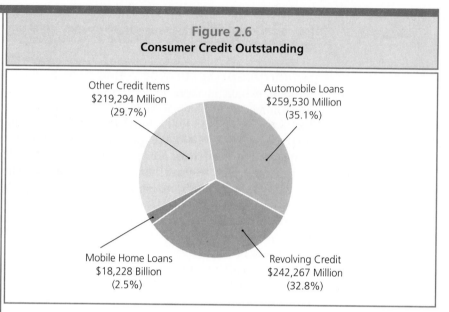

Figure 2.6
Consumer Credit Outstanding

Other Credit Items
$219,294 Million
(29.7%)

Automobile Loans
$259,530 Million
(35.1%)

Mobile Home Loans
$18,228 Billion
(2.5%)

Revolving Credit
$242,267 Million
(32.8%)

SOURCE: Board of Governors of the Federal Reserve System, *Federal Reserve Bulletin,* various issues and Citibase electronic database.

and states, but it is less active than the corporate and federal government bond markets. The bonds issued by smaller municipalities do not trade on a secondary market, which makes it very difficult for a holder to liquidate a bond prior to maturity.

International Financial Instruments

Tremendous growth has occurred in international financial instruments in recent years. For the most part, the financial instruments traded in international markets function like the instruments issued in the United States. The only difference is that the unit of account for these instruments is the local currency of the country in which they are issued. For instance, bonds issued in Britain are denominated in British pounds, while bonds issued in Germany are issued in German marks. Both are foreign bonds to U.S. residents. Eurobonds are an important exception. **Eurobonds** are bonds denominated in a currency other than that of the country of origin. For example, a bond issued in Germany but denominated (paying interest and its face value) in U.S. dollars is a Eurobond.

The recent surge in activity in world stock and bond markets has broadened the possibilities for investors and borrowers alike. A borrower no longer has to obtain funds from financial intermediaries in his or her own country; similarly, a lender need not lend funds only to borrowers in its own country.

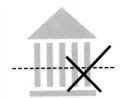

Inside Money

Box 2.4

Are All Bonds Created Equal?

Bonds differ with respect to their face amounts (the amounts paid when the bonds mature), maturities (the number of years before the face amounts are paid), and their tax status (whether interest income earned on the bonds is taxed by federal, state, or local government). Some bonds are callable; that is, the borrower may pay the face amount prior to maturity. In addition, bonds issued by different borrowers involve different risks. Corporate bonds are riskier than bonds issued by the federal government. Private rating companies, such as Moody's or Standard and Poor's, provide investors with a rating of the underlying risk associated with particular bonds. The table below summarizes features of some of the more common types of bonds.

Summary of Features of Various Bonds

	Corporate Bonds	U.S. Treasury Bonds and Notes	U.S. Treasury Bills	U.S. Agency Bonds (FNMA, GNMA, etc.)	Municipal Bonds
Face amount	$1,000	$1,000	$10,000	Varies	$5,000
Maturity	Varies	Bonds: over 10 years Notes: between 1 and 10 years	1 year or less	Varies	Varies
Tax status	Taxable	Exempt from state and local taxes	Exempt from state and local taxes	Some fully taxable, others exempt from state and local taxes	Exempt from federal taxes and sometimes from state and local taxes
Callable	Depends; often such provisions included	Not usually	No	No	Depends
Risk rated by private rating companies?	Yes	No; no risk of default	No; no risk of default	Sometimes	Yes

Because of time differences across the globe (when it is 4 A.M. in New York, it is 9 A.M. in London), international markets allow borrowers and lenders to make financial transactions at virtually any time of day. This fact has greatly enhanced the liquidity of financial assets that trade on exchanges around the world.

Summary
Exercise 2.3

For each of the following transactions, determine (1) the type of financial instrument and (2) whether the trade occurred through direct finance, a primary market transaction, or a secondary market transaction. (a) Exxon sells 1 million new shares of its stock through a broker. (b) Martha calls her broker and tells him to sell 100 shares of Exxon. (c) To increase its reserves, First City Bank contacts Second City Bank to borrow $1 million overnight. Second City Bank agrees, but the borrowed funds never leave the vaults of the Federal Reserve.

Answer: (a) The financial instrument is Exxon corporate stock and is sold in the primary market. Exxon receives cash when it issues stock in the primary market. (b) The financial instrument is Exxon corporate stock and is traded in the secondary market. Exxon receives no funds in this transaction. (c) The financial instrument is federal funds and was exchanged through direct finance.

OFFICIAL DEFINITIONS OF THE MONEY STOCK

In Chapter 1 we defined *money,* discussed various forms money has taken throughout history, and listed the desirable properties of money. Now that you have a basic understanding of various financial instruments, we focus on the definitions of the money stock used today by the Federal Reserve System. These measures of the **money stock**—the total amount of money in the economy—are the official definitions used by the U.S. government and its agencies.

Official definitions of the money stock are derived in two ways, which sometimes conflict. The first approach stresses the medium of exchange function of money and defines the money stock as only those assets that are reasonably regarded as media of exchange. The second approach stresses the liquidity of money and defines the money stock as the assets that are most liquid, or most easily converted into purchasing power. Besides currency and checkable deposits, the most liquid assets are those that are readily convertible into money. For assets that are not themselves the media of exchange, this requires a well-developed secondary market or some other guarantee of quick convertibity to money (such as the guarantee on savings accounts). A highly liquid marketable asset not only must have a secondary market; that market must handle a fairly high volume of transactions so that owners of the assets are fairly certain of their ability to sell them at the going market price. Moreover, the assets should be standardized so that the characteristics of assets offered for sale are readily ascertainable by purchasers not physically present at the market (i.e., those making purchases by phone).

The Federal Reserve System defines a series of **monetary aggregates**— ways of adding up the money in the economy into a measure of the money stock. The money aggregate based most closely on transactions considerations is known as *M1*. As we discussed in Box 1.1 of the previous chapter, M1 contains assets that serve as the media of exchange. Other monetary aggregates are M2, M3, and L. These are based on liquidity considerations and include various other assets considered to be more or less readily convertable into media of exchange.

M1

The monetary aggregate **M1** is defined as Currency + Demand deposits + Traveler's checks + Other checkable deposits. Notice that M1 contains only those assets that are readily accepted in exchange for goods and services. Thus, M1 is the most narrowly defined monetary aggregate.

M2

The monetary aggregate **M2** is defined as M1 + Savings deposits + Small time deposits + Money market deposit accounts + Money market mutual shares (not owned by institutions) + Overnight repurchase agreements + Overnight Eurodollars (specifically U.S. residents' holdings of overnight offshore deposits in U.S. branches). M2 includes all assets in M1 and adds savings and time deposits, money market deposit accounts, and money market mutual funds that can all be readily converted into purchasing power. Thus, while you cannot trade your savings passbook for a new pair of designer jeans, you can trade your savings account for currency or a checking account at your bank and then purchase the jeans. Similarly, a money market account has restrictions on the number and dollar amounts of checks you can write to withdraw funds, but you can deposit withdrawn funds in large dollar denominations into your checking account, from which you can purchase goods and services in any denomination. The last two items in the definition of M2—overnight repurchase agreements and Eurodollars—involve items not typically held by individuals, but they are included because they can be converted into M1 overnight.

M3

The monetary aggregate **M3** is defined as M2 + Large-denomination time deposits + Money market mutual shares (institutional) + Term repurchase agreements + Term Eurodollars. Thus, M3 includes everything in M2 and adds assets that are less liquid. For example, term repurchase agreements and term Eurodollars cannot be converted into M1 until the term, which is longer than overnight, expires. Likewise, large time deposits and institutional money market mutual shares are less easily converted into M1 than the assets included in M2 but not in M3.

L

The monetary aggregate **L** consists of M3 + Short-term Treasury securities + Commercial paper + U.S. savings bonds + Banker's acceptances. The broadest monetary aggregate defined here, L consists of M3 plus highly liquid assets that the Federal Reserve System does not consider money, such as U.S. savings bonds—hence the name L instead of M1, M2, or M3.

Recent attempts to provide alternative definitions of the money stock stress that there is no reason to simply add up the quantity of dollars held in various assets and name that sum M. Instead, some economists have argued that various assets should be weighted by their liquidity and then added together to obtain a monetary aggregate. While this approach to defining monetary aggregates is attractive on theoretical grounds, it has not led to a universally accepted alternative definition of the money stock.

Figure 2.7 shows trends in M1, M2, M3, and L for the period 1959 through early 1993. Notice that M1 is less than M2, which is less than M3 and L. This is, of course, due to the fact that the assets contained in M1 are also in M2, and so on for M3 and L. Furthermore, M2, M3, and L increased much more over this period than M1. The primary reason for this was the growing importance of financial instruments such as commercial paper, money market mutual funds, and the like, which are not included in M1.

A natural question is which of the official definitions of the Ms is best. The honest answer is that economists don't really know. Most economists think either M1 or M2 is the best definition of the four official Federal Reserve System definitions given here, but even here there is disagreement. In the 1970s, M1 appeared to be the best definition from a government policy standpoint; changes in M1 seemed to be linked to changes in unemployment or output. However, in the early 1980s this relationship broke down, and many economists looked to M2 as the more reliable policy variable. In the 1990s, this relationship too looks tenuous. In the next chapter, we will examine this issue in greater detail as we look at the relation between the money stock and what policymakers call the *price level* and *gross domestic product.*

Summary
Exercise 2.4

What is the primary difference in the monetary aggregates M1, M2, M3, and L?

Answer: M1 consists of the most liquid assets, M2 consists of M1 plus the next most liquid assets, M3 consists of M2 plus the next most liquid assets, and L consists of M3 plus the next most liquid assets. Thus, M1 is the narrowest of the four monetary aggregates (it does not include some assets that are included in M2, M3, and L). L is the broadest monetary aggregate (it includes everything in the other aggregates, plus some addi-

---

Figure 2.7
Alternative Monetary Aggregates for the U.S.

The Federal Reserve System measures the money stock in many ways. In the text, we define the monetary aggregates M1, M2, M3, and L. This figure plots these four aggregates from 1959 through the beginning of 1993. Notice how large M2, M3, and L are relative to M1. Notice too the general increasing trend in all four measures of the money stock. From 1960 to 1993, M1 averaged growth of 5.8 percent per year. That part of M2 not already included in M1 grew at 8.5 percent per year, while that part of M3 not included in M2 grew at 19 percent.

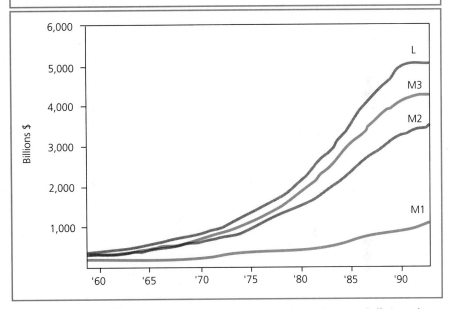

SOURCE: Board of Governors of the Federal Reserve System, *Federal Reserve Bulletin*, various issues and Citibase electronic database.

tional assets). Moreover, the assets included in M1 tend to serve as media of exchange, whereas many of the assets included in M2, M3, and L do not, although they can be easily converted into various forms of M1.

CONCLUSION

In this chapter, we overviewed money and banking in today's economy and saw how financial markets operate. We distinguished between the market for new issues of financial assets (the primary market) and the market for existing assets (the secondary market). Financial markets can be further distinguished by the characteristics of what is traded on the market (debt, equity, or financial services). The principal participants in financial markets are depository institutions (e.g., commercial banks and savings and loans) and nondepository institutions (e.g., insurance companies and pension funds). We noted that the recent deregulation of the banking industry has blurred the distinction between banks and other depository institutions, and today savings and loans, credit unions, and money market funds all perform many of the functions traditionally filled by commercial banks.

We also examined money market and capital market instruments. Money market instruments include assets that mature in one year or less, such as Treasury bills, commercial paper, and repurchase agreements. Capital market instruments have maturities exceeding one year and include mortgages, corporate stocks and bonds, and long-term government securities such as Treasury bonds.

Finally, we saw how the most liquid financial instruments are included in official definitions of the U.S. money stock. M1 is the most narrowly defined monetary aggregate and includes currency, demand deposits, traveler's checks, and other checkable deposits. M2 is a slightly broader measure; it consists of M1 plus various types of savings accounts, as well as overnight repurchase agreements and Eurodollars. The broadest measure of the money stock, known as L, includes a host of instruments like savings bonds and short-term Treasury securities. In the next chapter, we will see how changes in the money stock can affect factors like inflation and output.

KEY TERMS

financial market

primary market

secondary market

debt market

short-term asset

intermediate-term asset

long-term asset

equity market

financial service market

depository institution

commercial bank

savings and loan association (S&L)

mutual savings bank

certificate of deposit (CD)

Treasury bill (T-bill)

repurchase agreement (repo)

Eurodollars

banker's acceptance

federal funds

capital market instrument

corporate stock

corporate bond

mortgage

government security

consumer loan

commercial loan

KEY TERMS *continued*

credit union	municipal bond
money market mutual fund	Eurobond
nondepository institution	money stock
insurance company	monetary aggregates
pension fund	M1
brokerage firm	M2
money market	M3
commercial paper	L

QUESTIONS AND PROBLEMS

1. How are financial intermediaries similar to supermarkets? How do they differ?

2. Critically evaluate and interpret the following statement: ''Since corporate bondholders do not own a share of the underlying company, they don't care whether the company earns profits or makes losses.''

3. Critically evaluate and interpret the following statement: ''Since firms do not receive money when their stock is sold in the secondary stock market, they would benefit from the elimination of that market.''

4. How do depository financial institutions differ from nondepository institutions?

5. Rank the following financial instruments from most liquid to least liquid.
   (a). A $1 bill
   (b). A share of IBM stock
   (c). A municipal bond issued by a small town in Alaska
   (d). A U.S. Treasury bill

6. As we move toward a more global economy, would you expect Eurodollars to become more important sources of funds for banks? Why or why not?

7. Explain how a banker's acceptance differs from an ordinary bank draft.

8. ''Federal funds are dollars loaned to banks by the Federal Reserve at the federal funds rate.'' Is this statement true or false? Explain.

9. If a corporation needs short-term funds, does it obtain the funds in the money market or in the capital market?

10. Explain the terms of an 8 percent, 30-year fixed-rate mortgage that requires 10 percent down and 2 points to a person wishing to buy a $200,000 house.

11. A 30-year ARM with an initial interest rate of 8 percent, a 2 percent margin, a 15 percent ceiling, a 7 percent floor, and a 3-percent-per-year cap is available. The current interest rate index is 6 percent.
   (a). Explain these terms to a person wishing to purchase a $150,000 house.
   (b). If the interest rate index increases to 9 percent next year, what interest rate will be paid on the mortgage?

12. Why are municipal bonds attractive to individuals and corporations with high incomes or profits?

13. Which of the monetary aggregates contains only those financial instruments that serve as media of exchange?

14. Suppose the economy has $100 million in currency, $50 million in demand deposits, $150 million in savings deposits, $25 million in Eurodollars, and $75 million in Treasury securities. Determine the money stock as measured by
(a). M1
(b). M2
(c). M3
(d). L

15. Why are credit cards not included in any of the definitions of the money stock presented in this chapter?

SELECTIONS FOR FURTHER READING

Hutchinson, P. M., J. R. Ostas, and J. D. Reed. "A Survey and Comparison of Redlining Influences in Urban Mortgage Lending Markets." *American Real Estate and Urban Economics Association Journal,* 5 (Winter 1977), 463–472.

Knodell, J. "Open Market Operations: Evolution and Significance." *Journal of Economic Issues,* 21 (June 1987), 691–699.

Kopecky, K. J. "Nonmember Banks and Empirical Measures of the Variability of Reserves and Money: A Theoretical Appraisal." *Journal of Finance,* 33 (March 1978), 311–318.

Morrissey, T. F., and O. K. Gregory. "A Study of FHLB Advances and Their Limit under Efficient Intermediation." *Journal of Economics and Business,* 27 (Winter 1975), 122–130.

Ostas, J. R. "The Federal Home Loan Bank System: Cause or Cure for Disintermediation?" *Journal of Monetary Economics,* 8 (September 1981), 231–246.

Van Fenstermaker, J., J. E. Filer, and R. S. Herren. "Money Statistics of New England, 1785–1837." *Journal of Economic History,* 44 (June 1984), 441–453.

3

Money, Inflation, and Interest

*I*n 1970, the United States produced about $1 trillion worth of final goods and services—products like cars, homes, and textbooks. This year, more than $6 trillion worth of final goods and services will be produced. Does this mean six times more goods and services are available today than in 1970? Or does it mean you must pay six times more for goods and services than people paid in 1970? To address these questions, this chapter introduces what economists call *economic growth* and *inflation.* We will learn that inflation is a situation of generally rising prices. During the past quarter-century, much of the increase in the dollar value of goods and services produced was due to inflation—the fact that things cost about four times more today than in 1970. However, economic growth—the presence of more things to consume today than in 1970—also contributed to the increased dollar value of goods and services. In the first part of this chapter, we examine the major causes of inflation.

In the second part of the chapter, we overview interest rates and see how inflation affects the interest rate you pay on loans such as car loans and mortgages. We conclude with a look at how income taxes affect interest rates. Since the material in this chapter will play a key role in our economic analysis of financial markets and banks in the next three chapters, we encourage you to master the material presented in this chapter before continuing your study of money and banking.

DISTINGUISHING BETWEEN INFLATION AND ECONOMIC GROWTH

When your grandparents talk about paying a nickel for a loaf of bread or a quarter for a ticket to see *Gone With the Wind,* they are telling you prices that existed in the past. Today you might pay $6 or more for a movie ticket or $1.50 for a loaf of bread. A portion of the increase in prices of these items reflects inflation: a general rise in the level of prices in the economy. In contrast, when your parents tell you they didn't own a car or a TV when they got married, they are telling you about the real quantity of goods available in the past. The increased quantity and variety of things available to consume today reflects economic growth, and is the result of technological advances and increases in the pool of productive resources (e.g., the size of the work force).

The Price Level and Real Output

In this section, we look at how economists distinguish between inflation and economic growth. We begin by defining terms you may have heard on the evening news or read in the newspaper: the price level and real output. These definitions are not ends in themselves; rather, they are used at the end of this section, where we examine the relationship between money and inflation.

Measuring the Price Level. The **price level** is a measure of the average prices of goods and services in the economy. It serves as a gauge of the general purchasing power of money. The consumer price index (CPI) is the measure of the price level most familiar to Americans—and for good reason. The percentage change in the CPI is published each month in newspapers throughout the nation. Many union contracts have cost-of-living adjustments that are indexed to the CPI; that is, the contracts specify that wages will rise when the CPI increases. Social security benefits are also indexed to the CPI, and each year social security recipients find that their retirement benefits increase by the same percentage as the increase in the CPI.

The Bureau of Labor Statistics (BLS) calculates the CPI, which measures the cost of the "basket" of goods and services purchased by the average urban household. The items in the basket are determined from a survey conducted in the base year, which was 1987 at the time of this writing. Thus, the CPI reports how much more or less expensive the fixed base year basket of goods and services would be in different years. If the CPI is higher today than in 1987, it costs more to buy the basket of goods and services today than it did in 1987. A lower CPI means it costs less to buy the basket today than it did in 1987.

In addition to the CPI, economists use several other measures of the price level to track prices in the United States. These include the producer price index (PPI) and the implicit price deflator for gross domestic product. The primary difference between these alternative measures of the price level is the composition of the basket of goods and services used to measure price changes. Historically all these measures of the price level have provided similar measures of price movements, so we will not concern ourselves with the minor technical distinctions among them. All these measures share a common feature: Their values are normalized to equal 100 in the base year—the year corresponding to the basket of goods and services that is being priced over time. If the price level was 100 in 1987 and increased to 103 in 1988, the price of the average good in the United States increased by 3 percent between 1987 and 1988.

All three indices follow this custom of stating price levels with a base year value of 100. Thus, you will see something like "1987 = 100" to indicate that 1987 is the base year.

Measuring Nominal and Real Output. **Nominal output** refers to the current dollar value of the final goods and services produced in the economy. Gross domestic product (GDP), the most commonly used measure of nominal output, is the total dollar value of all final goods and services produced in the economy in one year. Recall from your principles course that GDP measures the current dollar value of final output; that is, it measures only the output of goods and services sold to final consumers of the products. Intermediate sales of, say, paper products from a sawmill to a book publisher such as Houghton Mifflin or of a book from Houghton Mifflin to a college bookstore are not incuded in GDP. The sale of a book by the bookstore to you, the final consumer, is included in GDP. Moreover, GDP includes only new output, not sales of used goods. If you sell your textbook as a used book at the end of the semester, your transaction is not included in GDP.

Since nominal output is the current dollar value of all final sales of newly produced goods and services in the United States, it is the summation of the quantities of final goods and services multiplied by the products' prices. We can represent this mathematically by using P to denote the price level and letting Y represent real output. **Real output** is a measure of the physical quantity of goods and services available to the final consumers of the items. In this case, the dollar (or nominal) value of the real goods and services in the economy is simply the price level times the real quantity of goods:

$$\text{Nominal output} = P \times Y.$$

Notice that if the price level (P) doubled but the level of real output (Y) remained the same, nominal output would double even though no additional goods and services are available. For this reason, when the price level increases, nominal output will increase even if real output remains constant. To avoid confounding growth and inflation, economists frequently use real output to measure the output of the economy. Real output is obtained by dividing nominal output by the price level:

$$Y = \frac{\text{Nominal output}}{P}.$$

In the United States, economists use GDP to measure nominal output and the implicit price deflator to measure the price level associated with GDP. If the base year is 1987, the price level effectively converts nominal values of output today into the dollar values that would prevail today if prices remained at their 1987 levels. In this case, real output is called *real GDP* and is obtained by dividing GDP in a given year by the price level in that year. For example, at the end of 1992, GDP was $6.061 trillion and the reported GDP deflator was 121.72. Consequently, real GDP in 1992 was

$$\text{Real GDP}_{1992} = \frac{\text{GDP}_{1992}}{P_{1992}} = \frac{6.061}{1.2172} = 4.979 \text{ trillion 1987 dollars.}$$

(We divided by 1.2172 instead of by 121.72 because the reported GDP deflator is the actual price level times 100.) Our calculation reveals that had prices in 1992 remained at their 1987 levels, the value of final goods and services produced in 1992 would have been $4.979 trillion—considerably less than the $6.061 trillion nominal value of output (GDP) in 1992.

Figure 3.1 provides historical trends in the nominal value of output (GDP), real output (real GDP), and the price level (GDP deflator) in the United States. Due to differences in the magnitude of the numbers, GDP and real GDP are measured on the scale on the right, while the GDP deflator is measured on the left. Notice that in 1987 (the base year), real GDP and GDP coincided, since the price level was 100 in the base year. Also notice that GDP was $6 trillion in 1992, which is considerably greater than the $1 trillion in final goods and services produced in 1970.

Why was GDP higher in 1992 than in 1970? Figure 3.1 reveals two reasons. First, real GDP was higher in 1992 than in 1970, which tended to increase GDP (remember that GDP = P × Real GDP). Second, the price level as measured by the GDP deflator increased from 34.5 in 1970 to 121.7 by the end of 1992. This reveals that average prices increased by 252.8 percent over this period.

Inflation and Economic Growth

Now that you have a basic understanding of the price level and real output, we will show you how to use these measures to calculate the rate of inflation and the rate of economic growth.

This graph shows GDP, real GDP, and the GDP deflator from 1959 through 1993. GDP is measured in billions of dollars and real GDP in billions of 1987 dollars, as shown on the right-hand scale. Note that GDP and real GDP were equal in 1987, when both were measured in 1987 dollars. The GDP deflator is measured on the left-hand scale and equaled 100 in 1987, the base year.

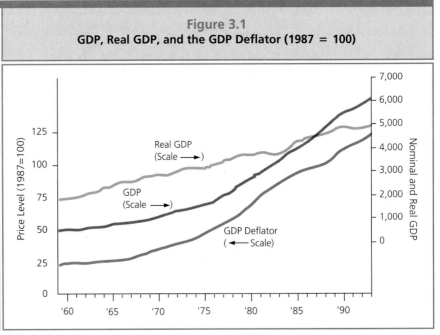

Figure 3.1
GDP, Real GDP, and the GDP Deflator (1987 = 100)

SOURCE: U.S. Department of Commerce, Bureau of Economic Analysis, *Survey of Current Business,* various issues, and Citibase electronic database.

Inflation.   The **inflation rate** is the rate of change in the price level. Inflation rates are stated as a percentage change on an annual basis. For instance, if the price level is P_t in year t and P_{t-1} in year $t - 1$, the inflation rate (π) between years t and $t - 1$ is defined as

$$\pi = \frac{P_t - P_{t-1}}{P_{t-1}}.$$

For example, the price level as measured by the implicit price deflator was 117.8 in 1991 and increased to 120.8 in 1992. Thus, the inflation rate between 1991 and 1992 was

$$\pi = \frac{P_{1992} - P_{1991}}{P_{1991}} = \frac{120.8 - 117.8}{117.8} = .025,$$

or 2.5 percent. In other words, average prices in the United States increased by 2.5 percent between 1991 and 1992.

We emphasize that inflation is a persistent, general rise in the average prices of all goods. Literally millions of goods can be purchased in our economy. If the price of only one good increases by 5 percent, that increase does not reflect inflation; rather, it is an increase in the price of that single commodity. But if the average prices of all goods in the economy increase each year by, say, 5 percent, then we say the inflation rate is 5 percent.

Box 3.1 describes the fall in inflation rates in five major economies between 1981 and 1991.

Economic Growth.   **Economic growth** is the rate of change in real output. The economic growth rate is usually stated as a percentage change on an annual basis. If real output was Y_t in year t and Y_{t-1} in year $t - 1$, the economic growth rate between years t and $t - 1$ is defined as

$$g_Y = \frac{Y_t - Y_{t-1}}{Y_{t-1}}.$$

For example, real output (real GDP) was \$4796.7 billion in 1991 and increased to \$4873.7 billion in 1992. Thus, the economic growth rate between 1991 and 1992 was

$$g_Y = \frac{Y_{1992} - Y_{1991}}{Y_{1991}} = \frac{4873.7 - 4796.7}{4796.7} = .016,$$

or 1.6 percent. In other words, between 1991 and 1992, the real quantity of final goods and services produced in the United States increased by 1.6 percent.

The Relationship Between Inflation and Economic Growth.
We can use a very simple formula to relate the rates of economic growth, growth in nominal output, and inflation. The growth rate of GDP equals the growth rate of real GDP *plus* the growth rate of prices (the inflation rate).

International Banking

Box 3.1

Inflation Rates Around the World

The United States experienced rapid inflation during the 1970s and early 1980s. In 1981, for instance, the U.S. inflation rate was 11.24 percent. This means that in the United States goods and services cost more than 11 percent more at the end of the year than at the beginning. Workers who did not receive wage increases of at least 11 percent found themselves unable to afford the same standard of living they enjoyed at the beginning of 1981. By 1991, the U.S. inflation rate had fallen to about 4 percent.

The accompanying figure reveals this experience was not purely an American phenomenon. All five of these major countries—the United States, Japan, Germany, the United Kingdom, and Canada—experienced higher inflation in 1981 than in 1991. In 1981, inflation rates in the U.K. and Canada rivaled those in the United States. But by 1991, these countries had experienced a dramatic decline in inflation, just as the United States had. Japan and Germany experienced lower inflation in 1981 than the other three major Western nations. Still, their inflation rates were lower in 1991 than in 1981.

The moral of the story is that some experiences of the U.S. economy are also the experiences in other nations. We truly live in a global economy.

_____

Source: U.S. Department of Commerce, Bureau of the Census, *Summary of U.S. Export-Import Merchandise Trade-FT900,* various issues, and Citibase electronic database.

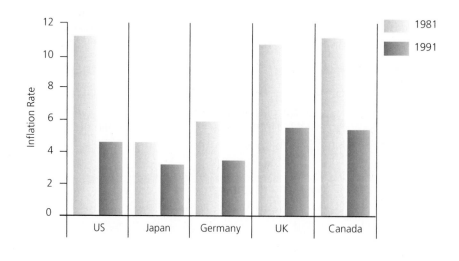

Thus, using g to represent growth rates, we can calculate the growth rate of real GDP as

$$g_{\text{real GDP}} = g_{\text{nominal GDP}} - g_{\text{price level}},$$

where the subscripts refer to what is growing.[1] This formula reveals that the growth rate in real GDP (the rate of economic growth) equals the growth rate in nominal GDP (called the *nominal growth rate*) minus the growth in the price level (inflation). For instance, if prices increase by 5 percent per year and nominal GDP increases by 7 percent per year, real output increases by only 2 percent per year, since $7\% - 5\% = 2\%$.

Figure 3.2 plots the growth rates of GDP, real GDP, and the GDP deflator for the period 1980–1992. As we showed earlier, the arithmetic difference between the growth rate of nominal GDP and the growth rate in the price level equals the rate of economic growth in each of these years. Notice the volatile movement in these growth rates over this period. For instance, in 1980 the inflation rate (as measured by the growth rate in the GDP deflator) was around 10 percent. By the end of 1992, the inflation rate was less than 3 percent. This reveals that inflation can vary considerably from year to year. In the remainder of this section, we will examine why inflation tends to vary over time. To do so, we must first look at the major causes of inflation.

Causes of Inflation

What causes inflation? As we see below, anything that causes the growth rate of the money supply to increase, the growth rate of velocity to increase, or the growth rate of output to decrease causes inflation.

Growth in the Money Stock.
Imagine that the room in which you are sitting is the economy and you are the sole consumer in that economy. Suppose one liter of soda is the only good in the room and the total money stock (the money in your pocket) is $1. Clearly, then, the maximum price you could pay for the soda is $1. Since the money in your pocket is fiat money, you cannot consume it; all you can consume is the one liter of soda.

Now suppose that by some miracle, another dollar appears in your pocket. The total money stock is now $2, but only one liter of soda is still available. You would now be willing to pay a price of $2 for the liter of soda (since you can't drink the $2 in fiat money). Since the money stock doubled, the price of soda doubled, and thus nominal output doubled as well. But since there is still only one liter of soda in the economy, real output is constant and you are no better off than before the extra dollar appeared. The increase in the money stock led to an increase in prices and nominal output

---

[1] This formula is an approximation. The exact formula is $g_{\text{real GDP}} = (g_{\text{nominal GDP}} - g_{\text{price level}})/(1 + g_{\text{price level}})$.

This graph shows the growth rates in GDP, real GDP, and the GDP deflator over the 1980–1993 period. All growth rates are the percentage change per year. The growth rate in GDP equals the growth rate of real GDP plus the growth rate of the GDP deflator. In the last quarter of 1992, the growth rate of GDP was 5.58 percent, of which the growth rate of real GDP was 3.75 percent and that of the GDP deflator was 1.83 percent.

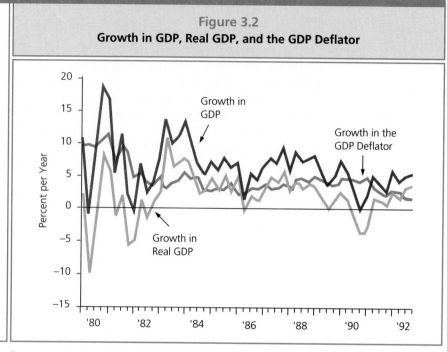

Figure 3.2
Growth in GDP, Real GDP, and the GDP Deflator

SOURCE: U.S. Department of Commerce, Bureau of Economic Analysis, *Survey of Current Business,* various issues, and Citibase electronic database.

but no increase in the real amount of goods available in the economy. In this sense, increases in the money stock lead to a higher price level.

You may wonder how such a simple story could explain something as complicated as inflation in the U.S. economy. Figure 3.3, which graphs two indices of the money stock (M1 and M2) and an index of the price level for the period 1959–1993, provides an answer. The figure suggests that periods of rising prices tend to be associated with periods of increases in the money stock. Such a relationship between growth in the money stock and inflation is precisely what we would expect based on our hypothetical example.

Velocity and Economic Growth.   Our one-soda economy is clearly an oversimplification. Yet the same logic explains the relationship between the money stock and the price level in an economy with many individuals and goods and services. The only additional complication is that with many people and goods and services, we have to take into account the **velocity** of money, which measures the number of times the average dollar changes hands in the economy in one year. Why does velocity matter? With many people and goods but only a single dollar in money, something remarkable happens: People can make more than $1 in purchases. You can use the $1 to buy something, the person you pay can in turn use the same $1 to buy something from someone else, and so on. If velocity is 2, the average dollar bill changes hands two times; $1 in money leads to $2 worth of purchases. If velocity is 10, $1 in money leads to 10 transactions, or $10 worth of purchases.

More generally, if the money stock is M and velocity is V, the total dollar value of transactions in the economy is MV. Similarly, if P is the price level and Y is real output, the dollar value of this output—nominal output—is $P \times Y$. Since the dollar value of transactions equals the dollar value of the goods and services in the economy, it follows that

$$MV = PY.$$

This fundamental relationship between the dollar value of exchanges (transactions) and nominal output is known as the **equation of exchange.**

The equation of exchange can be used to obtain a detailed picture of the causes of inflation. In particular, it implies that

$$\frac{\Delta M}{M} + \frac{\Delta V}{V} = \frac{\Delta P}{P} + \frac{\Delta Y}{Y},$$

This graph plots the measures of the money stock known as M1 and M2 and the price level from 1959 through 1993. The money stock is graphed on the right-hand scale in billions of dollars. The price level—the GDP deflator—is graphed on the left-hand scale and is set to equal 100 in 1987, the base year.

Figure 3.3

Relationship Between Money and the Price Level, 1959–1993

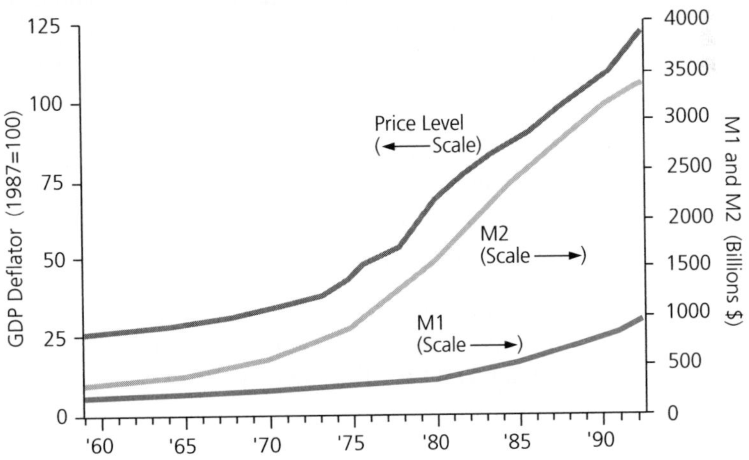

SOURCE: Board of Governors of the Federal Reserve System, *Federal Reserve Bulletin,* Table 1.21, various issues, U.S. Department of Commerce, Bureau of Economic Analysis, *Survey of Current Business,* various issues, and Citibase electronic database.

where Δ means "a change in." In words, $\Delta M/M$ is the percentage change in (or growth rate of) the money stock, $\Delta V/V$ is the percentage change in (or growth rate of) velocity, $\Delta P/P$ is the percentage change in prices (or the inflation rate), and $\Delta Y/Y$ is the percentage change in (or growth rate of) real output.[2]

This admittedly complicated relation is easier to visualize if we let g_M represent the growth rate in the money stock, g_V the growth rate in velocity, g_Y the growth rate in real output, and π the inflation rate and rewrite the above equation as

$$g_M + g_V = \pi + g_Y.$$

This equation simply says that the growth rate in the money stock (g_M) plus the growth rate in velocity (g_V) equals the inflation rate (π) plus the growth rate in real output (g_Y). We can rearrange this formula to obtain an expression for the inflation rate in terms of the growth rates of money, velocity, and real output:

$$\pi = g_M + g_V - g_Y.$$

The inflation rate thus equals the growth rate of the money stock, plus the growth rate of velocity, minus the growth of rate in real output. Changes in any of the three growth rates on the right-hand side of this equation can lead to changes in the inflation rate.

The so-called classical economists hypothesized that the growth rate of velocity and the growth rate of output are relatively constant and unaffected by changes in the growth rate of money. In this case, changes in the growth rate of money would lead directly to changes in the inflation rate. This is the simplest form of the famous *quantity theory,* which attributes rises in the price level to changes in the quantity of money. With regard to growth rates, changes in the growth rate of the money supply lead to changes in the inflation rate.

More generally, suppose velocity is constant so that its growth rate is zero. In this case, the inflation rate is simply the difference between the growth rate of the money stock and the growth rate of real output:

$$\pi = g_M - g_Y.$$

If the money stock increases at 10 percent per year but real output increases by only 3 percent annually, the inflation rate is $10\% - 3\% = 7\%$. This fundamental relation reveals that when velocity is constant, (positive) infla-

---

[2] This formula is also an approximation that holds for small percentage changes in M, V, P, and Y. The exact formula is

$$\frac{\Delta M}{M} + \frac{\Delta V}{V} + \left(\frac{\Delta M}{M} \times \frac{\Delta V}{V}\right) = \frac{\Delta P}{P} + \frac{\Delta Y}{Y} + \left(\frac{\Delta P}{P} \times \frac{\Delta Y}{Y}\right).$$

tion is caused by increases in the money stock that exceed the growth rate in real output: Too much money is chasing too few goods and services.

Of course, velocity need not be constant. During periods when individuals have **inflationary expectations**—that is, they expect prices to rise over time—velocity may grow. This is because inflationary expectations induce individuals to convert money into goods more rapidly in an attempt to buy things before prices increase. Since the inflation rate increases as the growth rate in velocity increases, growing inflationary expectations can in themselves fuel inflation.

We will say much more about these and other causes of inflation in the second half of this book. For now note that, as Figure 3.4 shows, velocity has not been constant in the United States. In fact, the velocity of M1 increased fairly steadily until 1980, after which its movements became more volatile. Currently the velocity of M1 is about 6.5, indicating that the average dollar of M1 changes hands 6.5 times each year. The velocity of M2 is more stable varying about a mean of around 1.7.

This graph plots the velocity of M1 and M2 over the 1959–1993 period. The velocity of M1 rose fairly steadily until about 1980, after which its behavior became more volatile. Note that M1 velocity is currently about 6.5, indicating that the average dollar of M1 changes hands 6.5 times in the course of one year. M2 velocity is much more stable at about 1.7.

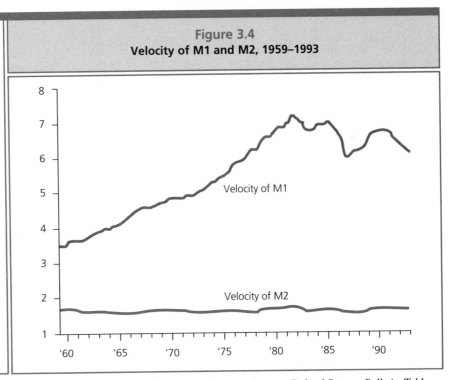

Figure 3.4
Velocity of M1 and M2, 1959–1993

SOURCE: Board of Governors of the Federal Reserve System, *Federal Reserve Bulletin,* Table 1.21, various issues, U.S. Department of Commerce, Bureau of Economic Analysis, *Survey of Current Business,* various issues, and Citibase electronic database.

In 1980 the price level was 71.73, M1 was $397.9 billion, and nominal output was $2,708 billion. In 1981 the price level increased to 78.88 and M1 increased to $426.8 billion. (a) Assuming the base year of the price level is 1987, what was real output in 1980? (b) What was the inflation rate between 1980 and 1981? (c) What do you think led to this inflation?

Answer: (a) Since the base year of the given price level is 1987, real output is measured in 1987 dollars. Specifically, real output in 1980, measured in 1987 dollars, was

$$\text{Real output}_{1980} = \frac{\text{Nominal output}_{1980}}{P_{1980}} = \frac{2{,}708}{.7173} = 3{,}775.3 \text{ billion 1987 dollars.}$$

(b) The inflation rate between 1980 and 1981 was

$$\pi = \frac{78.88 - 71.73}{71.73} = .0997,$$

or about 10 percent. (c) During the same period, the money stock increased at an annual rate of

$$g_M = \frac{426.8 - 397.9}{397.9} = .0726,$$

or about 7 percent. Since $\pi = g_M + g_V - g_Y$, we know that 7 percent of the 10 percent inflation was due to the 7 percent increase in the money stock. The other 3 percent was due to an increase in the difference, $g_V - g_Y$; the growth rate of velocity exceeded the growth rate of real output by 3 percent. This growth in velocity was probably due to growing inflationary expectations, brought on by rapid increases in the price level during the late 1970s.

INTEREST RATES

Up to this point, we have examined the relationship between the growth rates of money, output, and velocity and the inflation rate. We have seen that for constant growth rates of output and velocity, an increase in the growth rate of money will lead to an increase in the inflation rate. Now we introduce interest rates, which play an integral role in financial markets. There are many determinants of interest rates, among which is the rate of inflation. In this chapter, we draw out the relationship between the inflation rate and the interest rate. In Chapter 4, we will see how the market forces of supply and demand ultimately determine interest rates, such as the interest rate you pay on a car loan and the rate IBM pays when it issues a bond to obtain funds. Moreover, we will learn in later chapters that changes in the money stock can affect interest rates. Before we tackle these more complicated issues, we need a basic overview of interest rates.

In the first part of this section, we look at what interest is and examples of how interest is paid on a few common types of loans. Next, we examine the important principles of present value, future value, and the time value of money. Then we use these concepts to see how inflation affects the "real" interest received by those owning interest-bearing financial instruments.

What Is Interest?

When a bank or other financial institution lends you money, it requires you to repay the funds lent (the principal), plus an additional payment called *interest*. The timing of the payment of interest and principal are negotiable and vary from one loan to another. However, virtually all loans (except perhaps loans from close friends or relatives) require some payment in addition to the principal.

The interest rate on a loan is the ratio of the interest payments on the loan to the principal amount (the amount borrowed). In other words, it is the cost of borrowing funds as a percentage of the amount borrowed. If you borrow $500 to buy a fancy stereo and pay the money back next year plus $50 interest, you have paid an interest rate of 10 percent, calculated as $50/$500 = .10 or 10%. This example oversimplifies, however. To compare the interest rate on loans with different maturities (such as 1-year and 30-year loans), we need to calculate the interest rate for a given time span. For this reason, interest rates are stated as interest rates per year (the so-called "annual rate of interest" you have probably seen in TV ads or on a sign at your bank). The interest rate is the amount over and above the principal amount that is paid in a given year, expressed as a percentage of the principal amount. Also, interest can be indirect, as Box 3.2 shows.

When you consider interest charges on a loan, you need to realize that interest is charged because funds available for use today are more valuable than funds available for use in the future. This is because people prefer to satisfy their desires today to waiting until later. (Would you prefer to receive a $1,000 gift today or a $1,000 gift in 30 years?) Borrowers want funds for use today and promise to repay those funds in the future. But a lender requires more than that: A lender requires interest from the borrower as compensation for the lost use of the funds for the length of the loan. In essence, interest is the price of borrowing money. The interest rate expresses this price as the percentage of the principal amount that the borrower pays to use someone else's money. A brief description of how interest payments are structured on some common types of loan contracts follows.

A Simple Loan.   A *simple loan* allows the borrower the use of a given amount of funds (the principal) for a specified period of time. In exchange,

Inside Money

Box 3.2

Points and Mortgage Interest Rates

A telephone call to a mortgage company on April 12, 1993, allowed us to obtain the following interest rates on a 30-year, conventional fixed-rate mortgage (you might call a local lender today to see what the current rates are in your area):

Rate	Points
7⅝	0
7⅜	2

Notice that the interest rate varies depending on how many points are paid on the loan. Recall from Chapter 2 that points are the percentage of the loan amount that must be paid when the loan is obtained and is a form of prepaid interest. On a $100,000 loan, ½ points amount to $500 and 2 points equals $2,000. Other things equal, borrowers prefer mortgages that involve fewer points.

The catch, which the above table reveals, is that other things are *not* equal. The lower mortgage interest rate involves more points. A borrower can avoid paying points by paying a 7⅝ percent interest rate. In this case, the monthly payments on a 30-year, $100,000 loan are $707.79. If the borrower pays 2 points ($2,000 in this case), the interest rate is only 7⅜ percent, and the monthly mortgage payments drop to $690.68.

In effect, a home buyer shopping for a mortgage must decide whether to pay points now in exchange for lowering the mortgage payments by $17.11 each month over the life of the loan (360 months). If the borrower plans to stay in the house for 30 years and cannot invest the $2,000 at as high an interest rate, it is probably best to pay the points. In contrast, if the borrower can invest the $2,000 at a higher rate of interest or plans to sell the house in two or three years, it is best to pay the higher interest rate in lieu of the points.

---

the borrower must repay the principal on a specified date, at which point he or she also makes the full interest payment. For example, First National might lend you $1,000 and require you to pay back $1,050 (the principal plus a $50 interest payment) in six months.

A Fixed-Payment Loan.   With a *fixed-payment loan,* a borrower obtains funds in return for a series of fixed payments (usually monthly) that include both principal and interest. The interest rate is usually fixed for the length of the loan, and the regular payments are of equal amounts. Each fixed payment includes two parts: an interest payment and a payment to reduce the principal. Thus, with a fixed-payment loan, the outstanding balance (principal) declines during the life of the loan. The loan is paid in full when the principal balance declines to zero. Most auto loans are of this type, as are fixed-rate home mortgage loans. Box 3.3 illustrates how the payments on these loans will vary with the length of the loan, using 15 and 30 year mortgage loans as an example.

A Coupon Bond.

A *coupon bond* specifies (1) a face value, (2) a term, and (3) the coupon rate, which is the percentage of the face value that will be paid annually as interest when the holder redeems coupons attached to the bond at specified points in time (say, every six months). These coupons gave coupon bonds their name. Upon maturity, the bondholder redeems the bond for the face value. If the bond is sold to the lender at face value (or par), the face value is the principal and the coupons represent the interest on the bond. For example, suppose your bank purchases a 10 percent coupon bond at the face value of $10,000. In this case, the principal is $10,000—the price at which the bond is sold to the bank. Annual interest receipts are $1,000, or 10 percent of the principal amount. Sometimes coupon bonds sell at other than face value, as we will see in Chapter 8.

A Zero Coupon Bond.

As the term implies, the owner of a *zero coupon bond* receives no regular interest payments, since the bond has no coupons attached. Instead, the bond is sold at a discount from its face or redemption value. The change in value from its price at issue to its redemption value is implicit interest that the purchaser receives on the bond. For example, a zero coupon bond might have a redemption value of $1,000 one year from today. A lender might purchase this bond for $900, meaning the interest on the loan is effectively $100. The implicit interest rate is then $100/$900, or 11.11 percent.

The Time Value of Money

Now that you have a basic understanding of what interest is and how it is paid on several types of loans, we look at two basic tools used to evaluate the consequences of interest: present and future value analysis. Mastering future value analysis will simplify present value analysis, so we encourage you to make sure you fully understand the material in the next section before you read on.

Future Value Analysis.

Imagine that you put $1,000 in the bank today and the bank agrees to pay you an interest rate of 5 percent per year. Future value analysis provides a way to determine how much you will have in the future.

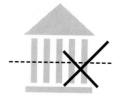

Inside Money

Box 3.3

15-Year Versus 30-Year Mortgages

Suppose you borrow $100,000 at 7 percent interest to buy your dream house. Your banker informs you that your monthly payments will be $665.30 for the next 30 years. How much would you have to pay each month if you wanted to pay off the loan in 15 years instead of 30? Most borrowers incorrectly believe the monthly payment required to pay off the loan in 15 years would be $1,330.60—twice the amount on the 30-year mortgage. In reality, it would cost you only $898.83 per month to pay off the loan in 15 years—only $233.53 more per month than with the 30-year payment schedule. How can this be?

To answer this question, suppose you take out a 30-year loan for $100,000 on January 1, 1995. The first year your payment schedule, which consists of interest and principal, will look as follows:

Date	Payment	Interest	Principal	Balance After
01/01/95	665.30	583.33	81.97	99,918.03
02/01/95	665.30	582.86	82.44	99,835.59
03/01/95	665.30	582.37	82.93	99,752.66
04/01/95	665.30	581.89	83.41	99,669.25
05/01/95	665.30	581.40	83.90	99,585.35
06/01/95	665.30	580.91	84.39	99,500.96
07/01/95	665.30	580.42	84.88	99,416.08
08/01/95	665.30	579.93	85.37	99,330.71
09/01/95	665.30	579.43	85.87	99,244.84
10/01/95	665.30	578.93	86.37	99,158.47
11/01/95	665.30	578.42	86.88	99,071.59
12/01/95	665.30	577.92	87.38	$98,984.21
Total for 1995	$7,983.60	$6,967.81	$1,015.79	

Continued on p. 77

After one year, the bank will pay you interest of 5 percent on the $1,000, which amounts to

$$.05 \times \$1,000 = \$50.$$

Thus, at the end of one year, you will have your principal of $1,000 plus $50 in interest for a total of $1,050. Notice that this amount can also be calculated as follows:

$$(1 + .05) \times \$1,000 = \$1,050;$$

Continued from p. 76

Thus, at the end of the first year, your $7,983.60 in payments reduced your loan balance by only $1,015.79. You still owe the bank $98,984.21.

Date	Payment	Interest	Principal	Balance After
01/01/95	898.83	583.33	315.50	99,684.50
02/01/95	898.83	581.49	317.34	99,367.16
03/01/95	898.83	579.64	319.19	99,047.97
04/01/95	898.83	577.78	321.05	98,726.92
05/01/95	898.83	575.91	322.92	98,404.00
06/01/95	898.83	574.02	324.81	98,079.19
07/01/95	898.83	572.13	326.70	97,752.49
08/01/95	898.83	570.22	328.61	97,423.88
09/01/95	898.83	568.31	330.52	97,093.36
10/01/95	898.83	566.38	332.45	96,760.91
11/01/95	898.83	564.44	334.39	96,426.52
12/01/95	898.83	562.49	336.34	$96,090.18
Total for 1995	$10,785.96	$6,876.14	$3,909.82	

In contrast, if you obtain a 15-year mortgage, your first-year payments will look like this:

With a 15-year payment schedule, a much greater portion of each payment made goes toward reducing the balance of the loan, thereby reducing the future interest you pay on the outstanding balance. The net effect of this after one year is that you have paid off $3,909.82 of the loan. Since your balance at the end of the first year is $96,090.18, your interest payments in the second year are even lower, allowing you to reduce your loan balance with each additional payment even further compared to the 30-year payment plan. The same is true for every year through the end of year 15, at which point your balance is zero. The end result is that by paying only $233.53 more each month, you pay off the $100,000 loan in half as much time.

the 1 in parentheses reflects the fact that you get your principal back, and the .05 is the interest rate on the principal. Thus, we see that the future value of $1,000 in one year when the interest rate is 5 percent is $1,050.

What is the future value of $1,000 in two years when the interest rate is 5 percent? As we just saw, at the end of the first year you will have

$$(1 + .05) \times \$1,000 = \$1,050.$$

This amount will earn interest of 5 percent for an additional year. Thus, at the end of two years you will have

$$(1 + .05) \times \$1,050 = \$1,102.50.$$

Notice that interest income earned during the second year is more than the amount earned during the first year. Why? During the second year, you earn interest of 5 percent not only on the original $1,000 but also on the $50 in interest you received during the first year. In the vernacular of financial markets, compounding of interest has occurred. In other words, it is interest earned in year 2 on your interest earnings from year 1. We can also express the future value of this investment with the formula

$$(1 + .05) \times (1 + .05) \times \$1,000 = \$1,102.50,$$

or, more simply,

$$(1 + .05)^2 \times \$1,000 = \$1,102.50.$$

The fact that $(1 + .05)$ is raised to the power of 2 reflects the fact that the original amount is invested for two years.

This basic principle for calculating the future value of an investment leads to the following general formula. If the interest rate is i and the present amount to be invested is PV, the **future value (FV)** of that amount in T years is

$$FV = PV \times (1 + i)^T.$$

Suppose you invest $2,000 today at an interest rate of 10 percent. How much will you have in 10 years?

Answer: To calculate the future value, set PV $= \$2,000$, $T = 10$, and $i = .1$ in the future value formula:

$$FV = PV \times (1 + i)^T = \$2,000 \times (1.1)^{10} = \$2,000 \times 2.5937423 = \$5,187.48.$$

Thus, in 10 years your $2,000 will have grown into $5,187.48.

Present Value Analysis. Future value analysis tells us how much a given sum invested at a specified interest rate will be worth at a future time. For example, future value analysis allows us to calculate how much money you would have at age 65 if you invested $1,000 today at a 5 percent interest rate. We might, however, be interested in knowing what the promise of a given sum of money in the future is worth to us today; that is, what is the value today of $100,000 when you turn 65? The ability to answer such a question is of immediate importance in pricing bonds, which entail the borrower's promise to pay a certain sum in the future. We have seen, for instance, that a zero coupon bond promises to pay the face value of the bond at a future date and has no explicit interest payments. How do you value such a bond? What is such a promise worth to you today? To answer these questions, we use present value analysis.

Simply put, the present value is the value today of funds available at some future date. Thus, $1,000 available today has a present value of $1,000.

What is the present value of an amount received not today but at some date in the future? Finding the answer is easy. All we have to do is rewrite our equation for future value so that PV is on the left-hand side. Recall that the future value formula is

$$FV = PV \times (1 + i)^T.$$

If we solve this equation for PV, we obtain the formula for the **present value (PV)** of an amount received T years in the future when the interest rate is i:

$$PV = \frac{FV}{(1 + i)^T}.$$

To see how to use this formula, let us calculate the present value of $1,050 available one year from today when the interest rate is 5 percent. According to the formula (here FV = $1,050, $T = 1$, and $i = .05$), the present value is

$$PV = \frac{FV}{(1 + i)^T} = \frac{\$1,050}{1.05} = \$1,000.$$

The answer should not surprise you. In the previous section, we saw that the future value of $1,000 invested for one year at 5 percent is $1,050. Thus, if the interest rate is 5 percent, you would need to invest $1,000 today to have $1,050 a year from now. In effect, present value is future value calculated in reverse.

Notice two things about the present value formula. First, as long as the interest rate is positive, $1 in the future is worth less than $1 today. This illustrates the time value of money: By waiting to receive money in the future, you forgo the use of the money (the interest you could have earned if you received the money today, for instance). Second, the present value of a given sum received in the future is inversely related to the interest rate. As the interest rate rises, the present value falls; conversely, the lower the interest rate, the greater the present value of a given future amount.

Summary Exercise 3.3

Recall that T-bills are zero coupon bonds issued by the federal government that are sold at a discount. Suppose a T-bill with a maturity of one year and a face value of $10,000 is offered for sale at a Treasury bill auction. The interest rate you could earn on an alternative one-year "safe" asset, such as a certificate of deposit, is 8 percent. What would be a reasonable price for this T-bill?

Answer: To answer this question, consider what you are purchasing. You are trading a purchase price (the present value, not yet determined) for a promise that the U.S. government will pay you $10,000 in one year. This promise is almost risk free, since it is extremely unlikely that the government will be unable to pay you this sum in one year. (For instance, as a last resort the government could always simply print paper money to pay you.) Since the interest rate on an alternative investment is 8 percent, the maximum price you should be willing to pay for the T-bill is the amount that, after earning 8 percent for one year, will equal $10,000. (This is exactly the definition of present value!) Thus, the highest price you will be willing to pay for the T-bill is the present value of $10,000 received one year in the future when the interest rate is 8 percent. Algebraically, the present value (PV) of the T-bill is

$$PV = \frac{\$10,000}{1.08} = \$9,259.26,$$

which is the highest price you would bid for the T-bill. If you bid lower and succeeded, your return on the T-bill would exceed 8 percent.

How Inflation and Taxes Affect Interest Rates

In the first part of this section, we look in more detail at how inflation affects interest rates and how to ensure that the interest rate you receive on an investment is high enough to protect your purchasing power from inflation. In the second part, we examine how to determine the aftertax interest rate received on investments and how current tax policy also affects the interest rate paid by borrowers who use funds to make purchases such as homes.

The Real Interest Rate

Suppose you make a $100, one-year loan to someone at a 5 percent interest rate. One year from now, you will have $105; this is the future value of the $100 loan. Before you conclude you will be able to purchase more one year from now than today due to the extra $5 you earned as interest, you had better think again. When you receive the future amount ($105), the prices you see in stores will be not today's prices but the prices one year from today. If the inflation rate is 7 percent, prices in one year will be 7 percent higher than they are today. The extra 5 percent you earned in interest will be more than offset by the 7 percent increase in prices.

To see why this is so, suppose that today you can buy a watch for $100. If the inflation rate is 7 percent, the same watch will cost $107 in one year. If you do not make the $100 loan, you can use the $100 to buy the watch at its current price of $100. But if you loan out the money at 5 percent interest, the $105 you will have in one year will be $2 short of what you need to buy the watch. In real terms, you will lose $2 in purchasing power (2 percent of the initial amount loaned) if you make the loan.

This example reveals that the presence of inflation can affect the real value of the money lenders receive in the future. A prudent investor should consider the real interest rate when making a loan. The *nominal interest rate* is the interest rate stated in the loan contract. The real interest rate is the nominal interest rate minus the expected rate of inflation. More formally, if i is the nominal interest rate and π^e is the expected rate of inflation, the **real interest rate,** r, is defined as[3]

$$r = i - \pi^e.$$

In the preceding example, the inflation rate is 7 percent and the nominal interest rate is 5 percent. According to this formula, the real interest rate is

$$-2\% = 5\% - 7\%.$$

The fact that the real interest rate is negative means that by loaning out money at 5 percent when prices are expected to rise by 7 percent, you will actually lose 2 percent of your purchasing power. This is precisely what you lost in the preceding example (the $2 loss in puchasing power as a fraction of the original $100 loan is 2 percent).

Of course, investors are not very likely to loan out money if they think they will earn a negative real interest rate. To induce lenders to give up the use of funds, borrowers must compensate them such that they receive a greater real value in the future. Notice that we can rewrite the equation for the real interest rate to see exactly what the nominal interest rate would have to be to ensure that the lender earned a given real interest rate:

$$i = r + \pi^e.$$

This is called the *Fisher equation,* after American economist Irving Fisher. It says that the nominal or stated interest rate on a loan (i) equals the real interest rate (r) plus the expected rate of inflation (π^e). In effect, lenders will charge an **inflation premium**—an amount over and above the real interest rate to compensate for the decline in purchasing power due to inflation. This inflation premium will equal the expected inflation rate during the period of the loan.

For instance, suppose a lender expects inflation to be 4 percent and wants to earn a 3 percent real rate of interest; that is, she wants the amount

---

[3] Technically, the real interest rate is

$$r = \frac{i - \pi^e}{1 + \pi^e}.$$

The formulas in the text are widely used approximations.

paid back to have 3 percent more purchasing power than the money loaned out. In this case, the interest rate the lender must charge on the loan is

$$7\% = 3\% + 4\%.$$

By charging 4 percent above her desired real interest rate, the lender obtains additional funds that offset her expectation of inflation. Notice that the higher the lender's expected inflation rate, the higher the nominal interest rate must be for her to receive a given real interest rate. Remember, however, that the lender does not know what the inflation rate will be. She has to form an educated guess—an expectation. As inflationary expectations change over time, nominal interest rates will also change.

One final note about real interest rates is that calculations and discussions of the real interest rate should make it clear whether the real interest rate being considered is an ex ante real interest rate or an ex post real interest rate. The *ex ante real interest rate* is the real interest rate we have been discussing: the nominal interest rate minus the expected inflation rate. It is called *ex ante* to signify that it is ''before the fact,'' meaning it is calculated from expected inflation rates and hence is itself an expectation of the real return from a given nominal interest rate. The *ex post real interest rate* is the nominal interest rate minus the actual inflation rate. *Ex post* means ''after the fact,'' and the ex post real interest rate is calculated using actual inflation rates, information that would be unavailable to an investor at the time he or she would make an investment decision.

Sometimes ex post real interest rates are used in discussions of the real interest rate, because the data on actual inflation rates are easier to get than data on expected inflation rates. For example, Figure 3.5 graphs U.S. inflation rates, nominal interest rates, and ex post real interest rates for the period 1960–1992. Note the link between nominal interest rates and the inflation rate, as well as the unusually high real interest rates of the early and middle 1980s. Notice too that between 1974 and 1980, the real interest rate was negative. During those years, lenders actually *lost* real purchasing power by loaning out money.

Are real interest rates the same in all countries? The answer is no, as shown in Box 3.4.

Anticipated Inflation. **Anticipated inflation** is inflation that participants in financial markets expect and thus take into account when making their plans. If a lender expects the inflation rate to be 4 percent and it turns out to be exactly 4 percent during the term of the loan, the inflation premium charged on the loan exactly offsets the inflation. In real terms, the lender receives a real return exactly equal to what led him to lend the money in the first place. The borrower pays back the loan with dollars that are worth exactly what she expected them to be worth.

Figure 3.5
U.S. Inflation and Nominal and Real Interest Rates, 1960–1992

This graph plots the U.S. inflation rate, the nominal interest rate on one-year U.S. Treasury bills, and the ex post real interest rate, the nominal interest rate minus the actual inflation rate. Notice that periods of high inflation also tend to be periods of high nominal interest rates, as is especially evident during the period 1960–1980. During this period, real interest rates were fairly steady at about 2 percent until the early 1970s and then fell sharply, becoming negative in 1974–1975. Real interest rates hovered around zero for the remainder of the 1970s. The 1980s saw a sharp rise in real interest rates in the early years—to the 5 percent range—followed by a gradual decline. By 1992, the real interest rate was around 1 percent.

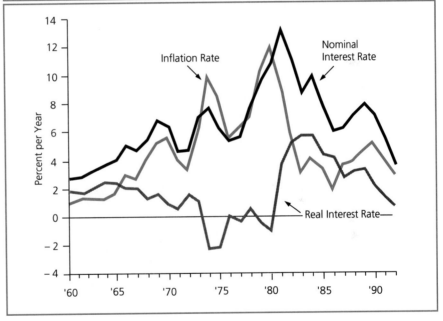

SOURCE: Board of Governors of the Federal Reserve System, *Federal Reserve Bulletin,* Table 1.35, various issues, U.S. Department of Labor, Bureau of Labor Statistics, *The Consumer Price Index,* various issues, and Citibase electronic database.

Unanticipated Inflation. **Unanticipated inflation,** on the other hand, is inflation over and above what participants in financial markets expected at the time funds were issued. Unanticpated inflation has a different impact on borrowers and lenders, as described next.

Suppose a lender expects the inflation rate to be 4 percent and thus adds an inflation premium of 4 percent to the real interest rate. And, suppose the actual inflation rate turns out to be 10 percent instead of the anticipated 4 percent. The lender expected prices to rise by 4 percent and charged an

International Banking

Box 3.4

Real Interest Rates Around the World

How do real interest rates compare among major Western industrialized nations? The answer depends on the point in time at which the comparisons are made. This point is illustrated in the accompanying diagram, which compares real interest rates in the United States, Japan, Germany, the United Kingdom, and Canada in 1981 and 1991.

This diagram reveals several interesting patterns. First, notice that real interest rates varied considerably across countries. In 1991, for instance, the real interest rate in the United States was 1.33 percent, considerably lower than the 5.9 percent rates in both Germany and the United Kingdom during that year. Second, notice how much real interest rates changed within each country between 1981 and 1991. In Canada, for instance, the real interest rate was 7.08 percent in 1981 but fell to 3.5 percent by 1991. Thus, real interest rates vary not only across countries but over time as well.

Source: OCED, various issues, U.S. Department of Commerce, Bureau of Economic Analysis, *Survey of Current Business,* various issues, and Citibase electronic database.

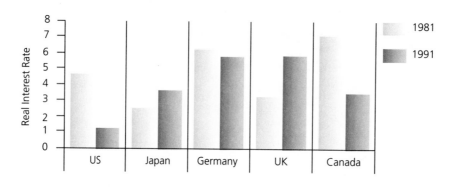

inflation premium to cover these expectations. Unfortunately for the lender, prices increased by 6 percent more than he anticipated, and he thus ends up with 6 percent less in purchasing power than he expected when he made the loan.

Is unanticipated inflation "bad"? It depends on whether you are a borrower or a lender. Clearly unanticipated inflation hurts lenders, since they are paid back with money that is less valuable than anticipated. Borrowers, on the other hand, are better off. They get to pay back the loan with money that is less valuable than they thought it would be.

Summary Exercise 3.4

In 1991, the prime interest rate was 8.46 percent. Between December 31, 1990, and December 31, 1991, the price level increased from 112.87 to 116.98. What was the real prime interest rate in 1991?

Answer: The inflation rate in 1991 was

$$\pi_{1991} = \frac{P_{1991} - P_{1990}}{P_{1990}} = \frac{116.98 - 112.87}{112.87} = .0364,$$

or 3.64 percent. Assuming this inflation was anticipated, the real prime interest rate in 1991 was $r = i - \pi^e = 8.46\% - 3.64\% = 4.82\%$.

The Aftertax Interest Rate

In the United States, interest income is subject to personal income tax. This means lenders must pay a fraction of interest earnings to the government in the form of income taxes. (We noted in the previous chapter that some exceptions exist. One exception is interest income from municipal bonds, which is exempt from federal income taxation.) Similarly, some forms of interest payments—mortgage interest payments, for instance—are tax deductible. Interest payments that are tax deductible reduce the taxes that a borrower would otherwise pay.

How do taxes affect the "effective" aftertax interest rate borrowers pay and lenders receive? Suppose your *marginal tax rate* is 30 percent; that is, you are in the 30 percent tax bracket and must pay 30 percent of each additional dollar you earn to the government as income tax. What will you earn if you make a $100, one-year loan at an interest rate of 10 percent? (For now, we keep things simple and ignore inflation.)

One year from today, you will receive $110 from the borrower. Of this amount, $100 is principal and $10 is interest income subject to the income tax at the 30 percent rate. You pay the government 30 percent of the $10, which is $3, and keep the remaining $7. In effect, you get to keep only the fraction $(1 - .3) = .7$, or 70 percent, of the interest income; the other 30 percent goes to the government. After taxes, you end up with $7 in interest on the $100 loan. In other words, your aftertax rate of interest is 7 percent, which is $(1 - .3) \times 10\%$.

We can state this finding much more generally. Suppose the marginal tax rate is τ and the pretax interest rate is i. Then the **aftertax interest rate** the lender earns is

$$i_\tau = (1 - \tau) \times i.$$

Summary Exercise 3.5

Your client is in the 38 percent tax bracket and thus pays $38 of every additional $100 she earns to the federal government. She has $10,000 to invest for one year and wants your advice in choosing between a corporate bond paying 9 percent interest and a municipal bond paying 6 percent interest. Interest on the municipal bond is exempt from taxation, whereas that on the corporate bond is not. Which bond should she purchase?

Answer: The aftertax interest rate is

$$i_\tau = (1 - \tau) \times i,$$

so the corporate bond pays an aftertax interest rate of $(1 - .38) \times (.09) = .0558$, or 5.58%. The municipal bond pays 6 percent before and after taxes. Therefore, your client should buy the municipal bond, since it yields a higher aftertax return.

HISTORICAL DATA ON INTEREST RATES

To acquaint you with past trends in interest rates, Table 3.1 provides historical data on various interest rates, including short-term Treasury securities (three-month and six-month Treasury bills), longer-term government bonds (three-year and ten-year bonds, converted to constant maturities), corporate bonds (both Aaa and Baa, where Baa bonds are riskier), municipal bonds, home mortgage rates, commercial paper and prime rates, the Federal Reserve discount rate, and the federal funds rate. These rates can be used to compare assets of different maturities and different assets with the same maturity, as well as to get a feel for historical movements in U.S. interest rates. As you look at the interest rates in Table 3.1, you should note two things (in the next chapter, we discuss these observations in more detail).

First, just as a supermarket has many prices, financial markets have many interest rates. We will look at the reason for this in the next chapter, but the basic reasons are simple to understand. First, financial instruments issued by different borrowers have different default risks. Riskier borrowers must offer higher interest rates to compensate lenders for the additional risk of default. Second, debt instruments differ with respect to their underlying liquidity. More liquid instruments tend to have lower interest rates than do less liquid instruments. Again, the higher interest rates paid on less liquid financial assets compensate lenders for the fact that they cannot as easily liquidate the assets prior to maturity. This makes less liquid assets attractive to investors seeking higher returns. Finally, different financial instruments have different terms to maturity; the interest rate on a 1-year loan generally does not equal the interest rate on a 30-year loan. Chapter 10 is entirely devoted to explaining this phenomenon, which is known as the *term structure of interest rates.*

The second thing to note about interest rates is that they vary over time. This is because inflation premiums, tax rates, the risk of default, and market conditions in debt markets all change over time, and changes in each of

Table 3.1												
Interest Rates on Various Financial Instruments, 1963–1992												

Year	U.S. Treasury Securities				Corporate Bonds (Moody's)		High-Grade Municipal Bonds (Standard & Poor's)	New-Home Mortgage Yields	Commercial Paper, 6 Months	Prime Rate Charged by Banks	Discount Rate, Federal Reserve Bank of New York	Federal Funds Rate
	Bills (new issues)		Constant Maturities		Aaa	Baa						
	3-Month	6-Month	3-Year	10-Year								
1963	3.157	3.253	3.67	4.00	4.26	4.86	3.23	5.89	3.55	4.50	3.23	3.18
1964	3.549	3.686	4.03	4.19	4.40	4.83	3.22	5.83	3.97	4.50	3.55	3.50
1965	3.954	4.055	4.22	4.28	4.49	4.87	3.27	5.81	4.38	4.54	4.04	4.07
1966	4.881	5.082	5.23	4.92	5.13	5.67	3.82	6.25	5.55	5.63	4.50	5.11
1967	4.321	4.630	5.03	5.07	5.51	6.23	3.98	6.46	5.10	5.61	4.19	4.22
1968	5.339	5.470	5.68	5.65	6.18	6.94	4.51	6.97	5.90	6.30	5.16	5.66
1969	6.677	6.853	7.02	6.67	7.03	7.81	5.81	7.81	7.83	7.96	5.87	8.20
1970	6.458	6.562	7.29	7.35	8.04	9.11	6.51	8.45	7.71	7.91	5.95	7.18
1971	4.348	4.511	5.65	6.16	7.39	8.56	5.70	7.74	5.11	5.72	4.88	4.66
1972	4.071	4.466	5.72	6.21	7.21	8.16	5.27	7.60	4.73	5.25	4.50	4.43
1973	7.041	7.178	6.95	6.84	7.44	8.24	5.18	7.96	8.15	8.03	6.44	8.73
1974	7.886	7.926	7.82	7.56	8.57	9.50	6.09	8.92	9.84	10.81	7.83	10.50
1975	5.838	6.122	7.49	7.99	8.83	10.61	6.89	9.00	6.32	7.86	6.25	5.82
1976	4.989	5.266	6.77	7.61	8.43	9.75	6.49	9.00	5.34	6.84	5.50	5.04
1977	5.265	5.510	6.69	7.42	8.02	8.97	5.56	9.02	5.61	6.83	5.46	5.54
1978	7.221	7.572	8.29	8.41	8.73	9.49	5.90	9.56	7.99	9.06	7.46	7.93
1979	10.041	10.017	9.71	9.44	9.63	10.69	6.39	10.78	10.91	12.67	10.28	11.19
1980	11.506	11.374	11.55	11.46	11.94	13.67	8.51	12.66	12.29	15.27	11.77	13.36
1981	14.029	13.776	14.44	13.91	14.17	16.04	11.23	14.70	14.76	18.87	13.42	16.38
1982	10.686	11.084	12.92	13.00	13.79	16.11	11.57	15.14	11.89	14.86	11.02	12.26
1983	8.63	8.75	10.45	11.10	12.04	13.55	9.47	12.57	8.89	10.79	8.50	9.09
1984	9.58	9.80	11.89	12.44	12.71	14.19	10.15	12.38	10.16	12.04	8.80	10.23
1985	7.48	7.66	9.64	10.62	11.37	12.72	9.18	11.55	8.01	9.93	7.69	8.10
1986	5.98	6.03	7.06	7.68	9.02	10.39	7.38	10.17	6.39	8.33	6.33	6.81
1987	5.82	6.05	7.68	8.39	9.38	10.58	7.73	9.31	6.85	8.21	5.66	6.66
1988	6.69	6.92	8.26	8.85	9.71	10.83	7.76	9.19	7.68	9.32	6.20	7.57
1989	8.12	8.04	8.55	8.49	9.26	10.18	7.24	10.13	8.80	10.87	6.93	9.21
1990	7.51	7.47	8.26	8.55	9.32	10.36	7.25	10.05	7.95	10.01	6.98	8.10
1991	5.42	5.49	6.82	7.86	8.77	9.80	6.89	9.32	5.85	8.46	5.45	5.69
1992	3.45	3.57	5.30	7.01	8.14	8.98	6.41	—	3.80	6.25	3.25	3.52

SOURCE: *Economic Report of the President* (Washington, D.C.: U.S. Government Printing Office, 1993), p. 428.

these factors affect interest rates. We briefly touched on the reasons inflation and taxes affect interest rates in this chapter. In the next chapter, we will take a closer look at these issues.

CONCLUSION

In this chapter, we focused on inflation and interest rates. We learned that inflation is growth in the overall price level and is caused by changes in the money stock and velocity that exceed changes in real output. We also saw how to use publicly available data to calculate such variables as nominal output, real output, and the rate of inflation.

Our study of interest rates provided examples of how interest is paid on different types of financial instruments. We also examined the basics of determining the present and future value of loans. We will use the basic tools of present value analysis extensively in Chapter 8 to see how a host of financial instruments are priced.

Finally, we saw how taxes and inflation affect the real purchasing power of lenders and borrowers. We also looked at historical data on interest rates for various financial assets; the data illustrate that interest rates vary considerably over time and across different financial instruments.

The material presented in this chapter will serve as our starting point in the next chapter, where we develop economic models we can use to understand and predict changes in interest rates over time.

KEY TERMS

price level

nominal output

real output

inflation rate

economic growth

velocity

equation of exchange

inflationary expectations

future value (FV)

present value (PV)

real interest rate

inflation premium

nominal interest rate

anticipated inflation

unanticipated inflation

aftertax interest rate

QUESTIONS AND PROBLEMS

1. If the price of a textbook increases by 7 percent, can you conclude that the inflation rate is 7 percent? Explain.

2. The price level was 26.02 in 1960 and 26.25 in 1961. What was the inflation rate between 1960 and 1961?

3. M1 was $167.9 billion in 1965 and $172.1 billion in 1966. Assuming velocity was constant during this period, how much would real output have had to grow for no inflation to have occurred? Explain.

4. A coupon bond with a face value of $1,000 pays $80 at the end of each year for five years and then matures. The interest rate on similar one-year investments is 8 percent. What is the present value of this bond?

5. **(a).** Determine the present value of $10,000 when the interest rate is 5 percent and the money is to be received in (1) 1 year, (2) 5 years, and (3) 10 years.
(b). What do you conclude about the relationship between when money is received and present value?

6. **(a).** Determine the present value of $10,000 to be received in five years when the interest rate is (1) zero percent, (2) 5 percent, and (3) 10 percent.
(b). What do you conclude about the relationship between the interest rate and the present value of a future amount?

7. If the interest rate is 10 percent, how much money would you have to put in the bank today to be a millionaire in 30 years?

8. "If you put $100 in a bank account that draws 5 percent interest, in one year you will have $105 and in two years you will have $110." Is this statement true or false? Explain.

9. Using Table 3.1, compare the six-month commercial paper rate with the six-month U.S. Treasury bill rate. Which is usually higher? Is this always the case? Can you explain why one rate is usually higher than the other?

10. "If the expected inflation rate is 5 percent and a lender loans out money at a 4 percent interest rate, he or she will end up with a 9 percent real return on the investment." Is this statement true or false? Explain.

11. Does inflation "hurt" borrowers or lenders? Explain carefully.

12. Joe issues a loan at an interest rate of 9 percent. Determine the "effective" interest rate Joe earns if
(a). Joe is in the 28 percent tax bracket and expects no inflation.
(b). Joe does not pay taxes but expects the inflation rate to be 6 percent.
(c). Joe is in the 28 percent tax bracket and expects the inflation rate to be 6 percent.

13. Suppose you just learned that the government plans to print more money to finance the federal budget deficit.
(a). How would this action affect your estimate of expected inflation? Why?
(b). How would this action affect the inflation premium you would charge on a loan? Why?
(c). How would this action affect the nominal interest rate you would charge on a loan? Why?

14. Briefly explain why interest rates vary (1) across different types of financial instruments and (2) over time.

SELECTIONS FOR FURTHER READING

Adams, R. D., and M. Moghaddam. "Searching for the Darby Effect in Tax Exempt and Taxable Interest Rate Data." *Quarterly Journal of Business and Economics,* 30 (Summer 1991), 48–63.

Allen, S. D. "The Determinants of the Tax-Adjusted Real Interest Rate." *Journal of Macroeconomics,* 14 (Winter 1992), 15–32.

Amsler, C. E. "What Determines Expected Real Interest Rates? *Quarterly Review of Economics and Business,* 25 (Winter 1985), 59–67.

Bach, G. L., and J. B. Stephenson. "Inflation and the Redistribution of Wealth." *Review of Economics and Statistics,* 56 (February 1974), 1–13.

Ball, L., and S. G. Cecchetti. "Inflation and Uncertainty at Short and Long Horizons." *Brookings Papers on Economic Activity* (1990), 215–245.

Biswas, B., and P. J. Saunders. "Money and Price Level in India: An Empirical Analysis." *Indian Economic Journal,* 38 (July–September 1990), 103–114.

Brunner, L. P., H. Beladi, and H. A. Zuberi. "Inflation and Indexation: An Empirical Approach." *Southern Economic Journal,* 52 (July 1985), 250–264.

Cecchetti, Stephen G. "The Case of the Negative Nominal Interest Rates: New Estimates of the Term Structure of Interest Rates During the Great Depression." *Journal of Political Economy,* 96 (December 1988), 1111–1141.

Gerdes, W. D. "Mr. Fisher and the Classics." *American Economist,* 30 (Spring 1986), 66–72.

Graham, F. C. "The Fisher Hypothesis: A Critique of Recent Results and Some New Evidence." *Southern Economic Journal,* 54 (April 1988), 961–968.

Grennes, T., and J. S. Lapp. "Neutrality of Inflation in the Agricultural Sector." *Journal of International Money and Finance,* 5 (June 1986), 231–243.

Hula, D. G. "The Phillips Curve and the Natural Rate of Inflation." *Policy Sciences,* 24 (November 1991), 357–366.

Ibrahim, I. B., and R. M. Williams. "The Fisher Relationship under Different Monetary Standards: A Note." *Journal of Money, Credit, and Banking,* 10 (August 1978), 363–370.

Mark, N. C. "Some Evidence on the International Inequality of Real Interest Rates." *Journal of International Money and Finance,* 4 (June 1985), 189–208.

Marquis, M. H., and K. L. Reffett. "Real Interest Rates and Endogenous Growth in a Monetary Economy." *Economics Letters,* 37 (October 1991), pp. 105–109.

Pelaez, R. F. "Interest Rates as Predictors of Inflation Revisited." *Southern Economic Journal,* 55 (April 1989), 1025–1028.

Ratti, R. A. "Sectoral Employment Variability and Unexpected Inflation." *Review of Economics and Statistics,* 67 (May 1985), 278–283.

Ring, R. J., Jr. "Variability of Inflation and Income across Income Classes." *Social Science Quarterly,* 66 (March 1985), 203–209.

Swofford, J. L., and G. A. Whitney. "The Composition and Construction of Monetary Aggregates." *Economic Inquiry,* 29 (October 1991), 752–761.

Thistle, P. D., R. W. McLeod, and B. L. Conrad. "Interest Rates and Bank Portfolio Adjustments." *Journal of Banking and Finance,* 13 (March 1989), 151–161.

Varghese, K. T. "Wage Indexation, Inflation, and Unemployment." *Journal of Economics and Business,* 32 (Fall 1979), pp. 51–55.

Wolf, H. A., and R. W. McEnally. "The Unemployment-Inflation Trade-off, 1948–1968: A Multiple Phillips Curve Analysis." *Social Science Quarterly,* 51 (September 1970), 275–284.

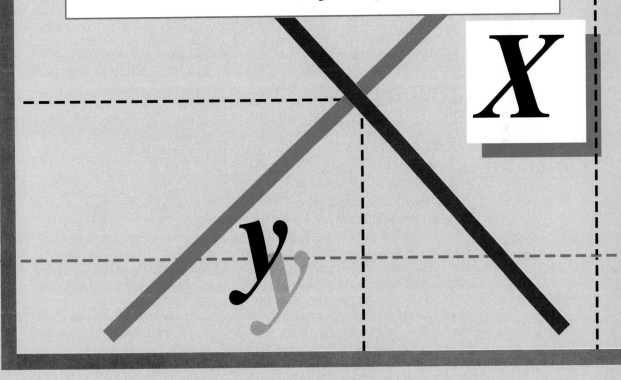

PART TWO

The Microeconomics of Banking and Financial Markets

CHAPTERS

4

Supply and Demand in Financial Markets

5

The Bank as a Firm: Loans

6

The Bank as a Firm: Deposits

7

The Banking Industry

4

Supply and Demand in Financial Markets

*L*ast week the *Wall Street Journal* reported that mortgage interest rates increased by .25 percent. What economic factors would have led to such a change? What impact will this change have on your ability to borrow funds for a house or a new car? This chapter presents the basic economic tool needed to answer these questions: supply and demand analysis.

Recall from your principles course that economists use supply and demand to analyze how market forces determine the price and quantity of a good or service. In the first part of this chapter, we review these basic tools and see how they can be used to explain how market forces determine the prices of ATM transactions, insurance policies, and other fee-based financial services. In the second part, we develop a supply and demand apparatus that is very useful for analyzing the market for loanable funds—the market that determines the interest rate charged for such loans as mortgages and car loans.

BASIC SUPPLY AND DEMAND ANALYSIS: A BRIEF REVIEW WITH APPLICATIONS TO FEE-BASED FINANCIAL SERVICES

If you took an introductory economics course, you probably learned how the supply and demand for products like gasoline ultimately determine the price you pay at the pump. Many financial services are priced like any other commodity. Just as the price of gasoline is quoted in terms of the amount you must pay for each gallon, the prices of **fee-based financial services,** such as withdrawals from an automatic teller machine (ATM), are quoted in terms of the amount you must pay for each withdrawal. Similarly, the price of an automobile insurance policy is quoted in terms of the amount you must pay to insure a given type of car. Accountants and bookkeepers price their services based on the amount you must pay for each hour of their services. Other examples of fee-based financial services are wire transfers, traveler's checks, credit reports, and the like.

Since prices of a fee-based financial service are quoted in terms of dollars per unit of the service purchased, we can use basic supply and demand analysis to see how the prices for these services are determined. Accordingly, the remainder of this section provides a brief review of basic principles of supply and demand analysis and uses them to analyze markets for fee-based financial services. We will use supply and demand analysis extensively throughout this book, so make sure you master this material before reading on.

Demand for Fee-Based Financial Services

Suppose you must determine whether or not to use an ATM to obtain cash from your checking account. Your decision will depend on a number of things, including the price charged for each withdrawal, your income, and the price of alternatives such as writing a check or withdrawing cash directly from the bank.[1]

The **demand curve** in Figure 4.1 shows the relationship between the price of ATM transactions and the quantity demanded of ATM transactions, holding other things constant. By the **law of demand,** an increase in the price of a fee-based financial service results in a decline in its quantity demanded. In Figure 4.1, we see that when the price of an ATM transaction is $1, 15 million in transactions are made each month. When the price rises to $2, consumers reduce the quantity of monthly ATM transactions to 10 million. The movement along a demand curve, such as the one from *A* to *B* in Figure 4.1, denotes a **change in quantity demanded.** In other words, a change in the price of a fee-based financial service leads to a change in the quantity demanded for that service.

Remember that the position of the demand curve in Figure 4.1 assumes that other things, such as income, prices of related goods, and consumer tastes, are held constant. If these things changed, the demand curve would shift to the right or the left depending on the nature of the change. A shift in the entire demand curve, such as the shift from D^1 to D^2 or D^3 in Figure 4.2, denotes a **change in demand** for fee-based services.

Determinants of Demand for Fee-Based Financial Services.
Economists call variables that affect the position of the demand curve **determinants of demand.** Changes in one or more of these determinants—including a change in the price of complementary or substitute goods, income, and tastes—shift the demand curve.

---

[1] This example has several complications. Banks sometimes offer their customers the "free" use of ATM machines located on their premises. Instead of paying a fee for each transaction, customers are required to keep a certain minimum balance in their accounts at the bank. Banks gain in two ways from this arrangement. First, they can hire fewer tellers, thus reducing labor costs. Second, they can earn interest by lending out the minimum balance customers are required to hold. Note, however, that even in these cases customers usually pay a fee for using ATM machines not located at their own banks. Our analysis of ATM transactions can be thought of as using ATM machines located away from the customer's bank.

The law of demand applies to financial services as well as to other goods and services. As the price of ATM transactions rises from $1 to $2, the quantity of ATM transactions demanded falls from 15 million to 10 million. The movement from point *A* to point *B* along the demand curve represents a change in quantity demanded.

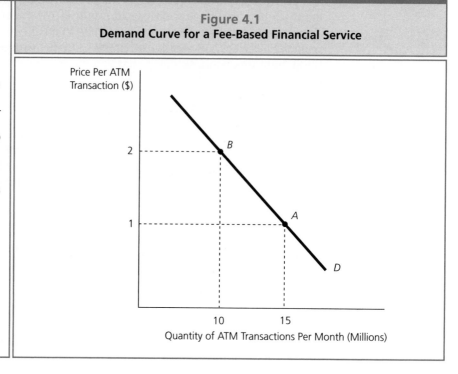

Figure 4.1
Demand Curve for a Fee-Based Financial Service

Prices of Substitutes.

One determinant of the demand for any good or service, including fee-based financial services, is the prices of substitutes. Goods or services are **substitutes** if, when the price of one increases, the demand for the other increases. For instance, withdrawing cash from an ATM is a substitute for writing a check. If your bank substantially increased the fee it charges you for each check you write, you would likely increase your use of ATMs. Figure 4.2 illustrates this increase in demand for ATMs by the shift from D^1 to D^3, which reflects the fact that consumers now make more ATM transactions than before at each price of an ATM withdrawal. A decrease in the price of a substitute good or service shifts the demand curve in the opposite direction, from D^1 to D^2.

Prices of Complements.

Another determinant of the demand for a financial service is the prices of complements. **Complements** are goods or services that tend to be used jointly. An easy way to see why the prices of complements affect the position of the demand curve for a given fee-based financial service is to consider car insurance, which is an example of such a service.[2] For a fee—the insurance premium—the insurance company agrees

---

[2] We analyze insurance more explicitly in Chapters 6, 7, and 9, where we look at insurance as a way to reduce risk.

to accept some of the financial responsibility for any accidents or other damages incurred by you or others. Car insurance and cars are complements: When the price of car insurance rises, fewer individuals will buy car insurance (due to the law of demand) and in turn will desire fewer cars (since insurance is usually a prerequisite for purchasing—or at least driving—a car). Indeed, many teenagers find they can more easily afford a car than they can afford the insurance on that car.

Since cars and car insurance are complements, an increase in the prices of cars reduces the demand for car insurance. This would be depicted as a shift to the left in the demand for car insurance. Similarly, a decrease in the prices of cars would lead to an increase in the demand for car insurance—a shift to the right in the demand for car insurance.

Income.   Income also influences the demand for fee-based financial services. Normally increases in income lead to increases in the demand for fee-based financial services, since the extra income affords individuals a greater opportunity to purchase these services. A decrease in income would lead to a decrease in the demand for financial services—a shift to the left in the demand curve.

Tastes.   Finally, a change in consumer tastes can change the position of the demand curve. For instance, if a change in tastes leads consumers to

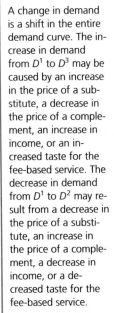

A change in demand is a shift in the entire demand curve. The increase in demand from D^1 to D^3 may be caused by an increase in the price of a substitute, a decrease in the price of a complement, an increase in income, or an increased taste for the fee-based service. The decrease in demand from D^1 to D^2 may result from a decrease in the price of a substitute, an increase in the price of a complement, a decrease in income, or a decreased taste for the fee-based service.

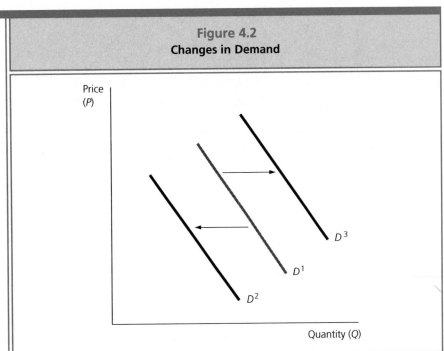

Figure 4.2
Changes in Demand

increase their use of cash and shun credit cards, the demand for ATM transactions will shift to the right. Conversely, if a taste change causes consumers to decrease their use of cash, the demand for ATM transactions will shift to the left.

Summary
Exercise 4.1

Homeowner's insurance is a fee-based financial service. Illustrate graphically the impact of the following on the demand for homeowner's insurance: (a) a reduction in the price of homeowner's insurance, (b) a reduction in income, and (c) a reduction in the price of new houses.

Answer: (a) By the law of demand, a reduction in the price of homeowner's insurance leads to an increase in the quantity demanded of homeowner's insurance. This corresponds to the movement from *A* to *B* in part a. (b) A reduction in income would decrease the demand for homeowner's insurance. This corresponds to the movement from D^1 to D^2 in part b. (c) Since new houses and homeowner's insurance are complements, a reduction in the price of new houses would increase the demand for homeowner's insurance. This corresponds to the shift from D^1 to D^2 in part c.

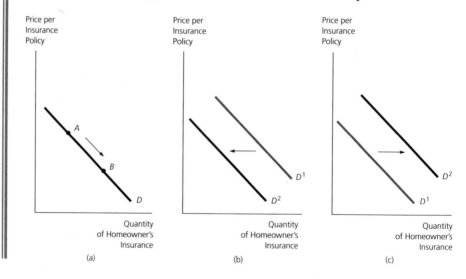

Supply of Fee-Based Financial Services

The **supply curve** for a fee-based financial service shows the quantity of financial services suppliers are willing and able to provide at alternative prices, holding everything else constant. Figure 4.3 depicts typical supply curves for ATM transactions. The movement along a supply curve, such as the one from *A* to *B* along S^1, is called a **change in quantity supplied.** The fact that the supply curve for fee-based financial services slopes upward simply reflects the **law of supply:** Providers of financial services provide more services when the price is high than when it is low.

A change in a variable other than the price of the financial service, such as input prices or a change in technolgy, leads to a **change in supply.** This corresponds to a shift in the entire supply curve, such as the shift in Figure 4.3 from S^1 to either S^2 or S^3.

Determinants of the Supply of Fee-Based Financial Services.

The **determinants of supply** are those factors that affect the position of the supply curve. They include input prices and the level of technology.

Input Prices.

A decrease in the price of an input (a decline in the price of electricity, for instance) shifts the supply curve to the right because suppliers of fee-based financial services are willing and able to provide more output at each price due to the lower input price. In Figure 4.3, suppose S^1 is the initial supply curve for ATM transactions. If the price of electricity falls, suppliers are willing to provide more ATM transactions at each price, so the supply curve shifts to the right to S^3. Conversely, an increase in the

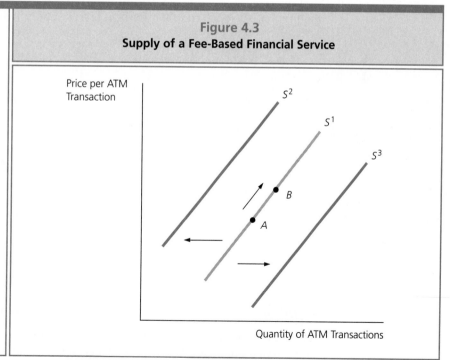

The law of supply states that as the price of a fee-based financial service rises, the quantity supplied of the service increases. This is represented by the movement from *A* to *B* along supply curve S^1. A change in a determinant of supply leads to a change in the position of the supply curve. An increase in supply is represented by a shift in the supply curve to the right from S^1 to S^3. A decrease in supply is reflected by a shift in the supply curve to the left from S^1 to S^2.

Figure 4.3
Supply of a Fee-Based Financial Service

Price per ATM Transaction

S^2

S^1

S^3

B

A

Quantity of ATM Transactions

price of an input (for example, an increase in the price of labor) shifts the supply curve to the left, such as the shift from S^1 to S^2 in Figure 4.3.

Technology.   Changes in technology also affect the position of the supply curve. Technological advances shift the supply curve to the right, since more of the services will be supplied at each price. This is reflected in Figure 4.3 as the increase in supply from S^1 to S^3. Indeed, improvements in computer technology have substantially increased the supply of ATMs, and banks provide more ATM transactions at each price today than they did five years ago.

Summary
Exercise 4.2

Many banks charge a fee for wire transfer services—the transfer of funds from one financial institution to another via telephone lines or other electronic media, including wireless communications. Illustrate graphically the impact on the supply of wire transfer services of (a) the innovation of satellites that replace telephone wires and (b) an increase in the wage paid to wire transfer operators.

Answer: Wire transfers are a fee-based financial service, since a charge is levied for each transfer. (a) The innovation of satellites is an improvement in technology, which leads to an increase in supply from S to S^1 in part a. (b) An increase in the wage paid to wire transfer operators is an increase in the price of an input and therefore decreases supply from S to S^2 in part b.

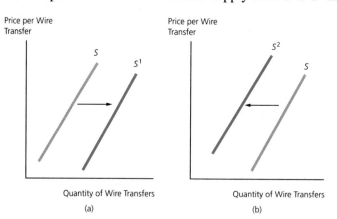

Equilibrium in the Market for Fee-Based Financial Services

Interactions among all buyers and sellers in the market determine the prices of fee-based financial services. More precisely, the interaction of supply and demand for a service determines its price.

Figure 4.4 shows hypothetical supply and demand curves for ATM transactions. To see how the market price is determined, suppose the price of ATM withdrawals is $1 per transaction. This price corresponds to point B on the demand curve, where consumers wish to make 15 million transactions per month. Similarly, the price of $1 corresponds to point A on the supply curve, so banks provide only 5 million ATM transactions per month at this price. When the price is $1, quantity demanded exceeds quantity supplied, creating a **shortage.** Shortages are associated with long lines; thus, when the price is $1, consumers experience higher transactions costs due to the inconvenience of having to wait in line to use an ATM.

Shortages put pressure on the price to rise. As the price rises from $1 to $2 in Figure 4.4, banks increase their quantity supplied of ATM services to accommodate 10 million transactions per month at this higher price. Similarly, as the price rises, consumers use ATMs less frequently. When the price rises to $2, the quantity demanded is 10 million transactions per month. At this price, banks provide just enough ATMs to accommodate all consumers willing and able to use them at that price; quantity demanded equals quantity supplied. The market is in **equilibrium,** meaning there is no tendency for the price to change any further.

Why wouldn't the price rise above $2 to, say, $3? At a price above the equilibrium level, there would be a **surplus** of ATM transactions because

At a price of $1, quantity demanded exceeds quantity supplied by 10 million. This shortage of ATM transactions causes the price to rise. At a price of $3, quantity demanded is less than quantity supplied by 10 million. This surplus of ATM transactions causes the price to fall. At a price of $2, quantity demanded equals quantity supplied, and no tendency exists for price to either rise or fall. This condition is called an *equilibrium.*

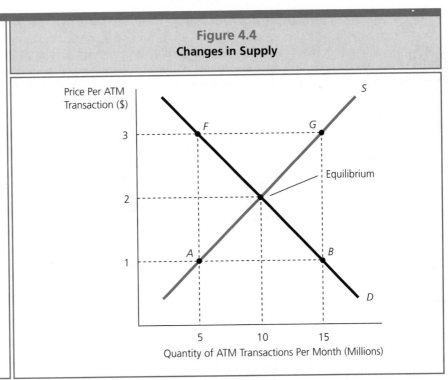

Figure 4.4
Changes in Supply

banks' quantity supplied of ATM transactions would exceed the quantity demanded by consumers. This underutilization of ATM machines would ultimately put pressure on banks to lower the price of ATM withdrawals. When the price falls to $2, the quantity demanded and the quantity supplied are both 10 million, and the market is in equilibrium.

Thus, the interaction of supply and demand ultimately determines a market price for the fee-based financial service—in this case, $2—such that neither a shortage nor a surplus of the good exists. This price is called the *equilibrium price*, and the corresponding quantity (10 million) is called the *equilibrium quantity* for the market. Once this price and quantity are realized, the market forces of supply and demand are balanced; there is no tendency for prices to either rise or fall until something changes the position of the demand or supply curve.

Changes in Equilibrium: Applications to the Insurance Market

The final step in our review of supply and demand is to show how changes in demand or supply can lead to changes in the prices of fee-based financial services. While the techniques described can be used to analyze markets for all types of fee-based financial services, we focus on the insurance market to provide a foundation for the analysis of insurance in Chapters 6, 7, and 9.

Impact of an Increase in the Demand for Insurance.   Imagine that an increase in the U.S. birth rate increases the demand for life insurance. How will this change affect the price of a typical life insurance policy? Figure 4.5 shows the initial supply (S^0) and demand (D^0) curves for life insurance. The initial equilibrium is at point A, where the equilibrium price of the average policy is $300 per year. Assuming other things remain unchanged, the increase in demand from D^0 to D^1 leads to a new equilibrium at point B. As a consequence of the increase in the demand for life insurance, the market price increases from $300 to $350, and the quantity of policies sold increases from 500 million to 600 million.

The reason for the change in equilibrium is as you would expect. When demand increases, there are too few insurance companies and agents to process applications at the old price to satisfy the number of consumers willing and able to buy policies at that price. This creates excess demand that puts pressure on the price to rise. As the price rises, insurance companies increase their quantity supplied (moving along S^0 from A to B) and consumers reduce their quantity demanded (moving along D^1 from C to B) until ultimately enough policies are offered at the new price of $350 to exactly equal quantity demanded.

Impact of a Decrease in the Supply of Insurance.   What would happen to the price of life insurance if rising costs in the insurance industry

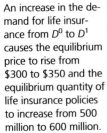

An increase in the demand for life insurance from D^0 to D^1 causes the equilibrium price to rise from $300 to $350 and the equilibrium quantity of life insurance policies to increase from 500 million to 600 million.

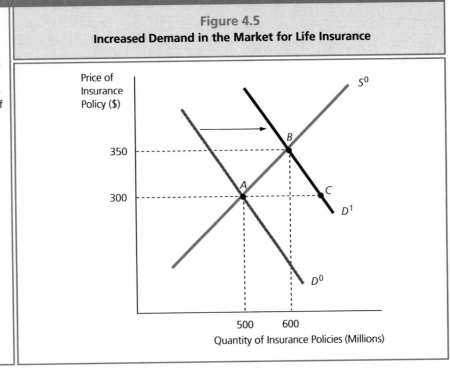

Figure 4.5

Increased Demand in the Market for Life Insurance

caused the supply to decrease? Point *A* in Figure 4.6 shows the initial equilibrium in the insurance market, where demand curve D^0 intersects the market supply curve S^0. The increase in the cost of providing insurance decreases the supply of insurance from S^0 to S^1, resulting in a new market equilibrium at point *B*. In this instance, the market price rises from $300 to $400, and the equilibrium quantity of insurance policies decreases from 500 million to 300 million. At the initial price of $300, consumers wish to buy more insurance than insurance companies provide at that price. The market mechanism eliminates the resulting shortage by raising the equilibrium price, in this case from $300 to $400 per policy.

Impact of a Simultaneous Increase in Demand and Decrease in the Supply of Insurance.   Finally, let us see what would happen to the price of life insurance if the supply and demand changed at the same time due to a simultaneous increase in the birth rate and costs in the insurance industry. In Figure 4.7, the insurance market is initially in equilibrium at point *A*, where demand curve D^0 intersects the market supply curve S^0. Supply decreases from S^0 to S^1 due to the higher costs of providing insurance, and demand increases from D^0 to D^1 as a result of the higher birth rate. In

A decrease in the supply of life insurance from S^0 to S^1 causes the equilibrium price to rise from $300 to $400 and the equilibrium number of policies to fall from 500 million to 300 million.

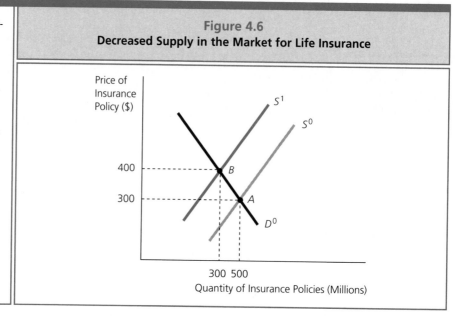

Figure 4.6
Decreased Supply in the Market for Life Insurance

this instance, a new equilibrium occurs at point B; the price increases from P^0 to P^1, and the quantity increases from Q^0 to Q^1.

Given the magnitude of the increase in demand and the decrease in supply in Figure 4.7, both the price and the quantity of insurance policies increase. Notice, however, that if the supply curve had shifted much farther to the left—say, to S^2—it would have intersected the new demand curve, D^1, at point C instead of B. In this case, the price (P^2) would still be higher than the initial equilibrium price of P^0. However, the resulting quantity (Q^2) would be lower than at the initial equilibrium quantity of Q^0, since at point C fewer insurance policies are bought and sold than at point A. Thus, when demand increases and supply decreases, the market price of fee-based financial services rises, but the market quantity may rise or fall depending on the relative magnitude of the shifts.

This example illustrates a general principle: Simultaneous changes in the demand and supply of fee-based financial services will lead to some ambiguity regarding whether price or quantity rises or falls. To determine the precise impact of simultaneous changes in demand and supply, we must take care that the conclusions we draw are not due to how far we have shifted the curves.

Summary
Exercise 4.3

Graphically illustrate what would happen in the market for traveler's checks if (a) due to a reduction in terrorist activity, families did more traveling; (b) a bank card was introduced that rebated 1 percent of all charges to the cardholder; and (c) the cost of issuing traveler's checks increased.

When demand increases from D^0 to D^1 and supply decreases by a small amount (from S^0 to S^1), the equilibrium quantity rises to Q^1 and the price rises to P^1. If the shift in supply is relatively large (a shift from S^0 to S^2), the equilibrium quantity falls to Q^2 and the price rises to P^2. In both cases, price rises but the effect on the equilibrium quantity depends on the magnitude of the decrease in supply.

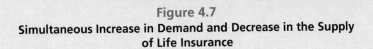

Figure 4.7
Simultaneous Increase in Demand and Decrease in the Supply of Life Insurance

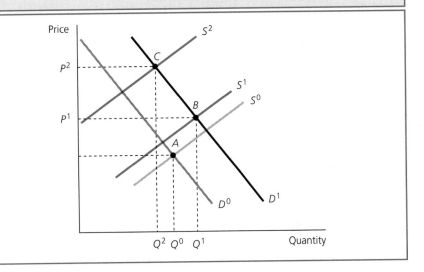

Answer: (a) This change in tastes for traveling would increase the demand for traveler's checks from D to D^1 in part a, resulting in an increase in both the equilibrium price and the equilibrium quantity of traveler's checks. (b) Since bank cards are a substitute for traveler's checks, a reduction in the price of using a bank card would decrease the demand for traveler's checks from D to D^2 in part b, reducing the equilibrium price and quantity of traveler's checks. (c) An increase in the cost of issuing traveler's checks would reduce the supply of traveler's checks in part c from S to S^1. This would increase the equilibrium price and reduce the equilibrium quantity of traveler's checks.

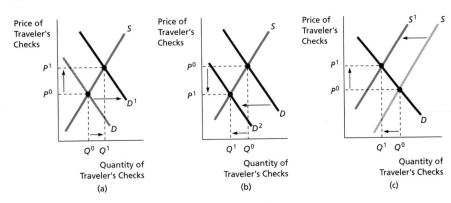

THE MARKET FOR LOANABLE FUNDS

In contrast to the prices of fee-based financial services, the price you pay for a mortgage or a car loan is not stated in terms of a dollar amount; rather, it is quoted as an interest rate. In shopping for a *car,* you generally wish to buy from the dealer that asks you to pay the lowest *dollar price.* When shopping for a *car loan,* you seek the lender offering the lowest *interest rate.* Financial services with prices expressed in terms of an interest rate are called **loanable funds.** You can think of the interest rate as the price of a dollar's worth of credit; that is, an interest rate of 10 percent means each dollar's worth of credit costs 10 cents. We can easily modify the supply and demand apparatus reviewed in the previous section to see how interest rates are determined in the market for loanable funds.

The Demand for Loanable Funds

Individuals borrow funds for such things as mortgages, car loans, personal loans, and education; businesses borrow funds to obtain capital equipment and working capital; and governments borrow funds to pay for government services, public investment in infrastructure, education, and so on. These three groups comprise the primary demanders of loanable funds in our economy.

Figure 4.8 shows a typical demand curve for loanable funds. This curve reflects the quantity of loanable funds that will be demanded at alternative *nominal* interest rates, holding everything else that might affect a borrower's

According to the law of demand, when the *nominal* interest rate falls from 10 to 5 percent and other things remain constant, the quantity demanded of loanable funds rises from $300 million to $600 million. Thus, the demand for loanable funds is downward sloping. The movement from point *A* to point *B* represents a change in quantity demanded.

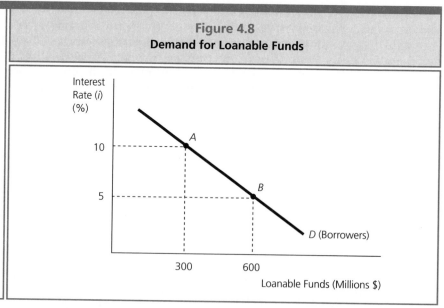

Figure 4.8
Demand for Loanable Funds

decision constant. When the interest rate on loanable funds is 10 percent, the quantity demanded of loanable funds is $300 million. When the interest rate falls to 5 percent, the quantity demanded of loanable funds increases to $600 million. Thus, the demand curve for loanable funds reflects the law of demand: The quantity demanded of loanable funds by borrowers increases as the price of credit (the interest rate) falls.

The demand curve for loanable funds holds everything constant except the interest rate on the particular type of loan. The movement along a demand curve, such as the one from *A* to *B* in Figure 4.8, denotes a change in quantity demanded. Whenever a variable other than the interest rate on a particular type of loan changes, it shifts the entire position of the demand curve. This shift in the entire demand curve, as from D^1 to either to D^2 or D^3 in Figure 4.9, reflects a change in demand.

Determinants of the Demand for Loanable Funds.   Table 4.1 summarizes the determinants of demand for loanable funds and shows the variables that can affect the willingness of either households, firms, or government to borrow funds. These variables are discussed next.

Interest on Alternative Sources of Funds.   Recall that the demand for a good or service depends on the prices of substitutes. The demand

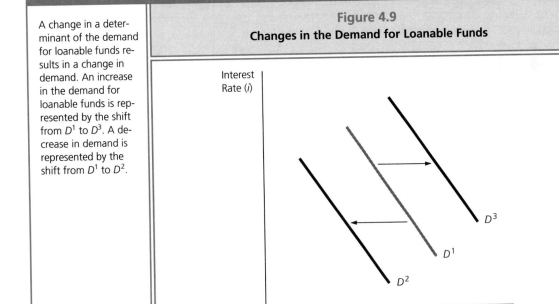

A change in a determinant of the demand for loanable funds results in a change in demand. An increase in the demand for loanable funds is represented by the shift from D^1 to D^3. A decrease in demand is represented by the shift from D^1 to D^2.

Figure 4.9
Changes in the Demand for Loanable Funds

Interest Rate (*i*)

D^3

D^1

D^2

Loanable Funds

> ### Table 4.1
> ### Determinants of Demand for Loanable Funds
>
> The position of the demand curve for loanable funds depends on the interest rate on alternative sources of funds, inflationary expectations, the tax deductibility of interest payments, the taste for borrowing, the profitability of business projects, and the size of the government budget deficit. The pluses in the right-hand column indicate that increases in any of these variables lead to a rightward shift in the demand for loanable funds.

Variable	Effect of an Increase in the Variable on the Demand For Loanable Funds
Interest rate on alternative sources of funds	+
Inflationary expectations	+
Tax deductibility of household interest payments	+
Taste for borrowing	+
Profitability of business projects	+
Size of government budget deficits	+

for loanable funds is no exception. A decrease in the interest rate on alternative sources of funds induces borrowers to substitute away from existing sources of funds and toward the sources with the lower interest rates.

Suppose a bank decides to offer a 1.9 percent interest rate on a new-car loan—a much lower rate than that offered at car dealerships. We would now expect fewer borrowers to obtain loans from car dealers and instead substitute toward the lower-priced funds at the bank. The reduction in interest rates offered by the bank thus leads to a decrease in the demand for loans from car dealers, since the two sources of car loans are substitutes.

This relation works the same way for firms, except that firms borrow to fund projects rather than buy cars. Regardless, the willingness of firms to acquire a given type of loanable funds still depends on the interest rate on substitute sources of funds. For instance, when IBM seeks funds for working capital, it can borrow funds in the bond market or directly from a bank. An increase in the rate IBM must pay on bonds will increase IBM's demand for bank loans; it substitutes toward them due to the higher cost of obtaining funds in the bond market.

Inflationary Expectations. Since borrowers receive current funds in exchange for the promise of future interest and principal payments, a borrower's inflationary expectations affect her or his perceived real cost of repaying the loan. For a given nominal interest rate, a higher expected inflation rate translates into a lower real cost of borrowing, since the borrower expects to pay back the loan with dollars that have lower purchasing power due to inflation. For a given nominal interest rate, borrowers will therefore increase their current demand for loanable funds whenever the expected rate of inflation increases.

Figure 4.9 on page 105 illustrates the impact of a change in inflationary expectations on the demand for loanable funds. The initial demand curve, D^1, represents the quantity of loanable funds demanded at alternative nominal interest rates, holding everything else (including the expected rate of inflation) constant. An increase in the expected rate of inflation shifts the demand curve to the right to D^3, where a greater quantity of funds is demanded at each interest rate. A decrease in inflationary expectations shifts the demand curve to the left to D^2, where fewer funds are desired at each interest rate.

Box 4.1 compares actual and expected inflation rates from 1982 to 1992.

Tax Deductibility of Household Interest Payments. In the United States and many other industrialized countries, governments allow households to deduct certain types of interest payments from income before computing their tax liability. For instance, in the United States, households can deduct mortgage interest payments from income before computing federal taxes. The demand for mortgage funds by households therefore depends in part on the marginal tax rate imposed on households.

To see why this is so, suppose a consumer with $100,000 in income borrows $50,000 at an interest rate of 10 percent. If the government taxes the consumer's income at 30 percent and interest payments are not tax deductible, the consumer pays $100,000 × .3 = $30,000 in taxes. However, if interest payments are tax deductible, the consumer deducts the interest payments (in this case, $50,000 × .1 = $5,000) from income before computing taxes:

Income	$100,000
Less interest	$5,000
Taxable income	$95,000

If interest is deductible, the consumer's tax liability is only $95,000 × .3 = $28,500, which is $1,500 less than it is when interest is not tax deductible. The tax deductibility of interest payments reduces a borrower's tax liability and thus encourages more borrowing.

More generally, we saw in Chapter 3 that when the nominal interest rate is i and the marginal tax rate is τ, the effective aftertax interest rate is

$$i_\tau = (1 - \tau) \times i.$$

The Data Bank

Box 4.1

Actual and Expected Rates of Inflation

How accurate are expectations of inflation? The accompanying figure graphs the actual and expected inflation rates in the United States from 1982 through 1992. These expected rates of inflation are based on surveys of economists who regularly forecast changes in the price level.

There are several things to notice about this graph. First, the actual and expected inflation rates tend to move together over time. Second, the expected inflation rate is much smoother and less volatile than the actual inflation rate. Third, during the period from 1982 through 1986, the expected inflation rate seems to have been systematically above the actual infla-

tion rate. During this period, the "experts" were making forecasts that on average were too high, or biased upward. From 1987 onward, there was a less strong bias in the expected inflation rates, although in the 1991–1992 period, a tendency to overstate the actual inflation rate recurred.

_____

Source: Citibase electronic database. For actual inflation rates, annual percentage change in the consumer price index. For expected inflation rates, forecasts of annual percentage change in the consumer price index by economists surveyed in the ASA-NBER *Business Outlook Survey.*

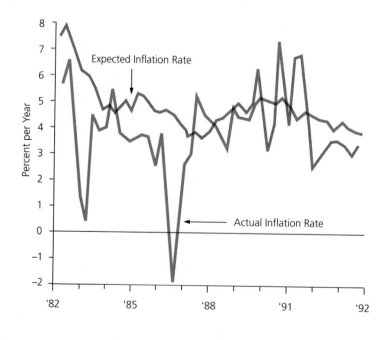

Notice that the aftertax interest rate (i_τ) decreases as the marginal tax rate (τ) increases. This illustrates that an increase in the marginal tax rate actually reduces the effective (aftertax) cost of borrowing and thus increases the demand for tax-deductible loanable funds such as mortgages.

Taste for Borrowing.

Tastes also affect the demand for loanable funds. Households, businesses, or governments may wish to borrow more or fewer funds at each interest rate due to changes in family composition, business status, or voter preferences. This change in tastes shifts the demand for loanable funds to the right or the left, depending on the nature of the change. Taste changes that result in a desire to borrow more at each interest rate shift the demand curve to the right. When borrowers desire fewer loanable funds at each interest rate, the demand curve shifts to the left.

Profitability of Business Projects.

Changes in the expected profitability of business projects alter the willingness of firms to borrow funds to finance the business projects and therefore affect the demand for loanable funds. An increase in the profitability of business projects shifts the demand for loanable funds to the right. This is because businesses now desire more loanable funds at each interest rate to be able to undertake the more profitable projects.

Magnitude of Government Budget Deficits.

Federal, state, and local governments also demand loanable funds to pay for expenses on such things as education, defense, welfare payments, and highways. The larger the projected budget deficit—that is, the greater the shortfall between tax receipts and government expenditures—the greater the amount the government must borrow to pay for the projects. For this reason, increases in the portion of the budget deficit financed through borrowing lead to increases in the government's demand for loanable funds. We will say much more about this important issue in Chapters 16 and 21.

Summary Exercise 4.4

Graphically illustrate the impact of the following on the demand for loanable funds: (a) a reduction in inflationary expectations, (b) an increase in the profitability of business projects, and (c) an increase in the size of the federal government budget deficit.

Answer: (a) A reduction in inflationary expectations decreases the demand for loanable funds from D^1 to D^2 in Figure 4.9 on page 105. (b) An increase in the profitability of projects funded through borrowing shifts the demand curve for loanable funds from D^1 to D^3 in Figure 4.9. (c) An increase in the budget deficit leads to an increase in the demand for loanable funds from D^1 to D^3 in Figure 4.9.

The Supply of Loanable Funds

Demand reflects only one side of the market for loanable funds; the other side of the market is supply. Suppliers of loanable funds give up the current use of funds in exchange for interest payments. The law of supply as it relates to loanable funds says that, holding other things constant, the higher the *nominal* interest rate, the greater the quantity of loanable funds supplied by lenders. Thus, a typical supply curve for loanable funds is upward sloping, as in Figure 4.10. When the nominal interest rate is 5 percent, lenders provide $200 million in loanable funds. When the interest rate rises to 10 percent, the quantity supplied increases to $300 million.

The movement along a given supply curve for loanable funds, such as the movement from *A* to *B* in Figure 4.10, denotes a change in the quantity of loanable funds supplied. A change in the position of the supply curve denotes a change in supply.

Determinants of the Supply of Loanable Funds. The major determinants of the supply of loanable funds—those factors that affect its position—are interest rates on alternative uses of funds, inflationary expectations, the tax rate on interest income, wealth, risk, and liquidity. Table 4.2

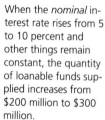

When the *nominal* interest rate rises from 5 to 10 percent and other things remain constant, the quantity of loanable funds supplied increases from $200 million to $300 million.

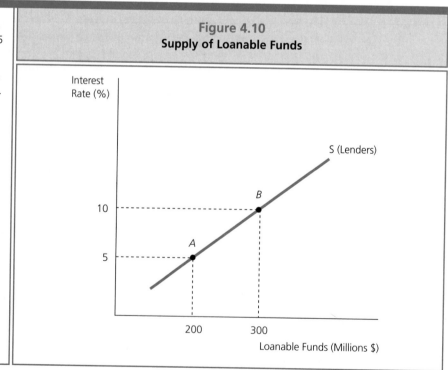

Figure 4.10
Supply of Loanable Funds

Table 4.2 Determinants of the Supply of Loanable Funds	
The position of the supply curve for loanable funds depends on the interest rate on alternative uses of funds, inflationary expectations, the tax rate on interest income, wealth, the riskiness of the loan, and the liquidity of the loan. The pluses in the right-hand column indicate that increases in wealth and liquidity shift the supply of loanable funds to the right. The minuses indicate that increases in interest rates on alternative uses of funds, inflationary expectations, the tax rate on interest income, or the riskiness of the loan shift the supply curve to the left.	
Variable	**Effect of an Increase in the Variable on the Supply of Loanable Funds**
Interest rate on alternative uses of funds	−
Inflationary expectations	−
Tax rate on interest income	−
Wealth	+
Riskiness of loan	−
Liquidity of loan	+

summarizes the impact of these variables on the position of the supply curve for loanable funds.

Interest on Alternative Use of Funds.
The greater the interest that could be earned by investing funds in some alternative use, the lower the supply of loanable funds. For instance, Figure 4.11 shows the initial supply of loanable funds, S^1. When the interest rate that could be earned by investing funds in an alternative investment rises, the supply of loanable funds shifts to the left to S^2. This means that at each interest rate, there is a lower quantity of loanable funds than before. Similarly, if the interest that could be earned on an alternative investment decreases, the supply curve shifts to the right, such as from S^1 to S^3 in Figure 4.11.

Inflationary Expectations.
Suppliers of loanable funds give up the use of money today in return for principal and interest at some future date. The higher the expected rate of inflation, the less that can be purchased when the principal and interest are repaid. Thus, increases in the expected rate of inflation reduce the willingness of suppliers of loanable funds to lend money

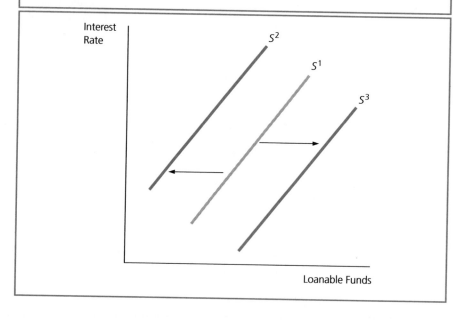

Figure 4.11
Changes in the Supply of Loanable Funds

Any of the following will cause a decrease in the supply of loanable funds from S^1 to S^2: a higher interest rate earned by investing funds in alternative uses, a higher expected inflation rate, an increase in the marginal tax rate, a decrease in wealth, an increase in the riskiness of the loan, and a decrease in the liquidity of the loan.

Any of the following will cause an increase in the supply of loanable funds from S^1 to S^3: a lower interest rate earned by investing funds in alternative uses, a lower expected inflation rate, a decrease in the marginal tax rate, an increase in wealth, a decrease in the riskiness of the loan, and an increase in the liquidity of the loan.

at the given interest rate. This is reflected in Figure 4.11 as the decrease in supply from S^1 to S^2. Conversely, a reduction in the expected rate of inflation increases supply from S^1 to S^3.

Tax Rate on Interest Income. Increases in the marginal tax rate reduce the amount of interest income lenders get to keep, which reduces the incentives to lend funds. In Figure 4.11, an increase in the marginal tax rate decreases the supply of loanable funds from S^1 to S^2, since lenders are willing to provide fewer funds at each interest rate. Similarly, a reduction in the marginal tax rate increases the supply of loanable funds from S^1 to S^3. As noted in Chapter 3, some forms of loanable funds (notably, municipal bonds) are exempt from federal taxes on interest income. Box 4.2 shows how this affects the relative rewards to investors on municipal versus other bonds.

Wealth. The wealth of lenders obviously affects their willingness and/or ability to supply loanable funds. In general, the greater a lender's wealth, the greater the lender's capacity to make loans, and thus the greater the supply of loanable funds. Graphically, an increase in wealth increases the supply of loanable funds, which is depicted in Figure 4.11 as the shift from S^1 to S^3. Similarly, a decrease in wealth decreases the supply of loanable funds from S^1 to S^2.

Risk. The level of risk associated with a loan affects the lender's willingness to make the loan, and thus affects the supply of loanable funds. We will deal more explicitly with various types of risk in Chapter 9. For now it will suffice to think of this risk as default risk. The greater the level of default risk, the greater the likelihood the borrower will fail to make interest and/or principal payments. This risk increases the interest rate necessary to induce the lender to make the loan. More generally, an increase in the riskiness of a loan decreases the supply of loanable funds, as the shift from S^1 to S^2 in Figure 4.11 shows. A reduction in risk has the opposite effect: It increases the supply of loanable funds from S^1 to S^3 in Figure 4.11.

Liquidity. The **liquidity** of an investment refers to the ease with which an investor can convert the loan into cash without loss. If a lender needs cash before the borrower is obligated to repay the loan, the lender can attempt to sell the loan to someone willing to pay for it now in return for the future principal and interest payments the initial borrower will make. The more liquid a loan, the easier it is to find a person willing to buy it.

The underlying liquidity of the loan thus affects the loan's supply. The more liquid the loan, the easier it is to sell at some future date, and thus the more willing a lender is to make the loan in the first place. Thus, an increase in the liquidity of loans will increase the supply of loanable funds, such as the shift from S^1 to S^3 in Figure 4.11. As you would expect, decreased liquidity shifts the curve in the opposite direction, from S^1 to S^2 in Figure 4.11.

Summary Exercise 4.5

One proposal that has floated around Washington, D.C., is to enact a transaction tax on financial transactions. This tax would be a fee of 1 percent or so on the value of specified financial transactions. Such a fee would discourage short-term investment. How would such a fee affect the supply of loanable funds? Would it have the same effect on the supply of one-year and two-year loans?

Answer: A transaction tax means the supplier of loanable funds would receive as payment the interest rate on loanable funds minus the tax. For example, a one-year loan of $1,000 might earn 10 percent interest, but after paying a 1 percent transaction tax, the net interest received by the supplier

Inside Money

Box 4.2

*Tax Rates and the Aftertax
Interest Rate in Two States*

Income taxes are levied not only by the federal government but also by state governments and sometimes county or city governments. Furthermore, the income tax rate on each additional dollar of income, called the *marginal tax rate*, varies with the level of income. For the U.S. federal income tax, the top marginal rate for 1992 taxes was 32 percent. Along with this, we will consider the top marginal tax rate for the two most populous states. The first, California, had a top marginal tax rate of 10 percent in 1992. The second, Texas, does not have a state income tax, so the marginal tax rate is zero.

The accompanying table illustrates what this means for aftertax interest rates. Consider a bond issued by Du Pont, which had a yield of 8.1 percent on April 30, 1993. What was the aftertax interest rate for a person living in Texas? The aftertax interest rate was the interest rate minus the total tax rate times the interest rate, or 8.1% − (.32 × 8.1%) = 5.51%. How does this compare to California? The aftertax interest rate for a person living in California was 8.1% − [(.32 + .10) × 8.1%] = 4.70%. Thus, a California resident would receive a lower aftertax return to investing in this Du Pont bond than a person living in Texas would.

Next, consider a U.S. Treasury bond, which is exempt from state and local taxes. A Treasury bond maturing in May 2003 yielded 6.11 percent on April 30, 1993. What was the aftertax rate of return in Texas? It was 6.11% − .32 × 6.11% = 4.15%. In California it was the same, since these bonds are exempt from state tax.

	Interest Rate	Aftertax Interest Rate	
		California	Texas
Du Pont, matures 2006	8.1%	4.70%	5.51%
U.S. Treasury bond, matures May 2003	6.11	4.15	4.15
San Antonio bond, matures August 2013	5.87	5.28	5.87
California government bond, matures April 2019	5.5	5.5	5.5

Source: The *Wall Street Journal,* May 3, 1993.

Finally, what about municipal bonds, which are exempt from federal income tax and from state tax in the state in which they are issued. We will look at two cases. First, consider a bond issued by the city of San Antonio, Texas. This bond yielded 5.87 percent on April 30, 1993. In Texas, which has no state tax, this bond also yielded 5.87 percent after tax. In California this bond's interest is still subject to a state tax of 10 percent, so the aftertax interest rate is 5.87% − (.1 × 5.87%) = 5.28%.

Second, consider a municipal bond issued by the state of California that matures on April 1, 2019, and yielded 5.5 percent on April 30, 1993. This bond is subject to neither federal nor state tax, so a California resident receives an aftertax rate of 5.5 percent. Moreover, the Texas resident pays no state income tax, so that person also receives an aftertax rate of 5.5 percent.

would be 9 percent. This would lead to a reduction in the supply of loanable funds.

Note, however, that on a two-year loan, the 1 percent transaction tax would be spread over two years in calculating net interest. For example, a two-year loan of $1,000 might earn 10 percent interest each year. After paying the 1 percent transaction tax, the supplier would receive net interest of 9 percent in year 1 and 10 percent in year 2, for an average of 9.5 percent. Thus, the supply of loanable funds for two-year loans also would be reduced, but by a smaller amount than the supply of one-year loans. Although both supply curves would be reduced by the transaction tax, the supply of short-term loans would decrease more than the supply of long-term loans.

Equilibrium in the Market for Loanable Funds

As in any market, equilibrium in the market for loanable funds is determined by the interaction of all suppliers of and demanders for those funds. Figure 4.12 graphs the demand for and supply of loanable funds. Suppose the interest rate is relatively low, say, 5 percent. At this rate, the quantity demanded of loanable funds is $400 million, while the quantity supplied is only $200 million; there is a shortage of $200 million in loanable funds. In contrast, when the interest rate is relatively high, such as 15 percent, the

Equilibrium in this market for loanable funds is achieved when the interest rate is 10 percent, where the supply and demand curves intersect. At this interest rate, the quantity supplied of loanable funds equals the quantity demanded. There is no tendency for the interest rate to rise above or fall below 10 percent unless something changes that shifts the position of the supply or demand curves.

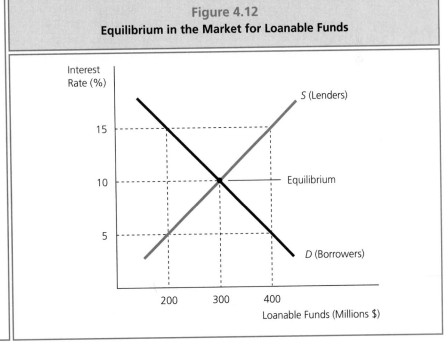

Figure 4.12
Equilibrium in the Market for Loanable Funds

quantity demanded of loans is only $200 million, but the quantity supplied is $400 million; thus, there is a surplus of loanable funds at this interest rate.

Notice, however, that when the interest rate is 10 percent, the quantity demanded of loanable funds is $300 million and the quantity supplied is $300 million. At this point the market is in equilibrium, with no tendency to change further. Everyone willing and able to pay an interest rate of 10 percent is able to obtain a loan, and everyone willing and able to provide loans at 10 percent is able to lend at this rate, so neither a shortage nor a surplus exists. Thus, the equilibrium interest rate is 10 percent, and the equilibrium quantity of loanable funds is $300 million.[3]

APPLICATIONS OF THE LOANABLE FUNDS MODEL

Now that you understand how the demand for and supply of loanable funds interact in a free market to reach a point of equilibrium, we may apply these tools to analyze how changes in the economic environment affect the equilibrium interest rates paid by households, businesses, and government.

The Tax Reform Act of 1982 and Interest Rates on Consumer Credit

Prior to the Tax Reform Act of 1982, interest paid by households on consumer loans (loans for car purchases, vacations, and other products) and credit card balances was fully tax deductible. The Tax Reform Act phased out the deductibility of interest on consumer loans and credit card balances, and, as of 1994, such interest payments are no longer tax deductible. How did this act affect the interest rate consumers pay for credit?

Figure 4.13 provides the answer. D^1 and S^1 represent, respectively, the demand for and supply of consumer credit when interest payments were tax deductible. The effect of eliminating the tax deductibility of interest payments on consumer loans was to decrease the demand for consumer loans to D^2, since households were willing and able to obtain fewer consumer loans at each interest rate when the interest payments are not tax deductible. Thus, the elimination of tax deductibility of consumer loans decreased the equilibrium interest rate on those loans from 21 to 15 percent and decreased the equilibrium quantity of the loans from $200 million to $150 million. Over the past decade, other changes (most notably drastic reductions in inflationary expectations) have led to further reductions in the interest rate on consumer credit.

---

[3] The loanable funds model used here determines the equilibrium stock (or quantity) of loanable funds at a point in time. In contrast, some economists use a loanable funds model that determines a flow of funds per unit of time. The flow model is more difficult to work with and will not be used in this text.

Eliminating the tax deductibility of interest payments on consumer loans reduces demand for these loans from D^1 to D^2. This leads to a lower equilibrium interest rate and fewer consumer loans.

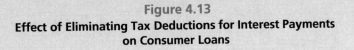

Figure 4.13
Effect of Eliminating Tax Deductions for Interest Payments on Consumer Loans

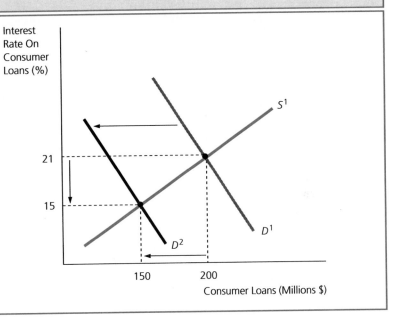

Inflationary Expectations and the Mortgage Interest Rate

As noted, one dramatic change during the past decade was a large reduction in the inflation rate and inflationary expectations. At the same time, mortgage interest rates fell substantially, reaching a 30-year low by 1994. We can use our loanable funds framework to see why reduced inflationary expectations contributed to the fall in mortgage rates.

Figure 4.14 presents an initial supply curve (S^1) and demand curve (D^1) for mortgages, with a corresponding equilibrium mortgage interest rate of 15 percent and equilibrium quantity of $400 million mortgages at point A. Since inflationary expectations are a determinant of both the demand for and supply of loanable funds, a reduction in inflationary expectations of 7 percent will affect both the demand for and supply of mortgages. In particular, a reduction in inflationary expectations decreases the demand for mortgages to D^2, since households are willing and able to obtain fewer mortgages at each interest rate. On the supply side, a reduction in inflationary expectations shifts the supply curve from S^1 to S^2 in Figure 4.14, since suppliers are willing to loan more funds at each interest rate. The intersection of the new demand curve D^2 and the new supply curve S^2 corresponds to a lower equilibrium interest rate of 8 percent at point B.

The initial equilibrium is at point A, where the nominal interest rate is 15 percent. A 7 percent decline in inflationary expectations decreases demand to D^2 but also shifts the supply curve from S^1 to S^2. The new equilibrium is at point B, with a lower nominal interest rate of 8 percent. Since the equilibrium nominal interest rate declined by the same amount as the reduction in inflationary expectations, the real interest rate is unchanged. Due to the Fisher effect, there is no change in the equilibrium quantity.

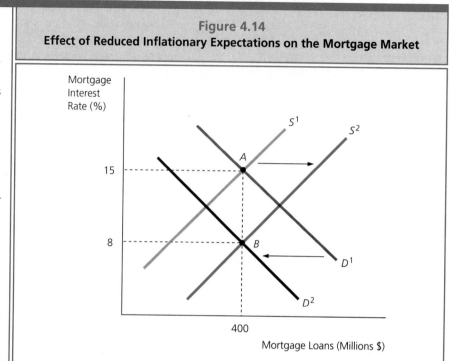

Figure 4.14
Effect of Reduced Inflationary Expectations on the Mortgage Market

Notice that a lower interest rate results regardless of how far we shift the demand and supply curves. In Figure 4.14, however, the supply and demand curves shift such that the equilibrium quantity of mortgages is the same as the initial level, and the equilibrium nominal interest rate declined by the same amount as the reduction in inflationary expectations (7 percent). As we discussed in Chapter 3, a situation where a 7 percent reduction in inflationary expectations leads to a 7 percent reduction in the equilibrium nominal interest rate (leaving the real interest rate unchanged) is known as the *Fisher effect*. Box 4.3 shows the link between inflationary expectations and nominal interest rates in the United States for the 1982–1992 period.

Returns on Real Estate Investments and Corporate Interest Rates

In the late 1970s and early 1980s, many investors began using their funds to invest in real estate, perceiving they could realize a greater return than they could by investing in other investments such as bonds. What was the impact of the shift into real estate on the corporate bond market, the major source of long-term business borrowing?

Figure 4.15 shows the market for corporate bonds with a face value of $1,000. The initial equilibrium is at point A, where S^1 and D^1 intersect at an interest rate of 10 percent. The increase in return on alternative investments

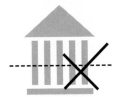

Inside Money

Box 4.3

*Nominal Interest Rates and
Expected Inflation Rates*

The accompanying figure shows the interest rate on one-year U.S. Treasury bills and the expected inflation rate from 1982 through 1992. Notice that the interest rate and the expected inflation rate tend to move together, but the relationship is not very tight. Thus, both the interest rate and the expected inflation rate were high in 1982. However, expected inflation rates declined from 1982 through 1987, while the nominal interest rate first declined and then rose sharply in 1984 before declining again. From 1987 to 1990, both the nominal interest and expected inflation rates increased, and both then declined through the end of 1992.

Another way to look at this graph is to calculate the implied real interest rate. The Fisher equation implies that the real interest rate is the nominal interest rate minus the expected rate of inflation, which is the difference between the graph of the interest rate and the graph of expected inflation. In 1984 the real interest rate was 5 percent, while by 1988 it had fallen to about 2.5 percent. By the end of 1992, the real interest rate was about zero. Thus, we find that the real interest rate has been quite variable over time.

Source: Citibase electronic database. For the interest rate, the one-year Treasury bill rate. For expected inflation, forecasts of annual percentage changes in the consumer price index by economists surveyed in the ASA-NBER *Business Outlook Survey.*

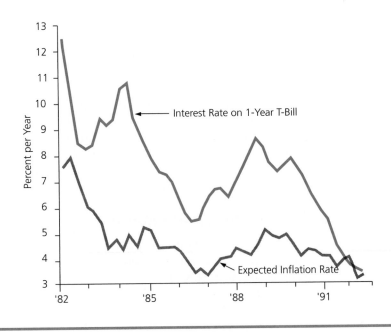

If lenders to corporations face an increase in the return on alternative investments such as real estate, the amount of funds they are willing to lend to corporations will fall at all levels of interest rates. This is represented by a decrease in supply from S^1 to S^2. The new equilibrium is at point B, where S^2 intersects D^1. The result is an increase in the equilibrium interest rate on business loans and a decrease in the equilibrium quantity of funds loaned to corporations.

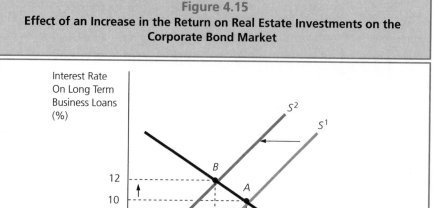

Figure 4.15

Effect of an Increase in the Return on Real Estate Investments on the Corporate Bond Market

such as real estate reduced the supply of funds in the corporate bond market, resulting in a shift in the supply of loanable funds in that market from S^1 to S^2. As we see, the impact of this shift was to increase the interest rate on corporate bonds to 12 percent.

Of course, between 1980 and 1994, the return on real estate investments was very low, and as a result investors have been leaving the real estate market in droves. This recent decline in the return on real estate has increased the supply of loanable funds in the corporate bond market, contributing (along with lower inflationary expectations) to the low interest rates on corporate bonds that prevail today.

Recessions and the Prime Interest Rate

Creditworthy businesses can obtain short-term funds to use as working capital in the prime lending market. The prime interest rate tends to vary over time, especially during periods of economic boom and recession. We can use our loanable funds model to see how a period of recession might affect the prime interest rate.

The market for prime lending is presented in Figure 4.16, which depicts the initial demand (D^1) and supply (S^1) of loanable funds, resulting in an equilibrium at point E, where the interest rate is 7 percent and the corresponding equilibrium quantity is $500 million. Let us suppose the economy is moving into a recession—a period of rising unemployment in which the profitability of business projects declines. What impact does this trend have on the market for prime lending? Since the profitability of business projects is a determinant of the demand for loanable funds, businesses decrease their demand for loanable funds to D^2. This results in a movement in equilibrium from point E to point A. The prime interest rate falls to 5 percent, and the equilibrium quantity of funds falls to $400 million.

Figure 4.16
Recessions and the Prime Interest Rate

The initial equilibrium is at point E. When a recession occurs, one effect is to decrease the demand for loanable funds due to a decline in the profitability of business projects. This is represented as a decrease in demand from D^1 to D^2, which tends to decrease the equilibrium interest rate and quantity of loanable funds to point A. However, recessions may also reduce suppliers' wealth, which would shift supply from S^1 to S^2, resulting in an equilibrium at point B. In addition, recessions may increase the risk of loaning funds, which could further decrease supply from S^2 to S^3. Notice that, depending on the magnitude of the shifts in supply and demand, the interest rate may go up (point C) or down (point A) during recessions. However, the equilibrium quantity of loans will clearly fall during recessions.

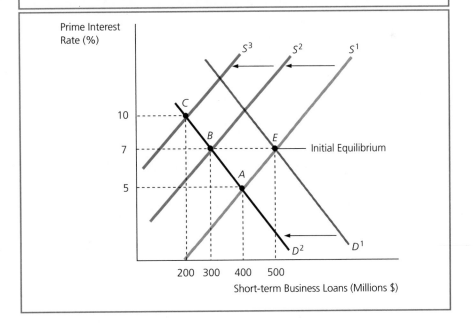

Do recessions necessarily result in a lower prime rate and less borrowing? If the only variable affected by recession is the profitability of business projects, the answer is yes. However, recessions also frequently affect two determinants of the supply of loanable funds: wealth and risk. Specifically, during recessions many lenders reduce their wealth as they draw on their assets. This decreases the supply of loanable funds—say, to S^2 in Figure 4.16. Furthermore, the reduced profitability of business projects increases the risk of lending in the prime market; this further decreases the supply of lending—say, to S^3. As we see, each of these changes tends to reduce the amount of borrowing during recessions. Whether the interest rate falls (point A), stays the same (point B), or rises (point C) depends on the relative magnitude of these effects, although the prime rate frequently rises during recessions.

The Federal Deficit and Interest Rates on Government Bonds

How does the growing federal budget deficit affect the interest rate the federal government must pay in the bond market? In Figure 4.17, the initial equilibrium in the government bond market is at point A, where S^1 and D^1

The initial equilibrium is at point A. An increase in the federal budget deficit increases the government's demand for loans from D^1 to D^2, resulting in a higher interest rate and quantity of loanable funds at the new equilibrium, point B.

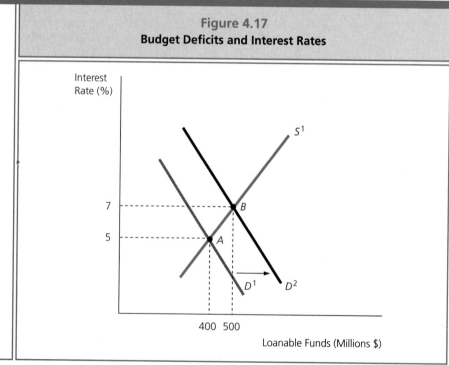

Figure 4.17
Budget Deficits and Interest Rates

intersect. A larger budget deficit increases the demand for loanable funds to the right to D^2 as the government attempts to obtain more funds to pay for its programs. This increases the equilibrium quantity of funds obtained from $400 million to $500 million, but at a higher interest rate. In this case, the increase in the budget deficit increased the interest rate from 5 to 7 percent. We examine this link between budget deficits and interest rates in more detail in Chapters 16 and 21.

Tax Policy and Interest Rates on Municipal Bonds

Municipal governments issue bonds to obtain funds to pay for local projects. One of the more interesting features of municipal bonds is that the interest lenders receive on the bonds is exempt from federal income taxes. This makes the bonds attractive to individuals in higher income brackets.

With all the debate in Washington about raising tax revenue to reduce the federal budget deficit, it is interesting to speculate what would happen if Congress eliminated the exemption on municipal bond interest in an attempt to gain additional federal income tax revenue. In other words, suppose Congress took action that made it necessary for lenders of funds in the municipal bond market to pay federal income taxes on municipal bond interest. This would raise tax revenue for the federal government, but what would be the impact on interest rates your state paid on its borrowing?

Point A in Figure 4.18 represents the initial equilibrium in the market for municipal bonds. S^1 and D^1 are drawn under the assumption that municipal bond interest is tax deductible. If municipal bond interest became subject to federal income taxes, lenders would provide fewer funds at each interest rate, because the taxes would lower the aftertax rate of interest. This would result in a decrease in the supply of funds in the municipal bond market, shifting the supply curve to the left to S^2 and moving equilibrium to point B. Thus, such a tax change would raise federal government revenue at the expense of municipal governments, which would have to pay a higher rate of 7 percent. In short, if the interest on municipal bonds were not tax deductible, municipal governments would pay a higher interest rate and obtain fewer loanable funds for municipal projects.

Interest Rate Ceilings

Until now, all of our applications have assumed that interest rates are free to rise or fall to achieve a point of equilibrium between the demand for and supply of loanable funds. This is not the case when interest rate ceilings are in effect. The term **interest rate ceiling** (also called a usury law) refers to a specified amount above which the interest rate is not permitted to rise. Until the early 1980s, interest rate ceilings were mandated by Regulation Q, which prohibited banks from paying interest on certain checking accounts and set maximum rates on savings and time deposit accounts. Although ceilings on deposits were phased out by the Depository Institution Deregulation and

Point *A* represents a situation where the interest on municipal bonds is tax deductible. If the federal government eliminates the tax deductibility of municipal bond interest, the supply of loanable funds shifts to S^2, resulting in a new equilibrium at point *B*. As a consequence, municipal governments will pay a higher interest rate.

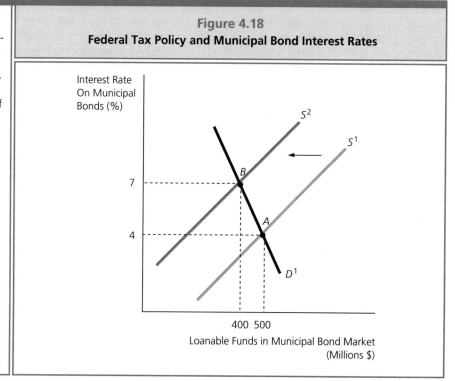

Figure 4.18
Federal Tax Policy and Municipal Bond Interest Rates

Monetary Control Act of 1980, some states still impose interest rate ceilings through state laws that regulate credit card and other types of interest.

When the interest rate is not allowed to rise to clear the market for loanable funds, a shortage results. This is illustrated in Figure 4.19, where we examine the impact of a 5 percent interest rate ceiling on the market for loanable funds. Given the ceiling of 5 percent, lenders provide only $100 million in funds, while the quantity demanded of loanable funds by borrowers is $400 million. There is a shortage of $300 million in loanable funds, indicating that some would-be borrowers are unable to obtain loans. We look at further ramifications of interest rate ceilings in Chapter 7.

Interest Rate Floors

Some financial instruments, such as U.S. savings bonds, have features that prevent the interest rate from falling below some specified amount, or **interest rate floor.** Other examples include pension funds that stipulate a minimum guaranteed interest rate and adjustable-rate mortgage contracts that stipulate that the interest rate, which varies throughout the term of the loan, cannot fall below some specified amount.

At an interest rate ceiling of 5 percent, quantity demanded exceeds quantity supplied by $300 million. Interest rate ceilings result in a shortage of loanable funds because they prevent interest rates from rising to clear the market.

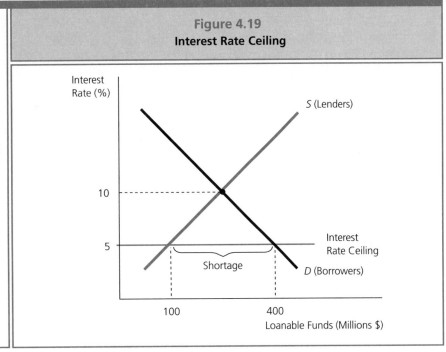

Figure 4.19
Interest Rate Ceiling

Figure 4.20 shows the impact of an interest rate floor of 15 percent on the market for loanable funds. When the interest rate is 15 percent, the quantity of funds supplied is $400 million, whereas only $100 million in funds is demanded at that interest rate. In other words, the interest rate floor creates a surplus of loanable funds of $300 million. Normally a free market automatically corrects this problem by driving down the interest rate until equilibrium between the quantity demanded of loanable funds and the quantity supplied is reached. The interest rate floor "disables" the mechanism that would eliminate the surplus.

Summary Exercise 4.6

The federal government is projected to have a large deficit next year. Suppose that, instead of borrowing funds to finance the deficit, the government raised the tax rates for all individuals, borrowers and lenders alike. What would happen to the equilibrium interest rate and quantity of loanable funds in (a) the government bond market and (b) the mortgage market?

Answer: (a) The initial equilibrium in the market for government bonds is at point E in part a. Since the government deficit is not funded through borrowing, the projected deficit does not affect the federal government's demand for loanable funds, which remains at D^0. However, higher tax rates

At an interest rate floor of 15 percent, the quantity supplied of loanable funds exceeds the quantity demanded by $300 million. Interest rate floors result in a surplus of loanable funds because they prevent interest rates from falling to clear the market.

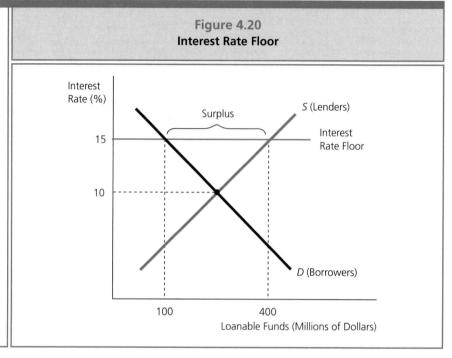

Figure 4.20
Interest Rate Floor

reduce the aftertax interest rate lenders (suppliers of loanable funds) receive at every interest rate. This decreases the supply of loanable funds from S^0 to S^1, resulting in a higher interest rate on government borrowing (i^1) and a lower quantity of loanable funds in the government bond market (L^1). (b) The initial equilibrium in the mortgage market is at point E in part b. An increase in the tax rate increases the demand for mortgages from D^0 to D^1, because mortgage interest is tax deductible. The higher tax rate means the aftertax interest rate paid by borrowers has fallen. Furthermore, the increase in the tax rate reduces the supply of loanable funds from S^0 to some curve to the left, such as S^1, S^2, or S^3. If the supply curve shifts by a small amount—say, to S^1—the new equilibrium occurs at point A (a higher interest rate and a greater quantity of mortgages). If the supply curve shifts farther to the left, such as to S^2, the equilibrium occurs at point B (a higher interest rate but the same quantity of mortgages as that before the tax increase). But if the supply curve shifts even farther to the left, such as to S^3, the new equilibrium is at point C (a higher interest rate and a lower quantity of mortgages). Thus, regardless of the magnitude of the shifts in the supply and demand curves, the mortgage interest rate rises. However, the impact of the increase in the marginal tax rate on the equilibrium quantity of mortgages is indeterminant; it could rise (point A), stay the same (point B), or fall (point C), depending on the relative magnitude of the increase in demand and the decrease in supply.

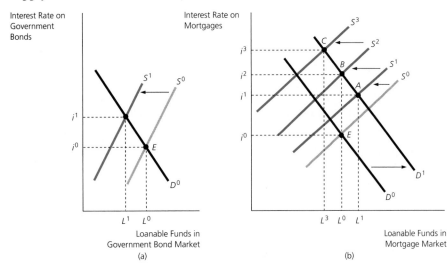

CONCLUSION

In this chapter, we examined the fundamental tools of supply and demand analysis in the context of financial markets. In particular, we analyzed the market for fee-based financial services and the loanable funds market. Equilibrium in each market is determined by the intersection of the supply and demand curves. In markets for fee-based financial services—markets for insurance, ATM transactions, wire transfers, and the like—equilibrium determines a price for the services such that quantity demanded equals quantity supplied. In markets for loanable funds, equilibrium determines the interest rate borrowers pay lenders for the use of funds.

We also discussed the major determinants of demand and supply and analyzed how changes in the determinants of supply and demand lead to changes in the equilibrium price and quantity, or interest rate and quantity, in these markets. These tools of supply and demand analysis will serve us well in the remainder of this text. We will have occasion to apply them in a wide variety of settings and to a broad array of markets.

KEY TERMS

fee-based financial service

demand curve

law of demand

change in quantity demanded

KEY TERMS *continued*

change in demand	determinants of supply
determinants of demand	shortage
substitutes	equilibrium
complements	surplus
supply curve	liquidity
change in quantity supplied	loanable funds
law of supply	interest rate ceiling
change in supply	interest rate floor

QUESTIONS AND PROBLEMS

1. What is the price of a fee-based financial service? What is the price of an interest-rate-based financial service? Is it possible to convert the interest-rate-based price of a given financial service into a fee-based price, and vice versa? Explain.

2. What is the difference between (a) an increase in demand and (b) an increase in quantity demanded? Explain and provide a diagram that illustrates the difference.

3. Mandatory seat belt laws have reduced the number of automobile liability insurance claims. What is the impact of this result on the market price and quantity of automobile liability insurance? Explain carefully.

4. During the late 1970s, the interest rate on money market mutual funds increased from 10 to 15 percent. Banks and savings and loans, however, continued to pay only $5\frac{1}{4}$ percent interest on savings accounts.
   (a). What impact did this increase in the interest rate have on the market for savings accounts at banks?
   (b). Graphically illustrate the impact of the Depository Institution Deregulation and Monetary Control Act of 1980 on the market for money market mutual funds.

5. During the 1980s, federal budget deficits were financed through borrowing. Graphically illustrate the impact of financing the budget deficit with federal borrowing on
   (a). The market for government bonds
   (b). The market for mortgages
   (c). The market for new-car loans

6. Other things being the same, would you expect the equilibrium interest rate to be higher on a 1-year loan or on a 20-year loan? Use supply and demand analysis to explain your answer.

7. Other things being the same, would you expect the equilibrium interest rate to be higher or lower on a small-business loan or on a large-business loan? Explain using supply and demand analysis.

8. Suppose the mortgage market is initially in equilibrium (label this point *A* in a supply and demand diagram). Lenders expect the inflation rate to decline, whereas borrowers expect it to rise. Show the new equilibrium in the market for mortgages, and label it point *B*. What can you say about the direction of the change in (a) the interest rate and (b) the quantity of mortgages?

9. Show the impact on the market for personal loans of

(a). A government law that permits borrowers to deduct interest payments on personal loans for tax purposes

(b). An increase in the marginal tax rate

(c). A simultaneous allowance for borrowers to deduct interest payments and a rise in the marginal tax rate

10. Use supply and demand analysis to explain the likely impact of a recession on the market for

(a). ATM transactions

(b). Life insurance

(c). Mortgages

(d). Savings deposits

(e). New-car loans

(f). Bank wire transfers

(g). Long-term business loans

11. Use supply and demand analysis to explain the likely impact of an increase in the marginal tax rate on

(a). ATM transactions

(b). Life insurance

(c). Mortgages

(d). Savings deposits

(e). New-car loans

(f). Bank wire transfers

(g). Long-term business loans

12. Use supply and demand analysis to explain the likely impact of a reduction in inflationary expectations on the market for

(a). ATM transactions

(b). Life insurance

(c). Mortgages

(d). Savings deposits

(e). New-car loans

(f). Bank wire transfers

(g). Long-term business loans

13. An article in the *Wall Street Journal* reported that the return on investing in stocks in 1996 is expected to be 5 percent higher than normal. Assuming investors believe this report, what would you expect to happen to (a) mortgage interest rates, (b) consumer loan rates, and (c) interest rates on federal and municipal borrowing?

14. Moody's bond rating service recently lowered its rating of bonds issued by several large insurance companies and pension funds, which means loans to these companies are now more risky. Graphically illustrate the impact of this action on the market for bonds issued by these companies.

15. Critically evaluate this statement: "An increase in the demand for mortgages increases the mortgage interest rate, which in turn leads to an increase in the supply of funds for mortgages. This increase in supply reduces the mortgage interest rate. Thus, an increase in the demand for mortgages leads to a self-correcting increase in supply, which tends to stabilize interest rates at their initial level."

16. Suppose the marginal tax rate is 33 percent. Determine the effective aftertax interest rate paid by a borrower with

(a). A 12 percent mortgage

(b). A 10 percent consumer loan

SELECTIONS FOR FURTHER READING

Fleisher, B. M., and K. J. Kopecky. "The Loanable Funds Approach to Teaching Principles of Macroeconomics." *Journal of Economic Education,* 18 (Winter 1987), pp. 19–33.

Henderson, J. V., and Y. M. Ioannides. "Dynamic Aspects of Consumer Decisions in Housing Markets." *Journal of Urban Economics,* 26 (September 1989), pp. 212–230.

Mitchell, W. E., and R. L. Sorensen. "Pricing, Price Dispersion, and Information: The Discount Brokerage Industry." *Journal of Economics and Business,* 38 (December 1986), pp. 273–282.

5

The Bank as a Firm: Loans

*I*n the previous chapter, we used the supply and demand model to analyze financial markets. We learned that the intersection of the supply and demand curves for funds determines the funds' market "price," the interest rate. How does this fact relate to banks, and in particular to the loan decisions of banks? In this chapter, we answer this question. We see how the market demand and supply for loans affects individual banks. We then focus on the behavior of individual banks, with particular emphasis on viewing banks as firms, similar to firms in other markets in the economy. Banks produce an output—loans—using inputs such as deposits, labor, and capital equipment.

The banking industry is heavily regulated, and in Chapter 7 we discuss how the regulation of banking has changed from the early days of the republic to the present. One important set of regulations that governed bank behavior since before World War II limited the ability of banks to change the interest rates offered to depositors or those charged for loans. The passage of the Depository Institution Deregulation and Monetary Control Act (DIDMCA) in 1980 altered these regulations and began a process of partial deregulation, eliminating many of the regulations on deposit interest rates. These tremendous changes in the banking industry make it necessary to look at individual bank behavior to analyze how these banks determine the most profitable quantity of and interest rates on loans and deposits.

Modern banks produce a variety of banking services, and in this chapter we focus on one of the most important outputs banks produce: loans. (In the next chapter, we examine bank decisions related to deposits.) We look at how banks determine the profit-maximizing quantity of loans to issue. As we will see, the quantity of loans and the interest rate charged depend on the degree of market power the bank enjoys. We begin by analyzing the situation where a bank is small relative to total loan demand and thus has no market power. Then we turn to the case where a bank is large relative to total loan demand and thus has some market power. Finally, we examine the impact on bank decisions of imperfect information regarding whether borrowers will repay loans.

PURELY COMPETITIVE BANKS

When individual banks are small relative to the market, they cannot influence the interest rates they charge for loans. In other words, they are price takers.

This situation typifies a model called **pure competition** among banks. The market for bank loans is purely competitive if

1. There are many buyers and sellers of bank loans, each of which is "small" relative to the whole market.
2. Each bank provides similar bank loans; that is, no product differentiation exists.
3. Buyers and sellers of banking services have full information about current market interest rates.
4. There are no transactions costs (the costs associated with securing and making loans).

The conditions for pure competition are unlikely to hold exactly, but they serve as a useful benchmark and may approximate reality in some cases. Many markets for banking services have numerous buyers and sellers (or demanders and suppliers) of loans, especially those in large cities. Moreover, loans made by different banking firms are similar in nature. It makes little difference in most cases whether a loan is provided by First City or First National. All that matters is the terms of the loan, which include the interest rate on the borrowed funds. Suppliers and demanders of loans are likely to be well informed about alternative sources of loans and the rates charged. Finally, while transactions costs are seldom zero, they are unlikely to be a dominant portion of the cost of demanding or supplying a loan.

If you remember the theory of perfect competition from your principles of economics course, you may notice a similarity between pure competition and an alternative industry model known as *perfect competition*. The key difference between these two models is that a perfectly competitive market has, in addition to the four characteristics listed above, a fifth characteristic known as *free entry and exit*. Pure competition does not require that there be free entry into and exit from the banking industry.

The reason we use the model of pure competition to analyze banks that lack market power is that there is no free entry into banking. Despite the deregulation of bank interest rates, entry into the banking industry is still heavily controlled by federal, state, and local regulations. Among other things, this implies that it is difficult for an entrepreneur to open a bank. A maze of applications and other red tape must be approved at many levels of government before a bank can be chartered. Exit is less of a problem, since banks can be sold or, with sufficient time and care, liquidated.

In a purely competitive banking market, no individual bank has market power and in effect must charge the "market-determined" interest rate. The reason is simple: Since there are many banks, each offering loans that are essentially identical, borrowers would just as soon obtain a loan from one bank as from any other. Since there are no transactions costs, borrowers will obtain loans from the bank that offers the lowest interest rate. If one bank attempted to charge a higher interest rate than all other banks, borrowers would go elsewhere for their loans.

Market Demand and the Demand for an Individual Bank's Loans

In a purely competitive banking market, the intersection of the market supply and demand curves determines the equilibrium interest rate on loans, as in part a of Figure 5.1. Banks supply loanable funds, while households, businesses, and government demand them. The equilibrium loan interest rate is 10 percent. The equilibrium dollar value of loans, measured on the horizontal axis, is $500 million.

Recall that in purely competitive markets, individual banks are price takers; that is, they take the market interest rate as given. This is illustrated in part b of Figure 5.1 by the horizontal demand for loans an individual bank faces. Individual banks must take the equilibrium interest rate on loans as given and can provide as many loans at this rate as they choose to make.

It is important to stress that the demand for loans at the market level is downward sloping, whereas the demand for loans provided by an individual purely competitive bank is horizontal. Borrowers are much more sensitive to a change in the interest rate an individual bank charges than to a change in the market interest rate, because at the market level, few substitute sources of funds exist. In contrast, there are many substitutes for loans provided by an individual bank (namely, loans at other banks).

Elasticity of Demand for Loans.
Economists use a concept called the *elasticity of demand* to measure the sensitivity of demand to price changes. In the loan market, the elasticity of demand for loans measures how responsive the quantity demanded of loans is to a change in the interest rate; it is the percentage change in the quantity demanded of loans divided by the percentage change in the interest rate on loans. Formally, if L is the quantity demanded of loans and i_L is the loan interest rate, the **interest elasticity of demand for loans** is

$$E = \frac{\%\Delta L}{\%\Delta i_L},$$

where Δ means "a change in." If E is greater than 1 in absolute value, a 1 percent increase in the interest rate leads to a greater than 1 percent reduction in the quantity demanded of loans. In this case, the demand for loans is elastic (that is, responsive) to a change in the interest rate. In contrast, if E is less than 1 in absolute value, a 1 percent increase in the interest rate reduces the quantity demanded of loans by less than 1 percent. In this case, the demand for loans is inelastic (that is, not very responsive) to a change in the interest rate.

The formula for interest elasticity of loan demand contains a pitfall you should avoid. In particular, since interest rates are stated in percentages, such as 5 percent or 10 percent, you may be tempted to think that an increase or decrease in the interest rate of 1 percent—say, from 5 to 6 percent—is a percentage change of 1 percent. This is not correct. The percentage change

Figure 5.1
Market and Individual Bank's Loan Demand in Pure Competition

This figure shows how the market determines the interest rate a purely competitive bank can charge on its loans. In part a, the market demand for loans is downward sloping, and the market supply curve for loans is upward sloping. The market-clearing interest rate is determined by the intersection of the market demand and supply curves. Part b shows the demand for loans at an individual bank. Demand is horizontal, or perfectly elastic, at the market interest rate of 10 percent, since an individual bank has no control over the interest rate it charges.

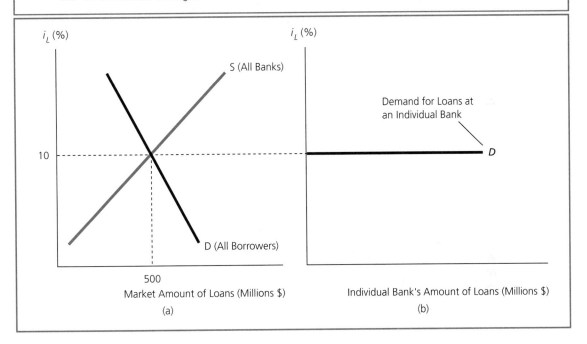

formula is $\Delta i_L/i_L$, just as it is for prices. Thus, an increase in the interest rate from 5 to 6 percent is a percentage change of $(6 - 5)/5 = .20$, or a 20 percent change.

The market demand for loans is more inelastic than the demand for loans by an individual bank. In fact, the demand for an individual bank's loans is perfectly elastic when the market is purely competitive. This is because if a purely competitive bank increases its interest rate even slightly above the market rate, it will lose all of its loan customers. Thus, the elasticity of demand for a purely competitive bank's loans is infinite in absolute value, or perfectly elastic. This is why the demand for the loans provided by an individual bank is horizontal at the market-determined interest rate on bank loans.

The Purely Competitive Bank's Loan Decision

Supply and demand at the market level determine the market interest rate on loans. A purely competitive bank must take this loan rate as given and determine how many loans to issue at this rate. Remember, the bank's goal is to maximize its profits. How many loans will a profit-maximizing bank issue? To answer this question, we must understand the nature of bank revenues and costs, since profits are the difference between revenues and costs. Remember too from your principles of economics course the distinction between accounting profits and economic profits. Economic profits are the difference between revenues and total opportunity cost. Since accounting costs do not include all opportunity costs, accounting profits are higher than economic profits. Thus, some banks can earn zero economic profits but report earning (accounting) profits on their income statements. These banks would be earning just enough accounting profits to cover the opportunity cost of resources tied up in the banks.

The bank's revenues from issuing L loans are given by

$$R = i_L \times L,$$

where i_L is the market interest rate on loans and L is the dollar value of loans provided by the individual bank; that is, revenues are merely the interest rate on loans times the dollar value of loans issued. For example, if a bank issues $1 million in loans at an interest rate of 10 percent, the bank's revenue (interest income) is $1,000,000 \times .10 = $100,000. Part a of Figure 5.2 graphs the revenues of an individual bank as a function of the dollar amount of loans on the horizontal axis. Notice that this relation is linear, since the bank receives the same interest rate, i_L, on each additional dollar in loans. Furthermore, revenues increase as more loans are made. When L_A loans are made, revenues are $150 million. When loans increase to L_M, revenues increase to $500 million.

The cost of issuing L loans is represented as $C(L)$ and consists of two components. The first is the cost of funds, since banks require funds in the form of reserves to make loans. These reserves can be obtained by attracting deposits, and the cost of deposits is the interest rate paid on deposits in the bank times the quantity of deposits. The second component is the general cost of administering the bank, which includes the cost of staffing the deposit window with tellers, the cost of the loan officers and staff needed to process loan applications, other operating costs such as the building and utilities, and the cost of covering loans that are in default. In part a of Figure 5.2, costs, $C(L)$, increase as more loans are made. For example, when L_A loans are made, costs are $150 million. When loans increase to L_M, costs increase to $200 million. Note too that the cost function intersects the vertical axis at a cost above zero. Even when the bank makes no loans, it must pay certain costs, such as the costs associated with the building and utilities. These are

Individual banks offer the quantity of loans that maximizes profits, where profits are the difference between total revenues and total costs. Part a shows bank revenues, R, and costs $C(L)$. Costs equal revenues at two levels of loans, L_A and L_B; at these points, the bank's profits are zero. When the bank issues L_M in loans, profits equal \$500 − \$200 = \$300 million, and this is the level of loans that maximizes profits. This can be seen more clearly in part b, where bank profits are graphed as a function of loans.

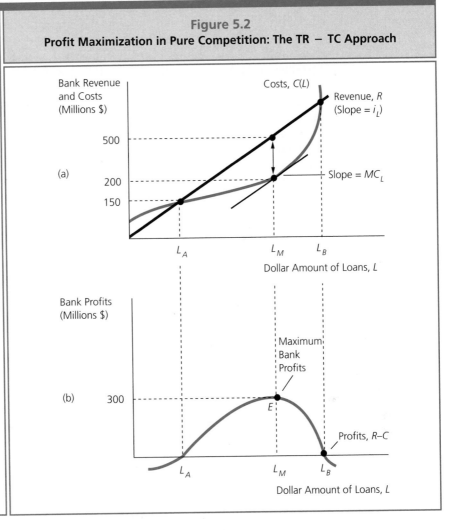

Figure 5.2
Profit Maximization in Pure Competition: The TR − TC Approach

called *fixed costs,* since they are paid at any level of loans, including zero. Costs that change when the bank changes the quantity of its loans are called *variable costs.*

Why is the revenue curve a straight line while the cost curve is not? Remember that the individual firm in pure competition cannot affect the market price, so revenue to that firm is simply the interest rate times the dollar amount of loans, or $i_L \times L$. This is a straight line through the origin, labeled R (for bank revenue), in Figure 5.2. The shape of the cost curve reflects the fact that as a bank makes more and more loans, costs first rise at a decreasing rate—up to loan amount L_A in the figure—and then begin rising at an increasing rate. Why? Consider a bank that opens up in a new building of a given size and has a given number of tellers, loan officers, and other workers. As the bank begins operations and starts accepting deposits and making loans, its costs rise somewhat, but due mostly to the cost of paying interest on deposits. The building and labor costs are being paid regardless of the number of deposits or loans. Thus, costs rise, but at a decreasing rate. At some point, however, the number of loans (and deposits) gets so large that costs start rising at an increasing rate. The number of loan applications and transactions engaged in to service depositors becomes so large that it taxes the ability of the bank's building and labor force to handle the work. At this point, the cost of making additional loans is not only the interest on deposits but also the cost of hiring and training more workers and the cost of expanding the bank building. Thus, the shape of the cost curve is based on the fact that as a bank makes a larger volume of loans, eventually the additional resources required to make each additional dollar of loans will increase, and hence costs will rise at ever increasing rates.

Using Total Revenue and Total Cost to Determine the Optimal Quantity of Loans.   The individual bank's profits are the difference between total revenues and total costs. In part a of Figure 5.2, profits are given by the vertical distance between the revenue and cost curves. Notice that when fewer than L_A loans are made, the cost curve lies above the revenue curve, and thus profits are negative (the bank experiences a loss). For loan amounts between L_A and L_B, the revenue curve lies above the cost curve, and the bank earns positive profits. But for loans in excess of L_B, costs again exceed revenues, and losses result at these levels of loans.

Part b of Figure 5.2 graphs the difference between the revenue and cost curves in part a. This profit curve summarizes the profits the bank could earn for different quantities of loans. Notice that profits are exactly zero at L_A and L_B. This is consistent with part a, since at these levels of loans costs exactly equal revenue. Furthermore, profits are maximized at point E, where the profit function $(R - C)$ is at its highest point. This level of loans, L_M, is the level that maximizes the bank's profits. Notice in part a that this point corresponds to the point where the vertical distance between revenue and costs is the greatest. Moreover, the slope of the cost curve at this level of loans equals the slope of the revenue curve.

It is no accident that the slope of the revenue curve equals the slope of the cost curve at the profit-maximizing level of loans. The slope of the cost curve is called **marginal cost** (MC_L) and reflects the cost to the bank of loaning out an additional dollar. For example, if the cost to the bank of making an additional \$1 loan is 7 cents, the marginal cost of the loan is .07. Similarly, the slope of the revenue curve is the interest rate on loans (i_L) and reflects the revenue the bank would generate if it loaned out an additional dollar. If the interest rate is 8 percent, for example, each dollar in loans yields the bank 8 cents in interest income.

To maximize profits, a bank in pure competition issues loans at the point where the marginal cost of a loan equals the interest rate on loans. The reason is simple: If the marginal cost were less than the interest rate (a point to the left of L_M in part a of Figure 5.2), the bank could add more to revenue than to cost by loaning out an additional dollar. This is why it is not profitable for the bank to make fewer than L_M loans. Similarly, if marginal cost were greater than the interest rate, the bank would reduce costs by more than it lowered revenue if it reduced its loans by $1. Thus, it would not be profitable for the bank to issue more than L_M loans. To summarize, to maximize profits a bank in pure competition produces the quantity of loans such that the interest rate on loans equals the marginal cost of loans:

$$i_L = \text{MC}_L.$$

This condition simply means that the revenues derived from issuing an additional $1 in loans ($i_L$) equals the cost to the bank of issuing an additional $1 in loans ($\text{MC}_L$).

Using Marginal Revenue and Marginal Cost to Determine the Quantity of Loans.
Figure 5.3 shows another way to summarize the profit-maximizing loan decision of an individual bank in pure competition. Here the interest rate on loans, $i_L = .10$ or 10%, is determined in the market and defines the demand curve for loans offered by an individual bank. The curve labeled MC_L represents the marginal cost to the bank of loaning out an additional dollar. Notice that at point A, marginal cost equals the interest rate on loans, which is the condition for maximizing profits. The level of loans that corresponds to this point is $L_M = \$100$ million, so the purely competitive bank maximizes profits by issuing $L_M = \$100$ million in loans. The bank issues the loans at the market interest rate, $i_L = 10\%$.

The curve labeled AC_L in Figure 5.3 represents the average cost to the individual bank of issuing loans. The average cost of issuing L loans is defined as the ratio of costs to the total dollar value of loans issued:

$$\text{AC}_L = \frac{C(L)}{L}.$$

For example, if the cost to a bank of issuing $100 million in loans is $5 million, the average cost of each $1 in loans is $\text{AC}_L = \$5,000,000/\$100,000,000 = 5\%$. Notice that the average cost of loans represents costs as a fraction of the dollar value of loans rather than a dollar amount. Like the interest rate, average cost is measured as a percentage of the dollar value of loans.

We can use Figure 5.3 to determine the profits of the individual bank. To maximize profits, the bank issues $L_M = \$100$ million in loans. The distance between points A and B reflects the spread between the interest rate received on loans (10 percent) and the average cost to the bank of issuing

To maximize profits, a purely competitive bank issues loans such that the marginal cost of an additional loan equals the marginal revenue from an additional loan. The marginal revenue from an additional loan is simply the market-determined interest rate, in this case, $i_L = .10$. The marginal cost is the upward-sloping curve labeled MC_L. Profits are maximized at point A, where marginal cost equals the market interest rate. This corresponds to $L_M = \$100$ million in loans. The shaded region reflects profits, which is total revenue minus total cost.

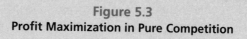

Figure 5.3
Profit Maximization in Pure Competition

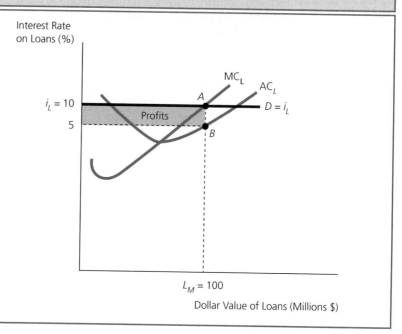

$L_M = \$100$ million in loans (5 percent). In this example, the spread is $.1 - .05 = 5\%$. Thus, net of costs, the bank earns an average of 5 percent on the $\$100$ million in loans it issues. The bank's profits when it produces the profit-maximizing level of loans is

$$.05 \times \$100,000,000 = \$5,000,000.$$

This corresponds to the shaded area of the rectangle in Figure 5.3. It is the base ($\$100$ million) times the height ($.05$), or $\$5$ million.

Summary
Exercise 5.1

Suppose the market demand for bank loans increases. Use a graph to illustrate what happens to the number of loans and the profits of an individual bank that operates in a purely competitive banking market.

Answer: In part a, the initial market equilibrium is at point A, where the market interest rate is i_L^0. Given this interest rate, the individual bank maximizes profits by issuing L_0 loans in part b to earn profits represented by the lightly shaded region. An increase in the demand for bank loans shifts the market demand for bank loans to the right from D^0 to D^1 in part a. This increases the market interest rate on bank loans from i_L^0 to i_L^1. The individual bank can now issue loans at a higher interest rate, which effectively shifts the demand for the bank's loans upward from D_F^0 to D_F^1 in part b. To maximize profits, the individual bank increases its loans from L_0 to L_1 and earns higher profits corresponding to the darker shaded region in part b.

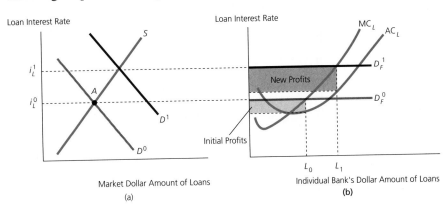

(a)

(b)

BANKS WITH MARKET POWER

In contrast to purely competitive banks, banks with market power have some control over the interest rate they charge for loans. The interest rate charged on loans by a bank with market power is not market determined but depends on the quantity of loans the bank chooses to issue. A bank with market power faces a downward-sloping demand curve, such as the demand curve for loans issued by Bank One in Figure 5.4. This downward-sloping demand curve indicates that some borrowers will obtain a loan from the bank even if the rate it charges is higher than the rates charged by other lenders of funds. For example, if Bank One charges an interest rate of 7 percent on loans, it will be able to issue \$150 million in loans. If it raises the interest rate to 10 percent, it will issue fewer loans—\$100 million—as some borrowers either decide not to borrow or choose to borrow from another bank. Thus, to issue more loans, a bank with market power must lower the interest rate it charges on loans.

Sources of Market Power for Banks

Before we examine how a bank with market power chooses which interest rate to charge for a loan, it is useful to briefly discuss factors that give rise to market power. A complete description of sources of market power is far beyond the scope of this text. Here we will review two sources of market

The demand curve for loans at a bank with market power is denoted *D*. If Bank One issues loans at 10 percent, it can sell $100 million in loans; if it lowers its rate to 7 percent, it can issue $150 million in loans.

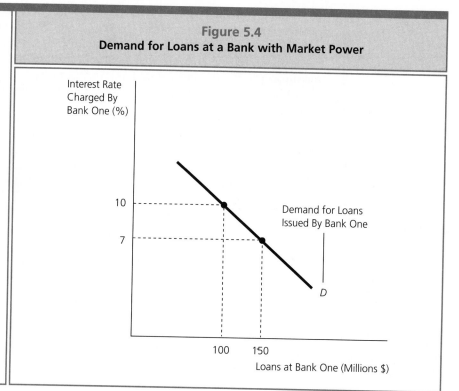

Figure 5.4
Demand for Loans at a Bank with Market Power

power that are important for understanding why some banks enjoy market power: economies of scale and location.

Economies of Scale and Monopoly Banks.

A **monopoly bank** is a single bank that effectively services the entire market for loans. Many small towns have a single bank, and the transactions costs of obtaining a loan from a bank located in some distant location make it impractical for households to obtain loans elsewhere. A natural question, however, is why small towns tend to have a single bank. The answer lies in what economists refer to as *economies of scale:* Larger banks can provide loans at lower average cost than smaller banks can. **Economies of scale** exist whenever the average cost curve decreases as the quantity of loans increases.

Consider the average cost curve for a bank illustrated in Figure 5.5, which exhibits economies of scale. Suppose borrowers desire $200 million in loanable funds. If a single bank provided these funds, the average cost to the bank of providing the loans would be 8 percent. (Remember, AC is not expressed as a dollar amount). To stay in business, this bank would have to receive an interest rate on loans of at least 8 percent to cover the costs of providing loans. In contrast, if two banks shared the market and each provided half of the $200 million in loans, the average cost for each bank of providing $100 million in loans would be 15 percent, because neither bank would be able to take advantage of the economies of scale reflected in the shape of the average cost curve.

What does all this imply about the number of banks in this hypothetical small town? If there were two banks, each charging 15 percent for loans, the banks would have an incentive to merge into a single bank (which would lower the average cost of loans). Alternatively, one of the banks could lower its interest rate on loans to attract customers from the other bank and drive its competitor out of business thanks to its lower average cost of servicing $200 million in loans. In short, when sufficient economies of scale exist, a single bank will dominate the market for loans. A monopoly bank faces a downward-sloping demand curve for loans to borrowers located in its vicinity and thus can issue more loans only if it lowers the interest rate. Box 5.1 discusses one study that looks at economies of scale in banking.

Location Advantages.   Market power does not necessarily imply that a single bank services the entire market. In many instances, borrowers value the convenience of using a bank that is close to their homes or offices. If a

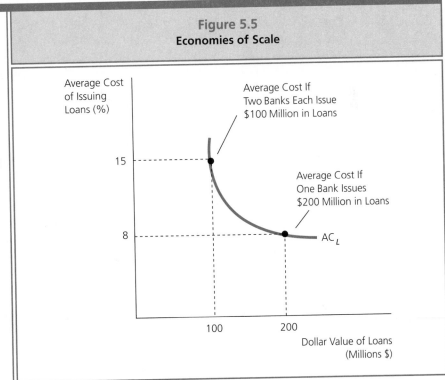

If the average cost of making loans exhibits economies of scale, a single bank can serve the market at a lower cost than can several banks serving the same market. When $200 million in loans is demanded this market, two banks sharing the market must charge 15 percent for each loan to cover costs, while one bank can provide the same number of loans at only 8 percent.

Figure 5.5
Economies of Scale

Average Cost of Issuing Loans (%)

Average Cost If Two Banks Each Issue $100 Million in Loans

Average Cost If One Bank Issues $200 Million in Loans

AC_L

15

8

100   200

Dollar Value of Loans (Millions $)

The Data Bank

Box 5.1

Economies of Scale in Banking

Economies of scale are one reason some industries are dominated by a few large firms. Do firms in the U.S. banking industry enjoy economies of scale? It turns out the evidence is rather mixed, but the main conclusion is that the average cost curves of banking firms have a flattened U shape, with slight economies of scale at small sizes and slight diseconomies of scale (an upward-sloping average cost curve) at large sizes. The accompanying figure illustrates this phenomenon.

Empirical data for 1984 suggest that for banks with $1 million in assets, average cost is about 10.5 cents per $1 of assets. For banks with $25 million in assets, average cost is 10 cents per $1 of assets. Thus, as banks grow from $1 million to $25 million in assets, average cost per dollar of assets falls by about one-half of 1 percent. As bank size grows from $25 million to $300 million, average cost fluctuates in the range of 10 cents per $1 of deposits, suggesting a flat average cost curve over this range. But as bank size grows to $5 billion, average cost rises to about 10.3 cents per $1 of assets.

During 1984, the prime interest rate was about 12 percent. Thus, banks received an inter-

Continued on p. 143

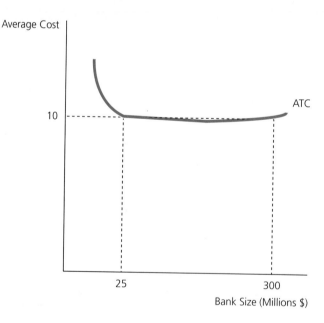

Continued from p. 142
est rate that was between 1.7 and 2 percent above average cost, depending on the economies of scale they enjoyed. The conclusion is that economies of scale in the U.S. banking industry are present but fairly modest and that

loan interest rates are relatively close to the average cost of funds to banks.

_____

Sources: David B. Humphrey, ''Why Do Estimates of Bank Scale Economies Differ?'' *Federal Reserve Bank of Richmond Economic Review* (September-October 1990), 38–50, *Economic Report of the President,* January 1993, 428.

bank across town offers a better deal on banking services, some borrowers will still choose to use the more convenient bank. Thus, by raising the interest rate on loans, a bank with a **location advantage** will lose some loan customers, but not all of them.

Of course, given modern technology such as the modem and the fax machine, the location advantage may be somewhat diminished. It is still important, however, if for no other reason than that bank customers still find it convenient to visit their local bank for a number of services. While possible, it is usually very inconvenient for a borrower to arrange a loan without visiting his or her bank. Perhaps it is possible to open accounts by mail, but this too is inconvenient. Ask yourself whether you would like to bank with First National Bank of Fairbanks, Alaska. The answer should convince you that location advantage is still important.

Profit-Maximizing Loan Decisions for Banks with Market Power

We can now examine how a bank with market power determines its profit-maximizing interest rate and level of loans. These decisions are a bit more complicated than those of purely competitive banks, because the interest rate a bank with market power receives on its loans depends on the number of loans it issues.

Consider the demand curve for loans at Bank One in part a of Figure 5.6. If the bank charges an interest rate of 30 percent, the quantity demanded of its loans is zero, so its revenues (graphed as a function of loans in part b) will also be zero, as shown by point *A*. On the other hand, part a reveals that if the bank lowers the interest rate on loans to 0 percent, it can issue $100 million in loans. But since nothing times something is nothing, its revenues will be zero, corresponding to point *B* in part b of Figure 5.6. For interest rates between zero and 30 percent, however, the bank is able to issue varying amounts in loans. The revenue function in part b of Figure 5.6 represents the revenues associated with these different levels of loans between $0 and $100 million. For example, if the bank charges an interest rate

Part a illustrates the demand curve for loans issued by Bank One. If Bank One charges an interest rate of 30 percent, no one will demand any loans. If it charges no interest for its loans, $100 million worth of loans will be demanded. Part b shows Bank One's revenue curve, which depends on the quantity of loans issued. An interest rate of 30 percent corresponds to point A in part b; an interest rate of zero corresponds to point B. As the interest rate increases from zero to 30 percent, revenues initially rise and then begin to decline.

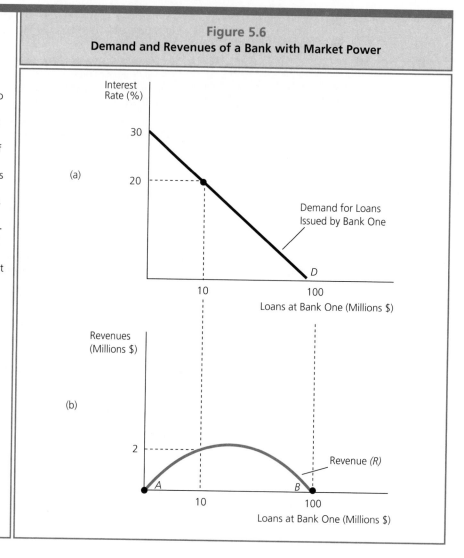

Figure 5.6
Demand and Revenues of a Bank with Market Power

of 20 percent, it can provide $10 million in loans and earn revenues of .20 × $10,000,000 = $2,000,000.

To determine the level of loans that maximizes Bank One's profits, we superimpose the revenue curve in part b of Figure 5.6 on the bank's cost curve to obtain the graph in part a of Figure 5.7. Notice that costs exceed revenues for points to the left of A or to the right of B, and the bank makes a loss. Part b of Figure 5.7 depicts these losses by graphing profits as a function of loans. At points A and B, revenues from loans exactly equal the bank's costs and profits are zero, which is consistent with the profit curve graphed in part b.

For loans between points *A* and *B*, revenues exceed costs and the bank earns profits. Notice that the vertical distance between revenues and costs is greatest at $40 million in loans. At this point, revenues are $3 million and costs are only $1 million. Profits are thus $2 million, which corresponds to point *C* in part b of Figure 5.7, where the profit curve achieves its maximum.

Notice that at the point of profit maximization, the slope of the bank's revenue curve (denoted MR_L in part a) equals the slope of the bank's cost curve (denoted MC_L). The slope of the revenue curve, MR_L, is the **marginal revenue** to the bank of issuing additional loans. For example, if by issuing

Figure 5.7
Profit-Maximizing Loan Decision for a Bank with Market Power

Part a shows the revenue and cost curves for Bank One, while part b shows the bank's profits as a function of loans. The slope of the revenue curve is marginal revenue (MR_L), and the slope of the cost curve is marginal cost (MC_L). The bank will maximize profits by expanding loans to the level where $MC_L = MR_L$. This is given by $40 million worth of loans. Note in part a that at the profit-maximizing quantity of loans, total revenue equals $3 million and total cost equals $1 million. In part b, we see that profits are indeed at their highest at point *C*, where they equal $2 million. Any level of loans other than $40 million will result in lower profits.

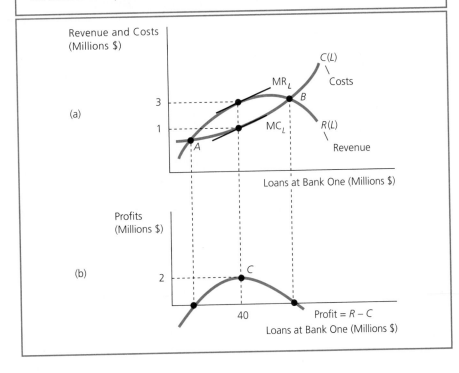

an additional $1 in loans the bank increases its revenue by 10 cents, the marginal revenue of additional loans is .10. Similarly, marginal cost (MC_L) reflects the cost to the bank of issuing an additional $1 in loans. At the point of profit maximization, $MR_L = MC_L$.

To understand why $MR_L = MC_L$ at the point of profit maximization, suppose the bank issues fewer than $40 million in loans. This corresponds to a point where the slope of the revenue function (MR_L) is greater than the slope of the cost function (MC_L). If $MR_L > MC_L$, the bank will be able to add more to revenue than to cost by offering more loans. As the bank expands loans up to $40 million, MR_L will equal MC_L. Would the bank want to continue issuing loans beyond $40 million? The answer is no. For loans in excess of $40 million, MR_L is less than MC_L: Issuing loans in excess of $40 million would increase costs more than it would increase revenues. In short, to maximize profits, a bank with market power issues loans such that marginal revenue equals marginal cost.

Figure 5.8 shows an alternative way to illustrate the profit-maximizing loan decision of a bank with market power. The demand curve for the bank's loans is given by D and is downward sloping since the bank has market power. The marginal revenue associated with loans is denoted MR_L and lies

A bank with market power issues the profit-maximizing quantity of loans where marginal revenue (MR_L) equals marginal cost (MC_L). This occurs at point A and corresponds to L_M worth of loans. The interest rate charged for these loans is given by the maximum interest rate borrowers will pay for L_M worth of loans. This interest rate, i_L^M, is above the marginal cost of issuing the loans, since the bank has market power. Profits are given by the shaded area.

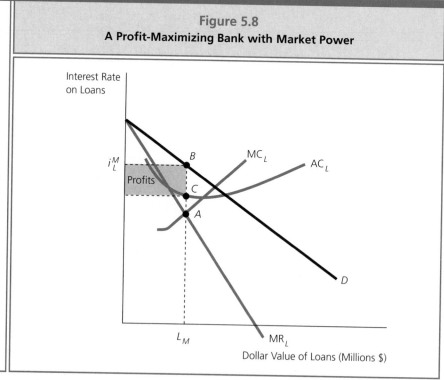

Figure 5.8
A Profit-Maximizing Bank with Market Power

below the demand curve. Notice that marginal revenue equals marginal cost at point A. Thus, the profit-maximizing level of loans for this bank is L_M.

The interest rate a bank with market power will charge for a loan is the maximum rate borrowers will pay for the profit-maximizing level of loans. This interest rate corresponds with point B on the demand curve, so the profit-maximizing interest rate charged by the bank is i_L^M. Notice that the bank charges an interest rate that exceeds its marginal cost of issuing loans, reflecting the bank's market power.

To determine bank profits, notice that the vertical distance BC in Figure 5.8 reflects the spread between the interest rate received on each loan and the average cost of issuing loans. Multiplying this spread by the total value of loans (L_M) determines the profits of the bank with market power. The shaded region in Figure 5.8 shows these profits.

Summary Exercise 5.2

Suppose a bank with market power has a constant marginal cost of issuing loans and that marginal cost equals the average cost at each level of output; that is, marginal and average costs are equal at every level of loans and also neither increase nor decrease as the number of loans expands. (a) Graph the bank's marginal and average cost curves. (b) Show the profit-maximizing value of loans, the interest rate on loans, and the bank's profits.

Answer: (a) The bank's marginal and average costs are a horizontal line, such as the one corresponding to $MC_L = AC_L$. (b) The profit-maximizing level of loans is that level where $MR_L = MC_L$. This corresponds to loans of L^0. The bank charges the maximum interest rate consistent with this level of loans, which is i_L^0. The bank's profits are given by the shaded region.

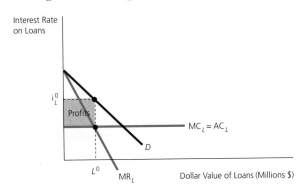

OLIGOPOLY BANKS

Oligopoly is a situation in which only a few firms in a market produce a good or service. Thus, an **oligopoly bank** competes for customers with only a few other banks. In this section, we focus on the case of duopoly banks: two banks that compete with each other for loan customers. (The basic principles apply even if there are, say, three to five banks in the relevant market.) The distinguishing feature of an oligopolistic market for banks is the high degree of interdependence among banks. One way to measure the degree of interdependence is to look at concentration ratios, as we discuss in Box 5.2.

The Nature of Oligopoly Interdependence

Let us first examine the nature of oligopolistic interdependence. Consider two banks that are located on the same block in a town, so neither bank has a location advantage over the other. In this instance, actions by one bank will have a dramatic impact on the profits of the other bank. For example, if one bank lowers its interest rate on loans below that of the other bank, shoppers for loans will switch to the bank offering the lower interest rate. This will drastically reduce the profits of the bank offering the higher interest rate. This effect characterizes oligopolistic interdependence.

Using Game Theory to Model Oligopolistic Interdependence

The interdependence of oligopolistic banks means the actions these banks take contain important strategic elements. Economists use *game theory* to analyze these strategic interactions, and we will use a simple game to illustrate these interactions between two banks. Table 5.1 depicts this oligopolistic interdependence between two banks, Bank One and Bank Two. For simplicity, we assume each bank has a choice between two interest rates on loans: a high interest rate of 15 percent and a low interest rate of 8 percent. The first entry of each cell of the matrix in Table 5.1 corresponds to the profits of Bank One, and the second entry corresponds to the profits of Bank Two. Looking at the table, we see that if both banks charge an interest rate of 8 percent, each bank earns zero profits. If Bank One charges 8 percent

Table 5.1
A Hypothetical Payoff Matrix

		Bank Two	
	Interest Rate	8%	15%
Bank One	8%	$0, $0	$40, −$10
	15%	−$10, $40	$10, $10

International Banking

Box 5.2

Concentration Ratios in Banking

One important determinant of market structure is the number of firms. For a monopoly, obviously, there is a single firm, while an oligopoly consists of several firms and a purely competitive market contains very many firms. To obtain a gauge of how concentrated a particular industry is, economists use a measure of the share of output or revenue belonging to the largest four or eight firms in the market. These statistics are called *concentration ratios.* In the case of banking, we might ask what percentage of banking industry assets are held by the four or eight largest firms. These data are called the *four-firm* and *eight-firm concentration ratios.*

An international comparison of concentration ratios reveals an interesting feature of the U.S. banking industry relative to other countries:

Continued on p. 150

	U.S.	Japan	U.K.	France	Germany
Total assets of four largest banks[1] (billions of U.S. dollars)	576.926	1,717.836	706.116	1,113.228	792.136
Total assets of eight largest banks[1] (billions of U.S. dollars)	916.258	3,157.847	947.335	1,649.382	1,316.312
Total assets of banking industry[2] (billions of U.S. dollars)	3,237.600	5,545.452	2,210.785	1,841.464	2,572.393
Concentration ratio of four largest banks	17.82%	30.97%	38.35%	60.45%	30.79%
Concentration ratio of eight largest banks	28.30%	56.94%	42.85%	89.57%	51.17%

[1] *The Banker,* July 1992.
[2] *International Financial Statistics,* February, 1993.

Continued from p. 149
In the United States, banking is less concentrated than in almost all other countries. The accompanying table reports the total assets held by the four and eight largest banks as well as the entire banking industry. Data are for the United States, Japan, the United Kingdom, France, and Germany, and all are converted into billions of U.S. dollars.

Notice that the four- and 8-firm concentration ratios are lower for the United States than those for any of the other four countries. For instance, the four largest U.S. banks account for 17.82 percent of American banking assets. In contrast, the four largest banks in France hold 60.45 percent of French banking assets. This illustrates the general feature of the U.S. banking system: It is relatively unconcentrated by international standards. One reason for this is the legacy of laws prohibiting interstate banking in the United States and some state laws prohibiting branch banking. These regulations severely limit concentration in the banking industry.

_____

Sources: _The Banker,_ July 1992; _International Financial Statistics,_ February 1993.

and Bank Two charges 15 percent, Bank One earns profits of $40, while Bank Two suffers losses of $10. Put simply, at the lower interest rate, Bank One steals Bank Two's customers and earns large profits at its rivals' expense. Likewise, if Bank One charges the high interest rate of 15 percent when Bank Two charges the low rate of 8 percent, Bank Two steals Bank One's customers. In this instance, Bank One loses $10, while Bank Two earns $40 in profits. But if both banks charge the high interest rate of 15 percent, each bank earns profits of $10 since they share the market equally.

Table 5.1 thus reveals that the profits Bank One earns depend not only on the interest rate it charges but also on the interest rate the rival bank charges. Given this situation, what interest rate would each bank choose to charge? Your initial answer might be 15 percent, since if each bank charged this rate, profits would be $10 for each bank. However, note that if Bank Two did charge an interest rate of 15 percent, Bank One could increase its profits from $10 to $40 by lowering its rate to 8 percent.

To determine the equilibrium outcome for this oligopoly, consider Table 5.1 from Bank One's perspective. If Bank Two charged 8 percent, Bank One would maximize profits by charging 8 percent, since the corresponding profits of zero are preferable to the loss of $10 it would incur by charging the high rate against the competitor's low rate. If Bank Two charged 15 percent, Bank One would still be better off charging 8 percent, since the profits of $40 are higher than the profits of $10 it would earn by charging the higher interest rate. In short, regardless of the rate Bank Two charges, in this example Bank One is always better off charging the lower interest rate. Notice that because the payoff matrix is symmetric, the same is true from the viewpoint of Bank Two. Thus, the equilibrium outcome for this oligopoly market is for each bank to charge the low interest rate to earn profits of zero.

This result may surprise you. Each bank finds it in its interest to charge a low interest rate, even though both banks would benefit if they agreed to each charge a high rate. Why wouldn't the banks conspire to charge a high rate? Conspiring to charge a high interest rate is an example of **collusion:** acting in concert to make both banks better off. In the United States, collusion is illegal; banks cannot conspire to set high interest rates. There are other reasons, however. Suppose the presidents of the banks secretly met and agreed to charge high interest rates. Would they have an incentive to live up to their promise? Consider Bank One's point of view. If it cheated on the collusive agreement by lowering its interest rate, it would increase its profits from $10 to $40. Thus, Bank One has an incentive to induce Bank Two to charge a high rate so that Bank One can cheat to earn higher profits. Of course, Bank Two recognizes this incentive, which reduces the likelihood that the agreement will be made in the first place.

Suppose, however, that the president of Bank One is honest and would never cheat on a promise to charge a high interest rate. (She is honest enough to keep her word to the other president, but not so honest as to obey the law against collusion.) What happens to Bank One if the president of Bank Two cheats on the collusive agreement? Bank One experiences losses of $10 when Bank Two cheats. When the stockholders ask the president of Bank One why they lost $10 when the rival bank earned profits of $40, how can the president answer? She cannot admit she was cheated on in a collusive agreement, for doing so would send her to jail for violating the law. Whatever her answer, she risks being fired or sent to jail, and this reduces her incentive to enter into a collusive agreement in the first place. Thus, the fact that only two banks service a market need not imply the banks have market power.

Repeated Interaction

Our description of the duopoly market for loans illustrates the difficulty banks have in reaching collusive agreements. An important feature of the analysis, however, is that a bank incurs no cost if it cheats on the collusive agreement; it receives only benefits. Technically, the reason this occurred in the previous section is that we assumed the underlying competition for customers was a "one-shot" (or one-time) interaction; that is, the banks faced the payoff matrix presented in Table 5.1 only once.

In reality, of course, banks compete for customers day after day and year after year. When banks repeatedly face a payoff matrix such as the one in Table 5.1, they can in some cases collude without fear of being cheated on. To see this, suppose Bank One and Bank Two secretly met and agreed to the following: "Let's each charge the high interest rate, provided neither of us has ever cheated before. If one of us cheats and charges the low interest rate, let's charge the low interest rate in every period thereafter." It turns out that if both banks agree to behave this way, conditions exist under which neither has an incentive to cheat. Before we look at this formally, let us examine the basic intuition. Under this agreement, a bank that cheats earns an immediate profit of $40 instead of $10. Thus, there is still the immediate benefit to a bank of cheating on the agreement. However, because the banks compete repeatedly over time, cheating has a future cost: The agreement stipulates that if either bank ever cheats, each bank will charge a low interest rate in all future periods. Thus, the bank that cheats will earn $0 instead of $10 in these periods. Hence, the benefit of cheating today on the collusive agreement is earning $40 instead of $10 today, but the cost is earning $0 instead of $10 in each future period. If the present value of the costs of cheating exceed the one-time benefit of cheating, it does not pay for a bank to cheat, and high interest rates can be sustained.

Now let us formalize this idea. Suppose the banks agreed to the collusive plan outlined earlier, and Bank One believes Bank Two will live up to the agreement. Does Bank One have an incentive to live up to the agreement? If Bank One cheats, its profits will be $40 today but $0 in all subsequent periods, since cheating today leads Bank Two to charge a low interest rate forever after. The best Bank One can do when Bank Two charges the low rate in these periods is earn $0. Thus, if Bank One cheats, the present value of its profits will be

$$\text{Profits if it does cheat} = \$40 + 0 + 0 + 0 + 0 + \ldots$$

If Bank One does not cheat, it will earn $10 each period forever. Thus, the present value of the profits of Bank One if it does not cheat will be

$$\text{Profits if it does not cheat} = 10 + \frac{10}{1 + r} + \frac{10}{(1 + r)^2} + \frac{10}{(1 + r)^3} + \ldots$$
$$= \frac{10(1 + r)}{r},$$

where r is the real interest rate the bank uses in its present value calculations.[1] Bank One has no incentive to cheat if its earnings from cheating will be less than its earnings when it does not cheat. In this example, there is no incentive to cheat if

$$\text{Profits if it does cheat} = \$40 < \frac{\$10(1 + r)}{r} = \text{Profits if it does not cheat,}$$

which is true if $r < 1/3$. In other words, if the real interest rate Bank One uses in its present value calculation is less than 33 percent (or 1/3), it will lose more (in present value) by cheating than it will gain. The same is true

---

[1] The above calculation uses a mathematical result from summing an infinite series. That result is

$$1 + x + x^2 + x^3 + \ldots + x^i + \ldots = \Sigma_{i = 0}^{\infty} x^i = 1/(1 - x)$$

for any fraction x that is greater than -1 and less than 1. In the present value calculation, x is $1/(1 + r)$. Substituting this for x, we find that the infinite sum is $(1 + r)/r$.

for Bank Two. Thus, since oligopoly banks compete repeatedly over time, they can collude and charge high loan interest rates to earn $10 each period. This benefits banks at the expense of borrowers, which explains why there are laws against collusion.

Summary
Exercise 5.3

Suppose Bank One and Bank Two repeatedly face the situation presented in Table 5.1 and that the interest rate they use in their present value calculations is 40 percent. (a) What are Bank One's profits if it cheats on the collusive agreement described earlier in the text? (b) What are Bank One's profits if it does not cheat on the collusive agreement? (c) Will both banks charge the high interest rate each period?

Answer: (a) If Bank Two lives up to the collusive agreement, Bank One will earn $40 today if it cheats and $0 forever after. (b) If Bank Two lives up to the collusive agreement and Bank One does not cheat, the present value of Bank One's profits will be

$$\$10 + \frac{\$10}{1 + .4} + \frac{\$10}{(1 + .4)^2} + \frac{\$10}{(1 + .4)^3} + \cdots = \frac{\$10(1 + .4)}{.4} = \$35.$$

(c) Since $40 > $35, the present value of Bank One's profits is higher if it cheats than if it does not cheat on the collusive agreement. Since the situation is symmetric, each bank has an incentive to cheat on the agreement, even if it believes the other bank will not cheat. In equilibrium, each bank will charge the low interest rate each period to earn profits of $0 each period.

BANKS WITH IMPERFECT INFORMATION

Thus far we have ignored an important consideration by individual banks in making loan decisions: We have assumed all borrowers are equally likely to repay their loans. In reality, some borrowers fail to repay loans, and this reduces bank profits. Of course, if a bank knows a particular borrower will not repay the loan, it will not agree to lend that person money in the first place. But banks suffer from **imperfect information:** They do not know for certain which borrowers will and which will not repay their loans. In this section, we analyze the impact of imperfect information on banks' loan decisions.

Symmetric Information

First, we assume there is **symmetric information;** that is, borrowers and banks have the same information about whether a loan will be repaid. Suppose the likelihood that a borrower with a low income is able to repay a loan is 10 percent, while the probability that a borrower with a high income will be able to repay a loan is 90 percent. Thus, on average only 1 out of every 10 low-income borrowers will repay loans, while 9 out of every 10 high-income borrowers will repay loans. In this case, symmetric information means that when a low-income borrower applies for a loan, both the bank and the borrower both know there is only a 10 percent chance the loan will be repaid. Similarly, when a high-income borrower applies for a loan, both the bank and the borrower know there is a 90 percent chance the borrower will repay the loan.

Therefore, when symmetric information exists, the expected return to the bank of lending to the high-income borrower at a given interest rate is greater than that of lending money to a low-income borrower. To be willing to lend money to a low-income borrower, the bank must receive a higher interest rate to compensate for the additional default risk associated with the loan. In short, the bank discriminates against low-income borrowers by requiring them to pay a higher interest rate for loans than high-income, more creditworthy borrowers pay. Individuals in each risk class pay an interest rate that fully compensates the bank for the riskiness of their own loans. Better credit risks do not subsidize poor credit risks when symmetric information exists.

Figure 5.9 illustrates why a bank with market power will charge a lower loan interest rate to borrowers who are good credit risks (part a) and a higher interest rate to borrowers who are bad credit risks (part b). For simplicity, we assume there is a constant marginal cost of providing loans. However, one component of the marginal cost of issuing loans is the likelihood of default, since defaults increase the cost to the bank of issuing loans. The marginal cost of issuing loans to good credit risks is denoted MC_G in part a, while the marginal cost of issuing loans to a bad credit risk is denoted MC_B in part b. Notice that $MC_B > MC_G$, reflecting the higher marginal cost of issuing more risky loans. The marginal revenue of issuing a loan to a good credit risk equals the corresponding marginal cost at point A in part a of Figure 5.9. Thus, L_G loans are issued to borrowers who are good credit risks at an interest rate of $i_G = 8\%$. Similarly, marginal revenue equals marginal cost for borrowers who are bad credit risks at point B in part b. Thus, the bank issues L_B loans to borrowers who are bad credit risks at an interest rate of $i_B = 15\%$. Since $i_B > i_G$, individuals who are bad credit risks obtain funds, but at a higher interest rate than do creditworthy borrowers.

Asymmetric Information and Adverse Selection

We now consider **asymmetric information,** the situation in which borrowers have better information about their ability to repay a loan than the bank does. To be concrete, suppose there are two types of borrowers, honest and dishonest. Honest and dishonest borrowers are identical in every observable respect (they have the same income, etc.) but differ in character, which is unobservable. For simplicity, assume honest borrowers repay loans 90 per-

Figure 5.9
Interest Rates Charged to Good and Bad Credit Risks

Here a bank with market power charges different interest rates to borrowers based on whether they are good or bad credit risks. Part a shows the demand and marginal cost of issuing loans to good credit risks, and part b shows the situation for bad credit risks. The lower marginal cost of issuing loans to good credit risks (MC_G) in part a results in a lower interest rate (i_G) than that charged to bad credit risks (i_B) in part b due to the higher marginal cost (MC_B) of issuing loans to bad credit risks.

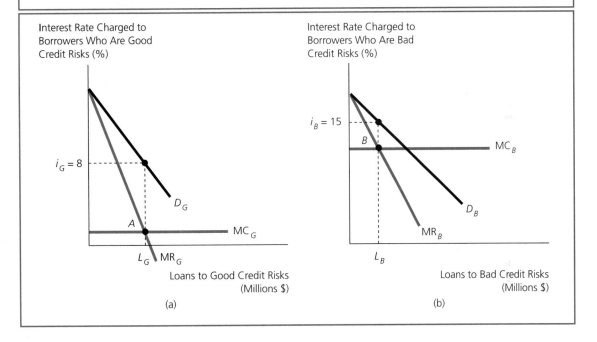

Interest Rate Charged to Borrowers Who Are Good Credit Risks (%)

$i_G = 8$

D_G

A

MC_G

L_G MR_G

Loans to Good Credit Risks (Millions $)

(a)

Interest Rate Charged to Borrowers Who Are Bad Credit Risks (%)

$i_B = 15$

B

MC_B

D_B

MR_B

L_B

Loans to Bad Credit Risks (Millions $)

(b)

cent of the time, whereas dishonest borrowers repay only 10 percent of the time. Asymmetric information arises because borrowers know how honest they are, but banks do not.

Because a bank cannot distinguish between honest and dishonest borrowers, it must charge the same interest rate to both types. This interest rate will be an average of the interest rates it would charge to each type of borrower if symmetric information existed. Asymmetric information creates a higher interest rate than the bank would charge to honest borrowers if there were symmetric information, but a lower rate than it would charge to dishonest borrowers if symmetric information were available. In short, honest borrowers pay a higher interest rate to compensate for the fact that dishonest borrowers default most of the time. Honest borrowers thus subsidize dishonest borrowers.

Unfortunately, this is not the end of the story. As the interest rate rises above the rate honest borrowers would have to pay in the presence of symmetric information, some honest borrowers decide not to borrow, and the quantity demanded of loans by honest borrowers falls. This increases the proportion of loans issued to dishonest borrowers, thus increasing the number of defaults as a fraction of all bank loans. As defaults increase, the bank further raises the interest rate to offset the higher marginal cost of issuing loans. Because of the higher interest rate, even fewer honest borrowers seek loans. Ultimately, by continuing to increase the interest rate, the bank ends up in a situation where it issues loans only to dishonest borrowers (who have no intention of repaying the loans in the first place), driving honest borrowers out of the market.[2]

This phenomenon is known as **adverse selection:** As the interest rate rises, honest borrowers decide not to borrow, and the bank is left with an adverse pool of borrowers—those who know they are more likely to default. When asymmetric information exists, an increase in the loan interest rate will raise the fraction of loans that will not be repaid.[3]

Adverse selection does not occur only because of asymmetric information about the honesty of borrowers. It also occurs because borrowers have inside information about the riskiness of the projects they are borrowing to finance. For example, suppose you have decided to open a small restaurant. Your aunt Alice has agreed to be your chef, and she has a great collection of Italian recipes. The bank knows most new restaurants fail but is convinced that your restaurant has a reasonable chance to succeed. It charges you a relatively high interest rate but agrees to make the loan. What the bank doesn't know, but you do, is that Aunt Alice has a weak heart and may not be able to work the long hours it will take to make the restaurant a success. Furthermore, you are not sure whether anyone else can replace Aunt Alice as chef. In this case, you have more information than the bank does. You know the restaurant is actually a riskier venture than the bank thinks because of the risk to your aunt's health.

Figure 5.10 illustrates the impact of adverse selection on the loan interest rate for a bank with market power. Since the bank cannot distinguish between good and bad credit risks, there is a single demand curve composed of good and bad credit risks alike. This demand curve is labeled $D_G + D_B$, signifying that it is the total demand by both types of borrowers. The corresponding marginal revenue curve is denoted simply as MR_L. Let MC_N denote the marginal cost of issuing loans in the absence of any defaults. If borrowers never defaulted, banks would choose to make a quantity of loans at point A, where MC_N intersects MR_L. We see that the bank would issue $200 million

---

[2] This analysis was first applied to the market for used cars by George Akerlof in "The Market for 'Lemons': Quality Uncertainty and the Market Mechanism," *Quarterly Journal of Economics,* August 1970, pp. 488–500.

[3] In the next chapter, we examine the related phenomenon of moral hazard.

Figure 5.10
Adverse Selection and Loans at a Bank with Market Power

When borrowers have better information about their status as credit risks than the bank does, the bank will face a single demand curve, $D = D_G + D_B$, composed of both honest and dishonest borrowers. In the absence of any defaults, the marginal cost curve would be MC_N. As dishonest borrowers default, the marginal cost increases to MC_D^1. This lowers the quantity of loans from $200 million to $150 million, and the interest rate goes up from 6 to 13 percent. In effect, honest borrowers must pay higher interest rates because of the behavior of dishonest borrowers. Since dishonest borrowers do not plan to pay back loans, they continue to seek loans even at the higher interest rate. Honest borrowers, on the other hand, are less likely to borrow at higher interest rates. Therefore, the proportion of dishonest borrowers increases, leading to an increase in defaults and further raising the marginal cost of making loans to MC_D^2. The result is an even higher rate of 13 percent. This phenomenon, known as *adverse selection,* leaves the bank with a pool of borrowers more likely to default.

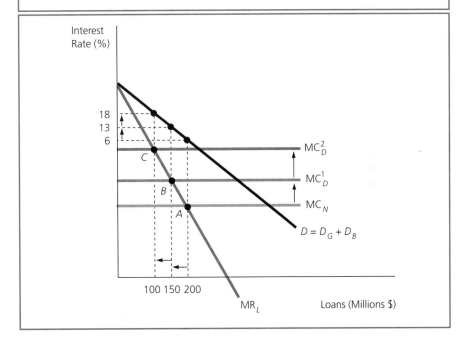

in loans and, with this quantity, the demand curve tells us the interest rate would be 6 percent.

Next, suppose dishonest borrowers default, but asymmetric information precludes the bank from distinguishing dishonest from honest borrowers. An increase in defaults raises the marginal cost of loans, since some loans now go unpaid. This higher marginal cost is represented in Figure 5.10 as MC_D^1, which lies above the marginal cost curve when there are no defaults (MC_N).

This increase in the marginal cost of issuing loans results in $MR_L = MC_D^1$ at point B. In turn, this increases the interest rate from 6 to 13 percent, resulting in a reduction in loans from \$200 million to \$150 million. Unfortunately, however, the reduction in quantity demanded consists solely of honest borrowers; dishonest borrowers have no intention of repaying loans and could care less what rate the bank charged. Thus, the fraction of loans issued to dishonest borrowers increases, leading to a further increase in marginal cost to MC_D^2. This new marginal cost equals marginal revenue at point C, resulting in a rise in the interest rate to 18 percent. In the presence of asymmetric information, increases in the interest rate can ultimately lead to a situation where the only individuals willing to pay the high rate are those who know they will default. In the absence of a mechanism for alleviating the problems generated by asymmetric information, banks would ultimately refuse to issue any loans at all.

Bank Strategies for Countering Asymmetric Information

We have seen the difference between symmetric imperfect information (imperfect because there is still uncertainty about whether a loan will be repaid, but this uncertainty is known by both borrower and lender) and asymmetric information (where borrowers have better information than lenders about ability or willingness to repay). We have also seen how information asymmetries can lead to problems of adverse selection. Yet, even though considerable information asymmetries exist in the banking industry, we all know that banks continue to make loans. In fact, as we saw in Chapter 1, loans are the engine that drives money creation in the economy. Because of this crucial role of loans, banks have developed several effective mechanisms to overcome default risks and other information asymmetries. We discuss these strategies in the next section.

Credit Reports. Banks rely heavily on credit reports for information about loan applicants' credit histories. By examining the past credit history of a potential borrower, a bank reduces the level of asymmetric information about that person. In effect, the bank can infer the probability that a potential borrower will (or will not) default on a new loan by examining the frequency with which that borrower has defaulted in the past. If the credit report is sufficiently accurate, symmetric information between the bank and the potential borrower exists. In this case, the bank can set an interest rate for the borrower that is consistent with his or her likelihood of default and charge individuals with poor credit reports higher interest rates than those with good reports.

Unfortunately, this is not always easy to do. Credit reports pose two problems. First, if they are inaccurate or incomplete, some asymmetric information will remain which will still lead to an adverse selection problem.

Second, some potential borrowers have no credit history because they have never borrowed funds before. In this case, credit reports tell the bank nothing and therefore do not help reduce asymmetric information. Some first-time borrowers may develop poor credit histories and others impeccable ones. The bank has no way of knowing which will be true for a given first-time borrower and thus needs some alternative strategy to deal with these cases.

Reputation.   In the absence of any credit history, banks need some other method to deal with the problem of asymmetric information. Many banks attempt to build a reputation for being tough on borrowers who default. Toughness might include foreclosing on the assets purchased with the loan money or seeking legal action to receive payment for the funds in default. In historical periods, being tough even included sending the defaulter to debtor's prison.

Is it "ethical" to be tough on those who default? Your answer might depend on whether you think the person who defaulted was dishonest (he or she was able to pay but chose not to) or was truly unable to pay back the loan. From the viewpoint of the bank, however, it is not always clear whether a defaulter is honest or dishonest. Dishonest defaulters can easily hide their assets to make themselves appear penniless. Asymmetric information makes it virtually impossible for a bank to determine the reason for default.

Given asymmetric information about the reason for default, suppose a bank adopts a policy of being relatively lenient on those who default. This, of course, will lead to an adverse selection problem. The policy will attract dishonest borrowers in droves, ultimately driving interest rates on loans so high that only dishonest borrowers will choose to borrow money from the bank.

In contrast, consider a bank that adopts a policy of always being tough on defaulters. This increases the cost to dishonest borrowers of doing business at the bank. Indeed, if the bank is tough enough, dishonest borrowers will either borrow funds from a "kinder, gentler" bank, do without borrowed funds, or actually behave honestly (i.e., repay loans). By investing in a reputation for being tough on defaulters, a bank can reduce the negative impact of asymmetric information. The bank benefits by having fewer defaults and, since a lower number of defaults reduces the loan interest rate, those who borrow from the bank benefit as well.

By adopting a policy of toughness, the bank rids itself of borrowers who default for reasons of dishonesty. Since anyone who defaults thereafter must really be unable to pay back the loan, why not let that person off easy? Unfortunately, if the bank started letting defaulters off easy, dishonest borrowers would again have an incentive to default. In the presence of asymmetric information, the only way the bank can avoid dishonest defaults is to be tough on everyone who defaults. In short, banks are tough on defaulters not because the banks are mean but because if they failed to do so, there would soon be no money available for honest borrowers due to adverse selection. Honest defaulters are, in effect, the sacrificial lamb that reduces the adverse selection problem, thus allowing all borrowers to obtain funds at a relatively low interest rate.

Collateral.   Many banks require borrowers to put up collateral to obtain a loan. **Collateral** is property or other assets pledged as security against default on a loan. If default occurs, the lender gets the collateral. Collateral is, in essence, a "hostage" the bank uses to induce the borrower to repay the loan. If the borrower does not repay the loan, the bank keeps the hostage; if the borrower does repay, the bank releases the hostage. New-car loans and mortgages typically use the underlying asset purchased with the loan money as collateral. If the borrower defaults on the loan, the bank can seize the car or the house and sell it to recoup some or all of the loan proceeds.

Down Payments.   To successfully induce borrowers not to default, the collateral must be valuable enough to give individuals an incentive to repay their loans. This can be a problem in the case of, say, a mortgage or a new-car loan. Suppose the only collateral put up for a mortgage loan is the house, and the money used to purchase the house comes solely from the bank. Then, in effect, no collateral exists. If the borrower defaults, the bank seizes the house, but the borrower receives the free use of it for the period up until the bank repossesses it. Clearly this strategy will not induce dishonest borrowers to repay loans.

One common mechanism banks use to counter this problem is to require a down payment. For example, suppose a bank agrees to lend a borrower 90 percent of the value of a house; the other 10 percent must come from the borrower's savings. In this case, the bank's stake in the house is only 90 percent of the house's market value. If the borrower defaults and the bank repossesses the house, it can sell it and use the proceeds to repay both the loan and the costs of foreclosing on the house. The borrower, in turn, loses the 10 percent down payment. Thus, a down payment reduces the incentive for even dishonest borrowers to default.

Does the use of down payments and collateral work in the real world? Mortgage lenders in the Southwest experienced numerous defaults in the late 1980s, despite the fact that loans required down payments and were collateralized. Is this consistent with our previous discussion? The answer is yes. During the late 1980s, real estate prices in the Southwest fell by as much as 50 percent in some places. To see the impact of this on the incentive to default, consider a borrower who obtained a mortgage on a $100,000 house. The bank required a 10 percent down payment, so the mortgage itself was $90,000, with the additional $10,000 coming from the borrower. As the above discussion indicates, when the market value of the house is $100,000, the borrower has no incentive to default; doing so would effectively give the bank an asset worth more than what was owed to the bank.

Now suppose that after the buyer has obtained the loan, the market price of the house falls, leaving the house worth only $50,000. The house is now worth less than the amount owed to the bank; thus, it is as if the bank had no down payment. If the borrower does not default, he pays the bank $90,000 in exchange for a house worth only $50,000. If the borrower defaults, he pays nothing, and the bank receives an asset worth only $50,000. Thus, since the price of the house fell below the value of the loan, the borrower has an incentive to default. To induce a borrower to repay the loans, the down payment must be sizable enough to keep the loan value below the market value of the house throughout the life of the loan. This did not happen in the Southwest, and consequently the number of defaults skyrocketed during that period.

Of course, lenders can always sue for damages, even after seizing collateral. Thus, banks in the Southwest could sue borrowers for losses not covered by the sale of the collateral. However, this process would be both expensive and time consuming. The value of collateral and down payments is that they are relatively inexpensive means of recovering losses from defaults on certain loans. However, when housing prices in the Southwest fell drastically, the value of collateral and down payments was insufficient to allow recovery of the loan amounts. As a result, banks and savings and loan institutions throughout the Southwest were severely weakened. Box 5.3 further illustrates the plight of savings and loans in the 1980s.

Summary Exercise 5.4

Banks that issue car loans require a much larger down payment on a used car than on a new one. Furthermore, interest rates on used-car loans are higher than rates on new cars. Why?

Answer: The seller of a car has better information about its condition than the buyer does. This leads to adverse selection: Car owners are more likely to keep good cars and sell bad ones, so the market for used cars will likely be composed of many "lemons." (This situation is similar to the loan market, in which the group of potential borrowers consists of many "lemons" who have a high probability of borrowing and not repaying). Before purchasing a used car, a buyer can hire a mechanic to inspect the car and determine whether it is a jewel, a lemon, or something in between. But ultimately, the true test of whether or not a used car is a lemon comes when the owner regularly drives the car.

Banks, of course, know this and recognize that a used-car buyer will have an incentive to default on a used-car loan if the car turns out to be a lemon. Therefore, the marginal cost to a bank of issuing a used-car loan is higher than the marginal cost of issuing a loan for a new car. As the figure shows, the higher marginal cost of issuing used-car loans (MC_U) leads to a higher interest rate (i_L^U) relative to the lower marginal cost for new-car loans (MC_N) and the corresponding interest rate on such loans (i_L^N).

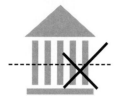

Inside Money

Box 5.3

*Going for Broke in the
Savings and Loan Industry*

In the early 1980s, many savings and loans experienced severe financial difficulty due to the rise in interest rates they had to pay on deposits, while the interest rates on outstanding mortgage loans were fixed and often below the interest paid on deposits. Thus, many savings and loans were insolvent according to Generally Accepted Accounting Practices. Bank managers faced perverse incentives to choose riskier investments, which tended to accentuate the insolvency of S&Ls.

An example will illustrate the nature of this perverse incentive. Consider a manager of an insolvent savings and loan with a net worth of −$50 million. This manager has only two investment alternatives. Alternative 1 yields a return of $25 million if things go well, which will happen 50 percent of the time, and a return of $0 if things go badly, which also will happen 50 percent of the time. Thus, this alternative yields an average (or expected) return of

$$(\$25,000,000 + \$0)/2 = \$12.5 \text{ million.}$$

If things go well, the savings and loan will earn $25 million, reducing its negative net worth to −$25 million, whereas if things go badly, the S&L's net worth will remain −$50 million.

However, there is another option, alternative 2, which is riskier than alternative 1. This alternative pays $50 million when things go well (50 percent of the time) but loses $100 million when things go badly (also 50 percent). The average return of this alternative is

$$(50,000,000 + -\$100,000,000)/2 = -\$25 \text{ million,}$$

which is negative and considerably lower than that of alternative 1. However, if things go well, the savings and loan will earn $50 million and end up solvent, with a net worth of zero. If things go badly, of course, it will have a net worth of −$150 million.

What do you think the manager facing these two hypothetical alternatives will do? You might think she would choose alternative 1, since it both pays a higher average return and involves less risk. However, because the savings and loan is already insolvent, the manager actually has an incentive to choose the riskier option, alternative 2. The reason is as follows. If things go well, the savings and loan will be restored to solvency, and the manager will be a hero. If things go badly, the S&L will still be insolvent, but more deeply in the hole. But the magnitude of the insolvency is not important, since the manager and stockholders are already in a position of negative net worth. The limited liability of corporations prevents stockholders from having to come up with funds to cover the negative net worth. Furthermore, the depositors are covered by federal deposit insurance, which guarantees their deposits will be made good with federal dollars if the savings and loan is insolvent.

Thus, neither the manager, shareholders, nor even depositors have a reason to object to

Continued on p. 163

Continued from p. 162

the go-for-broke strategy of alternative 2. In fact, if alternative 2 fails and things go badly, this will encourage an even riskier investment in the future. The problem is that no one except the Federal Deposit Insurance Corporation (and those ultimately responsible for paying for this insurance, the taxpayers) will have any incentive to prevent the savings and loan from taking on high risk in the hope that a lucky occurrence will restore it to solvency.

Although purely hypothetical, this example reflects the underlying incentives bank managers faced during the early 1980s. As a result of these go-for-broke decisions, numerous S&Ls failed in the 1980s, leading to the multibillion-dollar S&L bailout by the federal government.

Banks also reduce the likelihood that used-car buyers will default by requiring larger down payments on used cars. With a small down payment, a borrower will tend to default even if he or she learns the car has only minor quirks. But with a large down payment, the used-car buyer will have to learn the car is truly a lemon before he or she has an incentive to default.

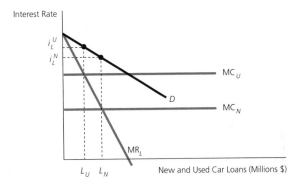

CONCLUSION

In this chapter, we looked at how banks behave in the loan market. The structure of the loan market, be it pure competition, monopoly, or oligopoly, influences this behavior. We stressed the importance of the strategic elements of actions by banks in oligopoly by modeling this behavior as a game between banks. Finally, we examined the impact of asymmetric information between banks and borrowers in the loan market.

In the next chapter, we look at the behavior of banks in the deposit market and how that behavior affects the structure of the deposit market. We also examine the important issues of deposit insurance and bank failure in connection with these topics.

KEY TERMS

pure competition

interest elasticity of demand for loans

marginal cost

marginal revenue

monopoly banks

economies of scale

location advantage

oligopoly bank

collusion

imperfect information

symmetric information

asymmetric information

adverse selection

collateral

QUESTIONS AND PROBLEMS

1. Who demands bank loans? Who supplies them?

2. Suppose the market interest rate on bank loans is 10 percent. How many loans will a purely competitive bank issue if it charges an interest rate on loans of 10.5 percent? Explain.

3. What is the impact on the costs to a bank if an increase occurs in (a) the interest rate paid to depositors for funds, (b) the frequency with which borrowers default, and (c) the wage paid to loan processors?

4. Suppose the market demand for bank loans increases in a purely competitive market for loans. Using words and a diagram, explain the impact of this on
   (a). The market interest rate
   (b). The demand for loans issued by an individual bank
   (c). The number of loans issued by an individual bank
   (d). The profits of an individual bank

5. Explain why a purely competitive bank issues a quantity of loans such that the interest rate on loans equals the marginal cost of issuing another dollar in loans.

6. Suppose the cost to a bank of issuing $100,000 in loans is $8,000.

(a). What is the bank's average cost of issuing $100,000 loans?
(b). How does one interpret this number?

7. Explain why a bank may have market power.

8. "If a bank with market power raises its interest rate above those charged by other banks, no borrowers will seek funds from that bank." Is this statement true or false? Explain.

9. Suppose a bank with market power experiences a decrease in the marginal cost of issuing loans.
   (a). Describe the factors that could lead to a decrease in the bank's marginal cost.
   (b). What is the impact of the decrease in marginal cost on the bank's profit-maximizing interest rate on loans and on the corresponding level of loans issued? Use a graph in your answer.
   (c). Do bank profits necessarily increase if the marginal cost of issuing loans decreases? Explain.

10. Why are there laws against collusion in banking?

   Answer questions 11–14 based on the following profit matrix for two duopoly banks:

Bank Two

Bank One	Interest Rate	8%	15%
	8%	0,0	25, −5
	15%	−5, 25	5, 5

11. What are Bank One's profits if it charges an interest rate of 8 percent when Bank Two charges an interest rate of (a) 8 percent and (b) 15 percent?

12. What are Bank Two's profits if it charges an interest rate of 15 percent when Bank One charges an interest rate of (a) 8 percent and (b) 15 percent?

13. Suppose the banks do not compete repeatedly. What are their equilibrium profits? Why?

14. Suppose the banks compete repeatedly over time. Determine whether (and if yes, how) they can earn profits of $5 each period if the interest rate used in their present value calculations is
    (a). 10 percent
    (b). 20 percent
    (c). 30 percent
    (d). 40 percent

15. Explain the difference between symmetric and asymmetric information.

16. In the presence of symmetric information about the ability of borrowers to repay loans, would you expect banks to charge a single interest rate to all borrowers? Why or why not?

17. In a recent television advertisement, a bank offered to issue a credit card to anyone regardless of his or her credit history. What would you expect the interest rate to be on credit card loans at this bank compared to those at other banks? Why?

18. Suppose you are the president of the bank in question 17. Given the bank's policy, what can you do to reduce or eliminate the problem of adverse selection?

SELECTIONS FOR FURTHER READING

Edmister, R. O., and H. E. Merriken. "Pricing Efficiency in the Mortgage Market." *American Real Estate and Urban Economics Association Journal,* 16 (Spring 1988), 50–62.

Gropper, D. M. "An Empirical Investigation of Changes in Scale Economies for the Commercial Banking Firm, 1979–1986." *Journal of Money, Credit, and Banking,* 23 (November 1991), 718–727.

Knudsen, J. W. "Consumer Spending and Economic Activity." *Federal Reserve Bank of Kansas City Monthly Review,* (February 1971), 3–10.

Kolari, J., and A. Zardkoohi. "Further Evidence on Economies of Scale and Scope in Commercial Banking." *Quarterly Journal of Business and Economics,* 30 (Autumn 1991) 82–107.

Ostas, J. R. "Effects of Usury Ceilings in the Mortgage Market." *Journal of Finance,* 31 (June 1976), 821–834.

Peterson, R. L., and D. A. Black. "Consumer Credit Search: A Note." *Journal of Money, Credit, and Banking,* 16 (November 1984), 527–535.

Shaaf, M., and P. A. Smith. "The Role of the Regional Economy in Oklahoma Bank Failures." *Journal of Economics,* 15 (1989), 86-91.

6

The Bank as a Firm: Deposits

Our study of loan decisions in the previous chapter may have left you wondering how deposits fit into this picture. After all, individual banks not only supply loans to borrowers but also attract deposits from savers, and in fact pay interest to those who have funds deposited in the banks. How do banks determine how many deposits they want to attract and how much interest to pay on deposits?

In this chapter, we address these issues by applying the theory of production to banking firms. Basically deposits are an input into the production of loans, and our task here is to examine how banks determine the interest rate and the amount of deposits that will maximize profits. As we will see, the answers to these questions depend on the degree of market power banks enjoy in both the loan market and the deposit market. In the final part of this chapter, we look at problems that arise due to uncertainty about when deposits will be withdrawn and discuss several strategies banks use to alleviate such difficulties.

DEPOSITS AS AN INPUT IN PRODUCING LOANS

Banks use many inputs to produce loans. Like any other firm, a bank uses labor (e.g., tellers, accountants, loan officers), buildings, computers, and utilities. It also issues commercial paper, stocks, and bonds to obtain financial and working capital. Unlike with other firms, however, the primary source of the funds a bank uses to produce its output is the reserves created when the bank accepts deposits. As we saw in Chapter 1, at the very minute you deposit $1,000 into your checking or savings account, the reserves at your bank increase by $1,000. By law, the bank must keep a fraction (say, 9 percent) of your deposit as required reserves. It may also hold an additional 1 percent as excess reserves against withdrawals. The remaining 90 percent will be used to supply loans in the loanable funds market, as discussed in Chapters 4 and 5, until the bank ends up with a balance sheet like that in Table 6.1.

Thus, the primary reason your bank wants your deposits is that they create reserves the bank can use to produce loans on which it earns interest income. Therefore, the individual bank's demand for deposits (and indeed the demand for any input into the production process) is called a **derived**

	Table 6.1	
	Balance Sheet for First Hypothetical Bank	
Assets		**Liabilities**
Reserves	$100	Deposits	$1,000
Loans	$900	Net Worth	$0

This bank has $1,000 worth of deposits (a liability), of which 10 percent is kept as reserves (an asset). The bank loans out the remaining $900 in assets in the loanable funds market.

demand—demand derived from the demand for loans that banks try to satisfy. To highlight the role deposits play in producing loans, we look at their productivity in producing loans by taking the levels of all other inputs, such as accountants, tellers, and loan officers, as given.

Total and Marginal Product

The demand for deposits depends in part on their productivity. **Total product** refers to the total level of output produced with a given quantity of an input. For example, if $100,000 in deposits permits a bank to issue $80,000 in loans, the total product of $100,000 in deposits is $80,000 in loans.

Marginal product is the change in total product (or total output) that results from a one-unit change in the usage of an input, holding the quantities of other inputs constant. For instance, if a $1 increase in deposits increases the amount of loans issued by 80 cents, the marginal product of deposits is 80 cents in loans.

In most production processes, initial increases in the use of an input will lead to successively larger increases in total output. In a hairstyling salon, for example, the first hairdresser hired increases the number of haircuts from zero to, say, two haircuts per hour. The marginal product of the first hairdresser is thus two haircuts. The second hairdresser hired increases the number of haircuts per hour from two to five. The marginal product of the second hairdresser is three haircuts, which is greater than the marginal product of the first hairdresser. The reason for the increase in the marginal product of the second hairdresser may be the fact that when the phone rings, one hairdresser can continue to cut hair while the other answers the phone. When there is only one worker, production stops when the phone rings.

For given levels of other inputs, as more and more of a specific input is used, its marginal product eventually begins to decline; that is, total product continues to increase, but at a *decreasing* rate. For example, hiring a third hairdresser may increase output from five to seven haircuts per hour. In this instance, the marginal product of the third hairdresser is two haircuts, which is less than the marginal product of the second hairdresser. Furthermore, as more and more hairdressers are packed into the salon, the marginal product of each additional hairdresser gets smaller and smaller. This phenomenon is known as the **law of diminishing marginal returns,** which states that if the amount of one input increases and the amounts of all other inputs remain constant, the marginal product of the input eventually begins to decline.

Applied to banking, the law of diminishing marginal returns says that for given quantities of other inputs, increasing the amount of deposits will eventually lead to a declining marginal product of deposits. Banks must hire labor and capital equipment (such as computers) to monitor loan payments, staff teller windows, collect bad debts, process loan applications, and keep the books on each deposit and each loan account. For given levels of these inputs, as the bank attracts more and more depositors, the desks of loan officers and accountants pile up with new-account forms and loan applications. As a result the amount of new loans the bank can issue eventually diminishes.

Part a of Figure 6.1 shows the total product curve for loans—the relationship between loans produced by a bank and the amount of deposits in the bank, holding other inputs constant. As deposits increase from $0 to $100 million, the amount of loans the bank issues rises at an increasing rate. For example, the first $50 million in deposits yields $40 million in loans, while the second $50 million increases loans by $45 million. The marginal product of the first $50 million in deposits is $40 million in loans, and the marginal product of the second $50 million in deposits is $45 million in loans. The "extra" $5 million in loans is reflected in the increasing slope of the total product curve as deposits rise from $0 to $100 million.

Part b graphs the marginal product of deposits (MP_D), which is less when deposits are $50 million than when deposits are $100 million. Note the relation between the marginal product of deposits graphed in part b and the slope of the total product curve in part a: As the total product curve gets steeper, its slope increases and the marginal product of deposits also rises. When the total product curve gets flatter, its slope declines and the marginal product of deposits falls.

Notice that as deposits increase beyond $100 million in part a of Figure 6.1, the total amount of loans increases, but at a decreasing rate. In particular, increasing deposits from $100 million to $200 million increases loans by only $45 million, $40 million less than the $85 million in loans that resulted from increasing deposits from $0 to $100 million. The slope of the total product curve declines as deposits increase beyond $100 million, indicating that the marginal product of each additional deposit declines over this range. This is consistent with the declining marginal product curve in part b for deposits beyond $100 million. In part b, the law of diminishing marginal returns applies when deposits exceed $100 million.

A Simple Technology for Producing Loans

We can more clearly see the link between bank loans and bank deposits by looking at a simple loan technology that builds on what we learned about

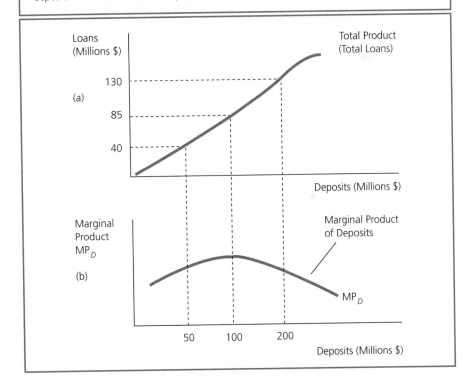

Figure 6.1
Total and Marginal Products of Deposits

This figure shows the production function for loans as a function of deposits, holding other banking inputs constant. As deposits increase from $0 to $200 million, the bank's loans (its total product, or output) increase from $0 to $130 million. This is shown in part a, where loans are graphed on the vertical axis and deposits on the horizontal axis. Part b graphs the marginal product of deposits—the slope of the production function in part a. As deposits increase, so do loans, but the rate of increase changes as the size of deposits changes. The first $100 million in deposits yields $85 million in loans, while the next $100 million in deposits yields only $45 million in additional loans. This is due to the law of diminishing marginal returns, which is illustrated by the declining marginal product of deposits when deposits exceed $100 million in part b.

fractional reserve banking in Chapter 1. Suppose the *required reserve ratio* is *rr*, meaning the bank is required by law to keep a constant fraction, *rr*, of its deposits on reserve. Thus if we let D denote deposits, the bank can legally lend up to $(1 - rr) \times D$ of its deposits. However, as deposits increase, the bank may not be able to immediately issue the quantity of loans allowed by law due to diminishing marginal returns. This is most likely to be the case at very small banks, where loan officers sometimes are unable to process sufficient loan applications to keep pace with rising deposits.

In this case, the production of loans is a function of the amount of deposits the bank can legally loan out:

$$L = F([1 - rr] \times D).$$

For instance, if the required reserve ratio is .09 and deposits are $1 million, the bank can legally issue up to $910,000 in loans. How much it will actually produce depends on its production function. Perhaps the bank will only issue $900,000 in loans. When deposits grow to $2 million, the bank will be legally able to issue up to $1,820,000 in loans, since $[1 - .09] \times \$2,000,000 = \$1,820,000$. However, because of diminishing marginal returns, the bank actually might transform deposits into only $1,750,000 in loans. Like the total product curve graphed in part a of Figure 6.1, these numbers illustrate that a doubling of bank deposits will not double the amount of loans when diminishing marginal returns to deposits exist. We will look more closely at how changes in the required reserve ratio affect the entire banking industry and the overall economy in Chapters 7, 13, and 14.

Suppose a large bank can produce loans according to the relation

$$L = (1 - rr) \times D,$$

where L is the amount of loans, rr is the constant required reserve ratio, and D is the level of deposits. (a) Graph this bank's total product curve as a function of deposits when the required reserve ratio is .1. (b) Graph the total product curve when the required reserve ratio is .2. What can you conclude about the impact of a change in the required reserve ratio on the production of loans? (c) Graph the bank's marginal product curve when the required reserve ratio is .1 and .2. What happens to marginal product when the required reserve ratio increases? (d) Does this bank's production of loans satisfy the law of diminishing marginal returns?

(a) When the required reserve ratio is .1, the formula for the total product curve is $L = .9 \times D$, which is graphed as the linear relation in part a. Notice that $100,000 in deposits produces $90,000 in loans. (b) When the required reserve ratio increases to .2, the total product curve becomes $L = .8 \times D$, which is also plotted in part a. Given the higher required reserve ratio, only $80,000 in loans can be produced with $100,000 in deposits. We conclude that an increase in the required reserve ratio decreases the total product curve for loans. (c) When the required reserve ratio is .1, each additional dollar in deposits increases loans by 90 cents, so the marginal product of deposits is .9. This is graphed in part b as the horizontal line $MP_D = .9$. When the required reserve ratio increases to .2, each additional dollar in deposits increases loans by 80 cents, so the marginal product of deposits is .8. This is graphed in part b as the horizontal line $MP_D = .8$. Thus, an increase in the required reserve ratio decreases the marginal product of deposits. (d) Since the marginal product curve is horizontal, the production process for this bank does *not* exhibit diminishing marginal returns. Here a doubling of bank deposits leads to a doubling of loans, since the bank is able to maintain the same level of excess reserves (zero) regardless of the size of its deposits.

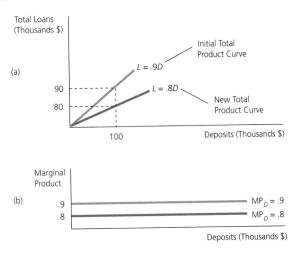

THE DEMAND FOR DEPOSITS BY PURELY COMPETITIVE BANKS

Now that we understand the production relationship between a bank's output (loans) and input (deposits), we look at how banks determine the interest rate on deposits and the level of deposits needed to produce loans. These figures vary with the market structure of the deposit market. Similar to what we saw in the loan market, purely competitive banks and banks with market power behave differently. We begin by looking at a bank in a purely competitive market.

Market Supply and the Supply of Deposits to an Individual Bank

In a **purely competitive deposit market,** individual banks are small relative to the entire market for deposits and must pay their depositors the market rate on deposits. Depositors would not choose to deposit funds in a bank that offered a lower rate on deposits than the rate other banks offered.

When the market for bank deposits is purely competitive, the intersection of the market demand and supply of deposits determines the market interest rate on deposits. All banks demand deposits to use as an input in producing loans. Households and businesses supply these deposits. Part a of Figure 6.2 illustrates equilibrium in the deposit market; the market interest rate on

Figure 6.2
Supply of Deposits to a Purely Competitive Bank

This figure shows how the deposit interest rate offered by purely competitive banks is determined. Part a shows the market demand (*D*) and supply (*S*) curves for deposits. The intersection of these curves determines the market rate of interest on deposits and the total market amount of deposits. Part b shows that the supply of deposits to any one bank is a horizontal line at the market rate of interest of 4 percent. If an individual bank attempts to offer an interest rate lower than 4 percent, it will receive no deposits because depositors will go to another bank that offers the market rate of interest.

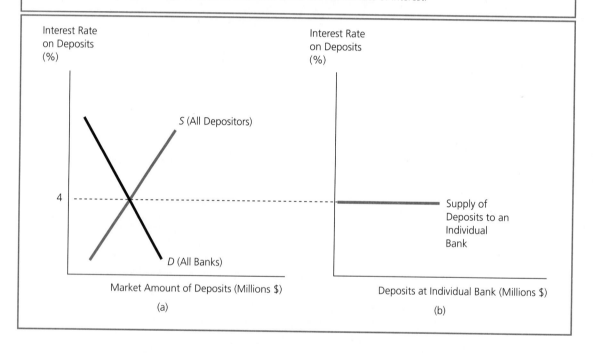

(a)

(b)

deposits—determined by the intersection of the market demand and supply curves—is 4 percent.

The supply of deposits to an *individual bank* is horizontal at the market interest rate on deposits, which is 4 percent in part b of Figure 6.2, because the individual bank must offer that rate. In contrast, the supply of deposits to *all banks* in the deposit market is upward sloping in Figure 6.2. The reason for the difference is that at the individual bank level, depositors are very sensitive to changes in the bank's interest rate. If a purely competitive bank reduced the rate it paid on deposits below the market rate its competitors paid, the bank would lose its depositors to other banks. Thus, the supply of deposits to an individual purely competitive bank is perfectly elastic at the market rate on deposits.

The Value Marginal Product of Deposits

Purely competitive banks must pay the market interest rate on deposits (i_D) to attract deposits. As we learned in the previous chapter, they also must charge the market interest rate on loans (i_L) if they wish to issue any loans. (Box 6.1 shows how bank profits are partly determined by the difference in these rates.) While purely competitive banks have no power over the interest rates charged for loans or paid on deposits, they can control the number of loans they issue at those rates. In Chapter 5, we saw how purely competitive banks determine the level of loans that maximizes profits. All that remains to complete our analysis of purely competitive banks is to see how banks determine the amount of deposits they need to generate these loans.

Let MP_D represent the marginal product of deposits—the additional amount of loans a bank can issue if it acquires an additional $1 in deposits. Since the bank loans out money at the market interest rate of i_L, the **value marginal product of deposits (VMP$_D$)** to the bank—the additional revenue it gets from an additional $1 of deposits—is

$$VMP_D = i_L \times MP_D.$$

The value marginal product of an additional $1 of deposits simply reflects the value of the interest income that will be generated by obtaining an additional $1 of deposits and converting the resulting reserves into loans. To maximize profits, a purely competitive bank continues to attract deposits up to the point where the value marginal product of deposits equals the bank's cost of acquiring an additional dollar of deposits:

$$VMP_D = i_D.$$

To see why, suppose a $1 increase in deposits increases loans by 80 cents so that the marginal product of the last deposit (the increase in loans) is .80. If the interest rate on loans is 10 percent, the value of the marginal product of the deposit is

$$VMP_D = .1 \times .80 = .08.$$

In other words, the last dollar in deposits earned the bank 8 cents in interest income. If the market interest rate the bank must pay on deposits is 4 percent, the cost to the bank of one more dollar in deposits is only $1 $\times$ .04, or 4 cents. It costs the bank less (4 cents) to attract another dollar in deposits than it will receive by converting the deposit into a loan (8 cents). Clearly it pays for the bank to obtain additional deposits and convert them into loans. But as the bank acquires more deposits, the law of diminishing marginal returns implies that the marginal product of deposits falls, which reduces the value marginal product. As the bank attracts additional deposits, VMP_D falls until it eventually equals the interest rate on deposits, i_D. The bank will not actively seek additional deposits, because doing so would reduce the value

The Data Bank

Loan and Deposit Interest Rates

Box 6.1

Banks make profits on the difference between the interest rate charged on loans and the interest rate paid on deposits. One key interest rate on loans is the prime interest rate—the rate banks charge to creditworthy commercial customers. As such, it is a benchmark of the rate at which such firms can borrow. Less creditworthy firms or individuals usually pay a rate in excess of the prime rate. On the deposit side, banks also pay a host of different rates, depending on the type of deposit. Some checking accounts receive no interest at all, while other deposits receive various rates depending mostly on how long a depositor is willing to commit to keeping the funds in the bank. The difference between

the rate charged on loans and the rate paid on deposits represents the bank's spread—the profit margin it earns on its funds.

The accompanying figure plots the deposit interest rate as measured by the rate on three-month certificates of deposit, along with the loan interest rate charged to commercial borrowers (the prime loan rate) for the period 1972–1992. With a few exceptions in the early 1970s, the loan rate exceeded the deposit rate, revealing a generally positive spread between the loan and deposit rates. The spread changed over time but has remained moderately steady since the early 1980s. At the end of

Continued on p. 175

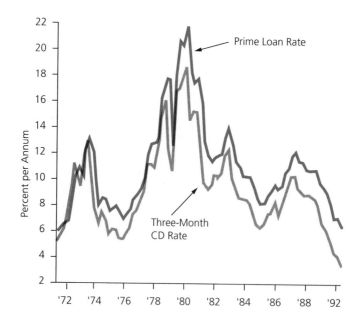

Continued from p. 174

1992, the prime rate was 6 percent and the three-month CD rate was 3.44 percent. Ignoring other costs, in 1992 a bank could take in $1,000 in a CD and pay a 3.44 percent annual rate to the depositor while lending out the entire amount if it so desired (because CD deposits are not subject to reserve requirements) at a 6 percent annual rate to a commercial customer such as AT&T. In doing so, the bank could not only link borrowers and lenders but earn 2.56 percent for its efforts as a financial intermediary.

Source: Citibase electronic database.

marginal product to a level below the interest rate on deposits. In that case, the bank would pay more for the last deposit than it could earn by converting it into a loan. Thus, to maximize profits, a purely competitive bank will aggressively seek deposits up to the point where $VMP_D = i_D$.

Figure 6.3 illustrates the profit-maximizing level of deposits for a purely competitive bank. The vertical axis measures the interest rate on deposits, and the horizontal axis measures the dollar amount of deposits. The supply of deposits to the individual bank is horizontal at the market interest rate of 4 percent. The point at which the value marginal product of deposits (VMP_D) equals the interest rate on deposits denotes the profit-maximizing level of deposits, D^*. Since the VMP_D curve determines the bank's quantity of

To maximize profits, the bank will attract enough deposits to equate the value marginal product of deposits to the interest rate on deposits. The value marginal product of deposits, given by the downward-sloping curve VMP_D, is the marginal product of an additional $1 of deposits times the interest rate the bank charges on loans. The VMP_D curve is a purely competitive bank's demand curve for deposits.

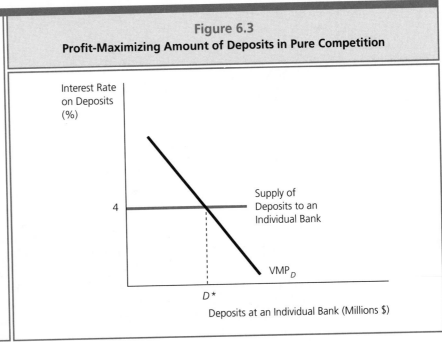

Figure 6.3
Profit-Maximizing Amount of Deposits in Pure Competition

deposits demanded at each interest rate on deposits, it is the individual purely competitive bank's demand curve for deposits. *The demand for deposits by a purely competitive bank is downward sloping due to the law of diminishing marginal returns.*

Summary Exercise 6.2

Graphically illustrate the effect on a purely competitive bank's profit-maximizing demand for deposits if (a) the interest rate on loans increases and (b) the required reserve ratio on deposits increases.

Answer: (a) An increase in the interest rate on loans (i_L) increases the value marginal product of deposits, since $\text{VMP}_D = i_L \times \text{MP}_D$. In part a, if the initial interest rate on loans is i_L^0, the initial value marginal product curve for deposits is $\text{VMP}_D^0 = i_L^0 \times \text{MP}_D$. Given the market interest rate on deposits (i_D), the bank attracts D_0 in deposits. An increase in the interest rate on loans to i_L^1 increases the value marginal product of deposits to $\text{VMP}_D^1 = i_L^1 \times \text{MP}_D$, which is a rightward shift in the demand for deposits in the figure. As shown, this increases the equilibrium quantity of deposits the bank desires to D_1. (b) An increase in the required reserve ratio reduces the marginal product of deposits from MP_D^0 to MP_D^1, since a greater fraction of deposits must be kept in reserve than before. Graphically, this shifts the demand for deposits to the left in part b, reducing the equilibrium amount of deposits from D_0 to D_1.

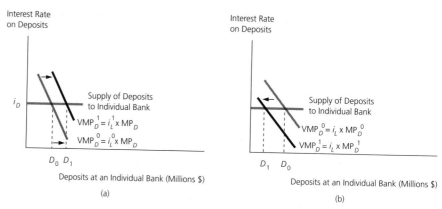

(a)

(b)

THE DEMAND FOR DEPOSITS BY BANKS WITH MARKET POWER

The preceding analysis is relevant only for very small banks that are unable to influence interest rates. In contrast, larger banks typically have power that enables them to raise loan rates or lower deposit rates without losing all of their customers. To determine the profit-maximizing level of deposits for banks with market power, we distinguish between two possible cases. In the first, the bank has market power in issuing loans but no market power in obtaining deposits. In the second, the bank has market power in both the market for loans and the market for deposits.

Market Power in the Loan Market Only

We first consider a bank that has market power in the loan market but not in the market for deposits. Thanks to its market power in the loan market, the bank faces a downward-sloping demand for loans, as we saw in the previous chapter. This means the bank must lower the interest rate on loans to issue additional loans. However, since the bank operates in a purely competitive deposit market, it can readily obtain deposits at the market interest rate on deposits.

Figure 6.4 illustrates this situation. In part a, demand for the individual bank's loans is downward sloping, which reflects the bank's market power in the loan market. In part b, the supply of deposits to the bank is perfectly

If a bank has market power in the market for loans, it must lower the interest rate it charges for loans to make more loans. This is illustrated in part a by a downward-sloping demand curve for loans. Since this bank operates in a purely competitive deposit market, it faces a horizontal deposit supply curve in part b. The bank need not change the interest rate on deposits to attract more deposits.

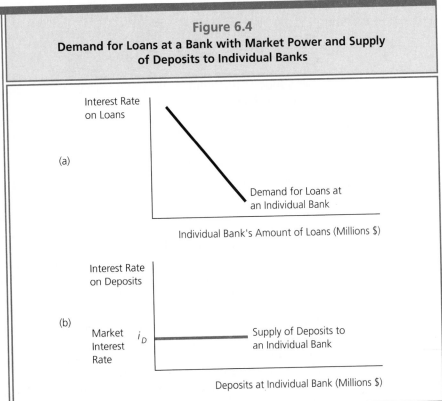

Figure 6.4

Demand for Loans at a Bank with Market Power and Supply of Deposits to Individual Banks

elastic at the market-determined interest rate, reflecting the fact that the bank obtains deposits in a purely competitive deposit market.

Each additional dollar in deposits the bank obtains increases loans by the marginal product of deposits, MP_D. Since the bank has market power in the loan market, to issue additional loans it must lower its loan interest rate. The additional revenue the bank receives when it issues another dollar in loans is the marginal revenue of a loan, MR_L. If we multiply the additional revenue received from a loan by the change in loans resulting from the receipt of an additional dollar in deposits, we obtain the **marginal revenue product of deposits (MRP_D):**

$$MRP_D = MR_L \times MP_D.$$

This tells us the additional interest income the bank will earn if it accepts another dollar in deposits and converts the corresponding reserves into loans.

How many deposits must a bank with market power in the loan market attract to maximize profits? When the interest rate on deposits is market determined and given by i_D, the bank attracts deposits until the marginal revenue of loans multiplied by the marginal product of deposits equals the interest rate on deposits:

$$MR_L \times MP_D = i_D,$$

or

$$MRP_D = i_D.$$

Let's look at the intuition behind this rule. MP_D is the additional amount of loans the bank can make with the reserves generated from an additional dollar of deposits. MR_L tells us how much the increase in loans will increase the bank's revenue. Multiplying marginal product by marginal revenue gives us the additional revenue from another dollar of deposits (since the marginal product tells us the additional loans, and multiplying by marginal revenue tells us the additional revenue from these additional loans). For profit maximization, MRP_D should equal the cost of an additional dollar of deposits, which is the interest rate on deposits (i_D). Thus, when the profit-maximizing level of deposits is achieved, the additional revenues from attracting the last dollar of deposits just equals the additional cost of the last dollar of deposits.

Table 6.2 illustrates this principle. Deposits vary from $0 to $200 million, and the associated level of loans varies from $0 to $130 million. The marginal product of deposits is calculated as the change in loans (ΔL) divided by the change in deposits (ΔD). For example, when deposits rise from $0 to $50 million, loans increase from $0 to $40 million, so the marginal product of deposits is $40/$50 $= .8$. When deposits increase from $50 million to $100 million, loans increase from $40 million to $85 million, and the marginal product of deposits is $45/$50 $= .9$.

Columns 2 and 4 in Table 6.2 show the demand for loans at this bank. When the interest rate in column 4 is high, such as 15 percent, the quantity of loans demanded in column 2 is $0. As the interest rate falls to 11 percent, the quantity of loans demanded rises to $40 million in accord with the law of demand. Multiplying each entry in column 2 by the corresponding entry in column 4 gives us column 5, the revenue (interest income) the bank earns from issuing different amounts of loans: $R = i_L \times L$. For instance, if the bank charges 11 percent, it will be able to issue $40 million in loans to earn revenues of $.11 \times $40 million, or $4.4 million. If the bank lowers its interest rate to 6.5 percent, the amount of loans it issues increases to $85 million and revenues increase to $5.525 million.

Column 6 summarizes the marginal revenue to the bank of issuing loans—the change in bank revenues divided by the change in the amount of loans. For instance, if the bank increases its loans from $0 to $40 million, the marginal revenue is ($4.4 − $0)/($40 − $0) = .11, or 11 percent. Thus, column 6 contains an entry of 11 percent when the bank issues $40 million in loans. When loans are $85 million, we calculate marginal revenue as ($5.525 − $4.4)/($85 − $40) = .025, or 2.5 percent. Notice that as the amount of loans increases from $40 million to $85 million, marginal revenue declines from 11 to 2.5 percent. Furthermore, if the bank increases its loans to $115 million, marginal revenue becomes negative. This indicates that after some point, as the bank issues more loans, its total revenues fall because the additional revenue from issuing more loans is more than offset by the revenue lost from the reduction in the interest rate the bank needed to issue more loans.

Finally, column 7 of Table 6.2 calculates the marginal revenue product for deposits as the marginal revenue of loans (column 6) multiplied by the marginal product of deposits (column 3). The bank maximizes profits by continuing to attract deposits up to the point where the marginal revenue product of deposits equals the interest rate on deposits. For example, if this bank can obtain all the deposits it wants at an interest rate of 2.25 percent, it will choose to attract $100 million in deposits to maximize profits. When deposits are $100 million, the interest rate on deposits of 2.25 percent will just equal the marginal revenue product of deposits. The bank will issue loans of $85 million at a loan interest rate of $i_L = 6.5$ percent. It will have revenue (interest income) of $85 million $\times$ .065 = $5.525 million, while its interest costs on deposits are $100 million $\times$ .0225 = $2.225 million.

Figure 6.5 graphs the tables' results. The MRP_D curve is the demand for deposits by this bank, which has market power only in the loan market. The vertical axis shows the interest rate on deposits (which is determined in the purely competitive deposit market), while the horizontal axis shows the amount of deposits. When the market interest rate on deposits is 2.25 percent, the profit-maximizing level of deposits is $100 million, where $i_D = MRP_D$.

There are two reasons the demand for deposits slopes downward in the case of a bank with market power in only the loan market. First, if diminishing marginal returns exist, the marginal product declines as additional deposits are obtained, causing MRP_D to decline. Second, because the mar-

Table 6.2
Calculating the Marginal Revenue Product of Deposits

The marginal revenue product of deposits in column 7 is the marginal product of deposits (column 3) times the marginal revenue of issuing loans (column 6). The marginal revenue product of deposits declines as the bank receives more deposits.

Deposits (Millions of Dollars)	Loans (Millions of Dollars)	Marginal Product of Deposits	Interest Rate on Loans	Revenue (Millions of Dollars)	Marginal Revenue	Marginal Revenue Product of Deposits
D	L	$MP_D = \dfrac{\Delta L}{\Delta D}$	i_L	$R = i_L \times L$	$MR_L = \dfrac{\Delta R}{\Delta L}$	$MRP_D = MR_L \times MP_D$
(1)	(2)	(3)	(4)	(5)	(6)	(7)
0	0	—	15%	0	—	—
50	40	.8	11%	4.4	11%	8.8%
100	85	.9	6.5%	5.525	2.5%	2.25%
150	115	.6	3.5%	4.025	−5%	−3%
200	130	.3	2%	2.60	−9.5%	−2.85%

ginal revenue of loans decreases as more loans are issued, MRP_D declines as deposits increase. The second factor is not present in the case of a purely competitive bank, since the bank need not lower the interest rate to issue more loans. *Thus, a bank with market power in the loan market will have a downward-sloping demand for deposits even if there are not diminishing marginal returns to deposits.*

Summary Exercise 6.3

Suppose the market for deposits is purely competitive. Illustrate the impact of an increase in the market supply of deposits on the profit-maximizing level of deposits at a bank that has market power in the loan market.

Answer: The initial equilibrium in the deposit market is at point A in part a, where the equilibrium interest rate on deposits is i_D^0. Given this interest rate, the individual bank obtains D^0 deposits in part b, where the marginal revenue product of deposits equals the market interest rate on deposits. An increase in the market supply of deposits shifts the market supply curve from S^0 to S^1 in part a, resulting in a lower interest rate on deposits of i_D^1. The individual bank now needs more deposits, D^1, to maximize profits.

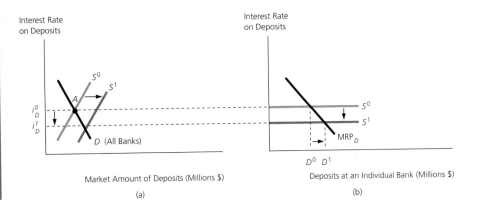

(a)

(b)

Market Power in Both the Loan and Deposit Markets

Large banks often have market power in both the loan market and the deposit market, and this tends to lower the interest rate they pay depositors. Let us see why.

Any profit-maximizing bank compares the benefits of obtaining an additional dollar in deposits with the corresponding costs. If a bank enjoys market power in the loan market, the relevant measure of the benefits to the bank of obtaining an additional dollar in deposits is the marginal revenue product of deposits (MRP_D):

$$MRP_D = MR_L \times MP_D.$$

However, the cost of obtaining an additional dollar in deposits differs when the bank has market power in the deposit market, since it faces an upward-sloping supply curve for deposits such as the one labeled S in Figure 6.6. This affects the bank's cost of obtaining additional deposits. For instance, if the bank currently obtains D_0 in deposits and wishes to increase deposits to D_1, it must increase the interest rate from i_D^0 to i_D^1. In this situation, the cost to the bank of obtaining an additional dollar in deposits is not the current interest rate on deposits but the **marginal resource cost of deposits (MRC$_D$),** the change in the cost of deposits due to a $1 change in the level of deposits.

Table 6.3, on page 184, shows how to calculate the marginal resource cost. The first two columns summarize the supply of deposits to this bank. As the interest rate on deposits rises, so does the quantity supplied. For example, if the bank pays .5 percent interest, it attracts $25 million in deposits, which costs the bank $0.125 million. If the bank wants to increase its deposits to $50 million, it must increase the interest rate on deposits to 1 percent. When it does so, its costs increase to $0.5 million. The change in cost divided by the change in deposits is the marginal resource cost. In this case, the marginal resource cost is $.375/$25 = 0.015, or 1.5 percent.

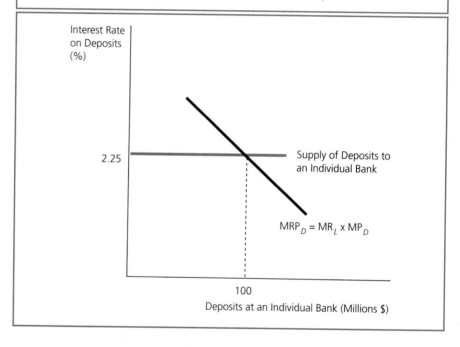

Figure 6.5
Profit-Maximizing Amount of Deposits in a Bank with Loan Market Power

Since this bank has market power in the loan market, the interest rate it receives on loans depends on the amount of loans it makes. The additional revenue the bank receives from making an additional loan is the marginal revenue of the loan, MR_L. To find the demand for deposits by the bank, we multiply the marginal revenue of the additional loan by the marginal product of an additional deposit to obtain the marginal revenue product ($MRP_D = MR_L \times MP_D$). With a market interest rate on deposits of $i_D = 2.25$ percent, the bank will set MRP_D equal to 2.25 percent and obtain $100 million in deposits.

Interest Rate on Deposits (%)

2.25

Supply of Deposits to an Individual Bank

$MRP_D = MR_L \times MP_D$

100

Deposits at an Individual Bank (Millions $)

The bank's MRC_D is greater than 1 percent, the interest rate on deposits, because the bank must raise the interest rate from .5 to 1 percent not just on the additional $25 million in deposits but also on the initial $25 million. Imagine what would happen if the bank announced it was going to pay 1 percent only on new deposits but existing deposits would still earn .5 percent! The existing deposits would likely be withdrawn and redeposited as new deposits. Thus, the concept of marginal resource cost takes into account the fact that a bank with market power can raise additional deposits only by increasing the market interest rate on *all* deposits, and this raises costs by more than just the amount paid on the additional deposits. In terms of Figure 6.6, the marginal resource cost curve, MRC_D, lies above the supply curve

This bank has market power in both the loan and deposit markets. Consequently, it must lower the interest rate on loans to make additional loans and must raise the interest rate on deposits to obtain additional deposits. The need to raise deposit interest rates to obtain more deposits is shown by the upward-sloping supply curve of deposits, S. The curve labeled MRC_D is the marginal resource cost of deposits. To increase deposits from D_0 to D_1, the bank must raise the interest rate it pays depositors from i_D^0 to i_D^1.

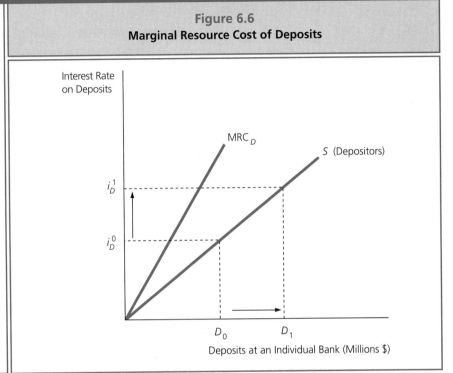

Figure 6.6
Marginal Resource Cost of Deposits

of deposits, because an increase in deposits raises resource costs by more than i_D.

Now that you understand the relevant benefits and costs to a bank of obtaining additional deposits, we can easily determine the level of deposits that maximizes bank profits. A bank with market power in both the loan and deposit markets will maximize profit by obtaining deposits up to the point where the additional costs of increasing deposits, MRC_D, just equals the additional revenue from increasing deposits, MRP_D, or

$$MRP_D = MRC_D.$$

For example, in Figure 6.7, the intersection of MRP_D and MRC_D occurs at point A, so the profit-maximizing quantity of deposits is D^*.

What interest rate on deposits will the bank pay to attract D^* deposits? Since the bank in Figure 6.7 has market power in the deposit market, it will pay the lowest possible interest rate that will generate D^* in deposits. This interest rate is determined by point B on the supply curve, which corresponds to an interest rate of i_D^*. In other words, if the bank offers depositors an interest rate of i_D^*, the quantity of deposits supplied will be D^*, which is the

---

Table 6.3
Calculating the Marginal Resource Cost of Deposits

The marginal resource cost of deposits is the change in deposit interest required to obtain an additional dollar in deposits. The marginal resource cost of deposits increases as additional deposits are received. This is because the only way a bank with market power in the deposit market can attract more deposits is to raise the interest rate paid to depositors.

Quantity Supplied of Deposits (Millions of Dollars)	Interest Rate on Deposits	Interest Cost (Millions of Dollars)	Marginal Resource Cost of Deposits
D	i_D	$C = i_D \times D$	$MRC_D = \dfrac{\Delta C}{\Delta D}$
25	0.5%	.125	—
50	1%	.5	1.5%
75	1.5%	1.125	2.5%
100	2%	2.0	3.5%
125	2.5%	3.125	4.5%
150	3%	4.5	5.5%

---

profit-maximizing level. If the bank offered a lower interest rate, it would attract fewer deposits than D^* and therefore would not maximize profits.

Summary Exercise 6.4

Suppose that due to a reduction in the required reserve ratio, the marginal product of deposits increases. Illustrate the impact of this change on the interest rate paid on deposits and the quantity of deposits obtained by a bank with market power in both the loan and deposit markets.

Answer: The initial level of deposits is given by D^0, where $MRP_D^0 = MRC_D$ at point A. The bank pays the lowest interest rate that will attract this level of deposits, which is i_D^0. The increase in the marginal product of deposits shifts the MRP_D curve to the right to MRP_D^1. The new profit-maximizing level of deposits is D^1, which corresponds with point B. The bank pays the lowest interest rate that will attract D^1 in deposits, or i_D^1. Thus, the increase in the marginal product of deposits induces the bank to obtain more deposits by offering a higher interest rate on deposits.

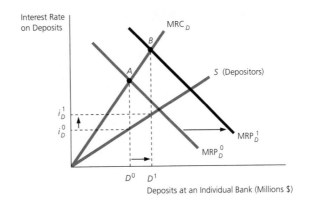

UNCERTAINTY AND BANK DEPOSITS

The final step in our analysis of deposits as an input into producing loans is to show how banks deal with uncertainty concerning when deposits will be withdrawn. We have seen that to maximize profits, a bank must convert the reserves generated by its optimal level of deposits into loans. In doing so, however, the bank converts liquid assets (reserves) into less liquid assets (loans). This raises the possibility that the bank will not have enough liquid assets to meet its depositors' demands. In this section, we examine how banks solve this problem and also how the failure to solve it can lead to bank panics.

Bank Withdrawals and the Law of Large Numbers

How can a bank dare to convert into a loan the liquid reserves created when you deposit money in your account? If you deposit $100 and the bank is certain you will not withdraw the funds for one year, it can loan out the reserves your deposit creates for one year without losing any sleep. In reality, however, banks do not know how long each depositor will leave their deposits in the bank before withdrawing funds. How do banks deal with this uncertainty?

The answer lies in what statisticians call the *law of large numbers*. When applied to banking, the **law of large numbers** says that if individual withdrawal decisions are independent and the number of depositors is large, the bank can determine very precisely how much it can afford to lend out and still cover the withdrawals of its many depositors. One of the best ways to grasp the law of large numbers is to illustrate what it implies about something we all understand: flipping a coin.

When you flip a fair coin, there is a 50–50 chance it will come up heads. If you flip a coin only once, you cannot be certain whether it will turn up

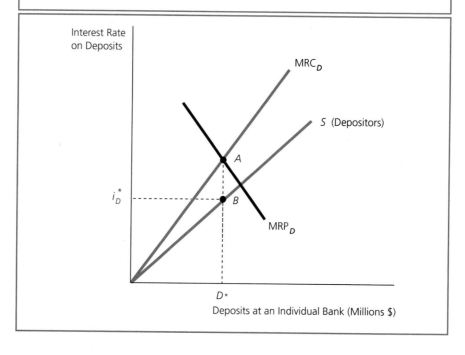

Figure 6.7
Profit-Maximizing Amount of Deposits: The Case of Market Power Both in the Loan and Deposit Markets

To determine the profit-maximizing level of deposits, a bank with market power in both the loan and deposit markets will equate the cost of obtaining an additional dollar of deposits with the benefits of obtaining an additional dollar of deposits. The benefit of an additional dollar of deposits is the marginal revenue product of deposits (MRP_D), and the cost is the marginal resource cost of deposits (MRC_D). These are equal at point A, which yields D^* worth of deposits. The interest rate on D^* deposits is given by the minimum interest rate depositors are willing to accept to provide that quantity of deposits. This is given by point B on the supply curve, S, or i_D^*.

heads or tails. However, if you flip a coin repeatedly, you will find that the ratio of the number of heads to the total number of flips gets closer and closer to the probability that any one toss will result in heads, which is 1/2. For instance, if you flip a coin 10 times, you may find that 4/10 of the flips are heads. If you flip a coin 100 times, maybe 47/100 of them will be heads. If you flip a coin 1,000 times, you can be very confident that close to 1/2 of the flips will turn up heads. Even though the outcome of any one coin toss is purely random, when the outcomes are averaged over a large number of tosses, the result can be predicted with great certainty.

Similarly as the number of depositors at a bank increases, the bank can predict with increasing accuracy the amount of withdrawals depositors will make in a given period of time. To be sure, the amount withdrawn by a single individual is uncertain, just as the outcome of a coin toss is. But when the bank averages over a large number of depositors, this randomness vanishes. The bank can then predict with great certainty the amount of reserves it needs to cover withdrawals.

To see why, suppose there are N depositors in the bank, each with an equal-size account. Thus, if the total deposits at the bank is D, any individual, i, has $D_i = D/N$ of these deposits in his or her name. If individual i withdraws W_i dollars of deposits, the fraction of deposits withdrawn, denoted d_i, is

$$d_i = \frac{W_i}{D_i} = \frac{W_i}{D/N}.$$

Notice that different individuals withdraw different fractions of their deposits; that is, d_i varies across different individuals in much the same way that different tosses of a coin result in different outcomes.

If we divide both sides of the above expression by the total number of depositors (N), we get

*Summary
Exercise 6.1*

$$\bar{d} = \frac{\Sigma d_i}{N} = \frac{\Sigma W_i}{D}$$

In other words, the average fraction of deposits withdrawn by all depositors ($\bar{d}$) equals the total withdrawals by all individuals (ΣW_i) divided by total deposits at the bank (D).

If withdrawal decisions are independent of one another and the number of depositors is large, the law of large numbers says that total withdrawals as a fraction of total deposits is very close to the probability that one depositor will withdraw her or his deposits. For example, if the probability that any one depositor will withdraw funds from the bank is p, then when N is very large,

Answer:

$$\bar{d} = p = \frac{\Sigma W_i}{D}.$$

This means that when a bank has a large number of depositors, it knows total withdrawals as a fraction of total deposits will be very close to the probability, p, that a single depositor will withdraw his or her funds from the bank. This is true even though the bank does not know whether any individual depositor will withdraw funds. For instance, if $p = .5$, there is a 50–50 chance that you will withdraw all of your deposits. Still, by keeping one-half of all deposits as reserves and loaning out the rest, a bank with many depositors can be reasonably sure of having enough reserves to cover withdrawals by you and other depositors (see Box 6.2).

Inside Money

Box 6.2

The Law of Large Numbers and Deposit Withdrawals

A simple illustration will show how the law of large numbers helps banks accurately predict withdrawals. We will consider the impact of four different scenarios on the bank's uncertainty about needed reserves. In the first, the bank has only a single depositor with $1 million. In the second, the bank has two depositors, each with $500,000. The third has four depositors, each with $250,000. Finally, the bank has 1,000 depositors, each with $1,000. In all four cases, total deposits at the bank are $1 million and there is a 90 percent chance that each individual depositor will leave deposits in the bank and a 10 percent chance that each will withdraw all deposits. The withdrawal decisions of one depositor are assumed to be independent of the decisions of other depositors.

What is the bank's reserve situation with only one depositor? In this case, the bank knows there is a 90 percent chance that it will have $1 million in deposits, but also a 10 percent chance that it will have no deposits at all. This is a very risky situation for the bank. It is risky to make loans, since chances are 1 out of 10 that the single depositor will withdraw all of its deposits.

With two depositors, the bank is a bit better off. Now the first depositor will keep her deposits in the bank with 90 percent probability, as will the second, so the probability that both will keep their deposits in the bank is .90 × .90 = 81 percent. The probability that the first will withdraw her deposits and the second will not withdraw his is .10 × .90 = 9 percent, and the probability that the first will not withdraw her

deposits and the second will withdraw his is also .90 × .10 = 9 percent. Finally, the probability that both will withdraw their deposits is .10 × .10 = 1 percent. Thus, the bank faces a situation in which it will have $1 million in deposits with 81 percent probability and $500,000 in deposits with 18 pecent probability. The bank will end up with no deposits only 1 percent of the time. Thus, by merely having two depositors instead of one, the bank reduces the probability of having no deposits from 10 to 1 percent.

With four depositors—the third scenario—the number of possibilities rises. All four depositors may keep their money in the bank, in which case the bank has $1 million in deposits. The odds of this happening are 65.61 percent. The odds that three depositors will keep their money in the bank and one will not, leaving deposits of $750,000, are 29.16 percent. The odds that two depositors will keep their money in the bank and two will withdraw theirs, so that deposits total $500,000, are 4.86 percent. The odds that only one depositor will keep his or her money in the bank, leaving deposits of $250,000, are 0.36 percent, and the odds of all four depositors withdrawing their deposits are 0.01 percent. Thus, by having four depositors instead of one, the odds that the bank will have no deposits have shrunk from 1 in 10 (10 percent) to 1 in 10,000 (.01 percent). Furthermore, the odds of the bank having less than $500,000 in deposits has fallen to .37 percent. Thus, the bank is fairly sure of having $500,000 or more in deposits.

Continued on p. 189

Continued from p. 188

Finally, what if there are 1,000 depositors, each with $1,000 in deposits? In this case, the odds that the bank will end up with less than $500,000 in deposits are, for all practical purposes, zero. In fact, the odds that the bank will end up with less than $800,000 in deposits are also zero. The odds that the bank will end up with less than $850,000 in deposits is a little less than 1 in 10 million! The odds that the bank will end up with less than $875,000 in deposits is about 4 in 1,000. Thus, with 1,000 depositors, the bank is almost certain it will have more than $850,000 in deposits, with only a small chance of having less than $875,000 in deposits. This is the impact of the law of large numbers on this bank.

Of course, this example has ignored many complicated real-world issues, such as the fact that different depositors have different probabilities of withdrawal and different sizes of deposits and that few withdraw their entire accounts. Still, the main point is that having a large number of depositors is a great aid to banks in predicting the amount of reserves they need to hold.

Differences in Withdrawal Rates Among Households. Some depositors are more likely to withdraw funds than others. For example, most students end up with a zero balance in their checking accounts virtually every month, while others tend to maintain large, positive balances. What impact does this have on banks?

First, note that if banks have better information about the likelihood of withdrawals, they can loan out more money. For example, the rate of withdrawals from savings accounts tends to be lower than the rate of withdrawals from checking accounts. This means banks can lend out a larger fraction of savings deposits relative to checking deposits and still have sufficient funds in reserve to accommodate withdrawals.

To manage the size of its reserves efficiently, a bank must have information about how often depositors will withdraw funds. One of the more common methods of obtaining this information is by sorting depositors. How is this done?

Banks tend to offer depositors a variety of options. For those depositing money in checking accounts, banks offer "no-fee" checking accounts, as well as "no-minimum-balance" accounts. With a no-fee account, there is no monthly fee, provided a minimum balance of, say, $1,000 is kept in the account. If the balance falls below $1,000, however, the bank might impose a hefty service charge ($10). In contrast, no-minimum-balance accounts typically charge depositors a fee (say, $5 per month), regardless of the account balance.

Given these options, individuals who usually end up with a zero balance have an incentive to open a no-minimum-balance account, while those with large balances have an incentive to open a "no-fee" account. Thus, individuals tend to sort themselves into different types of checking accounts according to the frequency with which they will drain their accounts. Banks know that no-minimum-balance accounts are preferred by individuals who tend to withdraw most of their deposits each month, and therefore they hold a greater fraction of such deposits in reserve.

Similar sorting occurs with savings deposits. Banks offer regular savings accounts, which pay a low interest rate but have no restrictions on the number of withdrawals permitted per statement period. They offer a moderate interest rate on accounts that limit the number of withdrawals or charge a penalty if the savings balance falls below some specified amount. The highest interest rates are paid on certificates of deposit (CDs). When a bank issues a certificate of deposit, it promises to pay a relatively high interest rate if the account is kept for the specified period of time (usually between six months and five years). However, it imposes a substantial penalty for early withdrawal.

Savings depositors sort themselves by selecting different types of savings accounts. Depositors who deplete their savings accounts during a given time period tend to deposit money in regular savings accounts to avoid the penalty for early withdrawal they would end up paying if they deposited funds in a CD and then withdrew them. Those who tend not to withdraw funds opt for CDs. The bank thus can lend out a greater fraction of CD deposits than it can regular savings deposits.

Recessions and Reserve Management.

In applying the law of large numbers to deposits, we assumed individuals' withdrawals were independent of one another. For instance, Mr. Jones's decision to make a withdrawal is independent of Ms. Smith's decision.

Unfortunately, changes in the economic environment can lead to a situation where many depositors decide to withdraw funds at the same time. In a recession, for example, many depositors deplete their savings accounts as they attempt to make ends meet. In severely depressed areas, this can drain a bank of its reserves and, in some instances, leave the bank illiquid. A bank is **illiquid** when it lacks enough liquid assets to meet the immediate demands of its creditors or depositors.

How does a bank respond when its reserves are too low? First, the bank may liquidate some of its assets. For example, it can sell some of its loans or securities (such as Treasury bills) to another bank or to an individual investor in return for cash. Since it takes time to sell assets, this practice is of limited help to the bank when an individual depositor wants cash today. Thus, banks continually monitor their reserves to determine whether they need to begin selling off assets to generate additional reserves. In addition, banks can borrow funds from other banks at what is known as the federal funds rate, to obtain funds on a short-term (overnight) basis. Banks can also borrow funds from the central bank, the Federal Reserve System. We cover these latter two sources of funds in more detail in Chapter 14.

Bank Panics

A **bank panic** occurs when the failure of one bank to honor its deposits leads the general public to fear that other banks will be unable to honor their deposits. When this occurs, depositors attempt to withdraw their deposits before their bank fails and in so doing may place it and other banks in jeopardy.

Imagine that a bank did not have enough cash on hand to satisfy withdrawals made by depositors on a given day. Telling a depositor "Sorry, we don't have enough cash for you to withdraw your funds today" could well set off a bank panic. Depositors will quickly line up at the bank, hoping to be the first in line to withdraw their deposits on the next day. This, of course, worsens the problem. As more and more depositors begin to withdraw funds, the bank must sell more and more assets to obtain cash. In extreme cases, a bank may be forced to sell assets at prices below their book value, leading to insolvency. A bank is **insolvent** if its total liabilities exceed the value of its assets. Even if the bank sold all its assets, it would not generate enough funds to pay all those to whom it owed money, including depositors.

Why Banks Are Vulnerable to Panics.

Two features of commercial banking make even otherwise healthy banks vulnerable to bank panics. First, as we learned in Chapter 1, the banking system operates on a fractional reserve system in which each bank maintains only a fraction of its deposits in reserves. Thus, banks literally lack enough cash in the vault to immediately cover all requests for withdrawals by depositors. Second, a large portion of bank liabilities is in the form of deposits payable on demand. Thus, banks face a potential calamity during a bank panic: They have promised their depositors payment on demand, but if too many depositors take them up on it, there is no way the banks can actually honor the promise. This condition snowballs into a bank panic, since depositors of otherwise healthy banks know of this danger and will want to be the first to withdraw their deposits before the bank has depleted its reserves.

Of course, the bank has sources of funds other than vault cash. It can call on its reserves on deposit at the Federal Reserve Bank. It may be able to sell off some of its portfolio of liquid assets, such as government bonds, to obtain the needed funds quickly. But in a banking panic many banks scramble for funds, and this will likely drive down the market prices of government bonds and other assets, further contributing to their problems. This scramble for funds across the banking system and the resulting decline in the prices of liquid securities may cause otherwise healthy banks to fail. This further exacerbates the banking panic, as depositors at healthy banks have reason to fear for the health of their banks after the decline in security prices.

Why Bank Panics Pose an Economic Problem.

The problem is not the failure of a single insolvent bank. After all, thousands of poorly run businesses go bankrupt each year. The real problem is that the failure of one insolvent bank spreads to other banks in the banking system, and the scramble for funds among healthy banks may set off failures that would not otherwise occur. Thus, bank panics are a problem because of their effect on

International Banking

Box 6.3

The Bank Panic of 1907

In October and November of 1907, the United States suffered a banking panic. The political response to this event led to the establishment of the Federal Reserve System, which began operations in 1914. In late 1906 and early 1907, European investors who had previously invested heavily in the United States began withdrawing funds, causing prices of U.S. stocks to fall sharply in the first half of 1907. By June 1907, the U.S. economy was in recession.

The panic of 1907 began when the Mercantile National Bank in New York City suffered large losses and depositors began withdrawing funds. In October, other New York City banks cooperated to help the Mercantile National Bank by supplying it with funds after it was put under new management. But this action was not sufficient to stop the bank panic. Instead depositors began withdrawing funds from other banks as the panic spread. By November 1907, banks in New York City had suspended cash payments on deposits. This suspension spread to other cities and did not end until early 1908. However, the recession deepened during this time, and bankruptcies of nonfinancial businesses increased. Both of these occurrences were blamed on the panic of 1907.

Source: R. Alton Gilbert and Geoffrey E. Wood, "Coping with Bank Failures: Some Lessons from the United States and the United Kingdom," *Federal Reserve Bank of St. Louis Review,* V. 68, December 1986, p. 5–14. Copyright © 1986. Used with permission.

otherwise healthy banks. They have an element of self-fulfilling prophecy, since a mere rumor that certain banks are in ill health can lead to withdrawal of deposits, thus actually causing the ill health of these and other banks.

Dealing with Bank Panics.   The time-honored method for dealing with bank panics is the suspension of cash payments of deposits (see Box 6.3). During a suspension of cash payments, banks do not pay cash for deposits, but otherwise they conduct business as usual, clearing checks, making loans, and accepting deposits. Tellers are allowed to resume payments after the panic subsides. Suspending cash payments deals with one of the two problems that lead to bank panics: Not having to pay cash on demand frees banks from the scramble to obtain funds.

Another method of dealing with bank panics is for the central bank, the Federal Reserve System in the United States, to act as the lender of last resort. The lender of last resort provides cash loans to banks during a bank panic. A bank can secure these loans with otherwise illiquid assets. An otherwise healthy bank can thus get the cash it needs to satisfy its depositors' demands. The main idea is that because the central bank stands willing to lend cash to its banks if necessary, it assures the public that no healthy bank will fail because of a panic begun by the failure of an unhealthy bank.

The Role of the FDIC. Today the existence of **federal deposit insurance,** which guarantees the full payment (up to $100,000) to owners of certain deposit accounts at failed banks, greatly reduces the likelihood of a bank panic. With deposit insurance, there is no reason to hurry even to an unhealthy bank to withdraw your deposits (unless your account contains more than $100,000), since the federal deposit insurance guarantees you will recover the amount of your deposit even from a failed bank. Indeed, even during the recent banking crisis, in which hundreds of banks and thrifts failed in 1989 alone, no bank panic occurred. The reason is that federal deposit insurance gives depositors little incentive to withdraw funds from insolvent banks or savings and loans. One of the authors of this text calmly watched as his insolvent savings and loan institution in a small Texas city changed hands three or four times in as many years, and countless others around the nation acted likewise.

Ironically, such calmness among depositors in the face of insolvency is a cause for concern among policymakers. Without deposit insurance, depositors would shift funds away from banks and savings and loans that appeared to be in danger of failure, and the fear of this happening would serve to discipline the actions of banks and S&Ls. Moreover, when these banks or savings and loans did get in trouble, the response of depositors would provide for the shrinkage or even quick failure of the institutions, and thereby limit the losses.

With deposit insurance, however, depositors are less likely to flee an insolvent bank or savings and loan, and the institution keeps operating, sometimes at ever growing losses. Then, by the time regulators get around to closing or otherwise dealing with the insolvent institution, the costs of so doing have skyrocketed. During the 1980s, many insolvent institutions offered the highest interest rates on deposits and, as we would expect, saw their deposits increase. This was an attempt to grow out of their problems, an effort that was made possible only by deposit insurance and by the slow movement to close insolvent institutions. As often as not, such attempts led to even greater losses and eventually to greater expense to the regulators and to those ultimately responsible—the taxpayers.

Moral Hazard

The presence of deposit insurance reduces the likelihood of bank panics and therefore lowers the risk to bank managers of massive withdrawals. Unfortunately, as we inferred earlier, it leads to another problem: moral hazard. **Moral hazard** arises when one party in a transaction is subjected to the risk (or hazard) that the other will take actions that are undesirable (immoral) from the first party's viewpoint. For instance, when a rental car company sells you insurance on a rental car, it is subjected to moral hazard because there is a chance you are the kind of customer that likes to "hot rod" in rental cars—an action the company views as undesirable.

How does deposit insurance lead to moral hazard? Since depositors are insured against the insolvency of a given bank, they are likely to spend less time scrutinizing the bank's health before opening a deposit account. This means banks that make excessive risky loans may attract as many deposits as those that make prudent loan decisions. As a result, the presence of federal deposit insurance creates the hazard that people will deposit in banks that make loans to poor credit risks. This can ultimately increase the number of insolvent banks and, consequently, the insurance payments made by the FDIC to depositors at those banks.

During the 1980s, many savings and loans—and some banks—were allowed to continue operating even though they were insolvent. Regulators failed to close these insolvent institutions for a number of reasons, including intercessions on behalf of troubled institutions by some members of Congress. Of course, in the absence of deposit insurance, the depositors of insolvent institutions would have withdrawn their funds and forced the institutions to shut down. But armed with the security of deposit insurance, depositors did not withdraw their funds and the insolvent institutions continued to operate. As we first saw in Box 5.3 in the previous chapter, this created perverse incentives. Insolvent institutions were tempted to invest in ways that had the potential to generate large returns, even if those investments were also very risky. For an insolvent institution, there is little downside risk. The worst that can happen if an investment fails is that the institution becomes "more insolvent" than before. As long as no laws are violated, the managers and owners are not personally responsible for any further losses, and, since the institution is already insolvent, the owners have already lost their invested funds. The limited liability of corporations protects these owners from losing more than their invested funds. Moreover, if the risky investment succeeds, the institution may become solvent again, and the owners may recover at least some of their investment. The only parties standing to lose from this behavior are the deposit insurance funds and, ultimately, the taxpayers. If the investment doesn't succeed, the deposit insurance fund will have to provide even more funds to reimburse depositors when the institution finally closes.

To be concrete, suppose an insolvent institution has a negative net worth of $100 million and is allowed to continue operating. It faces two investment choices: a safe investment and a risky investment. The safe investment is certain to net the bank $20 million, while the risky investment will net the bank $200 million in profits or $160 million in losses, with equal probability. On average, the risky investment will net the bank $20 million, the same amount the safe investment will. But the bank is just as likely to lose $160 million as it is to strike it rich and earn $200 million.

Since the bank has a negative net worth of $100 million, the safe investment will not earn the bank enough to pull it out of the hole. In contrast, the risky investment offers a 50 percent chance of earning $200 million, more than enough to put the bank in the black. But it is equally likely to put the bank deeper in the whole: Its net worth will decline by $160 million if the investment turns sour.

Given these alternatives, the insolvent institution has an incentive to choose the risky investment. If this investment succeeds in earning the $200 million, the insolvent institution will be restored to solvency and will no longer be a problem for the insurance fund. If the investment proves unsuccessful, the insolvent institution goes from a $100 million to a $260 million liability to the insurance fund. Moreover, a real asymmetry exists here, since the insurance fund will pay for the losses if things turn out bad but will not receive an offsetting amount if things go well. In other words, the insurance fund, on average, loses if this institution chooses the risky investment over the safe one. The presence of deposit insurance creates moral hazard; it allows savings and loans to gamble with other people's money and keep the winnings if they succeed. Investment decisions such as the one in this example exacerbated the S&L crisis in the 1980s and caused deposit insurance funds to more carefully scrutinize investments made by insured financial institutions. Box 6.4 shows the rise in the thrift and bank failures that occurred during the 1980s.

Summary Exercise 6.5

Suppose a bank has two types of depositors: A large depositor who has $10 million at the bank and many small depositors with deposits totaling $10 million. Each depositor withdraws all funds from his or her account with a probability of 1/4 and leaves all money in the account with a probability of 3/4. (a) What is the minimum amount of reserves the bank must keep to be certain of having enough cash on hand to cover withdrawals? (b) What strategy can the bank use to enable it to keep fewer reserves?

Answer: (a) Before we apply the law of large numbers, note that in this case, one depositor contributes $10 million of the bank's $20 million in deposits, but many small depositors together have $10 million deposited in the bank. Since not all depositors have equal-size deposits, we must determine the reserves needed for each type of depositor.

There is a 25 percent chance that the large depositor will withdraw all funds from the account. The only way to ensure having enough money to cover such a withdrawal is to keep the entire $10 million deposit in reserve. In contrast, we can apply the law of large numbers to the small depositors. The law of large numbers implies that the total withdrawals of the small depositors as a fraction of the deposits of all small depositors equals 1/4. Thus, the bank must keep $10,000,000 $\times$ .25 $=$ $2,500,000 in reserve to be certain of having enough cash to cover withdrawals by small depositors.

Inside Money

Box 6.4

*Failures of Insured Thrifts
and Banks, 1934–1989*

In 1933, the United States established the Federal Deposit Insurance Corporation (FDIC) to insure bank deposits and the Federal Savings and Loan Insurance Corporation (FSLIC) to insure savings and loan deposits. The accompanying graph shows the number of failures of insured banks and savings and loans from 1934 until 1989, when the FSLIC was eliminated and the FDIC began administering the insurance fund for both banks and savings and loans. Notice that the number of failures of insured banks during the 1930s reached a peak of 77 in 1937, when there were 13,797 insured banks. The number

of insured savings and loans that failed reached 13 in 1941, when 2,343 insured savings and loans existed.

Compare this to the experience of the 1980s. In 1988, 205 out of a total of 2,949 insured savings and loans failed. The assets of these failed institutions totaled $10,660,000. A similar number of bank failures occurred—206 out of 12,712 insured banks. Assets of these failed banks totaled $29,168,596.

_____

Source: Congressional Budget Office, *Reforming Federal Deposit Insurance* (September 1990), Tables C-1, C-2.

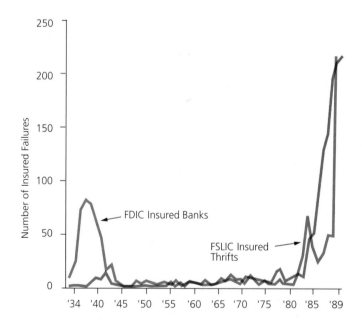

In total, then, the bank must keep $10,000,000 + $2,500,000 = $12,500,000 in reserves.

(b) The lion's share of the reserves is due to the large depositor. One strategy for reducing reserves is to induce the large depositor to purchase a certificate of deposit. For example, suppose the bank offered the large depositor a favorable interest rate on a one-year CD, with the stipulation that the money can be withdrawn early only by forfeiting 10 percent of the initial deposit. Then, even if the large depositor withdrew funds early, the bank would have to give the depositor only 90 percent of the deposit. Persuading the large depositor to do this would considerably reduce the bank's necessary reserves.

CONCLUSION

In this chapter, we learned how banks decide how many deposits to attract, and how market forces determine the interest rate banks pay on deposit. Combined with Chapter 5, in which we saw how banks decide how many loans to make and at what rate, we have now analyzed the behavior of banks in both the loan market and the deposit market. We also investigated in this chapter several related issues concerning the management of reserves, the importance of the law of large numbers for predicting withdrawals, the problem of bank panics, and the role of deposit insurance as a solution. Finally, we discussed the moral hazard problem implicit in the provision of deposit insurance and gave an example showing how deposit insurance and insolvency combined to create a severe moral hazard problem in the savings and loan industry in the 1980s.

Our emphasis in this chapter was on the behavior of individual banks. In the next chapter, we will look at the banking industry in more depth. There we will see more historical details about this industry, including the rules and regulations governing banks.

KEY TERMS

derived demand

total product

marginal product

law of diminishing marginal returns

required reserve ratio

excess reserve ratio

purely competitive deposit market

value marginal product of deposits (VMP_D)

marginal revenue product of deposits (MRP_D)

marginal resource cost of deposits (MRC_D)

law of large numbers

illiquid

bank panic

insolvent

federal deposit insurance

moral hazard

QUESTIONS AND PROBLEMS

1. Why is the demand for deposits by a bank called a *derived demand?*

2. Tenth National Bank is a small bank in a large city. How do you think Tenth National determines the interest rate to pay depositors and to charge for loans? Explain.

3. Is it possible for a bank to have market power in the deposit market but no market power in the loan market? Justify your answer.

4. Town Bank obtains deposits and issues loans in purely competitive markets where $r_D = 5$ percent and $r_L = 10$ percent. The bank manager has learned from the bank's research department that the marginal product of deposits is .2.
   (a). Explain what it means for the marginal product of deposits to be .2.
   (b). Based on these numbers, does an additional $1 in deposits increase loans by $1? Why or why not?
   (c). Is Town Bank attracting the profit-maximizing amount of deposits? Explain carefully.

5. Suppose the required reserve ratio is 15 percent. Can the marginal product of deposits ever be greater than 85 percent? Explain.

6. Major Bank is the sole supplier of loans in its market area but competes in a national market for deposits.
   (a). Why might Major Bank be a monopoly in the (local) loan market but a purely competitive bank in the deposit market?
   (b). Use a diagram to show how Major Bank determines the interest rate it pays on deposits to attract the profit-maximizing level of deposits.
   (c). If Major Bank's required reserve ratio decreased, what would happen to the in-

terest rate it pays on deposits? What would happen to the quantity of deposits it attracts? Use a diagram to illustrate your answer.

7. Stockholders at Bank One are concerned that management is not running the bank properly. The reason for their concern is that deposits at the bank have doubled in recent years, but the amount of loans issued has increased by only 30 percent. Are the stockholders' concerns justified? Explain.

8. Any Bank obtains deposits and issues loans in purely competitive markets where $r_D = 5$ percent and $r_L = 10$ percent.
   (a). Use a graph to illustrate how Any Bank determines the profit-maximizing level of deposits.
   (b). Use a graph to show what would happen to Any Bank's profit-maximizing level of deposits if the interest rate on deposits increased to 7 percent.
   (c). Use a graph to show what would happen to Any Bank's profit-maximizing level of deposits if the market interest rate on loans increased to 13 percent.

9. Bertha Bank is the sole user of deposits and issuer of loans in its market.
   (a). Explain how the incentive to maximize profits leads Bertha Bank to pay a positive interest rate on deposits, even though it is the only bank in the market.
   (b). "If the marginal productivity of deposits rises (due to a decline in the required reserve ratio), Bertha Bank will lower the interest rate it pays on deposits." Is this statement true or false?

10. Explain why the marginal resource cost of deposits is greater than the interest rate paid to depositors. (Assume, of course, that the bank has market power in the deposit market.)

11. Determine the likely impact of the following on an individual bank's value marginal product of deposits.

    (a). An increase in the market supply of deposits

    (b). An increase in the market demand for deposits

    (c). A reduction in the bank's required reserve ratio

    (d). A reduction in the fraction of borrowers who default

12. Suppose a bank has market power in the loan market. The bank can produce loans according to a total product curve, $L = (1 - rr) D,$ where rr is the required reserve ratio.

    (a). Does this bank's marginal product curve obey the law of diminishing marginal returns?

    (b). Graph the bank's marginal revenue product curve for deposits, and explain why it looks as it does.

13. Can a solvent bank be so short on cash that it cannot accommodate withdrawals? Explain.

14. Carefully explain why banks need not keep all deposits in reserve to cover withdrawals by depositors.

15. A bank with market power in both the deposit and loan markets is experiencing losses. The bank plans to reduce the rate it pays to depositors while increasing the rate it charges on loans.

    (a). Ignoring the consequences of "imperfect information" in the loan and deposit markets, will the bank's profits necessarily increase if it adopts this action? Explain carefully.

    (b). How would the presence of imperfect information alter your answer in part? Explain carefully.

16. Central Bank offers 8 different types of checking accounts and 24 different types of savings accounts. Why doesn't Central Bank reduce its bureaucracy by offering only one type of account?

17. Suppose a bank has market power in the deposit market. The law of supply reveals that if the bank reduces the interest rate it pays on deposits, it will attract fewer deposits. What does the economic principle of adverse selection suggest about which depositors will continue to leave their money in the bank? Explain carefully.

18. Some banks do not pay interest on deposits and, in fact, charge depositors a monthly maintenance fee, plus 10 cents for each check written. Does this policy contradict the analysis in this chapter? Explain.

19. Does the presence of federal deposit insurance lead to moral hazard in the banking industry? Explain.

20. Suzie has never written a bad check in her 30 years as a customer at Friendly Bank. The bank manager recently called Suzie to inform her that she has been given "automatic overdraft privileges." This is a fancy way of saying that the bank will automatically transfer funds from Suzie's savings account to her checking account to cover any checking account overdrafts.

    (a). "Automatic overdraft privileges are worthless to Suzie, since she never writes bad checks." Is this statement true or false? Explain.

    (b). Do you think automatic overdraft privileges lead to an increase in the number of checks bounced at a bank? (Remember: For a check to bounce with automatic overdraft privileges, it must exceed the amount in both the savings and checking accounts.) Explain.

SELECTIONS FOR FURTHER READING

Boughton, J. M., and E. R. Wicker. "The Behavior of the Currency Deposit Ratio during the Great Depression." *Journal of Money, Credit, and Banking,* 11 (November 1979), 405–418.

Day, A. E. "Reserve Ratios: A Proposal for Change." *Journal of Macroeconomics,* 8 (Fall 1986), 479–484.

Edmister, R. O. "Margin Analysis for Consumer Deposit Interest Rate Policy." *Journal of Bank Research,* 13 (Autumn 1982), 179–184.

Edmister, R. O., and H. E. Merriken. "Measuring Interest Rate Sensitivity of Consumer Depositors." *Journal of Financial Services Research,* 2 (June 1989), 133–145.

Froyen, R. T., and K. J. Kopecky. "A Note on Reserve Requirement and Monetary Control with a Flexible Deposit Rate." *Journal of Banking and Finance,* 7 (March 1983), 101–109.

McCulloch, J. H. "Bank Regulation and Deposit Insurance." *Journal of Business,* 59 (January 1986), 79–85.

Steindl, F. G., and M. D. Weinrobe. "Natural Hazards and Deposit Behavior at Financial Institutions: A Note." *Journal of Banking and Finance,* 7 (March 1983), 111–118.

Wells, D. R. "Security Reserve Requirements—A Possible Substitute for Deposit Insurance?" *Journal of Economics,* 14 (1988), 76–83.

The Banking Industry

*I*n the previous two chapters, we analyzed the economic decisions made by individual banks. In this chapter we broadly survey the banking industry, which is made up of numerous individual banks as well as savings and loans and credit unions.

In the United States and other industrialized nations, the government actively regulates the banking sector. In particular, the banking industry is subject to rules and regulations imposed by various state and federal regulatory agencies, including the Federal Reserve System, state banking commissions, the comptroller of the currency, and the Federal Deposit Insurance Corporation. State and federal legislative bodies also affect the banking industry.

In the first part of this chapter, we examine the evolution of the banking industry. We then turn to an economic analysis of the many rules and regulations supervisory agencies impose on the banking industry. As we will see, some past regulations had surprisingly adverse effects on the industry, giving regulators and banks powerful incentives to evolve and innovate to overcome them.

DUAL BANKING

We learned in Chapter 1 that money and banks existed in very early societies. While banks initially provided a safe place to store gold, bankers soon realized that most of the gold in their vaults was never withdrawn. Eventually banks began to issue bank notes, which were an early form of paper money.

Prior to 1863, each bank issued its own bank notes, which could be redeemed on demand for gold. Although banks were regulated by the states in which they operated, it was relatively easy for unscrupulous individuals to defraud banks and merchants by counterfeiting bank notes. Because each bank's bank notes differed in appearance from those of other banks, it was difficult to determine whether a particular bank note was genuine or counterfeit. Some banks issued bank notes that exceeded the value of the assets the banks held, while others defaulted on the bonds backing their bank notes. As a result of these and other problems, many state-chartered banks failed.

The *National Banking Act of 1863* was passed in an attempt to eliminate the problems associated with the state banking system and individual banks' bank notes. Under the new banking system this act created, the federal government issued charters to certain banks. These banks, known as **national banks,** still exist today under the regulatory supervision of the U.S. Treasury (more specifically, the comptroller of the currency). The intent of the act was to entirely eliminate state banks by imposing heavy taxes on the bank notes they issued. The bank notes of national banks, however, could be used as currency without having to pay such taxes, thus putting state banks at a competitive disadvantage. But the state banks quickly countered by creating a close substitute for currency, called *demand deposits,* which were the forerunners of the checks you use today. This innovation not only allowed state banks to survive but led national banks to adopt demand deposits as well.

As a consequence, today we have a **dual banking system** wherein state and national banks coexist. The comptroller of the currency, an office of the Treasury, grants charters to national banks. State banking commissions in each state grant charters to **state banks.** Currently about two-thirds of banks have state charters and the remainder have national charters.

ACQUIRING A BANK CHARTER

Opening a bank involves considerable red tape and financial capital. As we saw in Chapter 5, this condition restricts free entry and may reduce competition in the banking industry. To form a bank, the parties involved must obtain approval from the relevant regulatory body (the comptroller of the currency for a national bank and the state banking commission for a state bank). The process of obtaining such approval is known as acquiring a **bank charter.**

To obtain a charter, the potential owners of the bank must prove they have not only the required financial capital but also the qualifications needed to operate the bank. In addition, they must show that the area in which they propose to locate both needs and can support a new bank. If the chartering agency believes the proposed bank has insufficient capital, the applicants are not qualified, or the area does not need another bank, it will not approve the charter. Showing need is very subjective. One time-honored approach is to identify a geographic area or an interest group that is not being adequately served by existing banks and promising to serve that area's or group's banking needs. Box 7.1 discusses the criteria used by the comptroller of the currency in considering applications for national bank charters.

SUPERVISION AND EXAMINATION OF BANKS

Once a bank charter is granted, it is supervised and examined from time to time by various agencies, including the Federal Reserve System, the Federal

Inside Money

*Requirements for Obtaining
a Bank Charter*

Box 7.1

To illustrate the reasoning behind decisions by the comptroller of the currency to approve or deny a bank charter, we reproduce here three decisions made by that office as reported in the *Quarterly Journal.* These decisions highlight the importance of demonstrating a need for the proposed bank, an adequate organizational plan, and evidence of the qualifications of the organizers and proposed bank officers.

The first decision is an approval of a bank charter in California. The approval is conditional on a few items; it explicitly states that two of the proposed executive officers are not acceptable:

On August 4, 1988, the Office approved a new bank charter in California on the condition that two of the organizers be prohibited from serving as executive officers of the proposed institution. The individuals were involved with a company that had recently emerged from Chapter XI bankruptcy and it was the opinion of the Office that management of the company would require an inordinate amount of the individuals' time. As such, they would be unable to devote the necessary amount of time to the proposed bank to ensure that it would have a reasonable likelihood of success. The remaining organizers were considered excellent and the proposed chief executive officer possessed good credentials (page 15).

The second decision is a denial of a proposed charter in Arkansas due to intense competition already present in the relevant market and an inadequate organizational plan:

On August 19, 1988, the Office denied a charter application in Arkansas because of a weak and unrealistic operating plan and a weak organizing group. The organizers did not demonstrate that they possessed the qualifications to succeed in the market area where the economy was weak and competition was intense (page 15).

The final decision explicitly mentions that the bank will service a particular interest group (recall this is one way to establish a need for a new bank):

United Citizens Bank, National Association, Los Angeles, California was approved by the Office on June 30, 1988. The new bank was established in order to serve the Korean community in Los Angeles. The Office noted that the proposed chief executive officer had strong credentials, the organizers had very strong ties to the targeted community, and that similar new banks had been successful in the recent past (page 29).

Source: Quarterly Journal of the Comptroller of the Currency, Administrator of National Banks, (December 1988), pp. 15, 29.

Deposit Insurance Corporation (FDIC), the comptroller of the currency, and state banking authorities. Bank examinations typically focus on the status of the bank's loan portfolio and the bank's capitalization.

Status of the Loan Portfolio

One important purpose of supervision and examination is to reduce the hazards of asymmetric information between bank managers and the public regarding the riskiness of the bank's loan portfolio and thus assure depositors that the bank is a safe place to deposit funds. To this end, bank regulations require the examining agency to evaluate the quality of the bank's loan portfolio and verify that the bank has sufficient assets and reserves to cover its deposits. This monitoring helps alleviate depositors' concern about such things as the quality of loans issued by the bank.

Quality loans are loans with a high probability of being repaid. For example, suppose your bank claims to have $100 million in assets. It would be difficult (and costly) for you to verify this information, but a bank examiner does this for you. He or she examines the portfolio to determine whether the assets really are worth $100 million. If the assets consist solely of idle cash, the true value of the bank's assets is clear. However, since banks use reserves to issue loans, most of the bank's assets will be in the form of loans rather than cash.

In fact, two-thirds of the average bank's assets consist of loans. The true value of these loans depends on whether the borrowers are making their interest and principal payments on time (that is, on whether borrowers are paying off their debt). For instance, the value of a car loan on the books might be $10,000 even if the loan is in default. If the bank is forced to repossess the car and can sell it for only $6,000, the true value of the loan is $6,000, and the bank has overstated the loan's value by $4,000. A bank examiner, however, can require the bank to value such assets properly.

When a loan is in default, the bank examiner may require the bank to either write off the loan—that is, not include it as an asset—or liquidate the asset. Doing so reduces the bank's net worth, or capital. If this happens too often, the bank's capital may fail to satisfy minimum capital regulations. A bank in this situation (and any bank that is caught manipulating the books to hide information from the examiner) is classified as a "problem bank." Such a bank will be very heavily scrutinized in the future, and its officers may even face penalties and legal actions.

Bank Capitalization

As noted earlier, sufficient capital is required to obtain a charter and to continue operating a bank. Bank capital is the equity of stockholders; it serves as a buffer against bank insolvency when losses on loans or other securities occur. Prior to the 1980s no official capital requirements existed, but the various supervisory and regulatory agencies used informal means to encourage banks to maintain what they deemed a reasonable level of capitalization. Bank examiners began noticing that capitalization rates were falling in the late 1970s and early 1980s, in part due to bank losses on international loans to developing countries. The **International Lending Supervisory Act of 1983** authorized the Federal Reserve System, the FDIC, and the comptroller of the currency to set and enforce minimum capital requirements in an effort to stem the international debt crisis.

Under this act, regulatory capital limits were first put in place in 1985. The results were disappointing, however, and bank capital to asset ratios were still low by the late 1980s. In response, a whole new structure of capital requirements was imposed. These regulations applied to both core capital (stockholder equity in the bank) and supplemental capital (loan loss reserves up to 1.25 percent of the assets and subordinated debt issued by the bank). Subordinated debt is debt that is sold subject to the condition that, in the event of insolvency, all other liability holders have precedence. Thus, subordinated debt is in many ways similar to shares of stock, except the holder receives a stated interest payment instead of a share of residual profits.

In addition to imposing regulations on core and total (core plus supplemental) capital to asset ratios, the new regulations required examiners to weight assets by risk. Cash, U.S. government securities, and GNMA mortgage-backed securities were considered safe assets, and no risk adjustment occurred. Interbank deposits, general-obligation municipal securities, and FNMA and FHLMC mortgage-backed securities were considered to have a small default risk and were assigned a risk weight of 20 percent. First-home mortgages and municipal revenue bonds were assigned a risk weight of 50 percent. Finally, all other bank securities and loans were assigned a risk weight of 100 percent. Currently the risk-adjusted ratio of total capital to assets must be at least 8 percent.

The response of many banks to these requirements was to increase their capitalization by issuing more equity shares and more subordinated debt. This increased these banks' stake in their own fate, reducing to some extent their incentive to gamble by making risky loans. Unfortunately for stockholders, the large number of new issues of equity by banks may be responsible for the declines in prices of bank stocks in the early 1990s.

Overlapping Responsibilities

We have mentioned a host of agencies involved in chartering banks, supervising banks' operations, and examining banks' loan portfolios and capitalization. There is considerable overlap of responsibilities, as banks are subject to multiple layers of supervision and examination among agencies. In practice, however, these agencies divide their duties as follows. The comptroller of the currency charters, supervises, and examines all national banks. State banking commissions charter state banks, and the Federal Reserve System supervises and examines state banks that are members of the Fed. Similarly, the FDIC supervises and examines state banks that are members of the FDIC but are not part of the Federal Reserve System. State banking commissions supervise and examine banks that are neither Federal Reserve System nor FDIC members. Table 7.1 summarizes these responsibilities. In the next two sections, we look at how and why the supervisory powers of the Federal Reserve System and the FDIC have evolved over time.

THE FEDERAL RESERVE SYSTEM

Congress established the **Federal Reserve System** (the Fed) when it passed the *Federal Reserve Act* in 1913. The Fed was given the task of promoting stability in the banking industry and serving as the sole supplier of U.S. currency. This currency is now known as *Federal Reserve* notes—the dollar bills in your pocket or purse. Every national bank was required to be a member of the Federal Reserve System and to honor the Fed's rules and regulations. One benefit of membership was Fed services such as check clearing. State banks, on the other hand, could join the Federal Reserve System and enjoy similar services if they paid the required membership fee, but they were not obligated to do so.

Over time, shrinking membership reduced the Fed's influence on the banking system. Between the early 1950s and the 1980s, assets of member banks declined from 85 percent to about 50 percent of total banking system assets. Much of this decline occurred during the 1970s—when interest rates

Table 7.1
Responsibilities of Commercial Bank Regulatory Bodies

This table summarizes the responsibilities of the four bodies that regulate commercial banks in the United States.

Type of Bank	Chartered by	Supervised and Examined by	Insured by
National banks	Comptroller of the currency	Comptroller of the currency	FDIC
State banks that are members of the Fed	State banking commissions	Federal Reserve System	FDIC
State banks insured by the FDIC (nonmembers of the Fed)	State banking commissions	FDIC	FDIC
State banks not insured by the FDIC	State banking commissions	State banking commissions	State authorities

were high—because banks actually profited by avoiding or giving up Fed membership. The Federal Reserve System not only charged a membership fee but imposed tougher reserve requirements and other regulations than did the various state banking agencies. For instance, the Fed did not pay interest on member banks' reserves, whereas many states allowed state-chartered banks to hold reserves in interest-earning securities. Consequently banks found it profitable to obtain state charters and opt against Fed membership. This ultimately reduced the Fed's control over the banking system.

This situation changed in 1980 with the passage of the *Depository Institution Deregulation and Monetary Control Act (DIDMCA)*. While DIDMCA contained other provisions that we will discuss later in this chapter, a key provision enhanced the Fed's ability to stabilize the banking system. This provision created **uniform reserve requirements** that essentially required all depository institutions to meet Federal Reserve System reserve requirements in exchange for enjoying the privileges of membership. Specifically the act stated that all depository institutions were subject to the same set of reserve requirements, which would not earn interest, and gave the Federal Reserve System authority to set supplemental reserve requirements, which would pay interest. In exchange, all depository institutions were permitted to borrow from the Federal Reserve System (called *using the discount window*), and all could avail themselves of Fed services such as check clearing and wire transfers. However, these services, which had been free, would now be priced by the Federal Reserve System at cost. As a result of DIDMCA, the distinction between members and nonmembers has blurred, since both are now subject to many of the same regulations. In Chapter 13, we discuss the Fed in more detail.

THE FDIC

The **Federal Deposit Insurance Corporation (FDIC)** emerged as a result of the Fed's inability (or unwillingness) to stabilize the banking system during the Great Depression. When banks began getting into trouble, the Fed failed to serve as a lender of last resort and in fact raised the rate it charged banks for emergency funds. Ultimately one-third of all U.S. banks failed, and many depositors were left penniless. This crisis culminated with the Bank Holiday in March 1933, when President Roosevelt closed all U.S. banks for one week as a temporary measure to calm the panic. Longer-term measures were instituted when Congress passed the *Banking Act of 1933* (better known as the *Glass-Steagall Act*). Among other things, this legislation established the FDIC to insure depositors against bank failures. Today every national and state bank that is a member of the Federal Reserve System is required to purchase FDIC insurance to cover depositors. State banks that are not members of the Fed may choose not to purchase FDIC insurance, but membership in the FDIC is almost universal. Figure 7.1 illustrates the

Figure 7.1
Bank Charters, Fed Membership, and FDIC Coverage

Banks can acquire either a state or a national charter. National banks must join both the Fed and the FDIC. State banks can choose to join the Fed, in which case FDIC insurance is required. State banks that do not join the Fed have an option to either buy FDIC insurance or rely on their states' insurance authorities for coverage.

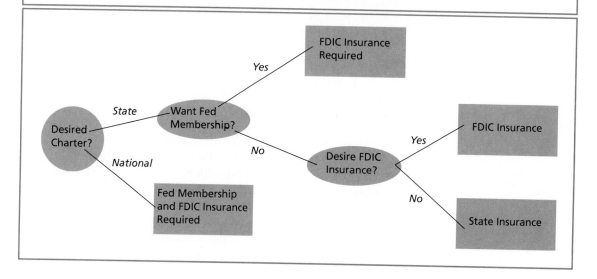

extent to which banks have a choice in purchasing FDIC insurance depending on their charter and membership in the Fed.

Today the FDIC insures depositors up to $100,000 against loss due to bank failure. In return for this insurance, a bank is required to pay an insurance premium and to adhere to rules and regulations on deposits and loans established by the FDIC. The FDIC currently charges .23 percent of the dollar value of bank deposits. Thus, if you open up an account at your bank for $100, your bank will pay 23 cents to the FDIC to insure your deposit.

In addition to insuring depositors against loss, deposit insurance reduces the likelihood of bank panics. To see why, suppose depositors at a bank without deposit insurance heard a rumor that their bank was about to fail. Some depositors would rush to the bank to withdraw their deposits before the bank ran out of funds. Since the bank keeps only a small fraction of deposits as excess reserves, these reserves would become depleted as more and more depositors withdrew funds. Eventually the bank would lack enough liquid assets to cover any further withdrawals. This situation could result in a bank panic, in which virtually every depositor would try to withdraw deposits. This, of course, would exacerbate the problem, because the bank would have to sell off illiquid assets at a very low price to obtain cash.

Deposit insurance reduces the likelihood of such an occurrence. In particular, since depositors know they will receive their deposits even if the bank fails (thanks to the insurance), they have a greatly reduced incentive to withdraw their funds if they hear a rumor that the bank is on the verge of failure. The FDIC will pay them the full value of their deposits in such an event. Consequently, bank panics are much less likely to occur when banks have deposit insurance.

During the past decade, however, many banks that were members of the FDIC failed because of the moral hazard problems created by deposit insurance (see Box 6.4 in the previous chapter). In 1989, at the height of the trend, more than 200 banks failed in the United States. In an attempt to cover the costs of the claims paid to depositors who otherwise would have lost their deposits, new proposals were pending in 1994 that would increase the cost to banks of FDIC insurance. Under the new plan, the cost to a bank of deposit insurance would rise to between 25 and 30 cents per $100 in deposits depending on the bank's financial health.

In the same way the FDIC insures depositors at commercial banks, the Federal Savings and Loan Insurance Corporation (FSLIC) insured depositors at savings and loans, but it went out of existence in 1989 as a result of the S&L crisis. Today the FDIC is the insurance agency for both commercial banks and savings institutions.[1] In the next section, we briefly examine the crisis that caused the FDIC to take over the responsibility for insuring S&Ls and discuss some recent legislation directed at improving the FDIC.

The S&L Crisis and Changes in the FDIC

The S&L crisis began with large losses in the thrift industry during the 1970s and 1980s. These losses were due in part to the high nominal interest rates at the time, which left many S&Ls paying more on deposits than they were receiving on (relatively old) mortgages. People who bought homes in the late 1960s were still paying 7 percent on their mortgages when their deposits at S&Ls were earning more than 10 percent. This created perverse incentives for S&Ls to gamble by making risky investments in the hope of big payoffs (see Box 5.3 in Chapter 5, "Going for Broke in the Savings and Loan Industry"). But the big payoffs never came. Rather, the S&Ls incurred big losses, and in the end the volume of failed S&Ls left the FSLIC with too few funds to cover their deposits. The result was the S&L "bailout," in which Congress picked up the tab at an estimated cost at the time of $680 for every person in the United States.

---

[1] A different agency, the National Credit Union Administration (NCUA), administers an insurance fund for credit unions. This fund is the National Credit Union Shareholders Insurance Fund (NCUSIF), and insures credit union depositors (called *shareholders*) up to $100,000.

FIRREA.   Congress abolished the bankrupt FSLIC and restructured the FDIC to insure depositors at both commercial banks and savings institutions when it passed the *Financial Institutions Reform, Recovery, and Enforcement Act of 1989 (FIRREA).* The FDIC now administers separate funds for the two types of institution. The fund for banks is the Bank Insurance Fund (BIF), while the Savings Association Insurance Fund (SAIF) insures depositors at S&Ls. FIRREA also abolished the Federal Home Loan Bank Board (FHLBB), which had regulated the savings and loan industry. To replace the FHLBB, this act created the Office of Thrift Supervision (OTS) at the U.S. Treasury.

FDICIA.   More recently, Congress took steps to reduce the moral hazard problems that bankrupted the FSLIC by passing the *Federal Deposit Insurance Corporation Improvement Act (FDICIA)* in 1991. This legislation required the FDIC to initiate proposals for risk-based insurance premiums by 1994, meaning that institutions with relatively risky loan portfolios will have to pay higher rates for deposit insurance than those with safer ones. This act will give banks stronger incentives to manage risk to avoid higher premiums. The act also mandated the FDIC to resolve problems at troubled institutions at the least possible long-term cost to the insurance fund. To do this, the FDIC must itself monitor banks and bank examiners. These incentive effects on both banks and the FDIC will reduce the potential for asymmetric information and moral hazard problems to bankrupt the FDIC.

Summary Exercise 7.1

You are considering opening an account in either First National Bank or First State Bank in your local city. Briefly explain the differences between these two banks. What specific information should you request before depositing funds in First State Bank? Explain.

Answer: First National, being a national bank, was chartered by the U.S. Treasury (the office of the comptroller of the currency). The regulations that guided its creation were established at the federal government level. In contrast, rules established by the state banking commission guided the chartering of First State Bank. First National is necessarily a member of both the Federal Reserve System and the FDIC. Your deposit (up to $100,000) in First National would be insured against loss by bank failure (or by theft). In contrast, First State Bank is not necessarily a member of the Federal Reserve, nor does it necessarily have FDIC deposit insurance. You should ask First State Bank whether it is a member of the Federal Reserve System. If the answer is yes, it is also a member of the FDIC, and your deposit in the bank will be insured. If it is not a member of the Federal Reserve, it may still be a member of the FDIC. By all means, find out. Otherwise you might end up like the grandmother of one of the authors: She lost $25,000 at a depository institution that didn't have FDIC coverage.

AN OVERVIEW OF BANKING REGULATION

We have seen that a host of regulatory bodies oversee the operations of the more than 11,000 commercial banks in the United States. The large number of banks, coupled with the numerous regulatory agencies and the many changes made in banking regulations each year, makes for a very confusing regulatory system. Not only is it difficult for the average citizen to understand the operation of the banking system, but even banks struggle to fully understand the nature and implications of regulations on their operations. A report by the Federal Financial Institutions Examination Council (which consists of regulatory agencies that include the Federal Reserve System, the comptroller of the currency, and the Federal Deposit Insurance Corporation) estimates that complying with banking regulations costs commercial banks and thrift institutions (savings and loans, credit unions, and mutual savings banks) anywhere from $7.5 billion to $17 billion each year. This includes the costs of paperwork, legal fees, and other costs of conforming to government mandates. As a result of the report, as of 1994 the Clinton administration was considering proposals to ease the regulatory burden on the banking industry.

Regulation of the banking industry aims to achieve several goals. The first is maintaining bank solvency or, alternatively, limiting bank failures. As we saw in Chapters 5 and 6, the presence of asymmetric information makes it difficult for the average depositor to know how safe his or her deposits are at a bank, and the mere rumor that a bank is on the verge of failure could cause a bank panic. Proponents of regulation argue that government's presence to regulate and monitor banks bolsters depositor confidence, thus enhancing the stability of the banking system.

Another goal of regulation is to ensure liquidity of the banking industry, making sure that banks can honor their promise to redeem demand deposits for currency on demand. As we saw in the previous chapter, the fact that the Fed is the lender of last resort and the FDIC insures depositors helps banks honor their promises to depositors.

The third goal is to promote economic efficiency, which includes providing deposit and loan services to people in local communities at competitive interest rates. Regulators have enacted myriad regulations designed to foster such competition by keeping banks from growing too big and gaining monopoly power in loan and deposit markets.

The banking system we know today has been shaped directly and indirectly by legislation designed to achieve one or more of these goals of regulation. As we will see in the next few sections, however, some pieces of legislation did not have their intended effect, and as a result multiple layers of new legislation have been added over the years to deal with the problems they created. Furthermore, we will see that banks have successfully gotten around many of the regulations through financial innovations and loopholes in the laws.

HOW BRANCHING RESTRICTIONS SHAPED THE BANKING INDUSTRY

A distinguishing feature of the U.S. banking system is the large number of small, local banks. This is the result of a long history of regulations that restricted banks from freely opening branches within states and across the nation. Imagine a law that allowed a shoe manufacturer to sell shoes only to consumers who lived in the same city as its plant! This is, in effect, what branching restrictions in many states required banks to do.

Branching restrictions grew out of fear that in their absence, banks would grow progressively larger and acquire excessive market power, making them less sympathetic to the needs of people and businesses in local communities. Consequently, numerous banks were formed across the states to service the needs of local communities. Many states (primarily those in the central United States) limited the ability of state-chartered banks to branch within their states' boundaries. This practice, called **limited branching,** restricted the number of branches a bank could have within a state. Some states took this to an extreme, enacting **unit banking** laws that allowed a bank to serve only a single location in its state. However, not all states limited the ability of their banks to open branches within their boundaries. Primarily along the West Coast, some states allowed **statewide branching,** which permitted banks to open branches throughout the state.

Initially national banks were not subject to the branching restrictions imposed by the states, and as a result they had an advantage over state banks. To level the playing field, Congress passed the *McFadden Act of 1927,* which made national banks subject to the same branching restrictions imposed by state regulators on state-chartered banks. Since most states had restrictions against branching, neither state nor national banks could freely establish branches across state lines. As a result, numerous small banks emerged across the country as individual states enacted laws that prevented entry by out-of-state banks. Box 7.2 contrasts this trend with the current move toward free trade within the boundaries of the European Community.

Over time, however, two financial innovations occurred that allowed banks to get around these laws to better serve their customers: bank holding companies and electronic banking. These innovations, along with recent changes in state laws that grew partly out of the S&L crisis of the 1980s, are discussed next.

Bank Holding Companies

Bank holding companies, such as Citicorp (which owns Citibank) and Mellon Bank Corp. (which owns Mellon Bank), are corporations that own the controlling interest in one or more banks. A bank holding company may also own other companies that are in businesses related to banking, such as credit card services and life insurance. Some bank holding companies, known as *nonbank banks,* do not provide the full array of services offered by full-service banks. For example, a nonbank bank might have an office that accepts

International Banking

Box 7.2

Banking in the European Community and the Principle of Mutual Recognition

Recently Gerald P. O'Driscoll, Jr., economist and vice president at the Federal Reserve Bank of Dallas, wrote about the lack of free trade within the United States. This is particularly a problem in services and financial markets, including banking. O'Driscoll contrasted this situation with the move toward free trade within the boundaries of the European Community (EC).

A guiding principle in Europe is that of mutual recognition. This principle stipulates that each member state will recognize the rules and regulations of other member states. The European Community will establish some minimum criteria that all member states must adopt. Other than those, each member state will make its own rules and regulations, and these will be recognized as valid by all other member states.

What exactly does this mean? It means that a bank established under the rule of the Netherlands is free to operate in Germany *under the rules that apply in the Netherlands* as long as it obeys the overall EC rules. Moreover, this applies even if the German banks are disadvantaged by more favorable banking rules in the Netherlands.

In the United States, federal banking guidelines apply to banks in all states. However, after meeting these requirements, states are free to add additional regulations. Under the principle of mutual recognition, though, a bank chartered in Texas would be free to operate in New York or California while obeying the state regulations of Texas even if those regulations differed from those of New York or California and even if they gave the Texas bank an "unfair" advantage.

What are the implications of adopting this principle of mutual recognition? First, it will certainly create a single market, with free entry across the 50 states. No longer will states be able to keep out banks chartered in other states or even to regulate them. Second, state banking rules and regulations will tend to evolve toward those of the most liberal state, subject only to the federal minimum standards. This will occur as banks naturally seek charters from the state that provides the most favorable regulations. This is exactly what happened in the United States for corporate charters. Delaware is the home of a disproportionate number of corporations because it provided more favorable treatment of corporations.

Source: O'Driscoll, Jr., Gerald P., What About Free Trade Within the United States?, from *Southwest Economy,* January/February 1992, 1–5. Copyright © 1992. Used with permission.

deposits but does not make loans and another office that makes loans but does not accept deposits.

Bank holding companies evolved as a financial innovation to enable banks to circumvent branching restrictions. By acquiring the controlling interest of banks located in different regions of the country, a bank holding company could effectively offer services to customers in different regions or states without violating branching laws. Congress responded to this innovation by passing the *Bank Holding Company Act of 1956,* which restricted bank holding companies from acquiring banks in other states without the consent of those states. Further innovations occurred due to a loophole in the law that allowed one-bank holding companies to cross state lines. Congress closed this loophole when it passed the *Bank Holding Company Act of 1970,* which extended restrictions on bank holding companies to one-bank holding companies. Despite these attempts to limit bank holding company acquisitions, bank holding companies today indirectly hold (through their subsidiaries) more than 90 percent of all bank deposits.

Electronic Banking

Automatic teller machines (ATMs) now make it possible for individuals located far from their banks to withdraw funds from their bank accounts via machines located in other cities, states, and even countries. However, most of these transactions take place within the same states as the banks holding the deposits. Many automatic teller machines are not owned by a particular bank but are paid for on a per-transaction basis. Consequently they technically are not branch banks and are not controlled by branching regulations. However, the regulatory decision not to count an ATM as a bank branch was made only after much discussion and negotiation. Today banks are free to place these machines where they please. Electronic banking thus represents a financial innovation that circumvents branching restrictions and allows depositors ready access to their deposits in areas far from their banks. Moreover, as Box 7.3 suggests, this innovation has not adversely affected employment in the banking system.

Current Status

During the 1980s, states gradually began relaxing their restrictions on interstate banking. This resulted in part from a need to allow out-of-state banks to acquire failed banks and S&Ls and to accommodate the needs of corporations that have offices in different regions. This trend has continued through the 1990s and has led to a dramatic change in the structure of banking. Most states now permit branching within their borders, and a few have reciprocal privileges that allow branches from other states to enter their states. As of July 1994, every state except Hawaii allows some form of interstate banking.

HOW GLASS-STEAGALL SHAPED THE BANKING INDUSTRY

Perhaps the piece of banking legislation that had the most profound impact on the evolution of the banking system into its present form was the Glass-Steagall Act of 1933. Although not all elements of this act are still in force,

The Data Bank

Box 7.3

Employment in Banking and ATM Machines

Many employees worry about the effect of automation on employment, and indeed automation can eliminate some jobs while creating others. The accompanying table shows the number of ATM machines, as well as employment in the banking industry as a percentage of total nonagricultural employment, during the early years of ATM growth. The 300 percent increase in the number of ATM machines between 1980 and 1986 did not reduce employment in banking relative to total employment. In fact, from 1980 to 1983, employment in banking increased slightly, as banks adjusted to the change in technology by hiring fewer bank tellers but more accountants and high-tech employees.

Year	Number of ATMs[1]	Employment in Banking as a Percentage of Nonagricultural Employment[2]
1980	19,858	1.74%
1983	53,332	1.84
1986	81,510	1.74

[1] *Magazine of Bank Administration,* May 1987.
[2] *Supplement to Employment and Earnings,* Bureau of Labor Statistics, 1983–1989.

Glass-Steagall led to fundamental changes in the structure of the banking industry that persist today.

As we already noted, Glass-Steagall was passed in response to the collapse of the financial system during the Great Depression, and one of its provisions created the FDIC in the hope of limiting incentives for depositors to engage in bank runs. In addition, Glass-Steagall imposed a number of restrictions on commercial banks, including restrictions against investment banking and limitations on deposit interest paid by banks. We now examine why these restrictions were enacted and how banks, courts, and even legislators responded to some of the problems they created.

Restrictions Against Investment Banking

The Glass-Steagall Act banned commercial banks from engaging in investment banking. An **investment bank** handles the administration, promotion, and distribution of securities and guarantees the issuer a certain price. It then sells the issue in the primary market and earns a profit on the difference. Prior to Glass-Steagall, banks freely engaged in these activities. Unfortunately, some banks experienced losses when they were unable to sell the securities in the primary market after the stock market crash of 1929. This created losses for some banks that exacerbated the banking crisis of the time.

In an effort to prevent such problems from recurring, the Glass-Steagall Act tied the hands of commercial banks, prohibiting them from engaging in investment banking activities. Its passage also stemmed fears that such activities by commercial banks could lead to conflicts of interest if the banks compromised the safety of their portfolios of assets to accommodate their own investment banking activities. Consequently, our banking system today differs substantially from those of many other countries. For instance, Germany, France, Switzerland, and the United Kingdom allow **unified banking;** that is, their banks serve as both commercial banks and investment banks.

In recent years, however, financial innovation in the U.S. banking industry has led to a wider array of services at both commercial and investment banks. Through bank holding companies, banks set up mutual funds, brokerage services, life insurance, and a host of other services. During the 1980s, investment banks acquired some of the failed S&Ls, and firms like Merrill Lynch offered money market funds with check-writing privileges. Furthermore, in 1988 the Supreme Court ruled that the Fed could allow banks to underwrite some types of bonds. As a result of financial innovation and court rulings, commercial and investment banks today can offer a wider array of services than originally allowed under the Glass-Steagall Act, although they are still not entirely free to do as they please.

Interest Rate Restrictions

The Glass-Steagall Act also prohibited banks from paying interest on demand deposits (i.e., checking accounts) and allowed the Federal Reserve System to regulate interest rates on saving and time deposits at commercial banks. The authors of Glass-Steagall reasoned that one cause of bank failures during the early 1930s was excessive competition for deposits by banks, which eroded their profits. The purpose of interest rate ceilings on deposits, known as **Regulation Q,** was to reduce the cost to banks of obtaining funds and thereby enhance their profits and the stability of the banking system. For many years, the Fed used its newly given authority to impose interest rate ceilings on saving and time deposits at commercial banks through Regulation Q, until the caps were phased out during the 1980s (see Box 7.4). The discussion that follows describes the events that led to the elimination of those ceilings.

Interest Rate Adjustment Act. An unintended consequence of Glass-Steagall's restrictions on bank interest payments was that banks were put at a competitive disadvantage relative to S&Ls. Under Glass-Steagall, interest rate ceilings applied only to deposits at commercial banks. Savings and loans were free to compete for deposits by paying higher interest rates on saving and time deposits (but not on demand deposits; at that time, savings

Inside Money

Box 7.4

The Long Phaseout of Regulation Q

The accompanying table shows the steps in the phaseout of Regulation Q. Note that by March 31, 1986, all interest rate ceilings had been eliminated except the restriction that no interest could be paid on demand deposits. (This restriction is no longer in force.)

Effective Date of Change	Nature of Change
June 1, 1978	MMCs established, with minimum denomination of $10,000 and maturities of 26 weeks. The floating ceiling rates for each week were set at the discount yield on six-month Treasury bills at S&Ls and MSBs, 25 basis points less at CBs.
November 1, 1978	CBs authorized to offer ATS accounts, allowing funds to be transferred automatically from savings to checking accounts as needed to avoid overdrafts. The ceiling rate on ATS accounts was set at 5.25 percent, the same as the ceiling rate on regular savings accounts at CBs.
July 1, 1979	SSCs established with no minimum denomination, maturity of 30 months or more and floating ceiling rates based on the yield on $2\frac{1}{2}$-year Treasury securities, but 25 basis points higher at S&Ls and MSBs. Maximums of 11.75 percent at CBs and 12 percent at S&Ls and MSBs.
June 2, 1980	The floating ceiling rates on SSCs raised 50 basis points relative to the yield on $2\frac{1}{2}$-year Treasury securities at S&Ls and MSBs and at CBs. The maximum ceiling rates set in June 1979 were retained.
June 5, 1980	New floating ceiling rates on MMCs. All depository institutions may pay the discount yield on 6-month Treasury bills plus 25 basis points when the bill rate is 8.75 percent or higher. The ceiling rate will be no lower than 7.75 percent. A rate differential of up to 25 basis points favors S&Ls and MSBs if the bill rate is between 7.75 percent and 8.75 percent
December 31, 1980	NOW accounts permitted nationwide at all depository institutions. Ceiling rates on NOW and ATS accounts set at 5.25 percent.
August 1, 1981	Caps on SSCs of 11.75 percent at CBs and 12 percent at S&Ls and MSBs eliminated. Ceiling rates float with the yield on $2\frac{1}{2}$-year Treasury securities.
October 1, 1981	Adopted rules for the All Savers Certificates specified in the Economic Recovery Act of 1981.
November 1, 1981	Floating ceiling rates on MMCs each week changed to the higher of the 6-month Treasury bill rate in the previous week or the average over the previous four weeks.
December 1, 1981	New category of IRA/Keogh accounts created with minimum maturity of $1\frac{1}{2}$ years, no regulated interest rate ceiling and no minimum denomination.
May 1, 1982	New time deposit created with no interest rate ceiling, no minimum denomination and an initial minimum maturity of $3\frac{1}{2}$ years.
	New short-term deposit instrument created with $7,500 minimum denomination and 91-day maturity. The floating ceiling rate is equal to the discount yield on 91-day Treasury bills for S&Ls and MSBs, 25 basis points less for CBs.
	Maturity range of SSCs adjusted to 30–42 months.
September 1, 1982	New deposit account created with a minimum denomination of $20,000 and maturity of 7 to 31 days. The floating ceiling rate is equal to the discount yield on 91-day Treasury bills for S&Ls and MSBs, 25 basis points less for CBs. These ceiling rates are suspended if the 91-day Treasury bill rate falls below 9 percent for four consecutive Treasury bill auctions.

Continued on p. 218

Continued from p. 217

December 14, 1982	MMDAs authorized with minimum balance of not less than $2,500, no interest ceiling, no minimum maturity, up to six transfers per month (no more than three by draft), and unlimited withdrawals by mail, messenger or in person.
January 5, 1983	Super NOW accounts authorized with same features as the MMDAs, except that unlimited transfers are permitted.
	Interest rate ceiling eliminated and minimum denomination reduced to $2,500 on 7- to 31-day accounts.
	Minimum denomination reduced to $2,500 on 91-day accounts and MMCs of less than $100,000.
April 1, 1983	Minimum maturity on SSCs reduced to 18 months.
October 1, 1983	All interest rate ceilings eliminated except those on passbook savings and regular NOW accounts. Minimum denomination of $2,500 established for time deposits with maturities of 31 days or less (below this minimum, passbook savings rates apply).
January 1, 1984	Rate differential between commercial banks and thrifts on passbook savings accounts and 7- to 31-day time deposits of less than $2,500 eliminated. All depository institutions may pay a maximum of 5.50 percent.
January 1, 1985	Minimum denominations on MMDAs, Super NOWs and 7- to 31-day ceiling-free time deposits reduced to $1,000.
January 1, 1986	Minimum denominations on MMDAs, Super NOWs and 7- to 31-day ceiling-free time deposits eliminated.
March 31, 1986	All interest rate ceilings eliminated, except for the requirement that no interest be paid on demand deposits.

Terms:

S&Ls—savings and loan associations	SSCs—small saver certificates
MSBs—mutual savings banks	ATS—automatic transfer service accounts
CBs—commercial banks	NOW accounts—negotiable order of withdrawal accounts
MMCs—money market certificates	MMDAs—money market deposit accounts

Source: Gilbert, R. Alton, Requiem for Regulation Q: What It Did and Why It Passed Away from *Federal* *Reserve Bank of St. Louis Review* February 1986, pp. 22–37. Copyright © 1986. Used with permission.

and loans did not offer checkable accounts). Over time many savers switched saving deposits from banks into thrift institutions, which paid higher interest rates. To level the playing field, Congress passed the *Interest Rate Adjustment Act of 1961*, which extended the Glass-Steagall interest rate limits to thrifts.

The Interest Rate Adjustment Act reduced the flow of deposits from banks to thrift institutions. However, the soaring interest rates of the 1970s ultimately led to a problem called **disintermediation:** The ceilings on deposit rates at banks and thrifts led depositors to pull funds out of banks and savings and loans and place those funds in alternative financial instruments that paid market interest rates, such as money market mutual funds. The impact of this drain of funds from banks and thrifts to money market mutual funds is difficult to overemphasize. Money market mutual funds grew from about $3 billion in assets in 1977 to nearly $190 billion in assets in 1981! This represents a very large volume of funds that would otherwise have been available to the banking industry had it been allowed to offer market rates on deposits.

DIDMCA. During the late 1970s, disintermediation was rapidly draining banks and thrifts of their deposits and reserves, reducing their ability to issue new loans that would have earned higher market interest rates. Furthermore, thrifts were saddled with long-term loans (such as mortgages) that were earning low, fixed interest rates. This problem was rapidly driving the entire savings and loan industry into insolvency.

Congress's response to these problems was to pass the Depository Institution Deregulation and Monetary Control Act (DIDMCA) in 1980. DIDMCA phased out interest rate ceilings on deposits and permitted nationwide NOW (negotiable order of withdrawal) accounts, which were essentially checking accounts at thrift institutions. This allowed banks and thrifts to attract new deposits by offering interest rates that were more in line with the market rates paid by money market funds. To allow thrifts to convert these new deposits into new loans at the relatively high market interest rates, DIDMCA permitted S&Ls to make some consumer loans, credit unions to make real estate loans, and thrifts to issue credit cards. As mentioned earlier in the chapter, DIDMCA also enacted uniform reserve requirements, which gave back to the Fed some of the power it had lost as a result of its declining membership.

Garn–St. Germain. DIDMCA blurred the distinction between thrifts and commercial banks, and Congress further obscured it when it passed the *Garn–St. Germain Act of 1982*. This act, which was directed at dealing with S&L failures that occurred between 1980 and 1982, contained a provision allowing the FDIC and FSLIC to arrange interstate mergers of troubled institutions. More important, it gave thrifts more freedom to issue loans and compete for deposits. For instance, thrifts were allowed to issue up to 10 percent commercial loans and 30 percent consumer loans, and depository institutions were authorized to offer money market deposit accounts (MMDAs) to compete with money market mutual funds. These MMDA accounts could offer competitive interest rates and, unlike money market mutual funds, were insured by federal deposit insurance. Today, as a result of all of these events since Glass-Steagall that ultimately culminated in the S&L crisis, commercial banks and thrifts are very similar in terms of both the types of loans they can make and the regulations to which they are subject.

Summary Exercise 7.2

(a) List some of the financial innovations that resulted from banks' attempts to circumvent banking restrictions. (b) List some of the legislative changes that blurred the distinction between commercial banks and S&Ls.

Answer: (a) Your list should include checkable deposits, bank holding companies, and electronic banking, among others. Make sure you understand the environment that led to each of these innovations. (b) Among other things, your list should include the following: (i) The FDIC now insures S&Ls and banks, (ii) all depository institutions are subject to uniform reserve requirements set by the Fed, and (iii) S&Ls and banks are now allowed to make similar types of loans. Make sure you know the legislation and chain of events that led to each of these changes.

THE ECONOMIC IMPACT OF BANKING REGULATIONS

As we have seen, legislative and regulatory bodies have imposed a variety of restrictions and regulations that shaped the banking industry into what it is today. While the primary aim of such regulations was to enhance the stability of the banking industry and protect depositors, some of the restrictions ultimately had the opposite effect. We have already seen that over the years, banks have come up with financial innovations that circumvent many of these laws. In this section, we examine some of the economic implications of various regulatory policies for the markets for loans, deposits, and credit. We will see that some regulations have had adverse effects on consumers and banks.

Bank Charters

The requirement that banks be chartered before they can operate distinguishes the banking industry from many other industries in the United States. As we have seen, the strict capital requirements and lengthy time period required for approval of a bank charter limits entry by new banks. This means that if existing banks are earning sizable economic profits, it is difficult for a new bank to quickly emerge and compete away some of those profits. We can use the model of bank behavior developed in Chapter 5 to see the implications of this condition.

Part a of Figure 7.2 shows the market supply and demand for loans in a purely competitive banking industry. The equilibrium interest rate—10 percent in this example—is determined by the intersection of the supply (S^0) and demand (D^0) curves for loans at point A in part a of Figure 7.2.

Part b illustrates the situation for an individual bank. An individual bank in a purely competitive market can issue loans at the market interest rate of 10 percent, so the demand for an individual bank's loans is horizontal and given by D_F^0. Since the interest rate is also the individual bank's marginal revenue curve, the bank maximizes profits by issuing the quantity of loans where the interest rate equals the marginal cost of loans, which is at point a in part b of Figure 7.2. This corresponds to L_F^0 loans issued by the individual bank, at an interest rate of 10 percent. The economic profits earned by this bank are given by the shaded rectangle.

If entry into the banking industry were unrestricted and existing banks were earning profits, new banks would enter the banking industry to reap

Figure 7.2
Effect of Entry into the Banking Industry

Part a shows the market for loans, where the initial interest rate is 10 percent at point *A*. Part b shows the situation for an individual competitive bank, which initially produces at point *a*. If new banks are allowed to enter this market, the supply of loans in part a shifts to S^1, lowering the market interest rate to 8 percent at point *B*. The individual bank adjusts its loans to point *b*, where it earns zero economic profits. Free entry into the banking industry thus results in lower interest rates on bank loans and banks earn zero economic profits.

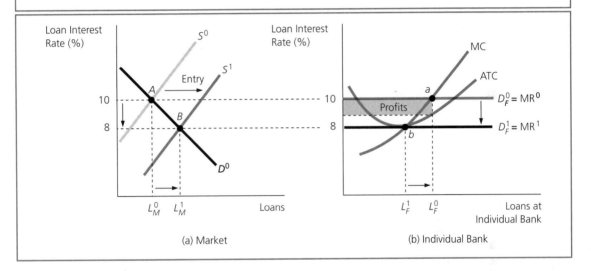

(a) Market   (b) Individual Bank

some of the profits. The entry of new banks would shift the market supply curve in part a of Figure 7.2 to the right to S^1, resulting in a new equilibrium at point *B*. Notice that as a result of the entry of new banks into the industry, the interest rate on loans falls to 8 percent. Borrowers now obtain loans at a lower interest rate due to increased competition in the banking industry.

The decline in the market interest rate shifts the demand for an individual bank's loans down to D_F^1 in part b of Figure 7.2. Marginal revenue now equals marginal cost at point *b*. Furthermore, at point *b* the interest rate on loans exactly equals the bank's average cost of issuing loans; the bank now earns zero economic profits. Thus, with free entry into the banking industry, new banks will enter the industry until the economic profits earned by existing banks are zero. Banks receive just enough interest payments on loans to cover the opportunity cost of the resources required to issue the loans. At this point, there is no further incentive for additional banks to form.

As you can see, free entry into the banking industry would ensure that banks charge an interest rate just high enough to cover the opportunity cost of the loaned funds. However, there is not free entry into the banking industry. Even when entry is allowed, it can take considerable time for a new bank to go through the process of obtaining a charter; in the meantime, interest rates and bank profits will remain at a high level.

In fact, limiting entry tends to keep bank profits and loan interest rates at a higher level than they would be otherwise. For example, in part a of Figure 7.2, the interest rate is 10 percent if new banks are not allowed to enter but falls to 8 percent if entry is allowed due to the increased supply of loans. Similarly, the shaded rectangle in part b shows profits if entry is not allowed, which fall to zero if entry is permitted.

Proponents of restrictions on entry into banking argue that the negative aspects of restricted entry (the higher interest rates to borrowers) are more than offset by the positive aspects. First, they argue that restricting entry of new banks means fewer banks will fail, since banks will earn greater profits. Second, by carefully screening applications for a bank charter, banking authorities can prevent the entry of banks that are likely to fail in the first place. Together these factors reduce the likelihood of bank failures and also decrease the size of the insurance claims that must be paid on those banks that do fail.

Branching Restrictions

Branching restrictions decrease the accessibility of bank deposits and loans outside the area serviced by a bank, which reduces competition among banks and inconveniences customers. Individuals keep fewer funds on deposit, since they need larger stashes of cash for unexpected trips outside of bank service areas. This decreases the market supply of deposits from S^0 to S^1 in Figure 7.3 and increases the interest rate on deposits from i_D^0 to i_D^1. (Remember, banks use deposits to produce loans; therefore, they are the demanders in the deposit market, and households are the suppliers.) Thus, because of branching restrictions, banks actually have to offer higher interest rates on deposits to attract customers than they would otherwise. These higher rates partially compensate depositors for the inconvenience of keeping deposits at banks. But since an increase in the interest rate paid on deposits increases a bank's marginal cost of issuing loans, interest rates on bank loans will rise as well. This rise is further exacerbated by lessened competition among banks for loan customers.

As we noted earlier, however, banks today are less adversely affected by branching restrictions than in the previous decade due to the emergence of automated teller machines. As a result, depositors are now willing to maintain larger balances in their accounts, knowing they can readily withdraw funds from ATMs in distant locations. The emergence of ATMs shifts the supply of loanable funds from S^1 back to S^0 in Figure 7.3, lowering the cost to banks of obtaining funds.

A subtler but more important aspect of branching restrictions is their effect on the riskiness of a bank's loan portfolio. When a bank is restricted

Restrictions on the number of branches banks can reduce the market supply of deposits from S^0 to S^1. This raises the interest rate on deposits from i_D^0 to i_D^1, resulting in fewer deposits at banks.

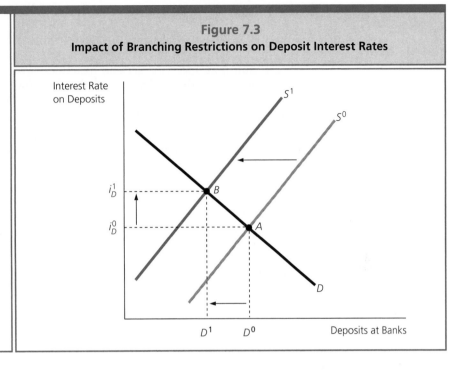

Figure 7.3

Impact of Branching Restrictions on Deposit Interest Rates

to making loans and obtaining deposits in a small geographic area, it is more sensitive to fluctuations in local market conditions than it would be if it were allowed to engage in banking activities across a larger geographic region. Consider a bank in a city on the Gulf Coast that is restricted from opening branches outside the city. If a hurricane hits and destroys the city, depositors are likely to withdraw sizable amounts of their savings from the bank. Moreover, loans to borrowers in the city may not be repaid. This can have disastrous effects on the bank. In contrast, if the bank is allowed to open branches throughout the United States, the local hurricane will not likely affect withdrawals in other regions of the country, and loans issued elsewhere will not be affected. Consequently, the bank will be diversified; the unanticipated withdrawals in the local area will likely be offset by unexpected deposits in other regions. In short, branching restrictions actually increase the likelihood of bank failures.

Bank holding companies, as we saw earlier, allow banks to circumvent these negative aspects of branching restrictions. A bank holding company that owns the controlling interest of many banks across the country owns a diversified portfolio of banks, just as an investor who owns shares of stock in many different companies is diversified. Largely for this reason, the 1990s have seen a movement toward allowing banks and bank holding companies more freedom in crossing regional boundaries as well as in the type of activities they can conduct.

Interest Rate Regulations

In addition to agencies specifically designed to supervise the banking industry, state and federal legislative bodies also pass laws that have an impact on the banking industry. This section examines laws and regulations that affect the interest rate banks may charge for loans and pay on deposits.

Usury Laws.   Many states have **usury laws,** which are ceilings that restrict the interest rate lenders can charge on loans and credit card balances. Figure 7.4 shows the impact of a usury law on the banking industry. Without a usury law, market forces determine the interest rate where the supply of and demand for loanable funds intersect at point *A*. At this point, the market interest rate is i_L^0, and the banking industry issues a total of L^0 loans. The usury law makes it illegal to charge an interest rate above i_L^1 for a loan. At this regulated interest rate, borrowers desire L^d loans, but the quantity supplied of loans is only L^s. The usury law results in a shortage of $L^d - L^s$

Figure 7.4
Usury Laws and Shortages of Loans

The market-clearing interest rate, i_L^0, is determined at point *A* by the intersection of the demand for and supply of loanable funds. A usury law requiring that the interest rate be no more than i_L^1 creates a shortage of loanable funds. The market-clearing amount of loans is L^0, but at an interest rate of i_L^1, the quantity supplied of loans is only L^s while the quantity demanded is L^d. This creates a shortage of $L^d - L^s$.

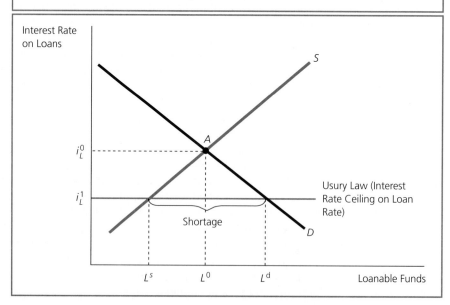

loans, and fewer loans are issued (L^s) than would be in the absence of the usury law (L^0).

By reducing the interest rate banks can legally charge on loans, usury laws result in lower profits for banks. In extreme instances, where the cost to a bank of obtaining funds exceeds the interest rate the bank can legally charge for loans, the bank may choose to issue no loans at all. In less extreme circumstances, such as those depicted in Figure 7.4, the bank issues loans, but to fewer borrowers than want them at the ceiling interest rate.

Since usury laws result in a shortage of loanable funds, banks respond by loaning funds to only the most creditworthy borrowers; in essence, they ration credit. The interest rate required to compensate a bank for the risk of loaning to a noncreditworthy individual (who is less likely to repay a loan) may exceed the rate allowed by law. Credit rationing can thus negatively affect borrowers whom banks view as bad credit risks. This is an unfortunate paradox, since the most common reason given for passing usury laws is to protect those borrowers who most need funds from having to pay high interest rates. Usury laws often prevent such individuals from borrowing any funds at all, at least from a bank.

Regulation Q.   Regulation Q restricted the maximum interest rate banks could pay on saving and time deposits. Fortunately for small savers, the gradual elimination of these restrictions began with DIDMCA in 1980. Earlier in this chapter, we examined Congress's rationale for including interest rate restrictions in the Glass-Steagall Act. We now look at how they affected borrowers and lenders.

Part a of Figure 7.5 shows the market for deposits, where households supply deposits to banks and banks demand them. In the absence of Regulation Q, equilibrium is at point A, the interest rate on deposits is 8 percent, and the resulting level of deposits is D^0. For simplicity, suppose banks convert all deposits to loans; thus, the supply of loans is given by the vertical line labeled $S = D^0$ in part b of Figure 7.5. In the absence of an interest rate ceiling on deposits, the equilibrium in the loan market is at point B and the interest rate on loans is 10 percent.

Now suppose an interest rate ceiling of 5 percent is imposed in the deposit market, as it was during the 1970s under Regulation Q. Let us use supply and demand analysis to illustrate the problem of disintermediation we discussed earlier in the chapter. At a rate of 5 percent, banks desire D^d in deposits, but households deposit only D^s in funds; the result is a shortage of deposits. Because of this shortage, banks can now issue fewer loans. In particular, since they can issue only D^s in loans, the supply curve of loans in part b of Figure 7.5 shifts to the left to $S = D^s$. The effect of this decrease in the supply of loans, due to the availability of fewer deposits, is to increase the interest rate charged on loans from 10 to 12 percent. Thus, interest rate ceilings on deposits—designed to keep bank costs low—actually increase the rate banks charge on loans. In fact, the law harms borrowers, lenders,

Figure 7.5
Regulation Q and Loan Interest Rates

Part a depicts the deposit market, where the market-determined interest rate on deposits is 8 percent and D^0 in deposits is provided to banks. Assuming for simplicity that the supply of loans equals the quantity of deposits, D^0 worth of deposits is converted into D^0 worth of loans by banks in part b. This is given by the vertical supply of loans curve $S = D^0$ and results in an interest rate charged on loans of 10 percent. If there is a restriction on the interest rate paid on deposits (as under Regulation Q) of 5 percent, the quantity of deposits falls to D^s in part a. This implies that the quantity of loans banks may offer also falls to $S = D^s$, and the interest rate on loans rises to 12 percent in part b. Thus, restrictions on the interest rate paid on deposits raises the interest rate charged on loans.

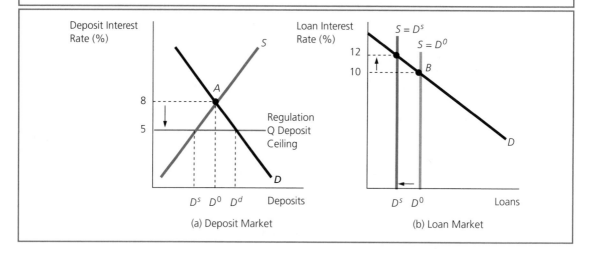

(a) Deposit Market

(b) Loan Market

and banks. Those depositing money in banks receive a lower interest rate (5 percent), while those borrowing money from banks pay a higher rate (12 percent). Banks make fewer loans. Of course, DIDMCA phased out ceilings on deposit rates, which had the opposite effect of lowering interest rates on loans and raising rates on bank deposits.

Uniform Reserve Requirements

Prior to DIDMCA, banks that were not members of the Fed were subject to lower reserve requirements than member banks. As a consequence of DIDMCA, uniform reserve requirements were instituted across all depository institutions. These uniform reserve requirements gave the Fed considerably more control over the money supply and the banking industry than was the case prior to DIDMCA.

To see this, look at Figure 7.6, which shows the market for loanable funds before uniform reserve requirements were in place. If states and other

Figure 7.6

Decreases in Reserve Requirements and Loan Interest Rates

Prior to DIDMCA, changes in reserve requirements by depository authorities other than the Fed could affect interest rates. Here a cut in the reserve requirement at depository institutions (such as thrifts or state banks) that are not members of the Fed increases the supply of loanable funds to S^1, resulting in a lower interest rate. DIDMCA changed this possibility by allowing the Fed to set uniform reserve requirements across all depository institutions, thus giving the Fed greater control over the banking system. The Fed used this power in the early 1990s when it reduced reserve requirements, resulting in lower interest rates as shown in this graph.

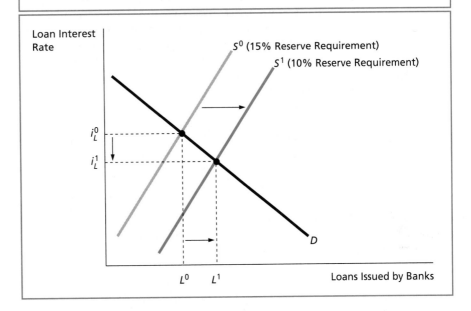

authorities controlling reserve requirements at nonmember banks and thrifts set reserve requirements at 15 percent, the supply of loanable funds is given by S^0. The equilibrium interest rate is i_L^0, and the quantity of loans issued by all banks is L^0. If authorities lower reserve requirements to 10 percent, their institutions can then issue more loans at any given interest rate, since a smaller fraction of deposits must be kept in reserve. Consequently the supply curve shifts to S^1, resulting in a lower interest rate (i_L^1) and more loans (L^1). Thus, prior to DIDMCA, changes in reserve requirements by authorities other than the Fed affected interest rates and the equilibrium quantity of loanable funds. This example illustrates that the Fed was not the only driver at the wheel of the banking system prior to DIDMCA.

Today the Fed controls reserve requirements at all depository institutions, and it alone has the authority to change them. For instance, between

1990 and 1992, the Fed decreased its average reserve requirement from 10.73 to 7.28 percent of total checkable deposits. Similar reductions occurred on April 2, 1992, when it lowered reserve requirements on transaction accounts from 12 to 10 percent. This had effects similar to those shown in Figure 7.6, resulting in lower interest rates.

We point out, however, that historically the Fed has been reluctant to change reserve requirements, and as a result they have tended to remain stable over time. There are two reasons for this stability. First, the Fed can use a host of other policies to affect the financial system; we will look at these policies in Chapter 13. Second, prior to DIDMCA the Fed was reluctant to change its reserve requirements because setting them below those of nonmember institutions would place those institutions at a disadvantage relative to member banks. While it remains to be seen whether the Fed will change reserve requirements more frequently now that uniform reserve requirements are in place, most economists believe it will not.

Deposit Insurance

Deposit insurance insulates depositors from losses due to a bank failure. As a consequence, even if you hear a rumor that your bank is about to fail, you have little reason to be concerned or withdraw funds from your account. This enhances the safety of the banking system by reducing the likelihood of a bank panic. Unfortunately, as we learned in Chapter 6, deposit insurance leads to moral hazard.

To be concrete, suppose you are considering depositing money in two banks. One bank offers a high interest rate on savings deposits, and the other bank offers a lower interest rate. One bank is more likely to fail than the other, but the only way for you to find out which one is to spend considerable time and money researching each bank's financial situation. In which bank would you choose to deposit money?

If the banks did not have deposit insurance, you would probably spend lots of time trying to find out how likely each bank is to fail before making a decision. But with deposit insurance, you need not spend time collecting this information; you can simply shop around for the highest rate on deposits. You would correctly reason, "So what if the bank fails? The FDIC will pay back every penny I have deposited." This is moral hazard: You can take action to avoid losing your deposits, but since you are insured you fail to do so.

What if the bank offering the higher interest rate does so because it knows it is more likely to fail than its rival? It reasons that, being on the brink of bankruptcy, its only hope is to attract additional deposits by offering higher interest rates than other banks so that it can increase the number of loans it issues. But to cover the higher cost of obtaining deposits, the bank will have to charge a higher interest rate on loans than other banks do. We saw in Chapter 5 that this can lead to adverse selection: The only people willing to pay the higher interest rate for a loan will be those who are unable to obtain funds at lower rates from other banks because they are bad credit risks. As the bank issues more and more loans to bad credit risks, the likelihood that it will fail actually increases.

Thus, we see that deposit insurance leads to both moral hazard (people don't carefully check out the financial status of a bank before depositing money and banks make risky loans) and adverse selection (the higher interest rate on loans tends to attract borrowers who know they are bad credit risks). Together these factors tend to increase the probability of bank failures and the cost to the FDIC of covering depositor losses.

Bank Examination as a Solution to Moral Hazard and Adverse Selection

To circumvent the problems of moral hazard and adverse selection, regulatory agencies frequently monitor the loan portfolios of individual banks. To be most effective, these examinations should be done on a random basis so that the banks cannot prepare for them or attempt to cover up any probems. Examining banks randomly over time instead of on prespecified dates enhances the effectiveness of bank examinations in reducing the asymmetric information that can lead to bank failures.

Summary
Exercise 7.3

The city council of a major city is concerned about the high interest rates local banks charge on automobile loans. The banks have argued that the high rates are necessary to cover their cost of obtaining loanable funds. In response, two proposals are before the city council: (a) an ordinance that would limit the interest local banks could legally pay on deposits and (b) an ordinance that would limit the rate local banks could charge on car loans. How would each ordinance affect the local market for car loans? Use a graph of the local deposit and loan market to answer this question.

Answer: (a) Suppose the initial equilibrium interest rate in the local deposit market is at point A in part a. The interest rate on deposits is 6 percent, and $12 million is deposited in the local banks. The first proposal is an interest rate ceiling on deposits of, say, 3 percent. This ceiling creates a shortage of $15 million in deposits. Given the prospect of earning a lower rate on deposits at local banks, large depositors would choose to deposit funds at banks in other cities or use their funds for investments not affected by the local ordinance. Given the ordinance, local banks collect only $5 million in deposits. Assuming for simplicity that banks use all of their deposits for car loans, the decrease in deposits leads to a decrease in the local supply of car loans from S^0 to S^1 in part b. The result is an increase in the interest rate local banks charge for car loans from 10 to 13 percent. Thus, the first proposal would lead to higher rather than lower interest rates on car loans. It might also lead to adverse selection: Customers with good credit ratings could obtain loans at the free market rate (10 percent) from lending institutions located outside the jurisdiction of their city council. This would leave local banks with a pool of riskier borrowers who would be willing to pay the higher local rate.

(b) The second ordinance is an interest rate ceiling in the local market for automobile loans. As in Figure 7.4, the result of such a ceiling would be a shortage of car loans. More car loans would be desired at the regulated interest rate than there would be funds available. Consequently the local banks would be forced to ration credit. People with average or marginal credit histories would be unlikely to qualify for a car loan. If the city regulated the interest rate on car loans at a level below that paid by banks to acquire deposits, the banks would refuse to issue car loans at all. It would make no sense for them to lend money at a rate lower than their marginal cost of obtaining funds. If the city council is not careful, it may create something worse than a shortage and credit rationing: A situation might result in which the city's residents cannot borrow funds locally to purchase cars.

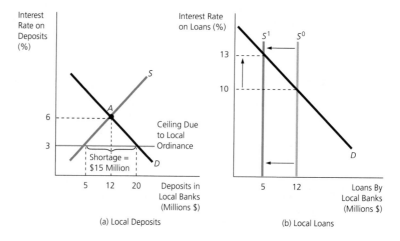

(a) Local Deposits

(b) Local Loans

CONCLUSION

In this chapter we detailed the regulation and supervision of the banking industry, tracing its evolution and highlighting the financial innovations and legislative changes that shaped today's banking system. Table 7.2 summarizes some of the important legislation. We also provided economic analyses of the impact of these rules and regulations on the banking industry.

The material in this chapter, coupled with that in the previous two chapters, has provided you with an understanding of how the banking in-

Table 7.2

Chronology of Important Banking Legislation

This table summarizes the chronology and key features of banking regulations in the United States between 1863 and 1991.

Year	Name	Legislation
1863	National Banking Act	Created national banks
1913	Federal Reserve Act	Created the Federal Reserve System
1927	McFadden Act	Required each bank to operate under the branching restrictions imposed by the state in which it operated; essentially allowed each state to restrict the operation (by restricting branching) of banks chartered nationally or in other states
1933	Glass-Steagall Act	Created the FDIC Prohibited commercial banks from engaging in investment banking (eventually weakened) Imposed various interest rate regulations (no longer in force)
1956	Bank Holding Company Act	Prohibited interstate acquisitions unless permitted by state in which acquired bank was located
1961	Interest Rate Adjustment Act	Extended interest rate regulations to thrifts (no longer in force)
1970	Bank Holding Company Act	Extended restrictions on bank holding companies to include one-bank holding companies
1980	Depository Institution De-regulation and Monetary Control Act (DIDMCA)	Phased out interest rate ceiling Extended Federal Reserve System reserve requirements to all institutions regardless of membership Made Federal Reserve System services available to all banks and thrifts; services must be priced to cover costs

Continued on p. 232

Continued from p. 231

1982	Garn–St. Germain Act	Expanded powers of thrifts Increased dollar amount of deposits covered by FDIC insurance Allowed money market deposit accounts Further increased powers of thrifts Allowed interstate mergers of troubled institutions
1983	International Lending Supervisory Act	Authorized national bank supervisory and regulatory agencies to set minimum capital requirements for banks
1989	Financial Institutions Reform, Recovery, and Enforcement Act (FIRREA)	Abolished the Federal Home Loan Bank Board and the FSLIC Restructured the FDIC to have bank insurance fund (BIF) and savings association insurance fund (SAIF) Increased deposit insurance premiums
1991	Federal Deposit Insurance Corporation Improvement Act (FDICIA)	Requires the FDIC to monitor examiners and minimize long-term cost to insurance fund of troubled banks Requires the FDIC to institute risk-based insurance premiums

dustry and individual banks operate. In the next chapter, we focus on financial markets and look at how the prices and yields of financial instruments such as stocks and bonds are determined.

KEY TERMS

national bank

dual banking system

state bank

bank charter

International Lending Supervisory Act of 1983

Federal Reserve System

unit banking

statewide branching

bank holding company

investment bank

unified banking

Regulation Q

KEY TERMS continued

uniform reserve requirements   disintermediation
Federal Deposit Insurance Corporation (FDIC)   usury law
limited branching

QUESTIONS AND PROBLEMS

1. What does the term *dual banking system* mean? Why does the United States operate under such a system?

2. Who is responsible for granting charters to national banks? To state banks?

3. Can state banks become members of the Federal Reserve System? Can they join the FDIC?

4. Can a national bank choose not to become a member of the Federal Reserve System? Can it refuse to become a member of the FDIC?

5. A current proposal would increase the premium banks pay for FDIC insurance from 25 cents to 31 cents per $100 in deposits. What impact, if any, would this have on (a) a national bank's decision to obtain FDIC insurance, (b) a state bank's decision to renew its FDIC insurance, and (c) the relative number of new banks that would open as state banks instead of national banks?

6. When was the FDIC established? Why?

7. Why are there more than 11,000 banks in the United States?

8. Why was the McFadden Act of 1927 enacted?

9. What is a bank holding company? Why are more than 90 percent of all banks in the United States owned by holding companies?

10. Explain the pros and cons of bank charter restrictions.

11. Suppose the government made bank holding companies illegal. What would you expect to happen to the number of bank failures? Why?

12. Do usury laws benefit or harm (a) well-to-do borrowers or (b) borrowers who are down on their luck?

13. What impact did Regulation Q have on the interest rates (a) earned on deposits and (b) charged on bank loans?

14. Explain how deposit insurance can actually increase the likelihood that a troubled bank will fail.

15. What practices do banking supervisory agencies undertake to mitigate the situation in problem 14?

SELECTIONS FOR FURTHER READING

Elyasiani, E., and S. Mehdian. "Efficiency in the Commercial Banking Industry: A Production Fron- tier Approach." *Applied Economics,* 22 (April 1990), 539–551.

Fenstermacker, J. V., R. P. Malone, and S. R. Stansell. "An Analysis of Commercial Bank Common Stock Returns: 1802–97." *Applied Economics,* 20 (June 1988), 813–841.

Fraser, D. R., and J. W. Kolari. "The 1982 Depository Institutions Act and Security Returns in the Savings and Loan Industry." *Journal of Financial Research,* 13 (Winter 1990), 339–347.

Graddy, D. B., and A. S. Karna. "Net Interest Margin Sensitivity among Banks of Different Sizes." *Journal of Bank Research,* 14 (Winter 1984), 283–290.

Graddy, D. B., and A. S. Karna. "Dividend Policy and the Return of Bank Holding Company Stock." *Quarterly Journal of Business and Economics,* 25 (Spring 1986), 3–21.

Graddy, D. B., and R. Kyle III. "The Simultaneity of Bank Decision-making, Market Structure, and Bank Performance." *Journal of Finance,* 34 (March 1979), 1–18.

Hester, D. D. "Instructional Simulation of a Commercial Banking System." *Journal of Economic Education,* 22 (Spring 1991), 111–143.

Ladenson, M. L., and K. J. Bombara. "Entry in Commercial Banking: 1962–78." *Journal of Money, Credit, and Banking,* 16 (May 1984), 165–174.

Lobue, M. "Categorical Bank Acquisitions." *Journal of Bank Research,* 14 (Winter 1984), 274–282.

Reidenbach, R. E., D. L. Moak, and R. E. Pitts. "The Impact of Marketing Operations on Bank Performance: A Structural Investigation." *Journal of Bank Research,* 17 (Spring 1986), 18–27.

Wells, D. R., and L. S. Cruggs. "Historical Insights into the Deregulation of Money and Banking." *Cato Journal,* 5 (Winter 1986), 899–910.

Witte, W. E. "Dynamic Adjustment in an Open Economy with Flexible Exchange Rates." *Southern Economic Journal,* 45 (April 1979), 1072–1090.

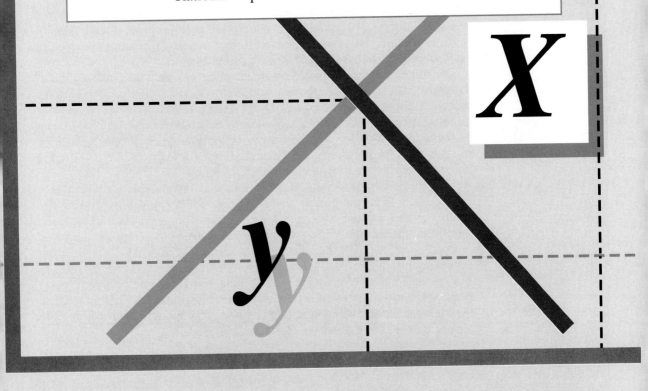

PART THREE

The Valuation of Financial Assets

CHAPTERS

8

The Time Value of Money and Asset Pricing

9

Risk, Uncertainty, and Portfolio Choice

10

The Term Structure of Interest Rates

11

Foreign Exchange Markets

12

Rational Expectations and Efficient Markets

The Time Value of Money and Asset Pricing

*H*ow do investors on Wall Street determine the value of a share of IBM stock or an AT&T bond? How do changes in taxes, inflation, risk, or other economic variables affect the price of NationsBank's stock or a Treasury bill in the firm's portfolio? This chapter and the next two chapters will answer these questions. In this chapter, we show that various financial instruments will have different prices due to differences in payment schedules (when and how much money is paid). In Chapter 9, we extend the analysis to situations where the interest rate depends on the riskiness of the asset. We will see that riskier financial assets tend to sell at lower prices than less risky ones. In Chapter 10, we further extend the analysis to situations where the interest rate varies based on the length of the loan.

In this chapter, we focus on financial assets such as Treasury bills, Treasury bonds, corporate bonds, and common stock that are bought and sold in well-established secondary markets at a dollar price (as opposed to an interest rate). You can think of the prices of these financial instruments as being analogous to the prices paid for various types of automobiles or refrigerators. In this chapter, we examine how these prices are determined and why they fluctuate with economic conditions.

The price of any asset, including financial instruments such as stocks and bonds, reflects the present value of the benefits enjoyed by owning the asset. For this reason, we begin with a review of present value analysis, introduced in Chapter 3. We then adapt this analysis to determine the value of bonds, stocks, and other financial instruments. Finally, we see how the basic supply and demand analysis developed in Chapter 4 can be used to analyze the impact of changes in such things as taxes and inflationary expectations on the prices of different financial instruments. This material is the building block for the next two chapters, which show how risk and the term structure of interest rates affect the analysis.

THE TIME VALUE OF MONEY

As we saw in Chapter 3, the time value of money reflects the fact that $1 received in the future is worth less than $1 today. By waiting until a future date to receive a given amount of money, you forgo the immediate use of the money, including the interest you would earn if you saved the money. Economists use present value analysis to determine the value today (in the present) of a future sum of money. The **present value** of an amount received in the future is the amount you would have to invest today, at the prevailing interest rate, to end up with the future amount.

In a sense, present value analysis is the reverse of future value analysis. If you deposit $100 today in a bank account that pays 5 percent interest per year, at the end of the year you will have $105. Thus, $105 is the future value of $100 today. Stated in reverse, $100 is the present value of $105 received in the future. The present value of a future sum of money depends on (1) the interest rate, (2) the length of time until you will receive the future amount, and (3) the size of the future amount.

To be more concrete, suppose you deposit $2,000 in the bank today and the bank agrees to pay you an interest rate of 4 percent per year. After one year, you will have

$$(1 + .04) \times \$2,000 = \$2,080.$$

The 1 in parentheses reflects the fact that you get your principal back, and the .04 is the interest rate on the principal. At the end of two years, you will have

$$[(1 + .04) \times \$2,000] \times (1 + .04) = (1 + .04)^2 \times \$2,000 = \$2,163.20.$$

The fact that $(1 + .04)$ is raised to the power of 2 reflects the fact that the original amount is invested for two years; you earn interest in the second year on the interest received in the first year.

More generally, suppose a single market interest rate, i, is available to all borrowers and lenders (we relax this assumption in the next two chapters, where we allow interest rates to vary depending on the riskiness and length of the loan). If the present amount to be invested at the interest rate is PV, the **future value** (FV) of the present amount in T years is

$$FV = PV \times (1 + i)^T. \tag{8.1}$$

This equation suggests that present value and future value are closely related. In particular, if we solve equation 8.1 for PV in terms of FV, we obtain

$$PV = \frac{FV}{(1 + i)^T}. \tag{8.2}$$

Equation 8.2 tells us the present value (PV) of an amount (FV) received T years in the future when the interest rate is i percent per year. For example, if FV = $1,050, $T = 1$, and $i = .05$, you will receive $1,050 one year in the future, and the prevailing interest rate is 5 percent. In this case, the present value of the future amount is

$$PV = \frac{FV}{(1 + i)^T} = \frac{\$1,050}{(1.05)^1} = \$1,000.$$

In other words, if the interest rate is 5 percent, you will need to invest $1,000 today (the present) to receive $1,050 a year from now.

Equation 8.2 illustrates the time value of money. The farther into the future a given dollar amount is to be received (the greater T is), the lower its present value. In other words, the present value of a future amount is inversely related to the time in which that amount is received. Moreover, note that the present value of an amount to be received at a given point in the future is inversely related to the interest rate. As the interest rate rises, the present value of a given future amount falls. Conversely, the lower the interest rate, the greater the present value.

We can easily apply the basic formula for computing the present value of a future amount to calculate the present value of a series of future values. Suppose varying amounts are to be received over time; FV_1 will be received at the end of the first year, FV_2 at the end of two years, and so on for T years. The present value of this stream of future payments is

$$PV = \frac{FV_1}{(1 + i)^1} + \frac{FV_2}{(1 + i)^2} + \frac{FV_3}{(1 + i)^3} + \cdots + \frac{FV_T}{(1 + i)^T}.$$

The first term on the right-hand side of the equality is the present value of the first future payment. To this we add the present value of the payment received two years in the future, three years in the future, and so on. By adding together the present value of each future payment, we end up with the present value of the series of future payments.

Summary Exercise 8.1

Your uncle plans to purchase a $50,000 Mercedes Benz when you graduate three years from now. If the interest rate is 5 percent, how much will he have to deposit in the bank today to be able to purchase the car when you graduate?

Answer: He must deposit the present value of the $50,000 needed in three years. Given the 5 percent interest rate, this amount is

$$PV = \frac{\$50,000}{(1.05)^3} = \$43,191.88.$$

THE VALUATION OF DEBT INSTRUMENTS

Let us now see how present value analysis determines the market price of debt instruments held by banks and other investors. Short-term debt instruments such as U.S. Treasury bills, commercial paper, and repurchase agreements are bought and sold at prices determined in the money market—the market for short-term debt. They comprise an important component of the portfolios of banks and other financial intermediaries such as pension funds and insurance companies. In contrast, debt instruments that are long term in nature, such as U.S. Treasury bonds and corporate bonds, are traded at prices determined in the capital market—the market for long-term debt. These debt instruments are held primarily by pension funds, insurance companies, mutual funds, and individual investors.

A **debt instrument** is simply a written promise by a borrower to pay the owner of the instrument a specified amount (or amounts) in the future. When a debt instrument is first issued by a borrower and sold to a lender in the primary market, the owner of the instrument is the original lender. However, debt instruments can often be resold in a secondary market, so the current owner is not necessarily the original lender.

Debt instruments take various forms. In some instances, a single amount will be paid in the future; in other cases, several future payments may be promised. In the following subsections we see how the payment schedule affects the valuation of a given type of debt instrument.

Treasury Bills and Other Debt Instruments Sold on a Discount Basis

Many debt instruments—including Treasury bills, banker's acceptances, and some forms of corporate bonds (called *discount bonds*)—do not pay interest directly. Instead they are sold on a discount basis, that is, at a price that is less than their face value. At maturity, the owner presents these bonds to the borrower, who pays the face value. For instance, the face value of a Treasury bill is $10,000; the U.S. Treasury promises to pay $10,000 to the owner of the Treasury bill when it matures—say, in a year. Treasury bills are sold in an auction at a price that is less than their face value, for example, $9,500. Thus, for these types of debt instruments, the return to the owner is the difference between the face value collected at maturity and the purchase price.

Discount Yield and Yield to Maturity. The yield on a Treasury bill or a discount bond is a measure of the percentage annual return earned by the owner of the instrument. There are two methods of measuring the yield of debt instruments sold on a discount basis: the discount yield method and the yield to maturity.

The **discount yield,** which is frequently used to measure yields on Treasury bills, is defined as

$$\text{Discount yield} = \frac{\text{FV} - P_{TB}}{\text{FV}} \times \frac{360}{\text{Days to maturity}},$$

where FV is the future value of the Treasury bill, or the **face value**—the amount paid when the bill matures—and P_{TB} is the price paid for the Treasury bill. For instance, a $10,000 Treasury bill that matures in 365 days and was purchased for $9,500 would have a discount yield of

$$\text{Discount yield} = \frac{\$10,000 - \$9,500}{\$10,000} \times \frac{360}{365} = .049,$$

which is 4.9 percent.

Two aspects of the discount yield formula cause it to understate the actual yield on a Treasury bill. First, note that the formula is based on a 360-day year, not on the standard 365-day year. Second, the discount yield formula uses the face value of the Treasury bill rather than its actual purchase price in the denominator. In other words, the term $(FV - P_{TB})/FV$ in the discount yield formula does not represent the actual percentage return to the investor; the actual return is $(FV - P_{TB})/P_{TB}$. Since P_{TB} is less than FV, the discount yield formula understates the actual yield on a Treasury bill.

A measure of yield that does not suffer from these two deficiencies is the yield to maturity. The **yield to maturity** is the interest rate at which the amount used to purchase the Treasury bill would have to be invested to grow to the face value paid at maturity. Consider the one-year, $10,000 Treasury bill purchased for $9,500. At what interest rate would one have to invest $9,500 today to end up with $10,000 at the end of one year? Mathematically, we must find the value of i that satisfies the following equation:

$$\$9,500 = \frac{\$10,000}{1 + i}.$$

Solving this equation for $(1 + i)$ gives us

$$1 + i = \frac{10}{9.5},$$

so $i = .053$. Thus, the yield to maturity on the Treasury bill is 5.3 percent, which is greater than the discount yield.

Box 8.1 describes how to interpret financial data for Treasury bills with various maturities.

Valuing Debt Instruments Sold on a Discount Basis.

How much will a bank or other investor pay for a debt instrument that is sold on a discount basis? The answer depends on the market interest rate. Consider a Treasury bill with a face value of $10,000 that matures in one year. Since Treasury bills are sold on a discount basis, the only thing the buyer will receive is $10,000 one year from today. The amount an investor would be willing to pay for this Treasury bill depends on the market interest rate. When the interest rate is low, the investor is willing to pay a relatively high price and earn a relatively low yield, since alternative investments also give a low return. Conversely, when the interest rate is high, the investor will pay a relatively low price and earn a relatively high return.

Inside Money

Box 8.1

*How to Read Information on Treasury Bills
in the* Wall Street Journal

The *Wall Street Journal* reports information on Treasury bills daily. The information reported here is from the Wednesday, February 16, 1994, edition and contains prices from Tuesday, February 15, 1994.

The first column, labeled *Maturity,* gives the date on which the Treasury bill matures. The second column, labeled *Days to Mat.,* indicates the days until maturity from the settlement date of the purchase until the maturity date. For instance, the last T-bill quoted had 357 days to maturity from the settlement date.

The third column, labeled *Bid,* reports the highest discount by buyers. It is reported as a percentage of the face value and then converted to an annual rate. Thus, for the last T-bill quoted, maturing on February 9, 1995, the highest discount bid by a buyer was a 3.68 percent discount from the face value. What does this mean? A T-bill with a $10,000 face value had a bid discount yield of .0368, which means the price bid satisfies ($10,000 − P_{TB})/$10,000 × (360/357) = .0368, or the bid price was $9,635.07.

The fourth column, labeled *Asked,* is the lowest discount asked by sellers. On the bill maturing on February 9, 1995, the asked discount yield of 3.66 percent means the seller offered to sell the $10,000 T-bill for a price satisfying ($10,000 − P_{TB}/$10,000) × (360/357) = .0366, or $9,637.05.

The fifth column, labeled *Chg.,* indicates the percentage change in the bid discount. For the

bill maturing on February 9, 1995, the bid discount did not change from the previous day.

The final column, *Ask Yld.,* tells the yield to maturity the investor would receive at the asked discount. For the Treasury bill, the yield to maturity was 3.82 percent.

TREASURY BILLS

Maturity	Days to Mat.	Bid	Asked	Chg.	Ask Yld.
Feb 17 '94	0	3.11	3.01	+ 0.16	0.00
Feb 24 '94	7	2.50	2.40	− 0.13	2.43
Mar 03 '94	14	2.96	2.86	− 0.03	2.90
Mar 10 '94	21	3.00	2.90	− 0.04	2.95
Mar 17 '94	28	2.94	2.90	− 0.07	2.95
Mar 24 '94	35	2.96	2.92	− 0.01	2.97
Mar 31 '94	42	3.01	2.97	− 0.02	3.02
Apr 07 '94	49	3.10	3.06	− 0.02	3.12
Apr 14 '94	56	3.11	3.07	− 0.01	3.13
Apr 21 '94	63	3.19	3.17	....	3.23
Apr 28 '94	70	3.22	3.20	....	3.26
May 05 '94	77	3.25	3.23	....	3.30
May 12 '94	84	3.25	3.23	− 0.01	3.30
May 19 '94	**91**	**3.27**	**3.25**	**....**	**3.32**
May 26 '94	98	3.28	3.26	....	3.33
Jun 02 '94	105	3.31	3.29	....	3.37
Jun 09 '94	112	3.31	3.29	− 0.01	3.37
Jun 16 '94	119	3.33	3.31	....	3.39
Jun 23 '94	126	3.34	3.32	....	3.41
Jun 30 '94	133	3.35	3.33	+ 0.01	3.42
Jul 07 '94	140	3.36	3.34	....	3.43
Jul 14 '94	147	3.37	3.35	+ 0.01	3.44
Jul 21 '94	154	3.38	3.36	+ 0.01	3.46
Jul 28 '94	161	3.39	3.37	....	3.47
Aug 04 '94	168	3.40	3.38	....	3.48
Aug 11 '94	175	3.40	3.38	− 0.01	3.48
Aug 18 '94	**182**	**3.41**	**3.39**	**− 0.02**	**3.50**
Aug 25 '94	189	3.44	3.42	+ 0.01	3.53
Sep 22 '94	217	3.47	3.45	....	3.56
Oct 20 '94	245	3.53	3.51	....	3.63
Nov 17 '94	273	3.56	3.54	− 0.01	3.67
Dec 15 '94	301	3.59	3.57	....	3.70
Jan 12 '95	329	3.64	3.62	....	3.76
Feb 09 '95	357	3.68	3.66	....	3.82

In the market for loanable funds, the interest rate is determined by the interaction of demand and supply. Consider the supply and demand curves for loanable funds given by S^1 and D^1 in Figure 8.1. The demanders of loanable funds are borrowers, and the suppliers are lenders. In this case, equilibrium is at point A and the market interest rate is 7 percent.

Given the scenario in Figure 8.1, we can determine the present value of the Treasury bill—the amount a typical investor would be willing to give up today to receive the promised $10,000 in one year. In particular, when the interest rate is 7 percent, the price of the Treasury bill (P_{TB}) is the present value of the $10,000 received one year in the future:

$$P_{TB} = \frac{\$10,000}{1.07} = \$9,345.79.$$

Thus, the maximum price the seller of the Treasury bill could obtain given the 7 percent market interest rate is $P_{TB} = \$9,345.79$. If the seller asked a higher price, investors would not purchase it; they could earn a higher return by investing their money in some alternative investment.

We learned in Chapter 4 that changes in determinants of demand or supply—factors like wealth, inflationary expectations, and tax rates—can shift demand or supply, resulting in changes in the interest rate. Table 8.1

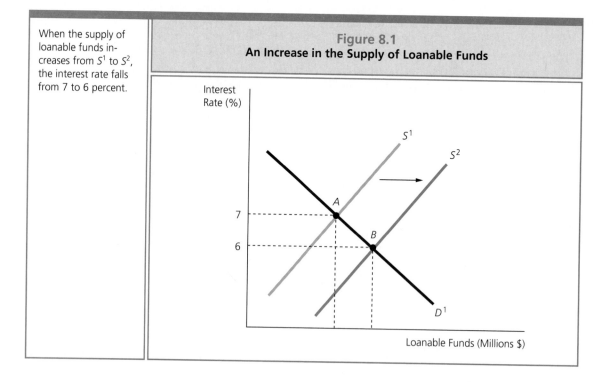

When the supply of loanable funds increases from S^1 to S^2, the interest rate falls from 7 to 6 percent.

**Figure 8.1
An Increase in the Supply of Loanable Funds**

Interest Rate (%)

Loanable Funds (Millions $)

Table 8.1
Variables that Shift the Demand and/or Supply of Loanable Funds

This table summarizes some of the important variables that can shift the demand or supply of loanable funds. A change in any of these variables will change the equilibrium interest rate and therefore affect the dollar prices of financial assets such as Treasury bills. Tables 4.1 and 4.2 in Chapter 4 present a complete list of determinants of the demand and supply of loanable funds.

An increase in	Shifts the Demand Curve for Loanable Funds	Shifts the Supply Curve for Loanable Funds
Inflationary expectations	$\longrightarrow$	$\longleftarrow$
Tax deductibility of household interest payments	$\longrightarrow$	No effect
Size of government budget deficit	$\longrightarrow$	No effect
Tax rate on interest income	No effect	$\longleftarrow$
Wealth	No effect	$\longrightarrow$

summarizes a few of these determinants and their impact on demand and supply (a more complete list appears in Tables 4.1 and 4.2 in Chapter 4).[1] We can use this information to see how a change in a determinant of demand or supply affects bond prices.

For instance, what do you think would happen to bond prices if wealth increased? The increase in wealth would increase lenders' willingness to loan out funds, thus increasing the supply of loanable funds to S^2 in Figure 8.1. In this case, equilibrium moves to point B, and the market interest rate falls from 7 to 6 percent. Given this lower interest rate, the price of the Treasury bill rises to

$$P_{TB} = \frac{\$10,000}{1.06} = \$9,433.96.$$

The increase in wealth led to a decline in the interest rate, which in turn increased the price of the Treasury bill.

This example illustrates a general principle: As the interest rate falls, the price of a debt instrument sold on a discount basis rises. This inverse relationship is shown in Figure 8.2, where each point on the horizontal axis indicates the price (present value) of the one-year Treasury bill at various

---

[1] Other determinants include risk, liquidity, and rates on substitute sources and uses of funds. These variables are not listed in Table 8.1 because they are not important in our discussion of identical risk-free loans. In the next chapter, we will see how allowances for risk change the analysis.

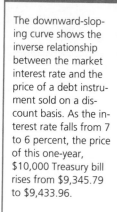

The downward-sloping curve shows the inverse relationship between the market interest rate and the price of a debt instrument sold on a discount basis. As the interest rate falls from 7 to 6 percent, the price of this one-year, $10,000 Treasury bill rises from $9,345.79 to $9,433.96.

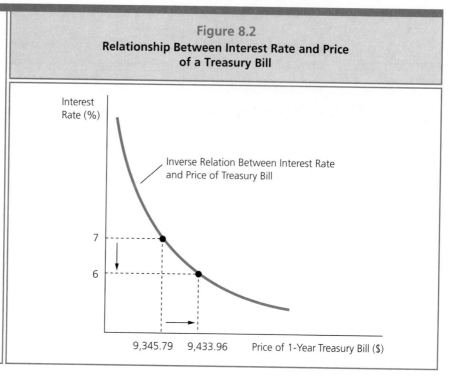

Figure 8.2
Relationship Between Interest Rate and Price of a Treasury Bill

Inverse Relation Between Interest Rate and Price of Treasury Bill

interest rates. The points on this curve correspond with our earlier calculations: When the interest rate is 7 percent, the price of the Treasury bill is $9,345.79; when the interest rate falls to 6 percent, the price of the Treasury bill rises to $9,433.96.

Coupon Bonds and Other Interest-Bearing Debt Instruments

Unlike discount bonds, some debt instruments—such as coupon bonds issued by both the U.S. Treasury (Treasury bonds) and corporations (corporate bonds)—provide regular interest payments in addition to paying their face value at maturity. The face value of a coupon bond is similar to that of a discount bond and a Treasury bill: It specifies the amount that will be paid when the bond matures. In addition, however, the face value of the bond indirectly determines how much the investor will receive in interest payments each year up to and including the bond's maturity date.

In particular, a coupon bond specifies a coupon rate of interest. This **coupon rate** determines the percentage of the face value that will be paid each year as interest. Consider a corporate bond with a face value of $1,000 and a coupon rate of 5 percent. If this bond matures in 20 years, the owner of the bond will receive 20 coupon payments of .05 × $1,000 = $50 each.[2] This annual payment of $50 is in effect an interest payment to the owner of the bond. In addition to these coupon payments, the bond pays the owner the face value of $1,000 at the end of 20 years. Note that the coupon rate of interest is applied to the face value of the bond rather than to its purchase price.

Box 8.2 explains how to interpret financial data on U.S. Treasury bonds and notes.

Current Yield and Yield to Maturity.

Because the coupon rate applies to the face value of the bond, it generally does not reflect the actual yield the owner will receive over the bond's life. This is because the owner may pay more or less for the bond than its face value, depending on the relationship between the coupon rate and the market interest rate. The coupon rate will exceed the yield on a bond when the price paid exceeds the bond's face value; the coupon rate will be less than the yield on a bond when the price paid is less than the face value. To see why this is the case, we now look at two measures of the yield on a coupon bond: current yield and yield to maturity.

The **current yield** is simply the ratio of the annual coupon payment to the price paid for the bond:

$$\text{Current yield} = \frac{\text{Annual coupon payment}}{P_{CB}},$$

where P_{CB} is the price paid for the coupon bond. To illustrate, suppose you pay $950 for a 6 percent coupon bond that has a face value of $1,000 and matures in one year. Then you will receive an annual coupon payment of .06 × $1,000 = $60. Since you paid $950 for the bond, the current yield is

$$\text{Current yield} = \frac{\$60}{\$950} = .063,$$

which is 6.3 percent. The current yield is higher than the coupon rate stated on the bond (6 percent) because you paid less than the bond's face value. Notice that the current yield does not take into account the fact that you receive $1,000 in addition to the $60 interest payment when the bond matures.

The *yield to maturity* on a coupon bond, like that on a discount bond or Treasury bill, is the interest rate at which the price paid for the bond would have to be invested to return the stream of payments generated by the bond.

---

[2] Most coupon bonds actually make interest payments every six months instead of once each year. Since this does not significantly affect the calculations, we ignore it for simplicity.

Inside Money

Box 8.2

How to Read Information on Treasury Bonds and Notes in the Wall Street Journal

The *Wall Street Journal* reports information on Treasury bonds and notes daily. The information reported here appeared in the Wednesday, February 16, 1994, edition and reports prices from Tuesday, February 15, 1994.

The first column, labeled *Rate,* gives the coupon rate on the bond or note. The second column, *Maturity Mo/Yr,* gives the date of maturity and indicates whether the instrument is a note (denoted n) or a bond. The bid and asked prices are reported next. Prices are given in number of dollars per $100 of face value, with "decimals" reporting 32nds of a dollar. The last two columns report the change in the bid price and the yield to maturity, annualized, calculated from the asked price.

As an example, consider the last note listed. The coupon rate is 10½, or 10.5 percent, and the note matures in August 1995. The bid price was 109:03, or $109³⁄₃₂ per $100 of face value; that is, $1,090.94 was bid on each $1,000 in face value. The asked price was 109:05, so $1,091.56 was asked on each $1,000 in face value. The yield maturity on this note, annualized, is 4.12 percent.

GOVT. BONDS & NOTES

Rate	Maturity Mo/Yr	Bid	Asked	Chg.	Ask Yld.
5³⁄₈	Feb 94n	100:02	100:04	....	1.23
5³⁄₄	Mar 94n	100:09	100:11	....	2.70
8½	Mar 94n	100:19	100:21	− 1	2.71
7	Apr 94n	100:18	100:20	....	2.92
5³⁄₈	Apr 94n	100:12	100:14	....	3.11
7	May 94n	100:27	100:29	....	3.14
9½	May 94n	101:14	101:16	....	3.13
13¹⁄₈	May 94n	102:10	102:12	....	3.07
5¹⁄₈	May 94n	100:15	100:17	....	3.20
5	Jun 94n	100:17	100:19	....	3.34
8½	Jun 94n	101:26	101:28	....	3.30
8	Jul 94n	101:25	101:27	....	3.40
4¹⁄₄	Jul 94n	100:09	100:11	....	3.47
6⁷⁄₈	Aug 94n	101:19	101:21	....	3.47
8⁵⁄₈	Aug 94n	102:14	102:16	....	3.48
8³⁄₄	Aug 94	102:16	102:18	....	3.48
12⁵⁄₈	Aug 94n	104:13	104:15	....	3.43
4¹⁄₄	Aug 94n	100:10	100:12	....	3.53
4	Sep 94n	100:06	100:08	....	3.59
8½	Sep 94n	102:29	102:31	....	3.59
9½	Oct 94n	103:22	103:24	....	3.68
4¹⁄₄	Oct 94n	100:11	100:13	....	3.66
6	Nov 94n	101:20	101:22	+ 1	3.67
8¹⁄₄	Nov 94n	103:07	103:09	....	3.72
10¹⁄₈	Nov 94	104:19	104:21	....	3.70
11⁵⁄₈	Nov 94n	105:22	105:24	....	3.69
4⁵⁄₈	Nov 94n	100:21	100:23	+ 1	3.69
4⁵⁄₈	Dec 94n	100:21	100:23	....	3.78
7⁵⁄₈	Dec 94n	103:06	103:08	− 1	3.78
8⁵⁄₈	Jan 95n	104:06	104:08	....	3.83
4¹⁄₄	Jan 95n	100:11	100:13	....	3.81
3	Feb 95	99:07	100:07	+ 1	2.78
5¹⁄₂	Feb 95n	101:17	101:19	....	3.85
7³⁄₄	Feb 95n	103:23	103:25	....	3.84
10¹⁄₂	Feb 95	106:12	106:14	− 1	3.84
11¹⁄₄	Feb 95n	107:05	107:07	....	3.79
3⁷⁄₈	Mar 95n	99:30	100:00	....	3.88
3⁷⁄₈	Mar 95n	99:28	99:30	....	3.93
8³⁄₈	Apr 95n	104:28	104:30	+ 1	3.97
3⁷⁄₈	Apr 95n	99:26	99:28	....	3.98
5⁷⁄₈	May 95n	102:05	102:07	....	4.03
8¹⁄₂	May 95n	105:10	105:12	....	4.02
10³⁄₈	May 95	107:19	107:21	− 1	3.99
11¹⁄₄	May 95n	108:21	108:23	− 2	3.98
12⁵⁄₈	May 95	110:11	110:15	....	3.90
4¹⁄₈	May 95n	100:02	100:04	+ 1	4.02
4¹⁄₈	Jun 95n	100:01	100:03	+ 1	4.05
8⁷⁄₈	Jul 95n	106:13	106:15	....	4.10
4¹⁄₄	Jul 95n	100:04	100:06	+ 1	4.12
4⁵⁄₈	Aug 95n	100:20	100:22	+ 1	4.15
8¹⁄₂	Aug 95n	106:06	106:08	....	4.14
10¹⁄₂	Aug 95n	109:03	109:05	....	4.12

The yield to maturity on a coupon bond takes into account not only the face value paid on maturity but also the annual coupon payments received during its term. More concretely, having paid $950 today for the coupon bond, in one year you will receive a $60 coupon payment, plus the $1,000 face value.

Thus, the yield to maturity on this coupon bond is the interest rate, i, that satisfies the following condition:

$$\$950 = \frac{\$60 + \$1,000}{1 + i}.$$

Solving this expression for i reveals that the yield to maturity on this bond is 11.58 percent, which is considerably higher than both the coupon rate stated on the bond (6 percent) and the current yield (6.3 percent). The reason is that the yield to maturity takes into account the money received from both the coupon payments and the face value payment. Since the face value of the bond exceeds the price paid for the bond, the yield to maturity is greater than both the coupon rate and the current yield. In contrast, if the face value of the bond were less than the bond's price, the yield to maturity would be lower than the coupon rate and the current yield.

Valuing Coupon Bonds.   How do financial intermediaries value coupon bonds? The price of a coupon bond reflects the present value of all future payments the bondholder receives. A coupon bond that pays its face value (F) in T years also generates a coupon payment (PMT) at the end of each year until maturity. If the market interest rate is i, the price of a coupon bond (P_{CB}) will be

$$P_{CB} = \frac{\text{PMT}}{(1 + i)^1} + \frac{\text{PMT}}{(1 + i)^2} + \frac{\text{PMT}}{(1 + i)^3} + \cdots + \frac{\text{PMT} + F}{(1 + i)^T}.$$

Notice that at the end of year T, when the bond matures, the owner receives a coupon payment plus the face value of the bond.

Suppose a coupon bond pays $100 each year for two years, plus the face value of $1,000 at the end of the second year. In this case, the owner will receive $100 at the end of the first year and $1,100 at the end of the second year ($100 in interest, plus the payment of the face value). The price of the coupon bond will depend on the market interest rate as determined by the supply of and demand for loanable funds. For instance, suppose the supply of and demand for loanable funds are given by S^1 and D^1 in Figure 8.3. Point A denotes the market equilibrium; the interest rate is 8 percent. What is the maximum price you would be willing to pay for the bond?

Given the 8 percent interest rate, the price of the coupon bond (P_{CB}) is the present value of all payments the owner receives:

$$P_{CB} = \frac{\$100}{1.08} + \frac{\$1,100}{1.08^2},$$

which is $1,035.66. In other words, given a market interest rate of 8 percent, you would be willing to pay up to $1,035.66 for this coupon bond. This shows that an investor is sometimes willing to pay more than face value for

At point *A*, the market interest rate is 8 percent. When the demand for loanable funds increases to D^2, the market interest rate rises to 10 percent.

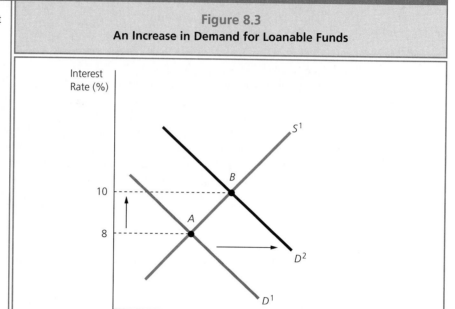

Figure 8.3
An Increase in Demand for Loanable Funds

a bond. Again, this occurs because the coupon rate, 10 percent, exceeds the market interest rate, 8 percent.

If the market interest rate changes, so will the price of the bond. For example, suppose the government needs to borrow additional loanable funds to finance the deficit. This causes the demand for loanable funds in Figure 8.3 to increase to D^2. The increased demand for loanable funds drives up the equilibrium interest rate to 10 percent at point *B*. Given this higher interest rate, the price of the coupon bond falls to

$$P_{CB} = \frac{\$100}{1.10} + \frac{\$1,100}{1.10^2}$$

or $1,000. Thus, as the interest rate rises, the price of the coupon bond falls, as the solid curve in Figure 8.4 shows. Here each point on the horizontal axis indicates the price (present value) of a coupon bond at various interest rates. When the interest rate is 8 percent, the price of the two-year bond is $1,035.66. When the interest rate rises to 10 percent, the price of the bond falls to $1,000. Thus, an inverse relationship exists between the price of a coupon bond and the market interest rate, just like that between the interest rate and the price of a discount bond. An investor who owns this two-year coupon bond would see it decline in value due to the higher interest rate caused by increased federal borrowing to finance the deficit.

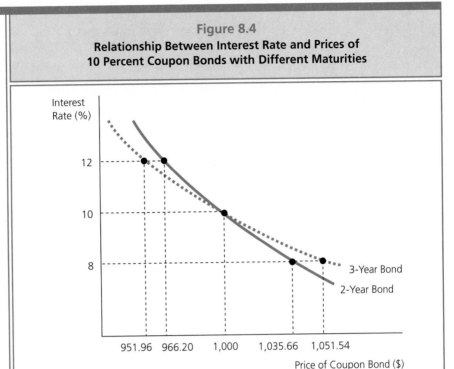

The solid curve shows the relationship between the interest rate and the price of a two-year coupon bond, while the dashed curve shows the relationship between the interest rate and the price of a three-year coupon bond. Both bonds have a face value of $1,000 and a coupon rate of 10 percent. As the market interest rate rises, the prices of both bonds fall, but the price of the three-year bond falls more rapidly than that of the two-year bond.

Figure 8.4

Relationship Between Interest Rate and Prices of 10 Percent Coupon Bonds with Different Maturities

In using Figure 8.4, it is important to remember that the solid curve is drawn holding constant both the future payments and the maturity of the bond (the date on which the bond issuer pays back the face amount). The dashed curve in Figure 8.4 shows the inverse relationship between the interest rate and the price of a coupon bond that matures in three years instead of two. The $1,000 face value and the 10 percent coupon rate on the three-year bond are identical to those on the two-year bond; all that differs are the maturity dates. Because of the longer maturity, the effect of a change in the market interest rate on the price of the three-year bond is greater than that for the two-year bond. When the interest rate is 10 percent, the price of both bonds is $1,000, since the coupon rate on both is also 10 percent. If the interest rate falls to 8 percent, the price of the two-year bond rises to $1,035.66 and the price of the three-year bond rises to $1,051.54. Similarly, when the interest rate rises from 10 to 12 percent, the price of the two-year bond falls to $966.20 and the price of the three-year bond falls further to $951.96. A change in the market interest rate has a greater effect on the prices of bonds with a longer remaining time to maturity.

Box 8.3 describes how to read financial information on corporate bonds.

Inside Money

Box 8.3

How to Read Information on Corporate Bonds in the Wall Street Journal

The *Wall Street Journal* reports information on corporate bonds daily. The information reported here is from the Wednesday, February 16, 1994, edition and reports prices from Tuesday, February 15, 1994.

The first column, labeled *Bonds,* gives the name of the company issuing the bond, followed by the coupon rate, then by the year in which the bond matures. If a zr appears where the coupon rate should be, it means this bond is a zero coupon bond.

The second column gives the current yield on the bond. Consider the last ATT bond listed. This bond pays a coupon rate of $8\frac{1}{8}$ (or 8.125 percent) and matures in 2024; ATT pays $81.25 per year in coupon interest payments for each $1,000 bond. The current yield of 7.4 percent means that if the bond was purchased on February 15, 1994, the coupon interest accruing from it would represent an interest rate of 7.4 percent of the price paid.

The third column gives the volume of bonds traded the previous business day. It is expressed in terms of the number of $1,000 bonds traded. Thus, 101 of these ATT bonds were traded the previous day.

The fourth column tells the price of the bond when trading stopped on the previous business day. It is expressed as a percentage of the face value of the bond. Thus, this ATT bond

had a closing price equal to $109\frac{3}{8}$ percent of its face value, or $1,093.75 for a bond with a $1,000 face value.

The final column reports the change in the closing price between the previous business day (February 15) and the day before that (February 14). It too is expressed as a percentage of the face value. The ATT bond was up five-eighths of a point, or .00625 × $1,000 = $6.25.

Note how the current yield is calculated with this information. The purchase price is $1,093.75, and the annual coupon is $81.25, so the current yield is $81.25/$1,093.75 = 0.074, or 7.4 percent.

CORPORATION BONDS
Volume, $33,870,000

Bonds	Cur Yld	Vol	Close	Net Chg.
AForP 5s30	7.3	63	68½ +	⅜
Actava 9½98	9.5	20	100 −	¼
Actava 10s99	9.8	24	101¾ −	¼
AlskAr 6⅞14	cv	84	87½	
AlskAr zr06	...	218	40⅜ +	⅜
AlbnyInf 5s02	cv	4	96 −	1
AlldC zr98	...	7	76⅜ −	⅛
AlldC zr97	...	100	83⅜ −	½
AlldC zr07	...	5	38¾	...
AlegCp 6½14	cv	10	103	...
AAirl 5¼98	5.5	20	95	...
ATT 4⅜96	4.4	30	99⅜ −	⅛
ATT 6s00	6.0	375	100¾	...
ATT 8⅝31	7.5	20	114¼ −	½
ATT 7⅛02	6.7	90	106⅛ +	¼
ATT 8⅛22	7.5	30	109	...
ATT 8⅛24	7.4	101	109⅜ +	⅝

Source: Reprinted by permission of the *Wall Street Journal,* © 1994 Dow Jones Company, Inc. All Rights Reserved Worldwide.

Summary
Exercise 8.2

Assuming the market interest rate is 9 percent, determine the price and yields of the following: (a) a $10,000 Treasury bill that matures in one year and (b) a $1,000 corporate bond that has a coupon rate of 10 percent and matures in one year.

Answer: (a) The price of the Treasury bill is

$$P_{TB} = \frac{\$10,000}{1.09} = \$9,174.31.$$

The discount yield on this bond is

$$\text{Discount yield} = \frac{10,000 - 9,174.31}{10,000} \times \frac{360}{365} = .081,$$

which is 8.1 percent. The yield to maturity is the interest rate, i, that satisfies

$$\$9,174.31 = \frac{\$10,000}{1 + i}.$$

Solving for i, the yield to maturity is 9 percent, the same as the market interest rate used in our present value calculations. This is to be expected, of course, since we used this interest rate in determining the price of the Treasury bill.

(b) The annual coupon payment for this bond is $100. This coupon payment, along with the face value, will be received in one year. Thus, the price of the corporate bond is the present value of these payments when the interest rate is 9 percent:

$$P_{CB} = \frac{\$100 + \$1,000}{1.09} = \$1,009.17.$$

Notice that this amount is greater than the face value of the bond because the coupon rate of interest ($100/$1,000 = 10 percent) is greater than the market rate of interest (9 percent). The current yield on this bond is

$$\text{Current yield} = \frac{\$100}{\$1,009.17} = .099,$$

or 9.9 percent. Since the price paid for this bond is based on the market rate of interest, the yield to maturity is the market rate of interest, 9 percent. Notice that the current yield is greater than the yield to maturity because the price of the bond exceeds the bond's face value.

THE EQUILIBRIUM PRICE AND QUANTITY OF BONDS

Our analysis of discounted corporate bonds and Treasury bills, as well as bonds with coupons such as Treasury bonds and corporate bonds, has revealed an important principle: An inverse relationship exists between the price of a bond and the market interest rate. For this reason, it is important to understand how changes in the economy affect interest rates and thus bond prices. We now introduce two different but equivalent methods of analyzing bond markets. One approach relates the interest rate to the supply of and demand for loanable funds; the other relates the prices of bonds to the supply of and demand for bonds. We also show the equivalence of the two approaches by demonstrating that for a given interest rate, the price of a bond can be determined from our graph of the inverse relationship between bond prices and interest rates.

Bond Prices: The Loanable Funds Approach

One way to analyze bond prices is to combine what we have already learned about interest rate determination and present value analysis into a convenient framework. Parts a and b of Figure 8.5 illustrate this approach. Part a depicts the supply of and demand for loanable funds, with the interest rate on the vertical axis and the dollar value of loanable funds on the horizontal axis. The supply of loanable funds is provided by lenders, who are willing to offer more loanable funds at higher interest rates. The supply of loanable funds is therefore an upward-sloping curve. Borrowers, on the other hand, seek more funds as the interest rate falls. Thus, the demand curve for loanable funds slopes downward. Equilibrium is determined by the intersection of the supply and demand curves for loanable funds and changes with fluctuations in either

Figure 8.5
Changes in the Supply of Loanable Funds and Bond Prices

In part a, the market interest rate is determined in the loanable funds market. With demand of D^1 and supply of S^1, the market interest rate is 10 percent. In part b, the price of a 10 percent coupon bond is $1,000 when the market interest rate is 10 percent. However, when the supply of loanable funds increases in part a to S^2, the market interest rate falls to 8 percent. In part b, this causes the price of the bond to rise to $1,035.66.

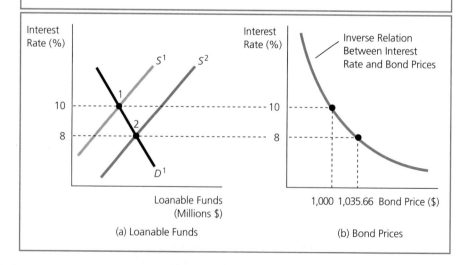

(a) Loanable Funds

(b) Bond Prices

supply or demand. For example, when the supply curve is S^1, equilibrium is at point 1 and the interest rate is 10 percent. If the supply of loanable funds increases to S^2, as would occur if the tax rate on interest income were reduced, equilibrium moves to point 2 and the equilibrium interest rate falls to 8 percent.

Part b of Figure 8.5 illustrates the inverse relationship between the interest rate and the price of a bond. When equilibrium is at point 1 in part a, the interest rate is 10 percent. Tracing this interest rate over to part b, we see that the corresponding price of a 10 percent coupon bond is $1,000. When equilibrium in part a shifts to point 2, the interest rate falls to 8 percent. Tracing this over to part b, we see that the price of the bond rises to $1,035.66.

Figure 8.5 shows a graphical technique for determining the impact of changes in the supply of and demand for loanable funds on bond prices. A change in any of the determinants of demand or supply listed in Table 8.1 that results in a higher interest rate in part a will lead to lower bond prices in part b. Conversely, any change in demand or supply that leads to a lower interest rate in part a will lead to higher bond prices in part b. Thus, bond prices will systematically fluctuate with changes in such variables as inflationary expectations, taxes, budget deficits, and wealth.

Box 8.4 uses a real-world example to illustrate the inverse relationship between bond prices and interest rates.

Bond Prices: The Suppy and Demand of Bonds Approach

An alternative way to determine the equilibrium prices of bonds is to directly graph the demand and supply curves for bonds as a function of a bond's price instead of using the two-part approach used in the previous section. We will base our analysis in this section on the same scenario that existed at point 1 in part a of Figure 8.5 to emphasize the equivalence of this approach to the loanable funds approach. Recall that at point 1 in that figure, the interest rate is 10 percent, the coupon rate is 10 percent, and the corresponding price of a bond in part b of Figure 8.5 is $1,000.

Since a bond is a promise to pay a set amount over the life of the bond and the coupon rate is assumed to be 10 percent, the lower the price of the bond, the higher the bond's yield to maturity. In turn, the higher the yield to maturity relative to the market interest rate, the more attractive the bond is to investors. For this reason, the demand for a bond is a decreasing function of the bond's price, as illustrated by the curve D^B in Figure 8.6, on page 255. Notice that this demand curve holds everything constant except the price and quantity of bonds sold. The demand curve for bonds is composed of those wishing to give up money today in return for the future stream of funds promised by the $1,000 bond with a coupon rate of 10 percent. The lower the price of the bond, the more bonds investors will want to hold.

The Data Bank

Box 8.4

The Inverse Relationship Between Bond Prices and Interest Rates

This table reports the asked prices and yields to maturity for each day during the first week of June 1993, for two $10,000 government bonds maturing in June 1994. The first bond carried a 5 percent coupon rate and the second an 8.5 percent coupon rate. Notice several things. First, the price of the bond with the 8.5 percent coupon interest rate was higher than the price of the 5 percent coupon rate bond, reflecting the higher coupon payments on the 8.5 percent bond. Second, despite the differences in coupons, the yields to maturity on these two bonds were very similar. Thus, the market price adjusted for the difference in coupon rates. Third, the asked price and the yield to maturity varied over the week. When the asked price increased, the yield to maturity decreased, and vice versa. This example illustrates the inverse relationship of bond prices and yields for an average week.

Date	5% Coupon Rate		8.5% Coupon Rate	
	Asked Price	Yield	Asked Price	Yield
Fri., 5/28/93	$10,140.63	3.66%	$10,509.38	3.64%
Tue., 6/1/93	10,143.75	3.62	10,512.50	3.60
Wed., 6/2/93	10,140.63	3.65	10,512.50	3.59
Thur., 6/3/93	10,143.75	3.61	10,512.50	3.55
Fri., 6/4/93	10,128.13	3.76	10,490.63	3.74

Source: Bond prices calculated on a one-year, $10,000 government bond maturing in June 1994. Data from the *Wall Street Journal,* June 1, 2, 3, 4, and 7, pp. C16, C19, C19, C14, and C14, respectively.

The suppliers of bonds, on the other hand, wish to sell the right to a specified amount over the life of the bond. Since the seller of a bond receives money today in return for future payments promised over the bond's life, the higher the price of a given bond, the more lucrative it is to sell the bond, holding other things constant. For this reason, the supply of bonds is an increasing function of the price of a bond, as illustrated by the curve S^B in Figure 8.6. Notice that this supply curve holds everything else constant; all that varies along the supply curve is the price and quantity of bonds.

Equilibrium in the bond market is determined by the intersection of the supply and demand for bonds, such as at point A in Figure 8.6. In this

The quantity demanded of bonds will increase as the price of bonds decreases, holding other things constant. The quantity supplied of bonds will increase as the price of bonds increases, holding other things constant. Equilibrium in the bond market occurs at point *A*, where demand equals supply. When the market interest rate is 10 percent, the equilibrium price of 10 percent coupon bonds is $1,000. In this case, 4,000 bonds trade in the market.

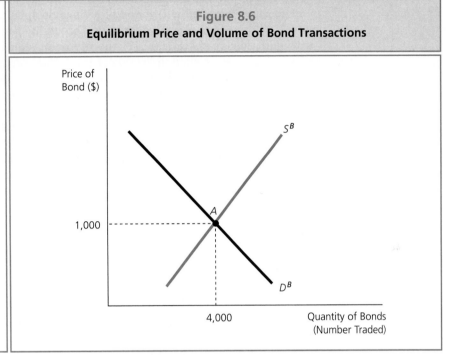

Figure 8.6
Equilibrium Price and Volume of Bond Transactions

example, the equilibrium price of bonds is $1,000 and the equilibrium quantity of bonds is 4,000. Notice that this equilibrium price of bonds is precisely the same as that in part b of Figure 8.5 when the market interest rate is 10 percent.

This analysis applies to both the primary and secondary markets. When bonds trade in the primary market (the market for new bonds), those demanding bonds are providing loanable funds to those issuing the bonds. When bonds trade in the secondary market (the market for existing bonds), the demander of a bond is providing funds to the party wishing to sell an existing bond. Likewise, in the primary market, the suppliers of bonds are corporations and governments. These parties issue bonds to obtain loanable funds. In the secondary market, the suppliers of bonds are those who own existing bonds and wish to sell them to obtain funds immediately.

Summary
Exercise 8.3

(a) Determine the impact of an increase in inflationary expectations on interest rates and bond prices. (b) Suppose the government passed a law that exempted interest income from federal taxes but the change left the size of the budget deficit unchanged. What would be the impact on the interest rate and bond prices? Illustrate your answers graphically.

Answer: (a) The initial equilibrium in the loanable funds market is at point 1 in part a below, where S^0 and D^0 intersect. Given the initial interest rate of i^0, the price of a bond is given by P_B^0 in part b. The increase in inflationary expectations decreases the supply of loanable funds from S^0 to S^1 in part a, since lenders now expect the future interest receipts and face value received at maturity to have less purchasing power. Similarly, increased inflationary expectations increase the demand for loanable funds from D^0 to D^1 in part a, since borrowers now expect to be able to pay back lenders with money that has less purchasing power than before. Thus, equilibrium moves from point 1 to point 2 in part a, and the interest rate rises to i^1. In part b, the higher interest rate translates into a decrease in bond prices from P_B^0 to P_B^1. Thus, increased inflationary expectations lead to higher interest rates and lower bond prices.

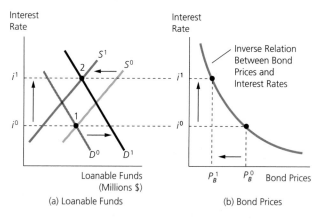

(b) The initial equilibrium in the loanable funds market is at point 1 in part a below, where the interest rate is i^1. Part b reveals that initially bond prices are given by P_B^1. When the government announces that interest income on bonds is exempt from federal taxes, the supply of loanable funds increases

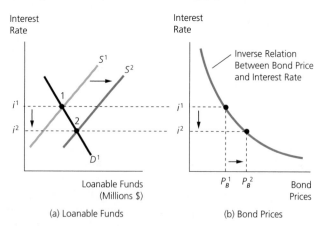

from S^1 to S^2 in part a. This is because at any interest rate, bondholders pay less taxes on bond income than before and are thus willing to lend more funds. Hence, equilibrium moves from point 1 to point 2 and the interest rate falls to i^2 in part a. In part b, this translates into an increase in bond prices to P_B^2. Thus, when bond income is exempted from federal taxes, the result is lower interest rates, higher bond prices, and a greater equilibrium quantity of loanable funds.

VALUING STOCKS AND OTHER ASSETS

Unlike debt instruments, **equity instruments** (such as common stock) represent the ownership of a share of a firm. Accordingly, the owner of a share of common stock owns a share of the future earnings (profits) of the company issuing the stock. Individuals, insurance companies, mutual funds, and pension funds hold stocks in their portfolios and continually seek out stocks that are undervalued. Most banks and bank holding companies are also owned by shareholders; you can buy a share of Chase Manhattan Bank, Chemical Bank, or Mellon Bank on the New York Stock Exchange. Box 8.5 describes how to interpret financial data for corporate stocks.

When is a stock a good buy? To answer this question, we must determine the value of a share of stock.

When a bank or other company has earnings, it can either (1) return them to shareholders in the form of dividends or (2) retain them within the firm. **Dividends** represent a direct payment to shareholders. Earnings that are retained by the firm increase the value of the firm in that they can either be invested in projects within the firm that will enhance future earnings or be invested elsewhere at the market interest rate and be paid out as dividends in the future.

The value of a firm at any point in time is the present value of all of the firm's future earnings:

$$\text{Value of a firm} = \frac{EE_1}{(1 + i)} + \frac{EE_2}{(1 + i)^2} + \cdots + \frac{EE_T}{(1 + i)^T}, \qquad (8.3)$$

where EE_t represents the firm's expected earnings at the end of year t, i is the interest rate, and T is the number of years over which the firm will operate.

Two aspects of corporate stock make stock valuation more difficult than valuing, say, a U.S. Treasury bond. First, if you purchase a U.S. Treasury bond, you purchase a stream of known future payments. When you purchase a stock, you purchase a share of the company's future earnings, which are far from known. Second, the maturity of a bond is known. The life of a firm, T, is not known; the firm may live on forever, or it may go bankrupt in one year. These elements make determining the value of a firm a complicated

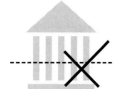

Inside Money

Box 8.5

How to Read Information on Stocks in the Wall Street Journal

The *Wall Street Journal* reports information on stock prices daily. The information reported here is from the Wednesday, February 16, 1994, edition and reports prices from the previous day.

The *Hi Low* columns give the highest and the lowest price, respectively, of the stock over the last 52 weeks. The *Stock* column reports the name of the issuing company. The *Sym* column indicates the company's ticker symbol.

The *Div* column tells the current annual dividends per share. Thus, for Du Pont, each share pays annual dividends of $1.76. The column labeled *Yld %* reports the annual dividend yield, calculated as a percentage of the price of a share. It is calculated as Div divided by the closing price (the *Close* column). For Du Pont the dividend yield was $1.76/$55, or 3.2 percent.

The column labeled *PE* is the price-earnings ratio. It is the closing price divided by the earning per share from the most recent four quarters. For Du Pont, the price of a share is 66 times as large as the earnings per share over the most recent four quarters. Since the price of a share is $55, this means earnings per share were $55/66 = $0.83 per share.

The eighth column, *Vol 100s,* is the number of shares traded the previous business day expressed in hundreds of shares. Thus, 936,900 shares of Du Pont stock were traded on February 15. The next three columns report the highest, lowest, and closing price of the stock for the day. For Du Pont, the high price was $55.125, the low price was $54.50, and the closing price was $55. The last column indicates the difference between the closing price on that day and the closing price on the previous day. Thus, the closing price of Du Pont stock on February 15 was five-eighths of a dollar (62.5 cents) higher than the closing price of the stock on February 14th.

52 Weeks Hi	Lo	Stock	Sym	Div	Yld %	PE	Vol 100s	Hi	Lo	Close	Net Chg
s 64⅛	39⅛	Diebold	DBD	1.20	2.3	21	1797	51⅝	51	51½	+ ⅜
49¼	28⅞	DigitalEqp	DEC		...	dd	5136	29⅜	29⅛	29⅛	− ¼
48¼	33⅛	DillardStrs	DDS	.08	.2	16	2549	35	34¾	35	+ ⅛
9⅛	6⅛	DimeSvgNY	DME		...	9	1684	8⅜	8¼	8¼	...
31⅛	20⅝	DiscountAuto	DAP		...	26	80	25⅛	24¼	24⅝	− ⅝
48⅜	36	Disney	DIS	.30f	.6	34	9318	46¾	46⅜	46¾	+ ⅜
37⅞	25⅞	DoleFood	DOL	.40	1.3	23	1087	30⅜	30	30⅛	− ⅛
49½	41⅛	DominRes	D	2.54f	6.0	13	1972	42½	42⅛	42¼	+ ½
6⅞	4¼	Domtar g	DTC		...	...	227	6⅜	6¼	6¼	+ ⅛
47⅞	33¼	Donaldson	DCI	.56f	1.2	22	44	47⅛	46¾	46⅞	− ⅝
31¾	26⅛	Donelley	DNY	.56	1.8	27	2459	31⅜	30¼	31¼	+ ¾
61⅞	44⅜	Dover	DOV	.92	1.5	22	682	61½	60¼	61½	+1¼
65	49	DowChem	DOW	2.60	4.1	27	5099	64⅛	63¼	64	+ ¼
40⅞	26¾	DowJones	DJ	.84f	2.1	27	2180	40⅛	39¾	40	− ¼
27¾	14¼	DowneySL	DSL	.48f	2.6	10	60	18¾	18⅛	18¼	− ½
26	14¼	DrPepper	DPS		...	17	1130	25⅛	24⅞	25	− ⅛
12½	8¾	Dravo	DRV		...	25	344	12⅜	12	12¼	+ ¼
25⅜	17⅞	DresserInd	DI	.60	2.6	25	8942	22¾	21½	22¾	+ ⅞
48½	35¾	Dreyfus	DRY	.76	1.6	17	1278	46⅝	46⅛	46⅜	...
12⅛	10	DreyfStrGvFd	DSI	.90	8.4	...	139	10¾	10⅝	10¾	+ ⅛
11	9¾	DreyfStrMunBd	DSM	.66	6.5	...	348	10⅛	10	10⅛	+ ⅛
11½	10¼	DreyfusMuni	LEO	.73	6.5	...	275	11¼	11⅛	11¼	+ ⅛
56¾	44½	DuPont	DD	1.76	3.2	66	9369	55⅛	54½	55	+ ⅝

Source: Reprinted by permission of the *Wall Street Journal,*

forecasting exercise. However, once this forecast of future earnings is made, determining the value of the price of a share of stock is a relatively straight-forward process.

In particular, the price of a share of stock is simply the value of the firm divided by the number of shares of stock issued by the company:

$$\text{Stock price} = \frac{\text{Value of the firm}}{\text{Number of shares}}. \qquad (8.4)$$

Notice in equation 8.3 that the higher the interest rate, the lower the value of the firm. Holding the number of shares of the stock constant, this implies a lower stock price in equation 8.4. Thus, holding everything else constant, the higher the interest rate, the lower the price of a given firm's stock.

We now examine in detail the valuation of two particular types of stocks: income stocks and growth stocks. **Income stocks** are the stocks of companies that have a low level of retained earnings and thus pay most of their earnings to shareholders. Earnings paid to shareholders are called dividends. An investor who purchases an income stock primarily purchases a future stream of dividend payments. In contrast, **growth stocks** are the stocks of companies that retain most of their earnings to reinvest them within the firm. The purchaser of a growth stock essentially purchases a company that acquires more and more assets today to pay higher dividends in the future.

Income Stocks

Income stocks have a low level of retained earnings and thus pay shareholders yearly dividends that are a very large fraction of the firm's earnings. As a consequence, income stocks tend to have relatively high dividend yields. The **dividend yield** on a stock is simply the ratio of the annual dividends per share to the stock price:

$$\text{Dividend yield} = \frac{\text{Annual dividends per share}}{P_S},$$

where P_S is the price of a share of the stock. For example, suppose a firm's stock sells for $10 per share and the firm pays out annual dividends of 60 cents per share. Then the stock's dividend yield is $0.60/$10, or 6 percent. The stocks of most electric utilities are income stocks; most of their earnings in any given year are paid out as dividends.

In practice, the valuation of an income stock can be difficult because the earnings and dividends paid out may vary considerably over time. While we postpone an analysis of risk until the next chapter, we can gain a basic understanding of how the price of an income stock is determined by making a few simplifying assumptions. Suppose a company does not retain any of its earnings but instead pays them all out as dividends. Furthermore, suppose the market for the firm's product is stable and annual earnings are expected to remain constant at a level of EE from now on. In this case, the firm is expected to pay out dividends per share of $d = EE/N$ each year, where N is the number of shares of stock issued by the firm. Effectively, the ownership of such a stock is a perpetuity that pays dividends per share of $d = EE/N$ in every year from now on. The value of this perpetuity is the price of a share of this income stock (P_{IS}):

$$P_{IS} = \frac{\text{Annual dividends per share}}{\text{Interest rate}} = \frac{d}{i}.$$

As an example, suppose an electric utility company is expected to have earnings of $1 million each year from now on and has issued 500,000 shares of stock. Thus, annual dividends per share are expected to be $d = \$1,000,000/500,000 = \$2$ per share. If the market interest rate is 5 percent, the price of a share of this utility stock will be

$$P_{IS} = \frac{\$2}{.05} = \$40.$$

Growth Stocks

Growth stocks differ from income stocks in that most or all of the firm's current earnings are reinvested in the firm. Consequently, the dividend yield on a growth stock will be considerably lower than that on an income stock; in fact, the stock may not pay current dividends at all (a zero dividend yield). Nonetheless, since the value of the firm is the present value of all future earnings and earnings invested back into the firm increase the firm's value, considerable growth in earnings will occur over time. As the firm matures, it ultimately begins to pay dividends to stockholders—much larger dividends, in fact, than it would have paid during its early years. Usually growth stocks are shares of relatively young companies.

Like valuing income stocks, valuing a growth stock can be difficult in practice because the firm's future earnings are far from certain. Again we can use a few simplifying assumptions to gain some basic insights into the pricing of growth stocks without getting bogged down with risk considerations.

Suppose a firm's earnings last year were EE, as investors expected. These earnings are expected to grow at a rate of g each year from now on. Thus, at the end of this year, expected earnings are $EE_1 = (1 + g)EE$, at the end of next year they are expected to be $EE_2 = (1 + g)^2EE$, at the end of three years they are expected to be $EE_3 = (1 + g)^3EE$, and so on. The present value of the growth firm in this case is given by

Value of growth firm

$$= \frac{EE_1}{(1 + i)} + \frac{EE_2}{(1 + i)^2} + \frac{EE_3}{(1 + i)^3} + \cdots = \sum_{t=1}^{\infty} \frac{EE_t}{(1 + i)^t}.$$

Using the fact that $EE_t = (1 + g)^t EE$, we can simplify this to

$$\text{Value of growth firm} = EE \times \Sigma_{t=1}^{\infty} \left[\frac{1 + g}{1 + i}\right]^t.$$

If expected earnings growth exceeded the interest rate ($g > i$), this expression would be infinite, reflecting the fact that the firm is infinitely valuable. Of course, this is unlikely since a firm cannot continue to grow forever at a rate that exceeds the market rate of interest. The more plausible case is that where the expected growth rate is less than the market rate of interest.

When $g < i$, the formula for the value of a growth firm can be simplified to[3]

$$\text{Value of growth firm} = EE \times \left[\frac{1 + g}{i - g}\right].$$

If N shares of stock are outstanding, the price of a share of the firm's stock will be the fraction $1/N$ of the value of the firm. In other words, the price of a growth stock will be

$$P_{GS} = \frac{EE}{N} \times \left[\frac{1 + g}{i - g}\right],$$

where EE is expected earnings last year, g is the expected annual growth in those earnings, i is the interest rate, and N is the number of shares of stock outstanding. For example, suppose a firm has expected earnings of $1 million and these earnings are expected to grow at an annual rate of 3 percent from now on. If 500,000 shares of stock are outstanding and the interest rate is 7 percent, the price of a share of this firm's stock will be

$$P_{GS} = \frac{\$1,000,000}{500,000} \times \left[\frac{1 + .03}{.07 - .03}\right] = \$51.50.$$

---

[3] To see why

$$\Sigma_{t=1}^{\infty} \left[\frac{1 + g}{1 + i}\right]^t = \frac{1 + g}{i - g},$$

let $\delta = (1 + g)/(1 + i)$. It is a well-known property of infinite series that

$$\Sigma_{t=1}^{\infty} \delta^t = \frac{\delta}{1 - \delta}$$

whenever $|\delta| < 1$. Since $(1 + g)/(1 + i)$ plays the same role as δ in this formula, it follows that

$$\Sigma_{t=1}^{\infty} \left[\frac{1 + g}{1 + i}\right]^t = \frac{\dfrac{1 + g}{1 + i}}{1 - \dfrac{(1 + g)}{(1 + i)}} = \frac{\dfrac{1 + g}{1 + i}}{\dfrac{1 + i - 1 - g}{1 + i}} = \frac{1 + g}{i - g},$$

as required.

If the interest rate falls to 5 percent, the stock price will increase to

$$P_{GS} = \frac{\$1,000,000}{500,000} \times \left[\frac{1 + .03}{.05 - .03} \right] = \$103.$$

This example illustrates that the price of a growth stock increases as the interest rate declines; an inverse relationship exists between the interest rate and the price of a share of growth stock. Similarly, the greater the growth rate in earnings, the higher the price of a growth stock.

Summary
Exercise 8.4

Suppose a firm's earnings were $5 million last year. There are 5 million shares of the company's stock outstanding, and the market interest rate is 4 percent. Determine the price of a share of this firm's stock if (a) earnings are expected to remain constant forever and the firm pays all earnings out as dividends and (b) the firm's earnings are expected to grow at an annual rate of 3 percent.

Answer: (a) Earnings per share are expected to be $5,000,000/5,000,000 = $1 and paid out as dividends each year forever. Thus, by purchasing a share of this firm, the investor buys a perpetual stream of $1 dividend payments. The price of this income stock is thus

$$P_{IS} = \frac{\$1}{.04} = \$25.$$

(b) Using our formula for the price of a growth stock (here EE = $5,000,000, N = 5,000,000, g = .03, and i = .04), we find the price of a share of the growth stock to be

$$P_{GS} = \frac{\$5,000,000}{5,000,000} \times \left[\frac{1 + .03}{.04 - .03} \right] = \$103.$$

EQUILIBRIUM PRICE AND VOLUME OF STOCK TRANSACTIONS

Our analysis of the valuation of stocks showed an inverse relationship between the price of a share of stock and the market interest rate, just as was the case for bond prices. Changes in the economy thus affect stock prices in much the same way that they affect bond prices.

Part a of Figure 8.7 depicts the supply of and demand for loanable funds, with the interest rate on the vertical axis and the quantity of loanable funds on the horizontal axis. When the supply curve is S^1 and the demand curve is D^1, equilibrium is at point 1 and the interest rate is 7 percent. To find the price of a share of stock, we trace this interest rate over to part b, where we graph the inverse relationship between the interest rate and stock prices.

Thus, at the 7 percent equilibrium interest rate in part a, the corresponding stock price is $51.50 in part b.

If the demand for loanable funds decreases to D^2 in part a of Figure 8.7, the new equilibrium is at point 2 and the market interest rate falls to 5 percent. Tracing this interest rate over to part b, we see that as a result of the decline in the interest rate, the price of a typical share of stock rises to $103. This method of determining the impact of changes in the supply of and demand for loanable funds on stock prices is virtually identical to the way we analyzed the determination of bond prices. Any change in demand or supply in part a of Figure 8.7 that results in a lower interest rate will lead to higher stock prices in part b, and vice versa.

We can also graph the demand and supply curves for the stock as a function of its price to determine the stock's equilibrium price. Since the ownership of a share of stock represents a share of the future earnings of the firm, holding constant other things such as the interest rate, the lower the price, the more desirable it is to purchase the stock. Consequently, graphing the demand for a stock as function of its price yields a downward-sloping demand curve like D^{Stock} in Figure 8.8. Notice that the interest rate is held constant at 7 percent along this demand curve.

On the other hand, the higher the price that can be received by selling a share of stock, the greater the amount of stock that will be offered for sale. Thus, the supply curve for a stock is an increasing function of the stock's

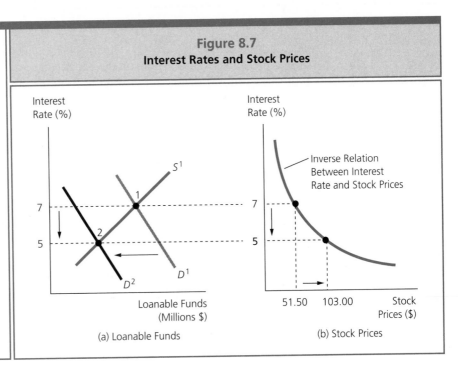

At point 1 in part a, the equilibrium interest rate for loanable funds is 7 percent. Part b shows that at a market interest rate of 7 percent, the price of the stock is $51.50. A decrease in the demand for loanable funds from D^1 to D^2 causes the market interest rate to fall to 5 percent. Part b shows that at a market interest rate of 5 percent, the price of the stock rises to $103.

Figure 8.7
Interest Rates and Stock Prices

(a) Loanable Funds

(b) Stock Prices

The demand for a stock is inversely related to the stock's price, while the supply of the stock is directly related to the price. The demand and supply curves are drawn holding constant all other relevant variables. One such variable is the market interest rate. When the interest rate is held constant at 7 percent, the resulting equilibrium has 5,000 shares of stock being traded at a price of $51.50 per share.

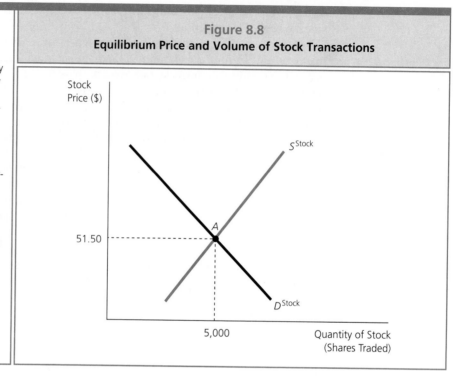

Figure 8.8
Equilibrium Price and Volume of Stock Transactions

price, such as S^{Stock} in Figure 8.8. The intersection of the supply and demand curves determines equilibrium in the stock market. Point A denotes the equilibrium price, $51.50, and the equilibrium quantity sold, 5,000 shares.

Summary Exercise 8.5

Suppose you read that the growth in Beta Company's earnings will be lower than expected. Looking at the stock market—the secondary market in stocks—and assuming other things remain the same, what would you expect to happen to the price of the stock? To the number of shares traded? Illustrate your answer with a graph.

Answer: One way to answer this question is to recall that the price of a share of stock is an increasing function of the growth in the firm's earnings. Thus, a decline in the growth rate of earnings will reduce the present value of the firm and lead to a lower stock price. However, this method does not answer the second part of the question; to do that we must graph the supply of and demand for a firm's stock in the secondary market before and after the announcement of lower-than-expected growth in earnings. This approach will allow us to see the impact of the announcement on both the price and volume of shares traded.

The figure illustrates the initial supply (S^0) and demand (D^0) for Beta's stock. The initial equilibrium is at point A, which means the equilibrium price of a share of Beta's stock is P^0 and the corresponding quantity of shares traded on a typical day is Q^0. When the lower-than-expected earnings growth is announced, the demand curve shifts to D^1. This occurs because buyers of the stock will now pay less for any given quantity of the stock due to the lower growth forecasts. Simultaneously, the supply of Beta's stock shifts to S^1 as owners of Beta stock attempt to get rid of their shares on the secondary market thanks to Beta's lower projected earnings. Since demand decreases and supply increases, the equilibrium price of the firm's stock clearly falls to a level such as P^1. However, the volume of shares traded may rise, fall, or remain the same depending on the relative magnitude of the shifts. This is the same ambiguity that typically arises when both demand and supply shift. The new equilibrium shown at point B assumes the increase in supply exactly offsets the decrease in demand, but this need not be the case.

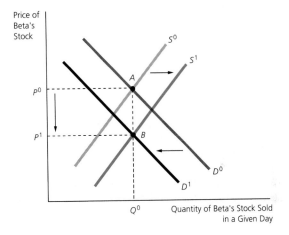

CONCLUSION

In this chapter, we used present value analysis to determine the prices of financial assets and found an inverse relationship between asset prices and the interest rate. This analysis not only provides a means of pricing financial assets like stocks and bonds but, coupled with the supply and demand analysis we learned in Chapter 4, also shows how these prices fluctuate with changes in inflationary expectations, budget deficits, tax rates, wealth, and other variables that shift the demand for or supply of loanable funds. In the next chapter, we extend this analysis by examining how risk affects asset prices.

KEY TERMS

present value

future value

debt instrument

discount yield

face value

yield to maturity

coupon rate

current yield

equity instrument

income stock

dividend

growth stock

dividend yield

QUESTIONS AND PROBLEMS

1. Suppose you plan to purchase a new house at the end of five years. How much would you have to deposit in the bank today to have enough for the $20,000 down payment if the interest rate is (a) 1 percent, (b) 5 percent, (c) 10 percent, (d) 15 percent, and (e) 20 percent?

2. Based on your results in problem 1, graph the relationship between the interest rate and the present value of $20,000 received in five years.

3. A recent advertisement offers a two-year subscription to a magazine for $20. If a one-year subscription costs $11 and you can invest your money at an interest rate of 9 percent, would you save money by sending in a check today for a two-year subscription? Explain.

4. Suppose you paid $9,000 for a Treasury bill that matures in one year. Determine (a) the discount yield and (b) the yield to maturity.

5. If the market interest rate is 8.5 percent, how much would you be willing to pay for a Treasury bill that matures in one year? Given this price, determine the discount yield and the yield to maturity, and explain why they differ.

6. Carefully explain what would happen to the price and quantity of Treasury bills traded in the money market if inflationary expectations increased.

7. You just purchased a coupon bond that has a face value of $1,000 and a coupon rate of 8 percent. The bond matures in one year.
(a). If the interest rate was 6 percent when you purchased the bond, how much did you have to pay for this bond? What was the current yield? The yield to maturity?
(b). Suppose that as soon as you purchased the bond at the price determined in part a, the interest rate soared to 10 percent. If you immediately sold the bond, what would you receive for it? As a holder of the bond, are you pleased that the interest rate increased to 10 percent? Explain.

8. Suppose the government enacted a policy that prevented corporations from deducting interest payments on coupon bonds from their income taxes. How would this affect prices of corporate coupon bonds traded in (a) the primary bond market and (b) the secondary bond market?

9. Suppose a one-year Treasury bill has a discount yield of 5 percent. If your alternative to purchasing this bond is to deposit the funds in a bank account that pays 5 percent interest, what will you do? Why?

10. A utility company is expected to have earnings of $5 million each year from now to eternity. The company pays out all of its annual earnings as dividends to owners of its 2 million shares of stock. If the interest rate is 6 percent,
(a). What is a reasonable price to pay for the stock?
(b). Based on the price in part a, what is the stock's dividend yield?
(c). Based on the price in part a, what is the ratio of the stock's price to earnings per share (called the P/E ratio on Wall Street)?

11. Why would anyone purchase a stock that does not pay dividends?

12. Young-R-Us Company presently does not pay out dividends, even though it had earnings of $2 per share last year. If the interest rate is 4 percent, what is the price of the firm's stock if earnings are expected to grow forever at an annual rate of

(a). 1 percent?
(b). 2 percent?
(c). 3 percent?
(d). Based on your results in parts a–c, graph the relationship between the growth rate and the price of Young-R-Us's stock price.

13. Young-R-Us Company (problem 12) presently pays no dividends, even though it had earnings of $2 per share last year. If the growth rate in earnings is expected to be 4 percent per year forever, what is the price of the firm's stock if the interest rate is
(a). 5 percent?
(b). 6 percent?
(c). 7 percent?
(d). Based on your results in parts a–c, graph the relationship between the interest rate and the price of Young-R-Us's stock price.

14. Suppose a firm announces a two-for-one stock split; that is, for every share of stock owned by investors, the firm gives them another share for free. What impact does this practice have on the price of the stock?

15. Who receives funds when a stock or a bond is purchased in the primary market? In the secondary market?

SELECTIONS FOR FURTHER READING

Bodurtha, J. N., Jr., and N. C. Mark. "Testing the CAPM with Time-Varying Risks and Returns." *Journal of Finance,* 46 (September 1991), 1485–1505.

Cecchetti, S. G. "Evaluating Empirical Tests of Asset Pricing Models: Alternative Interpretations." *American Economic Review,* 80 (May 1990), 48–51.

Cecchetti, S. G., P. Lam, and N. C. Mark. "Mean Reversion in Equilibrium Asset Prices." *American Economic Review,* 80 (June 1990), 398–418.

Craig, E. D. "Impact of Federal Policies on Municipal Bond Financing." *National Tax Journal,* 34 (September 1981), 389–394.

Continued on p. 268

Fabozzi, F. J., and T. B. Thurston. "State Taxes and Reserve Requirements as Major Determinants of Yield Spreads among Money Market Instruments." *Journal of Financial and Quantitative Analysis,* 21 (December 1986), 427–436.

Falk, B. "Formally Testing the Present Value Model of Farmland Prices." *American Journal of Agricultural Economics,* 73 (February 1991), 1–10.

James, C. M., and R. O. Edmister. "The Relation between Common Stock Returns Trading Activity and Market Value." *Journal of Finance,* 38 (September 1983), 1075–1086.

Lee, T. K. "Settlement System and the Day-of-the-Week Effect." *Economic Letters,* 26 (1988), 353–356.

McCulloch, J. H. "An Estimate of the Liquidity Premium." *Journal of Political Economy,* 83 (February 1975), 95–119.

Schilling, D. "Estimating the Present Value of Future Income Losses: An Historical Simulation, 1900–1982." *Journal of Risk and Insurance,* 52 (March 1985), 100–116.

Spatt, C. S., and F. P. Sterbenz. "Warrant Exercise, Dividends, and Reinvestment Policy." *Journal of Finance,* 43 (June 1988), 493–506.

Risk, Uncertainty, and Portfolio Choice

*I*n the previous chapter, we saw that interest rates affect the prices of financial assets that banks and individuals hold, such as stocks and bonds. We assumed there was a single interest rate and borrowers fully kept their promises to repay loans.

In reality, a host of factors affect the prices of financial assets, chief among them the various forms of risk. For example, default risk is the risk that a borrower will not fully repay the principal and interest on a loan. Market risk, the risk that the price of a security will fall between the time the security is purchased and the time the owner wants to sell it, can also affect an asset's price.

Different types of financial instruments by their nature entail different levels of risk. Moreover, financial instruments issued by various borrowers represent different degrees of risk due to variations in borrowers' ultimate ability to repay. Thus, there is generally no single interest rate in the market for loanable funds; instead, interest rates vary for different borrowers and for different types of financial instruments. A key reason for differential interest rates is different degrees and types of risk among various financial instruments.

Lending money always involves some form and some degree of risk. In this chapter, we see how different types of risk affect the prices banks and investors are willing to pay for financial assets and how those prices in turn affect the interest rates borrowers must pay to obtain funds. First, we define risk and describe the various types of risk that affect financial instruments. Then we see how risk affects asset prices and interest rates. Finally, we examine some methods banks and individuals use to reduce financial risk.

UNCERTAINTY AND RISK

Both *uncertainty* and *risk* are widely used words, and most of us understand their commonly used definitions. For instance, *The American Heritage Dictionary of the English Language* defines *uncertainty* as ''the condition of being uncertain, doubt'' and *uncertain* as ''not known or established; not determined, undecided; not having sure knowledge; subject to change, variable." It defines *risk* as the "possibility of suffering harm or loss; danger," but also as "the danger of probability of loss to an insurer; the variability of returns from an investment; the chance of nonpayment of a debt."[1]

In this chapter, we introduce the specialized definitions of these terms as economists use them. We begin with risk. Like the dictionary definition, economists think of risk as a possibility of loss. The term *risk* applies to outcomes that cannot be exactly predicted. However, economists distinguish between situations in which we cannot exactly predict outcomes, but know which outcomes might occur and are able to assign probabilities to those outcomes and situations in which we lack such information. The former situation is a situation of *risk* and the latter a situation of *uncertainty*.

As a simple example, consider a coin toss in which you bet $50 that heads will come up instead of tails. Before you toss the coin, you cannot exactly predict the outcome. However, you can list all possible outcomes—heads and you win $50 or tails and you lose $50—and the probability of each outcome occurring. In this example, there is a 50-50 chance of each outcome, or a probability of 1/2. These are objective probabilities—the true chance of the event occurring—and this is a situation of risk.

However, more complicated situations are still considered situations of risk. For instance, your grade in this course is an outcome that you cannot predict exactly. However, you can list the possible outcomes—A, B, C, D, or F—and you have an idea of the probabilities of each. In this case, the probabilities are perhaps a bit more difficult to determine and clearly depend on your willingness to expend resources (study time, money for books or tutors, etc.) to learn the material in this course. However, even here you can estimate the probabilities of the various outcomes. These probabilities are subjective, since they are formed by you and may not be the same as the true or objective probabilities of the various outcomes. (You may be more pessimistic or more optimistic than warranted.) However, as long as you think these probabilities are correct, you will act as though they are objective.

What distinguishes risk from uncertainty? Economists usually reserve the word **uncertainty** to describe a situation in which individuals cannot form probabilities for outcomes, either because they cannot identify the possible outcomes or because they cannot estimate the probabilities to assign to the outcomes. Such a situation occurs when we have no historical evidence and hence no ability to draw on past experience to help us assign probabilities to outcomes. Because of this, economists rarely analyze such situations, and examples seem rather far-fetched. Imagine trying to figure out the probability of global thermonuclear war. It is difficult to estimate this probability since, fortunately, no historical precedents exist. You might consider the probability of occurrence of world wars in general, but the very existence of nuclear

---

[1] Excerpted from *The American Heritage Dictionary of the English Language*, 3rd ed. (Boston: Houghton Mifflin, 1992).

weapons may have lessened the importance of these historical probabilities for predicting future wars, especially nuclear wars. In any case, we concern ourselves in this chapter with situations of risk, in which probabilities—at least subjective probabilities—can be assigned to the various outcomes. We will say more about the difference between subjective and objective probabilities in Chapter 12, when we introduce the concept of rational expectations.

In the following sections, we deal with situations of risk. In these situations, we can list the possible outcomes and assign a probability of occurrence to each. This allows us to formalize two concepts: risk and expected return. In financial markets, the outcomes might be various possible rates of return on a financial instrument and the expected return an appropriately defined average of these possible rates of return, an average that is weighted by the probability that each rate of return will actually occur. In this application, the concept of risk is the chance that the rate of return will differ from the expected or average return. The higher the probability that the rate of return that occurs will be far from the average return, the higher the risk. We also show that these concepts are simply special cases of two statistical concepts, expected value and variance, that we discuss next.

Expected Value

Imagine a coin toss in which you will receive $1 if the coin turns up heads but must pay $1 if it turns up tails. Each of the two possible outcomes is equally likely, which means the probability of each occurring is 1/2. The **expected value** (or **mean**) of this risky prospect is the sum of the outcomes weighted by their probabilities. Thus, for our example the expected value is

$$\text{Expected value} = \frac{1}{2}(\$1) + \frac{1}{2}(-\$1) = 0.$$

In other words, there is a probability of .5 (or 50 percent) that you will make $1 and a probability of .5 (or 50 percent) that you will lose $1. On average, you will neither make nor lose money by undertaking this risky prospect. Even though the expected value of this prospect is zero, you will never earn zero by making the bet; you will either make or lose $1.

More generally, suppose you own a risky asset. The value of the asset (x) is not certain. There is a probability p_1 that its value is x_1, a probability p_2 that its value is x_2, and so on up to a probability p_n that the value is x_n. We use p_i to denote the probabilities assigned to different values of the asset. These probabilities must sum up to 1 if we have listed all possible outcomes, since one of them must occur. Moreover, we *must* list all possible outcomes to be in a situation of risk as opposed to one of uncertainty. Using summation notation, we write this condition as

$$\sum_{i=1}^{n} p_i = p_1 + p_2 + \cdots + p_n = 1.$$

Remember, x_i denotes all the possible values of the asset and p_i denotes the corresponding probabilities, so the expected value (or mean) of this risky asset, denoted Ex, is the sum of the possible outcomes weighted by their probabilities of occurrence:

$$Ex = p_1x_1 + p_2x_2 + \cdots + p_nx_n = \sum_{i=1}^{n} p_ix_i.$$

Notice that the expected value of a risky asset collapses information about the possible value of the asset into a single number. This number measures the average value that would occur if a risky situation were played out many times (technically an infinite number of times).

Variance

When dealing with risky situations, we also want a measure of the risk: the possibility of values other than the expected value. For this we turn to the variance. In our coin-tossing example, the expected value of the risky prospect is zero; on average, you will neither make nor lose money by placing the bet. However, you will never earn exactly zero by betting $1 on the outcome of a coin flip; you will either make or lose $1. The only way you can earn zero for sure is by not placing the bet. Of course, the expected value of betting zero (i.e., not betting) is zero, since regardless of whether the coin comes up heads or tails, you earn zero:

$$\text{Expected value of not betting} = \frac{1}{2}(\$0) + \frac{1}{2}(\$0) = 0.$$

Thus, two prospects can have identical means but differ with respect to their underlying risks. Betting zero or betting $1 on a coin toss both have an expected value of zero, yet betting on the outcome of a coin toss is more risky than not betting.

A common measure of the risk of a risky prospect is its **variance** (σ^2), which is a weighted sum of the squared deviations of potential outcomes, x_i, from the expected value, Ex. The weights used are the probabilities of each outcome occurring—the p_i mentioned earlier. Thus, the variance of a risky prospect is defined as

$$\sigma^2 = p_1(x_1 - Ex)^2 + p_2(x_2 - Ex)^2 + \cdots + p_n(x_n - Ex)^2$$
$$= \sum_{i=1}^{n} [p_i(x_i - Ex)^2].$$

For example, when you bet $1 that a coin will turn up heads, $p_1 = 1/2$, $x_1 = 1$, $Ex = 0$, $p_2 = 1/2$, and $x_2 = -1$. The variance in your profit is

$$\sigma^2 = \frac{1}{2}(1 - 0)^2 + \frac{1}{2}(-1 - 0)^2 = 1.$$

In contrast, if you bet nothing, $p_1 = 1/2$, $x_1 = 0$, $Ex = 0$, $p_2 = 1/2$, and $x_2 = 0$. Now the variance is

$$\sigma^2 = \frac{1}{2}(0 - 0)^2 + \frac{1}{2}(0 - 0)^2 = 0.$$

The fact that the variance of betting \$1 is greater than the variance of betting \$0 means that betting \$1 is more risky than betting nothing.

Finally, some economists use a closely related measure of risk called the *standard deviation*. The standard deviation is simply the square root of the variance. Increases or decreases in the variance will also be increases or decreases in the standard deviation. Thus, when risk is changing, both measures tell us that risk is moving in the same direction. Hence we need look at only one of these measures; in this text, we will concentrate on the variance.

Risk Preference

Even if two bets had the same expected value and variance, not everyone would be indifferent when choosing between the two bets. Different people have different attitudes toward risk. Suppose there are two prospects, a risky one and a sure thing. Each prospect has the same expected value, but the riskier prospect has a higher variance. On average, you will earn the same amount from each. To be concrete, suppose you are offered one of two jobs in a company. Job 1 pays a salary of \$50,000 every year regardless of the company's profits that year. Job 2 pays a base salary of \$25,000 every year, plus a bonus that depends on the company's profits that year. Based on past history, these bonuses are \$0 with probability 1/4, \$25,000 with probability 1/2, and \$50,000 with probability 1/4. What is the expected value of job 1? Clearly it is \$50,000 per year. What about job 2? The expected value is \$25,000 + (1/4) × \$0 + (1/2) × \$25,000 + (1/4) × \$50,000, or \$50,000. These jobs have the same expected value, but job 2 is riskier than job 1 because it has a higher variance.

Some people will choose job 1 over job 2. These people are **risk averse:** They prefer a sure thing to a risky alternative with an identical expected value. Others will prefer job 2 to job 1. These people are **risk loving:** They prefer the risky prospect to the sure thing, even though both have identical expected values. Finally, some people will be indifferent between the two jobs. They are **risk neutral:** They differentiate between risky prospects only on the basis of expected value. A risk-neutral investor sees assets with identical expected values as equivalent, even if their variances differ.

Risk-averse individuals are willing to pay money to avoid a risky prospect. For instance, consider a person who owns a \$100,000 house. This is a risky prospect, for if the house burns down, it will be worth nothing. Most people are willing to pay several hundred dollars in fire insurance each year to avoid the risk of loss from fire. In effect, by purchasing fire insurance they are buying a sure thing: a house that is worth $100,000 regardless of whether or not it burns down. Of course, most mortgage companies require borrowers to carry fire insurance. But consider earthquake insurance. Mortgage companies often don't require earthquake insurance, and in the Los Angeles earthquake of 1994, only about 40 percent of homeowners had this coverage. Apparently there are quite a few risk-neutral or risk-loving homeowners in L.A.

Summary Exercise 9.1

You are considering two investments. Investment A (x_A) is certain to yield profits of $100. Investment B ($x_B$) will yield profits of $910 with probability .1 and $10 with probability .9. (a) What are the expected value and variance of each investment? (b) Which investment will you prefer if you are risk averse? (c) Which investment will you prefer if you are risk neutral?

Answer: (a) Since investment A is certain, its expected value is

$$Ex_A = \$100,$$

while its variance is $\sigma_A^2 = 0$. For investment B,

$$Ex_B = .1(\$910) + .9(\$10) = \$100$$

and

$$\sigma_B^2 = .1(910 - 100)^2 + .9(10 - 100)^2 = 72,900.$$

Thus, investment A has the same mean but a lower variance. (b) If you are risk averse, you will prefer a sure thing to an uncertain prospect with an identical expected value. Thus, you will prefer investment A. (c) If you are risk neutral, you will be indifferent between investment A and investment B.

VALUING RISKY FINANCIAL ASSETS

Now that you have a basic understanding of risk and the methods used to evaluate risky prospects, we examine the implications of risk for financial markets. In this section, we look at how different types of risk affect the pricing of financial instruments as well as interest rates, prices, and the yields of financial instruments such as bank loans, Treasury bills, corporate bonds, and municipal bonds.

Individuals will insist on paying less for a risky asset than for a risk-free asset for two reasons. First, a risk-free asset generally has a higher expected repayment than a risky asset. For instance, consider two bonds, one of which is certain to pay $1,000 to the holder at maturity while the other will pay $1,000 only if the issuing firm does not go bankrupt. If the probability of bankruptcy is, say, 10 percent, the expected value of the payment at maturity of the second bond is $.9 \times \$1,000 + .1 \times 0 = \$900$. The lower expected payment of the risky bond leads to a lower price (and a higher yield) than that of the risk-free bond.

Second, even if two financial assets have identical expected values, risk-averse individuals will insist on paying less for the riskier asset (the one with a higher variance) than for the less risky one. Since a lower price implies a higher interest rate (as we learned in Chapter 3, a risk-averse individual will demand a higher interest rate on riskier assets even if the expected value is identical to those on less risky assets). The difference between the interest rate on a risky asset and that on a risk-free asset is known as the *risk premium*.

Default Risk

Default risk is the risk that a borrower will fail to make the stipulated debt payments. For instance, suppose you purchase a 20-year corporate bond that has a face value of $1,000 and a coupon rate of 7 percent. The issuing corporation has promised to pay $70 each year to the bond owners and an additional $1,000 at maturity. Of course, many things can happen in 20 years; the corporation might suffer losses and be unable to make one or more of its interest payments or, even worse, be unable to pay the $1,000 face value at maturity. When the issuer of a debt instrument fails to make required payments when due, the instrument is in default.

Default risk is related to the creditworthiness of the issuer of a particular debt instrument. When the U.S. Treasury issues a Treasury bill or Treasury bond, default risk is very low; to obtain funds to meet its obligation, the federal government can collect additional tax revenue or print money.[2] For this reason, Treasury bills, Treasury bonds, and other debt instruments that are backed by the full faith and credit of the U.S. government are often referred to as *default-free* debt instruments. However, the growing federal debt may add some degree of default risk even to U.S. government–backed debt instruments, although that risk is minimal.

During the 1980s Mexico, Brazil, and other Latin American countries had difficulty meeting payment obligations on their government-issued debt. One reason for these defaults was that the debt was issued in a foreign currency, usually U.S. dollars. Since these countries were obligated to repay in U.S. dollars, they could not meet their obligation by simply printing more money. In contrast, U.S. government debt is denominated in U.S. currency, so the United States has the ability to repay its debt by printing money. Doing so would cause tremendous inflation, however, and would in effect be a de facto default, though not a default recognized as such by the courts. We discuss inflation risk later in this chapter. For now we simply note that

---

[2] Resorting to printing money to pay interest on the debt can lead to inflation, another risk that we consider later in this chapter.

the federal government's temptation to print fiat money to repay its debts is in essence a temptation to default on that debt.

Corporate bonds carry a higher default risk than U.S. government bonds. Since a firm's profits can vary significantly from year to year, the firm may lack enough funds to make required debt payments when they fall due. Obviously firms cannot print money or raise taxes to cover their deficiencies, which makes corporate bonds riskier than U.S. government bonds.

Firms in a strong financial position will have lower default risk than firms in weaker positions. Moody's and Standard and Poor's provide investors with ratings of the bonds issued by major corporations. Box 9.1 summarizes Moody's rating system. As we will see later in this chapter, low-quality bonds (junk bonds) have lower prices and higher yields than higher-quality bonds.

Bank loans also carry default risk, which varies depending on the type of loan. The typical individual who obtains a short-term consumer loan at a bank is more likely to default on the loan than, say, AT&T. To compensate the bank for the higher risk of default, this individual pays a higher interest rate than the bank charges creditworthy corporations (called the *prime rate*). Figure 9.1 illustrates this fact using the loanable funds model developed in Chapter 4. Part a shows the supply of and demand for consumer loans, and the equilibrium interest rate on consumer loans is 10 percent. Part b shows the supply of and demand for loans to the bank's more creditworthy corporations; the equilibrium interest rate—the prime interest rate—is 7 percent.

Default Risk Premium.   The difference between the 10 percent rate charged on consumer loans and the 7 percent prime rate charged to more creditworthy customers reflects a **default risk premium,** a premium a borrower must pay to compensate a lender for the risk of default. Here the default risk premium is the amount consumers pay to banks as compensation for the higher default risk on consumer loans. As we will see, however, even the most creditworthy customers pay a premium over and above the rate at which the U.S. government can obtain loanable funds.

The default risk premium applies not only to banks but also to bonds and other assets that are traded on major exchanges at a dollar price. For simplicity, we consider bonds that are identical in every respect except their default risk. Each bond is a one-year bond with a $1,000 face value and a coupon rate of 5 percent. Thus, each bond promises to pay the holder $1,050 at the end of one year (a $50 interest or coupon payment, plus $1,000 face value). We also assume individuals are risk neutral; at the end of this section, we examine the implications of risk aversion for the pricing of risky assets.

We begin by considering a default-free bond issued by the government. If the default-free interest rate (the interest rate charged to those who are known to never default on a debt obligation) is $i = 5$ percent, the price of

Inside Money

Box 9.1

What Bond Ratings Mean

There are two main sources of bond ratings: Moody's and Standard and Poor's. The accom-panying table shows Moody's ratings and their meanings.

Rating (Moody's)	Interpretation
Aaa	These bonds have the lowest risk of default.
Aa	These bonds carry a slightly higher long-term investment risk.
A	These bonds are still good investments, but they have a higher default risk.
Baa	These bonds are reliable at least in the short run, but are questionable over the long run.
Ba	These bonds have a relatively high degree of risk.
B	These bonds are considered undesirable investments due to their high degree of risk.
Caa	The issuers of these bonds are already or may soon be in default.
Ca	These bonds are often already in default; investment in such bonds would be only for speculative purposes.
C	This is the lowest rating given to bonds. The probability that these bonds will ever be considered a good investment is very low.

the government bond is simply the present value of $1,050, as we discussed in Chapter 8. Thus,

$$P_G = \frac{\$1,050}{1.05},$$

or $1,000. The price of the government bond equals the face value because the coupon rate is the same as the default-free rate of interest.

Now consider a bond issued by a corporation that has a bond rating of B. Given this rating, there is only, say, a 90 percent chance that the firm will pay its obligations in full, in which case the bondholder will receive $1,050 at the end of one year. There is a 10 percent chance that the firm will be unable to meet its debt obligations. This could mean the firm can only pay,

Figure 9.1
Default Risk Premium

Because consumers are more likely than business firms to default on their loans, consumers must pay a higher interest rate on their loans to offset this added risk. This situation is illustrated with the demand and supply curves in the consumer loan market (part a) and the prime business loan market (part b). Note that the equilibrium interest rate in the consumer loan market is 3 percent higher than the equilibrium prime interest rate. This additional 3 percent is called the *default risk premium* and represents the additional compensation banks require to loan money to consumers rather than to their more creditworthy customers such as corporations.

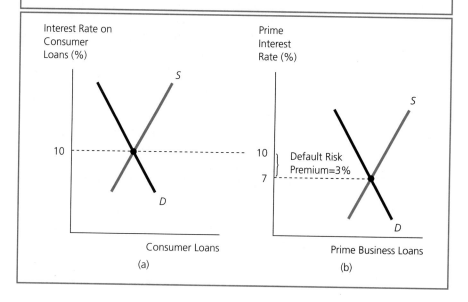

Interest Rate on Consumer Loans (%)

Prime Interest Rate (%)

Default Risk Premium=3%

Consumer Loans

Prime Business Loans

(a)

(b)

say, 50 cents on the dollar, but we will suppose it pays nothing to the bondholder in the event of default. Thus, the expected value of the payment received at the end of the year is

Expected value of payment $= .9 \,(\$1{,}050) + .1 \,(\$0) = \$945.$

Even though the bond states that $1,050 will be paid at the end of the year, the 10 percent chance of default lowers the expected value of the payment to $945.

Now suppose an investor considering the purchase of this bond wants to know how much she can pay for it and still earn the 5 percent interest rate she could earn on a default-free investment. The price this risk-neutral investor will be willing to pay for this B-rated bond is the present value of the expected payment:

$$P_B = \frac{\$945}{1.05},$$

or \$900. Notice the similarity between default-free bonds and risky bonds. However, the default risk on the B-rated corporate bond means the bond sells at a lower price than the default-free government bond does, even though both bonds promise to pay \$1,050 at the end of one year. The higher price investors are willing to pay for the government bond reflects the fact that the government will almost certainly keep its promise to repay.

The Inverse Relationship Between Bond Prices and Interest Rates Revisited.

The fact that these two bonds have different prices also implies that the interest rate for the default-free government bond will be lower than that for the risky B-rated corporate bond. To see this, consider Figure 9.2, which graphs the inverse relationship between bond prices and the interest rate. The interest rate associated with a bond price of $P_G = \$1,000$ is 5 percent; the interest rate associated with a bond price of $P_B = \$900$ is 16.7 percent. The difference between the interest rate on the B-rated corporate bond and that on the otherwise identical government bond is the default risk premium. In this case, the default risk premium is 11.7 percent. If the B-rated corporate bond does indeed meet its obligations, you will earn a return that is 11.7 percent higher than that on the government bond. Of course, since there is a 10 percent chance that the company will default, you require this premium to compensate for this risk.

Another way to look at the default risk premium associated with the B-rated corporate bond is to calculate the yield to maturity of each bond. These calculations assume both bonds do in fact meet their obligations. Recall from Chapter 8 that the yield to maturity on the government bond is the interest rate, i_G, that satisfies the condition

$$\$1,000 = \frac{\$1,050}{1 + i_G}.$$

Solving this expression for i_G reveals that the yield to maturity of the government bond is $i_G = 5$ percent—the default-free interest rate. In contrast, the yield to maturity on the B-rated corporate bond (assuming the company does not default) is

$$\$900 = \frac{\$1,050}{1 + i_B}.$$

Solving this expression for i_B reveals that the yield to maturity on the corporate bond is $i_B = 16.7$ percent.

In equilibrium, the yield to maturity on a bond will equal the market interest rate for loans issued to borrowers with similar credit risks. Figure 9.3 illustrates the market for default-free loans and for loans to companies

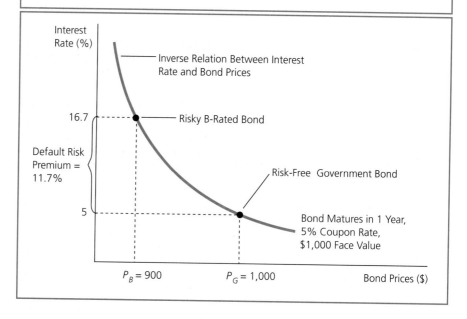

Figure 9.2
**Prices and Yields of a Government Bond and
a Low-Grade Corporate Bond**

This figure shows how two bonds with the same face value ($1,000), the same maturity (one year), and the same coupon rate (5 percent) differ in price and yield to maturity because of their differing risks of default. Each bond promises to pay $1,050 at the end of one year, but one bond is issued by a B-rated corporation and the other is a default-free bond issued by the government. If the default-free interest rate is 5 percent, the price of the government bond is $1,000 and its yield is 5 percent. In contrast, the B-rated corporate bond sells at a price of $900 and has a yield of 16.7 percent. The default risk premium on the B-rated bond is thus 11.7 percent.

with a credit rating of B (very risky loans). The market equilibrium interest rate for default-free government bonds is 5 percent. The market interest rate on loans issued to borrowers with a 10 percent chance of defaulting is 16.7 percent. The difference in the rates for default-free and risky loans reflects the default risk premium. The main reason for the default risk premium is that the supply of loanable funds shifts to the left on riskier loans. At every interest rate, the quantity of loanable funds supplied is lower on riskier loans.

The default risk premium will be lower on loans issued to borrowers less likely to default. Consider a very creditworthy corporation that has issued a Aaa-rated bond. This bond, like the earlier B-rated bond and government bond, has a face value of $1,000, matures in one year, and has a coupon rate of 5 percent. However, this firm has only a 1 percent chance of defaulting on the loan. Given this probability of default, the expected payment to the bondholder at the end of the year is

$$\text{Expected payment}_{\text{Aaa}} = .99\ (\$1{,}050) + .01\ (\$0) = \$1{,}039.50.$$

The present value of this expected payment given the 5 percent default-free interest rate is the price a risk-neutral investor would be willing to pay for the bond:

$$P_{Aaa} = \frac{\$1{,}039.50}{1.05},$$

or $990. A risk-neutral investor would pay more for this Aaa bond than for the B-rated bond, but slightly less than for a default-free government bond.

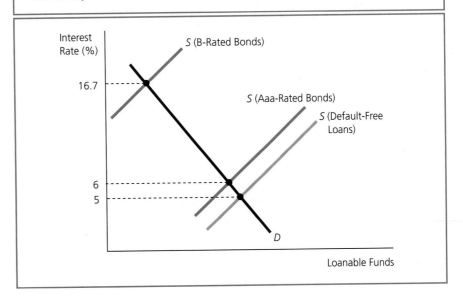

Figure 9.3
Default-Free and Risky Loans

Since the yield to maturity on a bond will equal the market rate of interest on loans issued to borrowers with similar credit risks, the default risk premium can be illustrated by the difference between the interest rate for risky loans and the interest rate for default-free loans. In this figure, the demand for risky and default-free loans is assumed to be the same for simplicity. The default-free interest rate is 5 percent, while the interest rate on B-rated bonds is 16.7 percent. The default risk premium—the difference between these two interest rates—is 11.7 percent and is the additional interest necessary to induce lenders to issue loans to risky borrowers.

Given this price, the yield to maturity if the Aaa bond does not default is

$$\$990 = \frac{\$1,050}{1 + i_{Aaa}}.$$

Solving for i_{Aaa} gives us the yield to maturity of this Aaa bond: $i_{Aaa} = .06$, or 6 percent. Thus, the less risky Aaa bond has a default risk premium of only 1 percent over the default-free government bond—a considerably lower default risk premium than the B-rated bond has. This 1 percent default risk premium is required to compensate the investor for the (small) chance that the company will default. Box 9.2 shows the interest rates on Aaa and Baa corporate bonds and on one-year Treasury bills.

Until now, our analysis of valuing risky assets assumed investors are risk neutral and care only about the expected value of a risky asset. Since a risk-averse investor prefers a sure thing to a risky prospect with an identical expected value, it follows that risk-averse investors will pay less for a risky bond than risk-neutral investors will. The lower price risk-averse investors will pay is equivalent to saying that risk-averse investors demand an even higher interest rate on risky assets. In other words, the default premiums in markets dominated by risk-averse investors will be even higher than the risk premiums required by risk-neutral investors.

One class of particularly risky bonds is the so-called junk bonds. Box 9.3 explains junk bonds and convertible bonds.

Liquidity Risk

As we saw in Chapter 2, debt instruments differ with respect to their underlying liquidity—the ease with which the owner can sell the debt instrument without loss to obtain money. Some bonds, such as federal government bonds, are widely held and easily sold in well-established secondary markets; thus, these bonds are very liquid. Other bonds, such as those issued by small companies and municipal governments, are not widely held and are less widely traded in secondary markets. We say the market for these bonds is "thin." When the secondary market for a bond is very thin, a person who wishes to sell a bond for cash could have a very difficult time. He or she may be able to do so only at a very low price or, in some cases, at no price at all.

Buying debt instruments that are not very liquid involves considerable liquidity risk. **Liquidity risk** is risk concerning the price an investor will receive if a bond or other debt instrument must be liquidated prior to maturity. As we will see in the next subsection, liquidity risk is closely related to interest rate risk, which affects the price at which a bond can be sold if liquidated prior to maturity.

While virtually all debt instruments carry some degree of liquidity risk, some are riskier than others. In general, liquidity risk is lower on debt instruments whose issuers are widely known to be creditworthy. For instance,

The Data Bank

Box 9.2

*Interest Rates on Aaa, Baa, and
U.S. Treasury Bills, 1971–1992*

The accompanying figure graphs the interest rates on one-year U.S. Treasury bills and two classes of corporate bonds, Aaa bonds and Baa bonds. Moody's assigns a rating of Aaa to bonds of the highest quality (those with the lowest degree of default risk); It assigns a rating of Baa to medium-grade bonds (bonds whose short-term prospects are adequate but whose long-term prospects are suspect). We would expect the Baa rate to exceed the Aaa rate to compensate investors for the additional risk of default on Baa bonds, and indeed this is the case. The government bond rate is generally below even the Aaa bond rate.

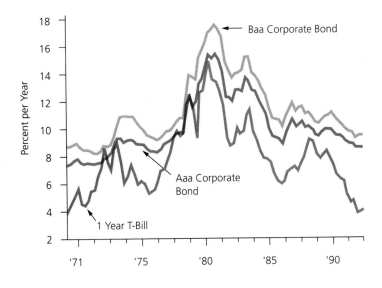

Source: Citibase electronic database.

U.S. government bonds tend to have relatively little liquidity risk, since millions of investors are familiar with their terms and the creditworthiness of the U.S. government. In contrast, bonds issued by a small town or a small company are not very liquid. Very few investors are familiar with the issuers' ability to repay the debt, and it is difficult to determine the specific terms on

Inside Money

Box 9.3

*What Are Junk Bonds and
Convertible Bonds?*

Junk bonds and convertible bonds are two very different things. A *junk bond* is a corporate bond that has a very low rating (or perhaps no rating at all). This, of course, implies that the market associates a very high element of risk with these bonds. In exchange for the high degree of risk, a junk bond will offer a high interest rate. Junk bonds became popular in the 1980s, when corporations issued these bonds and used the proceeds to purchase other companies. Thus, junk bonds were instrumental in the takeovers and mergers of that decade.

A *convertible bond* gives the bondholder the option to have the loan repaid with stock instead of cash. The date on which the bondholder can exercise this option and the number of shares of stock for which each bond can be exchanged are specified when the bond is issued. Convertible bonds are not necessarily junk bonds, nor are junk bonds always convertible bonds.

the bonds. Thus, it is more difficult for buyers and sellers to get together and agree on a price.

The more liquid an asset, the more attractive it is to buyers. Consider part a of Figure 9.4, which illustrates the supply of and demand for loanable funds to large U.S. corporations. Since corporate bonds are relatively liquid, the equilibrium interest rate is 6 percent. Part b of Figure 9.4 illustrates the supply of and demand for loanable funds to small corporations. Since bonds issued by small corporations are less liquid than those issued by larger ones, the equilibrium interest rate must be higher, even ignoring differences in default risk. In this case, the interest rate on the less liquid bonds is 8 percent. The difference in these rates reflects the **liquidity premium**—the additional interest rate lenders must receive as compensation for the liquidity risk.

Since a decrease in liquidity leads to a reduction in the supply of loanable funds, corporations whose bonds are not listed (or traded) on the secondary market for bonds (such as the New York Bond Exchange) can be adversely affected. To see this, consider part a of Figure 9.5, which illustrates the demand for and supply of loanable funds to a firm. When the firm's bonds are listed on a major exchange, equilibrium is at point *A,* and the interest rate the firm must pay for loanable funds is 8 percent. When the firm's bonds are not traded in the secondary bond market, their liquidity decreases, and lenders are less willing to lend to this firm. This decrease in liquidity shifts the supply of loanable funds to the left. The new equilibrium is at point *B*

Figure 9.4
Liquidity Premium

The more liquid an asset, the lower the interest rate needed to compensate lenders for their funds. In this figure, loans to large corporations (part a) are more liquid than loans to corporations (part b). Consequently, the equilibrium interest rate on loans to large corporations is 2 percent lower than that to small businesses because small-business loans are less liquid than corporate loans. This 2 percent liquidity premium is the additional interest rate lenders must receive as compensation for holding the less liquid asset.

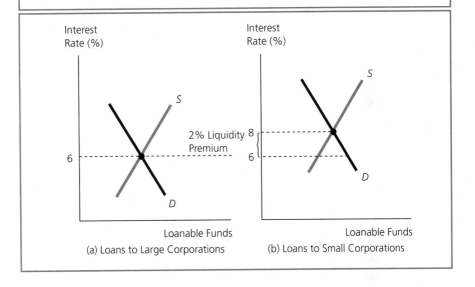

(a) Loans to Large Corporations   (b) Loans to Small Corporations

in Figure 9.5, where the interest rate is 12 percent. When the firm seeks additional funds, it will have to pay a higher interest rate.

Part b of Figure 9.5 illustrates the impact of the decrease in liquidity on bond prices (and thus on owners of existing bonds). When the firm is listed on the bond exchange, the interest rate of 8 percent translates into a bond price of $1,000. When the firm is not listed, the rise in the interest rate to 12 percent leads to a reduction in the price of an existing bond to $900. The value of an investor's loan portfolio will fall due to the decrease in liquidity of the bonds.

Interest Rate Risk and Call Risk

Variability in interest rates leads bond prices to fluctuate, creating risk to the value of an investor's bond holdings. This **interest rate risk**—the risk of a change in the overall level of interest rates—leads to greater liquidity risk. Interest rate risk also imposes an additional source of risk on bonds

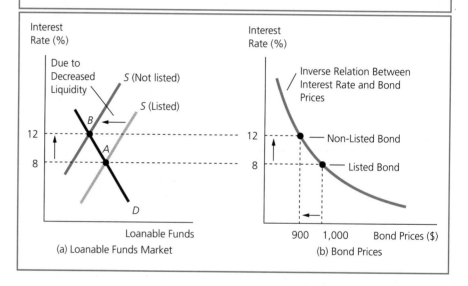

Figure 9.5

Prices and Yields for Bonds Listed and Bonds Not Listed on the Secondary Bond Market

A decrease in the liquidity of an asset will lower that asset's price and raise the interest rate necessary to compensate lenders who hold the asset. Such a situation occurs when a corporation's bonds are not listed on (not traded in) the secondary bond market. Part a shows the loanable funds market for such a corporation, and part b indicates the relationship between the bond's interest rate and the price. The original interest rate for the listed bond is 8 percent at point A in part a. This corresponds to a price for the listed bond of $1,000 in part b. When the bond is not listed, it thus becomes less liquid, the supply of loanable funds decreases, and equilibrium moves to point B in part a. This leads to a higher interest rate of 12 percent and a lower bond price of $900.

with call features. In particular, **callable bonds** are subject to the risk that the issuer will call the bond, that is, pay off the bond's face value prior to maturity. This happens when a bond is issued with a high coupon rate and the overall level of interest rates then declines, making it profitable for the bond issuer to call in the old bonds and reissue them with a lower coupon rate. In this case, the owner receives the face value earlier than anticipated, but will not receive the same amount in coupon payments that he or she would have received had the bond not been called.

If interest rates did not fluctuate, this **call risk** would not be a problem for investors. Regardless of when the bonds were paid off, the proceeds could be used to purchase bonds with identical coupon payments from some other issuer. Unfortunately, if the interest rate fell after the callable bond was purchased, it would not be possible to obtain a new bond that yielded as much as the old bonds. Let us see why this is the case.

Suppose you purchase a one-year bond with a coupon rate of 8 percent and a face value of $1,000. For simplicity, assume there is no default risk and this bond is not callable. If the market interest rate is 8 percent, the price of this bond is

$$P_B = \frac{\$80 + \$1,000}{1 + .08} = \$1,000.$$

Since the market interest rate of 8 percent equals the coupon rate, the yield to maturity of this bond is also 8 percent.

Now suppose that immediately after you purchase the bond, the interest rate drops to 4 percent. Since this bond is not callable, the interest rate change does not affect your 8 percent coupon payment; you will still receive an 8 percent yield to maturity on your initial investment despite the fall of the market rate to 4 percent. Notice, however, that investors who want to purchase the bond from you after the decline in the interest rate will be willing to pay

$$P_B = \frac{\$80 + \$1,000}{1 + .04} = \$1,038.46. \tag{9.1}$$

In effect, by purchasing the bond prior to the decline in the interest rate, you were able to buy the bond for $38.46 less than those who purchase this bond today. This is why your yield is still 8 percent when the market rate has fallen to 4 percent. Alternatively put, your bond has increased in value from $1,000 to $1,038.46 due to the decline in the interest rate.

Notice that the price change is even greater on bonds with longer times to maturity. Suppose you purchase a two-year bond with a coupon rate of 8 percent and a face value of $1,000. This bond will pay you $80 in one year and $1,080 in two years (the $80 in interest from year 2, plus the principal). When the market interest rate is also 8 percent, the price of this bond is

$$P_B = \frac{\$80}{1 + .08} + \frac{\$1,080}{(1 + .08)^2} = \$1,000.$$

Now what happens if immediately after you purchase this bond, the market interest rate drops to 4 percent? The price of the bond immediately changes to

$$P_B = \frac{\$80}{(1 + .04)} + \frac{\$1,080}{(1 + .04)^2} = \$1,075.44.$$

Thus, the price of the two-year bond increased by $75.44, whereas the price of the one-year bond increased by only $38.46. This difference is due to the different times to maturity. With the one-year bond, the higher interest rate is locked in only for one year, while the two-year bond locks in the higher interest rate for two years.

The story differs if interest rates rise right after you purchase the bond. To see why, suppose the interest rate rises to 12 percent immediately after you purchase a one-year bond. In this case, your bond will still yield 8 percent. However, when the interest rate is 12 percent, similar bonds now sell for

$$P_B = \frac{\$80 + \$1,000}{1 + .12} = \$964.29. \tag{9.2}$$

Your bond has declined in value due to the rise in interest rates.

This example illustrates the interest rate risk associated with purchasing a bond: If interest rates rise, your bond will fall in value (from $1,000 when the interest rate is 8 percent to $964.29 when it rises to 12 percent). If you liquidate your bond right after purchasing it, you will lose a hefty $35.71— nearly 4 percent of your initial $1,000 investment.

Capital Gains and Interest Income on a Bond. The preceding examples highlight a general feature of investing in the bond market. The owner of a bond actually receives income from two sources. One source is the interest income on the bond at the time of purchase. The other source is what is called the **capital gain.** The capital gain is the change in the price relative to the purchase price. In our example of the decline in the market interest rate, the initial coupon rate and the market interest rate were both 8 percent. An investor who purchased the one-year bond received an 8 percent yield to maturity. After the market interest rate fell to 4 percent, the price of the bond rose by $38.46. This is the capital gain on the bond created by the fall in the market interest rate, and the capital gain is itself a return over and above the 8 percent yield. The capital gain is a return of $38.46 on a purchase price of $1,000, or $38.46/$1,000 = 3.8 percent. The total return is the sum of the coupon interest rate and the capital gain, or

$$\text{Total return} = 8\% + 3.8\% = 11.8\%.$$

How does this scenario change if the bond has a call feature? If the interest rate rises from 8 to 12 percent and the bond is called, you will be in great shape; you will receive $1,000 (but no coupon payment, since the bond is paid off early). This $1,000 will be more than enough to let you purchase a bond from another firm. In fact, equation 9.2 reveals that when the interest rate rises to 12 percent, you can purchase a similar bond at $964.29 and earn a yield to maturity of 12 percent. You even have $35.71 left over! In short, if interest rates rise and your bond is called, you will do quite well.

On the other hand, if the market interest rate falls to 4 percent, the $1,000 you receive when the bond is called will not be enough to let you purchase another bond. Equation 9.1 reveals that at a 4 percent market interest rate, similar bonds are selling for $1,038.46—more than the $1,000 you are paid when your bond is called. Even if you scrape up an extra $38.46 to buy a bond, the yield to maturity will be only 4 percent—considerably lower than what you would have earned had your bond not been called.

This example might tempt you to conclude that you could gain or lose by purchasing this callable bond depending on whether interest rates are higher or lower when it is called. This is incorrect; you can only lose by purchasing this bond. To see why, notice that when the interest rate rises from 8 to 12 percent, the issuing company has no incentive to call your bond and pay you $1,000 for it. Instead it can buy back the bond in the secondary market at a much lower price of $964.29. In effect, since you are providing the firm with loanable funds at a lower rate (8 percent) than the current market rate (12 percent), it has no incentive to exercise the call feature!

In contrast, if interest rates fall to 4 percent, the firm will want to call your bond. The firm can issue a new bond—one identical to the bond you purchased—and receive $1,038.46 for it. The firm can use the proceeds of this bond to pay you $1,000 and call the bond. In the process, the firm gains $38.46 in immediate cash and now pays the lower market rate of 4 percent instead of the 8 percent it was paying you. Thus, the issuer will call a bond only when doing so is to your disadvantage; you are a victim of adverse selection.

Of course, investors in financial markets recognize this problem. As a result, they pay lower prices for callable bonds than for noncallable ones. The lower price compensates investors for the additional risk that the bond will be called. Figure 9.6 illustrates this principle using the inverse relationship between interest rates and bond prices. Point A represents a bond that is not callable, and point B represents a bond with a call feature. Since callable bonds sell at lower prices than noncallable ones, the interest rate on callable bonds (i_C) is higher than that on noncallable bonds (i_N). The difference between these two interest rates is the **call premium**—the additional yield purchasers of callable bonds must receive to be willing to expose themselves to call risk.

The Inflation Premium and Inflation Risk

When a lender provides current funds to a borrower, the borrower promises to pay back principal and interest in the future. Since inflation erodes the purchasing power of money, a dollar paid back in the future does not purchase the same real quantity of goods as a dollar loaned to the borrower today.

Because investors recognize the impact of inflation on the real value of the interest receipts they earn on loans, they require a premium to cover their expectation of inflation. This **inflation premium** can be seen in the Fisher equation we discussed in Chapter 3. To recap that discussion, suppose r is the interest rate that would be charged in the absence of any inflation; this is known as the *real interest rate*. If i is the nominal interest rate (the

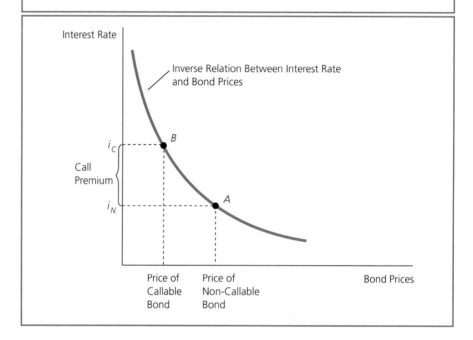

Figure 9.6
Call Premium

Some bonds give the issuer the option to pay off the bond before it reaches maturity. As a result, investors are willing to pay a lower price for callable bonds than for noncallable ones. The lower price compensates investors for the additional risk that the bond will be called if the interest rate falls. In this figure, the yield on a callable bond (i_C) is higher than that on a noncallable bond (i_N). This difference in interest rates on callable and noncallable bonds is the call premium—the additional yield purchasers of callable bonds must obtain to be willing to expose themselves to call risk.

interest rate stated in the loan contract) and π^e is the expected rate of inflation, then, by the Fisher equation we have

$$i = r + \pi^e.$$

Thus, the nominal (or stated) interest rate on a loan equals the real interest rate plus the expected rate of inflation. The higher the expected rate of inflation, the higher the nominal interest rate.

In addition to the inflation premium (or Fisher premium) due to expected inflation, there is an inflation risk premium. **Inflation risk** is the risk that the actual inflation rate will differ from the expected inflation rate. If the inflation rate is higher than expected, the real interest rate will be lower than expected. Recall that in Chapter 3 we distinguished between the ex ante and ex post real interest rates. The ex ante real interest rate is the nominal interest rate minus the expected inflation rate, while the ex post real interest rate is the nominal interest rate minus the actual inflation rate. When the actual inflation rate is higher than expected, the ex post real interest rate is lower than the ex ante real interest rate.

For example, suppose the expected inflation rate is 2 percent and the nominal interest rate on your mortgage loan is 7 percent. You expect the inflation rate to stay at 2 percent, and the nominal interest rate on your mortgage is fixed. The ex ante real interest rate on your mortgage loan is 5 percent. What happens if the actual inflation falls to 0 percent? In this case, the ex post or actual real interest rate on your mortgage loan is 7 percent, a higher rate than you intended to pay. You, the borrower, are worse off. However, if the actual inflation rate rises to 6 percent, the actual or ex post real interest rate on your mortgage loan will be 1 percent, a lower rate than you expected to pay. You are better off, whereas the lender is worse off.

Both borrowers and lenders face inflation risk. Borrowers benefit from unexpected increases in the inflation rate but are harmed by unexpected decreases, while lenders benefit from unexpected decreases but are harmed by unexpected increases. If risk averse, both will require an inflation risk premium when they borrow or lend funds.

Tax Risk

Finally, market interest rates and bond prices are affected by **tax risk**—the risk of changes in the tax treatment of interest income. In the United States, interest income on corporate and government bonds is subject to personal income tax. However, many municipal bonds are issued under a federal law that exempts interest earnings from federal income taxation. This allows municipalities to charge a lower interest rate and still give investors the same aftertax interest rate as other bonds whose interest is subject to federal taxation.

For example, suppose you are in the 38 percent tax bracket; out of each additional dollar you earn in interest income, you must pay 38 cents to the federal government. You have $10,000 to invest for one year and must choose between a corporate bond with a yield to maturity of 9 percent and a municipal bond with a yield to maturity of 6 percent. Which bond should you purchase?

Assume for simplicity that both bonds are free of default risk and the only difference between the bonds is the tax treatment of interest income. Since the interest received on the municipal bond is exempt from federal taxes, the aftertax yield on such a bond is simply the 6 percent nominal yield. For bonds with taxable interest, the aftertax yield is the nominal yield times $(1 - \text{Marginal tax rate})$. Since you must pay taxes on the income you receive from the corporate bond, the aftertax yield is $(.09)(1 - .38) =$

.0558, or 5.58 percent. The municipal bond pays a 6 percent yield before and after taxes, so you will earn a higher aftertax yield by purchasing the municipal bond.

Because changes in tax rates on interest income affect the aftertax return from an investment, the risk of future changes in tax policy indirectly leads to interest rate risk. As we already saw, this results in reduced prices for financial assets and higher market interest rates. However, since the interest income on municipal bonds is exempt from federal taxes, the prices of municipal bonds often rise during periods of increased uncertainty about federal tax policy.

One particularly interesting test of the impact of risk on interest rates is how the danger of war affects interest rates. Box 9.4 compares the interest rates on bonds of several European countries just prior to and after Germany's invasion of Poland at the start of World War II.

Summary Exercise 9.2

(a) National Trash Collection has $10 million in outstanding bonds that will mature in one year. Each bond has a coupon rate of 15 percent on its face value of $1,000, and the current default-free interest rate is 5 percent. A recent report reveals there is a 90 percent chance National Trash Collection will go bankrupt by year end. If this happens, the firm will be unable to make interest payments and will be able to pay only 10 cents on the dollar of the face value of its outstanding debt. What price would you expect its bonds to trade for after this announcement? (b) NewCorp, a relatively young company, has just had its bonds listed on the New York Bond Exchange. Your friend owns some of the firm's outstanding bonds and asks you what impact the listing will have on the value of her bonds. How do you respond? Explain your answer graphically.

Answer: (a) National Trash Collection is scheduled to pay $1,150 in one year ($150 in coupon payments, plus $1,000 in face value). But there is a 90 percent chance bondholders will receive no coupon payment and only 10 cents on the dollar of face value, or $100. Thus, the expected payment by National Trash Collection in one year is

$$.9(\$100) + .1(\$1,150) = \$205.$$

The present value of this expected payment given the default-free interest rate of 5 percent is

$$\text{Present value of expected payment} = \frac{\$205}{1 + .05} = \$195.24.$$

Thus, risk-neutral investors would pay $195.24 for this bond, and risk-averse investors would be willing to pay even less.

International Banking

Box 9.4

The Beginning of World War II and Interest Rates

History reveals that political events can affect yields and prices of financial assets. On September 1, 1939, Germany invaded Poland, leading quickly to declarations of war by France and Britain. While not totally unexpected, the exact timing of the invasion was a military secret, and diplomats hoped until the end to avoid the coming global conflagration. How did financial markets react to the outbreak of World War II? To find out, we gathered data on interest rates in London for bonds from countries in Europe and elsewhere for the week ending August 23, 1939, and again for the week ending September 27, 1939. These figures are reported in the accompanying table.

Type of Bond	Price (British Pounds)		Yield	
	Aug. 23, 1939	*Sept. 27, 1939*	*Aug. 23, 1939*	*Sept. 27, 1939*
British Consol 2.5%	63.5	62.0	6.2%	6.5%
British victory bonds 4%	103.0	102.0	3.7	3.8
Argentinean 4.5%	76.0	75.0	7.8	8.0
Belgian 4%	76.5	52.5	7.5	14.5
Danish 3%	96.5	95.0	3.2	3.3

The price of Belgian bonds fell from 76.5 to 52.5 pounds sterling in one month, and the corresponding yield increased from 7.5 to 14.5 percent. This reflected British investors' fears for the fate of Belgium in a continental war with Germany. If Germany invaded Belgium, the Belgian bonds would not be repaid. The higher yields following the invasion of Poland thus reflected a higher default premium on Belgian bonds.

Meanwhile investors appeared more sanguine about the fates of other countries. Danish bonds barely budged, with a 1.5 pound sterling decline in price and a yield increase of from 3.2 to 3.3 percent. Interestingly, Denmark was not directly involved in the initial hostilities on the continent. British bonds also changed very little: The yield on consol bonds (perpetuities) increased from 6.2 to 6.5 percent, and the yield on victory bonds rose from 3.7 to 3.8 percent. Argentinean bonds were equally stable.

_____

Source: The Economist, August 26, 1939, p. 428, and September 30, 1939, p. 624.

(b) NewCorp's bonds are now more liquid. This increases the willingness of lenders to loan funds to NewCorp, which in turn increases the supply of loanable funds to NewCorp from S^0 to S^1 in part a. This reduces the interest rate at which NewCorp can borrow from i_0 to i_1. Part b shows the inverse relationship between the interest rate and bond prices. The decline in the interest rate from i_0 to i_1 leads to an increase in the price of NewCorp's bonds from P_0 to P_1. Thus, your friend will have a more valuable bond portfolio.

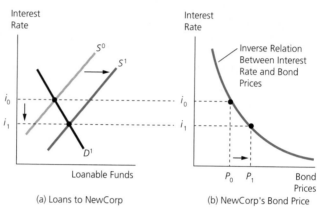

(a) Loans to NewCorp   (b) NewCorp's Bond Price

MINIMIZING FINANCIAL RISK

Having seen in the previous section the many risks inherent in financial markets, you may wonder why investors participate in them at all. One reason, of course, is the potential to earn income. Another is that investors can take steps to mitigate some of the risk. In this section, we examine some of those steps. In particular, we describe three methods: (1) diversification, (2) futures markets, and (3) options markets. The only way to eliminate *all* financial risk is to forgo participation in financial markets. This, however, is not what investors have in mind when they seek to minimize risk; after all, nothing ventured, nothing gained. Instead they wish to minimize the risk associated with obtaining any given levels of return on their investments.

For instance, suppose two assets have identical expected returns but different variances in returns (risk). If an investor can choose only one of these two investments, choosing the one with the lower variance will minimize the risk of obtaining a given level of return. As we will see next, however, it is not always in an investor's best interest to choose to make a single investment. An investor may be better able to reduce financial risk by making several investments simultaneously.

Diversification

Diversification means spreading your investment dollars over two or more assets; it is the investment analogue of not putting all your eggs in one basket. To reduce risk, you should make diversification a guiding principle behind your portfolio selection; that is, you should take into account how your choice of investment options will influence the riskiness of your portfolio.

To see how diversification can reduce financial risk, suppose you have $100 to invest and are considering two investment opportunities. The first option is to invest your entire $100 in a budget hotel chain. The risk lies in your not knowing how much profit this investment will earn. Suppose that during economic booms, budget hotels lose business to luxury hotels; your profit from investing in the budget hotel will be only $2. During recessions, however, budget hotels do much better; the $100 investment in a budget hotel will yield a profit of $10. If a recession and an economic boom are equally likely, your $100 investment will yield an expected profit of

$$\text{Expected profit from budget hotel} = .5(\$2) + .5(\$10) = \$6.$$

The variance in profits if you invest in the budget hotel is

$$\sigma^2_{\text{budget hotel}} = .5(2 - 6)^2 + .5(10 - 6)^2 = 16.$$

The first row of Table 9.1 summarizes this information.

The second option is to invest your entire $100 in a luxury hotel chain. This investment does better during economic booms, when your $100 investment will net you $10 in profits, whereas you can earn only $2 during a recession. Given the 50-50 chance of a boom or a recession, your $100 investment in a luxury hotel will yield an expected profit of

$$\text{Expected profit from luxury hotel} = .5(\$10) + .5(\$2) = \$6.$$

The variance in profits if you invest in the luxury hotel is

$$\sigma^2_{\text{luxury hotel}} = .5(10 - 6)^2 + .5(2 - 6)^2 = 16.$$

The second row of Table 9.1 summarizes this information.

Notice in Table 9.1 that by investing your entire $100 in either a budget hotel or a luxury hotel, you will earn the same expected profits of $6, which represents a 6 percent expected return ($6/$100 = .06). Notice too that the $100 investment in a budget hotel has exactly the same variance in profits as the investment in a luxury hotel. From the standpoint of risk and return, these two investments are identical. There is one important difference, however. The investment in a budget hotel will yield low profits during an economic boom but higher profits during a recession. In contrast, the luxury hotel will do better during booms than during recessions. As we will see, this difference in the investments gives rise to the benefits of diversifying.

	Table 9.1			
	Diversifying Risk			

This table illustrates the benefits of diversifying an investment portfolio. By sinking your entire $100 investment in either a budget hotel or a luxury hotel, you will make either $2 or $10 in profits. By investing $50 in both projects, you guarantee profits of $6.

Investment	**Profit During Economic Boom (Probability = 50%)**	**Profit During Recession (Probability = 50%)**	**Expected Profit**	**Variance in Profit**
$100 investment in budget hotel	$2	$10	$6	$16
$100 investment in luxury hotel	10	2	6	16
$50 investment in budget hotel and $50 investment in luxury hotel	6	6	6	0

Suppose you invested half of your $100 in the budget hotel and half in the luxury hotel. Your total investment is now diversified. During a boom you will earn $1 from the budget hotel, but you will also receive $5 from the luxury hotel. This amounts to total profits of $6 during an economic boom. During a recession, your investment in the budget hotel will yield $5 in profits, but your investment in the luxury hotel will net you only $1.

The third row of Table 9.1 summarizes the result of your diversified investment. Regardless of whether a boom or a recession occurs, your profits if you diversify will be $6 and the variance in those profits will be zero. By diversifying you have completely eliminated the risk associated with booms and recessions. Moreover, you have done so without lowering your expected profits. This example demonstrates the benefits to investors of owning a portfolio of different financial assets.

In reality, of course, it is generally not possible to completely eliminate risk by diversifying. As we saw in the previous section, real-world investments involve many types of risk, not simply the risk of a boom or a recession. Some risks are not diversifiable. To diversify, you must be able to purchase two or more securities whose individual returns move differently in response to a risky event. Some risks make the returns on all securities move in the same direction. As an extreme example, there is no way to diversify your portfolio against the effect of the sun going supernova and destroying all life on earth. Less extreme examples might be the risk of nuclear war or the risk of political insurrection (although you could keep some assets overseas).

Diversifying is not the only way to reduce financial risk. Investors may also use futures markets or options markets.

Futures Markets

A **futures contract** is a deal made now to take place at a specified future date at a price and quantity specified today. Futures contracts are traded in the **futures market.** We present a simple example that illustrates how futures markets reduce risk for buyers and sellers of assets.

Suppose Exxon wishes to expand its refinery this year so that it can produce more gasoline next year. The expansion project will be profitable only if Exxon can obtain a supply of oil for $20 per barrel next year. Given that the firm does not know what the price of oil will be next year, it decides not to make the investment. Furthermore, suppose the owner of an oil lease is considering installing additional wells today to increase next year's oil production. The new wells will be profitable only if the price of oil is at least $20 per barrel next year. Due to uncertainty about what price oil will be in one year, the lease owner decides not to invest in additional wells today.

This example reveals that uncertainty about future oil prices can keep both suppliers and demanders of oil from making investments today. Futures contracts, however, can eliminate the uncertainty about future oil prices, thus allowing both parties to profitably engage in investment activities today. If the two firms wrote a contract that specified Exxon's refinery would purchase, say, 5 billion barrels of oil from the owner of the oil lease in one year at a price of $20 per barrel, the two firms would eliminate some of the uncertainty about the price at which they can buy (and sell) oil in one year. The contracted price ensures that both parties will find it profitable to make their investments, and the contract enhances the investment by reducing uncertainty about future prices.

Futures contracts are traded in major markets, including the Chicago Board of Trade (CBOT), the Chicago Mercantile Exchange (CME), the International Monetary Market (IMM) in Chicago, the Commodities Exchange (COMEX) in New York, and the New York Futures Exchange (NYFE). Well-established futures markets exist not only for oil futures but also for many commodities and assets ranging from hog bellies to financial instruments (including certificates of deposit, Treasury bills, and Treasury bonds).

In addition to stock price listings, major newspapers print listings of future contracts. Box 9.5 gives an example of a futures contract listed in the *Wall Street Journal.* Financial futures contracts are similar to commodity

Inside Money

Box 9.5

How to Read Information on
Futures Markets in the Wall Street Journal

Information on futures markets is regularly reported in the *Wall Street Journal.* Consider the information presented in the February 8, 1994, edition, which reported prices for Feb. 7, 1994. In the table called *Futures Prices,* look at the first

item listed, corn. Written in parentheses next to *Corn* is *CBT,* which stands for the Chicago Board of Trade, the exchange on which this commodity trades. Next comes *5,000 bu.;* this

Continued on p. 299

FUTURES PRICES

Monday, February 7, 1994.
Open Interest Reflects Previous Trading Day.

	Open	High	Low	Settle	Change	Lifetime High	Low	Open Interest
Mar	77.60	77.80	75.30	75.60	− 1.63	78.36	55.62	18,557
May	77.65	77.75	75.80	76.00	− 1.55	77.75	57.47	15,464
July	77.84	77.94	76.00	76.36	− 1.29	77.94	58.30	9,555
Oct	72.15	72.25	71.50	71.55	− .70	72.25	59.81	1,999
Dec	69.70	69.75	68.85	69.08	− .71	69.99	59.48	6,811
Mr95	70.45	70.45	69.95	69.77	− .68	70.45	64.00	202

Est vol 13,500; vol Fri 9,027; open int 57,663, −454.

ORANGE JUICE (CTN)—15,000 lbs.; cents per lb.

	Open	High	Low	Settle	Change	Lifetime High	Low	Open Interest
Mar	104.00	104.50	103.20	103.30	....	134.25	84.50	10,588
May	107.00	107.10	106.15	106.15	....	134.50	89.00	3,709
July	109.50	109.80	109.45	109.15	+ .15	135.00	106.00	1,526
Sept	....	....		111.15	+ .15	133.65	107.50	830
Nov	....	....		113.15	+ .15	134.00	108.00	439
Ja95	....	....		115.15	+ .15	132.00	103.50	529

Est vol 1,400; vol Fri 1,500; open int 17,743, +435.

METALS AND PETROLEUM

COPPER-HIGH (CMX)—25,000 lbs.; cents per lb.

	Open	High	Low	Settle	Change	Lifetime High	Low	Open Interest
Feb	88.10	89.40	88.10	89.40	+ .25	99.20	73.00	514
Mar	88.40	89.40	87.85	89.30	+ .30	107.50	73.00	35,315
Apr				88.65	+ .45	90.10	74.50	782
May	87.70	88.55	87.20	88.55	+ .45	102.20	73.60	13,902
June	87.70	87.70	87.70	88.65	+ .55	89.50	74.10	847
July	87.90	88.70	87.30	88.70	+ .60	102.95	74.20	6,598
Aug	87.90	87.90	87.90	88.80	+ .60	88.70	75.30	380
Sept	87.70	87.90	87.70	88.85	+ .60	103.30	74.90	3,544
Oct	88.10	88.10	88.10	89.00	+ .55	88.30	75.20	138
Nov	88.00	88.30	88.00	89.15	+ .55	88.30	77.75	165
Dec	88.20	88.40	88.00	89.25	+ .50	101.90	75.75	3,460
Mr95	88.50	88.90	88.50	89.55	+ .50	89.70	76.30	1,143
May	89.40	89.40	89.40	89.65	+ .50	89.40	76.85	333
July	89.90	89.90	89.90	89.75	+ .50	89.90	78.00	225
Sept	90.30	90.30	90.30	89.85	+ .50	90.30	79.10	125

Est vol 6,700; vol Fri 14,213; open int 67,558, +89.

GOLD (CMX)—100 troy oz.; $ per troy oz.

	Open	High	Low	Settle	Change	Lifetime High	Low	Open Interest
Feb	382.50	383.70	379.00	378.90	− 7.70	415.70	333.80	1,073
Mar	386.30	384.30	384.30	379.40	− 7.70	398.30	376.50	13
Apr	385.80	386.50	380.50	380.70	− 7.60	418.50	335.20	67,609
June	387.50	388.60	382.50	382.70	− 7.60	417.20	339.40	29,093
Aug	389.30	389.60	385.50	384.80	− 7.60	415.00	341.50	5,016
Oct	392.10	392.30	391.80	387.10	− 7.50	417.00	344.00	4,063
Dec	393.50	394.50	389.50	389.40	− 7.50	426.50	343.00	13,153
Fb95	....	....		391.90	− 7.40	411.00	363.50	2,393
Apr	....	....		394.30	− 7.40	425.00	385.50	3,015
June	402.00	402.00	400.00	396.70	− 7.40	430.00	351.00	3,872
Aug	....	....		399.20	− 7.40	412.50	380.50	463
Oct	....	....		401.90	− 7.30	413.30	410.20	159
Dec	407.00	410.00	405.00	404.70	− 7.20	439.50	358.00	2,601
Ju96	....	....		413.40	− 7.00	447.00	370.90	830

GRAINS AND OILSEEDS

CORN (CBT) 5,000 bu.; cents per bu.

	Open	High	Low	Settle	Change	Lifetime High	Low	Open Interest
Mar	287½	292	287¼	291½	+ 3	311¾	232¾	91,682
May	293	297¼	292¾	296¾	+ 2¾	316¼	238½	94,345
July	293¾	298½	293¾	298	+ 2¾	316½	241	80,874
Sept	278¾	282	278¾	281½	+ 2	292¼	240½	17,692
Dec	263½	266	263½	265½	+ 1½	273¾	236½	45,018
Mr95	270	272¼	270	271½	+ 1½	279½	253½	2,934
May	275	275	275	275	+ 1½	282	273	263
July	275	276½	275	276½	+ 1½	282½	274¼	585

Est vol 38,000; vol Fri 40,434; open int 333,464, +584.

OATS (CBT) 5,000 bu.; cents per bu.

	Open	High	Low	Settle	Change	Lifetime High	Low	Open Interest
Mar	129¼	130½	129¼	129¾	....	163½	129	11,759
May	134¼	135¾	134	134¾	....	164	134	5,769
July	137	139	137	138½	+ ½	161¼	137¾	1,729
Sept	143	143	142¼	142¼	+ ½	154½	141	301
Dec	145½	145½	145½	145¾	+ ¼	157¼	143	419

Est vol 1,000; vol Fri 634; open int 19,978, +25.

SOYBEANS (CBT) 5,000 bu.; cents per bu.

	Open	High	Low	Settle	Change	Lifetime High	Low	Open Interest
Mar	573	678	670½	673¾	− ¾	754	589¾	59,318
May	677½	682½	675	677¾	− 1¾	751	592½	43,534
July	679	684	676½	679¼	− 1½	750	594½	35,226
Aug	669½	675	669½	671	− 1¾	735	628	6,792
Sept	651½	655	651	651¼	− 3¼	689¼	617	3,769
Nov	636½	640¼	635	635½	− 2½	665¾	581½	19,388
Ja95	642	644¾	642	641½	− 1½	670	618½	1,526
Mar	....	....		650½	+ 2	673	642	297
July	....	....		651¼	+ 1¾	672	642½	215
Nov	613	616	613	617	+ 1	636	613	881

Est vol 43,000; vol Fri 54,86; open int 170,946, −1,145.

SOYBEAN MEAL (CBT) 100 tons; $ per ton.

	Open	High	Low	Settle	Change	Lifetime High	Low	Open Interest
Mar	194.00	196.20	193.70	194.90	+ .60	237.50	185.20	32,879
May	193.90	196.10	193.80	194.70	+ .10	232.00	185.50	20,062
July	194.20	196.00	193.90	194.80	....	230.00	193.00	17,510
Aug	192.90	194.20	192.90	193.00	+ .40	225.00	191.50	7,051
Sept	190.20	192.00	190.20	190.90	+ .10	210.00	189.30	4,027
Oct	189.00	190.00	189.00	189.50	+ .50	206.00	187.10	2,186
Dec	187.80	189.60	187.80	188.30	+ .20	209.00	185.90	6,143
Ja95	190.00	190.00	189.00	189.00	+ .70	200.00	186.50	581

Est vol 14,000; vol Fri 15,101; open int 90,439, −746.

SOYBEAN OIL (CBT) 60,000 lbs.; cents per lb.

	Open	High	Low	Settle	Change	Lifetime High	Low	Open Interest
Mar	28.10	28.24	27.98	28.09	− .06	30.75	21.13	29,306
May	28.02	28.18	27.95	28.03	− .08	30.45	21.30	25,104
July	27.80	27.95	27.75	27.84	− .08	29.70	21.55	18,065

Continued from p. 298

tells the units in which corn trades (5,000 bushels). Next comes *cents per bu.*, which indicates that the prices quoted are in cents per bushel.

Beneath this initial information is data on prices, quantities, and delivery dates. The first column gives the month in which the contract expires (i.e., the month in which delivery is due). The next four columns provide price information. For example, for July 1995 the price per bushel of corn opened at $2.75 (275 cents), with a daily high of $2.765 and a low of $2.75 before closing at the settle (or closing) price of $2.765 per bushel. Note that the futures contract for 5,000 bushels at the settlement price of $2.765 per bushel would cost $13,825.

The sixth column gives the change in the closing price from the previous day. The closing price on February 7 was 1.5 cents per bushel higher than it was on February 4. The seventh column reports the highest price over the life of the July 1995 contract, $2.825 per bushel, and the eighth column the lowest lifetime price, $2.7425 per bushel. The last column reports the amount of open interest in this contract. *Open interest* is the number of contracts that involve actual delivery and have not been canceled by offsetting trades. As the expiration date rears, the open interest in the contract usually increases.

Below the information for all the months are data on estimated volume, volume on Friday (February 4), and open interest. These figures are total figures for all delivery dates. The estimated volume of all contracts traded on Monday, February 7, was 38,000. The number of contracts traded on Friday, February 4, was 40,434. The open interest in contracts for all months was 333,464. The +584 is the addition to outstanding contracts from the previous trading day.

futures contracts. In a financial futures contract for U.S. Treasury bills, a buyer might agree today to purchase $1 million in one-year Treasury bills to be delivered in three months at a price of 95. The price of 95 reflects that when the T-bills are delivered in three months, the buyer will pay $950,000. Notice that if the price of T-bills rises over the next three months (and yields on T-bills thus fall), the buyer is unaffected; she or he has locked in a price of $950,000 for the $1 million in T-bills (and thus has locked in a yield to maturity of 5.3 percent). The seller, however, has contracted to sell the T-bills for $950,000 and must do so even though the prevailing market price exceeds $950,000. Of course, the price of T-bills could have fallen, and the seller would have a contract to sell at $950,000 even though the market price was less than $950,000.

Options Markets

An **option contract** is a contract that gives its owner a right—but not an obligation—to sell or buy an item at a prespecified price, called the **strike price,** until the option expires. Options trade in **options markets** and, like futures, provide a way for individuals to reduce the financial risk of fluctuations in asset prices. Unlike with futures contracts, however, the buyer of an option contract does not have to exercise the option; that is, he or she need not buy the asset. Options are bought and sold at an options price, which is distinct from the price of the underlying financial asset. Options are traded for major stocks, debt instruments, foreign currency, and even market indexes such as the Standard and Poor's 500 Stock Index.

A **call option** gives a buyer the right to buy a financial asset at a stipulated price up to a specified expiration date. For stocks, options contracts are almost always for 100 shares. Suppose the current price of IBM stock is $57 per share. You pay $5 for a call option on IBM, with a strike price (the price at which you have the option to purchase the stock) of $60 and an expiration date of three months. Then you have paid $5 per share for the right to buy 100 shares of IBM stock at a price of $60 per share anytime between now and the expiration of the contract (three months). Clearly, if the price of the stock stays below $60, you will not find it profitable to exercise the option; it will be cheaper to buy the stock at the lower market price. But if the price of the stock rises above $60, you can buy the stock at $60 per share by exercising your option. In essence, a call option acts like insurance against a dramatic rise in the stock price. This feature is particularly useful when you want to buy IBM stock in the future and want to ensure you don't pay more than $60 for it.

A **put option** lets a buyer sell a financial asset at a specified price up to the option's expiration date. Suppose you pay $5 for a put option on IBM, with a strike price (the price at which you can sell the stock) of $60 and an expiration date of three months. Then you have paid $5 per share for the right to sell 100 shares of IBM stock at a price of $60 per share anytime in the next three months. Clearly, if the price of the stock stays below $60, you will find it profitable to exercise the option; you will earn more by exercising the option and selling the stock for $60 than by selling it at the lower market price. But if the price of the stock rises above $60, you can sell the stock for more than $60 by choosing not to exercise your option. The buyer of a put option thus buys insurance against a dramatic fall in the price of the stock.

Participants in futures and options markets can get information about their investments by looking at the tables printed in major newspapers. Box 9.6 explains the futures options listings in the *Wall Street Journal.*

Summary
Exercise 9.3

Natalie, a long-time family friend, has accumulated $3 million in her company's stock through an employee stock ownership plan. Under the terms of the agreement, she cannot liquidate the stock until she retires in three months. Natalie owns no other financial assets and has asked for your advice regarding what she should do. She is concerned that the value of her stock may fall in value during this three month period. Can the futures or options market help her? What do you tell her?

Inside Money

Box 9.6

How to Read Information on Futures Options Markets in the Wall Street Journal

In addition to stock options, the *Wall Street Journal* publishes information about options markets for agricultural products, precious metals, and foreign currency. Consider the information on corn presented in the first table under *Futures Options Prices* on February 8, 1994. As

in the futures market itself, we have the commodity listed, the exchange on which it trades, the units in which a contract is expressed, and the price per unit.

Continued on p. 302

FUTURES OPTIONS PRICES

Monday, February 7, 1994.

AGRICULTURAL

CORN (CBT)
5,000 bu.; cents per bu.

Strike Price	Calls–Settle Mar	May	Jly	Puts–Settle Mar	May	Jly
270	21½	27	30	⅛	1	2¾
280	11⅝	10¾	22½	¼	2½	5½
290	4	12	17	2½	5½	9¼
300	¾	7¾	12¾	9¼	10½	15
310	⅛	4¾	9½	18½	18	21½
320	⅛	2½	7	28½	26	29

Est vol 5,000   Fri 3,943 calls 1,615 puts
Op int Fri   100,091 calls 88,276 puts

SOYBEANS (CBT)
5,000 bu.; cents per bu.

Strike Price	Calls–Settle Mar	May	Jly	Puts–Settle Mar	May	Jly
625	48¾	54½	59	¼	1¾	4¾
650	24½	34	42½	⅝	6	12
675	6	20	29	7	17	25
700	1	11¼	20	27½	33¼	41
725	¼	6¾	14½	51½	53½	60
750	¼	3⅞	10¾	76½	75½	82

Est vol 11,000   Fri 7,135 calls 3,814 puts
Op int Fri   100,267 calls 65,658 puts

SOYBEAN MEAL (CBT)
100 tons; $ per ton

Strike Price	Calls–Settle Mar	May	Jly	Puts–Settle Mar	May	Jly
185	9.85	29.70	....	.10	.90	1.60
190	5.40	6.85	8.00	.60	2.15	3.10
195	2.15	4.30	5.80	2.25	4.60	5.85
200	.90	2.80	4.50	5.80	7.85	9.25
210	.20	1.50	2.65	15.20	16.45	17.50
220	.05	.75	1.60	25.10	....	....

Est vol 600   Fri 601 calls 204 puts
Op int Fri   26.365 calls 15,044 puts

SOYBEAN OIL (CBT)
60,000 lbs.; cents per lb.

Strike Price	Calls–Settle Mar	May	Jly	Puts–Settle Mar	May	Jly
26	2.100	2.170	2.140	.010	.150	.300
27	1.100	1.380	1.500	.020	.350	.650
28	.400	.840	1.050	.300	.800	1.200
29	.120	.550	.770	1.000	1.520	1.900
30	.060	.360	.550	1.950	2.350	2.700

LIVESTOCK

CATTLE-FEEDER (CME)
55,000 lbs.; cents per lb.

Strike Price	Calls–Settle Mar	Apr	May	Puts–Settle Mar	Apr	May
76	....	....	....	0.10	0.40	0.65
78	2.72	....	....	0.25	0.80	1.05
80	1.22	1.15	1.20	0.75	1.60	2.00
82	0.37	0.50	0.60	1.90	2.90	3.40
84	0.05	0.12	0.22	3.55	....	....
86	0.02	0.02	0.10	....	....	....

Est vol 234   Fri 99 calls 155 puts
Op int Fri   1,901 calls 5,787 puts

CATTLE-LIVE (CME)
40,000 lbs.; cents per lb.

Strike Price	Calls–Settle Apr	Jun	Aug	Puts–Settle Apr	Jun	Aug
70	5.00	....	....	0.20	0.52	0.77
72	3.22	2.52	....	0.42	1.15	1.45
74	1.80	1.40	1.15	0.97	2.00	2.45
76	0.85	0.65	0.57	2.02	....	....
78	0.32	0.27	0.20	3.47	....	....
80	0.07	0.07	....	5.22	....	....

Est vol 5,481   Fri 14,994 calls 6,476 puts
Op int Fri   10,815 calls 22,095 puts

HOGS–LIVE (CME)
40,000 lbs.; cents per lb.

Strike Price	Calls–Settle Apr	Jun	Jly	Puts–Settle Apr	Jun	Jly
46	4.87	....	....	0.17	0.05	....
48	3.10	7.50	....	0.40	0.15	0.30
50	1.77	5.70	....	1.05	0.32	0.55
52	0.85	4.07	3.40	2.12	0.70	1.05
54	0.30	2.67	2.25	....	1.25	1.85
56	0.12	1.60	1.35	....	2.17	....

Est vol 488   Fri 1,112 calls 1,660 puts
Op int Fri   4,203 calls 2,362 puts

METALS

COPPER (CMX)
25,000 lbs.; cents per lb.

Strike Price	Calls–Settle Mar	May	Jly	Puts–Settle Mar	May	Jly
86	4.15	4.95	5.65	0.85	2.40	2.95
88	2.80	3.85	4.55	1.50	3.55	3.85
90	1.80	3.00	3.65	2.50	4.45	4.95
92	0.85	2.20	2.90	3.55	5.65	6.20
94	0.45	1.75	2.25	5.15	7.20	7.60

Continued from p. 301

The first column tells the strike price, the price at which the option to buy or sell the futures contract may be exercised. The first option listed has a strike price of 270 cents per bushel. The next three columns give the prices of call contracts with various expiration dates. For corn at $2.70 per bushel, the price for the option expiring in March is $21.50; that is, for 21.50 cents per bushel, you can buy an option to purchase 5,000 bushels of corn at $2.70 per bushel. The current futures price is $2.915 per bushel (see the settle price of March corn futures in Box 9.5), so the option basically is priced so that you can purchase corn for the same price in the futures market ($2.915 per bushel) by purchasing the option for $2.70 per bushel for $.215 per bushel.

The third and fourth columns report prices of call options that do not expire until May and July, respectively. Notice that all prices are closing prices. Any blank would indicate that no call option exists at that price for that expiration date. See, for example, the blank for soybean meal calls at a strike price of 185 for July.

The fifth through seventh columns give the same information on put options, options to sell 5,000 bushels of corn at the listed strike prices. As before, these options expire in March, May, and July.

The information below the price summaries for each commodity is similar to that at the bottom of the *Corn* table in the *Futures Prices* section (Box 9.5). There is an estimated volume for all options on corn. Then Friday's volume is broken down into call and put options, and Friday's open interest (contracts outstanding) is broken down into call and put options.

Answer: There are three things for Natalie to consider: (1) the impact of a dramatic decline in her company's stock price before she retires, (2) the implications of having all her money tied up in a single financial asset when she retires; and (3) the impact of a decline in market interest rates before her retirement. More specifically, when Natalie retires, she should consider diversifying her risk by selling her stock and purchasing a portfolio of assets designed to generate retirement income. Such an income-generating portfolio would consist of various income stocks, corporate and U.S. government bonds, and certificates of deposit.

However, even if Natalie plans to acquire such a diversified portfolio of assets when she retires, she is subject to two types of risk over the next three months. First, for every 1 percent decline in her company's stock price, Natalie will lose $30,000 in retirement funds. Of course, a rise in the stock's price will increase her retirement income; the point is that she faces risk about the value of her retirement funds in three months. If Natalie is risk averse, she can avoid the risk of a price decline by purchasing a three-month put option on her company's stock. Such a put option would lock in a price at which she could sell her stock when she retires. Whether or not she should buy the put option depends on the market price of the put option and its strike price, as well as her own risk preferences.

Second, Natalie risks a decline in interest rates over the next three months. If interest rates decline, when she sells the stock to buy the diversified portfolio of income-generating assets, she will have to accept a lower return than she could earn today. To minimize this risk, Natalie may wish to consider using the futures or options markets to lock in today the price she will pay in three months for the portfolio of assets.

CONCLUSION

This chapter showed how six types of risk—default risk, liquidity risk, interest rate risk, call risk, inflation risk, and tax risk—affect interest rates and the prices of financial assets. We saw why risky financial assets tend to sell at lower prices and return higher yields than less risky assets do and illustrated this principle with graphs of the loanable funds market. We also looked at strategies for reducing risk, incuding diversification and uses of the futures and options markets. In the next chapter, we will complete our picture of the pricing of financial assets by examining how the length of loans can affect the prices and yields on financial assets.

KEY TERMS

uncertainty

risk

expected value (mean)

variance

risk averse

risk loving

risk neutral

default risk

default risk premium

liquidity risk

liquidity premium

interest rate risk

callable bond

call risk

call premium

inflation risk

inflation premium

tax risk

diversification

futures contract

futures market

capital gain

option contract

strike price

options market

call option

put option

QUESTIONS AND PROBLEMS

1. Briefly explain the difference between risk and uncertainty.

2. Suppose you roll a single die and receive $1 for each dot that appears on your first roll.
   (a). What is the expected value of this risky prospect?
   (b). What is the variance?
   (c). How much would a risk-neutral person be willing to pay to roll the die under the above terms?
   (d). What can you say about the amount a risk-averse person would be willing to pay to roll the die under the same terms?

3. Use supply and demand graphs to illustrate the impact of the following changes on the interest rate a firm pays for loanable funds.
   (a). An increase in the firm's default risk
   (b). A decrease in the liquidity risk of the firm's bonds
   (c). An increase in inflationary expectations
   (d). Increased uncertainty about the future tax treatment of interest income

4. At one point in the late 1970s, the interest rate on one-year U.S. Treasury bills was 12 percent, while the interest rate on one-year debt issued by the Swiss government was only 3 percent.
   (a). Use supply and demand curves to illustrate the equilibrium in the U.S. and Swiss markets for one-year government loans.
   (b). What could account for the differences in these interest rates?

5. Moody's recently downgraded XYZ's bonds from Aaa to C. What impact would you expect this to have on (a) the price of XYZ's bonds, (b) the interest rate XYZ must pay for additional loanable funds,

and (c) the default premium paid by XYZ?

6. Bonds issued by two different companies have the same face value, coupon rate, and maturity date, yet one bond is selling at a much higher price than the other bond.
   (a). Provide three potential reasons for these price differences.
   (b). Does the high-priced or the low-priced bond have the greater yield to maturity? Explain.

7. BUS, Inc., has a $1 million bond outstanding that will mature in one year. The bond pays a coupon rate of 10 percent, which equals the default-free market interest rate.
   (a). If investors believe BUS is certain to meet its payment obigations, how much will they be willing to pay for this bond?
   (b). What is the default risk premium in the market for BUS bonds?

8. Consider the same scenario in problem 7, but suppose a recent report reveals a 2 percent chance that BUS will not make any debt payments.
   (a). How much will a risk-neutral investor pay for a BUS bond?
   (b). What is the yield to maturity on this bond given the new information?
   (c). What is the default risk premium given the new information?
   (d). Would your answers in parts b and c differ if investors were risk averse? Explain.

9. Explain why an investor who purchases a callable bond requires a call premium.

10. One of the stocks in Joe's portfolio is selling at an all-time high. Joe would like to wait six months to sell to postpone paying taxes on his capital gains.

(a). What does Joe risk by waiting six months to sell his stock?

(b). What method for avoiding this risk can you suggest to Joe?

11. "If one person gains from a financial transaction, someone else loses. Thus, futures markets benefit either buyers or sellers, but not both." Is this statement true or false? Explain.

12. Provide two reasons risky bonds sell at lower prices (and higher yields) than default-free bonds.

13. "Risk-neutral investors do not care about the variance in returns; they care only about the expected value of a risky prospect. Thus, risk-neutral investors will pay the same amount for bonds with identical face values, coupon payments, and maturities even if the issuers have different probabilities of defaulting." Is this statement true or false? Explain.

14. What are the similarities between futures contracts and option contracts? What is the major difference?

15. You work for a major computer firm and face the risk that a rival company will earn huge profits at the expense of your firm. Can you suggest a method for diversifying the risk you face of losing your job? (Hint: Should you buy shares of your stock or of your rival's stock?) Explain carefully.

SELECTIONS FOR FURTHER READING

Allen, L., and T. Thurston. "Cash Futures Arbitrage and Forward Futures Spreads in the Treasury Bill Market." *Journal of Futures Markets,* 8 (October 1988), 563–573.

Berck, P., and S. G. Cecchetti. "Portfolio Diversification, Futures Markets and Uncertain Consumption Prices." *American Journal of Agricultural Economics,* 67 (August 1985), 497–507.

Boyle, G. W., and L. Young. "Asset Prices, Commodity Prices, and Money: A General Equilibrium, Rational Expectations Model." *American Economic Review,* 78 (March 1988), 24–45.

Dillingham, A. E. "The Influence of Risk Variable Definition on Value-of-Life Estimates." *Economic Inquiry,* 23 (April 1985), 277–294.

Driskill, R., S. McCafferty, and S. M. Sheffrin. "Speculative Intensity and Spot and Futures Price Variability." *Economic Inquiry,* 29 (October 1991), 737–751.

Harris, W. G. "Inflation Risk as a Determinant of the Discount Rate in Tort Settlements: Reply." *Journal of Risk and Insurance,* 52 (September 1985), 533–536.

Kaufman, H. M., and D. E. Schlagenhauf. "FNMA Auction Results as a Forecaster of Residential Mortgage Yield." *Journal of Money, Credit, and Banking,* 13 (August 1981), 352–364.

Kolari, J. W., and V. P. Apilado. "The Cyclical Effect of Default Risk on Industrial Bond Yields." *Journal of Economics and Business,* 37 (December 1985), 311–325.

Miller, M. A. "Age-Related Reductions in Workers' Life Insurance." *Monthly Labor Review,* 108 (September 1985), 29–34.

Perry, L. G., D. A. Evans, and P. Liu. "Bond Rating Discrepancies and the Effect on Municipal Bond Yields." *Quarterly Journal of Business and Economics,* 30 (Winter 1991), 110–127.

Roper, D. E. "The Role of Expected Value Analysis for Speculative Decisions in the Forward Currency Market: Comment." *Quarterly Journal of Economics,* 89 (February 1975), 157–169.

Tripathy, N., and R. L. Peterson. "Portfolio Risk, Adjustment Costs, and Security Dealers' Bid/Ask Spreads." *Journal of Financial Services Research,* 5 (October 1991), 131–142.

Witte, W. E. "A Short-Run Analysis of the Effects of Portfolio Realignments Due to Money Market Innovations." *Journal of Economics and Business,* 34 (1982), 193–199.

The Term Structure
of Interest Rates

*F*rom Chapter 9 we know that differences in yields between some financial assets, such as between government bonds and corporate bonds, are due to differences in the assets' risk of default. However, even bonds with identical default risks can have different yields. In this chapter, we examine how otherwise identical assets that mature at various times can have different yields. Economists propose three hypotheses to explain this phenomenon. Each theory attempts to explain some interesting data about the historical relationship between yields and terms to maturity. We begin by examining these data with the help of a tool known as the *yield curve.*

THE YIELD CURVE

In this chapter, we focus on debt issued by essentially identical lenders; the only differences we consider are differences in the times at which the debt instruments mature. For instance, in April of 1994 an investor (such as a bank or an individual) could purchase a Treasury bill maturing in August 1994 with a yield to maturity of 3.79 percent and a Treasury bill maturing in April 1995 with a yield to maturity of 4.66 percent. Since both assets are issued by the U.S. government, the only difference between them is their term to maturity, and it is the term to maturity that causes the difference in yields. This relationship is called the **term structure of interest rates.**

Suppose you are considering placing $100,000 in a certificate of deposit (CD) at an insured bank. You face virtually no default risk; the only issue you must address is whether to obtain a one-, two-, or six-month CD. On February 5, 1994, a typical bank offered the following rates on CDs with different terms to maturity: 3 percent on a one-month CD, 3.1 percent on a two-month CD, and 3.2 percent on a six-month CD. Thus, the interest rate depended on the CD's term to maturity. Graphing this relationship between the interest rates on these CDs and their terms to maturity generates the curve in part a of Figure 10.1. This is known as the **yield curve,** and it summarizes the yields one can earn by purchasing otherwise identical debt instruments of varying maturities.

Figure 10.1
Yield Curves at Different Points in Time

Part a graphs the yield curve for CDs on February 5, 1994. A CD maturing in one-month had an interest rate of 3 percent, a two-month CD paid 3.1 percent, and a six-month CD paid 3.2 percent. It is important to remember that each CD, regardless of its term to maturity, had the same risk of default. Thus, the only explanation for the differing interest rates is the term to maturity. Part b shows how the yield curve can shift over time. On April 19, 1990, a CD maturing in one month had an interest rate of 7.7 percent, a two-month CD paid 7.8 percent, and a six-month CD paid 7.9 percent.

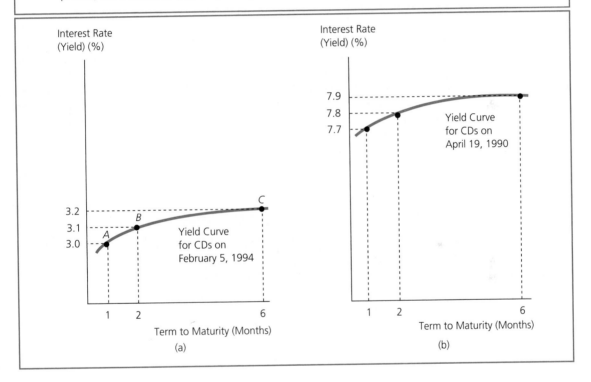

A yield curve is a snapshot taken at a given point in time. At another time, the term structure of interest rates will differ from that shown in part a of Figure 10.1. For instance, on April 19, 1990 (part b), the one-month rate for certificates of deposit was 7.7 percent, the two-month rate was 7.8 percent, and the six-month rate was 7.9 percent.

Yield curves can also be graphed for other debt instruments, such as Treasury bills or bonds. All you need remember when graphing a yield curve is to hold constant the date at which the yields are relevant and the default risk associated with the particular instrument.

To illustrate that yield curves can be graphed for other financial assets and are a snapshot at a given point in time, consider the picture for U.S. government securities in June 1983. For purposes of this discussion, we will refer to Treasury bills, notes, and bonds as simply government bonds. In June 1983, a government bond maturing in 1 year had a yield of 9.66 percent, a 3-year bond had a yield of 10.32 percent, a 7-year bond had a yield of 10.83 percent, a 10-year bond had a yield of 10.85 percent, and a 30-year bond paid 10.93 percent. Thus, in June 1983 you could purchase government bonds yielding anywhere from 9.66 to 10.93 percent, depending on the time to maturity. The yield curve for government bonds on June 1983 is the upward-sloping curve in part a of Figure 10.2.

The yield curves we have seen so far are all upward sloping: The longer the term to maturity, the higher the yield. While this has historically been the rule regarding yield curves, exceptions have occurred. In April 1990, for instance, there was little difference between the yields of assets with short terms to maturity and those with longer terms. Part b of Figure 10.2 illustrates the yield curve for government securities on April 1990, which was essentially flat. On this date, a 3-year Treasury note had the same yield as a 30-year Treasury note. Interestingly, a few episodes of downward-sloping yield curves have occurred. For instance, the yield curve for government bonds on February 1981 in part c of Figure 10.2 was downward sloping. This

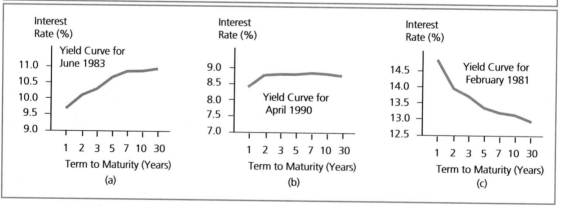

Figure 10.2
Upward-Sloping, Downward-Sloping, and Flat Yield Curves

These yield curves are for government securities at three different points in time. Part a shows that in June 1983, the yield curve for government securities was upward sloping. Part b shows that the yield curve was flat in April 1990. Part c shows a downward-sloping yield curve for February 1981.

SOURCE: Board of Governors of the Federal Reserve System, *Federal Reserve Bulletin,* various issues, and Citibase electronic database.

indicates that yields on longer-term bonds were lower than those on short-term bonds. The remainder of this chapter explains the factors that influence the shapes of yield curves, why they are normally upward sloping, and why they are sometimes flat or downward sloping. Box 10.1 shows yield curves for bonds issued by various countries as of June 10, 1993.

Summary
Exercise 10.1
Given the following information, graph the relevant yield curves: A three-year government bond yields 7 percent; a three-year Aaa corporate bond yields 8 percent; a seven-year government bond yields 9 percent; and a seven-year Aaa corporate bond yields 10 percent.

Answer: Since government bonds are less risky than Aaa corporate bonds, we must graph one yield curve for the corporate bonds and another for the government bonds. The figure plots these two yield curves. Notice that the yield curve for Aaa corporate bonds lies above the curve for government bonds. This reflects the default-risk premium on Aaa bonds and the differences in the tax treatment of the interest income these bonds generate. Recall that interest on Aaa corporate bonds is taxed by both the federal and state governments, while interest on U.S. government bonds is taxed only by the federal government.

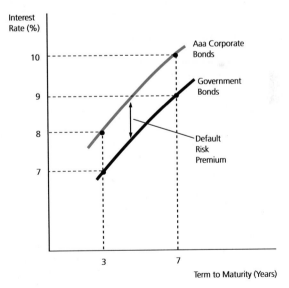

EXPLANATIONS OF THE TERM STRUCTURE OF INTEREST RATES

We now know three important facts: (1) Yields on financial assets differ according to their terms to maturity; (2) yield curves are usually upward

International Banking

Box 10.1

Yield Curves for Different Countries

The accompanying graph plots the yield curve for government bonds of the United States, Japan, Britain, and Germany on June 10, 1993. Because of the difference in maturity structures across countries, we include only 1-month, 3-month, 6-month, and 10-year (120-month) government bonds. Notice that while the United States, Japan, and Britain all had upward-sloping yield curves on this date, Germany's yield curve was downward sloping. Also, notice the difference in the level of interest rates between Japan and the United States on the one hand and Britain and Germany on the other. International interest rates often vary widely, and interest rates in Europe have been relatively high since the early 1990s as Germany strives to deal with its budget problems and its reunification with the former East Germany.

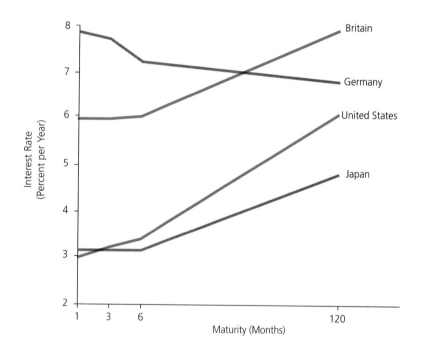

Source: International Herald Tribune, June 11, 1993; Financial Times, June 11, 1993.

sloping, reflecting higher interest rates on longer-term loans than on shorter-term ones; and (3) a few episodes of flat and even downward-sloping yield curves have occurred. We now look at why yield curves are shaped as they are and why their shapes may change over time. But first, Box 10.2 tells us how to read the data in the *Wall Street Journal* on yield curves.

We begin with two very different theories that economists have advanced to explain the shape of yield curves: the expectations hypothesis and the segmented-market hypothesis. The third theory—the preferred-habitat hypothesis—combines essential elements of the first two hypotheses. As we will see, the preferred-habitat hypothesis does the best job of explaining the shape of yield curves.

The Expectations Hypothesis

The **expectations hypothesis** asserts that longer-term interest rates are an average of the shorter-term interest rates expected to prevail during the life of the longer-term asset. For instance, if the current interest rate on a one-year bond is 5 percent and investors expect the interest rate on one-year bonds to be 7 percent next year, the current interest rate on a two-year bond will be (approximately) an average of the two one-year rates, or $(.05 + .07)/2 = 6$ percent. Let us see what lies behind this theory.

Assumptions.   Under the expectations hypothesis, we assume investors view a series of short-term bonds as perfect substitutes for long-term bonds. An investor who wishes to invest funds for, say, two years has a choice between (1) purchasing a bond that matures in two years and (2) purchasing a one-year bond and, when it matures, using the proceeds to purchase another one-year bond. In either case, the investor will have invested funds for two years. Since the expectations hypothesis assumes short- and long-term bonds are perfect substitutes, the only factor that will affect the investor's decision is the expected return to be earned from purchasing a two-year bond compared to that from purchasing the two one-year bonds. Thus, the expectations hypothesis also implicitly assumes investors are risk neutral and thus are not willing to pay a premium to lock in a two-year interest rate. In addition, it assumes transactions costs are zero so that the cost of buying, say, a two-year bond is the same as that of buying a series of one-year bonds: zero.

Implications for the Term Structure of Interest Rates.   Given the assumptions that short- and long-term financial assets are perfect substitutes and that investors care only about the expected return, the only way borrowers can attract long-term funds is to offer a long-term interest rate that gives investors the same expected return they could earn on a sequence of short-term investments. More specifically, suppose you have $10,000 in cash that you will not need for two years. The current interest rate on a one-year CD is 4 percent, and next year a one-year CD will pay interest of i_1

Inside Money

Box 10.2

How to Read Information on the Treasury Yield Curve in the Wall Street Journal

The yield curve in the accompanying figure is taken from the *Wall Street Journal* on February 8, 1994. It shows the yield curve on U.S. Treasury securities (bills, notes, and bonds) with maturities from 3 months to 30 years. On this day the yield curve was upward sloping, with the then current one-year rate at 3.8 percent and the two-year rate at 4.4 percent. According to the expectations hypothesis (which we look at in Chapter 12), the expected future one-year rate (in February 1995) was 5 percent. Since this box was written in February 1994, we do not know how accurate this forecast was. You will be able to check its accuracy by looking at a February 1995 issue of the *Wall Street Journal* to see if one-year rates were really 5 percent at that time.

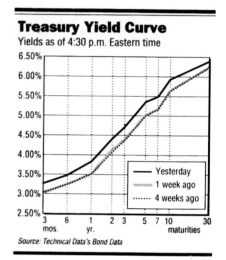

Treasury Yield Curve

Yields as of 4:30 p.m. Eastern time

— Yesterday
⋯⋯ 1 week ago
⋯⋯⋯ 4 weeks ago

Source: *Technical Data's Bond Data*

percent. Then, if you purchase a one-year CD today and, when it matures, purchase another CD that pays i_1 percent, in two years you will have

$$V_S = \$10{,}000(1 + .04)(1 + i_1).$$

Obviously your total return if you buy the series of one-year CDs depends on what the interest rate (i_1) is next year, when your first CD matures. Unfortunately, since interest rates fluctuate randomly due to changes in market conditions, you do not know with certainty what next year's rate on a one-year CD will be; all you (and other investors in the market) can do is form an expectation of what you think it will be. Suppose you and other investors expect the interest rate on a one-year CD to be $E_1 i$ next year. For example, if you expect the rate next year to be the same as this year's rate,

$E_1i = .04$. In this case, by purchasing a series of one-year CDs, you will compound the 4 percent interest rate for two years, giving you

$$V_S = \$10,000(1 + .04)(1 + .04) = \$10,816$$

at the end of two years. In contrast, if you expect the interest rate in one year to be $E_1i = .10$, you will earn

$$V_S = \$10,000(1 + .04)(1 + .10) = \$11,440$$

by purchasing a series of one-year CDs. The higher you expect the future one-year rate to be, the greater will be the value (V_S) to you of purchasing the series of one-year CDs.

Suppose the bank does not want all of its CDs to mature on the same date; it would like some investors to purchase one-year CDs and some to purchase two-year CDs. If the bank offers a rate of i_2 on a two-year CD, the total return to the purchaser of such a CD will be

$$V_L = \$10,000(1 + i_2)^2.$$

However, since investors view short- and long-term CDs as perfect substitutes and are risk neutral, they will not purchase short-term CDs if $V_S < V_L$; in that case, their expected return will be higher from purchasing the two-year CD. In contrast, if $V_S > V_L$, investors will not purchase long-term CDs; the expected return will be higher if they purchase the series of short-term CDs. In fact, under the expectations hypothesis, the only condition in which a bank can sell both one- and two-year CDs is that where investors are indifferent between purchasing one type or the other: $V_L = V_S$. In this case, the expected return from a two-year CD exactly equals that on the series of one-year CDs. Of course, the actual return on the series of one-year CDs may differ from what is expected, but risk-neutral investors don't concern themselves with this.

To see what this example implies about the term structure of interest rates, suppose the current rate on a one-year CD is 4 percent and investors expect the one-year rate to be 6 percent next year ($E_1i = .06$). In this case, the interest rate on a two-year CD that equates the expected return of holding a two-year CD with that of purchasing a series of one-year CDs satisfies the condition

$$V_L = V_S$$

or, substituting in for V_S and V_L,

$$\$10,000(1 + i_2)^2 = \$10,000(1 + .04)(1 + .06).$$

The $10,000 sum cancels out because it is on both sides of the equation. Thus, we see that investors will be indifferent between a one-year and a two-year CD if

$$(1 + i_2)^2 = (1 + .04)(1 + .06).$$

Taking the square root of both sides of this equation gives us

$$1 + i_2 = \sqrt{(1 + .04)(1 + .06)} = 1.05.$$

Since $i_2 = .05$, the only way the bank can induce investors to purchase a two-year CD, given the current one-year rate of 4 percent and investors' expectations of a 6 percent rate next year, is to pay 5 percent today on the two-year CD. At this rate, investors earn exactly the same return from both investments: $V_S = V_L = \$11,025$.

This analysis reveals that according to the expectations hypothesis, expectations about short-term rates determine long-term interest rates. If expectations about future short-term rates change, the current interest rate on long-term rates will change. For instance, if the current one-year rate is 4 percent and investors expect that rate to remain at 4 percent next year, the interest rate on a two-year CD will satisfy the condition

$$(1 + .04)(1 + .04) = (1 + i_2)^2.$$

Solving this equation for i_2 reveals that $i_2 = 4$ percent. Thus, if investors expect the interest rate to be constant, the rate on one-year CDs will equal that on two-year CDs.

Similarly, if investors expect the one-year rate to drop to 2 percent next year, the interest rate on a two-year CD must satisfy the condition

$$(1 + .04)(1 + .02) = (1 + i_2)^2.$$

Solving for i_2 reveals that the two-year interest rate is 3 percent.

Figure 10.3 illustrates the yield curves associated with the three cases we examined. Part a shows an upward-sloping yield curve, indicating that investors expect a higher one-year rate next year. Part b depicts a flat yield curve, indicating that investors expect the one-year rate to remain at 4 percent. Finally, part c illustrates a downward-sloping yield curve, indicating that investors expect a lower one-year rate next year.

A More General Formulation.   Now that you understand the basic implications of the expectations hypothesis, it is easy to extend the results to compare yields on financial instruments with various terms to maturity. More specifically, let i be the current interest rate on a one-year CD and $E_t i$ be the expected interest rate on a one-year CD purchased t years in the future. Then, if i_n is the current interest rate on a CD with n years to maturity, investors will be indifferent between a series of one-year CDs and the n-year CD if

$$(1 + i_n)^n = (1 + i)(1 + E_1 i)(1 + E_2 i) \cdots (1 + E_{n-1} i). \qquad (10.1)$$

The term on the left-hand side of this equation represents the total return (per dollar invested) if the investor purchased a CD that matures in n years and pays an interest rate of i_n percent per year. The right-hand side represents

Figure 10.3
Yield Curves and the Expectations Hypothesis

In part a, short-term interest rates are expected to increase, giving rise to an upward-sloping yield curve. In part b, short-term interest rates are expected to remain constant, generating a flat yield curve. In part c, the yield curve is downward sloping because short-term interest rates are expected to fall.

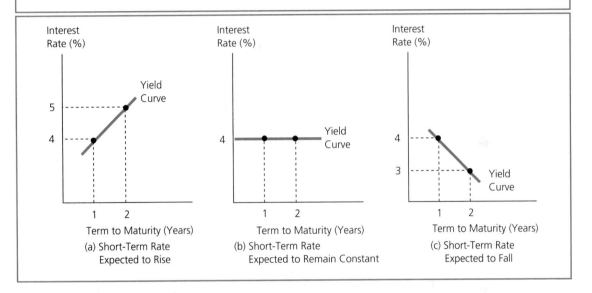

(a) Short-Term Rate Expected to Rise

(b) Short-Term Rate Expected to Remain Constant

(c) Short-Term Rate Expected to Fall

the expected return if the investor purchased a one-year CD that pays i percent, reinvested the proceeds at the end of the first year in another one-year CD that pays E_1i, reinvested those proceeds at the end of the second year in another one-year CD that pays E_2i, and so on. We may obtain an exact expression for the relationship between the interest rate on an n-year CD and the expected future rates on one-year CDs by taking the nth root of both sides of the equation 10.1 and solving for i_n:

$$i_n = \sqrt[n]{(1 + i)(1 + E_1i)(1 + E_2i) \cdots (1 + E_{n-1}i)} - 1. \quad (10.2)$$

For example, if the current one-year rate is 4 percent ($i = .04$) and the expected rate on a one-year CD next year is 6 percent ($E_1i = .06$), the interest rate on a two-year CD (i_2) will be

$$i_2 = \sqrt[2]{(1 + .04)(1 + .06)} - 1 = .04995,$$

or 4.995 percent. Notice that this amount is very close to the simple average of the current one-year rate ($i = .04$) and the expected one-year rate next year ($E_1 i = .06$):

$$i_n = .04995 \approx \frac{i + E_1 i}{2} = \frac{.04 + .06}{2} = .05.$$

In fact, a very useful approximation that we have already used for the exact formula in equation 10.2 is:[1]

$$i_n \approx \frac{i + E_1 i + E_2 i + E_3 i + \cdots + E_{n-1} i}{n}.$$

That is, the interest rate on an n-year CD (i_n) will, under the expectations hypothesis, approximately equal the simple average of current and expected one-year rates over the life of the n-year bond. We will use this approximation formula throughout the remainder of this chapter.

Using the Expectations Hypothesis to Forecast Future Interest Rates.   One of the more interesting aspects of the expectations hypothesis is that we can use it to obtain a market forecast of future interest rates. Let us see how we can accomplish this.

Suppose you have no idea whether short-term interest rates will rise or fall; all you know is that the yield on a bond with one year to maturity is $i = 4$ percent and the yield on a bond with two years to maturity is $i_2 = 8$ percent. Let us suppose other investors in the market expect the interest rate on a one-year bond to be $E_1 i$. Unfortunately, you do not know what $E_1 i$ is based on their forecasts; you know only the yields on one- and two-year bonds. However, given only this information, you can use the expectations hypothesis to determine what these other investors believe the future one-year rate will be, even if they do not directly report their estimate to you.

Specifically, under the expectations hypothesis, the rate on a two-year bond (i_2) must equal the average of the current one-year rate (i) and the market's expectation of the future one-year rate ($E_1 i$):

$$i_2 = \frac{i + E_1 i}{2}.$$

---

[1] In particular, if we take the logarithm of equation 10.1, we get

$$n \ln(1 + i_n) = \ln(1 + i) + \ln(1 + E_1 i) + \ln(1 + E_2 i) + \cdots + \ln(1 + E_{n-1} i).$$

Since the logarithm of $(1 + x)$ approximately equals x when x is small, this equation can be approximated by

$$n \times i_n \approx i + E_1 i + E_2 i + \cdots + E_{n-1} i.$$

Dividing through by n gives us

$$i_n \approx \frac{i + E_1 i + E_2 i + \cdots + E_{n-1} i}{n}.$$

Since you know $i = .04$ and $i_2 = .08$, we may plug these numbers into the equation to obtain

$$.08 = \frac{.04 + E_1 i}{2},$$

or, solving for $E_1 i$,

$$E_1 i = (.08)(2) - .04 = 0.12.$$

Thus, based on what you know about current yields on one- and two-year bonds, you can infer that the market thinks one-year bond yields will rise to 12 percent next year. Box 10.3 applies the expectations model to check whether the market predictions of April 1990 came to pass.

The Expectations Hypothesis and Yield Curves.   Our analysis of the expectations hypothesis provides a potential explanation for the shape of yield curves at different points in time: The varying shapes are due to different expectations of future one-year interest rates. Unfortunately, this explanation is far from complete. As noted earlier, with a few exceptions, yield curves have historically sloped upward. According to the expectations hypothesis, this would imply that investors almost always expect future rates to be higher than current rates—an outcome the actual data on interest rates have not borne out. In particular, short-term interest rates tend to fluctuate randomly over time; they are as likely to rise as they are to fall. Thus, the expectations hypothesis alone cannot fully account for the historical shapes of yield curves in the United States. Other hypotheses, presented in the following sections, were developed to better explain the historical yield curves.

Summary
Exercise 10.2

Suppose the interest rate on a one-year CD is 5 percent, on a two-year CD is 4 percent, and on a three-year CD is 8 percent. (a) Describe the shape of the yield curve. (b) Use the expectations hypothesis to determine the market's forecast of the one-year rate next year. (c) What is the market's forecast of the one-year rate in two years?

Answer: (a) The yield curve is V shaped; two-year rates are lower than both one-year and three-year rates. (b) Under the expectations hypothesis, the current interest rate on a two-year CD is the average of the expected one-year rates during the two-year term:

$$i_2 = \frac{i + E_1 i}{2}.$$

The Data Bank

Box 10.3

Calculating Expected Future Interest Rates

The expectations hypothesis asserts that long-term interest rates approximately equal the average of the expected one-year interest rates over the term to maturity of the long-term security:

$$i_n = \frac{i + E_1 i + E_2 i + E_3 i + \cdots + E_{n-1} i}{n}.$$

We use the data on the government securities yield curve summarized in the accompanying table from April 1990 to calculate various expected future one-year interest rates. We can get an idea about the accuracy of the expectations hypothesis by checking whether the short-term interest rates predicted in April 1990 by the expectations hypothesis actually came to pass.

Interest Rate in April 1990	Term to Maturity
8.40%	1 year
8.72	2 years
8.78	3 years
8.77	5 years
8.81	7 years
8.79	10 years
8.76	30 years

What did investors in 1990 think the interest rate would be in 1991? The expectations hypothesis asserts that the two-year interest rate in 1990, i_2, equaled the average of the current one-year rate, i, and the expected one-year rate for April 1991. Based on data for 1990, this means investors expected the one-year interest rate in April 1991 to be 9.04 percent. The actual one-year interest rate in April 1991 was 6.24 percent, so investors' expectations were too high. Similarly, investors using the expectations hypothesis in 1990 predicted that the one-year interest rate in April 1992 would be 8.9 percent. In reality, it was 4.3 percent. Thus, the expected one-year interest rates implied by the expectations hypothesis failed to detect the general downward movement in interest rates that occurred during the early 1990s.

Source: Board of Governors of the Federal Reserve System, *Federal Reserve Bulletin,* TI.35, various issues, and Citibase electronic database.

Since $i = .05$ and $i_2 = .04$, we have

$$.04 = \frac{.05 + E_1 i}{2},$$

so $E_1 i = .03$. Thus, the market expects a one-year CD to yield 3 percent next year. (c) Similarly, the current interest rate on a three-year CD is the average of the expected one-year CD rates during the three-year term:

$$i_3 = \frac{i + E_1 i + E_2 i}{3}.$$

We are given $i = .05$ and $i_3 = .08$, and from part b we know $E_1 i = .03$. Substituting these values in the preceding formula gives us

$$.08 = \frac{.05 + .03 + E_2 i}{3}.$$

Solving this for $E_2 i$ reveals that the market forecast of the interest rate on a one-year CD in two years is a whopping 16 percent!

The Segmented-Markets Hypothesis

The **segmented-markets hypothesis** is at the opposite end of the spectrum from the expectations hypothesis. It states that bonds with different maturities are not substitutable for one another; their yields are determined independently of one another. In effect, the segmented-markets hypothesis views the markets for bonds with varying maturities as separate. In each segmented market, the yield is determined by the intersection of the supply of and demand for each type of bond.

Part a of Figure 10.4 illustrates the market for loanable funds with a term to maturity of one year. Equilibrium in this market occurs where demand (D^0) intersects supply (S^0) at point A and the market rate of interest on one-year loans is 4 percent. In contrast, part b presents a separate market for loanable funds with a two-year term to maturity. The interest rate on these bonds is determined by the demand for and supply of funds with a two-year term to maturity and is 5 percent. Yet a third market exists for loanable funds, with a term to maturity of three years, in part c. The interest rate in this market is 6 percent, determined by the demand for and supply of three-year loans.

If the interest rate on one-year loans increased to 5 percent due to an increase in the demand in part a of Figure 10.4 from D^0 to D^1, then, according to the segmented-markets hypothesis, there would be no impact on the market for two- or three-year loans. The demand and supply curves in parts b and c would be unchanged, since participants in the financial markets do not base two- or three-year loanable funds decisions on other interest rates; the markets are viewed as segmented, or independent of one another. Thus,

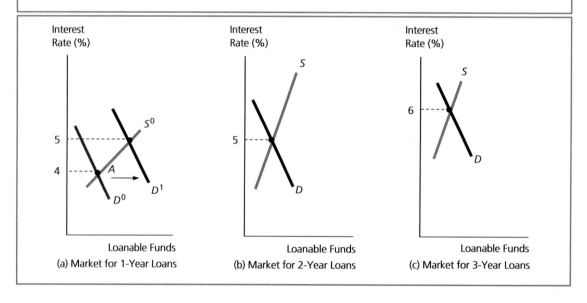

Figure 10.4
Determination of Short- and Long-Term Rates under the Segmented-Markets Hypothesis

According to the segmented-markets hypothesis, short-term bonds are not substitutes for long-term bonds. Thus, separate markets exist for one-year bonds, two-year bonds, and so on. Parts a through c show the markets for one-, two-, and three-year loans, respectively. The interest rate on a bond with a given maturity is determined in its specific market, independently of the interest rates on bonds with different terms to maturity. An increase in demand for one-year loans in part a, which raises the interest rate on one-year loans, affects neither the market for two-year bonds nor the market for three-year bonds.

(a) Market for 1-Year Loans

(b) Market for 2-Year Loans

(c) Market for 3-Year Loans

a change in short-term interest rates has no impact on long-term rates, and vice versa.

The Rationale for the Segmented-Markets Hypothesis.   The basic idea behind the segmented-markets hypothesis is that investors have preferences for financial instruments with particular terms to maturity. Suppose you have idle cash you will not need for two years, at which point you will need the money for retirement. According to the segmented-markets hypothesis, you will have a preference for instruments with a two-year maturity. Purchasing and holding a two-year bond to maturity is more attractive than buying a one-year bond in each of the next two years or purchasing a longer-term bond and selling it prior to maturity, because it minimizes transactions costs, the time and effort needed to make the investment decision, and interest rate risk. If interest rates rose after the initial purchase of the bond, the price of the bond would decline, potentially leading to a net loss when you sold it prior to maturity. You can eliminate this interest rate risk by purchasing a two-year bond and holding it to maturity. Effectively, by purchasing a bond with the desired term to maturity, you can lock in the yield for the term of the bond.

The Segmented-Markets Hypothesis and Yield Curves.   The segmented-markets hypothesis thus implies that the relative supply of and demand for bonds and other financial instruments of varying maturities determines the shape of the yield curve. For a given demand for loanable funds, when the supply of short-term loanable funds is greater than the supply of long-term loanable funds, short-term rates will be lower than long-term rates. For example, in part a of Figure 10.5 the equilibrium interest rate on one-year loans is 5 percent, and in part b the equilibrium interest rate on

Figure 10.5
The Segmented-Markets Hypothesis and an Upward-Sloping Yield Curve

In part a the equilibrium interest rate for one-year loans is 5 percent, and that for two-year loans is 6 percent in part b. This difference in interest rates is due to different conditions in the two segmented markets. In part c, the information from parts a and b is used to derive a yield curve. Loans with terms to maturity of one year pay a 5 percent interest rate, while loans with terms to maturity of two years pay a 6 percent rate. Thus, the yield curve is upward sloping.

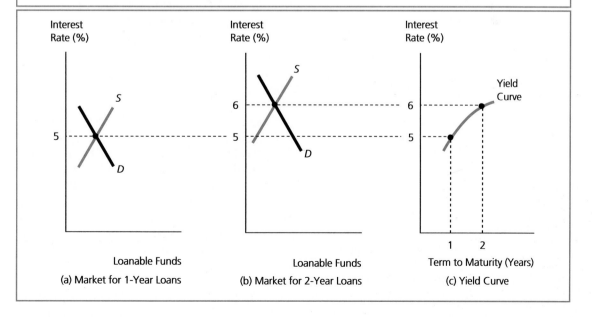

(a) Market for 1-Year Loans

(b) Market for 2-Year Loans

(c) Yield Curve

two-year loans is 6 percent. These interest rates give rise to the yield curve in part c. Notice that the vertical axis in part c is the same as that in parts a and b, but the horizontal axis is the term to maturity. The yield curve in part c slopes upward because the supply of one-year loans is relatively greater than that of two-year loans.

In contrast, if for a given demand the supply of short-term loanable funds is less than that for longer-term loans, short-term rates will exceed long-term interest rates as illustrated in parts a and b of Figure 10.6. This gives rise to the downward-sloping yield curve in part c.

While the segmented-markets hypothesis provides a possible explanation for both upward- and downward-sloping yield curves, it is subject to two criticisms. First, it is not very useful in predicting changes in the pattern of yields; it states only that changes in preferences for loans of different maturities will change the shape of the yield curve. Second, the theory implies that short-term and long-term interest rates are competely unrelated. Yet empirical evidence reveals that long- and short-term interest rates tend to move together; when short-term rates rise, long-term interest rates also tend to rise. For this reason, the segmented-markets hypothesis provides only an incomplete explanation of the term structure of interest rates.

The Preferred-Habitat Hypothesis

The **preferred-habitat hypothesis** combines key features of both the expectations and segmented-markets hypotheses. It says that while investors have a preference for loanable funds of a given term, they are willing to substitute away from their preferred terms if they are compensated for doing so. The compensation required to induce investors to purchase an asset with a different term to maturity than their preferred terms is known as the **term premium.**

The Rationale for the Preferred-Habitat Hypothesis.   The

rationale for the preferred-habitat hypothesis is a combination of the rationales for the expectations and segmented-markets hypotheses. Since we already examined the other two theories, let us look at the preferred-habitat hypothesis in the context of an analogy.

Suppose you must choose between two jobs: a job in the Bahamas or a job in Antarctica. The job descriptions are identical; the only difference is the habitat in which you will live. If we applied the expectations hypothesis to job choice, you would care only about the expected income from each job. Thus, in equilibrium an employer in the Bahamas must pay the same wage as an employer in Antarctica to get you to be indifferent between the two jobs. In contrast, if we applied the segmented-market hypothesis, you would have a preference for one job over the other independent of the pay differentials. For example, you would choose to work in the Bahamas regardless of how much more you could earn working in Antarctica. In other words, even if the job in the Bahamas paid $100 per year and the job in

Figure 10.6
The Segmented-Markets Hypothesis and a Downward-Sloping Yield Curve

The supply of loanable funds in the market for one-year loans (part a) is less than the supply of loanable funds in the market for two-year loans (part b). This leads to a lower interest rate on two-year loans than on one-year loans. Part c uses the information from parts a and b to derive a yield curve. Loans with terms to maturity of one year pay a 7 percent interest rate, while loans with terms to maturity of two years pay 6 percent. Thus, the yield curve is downward sloping.

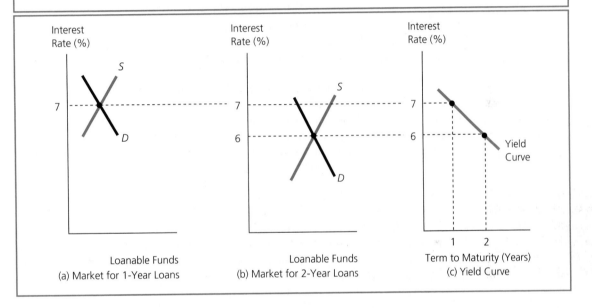

(a) Market for 1-Year Loans

(b) Market for 2-Year Loans

(c) Yield Curve

Antarctica paid $2 million annually, application of the segmented-markets hypothesis would lead you to choose the job in the Bahamas. You would have a preference for a particular job location and would be unwilling to substitute alternatives.

In contrast, the preferred-habitat hypothesis, when applied to job choice, combines these two features in the following way. You have a preference for the habitat of the Bahamas, but you also care about how much you expect to earn in your job. All else equal, you would prefer to work in the Bahamas. But if a company in Antarctica offered you a premium—say, $100,000 above what you expected to earn in the Bahamas—you would choose the job in Antarctica.[2] The premium the company offered would compensate you for the fact that Antarctica was not your preferred habitat.

---

[2] In the labor market, this premium is often called a *compensating wage differential*.

In the context of financial markets, the preferred-habitat hypothesis asserts that an investor will choose bonds on the basis of both the expected return of the bond and the investor's preference for bonds with a particular maturity. An investor will purchase a bond with an "undesirable" term to maturity only if he or she receives a term premium. The term premium is simply the additional yield required to induce the investor to purchase a bond with a term that is not exactly in line with the investor's preferences.

If we let α_n be the term premium required on a bond with a term to maturity of n years, the preferred-habitat hypothesis states that the yield on the bond, i_n, is determined by the term premium plus the average of the expected one-year interest rates over the life of the n-year bond:

$$i_n = \alpha_n + \frac{i + E_1 i + E_2 i + E_3 i + \cdots + E_{n-1} i}{n}, \qquad (10.3)$$

Here i is the interest rate on one-year bonds and $E_t i$ is the expected interest rate on one-year bonds in year t. Thus, the interest rate on an n-period bond equals the average of the one-year rates that are expected to prevail during the life of the long-term bond, plus the term premium required to induce investors to hold an n-period bond. The term premium is required to compensate the investor for the additional risk and/or transactions costs invoved in purchasing a bond that does not match his or her immediate preferences. For instance, suppose you have a preference for one-year bonds because you need funds at the end of the year. Buying a two-year bond and selling it at the end of one year (prior to maturity) involves risk; if interest rates rise between the time you purchase or sell the bond, you will be forced to sell the bond at a lower price than you would obtain otherwise. Moreover, you will have to pay additional sales commissions to a broker to liquidate the bond prior to maturity. (At maturity, the firm charges no commission to pay you the face value of the bond.) For these reasons, you must receive a term premium to buy longer-term bonds when your preference is for shorter term bonds.

The expectations and segmented-market hypotheses are actually extreme versions of the preferred-habitat hypothesis. Under the segmented-markets hypothesis, the term premium is effectively infinite; there is no finite interest rate that one can offer to induce an investor to purchase a bond whose maturity does not exactly match her or his preferences. Under the expectations hypothesis, the term premium is zero; i_n is simply the average of expected one-year rates during the term of the long-term bond. In this case, investors do not require any premium to be willing to hold bonds of different maturities.

The Preferred-Habitat Hypothesis and Yield Curves.   The beauty of the preferred-habitat hypothesis lies not only in its intuitive appeal in combining the best aspects of the other two hypotheses but also in its power in explaining the shapes of yield curves. The preferred-habitat hy-

pothesis explains not only upward-sloping yield curves but flat and down-ward-sloping ones as well. Unlike the other hypotheses, it also explains why yield curves are more frequently upward than downward sloping. Moreover, since an increase in the short-term interest rate (i) in equation 10.3 leads to an increase in the long-term interest rate (i_n), the preferred-habitat hypothesis implies that short-term and long-term interest rates will tend to move together. As noted earlier, this prediction is highly in accord with empirical data on interest rates and is also predicted by the expectations hypothesis. A simple example will illustrate these facts.

Suppose the term premium required on two-year bonds is $\alpha_2 = .01$ (1 percent). Further, assume the interest rate on a one-year bond is 6 percent. According to the preferred-habitat hypothesis, the interest rate on a bond that matures in two years will be

$$i_2 = .01 + \frac{.06 + E_1 i}{2}, \qquad (10.4)$$

where $E_1 i$ is the expected interest rate next year on a one-year bond. Let us calculate the interest rate on the two-year bond (i_2) under three different scenarios regarding expectations about future interest rates ($E_1 i$).

Case A: $E_1 i = .20$. In this case, investors expect a substantial increase in the future interest rate on one-year bonds. If we insert this expectation into equation 10.4, we get the corresponding interest rate on a two-year bond:

$$i_2 = .01 + \frac{.06 + .20}{2} = .14.$$

Since the current interest rate on a one-year bond is $i = .06$ and the interest rate on a two-year bond is $i_2 = .14$, the yield curve in this case is upward sloping, as illustrated in part a of Figure 10.7. The upward-sloping yield curve reflects the fact that short-term rates are expected to rise substantially in the future.

Case B: $E_1 i = .04$. In this case, investors expect the interest rate on one-year bonds to be slightly lower next year. Setting $E_1 i = .04$ in equation 10.4 gives us the interest rate on a two-year bond:

$$i_2 = .01 + \frac{.06 + .04}{2} = .06.$$

Since the current interest rate on a one-year bond is $i = .06$ and the interest rate on a two-year bond is $i_2 = .06$, the yield curve in this case is flat, as illustrated in part b of Figure 10.7. The flat yield curve reflects that short-term rates are expected to fall moderately. In fact, the expectations hypothesis would suggest that the interest rate on two-year bonds is 5 percent. But when

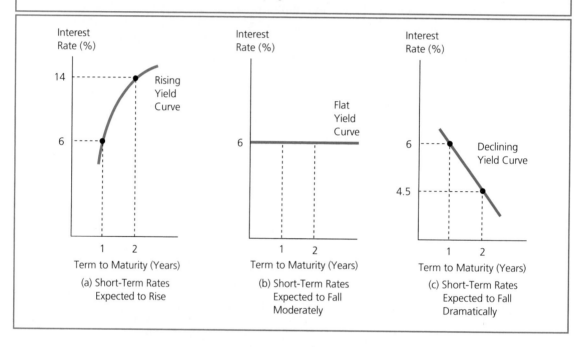

Figure 10.7
The Preferred-Habitat Hypothesis and Yield Curves

Part a shows that when the term premium is positive and short-term interest rates are expected to rise, the yield curve will be upward sloping. Part b shows that when the term premium is positive and short-term interest rates are expected to fall by only a small amount, the yield curve will be relatively flat. In part c, the term premium is positive and short-term interest rates are expected to fall by a substantial amount; thus, the yield curve is downward sloping.

(a) Short-Term Rates Expected to Rise

(b) Short-Term Rates Expected to Fall Moderately

(c) Short-Term Rates Expected to Fall Dramatically

the term premium of 1 percent is added in, the yield on the two-year bond is 6 percent—the same as that on the current one-year bond.

Case C: $E_1i = .01$.   In this case, investors expect the interest rate on one-year bonds to fall dramatically next year. Setting $E_1i = .01$ in equation 10.4 gives us the interest rate on a two-year bond:

$$i_2 = .01 + \frac{.06 + .01}{2} = .045.$$

Since the current interest rate on a one-year bond is $i = .06$ and the interest rate on a two-year bond is $i_2 = .045$, the yield curve is downward sloping in part c of Figure 10.7. The downward-sloping yield curve reflects the fact that short-term rates are expected to fall so sharply that even when a term premium is applied to the two-year bond, the current two-year rate is below the current one-year rate.

These three cases reveal that the preferred-habitat hypothesis is capable of explaining the various shapes yield curves take. Moreover, even if short-term interest rates are expected to remain constant or fall slightly, the yield curve will slope upward due to the term premium on longer-term bonds. A downward-sloping yield curve results only when investors expect future short-term interest rates to fall dramatically. Thus, in most instances yield curves will slope upward. Taken together, all the implications of the preferred-habitat hypothesis accord very well with the empirical data on interest rates presented at the beginning of this chapter.

Summary Exercise 10.3

Suppose investors prefer one-year bonds to three-year bonds and will purchase a three-year bond only if they expect to receive an additional 2 percent over the return from holding one-year bonds. Currently one-year bonds yield 3 percent, but investors expect this yield to rise to 4 percent next year and to 6 percent the year after. (a) Which of the three models of term structure is relevant in this case? (b) Is the yield curve upward sloping, flat, or downward sloping? (c) What is the yield on a three-year bond?

Answer: (a) Since investors have a preference for one-year bonds but are willing to hold three-year bonds if they receive a term premium of 2 percent, this scenario is consistent with the preferred-habitat hypothesis. Under the expectations hypothesis, investors would require no term premium; under the segmented-markets hypothesis, investors would not purchase three-year bonds for any premium. (b) Since short-term rates are expected to rise, the yield curve must be upward sloping. (Note: You should know this answer even before working part c of this exercise.) (c) Under the preferred-habitat hypothesis, the interest rate on a three-year bond is

$$i_3 = \alpha_3 + \frac{i + E_1 i + E_2 i}{3}.$$

Here $\alpha_3 = .02$, $i = .03$, $E_1 i = .04$, and $E_2 i = .06$. Thus, the yield on a three-year bond is

$$i_3 = .02 + \frac{.03 + .04 + .06}{3} = .063,$$

or 6.3 percent. Notice that the interest rate on a three-year bond is higher than that on a one-year bond, which means the yield curve is upward sloping.

CONCLUSION

In this chapter, we examined the relationship between the yield on a financial asset and the asset's term to maturity. Unlike in Chapter 9, where we saw that differences in risk can explain differences in asset prices, in this chapter we noted that the term structure of interest rates gives rise to different yields on financial instruments with identical risk characteristics. Together this and the last two chapters have provided insight on how the time value of money, risk, and the term structure of interest rates affect the prices and yields of financial assets held by banks and other investors. In the next chapter, we examine how this picture is affected by activities in the foreign exchange market—the market in which currencies like Japanese yen and British pounds are bought and sold.

KEY TERMS

term structure of interest rates

yield curve

expectations hypothesis

segmented-markets hypothesis

preferred-habitat hypothesis

term premium

QUESTIONS AND PROBLEMS

1. What is held constant along a yield curve? What is allowed to vary?

2. Explain the rationale for the expectations hypothesis. What are the theory's major weaknesses?

3. Suppose that on January 1, 1995, the interest rate on a one-year government bond is 5 percent, the interest rate on a two-year government bond is 6 percent, and the interest rate on a three-year government bond is 7 percent. According to the expectations theory of the term structure of interest rates, what is the expected interest rate on one- and two-year bonds issued on January 1, 1996? What is the expected interest rate on a one-year bond issued on January 1, 1997?

4. According to the expectations hypothesis, when would the yield curve slope upward? When would it slope downward?

5. Get a current issue of the *Wall Street Journal* and look up the interest rate on three-month, six-month, and one-year Treasury bills. Is the term structure of interest rates increasing, decreasing, or flat? Does this imply anything about expected future interest rates? Explain.

6. Explain the rationale for the segmented-markets hypothesis. What are this theory's major weaknesses?

7. According to the preferred-habitat hypothesis, if the market expects future one-year interest rates to be the same as today's one-year interest rate, will the term structure of interest rates be increasing, decreasing, or flat? Why?

8. Explain how the expectations and segmented-markets hypotheses are extreme versions of the preferred-habitat hypothesis. Give an example to illustrate your explanation.

9. The interest rate on a one-year government bond is 4 percent, the rate on a two-year CD is 7 percent, and the rate on a three-year corporate bond is 9 percent. What can you infer about the term structure of interest rates? Explain.

10. The interest rate on a one-year government bond is 4 percent, the rate on a two-year government bond is 7 percent, and the rate on a three-year government bond is 9 percent.

(a). Describe the shape of the yield curve.

(b). Use the expectations hypothesis to determine the market's forecast of the one-year rate next year.

(c). What is the market's forecast of the one-year rate in two years?

11. Suppose investors prefer one-year bonds to two-year bonds and will purchase a two-year bond only if they expect to receive an additional 4 percent over the return from holding one-year bonds. Currently one-year bonds yield 5 percent, but investors expect the yield to fall to 4 percent next year.

(a). What is the yield on a two-year bond?

(b). Is the yield curve upward sloping, flat, or downward sloping?

12. Determine whether the following scenarios are most consistent with the expectations, segmented-markets, or preferred-habitat hypothesis.

(a). Natalie's sole criteria in choosing among bonds with varying maturities is the expected yield she will earn on the bonds.

(b). Since Mitchell plans to retire in 20 years, he will purchase 20-year bonds.

(c). M'Lissa wishes to earn a high expected return on her investments but has a preference for five-year bonds. She will, however, consider purchasing shorter- or longer-term bonds if they offer a substantially higher yield.

(d). Jay prefers one-year bonds even if they have a lower yield than any other bond.

13. Suppose investors expect inflation to remain stable this year but increase dramatically next year.

(a). What impact will this have on expectations of next year's short-term interest rate? Explain.

(b). How will this expectation affect current one-year interest rates? Explain.

(c). How will this expectation affect current two-year interest rates? Explain.

14. Suppose a company's bonds have recently been downgraded from Aaa to C. Assuming the firm has outstanding bonds maturing in 1, 5, and 10 years, how will this announcement affect the yield curve for the company's bonds?

15. A mortgage applicant was perplexed when he learned that the mortgage company was charging a lower rate on a 15-year mortgage than on a 30-year mortgage. Explain to the applicant why a mortgage company might have such a term structure of mortgage rates.

SELECTIONS FOR FURTHER READING

Lee, T. K., and Y. K. Tse. "Term Structure of Interest Rates in the Singapore Asian Dollar Market." *Journal of Applied Econometrics,* 6 (April–June 1991), 143–152.

MacDonald, S. S., and S. E. Hein. "Futures Rates and Forward Rates as Predictors of Near-Term Treasury Bill Rates." *Journal of Futures Markets,* 9 (June 1989), 249–262.

Mankiw, N. G., and J. A. Miron. "The Changing Behavior of the Term Structure of Interest Rates." *Quarterly Journal of Economics,* 101 (May 1986), 211–228.

McCulloch, J. H. "The Tax-Adjusted Yield Curve." *Journal of Finance,* 30 (June 1975), 811–830.

Foreign Exchange Markets

$\mathcal{E}$ach morning, national TV and radio news programs begin their business reports with a quick rundown of the previous day's activity in the New York, Tokyo, and London stock markets. These reports usually include closing quotes for the Dow and Nikkei averages and a summary of exchange rates ("the yen closed at 107," "the pound dropped sharply in response to the jump in U.S. interest rates," "the Fed intervened to boost the dollar"). Perhaps you have wondered what these reports mean and why they change so frequently.

This chapter provides answers. First, we look at what exchange rates are and how changes in them affect prices of the foreign goods, such as cars, TVs, and CD players, that you purchase. Next, we examine why exchange rates change in response to changes in price levels or interest rates on foreign and domestic deposits and how currency traders' short-term incentives to hold U.S. or foreign bank deposits depend on their expectations. We also look at how interest rates, exchange rates, and price levels are linked by international arbitrage conditions and how central bank interventions affect exchange rates. We conclude by using our knowledge of exchange rates to examine the history of world exchange rate systems, including the European monetary system.

FUNDAMENTALS OF EXCHANGE RATES

Thus far, we have been concerned mainly with domestic financial markets in which U.S. residents hold dollar deposits at banks and/or purchase U.S. stocks or bonds. An important link between these markets and the global economy is the **foreign exchange market,** the market in which different currencies are bought and sold. This over-the-counter market is composed of hundreds of banks and other dealers in foreign currency that buy and sell deposits of foreign currency. A very small fraction of foreign exchange transactions—primarily those of tourists—is exchanges of actual dollar bills and notes issued by other governments. Most of the transactions occur over the phone or by computer and are merely bookkeeping entries that shift bank deposits denominated in one currency into another.

Foreign exchange markets arise because various countries have different monetary systems and require different currencies to buy goods, services, and financial assets. If your mutual fund wishes to purchase stocks or bonds in the British financial market, it must pay for them in British pounds (£). Similarly, a U.S. import dealer who wishes to buy Japanese cars to sell in the United States must pay for the cars in yen (¥). Transactions such as these have become increasingly important to the U.S. economy.

To put this importance in perspective, in 1993 U.S. gross domestic product, a measure of the total output of finished goods and services, was more than $6 trillion. Of that amount, more than 12 percent was exported to other countries, and our imports of foreign goods were even larger. The foreign exchange market makes all of these transactions possible by facilitating the exchange of other currencies into dollars, and vice versa. The number of units of one currency that must be given up to buy a unit of another currency is called the **exchange rate.** As Box 11.1 shows, these rates are published daily in some business newspapers.

Before we explain how market forces determine exchange rates, you need to understand how to interpret and use those rates. When you buy a loaf of bread, you probably see the $2 price tag without thinking about what it means. The price of $2 means each loaf of bread can be exchanged for $2. Stated differently, $1 buys one-half loaves of bread. In terms of value,

$$\frac{1}{2} \text{ loaves of bread } = \$1.$$

Just as the price of bread reveals how much bread you can buy for $1, an exchange rate reveals how much one unit of a particular currency costs in terms of another. For instance, suppose you plan to visit Germany and need German marks to make purchases there. If it costs 50 cents to buy one mark (DM), then, in terms of value we would say,

$$\$.50 = \text{DM1},$$

or there are .50 dollars per mark. The exchange rate of dollars in terms of marks is 50 cents per mark. Put another way, you can sell each dollar for two marks:

$$\$1 = \text{DM2}.$$

When expressed this way, we say the exchange rate of marks in terms of U.S. dollars is two marks per dollar. In the United States, it is more common to state the exchange rate as the number of marks (or other currency) one will receive per dollar. Thus, if the exchange rate for German marks is DM1.7/$1 (as it was in early 1994), there are 1.7 marks per dollar.

The exchange rate lets you determine how much it would cost in dollars to purchase a good whose price is quoted in another currency. For instance, suppose you were on a business trip in Japan in early 1993 and noticed that a camera you could buy for $90 in the United States was priced at 10,000 yen (¥10,000) in Tokyo. Should you have bought the camera in Tokyo or waited until you returned to the United States?

Inside Money

Exchange Rate Information in the Wall Street Journal

Box 11.1

Each edition of the *Wall Street Journal* contains a table of exchange rates such as that shown here. This table lists various countries, with their currencies in parentheses, followed by a series of exchange rates. The table reproduced here is from the Wednesday, March 2, 1994 edition, and the rates quoted are for both Tuesday and Monday.

Rates are given in both U.S. dollar equivalents (how many dollars you can purchase with a unit of the foreign currency) and currency per U.S. dollar (how many units of the foreign currency you can purchase with one U.S. dollar). The current market rate (called the *spot rate*) is given for all the countries listed. Forward rates are also given for the major currencies. The forward rate indicates the rate at which you can buy foreign currency to be delivered at a specified future date (usually 30, 90, and 180 days).

Consider the Canadian dollar. The exchange rate on Tuesday was .7403 U.S. dollars per Canadian dollar, or 1.3508 Canadian dollars for every U.S. dollar. The forward rates (in currency per U.S. dollar) were 1.3510 Canadian dollars per U.S. dollar 30 days forward, 1.3514 Canadian dollars per U.S. dollar 90 days forward, and 1.3524 Canadian dollars per U.S. dollar 180 days forward. The exchange market is predicting a depreciation of the Canadian dollar relative to the U.S. dollar, since the forward market is indicating that a U.S. dollar can buy even more Canadian dollars per U.S. dollar as we move into the future.

EXCHANGE RATES

Tuesday, March 1, 1994

The New York foreign exchange selling rates below apply to trading among banks in amounts of $1 million and more, as quoted at 3 p.m. Eastern time by Bankers Trust Co., Dow Jones Telerate Inc. and other sources. Retail transactions provide fewer units of foreign currency per dollar.

Country	U.S. $ equiv. Tues.	U.S. $ equiv. Mon.	Currency per U.S. $ Tues.	Currency per U.S. $ Mon.
Argentina (Peso)	1.01	1.01	.99	.99
Australia (Dollar)	.7130	.7133	1.4025	1.4019
Austria (Schilling)	.08325	.08350	12.01	11.98
Bahrain (Dinar)	2.6529	2.6529	.3770	.3770
Belgium (Franc)	.02845	.02853	35.15	35.05
Brazil (Cruzeiro real) .	.0015518	.0015710	644.40	636.55
Britain (Pound)	1.4896	1.4860	.6713	.6729
30-Day Forward	1.4875	1.4838	.6723	.6739
90-Day Forward	1.4845	1.4808	.6736	.6753
180-Day Forward	1.4812	1.4775	.6751	.6768
Canada (Dollar)	.7403	.7398	1.3508	1.3518
30-Day Forward	.7402	.7396	1.3510	1.3520
90-Day Forward	.7400	.7394	1.3514	1.3525
180-Day Forward	.7394	.7388	1.3524	1.3535
Czech. Rep. (Koruna)				
Commercial rate	.0334795	.0334795	29.8690	29.8690
Chile (Peso)	.002400	.002400	416.59	416.59
China (Renminbi)	.114882	.114882	8.7046	8.7046
Colombia (Peso)	.001220	.001220	819.71	819.71
Denmark (Krone)	.1494	.1499	6.6928	6.6701
Ecuador (Sucre)				
Floating rate	.000493	.000493	2030.00	2030.00
Finland (Markka)	.18056	.18076	5.5382	5.5321
France (Franc)	.17191	.17273	5.8170	5.7895
30-Day Forward	.17147	.17227	5.8320	5.8049
90-Day Forward	.17082	.17195	5.8540	5.8155
180-Day Forward	.17008	.17090	5.8795	5.8514
Germany (Mark)	.5855	.5870	1.7080	1.7035
30-Day Forward	.5841	.5856	1.7121	1.7077
90-Day Forward	.5822	.5837	1.7175	1.7132
180-Day Forward	.5802	.5817	1.7234	1.7190
Greece (Drachma)	.004034	.004052	247.90	246.80
Hong Kong (Dollar)	.12939	.12943	7.7287	7.7263
Hungary (Forint)	.0096740	.0096404	103.3700	103.7300
India (Rupee)	.03216	.03216	31.09	31.09
Indonesia (Rupiah)	.0004664	.0004664	2144.04	2144.04
Ireland (Punt)	1.4289	1.4291	.6998	.6997
Israel (Shekel)	.3339	.3339	2.9945	2.9945
Italy (Lira)	.0005910	.0005925	1691.96	1687.76

Obviously the answer to this question depends on the exchange rate. The exchange rate (on February 5, 1993) between yen and U.S. dollars was ¥134/US$. Taking the reciprocal of this tells us the number of dollars needed to buy one yen: 1/(¥134/US$) = US$.00746/¥. In other words, it costs a little less than a penny to buy one yen. If we multiply this figure by the number of yen needed to purchase the camera (¥10,000), we get

$$\$.00746/¥ \times ¥10,000 = \$74.60.$$

(Notice the ¥ signs cancel out on the left-hand side of this equation, which means we have converted yen to dollars). Thus, given the exchange rate on February 5, it would have been cheaper for you to purchase the camera in Japan than to purchase it when you returned to the United States. Yet if you had been in Japan in February of 1994, when the exchange rate was about ¥100/US$, you would have been better off buying the camera stateside.

When the exchange rate falls, even if the price of the camera remains the same (¥10,000), it will now cost you more in dollars to buy the camera in Japan. Why? Because the value of the dollar has depreciated against the yen. **Depreciation** of the U.S. dollar means the dollar sells for fewer units of foreign currency than before. For example, when the exchange rate between yen and U.S. dollars falls to ¥100/$, a dollar can be sold for only 100 yen. The reciprocal tells us the number of dollars it would take to buy one yen at this lower exchange rate: 1/(¥100/$) = $.01/¥. Due to the depreciation of the dollar, each yen now costs 1 cent. Multiplying the dollar cost per yen ($.01/¥) by the number of yen needed to purchase the camera (¥10,000) reveals that the cost of buying the camera in Japan rises to

$$\$.01/¥ \times ¥10,000 = \$100.$$

When the dollar depreciates relative to the yen, Japanese goods become relatively more expensive to Americans. In Chapter 17, we will see how the depreciation of the dollar affects the balance of trade.

The U.S. dollar might also appreciate relative to the Japanese yen. When the dollar **appreciates,** holders of foreign currency have to give up more of their currency to buy a dollar than before. As the dollar appreciates relative to the yen, not only will the dollar buy more yen than previously, but Japanese goods will also become less expensive in terms of U.S. dollars. Depreciation and appreciation are always relative to another currency. Thus, when the U.S. dollar appreciates relative to the yen, the yen *must* be depreciating relative to the dollar: If a U.S. dollar now buys more yen, a Japanese yen now must buy less of a U.S. dollar.

Finally, as Box 11.2 shows, the U.S. dollar can appreciate relative to one currency while simultaneously depreciating relative to another. In the next section, we look at the market for foreign exchange and see what causes the dollar to depreciate or appreciate relative to foreign currencies.

The Data Bank

Box 11.2

*Exchange Rate Movements
Between the U.S. Dollar and
Four Major Foreign Currencies*

The accompanying figure illustrates exchange rate movements between the U.S. dollar and four major currencies: the German mark, the Japanese yen, the British pound, and the Canadian dollar. There has been considerable volatility in all these exchange rates, and the long-run trends tend to vary across currencies. For instance, part a of the figure graphs the exchange rates with the Canadian dollar and the British pound. Notice that the general trend in exchange rates between U.S. dollars and these two currencies is upward, so the dollar has generally appreciated relative to the Canadian dollar and the British pound over the last three decades.

In contrast, part b shows the exchange rates with the German mark and the Japanese yen. Here the general trend for each rate is downward, so the dollar has generally depreciated relative to the mark and the yen. For instance, it took more than four German marks to purchase a dollar in the early 1960s, but by

Continued on p. 335

(a) Exchange Rates, Canadian Dollar per U.S. Dollar (Left Scale) and U.K. Pound per U.S. Dollar (Right Scale)

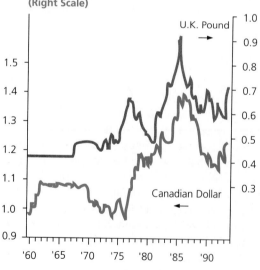

(b) Exchange Rates, German D-Mark per U.S. Dollar (Left Scale) and Japanese Yen per U.S. Dollar (Right Scale)

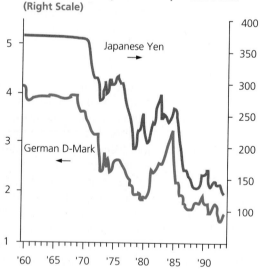

Continued from p. 334

1993 it took only 1.6 marks.

The graphs in the figure indicate not only that exchange rates are volatile over short periods of time but also that over long periods of time, the dollar may simultaneously appreciate relative to some currencies and depreciate relative to others.

_____

Source: Board of Governors of the Federal Reserve System, *Foreign Exchange Rates,* various issues; and Citibase electronic database.

Summary Exercise 11.1

(a) Suppose the exchange rate between British pounds (£) and U.S. dollars is .75 pounds per U.S. dollar. How much would it cost in dollars to purchase a watch that sells for 28 pounds? (b) If the exchange rate changes to one pound per U.S. dollar, how would your answer change?

Answer: (a) When the exchange rate is £.75/$, it costs $1/£.75 = $1.33/1£ to buy a pound. Consequently, it costs

$$\$1.33/£ \times £28 = \$37.24$$

to buy the watch. (b) When the exchange rate is 1£/$, it costs

$$\$1/£ \times £28 = \$28$$

to buy the watch. Since the dollar appreciated relative to the pound, the dollar cost of the British watch is now lower.

THE MARKET FOR FOREIGN EXCHANGE

With this understanding of how to use exchange rates to convert prices from one currency to another, we now look at how market forces determine exchange rates. Throughout this section, we will focus exclusively on the determination of the exchange rate between yen and dollars. The basic principles developed here are also valid for determining other exchange rates, such as that between British pounds and U.S. dollars or even that between Mexican pesos and Italian lire.

Before we begin, however, look at Figure 11.1. This figure shows that the exchange rate between yen and dollars has fluctuated widely during the past two decades. Between 1976 and 1979, the dollar depreciated from about 300 to 180 yen per dollar. Between 1979 and 1985, the dollar appreciated from 180 to 260 yen per dollar, only to depreciate once again to 120 yen per dollar by the end of 1988. Each of these periods reflects a long-run depreciation or appreciation of the dollar. However, notice that within each period, the exchange rate movements were very volatile. Between 1979 and 1985, for instance, the jagged curve in Figure 11.1 represents considerable

The vertical axis indicates the yen/dollar exchange rate. Between 1976 and 1979, the exchange rate showed a downward trend, reflecting depreciation of the dollar against the yen. Between 1979 and 1985, the dollar appreciated against the yen, although numerous short-term rises and falls occurred over the period. Between 1985 and 1988, the dollar again depreciated against the yen.

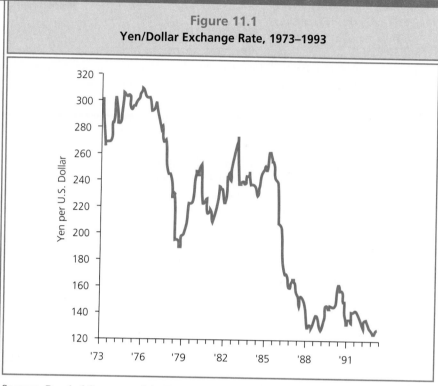

Figure 11.1
Yen/Dollar Exchange Rate, 1973–1993

SOURCE: Board of Governors of the Federal Reserve System, *Foreign Exchange Rates,* various issues; and Citibase electronic database.

exchange rate volatility, although the general trend over the period reflects the appreciation of the dollar.

In the first part of this section, we examine factors that can explain these longer-term trends in exchange rates. Then we look at why exchange rates can deviate from these trends over short periods of time, during which numerous rises and falls occur as shown in Figure 11.1.

Long-Run Exchange Rate Determination

In the long run, exchange rates are determined by economic fundamentals like price levels and real incomes in different countries. Figure 11.2 shows how the long-run exchange rate between yen and dollars is determined by the forces of supply and demand. As is customary, the vertical axis measures the "price" of dollars, while the horizontal axis measures the quantity of U.S. dollars. Since we are focusing on the foreign exchange market between yen and dollars, the price of dollars is the number of yen one must give up to purchase each dollar.

The vertical axis measures the price of dollars in the exchange market. This price is the yen/dollar exchange rate, the number of yen required to purchase a dollar. The demand for dollars consists of holders of yen deposits who want to use them to buy dollars. The supply of dollars is composed of those who hold dollars. Equilibrium in this figure occurs when the exchange rate is 100 yen per dollar.

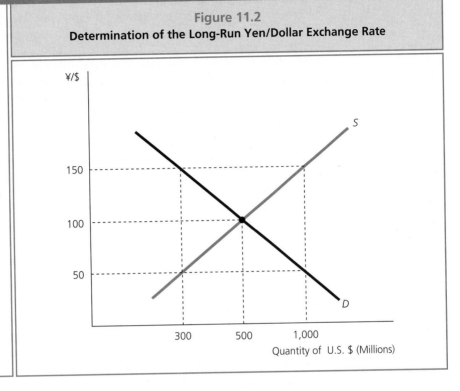

Figure 11.2
Determination of the Long-Run Yen/Dollar Exchange Rate

The downward-sloping curve, *D,* is the demand for U.S. dollars by Japanese residents and other holders of yen (including banks) who need dollars as a medium of exchange to buy U.S. products and financial assets such as stocks and bonds. When the exchange rate is 100 yen per dollar, these holders of yen have a quantity demanded of U.S. dollars of $500 million. When the exchange rate falls to 50 yen per dollar (the dollar depreciates), it becomes cheaper to convert yen into dollars to buy U.S. goods and assets, so the quantity demanded of dollars increases to $1 billion. This is as we would expect given the law of demand: Other things equal, the fewer yen required to purchase a dollar, the greater will be the quantity of dollars demanded by Japanese and other holders of yen.[1]

The upward-sloping curve, *S,* represents the supply of U.S. dollars by U.S. residents, banks, and other holders of dollars who wish to purchase Japanese goods or assets. Since these items must be paid for with foreign

---

[1] Advanced courses in international trade and finance typically introduce other factors (like import and export demand elasticities) that can alter the slopes of the supply and demand curves. We ignore these issues to focus on essential features of exchange markets.

currency, banks trade dollars in the foreign exchange market for foreign currency. When the exchange rate is 50 yen per dollar, the quantity supplied of U.S. dollars is $300 million. When the exchange rate rises to 100 yen per dollar (the dollar appreciates), the quantity supplied of dollars increases to $500 million, reflecting the law of supply. We can think of Americans and other holders of dollars as either demanding foreign currency or supplying dollars, but the latter interpretation allows us to more easily see how the exchange rate (in yen per dollar) is determined in the foreign exchange market.

In the long run, the equilibrium exchange rate is determined by the intersection of these demand and supply curves. In Figure 11.2, the equilibrium exchange rate is 100 yen per dollar and the equilibrium quantity of dollars bought and sold is 500 million. At the exchange rate of ¥100/$, the quantity demanded of dollars exactly equals the quantity supplied, and everyone willing and able to buy or sell dollars at this exchange rate can do so. If the exchange rate were below the equilibrium level, a shortage of U.S. dollars would arise in the exchange market, whereas an exchange rate above that level would create a surplus of dollars in the exchange market. Either situation would put pressure on the exchange rate, moving it back to equilibrium.

Factors That Shift Long-Run Demand or Supply.   Figure 11.1 shows that exchange rates often exhibit long-run trends. We now look at how these long-run trends can be explained by changes in the supply of and demand for currency brought on by changes in such factors as real income or price levels.

Real Income.   The level of real income in an economy ultimately reflects the productivity of the country's resources. Changes in real income at home relative to that abroad will shift the demand or supply curves in the foreign exchange market. For instance, the higher Japanese incomes are, the more U.S. goods and assets Japanese residents will desire, and thus the greater the amount of dollar deposits they will need to make these transactions. Hence the demand for U.S. dollar deposits tends to increase when real income in Japan rises and fall when it declines. Similarly, the supply of U.S. dollars increases when real income in the United States rises. This is because more Japanese goods and assets are desired due to higher real incomes in the United States, and this leads to a greater number of dollars sold in exchange for yen. The supply of U.S. dollars will decrease when U.S. incomes decline.

Since real incomes in Japan and the United States affect the demand for and supply of dollars in the exchange market, a change in Japanese or U.S. real incomes will affect the long-run exchange rate. Consider Figure 11.3, where the initial equilibrium in the exchange market is at point A, where D^0 and S^0 intersect. At the equilibrium exchange rate, e^0, suppliers of dollars

The initial equilibrium in the market for U.S. dollars is at point A, where the exchange rate between yen and dollars is e^0. An increase in U.S. real income raises the supply of dollars in the foreign exchange market from S^0 to S^1, resulting in a decrease in the equilibrium exchange rate from e^0 to e^1 (the dollar depreciates against the yen) and an increase in the equilibrium amount of dollars exchanged from F^0 to F^1.

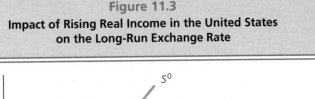

Figure 11.3

Impact of Rising Real Income in the United States on the Long-Run Exchange Rate

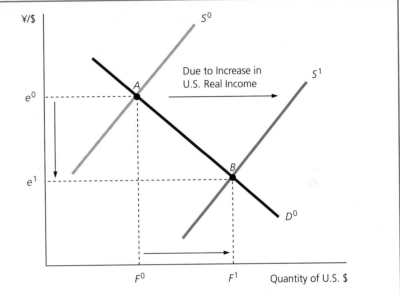

receive e^0 yen for each dollar they sell in the exchange market. Let us see what will happen if real incomes in the United States increase, but everything else (including real incomes in Japan) remains unchanged. With higher real incomes, people, businesses, and banks in the United States will want to purchase more Japanese goods and assets than before, which will require selling more dollars in exchange for yen. This increases the supply of dollars from S^0 to S^1 in Figure 11.3. Thus, as a result of an increase in real income in the United States, equilibrium moves from point A to point B, and the exchange rate falls from e^0 to e^1. The dollar depreciates against the yen because at point B, U.S. residents receive fewer yen for each dollar sold than before the increase in real U.S. income. Notice too that the equilibrium quantity of dollars sold in the foreign exchange market rises from F^0 to F^1.

Similarly, holding other things constant, an increase in Japanese real incomes will lead to an appreciation of the dollar relative to the yen due to the increased demand for dollars. Thus, changes in real income provide one explanation for discernible long-run trends in exchange rates. In fact, the depreciation of the dollar against the yen during the early 1990s that we saw in Figure 11.1 was due in part to the U.S. recession, which resulted in a decline in Americans' real incomes.

Price Levels.   Another important long-run determinant of exchange rates is the price level at home compared to that abroad. When the U.S. price level rises relative to that in Japan, U.S. goods and assets become more expensive relative to Japanese goods, potentially reducing Japan's need for dollars to buy U.S. goods and assets. Furthermore, during periods of continually rising U.S. prices, dollars become a poorer store of value compared to yen because the purchasing power of dollars is eroded more rapidly, allowing fewer goods to be purchased in the future for a given quantity of dollars. For these reasons, a rise in the U.S. price level relative to that in Japan tends to decrease the demand for dollars. Similarly, holders of dollars are more eager to sell them in exchange for yen. Thus, an increase in the U.S. price level relative to that in Japan will increase the supply of dollars.

Figure 11.4 shows how changes in relative price levels affect the long-run exchange rate between yen and dollars. The initial equilibrium is at point A, where the exchange rate (e^0) is determined by the intersection of the demand and supply curves D^0 and S^0. If the U.S. price level increases relative to that in Japan, both the demand for and supply of dollars will shift. In particular, a rise in the U.S. price level increases the supply of dollars from S^0 to S^1 in Figure 11.4 because holders of dollars are more eager to convert them into yen. The rise in the U.S. price level also makes holders of yen less willing to buy dollars, shifting the demand for dollars to the left. If the decrease in the demand for dollars is small relative to the increase in supply (the shift from D^0 to D^1 is small relative to the shift from S^0 to S^1), the new equilibrium will be at point B. In this case, the exchange rate falls from e^0 to e^B, and the equilibrium quantity of dollars traded rises from F^0 to F^B. However, if the decrease in demand is large relative to the increase in supply (the shift from D^0 to D^2 is large relative to the shift from S^0 to S^1), the new equilibrium will be at point C. In this case, the exchange rate falls to an even lower level, e^C, and the quantity of dollars traded falls to F^C.

This analysis reveals a very important principle in foreign exchange markets: All else equal, an increase in a country's price level will lead to long-run depreciation of the country's currency. In Figure 11.4, for instance, the rise in the U.S. price level leads to a decline in the exchange rate to either e^B or e^C. This depreciation of the dollar is due to two consequences of the rise in the U.S. price level: Although holders of dollars become more willing to sell their dollars in exchange for yen, holders of yen are less willing to use their yen to buy dollars. These two forces work together to reduce the exchange rate when the U.S. price level increases. In fact, the depreciation of the dollar against the yen during the last half of the 1970s shown in Figure 11.1 was partly due to the unusually high growth in the U.S. price level at the time.

Tariffs, Trade Barriers, and Preferences.   Tariffs and other trade barriers that restrict the amount of Japanese goods brought into the United States reduce the ability of Americans to purchase Japanese goods and

Figure 11.4
Impact of a Higher U.S. Price Level on the Long-Run Exchange Rate

The initial equilibrium is at point *A* with an exchange rate of e^0. An increase in the U.S. price level relative to that in Japan has two effects. The first is to increase the supply of dollars from S^0 to S^1, which tends to decrease the exchange rate and increase the amount of dollars exchanged. The second is to decrease the Japanese demand for dollars. If demand falls only from D^0 to D^1, the new equilibrium is at point *B*. However, if demand falls from D^0 to D^2, the new equilibrium is at point *C*. Regardless of whether the movement is to *B* or *C*, the higher U.S. price level results in the depreciation of the dollar.

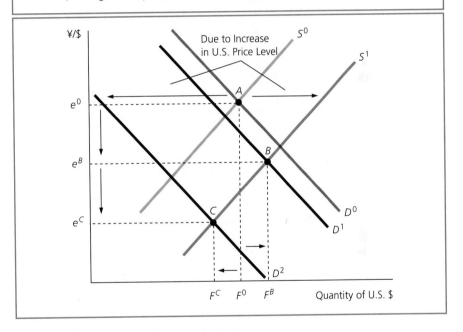

therefore reduce Americans' desire to convert dollars into yen. Thus, restrictions on imports from Japan decrease the supply of dollars, resulting in an increase in the exchange rate. Similarly, limitations on the amount of American goods that can be sold in Japan decrease the demand for dollars, resulting in a lower exchange rate. More generally, any change that reduces Americans' ability or desire to purchase Japanese goods leads to a reduction in the supply of dollars, while changes that reduce Japanese residents' ability or desire to buy U.S. goods decrease the demand for dollars.

The opposite is true of changes that enhance the willingness or ability of domestic consumers to buy foreign products. For example, during the 1980s many Americans perceived Japanese goods as being of better quality than goods made in the United States. These preferences led to increased demand for Japanese goods, most notably cars and electronic products. In turn, this increased demand for Japanese goods meant U.S. importers had to convert dollar deposits into yen to pay for those goods, which led to an increase in the supply of dollars in the foreign exchange market. This ultimately contributed to the depreciation of the dollar against the yen during the last half of the 1980s.

Interest Rates.   Foreign and domestic interest rates can also influence long-run exchange rates through their impact on the demand for and supply of currency. However, we will see shortly that if interest rate parity holds, the impact of interest rates will primarily be on short-run changes in exchange rates.

Why might interest rates affect the long-run exchange rate? Other things equal, the higher the interest rate in the United States relative to that in Japan, the more attractive holders of yen deposits find it to convert those deposits into U.S. dollar deposits to earn higher interest. For this reason, a rise in U.S. interest rates increases the demand for U.S. dollars. Similarly, those who hold dollar deposits become less willing to convert them into yen deposits as U.S. interest rates rise. Consequently, an increase in U.S. interest rates leads to a decrease in the supply of dollars in the exchange market.

Since changes in interest rates affect the demand for and supply of a currency, they affect the equilibrium exchange rate. To see this, suppose the exchange market for dollars is in equilibrium at point A in Figure 11.5. The exchange rate is e^0, which corresponds to the intersection of the demand and supply curves D^0 and S^0. Two things happen if interest rates in the United States rise relative to those in Japan while other things remain constant: First, people holding dollar deposits are now less willing to sell them in exchange for yen; second, people holding yen deposits are more willing to use them to buy dollars.

Thus, the effect of an increase in interest rates in the United States is to decrease the supply of dollars from S^0 to S^1 and increase Japanese consumers' demand for dollars from D^0 to D^1 in Figure 11.5. As a result of these two changes, the equilibrium exchange rate moves to point B, and the exchange rate rises from e^0 to e^B. (Since demand increased and supply decreased, the new equilibrium quantity of dollars traded may rise, fall, or remain the same.) At point A a dollar is worth only e^0 yen, but at point B it is worth e^B yen. The higher U.S. interest rates induce U.S. suppliers to sell fewer dollars at any given exchange rate, which exerts upward pressure on exchange rates. In addition, the higher U.S. interest rates induce Japanese residents to attempt to buy more dollars, which exerts even more upward pressure on the exchange rate. These two forces lead to a higher exchange rate and a more valuable dollar.

Purchasing Power Parity.   Our theory of exchange rates suggests that many factors contribute to the determination of exchange rates in the

The initial equilibrium is at point *A*, where the exchange rate is e^0. If U.S. interest rates rise relative to those in Japan, the supply of dollars falls from S^0 to S^1. In addition, the demand for dollars rises from D^0 to D^1. The new equilibrium is now at point *B*, with a higher exchange rate.

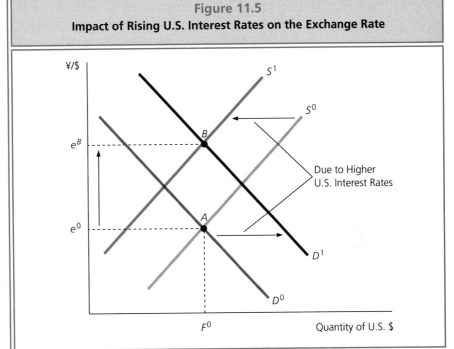

Figure 11.5
Impact of Rising U.S. Interest Rates on the Exchange Rate

long run. A simpler theory, called *purchasing power parity*, asserts that in the long run the exchange rate is determined solely by price levels in different countries. We conclude our analysis of long-run exchange rate determination by examining this theory and its limitations.

The idea of purchasing power parity (PPP) is derived from a consideration of the law of one price, which states simply that two identical goods within a relevant market must sell for the same price. The law of one price is based on the idea that violations of that law will be quickly corrected by buyers purchasing only the good with the lower price.

In international trade, the law of one price can be applied to two identical goods—say, a sweater made in the United States and an identical sweater made in France. For these two sweaters to be sold in the United States, they must sell for the same price, or consumers will buy only the cheaper one. Suppose the sweater costs $30 in the United States; then the sweater from France must also sell for $30 worth of francs. If the exchange rate is 5 French francs per dollar, the price of the sweater in French francs must be 150 francs.

The law of one price by itself applies to a set of identical goods, such as our two sweaters. But the idea has led to the notion of purchasing power parity, which is a relationship not between the prices of an identical good in the United States and in another country but between the price level in the United States and the price level in another country. **Purchasing power parity** states that the price level in the United States (P_{US}) times the exchange rate, e (expressed as foreign currency per dollar), equals the price level in a foreign country (P_F):

$$P_{US} \times e = P_F.$$

When purchasing power parity holds, the dollar has the same purchasing power in the United States and in any other country. By converting dollars into foreign currency at the market exchange rate, you would be able to buy exactly the same amount of foreign goods with your dollars that you would in the United States.

Purchasing power parity also implies that a foreign currency will depreciate if the country's price level rises relative to the foreign price level and appreciate if the foreign price level rises relative to the country's own price level. For instance, suppose the price levels in the United States and abroad are both 100. If purchasing power parity holds, the exchange rate must be unity in order for the purchasing power parity equation to hold. If the U.S. price level rises to 200 while the foreign price level remains unchanged, the dollar exchange rate must depreciate to .5 to balance the equation. More generally, purchasing power parity implies that, other things equal, a 10 percent increase in the U.S. price level will lead to a 10 percent depreciation of the dollar.

Does purchasing power parity hold? The answer is not exactly, especially in the short run (see, for instance, Box 11.3). One reason it fails to hold exactly is the presence of substantial transactions costs in the international trade of goods and services and the existence of nontraded goods—goods like real estate that are not traded internationally and for which there is therefore no tendency for market forces to eliminate international price differences. Another reason stems from the fact that many foreign and domestic goods are not identical; there is no reason to expect a Mercedes to sell for the same price as a Chevy. Finally, we will see shortly that short-run exchange rates are determined in great part by the expectations of traders in the foreign exchange market. Largely for these reasons, the historical evidence does not support the notion that a 10 percent rise in the U.S. price level relative to foreign price levels will result in a 10 percent depreciation of the dollar. However, the theory of purchasing power parity is nonetheless useful because it often accurately predicts the long-run *direction* of changes in exchange rates.

Exchange Rates in the Short Run

As we noted earlier, in the short run (seconds, minutes, hours, or days) exchange rates tend to fluctuate wildly. Since the long-run determinants of exchange rates discussed earlier (like price levels) do not change minute by

International Banking   Box 11.3

Purchasing Power Parity, the Big Mac Standard, and The Economist *Standard*

Economists frequently calculate purchasing power equivalent exchange rates—the exchange rates that would equalize purchasing power across countries. International firms often use these rates to determine the supplemental salaries employees living in high-cost countries require to be able to attain the U.S. standard of living while living abroad.

One of the more interesting measures is what the newsmagazine *The Economist* publishes under the name "Big Mac Standard." This measures what the exchange rates would have to be for the local currency price of a McDonald's Big Mac hamburger to be the same across countries. If the actual exchange rate equals the Big Mac Standard rate, purchasing power parity holds; you can convert the dollar price of a Big Mac in the United States into, say, yen and have enough yen to buy a Big Mac in Japan. Historically, however, actual exchange rates do not allow purchasing power parity to hold for Big Macs.

The accompanying table presents what we call "*The Economist* Standard." Similar to the Big Mac Standard, it contains the exchange rates that would allow you to convert the U.S. price of an issue of *The Economist* into a foreign currency and purchase the magazine at the foreign currency price published on the front cover. For example, in January 1993, the price of *The Economist* in Canadian dollars was C$4.25, and the price in German marks was DM7.00. The U.S. dollar price was US$3.50. These prices are summarized in the second column of the table.

The third column presents the implied purchasing power parity exchange rate on this date among the different currencies. For example, in 1993, C$4.25 would buy an issue of *The Economist,* as would US$3.50, so *The Economist* considered C$4.25 to be equivalent to US$3.50. Thus, the implied exchange rate between U.S. dollars and Canadian dollars that makes the local currency prices of this magazine the same is

Continued on p. 346

Country	Price of The Economist in Local Currency, January 23, 1993	Implied PPP Exchange Rate for One U.S. Dollar	Market Exchange Rate, February 9, 1993	Change in Exchange Rate Required for PPP to Hold	Market Exchange Rate, March 1, 1994
Canada	C$4.25	1.2143	1.2676	−	1.3508
France	FFr23	6.5714	5.5975	+	5.8170
Germany	DM7.00	2	1.6527	+	1.7080
Japan	¥850	242.86	121.25	+	104.55
U.K.	£1.80	.5143	.6985	−	.6713
U.S.	$3.50	—	—	—	—

Continued from p. 345
C\$4.25/US\$3.50 = 1.2143 Canadian dollars per U.S. dollar. Similarly, the implied exchange rate with the Japanese yen is ¥850/\$3.50 = 242.86 yen per U.S. dollar.

The fourth column lists the spot exchange rates on February 9, 1993. These exchange rates do not match up well with the implied rates based on purchasing power parity in column 3. This is consistent with the view that purchasing power parity tends not to hold in the short run. But in the long run, the idea of purchasing power parity is that the market exchange rates will move in the direction of the purchasing power parity rates. The fifth column indicates whether market exchange rates must increase or decrease relative to those in February 1993 for purchasing power parity to hold.

The final column shows the market exchange rates on March 1, 1994. Between 1993 and 1994, market exchange rates for French francs, German marks, and British pounds moved in the direction required by PPP, but this was not the case for Canadian dollars or Japanese yen. This illustrates that PPP is not aways a good predictor of exchange rate movements over short time periods like one year.

minute, they do not explain short-term fluctuations in exchange rates. What causes these short-run movements?

Since today's foreign exchange markets are linked by computers, banks and other dealers of foreign currency, as well as professional traders, can very quickly convert dollar deposits into deposits of foreign currency. In fact, these traders make their living by buying dollars at a low exchange rate one minute and selling them at a slightly higher rate the next. As we will see, this process often results in minute-by-minute changes in exchange rates due to changes in traders' expectations about future exchange rates.

Interest Rate Parity. To currency traders and banks, foreign bank deposits are very close substitutes for dollar deposits because they can easily be converted from one currency into another via the foreign exchange market. For this reason, currency traders and banks continually monitor movements in interest rates and exchange rates across countries to determine the most attractive form of deposits to hold. For instance, suppose a bank has \$1 million in U.S. deposits that pay interest of i_{US}. If the current exchange rate is 100 yen per dollar, the \$1 million can alternatively be converted into a 100-million-yen deposit that earns the foreign interest rate of i_F. Should the bank keep the funds as dollar deposits or convert them into yen deposits?

As we discussed in the section on the determination of long-term exchange rates, the higher the rate in Japan, the more attractive it is to hold Japanese deposits. However, another factor enters the picture in the short run because the rate of return of holding foreign deposits includes both the interest earned on those deposits and the expected appreciation of U.S. currency. If the dollar appreciates against the yen over the next few days, money will be lost when the yen are converted back into dollars. We can see this by letting Ee_{t+1} denote the trader's expectation of the future exchange rate and letting e_t represent the exchange rate right now. The expected rate of return of holding foreign deposits is thus

$$R_F = i_F - \frac{(Ee_{t+1} - e_t)}{e_t}.$$

Notice that $(Ee_{t+1} - e_t)/e_t$ is the expected appreciation of the dollar (in percentage terms) and must be subtracted from the foreign interest rate to account for the fact that an appreciating dollar means part of the interest earned on foreign deposits will be lost when the deposits are converted back into dollars. For instance, if the foreign interest rate is 5 percent and traders expect the dollar to appreciate 3 percent against the yen (that is, expect the exchange rate to increase from 100 yen to 103 yen per dollar), the expected rate of return of holding Japanese deposits is only 2 percent. While 5 percent interest is earned on the foreign account, 3 percent will be lost when the yen used to open the foreign account are converted back into dollars.

In deciding whether to hold dollar or yen deposits, traders continually compare the U.S. interest rate to the expected return they can earn on foreign deposits. If i_{US} exceeds, R_F, they expect to earn more by holding dollar deposits. Consequently these traders begin converting yen into dollars, which puts pressure on the exchange rate to rise. Conversely, if i_{US} is less than the expected return on foreign deposits, R_F, traders convert dollars into yen, which tends to drive down the exchange rate. The point is that traders constantly evaluate these returns and buy and sell currencies by the minute to capitalize on short-term profit opportunities. These short-term buy-and-sell decisions lead to short-term changes in the exchange rate.

Expressed differently, traders in currency markets continually look for profit opportunities that arise from short-term imbalances between the expected returns to holding U.S. versus foreign deposits. They switch deposits across countries to maximize their expected returns, and this practice ultimately leads to the returns being equal:

$$i_{US} = i_F - \frac{(Ee_{t+1} - e_t)}{e_t}.$$

This relation is called **interest rate parity,** because it means the interest rate on dollar deposits equals the expected return on foreign deposits. When interest rate parity holds, traders cannot profit by switching currency holdings, and this effectively determines the short-term exchange rate for the moment, e_t.

Figure 11.6 graphically illustrates interest rate parity. The horizontal axis measures the expected rate of return (in dollar terms), and the vertical axis measures the current exchange rate, e_t, expressed as yen per dollar. The line labeled R_F is the expected rate of return to holding foreign deposits, and the vertical line labeled i_{US} is the U.S. interest rate (the rate of return to holding

Figure 11.6
Interest Rate Parity and Determination of the Short-Term Exchange Rate

When the spot exchange rate is e_t^L, the return to holding dollar deposits (i_{US}) exceeds the return to holding foreign deposits (R_F) at point A. Currency traders quickly convert yen deposits into dollar deposits, which tends to drive up the spot exchange rate to e_t^*. Conversely, when the spot rate is e_t^H, the return to holding foreign deposits at point B exceeds that to holding dollar deposits. This induces currency traders to shift out of dollars and into yen, which drives the spot rate down to e_t^*. At point C interest rate parity holds, meaning the market is in short-run equilibrium because traders cannot make profits by converting one currency into another.

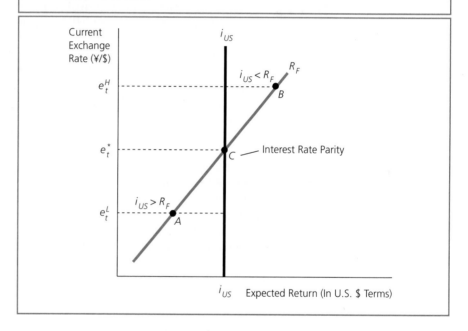

U.S. dollar deposits). At point A, the expected rate of return on dollar deposits exceeds that on foreign deposits ($i_{US} > R_F$), which means profits can be made by converting foreign deposits into dollar deposits. As traders do so, the exchange rate rises. Conversely, at point B the expected return is higher on foreign deposits. Consequently traders convert dollars into foreign deposits, which puts pressure on the exchange rate to fall. Only at point C, where the current (spot) exchange rate is e_t^*, are the expected returns on foreign and dollar deposits equal. At this point, traders cannot buy or sell dollar deposits to earn additional profits because interest rate parity holds; the market is in short run equilibrium.

Expectations of Future Exchange Rates.   We have seen that banks and other currency traders continually seek out profit opportunities.

Notice that these profit opportunities depend critically on the return to holding foreign deposits, which is

$$R_F = i_F - \frac{(Ee_{t+1} - e_t)}{e_t}.$$

This return depends not only on the current exchange rate (e_t) and the interest rate on foreign deposits (i_F) but also on traders' expectations of the future exchange rate (Ee_{t+1}). For this reason, traders' decisions about whether to buy or sell foreign deposits today depends in part on what they expect exchange rates to be in the future. Traders continually update these expectations based on new information, including minute-by-minute wire reports and rumors on the street.

What happens if new information surfaces that leads currency traders to increase their expectations of the future exchange rate? In this case, the expected return to holding foreign currency falls, inducing them to quickly sell yen and buy dollars. This puts upward pressure on the current exchange rate, and short-term appreciation of the dollar occurs. Graphically, an increase in the expected future exchange rate shifts the R_F curve in Figure 11.7 to the left, resulting in a higher exchange rate at which interest rate

The exchange market is initially in equilibrium at point A, where the expected return on foreign deposits equals that on U.S. deposits. An increase in the expected future exchange rate decreases the expected return on foreign deposits, shifting the R_F curve to the left. As you can see, this causes the spot exchange rate to rise to e_t^1 and creates a new short-run equilibrium at point B.

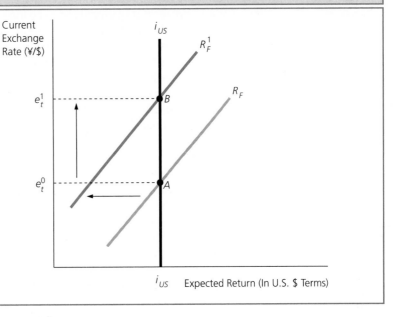

Figure 11.7
Impact of an Increase in the Expected Future Exchange Rate on the Short-Term Exchange Rate

parity holds. Conversely, if expectations of the future exchange rate fall, the R_F curve shifts rightward, and short-term depreciation of the dollar occurs.

You might think traders could profit by using our long-run supply and demand framework to aid in their forecasts of future exchange rates. For instance, suppose a report comes over the news wire that leads traders to expect a higher U.S. price level relative to that in Japan. As we saw earlier in this chapter, a higher price level, if it does materialize, will in the long run lead to the depreciation of the dollar. Does this mean currency traders could profit by immediately converting their dollar deposits into yen? The answer is no. The problem is that in the short run, uncertainty exists about not only whether the higher price level will materialize but, if so, just how high it will be and when its effect on exchange rates will be felt. Add to this the likelihood that other factors might change as well, which could offset the higher U.S. price level. Different traders are likely to form different expectations about all of these things. In addition, most currency traders have very short-term horizons and cannot afford to hold positions in foreign currency for two or three years to capitalize on a long-run devaluation of the dollar.

Consequently, in real life currency traders continually buy and sell currency based on their best guesses about how the latest news report or event will affect exchange rates over the next few days or even minutes. During the war in the Persian Gulf, for instance, exchange rates fluctuated wildly as traders bought and sold currency over very short spans of time based on their own expectations of how long the war would last and how it would affect exchange rate movements. Of course, each day the Department of Defense released new information, and each day these traders changed their buy-and-sell decisions based on their latest expectations.

Thus, short-term movements in exchange rates are largely unpredictable and arise primarily due to minute-by-minute changes in trader expectations that occur as new information becomes available. In the next chapter, we will take a deeper look at why the short-term returns on financial assets are so difficult to predict and discuss different views of how market participants form their expectations. We will use all of these tools extensively in Chapter 17, where we examine the macroeconomic ramifications of changes in exchange rates on such factors as the balance of payments.

Summary Exercise 11.2

(1) Assuming other things remain constant, determine the likely long-term impact of the following on the exchange rate between the U.S. dollar and the British pound. (a) Due to a long recession in both the United States and Britain, real incomes in both countries fall. (b) Interest rates in the United States fall by 2 percent. (2) Suppose the interest rates in the United States and Japan are both 6 percent, but the dollar is expected to depreciate by 2 percent relative to the yen. Does interest rate parity hold? In the short run, what would you expect to happen to the exchange rate?

Answer: (1) (a) Suppose the initial equilibrium in the exchange market between pounds and dollars is at point A in part a. Due to a decline in real income in the United States, the supply of dollars decreases from S^0 to S^1. The decline in real income in Britain reduces the demand for dollars from D^0 to either D^1 or D^2. Depending on the relative magnitude of the shifts, the exchange rate will either rise, fall, or remain the same. If the demand for dollars declines by less than the supply, the new equilibrium is at point B. In this case, the exchange rate rises from e^0 to e^B (the dollar appreciates against the pound). But if demand decreases by more than supply, the new equilibrium is at point C. In this case, the exchange rate falls from e^0 to e^C (the dollar depreciates against the pound).

(b) Suppose the initial equilibrium is at point A in part b. If interest rates in the United States decline, holders of dollar deposits find pound deposits relatively more attractive. This increases the supply of dollars from S^0 to S^1. The decrease in U.S. interest rates, however, makes those holding pound deposits less willing to convert them into dollar deposits. This leads to a decrease in the demand for dollars from D^0 to D^1. These two forces exert downward pressure on the exchange rate, and as a result the new equilibrium is at a point such as B. The exchange rate falls from e^0 to e^1 (the dollar depreciates against the pound).

(2) The expected rate of return (in dollars) of yen deposits is $R_F = 6\%$ $- (-2\%) = 8\%$, which exceeds that on U.S. deposits (6 percent). Since these returns are not equal, interest rate parity does not hold. In the short run, currency traders will attempt to profit by converting dollar deposits into yen deposits, leading to a short-term depreciation of the dollar against the yen.

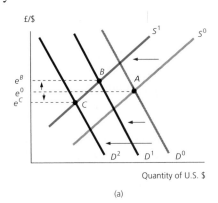

(a)

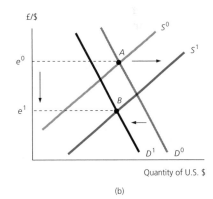

(b)

SPOT AND FORWARD EXCHANGE RATES

Our analysis of the short-term determination of exchange rates reveals that they are often driven by changes in expectations and, furthermore, that they can fluctuate considerably during a given day. This volatility in short-term exchange rates exposes users of foreign exchange markets to risk. In this section, we show how participants in the exchange market can reduce their exposure to risk by using the forward market and how doing so opens up arbitrage possibilities for traders seeking short-term profits in foreign exchange markets.

The **spot rate** is the current exchange rate, the rate at which you can exchange a foreign currency for U.S. dollars at this instant. The spot rate for foreign exchange is akin to getting a price quote on a share of Houghton Mifflin stock from your stockbroker; it is the price at which you can buy the asset in question right now. The forward rate is different. You can sign a forward contract today at an exchange rate and quantity of currency contracted for today. But the actual exchange will take place at a specific future date at a rate called the **forward exchange rate,** because the currency will actually be exchanged at some forward (future) date.

The forward exchange rates presented in Table 11.1 reveal they do not always move in concert with the spot rate. For example, the spot exchange rate for Canadian dollars is C$1.3508 for US$1, while the 180-day forward rate is C$1.3524 for US$1. It takes more Canadian dollars to purchase a given amount of U.S. dollars in a forward contract than on the spot market. Similar to our analysis of yield curves in the previous chapter, this means traders in the forward market expect the U.S. dollar to appreciate relative to the Canadian dollar over the next 180 days. In contrast, Table 11.1 reveals the spot rate for yen is greater than the 180-day forward rate. Since the spot rate of 104.55 yen per dollar exceeds the 180-day forward rate of 103.67 yen per dollar, the U.S. dollar is expected to depreciate relative to the yen over the next 180 days.

Participants in the Forward Market

Who would ever want to buy or sell currency in the forward market? The answer is hedgers, speculators, and arbitrageurs, each of whom we discuss next.

Hedgers.   **Hedgers** go to the forward market to buy or sell currency now to protect themselves against (hedge) fluctuations in exchange rates. Consider a grain dealer with an offer from Japan for a large quantity of soybeans. The Japanese insist on contracting in yen, and the contract offers the grain dealer 1 billion yen for a specified amount of soybeans. The grain dealer looks at the spot exchange rate of 104.55 yen per dollar and calculates that the Japanese are offering the equivalent of $9,564,801.50. The problem is that the Japanese will not pay until they receive the soybeans, half a year from now. The grain dealer wants to accept the deal, on which her costs are $8 million. If the exchange rate doesn't change, she will earn a profit of about 20 percent. However, she worries that the exchange rate could change

Table 11.1
Spot and Forward Exchange Rates

This table presents spot and forward exchange rates for six countries on March 1, 1994, as well as the market prediction of the future change in the exchange rate. For instance, on March 1 you could sell 1 U.S. dollar for 1.3508 Canadian dollars in the spot market. Alternatively, on this date you could sell 1 U.S. dollar on March 1 and in return receive 1.3524 Canadian dollars in 180 days. Since the forward rate is greater than the spot rate, the U.S. dollar is expected to appreciate relative to the Canadian dollar over the next 180 days. The + in the final column represents the market's prediction of this appreciation. Notice the − in the corresponding column for Japan, which indicates the market expects the dollar to depreciate relative to the yen over the next 180 days.

Country	Market Spot Exchange Rate, March 1, 1994	Market 180-Day Forward Exchange Rate, March 1, 1994	Forward Market Prediction for the Change in the Exchange Rate
Canada	1.3508	1.3524	+
France	5.8170	5.8795	+
Germany	1.7080	1.7234	+
Japan	104.55	103.67	−
Switzerland	1.4364	1.4374	+
U.K.	.6713	.6751	+

Source: The *Wall Street Journal*, March 2, 1994, p. C16.

drastically in half a year and destroy her profit margin. For example, if the exchange rate rises to 150 yen per dollar, her 1 billion yen will be worth only $6,666,666.67, and her tidy profit will turn into a loss.

What is the solution to this grain dealer's worries? She can hedge her position by contracting in the forward market for foreign exchange. She signs a contract now to exchange 1 billion yen for dollars in 180 days at the current 180-day forward exchange rate of 103.67 yen per dollar. In this way she locks in the sale and the price, and in 180 days she shows up with 1 billion yen and trades it for $9,645,992.10. This trade will be honored regardless of what the spot exchange rate happens to be in 180 days. Of course, our trader may end up kicking herself if the exchange rate falls or thanking her lucky stars if it rises, but the key point is that she can hedge her position and essentially eliminate the exchange rate risk in her transaction.

Speculators. **Speculators** also buy and sell in the forward market, not to hedge a position but to intentionally take a risky (or open) position. Speculators bet on the direction of the market. To be concrete, suppose the current spot exchange rate is C$1.3508 per U.S. dollar, and the speculator thinks the spot rate in 180 days will be C$1 for one U.S. dollar. Since the 180-day forward rate of C$1.3524 per U.S. dollar exceeds the market spot rate, the market thinks the U.S. dollar will appreciate relative to the Canadian dollar. The speculator can bet against the market by buying Canadian dollars on the forward market. If the market is wrong and the speculator right (i.e. the dollar depreciates), the speculator will be able to sell his Canadian dollars on the spot market in 180 days and make a handsome profit. For instance, if the speculator uses the forward market to buy C$1,000,000 in 180 days for C$1.3524 per U.S. dollar (at a total cost of US$739,426.20), if the spot rate falls to C$1 per U.S. dollar in 180 days, he can turn right around and sell his C$1,000,000 for US$1,000,000 in the spot market—a profit of about 35 percent. Of course, if the speculator is wrong and the market is right, he may lose money. Speculators make money by taking risky positions in the foreign exchange market.

There are other ways to speculate in the foreign exchange market, including going to the futures market instead of the forward market. We won't go into the details of such transactions here. We merely point out that speculators play an important role in these markets too and that these markets work similar to the futures markets we looked at in Chapter 9.

Arbitrageurs. A third group active in the forward market is arbitrageurs. **Arbitrageurs** are buyers and sellers who try to take advantage of temporary profit opportunities created by discrepancies among prices in various markets. They do not speculate; arbitrage possibilities are based not on outguessing the market but on taking advantage of pricing discrepancies. For example, if you notice that this textbook costs $65 at your bookstore but only $45 at a bookstore at another university, you have something like an arbitrage possibility. You could buy this book for $45 and sell it for almost $65 to a classmate. This might be risky, however, since you have only a small number of classmates and it might take considerable time to sell such a book. In contrast, the foreign exchange market involves millions of dollars in transactions virtually every minute. This allows arbitrage to occur very quickly in the exchange market, and at very little risk.

Triangular Arbitrage. One type of arbitrage in exchange markets is triangular arbitrage. **Triangular arbitrage** takes advantage of discrepancies between the spot exchange rate between two currencies and the exchange rate obtainable by first trading one of the two currencies for a third currency and then trading the third currency for the other of the two currencies. For example, suppose the spot rate between U.S. dollars and Canadian dollars is 1.30 Canadian dollars per U.S. dollar and the spot rate between U.S. dollars and British pounds is 1.50 U.S. dollars per 1 pound. One way to obtain British pounds from Canadian dollars is indirectly through purchases of U.S. dollars; that is, 1.95 Canadian dollars will purchase 1.50 U.S. dollars, which in turn will purchase 1 pound. If the exchange rate between Canadian dollars and British pounds differs from this rate, there is an arbitrage possibility—a riskless way to make profits.

For example, if the Canadian dollar were trading for 1.90 Canadian dollars per pound, an arbitrageur could use Canadian dollars to buy pounds and then trade the pounds for U.S. dollars and the U.S. dollars for Canadian dollars. For every 1.90 Canadian dollars, she would buy 1 pound, then buy 1.50 U.S. dollars, and then buy 1.95 Canadian dollars, for a profit of .05 Canadian dollars on every 1.90 Canadian dollars that she had initially. Since these transactions can be executed very quickly, this return can be compounded rapidly. If exchange rates were ever this far out of line, arbitrageurs would instantly trade millions of dollars using the above method, earning huge returns until the exchange rates adjusted to close off this arbitrage possibility.

Covered Interest Arbitrage.

Covered interest arbitrage is an arbitrage possibility that occurs when two countries have interest rates, a spot exchange rate, and a forward exchange rate that allow an arbitrageur to profit. Consider an investor with US$10,000. This investor is considering buying U.S. Treasury bills with these funds, and six-month Treasury bills are paying 5.9 percent interest. However, he is also looking into Canadian Treasury bills, which he reasons are just about as safe as U.S. T-bills and are paying 6 percent interest. His friends, of course, counsel him to take the 6 percent interest in the Canadian bills, but he is not one to quickly jump at things. Instead, he reasons that $10,000 in the U.S. Treasury bills, at 5.9 percent interest for half a year, will earn him $10,000 × 1.0295 = $10,295 after six months.

What about the Canadian investment? The investor can use the US$10,000 to buy Canadian dollars at the going exchange rate of C$1.3508 per U.S. dollar. His US$10,000 will give him US$10,000 × C$1.3508/US$ = C$13,508. He invests this at 6 percent interest for six months and earns C$13,508 × (1.03) = C$13,913.24. He is also worried about exchange rate risk, since six months is a long time away, so he decides to eliminate this risk by using the forward market. He knows that he will have these Canadian dollars in 180 days, so he also contracts forward to exchange this amount of Canadian dollars for U.S. dollars at the forward rate of C$1.3524 for one U.S. dollar. This process—covered interest arbitrage—gives him C$13,913.24/(C$1.3524/US$1) = US$10,287.81 in six months.

What does all this mean? The investment in Canada, even at a higher interest rate, pays a lower return after taking into account the forward exchange rate that would convert interest paid in Canadian dollars back into U.S. dollars in 180 days. Since these are equally safe investments, our investor earns more by investing in U.S. Treasury bills. In fact, so will all other investors in both the United States and Canada. They will flock to U.S.

Treasury bills, bidding up the price and lowering the yield, while at the same time the paucity of investors in Canadian Treasury bills will lower their price and raise their yield, until the return from these two alternative investments of equal risk are equalized. Covered interest arbitrage is the act of choosing between these two equally risky investments according to which pays the higher return, and the continual presence of covered interest arbitrageurs means departures from equality in these two alternative investments are very brief indeed, lasting only minutes at a time.

If we let i_{US} and i_C denote the risk-free interest rates in the United States and Canada and e_{spot} and $e_{forward}$ denote the spot and forward exchange rates (in foreign currency units per dollar), respectively, we can state the covered interest arbitrage condition as

$$1 + i_{US} = e_{spot} \times \frac{(1 + i_C)}{e_{forward}}.$$

The left-hand side is the total return from investing in the U.S. Treasury bill. The right-hand side is the total return from investing in the Canadian Treasury bill, which includes the interest rate in Canada times the spot rate divided by the forward rate. The spot rate divided by the forward rate is called the *foreign exchange term premium* and indicates how the forward market perceives the exchange rates will move. When this equation holds with equality, investors cannot profit from covered interest arbitrage. When the equality does not hold, covered interest arbitrage will lead to profits. If you plug the interest rates and exchange rates used in our earlier example, you will find this equality does not hold. In this example, Canadians can earn profits by investing in the United States via covered interest arbitrage, while Americans simply invest in the United States.

Covered interest arbitrage links the spot and forward exchange rates and the relative interest rates on equally risky investments between two countries. However, covered interest arbitrage does not determine the exchange rate, nor does it tell us how the spot rate will react to a change in the U.S. or Canadian interest rate. We know that if the U.S. interest rate rises, the covered interest arbitrage condition will hold after a very brief adjustment, but we don't know if it will hold because the spot rate will rise, the forward rate will fall, the Canadian interest rate will rise, or some or all of these events will occur.

Summary Exercise 11.3

The yield to maturity on a one-year U.S. Treasury bill is 4.5 percent, and that on an equally safe one-year Canadian Treasury bill is 7 percent. The spot exchange rate is 1.25 Canadian dollars per U.S. dollar, and the one year forward rate is 1.28 Canadian dollars per U.S. dollar. Which Treasury bill should you buy to maximize your return?

Answer: The U.S. Treasury bill yields 4.5 percent, or a return of 1.045. In Canada, you can invest with equal safety by first converting your funds into Canadian dollars at the spot exchange rate of C$1.25/US$1. Then you invest in the Canadian Treasury bill and earn 7 percent, and you contract in the forward market today to convert your funds back into U.S. dollars at the forward exchange rate of C$1.28/US$1. Your return on the Canadian bill is calculated as (C$1.25/US$1) $\times$ (1.07)/(C$1.28/US$1) = 1.0449. Thus, you are almost indifferent between the two investment options, although the U.S. T-bill pays an extra 1/100 of 1 percent.

FIXED AND FLEXIBLE EXCHANGE RATE SYSTEMS

Exchange rates can be flexible—that is, set by forces of supply and demand in the exchange market as discussed earlier in this chapter—or they can be controlled by central bank intervention. We now compare these systems and look at how the Fed can actually intervene in a flexible exchange rate system to influence the exchange rate.

Flexible Exchange Rates

When the exchange rate is determined strictly by the intersection of supply and demand, with no central bank intervention, we say we have **flexible (or floating) exchange rates.** This indicates the exchange rate is free to rise or fall as dictated by supply and demand in the market for foreign exchange, as we have thus far assumed in this chapter. Of course, exchange rates don't have to be flexible, and throughout much of history the world has had fixed exchange rates. We discuss this history a bit later in this chapter, but to put it into context, we first explain methods authorities like the Fed use to intervene in exchange markets.

Central Bank Intervention

Central bank intervention can occur in any foreign exchange market, even in a situation of flexible exchange rates. This situation, called a **dirty float,** occurs when the monetary authority (e.g., the Fed) buys or sells currency to influence the market-determined exchange rate. For instance, today the U.S. dollar exchange rate against the British pound is basically determined by the laws of supply and demand, but the Fed occasionally intervenes to influence the rate.

To see how central bank intervention works, consider a situation where the pound/dollar exchange rate is high by historical standards. The high exchange rate makes it difficult for U.S. exporters specializing in shipments to England to sell products there. This might lead to political pressure that ultimately persuades the Fed to intervene in the foreign exchange market.

What can the Fed do to help U.S. exporters? It can increase the supply of dollars by purchasing pounds. This adds to the total market supply of dollars and tends to lower the exchange rate. Figure 11.8 illustrates this situation. The initial equilibrium is at the intersection of the supply of and demand for dollars, S^0 and D^0, and the equilibrium exchange rate is e^0. The Fed seeks to lower this exchange rate by supplying additional dollars, which shifts the supply curve to S^1. This lowers the equilibrium exchange rate to e^1, the desired result (at least from the point of view of U.S. exporters). U.S. consumers who have a taste for British products, on the other hand, will be harmed by the Fed's actions, since they will now have to pay higher prices for British goods due to the depreciation of the dollar.

Notice that intervention to lower the exchange rate requires the Federal Reserve System to create dollar deposits, which it supplies to the foreign exchange market in return for pounds. Thus, the intervention means the Fed accumulates foreign reserves in the form of British pounds, while also increasing the supply of dollars in circulation. You might be tempted to conclude that these dollars, since they end up in the hands of non-Americans,

The initial supply of dollars is S^0, and demand is D^0. The equilibrium exchange rate is e^0 in the absence of government intervention. If the Fed wants to intervene to lower the exchange rate, it can do so by supplying additional U.S. dollars in the foreign exchange market, increasing the market supply from S^0 to S^1. By doing so, it reduces the equilibrium exchange rate to e^1. Notice that with exchange rates quoted in units of foreign currency per dollar, this reduction in the exchange rate reflects a depreciation of the dollar.

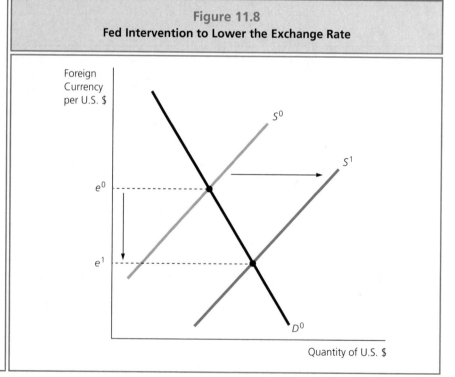

Figure 11.8
Fed Intervention to Lower the Exchange Rate

will not change the U.S. money supply. That is incorrect, however, because non–U.S. consumers generally purchase dollars not to hoard but to spend on U.S. goods or assets, and these dollars, once spent, are in circulation in the United States just like any other dollars. Thus, intervention in the foreign exchange market will tend to increase the U.S. money supply. As we learned in Chapter 3, this can lead to inflation in the United States. In Chapter 17, we look at this situation in more detail.

Would the Fed ever intervene if the exchange rate were too low? A low exchange rate also makes U.S. assets inexpensive relative to British assets, and hence there may be a large increase in purchases of U.S. assets by U.K. citizens. This can have severe political repercussions. Remember the concern a few years ago that the Japanese were ''buying up America''? To remedy this fear, the Fed might intervene to raise the exchange rate, making U.S. assets more expensive for non-Americans. To do so, the Fed would need to decrease the supply of dollars or increase the demand for dollars. But the Fed cannot directly reduce the number of dollars brought to the foreign exchange market, even though it can reduce the U.S. money supply. Thus, the Fed cannot easily shift the supply curve for dollars leftward. But it can add to the demand for dollars by also offering to sell British pounds in exchange for dollars. By doing so, the Fed in essence increases the demand for dollars to D^1 in Figure 11.9. This additional demand will raise the exchange rate from e^0 to e^1.

Of course, the Fed can act in this way only if it actually has a way to pay for the dollars with British pounds; that is, the Fed must have a stash of pounds, or so-called reserves of foreign exchange, before it can intervene in this manner. Also, unlike the situation in which the Fed was supplying dollars (something it can do in unlimited quantities if it so desires), the Fed cannot keep supplying pounds forever; it has only finite supplies of foreign currencies that it can use to intervene in the exchange markets. Thus, trying to raise the pound-per-dollar exchange rate is a different problem than trying to lower it.

Fixed Exchange Rates

How, then, do fixed exchange rates work? The answer depends partly on the exact system of fixed exchange rates adopted. For example, a nation can unilaterally decide to fix the exchange rate between its currency and another currency. Some nations fix the exchange rate between their currencies and the U.S. dollar, even though the dollar itself floats against other currencies. In this situation, the unilateral action requires that the country fixing the exchange rate buy or sell its currency or its foreign reserves to keep the exchange rate fixed. Alternatively, several nations may band together to set up a fixed exchange rate regime, in which the countries take on a mutual responsibility to maintain fixed rates. In this situation, there will be specific

The initial supply of dollars is S^0 and demand is D^0. The equilibrium exchange rate is e^0 in the absence of government intervention. If the Fed wants to intervene to raise the exchange rate, it can do so by demanding U.S. dollars. In effect, it must offer to buy U.S. dollars with its reserves of the foreign currency. This increases demand from D^0 to D^1 and raises the equilibrium exchange rate to e^1. Notice that with exchange rates quoted in units of foreign currency per dollar, this increase in the exchange rate reflects an appreciation of the dollar.

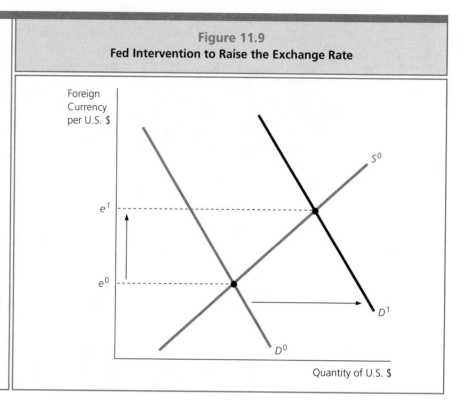

Figure 11.9
Fed Intervention to Raise the Exchange Rate

rules or understandings concerning each country's responsibilities in terms of interventions.

In all cases, **fixed exchange rates** result when a country or group of countries pledge to keep the exchange rate within a narrow band of a target level. To honor this pledge, these nations set up an upper and a lower limit on the exchange rate, then offer to buy or sell all the currency demanded or supplied at those limits. Figure 11.10 illustrates this system. There is an upper bound, e_U, a lower bound, e_L, and somewhere in between a target level, e_T. These bounds are usually fairly tight, such as plus or minus 1 to 3 percent of the target. When the exchange rate gets to the upper bound, e_U, the Fed and/or the foreign central bank agrees to supply more dollars to keep the exchange rate within the band. When the exchange rate gets to the lower bound, e_L, the foreign central bank agrees to demand dollars to keep the exchange rate within the band. A reasonable division of responsibilities might be for the Fed to supply dollars when the exchange rate gets near the upper band, because this is relatively easy for it to do, and the foreign central bank to supply its currency when the exchange rate gets near the lower band, because it is relatively easy for it to do so. The alternatives, such as the

Figure 11.10
Currency Bands and a Fixed Exchange Rate System

With a fixed exchange rate system, the central banks involved commit to maintaining the exchange rate within some band. In the figure, the upper and lower bounds of this band are labeled e_U and e_L, respectively, and the target level for the exchange rate is labeled e_T. As long as the demand for and supply of U.S. dollars results in an exchange rate within the band (as at point A), no action by the Fed is required. If the demand for and supply of dollars results in an equilibrium exchange rate above the upper bound, the Fed will have to supply dollars to reduce the exchange rate. If the equilibrium exchange rate is below the lower bound, the Fed will have to use its foreign currency reserves to demand dollars to increase the exchange rate.

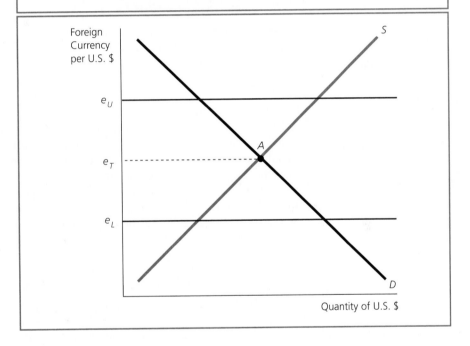

foreign central bank supplying dollars, will tend to drain that bank's reserves of U.S. dollars.

Fixed exchange rates require that monetary policy be devoted to maintaining the exchange rates within the fixed bands. Thus, the U.S. Federal Reserve System would find that its main task is not to maintain a stable money supply or a stable price level but to maintain a stable exchange rate. If this means a stable money supply or a stable price level, all the better. But under a fixed exchange rate system, the Fed must sacrifice its ability to pursue other goals to almost singlemindedly pursue the goal of exchange rate stability. For reasons we will see in Chapter 17, many nations do not want to give up their ability to use monetary policy for domestic purposes, and hence will not commit to a fixed exchange rate system.

A BRIEF HISTORY OF THE FOREIGN EXCHANGE RATE SYSTEM

You now have a basic understanding of how modern exchange markets work and how they are affected by central bank intervention. We conclude by taking a look at the history of exchange rate systems. As we will see, there have been a number of such systems, ranging from the gold standard to the present system in which many currencies float against one another.

The Classical Gold Standard

A **gold standard** pegs currency to a specified amount of gold—say, one ounce. During most of the 1700s and 1800s, England was on a gold standard, departing from it during the Napoleonic Wars and during World War I in 1914. England returned briefly to the gold standard in 1926, only to depart again in 1931 during the Great Depression. The United States was on a gold standard from 1879 until the midst of the Great Depression in 1933. The period 1890–1914 is considered the high point of the gold standard. During this period, countries announced they would buy or sell gold at stated prices. This would set, or peg, the value of the currency in terms of gold. For example, the United States pegged the dollar so that an ounce of gold was worth about 20 U.S. dollars.[2] Similarly, the British pegged the pound so that an ounce of gold was worth about four English pounds. In essence these actions not only set the value of the currencies in terms of gold but also set the exchange rates, since a U.S. citizen could exchange $20 for one ounce of gold and then use the gold to purchase four pounds. Thus, $20 was equal in value to 4 pounds; that is, the exchange rate was $5 for 1 pound, or .2 pounds for $1.

How did the governments maintain these gold equivalents? Basically, by standing willing to supply enough currency—dollars or pounds—to keep the supply of and demand for the currency relative to gold in equilibrium at the desired levels. What would happen, for example, if the U.S. dollar started to appreciate so that the dollar price of gold was falling? As the equilibrium price of gold was falling to $19 per ounce, the U.S. government would still buy or sell gold for $20 an ounce. In this case, domestic and foreign residents would trade the government gold for dollars, since the government would give them $20 per ounce while the market price was only $19 per ounce. Of course, the U.S. government would be accumulating gold. This increase in gold would lead to an increase in the money supply and an eventual rise in the price level. When the price level rose, the price of gold would rise,

---

[2] Actually, $20.672 per ounce of gold.

and this would tend to restore equilibrium. In practice the price of gold never departed much from the pegged levels, because the governments adjusted their money supplies to fluctuations in the stock of gold to keep its price at the pegged levels.

Like any fixed exchange rate system, the gold standard had its pluses and minuses. The biggest minus was perceived to be the constraint the gold standard imposed on monetary policy. Under a gold standard, a nation was not free to increase the money supply at will, since doing so would tend to destroy the pegged price of gold. Instead, any increases or decreases in the money supply ended up being governed by gold flows into and out of the government's treasury. Some viewed this as a plus, however, because it limited the government's ability to inflate the money supply and prices.

Bretton Woods

The Great Depression and World War II spelled the end of the classic gold standard. After World War II, the western nations operated under an exchange rate system called the **Bretton Woods** system, named after the town in New Hampshire in which the system was negotiated. Under this system, the United States agreed to peg the U.S. dollar so that an ounce of gold would sell for $35. Then each country fixed the exchange rate between its currency and the U.S. dollar. This was a modified gold standard in which each currency was indirectly pegged to gold via the dollar.

Unlike the classic gold standard, under the Bretton Woods system only the United States fixed the exchange rate between its currency and gold. All other nations bought or sold their currencies in terms of dollars, maintaining fixed exchange rates with the dollar. The Bretton Woods system operated until August 15, 1971, when President Nixon announced the United States would no longer honor requests to exchange dollars for gold at $35 per ounce.

What caused the demise of Bretton Woods? The basic problem was an overvalued dollar, caused in part by the unwillingness of the United States to pursue the policy required to maintain gold at $35 per ounce. This would have required a contractionary monetary policy, which, as we will see in Chapter 16, can cause temporary increases in unemployment and decreases in output. Not willing to pursue such a policy, the United States instead opted for more expansionary monetary policy that eventually led to the downfall of the Bretton Woods system. Other contributing factors were the unwillingness of other nations to adjust their exchange rates to correct the problem of an overvalued dollar and an institutional setup that provided no way for the United States to devalue its currency directly. Exchange rates between the United States and the war-torn industrialized countries of Japan and Europe became difficult to maintain as those nations recovered from their war wounds and became increasingly competitive with the United States on the economic front.

For a brief period, nations attempted to create alternatives to the defunct Bretton Woods system. But by February 12, 1973, the Japanese yen floated against the dollar, and by March 16, 1973, the European Community followed suit. The world embarked on a floating or flexible exchange rate system.

Post–Bretton Woods

From 1973 to the present, the United States has had a flexible exchange rate to one degree or another. Market forces set the exchange rate of the dollar against other currencies, with only occasional intervention by the Fed. However, some nations have unilaterally pegged their currencies to the dollar or to the currency of some other nation, and the European Community attempted a partial system of pegged exchange rates.

Some nations of the European Community started the **European Monetary System (EMS)** in 1979, in which exchange rates between member countries were pegged to narrow bands. This system pegged these currencies relative not to other currencies such as the dollar or the yen but only to one another. This system seemed to be working relatively well until 1992, when high German interest rates drove several currencies out of the EMS, most notably the English pound. Box 11.4 discusses the EMS in more detail.

Summary Exercise 11.4

Late in the summer of 1992, the EMS experienced difficulty because Germany raised its interest rates to new heights. The British government was under great pressure to devalue its currency, because Britain did not want to match Germany's increase in interest rates. Explain this situation using the foreign exchange market.

Answer: Graph the demand for and supply of British pounds, with the exchange rate being German marks per pound. The supply curve is the supply of pounds by Britons, while the demand curve is the demand for pounds by Germans. When Germany raised interest rates, German assets became more attractive than British assets, everything else constant. Thus, German demand for pounds declined, since fewer Germans wanted to buy assets in Britain. The British supply of pounds increased, however, because more Britons wanted to buy assets in Germany. The net effect was to reduce the exchange rate in marks per pound—a depreciation of the pound. To counter this, the British central bank would have had to raise British interest rates, which it refused to do in the midst of a recession. Instead, it chose to intervene heavily in the foreign exchange market, purchasing pounds with foreign reserves to increase demand and prop up the exchange rate. However, so great were the interest rate differential and the pressure on the pound that in the end Britain gave up and instead chose to let the pound float, effectively abandoning the EMS for the time being.

International Banking

Box 11.4

The European Monetary System

The European Community, which has been moving closer toward political and monetary union for some time, established the European Monetary System (EMS) in 1979. The EMS involves a system of fixed but adjustable exchange rates. The eventual goal was to establish full European Monetary Union (EMU), with a common European central bank and a common currency. These goals were framed by the DeLors report in 1989, which set goals of permanently fixed exchange rates (in effect, a common currency) and integrated capital markets (with monetary policy conducted not by the central banks of member nations but by a European central bank). More recently, the Maastricht Ac-

cord of 1991 confirmed the goals of the DeLors report and established a timetable for achieving those goals by January 1, 1999, at the latest.

The EMS is widely credited with reducing inflation rates in Europe, mostly because currencies are pegged to the German mark and Germany has maintained a low inflation rate. Because of this, other nations also must maintain a low inflation rate. If not, the ratio of the price level in Germany to the price level in another nation will fall, and the exchange rate with the German mark will move outside of the fixed rate. Thus, the EMS has imposed German monetary discipline on other nations.

Continued on p. 366

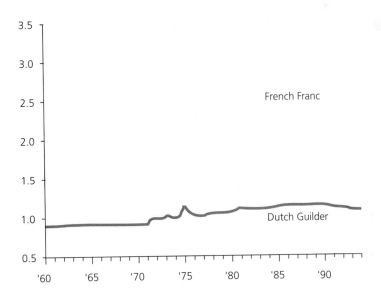

Continued from p. 365

The accompanying figure graphs the exchange rates between the French franc and the German mark and between the Dutch guilder and the German mark. Notice that the Dutch guilder has maintained a fairly constant exchange rate of about 1.12 guilders per mark since the early 1980s. In contrast, the French franc has a long history of depreciating relative to the mark; the exchange rate rose from fewer than 1.5 francs per mark in the 1960s to more than 3 francs per mark in the 1980s. As part of the EMS, the French franc was held at a fairly constant rate of about three francs per mark be-

ginning in early 1983 and lasting until early 1986. At this point the franc was devalued, and by early 1987 the franc had depreciated to about 3.33 francs per mark. This rate has been fairly closely maintained since then, so that in early 1993 the rate was 3.40 francs per mark. The stabilization of the franc after an initial false start was an EMS success story until the latter half of 1993, when the EMS once again encountered serious problems.

_____

Source: Board of Governors of the Federal Reserve System, *Foreign Exchange Rates,* various issues; Citibase electronic database, and authors' calculation.

CONCLUSION

In this chapter, we examined the role of foreign exchange markets and established a theoretical framework for predicting long-run exchange rate movements by using the model of supply and demand used throughout this text. We also looked at how purchasing power parity can be used to obtain a gauge of general long-run movements in exchange rates. We saw that short-term exchange rates are determined largely by arbitrage and interest rate parity, and that short-term movements in exchange rates are often difficult to predict because of the role of short-run expectations. We concluded by looking at how central banks intervene in currency markets and briefly overviewed the foreign exchange rate systems used during this century. In the next chapter, we take an in-depth look at how participants in financial markets form expectations and forecasts of economic variables like inflation and exchange rates.

KEY TERMS

foreign exchange market

exchange rate

depreciation

appreciation

purchasing power parity

interest rate parity

spot rate

forward exchange rate

hedger

speculator

arbitrageur

triangular arbitrage

KEY TERMS continued

covered interest arbitrage

flexible (floating) exchange rates

dirty float

fixed exchange rates

gold standard

Bretton Woods

European Monetary System (EMS)

QUESTIONS AND PROBLEMS

1. Based on what you learned in this chapter, why do you think exchange rates tend to fluctuate over long periods of time? Over short periods of time?

2. Suppose the exchange rate between Dutch guilders (DF) and U.S. dollars is 1.7 guilders per dollar.
   (a). How much would it cost in dollars to purchase a box of rare tulips that sell for 980 guilders?
   (b). How much would it cost in guilders to purchase a car that sells for $12,500?

3. How would your answer in problem 2 change if the exchange rate changed to three guilders per dollar? Has the dollar appreciated or depreciated against the guilder? Has the guilder appreciated or depreciated against the dollar?

4. How would your answer in problem 2 change if the exchange rate changed to 1.5 guilders per dollar? Has the dollar appreciated or depreciated against the guilder? Has the guilder appreciated or depreciated against the dollar?

5. Use a diagram to illustrate the impact of the following on the demand for dollars by Italians: (a) a decrease in Italians' real incomes, (b) an increase in the Italian price level, and (c) an increase in the interest rate in Italy.

6. Use a diagram to illustrate the impact of the following on the supply of dollars to Italians: (a) a decrease in Italians' real incomes, (b) a decrease in the Italian price level, and (c) a decrease in the interest rate in Italy.

7. Determine the impact of the following on the exchange rate between U.S. dollars and Italian lire:
   (a). Italy experiences a minor recession, while the U.S. enjoys an economic boom.
   (b). Interest rates in Italy fall by 3 percent.
   (c). Interest rates in the United States rise by 4 percent.
   (d). The price level in the United States increases by 10 percent.

8. Suppose interest rates in the United States increase from 4 to 8 percent, while those in Japan fall from 4 to 2 percent. What affect would you expect this to have on the long-run exchange rate between dollars and yen?

9. Suppose the government imposed a tax on income earned by non-residents on U.S. debt obligations. Would you expect the dollar to appreciate or depreciate relative to the yen? Explain.

10. Between 1985 and 1990, the dollar depreciated considerably against the British

pound. Do you think this contributed to a decline in the number of Americans who visited Britain? Explain.

11. Based on what you learned in this chapter, provide three possible explanations for each of the following events:
(a). Over the last four years, the dollar depreciated against the pound.
(b). Today the dollar appreciated against the mark.

12. During the past decade, the Mexican peso and various South American currencies have depreciated against the currency of virtually every western industrialized country. Why do you think this has happened? (Hint: Go to your library and obtain information about changes in the price level in Mexico and in various South American countries during the past 10 years.)

13. In light of problem 12, what actions could you recommend to the Mexican central bank to remedy the depreciation of the peso? Could your policy be sustained for very long? Explain.

SELECTIONS FOR FURTHER READING

Ahking, F. W. "The Dollar/Pound Exchange Rate in the 1920s: An Empirical Investigation." *Southern Economic Journal,* 55 (April 1989), 924–934.

Ahking, F. W. "Further Results on Long-run Purchasing Power Parity in the 1920s." *European Economic Review,* 34 (July 1990), 913–919.

Akgiray, V., et al. "A Causal Analysis of Black and Official Exchange Rates: The Turkish Case." *Weltwirtschaftliches Archiv,* 125 (1989), 337–345.

Antonovita, F., and R. D. Nelson. "Forward and Futures Markets and the Competitive Firm under Price Uncertainty." *Southern Economic Journal,* 55 (July 1988), 182–195.

Blenman, L. P. "A Model of Covered Interest Arbitrage under Market Segmentation." *Journal of Money, Credit, and Banking,* 23 (November 1991), 706–717.

Breece, J. H. "Devaluation, Money and Currency Substitution." *Economia Internazionale,* 40 (May/August 1987), 172–191.

Driskill, R., and S. McCafferty. "Exchange-Rate Determination: An Equilibrium Approach with Imperfect Capital Substitutability." *Journal of International Economics,* 23 (November 1987), 241–261.

Driskill, R., and S. McCafferty. "Speculation, Rational Expectations, and Stability of the Foreign Exchange Market." *Journal of International Economics,* 10 (February 1980), 91–102.

Feltenstein, A., and S. Morris. "Fiscal Stabilization and Exchange Rate Instability: A Theoretical Approach and Some Policy Conclusions Using Mexican Data." *Journal of Public Economics,* 42 (August 1990), 329–356.

Harrison, M. J., P. D. McNelis, and S. N. Neftci. "A Diagnostic Check for Model Specification: An Application to the Yen-Dollar Exchange Rate." *Economic Letters,* 33 (May 1990), 69–73.

Honohan, P., and P. McNelis. "Is the EMS a DM Zone?—Evidence from the Realignments." *Economic and Social Review,* 20 (January 1989), 97–110.

Kulkarni, K. G., and D. Chakraborty. "An Empirical Evidence of Purchasing Power Parity Theory: A Case of Indian Rupee and U.S. Dollar." *Margin,* 22 (October 1989–March 1990), 52–56.

Mark, N. C. "Real and Nominal Exchange Rates in the Long Run: An Empirical Investigation." *Journal of International Economics,* 28 (February 1990), 115–136.

McMillin, W. D., and F. Koray. "Does Government Debt Affect the Exchange Rate? An Empirical Analysis of the U.S.–Canadian Exchange Rate." *Journal of Economics and Business,* 42 (November 1990), 279–288.

Rogers, J. H. "Foreign Inflation Transmission under Flexible Exchange Rates and Currency Substitution." *Journal of Money, Credit, and Banking,* 22 (May 1990), 195–208.

Sayer, W. C., and R. L. Sprinkle. "Contractionary Effects of Devaluation in Mexico." *Social Science Quarterly,* 68 (December 1987), 885–893.

12

Rational Expectations and Efficient Markets

*T*hroughout the first half of this book, we have seen that expectations of consumers, banks, and other businesses have pronounced effects on supply and demand in financial markets. If inflationary expectations rise, the supply of and demand for loanable funds shift, and higher interest rates result. Similarly, we saw in the last chapter that when traders in the foreign exchange market expect the exchange rate to fall, the result is a rise in the cost of buying imports. Thus, changes in expectations affect the rate you pay on car loans and, if your car is an import, the sticker price of your car. We conclude the first part of the book by taking a closer look at how participants in financial markets form expectations and what might cause those expectations to change over time.

We learned in Chapter 9 that risk is present when individuals know the likelihood that different outcomes will occur. In many instances, however, individuals do not know the underlying probabilities of different outcomes. For instance, do you know the probability that the inflation rate will rise to 10 percent or fall to 1 percent next year? In such instances of uncertainty, you and other individuals must base your expectations on a subjective assessment of different future outcomes. In the first part of this chapter, we look at various methods used to form expectations under uncertainty. Then we deal with a related issue—the efficient markets hypothesis—which has profound implications for your ability to "beat" financial markets like the stock market. To put all of this in perspective, let us review the important role expectations play in financial markets.

THE ROLE OF EXPECTATIONS IN FINANCIAL MARKETS

Throughout this book you have seen how expectations affect financial markets and, more generally, the economy. Our analysis of the Fisher equation in Chapter 3, coupled with Chapter 4's model of loanable funds, showed how inflationary expectations influence interest rates. Chapters 5 and 6 revealed that a bank's portfolio of assets and liabilities depends in part on the expected return to various assets and the expected cost of various liabilities.

For example, a bank's amount of excess reserves is determined partly by the expected return on alternative assets such as loans and bonds and partly by expectations of the rate of deposit withdrawals. In Chapter 9, we saw that the price of a corporate bond will depend on investors' expectations about the bond's default risk. Chapter 10 revealed that the term structure of interest rates is affected by expectations, since long-term interest rates depend on expectations of future short-term interest rates. Chapter 11 showed how expectations influence short-term exchange rates.

In later chapters, we examine the implications of expectations on such factors as money creation (Chapter 14), the supply of and demand for money (Chapter 15), aggregate supply and demand (Chapter 16), and various aspects of monetary policy conducted by the Fed (Chapters 18 through 21). In fact, we will see that increases in the money supply have different effects on employment and real output depending on whether changes in the money supply are anticipated by workers or by firms.

As you can see, expectations play a central role not only in money and banking but in every aspect of economic life. In the next section, we look at methods people use to form expectations.

THREE THEORIES OF EXPECTATION FORMATION

Suppose you want to forecast the inflation rate for the current year to determine the expected real rate of interest on your saving deposits. By the Fisher equation, your expected real interest rate (r) is the difference between the nominal interest rate (i) paid by the bank and your inflationary expectations (π^e):

$$r = i - \pi^e.$$

If your bank pays 3 percent on saving deposits and you expect inflation to be 2 percent over the next year, your expected real interest rate is only 1 percent. If your inflationary expectations are higher—say, 5 percent—your expected real interest rate is -2 percent, meaning your deposits would lose 2 percent of its purchasing power while in the bank.

Obviously your incentives to deposit money in a savings account depend not only on the rate the bank offers but on your inflationary expectations as well. The same is true for other savers, including large investors like mutual funds, insurance companies, and traders on Wall Street. Furthermore, there is a cost to making errors in your inflationary expectations. If your inflationary expectations are too low on average during the course of your life, your errors may lead you to make investment decisions that yield a negative real return. How, then, do you go about forming expectations of inflation?

In this section we look at three ways to form expectations: the Markov expectations, adaptive expectations, and rational expectations hypotheses.

Each approach requires a different level of sophistication on the part of those forming expectations. To compare and contrast expectation formation under each theory, we focus on the formation of inflationary expectations, since they are an important determinant of virtually every financial market we have studied. As we will see, however, you may use similar methods to forecast other variables—your grade in this course, for instance.

Markov Expectations

The simplest way to form expectations about future events is to form Markov expectations. The **Markov expectations hypothesis** asserts that individuals expect the future to be like the most recent past. For instance, if the inflation rate last year was 3.5 percent, you can simply presume the future rate will be the same as last year's: 3.5 percent. With Markov expectations, individuals expect tomorrow to be exactly like today.

An obvious shortcoming of Markov expectations is that they do not take into account knowable events that might change the future environment. For instance, if the inflation rate is rising, Markov expectations will continually miss the mark. Each year you will expect the inflation rate to remain at its previous level, but each year you will be surprised to find it higher than expected. As we will see, another shortcoming is that this hypothesis ignores other information that might be useful in predicting the future. Markov expectations are based solely on the most recent value of the variable being forecast.

The Mechanics of Markov Expectations.   Under Markov expectations, the expected value of x_t, based on information available at time $t - 1$, is simply x_{t-1}:

$$x_t^e = x_{t-1}.$$

Thus, you simply use the most recent known value of x to forecast future values of x.

Although Markov expectations suffer from a number of deficiencies, they are a reasonable method of forming expectations when the forecasting environment is stable rather than changing over time. For instance, if inflation tends to be stable at 3.5 percent, as it was during much of the 1980s, using last year's rate of 3.5 percent to predict this year's inflation rate will not lead to any systematic error in your inflation forecast. In contrast, when the structure of the economy and economic variables are in a state of flux so that the inflation rate systematically rises or falls year after year as it did during the 1970s, Markov expectations tend to yield systematic errors. This is because the past is a poor predictor of the future during periods of change, and Markov expectations actually assume the future will be like the most recent past. In the next section, we take a deeper look at the deficiencies of Markov expectations during periods of change.

An Example: Markov Inflationary Expectations. If the inflation rate last year was 3.5 percent ($\pi_{t-1} = .035$), the **Markov inflationary expectation** is also 3.5 percent ($\pi_t^e = .035$). Clearly, forming Markov expectations of this year's inflation rate is a piece of cake: We simply obtain information about the most recent rate of inflation and use it as the forecast.

Table 12.1 shows that Markov expectations perform well when the economic environment is stable but can lead to systematic errors in an environment of change. The second column represents the actual inflation rate in each of 10 hypothetical periods. The third column gives the Markov expectation of these inflation rates, which are simply the previous period's inflation rate. The final column gives the forecast errors, the difference between the actual and expected rates of inflation. Notice that an individual with Markov expectations cannot form a forecast of the inflation rate in period 1, since there is no previous period on which to base the forecast. Once the individual observes that the actual inflation rate in period 1 is 5 percent, this value becomes the forecast of the inflation rate for period 2. No forecast errors occur for periods 2, 3, and 4 because the actual inflation rate did not change between periods.

In period 5, however, the actual inflation rate rises to 11 percent. This individual's expectation of the inflation rate in period 5 is the inflation rate in period 4, again 5 percent. Since the actual inflation rate in period 5 is 11 percent, the forecast error is 6 percent.

Once the individual observes the inflation rate in period 5 is 11 percent, the forecast of the inflation rate in period 6 becomes 11 percent. But in period 6, the actual inflation rate is 25 percent, so the forecast error is 14 percent. In periods 7 through 10, the actual inflation rate remains at 25 percent, so the forecast error is zero. Thus, Table 12.1 illustrates that Markov expectations work well in environments where inflation does not change from year to year but leads to systematic forecast errors in environments of change. In particular, when the inflation rate increases over time, Markov expectations will lead to systematic underestimates of inflation. Forecasters never learn from their past mistakes, and errors result each time the inflation rate rises.

Adaptive Expectations

The **adaptive expectations approach** assumes expectations evolve over time in light of past experience. It allows past trends in variables as well as previous forecast errors to affect future expectations as people slowly learn from past mistakes. For instance, a person may notice that her expectation of inflation was too high the previous period and thus revise downward her expectation of the future inflation rate. Since adaptive expectations look backward, they take into account the past history of a variable and of forecasts of that variable.

Table 12.1
Markov Expectations of Inflation

Markov expectations of inflation will be correct as long as the inflation rate does not change. This is the case in periods 2 through 4, where the forecast errors are zero. When the rate of inflation does change, as in periods 5 and 6, Markov expectations will lead to large forecast errors.

$$\pi_t^e = \pi_{t-1}$$

Period (t)	Actual Inflation Rate (π_t)	Expected Inflation Rate (π_t^e)	Forecast Error ($\pi_t - \pi_t^e$)
1	5%	—	—
2	5	5%	0%
3	5	5	0
4	5	5	0
5	11	5	6
6	25	11	14
7	25	25	0
8	25	25	0
9	25	25	0
10	25	25	0

A potential problem with adaptive expectations is that when the future is continually changing, past history is not always a good forecast of the future. Moreover, we will see that adaptive expectations do not use all the information that is useful in forecasting the future.

The Mechanics of Adaptive Expectations.   Adaptive expectations, like Markov expectations, are based on past experience. Unlike Markov expectations, however, adaptive expectations adjust current expectations based on information about the accuracy of prior forecasts. More specifically, the current adaptive expectation about x in period t given what is known in period $t - 1$, denoted x_t^e, is given by

$$x_t^e = x_{t-1}^e + \lambda(x_{t-1} - x_{t-1}^e).$$

This formula states that the current expectation of x, x_t^e, equals last period's expectation, x_{t-1}^e, plus a term that adjusts this expectation in light of past errors, $\lambda(x_{t-1} - x_{t-1}^e)$, where the expression in parentheses is last period's forecast error and λ is called the *adjustment factor*. More generally, adaptive expectations make current forecasts a weighted average of past observations.

The **speed of adjustment,** λ, determines how quickly expectations adjust to past errors. If λ is zero, expectations never adjust, and we always have $x_t^e = x_{t-1}^e$. In this case, the current expectation is identical to that in the previous period, regardless of how inaccurate the expectation was last period. In contrast, if λ is 1, expectations always adjust instantaneously to the previous value of the variable, and hence $x_t^e = x_{t-1}$. This illustrates that when $\lambda = 1$, we have a special case of adaptive expectations called *Markov expectations*.

An Example: Adaptive Inflationary Expectations.

Table 12.2 presents an example of **adaptive inflationary expectations** when the speed of adjustment, λ, is .5. The data in column 2 are hypothetical, but they illustrate a situation where inflation permanently increases from 5 to 10 percent in period 5. This is similar to what occurred in the United States during the last half of the 1970s, when the inflation rate doubled. To read this table, take as given the row for period 1; it simply says that we are starting from a point where the expectation of inflation is consistent with the actual inflation rate. Given that expectations were not in error in period 1, the adaptive expectation of the inflation rate in period 2 is

$$\pi_2^e = \pi_1^e + \lambda(\pi_1 - \pi_1^e) = .05 + .5(.05 - .05) = .05.$$

That is, since the forecast error in period 1 was zero, the inflation rate in period 2 is expected to be what was expected in period 1: 5 percent. When the inflation rate is announced in period 2, it is 5 percent—exactly what was expected. Given this, the forecast of the inflation rate for period 3 is

$$\pi_3^e = \pi_2^e + \lambda(\pi_2 - \pi_2^e) = .05 + .5(.05 - .05) = .05,$$

which is the same as we expected the previous period. Notice this situation continues through period 4.

In period 5, the forecast of the inflation rate for period 5 is again given by

$$\pi_5^e = \pi_4^e + \lambda(\pi_4 - \pi_4^e) = .05 + .5(.05 - .05) = .05.$$

Unfortunately, however, in period 5 the actual inflation rate is 10 percent, and the expectations are off by 5 percent. Consequently, when the forecast of inflation for period 6 is made, this error in expectation affects the estimate of inflation:

$$\pi_6^e = \pi_5^e + \lambda(\pi_5 - \pi_5^e) = .05 + .5(.10 - .05) = .075.$$

Notice that the expected rate of inflation in period 6 is higher than that in periods 1 through 5. The reason is that in period 5, the forecast error was $(.10 - .05) = .05$. This is multiplied by the speed of adjustment in expec-

---

Table 12.2
Adaptive Expectations with a Permanent Jump in Inflation: $\lambda = .50$

Like Markov expectations, adaptive expectations perform well when the inflation rate in column 2 is constant (periods 1 through 4). In period 5 the actual inflation rate increases to 10 percent, but the adaptive expectation of inflation for that period remains at 5 percent. Given the permanent jump in the inflation rate, the forecast error gradually declines in periods 7 through 10. The adaptive expectation of inflation is still off, however, even in period 10.

$$\pi_t^e = \pi_{t-1}^e + .5(\pi_{t-1} - \pi_{t-1}^e)$$

Period (t)	Actual Inflation Rate (π_t)	Expected Inflation Rate (π_t^e)	Expected Inflation Rate Last Period (π_{t-1}^e)	Actual Inflation Rate Last Period (π_{t-1})	Forecast Error Last Period ($\pi_{t-1} - \pi_{t-1}^e$)
1	5%	5%	5%	5%	0%
2	5	5	5	5	0
3	5	5	5	5	0
4	5	5	5	5	0
5	10	5	5	5	0
6	10	7.5	5	10	5
7	10	8.75	7.5	10	2.5
8	10	9.375	8.75	10	1.25
9	10	9.6875	9.375	10	0.625
10	10	9.84375	9.6875	10	0.3125

tations ($\lambda = .5$), which yields $.5(.10 - .05) = .025$. When this is added to the previous year's expectation of .05, the result is .075—a 7.5 percent expected inflation rate for period 6. This example illustrates how errors in past forecasts influence adaptive inflationary expectations as people attempt to learn from past mistakes.

The estimate of the inflation rate in period 7, given what is known in period 6, is the period 6 expectation (7.5 percent) plus half of the previous error in expectations (2.5 percent). Thus, the expected rate of inflation in period 7, formed in period 6, is 8.75 percent. This process continues, and with a constant actual inflation rate of 10 percent through period 10, the expectation in period 10 has reached 9.84375 percent—just slightly lower than the actual inflation rate in this period.

Figure 12.1 plots the results from Table 12.2 and reveals an important feature of adaptive inflationary expectations. When the actual rate of inflation jumps to 10 percent, expectations adjust slowly and only gradually get closer

Here inflation is stable until period 5, when it permanently jumps to 10 percent. Adaptive expectations only gradually adjust to the higher inflation rate, leading to systematic errors in period 5 and beyond.

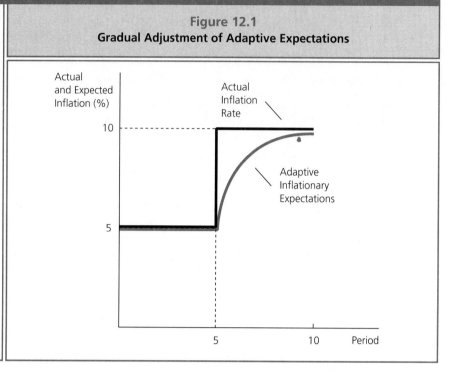

Figure 12.1
Gradual Adjustment of Adaptive Expectations

to the actual rate of inflation. This is because adaptive expectations make the current forecast a weighted average of past observations. During the adjustment process, systematic errors occur in inflationary expectations, since inflationary expectations are continually below the actual inflation rates in Figure 12.1 after the permanent jump in inflation in period 5.

The speed of adjustment, λ, determines just how quickly expectations adjust to the jump in inflation in period 5. To see this, suppose expectations adjust faster—$\lambda = .75$. Given the higher value of λ, expectations adjust much more quickly to the change in the inflation rate, as you can see by comparing Table 12.3 with Table 12.2. For instance, when $\lambda = .75$, the expected inflation rate in period 8 in Table 12.3 is roughly 9.92 percent, compared with 9.375 percent in Table 12.2.

Figure 12.2 illustrates how changes in the speed of adjustment affect inflationary expectations. The higher λ is, the more rapidly adaptive expectations converge to the true inflation rate of 10 percent. Similarly, the lower the value of λ, the slower expectations are to adjust. Still, Figure 12.2, on page 378, illustrates that even with a higher speed of adjustment, adaptive expectations lead to a systematic bias in inflationary expectations when a permanent jump in inflation occurs.

Table 12.3
Adaptive Expectations with a Permanent Jump in Inflation: $\lambda = .75$

This table shows how the numbers in Table 12.2 change with a faster speed of adjustment in expectations. As in Table 12.2, the inflation rate permanently changes in period 5, which leads to a forecast error. With a faster speed of adjustment, however, the forecast errors are smaller and the gap between actual and expected inflation closes much more quickly than that with a slower speed of adjustment.

$$\pi_t^e = \pi_{t-1}^e + .75(\pi_{t-1} - \pi_{t-1}^e)$$

Period (t)	Actual Inflation Rate (π_t)	Expected Inflation Rate (π_t^e)	Expected Inflation Rate Last Period (π_{t-1}^e)	Actual Inflation Rate Last Period (π_{t-1})	Forecast Error Last Period ($\pi_{t-1} - \pi_{t-1}^e$)
1	5%	5%	5%	5%	0%
2	5	5	5	5	0
3	5	5	5	5	0
4	5	5	5	5	0
5	10	5	5	5	0
6	10	8.75	5	10	5
7	10	9.6875	8.75	10	1.25
8	10	9.921875	9.6875	10	.3125
9	10	9.980469	9.921875	10	.078125
10	10	9.995117	9.980469	10	.019532

Since the speed of adjustment is important to adaptive expectations, you may be wondering why individuals don't react by setting λ as high as possible to get very quick adjustment to changes in the actual inflation rate. The reason is that not all changes are permanent as they are in Tables 12.2 and 12.3, where the increase in the inflation rate persists through time. Sometimes the inflation rate increases for a period but then returns to its previous level. This is precisely what occurred in the United States between 1946 and 1948, when the inflation rate more than doubled only to return to its previous level. Table 12.4, on page 379, shows how a one-time blip in inflation affects adaptive inflationary expectations when $\lambda = .5$. In this case, an error in expectations occurs in period 5, when the actual inflation rate is 10 percent but the expectation is only 5 percent, and another occurs in period 6, when the actual inflation rate returns to 5 percent but the expectation is 7.5 percent. Furthermore, if the speed of adjustment were faster—say, .75

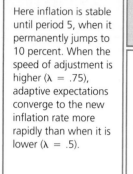

Here inflation is stable until period 5, when it permanently jumps to 10 percent. When the speed of adjustment is higher ($\lambda = .75$), adaptive expectations converge to the new inflation rate more rapidly than when it is lower ($\lambda = .5$).

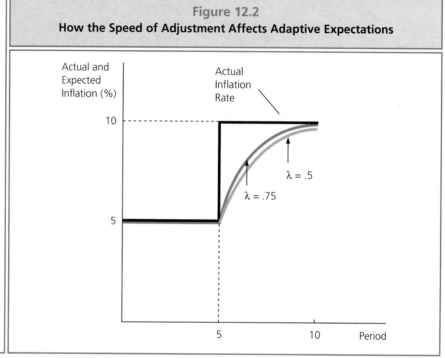

Figure 12.2

How the Speed of Adjustment Affects Adaptive Expectations

as it was in Table 12.3—the expectation in period 6 would be 8.75 percent instead of 7.5 percent, an even larger forecast error. Thus, there is a tradeoff between quickly responding to permanent changes in the level of the inflation rate, as in Tables 12.2 and 12.3, and not overreacting to one-time blips in the inflation rate, as in Table 12.4.

We should note some important features of adaptive expectations. First, like Markov expectations, adaptive expectations ignore other variables that might be useful in forecasting the future. For instance, based on what we learned about the effect of the money supply on the price level in Chapter 3, changes in the money supply might be useful in forecasting the inflation rate. Yet adaptive expectations (and Markov expectations) use only past values of the inflation rate to predict future rates of inflation. Second, even in response to a permanent change in the inflation rate, as in Tables 12.2 and 12.3, the adjustment of expectations is only gradual. After a permanent change in the actual inflation rate occurs, expectations take time to converge to the new inflation level. Yet when there is a one-time blip in the inflation rate, as in Table 12.4, expectations overreact and return to the actual inflation rate only gradually. Thus, whether a permanent change or a temporary blip occurs, adaptive expectations will systematically deviate from the actual inflation rate for several periods after the change.

Table 12.4
Adaptive Expectations with a Blip in Inflation: $\lambda = .5$

Even with a temporary change (a one-time blip) in the inflation rate in period 5, adaptive expectations only gradually lead to more accurate inflation forecasts. In period 5 the inflation forecast is too low, but in periods 6 through 10 the forecasts are too high.

$$\pi_t^e = \pi_{t-1}^e + .5(\pi_{t-1} - \pi_{t-1}^e)$$

Period (t)	Actual Inflation Rate (π_t)	Expected Inflation Rate (π_t^e)	Expected Inflation Rate Last Period (π_{t-1}^e)	Actual Inflation Rate Last Period (π_{t-1})	Forecast Error Last Period ($\pi_{t-1} - \pi_{t-1}^e$)
1	5%	5%	5%	5%	0%
2	5	5	5	5	0
3	5	5	5	5	0
4	5	5	5	5	0
5	10	5	5	5	0
6	5	7.5	5	10	5
7	5	6.25	7.5	5	−2.5
8	5	5.625	6.25	5	−1.25
9	5	5.3125	5.625	5	−.625
10	5	5.15625	5.3125	5	−.3125

Rational Expectations

The main criticism of Markov and adaptive expectations is that they may not be based on variables economic theory suggests are useful in forming more accurate expectations. This has led to the idea of rational expectations, which is the most sophisticated of the three methods of forming expectations. The **rational expectations hypothesis** asserts that when people form expectations, they use all knowable information, including variables economic theory suggests are relevant for making predictions. It is important to realize that rational expectations do not imply forecasts are always correct, only that no systematic errors in forecasts occur. Since rational expectations incorporate all relevant information, any deviations from what is expected are purely random in nature; any forecast errors that arise are just as likely to be positive as negative, as Box 12.1 shows.

Let us look at an example of rational expectations that is relevant to your performance in this money and banking course. Suppose you are at-

Inside Money

Box 12.1

Errors in the Inflationary Expectations of "Experts"

In Box 4.1, we looked at the inflationary expectations of so-called experts who sell their forecasts to businesses and governments. Do these experts make systematic errors in their forecasts, or are the forecasts correct, on average, with purely random errors? Look at the accompanying figure, which plots the difference between experts' expectations and the actual inflation rate, and see what you think.

Notice that the forecast errors do seem to randomly fluctuate around zero, so the experts' inflationary expectations tend to be correct on average. Still, the forecasts are seldom exactly right; that is, even professional forecasters of inflation are making predictions that are mostly wrong—and they know it. Being exactly right is less important than not making huge mistakes or systematic errors in forming inflationary expectations. Since the errors these experts make are purely random and are correct on average, these forecasters are not systematically surprised by high or low inflation. In other words, the experts appear to form rational inflationary expectations. As we will see later in this chapter when we look at the efficient markets hypothesis, this is not surprising because inflationary expectations play an important role in financial markets.

Source for data: ASA-NBER Business Outlook Survey, various issues, Citibase electronic database, and authors' calculations.

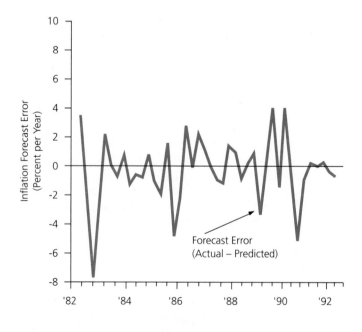

tempting to forecast the grade you will make on your final exam. If you have Markov expectations, your forecast will be the grade you earned on your last midterm exam. If you have adaptive expectations, your forecast will depend on what you expected to do on your last exam, as well as on your forecast error. If you did better on your last exam than you expected, your forecast of your final exam grade will be your previous forecast plus an additional amount to correct for your past error (underestimating your grade). In other words, you will expect to do better on the final than on the previous midterm.

In contrast, if you use rational expectations, your forecast will depend on all known variables that could theoretically affect your grade. These variables would include your propensity to excel in this subject (your past grades in the course), the number of other finals you have on the same day, how much time you plan to study, the tendency of your professor to give finals that are more difficult than midterms, and so on. Clearly each of these variables is important in forecasting your grade in the course; yet Markov and adaptive expectations ignore variables other than your past performance in this course.

The Mechanics of Rational Expectations.

In forming a rational expectation about interest rates, bond prices, or exchange rates, an individual would list all the determinants of demand and supply. All available information about these determinants would be used to help predict the location of demand and supply curves to form an expectation of the equilibrium interest rate, bond price, or exchange rate. In this way, rational expectations are based on the known variables economic theory views as relevant; thus, there are no systematic forecasting errors.

An Example: Rational Inflationary Expectations.

Since inflation is a key determinant of demand and supply in financial markets, we will look at how rational expectations can be used to form inflationary expectations. This will not only allow us to compare rational inflationary expectations with the Markov and adaptive expectations examined earlier but will also be useful for our analysis of macroeconomics and monetary policy in the second half of the book.

The first step in forming rational inflationary expectations is to determine the relevant theory that explains inflation. For instance, Chapter 3 described how classical economists developed the simple quantity theory of money that is based on the equation of exchange. According to this theory, velocity is constant, and changes in the money supply have no impact on the economy's real output. This theory, along with the equation of exchange, implies that the inflation rate equals the growth rate in the money supply (g_M) minus the rate of growth in real output (g_Y):

$$\pi = g_M - g_Y.$$

This is a theory, however, and as such it may not be the correct explanation for inflation (we will take a more careful look at competing theories and historical evidence in Chapters 16, 17, and 18). But if correct, this theory implies that a 10 percent increase in the money supply, coupled with a 3 percent increase in real output, will result in a $10\% - 3\% = 7\%$ rate of inflation. According to the simple quantity theory, inflation is caused by increases in the money supply that exceed the growth rate in real output: Too much money is chasing too few goods.

To make things as simple as possible, we first assume the growth rate in real output is zero and the inflation rate in the current period equals the growth rate in the money supply in the previous period. (In Chapter 18, we will see that it often takes many months for changes in the money supply to affect the price level). Given this simple economic model of inflation, including our simplifying assumption of no real output growth, the rational expectation of the inflation rate in period t depends only on the money growth rate in period $t - 1$. In fact, the inflation rate today is the money growth rate of last period. If this information is available, the **rational inflationary expectation** under the simple quantity theory is simply the money growth rate last period:

$$\pi_t^{RE} = g_{Mt-1}.$$

For instance, if the money supply increases by 7 percent in period $t - 1$, the rational expectation of the inflation rate in period t is 7 percent. Notice that this rational expectation does not depend on past inflation rates or previous errors in expectations.

Table 12.5 compares rational and adaptive expectations for a situation in which money growth is 5 percent for the first three periods and then jumps to 10 percent in periods 4 through 10. The actual inflation rate is 5 percent for the first four periods and then jumps to 10 percent in the remaining periods, just as it does in Tables 12.2 and 12.3.

For the first four periods inflation is stable, and so are everyone's expectations. What does a person forming a rational expectation under the simple quantity theory expect the inflation rate to be in period 5? Since the growth rate in the money supply in period 4 was 10 percent, this person's forecast of inflation in period 5 is

$$\pi_5^{RE} = g_{M4} = .10,$$

or 10 percent, which coincides with the actual inflation rate that occurs in period 5. As a point of contrast, Table 12.5 also includes the adaptive expectations first calculated in Table 12.2 for the same trend in inflation rates. In period 5, adaptive expectations miss the mark by 5 percent. Furthermore, they adjust to the permanent increase in the inflation rate only gradually, because adaptive expectations are not based on the economic theory that informs us that money growth is related to inflation.

In the example in Table 12.5, rational expectations result in inflation forecasts that are perfect. It is important to recognize that reality is more

---

Table 12.5
Rational Versus Adaptive Expectations with a Permanent Jump in Inflation

Since rational expectations of inflation incorporate information not used by adaptive expectations, they eliminate systematic errors in inflation forecasts. The simple quantity theory assumes velocity is constant. It predicts that when real output is also constant, increases in the money supply lead to inflation. Consequently rational expectations of inflation based on the simple quantity theory are based on the previous period's growth in the money supply. The rational expectations of inflation in column 4 coincide with the actual inflation rates in column 2, illustrating the absence of any forecasting errors in this simple case. In more complex environments, rational expectations do not entirely eliminate forecasting errors, but they do ensure that no systematic errors occur.

$$\pi_t^{RE} = g_{M_{t-1}}$$

$$\pi_t^e = \pi_{t-1}^e + .5(\pi_{t-1} - \pi_{t-1}^e)$$

Period (t)	Money Growth Rate (g_{M_t})	Actual Inflation Rate (π_t)	Rational Expectation of Inflation (π_t^{RE})	Adaptive Expectation of Inflation (π_t^e)
1	5%	5%	5%	5%
2	5	5	5	5
3	5	5	5	5
4	10	5	5	5
5	10	10	10	5
6	10	10	10	7.5
7	10	10	10	8.75
8	10	10	10	9.375
9	10	10	10	9.6875
10	10	10	10	9.84375

complicated than our simple example and that rational expectations do not require zero forecasting errors. As we noted earlier, rational expectations will sometimes lead to incorrect forecasts. The reason is that typically random, unpredictable events could occur that cause the inflation rate to rise or fall by more than expected based on available information. For instance, velocity might rise or fall randomly over time, resulting in errors in rational inflationary expectations that are unavoidable if changes in velocity are themselves unpredictable.

Part a of Figure 12.3 shows such a situation. Notice that the actual inflation rate fluctuates randomly about 5 percent, while expectations are consistently at 5 percent. But deviations between actual and expected inflation are purely random, and there are no systematic errors. In contrast, part b shows a situation where systematic errors in inflationary expectations occur

Figure 12.3
Nonsystematic and Systematic Errors in Inflation Forecasts

Part a shows a situation where inflationary expectations are correct on average and have no systematic errors. Even though inflation fluctuates around 5 percent, the resulting errors in expectations are purely random. In contrast, in part b systematic errors in inflationary expectations occur after period t, since they are too low on average.

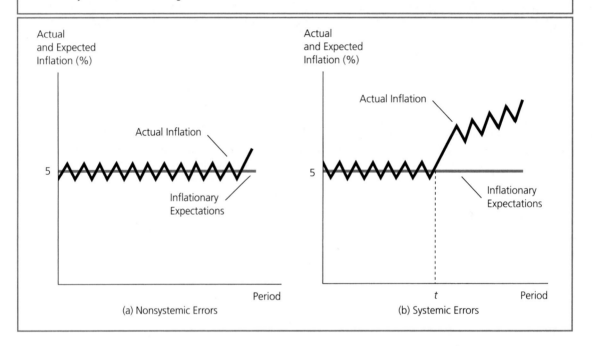

(a) Nonsystemic Errors

(b) Systemic Errors

after period t. In this case, inflationary expectations beyond period t always understate actual inflation, reflecting systematic errors in expectations. Even a person forming rational expectations cannot predict changes in inflation that are purely random, and therefore might make errors in forecasts like those in part a of Figure 12.3. But if all available information is being used, no systematic errors will arise in forecasts like those in part b. Thus, the advantage of rational expectations over other methods of forming expectations is not the elimination of all forecasting errors but the elimination of *systematic* forecasting errors.

The ability of rational expectations to eliminate systematic forecasting errors relative to those that would arise under adaptive expectations can be seen in yet another way. Consider a one-time blip in inflation, such as the one that occurred in the United States between 1946 and 1948. During this period, the inflation rate increased from about 3 to 13 percent and then fell back to about 3 percent thereafter. The rise in inflation was caused by increases in the money supply during World War II, and the subsequent decline in inflation was due to the reduced money growth that followed the war. Figure 12.4 presents a stylized diagram that illustrates how this type of change in the economic environment affects rational and adaptive expectations.

Notice that the inflation rate fluctuated around 3 percent until 1946; then it began fluctuating around 13 percent until 1948, when it returned to 3 percent. A person forming rational inflationary expectations would have noticed the increased growth in the money supply during the war and raised inflationary expectations for the 1946–1948 period accordingly. As part a of Figure 12.4 shows, this gave rise to inflationary expectations that contained no systematic errors prior to 1946, when inflation averaged 3 percent, and no systematic errors for the 1946–1948 period, when inflation averaged 13 percent. Furthermore, inflationary expectations returned back to 3 percent for 1948 and beyond, as people forming rational expectations fully anticipated inflation would decline due to reduced monetary growth following the war. Part a of the figure illustrates that people forming rational expectations formed correct inflationary expectations, on average, and were not surprised by the short-term blip in inflation between 1946 and 1948 caused by increased monetary growth.

Contrast this situation to the adaptive inflationary expectations shown in part b of Figure 12.4. The adaptive expectations worked well when inflation was stable prior to 1946, but missed the upward blip in inflation between 1946 and 1948 and also overreacted from 1948 and beyond. In effect, people forming adaptive expectations were surprised by the blip in inflation and were surprised again when inflation returned to its previous pattern. Notice that between 1946 and 1948 people systematically underestimated the rate of inflation, and from 1948 and beyond they systematically overestimated it. Once again we see that rational inflationary expectations have the advantage of eliminating these systematic errors—provided, of course, the expectations are based on the correct economic model. Box 12.2 shows what can happen when this isn't the case.

Our previous examples are based on the assumption that the rate of growth in real output is zero on average, as it was during the period immediately following World War II. When the growth rate in real output is not zero, the simple quantity theory implies the inflation rate is given by the difference between the monetary growth rate and the rate of growth in real output:

$$\pi = g_M - g_Y.$$

In this case, the rational expectation of inflation in period t based on the simple quantity theory is

$$\pi_t^{RE} = g_{M_{t-1}} - g_{Y_{t-1}}.$$

Let us see how those forming rational expectations can use this more general framework to respond to changes in the structure of the economy.

Part a shows how a one-time blip in inflation, caused by a short-term increase in monetary growth, led people forming rational expectations to anticipate the higher inflation and then expect lower inflation when money growth returned to its previous level. Notice that no systematic errors in rational inflationary expectations occurred because all relevant information was used to form expectations.

Part b shows that those forming adaptive inflationary expectations were surprised by the short period of higher inflation and then further surprised by its return to normal. Adaptive expectations led to systematic errors during both the period of high inflation and the period when inflation returned to its previous level.

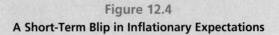

Figure 12.4
A Short-Term Blip in Inflationary Expectations

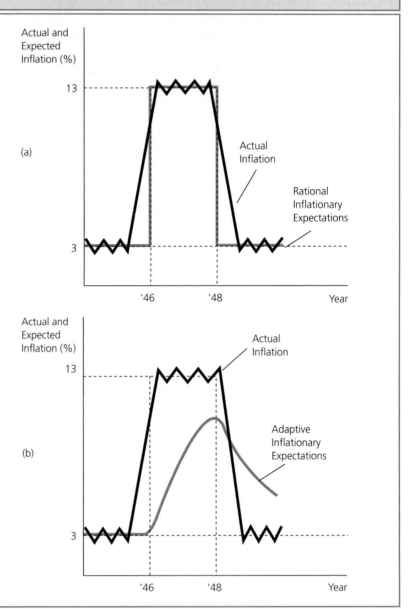

Inside Money

Box 12.2

*The Importance of Using
the Correct Model
When Forming Rational Expectations*

What happens if the economic model on which rational expectations are based is incorrect? The answer is that simpler expectations, like Markov expectations, may perform better. To illustrate this, we present two figures based on U.S. data for the period 1970 through 1993. The first one graphs the price level in a given period (P_t) against the price level in the previous period (P_{t-1}); the second graphs the price level in a given period against the money supply. The idea is to see whether the past price level or the money supply better explains the current price level.

In the first figure, the current price level is graphed as a function of the price level in the previous period, as it will be under Markov expectations. Notice the relation between these two variables lines up almost on a diagonal line, indicating that last period's price level does a very good job of explaining the current price level. Based on this time period, Markov expectations of the price level forecast the future price level quite adequately.

In the second graph, the current price level and the money supply do not line up so nicely, indicating the money supply by itself is not as good a predictor of the price level. This may seem strange to you; after all, shouldn't rational expectations of price increases incorporate all relevant information about things that cause prices to rise, like the money supply? Of course they should, but this information must be incorporated in a way that is consistent with correct economic theory. Even holding other factors (like real output) constant, the simple quantity theory does not predict that a $1 increase in the money supply will lead to a $1 increase in

(a) Price Level and Lagged Price Level 1970 – 1993

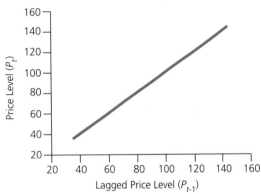

(b) Relationship Between the Money Supply and the Price Level 1970 – 1993

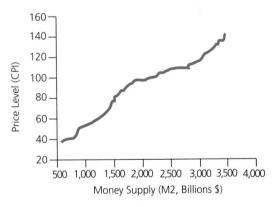

prices; it says that a 1 *percent* increase in the money supply will lead to a 1 *percent* increase in prices. The money supply is relevant for predicting future prices, but not in the way postu-

Continued on p. 388

CHAPTER 12 RATIONAL EXPECTATIONS AND EFFICIENT MARKETS

Continued from p. 387
lated in the graph. This is why the relationship in the second graph is less perfect than that in the first.

What should you make of all this? To form rational expectations of future variables, you must not only incorporate all relevant information into the forecast but also make sure the economic model into which you are incorporating the information is correct. If you are unsure of

the correct model or choose the wrong one, Markov expectations may lead to better forecasts than they would if you incorporated relevant information into the wrong model.

―――――――――

Source for data: U.S. Department of Labor, Bureau of Labor Statistics, *The Consumer Price Index,* various issues; Board of Governors of the Federal Reserve System, *Statistical Release and Federal Reserve Bulletin,* various issues; and Citibase electronic database.

Between 1979 and 1982, real output growth in the United States was sluggish, averaging zero. Things changed in 1983, when real output growth increased to about 3 percent per year and hovered around there through 1989. The rate of growth in the money supply declined during this period as well. Together these changes caused the inflation rate to decline from about 9 percent prior to 1982 to about 4 percent thereafter. Figure 12.5 presents two stylized diagrams showing this change in the inflation rate, along with the rational and adaptive inflationary expectations.

Based on the simple quantity theory, an increase in the growth in real output, coupled with a decline in monetary growth, reduces the inflation rate. Accordingly, part a of Figure 12.5 shows that those forming rational expectations lowered their inflationary expectations in response to these structural changes in the economy. The result is that rational expectations of inflation were 9 percent through 1982 and then fell to 4 percent beginning in 1983. In contrast, the adaptive expectations of inflation shown in part b of Figure 12.5 worked well until 1983, when they began to systematically overstate the actual inflation rate. These errors gradually diminished over time, but even by 1987 people with adaptive expectations were still forming forecasts of inflation that were too high. Thus, adaptive expectations adjust gradually to structural changes in the economy, just as they do to a change in the actual inflation rate. In contrast, rational expectations adjust quickly to structural changes, in this case the increased growth in real output accompanied by a decline in monetary growth.

Finally, it is important to stress that the rational inflationary expectations examined in this section are based on the simple quantity theory. If the underlying causes of inflation in the economy are consistent with the theory, no systematic errors in inflationary expectations will occur. However, one assumption underlying the simple quantity theory is that velocity is constant or, at the very least, changes in velocity are unpredictable. If velocity is not constant and in fact systematically rises or falls over time, there will be systematic errors in inflationary expectations that are based on the simple

Part a shows how people forming rational inflationary expectations used information about increased output growth and reduced money growth to lower their inflationary expectations. The result was the elimination of systematic errors in inflationary expectations. In contrast, those forming adaptive expectations in part b did so based only on past inflation rates, and as a result were surprised by the decline in inflation. Their forecast errors declined only gradually over time.

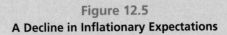

Figure 12.5
A Decline in Inflationary Expectations

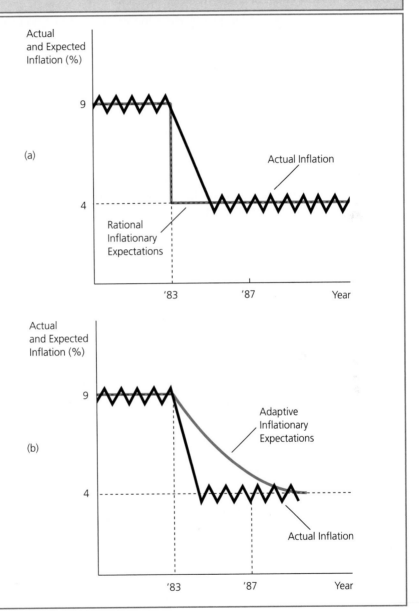

quantity theory. In effect, the errors are due to the fact that "rational" expectations are being formed based on an incorrect economic model. Rational expectations improve forecasts and lead to no systematic forecasting errors when they are based on the correct economic model. Expectations based on an incorrect theory, in contrast, may lead to systematic errors in forecasts. Given the importance of the underlying economic theory in forming rational expectations of inflation, in the second half of this book we take a closer look at the theoretical and empirical link among money, output, and inflation.

Summary *Exercise 12.1*

Last period, real output increased by 4 percent and the money supply increased by 5 percent. The inflation rate last period was 10 percent. (a) What is the Markov expectation of inflation this period? (b) If the adjustment factor is .3 and no forecast error occurred last period, what is the adaptive expectation of this period's inflation rate? (c) What is the rational expectation of the inflation rate? (Use the simple quantity theory as the relevant economic model.)

Answer: (a) The Markov expectation of inflation is $\pi_t^e = \pi_{t-1}$. Since last period inflation was 10 percent, the Markov expectation of inflation this period is $\pi_t^e = .10$, or 10 percent. (b) Since inflation last period was 10 percent and there were no errors in expectations, last period's adaptive expectation of inflation was $\pi_{t-1}^e = .1$. Given this and the fact that $\lambda = .3$, the adaptive expectation of inflation this period is

$$\pi_t^e = \pi_{t-1}^e + .3(\pi_{t-1} - \pi_{t-1}^e) = .1 + .3(.1 - .1) = .1,$$

or 10 percent. (c) Given the simple quantity theory and information about last period's growth rates in money and real output, the rational expectation of inflation this period is

$$\pi_t^{RE} = g_{Mt-1} - g_{Yt-1} = .05 - .04 = .01,$$

or 1 percent.

A CRITIQUE OF THE VIEWS OF EXPECTATIONS FORMATION

We conclude our discussion of expectations formation by pointing out some of the common criticisms levied against Markov, adaptive, and rational expectations. We do so with an analogy from American football to emphasize that the criticisms are potentially valid for expectations formed outside the normal realm of economics (although given the salaries of big-league players, economics is relevant even to football).

Consider an American football game in which a team is allowed four attempts (or downs) to gain 10 yards. If the team is unsuccessful, the opponent gets the ball. The usual play is to run or pass on the first three downs and, if unsuccessful at advancing 10 yards, use the fourth down to punt (kick the ball far down field so the opponent gets the ball far from your goal). What would you expect a team to do on third down and five yards to go?

With Markov expectations, you would expect the team to do what they did in the previous third-down-and-five situation; if they ran before, you would expect them to run again. If you used adaptive expectations, you would expect them to do what you thought they would do last time, but adjust your forecast based on your error in expectations last time. If you used rational expectations, you would form an expectation based on all available information: the players on the field just prior to the snap of the ball, their tendencies on previous downs in similar situations, the score, time left in the game, and so on.

What if the rules were changed to only allow only three attempts to gain 10 yards? Blind use of Markov or adaptive expectations would ignore this structural change in the rules of the game and form an expectation of the third-down play based on past experience with third downs. However, with such a rule change, past experience will be a very poor indicator of what the team will do given only three downs. With rational expectations, you would use your knowledge of the new rules of the game and conclude that a punt is now more likely. This is analogous to using your knowledge of the rules of the game in economics—economic theory—to sharpen your expectations about future values of economic variables.

This example highlights the weaknesses of Markov and adaptive expectations we alluded to in earlier sections, but also allows us to discuss by analogy some of the criticisms of rational expectations. One common criticism is that people do not know enough to form rational expectations. This criticism is actually a two-pronged attack. The claim is that they either don't know the relevant economic theory or simply find the required calculations too difficult. In our football example, this is analogous to saying that people either don't know the rules of football or just find it too difficult to figure out the strategy a coach would use in a certain situation. Critics of rational expectations would argue that the economy is certainly more complex than a football game; it is more reasonable to think people don't understand the rules of economics than it is to think people don't understand the rules of American football (though both may be true for most people).

The response from those espousing rational expectations is that people are willing to spend a lot of time learning the rules of the economy if doing so is important to their well-being. This is why coaches spend time gathering information about football—because it is valuable to them! Thus, those for whom an accurate expectation is important will devote considerable time, effort, and resources to learning the rules of the economy. This means not that they will always be right but that they will not make systematic errors in their forecasts. If they did make systematic errors, they could profit by figuring out how to better form expectations.

Another criticism of rational expectations is that people don't gather the necessary information. Defenders of rational expectations would argue that those people who don't gather the relevant information are the very ones who don't find it very important for their well-being. Again, those for whom the information is important will expend the effort and resources to gather it. As Box 12.1 showed, those who make a living forecasting inflation rates aren't systematically surprised by high or low inflation.

To critics of rational expectations, the clinching argument is that economists themselves do not always agree on the relevant economic theory, so how can noneconomists be expected to both know the relevant theory and gather and process the needed information? It is this argument that is often used to justify reliance on the more simplistic but more easily used adaptive or Markov expectations.

Summary Exercise 12.2

(a) Suppose money growth, inflation, and the growth in real output remain constant for a long period of time. Would inflationary expectations depend on which of the three methods were used to form expectations? (b) How would your answer to part a change if money growth, output growth, and inflation varied considerably over time? (c) Would your answer to part a change if there was a more complicated economic reason for inflation than the simple quantity theory suggests?

Answer: (a) If the economy started out in a situation where everyone's expectations were realized, each of the three methods would work equally well at forecasting future rates of inflation. However, if initial expectations were in error, adaptive expectations would only gradually lead to expectations of inflation that equaled the actual rate. In contrast, Markov expectations would adjust to the actual level of inflation after only one period of error. Rational expectations would lead to expectations that on average equaled the actual inflation rate, provided relevant information about past monetary and real output growth were available and the corresponding model of inflation was correct. (b) With considerable variation over time in inflation rates, money growth, and real output growth, Markov and adaptive expectations would continually have systematic forecast errors. Properly formed rational expectations, however, would be correct on average, with no systematic errors. (c) With a more complicated model of inflation, additional data would be needed to form rational expectations. If these data were not available, or if the complicated link between inflation and other variables could not be successfully modeled, rational expectations might perform more poorly than adaptive or Markov expectations. Rational expectations are no better than the validity of the model used to form expectations, whereas the other two methods are no better than the stability of the economic variable to be forecast.

EFFICIENT MARKETS

If you have ever dreamed of making a fortune in the stock market, this section is written just for you. Before you call your broker in an attempt to live out your dreams, however, we encourage you to read what we have to say about efficient markets—something related to but distinct from rational expectations.

The Efficient Markets Hypothesis

The **efficient markets hypothesis** states that the current price of an asset such as a share of stock reflects all available information about the value of the asset. Consider Figure 12.6, which plots the price of a share of stock between January 15, 1994, and January 15, 1995. Notice that the trend in this stock price is upward; the stock started out at $10 in 1994 and trades for $20 in 1995. A common temptation when reading the financial pages is to extrapolate beyond the current date to infer that the price of the stock will surely rise to $40 by next year. The extrapolation in Figure 12.6 is represented by the dotted line.

The efficient markets hypothesis asserts that on January 15, 1995, all available information about the value of the stock is contained in the price on that date, which is $20. This implies, among other things, that nothing can be gained by drawing a "trend line" to forecast the future stock price. To see why, simply notice that other investors also have access to a chart such as the one in Figure 12.6. If people knew the stock would be selling for $40 in 1996, do you really think it would be selling for $20 in 1995? If so, you and other investors would seek to purchase the stock today to earn a return of

$$R_{1996} = \frac{P_{1996} - P_{1995}}{P_{1995}} = \frac{\$40 - \$20}{\$20} = 1,$$

or 100 percent! But as you and other investors began purchasing the stock, the price would rise, thus reducing your return. This process would continue until the hefty return was no longer available.

More generally, according to the efficient markets hypothesis, the risk-adjusted expected return on all investments will be equal; that is, the return you should expect to earn on this stock exactly equals the return you could earn on any other asset with similar risk characteristics. The reason is that if one asset earns a higher risk-adjusted expected rate of return than another asset, investors will quickly attempt to purchase that asset, driving up its price and thus lowering its expected return. Recall from Chapter 10 that the expectations hypothesis of the term structure of interest rates postulates that the expected return from holding long-term bonds equals the average ex-

---

Figure 12.6
A Bad Method of Forecasting Stock Prices

If you are aware that a particular stock has increased in price from $10 to $20 over the past year, you might be tempted to expect this price to continue to rise to $40 next year. However, this extrapolation is generally a bad forecasting method, since it ignores economic determinants of stock prices such as taxes, interest rates, firm earnings, and so on. If markets are efficient, the price of any stock will be driven to an equilibrium level such that its return equals the return on other assets of similar risk. No one will be able to make money in the stock market by extrapolating or charting points using the method shown in this figure.

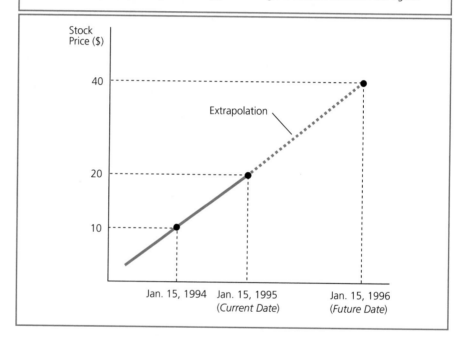

---

pected return from holding short-term bonds during the life of the long-term bonds. This is a form of the efficient markets hypothesis.

The efficient markets hypothesis has profound implications for your ability to make a killing in the stock market—or in any other financial market, for that matter. If the risk-adjusted returns on all financial assets are equal, you cannot systematically beat the market by picking a stock you think will outperform the market. All information that is relevant for forecasting the future returns on the stock are already reflected in its price. Of course, you might get lucky and pick a stock that does better than average, but you are equally likely to pick one that does worse than average. In general, you will earn the same return, and at lower risk, by purchasing a diversified portfolio of many stocks so that stocks that perform better than average offset those that do worse than average.

How should you determine which stocks to put in your portfolio? Believe it or not, research suggests that picking stocks by throwing darts at the financial pages does as well as spending lots of time (or money) researching particular stocks! Since the stock market is efficient, the only differences in returns on different stocks are due to risk, so riskier stocks earn higher returns than less risky ones. Which stocks you pick is less important than picking enough that you benefit from diversification, as we saw in Chapter 9.

For small investors like university professors, a more economical method of diversifying risk is to purchase shares in a diversified no-load mutual fund. These funds do not charge fees for buying or selling shares in their funds, and they pool the funds of many investors to purchase shares of hundreds of stocks. In contrast, broker commissions would bankrupt small investors who attempted to purchase single shares of hundreds of different stocks directly.

Rational Expectations and Efficient Markets

The efficient markets hypothesis is closely related to the notion of rational expectations. In fact, for a market to be efficient, expectations must be based on all known relevant information, which rational expectations require. Thus, rational expectations are necessary for efficient markets. Let us see why.

Consider again Figure 12.6. You want to forecast the price at which the stock will trade in 1996, but all you know is the current price and the past trend. Is this the only information you need to form an expectation of the future price? Clearly not. The price of the stock in 1996 will depend on a number of variables, including the earnings of the issuing firm, tax policy, interest rates, and the like. A forecast based on a trend line ignores all of this information.

Participants in the stock market who invest millions of dollars in stocks, such as pension funds and insurance companies, have a tremendous incentive to form accurate estimates of the company's future earnings. They also are likely to spend considerable time and money learning about government legislation that would affect the future price of the stock, the quality of the firm's management, and the like. An expectation of the stock price based on a simple trend line is a very poor substitute for this information.

Fortunately, however, if the market is efficient, the current stock price will already reflect this information. Those who invested considerable sums to gather the information they needed to form a rational expectation of the future stock price will, based on their information, buy the stock when it is underpriced and sell it when it is overpriced. In equilibrium, the price of the stock will rise or fall to reflect the relative demand for and supply of the stock given available information. You can hardly beat the professionals by drawing a line to connect the dots in Figure 12.6!

The idea that the risk-adjusted expected returns on alternative assets are equalized in equilibrium is based on the notion that market pressures will ensure that any temporary deviation from this equilibrium is corrected. These market pressures are based on the expectations of those who use all available information about the value of financial assets and continually revise their buy-and-sell decisions when new information becomes available. For instance, when people who make their living forecasting inflation expect it to rise, they will immediately attempt to sell off their bond portfolios. This leads to a very quick rise in interest rates, and this new information is quickly reflected in lower bond prices. By the time the information trickles down to you or you learn inflation is higher, bond prices already reflect this information. Similarly, stock prices tend to change very quickly in response to new information, and deviations from equilibrium are typically corrected in seconds or minutes rather than days or weeks.

Versions of the Efficient Markets Hypothesis

In its most general form, the idea of efficient markets is that asset prices tend to change very quickly in response to new information and thus the risk-adjusted returns on assets tend to be equal. Some economists believe in more specific forms of efficient markets: the weak form, the semi-strong form, and the strong form of market efficiency. As their names imply, these three statements of market efficiency make increasingly strong assumptions about asset market pricing.

Weak-Form Market Efficiency.   **Weak-form market efficiency** claims the best predictor of next period's asset price is this period's price. No other past information on the asset price can improve on this prediction. One implication of weak-form market efficiency is that the so-called **technical analysis** of asset prices—charting or plotting historical data on asset prices—cannot help predict future values of the asset price. As Box 12.3 shows, it is difficult at the very least to predict returns on stocks or Treasury bills by looking at historical data.

There is some evidence of *minor* departures from weak-form market efficiency in stock markets. For instance, a close look at stock prices sometimes reveals day-of-the-week effects (stock prices tend to rise on Monday and fall on Friday), time-of-year effects (stock prices tend to rise in January), and small-firm effects (small-firm prices typically rise by more than large-firm prices). But little evidence exists that average investors can use these effects to earn above-normal profits once transactions costs such as broker fees are taken into account.

The Data Bank

Box 12.3

The Random Nature of Stock Returns,
Interest Rates, and Inflation

Think you can make money predicting changes in stock prices or interest rates? If financial markets are efficient, stock returns and interest rates will fluctuate randomly, with no discernible trends in their movements over time. To check whether this is the case, the accompanying figure plots interest rates and returns on stocks for the period 1971–1992. The stock returns are based on a stock portfolio that mimics the Standard and Poor's 500 Index and includes price appreciation and dividends paid by the companies. The interest rate is that on one-year Treasury bills, a measure of the risk-free interest rate. The figure also plots the inflation rate over this period to show whether the returns were sufficient to offset increases in the cost of living during this time.

There are several things to notice in this graph. First, the interest rate on Treasury bills

and the inflation rate were usually fairly close to each other, although during the middle 1980s, the Treasury bill rate was substantially above the inflation rate. This indicates Treasury bills have mostly stayed just at or slightly above the inflation rate, but in the mid-1980s investors could earn a substantial return above the inflation rate by investing in T-bills. More important, notice there were no discernible trends in interest rates; they went up about as often as they went down, with increases and decreases randomly dispersed over the period.

The return on stocks was considerably more volatile, but also much greater on average than the risk-free interest rate and the rate of inflation. While stock returns were negative at times, especially in the middle 1970s, the positive returns far outweighed the negative returns. No-

Continued on p. 398

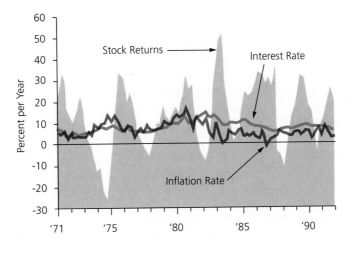

Continued from p. 397

tice too that some of the positive (and negative) returns were quite sizable. The largest positive return was 50 percent in early 1983, with numerous 30 percent returns randomly sprinkled throughout the 21-year span. There were also periods of negative returns, the most sizable one in early 1975. The higher expected returns on stocks merely compensated investors for the additional risk arising from the returns' higher volatility; no predictable patterns in the returns on stocks occurred over this period.

The main conclusion you should draw from this graph is that (1) on average, returns on the stock market exceeded the return on risk-free investments like Treasury bills; (2) stock returns were much more volatile, with periods of substantial negative returns interspersed among periods of substantial positive returns; and (3) there was no discernible trend in stock returns or interest rate movements.

Source for data: Board of Governors of the Federal Reserve System, *Federal Reserve Bulletin,* various issues; Standard and Poor, *The Outlook,* various issues; Bureau of Labor Statistics, *The Consumer Price Index,* various issues; and Citibase electronic database.

Semistrong-Form Market Efficiency.   **Semistrong-form market efficiency** asserts that no publicly available information will help predict future asset prices or returns better than the last known value of the asset. This includes not only past prices of the asset in question but also publicly available information on other asset prices, interest rates, profits, tax rates, business opportunities, and so on. Again the idea is that any useful publicly available information will be so quickly reflected in the market price that the current price is the best predictor of future prices.

However, this form of market efficiency leaves open the possibility that private information can be useful in predicting future asset prices. For instance, suppose you are an accountant at a major firm and, during an audit, learn that XXX Corporation understated its profits last year by $10 billion due to a bookkeeping error. When this information becomes public, the stock price will rise. In the meantime, you could buy shares of XXX Corporation and make a profit on your inside information. Your private information allows you to predict the future stock price better than the market can. This said, we note that it is illegal to act on this type of inside information. If you gain private information while in a fiduciary relationship, you cannot legally act on it, even though the information would allow you to form a better forecast of the future stock price than the market could.

The primary reason insider trading is illegal is that asymmetric information can destroy financial markets. Insiders have better information than outsiders do, and in a market dominated by insiders, outsiders stand only to lose by participating in the market.

To see why, suppose insiders know a stock is really worth $100 per share. As an outsider, you don't know for sure what the stock is worth.

Should you purchase the stock? Insiders will sell you shares only if you offer them more than $100. The only way you can buy the stock is by paying more than it is really worth, so you are better off staying out of the market altogether. If you and other investors fear the market is dominated by insiders, the market could collapse, leaving only those with the "best" inside information to buy and sell stocks. This reduces the number of market participants, decreases the liquidity of assets traded in the market, and potentially ruins the market for everyone. Laws against insider trading are designed to alleviate these problems.

Strong-Form Market Efficiency.

Strong-form market efficiency makes a very strong statement: that no current information, either publicly available or not, can improve on using the most recently known value of an asset price to predict the future value of that asset price. Thus, the strong-form version basically claims that even insider information cannot aid in predicting stock price movements.

There is evidence that the stock market does not meet the stringent conditions of strong-form market efficiency. For instance, Ivan Boesky earned millions of dollars year after year by trading on inside information about corporate takeovers, at least until the Securities and Exchange Commission (SEC) charged him with trading on such information. While Boesky ultimately paid $100 million in fines and was sentenced to three years in jail, his ability to "beat the market" for many years by using insider information makes strong-form market efficiency suspect. The weak and semi-strong forms of market efficiency, in contrast, are largely consistent with what one observes in most financial markets.

Efficient Markets and Expectations

One interesting feature of these last three hypotheses about market efficiency is that they insist on a version of Markov expectations for predicting asset prices. This is an example of a situation in which Markov expectations *are* rational expectations! In this case, the relevant economic theory of efficient markets implies that all information that is useful for predicting movements in asset prices are already contained in the current price. Any changes in the asset price will be purely random, so the rational expectation of tomorrow's asset price is today's price—its Markov expectation. Thus, we looked up the price of Microsoft stock in the paper on June 21, 1994, and saw the price was $53.50. Our best forecast of the price of Microsoft stock for July 3 was $53.50.

Even though this was our best forecast, it was still subject to a lot of uncertainty; that is, while we say $53.50 was our best forecast, we can also say there was a large chance that the price would differ from this number and that the probability that the actual value would differ from our forecast would increase over time. However, none of this contradicts the claim that $53.50 was the best forecast we could make. As with meteorologists, the best forecast we can make may be subject to a lot of uncertainty, especially as we forecast far into the future.

Summary
Exercise 12.3

Suppose two bonds with identical risks and terms to maturity have different yields. (a) If the market is efficient, what would you expect to happen to the yields and prices of these bonds? (b) If you observe two apparently identical bonds with different yields, should you buy the one with the higher yield?

Answer: (a) If the market is efficient, the prices of the bonds will adjust very quickly to equalize the bonds' yields. The view that the bonds have identical risks must, of course, be based on rational expectations, that is, all available information about the riskiness of each bond. (b) If you are confident the bonds are really identical, of course you should purchase the one with the higher yield. But chances are that by the time you call your broker, some other investor who makes his or her living looking for such profit opportunities will have already driven up its price and thus eliminated the higher yield. It is also possible—and arguably more likely—that the bonds are really not identical. The higher yield may reflect information by insiders that the bond involves higher risk. If this is the case, you can rest assured that the risk-adjusted return on this bond will be the same as those on other bonds.

CONCLUSION

In this chapter, we examined alternative methods of forming expectations and noted the pros and cons of each. Properly formed rational expectations contain no systematic errors and are correct on average, but they usually require more information than Markov or adaptive expectations do. We also saw that Markov expectations are sometimes exactly the expectations that economic theory suggests are rational expectations. Finally, we looked at the concept of efficient markets and its implications for asset prices.

The material in this chapter, coupled with that presented in the first 11 chapters, has given you a firm grasp of the workings of the specific financial markets in which banks, pension funds, insurance companies, and individuals such as yourself borrow and lend loanable funds. In the next half of the book, we use what we have learned about these specific markets and rational expectations to analyze macroeconomics and policy—the study of how all economic markets, aggregated together, are affected by government and Fed actions.

KEY TERMS

Markov expectations hypothesis
Markov inflationary expectations
adaptive expectations approach
speed of adjustment
adaptive inflationary expectations
rational expectations hypothesis

rational inflationary expectations
efficient markets hypothesis
weak-form market efficiency
technical analysis
semistrong-form market efficiency
strong-form market efficiency

QUESTIONS AND PROBLEMS

1. Provide, at an intuitive level, an explanation of Markov, adaptive, and rational expectations.

2. Determine whether the following examples most closely conform to Markov, adaptive, or rational expectations.

    (a). When Sue wakes up in the morning, she expects her husband to fix the same breakfast he made yesterday.
    (b). Sam always expects his wife to fix pancakes for breakfast.
    (c). Joe bases his expectation of dinner on what he observed thawing out in the sink when he left for work.

3. Last year, both real output and the money supply increased by 6 percent. The inflation rate was 10 percent.

    (a). What is the Markov expectation of inflation this year?
    (b). If the adjustment factor is 1, what is the adaptive expectation of this year's inflation rate?
    (c). If the adjustment factor is .5 and last year's forecast error was 6 percent, what is this year's adaptive expectation of inflation?

4. Last year, both real output and the money supply increased by 6 percent. The inflation rate was 10 percent. What would you expect the inflation rate to be this year? Why?

5. What are the primary advantages of Markov expectation formation? What are the primary disadvantages (i.e., when do they lead to systematic forecast errors)?

6. What are the primary advantages of adaptive expectation formation? What are the primary disadvantages (i.e., when do they lead to systematic forecast errors)?

7. What are the primary advantages of rational expectation formation? What are the primary disadvantages?

8. What is the efficient market hypothesis? What does it imply about using past trends to "beat the market?"

9. An investment banker forms Markov expectations of inflation for period t based on information available in period $t - 1$. Complete the following table for the banker. Are the expectations ever correct in periods 2 through 10? Why or why not?

Period (t)	Actual Inflation Rate (π_t)	Expected Inflation Rate (π_t^e)	Forecast Error ($\pi_t - \pi_t^e$)
1	1%	1%	0
2	2		
3	3		
4	4		
5	5		
6	4		
7	3		
8	2		
9	1		
10	0		

10. Suppose the investment banker in problem 9 forms adaptive expectations of inflation and the speed of adjustment parameter is

$\lambda = .5$. Complete the following table. Are the banker's expectations ever correct in periods 2 through 10? Why or why not?

Period (t)	Actual Inflation Rate (π_t)	Expected Inflation Rate (π_t^e)	Forecast Error ($\pi_t - \pi_t^e$)
1	1%	1%	0
2	2		
3	3		
4	4		
5	5		
6	4		
7	3		
8	2		
9	1		
10	0		

11. Now suppose the investment banker in problems 9 and 10 forms rational expectations of inflation based on the simple quantity theory, $\pi = g_M - g_Y$. Complete the following table. Are the banker's expectations ever correct in periods 2 through 10? Why or why not?

Period (t)	Money Growth Rate (g_{Mt})	Output Growth Rate (g_{Yt})	Actual Inflation Rate (π_t)	Rational Expectation of Inflation (π_t^{RE})	Forecast Error ($\pi_t^e - \pi_t$)
1	2%	0%	1%	1%	0%
2	3	0	2		
3	4	0	3		
4	5	0	4		
5	6	2	5		
6	7	4	4		
7	8	6	3		
8	9	8	2		
9	10	10	1		
10	11	12	0		

12. Complete the following table to illustrate how the speed of adjustment affects the formation of adaptive expectations. Describe verbally the difference in adaptive expectations when $\lambda = .2$ compared to the case where $\lambda = .8$.

Period (t)	Actual Inflation Rate (π_t)	Adaptive Expectation Inflation Rate (π_t^e) When $\lambda = .2$	Adaptive Expectation Inflation Rate (π_t^e) When $\lambda = .8$
1	0%	0%	0%
2	5		
3	5		
4	5		
5	5		
6	5		
7	5		
8	5		
9	5		
10	5		

13. Can it ever be "rational" to use something other than rational expectations to form future expectations? Explain carefully.

14. Suppose you wanted to form rational expectations of future short-term interest rates. What variables would economic theory suggest are relevant for this undertaking?

15. Suppose you used your model in problem 14 to predict future interest rates. Do you think you could make money by using this forecast in financial markets? Explain.

SELECTIONS FOR FURTHER READING

Balvers, R. J., and T. F. Cosimano. "Actively Learning about Demand and the Dynamics of Price Adjustment." *Economic Journal,* 100 (September 1990), 882–898.

Balvers, R. J., T. F. Cosimano, and B. McDonald. "Predicting Stock Returns in an Efficient Market." *Journal of Finance,* 45 (September 1990), 1109–1128.

Blenman, L. P. "Price Forecasts and Interest Rate Forecasts: An Extension of Levy's Hypothesis." *Journal of Futures Markets,* 10 (December 1990), 605–610.

Bonham, C. S., and D. C. Dacy. "In Search of a 'Strictly Rational' Forecast." *Review of Economics and Statistics,* 73 (May 1991), 245–253.

Brandon, C., R. Fritz, and J. Xander. "Econometric Forecasts: Evaluation and Revision." *Applied Economics,* 15 (April 1983), 187–201.

Carns, F., and R. E. Lombra. "Rational Expectations and Short-Run Neutrality." *Review of Economics and Statistics,* (November 1983), 639–643.

Cecchetti, S. G., R. E. Cumby, and S. Figlewski. "Estimation of the Optimal Futures Hedge." *Review of Economics and Statistics,* 70 (November 1988), 623–630.

Cho, D. W. "Formation of Inflationary Expectations by Business Economists." *Business Economics,* 21 (April 1986), 34–39.

Chung, Pham. "A Note on Policy Evaluation and Rational Expectations." *Public Finance,* 41 (1986), 139–146.

Darrat, A. F., and F. A. Lopez. "Price Instability and Inflation: Some Tests Based on Rational Expectations Models." *Eonomic Letters,* 26 (1988), 111–119.

Continued on p. 404

Driskill, R. and S. McCafferty. ''Spot and Forward
Rates in a Stochastic Model of the Foreign
Exchange Market.'' *Journal of International Economics,* 12 (May 1982), 313–331.

Driskill, R., and S. McCafferty. ''Exchange Market
Intervention under Rational Expectations with Imperfect Capital Substitutability.'' *Exchange Rate
Management under Uncertainty.* Cambridge,
Mass., and London: MIT Press, 1985, 83–95.

Hall, A., and R. J. Rossana. ''Estimating the Speed of
Adjustment in Partial Adjustment Models.'' *Journal of Business and Economic Statistics,* 9 (October 1991), 451–453.

Joutz, F. L. ''Information Efficiency Tests of Quarterly Macroeconomic GNP Forecasts from 1976 to
1985.'' *Managerial and Decision Economics,* 9
(December 1988), 311–330.

MacDonald, S. S., R. L. Peterson, and T. W. Koch.
''Using Futures to Improve Treasury Bill Portfolio
Performance.'' *Journal of Futures Markets,* 8
(April 1988), 167–184.

Mankiw, N. G., J. A. Miron, and D. N. Weil. ''The
Adjustment of Expectations to a Change in Regime: A Study of the Founding of the Federal Reserve.'' *American Economic Review,* 77 (June
1987), 358–374.

Pearce, D. K. ''Short-Term Inflation Expectations:
Evidence from a Monthly Survey: A Note.'' *Journal of Money, Credit, and Banking,* 19 (August
1987), 388–395.

Wible, J. R. ''An Epistemic Critique of Rational Expectations and the Neoclassical Macroeconomic
Research Program.'' *Journal of Post Keynesian
Economics,* 7 (Winter 1984–85), 269–281.

Wrightsman, D. ''Forecasting with Velocity.'' *Challenge,* 28 (July/August 1985), 58–60.

PART FOUR

The Creation of Money

CHAPTERS

13

The Federal Reserve System: History,
Modern Structure, and Policy Tools

14

The Money Supply Process

15

The Demand for Money and Equilibrium
in the Money Market

13

The Federal Reserve System: History, Modern Structure, and Policy Tools

On February 4, 1994, Fed chair Alan Greenspan released a written statement to the press saying the Fed would tighten credit to keep inflationary pressures in check. This news shook financial markets. Interest rates rose, bond prices fell, and the stock market plummeted, posting its largest daily decline in almost two years. The Fed's announcement marked the end of the steady decline in interest rates that began with Fed actions in 1989. These events highlight the Fed's power over the economy.

In the first part of this book, we focused largely on how financial markets function and how they are affected by changes in interest rates, expectations, and various types of risk. In the second half, we examine the overall functioning of the economy and in particular how actions by the Fed influence it. Why does the Fed tighten credit or raise interest rates? Do the Fed's efforts to keep inflation in check affect other aspects of the economy like investment, employment, or real output? We answer these and related questions in the remaining chapters. Before we do this, however, we need a broad overview of why and how the Fed functions as a central bank, how the Fed is structured, and the tools it uses to control the money supply.

We begin this chapter with a close look at the evolution of the central bank of the United States, the Federal Reserve System. In contrast to Chapter 7, in which we focused on how the Fed and other regulatory bodies like the FDIC regulate the banking industry, here we examine the Fed's role as the central banker and regulator of the money supply. Our look at the structure of today's Fed, both as central banker for the United States and as a quasi-independent policymaker, introduces you to the tools the Fed uses to influence the economic landscape that extends far beyond the banking system. In later chapters, we will see how the Fed uses these tools to affect the money supply (Chapter 14), interest rates (Chapter 15), and the overall economy, including inflation, unemployment, investment, and real GDP (Chapters 16 through 18).

A Brief History of Central Banking in the United States

A **central bank** is a bank for the government and a bank for banks. A central bank holds deposits for and loans reserves to private commercial banks like Citibank. It also holds deposits for the government and takes actions that facilitate government borrowing. In its role as a bank for banks and government, the Fed also regulates the money supply—the topic of the next chapter.

Throughout its history, the United States has had three central banks: the First Bank of the United States, the Second Bank of the United States, and the Federal Reserve system (the current central bank). As we will see, there have also been several periods during the past 200 years in which no central bank existed. In this section, we briefly review the history of banking and central banking in the United States.

Banking in the United States Before 1791

Before 1791, the United States had no central bank and relatively few commercial banks. The first institution that functioned like a modern commercial bank was established in Philadelphia in 1782. The Bank of North America was a private bank created primarily by merchants, who used it to pool their funds and provide short-term financing for commercial transactions. No central bank existed at this time, nor even a banking industry as such. The Revolutionary War had just ended, and the federal government had not yet formed.

In these early days, banking developed as an activity carried out by private banks with state charters. These banks were primarily in the business of making short-term commercial loans, which financed purchases of goods and were liquidated when the goods were sold.

One key difference between banking then and banking today was that the issuance of banknotes—that is, the issuance of currency by private banks—was the primary means by which early banks made loans. Today, when a bank makes a loan, it commonly gives the borrower a checking account containing the loaned amount or makes some equivalent transfer of funds. With a mortgage loan, for example, a bank might provide the loaned funds directly to the seller of the house, again in the form of a checkable account or a check written against such an account. Rarely does a bank today make a loan by actually providing a borrower with a substantial sum of currency.

The use of banknotes instead of checkable deposits in the early years of the United States can be explained by several features of that period. First, the acceptability of checks in trade requires facilities for quickly clearing checks among banks. These facilities were not readily available in a nation with a quickly expanding frontier and poorly developed transportation and communication routes. Second, the acceptability of checks requires confidence in the honesty of people writing the checks or an efficient means of policing the use of bad checks. These elements too were absent in the early years of the United States. Thus, banknotes, usually redeemable in gold at the bank of issue, were a superior form of money during that period. As long as the issuing bank was sound, the holder of a banknote was certain of redemption in gold. These notes passed from hand to hand, serving as money in various transactions, before eventually being returned to the issuing banks for redemption in gold.

There was a problem, however, in maintaining banknotes' convertibility into gold. First, banks were tempted to overissue notes, since this was their way of making loans and hence profits. The result of overissue was that these banks could not meet the promise to redeem notes for gold on demand. Second, the fractional reserve banking system meant the gold reserves banks held did not equal the value of notes in circulation. (This occurs even today, although modern banks hold reserves as vault cash and deposits at the Fed instead of gold). Fear of inconvertibility caused bank runs. In the early United States, this meant noteholders would rush to the bank in an attempt to redeem their notes for gold before the bank exhausted its reserves. These problems ultimately led to the development of the first central bank in the United States.

The First U.S. Central Bank: First Bank of the United States

The first institution to perform some of the roles of a central bank was the First Bank of the United States, chartered by Congress in 1791. The First Bank of the United States acted as the bank for the U.S. government, with a main office in Philadelphia and branches in the major cities of the day: New York, Boston, Baltimore, Washington, Norfolk, Charleston, Savannah, and New Orleans. The government owned stock in the bank, but British investors owned a greater than two-thirds share of the bank. This foreign ownership disturbed many Americans, but the bank nonetheless acted as fiscal agent for the federal government and in particular for the U.S. Treasury. The First Bank of the United States issued its own banknotes, which circulated side by side with banknotes issued by a number of state-chartered banks. The First Bank of the United States not only issued its own notes; it also played a part in discouraging excessive note issue by state banks, since it forced state-chartered banks to redeem their notes in gold by promptly presenting any such notes in its possession to the issuing banks. If these banks refused, the First Bank of the United States refused to accept their banknotes for U.S. Treasury transactions.

These actions were not popular among state banks. The political opposition they created, along with concerns about the constitutionality of a federal charter, led to the early demise of the First Bank of the United States.

Its original charter expired in 1811 and was not renewed. The first U.S. experience with central banking was thus short-lived.

The Second U.S. Central Bank: Second Bank of the United States

After the demise of the First Bank of the United States, banking was left for a time in the hands of state-chartered banks. By 1814, banks across the nation were refusing to redeem their notes for gold. This contributed to the creation of the Second Bank of the United States in 1816. This bank too served as fiscal agent for the U.S. government. It issued its own notes and, like the First Bank of the United States, forced state banks to redeem their banknotes in gold by presenting any such notes it received directly to the issuing banks for redemption. This bank also encountered severe political opposition from state banks, and it too was attacked on constitutional grounds. In the early 1830s, President Andrew Jackson took actions that substantially weakened the bank's powers, and its charter was not renewed when it expired in 1836.

The Absence of a Central Bank: 1836–1913

After the demise of Second Bank of the United States, the United States lacked a central bank until the creation of the Federal Reserve System in 1913. Between 1836 and 1913, the United States experimented with two major banking systems: the free banking system and the national banking system.

The Free Banking System.   After 1836, banking in the United States, was once again a business left to the states, which could charter banks and decide how to regulate them. The *free banking system* was an innovation that began in Michigan in 1837 and in New York in 1838. The free banking movement had two main goals. The first was to make entry into the banking industry "free," or at least less heavily regulated than before. Prior to free banking, the procedure for obtaining a state charter was complicated and highly politicized, requiring action by the state legislature. The second goal was to make banknotes safe. This was attempted by requiring collateral for note issues. Under the free banking system, anyone could open a bank and issue notes as long as that person provided the requisite collateral. This commonly meant a bank had to deposit with the state government bonds equal in value to the notes issued. Furthermore, banks had to redeem notes for gold on demand. Failure to do so resulted in the closure of the bank, with the sale of the bonds held as collateral to compensate the noteholders. In addition, most states stipulated that if the collateral was not sufficient, noteholders had first claim on the bank's remaining assets. Finally, some states made bank owners legally liable to noteholders to the extent of their ownership share in the bank. The idea was to make banknotes a safe form

of money. Even in the case of bank failure, sufficient assets had to be deposited with the state to redeem the notes of the failed bank.

Free banking spread rapidly among the states, although it was not universally adopted. The first goal of the free banking system was successfully obtained: The number of banks soared. In New York, for example, the number of banks almost doubled within three years, and other free banking states saw similar rapid increases.

The second objective, to provide a safe issue of banknotes, was much less successful, and the reasons are a matter of current debate among economists. Conventional wisdom has it that the free banking system was marked by fraud, wildcat banking, bank failures, and widespread losses to noteholders. The term **wildcat bank** was coined during this period to describe a bank that would purposely issue excessive notes and locate in remote places (near the "wildcats") to make redemption difficult. If substantial numbers of notes were presented for payment, the bank would close up and disappear, leaving noteholders with notes of dubious value at best. Conventional wisdom is supported by personal anecdotes and by a look at some statistics on bank failures.[1] For example, Michigan, a pioneer of free banking in 1837, saw 40 banks established in the first year, but only 4 remained by the end of 1839. Furthermore, some estimates place the losses to noteholders as high as 45 percent of Michigan's annual income! Minnesota had a similar experience. Minnesota allowed free banking in 1858; 16 new banks were formed, but only 5 survived through 1863. In addition, in seven of the bank closings, noteholders received 35 cents or less on the dollar.

Other states had more pleasant experiences, but still saw a number of bank failures. In Indiana, 57 out of 72 free banks went out of business within two years, although at least 14 managed to fully compensate noteholders. Wisconsin saw 79 out of 140 free banks go out of business by the early 1860s, and in 37 of these failures noteholders experienced losses. Even in New York, one-fourth of the free banks established in the first year were out of business by 1841, and noteholders experienced losses in about half of those cases.

The conclusion from such statistics and from personal anecdotes in the historical record is that the free banking era failed to maintain a safe banking system and a sound currency. The failure of free banking is often blamed on fraudulent practices and wildcatting. Counterfeiting also played a role. It was perhaps easier to engage in counterfeiting due to the large number of different notes in circulation; by the end of the 1860s, almost 5,400 types of counterfeit notes were in circulation. Finally, as Box 13.1 shows, some problems during the free banking era can be attributed to volatile bond prices and to a lack of diversity in the portfolios of the free banks.

---

[1] Statistics from Arthur J. Rolnick and Warren E. Weber, "Free Banking, Wildcat Banking, and Shinplasters," *Federal Reserve Bank of Minneapolis Quarterly Review* (Fall 1982), 10–19.

Inside Money

Box 13.1

*Declining Bond Prices and Bank Failures
During the Free Banking Era*

Arthur Rolnick and Warren Weber, economists at the Federal Reserve Bank of Minneapolis, have provided evidence that declining bond prices, rather than fraud and theft, were the primary cause of bank failures during the free banking era. Free banks were required to hold state bonds as collateral against their note issues. Some states valued bonds put up as collateral at face value, while others required bonds to be valued at market value. In either case, a substantial fall in the market price of those bonds made a bank's collateral worth less than its note issue. In that case, a bank run could begin. At least some noteholders, aware of the decline in bond prices—and hence in the collateral backing the bank notes—would attempt to redeem their bank notes for gold. At the same time, if bond prices had fallen far enough that a bank's assets were less than its liabilities, bank owners would have to raise additional funds from their personal wealth or elsewhere to be able to fully redeem the notes. The alternative was to refuse to redeem the notes, triggering a bank closure and the sale of the bonds held as collateral to compensate the noteholders. The

bank owners would lose the value of their investment in the bank—but nothing more—and the noteholders would be partially compensated from the sale of the bank's collateral. In this situation, bank owners and noteholders shared in the loss caused by the decline in bond prices.

Rolnick and Weber point out that during the period from 1852 to 1863, most bank closings occurred during times when bond prices declined sharply. For example, bond prices fell more than 20 percent in the last half of 1854, dropped more than 15 percent in the middle of 1857, and again fell more than 15 percent from late 1860 through the summer of 1861. Such large declines in the value of collateral could well have placed banks in a situation that would trigger noteholders to redeem their notes, and banks in such a position could have opted for closure.

Source: Federal Reserve Bank of Minneapolis Quarterly Review, Fall 1982, pp. 10–19. Copyright © 1982 Federal Reserve Bank of Minneapolis. Used with permission.

The National Banking System.   During the Civil War, the U.S. government found itself in need of funds. These funds were provided in part by the issue of a fiat currency called **greenbacks** (recall that fiat currency is not backed by gold or any other commodity). Greenbacks and related U.S. government notes made up about 75 percent of the money in circulation by the end of the Civil War and had supplanted state banknotes as the primary currency in circulation.

The experience of the free banking system and the problems of financing the expenditures of the Civil War led Congress to establish a sound national currency with passage of the National Banking Act of 1863. This act, along with several subsequent revisions and extensions, established the **national banking system.** The federal government again began regulating both the banking system and the circulation of banknotes and imposed a 10 percent tax on any bank or individual using state banknotes for transactions. As discussed in Chapter 7, this policy did not drive state banks out of existence as intended. Instead it led to the dual banking system of today because state banks innovated by introducing *demand deposits,* a close substitute for banknotes issued by national banks.

The national banking system, like the free banking system, had some successes. National banknotes succeeded in that they provided a sound and stable national currency. However, the national banking system was created at a time when deposits were replacing banknotes as the main method of holding money. In 1860 deposits and banknotes in circulation were roughly equal in amount, but by 1880 deposits were more than three times larger than bank notes. In a sense, the national banking system concentrated on providing a sound and stable currency, but it paid too little attention to deposits.

The main criticism of the national banking system was that it did not prove flexible in dealing with the seasonal variations in business activity, especially in agriculture. Periodic increases in the demand for loans and in the holding of currency occurred during the spring planting season and especially during the fall harvesting periods.

For example, rural banks held not only their legal reserves but also a portion of their extra reserves in correspondent banks in reserve cities. These reserve city banks treated these deposits as they did all other deposits, holding the legally mandated level of reserves against them but otherwise lending out a substantial portion. During periods of seasonal activity in agriculture, demand for currency increased at the rural banks, because many transactions were still made with currency, and demand for loans rose as well. Rural banks found themselves in need of funds to lend and thus withdrew the extra reserves they had deposited in reserve city banks. The reserve city banks then had to recall loans to meet their own reserve requirements.

At times this situation became more than just an inconvenience. When periods of seasonal demand coincided with periods of financial strain, the call of bank loans in reserve cities was often unsuccessful. The loans called in were actually called *call loans* and were overnight loans secured with common stock as collateral. These loans could be called on demand. However, if the common stock used as collateral had fallen in price, calling the loan might not have yielded full repayment. Also, calling the loan forced the sale of the stock, and if this happened on a large scale the result was an additional decline in the price of the common stock, further reducing the chance of repayment. Reserve city banks thus found themselves in a rather precarious situation. They could either respond to the withdrawal of deposits requested by rural banks and violate their reserve requirements or fail to honor the request for deposits and trigger a bank run.

If bank runs spread to many banks, a banking panic resulted. There would be a widespread demand for currency by the public, a demand the banking system could not meet. The result would be restrictions on the withdrawal of currency, called a *suspension of payments.* Such restrictions occurred in 1857, 1861, 1873, 1893, and 1907. During these times, banks remained open and processed checks much as usual, but they restricted payment of currency in exchange for deposits. Some customers were able to obtain small amounts of currency, or even receive currency in the usual amounts for business purposes, while other customers found the restrictions less flexible, and large-scale withdrawals were rarely permitted. (During this period, currency could actually be purchased, but at a premium. In New York City this premium was as high as 5 percent, but often less.)[2]

Other attempts were made to provide the demanded currency. The U.S. Treasury tried to handle some of the seasonal demand by depositing funds each autumn in certain chosen banks to give them additional funds to lend or to meet the demand for currency. In response to specific episodes in 1873, 1893, and 1907, the U.S. Treasury made large purchases of bonds in an attempt to disburse currency to the public. This action was a precursor of open market operations, discussed later in this chapter.

The national banking system was unable to provide an elastic banking system, one that could expand or contract currency and loans in response to seasonal and other variations in the demand for currency and loans. In the national banking system, no bank was able to issue additional notes in a time of high seasonal demand for currency and reserves. Thus, support grew for the creation of a central bank, one that would be able to supply reserves and loans elastically. The result was the birth of the Federal Reserve System.

The Third U.S. Central Bank: The Federal Reserve System

The **Federal Reserve System** (or simply *the Fed*) was established as the central bank for the United States by the Federal Reserve Act of 1913, during the presidency of Woodrow Wilson, and began operations in 1914. Chapter 7 provided a quick overview of the Fed's history; now we take a more detailed look.

The Fed was established as a central bank to ensure that commercial banks indeed kept reserves (which were required to be on deposit at the central bank) sufficient to cover withdrawals by depositors. The Federal Reserve System was to stand willing to meet systemwide increases in the

---

[2] See Gerald P. Dwyer, Jr., and R. Alton Gilbert, ''Bank Runs and Private Remedies,'' *Federal Reserve Bank of St. Louis Review* (May/June 1989), 43–61.

demand for currency by supplying currency to the banking system in the quantity desired. The Fed would make it possible for the public to always be able to change its desired ratio of currency to demand deposits without severely disrupting the banking system. In other words, one main goal in establishing the Fed was to provide an **elastic currency,** a money supply that could be easily converted from demand deposits to currency. Moreover, it was expected that the very availability of currency on demand would quell the fears that fueled bank runs or bank panics, especially those that became widespread. Thus, the very provision of an elastic currency was expected to vastly reduce or even eliminate the occasional bank panics that occurred under the national banking system.

In addition to providing an elastic currency, the Federal Reserve would serve as the nation's central bank, regulating money markets in general and having day-to-day regulatory oversight on some commercial banks, as well as managing the nation's money supply for macroeconomic policy purposes.

The Federal Reserve Act of 1913.

The Federal Reserve Act of 1913 set up the Federal Reserve System as a set of 12 separate institutions, the district Federal Reserve banks. The actions of these 12 separate entities were to be coordinated by the Federal Reserve Board in Washington, D.C. Each Federal Reserve bank was set up to administer to a specific geographic area or district, with branch banks to aid in administering the large areas in some districts.

The district Federal Reserve banks were established by the sale of stock to commercial banks that became members of the Federal Reserve System. Member banks were required to purchase stock in the Federal Reserve bank equal to 3 percent of their own net worth. These stock certificates paid a dividend restricted by law to be 6 percent or less. Earnings in excess of these dividends were remitted to the federal government.

In terms of membership, all national banks—which meant all banks that were part of the national banking system—were compelled to join the Federal Reserve System or give up their national charter. However, state-chartered banks were allowed to choose to be or not be members of the Federal Reserve System. All member banks were required to hold reserves at their district Federal Reserve bank or branch bank.

Benefits of membership included access to check-clearing services and aid in times of stress. Member banks could get the Fed to loan them funds using bills of exchange or promissory notes as collateral. This practice, called **discounting,** was the forerunner of the modern discount window.

The original organization of each of the district Federal Reserve banks was as follows. There were nine directors, six elected by the member banks. Three of these directors were to be bankers, and three were to be business-persons not in the banking business. The remaining three directors were appointed by the Federal Reserve Board, and one of them was appointed as chair of the board and executive officer of the bank.

The Federal Reserve Board itself was composed of seven members appointed by the president and approved by the Senate. One member was named governor and one deputy-governor. The secretary of the Treasury and the comptroller of the currency were made members. Also established was a group called the Federal Advisory Council, composed of one banker from each district, with the role of offering advice to the board.

The basic aim in establishing the Fed—an idea that can be seen in its structure—was that of cooperative regulation. The idea was that central banking could be accomplished fairly automatically. Cooperation among the Board of Governors, the Federal Reserve banks, and the member banks would ensure that the tasks of the central bank were successfully accomplished. Moreover, the gold standard of the time required fairly automatic responses to economic events. The job of the central bank was to maintain a constant ratio between gold reserves and the sum of deposits plus notes.

The other task of the Fed was to provide an elastic banking system. Indeed, this was a primary motivation in establishing the Federal Reserve System. Elasticity was to be achieved by following what has been called the **real bills doctrine.** According to this doctrine, the central bank would supply liquid reserves to the member banks whenever they needed funds to make productive business loans. These loans from the Fed to member banks were temporary in nature and were made only if the banks could show the funds would be used to increase loans to productive businesses. These loans were to be discount loans, in which the collateral was various forms of short-term, high-quality commercial paper.[3] They were discount loans because the Fed would purchase the commercial paper at a discount from its face value and the member bank would buy back the paper at face value. When business activity increased and there was a greater demand for liquidity as evidenced by an increase in commercial paper and bills of exchange, the central bank would supply the liquidity, lending notes and reserves to member banks that presented these real bills as collateral.

The creators of the Fed intended that reserves would be created by discounting real bills. Such actions would produce short-term increases in reserves that would end when the discount loan was repaid by the borrowing bank. However, during the 1920s the district banks found another way to increase banking system reserves: by purchasing government securities for their own portfolios. This method was discovered by accident, as the banks' intent was to increase earnings on otherwise idle balances. (This was a forerunner of open market operations, which are discussed in detail later in the chapter.) To coordinate this activity, the Conference of Governors, which included the governors of the 12 district banks, formed the Open Market Investment Committee. This committee acted independently of the Federal Reserve Board.

---

[3] Recall that commercial paper is a short-term (nine months or less) debt instrument that firms issue to obtain funds. Commercial paper is negotiable, meaning it can be sold to someone else.

How did the Fed function as a whole? Basically the district Federal Reserve banks acted with a large degree of autonomy. They pursued their own independent discounting policies. If anything, they followed the lead of the Federal Reserve Bank of New York, which held the largest percentage of system reserves. Indeed, the New York Fed assumed responsibility for relationships with all foreign central banks and sometimes acted without informing even the Board of Governors. The Board of Governors found itself with little real power.

The Great Depression.

Perhaps the defining event in the history of the Federal Reserve System was the debacle of the Fed's handling of the onset of the Great Depression. In 1929 the stock market crashed, and subsequently a tremendous wave of bank failures swept the nation. From 1929 to 1932 more than 5,000 banks failed, which amounted to one-third of all commercial banks. Banks were unable to supply the currency depositors demanded, and this failure only fueled the ongoing runs on banks across the nation. In essence, the situation was like that faced at times during the national banking system, only magnified many times over. The Federal Reserve System, which had been created to provide an elastic banking system—one that would stand able to provide currency during a crisis—failed miserably in this test, refusing or neglecting to provide the necessary reserves. In fact, the money supply actually fell by about one-third over this period. The effect on the economy was severe, as the nearly total collapse of the financial system led business to a standstill from which recovery came only slowly.

The cause of the Great Depression is an issue of ongoing debate. Whether the banking panics that followed the stock market crash were a cause or a symptom is one element of that debate. However, condemnation of the Fed's inaction over this period is nearly unanimous. Whether that inaction merely increased the severity of the Great Depression or directly caused it also remains a matter of debate. There seems little question, however, that the Fed failed to take the necessary and appropriate action during that crisis.

The Banking Act of 1935.

In response to the Great Depression and the failure of the Fed to supply the reserves needed to maintain stability in the banking system and in the money supply, Congress moved to reform the Fed. As we learned in Chapter 7, the Glass-Steagall Act of 1933 prohibited commercial banks from dealing in corporate securities and empowered the Fed to set margin requirements on stock purchases. This act allowed the Fed some indirect regulation of securities markets and kept commercial banks from investing in corporate bonds and stocks, which fluctuated too widely in value and were considered too risky for a safe banking system.

However, it was the Banking Act of 1935 that really made the Fed what it is today. It transformed the Fed from a cooperative with 12 independent offices to an institution with a real central authority located in the Board of Governors in Washington, D.C. The Federal Reserve banks were no longer able to set policy independently of the wishes of the Board of Governors. The board was given complete power over relations with foreign central banks, setting discount rates, and even the internal affairs and budgets of the Federal Reserve banks. Monetary policy would now be determined in Washington. The Federal Open Market Committee, derived from the governors' conference's Open Market Investment Committee, was created to buy and sell government securities.

There were structural reforms as well. The chief executive officers of the Federal Reserve banks were renamed from governors to presidents. They were still chosen by the directors but were subject to the veto power of the Board of Governors. The Board of Governors also was reformed. The secretary of the U.S. Treasury and the comptroller of the currency were no longer allowed to serve on the board, and members' terms were lengthened from 10 to 14 years.

We describe the function and structure of the modern Federal Reserve System in more detail later in this chapter. For now we simply note that the institutional structure of the Fed today was determined in most of its essential elements by the Banking Act of 1935.

The Accord of 1951.

In the early 1940s, the Federal Reserve System acted to keep the interest rate on government securities low and almost constant to help the U.S. Treasury finance the war effort at a low interest rate. The Fed could do this by buying or selling securities at the pegged interest rate. This practice continued for some time after the war ended, but the Fed was concerned it was becoming just an arm of the Treasury instead of an independent monetary policymaker. Thus, the Fed and the Treasury reached a friendly agreement in March 1951, known as the Federal Reserve–Treasury Accord, that ended the practice of the Fed fixing the interest rate to facilitate financing of the debt by the Treasury.

Between 1951 and 1980, the main problem the Fed faced was declining membership. As we learned in Chapter 7, declining membership meant the Fed's control over the money supply was diminishing.

The Depository Institutions Deregulation and Monetary Control Act of 1980.

The Depository Institutions Deregulation and Monetary Control Act of 1980, or DIDMCA, had a profound effect on the structure of the Federal Reserve System—not by changing the board of the Federal Reserve banks but by altering the membership status of commercial banks and other depository institutions. Prior to 1980, commercial banks could choose whether or not to be members of the Fed. Nationally chartered banks were members, but state-chartered banks could choose not to be members. Membership had both costs and benefits. Costs included purchasing shares in the Federal Reserve bank, being subject to Fed oversight, and holding reserves at the Federal Reserve bank. Benefits included access to check clearing at subsidized prices and access to the discount window. State-chartered banks, savings and loans, thrifts, and other depository institutions had no direct access to Fed services. DIDMCA changed all that. Basically it said that all federally insured depository institutions must meet Federal Reserve System reserve requirements. In exchange, it also granted these institutions access to the discount window and Fed check clearing. The act also stipulated, however, that the Fed could no longer subsidize the price of check-clearing services, so the value of this benefit lessened considerably.

As a result of DIDMCA, by 1987 the Fed's authority over required reserves extended to virtually all depository institutions, including commercial banks, savings and loans, credit unions, and any others accepting federal deposit insurance. This was a huge increase in the Fed's direct authority over the banking system. Since 1987, legislation has focused largely on reforms directed at the S&L crisis rather than at the Fed's direct authority over the money supply. Chapter 7 details these legislative actions.

Summary | Throughout banking history, there have been various calls for an end to
Exercise 13.1 | fractional reserve banking. The rationale for 100 percent reserve banking is that a run on the deposits of a bank would never occur since the bank would actually have reserves in currency, gold, or some other very liquid form equal to the quantity of deposits. This idea was circulated as an alternative to the national banking system and to the Federal Reserve System and, in a revised form, has recently been suggested as a way to reform the current U.S. banking system by Nobel prize–winning economist James Tobin. In what ways did the free banking system and the national banking system differ from a system of 100 percent reserves?

Answer: Both the free banking system and the national banking system required banks to deposit with a government agency bonds equal in value to the notes they issued. However, these bonds were not reserves usable in the day-to-day operation of a bank; in fact, they served merely as collateral against the issue of notes. Especially in the free banking system, the value of these bonds fluctuated so widely that they might not have equaled the value of the circulating bank notes. Thus, unlike 100 percent reserves in currency (or 100 percent reserves in gold under a gold standard), the collateral of free banks was neither readily available for redeeming notes nor necessarily in a form that would always maintain a value equal to the value of the deposits. The main point is that having collateral equal to the value of bank notes, or equal to the value of deposits, is not the same as having 100 percent reserves.

THE STRUCTURE AND ROLE OF THE MODERN FEDERAL RESERVE SYSTEM

From its inception, the Fed has been largely independent of both the legislative and executive branches of government, an independence shared by only a few other central banks worldwide. For example, the Bank of England, the world's oldest central bank, serves as an arm of the British government. The independence of the Fed is the source of ongoing controversy, and scarcely a session of Congress passes without someone introducing a bill to somehow limit or abolish this independence.

To understand the functioning of the Federal Reserve System and such issues as the debate over its independence, it is important to know how the Fed is structured today.

The Institutional Structure

Today the Federal Reserve System consists of four main elements: (1) the Board of Governors, (2) the 12 regional Federal Reserve banks, (3) the Federal Open Market Committee, and (4) the member banks and other depository institutions. We look at the first three elements in turn; we looked at the banking system in detail in earlier chapters.

The Board of Governors.   The **Board of Governors** consists of seven members appointed by the U.S. president and confirmed by the Senate. Each member serves a 14-year term. Moreover, no member is allowed to serve more than one full term, although reappointment after a partial term (to replace a resignation, for example) is possible. The terms are staggered so that one position is appointed every two years. This policy has several implications. First, the members know they can serve well beyond the term of the president who appoints them. Second, a president would have a difficult time appointing a majority of members to the Board of Governors, since presidential terms are limited to four years (or to eight with reelection). Thus, it is not easy to stack the board with sympathetic members in an attempt to influence policy. Members are often chosen from the banking or business community, and a fair number of economists have served among the governors.

One member of the Board of Governors is appointed by the president to serve as chairperson, again with Senate confirmation. The chair has a four-year term that begins near the midpoint of a presidential term. Thus, newly elected presidents inherit a chair of the Board of Governors for the first half of their administration. The chair's term can be renewed, and a chair whose term is not renewed can continue to serve on the board as a regular member, although this is rarely done.

It is fair to say that most of the real power at the Board of Governors—and indeed in the entire Federal Reserve System—is concentrated in the hands of the Fed chair (more formally known as the chair of the Board of Governors). The chair of the Board of Governors sets the agenda for meetings on monetary policy and has substantial control over the staff serving the board. Governors who are out of favor with the chair may find their staff allocations cut significantly. Without competent staff support, a governor would have a difficult time researching and keeping informed about current issues and therefore would suffer a loss of power and influence. The chair of the Board of Governors as of July 1994 is Alan Greenspan, who replaced Paul Volcker in 1987.

The institutional structure of the Board of Governors is supposed to insulate that body from political considerations, and to some extent it does. The Fed does not rely on any arm of government for paying its bills and is not audited by the Office of Management and Budget. This fact, coupled with long appointments of members that technically are not renewable, reduces the Fed's tendency to cower to political pressures. Short of major legislative changes or extreme presidential pressure, members of the Board of Governors are relatively free of partisan considerations.

However, the board is responsible to Congress, and indeed the entire Federal Reserve System is a creation of Congress. Even major changes in the structure of the Fed require only a majority vote in each house and the approval of the president (or a two-thirds vote in each house in the event of a presidential veto). It is fair to say that the Fed is keenly aware of this and is careful not to place itself at odds with Congress unnecessarily. As long as the economy and the banking system function well, Congress tends to leave monetary policymaking to the Fed. However, when things have not gone well, such as during the Great Depression, Congress and the president have been willing to greatly modify the structure and operation of the Fed.

Despite its independence, the Federal Reserve works closely with the U.S. Treasury on macroeconomic policy issues and on issues involving the foreign exchange market. The Board of Governors is also responsible for setting discount rate policy, setting reserve requirements, and supervising the entire Federal Reserve System, including the budgets and internal affairs of the Federal Reserve banks. To aid in these tasks, the board has a large staff, including many economists who advise the governors on monetary policymaking, regulation of the banking industry and the financial industry in general, and other topics that may arise.

The Federal Reserve Banks.

The structure of the district Federal Reserve banks is nearly the same as that determined at the creation of the Fed, but the Banking Act of 1935 stripped these banks of much of their autonomy in policy matters. Let us briefly review this current structure.

The Federal Reserve System divides the country into 12 districts, and each district contains a Federal Reserve bank. The boundaries of these districts have changed little from those in effect in 1917 and are shown in Figure 13.1. Today the Federal Reserve banks are in Boston, New York, Philadelphia, Cleveland, Richmond, Atlanta, Chicago, St. Louis, Minneapolis, Kansas City, Dallas, and San Francisco. The Federal Reserve banks are actually owned by commercial banks in their districts that are members of the Federal Reserve System. This is accomplished by requiring each member bank to buy shares in the district Federal Reserve bank, which pay a flat

Figure 13.1
Federal Reserve Districts

This map shows the locations of the 12 Federal Reserve banks and the districts served by each bank.

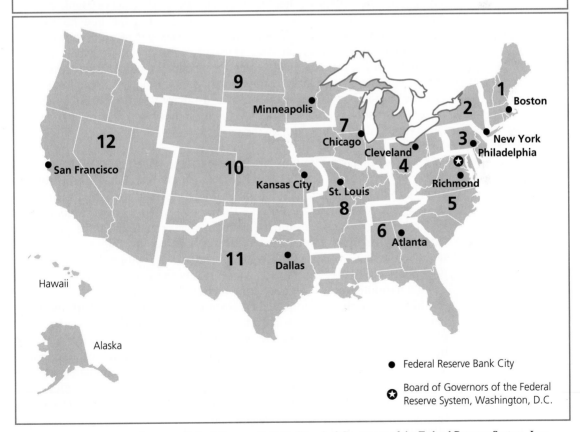

SOURCE: Federal Reserve *Bulletin,* Board of Governors of the Federal Reserve System, June 1993, A80.

dividend. Each Federal Reserve bank has nine directors, six chosen by the commercial banks in the district that are members of the Federal Reserve System and three appointed by the Board of Governors. The Board of Governors also names a director to be chair of the board at each regional bank. These directors nominate the presidents of the regional Federal Reserve banks, but their choices must be approved by the Board of Governors.

The regional banks are technically private corporations owned by commercial banks, but in reality they operate under the direction of the Board of Governors. In addition, any profits made over and above operating costs are remitted to the U.S. Treasury rather than to the commercial banks' shareholders. Most of these profits represent interest earnings on the Federal Reserve System's substantial holdings of U.S. government securities. The remittance to the Treasury is small by U.S. budget standards but not insignificant, being on the order of $30 billion per year.

The regional banks serve as regulatory agencies for banks in their districts and as check-clearing centers. Sometimes they have two or three branch offices in other cities in their region. The Federal Reserve Bank of New York serves as the primary location for carrying out the Federal Reserve System's monetary policy actions. It also carries out foreign exchange interventions on behalf of the U.S. Treasury. Finally, as we shall see, the presidents of the regional banks attend the Federal Open Market Committee meetings and sometimes vote on monetary policy issues. The regional banks provide research staffs of economists and others to advise their presidents on both monetary policy issues and issues involving the regulation and supervision of commercial banking.

The Federal Open Market Committee.   The Federal Reserve System's policymaking arm is the **Federal Open Market Committee,** or **FOMC.** The voting members of the FOMC consist of the seven governors, the president of the Federal Reserve Bank of New York, the president of the Federal Reserve Bank of either Chicago or Cleveland, and three presidents from the other nine regional Federal Reserve banks (see Figure 13.2). Note that five members of the FOMC—the presidents of regional Fed banks—are not appointed by elected officials or elected by the general population. This has led to controversy over the years, as Box 13.2 (page 424) explains.

Monetary policy actions, called *open market operations* and discussed later in this chapter, are carried out primarily at the Federal Reserve Bank of New York, which is why the president of that bank is always a voting member of the FOMC. The other bank presidents serve on a rotating basis, and the special positions accorded the Chicago and Cleveland banks are due to historical and political factors. All 12 regional bank presidents attend and discuss monetary policy issues at the FOMC meetings. Currently these meetings occur eight times per year, but only five of the bank presidents are allowed to vote at any one time.

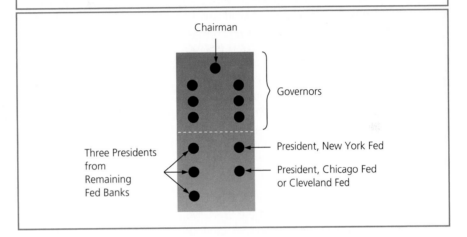

Figure 13.2
Composition of the Federal Open Market Committee

Except for the president of the New York Fed, who is a permanent member of the Federal Open Market Committee, the presidents of the other district Federal Reserve banks serve on the FOMC on a rotating basis. However, the president of either the Chicago or the Cleveland Fed always sits on the committee.

The Roles of the Fed

Originally the Fed was to provide an elastic currency and perform the fairly automatic tasks required to maintain the price of gold and keep the United States on the gold standard. Today its role has both expanded and become more complex. If nothing else, monetary policy is more difficult than it was under the gold standard.

The roles of the Fed are varied. They include

◆ Bank for bankers
◆ Bank for the federal government
◆ Regulator of banks
◆ Guardian of financial markets
◆ Keeper of the currency
◆ Gold depository
◆ Clearinghouse for checks and wire transfers
◆ Monetary policymaker

The Fed functions as the banker's bank in several ways. It holds the deposits of member banks, or reserves, and it makes loans to these banks at

Inside Money

Box 13.2

Making the Fed More Responsive to the Electorate: The Rebirth of an Old Idea

As recently as 1994, U.S. representative Henry B. Gonzales proposed legislation that would make members of the Fed, and particularly members of the FOMC, more accountable to the electorate. The idea of making those responsible for monetary policy accountable to those affected by their policies is not new. In 1964, for instance, the late Harry Johnson, then economist at the University of Chicago, testified before the Subcommittee on Domestic Finance, Committee on Banking and Currency, House of Representatives. According to Johnson,

> I believe that monetary policy should be brought under the control of the Executive and Legisature in the same way as other aspects of economic policy, with the administration bearing the ultimate responsibility for monetary policy as part of economic policy in general. In making this recommendation, I must admit there is a danger of

monetary mismanagement in the pursuit of political objectives; but I consider it preferable for such mismanagement to be a clear responsibility of the administration, and accountable to the electorate.

Johnson recognized that a potential danger of making the FOMC completely composed of presidential appointees is that it might lead the Fed to pursue short-term political objectives (like cranking up the money supply just before an election to stimulate the economy and win votes). Largely for this reason, past attempts to make all members of the FOMC appointed have failed.

———————————

Source: Harry G. Johnson, "Should There Be an Independent Monetary Authority?", in W. L. Smith and R. L. Teigen, eds., *Readings in Money, National Income, and Stabilization Policy,* 3rd ed. (Homewood: Irwin Press, 1974), 277.

the discount window. The Fed is also the bank of the federal government. The U.S. Treasury and other government agencies hold their accounts at the Federal Reserve banks and make deposits and withdrawals from these accounts just as a depositor in a commercial bank would. The Fed also handles the sale of U.S. savings bonds and U.S. Treasury bills for the government.

The Fed has regulatory power over depository institutions, including the ability to set reserve requirements. The job of providing auditing oversight is split between the Fed and other regulators, such as the FDIC. The Fed also has the broader responsibility of maintaining stability in financial markets, especially in the money markets.

The Fed is in charge of maintaining the supply of Federal Reserve notes, acting as a gold depository, and clearing checks. Maintaining the supply of

Federal Reserve notes means providing the supply of currency demanded by the public and keeping that supply in good condition. To this end, the Fed removes worn notes from circulation and adds new ones as required. The Fed, and in particular the Federal Reserve Bank of New York, serves as gold depository for the Federal Reserve System and holds gold for both the United States and other nations. Gold flows among nations are often no more than transfers of gold bars from a room or shelf holding the gold of one nation to a room or shelf holding the gold of another. Finally, the Fed provides check-clearing services. Under the DIDMCA of 1980, these services are priced at cost, so the Fed must compete with check-clearing services provided by private banks. Private check-clearing services can pick and choose the most profitable locations in which to provide these services. However, much as the post office must provide mail service to all locations in the United States, the Fed must provide check-clearing services to all U.S. banks.

Finally, the most important role of the Fed is that of the nation's monetary policymaker. The Fed is in charge of the money supply, which consists of not only Federal Reserve notes but also checkable deposits and other forms of money we looked at in Chapter 2. Moreover, the Fed is responsible for using its ability to change the money supply in ways that will benefit the economy. The Fed's overall policy goals are often listed as price level stability, full employment, economic growth, interest rate stability, stability of financial markets, and exchange rate stability. In our discussion of monetary policy in Chapters 19 through 21, we will see how the Fed might use monetary policy to help achieve some of these goals.

Figure 13.3 shows the informal structure of the Fed and how it uses its power to influence such things as discount rates, reserve requirements, and open market operations. The next section provides a broad overview of these monetary policy tools and how they affect the banking system. In Chapter 14, we examine in more detail how they affect the money supply.

Summary *Exercise 13.2*	The structure of the Fed is unique among central banks worldwide. The system of 12 Federal Reserve banks was originally set up to avoid concentrating too much power in Washington, although the Banking Act of 1935 changed this by centralizing much of the Fed's power in the Board of Governors. What do you think is the benefit of continuing to have 12 distinct Federal Reserve banks?

Answer: The Federal Reserve System needs branch offices to facilitate check clearing, regulation, discount window lending, and other routine tasks. The Federal Reserve banks and their branches fulfill this requirement. Thus, for most purposes the Federal Reserve banks serve a function that would still have to be performed in some way under an alternative Fed structure.

Figure 13.3
The Practical Structure of the Fed

In practice, the modern Fed sets monetary policy as illustrated here. The Board of Governors sets reserve requirements, establishes the discount rate, and sometimes sets selective credit controls or uses moral suasion. The Federal Open Market Committee (FOMC) directs open market operations.

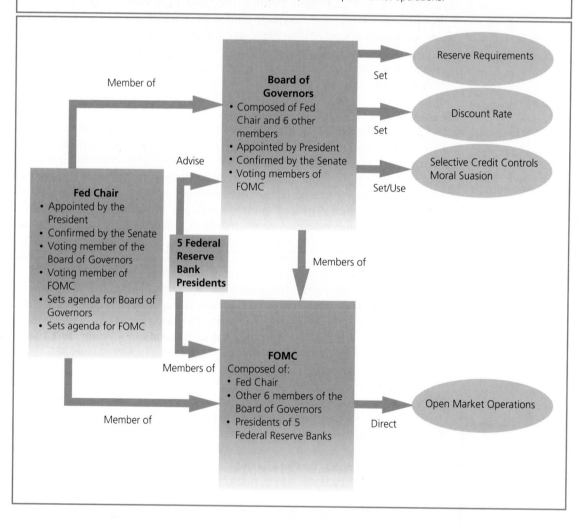

In monetary policy, however, the Federal Reserve banks play an important role. The presidents of five of the reserve banks participate in Federal Open Market Committee meetings and get 5 of the 12 votes on monetary policy decisions. Thus, they can be independent voices at the FOMC meetings.

Moreover, the Federal Reserve banks have their own research staffs that are independent of the board staff, allowing the bank presidents to more easily receive advice and keep informed about monetary and financial policy issues. Thus, the structure of the Fed, and particularly that of the FOMC, gives the Federal Reserve bank presidents the ability to present opinions on policy from outside the Board of Governors. When the Fed was first set up, there was a fear of concentrating too much power in Washington. Today the structure of the Fed shows the last vestiges of that fear in the provisions that voices from outside Washington be heard and sometimes vote on monetary policy actions.

TOOLS OF MONETARY POLICYMAKING

As Figure 13.3 suggests, there are three main tools or instruments of monetary policy and a few minor ones. The major tools are open market operations, discount window policy, and reserve requirements. Minor policy instruments are the ability to enact selective credit controls, including margin requirements, and the ability to use persuasion (sometimes called *moral suasion*) to lead banks and other depository institutions to act in a particular way.

Open Market Operations

Today the primary day-to-day means of conducting monetary policy actions is via open market operations. The Fed continually engages in open market operations, in which it buys U.S. government debt from securities dealers or sells government debt to dealers. We will see in the next few chapters that these open market operations affect, among other things, interest rates and the money supply. In an **open market purchase,** the Fed purchases U.S. government securities from a securities dealer, paying for the purchase with an electronic funds transfer or a check that promises to pay Federal Reserve notes.

When the Fed engages in an open market purchase, its assets increase, since it has additional government securities. But its liabilities also increase, since it has an outstanding check on which it will have to pay. The securities dealer, meanwhile, has merely traded one asset—government bonds, for instance—for another, the check from the Fed. Figure 13.4 illustrates this process.

When the securities dealer deposits the check in his or her bank, the dealer is again trading one asset, a check from the Fed, for another, deposits at the bank. Meanwhile the bank experiences an increase in both assets and liabilities. The check from the Fed is an asset, while the deposit account of the securities dealer is a liability.

Finally, the bank will itself transform its assets, since it will present the check to the Fed, depositing it in the bank's reserve account. For the bank,

Figure 13.4
Open Market Operations: Bond Purchases

This example shows how the Fed conducts an open market purchase of government bonds. First, the securities dealer sells $100 worth of government bonds to the Fed. The Fed writes the securities dealer a $100 check in payment for the bonds. Second, the securities dealer deposits the $100 check with a private bank. Finally, the bank deposits the check with the Fed and now has $100 on reserve at the Fed.

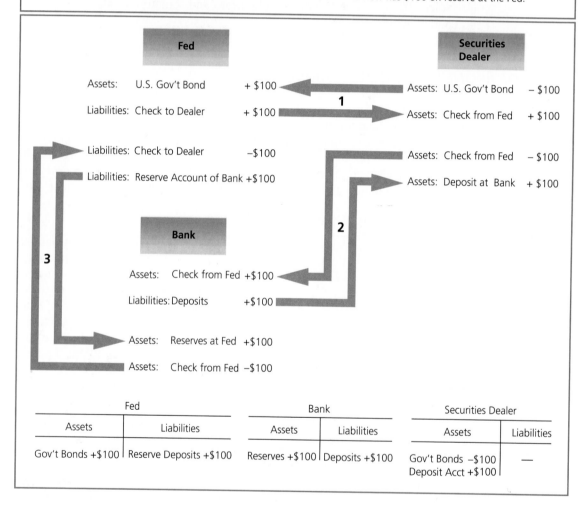

Fed				Securities Dealer		
Assets:	U.S. Gov't Bond	+ $100		Assets:	U.S. Gov't Bond	– $100
Liabilities:	Check to Dealer	+ $100	1	Assets:	Check from Fed	+ $100
Liabilities:	Check to Dealer	–$100		Assets:	Check from Fed	– $100
Liabilities:	Reserve Account of Bank	+$100		Assets:	Deposit at Bank	+ $100

Bank

			2
Assets:	Check from Fed	+$100	
Liabilities:	Deposits	+$100	
Assets:	Reserves at Fed	+$100	3
Assets:	Check from Fed	–$100	

Fed		Bank		Securities Dealer	
Assets	Liabilities	Assets	Liabilities	Assets	Liabilities
Gov't Bonds +$100	Reserve Deposits +$100	Reserves +$100	Deposits +$100	Gov't Bonds –$100 Deposit Acct +$100	—

this means exchanging one asset, a check, for another, a reserve account. For the Fed, this transaction transforms one of its liabilities from a check to a reserve account.

The bottom of Figure 13.4 shows the net effect on the three parties. As a result of the open market purchase, the Fed has gained an asset, the U.S. government bonds, and incurred a liability, reserve deposits of the bank. The securities dealer has merely traded one asset, the government bonds, for another, a deposit account at a bank. The bank has gained an asset, an increase in its reserve account, and incurred a liability, an increase in the securities dealer's deposit account.

How does this operation affect the money supply? An open market purchase affects the reserves of a bank, which in turn affects the amount of money it can loan out. In particular, the bank is required to hold reserves against deposits, but these reserves are only a small fraction of the size of the deposit account. With equal increases in reserves and deposits due to an open market purchase, the bank will have excess reserves that it can use to make loans. We will look at this process in much more detail in the next chapter; here an example will highlight how it works.

Suppose required reserves are 10 percent of deposits. The bank, which has just received an additional $100 worth of deposits, is required to hold only $10 in reserves and may loan out up to $90 of the other reserves. Thus, the bank's position shown in Figure 13.4 will change again, since the bank will seek to make loans of up to $90 with its new reserves. (We will see in Chapter 14 how the initial increase in loans and deposits actually gets multiplied by the actions of the banking system so that the increase in deposits and loans is much greater than just the initial $100 increase in deposits and $90 increase in loans.) In this way, open market purchases directly increase deposits and also increase excess reserves. When banks lend out these excess reserves, further increases in the money supply will occur. As we will see in Chapter 16, increases in the money supply can have a stimulative effect on the economy. Thus, open market purchases are considered an expansionary policy, a policy that tends to increase aggregate economic activity.

In an **open market sale,** the Fed sells government securities (bonds, bills, or notes) to a securities dealer. In Figure 13.5, for instance, the securities dealer gains an asset, government bonds, but loses another asset, its deposit account. The Fed loses an asset, the government bonds it sold, but it also loses a liability, since the bank's reserve account at the Fed decreases. The bank loses an asset, since its reserve account is reduced, and also loses a liability, because the securities dealer's deposit account decreases.

Again, however, this decrease in the bank's assets and liabilities has other effects. If the bank were holding reserves just equal to 10 percent of all deposits, the equal reduction in its reserves and deposits would mean the bank has too few reserves. For example, in Figure 13.5 the bank has lost $100 in deposits and reserves. Since it lost $100 in deposits, it can lose $10

Figure 13.5
Open Market Operations: Bond Sales

This example shows how the Fed conducts an open market sale of government bonds. First, the securities dealer buys $100 worth of government bonds from the Fed. The securities dealer writes the Fed a $100 check in payment for the bonds. Second, the Fed takes $100 out of the reserve account of the securities dealer's private bank. Finally, the private bank decreases the securities dealer's deposit account by $100.

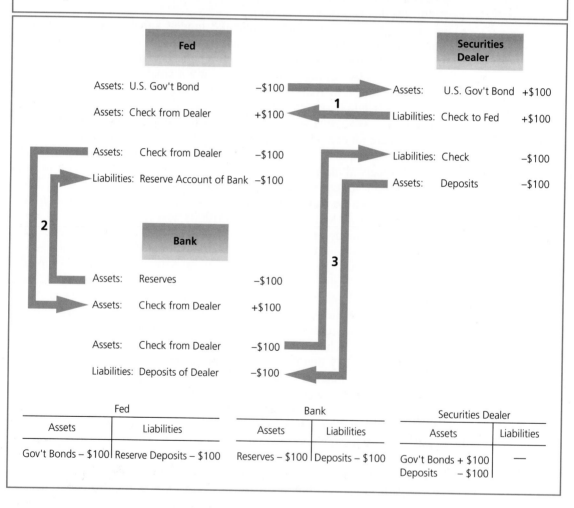

Fed

			Securities Dealer		
Assets: U.S. Gov't Bond	−$100	→	Assets: U.S. Gov't Bond	+$100
Assets: Check from Dealer	+$100	← 1	Liabilities: Check to Fed	+$100

Assets: Check from Dealer	−$100	Liabilities: Check	−$100
Liabilities: Reserve Account of Bank	−$100	Assets: Deposits	−$100

Bank

2

3

Assets: Reserves	−$100
Assets: Check from Dealer	+$100
Assets: Check from Dealer	−$100
Liabilities: Deposits of Dealer	−$100

Fed	
Assets	Liabilities
Gov't Bonds − $100	Reserve Deposits − $100

Bank	
Assets	Liabilities
Reserves − $100	Deposits − $100

Securities Dealer	
Assets	Liabilities
Gov't Bonds + $100 Deposits − $100	—

of reserves with no consequence to its reserve position. But the loss of $100 of reserves means the bank is $90 short of its reserve requirement. It must either recall some outstanding loans or sell some of its holdings of U.S. government bonds to receive sufficient reserves to cover the $90 loss. Thus, the open market sale has resulted in a decrease in deposits—that is, a decrease in the money supply—and a reduction in loans. This decrease in deposits, loans, and reserves at one bank reverberates throughout the banking system, leading to total decreases in deposits and loans that are multiples of the initial effects, as we shall see in Chapter 14. Thus, open market sales contract the money supply and exert a contractionary force on the economy. Box 13.3 on page 432 shows the magnitude of open market purchases and sales carried out by the Fed.

There are a few important institutional details regarding open market operations. First, the Fed and the securities dealers are dealing in a secondary market for securities. The U.S. government securities being bought and sold are not new issues by the Treasury; they are bonds that have been previously bought by someone other than the Fed. The Fed is prohibited from actually bidding on new issues of U.S. government securities.

Second, the purchase or sale of government securities from or to securities dealers is a voluntary activity; dealers do not have to buy or sell them at a set price. If the securities dealers don't want to sell at the offered price, they will simply refuse the Fed's offer. Of course, if the Fed wants to buy securities badly enough, it will merely offer a higher price, and eventually it will find a price at which someone will sell. Similarly, if it wants to sell securities badly enough, it will offer a lower price.

Reserve Requirements

The Board of Governors sets reserve requirements on all federally insured depository institutions within limits set by Congress. Reserve requirements are both an extremely powerful and a seldom used tool of monetary policy. The Fed has found other policy tools, especially open market operations, to be much more effective and controllable ways to change the money supply. When changes in reserve requirements do occur, they usually do so in conjunction with other structural changes in the banking industry, such as the DIDMCA of 1980, which imposed a new structure of reserve requirements across financial institutions. Such changes in reserve requirements are not conceived of as monetary actions per se but are made for purposes of regulation and stabilization of the banking industry. Still, changes in reserve requirements are a potential policy tool, and even when they are made for reasons not connected with monetary policy, they exert strong effects on the money supply.

How does an increase or a decrease in reserve requirements change the money supply? Consider a decrease in reserve requirements. A bank has

The Data Bank

Box 13.3

Open Market Operations and Churning

The accompanying table indicates the dollar volume of open market operations from May through November 1992. These transactions include what are called *outright transactions,* in which the Fed simply buys or sells securities; *matched transactions,* in which the Fed sells a security to a dealer and agrees to buy it back at a specified future date and price; and *repurchase agreements,* in which the Fed buys a security from a dealer and the dealer agrees to repurchase it in the future. Neither matched transactions nor repurchase agreements create permanent changes in reserves; rather, both change reserves only temporarily. The table shows, however, that the vast majority of open market purchases and sales are matched transactions or repurchase agreements.

Why the preponderance of temporary as opposed to permanent open market sales and purchases? Nobel Laureate Milton Friedman and other critics argue the answer is *churning*—the

intentional obscuring of the thrust of monetary policy by continual buying and selling of securities. According to this view, frequent buying and selling by the Fed hides the true intent of its monetary policy. This may indeed explain part of the large-scale use of temporary purchases and sales.

However, there are also good reasons for temporary changes in reserves. Part of the job of ensuring an elastic currency is to provide for the increased demand for currency during the Christmas season by increasing bank reserves and then reducing those reserves when the demand for currency returns to more normal levels after the holidays. One way to do this is through Fed repurchase agreements. The Fed buys securities in late November, and dealers agree to repurchase them a few weeks later, when the Christmas shopping rush is over, to increase banking system reserves for a short period of

Continued on p. 433

Month	Outright Transactions		Matched Transactions		Repurchase Agreements	
	Purchases	Sales	Purchases	Sales	Purchases	Sales
May	$4,310	0	$118,972	$117,524	$38,777	$38,533
June	3,836	0	126,977	129,216	10,792	11,036
July	0	0	127,051	126,137	12,224	12,224
August	866	0	104,873	102,575	39,484	31,868
September	5,927	0	116,331	115,579	68,697	59,628
October	4,272	0	116,024	114,917	18,698	35,383
November	7,820	0	115,020	117,020	42,373	39,117

Figures in millions of dollars.

Sources: Federal Reserve *Bulletin,* Board of Governors of the Federal Reserve System (March 1993), A10; *National Economic Trends* (April 1993), 21.

Continued from p. 432
time. However, critics point out that the Fed engaged in matched purchases on the order of $115 billion in November 1992 compared with total Fed holdings of government securities, which were $291 billion. More generally, the Fed buys and sells an amount of securities equal to roughly half of its portfolio in any given month! Critics like Friedman claim this volume of trading is not necessary to deal with seasonal changes in the demand for currency.

deposits against which it holds required reserves; it generally makes loans with the remainder. Thus, a bank might be in the position shown in part a of Table 13.1. The required reserve ratio is 10 percent. The bank has deposits of $1,000. It holds reserves equal to 10 percent of these deposits and has loaned $900. What if the required reserve ratio is reduced to 5 percent, as in part b of Table 13.1? Now the bank still has reserves of $100, but required reserves are only $50. There is $50 in extra reserves, called **excess reserves.** These reserves are now available for lending, and the bank will increase loans by $50. Furthermore, this happens at every bank. Not only do loans increase at every bank, but the interactions of these banks will produce a change in loans and deposits that is a multiple of this initial effect, as we will see in Chapter 14. The reduction in reserve requirements causes an expansion in the money supply and has an expansionary influence on the economy.

What about an increase in reserve requirements? A rise in reserve requirements will have a similar but opposite effect on each bank and on the banking system. Consider the situation in part a of Table 13.2. The bank initially faces a 10 percent reserve requirement. It has deposits of $1,000, reserves equal to the required $100, and loans of $900. An increase in reserve requirements to 20 percent creates the situation in part b of Table 13.2. The bank's required reserve amount increases to $200. Now excess reserves are −$100. In this situation, the bank's only recourse is to reduce loans by $100 or sell $100 in securities to obtain the required reserves. This causes a problem, of course, because calling in loans is always painful, and more so because this will happen at all banks. (A general sale of securities would also be painful, since it would cause the prices of those securities to decline.) In the end, not only will the initial reduction in loans occur, but the effect on loans and deposits will be magnified by the interactions of banks in the banking system. Thus, an increase in reserve requirements has a contractionary effect on the money supply and on the economy.

Discount Window Policy

We have seen that in the history of the Fed, discounting was once the primary means of conducting monetary policy. This has long since changed, as have

Table 13.1
Impact of a Decrease in Required Reserves on a Bank's Balance Sheet

A decrease in the required reserve ratio from 10 to 5 percent leads to excess reserves of $50 for this bank. This typically leads to an increase in loans.

(a) Required Reserve Ratio = 10%

Assets		Liabilities	
Reserves:	$100	Deposits:	$1,000
Loans:	$900		

(b) Required Reserve Ratio = 5%

Assets		Liabilities	
Reserves:	$100	Deposits:	$1,000
Required: $50			
Excess: $50			
Loans:	$900		

the procedures at the discount window. Originally the purpose of the **discount window** was to make loans against specific assets offered by banks, first commercial paper and later other assets. Today the discount window operates in somewhat the same way under procedures set by the Fed. Banks and other depository institutions can "go to the window" to borrow from the Fed. What the banks actually borrow are reserves. These reserves, called **borrowed reserves,** function in the same way as any other reserves of a bank. They can be used to meet reserve requirements, and excess reserves can be used to make loans. The only difference is that borrowed reserves must be repaid to the Fed, usually within a few weeks or months.

The interest rate the Fed charges is called the **discount rate.** It is not a market rate but a rate set by the Fed. Changes in the discount rate are widely publicized. Increases tend to discourage borrowing, reducing borrowed reserves. This reduction in borrowed reserves has the same effect on the banking system as any other reduction in reserves, such as that caused by an open market sale. Deposits and loans contract, and the money supply

Table 13.2

Impact of an Increase in Required Reserves on a Bank's Balance Sheet

An increase in the required reserve ratio from 10 to 20 percent leads to a decrease in excess reserves of − $100; that is, it increases the amount of required reserves. This typically leads to a decrease in loans.

(a) Required Reserve Ratio = 10%

Assets		Liabilities	
Reserves:	$100	Deposits:	$1,000
Loans:	$900		

(b) Required Reserve Ratio = 20%

Assets			Liabilities	
Reserves:		$100	Deposits:	$1,000
Required:	$200			
Excess:	− $100			
Loans:		$900		

falls. Thus, increases in the discount rate are considered a sign of contractionary monetary policy. Reductions in the discount rate tend to encourage borrowing, thus increasing borrowed reserves. This rise in reserves increases deposits and loans of the banking system and is considered a sign of an expansionary monetary policy.[4]

An important point to remember in evaluating discount window policy is that the Fed sets not only the discount rate but also the amount a bank can borrow. It is not the case that a bank can borrow all the reserves it wants at the discount rate. The actual effect of changes in the discount rate depends on the resulting change in reserves, so a reduction in the discount rate that

---

[4] The above analysis has an important qualification. The discount rate is set by the Fed and might be above or below other market-determined rates. If the discount rate is below other market rates, an increase in the discount rate may be seen as a "technical adjustment" to keep the discount rate in line with market rates and not as a sign of contractionary policy. Similarly, if the discount rate is above other market rates, a reduction in the discount rate may also be seen as a "technical adjustment" and not as a sign of expansionary policy.

does not lead to an increase in reserves will not be expansionary. There must be a reduction in the discount rate, accompanied by increased Fed lending at the window.

The discount window has traditionally been intended for short-term borrowing of reserves—what the Fed calls *adjustment credit* and *seasonal credit*. **Adjustment credit** is loans made to depository institutions to allow them to more gradually adjust their reserves and loan portfolios in response to changes in deposits. **Seasonal credit** is loans made to depository institutions facing strong seasonal variations in deposits and loans, such as banks in agricultural areas. A third category of borrowing is called **extended credit** and represents long-term lending to troubled depository institutions. In recent years, the dollar amount of extended credit has at times rivaled adjustment and seasonal credit as the Fed made long-term loans to troubled savings and loans and other depository institutions. In 1988 extended credit exploded to more than $3 billion, as Figure 13.6 shows, and, after returning to near $500 million in the second half of 1989, again peaked to more than $2 billion in 1990. By 1992 extended credit had returned to about $150 million, the same amount as the sum of seasonal plus adjustment credit.

Other Monetary Policy Tools

In addition to setting the discount rate, establishing reserve requirements, and directing open market operations, the Fed has other monetary policy tools. These include selective credit controls and moral suasion.

Selective Credit Controls.   The Fed is authorized to enact selective credit controls. It can, for example, set the **margin requirement** on stock purchases. Stocks are purchased *on margin* when the purchaser borrows a portion of the funds needed to buy the stock. A margin requirement of 40 percent would require that a buyer provide funds equal to 40 percent of the price of the stock. The Fed can raise margin requirements if it so chooses to prevent buyers from borrowing the entire amount of the purchase price. If margin purchases were widespread, a large reduction in the stock price could cause problems in the repayment of such loans and thus cause problems for the entire financial industry.

The Fed is also authorized to set selective credit controls on other loans. An example occurred in 1980, when President Carter asked the Fed to restrict unsecured consumer credit. This took the form of a 15 percent reserve requirement on credit card loans and other unsecured consumer loans and is widely blamed for reducing consumer spending and contributing to the recession of 1981–1982.

Moral Suasion.   As monetary policymaker and regulator of the banking industry, the Fed has considerable clout in persuading depository and other

This graph shows the large increase in extended credit that occurred during the late 1980s and early 1990s as the Fed increased its loans to troubled depository institutions.

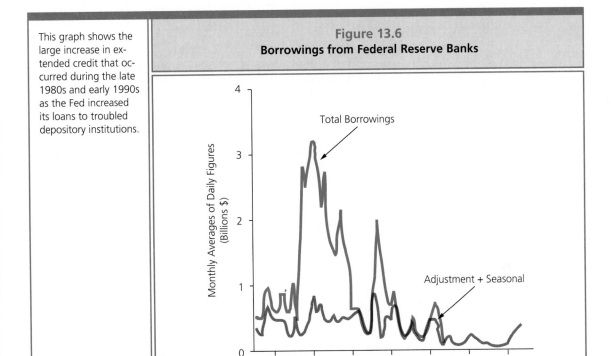

Figure 13.6
Borrowings from Federal Reserve Banks

SOURCE: Federal Reserve Bank of St. Louis *Monetary Trends* (October 1993), 12.

financial institutions to behave in what it regards as the public's best interest. **Moral suasion** is the term used for this persuasion, and the term itself indicates the response by banks is voluntary. The Fed can use moral suasion in attempts to lower interest rates or to get banks to impose looser or tighter standards on loan applicants. It is often difficult, however, to distinguish moral suasion from more direct pressure that the Fed can bring to bear on depository institutions. For example, depository institutions are well aware the Fed can use its discount window policies and even its auditing powers to punish noncooperative behavior.

Summary Exercise 13.3

Figure 13.4 showed the effects of an open market purchase on a bank's balance sheet. Now consider a bank that goes to the discount window to borrow $100 from the Fed, thus incurring a liability of $100—its IOU to the Fed. The bank also gets an increase in its reserve account, an asset, of $100. Show the balance sheet of this bank, and compare it to the balance sheet after the open market operation shown in Figure 13.4. Is there any difference?

Why might the Fed choose to use discount window lending instead of open market operations?

Answer: After the discount window borrowing, the bank has additional reserves of $100 and an additional liability, the $100 owed to the Fed. Thus, the change in its balance sheet looks like this:

Discount Window Borrowing		
Assets		**Liabilities**
Reserves:	+ $100	Loan from Fed: + $100

Recall that after the open market operation, the change in the balance sheet of the bank looked like this:

Open Market Purchase		
Assets		**Liabilities**
Reserves:	+ $100	Deposits: + $100

The only difference is in the type of liability incurred. Discount window borrowing leaves the bank with a loan it owes to the Fed of $100, whereas the open market operation leaves the bank with a deposit account of $100. The loan to the Fed is usually short term, meaning the bank knows the loan will have to be repaid, reversing the process and draining away the $100 in reserves. Thus, the bank will not make long-term loan commitments with the additional excess reserves. The open market operation, in contrast, has no such self-liquidating feature, giving the bank more flexibility in lending out its excess reserves. Of course, discount window borrowing can mimic open market operations if the borrowing is extended credit. In that case, the loan is much longer term, and the bank can be more flexible in using the reserves it obtains.

Why doesn't the Fed use open market operations instead of the discount window? If the Fed wants the change in reserves caused by an open market operation to be short term, it can always conduct an open market sale in the future.[5] However, open market operations are nonselective, affecting banks and the banking system but not targeted at any particular bank. The discount window is a way for the Fed to increase or even decrease reserves at a particular bank and as such is an instrument it can use to aid troubled banks or just banks that want to stretch out the process of adjusting to changes in reserves.

THE DEBATE OVER FEDERAL RESERVE INDEPENDENCE

Our description of the structure and history of the Fed demonstrates how the Fed is able to act at least somewhat independently of both the legislative and executive branches of government. However, it does not tell us whether or not that independence is a good thing. Is the Fed too independent, or is it not independent enough?

Two issues arise in any discussion of Fed independence. The first is whether or not the Fed should be allowed to pursue an independent monetary policy. By this we mean a policy independent of the dictates of fiscal policy. Fiscal policy is determined by the combined actions of the legislative and executive branches of government. The issue—whether the Fed should be able to pursue a monetary policy that directly contradicts or counteracts the government's fiscal policy—is discussed in detail in Chapter 19.

The second issue is whether monetary policy should be set in a discretionary way, meaning in each period the Fed decides what it currently determines as best for the economy, or be more automatic, following some set rule that limits discretion. More simply, should the Fed be able to set monetary policy independently of the stance of fiscal policy? Those answering yes usually base their arguments on the idea that Fed independence insulates the Fed from political pressure to inflate. The reasoning is as follows. Politicians are often shortsighted, worrying only about the next election. If they were allowed to determine monetary policy, their shortsightedness would prevent the pursuit of long-run price stability. Instead politicians would pursue a policy of inflation to gain a short-run benefit to the economy and enhance their reelection chances. According to this view, an independent Fed is a stalwart opponent of inflation and will maintain price stability if politicians are kept from having direct control of the Fed.

There is some evidence that the political manipulation of the Fed by elected officials has resulted in inflationary monetary policy by the Fed. In particular, some argue that during presidential election campaigns, the executive branch has successfully influenced the Fed to pursue an inflationary policy, temporarily stimulating the economy before the election to help the

---

[5] It could also use a repurchase agreement. In a repurchase agreement, the Fed buys securities but agrees to sell them back at a set price at a specified point in time. This creates a temporary increase in reserves that ends when the repurchase occurs.

incumbent's chances but resulting in longer-term inflation. Box 13.4 provides some international comparisons of inflation and the level of central bank independence.

The second argument in favor of Fed independence is that independence allows the Fed to resist pressure from the government to monetize the government debt. The Fed can *monetize* the debt by printing money and using it to buy outstanding government bonds. This action would reduce the size of the debt held by the public, but it would also be inflationary. According to proponents of independence, an independent Fed is again a bulwark against the inflationary impulses of the government.

Finally, some argue that an independent Fed is actually a useful public scapegoat for the executive and legislative branches of government; that is, the Fed is useful because it can be publicly blamed for a host of evils that might actually have their origin in the actions of others in the government. If the Fed were more clearly a branch of the executive, the president would have greater difficulty blaming the Fed for various ills.

These arguments view the Fed as the "good guy" in the battle against inflation and elected politicians (the government) as all too ready to inflate the money supply for their own short-run purposes if only the independence of the Fed didn't get in their way.

Of course, there are arguments on the other side. The need for policy coordination between fiscal and monetary policymakers is one argument for linking the Fed more closely to policymakers in the executive and legislative branches. An independent Fed certainly might choose to cooperate with the fiscal authority, but it might also choose the converse. By making the Fed a branch of the Treasury, for instance, there would be less potential for conflicting policy actions, whether inadvertent or otherwise.

Summary
Exercise 13.4

What is there in the structure of the Fed to explain why the Fed would be more opposed to inflation than a member of Congress would?

Answer: The main feature is the fact that the members of the FOMC, from the Board of Governors to the Federal Reserve bank presidents, do not have to run for reelection. Thus, they can take a longer-term view of policy actions. They will be less enamored with the short-run benefits of an expansionary monetary policy and more concerned with the long-run costs in terms of inflation.

CONCLUSION

In this chapter, we took a detailed look at the structure of the modern Fed, along with its historical roots. The creation of the Fed in 1914 was brought on by the failure of the free banking and national banking systems in the

International Banking   Box 13.4

The Benefits of Central Bank Independence: A Look at Inflation Around the World

An independent central bank has little reason to use monetary policy to stimulate the economy during elections. For this reason, proponents of central bank independence argue that this results in a more stable money supply and less inflation. Is this actually the case?

It is hard to tell by looking just at the United States, since it has never had a central bank that did not have a large degree of independence. One way to get information on this question is to look at the experience of other countries, especially other industrialized countries. Recently this was done by Alberto Alesina, who charted the average inflation rate for the 1973–1986

period for 17 nations and compared it to the degree of independence. The degree of independence was determined by taking account of the formal institutional relationship between the central bank and the national government, such as the presence of government officials on the central bank's governing board, whether the head of the central bank was appointed by the government, and the existence of rules requiring the central bank to help finance the deficit (i.e., requiring monetization of part of the deficit).

Alesina constructed four categories of independence and judged the most independent

Continued on p. 442

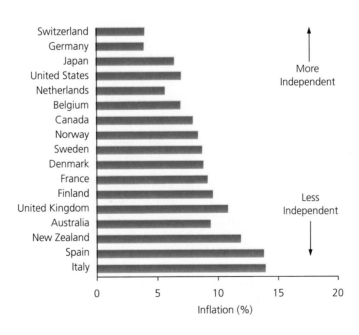

Continued from p. 441

central banks to be those of West Germany and Switzerland. Their average inflation rate over this period was 4 percent. The United States and Japan were determined to be in the category of the second most independent central banks, with average inflation rates of about 7 percent. Countries with the least independent central banks—Italy, New Zealand, Australia, and Spain—had average inflation rates of 12.5 percent. As the accompanying figure shows, the more independent central banks do seem to be a buttress against inflation. A danger of reducing the Fed's independence, as current proposals to make all members of FOMC appointed would do, is that doing so could lead to high inflation rates like those in Spain and Italy, which have less independent central banks.

Source: Alesina, Alberto, "Politics and Business Cycles in Industrial Democracies," *Economic Policy,* 8 (April 1989), p. 81 and W. Michael Cox, "Two Types of Paper: The Case for Federal Reserve Independence," *The Southwest Economy,* Federal Reserve Bank of Dallas, Nov–Dec 1992.

late 1800s to provide an elastic and stable currency. The Fed's role has changed over the past 50 years, largely in response to problems that arose during financial crises like the Great Depression. Today the Fed is charged with regulating the banking industry and controlling the nation's money supply. In the next chapter, we will see how Fed policies like reserve requirements and open market transactions affect the money supply.

KEY TERMS

central bank
wildcat bank
greenbacks
discounting
national banking system
Federal Reserve System
elastic currency
real bills doctrine
Board of Governors
Federal Open Market Committee (FOMC)
open market purchase

open market sale
excess reserves
discount window
borrowed reserves
discount rate
adjustment credit
seasonal credit
extended credit
margin requirement
moral suasion

QUESTIONS AND PROBLEMS

1. Describe the Board of Governors of the Federal Reserve System. With no resignations, how many members of the Board of Governors could a two-term president appoint?

2. Describe a Federal Reserve System regional bank. How is it like a private corporation? How is it like a government agency?

3. Describe the Federal Open Market Committee. How many voting members are on this committee? How often does a member of the Board of Governors get to vote on the FOMC? How often do the presidents of the Federal Reserve banks get to vote on the FOMC?

4. What features of its design tend to make the Federal Reserve System independent of the elected branches of government? What features detract from its independence?

5. Obtain a copy of the current *Economic Report of the President* and find out the current U.S. government deficit and tax receipts. Then obtain the *Bulletin* of the Federal Reserve System and find out the remittances from the Federal Reserve System to the U.S. Treasury. What fraction of U.S. government revenue is made up of remittances from the Federal Reserve System? What fraction of the U.S. government deficit? What fraction of the U.S. government debt does the Fed hold?

6. Considering question 5, what do you think of a proposal to raise more government revenue by instructing the Federal Reserve System to remit more money to the U.S. Treasury? Since the Federal Reserve System earns most of its profit on holdings of U.S. government bonds, it would have to purchase more such bonds. Would purchasing more bonds be possible? Would it be desirable? On what do you base your answer? Consider carefully what it takes to purchase more bonds and the likely effect on the economy.

7. First, state the case favoring a less independent Fed. Second, state the case favoring Fed independence. Which do you agree with, and why?

8. What were some benefits of the First and Second Banks of the United States?

9. Describe the chief features of the free banking system. Compare them with those of the national banking system.

10. What were the goals of advocates of the free banking system? Did the free banking system achieve those goals? Explain.

11. What were the goals behind setting up the national banking system? Did the national banking system achieve those goals? Explain.

12. The free banking system is used as an example of why banking needs to be regulated. What were the problems with the free banking system? What is the evidence that insufficient regulation caused those problems? Can one argue that the problem was inappropriate regulation rather than too little or too much regulation?

13. What were the goals of those who originally set up the Federal Reserve System in 1914? Were those goals achieved? Expain.

14. During the era of the national banking system, there continued to be occasional periods of bank runs in which deposits could not be redeemed for currency. Did the Federal Reserve Act of 1913 eliminate this problem?

15. What were the main reforms contained in the Banking Act of 1935?

16. What were the main changes made to the Fed by the DIDMCA of 1980?

17. Do banks like high reserve requirements? Why or why not? What about the U.S.

Continued on p. 444

Continued from p. 443

government? Ignoring the effects on the financial health of banks, does a revenue-maximizing government prefer a banking system with high or low reserves? In answering this question, consider how these reserves come into existence.

18. Is an open market operation that injects $1 million in reserves into the banking system more or less expansionary than a discount window operation that injects $1 million in borrowed reserves?

19. Assume you are a banker in the time of free banking. You start with $50,000 in gold, which you use to purchase government bonds for deposit in the state treasury. This transaction authorizes you to issue bank notes, and you use $10,000 of these notes to buy gold reserves and lend out the remaining $40,000. What does your balance sheet look like? How safe is your bank? Consider the following.
(a). If the value of bonds at the state treasury falls to zero but your loans remain sound, will your bank have to close? Will noteholders be at risk of suffering a loss?
(b). If the value of bonds at the state treasury stays at $50,000 but the value of the loans you have made falls to zero, will your bank have to close? Will noteholders be at risk of suffering a loss?
(c). If both the value of bonds at the state treasury and the value of your loans fall to zero, will your bank have to close? Will noteholders be at risk of suffering a loss?
(d). In many states, owners of free banks were liable not only for their initial investments but also for an additional sum equal to those investments. That is, the bank owner in our example would be liable for another $50,000 in personal funds to cover bank notes in the event of bank fail-

ure. Would this liability be sufficient to prevent noteholders from suffering losses in the above cases?

20. Assume you are a banker in the time of free banking. You start with $50,000 in gold, which you use to purchase government bonds for deposit in the state treasury. This transaction authorizes you to issue bank notes. You use these bank notes to purchase another $50,000 in government bonds, which you also deposit at the state treasury. This second deposit gives you the right to issue another $50,000 in bank notes. With this second $50,000, you use $10,000 to buy gold reserves and lend out the remaining $40,000. What does your balance sheet look like? How safe is your bank? Consider the following.
(a). If the value of bonds at the state treasury falls to zero but your loans remain sound, will your bank have to close? Will noteholders be at risk of suffering a loss?
(b). If the value of bonds at the state treasury stays at $100,000 but the value of the loans you have made falls to zero, will your bank have to close? Will noteholders be at risk of suffering a loss?
(c). If both the vaue of bonds at the state treasury and the value of your loans fall to zero, will your bank have to close? Will noteholders be at risk of suffering a loss?
(d). In many states, owners of free banks were liable not only for their initial investments but also for an additional sum equal to their initial investments. That is, the bank owner in our example would be liable for another $50,000 in personal funds to cover bank notes in the event of bank failure. Would this liability be sufficient to prevent noteholders from suffering losses in the above cases?

SELECTIONS FOR FURTHER READING

Bradley, M. D. and D. W. Jansen, "Federal Reserve Operating Procedures in the Eighties: A Dynamic Analysis." *Journal of Money, Credit, and Banking,* 18 (August 1986), 323–335.

Cosimano, T. F., and D. W. Jansen. "Federal Reserve Policy, 1975–1985: An Empirical Analysis." *Journal of Macroeconomics,* 10 (Winter 1988), 27–47.

Fenstermaker, J. V., and J. E. Filer. "Impact of the First and Second Banks of the United States and the Suffolk System on New England Bank Money: 1791–1837." *Journal of Money, Credit, and Banking,* 18 (February 1986), 28–40.

Jansen, D. W., "Ranking Federal Reserve Research Departments by Publications in Professional Journals." *Journal of Macroeconomics,* 13 (Fall 1991), 733–742.

Lawson, C. L., and L. L. Lawson. "Financial System Restructuring: Lessons from Veblen, Keynes, and Kalecki." *Journal of Economic Issues,* 24 (March 1990), 115–131.

Luckett, D. G. "A Pedagogical Note on the Use of Margin Credit." *Journal of Economic Education,* 19 (Fall 1988), 337–340.

Miron, J. A. "The Founding of the Fed and the Destabilization of the Post–1914 U.S. Economy." In *A European Central Bank? Perspectives on Monetary Unification after Ten Years of the EMS.* Cambridge; New York, and Melbourne: Cambridge University Press, 1989, 290–328.

Rockoff, H. "New Evidence on Free Banking in the United States." *American Economic Review,* 75 (September 1985), 886–889.

Rockoff, H. "Institutional Requirements for Stable Free Banking." *Cato Journal,* 6 (Fall 1986), 617–634.

Selgin, G. A. "Why Does Europe Want a Federal Reserve System?" *Cato Journal,* 10 (Fall 1990), 449–453.

Selgin, G. A., and L. H. White. "The Evaluation of a Free Banking System." *Economic Inquiry,* 25 (July 1987), 439–457.

Wells, D. R., and L. S. Scruggs. "Free Banking: The Ultimate Deregulation of the Financial System." *Atlantic Economic Journal,* 12 (September 1984), 80.

Wicker, E. "Colonial Monetary Standards Contrasted: Evidence from the Seven Years' War." *Journal of Economic History,* 45 (December 1985), 869–884.

Wicker, E. "Interest Rate and Expenditure Effects of the Banking Panic of 1930." *Explorations in Economic History,* 19 (October 1982), 435–445.

Yohe, W. P. "The Intellectual Milieu at the Federal Reserve Board in the 1920s." *History of Political Economy,* 22 (Fall 1990), 465–488.

14

The Money Supply Process

$\mathcal{F}$rom the beginning of this book, we have directly or indirectly discussed topics related to money and the money supply process. In Chapter 1 we defined money as *the* medium of exchange, something that is widely accepted in exchange for other goods. In Chapter 2 we looked at the practical definitions of money adopted by the Federal Reserve System, such as M1, M2, or M3. In the last chapter we discussed the Fed's policy instruments for controlling the money supply.

The nation's money supply has a vital impact on the performance of the overall economy. We have already seen that the rate of growth in the money supply affects the economy's rate of inflation. In the next few chapters, we will see that money can also affect interest rates, investment, real GDP, and employment.

Before we explore these important aspects of money, however, we need to look more closely at how money is created. We will see in this chapter that money creation is *not* simply the government's printing of the dollar bills you use to buy hamburgers and CDs. In fact, we will see that the entire banking system creates money with the aid of the Fed, which acts as the nation's central bank.

Our look at the Fed in the previous chapter gave you a broad overview of its central banking activities and pointed out that its primary function is to manage the nation's money supply. In this chapter we examine the *quantitative* impact on the money supply of Fed actions such as open market operations. Of course, if the Fed takes actions that change the nation's money supply too much or too little, it can have adverse effects on the economy, causing a rapid rise in the price level or even a recession. The techniques developed in this chapter, however, show that the Fed can reasonably ascertain how much its policies will change the money supply.

We begin our study by extending what we learned about money creation in Chapter 1 to our modern economy, in which the Fed actively manages the money creation process by supplying reserves to the banking system. Then we develop a graphical framework for analyzing monetary policy that will be very useful in the remainder of the book for analyzing the effects of the Fed's monetary policy on economic activity.

THE BALANCE SHEET OF BANKS AND MULTIPLE DEPOSIT CREATION

In Chapter 6, we saw that *individual* banks use deposits as an input to produce loans. In this chapter, we look at the maximum amount of loans the *entire banking system* can create given policies enacted by the Fed. Because new bank loans can affect the total amount of money in the hands of the public (in the form of either currency or deposits at other banks), the banking system's production of loans affects the amount of money in the economy. We will see in this section, however, that new loans issued by a bank create money only if the reserves used to create the loans come from outside the banking system.

Our basic tool of analysis in this chapter is the T-account, such as that shown in Table 14.1. Notice that total assets (the left-hand side of the T-account) equal the bank's liabilities plus net worth, since net worth is defined as the difference between assets and liabilities. Table 14.1 shows that our hypothetical bank, Bank One, has assets of $510 million consisting of $100 million in reserves, $400 million in loans, and a building worth $10 million. At the same time, the bank has liabilities of $500 million to depositors with accounts at the bank and $10 million of net worth.

Reserves consist of legally mandated reserves, called **required reserves,** and any additional reserves, called **excess reserves.** Required reserves can be held in two ways: as vault cash or as a deposit at the district Federal Reserve bank. (In fact, at least a portion of required reserves must be held

With deposits of $500 million and a required reserve ratio of 20 percent, the bank must hold $100 million of its assets as reserves. This bank is not holding any excess reserves.

Table 14.1

Balance Sheet of a Bank with a Required Reserve Ratio of 20 Percent

Balance Sheet of Bank One

Assets		Liabilities	
Reserves	$100,000,000	Deposits	$500,000,000
Required	$100,000,000		
Excess	0		
Loans	400,000,000	Net Worth	10,000,000
Building	10,000,000		
Total	$510,000,000	Total	$510,000,000

on deposit at the Fed.) Both vault cash and reserve deposits at the Federal Reserve banks are called *legal reserves*. A bank may also hold reserves not recognized by the Federal Reserve System as legal reserves such as deposits in other banks. Table 14.1 assumes the **required reserve ratio** is 20 percent. With deposits of $500 million and a required reserve ratio of 20 percent, required reserves are $100 million, so the bank has $100 million of required reserves and zero excess reserves. We would say the bank is fully "loaned up," because it has no excess reserves available to increase loans. Its reserves just equal the 20 percent of deposits specified by the reserve requirement.[1]

For simplicity, the T-account in Table 14.1 combines many of the assets and liabilities that comprise the balance sheets of real-world banks. As Box 14.1 shows, banks in the banking system own a variety of types of loans and hold deposits in forms that include savings deposits, small-denomination time deposits and CDs, large-denomination CDs, and borrowings from other banks or from the Fed. In Table 14.1, however, *loans* are the category of assets we use to include all financial instruments owned by the bank. As such, it includes consumer loans, mortgages, and government debt obligations (U.S. government securities). The category labeled *deposits* includes demand deposits and other forms of deposits.

Our simplified T-accounts will allow us to see how the entire banking system responds to a change in its reserves. In conducting this analysis, we will make the following assumptions (we will relax them in the next section):

1. All deposits are checkable deposits.
2. The reserve requirement is 20 percent of deposits.
3. Deposits are the only form of money (the public does not hold currency).
4. Loans are made only to private individuals and companies.
5. Banks do not want to hold any excess reserves.

How a Bank Responds to a Change in Reserves from Within the Banking System

Suppose your dear Aunt Bertha gives you a gift—a check for $1 million that is drawn from her account at Bank Two. You deposit the check in your account at Bank One. Your new deposit affects Bank One's balance sheet as shown in Table 14.2. Part a indicates how the balance sheet looks compared to the initial balance sheet shown in Table 14.1. Part b shows the *changes* in the balance sheet between Tables 14.1 and 14.2 to point out

---

[1] In Chapter 6, we learned that with given bank facilities and a fixed number of loan officers, a bank may be unable to immediately transform the reserves created from deposits into loans. In the short run, loan applications may stack up on the desks of loan officers. In the long run, however, banks can generally adjust to new deposits by increasing the use of other inputs such as labor and physical capital, allowing them to lend out funds to their legal maximum. Henceforth we concern ourselves with this long-run scenario where banks keep only those reserves prescribed by law.

The Data Bank

Box 14.1

The Balance Sheet of the Commercial Banking Sector

The accompanying table shows the balance sheet of the U.S. commercial banking sector in October 1992. Liabilities of the commercial banking sector included demand deposits ($718 billion), savings deposits ($739 billion), time deposits ($1,022 billion) and other liabilities, and net worth ($1,095 billion) for a total of $3,574 billion. Assets included reserves of $56 billion, which amounted to 7.8 percent of demand deposits. Liquid assets were $148 billion, investment securities were $822 billion, loans were $2,261 billion, and other assets accounted for the remaining $287 billion.

Balance Sheet of All Commercial Banks, October 1992

Assets (billions of dollars)			Liabilities (billions of dollars)	
Reserve Assets			Demand Deposits	718.2
Reserves with Federal				
Reserve Banks	24.5		Savings Deposits	738.9
Vault Cash	31.7		Small Time Deposits	645.0
Total Reserves		56.2	Large Time Deposits	376.7
Liquid Assets		147.5	Other Liabilities	1,095.2
Investment Securities		822.3		
Loans		2,260.8		
Other Assets		287.2		
Total		3,574.0	Total	3,574.0

Source: Federal Reserve Bulletin, January 1993, p. A19.

exactly which categories have changed. The $1 million check has increased the liabilities of Bank One, since it now owes depositors $501 million for their deposits. At the same time, the $1 million check will be cleared through the Federal Reserve System, resulting in an increase in Bank One's reserves of $1 million. (The $1 million will be subtracted from the issuing bank's [Bank Two's] reserve account at a Federal Reserve Bank, so *total banking system reserves are unchanged.* We will examine the impact of this reduction in reserves on Bank Two in a moment; for now we focus on how Bank One responds to the additional $1 million of reserves.)

Part a shows the balance sheet of Bank One after it receives $1 million in new deposits. Part b shows the *changes* in the bank's deposits, reserves, and loans after the bank receives the $1 million deposit. Note that the bank has yet to lend out any of the $1 million deposit, so it has excess reserves of $800,000.

Table 14.2
Effect of a $1 Million Deposit on a Bank

(a)   **Balance Sheet of Bank One**
Immediately after Receiving a $1 Million Deposit

Assets			Liabilities	
Reserves		$101,000,000	Deposits	$501,000,000
Required	$100,200,000			
Excess	800,000			
Loans		400,000,000	Net Worth	10,000,000
Building		10,000,000		
Total		$511,000,000	Total	$511,000,000

(b)   **Changes in Balance Sheet of Bank One**
Immediately after Receiving a $1 Million Deposit

Assets			Liabilities	
Reserves		+$1,000,000	Deposits	+$1,000,000
Required	+$200,000			
Excess	+ 800,000			
Loans		0	Net Worth	0
Building		0		
Total		+$1,000,000	Total	+$1,000,000

The additional reserves Bank One receives are not all required reserves. Since deposits increased by $1 million required reserves increased by 20 percent of $1 million, or $200,000. Since total reserves increased by $1 million the difference—$800,000—represents excess reserves, reserves held in excess of the legally prescribed minimum.

Of course, Bank One will not be satisfied with $800,000 in excess reserves. It earns no interest on cash sitting in the vault or on reserve deposits at the Fed. Thus, Bank One will eventually lend out the $800,000 of excess reserves, reducing reserves but increasing loans. This leads to the situation shown in Table 14.3. Again, part a indicates the balance sheet after the bank adjusts its loan and reserve holdings, while part b indicates the *change* in the balance sheet between the initial balance sheet shown in Table 14.1 and the balance sheet shown in part a of Table 14.3. Bank One now has reserves

This table shows Bank One's balance sheet after the bank has lent out the $800,000 of excess reserves. Part a shows the balance sheet adjusted for the deposit, the additional required reserves, and the additional loans of the bank. Part b shows the *changes* in the bank's balance sheet after lending out the $800,000.

Table 14.3
Effect of a $1 Million Deposit and the Resultant Expansion of Loans at a Bank

(a) Balance Sheet of Bank One after Receiving a $1 Million Deposit and Making Loans

Assets			Liabilities	
Reserves		$100,200,000	Deposits	$501,000,000
Required	$100,200,000			
Excess		0		
Loans		400,800,000	Net Worth	10,000,000
Building		10,000,000		
Total		$511,000,000	Total	$511,000,000

(b) Changes in Balance Sheet of Bank One after Receiving a $1 Million Deposit and Making Loans

Assets			Liabilities	
Reserves		+ $200,000	Deposits	+ $1,000,000
Required	+ $200,000			
Excess		+ 0		
Loans		+ 800,000	Net Worth	0
Building		0		
Total		+ $1,000,000	Total	+ $1,000,000

of $100,200,000, which just equals 20 percent of its deposits of $501 million. Excess reserves are zero, and loans are $400,800,000. Loans plus reserves equals deposits, and net worth still just equals the value of the physical bank building.

Notice that in going from Table 14.2 to Table 14.3, Bank One still holds $501 million of deposits. It has simply rearranged the way it holds its assets, transferring $800,000 from non-interest-bearing reserves to $800,000 of interest-bearing loans. At this point, Bank One is again completely ''loaned up,'' since it is holding the absolute minimum level of legal reserves. Any additional reduction of reserves to fund additional loans will bring the bank into violation of its legal reserve requirement. In this situation, it will be unable to make any additional loans without first attracting new deposits.

The preceding analysis pertains to a bank in the happy position of receiving a new deposit of $1 million. Remember, however, that the check was drawn on another bank, Bank Two. How does Bank Two respond when it faces the loss of $1 million of deposits?

Let us suppose that before the check was cashed, Bank Two's balance sheet was identical to the one in Table 14.1. When Aunt Bertha's check clears Bank Two, its deposits are reduced by this amount, as are its reserves. This loss of reserves occurs when the check clears against Bank One's reserve account at the Fed. When this happens, $1 million is transferred from Bank Two's reserve to Bank One's reserve account. For the bank losing reserves—Bank Two in this example—reserves decline by the same amount deposits decline, $1 million. Table 14.4 depicts this situation.

Part a shows the balance sheet of Bank Two after a withdrawal of $1 million in deposits. Part b shows the *changes* in the bank's deposits, reserves, and loans after it has lost the $1 million in deposits. Note that the bank has not yet adjusted its loans so that it will have enough reserves to meet its reserve requirement; that is, it has negative excess reserves, or excess reserves of −$800,000.

Table 14.4
Effect of a $1 Million Withdrawal on a Bank

(a) Balance Sheet of Bank Two
Immediately after Losing a $1 Million Deposit

Assets			Liabilities	
Reserves		$99,000,000	Deposits	$499,000,000
Required	$99,800,000			
Excess	− 800,000			
Loans		400,000,000	Net Worth	10,000,000
Building		10,000,000		
Total		$509,000,000	Total	$509,000,000

(b) Changes in Balance Sheet of Bank Two
Immediately after Losing a $1 Million Deposit

Assets			Liabilities	
Reserves		− $1,000,000	Deposits	− $1,000,000
Required	− $200,000			
Excess	− 800,000			
Loans		0	Net Worth	0
Building		0		
Total		− $1,000,000	Total	− $1,000,000

Deposits at Bank Two are now $499 million, and reserves are $99 million. This causes a problem for the bank, however, since at 20 percent of deposits required reserves are now $99,800,000 but actual reserves are only $99 million. Bank Two actually has *negative excess reserves,* meaning it is short of reserves. The only way to obtain additional reserves is to call in loans or borrow reserves from the Fed (at the discount rate) or from other banks (at the federal funds rate). We will concentrate here on the impact of calling in loans.

How does a bank call in loans? We tend to think of loans as long-term loans, such as 15- or 30-year mortgage loans or 4- or 5-year automobile loans. In fact, however, such loans make up only part of a bank's assets. Banks also make short-term loans to businesses, some of which are due "upon demand." Thus, a bank in a position of negative excess reserves can cover its reserve position by calling in the appropriate amount of loans, that is, by demanding payment of principal and interest. In addition, a large bank may have a whole series of short-term loans coming due each day and can simply decline to renew the appropriate amount of those loans to cover its shortage of reserves.

In Table 14.4, Bank Two needs $800,000 of additional reserves, which it obtains by calling in $800,000 in loans. After doing this, the bank finds itself in the position shown in Table 14.5. Reserves have increased to $99,800,000, just equal to 20 percent of deposits. Loans have fallen by $800,000 and now stand at $399,200,000.

Needless to say, this contraction of loans is painful for the bank. Calling in loans, or even failing to renew loans, is not a good way to make customers happy. The alternative is to borrow reserves, either from other banks in the federal funds market or from the Federal Reserve System, by going to the discount window.

We can summarize the effect of a change in deposits and reserves at a single bank very simply. An increase in deposits and reserves leads to excess reserves, which a bank will use to increase loans. A decrease in deposits and reserves leads to a shortfall of reserves, which a bank will meet by reducing loans or borrowing reserves.

What is the effect of these transactions on the money stock? Recall that the money stock is the sum of currency and checkable deposits, and we have been assuming people use only checks to make transactions. In this case, the total money stock is the amount of checkable deposits available. Since the $1 million check was written from a private account in one bank to a private account in another, one bank's loss is another's gain, and there is no net change in total banking system reserves, deposits, or loans. Thus, the total money stock remains constant when a check written at one bank is deposited in another bank. As we will see in the next section, the effect on the money stock differs when the initial deposit comes from outside the banking system rather than from another bank.

This table shows Bank Two's balance sheet after it has decreased its lending to gain reserves. Part a shows the balance sheet after the bank has recalled $800,000 in loans and used this amount to increase reserves. Part b shows the *changes* in the bank's balance sheet after decreasing its lending by $800,000.

Table 14.5

Effect of a $1 Million Withdrawal and the Resulting Contraction of Loans at a Bank

(a)   **Balance Sheet of Bank Two after Losing a $1 Million Deposit and Adjusting Loans**

Assets		Liabilities	
Reserves	$99,800,000	Deposits	$499,000,000
Required $99,800,000			
Excess 0			
Loans	399,200,000	Net Worth	10,000,000
Building	10,000,000		
Total	$509,000,000	Total	$509,000,000

(b)   **Changes in Balance Sheet of Bank Two Immediately after Losing a $1 Million Deposit and Adjusting Loans**

Assets		Liabilities	
Reserves	− $200,000	Deposits	− $1,000,000
Required − $200,000			
Excess 0			
Loans	− 800,000	Net Worth	0
Building	0		
Total	− $1,000,000	Total	− $1,000,000

Summary
Exercise 14.1

What is the effect on a bank's balance sheet of a withdrawal of $10,000? Assume the required reserve ratio is 5 percent, the bank held no excess reserves at the time of the withdrawal, and the bank is unable to borrow reserves.

Answer: The withdrawal of $10,000 reduces both bank reserves and bank deposits. Deposits fall by $10,000, which reduces required reserves by 5 percent of $10,000, or $500. Thus, the initial effect is to reduce reserves by $10,000, of which only $500 is a reduction in required reserves. The remaining $9,500 reduction is a reduction in excess reserves, indicating the bank has a shortfall of this amount of required reserves. The bank must call in loans of this amount to meet its reserve requirements. After calling in those loans, the bank's balance sheet will show that deposits declined by $10,000, reserves by $500, and loans by $9,500.

How the Banking System Responds to Infusions and Contractions of Reserves

As we just saw, a single bank that receives a new deposit will transfer the new reserves into loans to earn interest on its assets. We also saw that when the deposit comes from another bank, no change occurs in banking system deposits, reserves, or loans, since one bank's gain is another's loss. In this section, we will see that when a bank receives a new deposit from *outside the banking system*, such as from the Federal Reserve System, the additional deposit will increase the deposits, reserves, and loans of the *entire banking system*. We will also see that deposits and loans increase by a multiple of the initial infusion of reserves. Our focus on the entire banking system distinguishes this chapter, and indeed the rest of the book, from the micro analysis of individual banks in Chapters 5 and 6.

We emphasize that in contrast to the previous section, in which the initial change in deposits and reserves was merely a reshuffling of existing deposits and reserves among banks, this section examines the implications of an infusion (increase) or contraction (decrease) in *banking system* deposits and reserves. Such infusions or contractions are caused by the day-to-day operations of the Fed. For example, the Fed can alter total banking system reserves and deposits by (1) lending reserves to banks through the discount window or (2) engaging in an open market operation. (Recall that an open market operation is the purchase or sale of U.S. government securities by the Federal Reserve System in the open market.) Either of these actions will change a bank's reserves and deposits without creating a corresponding change in the opposite direction at another bank. As we will see next, such changes in reserves from outside the banking system will affect the total money stock; these transactions do not represent a reshuffling of reserves among banks.

Open Market Purchases: Multiple Deposit Expansion. In an open market purchase, the Federal Reserve System—more specifically, the Open Market Desk at the Federal Reserve Bank of New York—contracts to purchase a set amount of U.S. government securities. The Federal Reserve System pays for these securities with a check or an electronic transfer into the account of the securities dealer, and the dealer delivers the securities to the Fed. To be concrete, suppose the Fed purchases $1 million in bonds and pays by electronically transferring funds to the security dealer's bank account in a bank we will call Bank One. Then Bank One has an increase in both reserves and deposits of $1 million. The Fed has an increase in assets of $1 million and an increase in liabilities, since the bank's reserve account is a liability of the Fed.

The *change* in both the Fed's and Bank One's balance sheets is shown in Table 14.6. The Fed increases its holding of U.S. government securities, an asset, and its reserve deposits, a liability. Bank One increases both its deposits and its reserves. With a required reserve ratio of 20 percent, the increase in required reserves is $200,000, so the remainder of the increase in reserves, $800,000, is excess reserves.

Notice the similarity between the change in Bank One's balance sheet in Table 14.6 and that in part (b) of Table 14.2. In both cases, the bank received a deposit and new reserves of $1 million. The effect on the individual bank is the same. What is special about the situation in Table 14.6 is

---

Table 14.6
Effect of a $1 Million Open Market Purchase

Part a shows the *changes* in the Fed's balance sheet after purchasing $1 million worth of government securities. Its assets and liabilities rise by $1 million. The Fed pays the securities dealer, who deposits the payment in Bank One, where deposits increase by $1 million. Bank One itself sends the check to the Fed, where it is deposited in Bank One's reserve account, increasing its reserves by $1 million. Part b shows the changes in the balance sheet of Bank One after the Fed's $1 million open market purchase. Notice these changes occur before Bank One has lent out any of its $800,000 in excess reserves.

(a) Changes in Balance Sheet of the Fed Immediately after a $1 Million Open Market Purchase

Assets		Liabilities	
U.S. Government Bonds	+$1,000,000	Reserves	+$1,000,000

(b) Changes in Balance Sheet of Bank One Immediately after Gaining $1 Million Through a Fed Open Market Purchase

Assets			Liabilities	
Reserves		+$1,000,000	Deposits	+$1,000,000
Required	+$200,000			
Excess	+ 800,000			
Loans		0	Net Worth	0
Building		0		
Total		+$1,000,000	Total	+$1,000,000

that the increase in reserves at the bank shown there is not countered by a decrease in reserves at some other bank. Instead, the increase in reserves is due to a net infusion of new reserves into the banking system, an infusion caused by an action of the Federal Reserve System. This infusion of reserves creates a large adjustment throughout the banking system as banks scramble to adjust to the new level of reserves.

To see these adjustments, look again at part (b) of Table 14.6, and note that Bank One has $800,000 of excess reserves. The bank will lend out these reserves as it transforms non-interest-bearing reserves into interest-bearing loans. When it does so, it ends up in the position illustrated in part a of Table 14.7.

What happens to the $800,000 of excess reserves that Bank One just

Part a shows the *changes* in Bank One's balance sheet after the bank has lent out all of its $800,000 of excess reserves. This $800,000 ends up being deposited in Bank Two, where deposits and reserves increase by this amount. Bank Two now has $640,000 in excess reserves, as shown in part (b).

Table 14.7
**Effect of the Expansion of Loans at Bank One
and Initial Effect on Bank Two**

(a)   **Changes in Balance Sheet of Bank One
after a $1 Million Open Market Purchase and Adjusting Loans**

Assets		Liabilities	
Reserves	+ $200,000	Deposits	+ $1,000,000
Required + $200,000			
Excess + 0			
Loans	+ 800,000	Net Worth	0
Building	0		
Total	+ $1,000,000	Total	+ $1,000,000

(b)   **Changes in Balance Sheet of Bank Two
Immediately after Receiving an $800,000 Deposit**

Assets		Liabilities	
Reserves	+ $800,000	Deposits	+ $800,000
Required + $160,000			
Excess + 640,000			
Loans	0	Net Worth	0
Building	0		
Total	+ $800,000	Total	+ $800,000

lent out? Consider in particular the borrower, for example, a real estate developer who borrows the $800,000 to buy real estate in Florida. When she does so, she gains property worth (she hopes) $800,000 and the seller gains the $800,000. The seller himself will want to deposit the $800,000 in his bank, which we will call Bank Two. Thus, Bank One's loan ends up as a new deposit and new reserves in Bank Two. The *change* in Bank Two's balance sheet after this new deposit is shown in part b of Table 14.7. Note that the deposit increased both deposits and reserves at Bank Two by $800,000. Of course, with a required reserve ratio of 20 percent, the increase in required reserves is only $160,000, leaving the remaining $640,000 of new reserves as an increase in excess reserves.

Again, however, we note that excess reserves earn no interest and Bank Two will want to turn the $640,000 of excess reserves into loans. Once this is accomplished, the *change* in Bank Two's balance sheet is as illustrated in part a of Table 14.8. Notice that Bank Two behaved similarly to Bank One. Both received an influx of deposits and reserves, and since they are required to hold only 20 percent of deposits as reserves, both moved to lend out the influx of excess reserves. The only difference is that Bank One received a new deposit of $1 million, while Bank Two received a new deposit of $800,000, which was the amount lent out by Bank One.

Of course, the story doesn't end here. Bank Two has just lent $640,000 to someone. These funds will be spent—after all, few people would borrow such a sum without a specific purpose in mind—and, once spent, will be redeposited in someone else's bank account at, say, Bank Three. This will lead to excess reserves at Bank Three of $512,000, as shown in part b of Table 14.8. Bank Three will keep a fraction of the money as reserves and lend out the remainder, which will be deposited in yet another bank. This process will continue, and at each stage the bank receiving an increase in deposits and reserves will hold the required 20 percent of the additional deposits as required reserves and lend out the remaining 80 percent. Table 14.9 shows the final situation after all adjustments have been made in the entire banking system: Total reserves in the banking system increase by $1 million, total loans increase by $4 million, and total deposits increase by $5 million.

To summarize, the initial $1 million infusion of reserves into the banking system, caused by the Fed's open market purchase, leads to **multiple deposit expansion**—an increase in total banking system deposits that is a multiple of the initial $1 million. This expansion is due to the simple deposit multiplier process, also called the simple money multiplier process. Both terms are appropriate because in this simple case, all money is held in the form of deposits. (Since we assumed the public holds no currency, money and deposits are synonymous.) The terms indicate that this is the process by which *the commercial banking system creates money.* The raw material in the money creation process is reserves, and these are supplied by the Federal Reserve System. But the entire banking system transforms an injection of

Part a shows the *changes* in Bank Two's balance sheet after the bank has lent out all of the $640,000 of excess reserves. This $640,000 ends up being deposited in Bank Three, where deposits and reserves increase by this amount. Bank Three now has $512,000 in excess reserves.

Table 14.8
Effect of the Expansion of Loans at Bank Two and the Initial Effect on Bank Three

(a)   Changes in Balance Sheet of Bank Two after an $800,000 Deposit and Adjusting Loans

Assets			Liabilities	
Reserves		+$160,000	Deposits	+$800,000
Required	+$160,000			
Excess	+0			
Loans		+640,000	Net Worth	0
Building		0		
Total		+$800,000	Total	+$800,000

(b)   Changes in Balance Sheet of Bank Three Immediately after a $640,000 Deposit

Assets			Liabilities	
Reserves		+$640,000	Deposits	+$640,000
Required	+$128,000			
Excess	+512,000			
Loans		0	Net Worth	0
Building		0		
Total		+$640,000	Total	+$640,000

reserves into new loans that ultimately increase banking system deposits by a multiple of the increase in reserves, as summarized at the bottom of the last column in Table 14.9.

The Simple Deposit Multiplier.   How do we know the $1 million increase in reserves will lead to the final situation in Table 14.9, where total banking system deposits rise by $5 million? Very simply, the lending process will end only when all banks are fully loaned up so that excess reserves are zero. Since the banking system has received an inflow of $1 million of new reserves, all reserves will be required reserves when deposits grow by enough that $1 million is 20 percent of deposits. Using rr to signify the required reserve ratio, ΔD for the change in deposits, and ΔR for the initial change

This table summarizes how the balance sheets of banks are affected after each round of lending. It assumes banks hold no excess reserves, the required reserve ratio is 20 percent, the public does not hold currency, and the initial $1 million deposit at Bank One was due to an open market purchase.

Table 14.9

Summary of Deposit Expansion Process Across Banks

Bank	Change in Assets		Change in Liabilities
	Change in Reserves	**Change in Loans**	**Change in Deposits**
One	+ $200,000	+ $800,000	+ $1,000,000
Two	+ 160,000	+ 640,000	+ 800,000
Three	+ 128,000	+ 512,000	+ 640,000
Four	+ 102,400	+ 409,600	+ 512,000
.	.	.	.
.	.	.	.
.	.	.	.
Total for entire banking system	+ $1,000,000	+ $4,000,000	+ $5,000,000

in reserves, the banking system will no longer be able to make additional loans when

$$\Delta D \times rr = \Delta R.$$

Solving this equation for ΔD gives us

$$\Delta D = \frac{1}{rr} \times \Delta R. \tag{14.1}$$

In this case, $\Delta R = \$1,000,000$ and $rr = .20$, so

$$\Delta D = \frac{1}{.2} \times \$1,000,000$$
$$= 5 \times \$1,000,000 \tag{14.2}$$
$$= \$5,000,000.$$

That is, when deposits have increased to $5 million, the banking system will be in equilibrium, with no further lending activity possible.

Equation 14.1 incorporates the **simple deposit multiplier,** $1/rr$, which is the multiple by which deposits increase in response to any increase in reserves. The simple deposit multiplier is the inverse of the required reserve ratio, so increases in the required reserve ratio will lower the deposit multiplier, while decreases in the ratio will increase the deposit multiplier. In our example, the simple deposit multiplier is 5, meaning total banking system deposits increase by five times the initial change in reserves. A higher required reserve ratio—say, $rr = .5$—would lead to a lower simple deposit multiplier of 2 (= 1/.5). In other words, had the required reserve ratio been .5 instead of .2, total banking system deposits would have increased by only two times the initial change in reserves, or by $2 million. In case you're wondering, Box 14.2 shows the actual reserve requirements set by the Fed as of January 1993.

An alternative way to verify the final situation shown in Table 14.9 is to add up the changes in deposits at all banks. Notice in Table 14.9 that deposits at Bank One increase by $1 million, deposits at Bank Two increase by $800,000 (which is [1 − rr], or 80 percent of $1 million), deposits at Bank Three increase by $640,000 (80 percent of $800,000), and so on. In each round of lending, deposits at the next bank increase by 80 percent of the increase at the previous bank. If we write out the change in deposits at the first four banks and use ellipses to indicate the change in deposits at all remaining banks, we obtain

$$\Delta D = \$1,000,000 + \$800,000 + \$640,000 + \$512,000 + \cdots$$

$$= \$1,000,000 + (.8)\$1,000,000 + (.8)\$800,000 + (.8)\$640,000 + \cdots$$

$$= \$1,000,000 + (.8)\$1,000,000 + (.8)(.8)\$1,000,000$$

$$+ (.8)(.8)(.8)\$1,000,000 + \cdots$$

This may be further simplified as

$$\Delta D = (1 + .8 + .8^2 + .8^3 + \cdots) \times \$1,000,000$$

$$= \left[\frac{1}{1 - .8}\right] \times \$1,000,000$$

$$= 5 \times \$1,000,000$$

$$= \$5,000,000.^2$$

This approach thus tells us deposits increase by $5 million—the same answer we obtained using equation 14.2.

How do we know total banking system loans in Table 14.9 increase by $4 million? Since each bank has a balance sheet, and we can aggregate these balance sheets to construct a balance sheet for the entire banking sector, we know the change in assets must equal the change in liabilities. For the entire banking system, liabilities in the form of deposits have grown by $5 million.

---

[2] To calculate the total change in deposits, we need to know the value of the series $(1 + .8 + .8^2 + .8^3 + \ldots)$, where the ellipses signify that the series continues forever, with successively larger exponents on the fraction .8. This is called an *infinite series,* and there is a mathematical formula for calculating the sum of this series given by

$$(1 + x + x^2 + x^3 + \cdots) = \frac{1}{1 - x}.$$

This formula is valid for values of *x* less than 1. In our example, *x* = .8.

Inside Money

Box 14.2

Reserve Requirements in the United States

The Board of Governors of the Federal Reserve System establishes reserve requirements in the United States within limits set by Congress, and these reserves must be held as deposits with one of the 12 Federal Reserve banks or as vault cash. Under provisions of the Depository Deregulation and Monetary Control Act of 1980, depository institutions that must meet these reserve requirements include commercial banks, mutual savings banks, savings and loan associations, credit unions, and agencies and branches of foreign banks.

The accompanying table shows the reserve requirements in effect in early 1993. The reserve requirements on checking accounts require small banks (those with less than $46.8 million in deposits) to hold 3 percent of deposits as required reserves, while larger banks (those with more than $46.8 million in deposits) must hold 10 percent of deposits in reserve. Time deposits and other forms of deposits are not subject to reserve requirements.

Reserve Requirements

Type of Deposit	Reserve Requirement (percent of deposit)	Effective Since
Checking accounts at banks with more than $46.8 million	10%	April 4, 1992
Checking accounts at banks with less than $46.8 million	3	December 15, 1992
Other deposits (time deposits and Eurocurrency liabilities)	0	December 27, 1992

Source: Federal Reserve Bulletin, January 1993, p. A9.

Assets in the form of reserves have increased by $1 million. This means assets in the form of loans must have grown by $4 million. Indeed, after the initial increase in reserves due to the open market purchase, the growth in loans is what leads to the growth in deposits. Thus, apart from the initial $1 million, the change in loans should be the same as the change in deposits.

Open Market Sales: Multiple Deposit Contraction. An open market sale has the exactly opposite effect from an open market purchase: It leads to a contraction of banking system reserves. During an open market sale of $1 million in government bonds, the Fed sells securities to a securities dealer, who likely pays by check. When the Fed cashes that check, it reduces reserves and deposits at Bank One. This causes Bank One to have negative excess reserves of $800,000, which can be covered temporarily by borrowing but will eventually lead the bank to recall $800,000 of its outstanding loans. Table 14.10 illustrates the positions of the Fed and the bank after the open market sale.

How does this open market sale affect the entire banking system? When Bank One recalls $800,000 in loans, these loans are paid by borrowers writing checks on accounts at, say, Bank Two. Bank Two will thus see a

---

Table 14.10
Effect of a $1 Million Open Market Sale

Part a shows the *changes* in the Fed's balance sheet after it has sold $1 million in government bonds. Its assets are reduced by this amount, as are its liabilities. Part b shows the effect on Bank One, the securities dealer's bank. The dealer writes a check on her deposit account to purchase the bonds from the Fed, and the Fed cashes this check by reducing Bank One's reserve account. Thus, Bank One has a reduction in deposits and reserves of $1 million. Notice that with this reduction in reserves, the bank now has negative excess reserves, or excess reserves of − $800,000.

(a)

Balance Sheet of the Fed
Immediately after a $1 Million Open Market Sale

Assets		Liabilities	
U.S. Government Bonds	− $1,000,000	Reserves	− $1,000,000

(b)

Changes in Balance Sheet of Bank One
Immediately after a $1 Million Open Market Sale

Assets		Liabilities	
Reserves	− $1,000,000	Deposits	− $1,000,000
Required	− $200,000		
Excess	− 800,000		
Loans	0	Net Worth	0
Building	0		
Total	− $1,000,000	Total	− $1,000,000

reduction in its deposits and reserves of $800,000, meaning this bank has a $640,000 shortfall of required reserves that it must meet by recalling loans. This process continues and is exactly the opposite of what happened when reserves were added to the banking system. In fact, the same deposit multiplier holds in reverse; that is, when the banking system loses $1 million in reserves, we can still calculate the change in deposits as

$$\Delta D = \frac{1}{rr} \times \Delta R.$$

In this case, $\Delta R = -\$1,000,000$ and $rr = .2$, so

$$\Delta D = \frac{1}{.2} \times -\$1,000,000$$

$$= 5 \times -\$1,000,000$$

$$= -\$5,000,000.$$

The $5 million contraction of deposits is driven by the contraction in reserves thanks to the open market sale and the subsequent reduction in loans throughout the entire banking system.

An important feature of this analysis is that the reduction in reserves engineered by the Fed is not eliminated by the actions of any one bank. Indeed, this reduction in reserves stays at $1 million throughout the adjustment process. The adjustment process simply spreads this reduction throughout the banking system.

Summary Exercise 14.2 What is the total contraction of deposits, loans, and reserves in the entire banking system if the required reserve ratio is 5 percent and the Fed makes an open market sale of $150,000? What happens to the money stock? Remember, we are assuming banks do not want to hold any excess reserves, the public does not hold cash, and banks do not borrow reserves.

Answer: The open market sale decreases reserves by $150,000. As we have seen, this will be the total change in banking system reserves. We can calculate the change in deposits from our simple deposit multiplier formula:

$$\Delta D = \frac{1}{.05} \times -\$150,000$$

$$= 20 \times -\$150,000$$

$$= -\$3,000,000.$$

Notice that the simple deposit multiplier is 20, much higher than it was when the required reserve ratio was .2.

To calculate the change in loans, we simply note the change in loans plus the change in reserves must equal the change in deposits to keep the balance sheet in balance. The change in reserves is $-\$150,000$ and the change in deposits is $-\$3,000,000$, so the change in loans equals the change in deposits minus the change in reserves, or $-\$2,850,000$. Finally, recall that the money stock is the sum of currency holdings and checkable deposits. Since deposits are the only form of money in this example, the money stock decreases by the same amount as deposits, or by $3 million.

A GENERAL MODEL OF MONEY CREATION

In the previous section, we derived the simple deposit multiplier as the inverse of the required reserve ratio. We did this under the assumptions that all bank reserves are required reserves and the public does not hold currency. In this very simple setting, the money stock is simply the amount on deposit at banks; the simple deposit multiplier could equivalently be thought of as the simple money multiplier.

In reality, the public holds currency as well as deposits, so the total money stock (M) is the sum of currency (C) and deposits (D):

$$M = C + D. \tag{14.3}$$

In this section, we examine money creation in this more general context and see how the level of deposits and the amount of currency holdings are determined. Ultimately this will allow us to examine how actions of the Fed, including open market operations, affect the total stock of money in the economy.

We first relax the assumptions used in the previous section. In particular, we now assume the public desires to hold currency in proportion to deposits so that people who decide to hold more money would increase their cash and deposit holdings proportionally. This is in contrast to the previous section, where we assumed people held money only in the form of deposits. We indicate the **desired currency to deposit ratio,** c^d, so that

$$C = c^d \times D. \tag{14.4}$$

We also allow banks to hold excess reserves in addition to reserves required by law. Thus, total reserves (R) equal required reserves (RR) plus excess reserves (ER):

$$R = RR + ER. \tag{14.5}$$

Required reserves still equal the required reserve ratio, rr, times deposits:

$$RR = rr \times D. \tag{14.6}$$

Desired excess reserves are assumed to be proportional to deposits so that desired excess reserves are equal to the **desired excess reserve ratio,** e^d, times deposits:

$$ER = e^d \times D. \tag{14.7}$$

Together equations 14.5, 14.6, and 14.7 imply that total bank reserves are

$$R = RR + ER$$

$$= rr \times D + e^d \times D \qquad (14.8)$$

$$= (rr + e^d) \times D.$$

Equation 14.8 indicates that when the total banking system holds a constant fraction of banking system deposits as required and excess reserves, total banking system reserves are proportional to deposits.

The Monetary Base

Since the public holds currency, the Fed cannot supply funds that will be earmarked as commercial bank reserves. Instead, funds supplied by the Fed get divided among two uses: as commercial bank reserves and as currency in the hands of the public.

Because funds supplied by the Fed are split among these two uses, it is not correct to view all the funds the Fed supplies as reserves, since a portion winds up in currency held outside of banks. Instead these funds are called the *monetary base* (*MB*). The **monetary base** (sometimes also referred to as *high-powered money*) is currency in the hands of the public (*C*) plus commercial bank reserves (*R*):

$$MB = C + R. \qquad (14.9)$$

An example will illustrate why it is convenient to use the monetary base to analyze Fed open market operations and how currency holdings and excess reserves affect money creation. Suppose a Fed open market purchase leaves a securities dealer holding a check for $1 million, which he deposits in his bank. If the securities dealer did not wish to hold cash, this deposit would increase the bank's reserves by $1 million. Furthermore, if the required reserve ratio is 20 percent and the bank holds no excess reserves, it can lend out $800,000 of the new deposit. In the previous section, we saw how this is multiplied throughout the banking system through subsequent rounds of deposits to create money in the form of deposits.

Now suppose the securities dealer wants to keep his currency holdings equal to one-quarter of his checkable deposits (i.e., $c^d = .25$) so that when he deposits the $1 million check, he takes $200,000 out in currency.[3] Due to this cash withdrawal, the bank has gained reserves (deposits) of $800,000. This illustrates that the initial effect of an open market purchase of $1 million results not in $1 million in new reserves at the bank (as it did in the absence of currency holdings) but in new reserves of $800,000 and new cash holdings by the public of $200,000. For this reason, it is more

---

[3] Notice that by withdrawing $200,000, he has $800,000 left on deposit. Thus, his currency to deposit ratio is $200,000/$800,000, or .25.

convenient to think of the open market purchase as increasing currency plus reserves (the monetary base) than to figure out how much of the initial deposit is converted into currency and how much is in the form of reserves.

After forking over $200,000 of currency to the securities dealer, how much of the remaining $800,00 can the dealer's bank lend out? The required reserve ratio of 20 percent means $160,000 of this $800,000 must be kept on reserve, which leaves the bank only $640,000 to lend out. Furthermore, if the bank's policy is to keep excess reserves of 5 percent in case of an emergency, it will keep another $40,000 as reserves, resulting in even less available to lend out—$600,000. Moreover, in each subsequent round of lending and deposits of the loans in other banks, currency holdings and excess reserves continue to diminish the additional loans banks can make.

This example suggests that a $1 million open market purchase will increase bank loans (and hence deposits at other banks), but by less than would be the case in the absence of currency holdings and excess reserves. It also illustrates that such actions by the Fed will have the additional effect of increasing currency in the hands of the public. In the remainder of this section, we determine the precise impact of Fed open market operations on (1) total banking system deposits, (2) total currency holdings by the public, and (3) the total stock of money.

The Complete Deposit Multiplier

We now derive the relationship between the monetary base and total banking system deposits, being careful to take into account how currency holdings and excess reserves drain the banking system of reserves. First, we substitute equations 14.4 and 14.8 into equation 14.9 to express the monetary base as

$$MB = C + R = c^d D + (rr + e^d)D,$$

which may be rewritten as

$$MB = (rr + e^d + c^d) \times D. \tag{14.10}$$

That is, the monetary base is total banking system deposits (D) multiplied by the sum of the currency to deposit ratio (c^d), the required reserve ratio (rr), and the desired excess reserve ratio (e^d).

Next, we solve equation 14.10 for D to obtain the total amount of deposits that are generated with a given monetary base:

$$D = \left[\frac{1}{rr + e^d + c^d}\right] \times MB. \tag{14.11}$$

Equation 14.11 completely determines total banking system deposits given the parameters of the banking system. It says that the total amount of banking system deposits is actually a multiple of the monetary base. For instance, suppose the Fed sets the monetary base at $350 billion and required reserves at 20 percent of deposits. If banks hold 5 percent of deposits as excess reserves and the public holds 25 percent of deposits as currency, total banking system deposits are

$$D = \left[\frac{1}{.2 + .05 + .25}\right] \times \$350,000,000,000$$

$$= 2 \times \$350,000,000,000 \qquad (14.12)$$

$$= \$700,000,000,000.$$

Notice that total banking system deposits are two times the monetary base.

How would total banking system deposits change if the Fed increased or decreased the monetary base through open market operations? An open market purchase would increase the monetary base, allowing banks to issue more loans. This effect would multiply throughout the banking system to create additional deposits according to the relation

$$\Delta D = \left[\frac{1}{rr + e^d + c^d}\right] \times \Delta MB. \qquad (14.13)$$

The term in brackets in equation 14.13 is called the **complete deposit multiplier** and indicates the multiple by which a given change in the monetary base will increase total banking system deposits. It is a generalization of the simple deposit multiplier introduced in equation 14.1. To see this, notice that when the public does not hold currency and banks do not hold excess reserves, $c^d = e^d = 0$. In this case, the complete deposit multiplier in equation 14.13 reduces to the simple deposit multiplier, $1/rr$, presented in equation 14.1.

We can use the complete deposit multiplier to determine how much total banking system deposits increased when the Fed purchased $1 million in bonds from our securities dealer. Recall that this open market purchase increased the monetary base by $\Delta MB = \$1,000,000$. Plugging $rr = .2$, $e^d = .05$, and $c^d = .25$ into equation 14.13, we find total banking system deposits changed by

$$\Delta D = \left[\frac{1}{.2 + .05 + .25}\right] \times \$1,000,000$$

$$= 2 \times \$1,000 = \$2,000,000. \qquad (14.14)$$

Here the complete deposit multiplier is 2, and thus total banking system deposits increase by two times the change in the monetary base, or by $2 million. Notice this is considerably less than the increase in deposits we found in equation 14.2, which was relevant when $c^d = e^d = 0$. (In that case, recall deposits increased by a whopping $5 million.) Why the difference?

First, we now assume banks hold excess reserves in addition to the reserves required by law. This means banks keep more of their deposits on reserve and thus have less to lend out when the Fed increases banking system reserves through an open market purchase. The less lent out, the less will be deposited after each subsequent round of lending, leading to fewer deposits than was the case when banks held only required reserves.

Second, individuals now wish to hold currency as well as deposits. In particular, when the $1 million check is deposited at the securities dealer's bank, the securities dealer withdraws $200,000 to hold as currency. This reduces the reserves of the bank, thus allowing it to make fewer loans than it would otherwise be free to make. Excess reserves and currency held by the public drain banking system reserves, resulting in fewer total deposits than would otherwise be the case.

More generally, the complete deposit multiplier decreases with increases in either the currency to deposit ratio, the required reserve ratio, or the desired excess reserve ratio. This implies the complete deposit multiplier—which takes into account currency holdings and excess reserves—is less than the simple deposit multiplier.

The Complete Currency Multiplier

When the public holds currency, an open market purchase leads not only to an increase in banking system deposits (as shown above) but also to more currency in circulation. Just how much currency is put in the hands of the public when the Fed makes a $1 million open market purchase? To answer this question, we first derive a relationship between the monetary base and currency holdings.

To do this, we solve equation 14.4 for D and substitute the result into equation 14.11 to obtain the following relationship between the monetary base and currency:

$$C = \left[\frac{c^d}{rr + e^d + c^d} \right] \times MB. \qquad (14.15)$$

Given the parameters of the banking system, equation 14.15 completely determines the currency holdings of the public. It says the total amount of currency held by the public is a fraction of the monetary base. For instance, if MB = $350 billion, rr = .2, e^d = .05, and c^d = .25, total currency holdings by the public are

$$C = \left[\frac{.25}{.2 + .05 + .25} \right] \times \$350,000,000,000$$

$$= \frac{1}{2} \times \$350,000,000,000 \qquad (14.16)$$

$$= \$175,000,000,000.$$

In other words, the Fed must maintain a $350 billion monetary base to keep $175 billion in currency in the hands of the public. Remember, some of the monetary base ends up as reserves at banks (and at the Fed), which is why the currency held by the public is actually less than the monetary base.

A change in the monetary base will lead to a change in currency holdings that is a fraction of the initial increase in the monetary base:

$$\Delta C = \left[\frac{c^d}{rr + e^d + c^d} \right] \times \Delta MB. \tag{14.17}$$

The relationship between the change in the monetary base and the change in currency held by the public in equation 14.17 involves the **complete currency multiplier,** $c^d/(rr + e^d + c^d)$. We can use this multiplier to determine by how much currency holdings increase due to a change in the monetary base.

Suppose the Fed wants to increase the amount of currency in circulation. By how much would currency in the hands of the public increase if the Fed engaged in an open market purchase that raised the monetary base by $1 million? If $rr = .2$, $e^d = .05$, and $c^d = .25$, then

$$\Delta C = \left[\frac{.25}{.2 + .05 + .25} \right] \times \$1,000,000$$

$$= \frac{1}{2} \times \$1,000,000 = \$500,000. \tag{14.18}$$

In other words, the $1 million increase in the monetary base has resulted in an increase in total currency holdings of $500,000. Since the complete currency multiplier is 1/2, currency holdings increased by less than the increase in the monetary base. It is important to note that this $500,000 increase in currency holdings is in addition to the $2 million increase in deposits shown in equation 14.14 and thus is an additional increase in the money stock.

The Complete Money Multiplier

How is the money stock related to the monetary base? Since the money stock consists of currency in the hands of the public plus checkable deposits, we can use the preceding results to find the link. Recall that total banking system deposits are

$$D = \left[\frac{1}{rr + e^d + c^d} \right] \times MB \tag{14.19}$$

and total currency in the hands of the public is

$$C = \left[\frac{c^d}{rr + e^d + c^d} \right] \times MB. \tag{14.20}$$

Since the money stock is simply the sum of currency and deposits ($M = C + D$), we can add equations 14.19 and 14.20 together to get

$$M = \left[\frac{1 + c^d}{rr + e^d + c^d}\right] \times MB. \tag{14.21}$$

Equation 14.21 is very important because it shows how the total stock of money is a multiple of the monetary base. The multiple (the term in brackets) is called the **complete money multipier** and depends on the desired currency to deposit ratio, the required reserve ratio, and the desired excess reserve ratio. For instance, suppose the Fed maintains a monetary base of $350 billion and requires banks to keep 20 percent of deposits as required reserves. If banks keep 5 percent of their deposits as excess reserves and the public holds 25 percent of their deposits as cash, the total stock of money in the economy is

$$M = \left[\frac{1 + .25}{.2 + .05 + .25}\right] \times \$350,000,000,000$$

$$= 2.5 \times \$350,000,000,000$$

$$= \$875,000,000,000$$

This shows how actions of the Fed, banks, and the public determine the total stock of money in the economy. Since the money stock consists of currency plus deposits, it is no coincidence that this amount exactly equals the sum of currency and deposits we calculated earlier in equations 14.12 and 14.16:

$$M = C + D = \$175,000,000,000 + 700,000,000,000 = \$875,000,000,000.$$

In other words, by maintaining a monetary base of $350 billion, the Fed actually ensures that the economy has $875 billion in money (currency plus checkable deposits). Box 14.3 discusses how the complete money multiplier we just derived is related to the actual M1 and M2 money multipliers for the U.S. economy.

Naturally, if the Fed changes the monetary base, the amount of currency and checkable deposits will change, since banks will alter their reserves and the public will change their currency holdings. The change in the money stock that results from a change in the monetary base is given by

$$\Delta M = \left[\frac{1 + c^d}{rr + e^d + c^d}\right] \times \Delta MB. \tag{14.22}$$

Since the change in the monetary base is multiplied by the complete money multiplier, the money stock (currency plus deposits) changes by a multiple of the change in the monetary base.

Not only does this example demonstrate the power the Fed has in changing the total amount of money in the economy, we can also use this formula to calculate the total amount of money created when the Fed purchased $1

Inside Money

The M2 Multiplier

Box 14.3

Our analysis of the money multiplier illustrates that the total supply of money in the economy is actually a multiple of the monetary base. For simplicity, the analysis in the text is based on a very narrow definition of the money supply, one that resembles M1. Recall from Chapter 2 that M1 is defined as currency plus demand deposits and other forms of checkable deposits, as well as traveler's checks. The complete money multiplier discussed in the text is, for all practical purposes, the M1 multiplier, since it includes all of the components of M1 except traveler's checks (which tends to be small amounts).

A broader monetary aggregate is M2, which adds to M1 savings deposits and time deposits, money market funds (not owned by insti-

tutions), overnight repurchase agreements, and overnight Eurodollars. As we learned in Chapters 7 and 13, the DIDMCA blurred the distinction between banks and thrifts. This fact, coupled with the volatility of M1 during the 1980s, led the Fed to largely abandon M1 and use its policy tools to target M2. The multiplier analysis described in the text also applies to M2, but the M2 multiplier is larger because of the additional components it contains.

We can gain a feel for how the M2 multiplier differs from that for M1 by lumping together several components in M2 to write

$$M2 = C + D + T + MM,$$

Continued on p. 473

Continued from p. 472

where, as before, C represents currency, D is demand deposits, T represents time deposits, and MM is the remaining components of M2, including money market funds. If we let $c^t = T/D$ and $c^m = MM/D$, the broader M2 measure of the money supply is given by the M2 multiplier times the monetary base:

$$M2 = \left[\frac{1 + c^d + c^t + c^m}{rr + e^d + c^d} \right] \times MB.$$

The term in brackets is the M2 multiplier. Notice it is considerably larger than the M1 multiplier discussed in the text, because time deposits and other components give rise to two additional terms in the numerator of the M2 multiplier. Furthermore, the ratio of money market mutual funds and time deposits to demand deposits tends to be much greater than 1. Since there are no reserve requirements on these components of M2, financial institutions create loans with these types of deposits that expand more readily through the banking system, resulting ultimately in a much larger money supply as measured by M2.

The accompanying figure shows the M2 multiplier for the 1972–1993 period. Notice it generally exceeded 10 during this time, indicating that a given monetary base is multiplied throughout the banking system to create more than 10 times that amount in money in the form of M2. In contrast, the M1 multiplier shown in part a of Figure 14.1 (page 475) is much smaller, and in fact is less than 3.

Sources for data: Board of Governors of the Federal Reserve System, *Federal Reserve Bulletin,* various issues; Citibase electronic database; authors' calculations.

---

million in securities through open market operations. In this case, $\Delta MB = \$1,000,000$, $rr = .2$, $e^d = .05$, and $c^d = .25$. Thus, we see the total change in the money stock is

$$\Delta M = \left[\frac{1 + .25}{.2 + .05 + .25} \right] \times \$1,000,000$$

$$= 2.5 \times \$1,000,000 = \$2,500,000.$$

Since the complete money multiplier is 2.5, the total stock of money increased by a multiple of the increase in the monetary base, or by $2,500,000. In equations 14.14 and 14.18, we saw that $2 million of this increase was in the form of deposits and $500,000 was in the form of currency holdings. Notice that if you add up these changes in deposits and currency holdings, you get $2,500,000—the total change in the money stock. This is a general result, since it is always the case that

$$\Delta M = \Delta C + \Delta D.$$

Summary Exercise 14.3

What are the changes in deposits, currency holdings, and the money stock for an open market sale of $100,000? The required reserve ratio is 10 percent, the desired excess reserve ratio is 5 percent, and the desired currency to deposit ratio is 25 percent.

Answer: To answer this question, we first note that an open market sale is a reduction in the monetary base of $100,000. Thus, we will be looking at reductions in currency holdings, deposits, and the money stock. Next, we will use the complete multiplier formulas derived earlier:

$$\Delta D = \left[\frac{1}{rr + e^d + c^d} \right] \times \Delta MB$$

$$\Delta C = \left[\frac{c^d}{rr + e^d + c^d} \right] \times \Delta MB$$

and

$$\Delta M = \left[\frac{1 + c^d}{rr + e^d + c^d} \right] \times \Delta MB$$

Using the figures given in the problem, we find the complete deposit multiplier is 2.5, the complete currency multiplier is .625, and the complete money multiplier is 3.125. It follows that

$$\Delta D = 2.5 \times -\$100{,}000 = -\$250{,}000,$$

$$\Delta C = .625 \times -\$100{,}000 = -\$62{,}500,$$

and

$$\Delta M = 3.125 \times -\$100{,}000 = -\$312{,}500.$$

Thus, the open market operation causes deposits to decline by $250,000, currency holdings to decline by $62,500, and the money stock to decrease by $312,500. In fact, this example illustrates a general property of the complete money multiplier: It is the sum of the complete deposit multiplier and the complete currency multiplier (in this case, $2.5 + .625 = 3.125$). This observation provides a useful way for you (and us!) to double check the arithmetic.

DETERMINANTS OF THE MONEY SUPPLY

Based on our previous analysis, it is natural to define the money supply (M^s) as

$$M^s = \left[\frac{1 + c^d}{rr + e^d + c^d} \right] \times MB. \tag{14.23}$$

This relationship is called the **money supply equation,** because it indicates how much money is created (produced) in the economy for a given monetary base. In effect, the banking system and the public transform the monetary base into specific amounts of currency holdings and deposits. It is customary to refer to this transformation as the *money supply process* and the resulting amount of money as the *amount of money supplied.* The term *money stock* is usually reserved for the specific amount of money supplied, although the terms *money supply* and *money stock* are sometimes used interchangeably.

Equation 14.23 indicates the major determinants of the money supply are (1) the required reserve ratio (rr), (2) the currency to deposit ratio (c^d), (3) the desired excess reserve ratio (e^d), and (4) the monetary base (MB). A change in any of these determinants will change the amount of money—that is, currency plus checkable deposits—available in the economy.

Part a of Figure 14.1 shows recent movements in the monetary base and the M1 money multipier; part b shows actual movements in the money stock as measured by M1. Notice that M1 increased substantially from the middle of 1991 to 1993, reflecting growth in the money stock of almost 13 percent. Part a shows that this increase in the money stock was caused by two factors. First, the Fed increased the monetary base by about 10.5 percent over this

The changes in the money stock shown in part b are a result of the changes in the money multiplier, the monetary base, or both in part a.

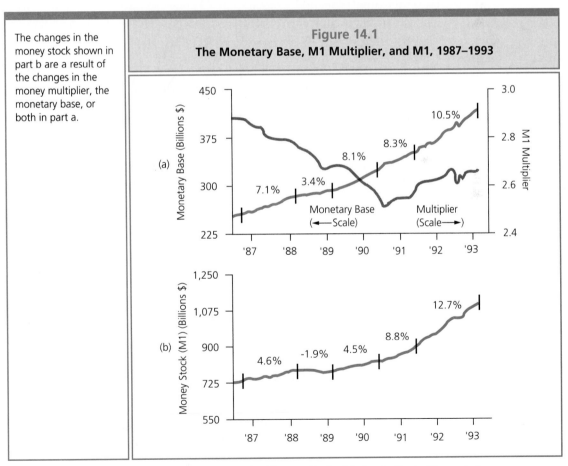

Figure 14.1

The Monetary Base, M1 Multiplier, and M1, 1987–1993

SOURCE: Copyright © Federal Reserve Bank of St. Louis. Used with permission.

period, which, as we saw earlier, results in an increase in the money stock. Second, notice the money multiplier also increased during this period, which accounts for the additional increase in the money stock.

This shows that changes in the monetary base and the money multiplier actually affect the amount of money in the economy. We will see next why the money supply might change due to changes in the behavior of (1) the Fed, (2) banks, or (3) the public.

Federal Reserve Determinants of the Money Supply

The Fed has two primary ways of influencing the money supply: (1) through the monetary base (*MB*) and (2) through the required reserve ratio (*rr*). During a period of economic expansion, the Fed sometimes takes actions that reduce the money supply to counter inflationary pressures. In contrast, the Fed often increases the money supply during economic downturns in the hope of stimulating the economy. In Chapter 16, we will examine why changes in the money supply affect the macroeconomy. Here we focus on the tools the Fed uses to change the money supply.

The Monetary Base. The Fed can increase (decrease) the monetary base by engaging in open market purchases (sales). An increase (decrease) in the monetary base leads to an increase (decrease) in the money supply that is a multiple of the increase (decrease) in the monetary base, thanks to the complete money multiplier.

To illustrate this, let us calculate the total money supply for two different levels of the monetary base. Suppose $rr = .2$, $e^d = .05$, $c^d = .25$, and $MB = \$350$ billion. In this case, the total money supply is

$$M^s = \left[\frac{1 + .25}{.2 + .05 + .25} \right] \times \$350{,}000{,}000{,}000$$

$$= 2.5 \times \$350{,}000{,}000{,}000$$

$$= \$875{,}000{,}000{,}000.$$

If the monetary base were lower—say, $300 billion—but the other parameters remained the same, the total money supply would be

$$M^s = \left[\frac{1 + .25}{.2 + .05 + .25} \right] \times \$300{,}000{,}000{,}000$$

$$= 2.5 \times \$300{,}000{,}000{,}000$$

$$= \$750{,}000{,}000{,}000.$$

This example illustrates that the Fed can decrease the money supply by reducing the monetary base through open market sales.

The Required Reserve Ratio. The Fed can also change the money supply by changing the required reserve ratio. By changing reserve requirements, the Fed alters the money multiplier, thereby changing the amount of money generated from a given monetary base. An increase in the required reserve ratio reduces the money multiplier and therefore leads to a reduction in the money supply, whereas a decrease in required reserves has the opposite effect.

To illustrate this, we calculate the total money supply for two different levels of the required reserve ratio. Suppose $MB = \$350$ billion, $rr = .2$, $e^d = .05$, and $c^d = .25$. In this case, the total money supply is

$$M^s = \left[\frac{1 + .25}{.2 + .05 + .25}\right] \times \$350,000,000,000$$

$$= 2.5 \times \$350,000,000,000$$

$$= \$875,000,000,000.$$

If the required reserve ratio were lower—say, $rr = .1$—but the other variables remained the same, the total money supply would be

$$M^s = \left[\frac{1 + .25}{.1 + .05 + .25}\right] \times \$350,000,000,000$$

$$= 3.125 \times \$350,000,000,000$$

$$= \$1,093.75 \text{ billion.}$$

This example illustrates that a reduction in the required reserve ratio leads to an increase in the money supply. The reason is that it increases the complete money multiplier, in this example from 2.5 to 3.125.

As a matter of practice, the Fed seldom uses this tool to influence the money supply; reserve requirements tend to remain fixed for long periods of time. Prior to the DIDMCA, the Fed lacked the power to set reserve requirements at S&Ls and other thrift institutions. Consequently the Fed could not affect the reserves of all depository institutions by changing the reserve requirements. Although the Fed now has the authority to set reserves at all depository institutions, it has little experience in using this tool to influence the money supply. A small change in reserve requirements leads to a large change in the money multiplier. Therefore, even a small mistake— setting reserve requirements a few percentage points too high, for instance— could drastically reduce the money supply, possibly creating a recession. For these reasons, the Fed relies primarily on open market operations to change the monetary base on a day-to-day basis.

Banking System Determinants of the Money Supply

The banking system helps determine the money supply by its choice of the ratio of excess reserves to deposits, e^d. Since higher excess reserves reduce the amount of loans the banking system creates from a given monetary base, increases in e^d lead to reductions in the money supply, whereas decreases in e^d lead to increases.

Figure 14.2 plots the actual excess reserve ratio of the banking system for the period 1972 to early 1993. Notice the ratio of excess reserves to deposits was very small, averaging less than .1 percent (or .001) during the 1970s but increasing to between .15 and .20 percent from the mid-1980s and into the 1990s. Thus, banks held very few excess reserves. In addition, the ratio of excess reserves to deposits showed a lot of volatility, with large upward and downward movements in only a few months.

What factors might cause a bank to raise or lower its desired excess reserve ratio? The major factors are changes in the market interest rate on loans, the risk of deposit withdrawals, and the interest rates on sources of borrowed reserves. We explain the link between these factors and the desired excess reserve ratio next.

Market Interest Rates on Loans. The market interest rates on loans influence the desired ratio of excess reserves to deposits because these interest rates are the opportunity cost of holding excess reserves. Recall that

The excess reserve ratios of banks tend to be very small but volatile.

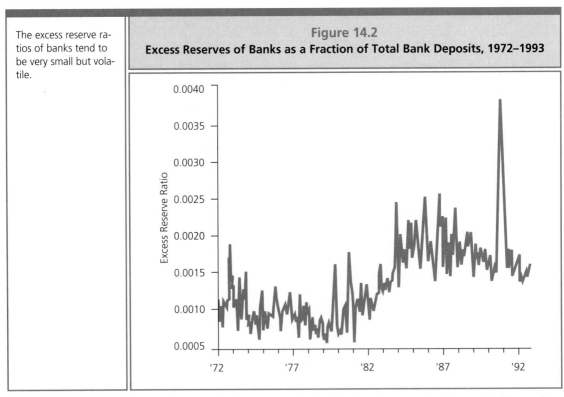

Figure 14.2
Excess Reserves of Banks as a Fraction of Total Bank Deposits, 1972–1993

SOURCES: Board of Governors of the Federal Reserve System, *Federal Reserve Bulletin,* various issues; Citibase electronic database.

excess reserves earn no interest. When a bank holds excess reserves, it forgoes the interest it could have earned by making a loan from those reserves. The higher the market interest rates on loans (or other securities a bank can purchase), the higher the opportunity cost of holding excess reserves. Thus, the desired ratio of excess reserves will decline with increases in the market interest rates on loans and other securities. In fact, the increase in the excess reserve ratio during the 1980s was due partly to the lower interest rates that prevailed during that period relative to the 1970s, which reduced the opportunity cost to banks of holding excess reserves.

Risk of Deposit Withdrawals.   Banks hold excess reserves mostly to help them deal with unexpected withdrawals. Having excess reserves available allows a bank to avoid calling in loans, selling securities, or borrowing reserves from either other banks or the Federal Reserve when it faces a withdrawal of deposits. For instance, an earthquake in California or a hurricane in Florida will generally lead banks in those areas to hold additional excess reserves in anticipation of people withdrawing funds to repair homes and the like. The higher the risk of such withdrawals, the greater the excess reserve ratio.

Interest Rate on Borrowed Reserves.   As we mentioned earlier, a bank facing a sudden need for reserves can avoid calling in loans, at least for awhile, by borrowing reserves from other banks (in the federal funds market) or from the Fed (through the discount window). Banks view the ability to borrow reserves in times of need as a substitute for holding excess reserves. Instead of holding excess reserves and giving up the market rate of interest on loans or securities, a bank can choose to be nearly "loaned up," with the intention of meeting any sudden need for reserves by borrowing. When the interest rates paid on borrowed reserves rise, as is the case when the federal funds rate or the discount rate increases, this option becomes relatively less attractive, and the excess reserve ratio increases. This tends to reduce the complete money multiplier and thus the money supply.

The Public's Determinants of the Money Supply

The public chooses its desired currency to deposit ratio, which also helps determine the money supply. If people want to make more cash transactions, the desired currency to deposit ratio will increase. This will reduce the complete money multiplier and thus lead to a reduction in the money supply. A decrease in c^d has the opposite effect.

To see how the currency to deposit ratio affects the money supply, suppose people initially hold 25 percent of their deposits as currency. Assuming $rr = .2$, $e^d = .05$, $c^d = .25$, and $MB = \$350$ billion, the total money supply is

$$M^s = \left[\frac{1 + .25}{.2 + .05 + .25} \right] \times \$350,000,000,000$$

$$= 2.5 \times \$350,000,000,000$$

$$= \$875,000,000,000.$$

If people increase their desired currency holdings to 50 percent of deposits, but the other parameters remain the same, the money supply decreases:

$$M^s = \left[\frac{1 + .5}{.2 + .05 + .5} \right] \times \$350,000,000,000$$

$$= 2 \times \$350,000,000,000$$

$$= \$700,000,000,000.$$

This example illustrates that an increase in the currency to deposit ratio leads to a reduction in the money supply, because it drains the banking system of some of its reserves. In this example, the rise in c^d reduces the multiplier from 2.5 to 2.

Figure 14.3 graphs the currency to deposit ratio for the 1972–1993 period. This ratio had an upward trend from about .3 in the early 1970s to around .4 in the early 1980s. A substantial decline occurred from about 1985 until 1987, followed by an even greater rise until about 1990. Since then there has been a further decline, back to a level of just over .4. This means the average depositor holds currency that is about 40 percent of his or her checkable deposits. Notice the substantial rise in the currency to deposit ratio from 1987 until 1990 translated into a decrease in the money multiplier during that period, as we saw in part a of Figure 14.1.

What factors might lead to a change in the public's desired currency to deposit ratio? This ratio depends on a number of factors, including the interest rate on checkable deposits, the fees on these deposits, income, the probability of bank failure, and the extent of illegal activity. We will discuss each of these factors in turn.

Interest Rates on Checkable Deposits.   Moneyholders face the choice of holding their money in the form of currency or checkable deposits. One cost of holding money in the form of currency is the forgone interest that might be earned on deposits. When the interest rate on checkable deposits rises, the attractiveness of holding currency declines, which reduces the currency to deposit ratio.

Fees on Checkable Deposits.   Moneyholders looking to choose between currency and checkable deposits will also be influenced by the fees charged on checking accounts, both monthly maintenance charges and fees assessed per check or ATM withdrawal. These fees are a cost of holding money in the form of deposits, as we learned in Chapter 4. When these fees

The public's currency to deposit ratio is currently about .4, indicating the public holds roughly 40 percent of demand deposits as currency.

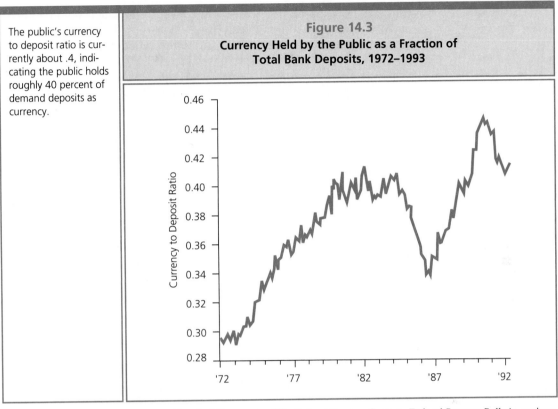

Figure 14.3

Currency Held by the Public as a Fraction of Total Bank Deposits, 1972–1993

SOURCES: Board of Governors of the Federal Reserve System, *Federal Reserve Bulletin,* various issues; Citibase electronic database.

increase, the attractiveness of holding money in the form of currency increases, which raises the currency to deposit ratio.

Income.   The income of moneyholders also has some influence on the currency to deposit ratio. In general, the currency to deposit ratio declines with income. Those with higher incomes tend to be more sophisticated users of the financial system and rely more on the financial system than on currency. Those with lower incomes are more likely to use currency in their transactions. Thus, the higher the income in an economy, the lower the currency to deposit ratio and the larger the money supply.

The Probability of Bank Failure.   When the probability of a bank failure rises, moneyholders tend to abandon deposits in favor of currency, even though deposit insurance in the United States makes bank failures and failures of other depository institutions such as savings and loans much less costly than during earlier times. In recent years, in fact, failures of depository institutions have caused little or no discomfort to most depositors and have frequently gone almost unnoticed. However, any widespread incidence of bank failures affecting numerous institutions, called a *bank panic,* would likely trigger a movement toward cash, increasing the currency to deposit ratio and reducing the money supply. Indeed, this is precisely what happened in the United States during the Great Depression.

Illegal Activity.   Since cash can be used to make unrecorded transactions, it is the medium of choice for illegal activities such as drug dealing, illegal gambling, and tax evasion. Economists and policymakers often speak of the **underground economy,** meaning that part of the economy that is unrecorded in official measurements of economic activity because it consists of illegal activities and unrecorded cash transactions. Any increase in the dollar amount of transactions that take place in the underground economy will tend to increase the currency to deposit ratio and thus decrease the money supply.

Summary Exercise 14.4

Assuming other things remain constant, determine the impact of each of the following events on the money supply: (a) The Fed lowers the required reserve ratio; (b) the interest rate paid on deposits rises; (c) the Fed raises the discount rate.

Answer: (a) A reduction in the required reserve ratio increases the complete money multiplier and thus leads to an increase in the money supply. (b) An increase in the deposit interest rate will lead to a lower currency to deposit ratio. This increases the complete money multiplier and thus increases the money supply. (b) An increase in the discount rate leads banks to increase their desired excess reserve ratios. This reduces the complete money multiplier and therefore decreases the money supply.

THE MONEY SUPPLY CURVE

Our analysis of the money supply in the previous section showed the amount of money in the economy ultimately depends on the monetary base, the excess reserve ratio, the required reserve ratio, and the currency to deposit ratio. The monetary base and the required reserve ratio are determined by the Fed, while banks and depositors determine the excess reserve and currency to deposit ratios. We conclude our analysis of the money supply process by graphically depicting the **money supply curve,** the amount of money suppliers are willing and able to supply at various interest rates.

Because economists disagree about the impact of interest rates on the determinants of the money supply, we will distinguish between two views. One is that the determinants of the money supply in equation 14.23 are exogenous, that is, determined by outside forces and do not depend on such variables as interest rates. According to this view, there is an **exogenous money supply:** Changes in interest rates do not alter the currency to deposit ratio or the desired excess reserve ratios of banks. The second view is that an **endogenous money supply** exists: The determinants of the money supply—most notably the currency to deposit ratio and the desired excess reserve ratio—are endogenous and depend on economic variables like interest rates. We will now see how these two views affect the picture of the money supply curve.

Exogenous Money Supply Curve

Suppose banks wish to hold a fixed fraction of deposits as excess reserves and depositors hold a fixed fraction of deposits as cash. In this case, the excess reserve and deposit ratios are exogenous, that is, independent of interest rates and other economic variables. Since these ratios are constants, the money supply curve is vertical as in Figure 14.4 and called an *exogenous money supply curve.*

The term *exogenous money supply curve* refers to the situation where the supply of money in the economy is determined by banks' preferences

When the excess reserve ratio and the currency to deposit ratio are constant, the money supply curve is exogenous—a vertical function of interest rates. The money supply curve increases (shifts to the right) when the monetary base increases and decreases (shifts to the left) when the monetary base declines. An increase (decrease) in the required reserve, excess reserve, or currency to deposit ratio will cause the money supply curve to shift to the left (right).

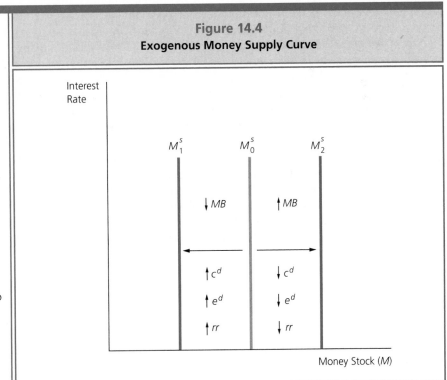

Figure 14.4
Exogenous Money Supply Curve

for excess reserves and depositors' preferences for holding cash, and these preferences are not affected by changes in economic variables like interest rates. In this case, the complete money multiplier is constant. Consequently the amount of money supplied along the money supply curve does not vary with interest rates; it is vertical, as is the case for the curve labeled M_0^s in Figure 14.4. Our analysis of the simple money multiplier, which assumed depositors never hold cash (a constant currency to deposit ratio of zero) and banks never hold excess reserves (a constant excess reserve ratio of zero), is an example of a situation where the money supply curve is vertical.

How do changes in c^d, e^d, rr, and MB affect the position of an exogenous money supply curve? Increases in c^d, e^d, and rr shift the money supply curve to the left (from M_0^s to M_1^s in Figure 14.4), since a rise in any of these variables leads to a lower complete money multiplier and thus a lower money supply. A decrease in any of these variables has the opposite effect, shifting the money supply curve from M_0^s to M_2^s. The monetary base has a direct effect on the money supply: An increase in MB shifts the money supply curve to the right, whereas a decrease shifts it to the left.

Endogenous Money Supply Curve

As noted earlier, some economists believe the excess reserve and currency to deposit ratios are not constant but vary systematically with economic conditions. For instance, as interest rates rise, many banks will decrease their excess reserves to be able to lend out additional funds at the higher rates. Similarly, many depositors will wish to hold less currency and more interest-bearing deposits to earn greater interest income. In these instances, the money multiplier is not a constant but an increasing function of interest rates. This gives rise to a money supply curve that is endogenous and upward sloping, such as the curve labeled M_0^s in Figure 14.5.

Why is the money supply curve upward sloping in the case of an endogenous money supply? As interest rates rise, excess reserves fall, and the amount of money in the economy increases due to the complete money multiplier. (Recall that a decrease in the excess reserve ratio leads to a higher complete money multiplier.) Similarly, higher interest rates lead to a lower currency to deposit ratio, which works through the complete money multiplier to further increase the money supply. Thus, when we graph the money supply as a function of interest rates as in Figure 14.5, it is an upward sloping curve. Higher interest rates lead to a greater quantity of money supplied when the money supply curve is endogenous. We will say more about this in the next chapter, where we look at how to determine the equilibrium stock of money in the economy.

When the money supply is endogenous, it is not appropriate to consider the effect of exogenous changes in c^d or e^d on the money supply, since they are functions of the interest rate graphed on the vertical axis. In fact, it is

When the excess re-
serve and currency to
deposit ratios decrease
as interest rates rise,
the money supply
curve is endogenous.
In this case, the
money supply curve is
an upward-sloping
function of interest
rates. An increase in
the monetary base or
a decrease in the re-
quired reserve ratio
shifts the money sup-
ply curve to the right.
Similarly, a decrease in
the monetary base or
an increase in the re-
quired reserve ratio
shifts the money sup-
ply curve to the left.

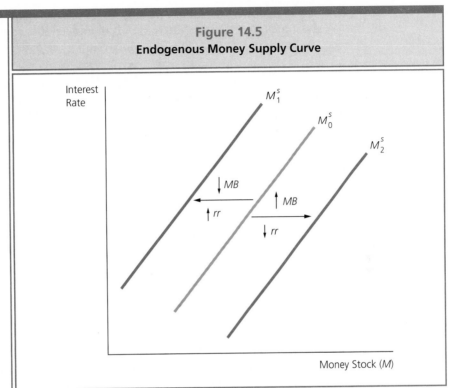

Figure 14.5
Endogenous Money Supply Curve

because of this functional relationship that the money supply curve slopes
upward in the first place: *Higher interest rates* lead to a lower c^d and e^d and
thus a higher money multiplier and a greater quantity of money supplied.

Changes in the required reserve ratio (rr) or the monetary base (MB),
however, will shift the money supply curve, and in the same direction as in
the case of an exogenous money supply curve. For instance, in Figure 14.5
we see that an increase in the required reserve ratio shifts the money supply
curve to the left, resulting in a lower money stock at each interest rate. A
decrease in the monetary base also shifts the money supply curve to the left,
resulting in a lower stock of money at each interest rate.

Summary
Exercise 14.5

Suppose the Fed engages in an open market purchase (it purchases government securities from a securities dealer). Graphically illustrate the impact of
this action on the money supply when (a) the money supply is exogenous
and (b) the money supply is endogenous.

Answer: Regardless of whether the money supply is endogenous or exogenous, the open market purchase leads to an increase in the monetary base

and thus shifts the money supply curve to the right. Part a of the figure illustrates the result for the case of an exogenous money supply. Part b of the figure is relevant when the money supply is endogenous.

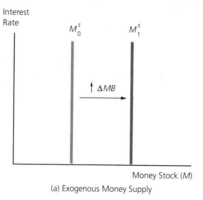

(a) Exogenous Money Supply

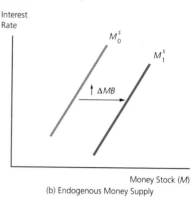

(b) Endogenous Money Supply

CONCLUSION

In this chapter, we developed algebraic and graphical models of the money supply. We discussed the determinants of the money supply, from those controlled by the Federal Reserve System to those elements determined by the behavior of banks or the public. In the next chapter, we look at the other side of the money market, money demand, and examine how equilibrium between the supply of and demand for money is determined.

KEY TERMS

required reserves

excess reserves

legal reserves

required reserve ratio

multiple deposit expansion

simple deposit multiplier

desired currency to deposit ratio

desired excess reserve ratio

monetary base

high-powered money

complete deposit multiplier

complete currency multiplier

complete money multiplier

underground economy

money supply curve

exogenous money supply

endogenous money supply

QUESTIONS AND PROBLEMS

1. The required reserve ratio is 12 percent. The desired currency to deposit ratio and the desired excess reserve ratio are both zero. If there is an open market purchase of $100,000, what will happen to the total deposits of the banking system? To the total loans? To the total reserves?

2. Consider a situation in which the required reserve ratio is 15 percent and each bank individually decides to hold 5 percent of every deposit against emergency withdrawals, in addition to the legally mandated reserves. There is no holding of cash. What happens to total banking system deposits if an open market purchase of $500,000 occurs?

3. The required reserve ratio is 10 percent. The excess reserve ratio is zero, but the public desires to hold currency equal to 5 percent of deposits. If an open market purchase of $250,000 occurs, what will happen to total banking system deposits?

4. Obviously deposits are a crucial input into the production of loans by banks. What other resources is a bank likely to require to be able to produce (or supply) loans?

5. If the legal reserve ratio is zero and banks hold no excess reserves, what will happen if the level of banking system reserves increases by $100? Does the currency to deposit ratio matter for your answer?

6. Explain how the Federal Reserve System creates money by buying U.S. government securities in the open market.

7. A substantial amount of U.S. dollars is in circulation outside the United States. Dollars are often accepted in exchange—that is, as money—in countries around the world. Suppose something occurs that makes foreign nationals no longer willing to hold dollars so those dollars, once outside the U.S. banking system, now get deposited in U.S. banks. What is the effect on the U.S. banking system?

8. Go back to 1913, when the Fed was just created. Could the Fed easily conduct open market purchases? What about open market sales?

9. Suppose an eccentric millionaire buries $1 million in a time capsule in 1994. This time capsule will be opened by her heir, her great-granddaughter, in the year 2014. What is the effect on the banking system in 1994? What will be the effect when her great-granddaughter opens the capsule in 2014?

10. In the early 1980s, the Federal Reserve System lowered the required reserve ratio on deposits. What was the predicted effect on the banking system?

11. Recently the government warned of an increase in drug trafficking. Assuming drugs are purchased solely with cash, what is the predicted effect on the banking system?

12. Historically an increase in the number of bank failures has been linked with an increase in the currency to deposit ratio. However, the recent savings and loan crisis, in which thousands of savings and loans failed, and the more recent trouble in the banking industry have not led to an increase in the currency to deposit ratio. Why not?

13. In the early 1980s, interest rates such as the prime rate and even the rate on U.S. Treasury bills reached unheard-of heights, nearing or even exceeding 20 percent. What do you think happened to the excess reserve ratio? Why? Would this have tended to increase or decrease the money supply?

14. President Clinton has suggested that taxes are going to increase. What do you predict will be the impact on the currency to deposit ratio? Why? What impact will this prediction tend to have on the money supply? Can the Fed offset this effect? If so, how?

15. The Fed receives interest income from its holdings of U.S. government bonds. When the Fed increases the monetary base, does this action increase or decrease the Fed's income from its securities portfolio? Other things equal, would you expect the Fed to favor increases in the monetary base or decreases in the reserve ratio as a means of increasing the money supply?

16. If you read in the paper that the discount rate has increased, do you think this will tend to increase or decrease the money supply? Why?

17. If loan rates and deposit rates both increase, what is the expected effect on the banking system?

18. Assume the currency to deposit ratio has increased. What is the effect on banking system reserves, deposits, loans, and the money supply? Can the Fed adjust the required reserve ratio and/or the monetary base to restore the money supply to its initial level? Can the Fed also restore deposits, loans, and reserves to their initial levels? Explain.

19. Some states have a tax on wealth, in which they charge a tax on bank deposits. What effect would this tax have on the banking system if it were adopted nationwide?

20. If the Fed has decided to try to minimize currency holdings because it has become too costly to maintain the stock of Federal Reserve notes, what actions might it take?

SELECTIONS FOR FURTHER READING

Garfinkel, M., and D. L. Thorton. "The Multiplier Approach to the Money Supply Process: A Precautionary Note." *Federal Reserve Bank of St. Louis Review,* (July/August 1991), 47–64.

Kopecky, K. J. "Required Reserve Ratios and Monetary Control." *Journal of Economics and Business,* 33 (Spring/Summer 1981), 212–217.

Meyer, P. A. "Money Multipliers and the Slopes of IS-LM." *Southern Economic Journal,* 50 (July 1983), 226–229.

Ross, M. H., and R. E. Zelder. "The Discount Rate: A Phantom Policy Tool?" *Western Economic Journal,* 7 (December 1969), 341–348.

Tiwari, K. N. "The Money Supply Process under Deregulation." *Financial Review,* 21 (February 1986), 111–123.

Trescott, P. B. "The Behavior of the Currency Deposit Ratio during the Great Depression: A Comment." *Journal of Money, Credit, and Banking,* 16 (August 1984), 362–365.

15

The Demand for Money and Equilibrium in the Money Market

*I*n the previous two chapters, we examined the institutional arrangements within the U.S. banking system, particularly the role of the Federal Reserve System and the money supply process. We now turn to a discussion of the other side of the market: the demand for money. We identify factors that determine how much money you and other actors in the economy—including businesses—keep in your pockets, checking accounts, and cash registers. Our analysis will enable you to predict the effect on interest rates of Fed policies that increase the money supply.

We begin this chapter with a look at three views of money demand: the classical view, the Keynesian view, and the modern quantity theory of money. We will see that classical economists believed people hold money primarily to make transactions (buy goods). This transactions view of money demand led the classical economists to conclude that income is the primary determinant of money demand. This view was later modified by John Maynard Keynes, who reasoned that people consider the costs of holding money when they decide how much to hold. You may think the costs of holding money are zero; after all, you pay no fees to carry currency in your pocket. Other forms of money, however, do involve direct costs. Traveler's checks often contain a fee of 1 percent of their amount, and many checking accounts charge fees. While the fees on checkable deposits vary, even ''free'' checking accounts usually require you to purchase the checks you will use. More important, there are also indirect costs of holding money in the form of currency, traveler's checks, or checkable deposits. These costs arise because you earn a lower interest rate on these holdings than you can earn by holding wealth in some other form. Even checking accounts that pay interest do not pay as much as you could earn by holding another asset such as a government bond or even a U.S. savings bond. Thus, holding money has an opportunity cost, since you lose out on potential interest earnings. This fact led Keynes to reason that the higher the interest rate, the less money people will hold. Milton Friedman further developed this view of money in what is known as the modern quantity theory of money. This theory combines features of the classical and Keynesian views of money and includes wealth, interest rates, and a host of other factors as determinants of money demand.

After we examine the historical origins and current thought on money demand, we look at how modern theories and the money supply apparatus developed in Chapter 14 can be used to predict the effects of monetary policy on interest rates. We conclude with a discussion of differences between monetarist and Keynesian views of monetary policy and examine the relationship between the analysis in this chapter and the loanable funds approach we developed in Chapter 4.

THE CLASSICAL VIEW OF MONEY DEMAND

The **classical view of money demand** considers income to be the primary determinant of money demand: The higher your income, the greater the amount of money you will hold. In this section, we look at two versions of the classical view of money demand: the simple quantity theory and the Cambridge theory. The simple quantity theory is based purely on the transactions motive for holding money, that is, the need for money to buy goods and services. The Cambridge theory views money as useful for transactions purposes and as a store of wealth. But as we will see, both theories imply similar demand functions for money.

The Simple Quantity Theory

In the early 1900s, Irving Fisher developed the **simple quantity theory of money demand,** which views transactions as the primary motive for holding money.[1] It has its roots in the equation of exchange. The **equation of exchange,** introduced in Chapter 3, links aggregate spending in an economy and the stock of money.

To illustrate the development of Fisher's ideas about money demand, we consider a simple economy in which total spending in a year, TS, is $1,000. Furthermore, the stock of money, M, is $200. Why can individuals in the economy buy $1,000 worth of goods and services if the money stock is only $200? The answer is that on average, each dollar is used more than once in a year. In fact, in this example each dollar must be used an average of five times in a year for a money supply of $200 to support $1,000 of spending.

The number of times an average unit of money changes hands in one year is called **velocity,** or V. We can then write the equation of exchange as

$$M \times V = TS.$$

---

[1] Later in this chapter, we will trace the origins back to the 1600s.

This equation states that the quantity of money in an economy, M, multiplied by the number of times the average unit of money changes hands in one year, V, will equal the value of annual total spending, TS.

The equation of exchange provides a useful way to think about money and the economy, but it is not a theory. In fact, the equation of exchange is an identity. It must be true, because velocity is defined so as to make it true. We do not really observe velocity. Instead we simply divide total spending by the money supply and call the result velocity.

This doesn't mean the equation of exchange is useless. For example, it tells us that if the quantity of money increases, either total spending will increase, velocity will fall, or both. In our example total spending is $1,000, velocity is 5, and the quantity of money is $200. If the quantity of money increases to $400 and velocity stays constant, total spending must increase to $2,000. Why? Because the economy now has $400 of money, and if everyone spends this money at a rate that causes it to change hands five times in a year, spending will have to be $400 \times 5 = 2,000$.

What if the money supply increases to $400 but total spending stays at $1,000? Then we know velocity has fallen to 2.5. With $400 of money and spending at $1,000, money must change hands 2.5 times in one year, on average.

The equation of exchange does not tell us whether an increase in the quantity of money will increase total spending or reduce velocity. Likewise, it is not clear whether an increase in income will raise the quantity of money or increase velocity.

To develop a theory of money demand, Fisher reasoned that velocity would be constant since it depends on slowly moving variables such as the frequency with which people are paid and institutional characteristics of the payments system. During Fisher's time the financial system was just developing, and it was probably reasonable to view velocity as determined primarily by the banking system of the day rather than varying in response to changes in the quantity of money or total spending. At any rate, this line of reasoning implies the equation of exchange can be used to write money demand as

$$M^d = \frac{TS}{V}.$$

Since velocity was thought to be constant, any increase in total spending would lead to an increase in the demand for money. The idea was that with constant velocity, an increase in spending required greater money holdings to satisfy the equation of exchange. Thus, money demand was linked to the desire to make transactions. This is why we say the simple quantity theory is based on the transactions motive for holding money.

Fisher had a further insight into money demand, which he got from considering how total spending could change. In our example, we know total spending is $1,000. What we don't know is whether this amount consists of the purchase of 1,000 goods costing $1 each, 2,000 goods costing $.50 each, or 500 goods costing $2 each. Thus, Fisher separated total spending, *TS*, into the quantity of goods purchased, *Y*, and the price of those goods, *P*, or

$$TS = P \times Y.$$

Using this formula, we can write the equation of exchange in its most familiar form as

$$M \times V = P \times Y.$$

Then the simple quantity theory of money demand becomes

$$M^d = \frac{P \times Y}{V}. \tag{15.1}$$

This version of the quantity theory of money demand stresses that people will want to hold more money if either the prices of the goods they purchase increase or the quantities they want to purchase increase. In either case, the amount of money required to pay for the purchase of these goods will increase.

Suppose people are purchasing 1,000 goods at a price of $1 each. From our previous example velocity is 5, so money demand is $200, calculated as $1,000/5. What happens if the price of the goods doubles to $2 each? If people still want to purchase 1,000 goods, they will now make purchases in the amount of $2,000 per year. With velocity constant at 5, this increases money demand to $400 ($2,000/5).

Alternatively, consider what happens if the number of goods people want to purchase rises to 2,000, but the price of each stays at $1. In this case, the dollar amount of purchases is also $2,000, so with velocity at 5, money demand is again $400. Thus, with velocity constant, increases in the price level have the same effect on money demand as do increases in the number of goods and services purchased. In fact, as our examples show, when the price level doubles, so does money demand. When prices rise from $1 to $2, money demand increases from $200 to $400. This is a general property of the simple quantity theory of money demand. As long as the physical amount of purchases stays constant, any increase in prices will be matched by a proportional change in money demand. Thus, the simple quantity theory of money demand is often called a theory of the demand for *real money balances*. **Real money balances** are the nominal money stock divided by the price level, *M/P*, and are a measure of the purchasing power of money. For a given quantity of dollars, *M*, increases in the price level mean less can be purchased. Increases in purchasing power come about from either an increase in the money stock, *M*, or a reduction in the price level, *P*, while decreases in purchasing power result from either a decrease in the money stock or an increase in the price level. To write the simple quantity theory of money demand in terms of the demand for real money balances, we simply divide both sides of equation 15.1 by the price level, P, to obtain

$$\frac{M^d}{P} = \frac{Y}{V}. \tag{15.2}$$

Since the simple quantity theory of money views velocity in equation 15.2 as constant, the demand for real money balances depends solely on real income. If real income doubled, real money balances would double as well; twice as much real money balances would be needed to make transactions. Box 15.1 examines the extent to which this hypothesized relationship holds for Mexico. Later we will look at data for the United States.

The Cambridge Theory

The **Cambridge theory of money demand** was developed by economists in Cambridge, England, at roughly the same time Irving Fisher was pioneering his views on the simple quantity theory of money. The Cambridge theory says people have two motives for holding money: to make transactions and to store wealth. Like Fisher, the Cambridge economists viewed the demand for real money balances as being proportional to real income:

$$\frac{M^d}{P} = k \, Y, \tag{15.3}$$

where k is called the **Cambridge constant.** According to the Cambridge view of money demand, a doubling of real income leads to a doubling of real money balances. In particular, with a given price level twice the amount of money would be desired for making transactions, and twice the amount would be desired as a store of wealth. Even though the Cambridge economists considered a second motive for holding money (storing wealth), they still ended up with a demand for money that was proportional to income, just as in the simple quantity theory.

In fact, the Cambridge view of money demand may be rewritten in a form that is identical to the simple quantity theory. If we take the Cambridge constant to be the reciprocal of velocity, $k = 1/V$, we can rewrite the Cambridge demand function for real money balances in equation 15.3 as

$$\frac{M^d}{P} = k \, Y = \frac{1}{V} Y, \tag{15.4}$$

which is identical to the simple quantity theory specification presented in equation 15.2.

Both the simple quantity and Cambridge theories view real money demand as depending primarily on real income. This view would be justified if k (or, equivalently, velocity) were constant. While the Cambridge economists usually treated k as a constant, they recognized that it might in fact

International Banking

Box 15.1

Money Demand in Mexico

The simple quantity theory of money says people hold real money balances because they want to purchase real goods and services (real GDP). The higher real GDP is, the higher will be the demand for real money balances. The accompanying figure shows real money balances and real GDP for Mexico from 1948 to 1990. Notice the close relationship between increases in real GDP and increases in real money balances from 1948 until about 1979. During the early 1980s, real GDP in Mexico remained relatively constant, but real money balances declined substantially. Thus, the simple quantity theory did a reasonably good job of explaining movements in real money balances in Mexico until the 1980s. After 1980, factors other than real GDP led to reductions in Mexican real money balances.

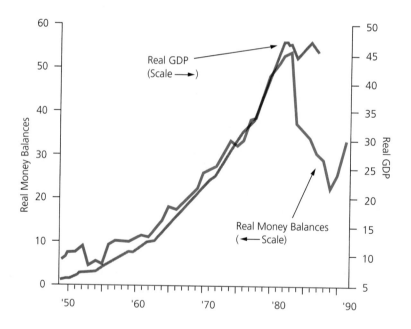

Sources: International Monetary Fund, *International Financial Statistics,* various years; Citibase electronic database.

vary as individuals altered the amounts of money they chose to hold as a store of wealth. This subtle difference ultimately led John Maynard Keynes, also a Cambridge economist, to consider factors other than income that might cause individuals to hold more or less money.

KEYNES'S VIEW OF MONEY DEMAND

The modern view of money demand owes much to the work of John Maynard Keynes in the 1930s.[2] While classical economists tended to emphasize the use of money in making transactions, Keynes identified three motives for holding money: the transactions motive, the precautionary motive, and the speculative motive. As with the classical economists, Keynes's **transactions motive** suggested that people hold money because it is useful in making purchases. Naturally the transactions motive for holding money would give rise to money demand that is positively related to income: People with higher incomes typically make more transactions and thus will hold more money. In fact, like the classical economists, Keynes viewed money held for transaction purposes as being proportional to income.

The **precautionary motive** for holding money is the desire to hold money to meet unexpected expenditure requirements, such as for emergencies or the proverbial rainy day. This motive is a refinement of the store of wealth function emphasized in the Cambridge theory. Indeed, Keynes also viewed money held for precautionary purposes as being proportional to income.

The most novel idea in Keynes's theory of money demand was the **speculative motive,** which implied money demand depends on interest rates. Keynes recognized that many assets other than money, such as bonds, can serve as a store of wealth. However, the return on a bond includes not only the interest payments received during the bond's term but also any capital gain or loss resulting from a change in the bond's price. As we learned in Chapter 8, when interest rates fall, bond prices rise, resulting in capital gains to bondholders. Keynes reasoned that when interest rates are above their ''normal'' levels, people will hold less money and more bonds because they expect bond prices to rise when interest rates return to lower, ''normal'' levels. This reasoning led Keynes to conclude that money demand is inversely related to the interest rate: The higher the interest rate, the less money (and more bonds) people will want to hold, since they speculate that bond prices will rise when interest rates return to normal. The focus on interest rates is the feature of *Keynes's view of money demand* that distinguishes it from the classical view.

---

[2] See John Maynard Keynes, *The General Theory of Employment, Interest, and Money* (New York: Macmillan, 1936).

While the view that interest rates inevitably return to "normal" is no longer generally accepted, we will see next that economists today do view interest rates on nonmoney assets as an important determinant of money demand for reasons somewhat different than those Keynes suggested.

The Modified Cambridge Theory

One major criticism of the classical view of money demand is that it assumes velocity is constant. As Box 15.2 shows, velocity tends to fluctuate over time, and these changes appear to be related to changes in interest rates. Keynes's view that money demand depends on interest rates provides a way to explain fluctuations in money demand that changes in income cannot account for.

To see this, let us modify the Cambridge theory to allow the Cambridge constant to decrease when interest rates rise according to the functional relation $k = k(i)$. Under this view, k is no longer a constant but varies with interest rates. In this case, we will call k the **Cambridge k** instead of the *Cambridge constant* to emphasize that it is no longer assumed to be constant. This **modified Cambridge theory** gives rise to a demand for real money balances of the form

$$\frac{M^d}{P} = k(i)\, Y.$$

Since $k(i)$ is assumed to be a decreasing function of interest rates, we see that money demand is inversely related to interest rates: As interest rates rise, individuals will hold a smaller fraction of their real incomes in real money balances and more in bonds (k decreases), and the quantity demanded of real balances will decline. This modification of the Cambridge model is clearly consistent with Keynes's view of money demand. It also suggests that fluctuations in interest rates will give rise to fluctuations in the demand for real money balances—something the classical view does not imply.

How is the modified Cambridge theory related to the evidence that velocity is not constant? The Cambridge k may be viewed as the reciprocal of velocity: $k(i) = 1/V(i)$. When interest rates rise, the Cambridge k falls, which means velocity must rise. Intuitively, the higher the interest rate, the more rapidly individuals will convert idle money balances into goods or other assets, since the opportunity cost of holding money has increased. This higher velocity, in turn, reduces the quantity demanded of real money balances. We can more clearly see this link by using equation 15.4 and the relation $k(i) = 1/V(i)$ to write the modified Cambridge specification of money demand in terms of velocity:

$$\frac{M^d}{P} = k(i)\, Y = \frac{1}{V(i)}\, Y.$$

The Data Bank

Box 15.2

Velocity and Interest Rates

Is velocity constant as the classical economists argued, or does it rise when interest rates rise as Keynes's theory of money demand suggested? The accompanying figure shows the relationship between the velocity of M1 and the interest rate on six-month commercial paper over the period

1975 to 1992. Notice velocity tended to rise when interest rates rose and decline as interest rates fell. Velocity peaked in 1981, when interest rates were near an all-time high. Since then interest rates have declined substantially, as has velocity.

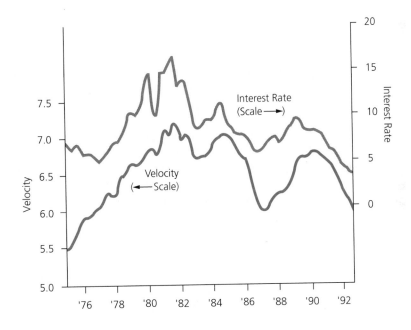

Sources for data: U.S. Department of Commerce, Bureau of Economic Analysis, *Survey of Current Business,* various issues. Board of Governors of the Federal Reserve System, *Federal Reserve Bulletin,* various issues; Citibase electronic database.

The modified Cambridge theory generalizes the earlier views of money demand. First, it allows real income and interest rates to affect the demand for real money balances, just as Keynes argued in his writings. Second, it provides an explanation for why velocity is not constant: Velocity rises when interest rates rise and declines when interest rates fall, as Box 15.2 shows.

Despite this feature of the modified Cambridge theory, the theory has been criticized because it is an ad hoc justification for interest rates to affect money demand. For this reason, economists began searching for microeconomic justifications for Keynes's view that interest rates affect money demand. The two most important such models are the inventory approach and the portfolio approach, which we discuss next.

The Inventory Approach to Money Demand

The **inventory approach to money demand,** pioneered by William Baumol and James Tobin in the 1950s,[3] provides a microeconomic justification for including interest rates as a determinant of money demand. Like the simple quantity theory and the Cambridge theory, this approach also stresses the importance of using money for transaction purposes. In fact, it says money is held only because it is useful for making transactions. But the inventory approach also considers the direct and indirect costs of holding money for transaction purposes and explains how changes in those costs will affect money demand.

The inventory approach is perhaps most relevant for flow-of-funds managers at multimillion-dollar corporations. But to keep dollar figures manageable, we will use a very simple example to illustrate the basic ideas. Our example focuses on the demand for money in the form of M1, but the basic ideas can be extended to the demand for broader monetary aggregates.

Consider Sue, a worker who is paid monthly. She is paid on the first day of the month and receives $3,000. Her monthly expenditures are also $3,000 and are spread evenly throughout the month, so she spends $100 per day. Sue's question is how much of her check to keep as money (in the form of M1) and how much to keep in less liquid assets. One answer might be to keep the entire $3,000 in M1 (cash or checkable deposits), since she knows she will spend it by the end of the month. This has some benefits, as we will see, but it also has some costs. The costs are that Sue will lose whatever interest she could have earned by using some of the funds to invest in another asset (like a bond or a savings account) for part of the month. The benefits are that she avoids the cost and bother of investing in some other asset and then disinvesting a few weeks later, when she needs money for purchases.

---

[3] See William J. Baumol, "The Transactions Approach to Demand for Cash: An Inventory Theoretic Approach," *Quarterly Journal of Economics,* 66 (November 1952), 545–556, and James Tobin, "The Interest Elasticity of Transactions Demand for Cash," *Review of Economics and Statistics,* 38 (August 1956), 241–247.

To be more specific, suppose the interest rate on a savings account is 1 percent each month, or .01. This translates into about 12 percent annual interest; this is a fairly high rate, but it will keep our calculations simple. Assume money in the form of currency or checkable deposits pays no interest. Also assume the cost of going to the bank or otherwise transferring funds from the savings account into money is $15. This can be a fee the bank charges or simply a dollar value of hassling with the bank. How should Sue manage her income?

Suppose Sue keeps the entire $3,000 in the form of M1. If she does so, she pays only one fee—the $15 for cashing her check—and gives up the potential to earn interest on her funds. In fact, with $3,000 at the start of the month, her average money holdings are $1,500, so her lost interest earnings are $1,500 × .01 = $15. The fact that her average money holdings are one-half her initial money holdings is evident in part a of Figure 15.1. Here Sue's money holdings are plotted on the vertical axis, while the days of the month are on the horizontal axis. She starts with $3,000, and spends $100 per day every day of the month. Halfway through the month she has $1,500 left, which is her average holdings over the month. By the end of the month she has no money holdings, but she will receive another paycheck and can start the process anew. Since her average money holdings are $1,500, she *gives up* $15 each month in potential interest earnings by choosing to hold all her income in the form of M1. Of course, she also pays $15 in fees at the beginning of the month, so her total cost of holding M1 is $30.

An alternative Sue might want to consider is to take her check for $3,000 and split it into two equal amounts. The first $1,500 is held as M1, and the second $1,500 is deposited in her savings account. After 15 days she will have spent the first $1,500, so she returns to the bank and withdraws the remaining $1,500 from her savings account, using these funds to pay for her purchases in the remaining 15 days. What are the costs of this plan? First, she has to visit the bank twice, and these costs are $15 × 2, or $30. Second, she gives up interest on $1,500 for an entire month and interest on the other $1,500 for half a month. We can calculate her average money holdings using part b of Figure 15.1. When the month begins, she holds $1,500 in money, which she spends at $100 a day until the money is exhausted on day 15. Then she goes to the bank and withdraws the remaining $1,500, which she also spends at $100 per day until the end of the month. Her average money holdings in this case are $750, or $1,500/2 (or, for later reference, $3,000/4), so the interest costs are $750 × .01 = $7.50. Her total cost of holding M1, including the $30 in bank fees, is $37.50.

Still another alternative is for Sue to split her $3,000 into three equal amounts. She holds the first $1,000 as M1 and then uses the remaining $2,000 to deposit in her savings account. After 10 days she will have spent the first $1,000, so she returns to the bank and withdraws $1,000 from her savings account. This lasts her until day 20, at which time she returns to the bank and withdraws the remaining $1,000 from her savings account. For

Figure 15.1
Money Holdings and the Inventory Approach

In part a, Sue holds all $3,000 of income as money at the beginning of the month. Every day she spends $100, until by the end of the month she has spent the entire $3,000 and the money is replenished by another payday. In this case, average money holdings during the month are $1,500.

In part b, Sue holds only $1,500 of income in the form of money at the beginning of the month and holds the remaining $1,500 as an interest-bearing asset. Every day she spends $100, until by the end of the 15th day she has spent the entire $1,500. On this day the $1,500 nonmoney asset is converted into money, and Sue spends $100 per day until the 30th day, when this sum too is exhausted and the funds are replenished by another payday. The average money holdings during the month are $750.

In part c, Sue holds only $1,000 of income as money at the beginning of the month and holds the remaining $2,000 as an interest-bearing asset. Sue spends $100 every day, so by the end of the 10th day the initial $1,000 is exhausted. On this day, Sue withdraws $1,000 of the interest-bearing asset to hold as money. This lasts until the 20th day, at which time she again withdraws $1,000 to hold as money. Average money holdings during the month are $500.

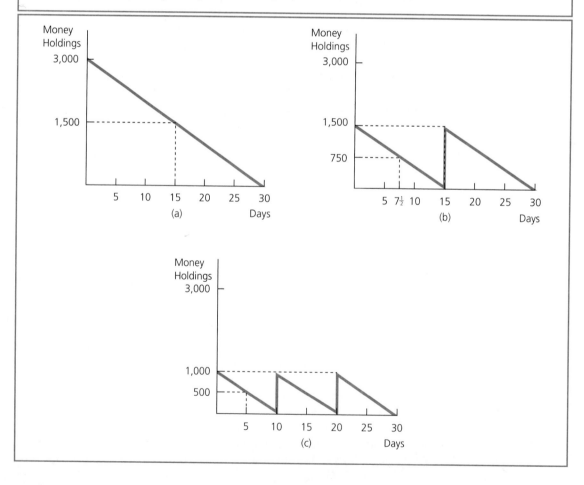

this plan, her costs include three trips to the bank, or $45 ($15 $\times$ 3). Also, her lost interest earnings are calculated as follows. First, as part c of Figure 15.1 shows, her money holdings over any 10-day period start at $1,000 and decline to zero, so her average holdings are $1,000/2, or $500. (For later reference, note that we can calculate this as $3,000/6.) The interest cost of holding this money is $500 $\times$ .01, or $5. Her costs also include $45 in bank fees, for a total cost of $50.

By now a pattern has emerged. The more trips Sue makes to the bank, the higher is her cost in terms of bank fees. But the more trips she makes, the lower are her holdings of M1 and hence the lower is her opportunity cost of lost interest. We can formalize our example as follows. If we let the number of trips to the bank be N, the cost of bank fees is $15 \times N$. Interest costs are the interest rate times her average money holdings. Average money holdings can be determined by the formula $3,000/2N$, so the costs of lost interest are .01 $\times$ $3,000/2N$. (You can verify the formula for average money holdings by letting N equal 1, 2, or 3 and comparing the results with our earlier calculations.) The total costs of one trip are $30, which is lower than that for two trips ($37.50) or for three trips ($50). Thus, given the bank's fees, the interest rate, and her income, Sue minimizes the cost of holding money in the form of M1 by making one trip to the bank each month.

Now let's see what happens if Sue's monthly income, and thus her spending, increases. Suppose Sue gets a hefty raise and her income rises from $3,000 to $12,000 per month. Thus, Sue now earns $12,000 per month and spends $12,000 per month. We can use our formulas to find the interest costs of holding money in the form of M1. The interest cost of making one trip to the bank is .01 $\times$ $12,000/2 = $60, that of two trips is .01 $\times$ $12,000/4 = $30, and that of three trips is .01 $\times$ $12,000/6 = $20. Adding these interest costs to the bank fees per trip reveals that the total cost of one trip to the bank is $60 + $15 = $75, that of two trips is $30 + $30 = $60, and that of three trips is $20 + $45 = $65. (Four trips would cost $15 + $60 = $75.) Obviously two trips minimizes Sue's total costs of holding M1, and with two trips her average holdings of M1 rise to $12,000/4 = $3,000.

What do we conclude about the effect of the increase in income on Sue's optimal money holdings? The increase in income (and in spending) led to an increase in her average holdings of M1. This is in accord with the basic idea of the simple quantity theory of money demand, and more generally, the transactions motive for holding money: Increases in spending will require larger amounts of money. However, the view of Keynes and the classical economists was that an increase in spending leads to a proportional increase in money demand. Thus, a doubling of spending would lead to a doubling of money demand. This is not the case in the inventory approach. In our example, for instance, we had a fourfold increase in income and spending, from $3,000 to $12,000. In this inventory approach, average money holdings increased only from $1,500 to $3,000, or by a factor of 2. This is but an example of a general feature of the inventory approach: Money demand increases only with the square root of the increase in income. Thus, if income doubles, money demand increases by $\sqrt{2}$, or by a factor of about 1.4. If income increases by a factor of 4, money demand increases by a factor of $\sqrt{4}$, or 2.

How does a rise in interest rates affect money demand under the inventory approach? It increases the opportunity cost of holding money and therefore leads to lower real money balances. When the interest rate increases, the cost of holding money rises, and we can calculate this cost for each number of trips to the bank from our previous formula for the interest costs. That formula was $.01 \times \$3,000/2N$, and we merely replace the interest rate with the higher rate of .04. Thus, interest costs rise to $.04 \times \$3,000/2N$. With one trip to the bank, interest costs are $60. Two trips lower interest costs to $30, and three trips lower them still further, to $20. With the higher interest rate, total costs of one trip to the bank are $60 + $15 = $75, while two trips cost $30 + $30 = $60 and three trips cost $20 + $45 = $65. Due to the higher interest rate, it pays Sue to make two trips to the bank each month instead of one to minimize her total cost of holding money.

What does the rise in the interest rate imply about Sue's holdings of M1? Average money holdings with two trips to the bank fall from $1,500 to $3,000/4 = $750. Thus, the increase in the interest rate caused Sue to hold less M1 and to hold more funds in her savings account. This is a general implication of the inventory approach: Increases in the interest rate result in a reduction in money demand.

The inventory approach we outlined here thus provides a microeconomic justification for Keynes's view of money demand. First, money demand is inversely related to the interest rate. Second, when income increases, real money demand rises as well. But in contrast to the classical view (and even the view of Keynes himself), when income rises by some percentage—say, 100 percent—money demand rises by less than 100 percent; as income increases, money holdings rise, but not as quickly. This finding is in part due to the assumption that the fee for converting the nonmoney asset into money does not change with income, nor does it change with the size of the transfer from the nonmoney asset into money. Changing either assumption would alter somewhat the prediction that money demand rises with the square root of the rise in income, but it would not alter the main qualitative result that money demand both increases with rises in income and decreases with rises in the interest rate.

The Portfolio Approach to Money Demand

The **portfolio approach to money demand** (also called the *asset approach*) was developed in the 1950s by James Tobin[4] and provides an alternative

---

[4] See James Tobin, "Liquidity Preference as Behavior Towards Risk," *Review of Economics Studies,* 25 (February 1958), 65–86.

justification for Keynes's view that interest rates affect money demand. The portfolio approach analyzes the decision by moneyholders to allocate their wealth between other assets and money. Other assets like bonds pay interest but are subject to the risk of price fluctuations and/or default. In contrast, money bears little or no interest but is not subject to these types of risk.

The Cambridge economists and Keynes argued that money is also held because it is a store of wealth, but they did not formally analyze how an individual would go about determining how much money to hold. Moreover, they did not consider the effects of risk on the desire to hold bonds or money. Tobin formally modeled the decision to hold money in an environment of risk and found that wealth and interest rates are key determinants of money demand.

The portfolio approach assumes the only reason money is held is that it is a safe asset. Stocks or bonds may go up or down in value, and investors will experience capital gains or losses when this happens, but this does not occur when they hold money. The portfolio approach stresses that unlike risky assets like bonds, money is not subject to such risk.

How does the presence of an asset that is not subject to these types of risk, like money, affect how individuals allocate their wealth between money and other assets? Most people like the return they could get from holding stocks or bonds but dislike risk. As we learned in Chapter 9, such people are called *risk averse*. They may choose to invest a portion of their portfolios in a safe asset like money. The key idea is that the proportion of money and bonds in a person's portfolio determines both the average return and the risk of that portfolio. The more money, the lower the average return, but also the lower the risk. The more bonds or stocks, the greater the average return, but also the greater the risk. Individuals with differing degrees of risk aversion will choose different mixes of money and risky assets to hold in their portfolios. Those who are very risk averse may choose to hold only money, while those who are risk neutral may prefer to hold only stocks.

Tobin used this reasoning to examine what happens to money holdings when the average rates of return on bonds and stocks changes. For example, if the average returns on bonds and stocks increases, what will happen to the proportion of money holdings in a portfolio? In this case, two effects may counteract. One effect is the **substitution effect,** in which the higher return on bonds and stocks means that now a higher reward—that is, a higher return—is available to investors for accepting any given level of risk. This higher return means the rewards for accepting risk have increased, and investors are induced to hold more stocks and bonds. Thus, the substitution effect unambiguously predicts that an increase in returns on stocks and bonds will tend to reduce money holdings.

The second effect is the **income effect** (sometimes called a *wealth effect* in this context), in which the higher returns on stocks and bonds leave a person with more income (or more wealth). When wealth increases, people may decide to accept more or less risk, depending on their preferences. Intuition suggests what is regarded as the usual case: The increase in wealth will lead individuals to accept more risk. But this need not be the case. If higher wealth leads an individual to accept more risk, the wealth effect occurs in the same direction as the substitution effect, indicating a higher return on stocks and bonds will lead to reduced money holdings. However, if higher wealth leads an individual to desire less risk, the wealth effect occurs in the direction opposite that of the substitution effect, and the net effect is ambiguous.

The portfolio approach thus implies that money demand depends on interest rates and that money is an important component of a portfolio only because it is a safe asset, not because it is useful as a medium of exchange. Critics naturally argue that many assets dominate the return to holding money, especially assets that dominate the return on money in the form of currency or demand deposits (M1). For example, savings deposits at insured banks are as risk free as checking accounts and currency, but they earn higher interest. The logical conclusion, based on the portfolio approach, is that individuals would never choose to hold assets in the form of M1, because they could earn a higher interest rate on other risk-free assets like those included in M2. Doing so would increase the overall return on the portfolio, with no increase in risk.

The punch is that Tobin's portfolio approach does not explain why people hold currency and demand deposits that are dominated in return by other risk-free assets. The only explanation for holding these forms of money lies in the transactions motive, which is absent in the portfolio approach to money demand. The portfolio approach can, however, explain the demand for monetary assets like savings deposits or Treasury bills, which are included in broader measures of the money stock like M2 or L. For these reasons, the portfolio approach provides an incomplete explanation of why people hold money and does not explain why the demand for narrow measures of the money stock (like M1) vary with interest rates.[5] Box 15.3 discusses an extension of the portfolio approach.

Summary Exercise 15.1

In our example of the inventory approach, we started with income of $3,000, an interest rate of .01, and fees of $15 per transaction. We asked what happens if income increases to $12,000 while fees and interest rates stay constant. However, in one interpretation the fees on transactions are the cost to the individual of the time and effort expended in going to the bank and switching funds from savings into money in the form of currency or checkable deposits. This opportunity cost of time may be proportional to income. Thus, if the fee is $15 when income is $3,000, it should be $60 when income

---

[5] Recently economists have developed cash-in-advance models that extend Tobin's model along these lines. These models are based on the notion that some purchases (e.g., hamburgers from McDonald's or Wendy's) require cash payment, thus providing a reason people might hold forms of M1 even though they are dominated in return by assets contained in M2.

Inside Money

Box 15.3

Currency Substitution

Currency substitution is the idea that domestic residents consider domestic and foreign currencies to be relatively close substitutes. Because of this, demand for the domestic money depends not only on domestic spending and opportunity cost variables but also on the rate of return on the foreign currency. The idea of currency substitution is a bold extension of the portfolio view of money demand. In this case, the demand for the domestic currency depends on factors external to the domestic economy, including influences from foreign policy decisions.

The currency substitution hypothesis has been extensively investigated. This is due partly to its policy implications. In a world of flexible exchange rates, the domestic central bank is supposed to be able to pursue monetary policy independently of the policy pursued by foreign central banks. The idea is that differential monetary policies will cause exchange rate movements but will not affect real output or employment. However, the currency substitution hypothesis restores the ability of foreign policy actions to affect the domestic economy. Under this hypothesis, changes in foreign monetary policy that alter the relative rate of return on the foreign currency will lead to changes in demand for the domestic currency and hence changes in the domestic interest rate or the level of real money balances.

Does currency substitution really exist? It does not seem reasonable to presume the average U.S. citizen holds much foreign currency or responds to changes in the rate of return on foreign currency. At the same time, other countries may have a different experience. Indeed, casual empirical evidence suggests that countries experiencing high rates of inflation—high rates of depreciation in the values of their currencies—often see their citizens begin holding and using a foreign currency for portfolio reasons and even for transactions. Thus, several South American countries experiencing high inflation in the 1980s saw an increased use of the U.S. dollar as citizens substituted away from the domestic currency.

Formal studies of currency substitution have yielded mixed results. One study by Bana and Handa reports finding currency substitution in Canada under the flexible exchange rate regime, in which Canadian money demand responded to the rate of return on the U.S. dollar. Bergstrand and Bundt also report evidence of currency substitution between a number of currencies and the U.S. dollar. Their study included the currencies of Canada, Italy, Switzerland, the United Kingdom, and West Germany and emphasizes that evidence of currency substitution is most likely to be found when looking at relationships over long time spans. Over short spans, the evidence is less supportive of the currency substitution hypothesis.

Sources: Ismail Mahomed Bana and Jagdish Handa, "Currency Substitution: A Multicountry Study for Canada," *International Economic Journal,* 1 (Autumn 1987), 71–85; Dallas S. Batten and R. W. Hafer, "Money, Income, and Currency Substitution: Evidence from Three Countries," *Federal Reserve Bank of St. Louis Review,* 67 (May 1985), 27–35; Jeffrey H. Bergstrand and Thomas P. Bundt, "Currency Substitution and Monetary Autonomy: The Foreign Demand for U.S. Demand Deposits," *Journal of International Money and Finance,* 9 (1990), 325–334.

is $12,000. (a) If fees and income rise by the same factor of 4 (to $60 and $12,000 respectively) what happens to average money holdings and to the number of trips to the bank under the inventory approach? (b) Is your finding in part a consistent with what the modified Cambridge theory would predict?

Answer: (a) The increase in income raises interest costs to .01 × $12,000/2N. One trip to the bank costs $60 in lost interest, two trips cost $30, three trips cost $20, and four trips cost $15. Fees for trips to the bank also rise to $60 × N, or $60, for one trip, $120 for two trips, $180 for three trips, and so on. The total cost of one trip is $60 + $60 = $120, that of two trips is $30 + $120 = $150, and that of three trips is $20 + $180 = $200. Clearly one trip to the bank is the best choice. Average money holdings increase to $12,000/2 = $6,000. (b) Notice that income has increased by a factor of 4, and so have average money holdings, from $1,500 to $6,000. Thus, in this case the inventory model predicts that money demand will increase in the same proportion as income. That is, with fees proportional to income, money demand will be proportional to income just as in the modified Cambridge theory (and the classical theories, for that matter).

THE MODERN QUANTITY THEORY OF MONEY DEMAND

Our discussion of the classical and Keynesian views of money demand has demonstrated some of the properties we would expect money demand to satisfy. In particular, money demand should increase when income rises, decline when interest rates increase, and increase when the risk of holding other assets increases. The **modern quantity theory of money demand** builds on the simple quantity theory by emphasizing the unique property of money as the medium of exchange. However, the modern quantity theory combines this emphasis on transactions motives for holding money with a consideration of the other determinants of money demand that are present in Keynes's view and in Tobin's portfolio approach to money demand. Thus, the modern quantity theory incorporates the insights gained from these alternative approaches to money demand while maintaining the concept of money as being uniquely valuable as the medium of exchange.

The modern quantity theory was pioneered by Milton Friedman in the mid-1950s.[6] It describes the determinants of money demand, the factors that indicate how much money households and businesses will demand. Friedman viewed money demand as being similar to the demand for any durable good. For example, a car is valued because it provides a stream of transportation services that lasts many years. A house is valued because it provides a stream

---

[6] Milton Friedman, "The Quantity Theory of Money: A Restatement," in M. Friedman, ed., *Studies in the Quantity Theory of Money* (Chicago: University of Chicago Press, 1956).

of housing services for many years. Money is valued because it provides a stream of purchasing power services; that is, it can be used to purchase goods and services.

Friedman emphasized that both individuals and businesses demand money. Individuals hold money to buy goods, but it is just one of a number of assets in their portfolios. Businesses hold money because it serves as a factor of production, making it easier for them to pay for inputs needed in production. To buy inputs, it is easier for firms to send a check or electronically wire funds than to engage in nonmonetary exchanges like barter. Firms also need money to facilitate sales. Imagine how few Big Macs your local McDonald's would sell if it didn't have cash on hand to make change!

Friedman organized the factors that influence individual and business demand for real money balances into three broad categories: (1) individual wealth and the scale of business activities, (2) factors that influence the opportunity cost of holding money, and (3) tastes and preferences.

Individual Wealth and the Scale of Business Activity

In the tradition of the quantity theory, Friedman viewed the primary motive for holding money to be its use in facilitating transactions. However, Friedman broadened the classical economists' view of variables that are related to this transactions demand for money. He reasoned that the *real wealth* of individuals determines the size of their portfolios, which are allocated among money and other assets. It also determines how many transactions can be made. In fact, wealth plays the same role here as income does in the classical theory of money demand. But the role of wealth is broader in that it allows individuals to spend more than their current incomes on goods. The reason is that wealth is a stock—the accumulation of assets over time. You can spend more than your current income if you draw on your wealth (by selling your car or using past savings). Like increases in income in the classical view, increases in wealth in the modern quantity theory lead to increases in purchasing power and spending and thus to a rise in the demand for real money balances.

Friedman also discussed the importance of the liquidity of wealth, that is, the ease with which wealth can be transformed into money. The easier it is to convert wealth held as stocks, bonds, houses, or cars into money, the less attractive it will be to hold money, and vice versa. Friedman acknowledged that much of an individual's wealth is in the form of **human capital,** the skills and training an individual acquires that makes her or him a productive employee or entrepreneur. Such wealth is not liquid. It can be rented at a wage rate to an employer, but it cannot be sold outright because human capital cannot be separated from the individual, and slavery is illegal. Because human capital is illiquid, it may have less of an effect on money demand than do other, more liquid forms of wealth. If an individual decides to switch between bonds and money, this is relatively easy to do, but it is much less easy to switch between the person's human capital and money.

Friedman further broadened the classical view by recognizing the utility of real money balances for business operations. Unlike the individual, the business firm is not constrained by a wealth variable. However, businesses' demand for real money balances depends on a variable that measures the scale of the business, such as the total value of the firm, the firm's total revenue, or some similar measure that indicates the firm's size. Increases in the size of the firm lead to increased numbers of transactions and hence to increased real money balances.

Factors That Influence the Opportunity Cost of Holding Money

While Friedman viewed real wealth as the primary determinant of money demand, he admitted that other factors also influence money demand. He noted, for instance, that individuals and businesses give up the interest they could earn on other assets when they hold money. The interest forgone is the opportunity cost of holding money. Increases in the interest rates on these alternative assets will reduce the amount of money people and businesses hold as they substitute away from money and toward these other assets.

Like Tobin, Friedman also realized that when the risk of holding other assets such as stocks and bonds increases, people will generally want to concentrate more of their portfolios in safe assets such as money. Thus, Friedman reasoned that in times of widespread uncertainty and volatility in financial markets, people will increase their holdings of money.

Furthermore, Friedman pointed out that inflationary expectations might influence the demand for money. Inflation is an ongoing increase in the price level and as such represents an ongoing increase in the prices of goods. When the prices of goods increase at a substantially higher rate than does interest on money holdings, people will tend to hold goods instead of money to earn a higher return. In periods of **hyperinflation,** such as existed in Germany in the 1920s, when the inflation rate exceeded 1 million percent, people may actually resort to barter rather than hold money. Carrying around loaves of bread to trade for steak is certainly an inconvenience. But during periods of hyperinflation, it is much more costly to leave your house to buy a $100 steak, only to find that it costs $200 by the time you arrive at the butcher. If you hold bread instead of money, the price of bread will grow at the rate of inflation while you are on your way to the butcher. For these reasons, Friedman believed a rise in the expected inflation rate increases the expected opportunity cost of holding money and results in a reduction in the amount of real money balances people will hold.

Tastes and Preferences

Finally, Friedman included a catch-all category called *tastes* that influences the demand for real money balances. For instance, if people's tastes or preferences for risk change, this will change how they split their portfolios of assets among safe assets like money and risky assets like stocks or bonds. If people become more willing to accept risk, they might hold more bonds and less money.

MONEY DEMAND: AN HISTORICAL NOTE AND CURRENT THOUGHT

We conclude our survey of money demand by noting the considerable overlap in the theories of Fisher, Keynes, and Friedman, and by pointing out that their views were shaped by the work of economists over several hundred years. We also present the main model of money demand that is widely accepted and used by economists today to analyze the effects of monetary policy.

An Historical Note[7]

While Fisher, Keynes, and Friedman were the first economists to formalize money demand in the modern era of checkable deposits, we need to understand two points to put their views in context. First, their theories are in many respects only refinements of the verbal arguments of economists in the seventeenth, eighteenth, and nineteenth centuries, who discussed money demand at a time when money consisted of gold and silver coins. The first discussion of velocity and its determinants appeared in Sir William Petty's writings in the 1660s. He identified *income,* among other things, as a key determinant of velocity. In the 1690s, John Locke made the link between velocity and money demand more explicit and introduced the *interest rate* as an important determinant since it represents the opportunity cost of holding money. Richard Cantillon extended the work of Petty and Locke in 1775 by introducing *expectations* into velocity, and Henry Thorton, J. B. Say, and Nassau Senior incorporated inflationary expectations in the early 1800s. Thus, by the 1800s most of the variables that might influence the demand for money were already known. In a sense, all Fisher, Keynes, and Friedman did was popularize and refine the ideas of their predecessors.

The second point is that our earlier presentations of Fisher's, Keynes's, and Friedman's views on money demand are very simplified in that we merely highlighted what each viewed as the *primary* determinants of money demand. Fisher tended to emphasize the impact of *real income* on money demand, Keynes stressed the *interest rate,* and Friedman emphasized *real wealth* (in later writings, Friedman referred to real wealth as *permanent income*). A closer look at their writings, however, reveals they all recognized that other variables could influence money demand. For instance, Fisher's

---

[7] This section is based on the excellent survey by Thomas M. Humphrey, ''The Origins of Velocity Functions,'' *Economic Quarterly,* 79 (Fall 1993), 1–17.

specification of velocity actually included most of the variables contained in Friedman's modern quantity theory, including interest rates, expected inflation, real income, and tastes. Indeed, there is considerable overlap among each of these views of money demand; the primary differences are in their emphasis.

Current Thought

After centuries of reflection, economists today recognize that many variables might influence money demand. However, the evidence suggests that two main variables influence the demand for real money balances, be it in the form of M1 or M2 (see Box 15.4). The first is a scale variable, such as real wealth or income. This affects money demand because greater real wealth or income leads to more purchases, which in turn require additional real money balances. The second variable reflects the opportunity cost of holding real money balances, such as the interest rate. Thus, the conventional demand function for real money balances used today can be summarized by

$$(M/P)^d = L^d(Y, i),$$

where Y is real income and i is the interest rate.

Notice that the demand for money can be expressed in nominal or in real terms. Money is demanded in part to purchase goods and services, so increases in the price level raise the amount of money required to purchase a given amount of goods. If the price level increases, money demand rises proportionally. But if we write money demand in real terms as above, then, if everything else remains the same, an increase in the price level, P, leads to a proportional increase in the quantity of money demanded, M, so that real money demand—the ratio of M to P—stays the same.

Figure 15.2 illustrates real money demand. On the vertical axis is the interest rate on nonmonetary assets (like bonds), while on the horizontal axis we graph the real quantity of money demanded. For reasons we explained throughout the chapter, a rise in the interest rate increases the opportunity cost of holding money and therefore leads to a reduction in the quantity of real money balances demanded. This gives the demand for real money balances its downward slope. Notice that a rise in real income increases the demand for real money balances, as represented by a rightward shift in the demand curve. The reason is that greater real income generally implies more purchases, thus requiring more real money balances at each interest rate.

EQUILIBRIUM IN THE MONEY MARKET

Our analysis of money demand in this chapter, along with the model of money supply we developed in Chapter 14, now allows us to determine equilibrium between the demand for and supply of money. Recall there are

The Data Bank

Box 15.4

Money Demand in the United States

The theories of money demand examined in the text suggest that many variables might affect money demand. Empirical evidence suggests, however, that real income (GDP) and interest rates are the primary factors influencing the demand for real money balances. Since we explored M1 in Box 15.2, we now look at how well these theories stack up when we look at a broader measure of the money supply, that measured by M2. The accompanying figure

plots real money balances in the United States (defined as the money aggregate M2 divided by the price level) along with real GDP (part a). Part b shows the relationship between real money balances and the six-month commercial paper interest rate.

In part a, we see that the hypothesized relationship between real M2 demand and real income holds fairly closely: Decreases in real M2

Continued on p. 512

(a) U.S. Recessions and the Behavior of Real GDP and Real M2, 1972–1992

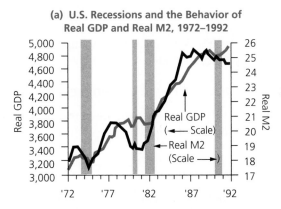

(b) Real M2 Money Balances and Six–Month Commercial Paper Rate, 1972–1992

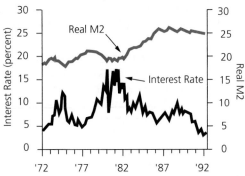

Continued from p. 511

accompany periods of slow growth or declines in real GDP. The shaded regions correspond with periods of recession. Notice that with the exception of the recession in the early 1980s, the decline in real GDP during those recessions was accompanied by a fall in real money balances.

Part b shows the extent to which changes in interest rates affect real M2 balances. The graph indicates that increases in the interest rate such as that in the mid-1970s or the late 1970s and early 1980s were accompanied by reductions in real M2, just as we would predict from our theories of money demand. However, since

many assets in M2 (like savings and time deposits) pay interest, the effect of changes in interest rates on M2 was less pronounced than that we saw when we looked at M1 in Box 15.2. In effect, higher interest rates affected the opportunity cost of holding M1 more than it did that of holding M2, since the rates paid on M2 balances tended to rise when rates paid on commercial paper and bonds increased.

———————————

Sources: Board of Governors of the Federal Reserve System, *Federal Reserve Bulletin,* various issues; U.S. Department of Commerce, Bureau of Economic Analysis, *Survey of Current Business,* various issues; Citibase electronic database.

two views on money supply. The first is that the money supply is exogenous; the quantity of money supplied does not change with changes in the interest rate. The second is that the money supply is endogenous; the quantity of money supplied fluctuates with changes in the interest rate.

Equilibrium with an Exogenous Money Supply

In Chapter 14, we saw that the money supply equals the money multiplier times the monetary base, or

$$M^s = \left[\frac{1 + c^d}{rr + e^d + c^d} \right] MB,$$

where c^d is the desired currency to deposit ratio, rr is the required reserve ratio, and e^d is the desired excess reserve ratio. If the money multiplier is exogenous, and in particular does not respond to changes in the interest rate, the money supply does not vary with changes in the interest rate.

The real money supply curve is the exogenous money supply, M^s, divided by the price level, P, or M^s/P. In this case, the real money supply is perfectly inelastic; the money supply curve is vertical as shown in Figure 15.3. In this graph, the vertical axis measures the interest rate on nonmonetary assets like bonds, while the quantity of real money balances, M/P, is measured on the horizontal axis. The money demand curve is downward sloping as it is in Figure 15.2. The intersection of the real money supply and demand curves at point A determines the equilibrium interest rate, i_0. With an exogenous money supply, the equilibrium quantity of real money balances is determined solely by the position of the real money supply curve.

Figure 15.2
Demand for Real Money Balances

Movements along the real money demand curve are caused by a change in the interest rate, which alters the opportunity cost of holding money. For example, starting from point A on $(M/P)^d$, an increase in the interest rate raises the opportunity cost of holding money. This leads to a movement along the money demand curve to point B, where the quantity demanded of real money balances is lower. An increase in real income shifts real money demand to the right, since more real money balances are desired at each interest rate to accommodate more transactions. A decline in real income shifts the demand for real money balances to the left.

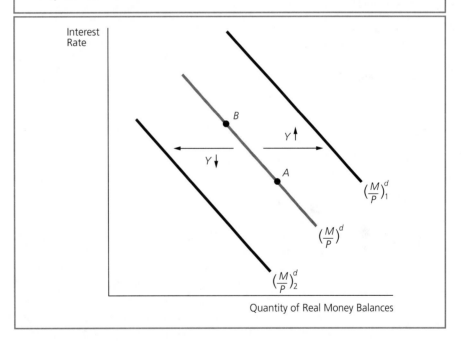

Notice that an interest rate below i_0 would result in a shortage of real money balances, since individuals and businesses would want to hold more real money balances than the amount supplied at that interest rate. This would put pressure on the interest rate to rise. As the interest rate increased, the quantity demanded of real money balances would fall, because individuals and firms would find it more attractive to hold less money and more assets earning the higher interest rate, like bonds. Ultimately the interest rate would rise until this imbalance was corrected. Similarly, if the interest rate were above i_0, a surplus of real money balances would occur, putting pressure on the interest rate to fall. Only at point A would there be neither a shortage nor a surplus of real money balances.

The money supply is exogenous in this graph; that is, it is not affected by changes in the interest rate. Thus, the equilibrium quantity of real money balances is determined solely by the position of the money supply curve. The equilibrium interest rate is determined by the intersection of real money demand and real money supply at point A.

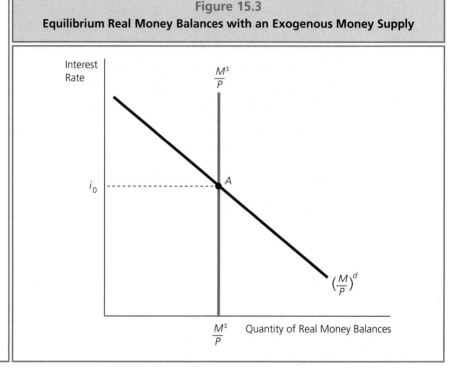

Figure 15.3

Equilibrium Real Money Balances with an Exogenous Money Supply

The real power of our money demand and supply framework is that it provides an easy way to show how monetary policy affects interest rates. As we learned in the previous chapter, the Fed can change the money supply by changing the monetary base (through open market operations) or by taking other actions that affect the money multiplier (like changing reserve requirements or the discount rate). Increases in the monetary base or the money multiplier will shift the real money supply to the right, as will decreases in the price level. Decreases in the monetary base or multiplier, or increases in the price level, will reduce the real money supply, shifting it to the left. Table 15.1 summarizes these variables.

Figure 15.4 illustrates how changes in the money supply affect interest rates. Starting at the initial equilibrium at point A, suppose the Fed increases the money supply through an open market purchase. This shifts the real money supply curve to the right as banks ultimately convert the increase in reserves created by the open market purchase into loans that wind up as new deposits at banks. The result is a new equilibrium at point B, where the equilibrium interest rate falls to i_1 as a result of the Fed's easing of credit. Notice that the quantity of real money balances rises to M_1^s/P.

If the Fed tightens credit by reducing the money supply, the result is just the opposite. The equilibrium changes from point A to point C in Figure

> ### Table 15.1
> #### Determinants of the Real Supply of Money
>
> The position of the supply curve for real money balances depends on the monetary base, the required reserve ratio, the excess reserve ratio, the currency to deposit ratio, and the price level. Increases in the monetary base raise the real money supply, while an increase in the required reserve, excess reserve, or currency to deposit ratio or in the price level leads to a decrease in the real money supply.
>
> | Variable | Effect of an Increase in the Variable on the Real Money Supply |
> |---|:---:|
> | Monetary base | + |
> | Required reserve ratio | − |
> | Excess reserve ratio | − |
> | Currency to deposit ratio | − |
> | Price level | − |

15.4, meaning the interest rate rises to i_2 and the equilibrium quantity of real money balances falls to M_2^s/P. The interest rate rises because the Fed's action reduces banking system reserves, which decreases the amount of loans banks make. Thus, our money demand and supply framework shows how actions by the Fed influence interest rates in the economy.

Notice that changes in the price level also change the real supply of money, even if the nominal money supply remains unchanged. For instance, holding the nominal money supply constant, a decrease in the price level increases the ratio of M^s to P, thus shifting the real money supply curve to the right. This results in lower interest rates. In particular, when the price level falls goods become cheaper, and if the interest rate did not fall the economy would have more real money balances than needed to make transactions. As idle real money balances are converted into other assets like bonds, downward pressure is exerted on the interest rate until a new equilibrium occurs at a lower interest rate.

Equilibrium with an Endogenous Money Supply

In Chapter 14 we developed our model of the endogenous money supply curve, which views the currency to deposit ratio, c^d, and the excess reserve ratio, e^d, as decreasing functions of interest rates. This gives rise to an upward-sloping money supply curve. Figure 15.5 graphs the endogenous real money supply and real money demand. Again the interest rate on loans is on the vertical axis. The real money supply curve is upward sloping, because increases in the interest rate lead to a higher money multiplier and

Figure 15.4
Impact of Changes in an Exogenous Money Supply on Equilibrium

Changes in the exogenous money supply will cause changes in the equilibrium interest rate and the equilibrium quantity of real money balances. An increase in the real money supply from M^s/P to M_1^s/P will shift the equilibrium from point A to point B, reducing the equilibrium interest rate but increasing the equilibrium quantity of real money balances. A decrease in the real money supply from M^s/P to M_2^s/P will cause the equilibrium to shift from point A to point C, increasing the interest rate and reducing the equilibrium real money stock.

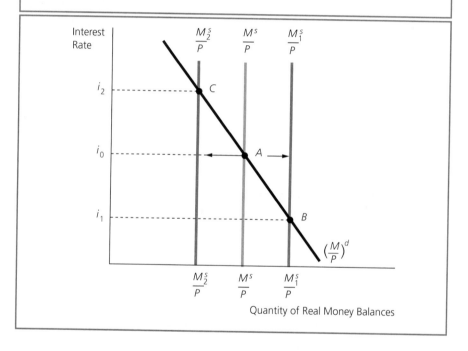

thus to an increase in the quantity of money supplied. The equilibrium in Figure 15.5 is at the intersection of money supply and money demand at point A, where the interest rate is i_0 and M_0/P is the equilibrium quantity of real money balances.

Our analysis of changes in an exogenous money supply is similar to what we learned for the case of an exogenous money supply. A Fed open market purchases increases the monetary base, which shifts the real money supply curve to the right as illustrated in Figure 15.6. The initial equilibrium is at point A, with a real money supply of M^s/P. The increase in the monetary base shifts the real money supply to M_1^s/P, moving equilibrium to point B, where the equilibrium interest rate is lower and the equilibrium quantity of real money balances higher than at point A. Likewise, we can also see the impact of any reduction in the money supply in Figure 15.6. Starting at the

When the money supply curve is endogenous, it slopes upward because a higher interest rate leads to a lower currency to deposit ratio and a lower excess reserve ratio. However, the equilibrium interest rate and the real money stock are still determined by the intersection of the money demand and money supply curves.

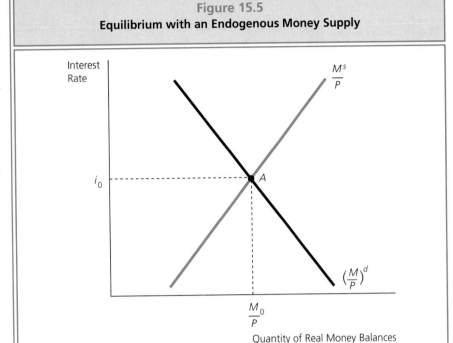

Figure 15.5
Equilibrium with an Endogenous Money Supply

initial equilibrium at point *A*, a reduction in the real money supply causes a leftward shift in the real money supply from M^s/P to M^s_2/P. The new equilibrium that occurs at point *C* has a higher interest rate and a lower equilibrium quantity of real money balances. Thus, we see that the effects of changes in an endogenous money supply are qualitatively the same as those for an endogenous money supply: Increases in the real money supply lead to lower interest rates.[8] For simplicity, we will assume an exogenous money supply in the remainder of our analysis.

Summary Exercise 15.2

If tax rates increase and lead to a rise in tax avoidance activity, how might this affect money supply? How might it affect the interest rate and real money balances? Assume the money supply is exogenous.

Answer: An increase in tax avoidance activity usually means, in part, an increase in cash transactions. This is an increase in the currency to deposit ratio, which lowers the money multiplier and hence the money supply. This

---

[8] However, when the money supply is endogenous, a given change in the money supply results in a smaller change in the interest rate than would occur if the money supply were exogenous.

With an endogenous money supply, increases in the money supply (a rightward shift of the money supply curve) decrease the equilibrium interest rate and raise the equilibrium money stock. Decreases in the money supply (a leftward shift of the money supply curve) increase the equilibrium interest rate and lower the equilibrium money stock.

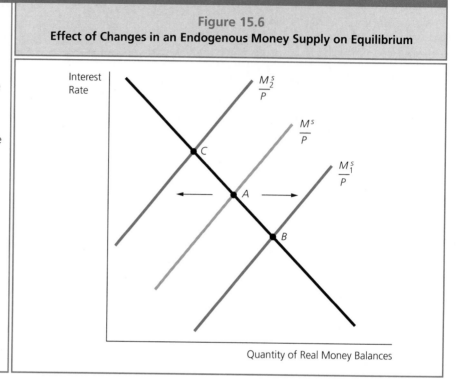

Figure 15.6

Effect of Changes in an Endogenous Money Supply on Equilibrium

reduction in the money supply causes a leftward shift in the real money supply, as illustrated in Figure 15.4 by the shift from M^s/P to M^s_2/P. The interest rate would increase, and the quantity of real money balances would decline.

KEYNESIAN AND MONETARIST VIEWS ON MONEY DEMAND

We have seen that both Keynes and Friedman viewed the demand for real money balances as a decreasing function of interest rates. Despite this similarity, there is considerable disagreement about exactly how much the quantity demanded of money rises when interest rates fall. Followers of John Maynard Keynes, called **Keynesians,** view money demand as relatively sensitive to the interest rate. In contrast, Milton Friedman and other **monetarists** admit that interest rates affect money demand, but view the effect as relatively small. Expressed differently, Keynesians view interest rates as a very important determinant of money demand, whereas monetarists consider it a relatively minor determinant.

We can use our demand and supply framework to shed light on how this seemingly minor difference between Keynesians and monetarists actually leads to a major difference in opinion about the impact of monetary policy. Suppose the Fed decides to increase the money supply in an attempt to lower interest rates and stimulate the economy. Would Keynesians and monetarists agree on the *quantitative* impact of this monetary policy?

Part a of Figure 15.7 illustrates the monetarist view of equilibrium in the money market, and part b shows the Keynesian view. The money demand curve in part a is much steeper than that in part b, reflecting that monetarists believe the quantity demanded of money is not very sensitive to changes in the interest rate. In both cases the initial equilibrium is at point 1 in each part, where the equilibrium interest rate is 5 percent.

Now suppose the monetary base increases due to an open market purchase by the Fed and everything else remains constant (including the price level). Both Keynesians and monetarists would expect this activity to shift

Part a shows the monetarist view of money demand, while part b shows the Keynesian view. Under the monetarist view, an increase in the money supply leads to a large decline in the interest rate, here from 5 to 2 percent. Under the Keynesian view, an increase in the money supply has little effect on interest rates; here it declines only from 5 to 4.5 percent.

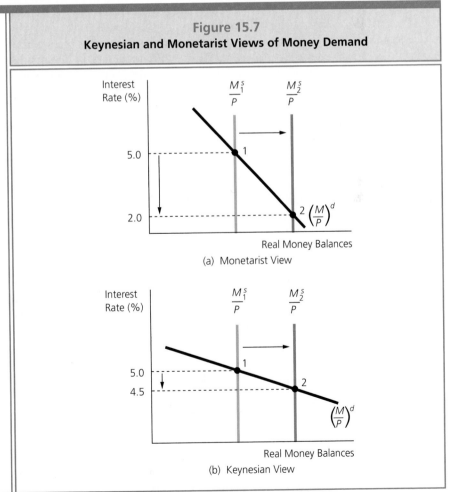

Figure 15.7
Keynesian and Monetarist Views of Money Demand

(a) Monetarist View

(b) Keynesian View

the money supply curve to the right, resulting in a new equilibrium at point 2 in each part of Figure 15.7. But now we see a major difference caused by the seemingly minor differences in the Keynesian and monetarist views of money demand. In part a the interest rate falls to 2 percent, but in part b it falls only to 4.5 percent. Since Keynesians believe the quantity demanded of money is less sensitive to interest rates than monetarists do, Keynesians expect monetary policy to have a relatively minor quantitative impact on interest rates. This illustrates what many view to be an important difference between Keynesians and monetarists. Monetarists view monetary policy as having pronounced effects on the economy (in this case, on interest rates), whereas Keynesians consider the effects of monetary policy to be relatively minor.

We emphasize that the analysis of a one-shot increase in the money supply illustrated in Figure 15.7 assumes everything else remains constant, including the price level. But in Chapter 3, we learned that increases in the money supply eventually lead to rises in the price level. When the price level rises, the real money supply shifts back to the left (since as P increases, M^s/P declines). This ultimately raises interest rates back toward their previous level of 5 percent. Thus, while monetary policy can have a short-run impact on interest rates, in the long run a one-shot increase in the money supply leads to a higher price level, which may ultimately return interest rates to their previous level. Monetarists and many Keynesians believe monetary policy has no long-term effects on interest rates. The disagreement concerns primarily the short-run effects of monetary policy on macroeconomic variables like interest rates.

Summary Exercise 15.3

Would the Keynesian and monetarist views of money demand lead to different conclusions regarding the impact of a reduction in the money supply on interest rates? Explain.

Answer: While both Keynesians and monetarists believe a reduction in the money supply would lead to higher interest rates in the short run, monetarists would expect rates to increase more. In the long run, however, monetarists and Keynesians would agree that the price level would fall and therefore interest rates would tend to rise toward their previous level.

USING THE LOANABLE FUNDS MODEL TO ANALYZE MONETARY POLICY

There is another, equivalent way to look at the impact of monetary policy on interest rates: the loanable funds model we developed in Chapter 4. The money demand/supply and loanable funds frameworks are related because when people demand more money, they in effect supply fewer loanable funds. The more money you hold, the less you have to lend in the bond market. Let us briefly see how the loanable funds approach is an alternative to the money demand/money supply approach we developed earlier.

Suppose the Fed increases the money supply. As we learned in Chapter 14, the primary way the Fed accomplishes this goal is through an open market purchase, which increases the monetary base. The loanable funds approach focuses on the impact of this Fed action in the loanable funds market. In particular, in an open market purchase the Fed purchases existing government securities, effectively financing government debt by "printing money." This reduces the amount of government debt instruments in the loanable funds market, effectively reducing the demand for loanable funds. (Wouldn't your demand for loanable funds decline too if you had the ability to print money?) This is represented by a decrease in the demand for loanable funds in Figure 15.8, which leads to a new equilibrium in the loanable funds market at point B and a lower interest rate. Thus, we reach the same conclusion using the loanable funds approach that we reached earlier with our money demand/money supply framework: An increase in the money supply (caused by an open market purchase) leads to a decline in the interest rate.

Even though both approaches are equivalent, there are advantages to using money demand and supply analysis to evaluate the effects of monetary

The loanable funds approach can also be used to analyze the effects of monetary policy. An increase in the money supply due to an open market purchase reduces the demand for loanable funds. This decreases the interest rate from i_0 to i_1.

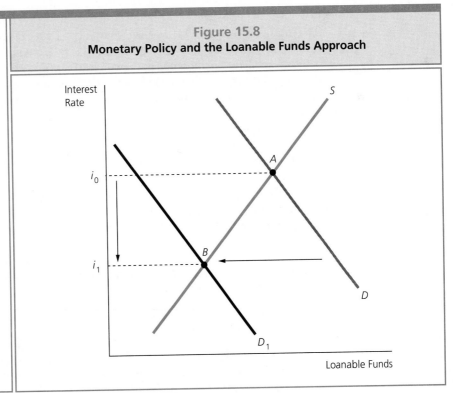

Figure 15.8
Monetary Policy and the Loanable Funds Approach

policy.[9] First, this approach explicitly incorporates factors that cause changes in the money supply and explicitly shows that changes in the *money supply* affect interest rates through its effect on the amount of money supplied. Second, the loanable funds approach focuses on how changes in monetary policy affect interest rates through its effect on the demand for loanable funds, but says nothing about what happens to the equilibrium stock of money in the economy as a result of an open market purchase. Since the amount of money in the economy has far-reaching effects on such variables as the price level, it is more informative to use money demand and supply analysis to see the effects of monetary policy on both the interest rate and the equilibrium stock of money.

While the money demand and supply framework is the easiest way to see how monetary policy or changes in the price level affect interest rates, the loanable funds framework developed in Chapter 4 is the simplest way to see how other changes affect interest rates. For instance, it is generally easier to use the loanable funds framework to see how changes in inflationary expectations or risk affect interest rates. For this reason, the loanable funds and money demand/supply frameworks are complementary tools in analyzing the banking and financial system.

CONCLUSION

The classical economists viewed income as the primary determinant of money demand. Keynes reasoned that money demand depends on interest rates as well as on income, and over the years several models have been developed that provide microeconomic justifications for Keynes's view. The two major models are the inventory approach and the portfolio approach. The modern quantity theory has broadened the view of money demand to include not only income and interest rates but other determinants as well.

Our analysis in this chapter showed how the money demand and money supply framework can be used to analyze monetary policy. The major conclusion from using this approach is that an increase in the money supply leads to a reduction in interest rates, at least in the short run. We also pointed out some disagreements about the magnitude of such effects. Monetarists view monetary policy as having pronounced effects on interest rates in the short run, whereas Keynesians take the view that the short-run effects are small. In Chapters 16, 19, and 20, we discuss monetary policy in more detail and we examine the extent to which Fed policies affect real GDP, the level of employment, and the price level.

---

[9] If you are puzzled by the fact that these seemingly different approaches give identical results, an analogy from arithmetic might help. There are two ways to calculate $1/2 \times 100$. One way is to divide 100 by 2; the other is to multiply 100 by .5. Both methods are equivalent, but sometimes it is easier to divide than to multiply. Similarly, sometimes it is easier to use the money supply and demand framework to look at the determination of interest rates.

KEY TERMS

classical view of money demand
simple quantity theory of money demand
real money balances
Cambridge theory of money demand
Cambridge constant
transactions motive
precautionary motive
speculative motive
Cambridge k

modified Cambridge theory
inventory approach to money demand
portfolio approach to money demand
modern quantity theory of money demand
human capital
hyperinflation
Keynesians
monetarists

QUESTIONS AND PROBLEMS

1. Describe the simple quantity theory of money demand. Explain how this theory is based on the transactions motive for holding money and how changes in income and prices affect money demand under this view.

2. Describe the inventory approach to money demand. Explain how this theory is based on the transactions motive for holding money and how interest rates and bank fees affect money demand under this approach.

3. Describe the portfolio approach to money demand. Does the transactions motive play any role in money demand under this approach? Explain.

4. What are the determinants of money demand under the inventory approach? Under the portfolio approach?

5. How does the modern quantity theory expand on the simple quantity theory, on the inventory approach, and on the portfolio approach to money demand?

6. What are the determinants of money demand in the modern quantity theory? How

do they affect the demand for real money balances? Why?

7. What are the determinants of money supply in the model used in this chapter and adapted from the one in Chapter 14? How and why does each determinant shift the real money supply curve?

8. What is the effect of an increase in the price level on real money demand? On the real money supply? On equilibrium in the money market?

9. What are the effects of an increase in fees on deposits in the inventory model of money demand?

10. What is the effect of an increase in wealth on money demand in the portfolio approach?

11. There has been some discussion about adding a transactions tax to all securities market purchases or sales. This would be much like an additional broker's fee, but would be paid to the federal government. What effects might this tax have on money demand?

12. Suppose the price level increases. Assuming other things remain unchanged, what impact will this change have on the equilibrium interest rate? Could the Fed change the monetary base in such a way as to offset the higher price level's effect on the interest rate? Explain.

13. Suppose real income increases. Assuming other things remain unchanged, what impact will this change have on the equilibrium interest rate? Could the Fed change the monetary base in such a way as to offset the effect of higher real income on the interest rate? Explain.

14. The Fed wants to achieve an interest rate of 3 percent and a money stock of $700 billion. The economy is currently in equilibrium, with an interest rate and a money stock that are both below the Fed's targets. Can the Fed use its policy instruments (like open market operations or reserve requirements) to raise interest rates and the equilibrium stock of money to their desired levels? Explain.

15. Why do Keynesians and monetarists sometimes disagree about the effects of monetary policy on interest rates?

SELECTIONS FOR FURTHER READING

Ahking, F. W. "International Currency Substitution: A Reexamination of Britain's Econometric Evidence: A Comment." *Journal of Money, Credit, and Banking,* 16 (November 1984), 546–556.

Amsler, C. "A 'Pure' Long-Term Interest Rate and the Demand for Money." *Journal of Economics and Business,* 36 (August 1984), 359–370.

Douglas, R. W., Jr. "A Three-Asset Determination of the Transactions Demand for Money." *Journal of Macroeconomics,* 11 (Winter 1989), 95–108.

Dutton, D. S., and W. P. Gramm. "Transactions Costs, the Wage Rate, and the Demand for Money." *American Economic Review,* 63 (September 1973), 652–665.

Falls, G. A., and H. Zangeneh. "The Interest Rate Volatility and the Demand for Money: The Empirical Evidence." *Quarterly Journal of Business and Economics,* 28 (Winter 1989), 26–42.

Gerdes, W. D. "The Demand for Money in Socialist Tanzania." *Atlantic Economic Journal,* 18 (September 1990), 68–73.

Girton, L., and D. Roper. "Theory and Implications of Currency Substitution." *The Monetary Approach to International Adjustment.* New York and London: Greenwood Press, Praeger 1986, 212–235.

Goldberg, M., and T. B. Thurston. "Monetarism, Overshooting, and the Procyclical Movement of Velocity." *Economic Inquiry,* 15 (January 1977), 26–32.

Goldstein, H. N., and S. E. Haynes. "A Critical Appraisal of McKinnon's World Money Supply Hypothesis [Currency Substitution and Instability in the World Dollar Standard]." *American Economic Review,* 74 (March 1984), 217–224.

Graham, F. C. "A Note on the Vanishing Liquidity Effect of Money on Interest." *Economic Inquiry,* 24 (July 1986), 497–503.

Hafer, R. W., and D. W. Jansen. "The Demand for Money in the United States: Evidence from Cointegration Tests." *Journal of Money, Credit, and Banking,* 23 (May 1991), 155–168.

Hoffman, D., and R. H. Rasche. "Long-Run Income and Interest Elasticities of Money Demand in the United States." *Review of Economics and Statistics,* 78 (1991), 665–674.

Marquis, M. H., and W. E. Witte. "Cash Management and the Demand for Money by Firms." *Journal of Macroeconomics,* 11 (Summer 1989), 333–350.

Meyer, P. A., and J. A. Neri. "A Keynes-Friedman Money Demand Function." *American Economic Review,* 65 (September 1975), 610–623.

Swofford, J. L., and G. A. Whitney. "Nominal Costs and the Demand for Real Transactions Balances." *Economic Inquiry,* 23 (October 1985), 725–740.

PART FIVE

Money and the Macro Economy

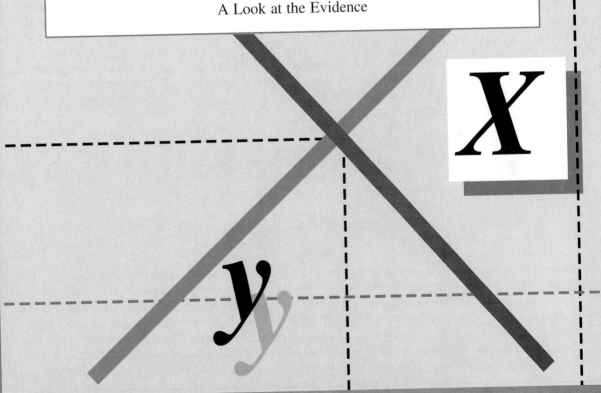

CHAPTERS

16

A Simple Macroeconomic Model

17

Open Economy Macroeconomics

18

Money and Economic Activity:
A Look at the Evidence

X

y

16

A Simple Macroeconomic Model

*T*he United States is one of the most productive and prosperous nations in the world, producing more than one-fourth of the world's total output with a mere 5 percent of the world's population. Despite this prosperity, periods of recession occur during which the real output produced in the United States declines. During these hard times, politicians and economists frequently propose policies designed to stimulate the economy. Undoubtedly you have heard commentators debate the pros and cons of boosting the economy by changing government spending or taxes, lowering interest rates, or expanding the money supply. Have you ever wondered precisely how and why these policies affect prices and output in the economy, or why so much disagreement exists about the ''best'' policy? In this chapter, we synthesize much of what we learned in previous chapters into a single, simple framework that allows us to answer this question.

We begin by developing a model of the aggregate demand and supply of goods and services in the economy that explains how variables such as the money supply, government borrowing, and taxes affect interest rates, the price level, and real output (real GDP). We then use our model of the macroeconomy to examine the impact of government policies designed to stimulate the economy.

When you study the macroeconomic model we develop, you should be aware that there are competing approaches to developing both aggregate demand and aggregate supply frameworks. For example, we looked at the equation of exchange and the quantity theory of money in Chapter 3. We can use these concepts to develop an aggregate demand curve that emphasizes the importance of the nominal money supply and velocity. We will use an alternative approach that is fairly simple yet flexible and can be adapted in various ways to address important economic issues. There are still other approaches, however, including one that develops aggregate demand from what is known as the *IS-LM model.* In the appendix to this chapter, we see how the approach we use in the text can be used to construct an IS-LM model and then to derive aggregate demand from that model.

Finally, we concentrate on a model in which net exports are exogenous. If net exports are zero, this is called a **closed economy model,** a model that does not analyze the impact of international trade on the aggregate economy. We consider this model first to avoid the complications introduced by endogenous net exports when first presenting our macroeconomic model. After developing this essentially closed economy model, we expand it to an open economy model that does consider the impact of international trade on the aggregate economy in Chapter 17.

AGGREGATE DEMAND

The first step in building a macroeconomic model of the economy is to describe aggregate demand, the total demand for all goods and services in the economy. Aggregate demand is, in essence, the demand for real gross domestic product (the sum of consumption, investment, government purchases, and net exports). **Consumption goods** are the goods and services demanded by households—goods such as food and medicine, rental payments on housing, and purchases of leisure items. **Investment goods** represent outlays for the purchase of new machines, buildings, and structures, things economists call **physical capital.** Goods and services demanded by government make up the third category, called **government purchases.** Government purchases include spending on national defense, highways, and other goods and services. However, not all government spending is government purchases. A government *transfer payment* is government spending, but it is not the purchase of goods and services. Instead, **transfer payments** are funds dispensed to individuals with no required exchange of goods, services, or labor. Transfer payments include such things as unemployment insurance payments and welfare payments. The final category of aggregate demand is **net exports,** the difference between exports and imports. For the United States, exports are sales of U.S. goods and services overseas, while imports are purchases of foreign-made goods and services by U.S. residents. The difference, net exports, represents the net demand for goods and services produced by the United States from international trade and may be positive or negative. We say more about net exports in Chapter 17.

Aggregate demand (*AD*) in the economy is defined as the total demand for all four categories of goods and services:

$$AD = C^d + I^d + G^d + NX^d,$$

where C^d is the total demand for consumption goods, I^d is total investment demand, G^d is government demand for goods and services, and NX^d is net demand for exports.

In microeconomics, we define a demand curve as the graph of the relationship between the price of a good and the quantity demanded of the good, holding all other variables constant. Similarly, we define an **aggregate demand curve** as the relationship between the aggregate price level (P) and the aggregate quantity of goods and services demanded (Y), holding other variables constant.

Figure 16.1 shows an aggregate demand curve. Note that an increase in the price level from P_0 to P_1 leads to a decrease in the aggregate quantity demanded of all goods and services from Y_0 to Y_1.

Why the Aggregate Demand Curve Slopes Downward

One of the most important ideas in economics is the law of demand, which states that as the price of a good rises and other prices remain the same, consumers will purchase less of that good. There are two reasons for this. First, the good has become more expensive relative to other goods, making it attractive for the consumer to substitute toward other goods. This is called the **substitution effect.** Second, the increase in price reduces the consumer's purchasing power, since any given income level purchases a smaller quantity of the good whose price has increased. This is called the **income effect.**

While it is tempting to apply the law of demand to the aggregate demand curve to explain its downward slope, a word of caution is in order. The aggregate demand curve is a relationship between the aggregate price level, P, and the quantity demanded of all goods and services in the economy, Y. Since the price level is a measure of the prices of all goods and services in

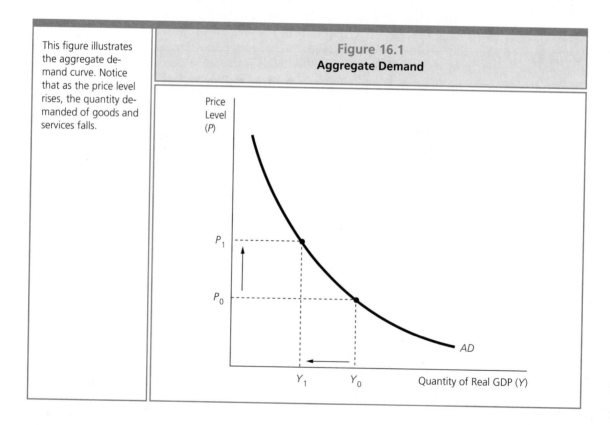

This figure illustrates the aggregate demand curve. Notice that as the price level rises, the quantity demanded of goods and services falls.

Figure 16.1
Aggregate Demand

the economy, an increase in the price level is an increase in all prices; this increase does not lead to substitution toward other goods.

Why, then, is the aggregate demand curve downward sloping? There are three reasons, two of which we will discuss here and one that we reserve until the next chapter. The first is a wealth effect, similar in some ways to the income effect just mentioned. This effect arises because an increase in the overall price level reduces the purchasing power of a consumer's money. For example, suppose you have $1,000 in your checking account. Your $1,000 gives you more purchasing power when the price level is 100 than when it is 200 and all goods are twice as expensive. Keeping other things the same, an increase in the price level reduces the purchasing power of your money holdings and leads to a decrease in the quantity of goods and services you demand. Moreover, an increase in the price level reduces the purchasing power of everyone's money holdings, so the aggregate quantity demanded of goods and services is decreased. Thus, one reason the aggregate demand curve is downward sloping is due to this wealth effect: A higher price level reduces the purchasing power of money holdings, leading to a lower aggregate quantity demanded.[1]

A second reason the aggregate demand curve slopes downward is due to a real interest rate effect. Recall from Chapter 15 that we can look at equilibrium between money demand and money supply as determining the interest rate. In that chapter, we presented money demand and money supply as demand for and supply of real money balances. An increase in the price level lowers the real money supply, shifting the money supply curve to the left and creating a higher equilibrium interest rate. Holding other variables constant (including the expected inflation rate), this higher interest rate is a higher real interest rate and causes a reduction in aggregate demand. Both investment demand and demand for consumption spending on durable goods will decline. While low interest rates encourage borrowing and spending on capital goods such as factories, houses, and consumer durables, high interest rates discourage this borrowing and spending and thus reduce the aggregate quantity demanded.[2] Hence, a higher price level results in a lower real money supply, which directly reduces aggregate quantity demanded via a wealth effect and indirectly reduces aggregate quantity demanded through an increase in the interest rate, which discourages borrowing and spending.

There is a final reason for downward-sloping aggregate demand, which arises from the effect of the price level on net export demand. We discuss

---

[1] Because this wealth effect works through changes in the purchasing power of money holdings, it is often called a *real balance effect*. Real money balances, *M/P,* are reduced when the price level increases, and hence the aggregate quantity of goods and services demanded declines.

[2] This is sometimes called the *intertemporal substitution effect* to stress the fact that a higher interest rate encourages a substitution of fewer goods purchased today in exchange for more goods purchased in the future.

this effect in the next chapter, where we look at net export demand and the open economy in detail.

The Components of Aggregate Demand and Their Determinants

Just as the demand by a consumer for an automobile depends on factors other than the price of the car (such as the consumer's income), so does aggregate demand depend on factors other than the price level. These factors, which ultimately determine the position of the aggregate demand curve, are known as the *determinants of aggregate demand*. The easiest way to understand the determinants of aggregate demand is to consider the determinants of each component of aggregate demand: consumption, investment, and government purchases, which we turn to next. We will discuss determinants of the final component of aggregate demand, net exports, in Chapter 17. Box 16.1 shows the relative sizes of the four components of aggregate demand for the U.S. economy.

Determinants of Consumption Demand.
The consumption component of aggregate demand consists of spending by households on goods and services that directly satisfy their wants, such as food, medicine, rental payments on housing, and leisure items. We will look at consumption demand, and indeed at all components of aggregate demand, in real terms. Thus, consumption demand is the real quantity demanded of consumption goods and services.

Consumption demand depends on many variables, including the price level, wealth, the real interest rate, and taxes, as well as household tastes and expectations. It is convenient to summarize all the factors that influence consumption demand with the consumption demand function

$$C^d = C(P, W, r, \pi^e, T_H),$$

where C^d is the total quantity demanded of all consumption goods, P is the price level, W is household real wealth (including consumer holdings of money, bonds, stocks, and other assets like real estate), r is the ex ante (or expected) real interest rate calculated as $r = i - \pi^e$, π^e is the expected inflation rate, and T_H is taxes paid by households. Consumer tastes or preferences also affect consumption demand but are not included as a separate variable.

You may notice that one important variable is missing from this list: income. We have all seen simple consumption functions specifying that consumption is a function of income. Why is income not listed in the above specification? The answer is that consumption does depend on income, but our specification of aggregate demand already takes into account the effect of income on consumption demand. We will demonstrate how this works when we discuss aggregate demand as the sum of these four components; for now we simply outline the argument. Aggregate consumption does de-

The Data Bank

Box 16.1

Components of Aggregate Demand

We divide up total spending in the economy, GDP, into four components: consumption, investment, government purchases, and net exports. The accompanying figure shows values in 1987 dollars for these four components in 1992. Consumption was by far the largest component, equal to $3,354 billion. Government purchases of goods and services (*not* transfer payments) were $939 billion, while gross investment in new capital (not subtracting depreciation) was $742 billion. Net exports were a negative number, − $55 billion, reflecting the U.S. international trade deficit.

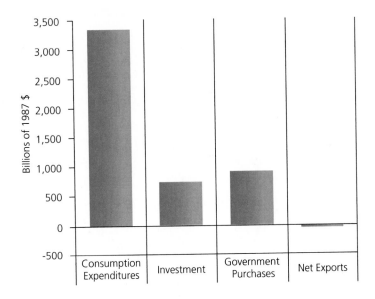

Source: U.S. Department of Commerce, Bureau of Economic Analysis, *Survey of Current Business,* various issues, and Citibase electronic database.

pend on aggregate income, and in equilibrium aggregate income equals aggregate spending, or GDP. But GDP equals consumption plus investment, government purchases, and net exports. Thus, we have a somewhat circular situation in which consumption depends on income and income depends on consumption plus other components of GDP. We demonstrate later that our specification of aggregate demand—and our specification of consumption demand—can be written in a form that already incorporates the effect of income on consumption. As we will see, this effect makes consumption demand and aggregate demand less steep than it would appear with income held fixed, but otherwise does not change the basic downward slope of these curves or the effects of changes in the determinants of consumption demand or aggregate demand on these curves.

If we hold everything constant except the price level and consumption, we obtain the relationship between the price level and real expenditures graphed as the curve C^d in Figure 16.2. This consumption demand curve

Figure 16.2
Consumption Demand

The demand curve for consumption goods shows the inverse relationship between consumption demand—consumption expenditures—and the price level. A rise in the price level will lead to a decrease in quantity demanded, such as a change from point A to point B. A change in the determinants of consumption demand other than the price level will change the position of the consumption demand curve. The consumption demand curve will shift to the right if there is an increase in wealth, a decrease in the real interest rate, a decrease in household taxes, or an increase in inflationary expectations. The consumption demand curve will shift to the left if there is a decrease in wealth, an increase in the real interest rate, an increase in taxes, or a decrease in inflationary expectations.

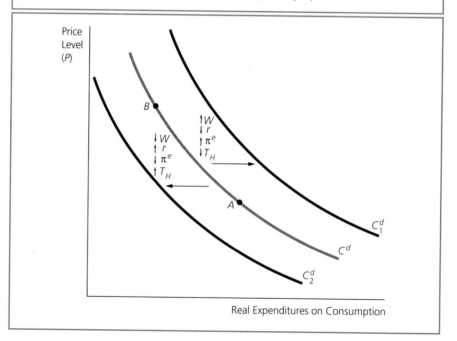

indicates that, holding other things constant, an increase in the price level will reduce demand for real expenditures on consumption goods as illustrated by the movement from A to B in Figure 16.2. This occurs because an increase in the price level reduces the real value of consumer wealth, especially money holdings, and thereby reduces the quantity demanded of aggregate consumption goods and services. Thus, from changes in the price level, a wealth effect occurs that operates through consumption. In addition, changes in the price level will change the real money supply and hence change the equilibrium interest rate in the money market, resulting in a further change in the quantity demanded of aggregate consumption goods and services. Both of these effects are summarized by the price level, P, in the consumption demand function.

In contrast, whenever there is a change in wealth or the real interest rate that is not due to changes in the price level, or whenever changes in the expected inflation rate, taxes paid by households, or tastes occur, the entire consumption demand curve will shift. This is illustrated in Figure 16.2 by a shift from C^d to either C_1^d or C_2^d. Now we look at how and why these determinants shift the consumption demand curve.

Wealth.
An increase in household real wealth—be it in the form of money, bonds, stocks, real estate, or other assets—increases the opportunities households enjoy for purchasing goods and services. Consequently, an increase in aggregate household wealth from sources other than a change in the price level will tend to increase the total demand for consumption goods. This is represented by a rightward shift in the consumption demand curve in Figure 16.2 from C^d to C_1^d.

Wealth can change for any number of reasons. Wealth tomorrow is wealth today, plus any income generated by that wealth, plus other income such as wage and salary income, minus consumption spending and taxes. Wealth may change if there is an increase in the money stock, holding the price level constant, or if an appreciation in value of real estate or stock market holdings occurs, both of which will be income in the form of capital gains. Any of these increases in wealth will make consumers feel wealthier and lead to increased consumption demand.

The Real Interest Rate.
Not all changes in the interest rate are due to changes in the price level. Changes in the real interest rate may arise for any number of reasons and will alter households' incentives to save or spend. While changes in the real interest rate have both an income and a substitution effect, we will assume higher real interest rates lead you and other consumers to save more, since the return to saving is now higher. However, when you save more at a given level of income, you have less left over for consumption spending. Similarly, the lower the real interest rate, the greater will be consumer spending. Graphically, an increase in the real interest rate shifts the consumption demand curve to the left, whereas a decrease in the real interest rate shifts the consumption demand curve to the right.

Expected Inflation.   If the expected inflation rate increases, consumers will tend to purchase more consumption goods today, before prices rise. Thus, increases in expected inflation will raise consumption demand (shifting it to the right), whereas a decrease in expected inflation will lower consumption demand.

Taxes.   Taxes on consumption have the obvious effect of decreasing consumption demand, but other taxes affect consumption demand as well. Taxes on income, such as federal and state income taxes and the social security tax, have an indirect effect on household wealth. Income taxes reduce households' ability to save for any given income level, which may reduce their ability to purchase consumer goods. Thus, increases in household income taxes may reduce consumption demand, shifting consumption demand to the left. A decrease in taxes would have the opposite effect, increasing consumption demand (a shift to the right).

Tastes.   Consumer tastes can also affect consumption demand. For example, households may experience an increase in thriftiness. This will decrease consumption demand, which is represented by a leftward shift in the consumption demand curve.

Determinants of Investment Demand.   The second component of aggregate demand is investment, the purchase of new physical capital. Firms buy physical capital today to increase their future profits, by either expanding their productive capacity or making their current productive capacity more efficient. Thus, the gain firms realize from investing in physical capital is the expectation of higher future profits. The greater the expected future value from a given expenditure today, the greater will be investment demand.

There is another side to investment: the cost of paying for physical capital today. To pay for investment, a firm might borrow loanable funds. In this case, investment has a very explicit cost: the interest payments on the borrowed funds. Alternatively, the firm might use internal funds such as retained earnings to fund investment. Then the cost to the firm of the investment is the implicit interest it forgoes by not investing the funds in the loanable funds market. Thus, regardless of whether a firm uses retained earnings or the capital market to fund investments, the relevant price of an investment is the real interest rate. The higher the real interest rate, the less desirable firms will find it to engage in investment.

To see why the real interest rate plays a central role in determining the level of investment, consider the following investment opportunity faced by a firm. The firm can purchase a new machine for $150 million today, year 1, which it expects will generate returns in real terms, adjusted for inflation, of $100 million in year 2 and another $100 million in year 3. After year 3 the machine will have no value, and the firm plans to give it to the junkyard in exchange for hauling it away. Will the firm choose to purchase this machine? The answer depends on the present value of the costs and earnings of the investment. The present value of the cost is simply the $150 million spent in year 1. The present value of the earnings depends on the real interest rate and is calculated as

$$PV = \frac{\$100,000,000}{(1 + r)} + \frac{\$100,000,000}{(1 + r)^2}.$$

For instance, if the real interest rate is zero, the present value of earnings is just $200 million and the present value of the firm's profits is $200 million − $150 million, or $50 million. If the real interest rate is 10 percent, or r = .10, the present value of earnings is $173.55 million and the present value of profit is $23.55 million. If the real interest rate is 20 percent, the present value of earnings is $152.78 million and the firm earns a profit of $2.78 million in present value terms. This example illustrates how a rise in the real interest rate reduces the profits from an investment.

Another way to describe the firm's decision is to calculate the rate of return on the investment project that makes the present value of earnings equal to the present value of costs; that is, what is the real interest rate that just makes

$$\frac{\$100,000,000}{(1 + r)} + \frac{\$100,000,000}{(1 + r)^2} = \$150,000,000?$$

The answer is that a real interest rate of about 21.5 percent will make the costs equal to the present value of earnings, so profits are zero. At any higher real interest rate, this firm will not pursue the investment opportunity, because the cost of the investment will exceed the present value of the firm's earnings. More generally, for an investment yielding a given stream of expected future earnings and expected costs, the higher the real interest rate, the less likely a firm is to make the investment. For the entire economy, with many firms facing different investment opportunities, increases in the real interest rate will make some investment opportunities unprofitable. The higher the real interest rate, the fewer will be the investment opportunities that remain profitable for firms.

Taxes on the earnings of firms—either corporate profits taxes or individual income taxes on business owners—will also reduce investment. Continuing with the preceding example, suppose the government imposes a 10 percent income tax on the earnings of the firm over and above the initial cost of the investment. In year 1 no tax is due, since the $100 million in earnings has not yet covered the initial cost of $150 million. In year 2 the first $50 million in earnings is also exempt from taxation, but the next $50 million is subject to the 10 percent tax, since earnings will exceed the cost of the machine. Thus, after taxes the firm will earn $95 million in year 2— the pretax earnings of $100 million minus the 10 percent tax on the $50 million of net earnings, or $5 million.

What is the present value of the aftertax profits in this example? With a real interest rate of zero, the present value of aftertax earnings is $195 million and the present value of costs is $150 million, so the present value of aftertax profits is $45 million. If the real interest rate is 10 percent, the present value of aftertax earnings is $100 million/1.10 + $95 million/1.10^2, or $169.42 million, so the present value of aftertax profits is $19.42 million. Finally, if the real interest rate is 20 percent, the present value of aftertax earnings is $149.31 million, so the present value of aftertax profits is −$0.69 million—a loss. The income tax has transformed an investment that was profitable at 20 percent interest into one that is unprofitable at that real interest rate. This is generally the case: The higher the tax rate on income or earnings, the less likely the firm will be to make an investment at any given real interest rate.

Since investment demand depends on expected future profits, the real interest rate, and income taxes, we can summarize the relationship between investment demand and its determinants with the following investment demand function:

$$I^d = I(P, \text{EE}, r, T_F,).$$

Here I^d is the real quantity demanded of total investment goods, r is the ex ante real interest rate, EE is expected earnings, and T_F is income taxes paid by owners of firms.

Figure 16.3 illustrates the inverse relationship between the real interest rate and investment by firms. When the real interest rate is 5 percent, 200 billion real dollars of investment spending will occur. If the real interest rate increases to 10 percent, only 150 billion real dollars of investment spending will occur. Based on Figure 16.3, we see that the higher the real interest rate, the lower the real quantity demanded of investment goods.

Why does investment demand depend on the price level? Our investment demand function contains no wealth effect. However, we have already seen how changes in the price level change the real money supply and hence the equilibrium interest rate in the money market. An increase in the price level, by lowering real money supply, will raise the interest rate and, for a given level of expected inflation, increase the real interest rate. This results in a reduction in the quantity demanded of aggregate investment goods and services.

Of course, it is important to remember that the price level effect via changes in the interest rate is only one way interest rates can change and thereby alter investment demand. Changes in the real interest rate due to factors other than a change in the price level are represented by the real interest rate variable in the investment demand function.

We can also graph investment demand, I^d, as a function of the *price level*, as we do in Figure 16.4. Here the price level is measured on the vertical axis and real expenditures for investment goods and services on the horizontal axis. The downward slope of the investment demand curve is due

The investment demand curve shows the inverse relationship between the real interest rate and investment demand, holding constant any other factors that might affect investment demand. Here a rise in the real interest rate from 5 to 10 percent causes a decline in the quantity demanded of investment goods from $200 billion to $150 billion (in real dollars).

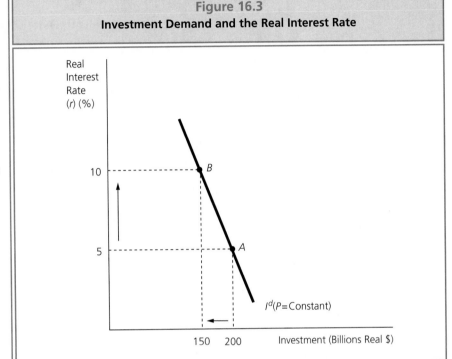

Figure 16.3

Investment Demand and the Real Interest Rate

to the effect of changes in the price level on the interest rate and hence on investment demand. Changes in expected future profits, in the real interest rate (due to factors other than the price level), or in income taxes will all shift the investment demand curve in Figure 16.4 to the right (to I_1^d) or to the left (to I_2^d). We summarize the causes of such shifts next.

Expected Earnings.   Expected earnings are the reason a firm invests. The higher the level of future expected earnings, the greater is the firm's interest in investment spending. This would be represented by a rightward shift in investment demand. A decrease in expected future earnings would shift investment demand leftward.

The Real Interest Rate.   The real interest rate is the opportunity cost of purchasing physical capital, so an increase in the real interest rate results in a reduction in real investment demand. This is represented by a leftward shift in investment demand. Similarly, a decrease in the real interest rate reduces the opportunity cost of investment and leads to a rightward shift in investment demand.

If we graph investment demand as a function of the price level, the investment demand curve is downward sloping. The position of investment demand depends on the real interest rate, expected earnings, and tax policy. A rise in the real interest rate or income taxes will shift the investment demand curve to the left. However, a decline in the real interest rate or income taxes will shift it to the right.

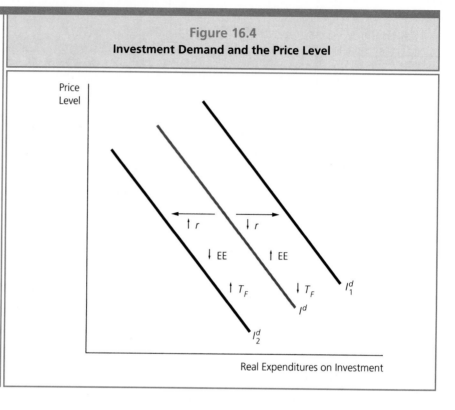

Figure 16.4

Investment Demand and the Price Level

Price Level

Real Expenditures on Investment

Taxes on Income from Investment in Physical Capital.
If government tax policy reduces the expected aftertax profitability of investing, firms will make fewer investments. This shifts the investment demand curve to the left. Conversely, tax policies that increase the aftertax profitability of investments (such as investment tax credits) shift the investment demand curve to the right.

Government Purchases.
Government purchases of goods and services are the third component of aggregate demand and result from the political process. For now we take this process to be exogenous, meaning government purchases of goods and services do not depend on interest rates, prices, or any other variable. Box 16.2 describes how government spending has been divided among government purchases, interest payments on the debt, and government transfer payments in various past years.

When we graph government purchases against the price level, the government's demand for goods and services is vertical, or perfectly inelastic, as illustrated by the curve G^d in Figure 16.5. We will assume the government demand for goods and services is

$$G^d = G,$$

The Data Bank

Box 16.2

*Components of Government Spending,
1962, 1977, and 1992*

Total government spending includes government demand for goods and services, labeled G^d in the text, plus government transfer payments and net interest payments on the national debt. In 1962, purchases of goods and services made up 58.9 percent of government spending, followed by transfer payments (25.1 percent) and interest payments (6.3 percent). By

1977, government purchases were 34.5 percent of government spending, while transfer payments had climbed to 40.1 percent and interest payments to 7 percent. In 1992, transfer payments were 42.9 percent of government spending, purchases of goods and services were 30.5 percent, and interest payments had risen to

Continued on p. 540

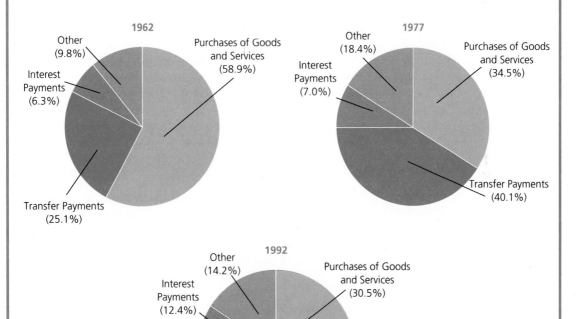

Continued from p. 539
12.4 percent. Thus, there has been a large in-crease in government transfer payments relative to government purchases over the last three decades, as well as a rising percentage of gov-ernment spending devoted to paying interest on the national debt.

Source: U.S. Department of Commerce, Bureau of Economic Analysis, *Survey of Current Business,* various issues, and Citibase electronic database.

where G is the exogenous level of government purchases. Given these assumptions, an increase in government purchases shifts the government demand for goods and services to the right (to G_1^d), whereas a decrease in government purchases shifts government demand to the left (to G_2^d), as in Figure 16.5.

Net Exports.   Net exports depend on several factors that we explore in Chapter 17. For now we take net exports as given and not a function of either the interest rate or the price level. When we graph net export demand against the price level, we get a vertical line, indicating net export expenditures do not change with changes in the price level. In this way, net exports are treated in this chapter in the same way government purchases are—as exogenous. Hence we write

$$NX^d = NX.$$

Adding Up the Components to Obtain Aggregate Demand

We have outlined the four major components of aggregate demand: consumption, investment, government purchases, and net exports. We have also discussed the determinants of each component and examined the effects of changes in the determinants of each. Now we turn our attention to aggregate demand, which is the sum of these components:

$$AD = C^d + I^d + G^d + NX^d.$$

Figure 16.6 illustrates that aggregate demand is the sum of consumption, investment, government, and net export demand by combining them in one graph. The aggregate demand curve is the horizontal summation of consumption demand, investment demand, government purchases demand, and net export demand. For example, when the price level is P_0, investment demand is at point I on the I^d curve, government demand is at point G on the G^d curve, net export demand is at point NX on the NX^d curve, and consumption demand is at point C on the C^d curve. If we add the horizontal distances together, we get the point labeled $I + NX + G + C$ on the AD curve, which represents aggregate demand when the price level is P_0. Notice

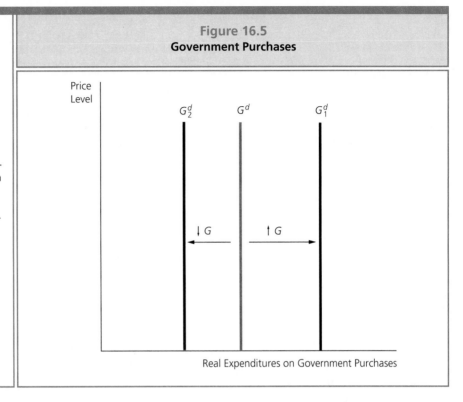

Government purchases of goods and services are assumed to be the result of a political process and independent of any economic variable. Therefore, government demand for goods and services is represented by a vertical line. An increase in government demand is reflected in a rightward shift in the vertical line, such as from G^d to G^d_1. A decrease in government demand is represented by a leftward shift in the vertical line, such as from G^d to G^d_2.

Figure 16.5
Government Purchases

that the aggregate demand curve is downward sloping because consumption and investment demand are downward sloping.

Why Aggregate Demand Does Not Depend on Income

We use an aggregate demand curve that subsumes the effect of income on aggregate demand. Figure 16.7 shows how we can justify this approach. Consider first the curve labeled $ad(Y_0)$, which is desired aggregate expenditures when income is Y_0. Suppose we start at point A, where the price level is P_0. What happens when the price level falls to P_1?

On $ad(Y_0)$ we move to point B, with a price level of P_1. However, on $ad(Y_0)$ spending is a function of income, and income is held constant at Y_0. But this is not an equilibrium position, since in equilibrium aggregate income must equal aggregate real expenditures. When real expenditures increase to Y_1, aggregate income in the desired aggregate spending equation also increases to Y_1 in equilibrium. This increase in income raises consumption and shifts aggregate expenditures to the right from $ad(Y_0)$ to $ad(Y_1)$. Thus, when real expenditures and income increase to Y_1, increasing consumption

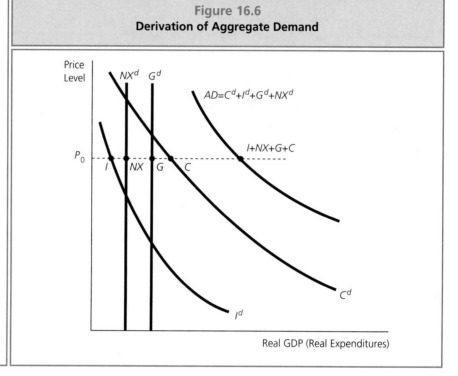

Aggregate demand is the summation of investment demand, government purchases demand, consumption demand, and net export demand. Notice the aggregate demand curve slopes downward due to the consumption and investment demand curves.

Figure 16.6
Derivation of Aggregate Demand

and hence aggregate spending, we are at point B' on $ad(Y_1)$, with a price level of P'_1.

Similarly, starting at point A and with real expenditures equal to real income of Y_0, we ask what will happen when real expenditures decline to Y_2. When real expenditures fall to Y_2 but aggregate income is held constant at Y_0, we move to point C on $ad(Y_0)$, where the price level is P_2. As before, however, this is not an equilibrium, since total real spending must equal total real income in macroeconomic equilibrium. Thus, when real expenditures decline to Y_2, we want real income to also drop to Y_2. This reduces consumption and hence aggregate spending, shifting us to $ad(Y_2)$. On $ad(Y_2)$, real expenditures of Y_2 place us at point C', where the price level is P'_2.

To summarize, we have found three equilibrium points where total real expenditures equal total real income: C', A, and B'. We draw a curve connecting these points and call it aggregate demand, or AD. However, this AD curve does not depend on the level of income. Instead it is the AD curve we derive under the condition that total expenditures and total income must be equal. In this way, we derive consumption demand $C^d(r, W)$ and hence aggregate demand AD, which do not depend on income.

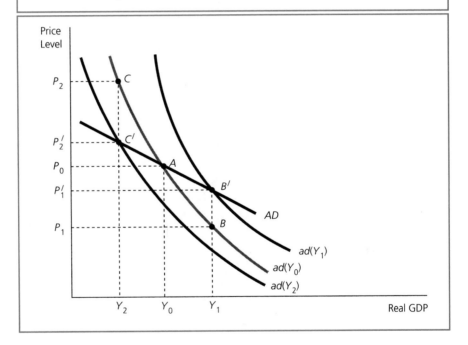

Figure 16.7
Deriving Aggregate Demand

Here $ad(Y_0)$ shows desired aggregate expenditures when income is Y_0. When real expenditures (real GDP) equal Y_0, we are at point A. When desired expenditures increase to Y_1, we move to point B. But this cannot be an equilibrium because the higher income Y_1 increases desired aggregate expenditures to $ad(Y_1)$. Thus, when income and expenditures both equal Y_1, we are at point B' on $ad(Y_1)$. Similar reasoning gets us to point C' on $ad(Y_2)$ when income and expenditures both equal Y_2. The aggregate demand curve labeled AD that passes through points A, B', and C' is the aggregate demand curve we use in this text, and it is drawn assuming income in the consumption equation adjusts to equal real GDP.

Changes in Aggregate Demand

Changes in the price level lead to a movement along the aggregate demand curve (such as the movement from A to B in Figure 16.8), whereas a change in the determinants of any component of aggregate demand causes a shift in the aggregate demand curve to either AD_1 or AD_2. Thus, the determinants of aggregate demand are simply the determinants of the components of aggregate demand.

We can emphasize these determinants by writing aggregate demand as

$$AD = AD(P, r, \pi^e, W, T_H, T_F, EE, G, NX).$$

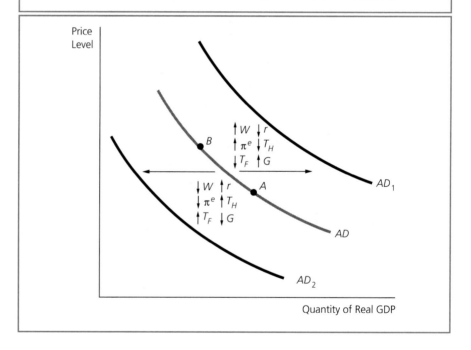

Figure 16.8
Changes in Aggregate Demand

Since aggregate demand is the sum of investment demand, government demand, net export demand, and consumption demand, any factors that cause these to shift will also cause the aggregate demand curve to shift. Therefore, the aggregate demand curve will shift to the right if there is an increase in wealth, an increase in government purchases, a rise in inflationary expectations, an increase in expected future profits, a decrease in the real interest rate, a decrease in taxes, or an increase in net exports. The aggregate demand curve will shift to the left if there is a decrease in wealth, a decline in government purchases, a decrease in inflationary expectations, a reduction in expected future profits, an increase in the real interest rate, an increase in taxes, or a reduction in net exports.

The effect of each variable in parentheses on aggregate demand is determined by its impact on the three components of aggregate demand discussed above. Table 16.1 summarizes these effects.

Before concluding this section, we again point out there are alternative ways to derive aggregate demand. Some might prefer the quantity equation of Chapter 3 and others what is known as the *IS-LM model*. In the appendix to this chapter, we outline a version of the IS-LM model that builds on the four components of aggregate expenditures we introduced in this chapter.

Summary
Exercise 16.1

Holding other things constant, determine the impact of each of the following scenarios on consumption demand, investment demand, and aggregate demand: (a) an increase in the real interest rate not caused by a change in the price level, (b) an increase in taxes paid by households, and (c) an investment tax credit for businesses.

Answer: (a) An increase in the real interest rate dereases both consumption demand and investment demand. Thus, an increase in the real interest rate decreases aggregate demand (shifts aggregate demand to the left). (b)

	Table 16.1	
Determinants of Aggregate Demand		
Change in Determinant of Consumption Demand	**Effect on Consumption Demand**	**Effect on Aggregate Demand**
Increase in wealth (W)	Shifts right	Shifts right
Increase in real interest rate (r)	Shifts left	Shifts left
Increase in expected inflation rate (π^e)	Shifts right	Shifts right
Increase in taxes on households (T_H)	Shifts left	Shifts left
Change in Determinant of Investment Demand	**Effect on Investment Demand**	**Effect on Aggregate Demand**
Increase in real interest rate (r)	Shifts left	Shifts left
Increase in expected earnings (EE)	Shifts right	Shifts right
Increases in taxes on firms (T_F)	Shifts left	Shifts left
Change in Determinant of Government Demand	**Effect on Government Demand**	**Effect on Aggregate Demand**
Exogenous increase in government purchases (G)	Shifts right	Shifts right
Change in Determinant of Net Exports	**Effect on Net Exports**	**Effect on Aggregate Demand**
Exogenous increase in net exports (NX)	Shifts right	Shifts right

An increase in taxes paid by households decreases consumption demand, but has no effect on investment demand. Thus, an increase in taxes paid by households decreases aggregate demand (shifts aggregate demand to the left). (c) An investment tax credit increases the expected aftertax profits of businesses, thus increasing investment demand. It has no effect on consumption demand. Thus, an investment tax credit increases aggregate demand (shifts aggregate demand to the right).

SHORT-RUN AGGREGATE SUPPLY

Short-run aggregate supply (SRAS) characterizes the supply side of the macroeconomy in the short run. More specifically, short-run aggregate supply summarizes the total quantity of goods and services an economy will produce at various price levels, holding constant such things as the prices of inputs, taxes, the stock of physical capital available to firms, and the level of technology. We can summarize the dependence of short-run aggregate supply on these variables by the relation

$$SRAS = SRAS(P, w_L, Z, T_L, K, \text{Tech}),$$

where $SRAS$ represents the total (or aggregate) real quantity of goods and services supplied, P is the price level, w_L represents nominal wages paid to labor, Z denotes the price of variable inputs other than labor (such as materials or energy inputs), T_L represents taxes on labor, K stands for the capital stock (which is fixed in the short run), and Tech represents the available technology.

The short-run aggregate supply curve holds everything but the price level constant and is sketched in Figure 16.9. An increase in the price level leads to a movement along a given short-run aggregate supply curve, such as from point A to point B along the curve labeled $SRAS$. A change in one of the other variables that influence aggregate supply, such as a change in the price of inputs, shifts the short-run aggregate supply curve to the right (to $SRAS_1$) or to the left (to $SRAS_2$). Next, we explain why the short-run aggregate supply curve slopes upward and how changes in input prices, taxes, the capital stock, or technology affect the position of the short-run aggregate supply curve.

Why the Short-Run Aggregate Supply Curve Slopes Upward

The reason the short-run aggregate supply curves in Figure 16.9 slope upward is that we are holding the nominal wage rate and other nominal input prices constant along each aggregate supply curve. As the price level increases, firms are able to sell their goods at higher prices, while continuing to pay the same nominal wage to workers or the same prices for other inputs. Consider what this means to workers. With their nominal wages held constant and the price level increasing, their real wages—the ratio of the nominal

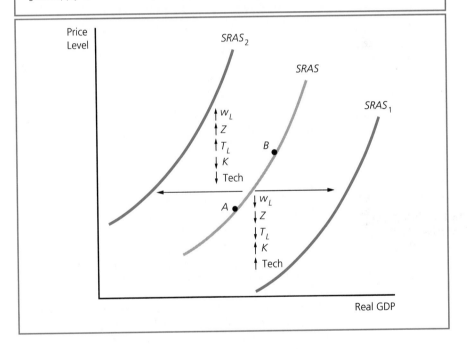

Figure 16.9
Changes in Short-Run Aggregate Supply

A short-run aggregate supply curve holds constant all variables other than the price level that may affect aggregate supply. The upward-sloping short-run aggregate supply curve shows that if input prices remain constant as the price level rises, the quantity supplied of goods and services will rise, such as from point *A* to point *B* on *SRAS*. A change in a variable that affects short-run aggregate supply other than the price level will shift the short-run aggregate supply curve. For example, a decrease in nominal wages, the cost of other inputs, or taxes on labor will shift the short-run aggregate supply curve to the right, as will an increase in the capital stock or available technology. Conversely, an increase in nominal wages, the cost of other inputs, or taxes on labor will shift the short-run aggregate supply curve to the left, as will a decrease in the capital stock or available technology.

wage to the price level, or w_L/P—will decline. Thus, the increase in the price level results in higher output along the short-run aggregate supply curve precisely because firms find it less expensive in real terms to hire workers and buy other inputs. This induces firms to use more of these inputs and leads to greater aggregate output. As we will see later in this chapter, if nominal input prices (such as nominal wages paid to workers) increase in the same proportion as the rise in the price level, firms will not use more of these inputs, output will not increase, and the aggregate supply curve will be vertical.

You may be thinking that if the price level rises by 10 percent, workers will receive a 10 percent cost-of-living adjustment to compensate for higher prices, and this will keep real wages constant. However, many economists stress that in the short run, wages adjust more slowly than does the overall price level. This view has a long history in economics and has come to be considered a Keynesian view, since Keynes argued that nominal wages are rigid—unresponsive to changes in the price level. However, not only Keynesians suggest nominal wages are not perfectly flexible in response to price level changes. Friedman and other monetarists have also made such claims, and both new Keynesians and new classical economists have made relatively sophisticated arguments to this effect.

One reason wages do not adjust instantaneously to changes in the price level is that many wages are set by formal contract between workers and firms and adjusted only at set intervals, say, every six months or every year. Union workers have contracts that often set wages for a period of three years. Even workers without formal contracts often receive wages that are adjusted only at intervals. If you have ever had a summer or part-time job, you were probably offered a certain nominal wage that was adjusted only at regular intervals, if at all, and did not adjust each month when the government announced new values for the consumer price index. Thus, we see that both formal and informal contracts mean nominal wages adjust only periodically, and we say there is **nominal wage rigidity** (or *nominal wage stickiness*). Due to this nominal wage rigidity, the price level can increase and at least temporarily depress the real wage, giving rise to an upward-sloping aggregate supply curve in the short run. A similar argument may be made about other input prices, since firms often have contracts with suppliers that specify prices over months or even years.

An alternative argument about nominal wage rigidity can be made based on price expectations. According to this argument, nominal wages are flexible, but firms and workers are not equally informed about the price level. In particular, workers are seen as having imperfect information about the current price level. They form an expectation of the price level and use this expectation, along with the known nominal wage, to form an expectation of the real wage. If the actual price level changes but workers' expectations of the price level do not adjust fully, workers are slow to realize the full extent of the change in their real wages. In this situation, an increase in the actual price level may lower real wages more than workers realize, allowing firms to temporarily hire workers at a lower real wage, thus inducing an increase in employment and output.

In this explanation for the slope of short-run aggregate supply, the extent of the nominal wage rigidity depends heavily on how expectations are formed. Friedman presented this argument assuming price expectations are formed using the adaptive expectations hypothesis we examined in Chapter 12. New classical economists have presented this argument assuming price expectations are formed using rational expectations, again as we saw in

Chapter 12. With rational expectations, the deviation of the actual price level from the expected price level must be unpredictable, and this leads to the presumption that the short-run aggregate supply curve holds for very short periods of time.

Determinants of Short-Run Aggregate Supply

The determinants of short-run aggregate supply are the factors that cause it to shift. As noted earlier, these determinants include the nominal wage rate, the prices of other inputs, the stock of physical capital available for use in production, and the state of technology. It may also include the expected price level. We now look at how each of these factors affects the position of the aggregate supply curve.

Nominal Wages. The nominal wage (w_L) is the payment to labor, and labor is the major input for most firms. Holding other things constant (including the price level), an increase in the nominal wage rate raises the cost of production and leads firms to cut back on the amounts they are willing to produce at each price level. Graphically, the reduction in short-run aggregate supply induced by an increase in nominal wages is depicted by a leftward shift in the short-run aggregate supply curve. A reduction in the wage rate has the opposite effect: It increases short-run aggregate supply (shifts the curve to the right).

Prices of Other Inputs. Changes in other input prices, including the prices of raw material inputs such as iron ore and bauxite, and the prices of energy inputs, such as the price of electricity per kilowatt hour or the price of natural gas, also affect short-run aggregate supply. Increases in the prices of these inputs affect short-run aggregate supply in the same manner as an increase in the wage rate. Thus, increases in input prices (Z) lead to a reduction in short-run aggregate supply, shown by a leftward shift from *SRAS* to $SRAS_2$ in Figure 16.9. Decreases in the prices of inputs lead to an increase in short-run aggregate supply.

Taxes on Labor. Taxes on labor, which include the income tax and social security taxes, can also affect short-run aggregate supply. Social security taxes, for example, are paid by both employers and employees. An increase in this tax makes labor more expensive to firms and also lowers the aftertax wage workers earn. Consequently, an increase in such taxes reduces the quantity of labor demanded by firms and may also decrease workers' willingness to provide labor services. (In the extreme case of 100 percent taxation, it is clear that few, if any, will choose to work.) For these reasons, increases in the tax rate on labor (T_L) reduce the amount of labor used in production, which in turn shifts the short-run aggregate supply curve to the left. Reducing tax rates on labor has the opposite effect: It shifts the short-run aggregate supply curve to the right.

Stock of Physical Capital.   The economy's physical capital stock (K) is a variable that is fixed in the short run, because it takes time to add new structures or machinery to the nation's productive capital stock. Nonetheless, the capital stock is an important determinant of short-run aggregate supply. A greater capital stock increases the productive capacity of the economy and leads to higher output at every price level. An increase in the capital stock also exerts an indirect effect on output through its effect on labor. In particular, a rise in the capital stock increases labor demand because the additional capital makes any given quantity of labor more productive. This causes an increase in the demand for labor, and the increase in the equilibrium level of employment also contributes to higher output at every price level. Thus, an increase in the capital stock causes the short-run aggregate supply curve to shift to the right. A decrease in the capital stock works in the opposite direction, leading to a reduction in short-run aggregate supply.

Technology.   The state of technology (Tech) is the method by which a firm combines inputs of labor, capital, raw materials, and energy to produce output. Improvements in technology occur when a firm can take a given amount of inputs and produce more output than previously. For example, the recent widespread adoption of personal computers is a technological advance that allows substitution of the inexpensive and flexible computing power of PCs for expensive and inflexible mainframe or human computing power. Technological advances allow more output to be produced at each price level and hence shift short-run aggregate supply to the right.

Summary Exercise 16.2

Explain the impact of the following events on the position of the short-run aggregate supply curve. (a) A war in the Persian Gulf breaks out, drastically increasing the price of crude oil. (b) Congress raises the social security tax to 20 percent to finance the social security trust fund in the wake of an aging population.

Answer: (a) The rise in the price of crude oil—a raw material used to produce gasoline—decreases short-run aggregate supply (shifts it to the left). Changes in the overall price level also may occur, but they lead to a movement along the short-run aggregate supply curve. (b) An increase in the social security tax decreases short-run aggregate supply.

SHORT-RUN MACROECONOMIC EQUILIBRIUM

Our next step is to describe **short-run macroeconomic equilibrium**—the determination of the equilibrium interest rate, price level, and level of real GDP for the economy. As we saw in Chapter 15, the equilibrium interest rate can be analyzed using either money supply and money demand in the

The nominal interest rate is determined in the money market by the intersection of the demand and supply curves for real money balances. This in turn implies a real interest rate, $r^* = i^* - \pi^e$, which determines the level of investment and consumption demand.

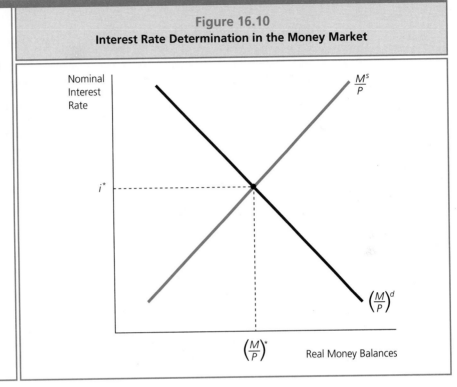

Figure 16.10

Interest Rate Determination in the Money Market

money market or the loanable funds market developed in Chapter 4.[3] Figure 16.10 shows the equilibrium interest rate determined in the money market, i^*, as the nominal interest rate that equilibrates money supply and money demand. For a given exogenous expectation of inflation, π^e, this nominal rate implies a real interest rate, r^*, such that $r^* = i^* - \pi^e$. Thus, the nominal rate determined in the money market minus the expected inflation rate gives us the real rate of interest, r^*.

The real interest rate, in turn, determines the position of both the consumption and investment demand curves, as we discussed earlier. Given the real interest rate determined in the money market, we can graph aggregate demand (which depends on the real interest rate) and short-run aggregate supply as in Figure 16.11. The short-run equilibrium price level and the level of real GDP are determined in the goods market by the intersection of the aggregate demand and short-run aggregate supply curves. Equilibrium

---

[3] In Chapter 15, we saw that these approaches are equivalent but there are advantages to using the money market to discuss the effect of changes in the money supply while using the loanable funds approach to discuss the effects of other changes, such as changes in the government deficit.

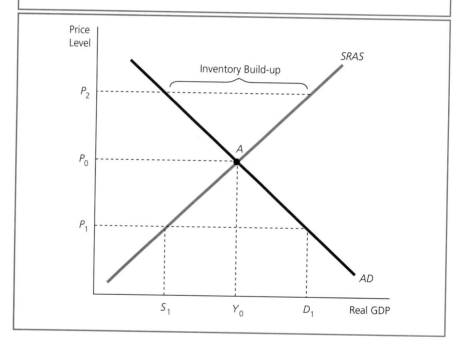

Figure 16.11
Short-Run Macroeconomic Equilibrium

Short-run equilibrium real GDP is determined by the intersection of short-run aggregate supply and aggregate demand at point A. The equilibrium price level and real GDP are P_0 and Y_0, respectively. Notice that at a price level higher than P_0, such as P_2, there is excess supply and inventories build up. The excess supply will be eliminated only if the price level falls, which will reduce the quantity supplied while increasing the quantity demanded for reasons described in the text. Similarly, if the price level is lower than P_0, such as P_1, there is excess demand for goods and services. In this case the price level rises, stimulating the quantity supplied while reducing the quantity demanded until the price rises enough that short-run aggregate supply equals aggregate demand.

is at point A in Figure 16.11, so the equilibrium price level is P_0 and equilibrium real GDP is Y_0.

To summarize, the equilibrium nominal interest rate is determined in the money market at the intersection of the supply and demand for real money balances. This implies a real interest rate, and the real interest rate in turn determines consumption demand and investment demand and hence the position of aggregate demand. Thus, equilibrium in the money market is an important determinant of the position of the aggregate demand curve in the goods market. The short-run equilibrium price level and real GDP are determined in the goods market by the intersection of the AD and SRAS curves.

Achieving Equilibrium

How does the economy get to equilibrium at point A in Figure 16.11? To answer this, suppose the price level is below the equilibrium price level, say, at P_1. When the price level is P_1, the aggregate quantity supplied is only S_1, while the aggregate quantity demanded is D_1. There is an excess demand for total output of $D_1 - S_1$. Some component of aggregate demand (either consumption demand, investment demand, or government demand) is not being satisfied at this price level; consumers, investors, and government desire more goods at this price level than there are goods available. This excess demand exerts upward pressure on prices in the economy until the price level eventually reaches P_0. Notice that as the price level begins to rise above P_1, aggregate quantity supplied increases and aggregate quantity demanded decreases. But as long as the price level is below P_0, an excess demand will remain (and hence pressure on the price level to move toward P_0 will remain). Once the price level reaches P_0, the upward pressure on the price level is eliminated as aggregate quantity supplied equals aggregate quantity demanded.

Had the price level started at a higher level—say, P_2—there would have been an excess supply of output. In the aggregate, firms would begin to accumulate larger inventories than they wanted. They would begin to lower prices, leading to a lower overall price level. As the price level declined, inventories would begin to shrink. Once the price level reached P_0, suppliers would have no further incentive to lower prices, and the price level would remain at P_0.

Changes in Equilibrium

How do changes in aggregate demand or short-run aggregate supply affect the equilibrium price level and real GDP? To answer this question, we look at changes first in aggregate demand and then in short-run aggregate supply.

Changes in Aggregate Demand.
During the first part of the 1980s, the U.S. government embarked on an extended program of expanded defense purchases. Federal government purchases for defense rose from $143 billion in 1980 to $259 billion in 1985, an increase of 81 percent in nominal terms and 37 percent after inflation. This increase was substantial even when measured against total GDP. In 1980 federal defense purchases were 5.3 percent of GDP, and by 1985 they were 6.4 percent. What is the effect of such an increase in defense spending?

To answer this question, we will hold all variables constant except government purchases. This will show us how an increase in government purchases affects the economy. However, we will ignore important features of the increase in government purchases that have to do with how the spending is financed. The government can increase purchases and thus affect the economy, but it also must decide how that spending will be financed, and this too will have an effect on the economy. For now we ignore the financing decision and take it up later in the chapter.

Figure 16.12 shows an initial equilibrium, where short-run aggregate supply ($SRAS_0$) and aggregate demand (AD_0) intersect at point A. At the initial equilibrium, the price level is P_0 and the quantity of output—real GDP—is Y_0. When aggregate demand increases to AD_1—as it did due to the increased defense purchases in the early 1980s—the new equilibrium is at the intersection of AD_1 and $SRAS_0$ at point B. Thus, we see that in the short run, an increase in aggregate demand will lead to a higher price level (P_1) and a higher level of real GDP (Y_1). We conclude that the defense buildup in the first half of the 1980s tended to raise both real GDP and the price level.

We can state these results more generally as follows. Any change in a determinant of aggregate demand that shifts AD to the right will have the short-run effect of increasing the price level and increasing the quantity of output. Similarly, any change in a determinant of aggregate demand that shifts AD to the left will have the short-run effect of reducing the price level and decreasing real GDP.

An increase in aggregate demand from AD_0 to AD_1 causes the short-run equilibrium to change from point A to point B. Note the new equilibrium is at a higher price level and a higher level of real GDP.

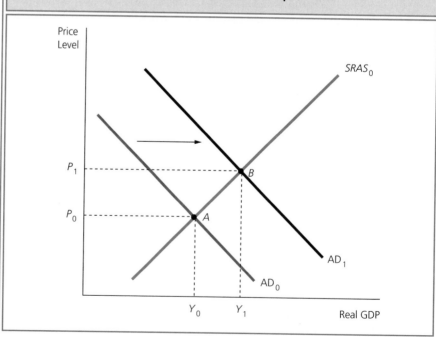

Figure 16.12
Effect of a Rise in Aggregate Demand on Short-Run Macroeconomic Equilibrium

Changes in Short-Run Aggregate Supply.   The summer of 1993 was marked by widespread flooding along the Mississippi and Missouri rivers and their tributaries. The flooding caused damage to the nation's capital stock as houses and factories were damaged or destroyed by floods and flooded farmland was rendered incapable of producing crops for the 1993 season. Then, in January 1994, Los Angeles and surrounding areas were struck by a major earthquake that severely damaged houses, factories, and the cities' infrastructures of roads, utility lines, and sewer systems. These events—natural occurrences that damage the nation's capital stock and ability to produce output—are one example of a negative supply shock, an event that shifts short run aggregate supply to the left. What is the impact of such a supply shock on real GDP and the price level?

To answer this question we turn to Figure 16.13, which illustrates an initial equilibrium between short-run aggregate supply ($SRAS_0$) and aggregate demand (AD_0) at point A. The corresponding price level is P_0, and the quantity of output—real GDP—is Y_0. This situation represents the economy before the supply shock. The supply shock is a change in one of the determinants of short-run aggregate supply that causes it to decrease to, say,

A decrease in short-run aggregate supply from $SRAS_0$ to $SRAS_1$ causes the equilibrium to change from point A to point B. Note the new equilibrium is at a higher price level and a lower level of real GDP.

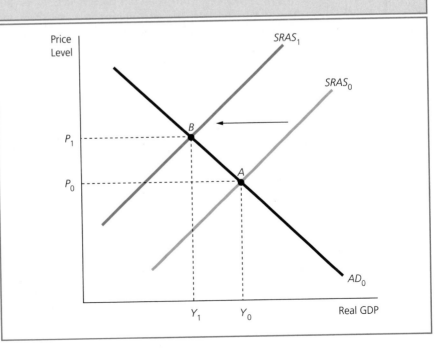

Figure 16.13

Effect of a Decrease in Aggregate Supply on Short-Run Macroeconomic Equilibrium

$SRAS_1$. The new equilibrium between $SRAS_1$ and AD_0 is at point B, with a higher price level of P_1 and lower real GDP of Y_1. Thus, a decrease in short-run aggregate supply results in a higher price level and lower equilibrium real GDP. Our model predicts that the flood of 1993 and the Los Angeles earthquake of January 1994 caused real GDP to fall and the price level to rise relative to what they otherwise would have been.

More generally, any change in a determinant of short-run aggregate supply that decreases SRAS—that is, shifts short-run aggregate supply to the left—will have the short-run effect of increasing the price level and decreasing real GDP. Any change in a determinant of short-run aggregate supply that causes it to increase—shifts short-run aggregate supply to the right—will decrease the price level and increase real GDP.

Summary Exercise 16.3

(a) Suppose the nominal equilibrium interest rate falls. What happens to the short-run equilibrium price level and real GDP assuming all other determinants of AD and SRAS remain the same? (b) The computer industry is constantly improving the speed and power of personal computers. Intel's 486 and Pentium processors are able to outperform the original 8088 chips of a decade ago by orders of magnitude. Holding other things constant, what is the impact of this technological advance on the equilibrium price level and the level of real GDP?

Answer: (a) Holding other things constant, a reduction in the nominal interest rate leads to a lower real interest rate. This increases investment and consumption demand, which shifts the aggregate demand curve to the right as in Figure 16.12. The reduction in the interest rate thus leads to a higher price level and higher real GDP in the short run. (b) Technological advances in general shift aggregate supply to the right. The technological advances in the computer industry shift short-run aggregate supply to the right. Holding everything else constant, including the determinants of aggregate demand, the result is an increase in real output and a lower price level than would otherwise be the case.

VERTICAL LONG-RUN AGGREGATE SUPPLY AND LONG-RUN EQUILIBRIUM

So far we have discussed short-run aggregate supply, a situation in which nominal wages and other input prices are fixed and price expectations have not adjusted to fully account for any changes in the price level. In the long run, however, nominal wages typically adjust to changes in the price level, as do the prices of other inputs, and price expectations adjust to match movements in the price level. When wages, other input prices, and price expectations rise in response to a higher price level, the short-run aggregate supply curve shifts to the left, eliminating some of the increase in output that occurs when the price level increases.

To see this, we will focus on the adjustment in nominal wages. For simplicity we will assume other input prices and price expectations adjust instantaneously, so only nominal wages are slow to adjust to price changes. Consider part a of Figure 16.14, which shows an initial short-run aggregate supply curve as $SRAS_0(w_L = 5)$ for a given value of the wage rate, $w_L = 5. If the price level is 100, real GDP is $4 trillion, as illustrated at point A.

Figure 16.14
The Long-Run Aggregate Supply Curve

The short-run aggregate supply curve is drawn with input prices constant. In part a the initial situation is at point A, with a price level of 100. As the price level rises to 120, short-run aggregate quantity supplied rises to point B. Notice that initially wages were 5 percent of the price level. At point B, wages are only about 4 percent of the price level. This fall in the *relative* input costs led to the increase in output. However, over time wages will adjust to give workers the same purchasing power they had before the price change; that is, wages will equal 5 percent of the price level. At a price level of 120, a wage of $6 will equal 5 percent of the price level, which shifts the short-run aggregate supply curve to the left.

Part b shows the adjustment between the short-run and long-run equilibria. The economy is initially in equilibrium at point A. Aggregate demand increases from AD_0 to AD_1, moving the short-run equilibrium to point B. In the long run wages will rise, thereby shifting back the short-run aggregate supply curve. This process will continue until the purchasing power of wages has been restored to its earlier level at point A. This occurs at point D, with wages equal to $6, a price level equal to 120, and output at the long-run level of $4 trillion in 1987 dollars; that is, the increase in aggregate demand is ultimately offset by a decrease in short-run aggregate supply. The vertical line through points A and D, denoted *LRAS*, is the long-run aggregate supply curve.

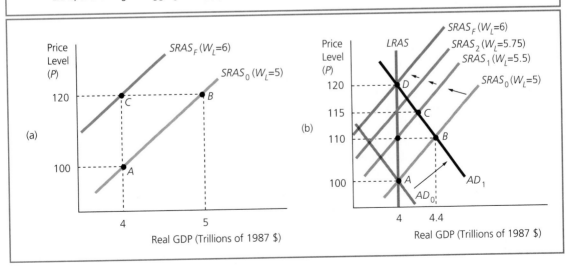

What happens when the price level increases to 120? In the short run (when the wage remains at $5), the quantity supplied increases as we move up the aggregate supply curve to point B, where real GDP is $5 trillion. This movement from A to B is the increase in quantity supplied, holding constant the nominal wage rate.

In the long run, workers observe the higher price level and must receive higher wages if the purchasing power of their wages is to remain the same. When wages increase, the short-run aggregate supply curve decreases, or shifts to the left. If the price level is still at 120, the increase in wages will shift short-run aggregate supply leftward. How much will wages rise? For the purchasing power of wages to remain constant, wages must rise proportionally with prices. Since the price level increased from 100 to 120, or 20 percent, wages must increase by 20 percent. Thus, wages would increase from $5 to $6, shifting the short-run aggregate supply curve to $SRAS_F(W_L = 6)$.

Once wages increase to $6, we are at point C in part a of Figure 16.14, and the wage rate stands in the same proportion to the price level as at point A; that is, at point A wages were $5 when the price level was 100, and now at point C wages are $6 when the price level is 120. The ratio of wages to prices is unchanged. Thus, workers now cost the same *relative to output prices* as they did at point A. Consequently, firms will hire only as many workers as they hired in the initial situation, and output will be the same as at point A. In other words, the increase in the wage rate to $6 shifts short-run aggregate supply to $SRAS_F(w_L = 6)$. At a price level of 120, this indicates real GDP will again be $4 trillion (point C). Thus, in the long run, after all adjustments in input prices, the change in output is zero.

Another way to see this, and to see just how the adjustment between the long run and the short run takes place, is illustrated in part b of Figure 16.14. The initial equilibrium is at point A, where AD_0 and $SRAS_0(w_L = 5)$ intersect. The price level is 100, and real GDP is $4 trillion. From this starting point, consider an increase in aggregate demand to AD_1. In the short run, with fixed wages and input prices, the equilibrium moves to point B, where the price level is 110 and real GDP is $4.4 trillion. This is the short-run impact of the increase in aggregate demand.

At point B, the price level has increased but wages remain fixed. In moving from A to B, prices rise from 100 to 110, or by 10 percent. Workers will ultimately require a 10 percent increase in wages to keep their purchasing power constant, and the wage will rise to $5.5. This increase in wages shifts aggregate supply to $SRAS_1(w_L = 5.5)$. If the price level stayed at 110, this would reduce real GDP back to the initial equilibrium value, 4. However, this leftward shift in aggregate supply, due to higher wages, results in an equilibrium at point C, where the price level has risen further to 115. At point C, the price level is 15 percent above the initial price level at point A, but wages and other input prices are only 10 percent above their initial values. Wages have still fallen in real terms, though not by as much as they did at point B. At point C real GDP is still above its initial level of \$4 trillion, but is now below the level it was at point B, \$4.4 trillion.

Once again workers observe their wages have not kept up with the price level, and they must receive higher wages to maintain their purchasing power. This again shifts aggregate supply to the left. This process continues until aggregate supply shifts to $SRAS_F(w_L = 6)$, where it intersects AD_1 at point D. In the long run, real GDP is \$4 trillion, the same output level as at point A. Points A and D, and all points on the line labeled $LRAS$, are called the **long-run aggregate supply curve** to indicate that changes in the price level do not affect real GDP when wages and other input prices are not fixed.

Thus, we see that increases in aggregate demand can raise output in the short run provided wages, price expectations, and other input prices do not adjust to increases in the price level. But in the long run, wages, price expectations, and other input prices increase with the price level, and real GDP will fall to its long-run equilibrium level. Of course, as the adjustment process illustrated in part b of Figure 16.14 indicates, the adjustment to the long-run equilibrium may take a considerable amount of time, depending on how quickly nominal wages adjust at each step. Also, although Figure 16.14 focuses on nominal wages, input prices and price expectations must also adjust.

Keynesian economists and others who stress nominal wage rigidity—including many so-called new Keynesians who stress the infrequent adjustment of nominal wages in labor contracts—tend to stress that this adjustment process (the movement from point B to D in part b of Figure 16.14) can be very slow. Keynes himself spoke disparagingly of economists who looked only at the long run and is reported to have said that in the long run, we are all dead. Other economists—notably monetarists (who stress the role of money in economic activity) and **new classical economists** (who stress rational expectations and market clearing)—are much more comfortable with long-run analysis and think wages adjust fairly quickly to get the economy to long-run equilibrium. New classical economists in particular often stress that only unexpected increases in the price level cause differences between short-run and long-run aggregate supply and that with rational expectations, these differences should be both unpredictable and temporary. Thus, new classical economists tend to be very comfortable with quick adjustment to the long run.

Does the preceding analysis mean real GDP cannot change in the long run? Not at all! It means real GDP does not change *in the long run* due to aggregate demand factors. The output level indicated by the long-run aggregate supply curve is also called the **natural rate of output,** the amount of goods and services the economy can produce with available technology and the full employment of its resources, including capital and labor. In the long run, firms can produce more only if the capital stock or the size of the work force increases or technological advances occur. For instance, increases in the capital stock shift long-run aggregate supply to the right, as does any improvement in technology. Lowering the tax rate on labor also shifts long-run aggregate supply to the right, since it encourages more people to enter the work force. Similarly, decreases in the capital stock, technological regress, or increasing the tax rate on labor all shift long-run aggregate supply to the left.

When economists talk about full employment, they do not mean a situation in which the unemployment rate is literally zero. Some unemployment is **frictional unemployment,** which occurs as people seek their first jobs, quit one job to seek another, or are displaced from jobs due to technological changes and must seek other jobs. If only frictional and structural unemployment exist, we say the economy is in a state of full employment. Another way to say this is that the economy is at the **natural rate of employment,** the level of employment that exists when there is only frictional unemployment. The **natural rate of output** is the level of output that occurs when employment is at the natural rate of employment so that only frictional unemployment exists. Thus, the level of output indicated by the position of the long-run aggregate supply curve is the natural rate of output.

More generally, the vertical long-run aggregate supply curve means that in the long run, **economic growth**—increases in the real output produced by an economy—requires a rightward shift in long-run aggregate supply. This fact has important implications for policy. For example, policies that directly encourage investment, or that encourage saving and indirectly encourage investment, will lead to faster growth of the capital stock and thus of long-run output. Policies that encourage technological change, such as subsidies or tax breaks for research and development activities, can also increase long-run aggregate supply. Finally, policies that encourage greater labor force participation by workers and higher labor demand by firms will lead to higher levels of employment and hence increase long-run aggregate supply. Such policies might be reductions in the tax rates on labor income to encourage an increase in labor supply or reductions in taxes paid by employers hiring labor, such as social security taxes.

Summary Exercise 16.4

Prior to elections, government often pursues policies that stimulate the economy, such as increasing government purchases or increasing the money supply. For example, it is claimed that in the United States, real output tends to rise just before presidential elections and to decline after those elections. Some analysts claim this is due to expansionary policy actions undertaken by incumbent presidents who are trying to get reelected or to get their parties' nominees elected. This phenomenon has been called the *political business cycle.* Describe how our model of aggregate demand and supply can explain how this political business cycle works.

Answer: In the short run, when wages are fixed, expansionary government policies increase aggregate demand, thus leading to greater real GDP (like the movement from *A* to *B* in part b of Figure 16.14). If the government times the expansionary policy correctly, this should occur right before the election. This would explain why the economy flourishes just prior to an election: Incumbents stimulate the economy to increase real GDP, thus enhancing their chances for reelection. In the long run, however (sometime after the election is over), wages and other input prices begin to rise, which shifts short-run aggregate supply to the left. This corresponds to a movement from *B* to *D* in part b of Figure 16.14. As we move from *B* to *D,* real output falls until real GDP returns to the natural rate.

FISCAL POLICY AND THE GOVERNMENT BUDGET CONSTRAINT

Summary Exercise 16.4 considered the impact of an increase in government purchases on short-run and long-run equilibrium. To keep the analysis simple, we didn't consider where the government obtained funds for the increased spending. In reality, to pay for additional spending the government must either raise taxes, borrow, or print new money. We will see that the way government chooses to finance its spending has important consequences for the economy. To understand the workings of **fiscal policy**—government spending or tax policy—we first look at the concept of the government budget constraint.

What Is the Government Budget Constraint?

The **government budget constraint** is the restriction that the government cannot purchase goods and services without having a source of funds to pay for these purchases. Of course, you are probably thinking the federal government continually purchases goods and services without immediately paying for them with tax revenue, and you are partially correct. However, the government does have to obtain funds to pay for programs.

One way it does so is to borrow funds in the loanable funds market, much as you might use a credit card to borrow funds for your expenses. The fact that you have a credit card doesn't mean you get to buy goods and services without paying for them, just as the government's ability to borrow doesn't mean it obtains goods and services without paying for them. However, the government has two ways to finance current spending that are not available to you: It can collect funds through taxes, and it can print money to pay for its purchases. Thus, the basic idea behind the government budget constraint is that to pay for increased spending, the government must either (1) raise tax revenues, (2) borrow funds by selling government bonds, or (3) print money. We will see next that when the government raises taxes or borrows funds to pay for spending increases, it dampens the short-run stimulating effects of higher government purchases on the economy.

Government Purchases Financed by Taxes

If an increase in government purchases is matched by an equal increase in taxes to pay for the spending, the government does not need to borrow any additional funds or print additional new money. We can analyze this case as a simultaneous increase in government purchases and in taxes. We first consider taxes that affect only aggregate demand and then look at taxes that affect both demand and supply.

Consumption Taxes.

Periodically there is talk in Washington about using a consumption tax—in particular, a value-added tax, or VAT—to raise additional tax revenue. For example, this idea was floated in the first year of President Clinton's term during the discussions surrounding his budget proposal. How would such a tax affect the economy? While this is a very complicated issue, we can use our aggregate demand and supply model to get some idea of the effect on real GDP and the price level.

Point A in Figure 16.15 illustrates the initial equilibrium in the economy. Suppose the government raises consumption taxes to finance an increase in government purchases of goods and services. Such a tax does not affect workers' take-home pay, so to keep things simple let us suppose it does not affect the position of the aggregate supply curve.[4] The increase in government purchases of goods and services raises aggregate demand from AD_0 to AD_1. But the rise in consumption taxes discourages consumption, which tends to shift aggregate demand back to the left. Does the increase in taxes totally cancel the increase in government purchases so that the net effect on aggregate demand is zero? Most economists say the answer is no. Every \$1 increase in government purchases causes government demand, and hence aggregate demand, to shift to the right by \$1. Every increase in taxes reduces consumers' aftertax income and thus reduces consumption demand—but by less than \$1, since consumers might pay the \$1 in taxes partly by reducing consumption and partly by reducing saving. Hence, the net effect is that the tax increase only partly counteracts the increase in government purchases, and the aggregate demand curve ends up in a position such as AD_2. Thus, the net short-run effect is that the equilibrium moves to point C, where the price level and real GDP are higher than at point A (but lower than at point B, which ignores the effect of the consumption tax on aggregate demand). This example illustrates that in the short run, an increase in government purchases financed by a consumption tax may actually stimulate the economy, that is, cause real GDP to rise.

In the long run, however, nominal wages and other input prices will rise due to the increase in the price level. This causes short-run aggregate supply

---

[4] In reality, all taxes are distortionary and thus are likely to affect aggregate supply. Even a lump-sum head tax reduces the incentive to have children, which will decrease the size of the work force and decrease aggregate supply.

Figure 16.15

Tax-Financed Government Purchases That Do Not Affect Long-Run Aggregate Supply

This graph shows the effect of an increase in government purchases financed by an increase in taxes when the taxes do not affect aggregate supply. The initial equilibrium is at point A. The increase in government purchases causes aggregate demand to rise from AD_0 to AD_1. The increase in taxes, however, causes aggregate demand to decrease to AD_2. Thus, short-run equilibrium is at point C, where the price level and real GDP are higher than at point A. In the long run wages rise, which results in a long-run equilibrium at point E. Thus, in the long run, aggregate output is unaffected by the increased government purchases financed by taxes, but the price level rises.

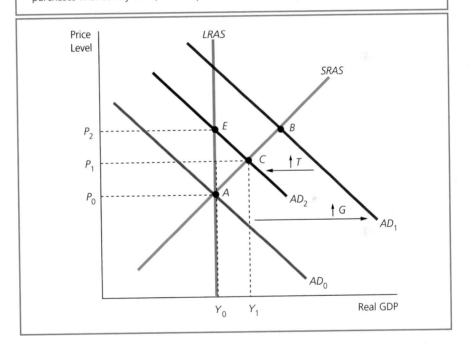

to shift to the left and ultimately results in a new long-run equilibrium at point E. At point E, real GDP is the same as it was before the increase in government purchases and taxes.

Income Taxes.   The primary source of federal government tax revenue is the income tax. What happens if the government raises income taxes to fund an increase in government purchases of goods and services? The increase in government purchases tends to raise aggregate demand. But the higher income taxes tend to reduce aggregate demand, for two reasons. First,

Inside Money

Box 16.3

*Did Indexation Cause the Budget
Deficits of the 1980s?*

It has become popular in some quarters to blame the indexation of the tax code during the Reagan tax cuts for the ongoing federal budget deficits. The argument is that indexing the tax brackets to inflation, coupled with indexing spending to inflation, caused the budget deficit to expand.

Does this argument make sense? It is true that if the tax brackets had not been indexed, the U.S. Treasury would have had more revenue solely because inflation pushed taxpayers into higher brackets. But the argument is stronger than this. It claims that this indexing means inflation caused an increase in the deficit, with spending rising faster than tax collections. Is this correct?

Consider a very simple example. You earn $10,000 and pay 10 percent tax. Every dollar over $10,000 is taxed at a higher rate, say, 20 percent. Your tax bill, $1,000, pays for some-one's social security check. Now suppose there is 20 percent inflation. If your earnings keep up with inflation, you now earn $12,000. With indexed tax brackets, you still pay only 10 percent tax on this income, which now comes to $1,200. (Without indexing, you would be pushed into a higher tax bracket and pay $1,400 in taxes—10 percent on the first $10,000 of income and 20 percent on the next $2,000.) Social security is also indexed to inflation, and the payment to recipients rises from $1,000 to $1,200. Thus, before inflation your taxes just paid for the social security payment, and after inflation your taxes just paid for the social security payment. Thus, indexing of tax brackets and of spending does not cause a budget deficit. Indeed, the increase in your tax bill increased by just enough to cover the increased social security spending.

the higher income tax leads to a reduction in consumption, as households have less to spend on consumer goods. Second, investment declines since firms will find fewer profitable investments at the higher tax rates.[5] This is not the end of the story, however. Higher income taxes also affect aggregate supply. The increase in the income tax reduces people's incentive to enter the work force, since they get to keep less of each additional dollar they earn. This lowers the natural rate of employment, which results in a reduction in both short-run and long-run aggregate supply.

---

[5] These decreases in consumption and investment may be further reduced if the higher income tax rates decrease the supply of loanable funds. In this case, interest rates rise, which further reduces both consumption and investment.

The ultimate magnitude of these effects is a source of much political debate, and we can see why by using our aggregate supply and demand framework. In Figure 16.16, the initial equilibrium is at point A at the intersection of AD_0 and $SRAS_0$. The increase in government purchases shifts aggregate demand to the right to AD_1, but the increase in taxes reduces investment and consumption, which shifts aggregate demand to the left, to AD_2. The rise in the income tax also decreases short-run aggregate supply to $SRAS_1$ and decreases long-run aggregate supply to $LRAS_1$.

If the rise in government purchases of goods and services more than offsets the decline in investment and consumption, the short-run equilibrium

Figure 16.16
Tax-Financed Government Purchases That Affect Aggregate Supply

This graph shows the effect of an increase in government purchases financed by an income tax, which does affect aggregate supply. The initial equilibrium is at point A. When the government increases purchases of goods and services, aggregate demand shifts to AD_1, but the income tax reduces consumption and investment, which causes aggregate demand to shift to the left to either AD_2 or AD_0. In addition, the increase in income taxes reduces short-run aggregate supply from $SRAS_0$ to $SRAS_1$. The new short-run equilibrium is at either point B or point C, indicating short-run real GDP may rise or fall. In the long run input prices rise, which ultimately leads to an equilibrium at point E or F. Thus, regardless of the short-run effects, the long-run effect is a reduction in real output to Y_{LR}.

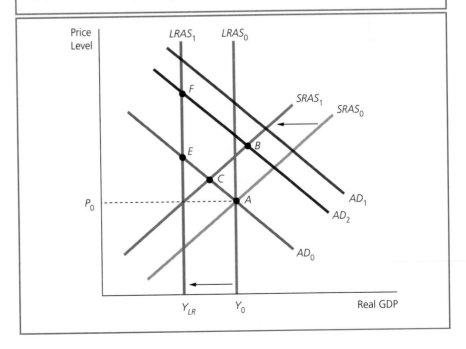

will be at point B, where AD_2 and $SRAS_1$ intersect. In this case, the "tax and spend" policy has the short-run effect of increasing real GDP and the price level compared with the initial situation at point A. However, if the reduction in investment and consumption exactly offsets the rise in government purchases, aggregate demand will remain at AD_0. In this case, the short-run equilibrium is at point C, where real GDP is lower than at point A. This example illustrates that a rise in government purchases financed by an increase in the income tax may either increase or decrease real GDP in the short run, depending on how much investment declines. Obviously those who believe the short-run effect of the "tax and spend" policy is to move the economy to point B are more likely to favor the policy than those who view point C as the likely equilibrium. Most income tax legislation has special provisions, called *investment tax credits,* that are designed to keep investment from drastically declining due to higher taxes, thereby increasing the likelihood that the actual short-run equilibrium will occur at point B.

The long-run effect of government purchases financed with income taxes is clearer. If taxes reduce long-run aggregate supply, then, regardless of the short-run effect, the long-run effect is to reduce real GDP and raise the price level. We can readily see this in Figure 16.16. If long-run aggregate supply declines from $LRAS_0$ to $LRAS_1$, then, whether the short-run equilibrium is at B (along AD_2) or C (along AD_0) is of little importance in the long run. In long-run equilibrium, the economy will be at either F (along AD_2) or E (along AD_0), and in either case real GDP will fall to Y_{LR}, since both AD_0 and AD_2 intersect $LRAS_1$ at the same level of real GDP. Thus, we see that in the long run, if higher income taxes decrease long-run aggregate supply by reducing incentives to enter the work force, this reduction in the natural rate of employment will decrease the natural rate of output of the economy.

Will taxes reduce long-run aggregate supply? Much debate exists over how much the natural rate of output declines as a result of higher income taxes. The popular press often uses the label **supply sider** to describe those who view the effect on aggregate supply as being important. Some economists dismiss the notion that tax rates have much to do with long-run aggregate supply. They claim long-run supply is mostly unaffected by tax rate changes of the sort usually proposed for the U.S. economy.

The Tradeoff: Higher Real GDP or Greater Income Equality.

Our analysis of the long-run effects of tax-financed government purchases suggests income taxes may have an adverse effect on long-run GDP. You may wonder why there is any debate at all about abolishing the income tax and replacing it with other forms of taxation, like a lump-sum or consumption tax. The answer is surprisingly simple. First, some argue income taxes have little effect on long-run GDP. Second, and probably equally important, is the fact that the U.S. income tax serves a dual purpose: to fund government programs and to decrease the degree of income inequality. Those who favor the consumption tax tend to stress that it results in higher long-run real GDP than under an income tax. Proponents of the income tax may even acknowledge its adverse effects on long-run real GDP but view the effect as small compared to the benefits of greater income equality.

Since the progressive income tax in the United States taxes the rich at higher rates than the poor, it tends to reduce the relative difference in incomes between the classes. Consumption taxes, on the other hand, tend to be regressive, meaning the poor actually pay a greater fraction of their income in taxes than the rich do. For the poor who spend all of their incomes on consumer goods, a consumption tax is an income tax. The rich, who spend a smaller fraction of their incomes on consumer goods, end up paying taxes only on the smaller percentage of income actually spent on consumption goods. For these reasons, consumption taxes tend to increase the level of income inequality, whereas the progressive income tax tends to reduce it.

Advocates of consumption taxes believe the benefits of higher long-run real GDP more than outweigh the negative effects on the distribution of income, whereas advocates of the income tax do not. Which view is "correct?" We cannot provide an answer to this question. We can only point out the tradeoff: The cost of using an income tax to equalize the distribution of income is lower long-run GDP.

Government Purchases Financed by Borrowing: Deficit Finance

In the 1980s, the U.S. government ran deficits of huge magnitudes when judged against its own history of peacetime government budgets, and financed these shortfalls with government bond sales. Did it make any difference to the economy that the government chose to finance its spending by borrowing instead of raising taxes? Two schools of thought exist on this question. The traditional **Keynesian view** is that deficit financing is more expansionary than tax financing, because taxpayers don't recognize that government debt is simply deferred tax liabilities and that taxes will someday be raised to pay for the accumulated debt. Another view, called the **Ricardian view,** is that borrowing and tax financing are equivalent. According to the Ricardian view, our analysis of tax-financed government purchases in the previous section also applies to deficit-financed government spending. We will examine the traditional Keynesian analysis here, deferring further discussion of Ricardian ideas until Chapter 21.

What happens when the government borrows to finance an increase in purchases of goods and services? In this case, government purchases rise (increasing aggregate demand), and there is no decline in consumption from raising taxes. However, government borrowing will increase the interest rate, which reduces investment and consumption. To see why, consider the loanable funds market introduced in Chapter 4. This market is illustrated in Figure 16.17, where the initial equilibrium is at point *A,* with an equilibrium interest rate of 5 percent. When the government increases its borrowing to

This figure shows how a deficit-financed increase in government purchases affects the market for loanable funds. When the government borrows funds, the demand for loanable funds rises from D_0 to D_1. The equilibrium then moves from point A to point B, and the interest rate rises from 5 to 7 percent.

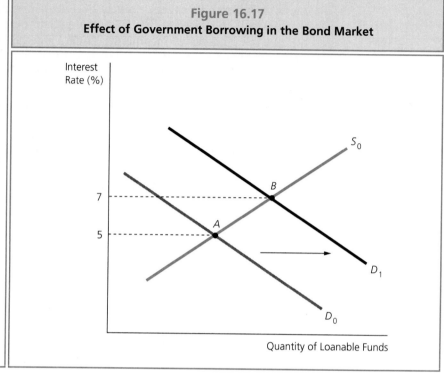

Figure 16.17
Effect of Government Borrowing in the Bond Market

Interest Rate (%)

Quantity of Loanable Funds

finance increased expenditures on goods and services, an increase occurs in the demand for loanable funds, represented by a shift from D_0 to D_1. This changes the equilibrium to point B and raises the equilibrium interest rate to 7 percent. This example illustrates that government borrowing raises the nominal interest rate.

However, this is not the end of the story. The increase in the nominal interest rate is, holding other things constant, a rise in the real interest rate. With no change in expected inflation, the increase in the real interest rate represents a rise in the real cost of borrowing funds for investment purposes or to finance the purchase of consumer durables. This, in turn, tends to reduce consumption and investment spending and hence reduce aggregate demand. This effect of government borrowing on interest rates and hence on nongovernment spending is called **crowding out.** Due to crowding out, the increase in government purchases financed by borrowing results in a smaller increase in aggregate demand than would at first appear to be the case. The case of **partial crowding out** is illustrated in Figure 16.18, where the increase in government purchases shifts aggregate demand from AD_0 to AD_1, but the increase in the interest rate from government borrowing reduces

> ### Figure 16.18
> ### Crowding Out
>
> An increase in government purchases shifts aggregate demand from AD_0 to AD_1. However, the interest rate rises when the government borrows funds to pay for spending. This causes both consumption and investment demand to fall. The result is a decrease in aggregate demand from AD_1. Partial crowding out occurs when aggregate demand shifts back only to AD_2 and the new short-run equilibrium is at point C. In the long run, input prices adjust and the equilibrium will be at point D. Complete crowding out occurs when aggregate demand shifts all the way back to AD_0 so that both the short- and long-run equilibria remain at point A.

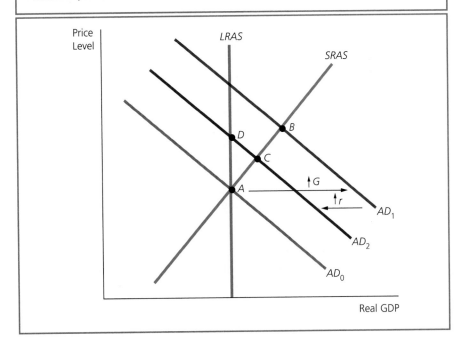

investment and consumption demand and hence decreases aggregate demand to AD_2. In this case, the net short-run effect of an increase in government purchases financed by borrowing is the movement from point A to point C in Figure 16.18, and real GDP increases. In the long run the economy moves to point D, where output returns to its initial level and the price level rises further.

We note that for a large enough reduction in consumption and investment due to the higher interest rate, it is possible that the interest rate effect completely offsets the increase in government purchases—an effect known as **complete crowding out.** In this case, government purchases of goods and services increase aggregate demand to AD_1, but the higher interest rates caused by government borrowing lead to reductions in consumption and investment that shift it back to AD_0. Here both the short-run and long-run equilibria remain at point A in Figure 16.18. It is important to realize that crowding out (partial or complete) reduces the impact of deficit-financed government purchases on short-run GDP.

Differing views exist on the magnitude of this crowding-out phenomenon, and this tends to spice up political debates about the merits of using fiscal policy to stimulate the economy. Keynesians believe crowding out is not a major detriment to deficit-financed fiscal policy, whereas monetarists and new classical economists tend to believe crowding out is more nearly complete. Hence, Keynesians are advocates of fiscal policy, whereas monetarists and others are not.

One interesting claim made by several influential commentators such as Edwin Yoder and Sam Donaldson is that indexing the Federal tax code was a leading cause of the budget deficits of the 1980s. Box 16.3 discussed this claim (see p. 564).

Government Purchases Financed by Money Creation

Government purchases can also be financed by money creation, and this approach has very strong short-run effects on macroeconomic equilibrium. While the U.S. government did not choose to finance government purchases with large-scale money creation in the 1980s, other countries have at times resorted to money creation to finance large portions of government purchases. Historical examples include the German hyperinflation of the 1930s. A current example is the government in Belgrade, Serbia (once the capital of Yugoslavia), where government money creation has led to inflation rates that reached 300 million percent per month in 1994!

What are the effects of financing government purchases with money creation? First, the increase in government purchases increases aggregate demand directly. Second, the increase in the money supply itself has two effects. First, the increase in the nominal money supply increases the real money supply and tends to lower the interest rate. Holding everything else constant, including the expected inflation rate, this fall in the interest rate translates into a decline in the real interest rate, which stimulates investment spending and consumption spending on durable goods and hence further increases aggregate demand. Second, the rise in the money supply increases the wealth of consumers, which directly stimulates consumption demand via the wealth effect and again increases aggregate demand.

Figure 16.19 illustrates government purchases financed by money creation. The initial equilibrium is at point A, with aggregate demand given by AD_0. The increase in government purchases raises aggregate demand to AD_1. The increase in the money supply, then, has two effects. First, it lowers interest rates and thus stimulates investment spending and consumer spending. Second, it increases consumer wealth, which exerts a positive effect on

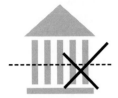

Inside Money

Box 16.4

*Using Aggregate Demand and Supply:
The Recession of 1990–1991*

The U.S. economy experienced negative real GDP growth—a recession—during the third and fourth quarters of 1990 and the first quarter of 1991. Real GDP declined from $4,878 billion (in 1987 dollars) in 1990 to $4,821 billion in 1991. What caused this recession? Several answers have been offered.

First, monetary policy was somewhat restrictive in 1989, and this restricted growth in aggregate demand. The monetary base grew at 7.1 percent in 1988 but slowed to 4.2 percent in 1989. The M1 measure of the money supply grew by only 1 percent in 1989 after growing by 5 percent in 1988. M2 still grew at 5.1 percent in 1989, down slightly from 5.5 percent in 1988, but slowed to 3.5 percent in 1990. Inter-

est rates responded as expected. The interest rate on three-month T-bills was 6.7 percent in 1988, and with an inflation rate of 3.9 percent, this was a 2.8 percent ex post real interest rate. The slow growth in the monetary base in 1989 had its intended effects: the three-month T-bill rate rose to 8.1 percent in 1989, and with an inflation rate of 4.4 percent, this was a 3.7 percent ex post real interest rate. Thus, the Fed took actions to restrict money growth and increase interest rates in 1989, and our aggregate demand and supply model suggests aggregate demand would grow more slowly because of these measures. You may wonder why a restrictive monetary policy in 1989 would cause a re-

Continued on p. 572

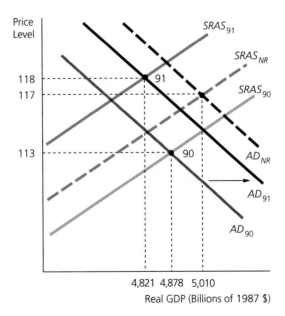

Price Level

Real GDP (Billions of 1987 $)

Continued from p. 571

cession in the last half of 1990. The reason is that it takes time for monetary policy actions to affect the economy. These lags are not incorporated in our model, but students of monetary history have observed repeatedly that it seems to take about 12 months or more for monetary policy to have its desired effects. We discuss lags in policymaking in more detail in Chapter 19.

The second restrictive action was the reduction in federal government purchases for national defense. With the winding down of the Cold War, these purchases actually declined between 1988 and 1990 from $287 billion (in 1987 dollars) to $283 billion. Total federal government purchases (defense plus nondefense) also declined in 1989, from $377 billion to $376 billion, before rising slightly in 1990. This reduction in federal government purchases, G, also restricted growth in aggregate demand.

Finally, aggregate supply also played a role. When Iraq invaded Kuwait and at least implicitly threatened Saudi Arabia in early 1990, the price of crude oil skyrocketed. From the spring to fall of 1990, crude oil prices doubled. This increase in the price of an important input to production caused aggregate supply to shift to the left.

What was the effect of all this? In the accompanying figure, AD_{90} and $SRAS_{90}$ intersect at a real GDP of $4,878 billion (in 1987 dollars) and a price level of 113. In 1991, aggregate demand increased, but only to AD_{91}, and aggregate supply shifted left to $SRAS_{91}$. The intersection occurs at a real GDP of $4,821 billion and a price level of 118. Had monetary policy and government purchases been less restrictive, aggregate demand might have grown to AD_{NR} (where NR stands for "no recession"). If oil prices had not doubled, aggregate supply might have shifted only to $SRAS_{NR}$. Had these shifts increased real GDP by its postwar average growth rate of about 2.7 percent, real GDP in 1991 might have been $5,010 billion. Instead, 1990–1991 was a period marked by a recession—one with widespread causes.

consumer spending. Both effects tend to increase aggregate demand further, to AD_2 in the figure. Thus, the short-run effect of government purchases financed by money creation is the movement from point A to point C, which implies a higher price level (P_1) and greater real GDP. Monetarists view the shift from B to C as relatively large, whereas Keynesians view it as rather small. The movement from A to C illustrates that government purchases financed by an increase in the money supply has a strong stimulating effect on real GDP in the short run. Note, however, that the price level also rises considerably in the short run due to the increase in the money supply.

Of course, only in the short run is aggregate supply responsive to changes in the price level. In the long run, the increase in aggregate demand will result in a higher price level but no change in real GDP. In Figure 16.19, for example, the long-run impact of the increase in aggregate demand to AD_2 will be to change the equilibrium to point D, where the price level has risen to P_2 but real GDP has returned to Y_0. Thus, the long-run effect of paying for government purchases by increasing the money supply is to raise prices. Moreover, since the short-run effect is a large shift in aggregate demand, the long-run effect is a large increase in the price level.

An increase in government purchases of goods and services increases aggregate demand from AD_0 to AD_1. The increase in the money supply that financed the increase in government purchases leads to lower interest rates, which further raises aggregate demand from AD_1 to AD_2. Thus, the short-run equilibrium moves from point A to point C. The long-run result is an increase in the price level but no change in output (point D).

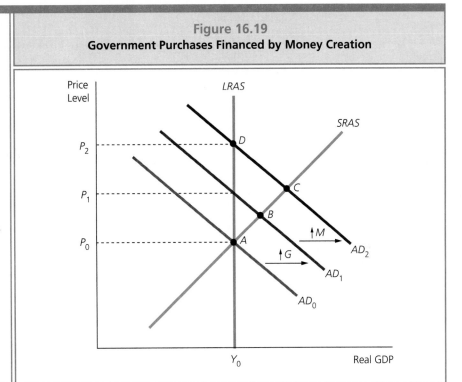

Figure 16.19
Government Purchases Financed by Money Creation

Box 16.4 shows how our aggregate demand and supply model can be used to explain the U.S. recession of 1990–1991.

MONETARY POLICY: OPEN MARKET OPERATIONS

In the previous section, we saw that government spending may be financed by increases in the money supply. Can the government change the money supply without changing taxes or spending? In other words, is it possible for government to pursue an *independent monetary policy*? The answer is yes; it can do so through open market operations. In this section, we examine the effect of an expansionary monetary policy conducted via an open market operation and how this policy relates to the government budget constraint.

Recall from Chapters 13 and 14 that an open market operation is the sale or purchase of government bonds by the Federal Reserve System. Consider an open market purchase. The Fed prints money and uses this money to purchase government bonds. Thus, the public now holds more money but fewer bonds, and in fact the increase in money holdings is equal in value to

When the Fed purchases bonds, it increases the monetary base. Thus, the supply of money increases from M_0^s/P to M_1^s/P. The equilibrium in the money market moves from point A to point B. The result is a decrease in the equilibrium interest rate from i_0 to i_1.

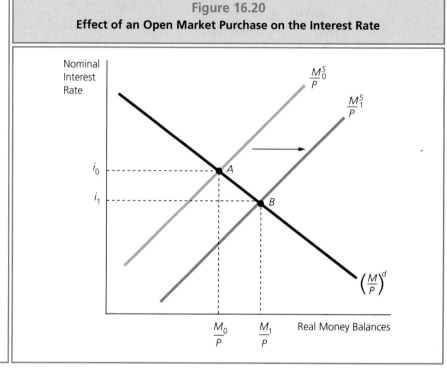

Figure 16.20

Effect of an Open Market Purchase on the Interest Rate

the reduction in bond holdings; thus, the wealth of the public is unchanged. How does this influence aggregate demand? As Figure 16.20 illustrates, holding other things constant the increase in the money supply reduces the interest rate.[6] Here the initial equilibrium is at point A, with an equilibrium interest rate of i_0. The increase in the supply of money from M_0^s to M_1^s changes the equilibrium to point B, where the interest rate falls to i_1. Thus, the effect of an open market purchase is that the Federal Reserve System increases the money supply, lowering the equilibrium interest rate.

The effect of open market operations on aggregate demand, then, follows from the change in the interest rate. Holding the expected inflation rate constant, the decrease in the nominal interest rate is a decrease in the real interest rate and leads to a rise in both consumption and investment demand and hence in aggregate demand. Figure 16.21 illustrates this effect. Aggregate demand is initially at AD_0, and the initial equilibrium is at point A. The

---

[6] We could also see this effect in the loanable funds market, where the Fed in effect acts as a lender, increasing the supply of loanable funds and reducing the interest rate.

An open market pur-
chase of bonds causes
the interest rate to
fall. This in turn in-
creases consumption
and investment, rais-
ing aggregate demand
from AD_0 to AD_1. The
short-run equilibrium
moves from point A to
point B. In the long
run, input prices rise
and the long-run equi-
librium moves to point
C.

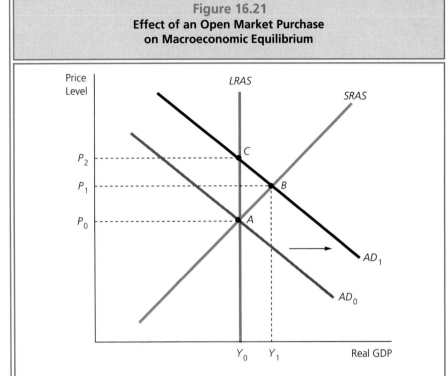

Figure 16.21
**Effect of an Open Market Purchase
on Macroeconomic Equilibrium**

open market purchase lowers the interest rate, shifting aggregate demand to
AD_1 and moving the equilibrium to point B in the short run, increasing the
price level to P_1 and the level of real GDP to Y_1. In the long run, however,
the economy moves to point C, where the price level rises further to P_2 and
real GDP returns to its natural rate, Y_0.

How does this open market purchase relate to the government budget
constraint? It turns out that an open market operation is in perfect accord
with the government budget constraint. The government budget constraint
merely restricts the change in government spending to equal changes in tax
revenue, plus changes in bonds, plus changes in money. If government
spending and tax revenue are unchanged, as they are in an open market
operation, the government budget constraint merely says that any increase
in bonds must be met by a reduction in the money supply, and vice versa.
But that is exactly what happens in an open market operation: The stock of
bonds changes by an equal but opposite amount from the stock of money.
Thus, an open market operation is a monetary policy action that takes place
with no change in government spending or tax collection.

Summary | (a) Suppose the government increases purchases of goods and services and
Exercise 16.5 | finances the spending by issuing bonds. What will be the short-run and long-run effects of this policy? (b) What will be the effect of this policy if the government funds the increase in purchases by raising the money supply?

Answer: (a) Government borrowing—deficit finance—leads to an increase in the demand for loanable funds, which in turn raises the interest rate. This increase in the interest rate decreases the level of investment and consumption in the economy, which tends to shift aggregate demand to the left. The increase in government purchases shifts aggregate demand to the right. If there is complete crowding out, these two effects perfectly cancel each other out, and no change in the price level or aggregate output occurs, although the interest rate does rise. If only partial crowding out exists, the increase in government purchases will more than offset the reduced consumption and investment, and aggregate demand will increase. In the short run, this will lead to greater output and a higher price level. In the long run, however, wages and other input prices will adjust, which will shift short-run aggregate supply to the left. In the long run, the policy will have no effect on real output; it will only raise the price level. (b) An increase in the money supply decreases interest rates, which for given inflationary expectations leads to greater investment and consumption demand. Likewise, the increase in government purchases raises aggregate demand. Thus, the short-run effect of this policy is to increase the price level and real GDP. In the long run, wages and other input prices rise, leading to a higher price level and returning real GDP to its natural rate.

CONCLUSION

In this chapter, we looked at a simple macroeconomic model that links together the determination of interest rates, the price level, and real output. Interest rates are determined in the money (or loanable funds) market, while real GDP and the price level are determined by aggregate demand and supply. We saw that government purchases of goods and services and monetary policy can stimulate the economy in the short run, but these policies do not have long-term effects on real GDP. Keynesians tend to advocate fiscal policy as a means of stimulating the economy in the short run, whereas monetarists advocate monetary policy. In the next chapter, we turn to a discussion of the open economy macroeconomic model and see how international trade affects the domestic economy.

KEY TERMS

closed economic model

consumption goods

new classical economists

natural rate of output

KEY TERMS continued

investment goods	frictional unemployment
physical capital	natural rate of employment
government purchases	economic growth
transfer payments	fiscal policy
net exports	government budget constraint
aggregate demand curve	Keynesian view
substitution effect	Ricardian equivalence
income effect	crowding out
short-run aggregate supply (SRAS)	partial crowding out
nominal wage rigidity	complete crowding out
short-run macroeconomic equilibrium	independent monetary policy
long-run aggregate supply curve	

QUESTIONS AND PROBLEMS

1. Show how the aggregate demand curve is derived from the investment demand, consumption demand, and government demand curves.

2. Explain why investment demand is graphed as downward sloping in Figure 16.4.

3. Holding other things constant, determine the impact (if any) of the following on consumption demand.
   (a). An increase in the interest rate
   (b). An increase in household taxes
   (c). Increased consumer optimism
   (d). Technological improvements

4. Holding other things constant, determine the impact (if any) of the following on government demand.
   (a). An increase in the interest rate
   (b). A decrease in the money supply
   (c). An increase in household taxes

   (d). Increased consumer optimism
   (e). Technological improvements
   (f). A tax on labor income
   (g). A decrease in government purchases

5. Holding other things constant, determine the impact (if any) of the following on investment demand.
   (a). An increase in the real interest rate
   (b). A decrease in the money supply
   (c). The elimination of investment tax credits
   (d). An income tax

6. Determine the impact of the following on aggregate demand.
   (a). An increase in the real interest rate
   (b). A decrease in the money supply
   (c). An increase in household taxes
   (d). An investment tax credit

7. Holding everything else constant, determine the short-run impact of the following

on the equilibrium price level and real GDP.

(a). An increase in the interest rate

(b). A decrease in the money supply

(c). An increase in the income tax

(d). Technological improvements

8. Explain why the short-run aggregate supply curve slopes upward.

9. Explain why the long-run aggregate supply curve is vertical.

10. Suppose the government cuts spending and finances the spending cuts by *lowering taxes*. What are the short-run and long-run macroeconomic effects assuming (a) the tax solely affects consumption, (b) the tax solely affects aggregate supply, and (c) the tax affects both aggregate demand and aggregate supply?

11. Suppose the government cuts spending and finances the spending cuts by *reducing borrowing*. What are the short-run and long-run macroeconomic effects on the interest rate, the price level, and real GDP?

12. Suppose the government reduces spending and finances the spending cuts by *printing less money*. What are the short-run and long-run macroeconomic effects on the interest rate, the price level, and real GDP?

13. Explain why open market operations can have a short-run effect on the economy even if government spending remains fixed.

14. Explain how the possibility of complete crowding out and partial crowding out gives rise to potential disagreements among policymakers about the desirability of using deficit-financed government purchases to stimulate the economy.

15. How can real GDP be increased in the long run?

SELECTIONS FOR FURTHER READING

Allen, S. D., J. M. Sulock, and W. A. Sabo. "The Political Business Cycle: How Significant?" *Public Finance Quarterly,* 14 (January 1986), 107–112.

Beard, T. R., and W. D. McMillin. "Government Budgets and Money: How Are They Related?" *Journal of Economic Education,* 17 (Spring 1986), 107–119.

Cecchetti, S. G. "Seigniorage as a Tax: A Quantitative Evaluation: Comment." *Journal of Money, Credit, and Banking,* 23 (August 1991), 476–480.

Fackler, J. S., and W. D. McMillin. "Federal Debt and Macroeconomic Activity." *Southern Economic Journal,* 55 (April 1989), 994–1003.

Kandil, M. "Variations in the Response of Real Output to Aggregate Demand Shocks: A Cross-Industry Analysis." *Review of Economics and Statistics,* 73 (August 1991), 480–488.

Kojima, K., and T. Ozawa. "Micro- and Macro-Economic Models of Direct Foreign Investment: Toward a Synthesis." *Hitotsubashi Journal of Economics,* 25 (June 1984), 1–20.

Koray, F., and P. Chan. "Government Spending and the Exchange Rate." *Applied Economics,* 23 (September 1991), 1551–1558.

McNelis, P. D. "Irrepressible Monetarist Conclusions from a Non-Monetarist Model." *Journal of Monetary Economics,* 6 (January 1980), 121–127.

Ratti, R. A. "A Descriptive Analysis of Economic Indicators." Federal Reserve Bank of St. Louis *Review,* 67 (January 1985), 14–24.

Ratti, R. A. "The Effects of Inflation Surprises and Uncertainty on Real Wages." *Review of Economics and Statistics,* 67 (May 1985), 309–314.

Raynold, P., W. D. McMillin, and T. R. Beard. "The Impact of Federal Government Expenditures in the 1930s." *Southern Economic Journal,* 58 (July 1991), 15–28.

Salemi, M. K. "On Teaching a Fractured Macroeconomics: Thoughts." *Journal of Economic Education,* 18 (Spring 1987), 227–231.

Scaperlanda, A. "Factors Affecting Private Investment." *Business Economics,* 15 (May 1980), 73–74.

Wallace, F. H., and H. Blanco. "The Effects of Real and Nominal Shocks on Union-Firm Contract Duration." *Journal of Monetary Economics,* 27 (June 1991), 361–380.

Wulwick, N. J. "The Phillips Curve: Which? Whose? To Do What? How?" *Southern Economic Journal,* 53 (April 1987), 834–857.

APPENDIX AN IS-LM MODEL OF AGGREGATE DEMAND

In the text, we develop a model of aggregate demand from four components of aggregate spending: consumption, investment, government purchases, and net exports. In this model aggregate demand is downward sloping, for two reasons. First, there is a wealth effect on consumption from any decrease in the price level that leads to an increase in consumer expenditures. Second, any decrease in the price level leads to an increase in the real money supply that will cause a decline in the interest rate, thus stimulating investment and consumption spending. Due to these two effects, consumption demand and investment demand depend on the price level, and hence aggregate demand depends on the price level.

The relationship between changes in the price level and changes in the quantity demanded of aggregate real goods and services can be derived more formally using what is called the *IS-LM model.* To develop this model, we first derive the IS curve.

THE IS CURVE

The *IS curve* is defined as the set of real GDP and real interest rate values consistent with equilibrium between aggregate spending and aggregate income. (The name IS signifies that this curve is the set of points at which Investment equals Saving, an alternative way of looking at equilibrium between spending and income.) Recall that in Figure 16.7 we derived a relationship that we labeled aggregate demand, or AD, from the relationship $Y = C^d + I^d + G^d + NX^d$. We showed that the requirement that the income variable affecting C^d be the same value as aggregate expenditures (or real GDP) allowed us to derive an aggregate demand curve that held whenever income equals aggregate spending.

The curve we derived, which we labeled *AD,* is very similar to the curve we call IS here. The IS curve is essentially our aggregate demand curve graphed as a function of the real interest rate: IS = IS $(r, P, \pi^e, W, T_H, T_F, EE, G, NX)$. This function is the IS equation, and we can graph this curve as we do in Figure 16A.1, with the real interest rate on the vertical axis and

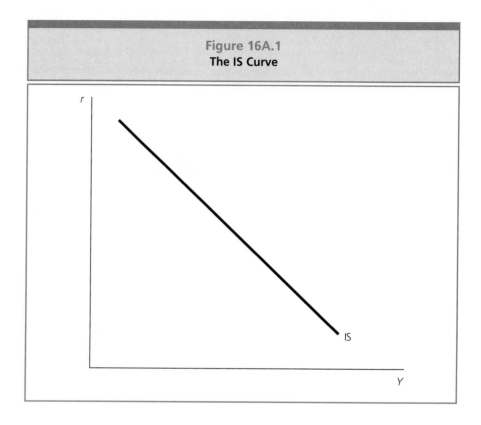

Figure 16A.1
The IS Curve

real output, Y, on the horizontal axis. The IS curve is downward sloping because increases in the real interest rate lead to reductions in investment and consumption spending. Increases in the other variables cause shifts in the IS curve. For example, an increase in government purchases, G, causes income to increase at every level of the real interest rate, so IS shifts to the right. An increase in the price level, P, while holding nominal wealth constant will cause real wealth to decline for every level of the real interest rate, which reduces consumption spending and hence real GDP, so IS shifts to the left.

THE LM CURVE

The *LM curve* is the set of real interest rates and real output values consistent with equilibrium in the money market. (The name LM signifies that this curve is the set of points at which liquidity demand—i.e. money demand—

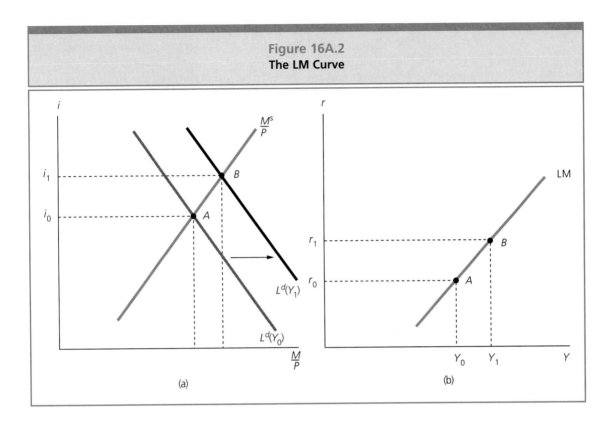

Figure 16A.2
The LM Curve

equals the supply of money.) We derive LM from the money market equilibrium as in Figure 16A.2. Here money demand, a function of real income Y_0, intersects real money supply at point A, where the interest rate is i_0. For a given expected inflation rate π^e, the real interest rate is then $r_0 = i_0 - \pi^e$. Thus, holding everything else constant, the money market equilibrium at point A has a real interest rate of r_0 and real output of Y_0.

What happens if income increases to Y_1? Money demand increases to $L^d(Y_1)$, and money market equilibrium moves to point B, with an interest rate of i_1 and a real interest rate of $r_1 = i_1 - \pi^e$. Thus we continue to hold everything else constant and find that the higher income level Y_1 and higher real interest rate r_1 occur in the equilibrium at point B.

We can continue to change real income and observe what happens to the interest rate—and the real interest rate—due to the money market. By doing so, we can find all combinations of real income and the real interest rate consistent with equilibrium in the money market when we hold constant all other determinants of either money supply or money demand. This gives us the LM curve in part b of Figure 16A.2.

The LM curve is upward sloping, reflecting the relationship between equilibrium real income and equilibrium real interest rates in the money market. The LM curve holds constant a number of variables, including the expected inflation rate, the nominal money supply, and the price level. An increase in the nominal money supply, a reduction in the price level, or an increase in the expected inflation rate will shift LM to the right.

IS-LM EQUILIBRIUM

IS tells us the set of equilibrium real interest rates and real income levels that can occur when aggregate demand (or aggregate spending) equals aggregate income. The LM curve tells us the set of equilibrium real interest rates and real income levels that can occur when real money supply equals real money demand. The intersection of IS and LM when both curves are placed on the same graph tells us the real interest rate and real income level that are consistent with equilibrium both between expenditures and income and between money supply and money demand. This is shown in Figure 16A.3. Changes in any of the determinants of IS or LM will result in changes

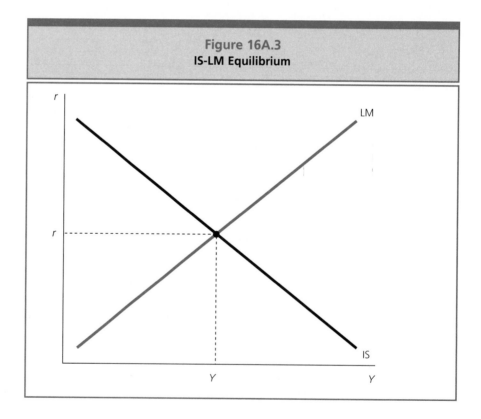

Figure 16A.3
IS-LM Equilibrium

in both the real interest rate and real income. For example, an increase in the nominal money supply will shift LM to the right, reducing the real interest rate and increasing real income. An increase in government purchases will shift IS to the right, increasing both the real interest rate and real income.[1]

AGGREGATE DEMAND

One criticism of the IS-LM model is that it holds the price level constant. To counter this criticism, we can use IS-LM to derive an aggregate demand curve. We do this by asking how the equilibrium between IS and LM might change with changes in the price level. For example, in part a of Figure 16A.4 we graph both $LM(P_0)$ and $IS(P_0)$ and note their intersection at point A, with a real interest rate of r_0 and real income of Y_0. What happens if the price level increases to P_1? This reduces real money balances to M/P_1, so LM shifts to the left. It also reduces real wealth, which shifts IS to the left. The new intersection is at point B, where real output has fallen to Y_1. At point B, the real interest rate may rise or fall depending on the magnitude of the shifts in IS and LM, but we have drawn the shifts so that the real interest rate rises to r_1. In any case, the key is that the increase in the price level to P_1 has resulted in a fall in real output to Y_1. In fact, every time the price level increases, IS and LM shift leftward, reducing real output. Every time the price level decreases, IS and LM shift rightward, and real output increases. In part b of Figure 16A.4, we draw this inverse relationship between the price level and real output as the aggregate demand curve, *AD*.

Why does this *AD* curve slope downward? There are two reasons. First, as the price level rises, real money balances decline, and this reduces real money supply and leads to a higher real interest rate, which tends to reduce investment and consumption spending and hence lower aggregate demand. This is the leftward shift in LM. Second, as the price level rises, real wealth declines, which directly reduces real consumption spending. This is the leftward shift in IS. In terms of changes in real income, the shifts in IS and LM reinforce each other, reducing real income to Y_1. Thus, *AD* slopes downward in the IS-LM scenario for the same reasons given in the text.

This *AD* curve can be used, along with the aggregate supply curves developed in the text, to analyze the effects of changes in the determinants of IS or LM on the price level and real income. One advantage of the IS-LM approach is that it more clearly ties together the equilibrium relationship between real income and real spending—the IS curve—and the

---

[1] Notice that these results for interest rates and for real output are the same as we find in the body of the text for an increase in government purchases or an increase in the money supply.

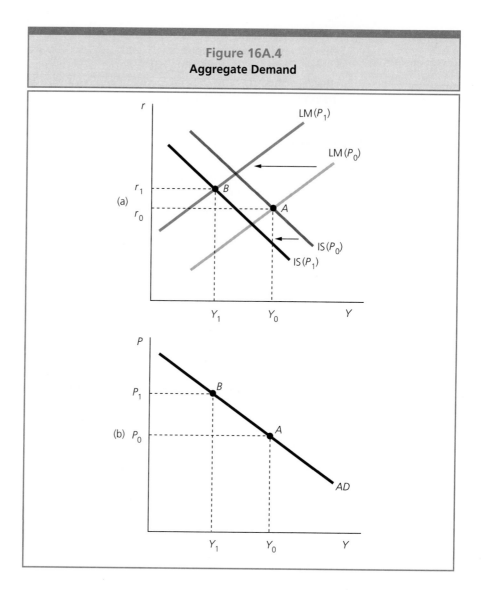

Figure 16A.4

Aggregate Demand

money market equilibrium—the LM curve. This allows us to see how changes in the price level and real output can lead to changes in the equilibrium real interest rate. However, the results we got in the text are basically the same as those that can be derived using the IS-LM approach, at least in terms of the directions of movement in the variables due to changes in the determinants of *AD*.

IS-LM is not without its critics or disadvantages. One disadvantage is that the IS-LM model relies on the money market equilibrium for any analysis of changes in the interest rate. However, we saw in Chapter 15 and in this chapter that the loanable funds market is often more convenient for analyzing the effects on the interest rate of changes in variables other than the money supply. For example, the effects on real interest rates of increases in the government deficit are most easily analyzed in the loanable funds market, as are the effects of increases in the expected inflation rate.

Open Economy Macroeconomics

*I*n Chapter 16, we examined a simple but useful model of the macro economy. The model presented there is a model with exogenous net exports, essentially a modest extension of a *closed economy model,* one that does not consider the impact of changes in international trade on the economy. For many years it was considered acceptable to model the United States in this way, since international trade was only a small part of the U.S. economy. However, international trade and investment flows have become increasingly important to the United States. In 1990, gross domestic product was $5,465 billion, while U.S. exports to other countries were valued at $653 billion, or more than 10 percent of output. Imports of foreign goods into the United States totaled $723 billion, an even larger percentage of GDP. Thus, foreign trade in goods and services is an important component of the U.S. economy today. Foreign investment is also becoming increasingly important. In 1990, U.S. direct investment in other countries totaled $421 billion, while foreign investment in the United States totaled $404 billion. This amounts to about 8 percent of GDP, indicating a substantial flow of funds between the United States and other countries.

Because of the growing importance of international trade and finance in the United States, we now extend the model of Chapter 16 to take account of international trade. The model we build in this chapter has endogenous net exports and is an **open economy model,** a model of an economy that is open to international trade. In Chapter 16, aggregate demand consisted of consumption demand, investment demand, government demand, and exogenous net exports. In this chapter, our model includes endogenous net exports. This not only affects the slope of the aggregate demand curve, giving yet another reason for downward-sloping aggregate demand, but also adds to the list of variables that shift aggregate demand.

We also look at the relationship between aggregate demand and aggregate supply in the open economy, with the particular aim of seeing how international trade affects macroeconomic equilibrium. We will explore the importance of open economy considerations in the loanable funds market and see how international borrowing and lending of loanable funds has important implications for the interest rate effects of government finance. We will also see that the effectiveness of monetary and fiscal policy in stimulating the economy depends on whether exchange rates are fixed or flexible. Throughout this chapter, we will pay close attention to the effects of policies that spring from special features of the open economy.

THE BALANCE OF PAYMENTS

The **balance of payments** summarizes the value of payments between households, firms, and governments in one country and the rest of the world. For the United States, this includes an accounting of imports and exports of goods and services, financial capital flows that include lending to and borrowing from other countries, and transfers and gifts between U.S. households, firms, or governments and the rest of the world. U.S. imports are goods and services produced in other countries and purchased by U.S. residents. When you buy a TV made in Taiwan, you are purchasing an **import,** a good or service that is made overseas but is purchased by a U.S. resident. U.S. **exports** are goods and services produced in the United States and purchased by the rest of the world. When a French business purchases computer software produced in the United States, this transaction represents an export from the United States.

In the balance of payments calculations, any transactions that result in a receipt of payments by a U.S. firm, household, or government is a positive entry—a credit. Likewise, any transaction that results in a payment by a U.S. firm, household, or government to a foreign party is a negative entry—a debit. Thus, exports are a positive entry, since the sale of U.S. products overseas results in the receipt of funds by the United States. Imports are a negative entry, since payment for imports by parties in the United States results in funds being received overseas.

Flows of financial assets also affect the balance of payments. When U.S. firms, households, or governments borrow from overseas, funds flow from abroad to the United States, resulting in a positive entry in the balance of payments. U.S. residents receive funds, while the rest of the world receives an asset, an IOU payable in the future. Similarly, when the United States lends funds to the rest of the world, the result is a negative entry in the balance of payments, because funds flow out of the United States into the hands of overseas parties.

How do purchases of stocks or bonds in other countries affect the balance of payments account? When a U.S. investor purchases stock on the London stock exchange, a negative entry in the U.S. balance of payments results because funds flow from the United States to the United Kingdom. Similarly, when a Japanese investor purchases a U.S. government bond, the result is a positive entry in the U.S. balance of payments because funds enter the United States from Japan. The key in all these examples is to remember that it is the direction of the flow of funds that determines whether a transaction is a positive or a negative entry in the balance of payments.

The balance of payments accounts are constructed so that the total of all funds flowing overseas should equal the total of all funds flowing to the United States. The idea is the same as any double-entry bookkeeping system. In the balance of payments accounts, an inflow of funds from the sale of U.S. exports will be matched by an outflow of funds as U.S. producers buy assets or goods in other countries. Thus, the overall balance of payments should be zero. In practice, however, the overall balance is not zero due to measurement errors and omissions, called the **statistical discrepancy,** in the balance of payments accounts. The statistical discrepancy can be rather substantial, indicating the difficulty governments have in keeping track of international transactions.

The balance of payments accounts are divided into two major sub-accounts. The first is called the *current account* and the second the *capital account.* The current account records the net flow of funds due to trade in goods and services, investment income, and gifts (unilateral transfers). As always, actions that generate a flow of funds to the United States are credits (positive entries), and actions that create a flow of funds out of the United States are debits (negative entries). The capital account records the net flow of funds due to changes in the levels of capital and financial assets between the United States and the rest of the world. When U.S. residents or the U.S. government increase their holdings of foreign assets, funds flow from the United States overseas to purchase those assets, so a debit or a negative entry in the capital account occurs. When foreign residents or governments increase their holding of U.S. assets, funds flow to the United States to purchase those assets, and a credit or a positive entry in the capital account results.

We cannot stress too much that aside from the statistical discrepancy, the sum of the current account and the capital account should be zero by construction. Thus, when news commentators report a balance of payments deficit or surplus, they cannot be referring to the overall balance of payments. Instead they are referring to one of the subaccounts, most likely the current account balance or even the merchandise trade balance (net exports of goods).

The balance of payments are reported in a table such as Table 17.1. Here we see the main categories in the balance of payments—the current account and the capital account—as well as details of the components of these accounts. We look at these accounts in more detail in the following sections.

The Current Account

The **current account** consists of the merchandise trade balance, the balance on services, the net flow of income on investments, and the net flow of unilateral transfers. The *merchandise account* consists of exports and imports of goods, where exports are a positive entry (funds flow to the United States) and imports a negative entry (funds flow abroad). The difference between

The balance of payments accounts consist of the current account balance and the capital account balance.

Table 17.1
The Balance of Payments Accounts

1. Current Account
   A. Merchandise Trade
       i. Exports ($+$)
       ii. Imports ($-$)
   B. Services
       i. Exports ($+$)
       ii. Imports ($-$)
   B1. Net Military Transactions
       (included in B)
   C. Income on Investments
       i. Receipts ($+$)
       ii. Payments ($-$)
   D. Unilateral Transfers
2. Capital Account
   A. U.S. investment overseas (increase of capital outflows)
       i. U.S. private assets, net
       ii. U.S. government assets other than official reserve assets
       iii. U.S. official reserve assets (ORAs)
   B. Foreign investment in the United States (increase in capital inflows)
       i. Private and other (non-ORA) foreign assets, net
       ii. Foreign official reserve assets (ORAs)

---

merchandise exports and merchandise imports is called the *merchandise trade balance*.[1] A positive trade balance simply means the United States exported more goods than it imported; a negative balance of trade indicates the United States imported more goods than it exported.

The *balance on services* consists of exports minus imports of services, including such items as military transactions, tourism, and transportation services. The category net military transactions includes military grants as well as sales, which we include as a separate category for later use.

Net income on investments includes the net flow of investment income such as dividends, interest income, and royalties. Income on foreign assets owned by U.S. residents is an inflow of funds to the United States—a credit. Income paid to foreign owners of U.S. assets is an outflow of funds from the United States—a debit.

Finally, the category *unilateral transfers* is the net flow of funds from gifts between U.S. and foreign residents. These are transfers of funds or

---

[1] News commentators sometimes mistakenly refer to this as the *balance of payments*. As discussed earlier, the balance of payments is always zero by construction.

goods for which no payment is expected in return. They include government grants (essentially foreign aid), private gifts sent to and received from other countries, and pension payments made to households overseas. If U.S. residents are net recipients of such gifts, this entry will be positive. In the usual case this entry is negative for the United States, representing that on net the United States is a donor of gifts to overseas residents.

The current account balance is the sum of the merchandise trade balance, the balance on services, net income on investments, and unilateral transfers. The current account balance is closely related to but not exactly the same as what we call **net exports** in aggregate demand. The category net exports includes net exports of merchandise—the merchandise trade balance—and net exports of services. However, the balance on services includes one category, net military expenditures, which consists of grants of military equipment and supplies from the U.S. government. Since this category does not represent actual sales of military goods abroad, we would exclude it from the calculation of net exports. Hence, net exports is the sum of the merchandise trade balance and the balance on services, minus net military transactions. Thus, net exports in aggregate demand differs from the current account balance in that net exports does not include net military transactions, net income on investments, or unilateral transfers.

The Capital Account

The second major category in the balance of payments is the capital account. The **capital account** keeps track of investments by U.S. firms, households, and governments overseas and investments by foreign residents in the United States. These international movements of loanable funds are called *international financial capital movements,* or simply *international capital movements.* They represent the lendings and borrowings by U.S. households, firms, and government. If U.S. households and firms lend to a foreign country, they receive foreign securities (such as stocks and bonds) in exchange for funds sent overseas. Since funds flow out of the United States, these movements are a negative entry in the capital account. Borrowing by U.S. firms and households from foreign sources is a positive entry in the capital account, because funds flow into the United States in exchange for securities flowing to overseas lenders. A positive capital account balance indicates the United States borrows more funds from abroad than it lends overseas; there is a net inflow of loanable funds into the United States.

One set of entries in the capital account is changes in U.S. official reserve assets and changes in foreign official reserve assets. *U.S. official reserve assets* are assets held by the U.S. Treasury or by the Federal Reserve System that consist primarily of gold and holdings of foreign currencies. Foreign currency is obtained when the Federal Reserve or the Treasury purchases it to influence exchange rates. When the Federal Reserve buys foreign currency and official reserve assets increase, this is a debit—a negative entry—because dollar funds flow out of the United States. Similarly, if the Federal Reserve sells foreign currency, obtaining dollars but reducing its holding of official reserve assets, the result would be a credit, because dollar funds would flow into the United States.

Recent U.S. Balance of Payments Accounts

Table 17.2 presents the U.S. balance of payments accounts for 1990, 1991, and the first nine months of 1992. Notice the U.S. current account was in deficit in all three years. The current account balance was − $90.4 billion in 1990 but moved dramatically toward balance in 1991, when it was − $3.7 billion. A large portion of this move was due to the change in unilateral transfers from − $32.9 billion to + $8.0 billion as countries around the world made unilateral transfers to the United States to help pay for the Persian Gulf War. In 1992 the current account balance moved back to a larger deficit position, − $37.9 billion in the first nine months.

The components of the current account provide interesting information about the U.S. trade situation. Notice in Table 17.2 that the merchandise trade balance was negative in all three years, meaning the United States imported more goods than it exported. However, the balance on services was positive; the United States exported more services than it imported. Income on overseas investments was also positive, indicating U.S. residents received more income from their investments abroad than foreign residents received from their investments in the United States. Finally, with the exception of the Persian Gulf War payments in 1991, the United States was a net donor of unilateral transfers to foreign residents.

What about the capital account? The U.S. capital account was in surplus each year, especially in 1990 and 1992. In each year, overseas residents increased their assets held in the United States by more than the United States increased its assets held overseas. This resulted in an inflow of funds to the United States and a positive capital account balance as foreign residents purchased U.S. assets.

One special type of official reserve asset is called SDRs, or *special drawing rights*. Special drawing rights are an international reserve asset created by the International Monetary Fund (IMF) as a substitute for gold. A country in need of international reserves could obtain an allocation of SDRs from the IMF that other countries would agree to honor as an international reserve asset, valid for trade in the currency markets. Entry 3 in Table 17.2 shows that SDRs were zero in these three years, indicating that the U.S. did not obtain international reserves from the I.M.F.

Entry 4 shows a discouraging feature of the U.S. balance of payments accounts: the size of the statistical discrepancy. This measure was attributed to such factors as illegal international trade in drugs and other contraband, unreported international trade in goods and services (to avoid tariffs or other trade restrictions), or unreported international borrowing and lend-

Table 17.2

U.S. Balance of Payments Accounts for 1990, 1991, and 1992 (partial) (billions of dollars)

	1990	**1991**	**1992 (Jan.–Sept.)**
1. Current Account	−90.4	−3.7	−37.9
A. Merchandise Trade Balance	−108.9	−73.4	−68.3
i. Exports (+)	388.7	416.0	326.2
ii. Imports (−)	−497.6	−489.4	−394.5
B. Services	32.0	45.3	42.1
i. Exports (+)	148.5	163.6	133.7
ii. Imports (−)	−116.5	−118.3	−91.6
Net Military Transactions (included in B)	−7.8	−5.5	−1.8
C. Income on Investments	19.3	16.4	10.0
i. Receipts (+)	143.5	125.6	84.7
ii. Payments (−)	−124.3	−108.9	−74.8
D. Unilateral Transfers	−32.9	8.0	−21.7
2. Capital Account	43.1	4.8	58.9
A. U.S. investment overseas	−56.3	−62.2	−24.4
i. U.S. private assets, net	−56.5	−71.4	−26.0
ii. U.S. government assets other than ORAs	2.3	3.4	2.4
iii. U.S. ORAs	−2.2	5.8	−0.7
B. Foreign investment in U.S.	99.4	67.0	83.3
i. Private and other	65.4	48.6	48.9
ii. Foreign ORAs	33.9	18.4	34.3
3. Allocation of SDRs	0.0	0.0	0.0
4. Statistical Discrepancy	47.4	−1.1	−21.0
5. Net Exports of Goods and Services	−69.1	−22.6	−24.4
6. Official Settlements Balance	31.7	24.2	33.6

Note: Numbers may not add to reported sums due to rounding. Data for 1992 is for first nine months only.

Sources: Economic Report of the President, (Washington, D.C.: U.S. Government Printing Office, January 1993), pp. 462–463; U.S. Commerce Department, *Survey of Current Business,* various issues; Citibase electronic database.

ing. The size of the statistical discrepancy was large relative to the other entries in the balance of payments accounts, indicating the difficulty government accountants have in keeping track of international transactions. In 1990, for instance, the statistical discrepancy was $47.4 billion, larger than the entire surplus on the capital account!

Entry 5 in Table 17.2 also reports net exports of goods and services, the variable that enters aggregate demand calculations. This measure is the sum of the merchandise trade balance and the balance on services, minus net military transactions (which are largely grants and aid without repayment and hence not sales of goods and services). Net exports were negative but grew closer to balance, from −$69.1 billion in 1990 to −$22.6 billion in 1991, before moving further from balance, to −$24.4 billion over the first nine months of 1992.

Finally, Entry 6 shows that the *official settlements balance,* the sum of the change in U.S. official reserve assets and the change in foreign official reserve assets, was positive in each year.

Summary Exercise 17.1

How would the following transactions affect the balance of payments? (a) A U.S. household purchases a car from Germany. (b) A U.S. firm sells a bond to a Dutch investor. (c) A Japanese citizen tours the United States, spending funds on lodging, food, and souvenirs. (d) The U.S. government makes a gift of wheat to Somalia.

Answer: (a) This is a negative entry in the current account, since funds flow from the U.S. household to Germany in exchange for the car. (b) In this case, the sale of the bond leads to an inflow of funds to the United States, so this sale is recorded as a positive entry in the capital account. (c) The Japanese tourist is buying goods and services from the United States, creating a flow of funds into the United States, so this is a positive entry in the current account. (d) The dollar value of the gift of wheat shows up as a negative entry in the unilateral transfers component of the current account.

THE DEMAND FOR NET EXPORTS

We have seen that net exports have fluctuated in recent years. Why do these movements occur, and how do they affect aggregate demand and macroeconomic equilibrium? To answer these questions, we now look at the *demand for net exports*—the demand for exports minus the demand for imports. The demand for net exports has two components: the demand for U.S. exports (the demand by foreign residents for U.S. goods and services) and the demand for imports (the U.S. demand for foreign goods and services). We begin with two examples that illustrate why the domestic price level, the foreign price level, and the exchange rate are primary deteminants of import and export demand.

Suppose a Japanese student is considering the purchase of word processing software made by a U.S. producer. The list price is $400 (including shipping). If the exchange rate in yen per dollar is 110, this software costs $400 × ¥110/$ = ¥44,000 for the Japanese student. In deciding whether to purchase this software or another product, the student is concerned about the price in Japanese yen, which is the dollar price times the exchange rate.

The higher either the exchange rate or the dollar price, the less likely the Japanese student is to buy U.S.-made software. More generally, a rise in either the exchange rate or the U.S. price level will lower the demand for U.S. exports, since it will make U.S. goods more expensive relative to foreign goods.

Similarly, suppose you are considering purchasing a car imported from Japan. You look at the price of the Japanese car relative to the price of cars made in the United States. In this case, any increase in the price of the Japanese car will tend to reduce your desire to buy it, thus reducing U.S. imports. But the price you have to pay for the Japanese car depends on the price in Japan, in yen, divided by the exchange rate in yen per dollar. For example, consider a car that costs ¥1,100,000 in Japan and an exchange rate of ¥110 per dollar. The price in dollars is ¥1,100,000/(¥110/$) = $10,000. If the price in yen rises or the exchange rate falls, the dollar price of the Japanese car will rise, making it less attractive for you to purchase it. More generally, the higher the foreign price level or the lower the exchange rate, the lower will be the U.S. demand for imports.

These examples explain why changes in price levels and exchange rates affect imports and exports. Since the demand for net exports is defined as export demand minus the demand for imports, the examples also suggest that net export demand depends on price levels and exchange rates. This is indeed the case, and in fact there are several other important determinants of net export demand. We summarize all of these determinants next.

The Domestic Price Level.

If we hold everything constant except the domestic price level and net exports, we obtain a relationship between the price level and expenditures for net exports called the *net export demand curve*. This relationship is the curve labeled NX^d in Figure 17.1 and indicates that, holding other things constant, an increase in the domestic price level will reduce the amount of real spending on net exports demanded. This is represented by the movement from A to B along net export demand curve NX^d. The downward slope reflects the impact of a rise in the domestic price level on exports and imports: Exports fall (since U.S. goods and services are more expensive for overseas residents) and imports rise (since foreign goods and services are now cheaper relative to U.S. goods and services). The decline in exports and rise in imports reduce net exports.

One unusual feature of the net export demand curve is that it can be negative. Usually we think demand must be positive or zero. However, net exports is exports minus imports. When imports exceed exports, net exports is negative, which simply means that (ignoring net income on investments and transfers) there is a current account deficit in the balance of payments. In contrast, when exports exceed imports, a current account surplus exists: Exports of U.S. goods and services exceed imports.

Figure 17.1 reveals that, holding other things constant, the magnitude of the current account deficit depends on the domestic price level. When the domestic price level is P_0, net exports are zero on the curve labeled NX^d. If

Figure 17.1
Demand for Net Exports

Net export demand, NX^d, depends on the domestic price level. Increases in the domestic price level cause a movement along NX^d to a lower quantity of real expenditures on net exports. Changes in the determinants of net exports will shift the curve. A shift to NX^d_1 would represent an increase in the demand for net exports, whereas a shift to NX^d_2 would indicate a decrease in the demand for net exports. Notice that with the demand for net exports given by NX^d, any domestic price level higher than P_0 results in a *negative* demand for net exports (a current account deficit), and any domestic price level lower than P_0 results in a positive demand for net exports (a current account surplus).

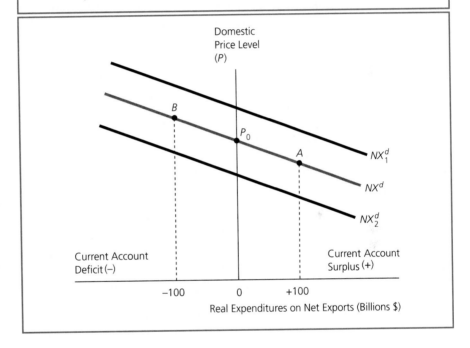

the domestic price level falls below P_0 and we move to point A, U.S. goods and services become cheaper relative to foreign ones. At point A net exports are +$100 billion, indicating a positive current account balance: The United States exports $100 billion more in real goods and services than it imports. Similarly, if the domestic price level rises above P_0 to point B on the NX^d curve, U.S. goods and services become more expensive relative to foreign ones. At point B net exports are −$100 billion, indicating a current account deficit.

Whenever there is a change in a determinant of net export demand— say, a change in the foreign price level—the entire net export demand curve shifts to the left or to the right. This is called a *change in net export demand* and is illustrated in Figure 17.1 by shifts from NX^d to either NX^d_1 or NX^d_2.

Next we look at how changes in the foreign price level and other determinants of net export demand can shift the net export demand curve.

The Foreign Price Level.   Suppose the price level in Japan rises so that the yen prices of Japanese goods increase. For a given exchange rate and U.S. price level, this makes Japanese goods more expensive to both Japanese and U.S. buyers. Japanese buyers will therefore tend to substitute toward U.S. goods, and U.S. exports will rise. Meanwhile you and other U.S. consumers will find it more costly to buy cars and other goods imported from Japan and will likely substitute toward U.S. goods, so imports from Japan will fall. Together the rise in exports and the decline in imports mean the difference, net exports, increases. More generally, a rise in the foreign price level increases the demand for net exports. This is represented by a rightward shift from NX^d to NX_1^d in Figure 17.1. A decrease in the foreign price level shifts the net export demand curve to the left to NX_2^d.

The Exchange Rate.   Changes in the exchange rate function in much the same way as changes in the foreign price level. A rise in the exchange rate (given as the number of units of a foreign currency needed to buy a single U.S. dollar, such as 100 yen per dollar) means foreign residents need more of their currency to buy a dollar. We say their currency has *depreciated* relative to the dollar. Holding everything else constant, including the U.S. price level, this means they need more of their currency to buy any U.S. good, making it less desirable to do so. Thus, their demand for U.S. goods and services will decline when the exchange rate rises, and export demand will fall. In like fashion, U.S. consumers compare the prices of U.S. and foreign goods. For a given U.S. price level and foreign price level, the increase in the exchange rate means it takes fewer U.S. dollars to buy foreign goods, so U.S. demand for imports increases. We say that the dollar has *appreciated* relative to the foreign currency.

For example, suppose a student in Britain is considering the purchase of a sweater that costs $20 in the United States. If the exchange rate is .5 English pounds per dollar, then, ignoring shipping costs, the student can buy this sweater for 10 pounds ($20 × .5 pounds/dollar = 10 pounds). If the exchange rate increases to 1 pound per dollar, the British student must pay 20 pounds ($20 × 1 pound/dollar = 20 pounds) for the sweater. Thus, as the exchange rate increases (i.e., as the pound depreciates relative to the dollar), U.S. goods become more expensive in Britain and British consumers will buy fewer of them, reducing export demand.

A similar analysis holds for imports. Consider the price you would have to pay for a British car costing 10,000 pounds. If the exchange rate is .5 pounds per dollar, you will need $20,000 to purchase the car (since $20,000 × .5 pounds/dollar = 10,000 pounds). If the exchange rate rises to one pound per dollar (i.e., the dollar appreciates relative to the pound), your cost will be only $10,000. The increase in the exchange rate reduces the price of the car to you, a U.S. resident, which leads to an increase in imports.

Thus, we see that an increase in the exchange rate (an appreciation of the dollar) will reduce export demand and raise import demand, which means net export demand must decline. This is illustrated by leftward shift in the entire net export demand curve. Likewise, a decrease in the exchange rate (a depreciation of the dollar) will increase net export demand (shift the entire net export demand curve to the right). How well does this prediction hold up in the historical record? Box 17.1 shows U.S. net exports and a weighted average exchange rate between the currencies of the major U.S. trading partners and the dollar.

Domestic Wealth.   An increase in domestic wealth decreases net export demand through its effect on the demand for imports. A rise in domestic wealth increases the ability of U.S. residents to buy imported goods, thus increasing the demand for imports. Consequently a rise in domestic wealth leads to a decrease in net export demand, as represented by a leftward shift in the net export demand curve.

Foreign Wealth.   An increase in foreign wealth increases net export demand through its effect on the demand for U.S. exports. An increase in foreign wealth increases overseas residents' demand for U.S. products, which raise their demand for our exports. Thus, a rise (decline) in foreign wealth leads to an increase (decrease) in net export demand, as represented by a rightward (leftward) shift in the net export demand curve.

The Real Domestic Interest Rate.   Holding other things constant, a higher real domestic interest rate induces people in the United States to save more, which leaves them less for purchasing imports. As a consequence net exports rise, which is represented by a rightward shift in the net export demand curve. A decline in the domestic real interest rate shifts the net export demand curve to the left.

The Foreign Real Interest Rate.   When the foreign real interest rate increases, foreign households tend to save more and thus have less to spend on U.S. goods. Their demand for U.S. exports will decline, as will U.S. net export demand. Similarly, the lower the foreign real interest rate, the greater will be foreign spending on consumer goods and services, including U.S. products, and this will increase U.S. net export demand. Graphically, an increase in the foreign real interest rate shifts the net export demand curve to the left, whereas a decrease in the rate shifts the curve to the right.

Tariffs.   Tariffs are taxes on imports and can be levied by both the United States and other countries. When the United States imposes a tariff, it raises

The Data Bank

Box 17.1

Net Exports and the Exchange Rate

Do U.S. net exports respond to exchange rate movements? The answer is yes, but they do so slowly and with lags. The accompanying graph shows U.S. net exports and an exchange rate measure that averages together the exchange rate between the dollar and the currencies of the United States' major trading partners. Net exports are given in billions of dollars on the left-hand scale, and the exchange rate is measured on the right-hand scale. Notice that when the dollar appreciated in the early 1980s, peaking in 1985, net exports were declining, and reached a record deficit of about − $140 billion in 1987. The exchange rate sank quickly from its 1985 peak. After 1987 net exports began rising, and by 1991 they were around − $20 billion.

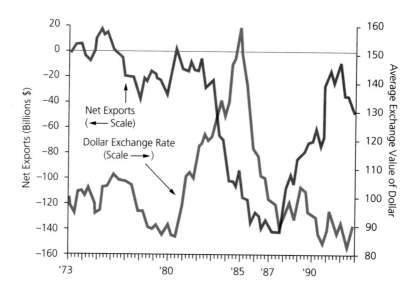

Source: Citibase electronic database

the aftertax price of imports to U.S. consumers. This reduces the relative attractiveness of imported goods and lowers import demand. In turn, net export demand increases. Graphically, an increase in tariffs levied by the United States shifts the demand for net exports to the right, whereas a reduction in U.S. tariffs shifts net export demand to the left.

When another country imposes a tariff on U.S. goods, it raises the prices of those goods to its citizens. This tends to reduce their demand for U.S. exports, making U.S. net exports decline. Thus, increases in foreign tariffs on U.S. goods will reduce net export demand, shifting the net export demand curve to the left. Decreases in foreign tariffs will increase net export demand and shift the net export demand curve to the right.

Quotas and Other Nontariff Barriers.

Quotas are one of several possible nontariff barriers to trade. A tariff raises the price of imported goods and thus reduces demand for them. A quota also reduces imports, but by directly restricting their quantity. For example, the United States negotiated a ''voluntary'' quota with Japanese auto companies on the quantity of Japanese cars allowed into the United States. This quantity restriction reduced the number of Japanese autos imported to the United States. Other nontariff barriers are restrictions or regulations on the import of certain goods for a variety of reasons, ranging from restrictions on imports of medicines without Food and Drug Administration approval to restrictions on imports of goods from certain countries, such as cigars from Cuba, for political reasons. These restrictions may serve legitimate public policy or national security concerns, but they also restrict imports. Indeed, some restrictions that were once considered important for these purposes have become difficult to remove even after these justifications are no longer warranted, because some domestic industry has prospered under the regulation and doesn't want to face increased competition. An example from overseas is Japan, which has quotas and other restrictions to protect its domestic rice farmers from foreign competition. The Japanese government claims these measures are important for national security reasons, although there has been a move recently to loosen some of these restrictions.

Quotas and other nontariff barriers imposed by the United States tend to reduce imports to the United States and thus to increase net export demand. This is illustrated by a rightward shift in net export demand. Quotas and nontariff barriers imposed by other countries on United States goods tend to reduce U.S. exports. This causes a decline in net export demand, or a leftward shift.

One way tariffs and nontariff barriers such as quotas are relaxed is through treaties among countries designed to free up trade among them. Recently the United States, Canada, and Mexico signed the North America Free Trade Agreement (NAFTA) to establish freer trade among these three countries, as discussed in Box 17.2.

Tastes and Expectations.

Finally, tastes and expectations of both U.S. and foreign residents can affect net export demand. During the 1980s, for example, a popular campaign in TV commercials was ''buy American.'' This slogan was designed by U.S. workers and producers to encourage U.S. consumers to shun foreign products. If successful, such advertisements reduce import demand, thus increasing the demand for net exports.

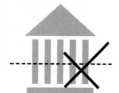

Inside Money

Box 17.2

The Impact of NAFTA on Output and Employment

The North America Free Trade Agreement, or NAFTA, is a treaty between Canada, the United States, and Mexico to establish a free trade zone in North America. NAFTA will require that the three partners lower the tariffs and trade barriers that apply to one another's goods and services. What will be the result for the U.S. economy? The standard theory of international trade presented in economics textbooks is that free trade will make all countries better off. This result is based on the idea that free trade allows greater specialization and thus increases overall economic efficiency. As each country specializes in the production of those goods in which it has a comparative advantage, the greater quantity and quality of goods available will benefit all countries.

In the economy as a whole, an increase in specialization and economic efficiency raises the natural rate of output. A rise in international trade allow firms to use domestic factors of production more efficiently. This means an economy can produce a larger quantity of output than previously. Moreover, if labor is now more efficient in production, the increase in labor demand should translate into higher employment. Free trade also increases the consumption opportunities for a country, because goods are now produced more efficiently, thus lowering the costs of final goods and services to consumers. Hence free trade will push the long-run aggregate supply curve to the right.

If free trade is such a good thing, why was there so much opposition to NAFTA? The problem is that while free trade may be good for the country as a whole, in terms of a higher long-run natural rate of output, it may well have adverse effects on individual firms or households. For example, NAFTA will result in some changes in the locations of various firms. Some U.S. firms and workers will benefit from increased access to Canadian and Mexican markets, but others will be hurt by increased competition from these countries. During the adjustment period, as production moves to the country with the comparative advantage, those firms and workers displaced by more efficient production elsewhere will have to find new jobs or new goods and services to produce. Even though the final result is more efficient production and expanded consumption possibilities, during the adjustment process some serious economic difficulties may arise. Those who see their jobs or firms in danger from increased competition abroad were understandably reluctant to see NAFTA enacted.

Summary Exercise 17.2

Holding other things constant, determine the impact of each of the following on net export demand: (a) a decrease in the exchange rate, (b) a decrease in the U.S. interest rate, (c) an increase in tariffs on Japanese goods, and (d) a European quota limiting the number of personal computers U.S. firms can sell in Europe.

Answer: (a) A decrease in the exchange rate means it takes fewer units of a foreign currency to buy a dollar or, equivalently, more dollars to buy a unit of the foreign currency. This makes U.S. exports less expensive to foreign residents, thus increasing demand for U.S. exports. It also makes imported goods more expensive in the United States. Thus, net export demand increases. (b) A decrease in the U.S. interest rate will increase net export demand. (c) An increase in tariffs on Japanese goods will reduce U.S. demand for imports and hence increase net export demand. (d) A European quota on U.S. goods will reduce demand for U.S. exports and hence reduce U.S. net export demand.

OPEN ECONOMY MACROECONOMIC EQUILIBRIUM

We are now ready to see how international trade affects macroeconomic equilibrium. We will want to know about (1) U.S. (or domestic) interest rates, (2) the exchange rate between U.S. dollars and other currencies, (3) the U.S. price level, and (4) U.S. real GDP. The equilibrium interest rate is determined in the money market or, equivalently, in the market for loanable funds. The equilibrium exchange rate is determined in the foreign exchange market, which we examined in detail in Chapter 11. Here we focus on determining the final two elements of macroeconomic equilibrium: the U.S. price level and real GDP.

As in a closed economy, in an open economy the equilibrium U.S. price level and real GDP are determined in the market for U.S. goods and services by the intersection of the aggregate demand and supply curves. Figure 17.2 shows such an equilibrium at point A, where the equilibrium price level is P_0 and the equilibrium level of real GDP is Y_0. While this picture looks identical to that for a closed economy, we need to address several aspects of these aggregate demand and supply curves before we examine the effects of fiscal and monetary policy in an open economy.

Aggregate Demand in an Open Economy

Aggregate demand in our open economy includes consumption demand, investment demand, government purchases, *and* an endogenous net export demand; that is, aggregate demand for U.S. goods in an open economy may be written as

$$AD = C^d + I^d + G^d + NX^d.$$

The aggregate demand curve for an open economy is downward sloping due not only to the wealth effect and interest rate (or intertemporal substitution) effect described in Chapter 16 but also to the effect of the price level on net export demand. We saw in Figure 17.1 that net export demand is negatively related to the price level in our open economy model. Changes in the domestic price level cause changes in the relative attractiveness of domestic and foreign products, and this leads to changes in the quantity demanded of domestic consumption (C^d), investment (I^d), and net exports (NX^d) when the price level changes. This is the third reason for downward-sloping aggregate demand, which we alluded to in Chapter 16 but postponed discussion of until this chapter. Net export demand may also change because changes in the price level alter the interest rate, as we saw in Chapter 16, and these changes in the interest rate can lead to changes in exchange rates and hence in net export demand. Thus, an increase in the price level will reduce real money supply and hence lower the interest rate. As we saw in Chapter 11, this will lead to a reduction in the exchange rate as international investors find the United States a less rewarding place in which to invest. This reduction in the exchange rate, in turn, leads to a decrease in net exports. This is yet another reason net export demand is downward sloping. Thus, the slope of net export demand and hence the slope of aggregate demand already incorporates the effect of changes in the interest rate and the exchange rate caused by changes in the price level. Of course, the effect of changes in the interest rate or the exchange rate not caused by changes in the price level will still shift aggregate demand.

As in a closed economy, macroeconomic equilibrium in the goods market occurs at point *A*, where aggregate demand equals aggregate supply. In our open economy, however, net exports are endogenous, and aggregate demand consists of consumption demand, investment demand, government purchases, *and* endogenous demand for net exports.

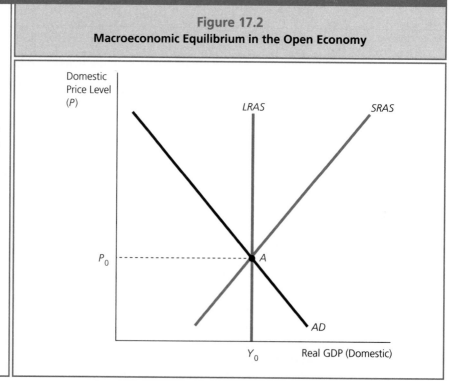

Figure 17.2
Macroeconomic Equilibrium in the Open Economy

What are the determinants of aggregate demand? These include not only the determinants of consumption demand, investment demand, and government purchases (all of which we discussed in detail in Chapter 16) but also the determinants of net export demand just discussed. For instance, in an open economy, an increase in U.S. tariffs increases net exports and thus leads to an increase in aggregate demand. More generally, a change in any determinant of C^d, I^d, G^d, or NX^d will change aggregate demand. Table 17.3 summarizes each of these determinants, along with their impact on aggregate demand.

Short-Run Aggregate Supply in an Open Economy

In our model of the closed economy, we saw that the major determinants of short-run aggregate supply are (1) the wage rate, (2) prices of other inputs, (3) taxes, (4) the stock of physical capital, and (5) the level of technology. In the open economy, two additional determinants come into play: (6) prices of foreign inputs and (7) tariffs.

Prices of Imported Inputs.   Not all inputs are from domestic suppliers. U.S. firms import a variety of inputs from around the world, including oil from the Middle East; industrial diamonds from South Africa and the former Soviet Union; computer chips from Japan; steel from Europe, Japan, and South Korea; transistors and other electronic components from Taiwan or Hong Kong; and so on. Increases in the prices of these imported inputs shift short-run aggregate supply to the left.

The major imported U.S. input is oil and, interestingly, oil trades on world markets in U.S. dollars. Some inputs, however, are priced in foreign currencies, and in those cases the price to a U.S. firm is the foreign currency price divided by the exchange rate (in foreign currency per U.S. dollar). For example, if a computer chip costs 1,000 yen and the exchange rate is 125 yen per dollar, the price of each computer chip to a U.S. computer manufacturer is 1,000 yen/(125 Yen/US\$) = \$8. Changes in the exchange rate obviously can affect the dollar price to U.S. firms of such inputs, even if the foreign price remains constant.

For simplicity, we will assume either that imported inputs trade in the world market at dollar prices (like oil) or that firms obtaining inputs from abroad hedge against short-run movements in exchange rates by using the futures market (as discussed in Chapter 9). Under either of these scenarios, short-run changes in the exchange rate will not affect the dollar price of foreign inputs, and the short-run aggregate supply curve will not vary with changes in the exchange rate.

Tariffs.   We saw earlier in the chapter that tariffs on imported finished goods raise the goods' prices. However, not all tariffs are on imports of finished goods. Many are on imported intermediate goods, such as steel or

Table 17.3
Determinants of Aggregate Demand in an Open Economy

Change in Determinant of Consumption Demand	Effect on Consumption Demand	Effect on Aggregate Demand
Increase in domestic wealth	Shifts right	Shifts right
Increase in domestic real interest rate	Shifts left	Shifts left
Increase in domestic expected inflation rate	Shifts right	Shifts right
Increase in taxes on domestic households	Shifts left	Shifts left
Change in Determinant of Investment Demand	**Effect on Investment Demand**	**Effect on Aggregate Demand**
Increase in domestic real interest rate	Shifts left	Shifts left
Increase in taxes on domestic firms	Shifts left	Shifts left
Change in Determinant of Government Purchases	**Effect on Government Demand**	**Effect on Aggregate Demand**
Exogenous increase in domestic government purchases	Shifts right	Shifts right
Change in Determinant of Net Export Demand	**Effect on Net Export Demand**	**Effect on Aggregate Demand**
Increase in foreign price level	Shifts right	Shifts right
Increase in exchange rate	Shifts left	Shifts left
Increase in domestic wealth	Shifts left	Shifts left
Increase in foreign wealth	Shifts right	Shifts right
Increase in domestic real interest rate	Shifts right	Shifts right
Increase in foreign real interest rate	Shifts left	Shifts left
Increase in domestic tariffs or quotas	Shifts right	Shifts right
Increase in foreign tariffs or quotas	Shifts left	Shifts left

computer chips. In addition, the Clinton administration at one time considered a tariff on oil imports. Such tariffs raise the prices of inputs to U.S. firms, which in turn shifts the short-run aggregate supply curve to the left. Reducing tariffs on imported inputs has the opposite effect: It shifts the short-run aggregate supply curve to the right.

Long-Run Aggregate Supply in an Open Economy

The final feature of macroeconomic equilibrium that is affected by international trade is long-run aggregate supply—the supply of domestic goods and services after wages and other input prices have adjusted to any change in the domestic price level. As we discussed in Chapter 16, in the short run input prices tend to be sticky, or slow to adjust. Consequently, as the price level rises in the short run, the real cost of inputs to firms declines, and firms increase real output as the price level increases. This gives the short-run aggregate supply curve its upward slope. Over time, however, wages and input prices increase, shifting the short-run aggregate supply curve to the left until long-run equilibrium is achieved. In the long run, after all input prices have fully adjusted to changes in the price level, the ratio of input to output prices remains constant. This, in turn, implies that in the long run the quantity of inputs used in production will be determined by the economy's natural rate of employment, giving rise to a vertical long-run aggregate supply curve at the natural rate of output.

If foreign inputs are priced in dollars, the same reasoning gives rise to a vertical long-run aggregate supply curve in a closed economy. In the long run, increases in the U.S. price level will lead to proportional changes in contracted prices of foreign inputs, leaving their relative prices unchanged. Thus, when the prices of foreign inputs are in U.S. dollars, the long-run aggregate supply curve in the open economy is also vertical, determined by the natural rate of output.

What if foreign input prices are in foreign currency units? The long-run aggregate supply curve will still be vertical, provided purchasing power parity holds. Recall from Chapter 11 that purchasing power parity is the idea that the exchange rate adjusts so that the U.S. price level is proportional to the foreign price level divided by the exchange rate. According to purchasing power parity, the exchange rate between the German mark and the U.S. dollar would adjust in the long run to keep the ratio of the German price level to the U.S. price level constant.

How would this work for an imported input price? Suppose a U.S. computer manufacturer buys computer chips from a Mexican firm under a contract specified in Mexican pesos—say, 100 pesos per chip. The cost of the chips to the U.S. firm is the peso price divided by the exchange rate in Mexican pesos per U.S. dollar—say, 3 pesos per dollar. Thus, the dollar cost to the U.S. firm is 100 pesos/(3 pesos per dollar) = \$33.33. The real cost to the U.S. firm is this dollar cost divided by the price of the firm's output. For the overall economy, we simply divide the dollar cost of the inputs by the U.S. price level, which might be taken to be 1.

What happens if the U.S. price level rises—say, to 2? In the short run, if the Mexican price level and the exchange rate are held constant, the real cost of the Mexican chips will fall, and U.S. firms will tend to purchase more of them. This will lead to an increase in U.S. output and partly explains why short-run aggregate supply is not vertical. If purchasing power parity holds, however, in the long run the exchange rate will adjust to keep the ratio of the Mexican price level to the U.S. price level constant.

Suppose the Mexican price level remains constant and the price of the chips remains a constant 100 pesos per chip. Since the U.S. price level doubled, the exchange rate will have to change from 3 to 1.5 pesos per dollar. But this means the dollar cost to the U.S. firm changes to 100 pesos/ (1.5 pesos per dollar) = $66.67. Thus, the dollar cost doubles. However, since the U.S. price level doubled, this means the real cost to the U.S. firm has just returned to its original level. Purchasing power parity leads to a vertical long-run supply curve in an open economy even if some input prices are quoted in foreign currency units.

Finally, we note that in an open economy, quotas and tariffs on inputs affect the natural rate of output, because they change the long-run level of productive resources that can be used to produce in the United States. Increases in U.S. tariffs or quotas on inputs reduce long-run aggregate supply, whereas reductions in these trade barriers increase it.

Summary
Exercise 17.3

Suppose the U.S. government imposes quotas on all items imported into the United States. Why might real GDP first increase and then decrease?

Answer: As the figure shows, the imposition of quotas affects both aggregate supply and aggregate demand. Quotas reduce imports and hence increase net export demand and aggregate demand from AD_0 to AD_1. The quotas reduce the availability of imported inputs, and this decreases both short-run and long-run aggregate supply, from $SRAS_0$ to $SRAS_1$ and $LRAS_0$ to $LRAS_1$, respectively. The increase in aggregate demand and the reduction in short-run aggregate supply will definitely raise the domestic price level, and in the short run it may also increase real GDP as the economy moves from point A to point B. In the long run, however, wages and other input prices will begin to rise in response to the increase in the price level, shifting short-run aggregate supply to the left. If long-run aggregate supply were unaffected, the long-run equilibrium would eventually return to the original

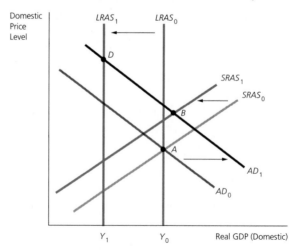

level of real GDP. However, because long-run aggregate supply itself shifts to the left due to the quotas, the long-run effect will be to reduce real GDP, as the economy utimately moves to point D.

FIXED EXCHANGE RATES, FLEXIBLE EXCHANGE RATES, AND POLICY EFFECTIVENESS

One important feature of the open economy that has large implications for policy is the choice between fixed and flexible exchange rates. In Chapter 11 we learned that under fixed exchange rates, monetary policy is dedicated to keeping the exchange rate fixed relative to some other currency. This means monetary policymakers must adjust the money supply to keep the exchange rate at the desired level instead of to achieve other macroeconomic goals such as full employment or price stability. When the demand for dollars is high, the Fed must increase the money supply to keep the exchange rate from rising; when demand is low, it must decrease the money supply to keep exchange rates from falling. A government participating in a fixed exchange rate system gives up its ability to use monetary policy to stimulate the economy. However, it can use fiscal policy.

In contrast, if the exchange rate is flexible, monetary policy is not tied to maintaining the exchange rate. In this case, the Fed can use monetary policy to achieve other macroeconomic goals or to stimulate the economy. However, while having flexible exchange rates frees up monetary policy, it restricts the use of fiscal policy. This restriction is not direct but is due to the way fiscal policy works in the economy. In a closed economy, the crowding-out effect discussed in Chapter 16 tends to at least partially counteract the effects of any increase in government purchases financed with borrowing, because the increase in demand for loanable funds used to finance the spending drives up the interest rate and reduces consumption and investment. In an open economy, this crowding out occurs in consumption, investment and net exports. Increases in the interest rate reduce consumption and investment just as in a closed economy. Increases in the interest rate attract foreign funds, which increases the capital account. These increases in the capital account are balanced by reductions in the current account, meaning net exports decline. This occurs because increased foreign capital inflows result in a rising demand for dollars, driving the exchange rate in foreign currency per U.S. dollar upward (an appreciation of the dollar) and reducing net exports. Thus, any increase in the interest rate reduces not only consumption and investment but also net exports. These three reductions counteract the increase in government purchases. The result is called *crowding out in the open economy* and is most severe when exchange rates are flexible. If exchange rates are fixed, net exports will not decline because of a higher exchange rate, and crowding out is less severe.

Thus, a country must choose between fixed and flexible exchange rates, and this choice will determine whether monetary or fiscal policy is more effective. Under flexible exchange rates, monetary policy can be effective at changing aggregate demand, while the effects of fiscal policy are diminished. Under fixed exchange rates, monetary policy is tied to exchange rate management and is not available for use in pursuing other policy goals. Fiscal policy, however, is less subject to crowding out and therefore more effective. Thus, the choice of fixed or flexible exchange rates has important implications not only for international traders and financiers themselves but also for the effectiveness of various macroeconomic policy tools. The United States has chosen to have a flexible exchange rate for a number of reasons, one being the additional flexibility it gives to the use of monetary policy. Box 17.3 describes the choice between fixed and flexible exchange rates in several European countries.

FISCAL POLICY IN AN OPEN ECONOMY

As we discussed in Chapter 16, fiscal policy actions are directed by the government budget constraint: The government must obtain funds to finance any government purchases. In an open economy, the only difference is that the sources of funds have expanded to include both taxes on international trade and international borrowing. However, we can still classify the methods of financing government purchases into three categories: (1) Raise tax revenues, including revenues from tariffs; (2) borrow funds by selling government bonds to U.S. or foreign residents; or (3) print money. The method of financing can affect the exchange rate; the interest rate, the price level, and real output. We now look at how different methods of financing government purchases affects the open economy.

Tax- and Tariff-Financed Increases in Government Purchases

Taxes available to the government include taxes such as the income tax and the social security tax and taxes such as tariffs on imports. We considered government purchases financed by an income tax in Chapter 16. Now we look at an increase in government purchases financed solely by a rise in tariffs. Such a consideration would have been very realistic in the early days of the United States, when tariffs were a major source of revenue and income taxes were unconstitutional. If an increase in government purchases is matched by an equal increase in tariffs, the government does not borrow any additional funds or print additional new money. We can analyze this situation as a simultaneous increase in government purchases, G, and in tariffs. The increase in government purchases has the direct effect of raising aggregate demand. The increase in tariffs raises the costs of imports, reducing demand for imports and raising net export demand. Thus, a tariff increase raises both net exports and aggregate demand! This is quite the opposite of the increase

International Banking

Box 17.3

*Fixed Versus Flexible Exchange Rates:
The European Experience*

The European Economic Community (EC) has been moving toward greater economic, political, and monetary union for more than two decades. During this time, many plans have been proposed for establishing a common currency for Europe or, more accurately, for the EC members. In 1971, a plan called the Werner Report called for a common currency by 1980. Most recently, the 1991 Maastricht treaty calls for a common currency by as early as 1997 and no later than 1999. As a step in this direction, the European Monetary System has had in place an exchange rate system known as the *exchange rate mechanism* (*ERM*) since March 1979. In this system, members of the European Monetary System pledged to maintain exchange rates within relatively narrow bands of target levels. At first, there were many revaluations of the targets as the various members adjusted to the ERM, including a series of major realignments in the early 1980s and again in 1986 and 1987. From then until late in the summer of 1992, the ERM was fairly stable, with most member countries' currencies keeping within narrow bands of ±2.25 percent around the target (or central) rates and others within ±6 percent bands. The United Kingdom, long a holdout from the ERM, finally joined in 1990.

However, in 1992 the effects of German reunification were being felt in Germany, which had experienced large budget deficits and inflation. The German central bank, the Bundesbank, responded by restricting money growth, which caused interest rates to rise. This is the time-honored response to inflation and was used by the U.S. Federal Reserve System in the early 1980s to reduce the U.S. inflation rate. But when Germany raised its interest rates, other ERM nations had to respond by raising their interest rates. If they didn't, the higher German rates would lead to capital inflows to Germany, and, as we saw in Chapter 11, the increased demand for German marks would cause the mark to appreciate and the other currencies to depreciate, thus violating the ERM bands. The fixed exchange rate system hence transmitted Germany's restrictive monetary policy to the rest of the EC. Moreover, other countries, such as France and the United Kingdom, found themselves unable to respond to domestic macroeconomic events with monetary policy, since they were forced to maintain high interest rates—which reduced investment and consumption—to maintain the exchange rate system. The problem was exacerbated by a worldwide recession in 1991 and 1992. Late in the summer of 1992, the United Kingdom pulled out of the ERM, refusing to suffer further under high interest rates to maintain the exchange rate with the German mark. Then, in the summer of 1993, the bottom fell out: The currencies of many countries were near the bottom of their bands against the mark. The European Monetary System's response was to widen the bands to ±15 percent, which effectively ended, at least temporarily, the fixed exchange rates of the ERM.

What had gone wrong? Basically the worldwide recession put pressure on European governments to lower interest rates at the same

Continued on p. 610

Continued from p. 609

time Germany was raising its rates to counter in- flation caused by increased government spend- ing due to reunification. Germany was unwilling to lower its interest rates, and other ERM mem- bers were unwilling to maintain high enough in- terest rates to keep the exchange rates within the agreed-upon bands. This example illustrates the cost of fixed exchange rates: They deprive a country of the ability to use monetary policy to achieve domestic policy goals.

Will the European Monetary System return to the tight ERM bands and to its goal of even- tual monetary union? The answer is not clear. It will take some time to move back to ERM bands of 2 or 3 percent, and the goal of monetary union by 1997 is extremely unlikely to be achieved. Whether this experience will dampen the enthusiasm for eventual monetary union re- mains to be seen.

in the consumption tax we analyzed in Chapter 16. But in an open economy, an increase in tariffs on imported inputs also might reduce aggregate supply. In this case, the increase in aggregate demand will be offset to some extent by the decrease in aggregate supply.

Figure 17.3 illustrates a tariff-financed increase in government purchases for the case where the tariffs do not affect aggregate supply. This case is most likely if the tariffs are imposed on consumer goods but not on imported inputs. Point A is the initial equilibrium. An increase in government pur- chases raises aggregate demand from AD_0 to AD_1, and the increased tariffs also raise it, from AD_1 to AD_2. In this case, the short-run equilibrium moves from point A to point C, illustrating a short-run rise in real GDP and prices. In the long run, however, wages and other input prices adjust, and the economy moves to point D. The long-run effect of a tariff that does not affect aggregate supply is to raise the domestic price level but leave real GDP at its natural rate.

Figure 17.4 illustrates the effect of an increase in government purchases financed by tariffs imposed on all foreign goods, including inputs. In this case the initial equilibrium is at point A, at the intersection of AD_0 and $SRAS_0$. The increase in government purchases shifts aggregate demand to the right to AD_1, and the increase in tariffs raises net exports, which further increases aggregate demand to AD_2. But the increase in tariffs on inputs raises production costs and reduces short-run aggregate supply from $SRAS_0$ to $SRAS_1$, and long-run aggregate supply declines from $LRAS_0$ to $LRAS_1$. The short-run effect is that the equilibrium moves to point B, with a higher price level and a higher level of real GDP than at point A. (Of course, this depends on the magnitude of the shifts in aggregate demand and short-run aggregate supply; real GDP could fall even in the short run.) In the long run, the adverse effects are compounded as the economy moves to point C. Prices rise even more, and output falls below the initial level at point A. Thus,

When an increase in government purchases is financed by an increase in tariffs on consumer goods but not in tariffs on imported inputs, the short-run and long-run aggregate supply may be unaffected. The increase in government purchases raises aggregate demand from AD_0 to AD_1. The increase in tariffs further increases aggregate demand from AD_1 to AD_2, since it increases net exports. Thus, the short-run equilibrium moves from point A to point C. The long-run equilibrium moves from point A to point D.

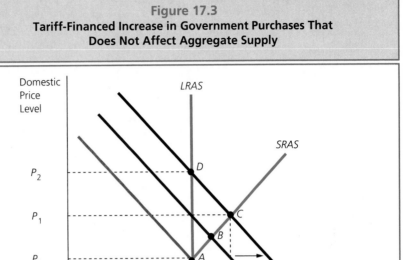

Figure 17.3
Tariff-Financed Increase in Government Purchases That Does Not Affect Aggregate Supply

tariffs on inputs reduce the natural rate of output; tariff-financed government purchases result in lower long-run GDP. This raises a dilemma for policymakers, particularly politicians: The short-run temptation is often to stimulate the economy now by imposing such tariffs, but the long-run effect will be a decline in real output.

Government Purchases Financed by Borrowing: Deficit Finance

What happens when the government borrows to finance spending in an open economy? As we saw in Chapter 16, the United States borrowed large amounts to finance government purchases in the early 1980s. How does our analysis of this policy change when we take account of the open economy? When government purchases rise, aggregate demand increases. There is no increase in taxes to reduce consumption. However, there is an increase in government borrowing, which results in crowding out. In the loanable funds market, the rise in government borrowing is an increased demand for loan-

When a tariff is imposed on all imports, including inputs, short-run aggregate supply falls from $SRAS_0$ to $SRAS_1$ and long-run aggregate supply falls from $LRAS_0$ to $LRAS_1$. Aggregate demand rises from AD_0 to AD_2. The short-run equilibrium moves from point A to point B, and the long-run equilibrium moves from point A to point C. Note that the effect of the tariff on aggregate supply diminishes any positive short-run effects of the fiscal policy and decreases output in the long run.

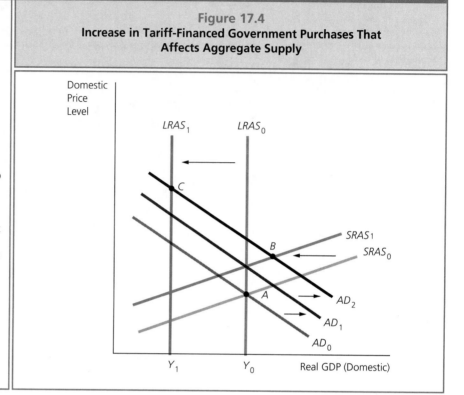

Figure 17.4
Increase in Tariff-Financed Government Purchases That Affects Aggregate Supply

able funds, which leads to an increase in the interest rate. This reduces investment and consumption just as we saw in the closed economy in Chapter 16. Furthermore, in an open economy, the increased demand for loanable funds is met in part by foreign lending. But the increase in the U.S. interest rate attracts foreign investors, who must first obtain additional U.S. dollars to purchase U.S. assets. This drives up the exchange rate, leading to a reduction in net exports and a worsening of the current account balance. Thus, the rise in aggregate demand due to the increase in government purchases is countered by two effects in an open economy: (1) an interest-rate-induced decrease in investment, consumption, and net exports and (2) a decline in net exports due to a higher exchange rate. This is crowding out in the open economy.

The case of partial crowding out is illustrated in Figure 17.5, where the increase in government purchases shifts aggregate demand from AD_0 to AD_1, but the increase in the interest rate from government borrowing and the rise in the exchange rate jointly cause a reduction in aggregate demand to AD_2. In this case, the short-run effect of an increase in government purchases financed by borrowing is the movement from point *A* to point *C*, where the price level and real GDP rise. In the long run, wages and other input prices increase, which moves us to point *D*. At point *D*, output returns to its natural rate, but the price level is higher.

It is important to remember that crowding out in an open economy occurs because of increases in both interest rates and the exchange rate. In contrast, in a closed economy crowding out occurs due only to rising interest rates. The magnitude of the crowding out depends on whether exchange rates are fixed or flexible. Figure 17.5 is drawn for the case of a flexible exchange rate, in which the increased exchange rate reduces net exports and further

Figure 17.5
Crowding Out in the Open Economy

This graph shows the effect of a deficit-financed increase in government purchases in an open economy. The increase in government purchases causes aggregate demand to rise from AD_0 to AD_1. However, the rise in the interest rate that accompanies the additional government borrowing will have a negative impact on aggregate demand, both because it reduces consumption and investment and because higher interest rates increase the exchange rate, which lowers net exports. These adverse effects reduce aggregate demand from AD_1 to AD_2. The short-run equilibrium moves from point *A* to point *C*, while the long-run equilibrium moves from point *A* to point *D*.

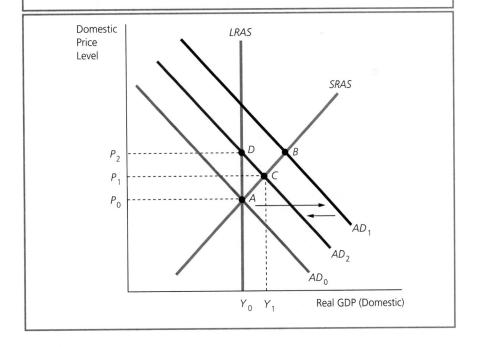

crowds out the increase in government purchases. If the exchange rate were fixed, the Fed would intervene in the exchange market by supplying U.S. dollars to keep the exchange rate, and thus net exports, unchanged.

Government Purchases Financed by Money Creation

Just as in the closed economy, one of the most expansionary ways to increase government purchases is to finance the spending by money creation. However, this method of finance is available only in the case of flexible exchange rates. With fixed exchange rates, the money supply cannot be increased to finance government purchases because doing so would lower the exchange rate. Thus, the analysis in this section pertains only to a regime of flexible exchange rates, as currently exists in the United States.

Government purchases financed by money creation has several effects on the economy. First, the increase in government purchases raises aggregate demand directly. Second, the increase in the money supply reduces the domestic interest rate. This increases domestic consumption and investment, further raising aggregate demand. Finally, the lower domestic interest rates reduce foreign demand for U.S. assets, which in turn reduces their demand for U.S. dollars. The result is a decrease in the exchange rate, making domestic goods cheaper relative to foreign goods, which raises net exports and improves the balance of trade. Thus, all three effects tend to increase aggregate demand.

Figure 17.6 illustrates these effects. The initial equilibrium is at point A, with aggregate demand given by AD_0. The increase in government purchases raises aggregate demand to AD_1. The increase in the money supply lowers interest rates and the exchange rate, which increases aggregate demand to AD_2. Thus, the short-run effect of government purchases financed by money creation is the movement from point A to point C, which implies a higher price level and higher short-run real GDP. In the long run input prices rise, and equilibrium moves to point D. Thus, the long-run effect is merely to raise the price level.

THE TWIN DEFICITS: THE BUDGET AND CURRENT ACCOUNT DEFICITS

During the 1980s, the United States had large government budget deficits, accompanied by large current account deficits. These deficits were labeled the *twin deficits* to indicate that they seemed to move together much of the time. These twin deficits are graphed in Figure 17.7, where we see that they both increased greatly from 1980 to 1985. From 1985 through 1989 there was a trend toward a reduction in both deficits, but in the 1990s the government budget deficit again increased sharply while the current account con-

This graph shows government purchases financed by money creation. The increase in government purchases increases aggregate demand from AD_0 to AD_1. In addition, the increase in the money supply lowers interest rates, which increases consumption, investment, and net exports. This further shifts aggregate demand from AD_1 to AD_2. The short-run equilibrium moves from point A to point C, and both the price level and real GDP rise. The long-run equilibrium is at point D, where output returns to its natural rate.

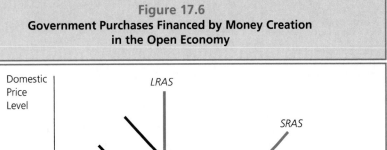

Figure 17.6
Government Purchases Financed by Money Creation in the Open Economy

tinued to improve. In this section, we explore the relationship among investment, saving, the government budget deficit, and the current account deficit and see why these twin deficits have moved together in recent years.

Investment, Saving, and the Budget Deficit

In an open economy, total spending on domestic output, Y, can be divided into consumption purchases (C), investment purchases (I), government purchases (G), and net exports (NX). Thus, we have the following relationship between total output and the various spending categories:

$$Y = C + I + G + NX. \tag{17.1}$$

Equation 17.1 provides one relationship between economic output and spending. Now consider individuals in the economy. Individuals receive income that equals the value of total output, Y, and they dispose of that income by buying consumption goods, C, by saving it, S, and paying taxes with it, T. Thus, we also have the relationship

$$Y = C + S + T. \tag{17.2}$$

This figure graphs real net exports (the balance of trade) and the real government deficit for 1976 through 1992 (both are in 1987 dollars). Since both deficits are negative and move together, they are often called the *twin deficits*. The government deficit shown here indicates federal, state, and local governments spent more between 1976 and 1992 than they collected in taxes.

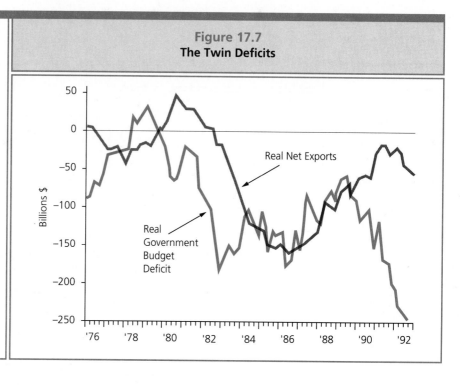

Figure 17.7
The Twin Deficits

Substituting Y in equation 17.2 for Y in equation 17.1 gives us

$$C + S + T = C + I + G + NX,$$

which can be simplified to

$$I + (G - T) = S - NX. \tag{17.3}$$

Equation 17.3 gives a relationship stating that investment spending (I) plus the government deficit ($G - T$) must equal private sector saving (S) minus net exports (NX). At first this relationship may look a bit strange, but in a closed economy, where net exports are zero, this relationship merely states that the demand for funds for investment and for financing the government deficit must equal the supply of funds available from private sector saving. In a closed economy, any increase in investment spending or in the government deficit must be matched by an increase in private saving. The left-hand side of equation 17.3 is essentially the demand for loanable funds, and the right-hand side is the supply of loanable funds, which in a closed economy is simply private sector saving.

In an open economy, equation 17.3 subtracts net exports from private sector saving. If we ignore income flows and unilateral transfers, net exports are essentially the current account in the balance of payments. Furthermore, the current account equals the opposite of the capital account. Thus, ignoring income flows, unilateral transfers, and statistical discrepancies, net exports indicate the size and magnitude of the capital account. If net exports are $-\$100$ billion, the capital account must be $+\$100$ billion. In effect, negative net exports—a current account deficit—are an outflow of funds to purchase goods and services produced abroad. This outflow is balanced by a capital account surplus, an equal-sized inflow of funds from abroad. This is an inflow of loanable funds used to finance both private investment and the government deficit. For given levels of private saving and investment, the greater the government deficit, the greater the amount of loanable funds needed to finance it and the greater the current account deficit. In an open economy, a current account deficit provides an additional source of loanable funds to the U.S. financial markets.

The Supply of Loanable Funds in an Open Economy

There is another way to look at the relationship between a current account deficit and the supply of loanable funds in the United States. Negative net exports means the United States is buying more goods from abroad than it sells abroad. There will be a net outflow of dollars from the United States, which will accumulate in the hands of overseas producers. These producers do not want to hold idle dollar balances, so they use these accumulated funds to purchase U.S. assets; that is, they trade them to U.S. borrowers in return for stocks, bonds, or other assets. In essence, they supply loanable funds in the U.S. loanable funds market.

Figure 17.8 provides a graphical view of the difference between an open and a closed economy in the loanable funds market. The graph explicitly indicates that the demand for loanable funds, D^{LF}, is to finance investment (I) and the government deficit ($G - T$). The supply of loanable funds in the closed economy (S_0^{LF}) is simply private domestic saving, S. The supply of loanable funds in the open economy is private domestic saving plus the supply of foreign funds as indicated by the balance on the capital account. Since the negative of the current account, or $-NX$, equals the capital account balance, the total supply of loanable funds to the United States in the open economy is $S - NX$, or S_1^{LF}.

Loanable funds equilibrium in the closed economy is at point A at the intersection of S_0^{LF} and D^{LF}, whereas equilibrium in the open economy is at point B, at the intersection of S_1^{LF} and D^{LF}. Notice that when there is a surplus on the capital account (or, equivalently, a deficit on the current account), net exports are negative. In this case additional loanable funds enter the United States from abroad, and the interest rate in the open economy (i_B) is below that in the closed economy (i_A).

International trade also has a more subtle effect on the total supply of loanable funds. Because both the private saving schedule and the supply of foreign funds are sensitive to interest rate movements, the slope of loanable funds supply in the closed economy is steeper than that in the open economy.

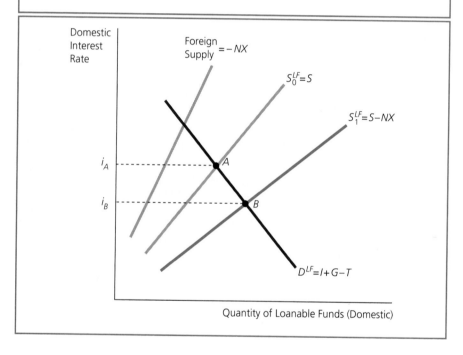

Figure 17.8
The Loanable Funds Market in an Open Economy

In a closed economy the supply of loanable funds is private saving, S, whereas in an open economy the supply is private saving, S, plus the foreign supply of loanable funds. Equilibrium in a closed economy is thus at point A, where the interest rate is i_A. In an economy such as the United States, where net exports are negative, equilibrium is at point B. Thus, interest rates are lower because the capital account surplus provides an additional supply of loanable funds. The foreign supply is given by the capital account, which is $-NX$ in the absence of central bank intervention. Hence, in the open economy, the supply of loanable funds is $S - NX$.

This means any increase in the U.S. demand for loanable funds will result in a larger increase in the interest rate in the closed economy than in the open economy. This implies, among other things, that a government deficit financed by borrowing will result in a smaller increase in the interest rate in the open economy, because foreign sources of loanable funds will help meet the increased demand for loanable funds. The flip side of this coin is that increases in the government deficit will result in a greater surplus on the capital account and hence a greater deficit on the current account, or greater negative net exports.

Explaining the Movement in the Twin Deficits

What can explain the close movements in the budget deficit $(G - T)$ and the current account deficit $(-NX)$ shown earlier in Figure 17.1? Many have argued that the high government budget deficit in the 1980s caused the high current account deficit during those years. Equation 17.3 does suggest that the budget deficit and the capital account deficit will move together, but only if both investment and private saving are held fixed, or at least if the difference between investment and private saving fails to adjust to the government budget deficit. For example, if we hold investment and private saving constant, any increase in the U.S. government budget deficit must be matched by a reduction in net exports (an increased deficit position in the current account). Note, however, that the validity of this argument depends on the crucial assumption that private saving and investment do not adjust to counter the government budget deficit.

In reality, domestic investment and private saving were not constant in the early 1980s, and in fact investment grew almost twice as fast during this period as private saving. This increase in real domestic investment was caused in part by drastic changes in tax laws that created a more favorable climate for investing in the United States. Domestic private saving did not keep up with investment; instead the funds required to finance this increase in investment came from abroad. To obtain dollars to lend in the United States, overseas producers increased their sales of goods in the United States, which increased the current account deficit. Concurrently, government spending in the 1980s increased at a faster rate than tax revenues (due largely to changes in tax laws), which led to an increase in the budget deficit.

Thus, we see that the high current account deficits in the early 1980s were caused by two factors: an increase in the government deficit and a rise in domestic investment relative to domestic private saving. Tax changes in the early 1980s contributed to both of these factors. Hence it is probably misleading to say that the increased government budget deficits were the sole cause of the current account deficits. Instead government budget deficits played a role in the rise of the current account deficits, a role shared by the rise in investment demand.

MONETARY POLICY: OPEN MARKET OPERATIONS

What is the effect of open market operations in an open economy? With fixed exchange rates, monetary policy must focus on keeping the exchange rate fixed; the Fed supplies U.S. dollars when the demand for dollars is high and buys U.S. dollars when demand for dollars is low. Such monetary policy keeps the exchange rate constant, or at least within some narrow band. This means, however, that the Fed cannot freely use open market operations as a means of stimulating the domestic economy.

The story differs with flexible exchange rates. In this case, the exchange rate is determined by market forces, and the Fed does not intervene to keep it from rising or falling. In other words, with flexible exchange rates, the Fed can use monetary policy to affect the domestic economy. Let us see how this works in an open economy.

In an open market purchase, the Federal Reserve System prints money and uses it to purchase bonds. This lowers the interest rate. The effect of open market operations on aggregate demand then follows from the change in the interest rate. The decrease in the interest rate leads to an increase in domestic consumption and investment and hence a rise in aggregate demand. Furthermore, in an open economy the reduction in the interest rate leads to a decrease in the foreign demand for U.S. assets and hence in the foreign demand for dollars on the market for foreign exchange. This tends to lower the exchange rate, making U.S. goods cheaper relative to foreign goods. This effect increases net exports (and improves the balance of trade), which further raises aggregate demand. Thus, we see that in an open economy, monetary policy has an effect on net exports, which tends to reinforce the effects present in a closed economy.

Figure 17.9 illustrates this effect. Aggregate demand is initially at AD_0, and the initial equilibrium is at point A. The open market purchase lowers the interest rate and the exchange rate, shifting aggregate demand to AD_1 and moving the equilibrium to point B in the short run, increasing both the price level and level of real GDP. Keynesians view the shift to point B as relatively small, whereas monetarists see it as more pronounced. In the long run, the economy moves to point C, where the price level is higher and real output returns to its natural rate.

Summary Exercise 17.4

(a) Suppose the government reduces spending and finances the spending by issuing fewer bonds. What will be the short-run and long-run effects of this policy on the interest rate, the exchange rate, the price level, real GDP, and the balance of trade? (b) How will the impact change if the government funds the spending cuts by decreasing the money supply?

Answer: (a) A reduction in government spending leads to a decrease in the demand for loanable funds, which in turn lowers the interest rate. This decrease in the interest rate increases the level of investment and consumption in the economy, which tends to shift aggregate demand to the right. In addition, the decrease in the interest rate lowers the exchange rate and tends to increase net exports (and the balance of trade), which further shifts aggregate demand to the right. The decrease in government purchases, how-

The decrease in interest rates resulting from an open market purchase of bonds causes aggregate demand to rise for two reasons. First, the decrease in interest rates causes both consumption and investment to increase. Second, the decrease in the interest rate causes the exchange rate to fall. This in turn increases net exports. Thus, aggregate demand increases from AD_0 to AD_1, resulting in a short-run equilibrium at point B. In the long run, equilibrium is at point C, with no effect on output.

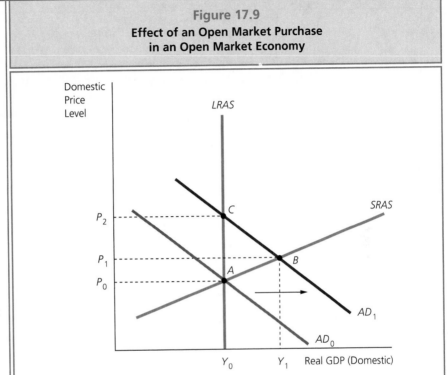

Figure 17.9
Effect of an Open Market Purchase in an Open Market Economy

ever, shifts aggregate demand to the left. If there is complete crowding out, these effects perfectly cancel each other out, and no change in the price level or aggregate output occurs, although the interest rate and exchange rate fall. If there is only partial crowding out, the decrease in government purchases will more than offset the increase in consumption, investment, and net exports, so aggregate demand will decrease. In the short run, this will lead to a lower real GDP and price level. In the long run, however, wages and other input prices will fall, shifting aggregate supply to the right. In the long run, the policy has no effect on real output; it only lowers the price level. (b) A decrease in the money supply increases domestic interest rates and thus the exchange rate. This leads to a reduction in consumption, investment, and net export demand (worsening the balance of trade). The decrease in government purchases further lowers aggregate demand, so net aggregate demand shifts to the left. The short-run effect of this policy is to decrease the price level and real GDP. In the long run, wages and other input prices fall, leading to a lower price level and the original level of output.

CONCLUSION

In this chapter, we explored the implications of international trade and international finance for the macro economy. We saw how features of the open economy modify our analysis of Chapter 16 and alter the effectiveness of monetary and fiscal policy. In the final three chapters of this book, we build on these basic models to look more closely at monetary and fiscal policy. But first, in Chapter 18, we look at the data illustrating the relationship between money and the economy.

KEY TERMS

open economy model

balance of payments

import

export

statistical discrepancy

current account

net exports

capital account

QUESTIONS AND PROBLEMS

1. Suppose a U.S. resident buys a case of French wine for $1,000. The owner of the French vineyard uses this money to buy $1,000 worth of IBM stock.
   (a). How do these transactions show up in the balance of payments?
   (b). If these are the only transactions in the economy, will there be a balance of payments deficit? A balance of trade deficit?

2. Explain why net exports can be positive or negative and why a higher (U.S.) price level results in a reduction in the quantity demanded of net exports.

3. Determine the impact of the following on the demand for imports:
   (a). An increase in the U.S. price level
   (b). An increase in the foreign price level
   (c). A decrease in the exchange rate

4. Determine the impact of the following on the demand for net exports:
   (a). An increase in the U.S. interest rate
   (b). An increase in the foreign price level
   (c). An increased taste for U.S. goods sold in Japan
   (d). A decrease in the exchange rate

5. Determine the impact of the following on the demand for net exports:
   (a). An increase in both the U.S. and foreign interest rates
   (b). An increase in both U.S. and foreign wealth

6. Determine the impact of the following on aggregate demand:
   (a). An increase in the foreign interest rate
   (b). A decrease in the money supply
   (c). An increase in tariffs on imported consumer goods

(d). Improved consumer optimism

(e). Technological improvement

(f). A tariff on imported raw materials for industry

7. Holding everything else constant, determine the short-run impact of the following on the equilibrium price level and real GDP:

   (a). An increase in the exchange rate

   (b). A decrease in the foreign interest rate

   (c). An increase in U.S. tariffs on imported household goods

   (d). Technological improvement

   (e). A tariff on imported raw materials

8. Explain why the exchange rate might affect the position of short-run aggregate supply. Under what conditions will changes in the exchange rate *not* affect short-run aggregate supply?

9. Explain why the tariffs on imported raw materials will affect the positions of both short-run and long-run aggregate supply.

10. Suppose the government increases spending and finances the spending by raising tariffs. What are the short-run and long-run macroeconomic effects assuming the tariff increase (a) affects only consumption, (b) affects only aggregate supply, and (c) affects both aggregate demand and aggregate supply?

11. Suppose the government increases spending and finances the spending by borrowing. What are the short-run and long-run macroeconomic effects on (a) the interest rate, (b) the exchange rate, (c) the price level, and (d) real GDP?

12. Suppose the government increases spending and finances the spending by printing money. What are the short-run and long-run macroeconomic effects on (a) the interest rate, (b) the exchange rate, (c) the price level, and (d) real GDP?

13. Assume the U.S. government is concerned about the fact that net exports in the United States are negative. What types of policies could improve the balance of trade?

SELECTIONS FOR FURTHER READING

Ahmed, S., B. Ickes, P. Wang, and S. Yoo. "International Business Cycles." *American Economic Review,* 83 (June 1993), 335–359.

Beladi, H., B. Biswas, and G. Tribedy. "Growth of Income and the Balance of Payments: Keynesian and Monetary Theories." *Journal of Economic Studies,* 13 (1986), 44–45.

Davila, A. E., and J. P. Mattila. "Do Workers Earn Less Along the U.S.–Mexico Border?" *Social Science Quarterly,* 66 (June 1985), 310–318.

Deyak, T. A., W. C. Sawyer, and R. L. Sprinkle. "An Empirical Examination of the Structural Stability of Disaggregated U.S. Import Demand." *Review of Economics and Statistics,* 71 (May 1989), 337–341.

Himarios, D. "The Impact of the Exchange Rate on U.S. Inflation and GNP Growth: Comment." *Southern Economic Journal,* 55 (April 1989), 1044–1051.

Honohan, P., and P. McNelis. "Is the EMS a DM Zone?—Evidence from the Realignments." *Economic and Social Review,* 20 (January 1989), 97–110.

Kim, B. J. C. "A Time-Series Study of the Employment Real Wage Relationship: An International

Continued on p. 624

Continued from p. 623

Comparison.'' *Journal of Economics and Business,* 40 (February 1988), 67–78.

Lowinger, T. C., C. Wihlborg, and E. S. Willman. ''OPEC in World Financial Markets: Oil Prices and Interest Rates.'' *Journal of International Money and Finance,* 4 (June 1985), 253–266.

Ozawa, T. ''Japan in a New Phase of Multinationalism and Industrial Upgrading: Functional Integration of Trade, Growth and FDI.'' *Journal of World Trade,* 25 (February 1991), 43–60.

Reichenstein, W. R., and F. J. Bonello. ''Aggregate Supply Considerations and the St. Louis Equation.'' *Journal of Economics and Business,* 34 (1982), 253–262.

Romans, J. T., and S. A. Warren. ''A Balance of Payments Analysis of the Latin American Debt Crisis.'' *Review of Income and Wealth,* 36 (June 1990), 207–213.

Money and Economic Activity: A Look at the Evidence

*I*magine that you work for a major Wall Street investment firm. Your boss calls you in and asks you about the likely impact on the economy of a recent rise in the money supply. How will you reply? The aggregate demand and supply model we developed in Chapters 16 and 17 suggests that in the short run (when input prices are fixed), an increase in the money supply may cause real output (real GDP) and the price level to rise. However, the model also suggests that in the long run (after input prices fully adjust), increases in the money stock will not change real output; it will only raise the price level. In the long run, an economy cannot produce more real output simply by printing more money.

These results are only theoretical, however, and you may wonder whether your boss would understand the diagrams you might use to illustrate these effects. You may even wonder yourself whether these theoretical ideas line up with the real-world facts. This chapter provides the answer as we look at the data on money and other economic variables to see the empirical relationship between money and such variables as real output, inflation, and interest rates.

THE LONG-RUN RELATIONSHIP AMONG MONEY, PRICES, AND REAL OUTPUT

Our model of aggregate demand and supply makes predictions about the relationship between money and other economic variables for both the long run and the short run. In this section, we examine three propositions that summarize the predictions about the long-run relationship among money, output, and prices. Then we look at some empirical evidence on these relationships, from both the United States and abroad, to see how well they hold up in reality.

Theoretical Relationships Between Money and Economic Activity

Recall from Chapters 16 and 17 that our long-run macroeconomic model has a vertical aggregate supply curve. This indicates that in the long run, after all input prices fully adjust to changes in the price level, changes in aggregate demand do *not* affect output since any increase or decrease in aggregate demand will merely result in movements up or down the vertical long-run aggregate supply curve. Changes in aggregate demand *do* affect the price level in the long run. Recall too that one important determinant of aggregate demand is the money stock. Changes in the money stock cause changes in aggregate demand, which in turn cause changes in the price level or output in the short run and changes in the price level in the long run. In this section, we elaborate on the relationship among money, prices, real output, and nominal GDP in the long run.

To begin, remember that aggregate demand is the sum of consumption demand, investment demand, government demand, and net export demand; the determinants of aggregate demand are simply the determinants of these components. Thus, the determinants of aggregate demand include wealth, the interest rate, taxes and tariffs, and the exchange rate. Anything that causes these determinants to change causes changes in aggregate demand, and thus changes in the price level or in real output.

Concentrating on the long run, we want to consider which of these determinants might be responsible for long-run movements in aggregate demand, that is, which determinant could create increases or decreases in aggregate demand that persist over years or even decades. A number of possibilities exist, but a traditional answer to this question that extends back to the classical economists such as Adam Smith and Alfred Marshall is that ongoing changes in the money supply cause ongoing changes in aggregate demand. In fact, this idea is formalized in the equation of exchange, first discussed in Chapter 3:

$$MV = PY.$$

The left-hand side of this equation is the product of the money stock, M, and the velocity of money, V (the number of times the average unit of money changes hands in one year). The right-hand side is the product of the price level, P, and real output (or real GDP), Y. The product of the price level and real GDP is also known as nominal GDP, or simply GDP.

We can use the equation of exchange to develop the quantity theory of money. As we saw in Chapter 3, this involves making assumptions about the behavior of velocity and real GDP. In particular, we assumed velocity to be fairly stable and changes in velocity were not related to changes in the money stock. Using the quantity theory, we can develop a model of aggregate demand that greatly simplifies the model developed in Chapters 16 and 17. The quantity theory emphasizes the importance of the money stock, which we recognized as being but one of a number of factors that could shift aggregate demand. The quantity theory consolidates all other determinants of aggregate demand into velocity so that changes in taxes, interest rates, or tastes are all considered changes in velocity. The classical economists thought these other determinants of demand are relatively stable and, more important, were not likely to have sustained movements in one direction or another over long periods of time. Thus, over the long run these other components may occasionally cause a change in aggregate demand, but they would not continually increase or decrease year after year and thus would not be responsible for ongoing movements in aggregate demand.

Changes in the money stock, on the other hand, do tend to be systematic; governments regularly print more money over time. The equation of exchange emphasizes the importance of such changes in the money stock. It also allows us to easily discuss another idea: that increases in the money stock lead to changes in nominal income (nominal GDP). For example, the equation of exchange can be written in terms of growth rates as

$$g_M + g_V = g_{\text{nominal GDP}} = \pi + g_Y.$$

This equation indicates that the growth rate of the money stock (g_M, or $\Delta M/M$) plus the growth rate of velocity (g_V, or $\Delta V/V$) equals the growth rate of nominal GDP ($g_{\text{nominal GDP}}$, or $\Delta \text{GDP}/\text{GDP}$). Furthermore, it separates the growth of nominal GDP into the inflation rate (π, or $\Delta P/P$) and the growth of real output (g_Y, or $\Delta Y/Y$).

As we mentioned earlier, one assumption the classical economists made was that the growth rate of velocity is fairly stable and is unaffected by changes in the growth rate of the money stock. We can simplify this to say that the growth rate of velocity is on average equal to zero. As we will see, this is approximately true for the velocity of M2, although it is not true for the velocity of M1. This is one reason this chapter stresses looking at M2 instead of M1: The velocity of M2 more closely corresponds to the classical assumptions.

If velocity growth is zero, we have the classical relationship between money growth and nominal income growth:

$$g_M = g_{\text{nominal GDP}} = \pi + g_Y.$$

This equation, along with the vertical long-run aggregate supply curve, gives us a host of propositions about money growth, nominal income growth, real output, and inflation. It links money growth (g_M) to nominal income growth ($g_{\text{nominal GDP}}$), which itself is the sum of output growth (g_Y) and inflation (π). The vertical long-run aggregate supply curve means that changes in aggregate demand, including those caused by changes in the money stock, cannot lead to changes in real output in the long run. Thus, increases in money growth in the long run must lead to increases in the inflation rate. We summarize the implications of these ideas in the following three propositions:

Proposition 1: In the long run, an increase in the growth rate of money will lead to an equal increase in the growth rate of nominal GDP.

Proposition 2: In the long run, an increase in the growth rate of money will lead to an equal increase in the inflation rate.

Proposition 3: In the long run, an increase in the growth rate of money will not lead to any change in the growth rate of real GDP.

We stress that these are long-run propositions. They need not apply to the short run. In the short run, aggregate supply is not vertical, so propositions 2 and 3 need not hold. Furthermore, in the short run the other determinants of aggregate demand continually lead to rises or falls in velocity, and these results detract from the relationship specified in proposition 1. We will discuss the short-run relationships between money and economic activity later. For now, we look at the evidence for these long-run propositions. We first look at evidence in the United States and then see whether or not the experience in other countries is similar.

U.S. Evidence on the Long-Run Relationships Between Money and Economic Activity

To investigate our three propositions, we first look at the evidence from 120 years of U.S. history on the impact of changes in the growth rate of the money stock on the inflation rate, the growth rate of real GDP, and the growth rate in nominal GDP for the 1869–1989 period. We divide these data into 10-year periods. For each period, we calculate the average growth in the money supply and compare it to the corresponding decade average inflation rate, nominal GDP growth rate, and real GDP growth rate. This allows us to see whether money growth over a 10-year period affected economic activity over the same decade. We will use a technique that allows us to visualize the relationship between money growth rates in these different decades to the growth in the price level, nominal GDP, and real GDP over the same period.

The first proposition states that increases in the growth rate of the money stock should lead to equal increases in the growth of nominal GDP. Is this proposition confirmed by 120 years of U.S. history? Part a of Figure 18.1(a) shows the growth rates of nominal GDP and the M2 money stock for each of 12 decades ranging from 1869–1879 to 1979–1989. This plot of points is called a **scatter diagram;** each point corresponds with the growth in nominal GDP and money growth in a given decade. This scatter diagram reveals that during decades in which money growth was high, the growth in nominal GDP also tended to be high. This is consistent with proposition 1: An increase in the growth rate of money leads to an increase in the growth rate of nominal GDP. The line drawn through these points is called a **best fit line;** it is chosen by a statistical procedure to fit the best straight line to the scatter of points. The slope of this line is 1, indicating that increases in the rate of money growth over these decades tended to lead to an equal rise in the rate of nominal GDP growth. Clearly the points do not lie exactly on the line, so proposition 1 did not hold exactly for every decade. Instead, the figure indicates that over time, increases in money growth tended to raise nominal GDP growth by an equal amount.

There are two rather large deviations from the best fit line in Figure 18.1. The one that lies farthest above this line has nominal GDP growth of 6.56 percent and money growth of 3.74 percent and represents the decade

Each point on this scatter diagram represents the growth in the money supply (M2) and growth in nominal GDP for each decade between 1869 and 1989 in the United States. The positive slope reveals support for proposition 1.

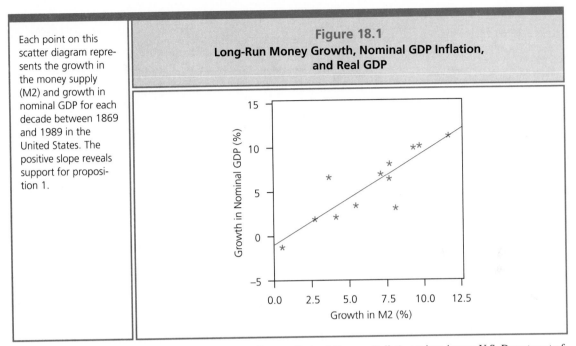

Figure 18.1
Long-Run Money Growth, Nominal GDP Inflation, and Real GDP

SOURCES: Board of Governors of the Federal Reserve System, *Federal Reserve Bulletin*, various issues; U.S. Department of Commerce, Bureau of Economic Analysis, *Survey of Current Business*, various issues; Citibase electronic database.

1949–1959. The one farthest below the line has nominal GDP growth of 2.99 percent and money growth of 8.00 percent and represents the decade 1879–1889. Remember, however, that the proposition concerns the long run, and over our sample of 120 years of U.S. history, the scatter of points in Figure 18.1 indicates that in the long run, increases in the growth rate of money led to increases in the growth of nominal GDP.

The second proposition states that increases in the growth rate of the money stock should lead to equal increases in the inflation rate. This proposition builds on proposition 1 and on the idea of a vertical long-run aggregate supply curve. Figure 18.2 shows the inflation rate and the growth rate of the money stock in the United States for 12 decades, ranging from 1869–1879 to 1979–1989. This scatter of points is consistent with proposition 2, since decades with higher growth rates of money tend to have higher inflation rates.

The line drawn through the scatter of points is again the best fit line, and the slope of this line is about .9, which is not statistically different from 1. This suggests that increases in the rate of money growth over these decades led to equal or nearly equal increases in the rate of inflation.[1] As in Figure

---

[1] The appendix to this chapter contains the regressions used to estimate the best fit lines.

Each point on this scatter diagram represents the growth in the money supply (M2) and the inflation rate in a given decade between 1869 and 1989 for the United States. The slope of the best fit line is 0.9, which is not statistically different from 1. This implies that in the long run, increases in the growth of money led to equal increases in the inflation rate. Thus, U.S. data support proposition 2.

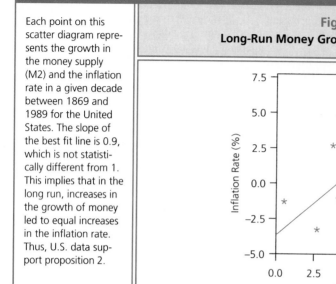

Figure 18.2
Long-Run Money Growth and Long-Run Inflation

SOURCES: Board of Governors of the Federal Reserve System, *Federal Reserve Bulletin,* various issues; U.S. Department of Commerce, Bureau of Economic Analysis, *Survey of Current Business,* various issues; Citibase electronic database.

18.1, it is clear that the points in Figure 2 do not lie exactly on the line, so proposition 2 did not hold exactly for every decade. Instead, over time increases in the rate of money growth caused equal or nearly equal increases in the inflation rate, with possible substantial deviations in any one decade.

An interesting feature of the relationship between inflation and money growth is that the best fit line does not pass through the point with zero inflation and zero money growth. This is because the equation of exchange, in growth rate form, links the rate of money growth to the rate of inflation plus the rate of output growth. Since output growth averaged more than 3 percent during 1869–1989, the inflation rate was on average about 3 percent less than the rate of money growth. Of course, output growth varied considerably over our sample due to changes in the capital stock and technology and to periods of recession, especially the Great Depression of the 1930s.

The third proposition states that increases in the growth rate of the money stock should have no effect on the growth rate of output, which we measure as growth in real GDP. Like proposition 2, this proposition is derived from proposition 1 and the idea of a vertical long-run aggregate supply curve. In the case of real GDP, the vertical long-run aggregate supply curve means that in the long run, real GDP was unaffected by changes in determinants of aggregate demand in general and by the money supply in particular.

Figure 18.3 graphs the rate of growth of real GDP and the growth rate of the money stock for 12 U.S. decades. This scatter of points is consistent with the notion that increases in the growth rate of money *do not* lead to increases in the rate of growth of real GDP. Indeed, except for the point at the origin, the points actually show a slight negative relationship between real GDP growth and money growth. We do not draw a best fit line because the slope cannot be distinguished statistically from zero. We conclude that proposition 3 held, since the figure shows no link between the rate of money growth and the rate of growth of real GDP. As in Figures 18.1 and 18.2, it is clear that the points do not lie on a straight line and that real GDP was not constant over this period. Real GDP growth was almost zero during the decade that included the Great Depression, but even leaving this point aside, the real GDP growth rates varied from just over 2 percent to more than 5 percent during this period, with no systematic relationship to the rate of money growth.

We conclude that U.S. evidence generally supports propositions 1 through 3. Data from 12 decades of U.S. history show that: first, decades with higher money growth had higher growth in nominal GDP, and furthermore this relationship was one to one. For example, decades with 5 percent higher money growth on average had 5 percent higher growth in nominal GDP. Second, decades with higher money growth rates tended to also have higher inflation rates. Moreover, this relationship was one to one; decades

The points on this scatter diagram represent the growth in the money supply (M2) and the rate of growth in real output for given decades between 1869 and 1989 for the United States. Notice that there appears to have been no relationship among the scattered points; in the long run, the growth rate in the money supply did not affect growth in real output. Thus, U.S. data tend to support proposition 3.

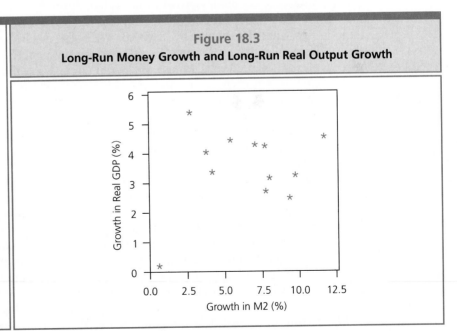

Figure 18.3
Long-Run Money Growth and Long-Run Real Output Growth

SOURCES: Board of Governors of the Federal Reserve System, *Federal Reserve Bulletin*, various issues; U.S. Department of Commerce, Bureau of Economic Analysis, *Survey of Current Business*, various issues; Citibase electronic database.

with 5 percent higher money growth generally had inflation rates that were 5 percent higher. Third, the growth rate of real GDP and the growth rate of money were not related. Decades with high money growth had, on average, the same growth in real GDP as did decades with lower money growth. Again we stress that these are long-run relationships that did not hold in any one year or, as we have seen, even in any one decade. Instead, they held over more than a century of U.S. history.

International Evidence on the Long-Run Relationships Between Money and Economic Activity

Before looking at short-run evidence on money and economic activity, we will examine another type of long-run evidence on our three propositions. Our previous evidence from the United States compared money growth and measures of economic activity over 12 consecutive decades. An alternative is to use data from a single timespan and gather them for several countries. This method gives us data on a large number of different experiences of money growth rates, all from a comparable period of time. The advantage of this approach over looking at only one nation is that we can gather much more information and examine all countries at the same point in time. A disadvantage is that we must compare nations with different institutional details and different values for velocity and the other determinants of aggregate demand. But in a way this is a plus, because our intent is to see whether differences in money growth can explain differences in nominal income and inflation rather than differences in real GDP growth.

Gerald P. Dwyer, Jr., and Rik W. Hafer conducted just such a study. Using data from 62 countries gathered for the period 1979–1984, they employed the scatter technique used in Figures 18.1 through 18.3. The difference is that each point represents a different decade in U.S. history, while each point in their figures represents the experience of a different country over the same time span.

Recall that our first proposition is that increases in the growth rate of the money stock should lead to equal increases in the growth rate of nominal income. Figure 18.4 graphs the average growth rate of nominal GDP and the average growth rate of the money stock for 62 countries for the time period 1979–1984. The scatter of points is consistent with proposition 1. The rates of money growth and GDP growth lie along the reference line drawn with a slope of 1, as suggested by proposition one. It is not the best fit line, which actually has a slope of 1.01. Thus, countries with higher money growth rates tended to have higher inflation rates.

Notice in Figure 18.4 that there is quite a bit more variation in international money growth rates than we saw when looking at historical U.S. data. In the 12 most recent decades of U.S. history, the highest rate of money growth was less than 12 percent and the lowest was above 0 percent. The 62 countries in Figure 18.4 showed a much wider range of money growth rates, ranging from a bit more than 0 percent to 220 percent in

Each point represents the average money growth and nominal GDP growth in 62 countries during the period 1979–1984. Notice that countries with higher money growth tended to have higher growth rates in nominal GDP.

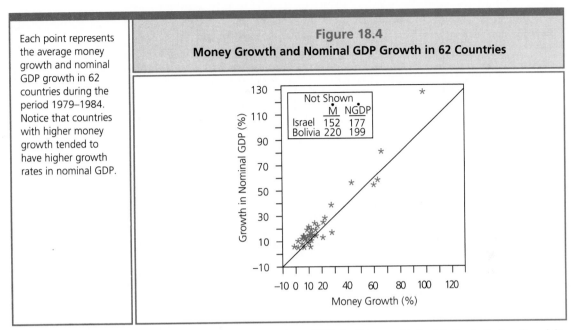

Figure 18.4
Money Growth and Nominal GDP Growth in 62 Countries

SOURCE: Dwyer, Gerald P. and R. W. Hafer, "Is Money Irrelevant?" Federal Reserve Bank of St. Louis *Review*. Copyright © 1988. Used with permission.

Bolivia. Likewise, they showed a much wider range of growth rates in nominal GDP and more evidence on whether proposition 1 held throughout this broader range. The answer is that it did seem to hold. The scatter plot suggests that countries with a higher rate of money growth did on average have higher rates of nominal GDP growth. It is also clear that, just as for the United States, the points do not lie exactly on the line, so proposition 1 did not hold exactly for every country over these five years. Instead, the figure indicates that those with 5 percent higher money growth tended to have 5 percent higher nominal GDP growth.

Proposition 2 states that increases in the growth rate of the money stock should lead to equal increases in the inflation rate. Figure 18.5 graphs the inflation rate and the growth rate of the money stock for the same 62 countries over the same time span. Also drawn is a reference line with a slope of 1. This scatter of points is consistent with proposition 2, since countries with higher money growth rates tend to have higher inflation rates. This gives rise to the upward-sloping best fit line, which has a slope of 1.03. This indicates that increases in the rate of money growth and increases in the inflation rate occurred essentially one for one. Again it is clear that the points do not lie exactly on the line, so proposition 2 did not hold exactly for every country. However, there is evidence supporting the idea that in-

This figure provides international evidence supporting proposition 2. Each point represents the average money growth and inflation rate in 62 countries during the period 1979–1984. Countries with higher money growth tended to have higher rates of inflation.

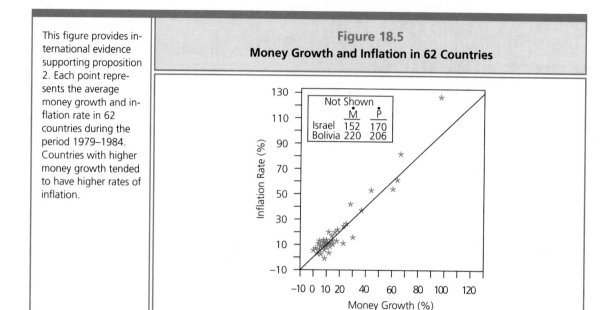

Figure 18.5

Money Growth and Inflation in 62 Countries

	Not Shown	
	M	P
Israel	152	170
Bolivia	220	206

SOURCE: Dwyer, Gerald P. and R. W. Hafer, "Is Money Irrelevant?" Federal Reserve Bank of St. Louis *Review*. Copyright © 1988. Used with permission.

creases in money growth cause equal increases in the inflation rate, as proposition 2 claims. Notice too that the country with the highest inflation rate (Bolivia, with 206 percent inflation) also had the highest growth in the money supply (220 percent).

Finally, the third proposition states that increases in the growth rate of the money stock have no effect on the growth rate of real GDP. Figure 18.6 graphs the rate of growth of real GDP and the growth rate of the money stock for 62 countries. This scatter of points shows little relationship between a country's real GDP growth and its money growth. The reference line has a slope of zero and is drawn at the average rate of growth of real GDP across the 62 countries, a bit more than 2 percent. The best fit line (not shown) has a slope of −.02, which is very close to zero. As in the previous figures, it is clear that the points do not lie on a straight line and that real GDP growth varied over the countries in the sample. It is also clear that the money growth rate had little effect on growth in real GDP. Indeed, even nations with very high money growth, such as Bolivia (220 percent) and Israel (152 percent) had rates of growth in real GDP that were similar to those of other countries.

We can conclude that international evidence also generally supports propositions 1 through 3. The data from 62 countries for the 1979–1984 period indicate that in the long run, first, countries with higher money growth rates tended to have higher growth rates of nominal GDP, and this relationship was one to one. Second, countries with higher money growth rates tended to have higher inflation rates. Finally, countries with higher money growth rates experienced roughly the same growth rates in real GDP as those with lower ones; money growth and real output growth were not related. Again we stress that these are long-run relationships that did not hold precisely for any one country but did hold on average for the countries in our sample. Box 18.1 examines how well these relationships held for historical data from the United Kingdom.

Summary
Exercise 18.1

Show how aggregate supply and demand analysis can explain the empirical relationships between money growth and growth in real GDP, the price level, and nominal GDP seen over the most recent 12 decades in U.S. history.

Answer: Suppose the economy is initially in long-run equilibrium at point *A*. For convenience, let us suppose the initial money stock is 200, the price level is 100, and real GDP is 4. Now suppose that over a 10-year period, the Fed increases the money supply by 10 percent to 220, which amounts to an average of 1 percent per year. This increase in the money supply will raise aggregate demand to AD_1, and in the long run the economy will move

This figure provides international evidence supporting proposition 3. Each point represents the average money growth and real output growth in 62 countries during the period 1979–1984. As you can see, countries with higher money supply growth rates on average had no higher or lower growth in real GDP.

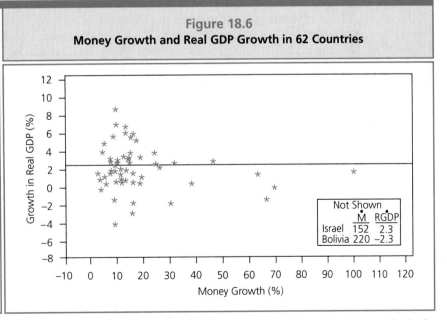

Figure 18.6
Money Growth and Real GDP Growth in 62 Countries

International Banking

Box 18.1

*Money Growth, GDP Growth, and Inflation
in the United Kingdom: 1*

In the text, we examined evidence on our three propositions from a series of historical U.S. data and also looked at the results from Dwyer and Hafer's study of 62 countries. This evidence strongly supports the three propositions. Here we look at evidence on these three propositions from the United Kingdom. Our data set consists of observations from 1963 to 1991, a much shorter series than the U.S. data.

Part a graphs nominal GDP growth against money growth in the United Kingdom. We find the expected positive relationship, but the slope of the best fit line is only .3, which is much less than one.

We find a similar result for the relationship

Continued on p. 637

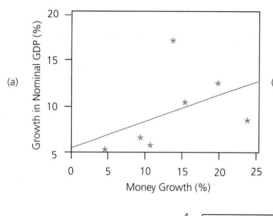

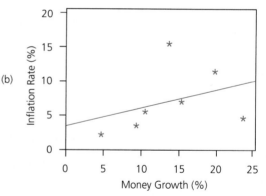

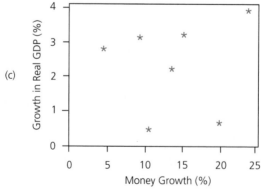

Continued from p. 636

between monetary growth and the inflation rate in part b. There is the expected positive relationship between money growth rates and inflation, but the best fit line has a slope of only about .3 instead of unity.

Part c plots real GDP growth rates against money growth rates, and we see there is very little relationship between these two variables. The best fit line is not shown, but it has a slope of only .02, which is insignificantly different from zero.

We conclude that the U.K. data provide less support for propositions 1 and 2, since the best fit line did not indicate that increases in money growth rates would show up one for one in nominal GDP growth and inflation. However, since we also find that increased money growth did not show up in an increase in real GDP growth, we must conclude that velocity in the United Kingdom was responding to money growth rate changes over this sample. Finally, we note that the results from the United Kingdom may be due to the short span of data used and that a longer series of data would be more helpful in comparing the U.K. and U.S. experiences.

Source for data: International Monetary Fund, *International Financial Statistics,* various issues.

---

to a new equilibrium at point *B*. At *B* the price level is 110, which indicates prices have increased by 10 percent over this 10-year period, or by 1 percent per year. Thus, we see that in the long run, increasing the growth rate of money by 1 percent raises the inflation rate by 1 percent. Real output remains at 4, indicating that increased money growth has no long-term impact on growth in real GDP. Finally, notice that nominal GDP at point *A* is 100 $\times$ 4 = 400, while at point *B* it is 110 $\times$ 4 = 440. Nominal GDP increased by 10 percent over this period, or by 1 percent per year. This explains why, in the long run, an increase in the growth of the money supply leads to an increase in the growth of nominal GDP.

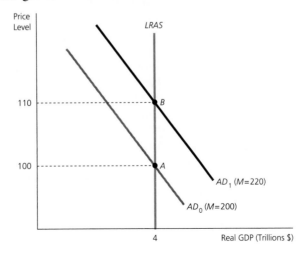

The Short-Run Relationship among Money, Prices, and Real Output

We have seen that in the long run, there is substantial support for our three propositions about the relationship of money to economic activity. What is the evidence on the short-run relationship between money and economic activity? To answer this question, we first ask what our aggregate demand and supply model predicts for the short-run relationship among money, the price level, and real output. Then we return to U.S. history to see how well this short-run model explains actual data on these variables.

Theoretical Relationships Between Money and Economic Activity

In Chapters 16 and 17, we learned that the long-run aggregate supply curve is vertical, since in the long run an economy can have increased output only if the natural rate of output rises. In the short run however, when wages and prices of other inputs are fixed, the aggregate supply cuve is upward sloping. This implies that in the short run, an increase in aggregate demand will lead to an increase in both the price level and the level of output.

What can change aggregate demand? As we first saw in Chapter 16, there is a whole list of determinants of aggregate demand, which we added to when we considered the open economy in Chapter 17. Changes in any of these determinants will shift the location of aggregate demand and cause changes in the price level and real output. In the previous section, we saw that persistent changes in aggregate demand are most frequently caused by ongoing increases in the money stock when we examined decade-long averages of historical data.

The short run, however, has many determinants of aggregate demand, and changes in any one of them can alter the price level and real output. Moreover, two or more determinants (like taxes and the money supply) often change at the same time, so the net effect on aggregate demand, and hence on the price level and real output, is unclear. Thus, we have no reason to believe the relationship between money and other economic variables will be as strong in the short run as we found it to be in the long run. Nonetheless, it is useful to see what happens to our scatter diagrams when we look not at decade-long averages but at quarterly observations of money growth rates, nominal GDP growth rates, inflation rates, and real output (real GDP) growth rates. This will not only provide information on the short-run relationship between money growth rates and these variables but also give us an idea of the types of problems faced by monetary policymakers, who must respond to short-run movements in the economy with changes in the money growth rate that may be tied only loosely to policy goals such as growth in real output.

Empirical Evidence on the Short-Run Relationship Between Money and Economic Activity

To examine the short-run empirical relationships, we will look at quarterly data on money growth, inflation, real GDP growth, and nominal GDP growth from 1959 to 1992. Then we will duplicate our scatter diagrams that previously used a decade-long data set. This will allow us to see whether growth in the money supply during a given quarter had any effect on economic activity during the same period.

Figure 18.7 looks at the relationship on a quarter-to-quarter basis between the rate of growth of nominal GDP and the rate of growth of the money stock, measured using both M2 (part a) and M1 (part b). It also shows an estimated line of best fit. It is clear from the scatter of points that the relationship between nominal GDP growth and money growth is much more

---

Figure 18.7
Short-Run Money Growth and Short-Run Growth in Nominal GDP

The points on this scatter diagram represent the quarterly growth rate in M1 and M2 and the quarterly growth in nominal GDP for the period 1959–1992 in the United States. While there appears to have been some relationship between short-term money supply growth and nominal GDP growth, the relationship was not nearly as great as it was in the long run. The lines of best fit have a slope much less than 1.

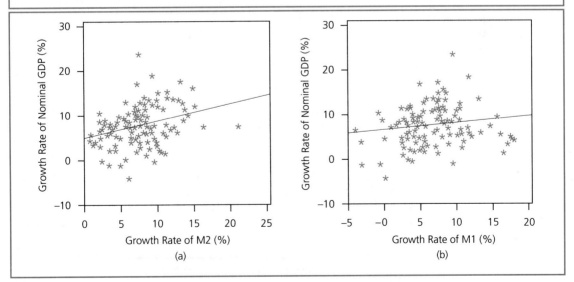

(a)

(b)

SOURCES: Board of Governors of the Federal Reserve System, *Federal Reserve Bulletin,* various issues; U.S. Department of Commerce, Bureau of Economic Analysis, *Survey of Current Business,* various issues; Citibase electronic database.

tenuous on a quarter-to-quarter basis. In fact, the best fit line has an estimated slope of .39 for M2, which is statistically larger than zero but also statistically smaller than 1. This means a 10 percent increase in money growth this quarter increased this quarter's nominal GDP growth by only 3.9 percent. For M1, the estimated slope of the best fit line is even smaller—.17—meaning a 10 percent increase in M1 money growth this quarter increased this quarter's nominal GDP by only 1.7 percent. Thus, we find that money growth in a given three-month period was positively related to the rate of nominal GDP growth during that period, but the relationship was much weaker than the one-to-one relationship we found over the 10-year periods. Thus, we see that short-run (quarter-to-quarter) growth in the money supply leads to small but positive increases in the growth of nominal GDP.

The short-run effects of money growth on inflation and real GDP also differ from the long-term effects we saw in the previous section. Figure 18.8 considers the short-run effects of increases in money growth on the inflation rate. The money growth rates and inflation rates are for each quarter from 1959 through 1992. Several things are very apparent in this graph. First, there is not a strong positive relationship between money growth and inflation like that in our long-run study. Second, the best fit line for M2 growth has an estimated slope of .15, and for M1 growth the estimated slope is .04, although the slope of M1 growth is not statistically different from zero. We conclude that in the short run, on a quarter-to-quarter basis, the inflation rate and the rate of money growth are not very closely related. This suggests that short-run increases in the growth of the money supply do not lead to immediate increases in the rate of inflation. This result is quite different from our long-run analysis, and indeed different from the predictions suggested by our short-run aggregate supply and demand analysis.

What is the short-run relationship between the rate of growth of real output and the rate of money supply growth? Figure 18.9 plots quarter-to-quarter real GDP growth and short-term money supply growth. The best fit line is actually estimated to have a positive slope of .23 for M2, which is statistically different from zero and statistically less than 1, and .13 for M1. Real GDP growth was positively related to money growth. This indicates that short-run increases in money supply growth do lead to short-run increases in real output. Together, Figures 18.8 and 18.9 suggest that in the short run, the Fed can increase the money supply and increase real output with very little impact on the price level. However, the results presented in the previous section suggest that the long-run effects of such an increase will be merely to increase the price level and inflation. This presents an obvious dilemma for the Fed and policymakers: Increasing the growth rate of the money supply may lead to greater economic growth in the short run, but in the long run economic growth will fall to its natural rate and inflation rates will rise.

To summarize our short-run findings, we have found that nominal GDP growth, the inflation rate, and real GDP growth are positively related to the

Figure 18.8
Short-Run Money Growth and Short-Run Inflation

The points on these scatter diagrams represent the quarterly growth rate in the money supply (either M1 or M2) and the quarterly rate of inflation for the period 1959–1992 in the United States.

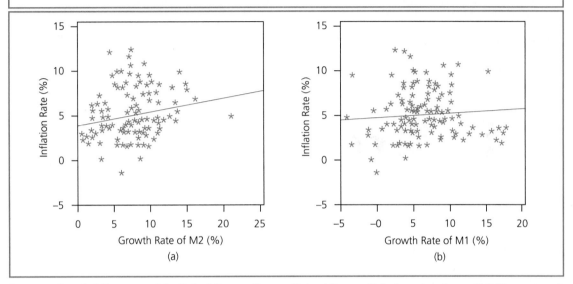

(a)

(b)

SOURCES: Board of Governors of the Federal Reserve System, *Federal Reserve Bulletin,* various issues; U.S. Department of Commerce, Bureau of Economic Analysis, *Survey of Current Business,* various issues; Citibase electronic database.

rate of money growth in the short run, and the best fit line describing this relationship for M2 is estimated to have a slope of .39 for GDP, .15 for inflation, and .23 for real GDP. The relationship between M1 growth and these three variables is even weaker. Thus, in contrast to the long run, in the short run changes in monetary growth do affect the real output produced in the economy but have little or no effect on the price level.

Summary Exercise 18.2

Our short-run empirical evidence suggests that increases in money growth do not affect the short-run inflation rate but do increase the growth in real output. Use aggregate demand and supply analysis to explain how this can occur.

Answer: Suppose the economy is in equilibrium at point *A* and the Fed increases the money supply by 3 percent during one quarter. This leads to an increase in aggregate demand from AD_0 to AD_1. If the short-run aggregate supply curve is flat, the new short-run equilibrium will be at *B*, where the

Figure 18.9
Short-Run Money Growth and Short-Run Real GDP

The points on these scatter diagrams represent the quarterly growth rate in the money supply (either M1 or M2) and the quarterly rate of real output growth for the period 1959–1992 in the United States. Unlike in the long run, there is a positive relationship between this quarter's money growth and this quarter's growth in real GDP.

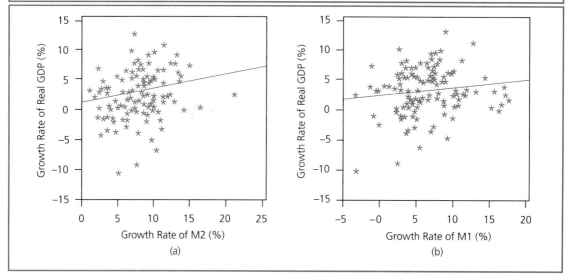

(a) (b)

SOURCES: Board of Governors of the Federal Reserve System, *Federal Reserve Bulletin,* various issues; U.S. Department of Commerce, Bureau of Economic Analysis, *Survey of Current Business,* various issues; Citibase electronic database.

price level remains at P_0 but real output rises from Y_0 to Y_1. Thus, when the short-run aggregate supply curve is flat, increases in monetary growth will

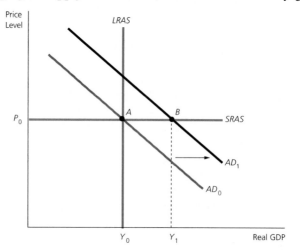

lead to short-run increases in real output but no change in the price level or the rate of inflation.

RECONCILING THE LONG-RUN AND SHORT-RUN RESULTS

U.S and international data reveal that the short-term and long-term effects of monetary growth are quite different. In the short run, increases in the growth rate of money are related to increases in the growth rate of real GDP but are not related to the inflation rate. Yet in the long run, increases in the growth rate of money are related to increases in the inflation rate but not to increases in the growth rate of real GDP. How does this happen?

The explanation involves several elements. First, many things change in the economy on a day-to-day basis, including many of the determinants of aggregate demand. These short-run changes can lead to changes in the price level, output, and nominal GDP that are not accounted for in our three propositions, which all concern the long-run effects of changes in the money growth rate. Some of these changes in demand will be changes in velocity, and these changes will alter the relationship between money growth and nominal income growth.

Second, there are lags in the effects of changes in money growth on changes in aggregate demand and hence in nominal income. These lags are due to the way money affects the economy. Changes in the money stock can exert powerful influences on aggregate demand, but these influences do not occur instantaneously. Instead, increases in the money supply first show up as additional money balances in the hands of individuals. These increased money holdings raise consumers' spending power, but individuals often react somewhat slowly to such increases. Increases in the money supply also temporarily lower the interest rate and stimulate investment spending.

Once aggregate demand shifts, the effects on the economy also depend on the slope of the short-run aggregate supply curve. If that curve is very flat, a change in aggregate demand will have a larger effect on real output than on the price level. If the short-run aggregate supply curve is very steep, a change in aggregate demand will have a larger effect on the price level than on real output. The short-run evidence seems to suggest that the short-run aggregate supply curve is fairly flat, since in the short run increases in the money growth rate affect real output growth but not the inflation rate. Another interpretation, however, is that the quarter-to-quarter movements in money growth are themselves responses to movements in real output. The scatter diagrams indicate only that money growth and output growth are related, not which causes which. It may be that in the short run, increases in real output growth raise money demand and hence increase money growth due to an endogenous money supply. Box 18.2 expands on this possibility.

For the above reasons, increases in the rate of money growth take time to affect the economy. Renowned monetary economist Milton Friedman has

Inside Money

Box 18.2

*Does Money Create Income, or
Does Income Create Money?*

A considerable amount of economic research has concentrated on the effects of nominal money balances on income. One of the best-documented facts in economics is that money and income tend to move together over time. Traditionally this has been explained by changes in the money supply causing changes in income. But this relationship could be the result of changes in income causing changes in the money supply.

One of the first attempts to analyze the money-income relationship was the seminal work by Milton Friedman and Anna Schwartz titled *A Monetary History of the United States, 1867–1960* (Princeton, N.J.: Princeton University Press, 1963). By examining historical episodes of monetary policy in the United States, they were able to isolate cases in which changes in money growth had an independent origin, that is, an origin that was not a response to changes in macroeconomic conditions. These changes in money growth resulted from factors such as gold discoveries (which increased the money supply under the gold standard), changes in Federal Reserve leadership, or changes in monetary institutions. In most of these cases, Friedman and Schwartz could document that changes in money growth occurred prior to changes in income, supporting the idea that changes in money caused changes in income and not vice versa.

More recently, there have been formal tests of the hypothesis that changes in the money supply cause changes in income. The first and probably best known of these tests is probably the work by Christopher Sims, who found that

changes in money predate changes in income.[1] However, subsequent work by Sims and others (e.g., Robert Litterman and Laurence Weiss[2]) found that the results are not so clear when the study includes interest rates along with money and income. In fact, when interest rates are included, money no longer plays a significant role in explaining changes in income. Instead, it is interest rate changes that precede changes in both money and income. The meaning of this result is not clear, and many interpretations have been offered.

Bennett McCallum argues that the monetary authority may be following an interest rate target, so changes in the interest rate indicate policy actions.[3] According to this view, the results of interest rate changes preceding income changes still favor the importance of monetary policy. Consider, for example, a situation in which the Fed has decided to keep the interest rate constant at 6 percent. To maintain that interest rate, the Fed must supply any amount of money the economy demands at that interest rate. Since the demand for money is a function of the level of income, any increase in income will lead to a higher demand for money. When this happens, the Fed will have to increase the

Continued on p. 645

[1] Christopher Sims, "Money, Income, and Causality," *American Economic Review* (September, 1972), 540–555.
[2] Robert Litterman and Laurence Weiss, "Money, Real Interest Rates, and Output: A Reinterpretation of Postwar U.S. Data," *Econometrica* (January, 1985), 129–156.
[3] Bennett McCallum, "A Reconsideration of Sims' Evidence Concerning Monetarism," *Economics Letters* (1983), 167–171.

Continued from p. 644

money supply to keep the interest rate constant. Thus, increases in income will lead to an increase in the money supply—exactly the reverse of Friedman and Schwartz's results. Moreover, any increase in the interest rate peg—say, from 6 to 8 percent—will require the Fed to reduce the money supply, and this could lead to a lower income level. Thus, the interest rate changes could lead to changes in income and the money supply not because money is unimportant but because the Fed's interest rate peg obscures the role of the money supply in causing income.

suggested that long and variable lags link changes in the money supply to changes in other macroeconomic variables. Hence, the quarterly scatter plots shown earlier can show no relationship between, say, money growth and inflation, whereas the long-run scatter plots show a clear one-to-one relationship between these two variables. The problem is that the initial increase in money growth has little or no effect on inflation. Only after individuals accumulate these money balances do they begin to spend these funds, and this is the cause of the increased aggregate demand. Moreover, in the short run aggregate supply is not vertical, so increases in aggregate demand raise output. Only in the long run do we get the predicted link among money growth, inflation, and growth in real output.

How can we see the movement from the short run to the long run in our U.S. data? One way is to take account of the fact that changes in the money growth rate affect only variables like the inflation rate or the rate of growth of nominal GDP with a lag. To do this, we use a measure of money growth that is not the current quarter's value but instead is an average of money growth rates over the previous 16 quarters. In this way, we compare average money growth over several years, rather than the money growth rate this quarter, to other variables.

This measure of average money growth is called a **moving average.** Its name comes from the fact that it is an average—in our case, of 16 quarters—and that the value of the average changes as we move through time. Every period we recalculate this average, using only the 16 most recent data points.

We now look at a final set of scatter plots of money growth rates against nominal GDP growth, inflation, and real GDP growth, using a moving-average measure of money growth rates. The idea is to see whether using the moving average to take account of the lags in the effect of money growth rates on the economy can begin to reveal results more like the long-run results from our decade-long averages in Figures 18.1 through 18.3.

Figure 18.10 looks at the relationship of nominal GDP growth to the moving averages of M2 and M1 money growth. It also includes the estimated line of best fit. The scatter of points clearly indicates that the relationship between the nominal GDP growth and the moving average of M2 money growth is more like the long-run results in Figure 18.1 than the short-run results in Figure 18.7. Indeed, the slope of the best fit line is .98, which is statistically indistinguishable from 1. Of course, a lot of variation occurs

Figure 18.10
Moving-Average Money Growth and Growth in Short-Run Nominal GDP

If money growth affects nominal GDP with a lag, there will be a positive relationship between the moving average of past money growth rates and this quarter's growth in nominal GDP. In part a this graph for the United States uses data from 1965 through 1992 and suggests that the 16-month average of past quarterly M2 money growth rates was positively related to this quarter's growth in nominal GDP. This suggests that money has lagged effects on nominal GDP. The relationship of the moving average of quarterly M1 growth rates to nominal GDP (part b) is positive but much weaker, and is not statistically significant.

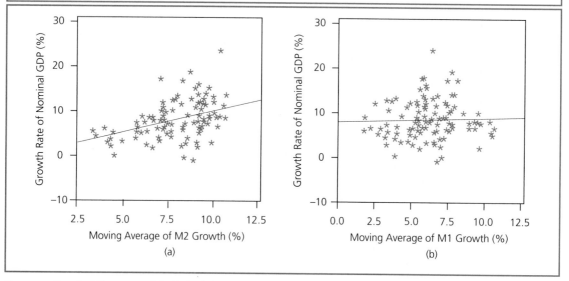

(a)   (b)

SOURCES: Board of Governors of the Federal Reserve System, *Federal Reserve Bulletin,* various issues; U.S. Department of Commerce, Bureau of Economic Analysis, *Survey of Current Business,* various issues; Citibase electronic database.

about the best fit line, but over time changes in the moving average of M2 money growth rates tend on average to be matched by changes in the rate of nominal GDP growth. Notice that the link between M1 growth and nominal GDP is not very striking. This is one reason many economists consider M2 a better measure of the money supply.

What about the relationship between the moving average of money growth and inflation? Figure 18.11 plots inflation against our moving-average measures of M2 and M1 money growth. As in Figure 18.10, we see a lot of variability, but we also see a positive relationship between inflation and money growth rates. Indeed, the best fit line for M2 has an estimated slope of .73, which is not quite 1 (and statistically less than 1) but is much higher than the .15 slope coefficient on the link between inflation and M2 money growth in Figure 18.8. Thus, our moving average of M2 money

---

Figure 18.11
Moving Average of Money Growth and Short-Run Inflation

If money growth affects the price level with a lag, there will be a positive relationship between the moving average of past money growth rates and this quarter's inflation rate. These graphs are based on U.S. data from 1965 through 1992 and suggests that the 16-month average of past quarterly money growth rates is positively related to this quarter's inflation rate. This suggests that money has lagged effects on the price level.

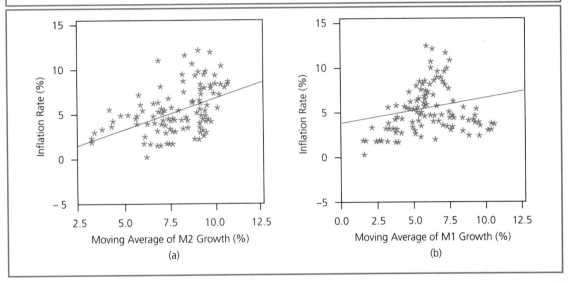

(a)

(b)

SOURCES: Board of Governors of the Federal Reserve System, *Federal Reserve Bulletin,* various issues; U.S. Department of Commerce, Bureau of Economic Analysis, *Survey of Current Business,* various issues; Citibase electronic database.

growth rates is much more closely related to the inflation rate than just the current quarter's M2 money growth rate. This suggests that the average M2 money growth over the past 16 (or more) quarters is what affects this quarter's inflation rate. Again, the case for M1 is less strong.

Finally, what is the relationship between the moving average of money growth rates and this quarter's real output growth? Figure 18.12 plots real GDP growth and our moving-average measure of money growth. The best fit line for M2 is estimated to have a slope of .25, which cannot be statistically distinguished from zero. Thus, real GDP growth in any current quarter is only weakly related to the moving average of M2 money growth over the past 16 quarters. The moving average of M2 money growth does affect inflation, but has a much smaller effect on the growth in real output. For M1, the relationship is negative. These results are more similar to those we found for the long run

To summarize, we have found that propositions 1 through 3 hold in the

Figure 18.12

Moving Average of Money Growth and Short-Run Growth in Real GDP

If it takes time for the economy to fully adjust to changes in real output, lagged changes in money growth should have little effect on this quarter's growth in real output. This graph, which is based on U.S. data from 1965 through 1992, suggests that the 16-month average of past quarterly money growth rates has little effect on this quarter's growth in real output.

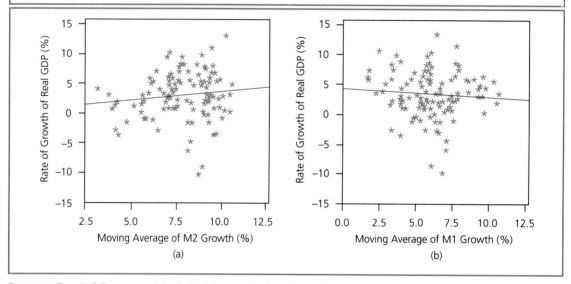

SOURCES: Board of Governors of the Federal Reserve System, *Federal Reserve Bulletin,* various issues; U.S. Department of Commerce, Bureau of Economic Analysis, *Survey of Current Business,* various issues; Citibase electronic database.

long run but not in the short run. We have also found that if we average M2 money growth rates over a number of periods, we can move a long way toward our long-run results even by looking at quarterly data on the inflation rate or real GDP growth rates. It seems high money growth in any one period just doesn't matter very much, while high growth over a year or two matters a lot for both nominal GDP and inflation. Box 18.3 looks at the United Kingdom data to see whether the moving-average calculations of money growth help us better understand the relationship of money growth to nominal and real GDP and the inflation rate in the United Kingdom.

Summary Exercise 18.3

Some economists have suggested that prices are sticky, or slow to adjust, in the short run. In that case, any increase in money growth will first raise real GDP and nominal GDP but will not change prices. Over time, however, the increase in money growth will raise the inflation rate but not affect real GDP; thus, absent any other changes, real GDP will return to its initial level.

International Banking

Box 18.3

*Money Growth, GDP Growth, and Inflation
in the United Kingdom: 2*

In the text, we looked at evidence on the relationship between a moving average of money growth and inflation, GDP growth, and nominal GDP growth in the United States. Here we follow up on Box 18.1 and present similar measures from our U.K. data. Part a of the accompanying figure presents the scatter plot of inflation rates and our moving-average measure of U.K. money growth rates. Again we find a positive relationship, but our best fit line has a slope of .22, which is significantly less than one. When we plot real GDP growth against money growth in part b, we find a best fit line that has a slope not significantly different from zero. The evidence is that the U.K. data provide less support for proposition 2 than did our long-run series of U.S. data or the international data of Dwyer and Hafer. The data do, however, tend to support proposition 3.

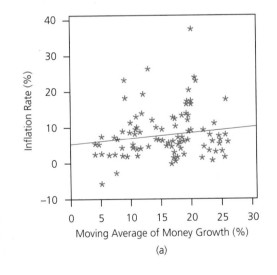

(a)

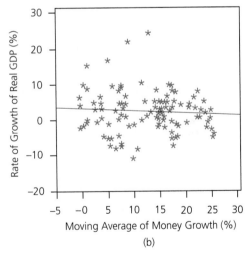

(b)

(a) If this is the case, how will real GDP respond to an increase in money growth in the short run and in the long run? (b) Suppose the money supply increased at 5 percent during the first two quarters of 1994 and by 10 percent over the second two quarters. What was the moving average of the quarterly money growth rate during this one-year period? (c) If money growth increases further to 15 percent in each of the first two quarters of 1995, what happens to the one-year moving-average growth rate of the money supply?

Answer: (a) An increase in money growth will first raise real GDP growth rates, as the question indicates. This is the short-run effect. Over time, as prices start to react and the inflation rate rises, real GDP will return to its initial level, so the GDP growth rate must fall. Thus, an increase in money growth first causes an increase in growth of real GDP, but after a time real GDP growth declines until it is restored to its initial level. After this, real GDP growth continues at its usual pace. Money growth causes real GDP growth to first rise, then fall, and then settle back down to its original rate. (b) The one-year moving average of the money growth rate is the average growth in the money supply over the most recent four quarters. Thus, the moving average in 1994 was (.05 + .05 + .1 + .1)/4, or 7.5 percent (c) Based on the most recent four quarters, the moving average of money growth is now (.1 + .1 + .15 + .15)/4, or 12.5 percent.

INFLATION, MONEY GROWTH, AND INTEREST RATES

An important issue in monetary economics is the relationship among money growth rates, inflation, and interest rates. We already examined the link between money growth rates and inflation and concluded that in the long run, increases in money growth rates lead to increases in the inflation rate, while in the short run increases in money growth rates in any one period have little or no impact on the inflation rate. Now we examine how changes in the inflation rate affect the interest rate.

Irving Fisher, a famous economist from the early part of this century, postulated a one-to-one relationship between the interest rate and the *expected* inflation rate, a relationship now known as the Fisher equation. As we saw in Chapter 3, the *Fisher equation* is

$$i = r + \pi^e,$$

where i is the nominal interest rate, r is the real interest rate, and π^e is the expected inflation rate.

In using this relationship, Fisher argued that the real interest rate could be taken as constant, at least for the most part. If so, the Fisher equation predicts that an increase in the inflation rate would show up as an equal increase in the nominal interest rate. The link from money growth rates to interest rates would then occur through expected inflation. Increasing the money growth rate, at least over an extended period of time, would raise the inflation rate and the expected inflation rate and thereby increase the nominal interest rate. The real interest rate would remain constant by assumption.

Does this really happen when the inflation rate increases? Part a of Figure 18.13 plots the inflation rate and the nominal interest rate from 1959 to 1992. Notice that the nominal interest rate and the inflation rate tracked fairly closely until about 1980. After 1980 the inflation rate declined rather sharply, but interest rates fell much more slowly, and not until the early 1990s did the two rates approach each other. Thus, there appears to be a relationship

Figure 18.13
Inflation and the Interest Rate

According to Irving Fisher's theory of nominal interest rate determination, the interest rate and the inflation rate should move together over time. U.S. data on the inflation rate and the interest rate on one-year Treasury Notes are plotted in part a for the period 1959–1990. Notice that rises in the inflation rate are associated with increases in the interest rate, and vice versa. Thus, empirical evidence does suggest that higher inflation rates lead to higher nominal interest rates. The scatter diagram in part b also corroborates this link.

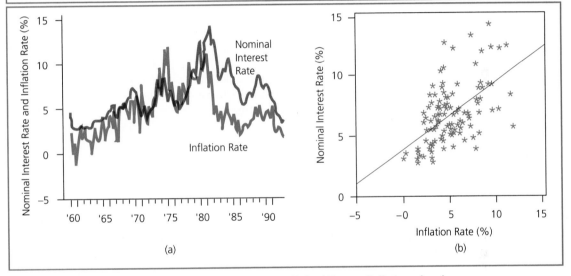

(a)   (b)

SOURCES: Board of Governors of the Federal Reserve System, *Federal Reserve Bulletin,* various issues; U.S. Department of Commerce, Bureau of Economic Analysis, *Survey of Current Business,* various issues; Citibase electronic database.

between the inflation rate and nominal interest rates, but it is by no means a steadfast rule that nominal interest rates mimic increases or decreases in the inflation rate. Part b of Figure 18.13 provides a scatter diagram and the best fit line for the relationship between the one-year T-bill rate and the inflation rate. The slope of the best fit line is .58, not the 1 predicted by the Fisher relationship. Using a moving-average measure of inflation rates would make this slope closer to unity. However, the scatter plot also shows quite a lot of variation around the best fit line, indicating the relationship between interest rates and inflation rates is not the neat and tidy one the Fisher equation would lead us to believe.

The slow decline of nominal interest rates and the quick drop in the inflation rate in the 1980s meant the real interest rate during this time was higher than it had been in recent history; that is, the real interest rate, calculated as the nominal interest rate minus the actual inflation rate, was not constant. Of course, the Fisher equation suggests the real interest rate is the nominal interest rate minus the *expected* inflation rate, but expected and actual inflation rates would have to differ for quite some time to keep the real interest rate constant. A more likely explanation, and one that supports other empirical research, is that real interest rates do vary over time, especially in the short run.

Why were real interest rates higher in the 1980s? Several explanations have been offered. One is that real interest rates were high due to the large budget deficits of that period. Increased government borrowing in the loanable funds market raised demand for loanable funds and pushed up interest rates even as inflation rates were declining, yielding higher real interest rates. Another explanation is that expected inflation rates did differ from actual inflation rates for an extended period in the 1980s. According to this view, actual inflation rates fell much more rapidly than expected, and expected inflation rates adjusted slowly to those changes. Thus, the real interest rate in the Fisher equation, defined as the nominal interest rate minus the expected inflation rate, may well have remained constant.

Instead of looking at the effect of inflation on interest rates, let us examine the effect of money growth on interest rates. Part a of Figure 18.14 plots the nominal interest rate against the rate of money growth. Notice the best fit line is upward sloping, although the estimated slope for M2 growth is .03, which is not statistically different from zero. (The results for M1 are similar but are not given here.) Thus, we find that money growth has a weak effect on interest rates.

If we look at the relationship between the interest rate and a moving average of money growth rates (part b), we see a much stronger relationship. The estimated slope coefficient of the best fit line is .56, which is statistically significant. It seems that increases in the money growth rate lead to rises in the interest rate, but the effect is not immediate; instead it requires a sustained period of increased money growth. One puzzling feature is that the increase in money growth rates does not cause the interest rate to decline, even when comparing the current-quarter money growth rate to the interest rate. We will say more about this particular result in the next section.

In summary, what do our data suggest about the effects of changes in monetary growth on interest rates? The effect of changes in the current quarter's money growth rate on the expected inflation rate in the Fisher equation is rather tenuous. This is partly because any increase in money growth causes inflation only in the long run and partly because the link between inflation and expected inflation may not be exact. The lesson for monetary policy is that in the short run, changes in the money growth rate may have little effect on the expected inflation rate and thus may not raise interest rates. In the long run, however, a persistent increase in the money growth rate will cause inflation, and increases in inflation will tend to cause nominal interest rates to rise. Thus, policy actions taken in the short run may have very different long-run effects.

Figure 18.14
Money Growth and the Interest Rate

This graph plots U.S. data on the rate of M2 money growth and the interest rate on one-year Treasury bills for the period 1959–1992. Notice in part a that the rate of M2 growth had little effect on the interest rate, whereas part b shows that the moving average of money growth showed a more substantial effect.

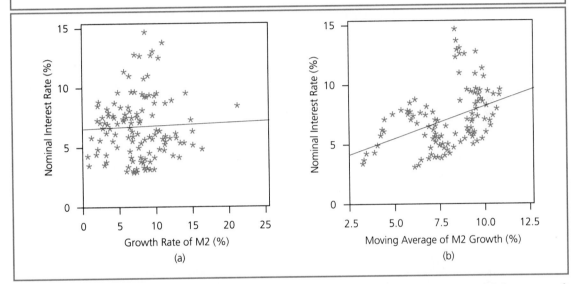

(a)

(b)

SOURCES: Board of Governors of the Federal Reserve System, *Federal Reserve Bulletin,* various issues; U.S. Department of Commerce, Bureau of Economic Analysis, *Survey of Current Business,* various issues; Citibase electronic database.

Summary
Exercise 18.4

(a) How do considerations of income taxes affect the Fisher relationship? (Remember, income taxes are paid on interest income.) (b) How might this relationship partially explain the rising real interest rate and declining nominal interest rate during the early 1980s?

Answer: The Fisher relationship states that the real interest rate equals the nominal interest rate minus the expected inflation rate. However, this is the relationship in the absence of taxation. If lenders are required to pay a tax rate of τ on their interest earnings, they will calculate their aftertax real interest rate as the nominal interest rate, i, times the portion of this income that they get to keep after taxes, $(1 - \tau)$, minus the expected inflation rate; that is, the aftertax real rate is

$$r = i(1 - \tau) - \pi^e.$$

(b) Tax rates were significantly reduced during the early 1980s. The analysis in part a reveals that a decrease in the tax rate will, holding other things constant, increase the real interest rate. Alternatively, holding the real interest rate constant, it will lower the nominal interest rate. Figure 18.13 reveals that both effects occurred during the 1980s. The gap between the nominal interest rate and the inflation rate widened during this period, even though the nominal interest rate declined.

REAL MONEY BALANCES, VELOCITY, AND INTEREST RATES

In Chapter 15 we discussed money demand at length, beginning with the equation of exchange and covering several other views on money demand. One was the modified Cambridge view that money demand can be written as

$$\frac{M^d}{P} = \frac{Y}{V(i)}. \tag{18.1}$$

We now investigate how well this relatively simple view of money demand can explain the U.S. historical experience. Then we turn to some policy implications of this view.

Real Money Balances, Real Income, and the Interest Rate

The modified Cambridge view of money demand has two determinants. The first is real income, a measure of the desired amount of transactions. The second is the interest rate, a measure of the opportunity cost of holding money. How well do these two variables explain movements in real money balances? Figure 18.15 presents two graphs using U.S. data from 1959 to 1992. Part a is a scatter diagram of real M2 money balances and real GDP. This plot indicates a strong positive relationship between real money balances and real GDP. The graph includes an estimated best fit line, and the points lie very close to this line over the entire sample. Thus, we see that increases in real income indeed lead to rises in real money balances, just as our theory of money demand would suggest. Increased real income raises the amount of purchases consumers will make, which increases their desire to hold money to use in making transactions.

Part b of Figure 18.15 graphs real M2 balances and real GDP over time. Notice how closely they track each other's movements through time. The downturns in real GDP are recessions, which are mimicked by downturns in real money balances. It appears real GDP can explain much about real M2 holdings, just as the modified Cambridge money demand equation would suggest.

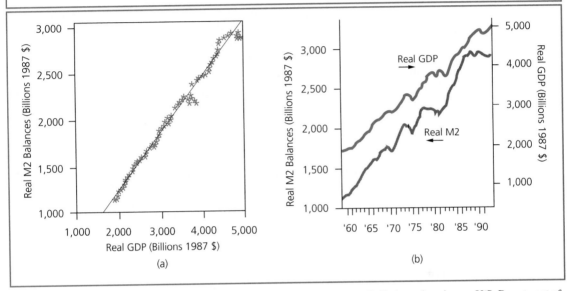

Figure 18.15
Real Money Balances and Real GDP

This figure presents a scatter diagram (part a) and plot (part b) of quarterly real money balances and quarterly real GDP for the period 1959–1992 in the United States. Notice these variables tended to be closely related; points with higher real GDP were associated with the higher real money balances.

SOURCES: Board of Governors of the Federal Reserve System, *Federal Reserve Bulletin,* various issues; U.S. Department of Commerce, Bureau of Economic Analysis, *Survey of Current Business,* various issues; Citibase electronic database.

Taking the modified Cambridge view further, we see that equation 18.1 can be rearranged by dividing both sides by income to yield

$$\frac{1}{V(i)} = k(i) = \frac{M^d}{PY}.$$

Here the inverse of velocity, $1/V$, is also called the Cambridge k and is simply real money balances divided by real income. Moreover, velocity, and hence the Cambridge k, depends on the nominal interest rate. An increase in the nominal interest rate raises the opportunity cost of holding money balances. This causes money users to try to get by using fewer money balances. As they attempt this, money will change hands more frequently and velocity will increase. The Cambridge k will then decrease. Thus, velocity rises and the Cambridge k decreases with increases in the interest rate.

We investigate this interest rate effect on velocity by plotting movements in velocity over time along with the nominal interest rate in Figure 18.16.

Notice first that the velocity of M2 is not constant but varies between 1.55 and 1.75. Second, the velocity of M2 shows no long-run tendencies to move either upward or downward.

Can we explain the short-run movements in velocity by changes in the opportunity cost of holding money? Early in the sample period it appears that movements in interest rates were only weakly related to movements in velocity, but during the late 1970s and early 1980s interest rates soared, and this corresponded to an unusually large rise in velocity. This means that when interest rates became unusually high, real M2 holdings fell, since individuals desired to hold fewer real money balances due to the higher opportunity cost (lost interest) of holding money.

The results for M1 velocity are similar to those for M2. Figure 18.17 graphs the velocity of M1 along with the interest rate. The velocity of M1 had a decided upward trend until about 1980 and afterward exhibited a slight downward trend. This change caused some economic models to severely mispredict at that time and, as we hinted earlier, led the Federal Reserve

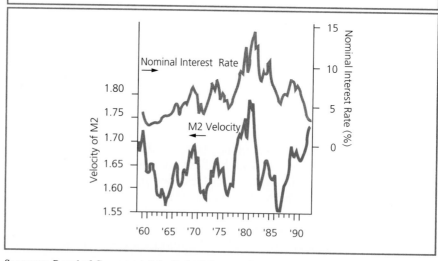

Figure 18.16
The Interest Rate and M2 Velocity, 1959–1992

This figure plots the velocity of M2 and the interest rate on one-year Treasury bills. Notice that when the interest rate rose, so did velocity.

SOURCES: Board of Governors of the Federal Reserve System, *Federal Reserve Bulletin,* various issues; U.S. Department of Commerce, Bureau of Economic Analysis, *Survey of Current Business,* various issues; Citibase electronic database.

System to turn away from M1 as a reliable measure of the money stock. In its place, the Fed began emphasizing M2, constructing targets for M2 growth and looking at M2 to gauge the impact of monetary policy actions on the economy. However, M2 is not perfect, and some early indications of instability in the velocity of M2 led the Fed to announce in the summer of 1993 that it was deemphasizing money stock targets.

Inflation, Velocity, and Real Money Balances

The quantity equation implies that the percentage increase in the money supply (g_M) plus the percentage increase in velocity (g_V) must equal the percentage increase in the price level (π) plus the percentage increase in real GDP (G_Y):

$$g_M + g_V = \pi + g_Y.$$

Figure 18.16 suggests that while M2 velocity does fluctuate over short time periods, in the long run no systematic trend upward or downward occurs.

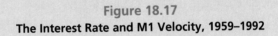

Figure 18.17
The Interest Rate and M1 Velocity, 1959–1992

This figure plots the velocity of M1 and the interest rate on one-year Treasury bills. Notice that when the interest rate rose, so did velocity.

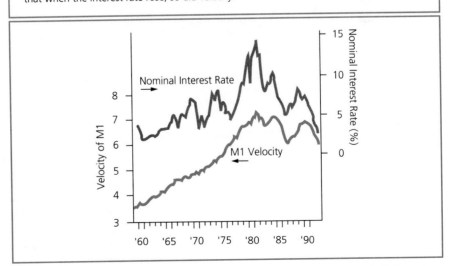

SOURCES: Board of Governors of the Federal Reserve System, *Federal Reserve Bulletin,* various issues; U.S. Department of Commerce, Bureau of Economic Analysis, *Survey of Current Business,* various issues; Citibase electronic database.

Thus, in the long run velocity tends to be constant (short-term fluctuations average to zero), which means its growth rate is zero. In this case, we see that the percentage growth rate of the M2 money supply equals the percentage growth rate of the price level plus the percentage growth rate of real GDP.

Do U.S. data support the view that in the long run g_V is zero? To answer this question, let us look at data for the U.S. economy over the 1960s, the 1970s, and the 1980s. Table 18.1 provides data on g_M, π, and g_Y for these decades. In the 1960s M2 money growth averaged 6.9 percent per year, the inflation rate averaged 2.7 percent, and output growth averaged 4 percent. Note that the percentage change in velocity was only two-tenths of a percent—almost zero. In the 1970s M2 money growth averaged 9.7 percent, substantially higher than in the 1960s. Output growth averaged only 3.2 percent, and inflation averaged 6.5 percent, again much higher than in the 1960s. Velocity growth averaged less than one-tenth of a percent in the 1970s. Finally, in the volatile 1980s M2 money growth averaged 7.9 percent, falling between the levels of the 1960s and 1970s. Output growth fell further, averaging 2.7 percent. The inflation rate thus averaged 4.7 percent, falling between the rate in the low-inflation 1960s and that in the high-inflation 1970s. In the 1980s, velocity growth was again less than 1 percent.

The data in Table 18.1 have several implications. First, the link among

---

Table 18.1

Decade Averages of Money Growth, Inflation, Growth in Real GDP, and Growth in Velocity, 1960–1990

This table shows average money growth, inflation, real GDP growth, and growth in velocity by decade. Notice that the growth in velocity was nearly zero in each decade, meaning growth in the money supply roughly equaled the inflation rate plus the growth in real output.

Decade	Growth in Money Supply (g_M)	Inflation Rate (π)	Growth in Real Output (g_Y)	Growth in Velocity (g_V)
1960s	6.9%	2.7%	4.0%	−0.2%
1970s	9.7	6.5	3.2	0.0
1980s	7.9	4.7	2.7	−0.5

SOURCES: Board of Governors of the Federal Reserve System, *Federal Reserve Bulletin*, various issues; U.S. Department of Commerce, Bureau of Economic Analysis, *Survey of Current Business*, various issues; Citibase electronic database.

This figure shows the average growth rates of the money supply (g_M), inflation (π), and real output (g_Y) during the 1970s and 1980s. The graph abstracts from year-to-year movements in these variables. Notice that real output grew at roughly the same rate (3 percent) during both decades, while the growth rate of the money supply declined from 10 percent in the 1970s to 8 percent in the 1980s. This translated into a significant decline in the inflation rate, from 7 percent in the 1970s to 5 percent in the 1980s.

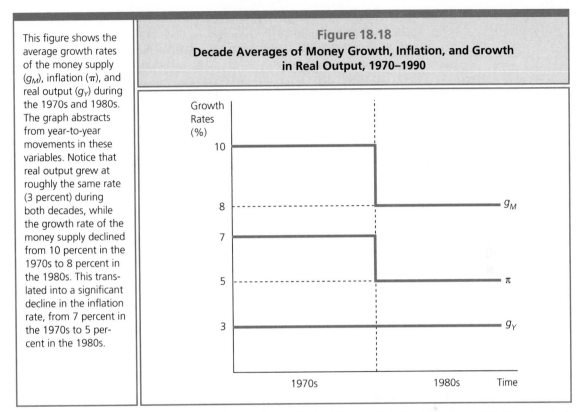

Figure 18.18

Decade Averages of Money Growth, Inflation, and Growth in Real Output, 1970–1990

SOURCES: Board of Governors of the Federal Reserve System, *Federal Reserve Bulletin,* various issues; U.S. Department of Commerce, Bureau of Economic Analysis, *Survey of Current Business,* various issues; Citibase electronic database.

money growth, inflation, and output growth seems to have held up well. Velocity seemed to be stable over these decades, so money growth equaled the sum of inflation and output growth. Moreover, Table 18.1 supports Milton Friedman's claim that inflation is a monetary phenomenon. Clearly the growth rate of output changed between the 1960s and the 1980s, and this would account for about 1.3 percent of the inflation differential between those decades. But the increase in the money growth rate from 6.9 to 7.9 percent accounted for much of the remainder. As Table 18.1 indicates, increases in the rate of growth of the money stock tended to lead to increases in the inflation rate, and reductions in the money stock growth rate tended to lead to reductions in the inflation rate. Velocity played a negligible role during this period.

Figure 18.18 presents the growth rates of M2, prices, and real GDP for the 1970s and 1980s, rounding off to the nearest 1 percent. In the 1970s money growth was 10 percent and output growth was 3 percent, so inflation was 7 percent. In the 1980s money growth declined to 8 percent and output growth was approximately unchanged at 3 percent, so inflation dropped to

5 percent. Thus, Figure 18.18 graphically illustrates the data in Table 18.1. The reduction in money growth rates had to lead to a decrease in inflation or in output growth. Since output growth remained fairly constant, it led to a reduction in inflation.

Summary Exercise 18.5

In the United States, the growth of M2 was 4.8 percent in 1989, 4 percent in 1990, and 2.8 percent in 1991. For 1992, M2 growth was barely 1 percent. If the rate of M2 growth stays in the range of 1 to 3 percent for many years, what is the predicted effect on nominal GDP, real GDP, and the inflation rate?

Answer: The evidence presented in this chapter supports our propositions 1 through 3. If M2 growth stays around 2 percent, nominal GDP growth will slow one for one with the decrease in money growth. Inflation will also slow down one for one with the decrease in money growth. With money growth at 2 percent inflation may well turn negative, since output growth is usually near 3 percent. Finally, real GDP is not affected by money growth in the long run, so the slowdown in M2 growth should not affect real GDP growth over time.

CONCLUSION

In this chapter we examined the evidence linking money to prices, real output, the inflation rate, interest rates, and velocity. We saw that in the long run money growth can explain the growth rate of nominal GDP and inflation, but in the short run changes in the money growth rate may have little effect on the inflation rate and may lead to increases in real GDP. These results are consistent with our model in Chapters 16 and 17, which distinguished short-run and long-run effects of changes in the money supply.

We also looked at data on the relationship between the inflation rate and the interest rate, using the Fisher equation to link these two variables. We saw that prolonged changes in the money growth rate can change the inflation rate and hence the nominal interest rate, and this would change velocity and real money demand. In the next chapter, we use this result to explore some of the issues involved in monetary policymaking. We will see that this result has important implications for linking changes in money growth rates back to changes in the demand for real money balances.

KEY TERMS

scatter diagram
best fit line

moving average

QUESTIONS AND PROBLEMS

1. How can propositions 1 through 3 apply in the long run but not in the short run?

2. The text provided long-run and short-run evidence on the effect of an increase in the money growth rate on the inflation rate and on the rate of growth of real GDP. Is this evidence consistent with the long-run and short-run effects predicted with our aggregate demand and supply model of Chapter 16?

3. How might lags in the impact of money growth on the economy help explain any disparities between the short-run and long-run effects of money growth on the economy?

4. Our short-run evidence seems to indicate that increased money growth has little or no effect on the inflation rate but does increase real GDP growth. What would this mean for the shape of the short-run aggregate supply curve?

5. Does the long-run evidence on the effect of increases in the money growth rate support the idea of a vertical long-run aggregate supply curve? Why or why not?

6. In 1992, M2 grew at 0.1 percent while the CPI grew at 2.9 percent. Does this mean that money growth does not influence the inflation rate? Why or why not?

7. In 1992, the U.S. inflation rate as measured by the CPI was 2.9 percent. The prime interest rate was 6 percent. What was the real interest rate?

8. If the inflation rate increases and the Fisher relationship holds, the nominal interest rate will rise. What will happen to real money balances?

9. In 1992, U.S. GDP increased to 2.9 percent. Based on the evidence in the text, what is your best prediction for the increase in real money balances in the United States over this period?

10. Suppose the Fed decides to stimulate the economy by raising M2 growth. What will happen in the short run? In the long run?

SELECTIONS FOR FURTHER READING

Abdullah, D. A., and P. C. Rangazas. "Money and the Business Cycle: Another Look." *Review of Economics and Statistics,* 70 (November 1988), 680–685.

Cecchetti, S. G. "Testing Short-run Neutrality: International Evidence." *Review of Economics and Statistics,* 69 (February 1987), 135–140.

Dickey, David A., D. W. Jansen, and D. L. Thornton. "A Primer on Cointegration with an Application to Money and Income." Federal Reserve Bank of St. Louis *Review* (March/April 1991), 58–78.

Dwyer, Gerald P. Jr., and R. W. Hafer. "Is Money Irrelevant," Federal Reserve Bank of St. Louis *Review* (May/June 1988), 3–17.

Enders, W., and B. Falk. "A Microeconomic Test of Money Neutrality." *Review of Economics and Statistics,* 66 (November 1984), 666–669.

Hafer, R. W., and D. W. Jansen. "The Demand for Money in the United States: Evidence from Cointegration Tests." *Journal of Money, Credit, and Banking,* 23 (May 1991), 155–168.

Hoffman, D. L., and R. H. Rasche. "Long-Run Income and Interest Elasticities of Money Demand in the United States." *Review of Economics and Statistics,* 73 (November 1991), 665–674.

Hoffman, D. L., and D. E. Schlagenhauf. "An Econometric Investigation of the Monetary Neutrality and Rationality Propositions from an International

Perspective." *Review of Economics and Statistics,* 64 (November 1982), 562–571.

Hoffman, D. L., and D. E. Schlagenhauf. "Real Interest Rates, Anticipated Inflation, and Unanticipated Money: A Multi-country Study." *Review of Economics and Statistics,* 67 (May 1985), 284–296.

Rangazas, P., and D. Abdullah. "Testing Some Monetarist Propositions." *Review of Economics and Statistics,* 70 (February 1988), 173–177.

APPENDIX

Regression Results or Estimates of Best Fit Lines

This appendix reports the regression results that generated the best fit lines in some of the scatter diagrams presented in the text. If you have not studied econometrics, the estimated regression lines or best fit lines are simply equations describing the line we can draw through the data points that fits best, where *best fit* is precisely defined as minimizing the sum of squared differences between the values of the left-hand side variable according to the best fit line and the actual values of the left-hand side variable. The numbers in paentheses are absolute values of *t*-statistics. If the *t*-statistic is above a certain value (approximately 2.00), the estimated coefficient is judged to be statistically significant. The R^2 number is a statistic that indicates how well the best fit line explains the left-hand side variable. R^2 varies from 0 to 1, with 0 indicating that the best fit line explains nothing about the left-hand side variable and 1 indicating that the best fit line explains the left-hand side variable perfectly. These concepts are explained in more detail in econometrics courses. Finally, MA indicates a moving average.

1. Nominal GDP (1960–1992)

$$\%\Delta GDP = 4.67 + 0.39 \times \%\Delta M2; R^2 = .10$$
$$(5.64)\ (3.86)$$

$$\%\Delta GDP = 6.56 + 0.17 \times \%\Delta M1; R^2 = .03$$
$$(10.37)\ (1.97)$$

$$\%\Delta GDP = 0.18 + 0.98 \times MA(\%M2); R^2 = .17$$
$$(0.11)\ (4.99)$$

$$\%\Delta GDP = 7.10 + 0.14 \times MA(\%\Delta M1); R^2 = .00$$
$$(5.88)\ (0.72)$$

2. Inflation (1960–1992)

$$\%\Delta Price = 3.54 + 0.15 \times \%\Delta M2; R^2 = .04$$
$$(6.52)\ (2.31)$$

$$\%\Delta Price = 4.42 + 0.04 \times \%\Delta M1; R^2 = .00$$
$$(10.37)\ (1.97)$$

$$\%\Delta Price = -0.70 + 0.73 \times MA(\%\Delta M2); R^2 = .24$$
$$(0.73)\ (6.16)$$

$$\%\Delta Price = 3.35 + 0.28 \times MA(\%\Delta M1); R^2 = .05$$
$$(4.52)\ (2.42)$$

3. Real GDP (1960–1992)

$$\%\Delta Real\ GDP = 1.14 + 0.23 \times \%\Delta M2; R^2 = .05$$
$$(1.51)\ (2.53)$$

$$\%\Delta\text{Real GDP} = 2.13 + 0.13 \times \%\Delta\text{M1}; R^2 = .02$$
$$(3.79)\ (1.62)$$

$$\%\Delta\text{Real GDP} = 0.90 + 0.25 \times \text{MA}(\%\Delta\text{M2}); R^2 = .01$$
$$(0.56)\ (1.23)$$

$$\%\Delta\text{Real GDP} = 3.72 - 0.15 \times \text{MA}(\%\Delta\text{M1}); R^2 = .01$$
$$(3.34)\ (0.83)$$

4. Interest rate, one-year T-bill (1960–1992)

$$\%\Delta\text{Interest rate} = 3.74 + 0.58 \times \%\Delta\text{Price}; R^2 = .36$$
$$(10.19)\ (8.53)$$

$$\%\Delta\text{Interest rate} = 6.27 + 0.03 \times \%\Delta\text{M2}; R^2 = .00$$
$$(11.52)\ (0.41)$$

$$\%\Delta\text{Interest rate} = 6.11 + 0.06 \times \%\Delta\text{M1}; R^2 = .01$$
$$(15.17)\ (1.08)$$

$$\%\Delta\text{Interest rate} = 2.39 + 0.56 \times \text{MA}(\%\Delta\text{M2}); R^2 = .16$$
$$(2.47)\ (4.69)$$

$$\%\Delta\text{Interest rate} = 2.77 + 0.67 \times \text{MA}(\%\Delta\text{M1}); R^2 = .29$$
$$(4.53)\ (6.93)$$

5. Velocity (1960–1992)

$$\text{Velocity of M2} = 1.57 + 0.01 \times \text{Interest rate}; R^2 = .32$$
$$(166.9)\ (7.83)$$

$$\text{Velocity of M1} = 3.43 + 0.34 \times \text{Interest rate}; R^2 = .13$$
$$(20.62)\ (14.10)$$

PART SIX

Special Issues in Monetary Economics

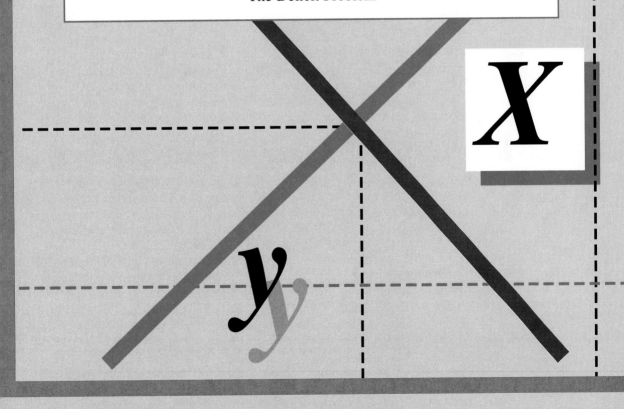

CHAPTERS

19

An Introduction to Monetary Policy

20

Monetary Policy: Rules, Discretion, and Games

21

Government Spending and Finance:
The Deficit Problem

An Introduction to Monetary Policy

*I*n this chapter, we begin a three-chapter discussion of the theory of monetary policymaking. We focus on the relationship between variables the central bank can control—the instruments of policy—and variables the Fed ultimately aims at influencing—the goals of policy.

The link between the instruments of policy and the goals of policy is described by the macroeconomic models we developed in Chapters 16 and 17. The short run and long run models lead to different implications for the effects of changes in monetary policy on the economy. Therefore, any discussion of policymaking must make it clear which macroeconomic model is being used. In this chapter, we will take care to note which model we are using to reach our conclusions about the formulation and effectiveness of policy. We will see that disagreements among economists who give policy advice is due mostly to disagreements about the macroeconomic model underlying that advice.

In this chapter, we also discuss some practical issues in policymaking. If the central bank wants to keep the money supply constant, just how should it do so? There are alternative instruments the Fed can manipulate, and these may have different effects on the economy. We characterize the central bank's choice of procedures as a policy regime and look at relevant examples. This discussion will include a description of both past and present policy regimes.

Finally, to avoid getting a misleading impression about the ease with which policy is made, we examine the recent history of monetary policy and discuss some problems concerning the effectiveness of policymaking.

TARGETS AND INSTRUMENTS

The study of policymaking requires a special vocabulary, with terms such as *policy instruments, targets, intermediate targets,* and *policy regimes.* We need to define these and a few other terms. We begin with monetary policy itself. Macroeconomic policymaking can involve several variables, such as government spending, taxes, and transfers, in addition to the money supply. Government actions to change any of the first three variables are called fiscal policy actions, to distinguish them from actions to change the money supply, which are **monetary policy actions.** In Chapter 21 we will have occasion to discuss the link between monetary and fiscal policy. For now we consider only monetary policy and hence look only at changes in the level or growth rate of the money supply or changes in variables that will in turn lead to these changes.

In discussing policy, we distinguish variables the policymaker can control from variables that represent the policymaker's goals. The former are called policy **instruments,** the latter policy *goals* or **targets.** The distinguishing characteristic of policy instruments is that they are under the direct control of the policymaker (the Fed), whereas policy targets are goals for variables the policymaker cannot directly control. One useful analogy is getting to a dinner party to which you are invited. It is across town, and your goal (or target) is to get to the dinner party by 8:00 P.M. The instrument you use is your automobile. We can get into even finer detail and say the instruments are the steering wheel, the brakes, and the accelerator. You must manipulate these instruments to get to the dinner party. Notice that there is randomness in the link between your instruments and targets. You face the possibility of road construction, traffic accidents, and possible mechanical problems that will influence the success of your efforts.

Instead of directly aiming instruments at a target, the Fed might adopt an intermediate target. The term **intermediate target** comes from the fact that it lies between the instruments of policy and the final target. The Fed sometimes finds it convenient to control instruments to achieve an intermediate target, which is set so that hitting it helps to achieve the final target. The intermediate target need not be a desirable policy goal in and of itself, but is a means of achieving the final target more easily.

In our automobile analogy, the final target is to arrive at the dinner party, and the instruments are the steering wheel, brakes, and accelerator. We can introduce an intermediate target into this analogy as follows. In planning your trip, you decide on a route from your house to the party. You will follow this route very carefully, and by doing so you will get to the party. This route is an intermediate target. Achieving this intermediate target, following the route, will help you to get to your party, but following the route will not in and of itself make you better off. It is only as a device that will help you get to the party that you desire to follow this route.

In monetary policy discussions, the instruments are often such variables as the sale or purchase of government bonds via open market operations, while the final target might be a 4 percent unemployment rate, a 3 percent rate of output growth, or a 5 percent inflation rate. The linkage between instruments and final targets is long and complex, making it convenient to describe policy via an intermediate target such as the money stock.

Why would the Fed use an intermediate target? The answer is that it may aid in achieving the final target, but this is a matter of some controversy. We examine the intermediate targeting issue in more detail later in this chapter.

Finally, we will look at operating procedures, also known as *operating* or *policy regimes*. An **operating procedure** is a combination of intermediate targets and procedures for using the policy instruments to achieve the targets. For example, the Fed might choose a particular level of the money supply, M1, as an intermediate target and use certain open market operations to achieve it. We examine several recent operating procedures later in this chapter. First, we turn to a discussion of the goals of policy and then to a discussion of policy instruments.

Monetary Policy Goals or Targets

There are many possible goals of monetary policy. We will narrow our consideration to those that are both feasible and in the proper domain of monetary policy. Also, we will use the terms *policy goal* and *policy target* interchangeably. *Policy target,* or just *target,* means the *final* target or goal and should be distinguished from *intermediate target.*

We will characterize monetary policy goals in two different ways. There are macroeconomic goals—goals for the entire economy—and there are goals for the financial sector, since the Federal Reserve System is charged with maintaining stability in this sector. This second goal is more microeconomic in nature and was discussed in Chapters 7 and 13. In this section, we focus on the macroeconomic goals of policy. However, the goal of financial market stability is sometimes interpreted as that of maintaining some type of stability in interest rates, and hence even this goal has macroeconomic implications.

We consider four categories of macroeconomic goals. The first is economic growth, which might be measured as the growth rate of real GDP, real personal income, or even the size of investment in capital structures and equipment that will lead to future growth. The government, and hence the Federal Reserve System, benefits from a growing economy and wants to stimulate growth.

The second goal is **price stability** and might be measured by the stability of the inflation rate and by the amount by which inflation exceeds a target level. Thus, price stability entails both a low inflation rate—perhaps zero— and a stable inflation rate so that the inflation rate is not jumping from 2 to 4 to 6 percent and back to 2 percent in successive months.

A third category of macroeconomic goals is stabilization of the business cycle. The Federal Reserve System wants to counteract the effects of the business cycle, especially the rise in unemployment and the fall in output during recessions. Policy actions aimed at counteracting business cycle influences on the economy are called **countercyclical policy** and are a major concern of the Fed.

The fourth category is a set of *all other goals* not contained in the first three categories. We already mentioned one such goal, interest rate stability. This might be desirable as an intermediate target for helping to achieve one or more of the first three goals, but it may also be a goal in and of itself, perhaps motivated by considerations of financial sector stability as described above. Another variable the Federal Reserve System might consider is the exchange rate. Because the exchange rate influences exports and imports and hence the trade balance, the Fed may have as a goal the stability of the exchange rate or even a target level of the exchange rate. This is especially true because wide fluctuations in the exchange rate can also contribute to financial market instability. It is important to point out, however, that the U.S. Treasury takes first responsibility for direct intervention in the exchange market. The Federal Reserve System's role is less direct. It stands by to counteract domestic money supply influences of Treasury actions in the foreign exchange market, and these monetary actions can have an indirect influence on the exchange rate.

Monetary Policy Instruments

What are the instruments of monetary policy—the tools the central bank can use to achieve its targets? The answer depends on the institutional setup of the central bank. For the Fed, the instruments of policy are fourfold: (1) open market operations, (2) the discount rate and discount window policy, (3) the required reserve ratio, and (4) selective credit controls. Changes in these instruments will change either the monetary base or the money multiplier and hence change the money supply. Thus, while the Fed has four instruments, they all affect the money supply.

Open market operations were described in Chapters 13 and 14. Basically an open market operation is a purchase or sale of government securities by the Fed via the Federal Reserve Bank of New York. An open market purchase occurs when the Fed buys securities, thereby increasing the monetary base (reserves plus currency in the hands of the public). An open market sale occurs when the Fed sells securities and thereby decreases the monetary base.

The discount rate is the interest rate the Federal Reserve System charges commercial banks and other depository institutions to allow them to borrow reserves directly from the Fed. Raising the discount rate tends to reduce discount borrowing, whereas lowering it tends to increase discount borrowing. Also, the Fed regulates both the interest rate *and* the quantity that can be borrowed, thus imposing both price and quantity controls on discount borrowing! The more expensive it is to borrow reserves, the more excess reserves banks will keep, thus lowering the money multiplier and the money supply.

The required reserve ratio is a powerful but rather imprecise policy instrument, since small changes in the reserve ratio can have large effects on the money multiplier and the money supply and large short-run effects on bank profitability and the stability of the financial sector. Due to their strong impact, required reserve ratios are seldom used as a macroeconomic policy instrument. Instead, their use tends to be tied to concerns with financial market stability and the health of the banking system, especially relative to other financial institutions.

Finally, the Federal Reserve System has at its disposal the ability to enact or alter selective credit controls. These are price ceilings or price floors on interest rates in selected financial markets or quantity restrictions in selected markets. For example, the Federal Reserve System's infamous Regulation Q imposed interest rate ceilings on various classes of deposits. Time deposits and savings deposits were restricted to paying no more than 5 percent interest at a time when market interest rates were much higher. Likewise, checking deposits could pay no interest at all. This regulation was phased out in the middle 1980s after the passage of DIDMCA (see Chapters 7 and 13), but it serves as an example of selective credit controls. Another control is margin requirements on stock purchases. If you purchase stock on margin, you are borrowing the funds that allow you to purchase the stock. The Federal Reserve System sets the margin requirement—the percentage of the value of the stock you are allowed to borrow. For example, if the margin requirement is 50 percent, you are allowed to borrow only 50 percent of the value of the stock purchase and must finance 50 percent from other sources. Margin requirements are an example of a quantity restriction imposed by the Federal Reserve System under its authority to set selective credit controls.

These four policy instruments, plus the Fed's ability to influence the financial markets via pronouncements or ''moral suasion,'' allow the Federal Reserve System to influence the economy. The instrument it uses most often—usually daily—is open market operations, through which the Fed exerts close control over the monetary base—the sum of bank reserves and currency in the hands of the public. The discount window is an ancillary tool, and reserve ratios are a blunt and seldom used policy instrument. Selective credit controls are also rarely used, although they can be a very powerful tool of policy. By restricting credit the Federal Reserve System can have a large negative impact on a given sector of the economy, and by relaxing a restriction it can have a large positive impact. In the long run, the economy adjusts to credit controls and often finds ways to circumvent them, but *changes* in selective credit controls can have very large initial effects on the economy.

The important issue for monetary policy is how successful the Federal Reserve System can be in achieving its policy goals with these four instruments of policy. On a day-to-day basis, this issue really concerns how successful the Fed can be in achieving its policy goals via open market operations, since this is the primary instrument of monetary policy. We now turn to an analysis of this issue.

The Number of Independent Instruments and Targets

Does the Fed have enough instruments to achieve any desired policy targets or goals? In 1952, economist Jan Tinbergen pointed out that to achieve a certain number of targets requires *at least* the same number of instruments as targets. Moreover, if the targets are distinct, the instruments must exert distinct influences on them. Thus, one target can be achieved with one instrument, two targets with two instruments, and so on, provided the instruments exert distinct influences on the targeted variables.

The impact of this on the Fed's ability to achieve targets is illustrated in the aggregate demand and supply diagram in Figure 19.1. The economy is initially at the intersection of *AD* and *SRAS* at point *A*, with a price level of P_0 and real output of Y_0. (Notice we have drawn a short-run or upward-sloping aggregate supply curve rather than a vertical long-run aggregate supply curve. This has no impact on the issue we are discussing, as you can verify by redrawing the figure and redoing this analysis with a vertical aggregate supply curve. We encourage you to do this as a check of your understanding of this point.) We assume the policymaker has two targets, one for the price level and one for real output. The target for the price level is P_T, and the target for output is Y_T, as indicated by point *T* in the figure. How can policy move the economy from its initial equilibrium at point *A* to the target equilibrium at point *T*? The answer depends on the number and effect of the Fed's policy instruments on supply and demand. Let us assume (although it is not true) the Fed has available two instruments, one that can shift aggregate demand and one that can shift aggregate supply. Then the move from the equilibrium at point *A* to the equilibrium at point *T* requires shifting aggregate demand to the right, from *AD* to AD_1, and shifting aggregate supply to the right, from *SRAS* to $SRAS_1$. If the Fed changes its instruments appropriately to shift aggregate demand and supply in this manner, and if no other changes in variables occur that influence aggregate demand and supply, the economy will reach the target equilibrium at point *T*. Thus, in this example two instruments, one that changes aggregate demand and one that changes aggregate supply, are sufficient to achieve two targets.

The example in Figure 19.1 is a good one for illustrating the situation where there is an equal number of targets and instruments, but it does not adequately describe actual policymaking. In reality, the Federal Reserve System has more than two instruments, but they all affect only aggregate demand. The Fed does not have control of an instrument that can alter aggregate supply. This has important implications for its ability to achieve both a price level and an output target, as Figure 19.2 illustrates.

To achieve the target price level (P_T) and output (Y_T), the Fed must have one instrument to shift aggregate demand from AD to AD_1 and a second instrument to shift aggregate supply from $SRAS$ to $SRAS_1$. While the Fed has more than two instruments, they influence only aggregate demand. Thus, the Fed cannot achieve both a price level target and an output target.

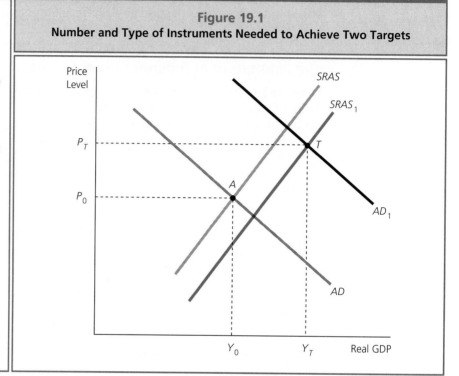

Figure 19.1
Number and Type of Instruments Needed to Achieve Two Targets

In Figure 19.2, the economy is at initial equilibrium where AD and $SRAS$ intersect at point A, with a price level of P_0 and an output level of Y_0. Suppose the target price level and output are P_T and Y_T, respectively, as given by point T. Can the Federal Reserve System achieve the targeted equilibrium of point T given that it is able to shift only the aggregate demand curve?

As you can see with a few attempts at curve shifting, no shift in aggregate demand alone, with aggregate supply fixed, will move the economy from point A to point T. It is simply impossible, which was Tinbergen's point more than 40 years ago. The Fed can achieve the targeted price level of P_T by shifting aggregate demand to AD_3, but the equilibrium at point D achieves the price level target with output Y_D, which is below the target level of Y_T. The Fed can achieve output level Y_T by shifting aggregate demand to AD_2, but the equilibrium at point C achieves the output target with a price level, P_C, that is above the targeted price level. Finally, the Fed may choose an equilibrium such as point B, with a price level of P_B and an output level of Y_B. Here both price and output targets are missed, but the output miss is less than at point D, and the price level miss is less than at point C. Notice, though, that all points lie on the original aggregate supply curve, $SRAS$. It

---

Figure 19.2
Fed Instruments Allowing Only One Target

Since the instruments available to the Fed can influence only aggregate demand, it can reach only one target. Starting at point A, the target equilibrium at T cannot be reached. If the Fed increases the money supply to shift aggregate demand to AD_3, the target price level is reached, but output is below the target. If it increases the money supply to shift aggregate demand to AD_2, the target for output is reached, but the price level is above the target. The Fed might decide to shift aggregate demand to a middle level, AD_1, where both targets are missed by a smaller amount.

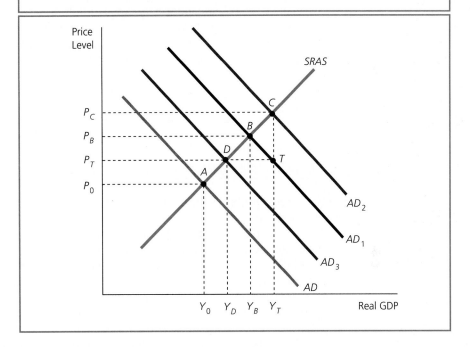

---

is the inability to shift *SRAS* that forces the Fed to choose between hitting one target and missing the other by a relatively large margin, such as at point *C* or *D*, and missing both targets by a relatively smaller margin, such as at point *B*.

Figures 19.1 and 19.2 illustrate Tinbergen's claim that it is not merely the number of instruments that is important, but the number of instruments exerting independent effects *on the target variables*. With no instrument to control aggregate supply, the Federal Reserve System is unable to achieve both a price level target and an output target. We say the Fed faces a shortage of policy instruments, since it lacks enough instruments to achieve its targets. For this reason, the Fed (and politicians) are always trading off the achievement of one set of goals for the achievement of another set. In the next section, we discuss these tradeoffs in more detail.

Summary
Exercise 19.1

We have seen that policy may have both a final real GDP target and a final price level target. If so, the monetary policymaker faces an instrument shortage. Can fiscal policy help solve this problem?

Answer: The answer depends on how you view the effect of fiscal policy. Remember that the instrument shortage problem here is due to the inability of monetary policy to shift aggregate supply. If fiscal policy affects only aggregate demand, it cannot help achieve both the price level and real GDP targets. However, we have seen that the marginal tax rates imposed by the fiscal authority might affect aggregate supply. If so, this enables fiscal policy to manipulate aggregate supply, with lower marginal tax rates shifting it to the right and higher rates shifting it to the left. In such a situation, fiscal policy might work in concert with monetary policy to better achieve the dual final targets.

THE LINK BETWEEN MONEY AND POLICY TARGETS

The policy problem the Federal Reserve System faces is twofold: how to control the money supply and how to alter the money supply in response to changes in the economy. We now deal with the second question, having discussed the first one earlier in Chapter 14.

In discussing how the Fed should change the money supply to deal with economic upheavals, it is important to keep the underlying economic model in mind. Remember that we have two models: a long-run model with vertical aggregate supply and a short-run model with upward-sloping aggregate supply. The effects of changes in the money supply differ in these models.

Figure 19.3 illustrates the achievement of a price level target in the long-run model. Remember that increases in the money supply shift aggregate demand to the right and reductions in the money supply shift it to the left. The price level target is P_T, and the economy starts in equilibrium at either point A, with aggregate demand AD, or point B, with aggregate demand AD_1. At either A or B, equilibrium output is Y_0. If the initial equilibrium is at point A, aggregate demand must be increased to AD_T to achieve the target price level, P_T, whereas if the initial equilibrium is at point B, aggregate demand must be decreased to AD_T to achieve this target. In either situation, appropriate changes in the money supply can be used to shift aggregate demand and achieve the price target.

What about an output level target greater than Y_0? In the long run, output is determined by the vertical aggregate supply curve. The Fed has no control

The Fed can achieve the target price level, P_T, in the long run, when the aggregate supply curve is vertical. If the initial equilibrium is at point A, the Fed can increase the money supply to cause aggregate demand to shift from AD to AD_T to reach the target price level. If the initial equilibrium is at point B, the Fed can decrease the money supply to lower aggregate demand from AD_1 to AD_T.

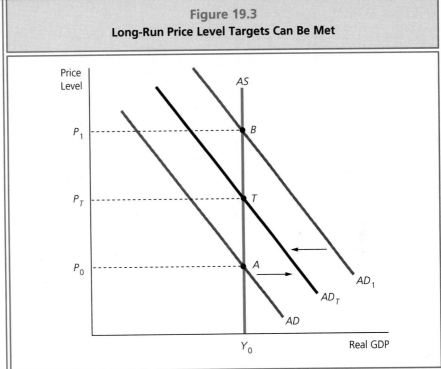

Figure 19.3
Long-Run Price Level Targets Can Be Met

over aggregate supply, and hence has no way to achieve a higher output level target. This is illustrated in Figure 19.4. The economy starts in equilibrium at point A, with a price level of P_0 and an output level of Y_0. The target level of output Y_T is above Y_0. In an effort to increase output toward the target level, the Fed might increase the money supply and hence aggregate demand, shifting AD to the right. But with a vertical aggregate supply curve, this merely drives up the price level to P_1; long-run output stays at Y_0. Thus, the message is that output targets cannot be achieved in the long run. The Fed would waste its time—and drive up the price level—if it attempted to use monetary policy to increase output in the long run. For this reason, many analysts have suggested that price level stability is the overriding long-run goal of monetary policy. Box 19.1 discusses a modern economy in which the goal of price stability has been completely abandoned.

What about the short run? In this case short-run aggregate supply is not vertical, as Figure 19.5 illustrates. Here the economy starts in equilibrium at point A, with price level P_0 and output Y_0. The target level of output is Y_T. Now the Fed can increase the money supply, thereby shifting aggregate demand to the right and moving the equilibrium to point T, where output equals the target, Y_T.

In the long run, when the aggregate supply curve is vertical, the Fed cannot influence output. Any policy that shifts aggregate demand will lead only to changes in the price level. Thus, in the long run an output target of Y_T cannot be met.

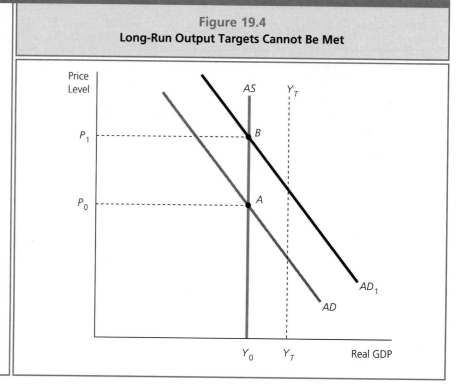

Figure 19.4
Long-Run Output Targets Cannot Be Met

It is important to remember that the position of the short-run aggregate supply curve in Figure 19.5 is influenced by the fact that input prices (especially nominal wage rates) are held constant and the level of input prices is determined largely by expectations about the price level. When workers and firms expect a rising price level, they are more likely to agree to rising nominal wage rates. Thus, expectations about the actions of monetary policymakers are important. If workers expect the Fed to attempt to raise the price level to reduce their real wage and increase output, they are likely to demand higher nominal wages, shifting short-run aggregate supply to the left and countering some or all of the influence of monetary policy. Thus, policymakers cannot regard the short-run aggregate supply curve as fixed and must be concerned about shifts in short-run aggregate supply even in the short run. In Chapter 20, we examine in more detail how expectations of policy actions can lessen the effectiveness of monetary policy.

It also bears remembering that even in Figure 19.5 it is not possible to achieve two targets. For example, if there are two targets, Y_T and P_0, the target of policy is the point labeled T'. The Fed cannot achieve both Y_T and P_0 by manipulating the money supply and hence aggregate demand. In this

International Banking   Box 19.1

*Monetary Policy Gone Awry:
Hyperinflation in Yugoslavia*

A common theme linking monetary policy in the United States, Germany, Japan, and many other nations is the belief that monetary policymakers should have a firm commitment to a stable price level. Other policy goals may coexist with this goal, and the instrument shortage problem may mean some nations are better than others at achieving the goal of stable prices. But all still claim price stability as a goal.

Why, then, do exceedingly high inflation rates occur? The state of Serbia, formerly part of Yugoslavia, provides a current example of inflation rates that are so high they are called *hyperinflation*. There the inflation rate runs more than 10 percent a day. At 10 percent daily, the annual rate of inflation will exceed 100 trillion percent. At 11 percent daily, it will exceed 1 quadrillion percent. One way to see what this means is to look at exchange rates. As we saw in Chapter 11, relative price levels in two countries help determine the exchange rates. At the end of 1985, the Yugoslavian dinar exchanged for about US$313. In early August 1993, the exchange rate reported in the *Wall Street Journal* varied from 10 million dinars per U.S. dollar at a Hyatt hotel to 17 million dinars per U.S. dollar at an underworld bank.

The rates of inflation just mentioned are incomprehensible to us, but some examples clearly illustrate the problem. A Snickers bar costs 6 million dinars and diapers 152 million dinars. Of course, had salaries risen at the same rate as the inflation rate, the higher prices

should not matter, but the same *Wall Street Journal* article reported that the average Serbian salary is about 200 million dinars per month, or US$20 at the Hyatt's exchange rate.

Serbian officials blame the United Nations trade embargo for this inflation, and the embargo certainly has had a negative impact on the Serbian economy, reducing aggregate supply and raising the price level. But the embargo is not the direct cause of inflation rates of 100 trillion or more per year. The cause of the inflation is the huge quantities of dinars being printed by the Serbian government. Indeed, the *Wall Street Journal* reports that the printing presses run at a furious pace around the clock, and rumors claim the government has even contracted out the printing of dinars. It is this huge increase in the supply of dinars that has caused the inflation and in turn created the tremendous depreciation of the dinar in currency markets.

Why did the Serbian government choose to print dinars in such quantities? No one is saying, but the answer must lie in the government budget constraint. Government spending must be paid for by taxes, borrowing, or money creation. The Serbian government has obviously decided to finance its spending via money creation, and the result is obvious. Why it chose this method of finance is less clear, but it may have to do with difficulties in collecting taxes and in borrowing due to the breakup of Yugoslavia, the ongoing war between Serbs and Croats in

Continued on p. 678

Continued from p. 677
Bosnia-Herzegovina and Croatia, and the U.N. trade embargo. But whatever the reason, the government and people of Serbia are now finding out that monetary finance of government spending is also not without cost.

case, the Fed faces a choice between point *A*, where the price level target is achieved but the output target missed; point *T*, where the output target is achieved but the price level target is missed; or some point on the line segment *AT* on the aggregate supply curve, where both targets are missed by some amount smaller than the largest miss at *A* or *T*.

To summarize, in the long run an output target is a quixotic goal for monetary policy, since it cannot be attained. Monetary policy can, however, achieve a price level target. In the short run, however, monetary policy might be able to achieve *either* a price level target or an output target, but not both. With instruments that directly affect only the money supply, the Fed can achieve only one target.

This discussion points out the importance of the shape of aggregate supply to monetary policymaking. It also indicates that monetary policy actions by the Fed can have much different effects in the short run than those in the long run. In the long run, with a vertical aggregate supply curve, output targets are not practical. Long-run monetary policy that attempts to set output above the level determined by long-run aggregate supply is ineffectual at best. In the short run, however, aggregate supply is upward sloping and output targets are appropriate, although even in this case the Fed, with both output and price level targets, has a shortage of instruments. Furthermore, the Fed faces a tough choice in making decisions based on the short-run aggregate supply curve, for it knows that in the end the long-run aggregate supply curve will determine output.

Summary Exercise 19.2

You are the monetary policymaker, and your price level and output targets are currently being met in the short run. You have an equal desire to achieve each target. You learn the U.S. economy has experienced an increase in the price level and in output. What do you do?

Answer: This is a realistic scenario. No one tells you the location of supply or demand; it is just you and the data. To decide how to respond, you should

Although the Fed cannot influence output in the long run, it can affect it in the short run, when the aggregate supply curve is upward sloping. Here the economy is initially at point A. If the Fed's target level of output is Y_T, an increase in the money supply would cause aggregate demand to increase from AD to AD_1, thereby achieving the output target.

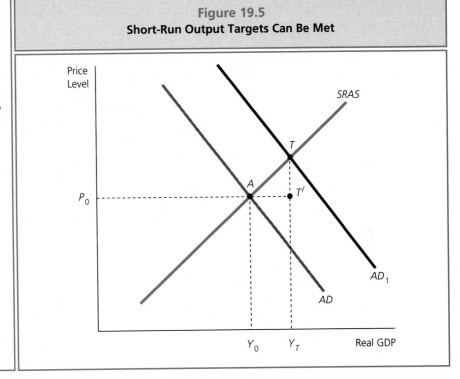

Figure 19.5
Short-Run Output Targets Can Be Met

first try to see why the price level and output could increase. If you look at aggregate demand and supply, you will see that this requires an increase in aggregate demand. For a given aggregate supply curve, an increase in aggregate demand will raise both price and output. You should try other shifts to convince yourself of this. (An increase in aggregate supply would lower the price level as output increased, while decreases in aggregate demand or supply would lower output.) Thus, since aggregate demand has increased, you should take the appropriate action to begin reducing it. This will reduce the price level and output, counteracting the increases reported to you. You can reduce aggregate demand by conducting monetary policies that decrease the money supply.

INTERMEDIATE TARGETS

Intermediate targets are targets that the Fed attempts to achieve because doing so will help attain the final targets of policy. But if the final target is the goal of policy, why have intermediate targets? That is, why aim at an intermediate target when the final target is the true goal? You might think the only reason for aiming at an intermediate target is to assure you of your best chance of hitting the final target, but we will see that this is not always the case.

The answer to the question of why the Fed adopts intermediate targets has several parts. One is that intermediate targets change the monetary policy debate from a debate over difficult issues like the unemployment rate goal, the output growth goal, or the inflation rate goal to a debate over the goal for the intermediate target. It is easier to discuss whether the money supply growth rate should be 2 or 4 percent than whether the Fed should try to achieve an unemployment rate target of 6 or 10 percent. In this view, then, the Fed adopts an intermediate target to make discussions of monetary policy less of a political and ideological contest.

Another view is that intermediate targets provide timely information on the state of the economy, and the Fed's success or failure at achieving those targets is useful information for the Fed. According to this view, it is no surprise that the Fed's choices of intermediate targets have been variables such as the interest rate (observed every few seconds) and the money supply (observed every week). The final goals of policy are variables observed monthly in the case of the unemployment rate and the consumer price index and quarterly in the case of real GDP or the GDP deflator. Since the intermediate target is observed more frequently, the Fed can collect more timely information on how well it is achieving its (intermediate target) goals. Of course, we saw in Chapter 18 that changes in the money supply do not immediately translate into changes in prices or even nominal GDP. Instead, it is prolonged changes in the growth rate of the money supply that eventually translate into the expected movements in the price level or nominal GDP. Thus, observing the money supply every week or interest rates every few seconds does not make it desirable to respond to every change in one of these variables.

What properties does the Fed look for in selecting a variable to serve as an intermediate target? First, achieving the intermediate target must be consistent with the Fed's final goals for policy. Second, the intermediate target must be accurately measurable on a timely basis. This provides the Fed with quick and accurate information about which monetary policy actions are needed to achieve the intermediate target. Finally, the intermediate target must be controllable so that the Fed can actually hope to achieve it, or at least move in the direction of achieving it.

The Fed has experience with several intermediate targets and faces proposals for several others. The traditional intermediate targets of Fed policy include both the money supply (either the monetary base, M1, or M2) and the interest rate (usually a short-term rate, such as a Treasury bill rate). Recently, however, there have been proposals to use prices or nominal GDP as intermediate targets. We will discuss these targets in turn.

A Money Aggregate as an Intermediate Target

Consider a situation in which the Fed wants the inflation rate to be 4 percent and expects real GDP to grow at 3 percent. In this case, nominal GDP would grow at 7 percent. The Fed might expect the nominal interest rate to be fairly stable at 6 percent, a 2 percent real interest rate, and a 4 percent expected inflation rate. Real money demand would grow at the rate of real GDP growth, 3 percent, and demand for nominal money balances would grow at the rate of nominal GDP growth, 7 percent. If all this worked out as expected, velocity would be stable, showing no growth or decline over the year.

With these goals and expectations, the Fed might decide to adopt an intermediate money target. Using the quantity equation in its growth rate formulation, the Fed reasons that 7 percent nominal GDP growth and 0 percent velocity growth means money growth should be 7 percent. Thus, the Fed might adopt an intermediate money target of 7 percent more money than last year. This target level of the money supply is labeled M_T in Figure 19.6, where the economy is initially in equilibrium at point A. Notice that the money demand and supply curves are drawn with the nominal money stock on the horizontal axis. In this graph, increases in the price level will shift money demand to the right, and vice versa for decreases in the price level.

Once the Fed adopts an intermediate target, it manipulates its policy instruments to keep the money supply at the intermediate target level. Thus, if money demand increases, from M^d to M_1^d, the equilibrium tends to change from point A to point B, with a higher equilibrium money stock. The Fed will counter this by reducing money supply to M_1^S, changing the equilibrium to point C. Notice that the Fed keeps the money supply at its intermediate target level, but doing so entails a rise in the interest rate from i^* to i_1. Thus, the Fed keeps the money stock at target by accepting an interest rate above the level it expected would occur.

Again starting at point A, if money demand decreases, the equilibrium shifts to point D, with a lower money stock. The Fed counters this by increasing the money supply to M_2^S, which moves the equilibrium to point E. This restores the money stock to target but causes a decline in the interest rate from i^* to i_2.

The key result in Figure 19.6 is that an intermediate money target can be achieved, but only if the Fed gives up control of the nominal interest rate. Thus, when the Fed chooses an intermediate money target, there will be greater interest rate variability than otherwise. Notice too that Figure 19.6 illustrates Tinbergen's point once again. The Fed can control only the money supply and therefore cannot hit both an interest rate and a money stock target.

Does the Fed actually achieve its money targets? Box 19.2 provides information on this question for the 1980s and early 1990s.

Figure 19.6
An Intermediate Money Stock Target

The intermediate target for the money stock is M_T. Beginning at point A, an increase in money demand to M_1^d moves the economy to a new equilibrium at point B, increasing both the money stock and the interest rate. However, with an intermediate money target of M_T, the Fed reduces the money supply to M_1^s, shifting equilibrium to point C. This further raises the interest rate but restores the money stock to its target value. A reduction in money demand works in the opposite direction, first moving the economy toward point D and then, after the Fed increases the money supply, toward point E. Intermediate money targets thus can lead to variability in interest rates.

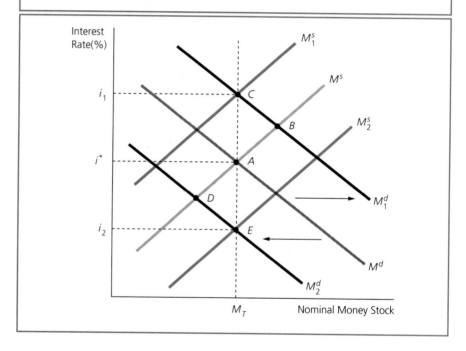

An Interest Rate as an Intermediate Target

Now consider the same situation outlined above for the case of an intermediate interest rate target. In particular, the Fed wants 4 percent inflation, expects 3 percent real GDP growth, and expects the nominal interest rate to be 6 percent. Again money demand is expected to grow at the rate of nominal GDP growth, 7 percent. Instead of worrying about money growth, the Fed decides to adopt an intermediate target of a 6 percent interest rate. As long as the Fed's forecast of money demand is accurate, this interest rate will result in a quantity demanded of money that is 7 percent greater than last year's money stock. How does this result differ from an intermediate money target?

The Data Bank

Box 19.2

Does the Fed Hit Its Money Targets?

The Fed began listing intermediate money targets in the 1970s, when it produced targets for various money aggregates. Since the early 1980s the Fed has concentrated on targets for M2, in part because the relationship of M1 and the final targets of policy seemed to break down, while M2 maintained a seemingly stable relationship to economic activity.

How well has the Fed done in achieving these M2 targets? The accompanying graph shows actual and targeted M2 growth from 1983 through 1992. Notice that the Fed's target for M2 was actually a range of upper-limit and lower-limit values rather than a single value. For example, at the end of 1992 the Fed's target range for M2 growth was 2.5 to 6.5 percent.

Did the Fed manage to keep M2 in the taret range? In the 10 years included in the graph, M2 growth exceeded the target range twice and fell below it twice. Interestingly, M2 growth stayed near the upper limit from 1983 through 1986 and then began hovering near the lower limit. Thus, the Fed managed to keep M2 growth at least close to its (rather wide) target ranges, but it actually achieved even these wide target bands only 60 percent of the time.

One interesting feature of M2 growth in 1992 is what it meant for prices and output growth. For 1992, M2 growth was about 2 percent. If velocity was stable, nominal GDP growth was the same 2 percent. The Fed's slow M2

Continued on p. 684

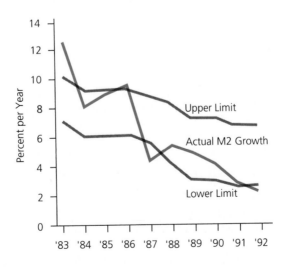

By choosing an intermediate interest rate target, the Fed has decided to manipulate the money supply to keep the interest rate at 6 percent. This is illustrated in Figure 19.7. If money demand is as expected, equilibrium is at point A; the intermediate interest rate target will achieve an interest rate of i^T and a money stock of M_0. However, if money demand increases to M_1^d, the equilibrium will tend to shift from point A to point B, with a rise in the interest rate. In response the Fed will increase the money supply, moving the equilibrium to point C, where the interest rate is i_T but the nominal money stock is M_1. Thus, the intermediate interest rate target is maintained at the cost of an increase in the money stock. Similarly, a fall in money demand to M_2^d would require a decrease in the money supply to M_2^S to maintain the interest rate at the target level at point E, but as a result the money stock would fall to M_2.

We conclude that an intermediate interest rate target can be achieved only at the cost of losing short-run control of the money stock. Of course, in the long run the intermediate interest rate target can be adjusted so that the expected level of the money stock is again M_0 if that is still a desirable level. But until the intermediate target is adjusted, money stock control is lost.

The Choice Between Interest Rates and Money as an Intermediate Target

We have seen that by choosing an intermediate target, the Fed confronts a choice of achieving either a money target or an interest rate target. Which is better? The answer depends on various aspects of the economy.

The Case for an Intermediate Interest Rate Target.   One important effect of interest rates is that on consumption and investment demand,

Figure 19.7
An Intermediate Interest Rate Target

The intermediate interest rate target is i_T. Beginning at point A, an increase in money demand to M_1^d moves the economy to point B. To counteract this increase in the interest rate, the Fed raises the money supply to M_1^s, moving the equilibrium to point C, where the interest rate stays at target but the money stock has increased. A reduction in money demand works in the opposite direction, moving the economy first toward point D and eventually to point E after the Fed reduces the money supply. Interest rate targets result in fluctuations in the money stock.

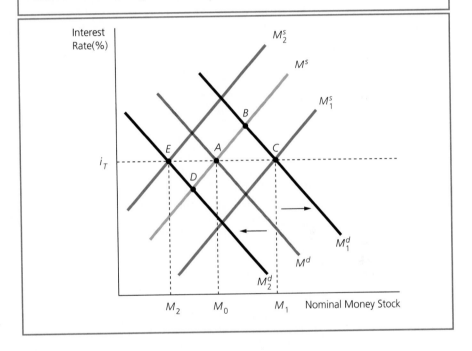

two large components of aggregate demand. Increases or decreases in the interest rate affect these components and hence lead to shifts in aggregate demand, resulting in changes in the short run to both the price level and the level of real output. Intermediate interest rate targets hold the interest rate constant and tend to reduce variations in consumption and investment due to interest rate changes. In addition, keeping the interest rate stable reduces the impact of changes in money demand on real GDP and the price level. A change in money demand leads to a change in the interest rate, and this in turn shifts aggregate demand. Thus, variations or instabilities in money demand translate into movements in the price level and real GDP. An intermediate interest rate target can eliminate this problem, since the Fed counters the shift in money demand with a shift in the money supply to keep the interest rate at its intermediate target value. With a stable interest rate, the economy is insulated from any variations in money demand. In fact, the more volatile money demand is, the greater is the case for an intermediate interest rate target.

The Case Against an Intermediate Interest Rate Target.

The case against intermediate interest rate targets is threefold. First, if consumption or investment demand increases for reasons other than interest rate changes (such as a change in tax rates), the intermediate interest rate target will actually exacerbate the effect on aggregate demand. To see this, consider an increase in investment demand, which also shows up in the loanable funds market as an increased demand for loanable funds. This raises the interest rate, and the Fed responds by increasing the money supply, which reduces the interest rate. By doing so, investment demand increases even further than previously, as does aggregate demand. Some blame the inflation rates of the late 1960s and early 1970s at least partly on the Fed's unwillingness to raise interest rates in the late 1960s, when aggregate demand was high as President Johnson tried to fight the Vietnam War and expand domestic transfer payments.

The second argument is a political one. Intermediate interest rate targets tend to take on a life of their own, becoming a final target instead of an intermediate target. Because many voters favor low interest rates, any move by the Fed to raise its intermediate interest rate target is likely to incur the wrath of voters and perhaps Congress. For example, even when the Fed gradually raised interest rates by a total of 1% in early 1994, there were grumblings from the White House and Congress.

The third argument is that interest rate targets cannot be maintained indefinitely. Basically the argument is based on the Fisher equation and the idea that in the long run, the real interest rate is determined by real factors in the economy that the Fed cannot control. Because the nominal interest rate equals the real rate plus the expected inflation rate, any successful long-run intermediate interest rate target must imply a stable expected inflation rate at a rate implied by the interest rate target and the real interest rate. Economists are very much divided on the issue of whether this is practical, especially in the long run.

The Case for an Intermediate Money Target.

The argument favoring an intermediate money target builds on the case against an intermediate interest rate target. First, an intermediate money target allows the interest rate to rise in response to shifts in investment demand or consumption demand not caused by interest rate movements, thus reducing fluctuations in aggregate demand from those causes. For example, suppose consumption demand decreases due to an unexpected widespread increase in thriftiness. This will reduce aggregate demand and lower both the price level and real GDP. If there is an intermediate money target, the reduction in real GDP will lower money demand, decreasing the interest rate, stimulating consumption and investment demand, and countering to some extent the initial decline in aggregate demand. Thus, the more volatile the components of aggregate demand are, the stronger is the case for an intermediate money target.

In addition, an intermediate money target is less likely to take on aspects of a final target, because voters are not very concerned about the size of the aggregate money stock. Finally, there are no reasons to think the Fed will be unable to achieve an intermediate money target even in the long run.

The Case Against an Intermediate Money Target.

There are two arguments against an intermediate money target. The first concerns choosing among the alternative money aggregates. The Fed defines a monetary base, M1, M2, and M3 and even these definitions change over time. We have seen that economists differ over which is the best. Thus, there is considerable debate over which should be chosen as the aggregate to target. This is a particular concern because, as we have seen, the various measures often do not indicate that policy is moving in the same direction.

The second argument against intermediate money targets is that they can lead to much interest rate variability. This is particularly true if money demand is itself variable, as shown earlier in Figure 19.6. Variability in interest rates leads to variability in both investment demand and consumption demand.

Other Suggested Intermediate Targets

Two suggestions for intermediate targets that the Fed has not tried are commodity price targets and nominal GDP targets. We discuss these briefly here.

A Commodity Price Target.

Some proposals call for the Fed to adopt an index of commodity prices as its intermediate target. Others have a single commodity price in mind, usually the price of gold. All of these proposals have in common a desire for a greater focus on price stability. The idea is that by targeting a price index of some kind, the Fed will better maintain a low and stable inflation rate.

If the Fed adopted a commodity price target, it would use the instruments under its control to adjust the money supply to offset deviations of the commodity price from target. This is easiest to do with a single commodity. For instance, the Fed could target the price of gold by offering to buy or sell gold at an announced price. If the target price is below the market equilibrium price, there is an excess demand for gold at the target price, and the Fed ends up selling gold to the public. In the process the Fed accumulates dollars, which are removed from circulation, reducing the monetary base and hence the money supply, and this leads to a decline in the overall price level. The decline in the overall price level shifts the demand for gold to the left; that is, at every price of gold, demanders want to buy a smaller amount of gold when the overall price level declines. The fall in the price level also shifts the supply of gold to the right, as suppliers are willing to supply more gold at every dollar price of gold. The net effect is to eventually reduce the amount of gold the public buys from the Fed to zero.

Figure 19.8 illustrates this scenario. The initial equilibrium is at point A, where the price of gold is P^0_{gold}. Suppose the Fed's target price is P^T_{gold}. The excess demand, $D_0 - S_0$, is the amount of gold the Fed sells to the public to satisfy demand. These gold sales, like open market sales of bonds, reduce the money supply and eventually the price level, and this leads to leftward shifts in demand for gold and rightward shifts in supply until the equilibrium price of gold is equal to the target price at point B.

A disadvantage of targeting the price of gold is that any change in the demand for or supply of gold will lead to a change in the equilibrium price, which in turn will lead to changes in the money supply and the overall price level to restore equilibrium to the target price. For example, a large gold discovery would lead to a large increase in the supply of gold, shifting

Equilibrium in the gold market is at point A. The target price of gold, P^T_{gold}, is below the initial equilibrium, meaning there is an excess demand for gold that the Fed must fulfill by selling gold to the public. As the public trades dollars for gold, the money supply is reduced. Eventually the overall price level declines, shifting gold supply to S_1 and gold demand to D_1, with an equilibrium price of gold equal to the target price at point B.

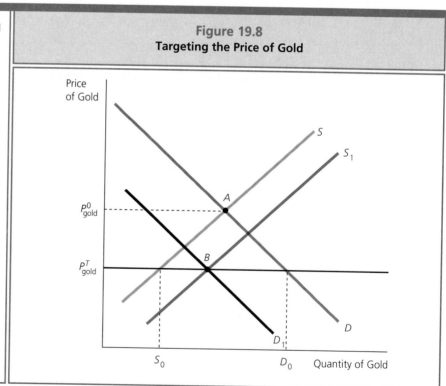

Figure 19.8
Targeting the Price of Gold

supply to the right. This would reduce the equilibrium price of gold below the target price. An excess supply would occur at the target price, and the Fed would buy gold, causing an increase in the monetary base and hence in the overall price level. Thus, a gold discovery would be inflationary.

What about more complex price targets? Various types of commodity price indexes have been proposed. The advantage of a larger group of commodities is that the money supply will not have to adjust as much to changes in the demand for or supply of any one commodity. If the index consists of gold, silver, and other metals, a large gold discovery will have less of an impact than it would if just the price of gold were being targeted. The disadvantage of such targeting is that it would involve the Fed in buying and selling a bundle of commodities. This process is more complex than buying or selling a single commodity such as gold.

Another disadvantage of targeting commodity prices is that the link between changes in commodity prices and changes in the final targets of policy, such as the overall price level or the level of real GDP, is poorly understood. Indeed, this is the primary problem with targeting commodity prices. If we don't know how commodity price changes get reflected in the unemployment rate or the overall price level, it is difficult to know how we should set the intermediate target.

A Nominal GDP Target.   Another proposal is to target nominal GDP, a strategy sometimes called *nominal income targeting*. In some ways, this proposal is related to that of targeting an overall price index. However, the nominal GDP target might be best thought of by recalling the equation of exchange from Chapter 3, $MV = PY$. The right-hand side of that equation is nominal income or nominal GDP, and the left-hand side is the product of the money supply and velocity. The basic idea is for the Fed to adjust the money supply to keep nominal GDP at a targeted level. If velocity is constant, the Fed can do this as long as it can control the money supply.

There are several benefits to nominal GDP targeting. One is that by targeting nominal GDP, the Fed is able to promote some stability in the price level. Recall that the growth rate of nominal GDP is simply the growth rate of real GDP plus the inflation rate. If the Fed targets a nominal GDP growth rate of 5 percent and real GDP is forecast to grow at 3 percent, the Fed is implicitly targeting an inflation rate of 2 percent.

A second benefit is that nominal GDP targeting provides a certain amount of built-in stabilization against changes in aggregate supply. Monetary policy is directed at controlling aggregate demand, and most policy advice is directed, at least implicitly, at keeping aggregate demand at some desired level. However, this will achieve a price level and/or real GDP target only if aggregate supply is stable. If aggregate supply shifts, both the price level and real GDP will change.

Nominal GDP targeting can partially stabilize the economy in the face of shifts to short-run aggregate supply while also stabilizing aggregate demand. We can best see this with the aid of Figure 19.9. The nominal GDP target is the curve drawn so that the product of the price level and real GDP, $P \times Y$, equals a target value, T. By adopting a nominal GDP target, the Fed is saying it wants the economy to be somewhere on the curve $P \times Y = T$, but it doesn't care where on that curve.

Suppose the economy is in equilibrium at point A, where $SRAS$ and AD intersect. The initial price level is P_0 and real GDP is Y_0. This equilibrium satisfies the nominal GDP target, since it lies on the curve $P \times Y = T$. What happens if aggregate demand increases to AD_1? The equilibrium price level and real GDP both increase to point B, causing the nominal GDP target to be violated. The Fed responds by reducing the money supply, shifting aggregate demand back to AD, which restores the economy back to the initial equilibrium at A. Thus, under a nominal GDP target, the Fed will attempt to completely offset any changes in aggregate demand.

What about changes in aggregate supply? If aggregate supply shifts right, the equilibrium price level will fall and the equilibrium level of real GDP will rise. In Figure 19.10, this effect is shown as the movement from equilibrium at point A to point B. However, at point B the nominal GDP target is violated. The Fed responds by increasing the money supply and aggregate

The nominal GDP target is $P \times Y = T$. An increase in aggregate demand from AD to AD_1 moves the economy to point B in the short run. The resulting increases in the price level and real GDP violate the nominal GDP target. A reduction in the money supply will shift aggregate demand back toward AD and restore the target value of nominal GDP.

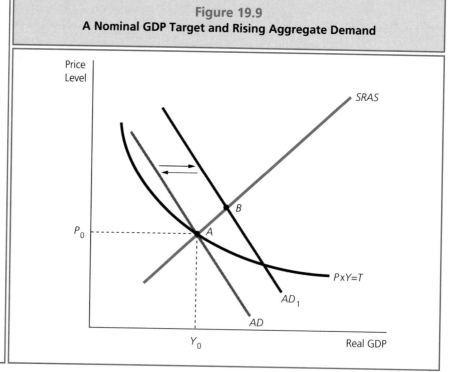

Figure 19.9
A Nominal GDP Target and Rising Aggregate Demand

Figure 19.10
A Nominal GDP Target and Rising Aggregate Supply

Starting at point *A*, a rightward shift in aggregate supply causes the price level to decline and real GDP to rise. The new short-run equilibrium at point *B* violates the nominal GDP target and calls for the Fed to increase the money supply and hence raise aggregate demand to AD_1. The result is point *C*, which satisfies the nominal GDP target and results in higher real GDP and a smaller decrease in the price level than at point *B*. Note too that the equilibrium at point *C* is closer to the new long-run level of real output (Y_1) than is the equilibrium at point *B*. Nominal GDP targeting speeds the economy's movement toward the new long-run equilibrium level of output.

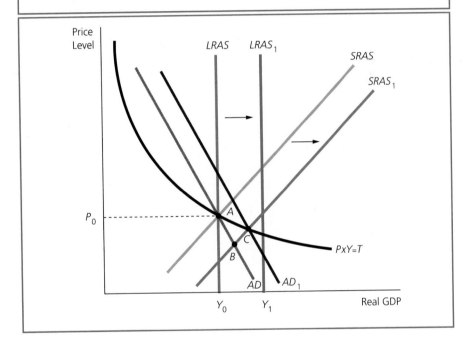

demand to achieve equilibrium at point *C*, where nominal GDP is restored to the target level, *T*. In this case, the Fed moves to generate a greater increase in real GDP and a smaller decline in the price level than would have occurred had aggregate demand remained constant. Notice too that the nominal GDP target moves the short-run equilibrium closer to its eventual long-run equilibrium, which will be at an even greater level of real GDP. Thus, the nominal GDP target encourages quicker short-run adjustment toward the long-run level of real output.

Nominal GDP targeting has much to recommend it. It stabilizes aggregate demand and hence the price level if aggregate supply is stable, and it helps the economy adjust more quickly to changes in aggregate supply.

However, nominal GDP targeting has several disadvantages. First, nominal GDP is announced only every quarter; other variables are known at much more frequent intervals. Second, it is difficult for the Fed to control nominal GDP; that is, changes in the money supply do not immediately show up as changes in nominal GDP. In fact, we saw in Chapter 18 that only in the long run are changes in the money supply reliably linked to equal percentage changes in nominal GDP. In the short run, the link is much more tenuous. Thus, there are problems with nominal GDP targeting that echo those with price level targeting, and these difficulties may continue to preclude the Fed's use of nominal GDP as an intermediate target.

Summary Exercise 19.3

Suppose you are in charge of setting the intermediate targets for the Fed. You are told the Fed has decided to increase its short-run final target for output. For the following choices of an intermediate target, tell how you would adjust the target to help in achieving the new, higher final target for output: (a) the money stock, (b) a short-run interest rate, (c) the price level, and (d) nominal GDP.

Answer: (a) If the intermediate target is a money target, the target level must be adjusted upward. An increase in the money stock should raise aggregate demand and hence equilibrium real output in the short run. (b) For an intermediate interest rate target, the target level must be lowered. A lower interest rate should lead to greater consumption and investment and hence greater aggregate demand, increasing short-run equilibrium real output. (c) An intermediate price level target would have to be increased, since this would allow the money supply to expand (thus increasing aggregate demand and real GDP). (d) The intermediate nominal GDP target would have to be increased for the same reason given in (c).

FEDERAL RESERVE OPERATING PROCEDURES

How does the Fed actually carry out monetary policy? What instruments does it use, and what is its intermediate target? These questions address the Fed's operating procedures, the combination of policy instruments and intermediate targets that describe how the Fed actually conducts policy.

Here we briefly discuss three operating procedures the Fed has actually used at various times in its history. To keep straight the relationship between policy instruments and the various targets, Figure 19.11 provides a schematic guide to Fed policymaking. On the far left are the policy instruments the Fed can use in conducting monetary policy, such as open market operations. On the far right are the final targets of policy, such as low inflation, low unemployment, and a high rate of growth in real GDP. In between are operating targets and intermediate targets. Intermediate targets are to the left

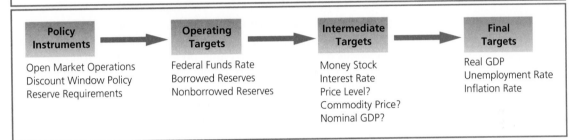

Figure 19.11
A Schematic Guide to Fed Policymaking

The Fed directly controls its policy instruments, which it uses to achieve operating targets that themselves are useful in achieving intermediate targets. These intermediate targets are in turn useful for achieving the final targets of monetary policy.

Policy Instruments	Operating Targets	Intermediate Targets	Final Targets
Open Market Operations	Federal Funds Rate	Money Stock	Real GDP
Discount Window Policy	Borrowed Reserves	Interest Rate	Unemployment Rate
Reserve Requirements	Nonborrowed Reserves	Price Level?	Inflation Rate
		Commodity Price?	
		Nominal GDP?	

of the final targets, indicating the Fed tries to achieve an intermediate target that will in turn help it achieve the final target. Operating targets lie between the policy instruments and the intermediate target. An **operating target** is an immediate target of policy—a target for a variable the Fed can definitely control on a daily or weekly basis, such as a category of reserves or a short-run interest rate. Just as the intermediate target is set so that achieving the intermediate target helps attain the final targets, the operating target is set so that reaching the operating target helps achieve the intermediate target.

Why does so much stand between policy instruments and final targets? The basic answer is that lags and lack of precise knowledge of their length and the response of the economy to any particular event makes it very difficult to aim policy instruments directly at final targets. At times the link between policy instruments and final targets seems very tenuous, and information on how well the current policy is achieving the final targets is slow to arrive at the Fed. Thus, the Fed adopts intermediate targets to focus on a variable that it better understands and is more closely related to the policy instruments. But even the intermediate target is not always linked tightly enough to the policy instruments, so at times the Fed tries to expand the money supply and the intermediate target variable is slow to respond. Thus, the Fed adopts operating targets—variables it *knows* it can control—and uses them to guide policy.

It is important to remember that both operating targets and intermediate targets are useful only as an aid in achieving the ultimate objectives of policy, the final targets. Operating targets and intermediate targets are adjusted as needed so that achieving them helps reach the final targets. If an operating or intermediate target takes on a life of its own, it becomes another final target—an end in itself instead of a means to an end. This is sometimes a danger of using interest rates as operating or intermediate targets; the Fed has difficulty making large changes in such targets even when such actions are indicated by the behavior of the final target variables.

We now discuss three operating procedures used by the Fed in recent years: federal funds rate targeting, nonborrowed reserve targeting, and borrowed reserve targeting.

Federal Funds Rate Targeting

During the 1970s, the Fed's operating procedure was to use its policy instruments to target the federal funds rate in such a manner as to achieve an intermediate money target. Basically this process works as follows. First, the Fed chooses a value for the intermediate money target, M^*. We need not be concerned with exactly how M^* is determined, except that it is chosen to be consistent with some final targets for output, inflation, the unemployment rate, or other goals. Once the money target is identified, the Fed uses an estimate of money demand to find out the interest rate that will make the quantity demanded of money equal to M^*. That is, the Fed works backward, first deciding on a quantity of money that it wants to achieve and then determining what interest rate will make money demand equal to that quantity of money. This interest rate becomes an operating target, a target for the instruments of policy. The Fed conducts open market operations to keep the interest rate, and in particular the federal funds rate, at the target level. If money demand stays at its estimated position, at this interest rate the quantity demanded of money will be M^*, the intermediate target level. Note, however, that under this procedure the Fed is targeting the interest rate, meaning the money stock just equals whatever quantity of money is demanded.

What if money demand has increased? Between meetings of the Federal Open Market Committee, the Fed would usually stick close to the federal funds rate operating target, meaning the increase in money demand would lead to an increase in the quantity demanded of money. In this case, the Fed would not achieve its intermediate money target.

One disadvantage this procedure had in the 1970s was that the Fed was often reluctant to adjust its operating targets for the federal funds rate. Thus, an increase in income would increase money demand, and under a federal funds rate procedure this would lead to a greater money stock. The Fed would miss its intermediate target for the money stock, and the response could have been to increase the operating target for the funds rate to reduce the quantity demanded of money. Adjustments in the operating target were often too little and too late, however, and the Fed was frequently in danger of exceeding its targets for money growth. This gave an inflationary bias to policy during the 1970s.

Another disadvantage of this procedure is that it tends to result in procyclical policy. **Procyclical policy** is policy that stimulates the economy during an expansion and restrains it during a recession. As we just noted, an increase in income would lead to an increase in the money stock under the federal funds rate target, giving a further stimulus to aggregate demand. Likewise, a reduction in income would reduce money demand and hence the money stock, further lowering aggregate demand. Unless the federal funds rate targets were adjusted to counter this, policy would end up exaggerating business cycle movements in aggregate income.

Nonborrowed Reserves Targeting

After using federal funds rate targeting during much of the 1970s, the Fed adopted a nonborrowed reserves targeting procedure in October 1979. Under this procedure, the Fed had an intermediate money target and used the money multiplier relationship (see Chapter 14) to estimate how large the monetary base would have to be to achieve the money target. From the monetary base, the Fed subtracted an estimate of currency holdings and borrowed reserves, giving it a value for the nonborrowed reserves required for its money target. This value was the Fed's nonborrowed reserves target, and the Fed conducted open market operations to keep nonborrowed reserves at this value.

Under this procedure, if borrowed reserves and currency holdings were estimated correctly, if the nonborrowed reserves target was achieved, and if the money multiplier was constant, the intermediate money target would be achieved. The idea behind this procedure was to have the money stock be determined more closely by money supply considerations.

How well did this procedure work? It should have resulted in a less volatile money stock in exchange for greater volatility in interest rates, which were no longer being targeted. In fact, however, the volatility of *both* the money stock and interest rates increased. In addition, the Fed proved no better able to hit its intermediate money targets under this procedure than previously. It abandoned this procedure in 1982.

Why did this procedure not work as expected? It may be that a large number of financial innovations (NOW accounts, ATM machines) and financial market deregulation caused the link between reserves and the money stock to break down over this period. Another explanation is that nonborrowed reserve targets were difficult to maintain when the Fed was imposing reserve requirements against deposits held two weeks earlier. This so-called lagged reserve accounting meant that banks were unable to alter their current levels of deposits to change their current reserve requirements.

Finally, many argue that the Fed had no real desire to use the nonborrowed reserve procedure but instead used it as a smokescreen behind which it could raise interest rates in its attempt to lower the inflation rate. According to this view, the Fed knew it would be politically unacceptable to target the interest rate at the high levels needed to slow inflation, so it adopted a policy procedure that required no mention of interest rates. This gave the Fed some cover from the intense political pressure generated by the record interest rates of that time.

For whatever reason, the experiment with nonborrowed reserves targeting was short-lived, and in 1982 the Fed turned to yet another policy procedure: borrowed reserves targeting.

Borrowed Reserves Targeting

Borrowed reserve targeting still had an intermediate money target, and like nonborrowed reserve targeting the borrowed reserve targeting procedure made use of the link between the money stock and the reserves. However, the target was a level of borrowed reserves that, together with nonborrowed reserves and currency, made up the monetary base.

Borrowed reserves targeting generated interest rate smoothing, since it led the Fed to partially counteract changes in the interest rate. For example, when interest rates were rising, banks were tempted to make more loans, and to do this they attempted to increase borrowing from the Fed. This increased demand for borrowed reserves raised borrowed reserves over the Fed's target, and the Fed had to respond by supplying more nonborrowed reserves via open market purchases to meet the demand for nonborrowed reserves. But the very act of conducting open market purchases increased reserves and the money supply and tended to counteract the initial rise in interest rates. Thus, the borrowed reserves procedure was a move back toward interest rate targeting. Indeed, some suggest this procedure was merely interest rate targeting in disguise. According to this view, the Fed wanted to return to interest rate targeting after the nonborrowed reserves procedure of 1979 to 1982, but did not want to admit that adopting the nonborrowed reserves procedure had been either a mistake or a smokescreen for the high interest rates of the period. Hence, the Fed disguised its interest rate targeting procedure as a borrowed reserves targeting procedure.

The 1990s: A Return to Interest Rate Targeting

During the 1990s, the Fed has more explicitly returned to the interest rate targeting procedures of the 1970s. It again targets an interest rate in an attempt to achieve an intermediate money target. Presumably the Fed has decided this procedure works best at achieving its objectives, either its intermediate money target or at least its final targets. As the decade unfolds, we will see whether the Fed has also learned the lessons of the 1970s experience with interest rate targeting. In particular, we will see if the interest rate targeting results in procyclical policy and if the tendency for an inflationary bias reemerges.

The Fed announced in July 1993 that it was de-emphasizing its monetary targets too. This announcement suggests that the Fed either will assign a smaller weight to achieving an intermediate money target or will abandon money as an intermediate target. In either case, this move away from money targets and toward interest rate targets is an interesting development in Fed policymaking.

Finally, in the late 1980s and early 1990s, the Fed publicized a new variable it called *P-star* as a guide to forecasting inflation and hence as a guide to the Fed in taking actions now to combat future inflation. Box 19.3 discusses P-star.

Summary
Exercise 19.4

Several variables can be placed in one or more of the following categories: policy instruments, operating targets, intermediate targets, or final targets. Which of the following variables—(a) nonborrowed reserves, (b) the interest rate, and (c) the money stock—can be placed in which of these categories, and why?

Answer: (a) We have seen that nonborrowed reserves have been an operating target of policy. The Fed can directly set the level of nonborrowed reserves via open market operations. Nonborrowed reserves have not been preferred as an intermediate target, and certainly make no sense as a final target of policy. (b) The interest rate is one variable that might fit all three target categories. It has been an operating target. Alternatively, interest rates can be an intermediate target, because achieving a certain interest rate might help attain a certain level of aggregate demand and hence aid in achieving final targets. Finally, an interest rate might be a final target of policy, especially if the Fed's ultimate objective is to maintain stability in the financial sector, interpreted as low volatility of interest rates. (c) The money stock is sometimes considered an operating target of monetary policy, although it is doubtful that the Federal Reserve System can directly control it. The assumption that the money stock is an instrument of policy is often made in theoretical analyses to avoid explicitly modeling the link between actual policy instruments and the money stock, especially when the purpose of the anaysis is to discuss the achievement of final targets. However, the money stock is most often taken to be an intermediate target of policy. It is not a reasonable final target of policy.

PROBLEMS IN MONETARY POLICYMAKING

In the previous section, we analyzed the choice of operating procedure to achieve an intermediate target. We have assumed changes in the money supply translate into changes in aggregate demand in a timely manner. We now turn to some additional practical issues in policymaking. These include the time lags between economic events that call for a policy response and the eventual response of the macroeconomy, as well as problems caused by conflicting goals held by a single policymaker and even conflicts among policymakers.

Inside Money

Box 19.3

P-Star: A New Target for Monetary Policy?

In the latter half of the 1980s, the Fed announced a new variable that was useful for predicting inflation and therefore might be a feasible guide for monetary policy. This variable, labeled P-star (or $P*$), was derived from equation of exchange considerations.

To derive $P*$, we begin with the equation of exchange, $MV = PY$. Next, we incorporate the empirical finding that the velocity of M2 is fairly stable at a value of about 1.64. Then we distinguish between the long run and the short run. In the long run real GDP, Y, is set by long-run aggregate supply, and we might measure this long-run level of real GDP by what is called *potential real GDP*—the level of real GDP the economy is capable of producing if labor and

capital resources are fully employed. In the long run, real GDP tends to equal this potential level of real GDP, Y^p.

Part a of the accompanying figure shows actual and potential real GDP from 1959 through 1992. Real GDP is sometimes above and sometimes below its potential level. After a drop during the recessions in the early 1980s, real GDP was at its potential level during the rest of the 1980s, then fell below potential again during the recession of 1990.

Using this reasoning, we can calculate the long-run price level that is consistent with today's money stock, taking velocity as constant and real GDP as equal to its long-run value,

Continued on p. 699

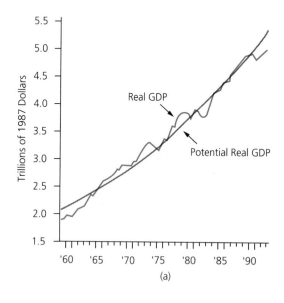

(a)

Continued from p. 698

measured by potential real GDP. We call this long-run price level P* and calculate it as

$$P\star = \frac{MV}{Y^p}.$$

How does this formula help predict inflation? This measure is an estimate of the long-run price level that will occur once output returns to its potential level. We also know that actual current price level, P, which using the equation of exchange, can be written as

$$P = \frac{MV}{Y}.$$

Differences between the current (short-run) price level, P, and the long-run price level, P*, are due to only two factors: Either velocity is temporarily away from its average value of 1.64, or output is temporarily away from its potential level, Y^p. In either case, if the current price level is below the long-run price level (P*), this indicates that the price level must rise or the economy will experience inflation. Similarly, if the current price level is above the long-run price level, this indicates the price level must decline.

How does this calculation aid policymakers? Because of lags in the effects of monetary policy, it is always useful to improve policymakers' ability to forecast the final impact of money growth on the economy. If the value of the P-star calculation suggests that the price level will rise in the future, the monetary policymaker intent on preventing this can reduce the money supply, thereby lowering P* and countering part of this increase in the price level.

Does P-star work as a predictor of inflation? Part b of the accompanying figure provides some evidence that it does. For example, P-star exceeded the price level (P) almost continually from about 1963 through 1980, and during this time there was an upward trend in the inflation rate. In 1980 P-star fell below the price level, and the inflation rate declined. From 1985 through 1988 P-star exceeded the price level, and indeed some slight upward movement oc-

Continued on p. 700

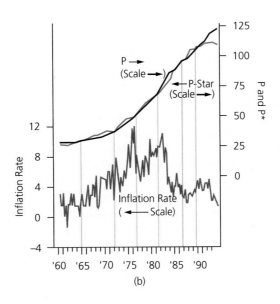

(b)

Continued from p. 699
curred in the inflation rate. Finally, since 1989 P-star has been below the price level, and we have seen a rather substantial reduction in the inflation rate. Thus, P-star does seem to work as a predictor of inflation. Is it better than other models of inflation? Here the evidence is much less clear. Several studies have indicated alternative models can forecast the inflation rate at least as well as P-star can. Thus, it is not all that clear that P-star is a uniquely valuable tool for

the Fed. Remember too that its usefulnesss depends on the stability of M2 velocity and on the assumption that real GDP will return to its estimated potential level. If these assumptions are violated, P-star loses much of its appeal. Time will tell whether P-star remains a useful aid to Fed policymaking.

_____

Source: Citibase electronic database; authors' calculations of potential real GDP and P-star.

Lags

There are a number of sources of lags between the occurrence of an event that brings forth a policy response and the eventual response of the economy. These lags are called *implementation lags* and *effectiveness lags*.

Implementation Lags. Lags occur between the time a policy action is needed and the time the action occurs. Such lags are called **implementation lags** and can be subdivided into three categories. The first category is **information lags**—lags in the availability of information about the state of the economy. The second is **recognition lags,** or lags in the recognition by the monetary policymaker that a policy action is needed, based on the information available to it. The third is **legislative lags**—lags in the enactment of the appropriate legislation needed for a policy action to occur.

To take the appropriate policy action, the policymaker must have information about the state of the economy. For example, consider a policymaker with a final target for inflation, real output, and unemployment. In this situation, the policymaker must know the price level, real GDP, and the unemployment rate before it can respond with an appropriate policy action. But lags occur between a change in the state of the economy and the indicators of that change. For instance, the price level in the United States is measured monthly in the case of the consumer price index (CPI) and quarterly in the case of the GDP deflator. Output can be measured by industrial production (measured monthly) or the broader measure, real GDP (measured quarterly). Unemployment, which is related to output, is measured monthly. Thus, the monetary policymaker is in a situation where at best it can get only monthly updates on prices and output and quarterly updates on the broadest measures of prices and output. Moreover, these updates occur quite some time *after* the month or quarter they are measuring. For example, the consumer price index for a given month is announced in the middle of the following month; that is, the CPI for January is announced in the middle of February. Information on the GDP deflator and real GDP is even more delayed. GDP and the GDP deflator for the first quarter of the year—January through March—are announced in a preliminary release in the first week of May, with revisions in June and again in July. Thus, the monetary authority does not have even a preliminary estimate of GDP available until a month after the quarter ends. Of course, there are monthly data on industrial production and unemployment, which give indications of what is happening to real GDP, but even these are announced several weeks after the end of the month to which they apply. Thus, these information lags cause lags in the enactment of monetary policy, since the Fed can hardly respond to events of which it is not aware.

Even after the data become available, lags occur in the policymaker's recognition of the state of the economy. These recognition lags are compounded by the fact that some data arrive monthly while other data arrive only quarterly. Sometimes it is clear that output has fallen or that the price level has increased, but other times the data give conflicting messages. For example, the consumer price index might have increased but the producer price index decreased, and the GDP deflator will not be available for another month or more. Or industrial production might have fallen but unemployment remained constant, so the output situation is uncertain, and real GDP won't be known for weeks or even months. In such situations, there is a lag in recognition by the monetary authority of the true state of the economy.

Finally, for some policymakers there may be significant legislative lags—lags in policy actions due to lags in enacting any required legislation. For monetary policy, legislative lags are seldom an issue. They are important in fiscal policy, as we will see in Chapter 21.

Effectiveness Lags.

An **effectiveness lag** is the time between when a policy action is made and when the action results in changes in the economy. For example, if the Fed is trying to target the price level, it might respond to a decline in the consumer price index by increasing the money supply. In our theoretical models this action immediately increases aggregate demand and the price level, but in practical applications of monetary policy things do not occur so quickly. Sometimes it takes many months for a policy action to have the desired effect, and these months make up the effectiveness lag. In Chapter 18 we saw that monetary policy has been estimated to take 12 or 13 months or more to exert its full effect on the economy, so the effectiveness lags in monetary policy can be substantial.

Lags in the effectiveness of monetary policy actions are a severe problem for the Fed. The effectiveness lag for monetary policy can last a year or more. On top of that, the average length of recessions in the United States since World War II has been less than one year. If a recession started today, we would expect it to be over before any monetary policy taken today could begin to counteract it. In fact, the monetary policy action would start exerting its stimulative effect just as the economy was recovering from the recession, making policy procyclical. This is the type of reasoning that led Milton Friedman to advocate increasing the money supply at a constant rate of 3 percent, regardless of business cycle conditions.

One solution to the problem of effectiveness lags would be for the Fed to forecast where the economy will be a year from now so that it can take the appropriate action today. An action taken today would exert its influence a year from now. If the forecast was accurate, the policy action taken today could help achieve the final targets for the economy in a year's time. Unfortunately, economic forecasts over horizons of a year or more are not very accurate. In particular, it is difficult to forecast business cycle turning points, that is, precisely when the economy will move from expansion to recession and vice versa. Thus, the Fed cannot look ahead from today and say with certainty that there will or won't be a recession in a year. Hence it doesn't know how it should change monetary policy today to counter any future business cycle movements.

We might make the following analogy to monetary policymaking with implementation and effectiveness lags, an analogy adapted from one made by Milton Friedman. The monetary policymaker is like the driver of a car, whose job is to keep the car on the road, perhaps one that twists and turns around mountain peaks. However, this driver cannot see out the front window of the car what is approaching. In fact, the driver cannot even see out the side windows to see the current road situation. Instead, the driver can see only out the rear window, receiving data on where she or he has already been. (This is the information lag.) To make things worse, the driver has very slowly responding instruments. The brake starts working only several seconds after the pedal is depressed, the steering wheel turns the car only after several seconds, and even stepping on the accelerator starts accelerating the car only after several seconds. (This is the effectiveness lag.)

Finally, Friedman has emphasized that the lags between a monetary policy action and changes in macroeconomic variables such as real GDP or the price level are not only long but also variable in length. In terms of our analogy, this means that when our driver steps on the brakes, not only does the car take several seconds to begin slowing but the number of seconds varies over time. One time it may take five seconds, and at another time it may take eight seconds. In monetary policymaking, reducing the money supply growth rate sometimes seems to take 7 months to begin slowing the inflation rate, while at other times it seems to take 14 months. This obviously compounds the problems the policymaker faces.

This analogy is particularly effective at communicating the constraints faced by the Fed. In such a situation, it is no surprise that the Fed reacts cautiously to any new development. It is also no surprise that policymakers prefer the slow and steady approach, even to the point of excessive caution, over the speedy but perhaps brash approach.

Instrument Instability

If the Fed decides to pursue an intermediate target, it will have to adjust its instruments and operating targets to achieve it. Consider what might happen if the Fed chooses a price level intermediate target. The Fed will conduct open market purchases to increase the money supply whenever the price level falls below target and conduct open market sales to reduce the money supply when the price level rises above target. In this way, the Fed hopes to keep the price level near the targeted value.

Instrument instability can arise when a change in the instrument affects the targeted variable over a number of future periods. For instance, suppose an open market purchase causes the price level to rise, but not immediately. Instead, this effect takes place only gradually over a period of 12 months. Suppose further that the Fed wants to keep the price level constant from quarter to quarter. Then, if the price level is below target today, the Fed will conduct an open market purchase sufficient to raise the price level to the targeted value within three months. If the Fed is successful, the price level will be at target three months from now.

In the following three months, however, the increase in the money supply due to the open market purchase in the first three months continues to exert its influence on prices, causing the price level to rise further. The Fed can counteract this only through an open market sale to decrease the money supply. Furthermore, in the third three months, the initial increase in the money supply continues to cause prices to rise, while the reduction in the money supply during the second three months causes prices to fall. This dynamic continues, and the required open market operations necessary to merely counteract the previous changes in the money supply to keep the price level constant may dampen down to zero as the effects of past changes gradually wear off. Alternatively, they may increase over time so that even larger swings in the money supply, from positive to negative and back again, are required to hold the price level at target. The latter case is a situation of instrument instability, where the Fed must tolerate ever larger changes in the instrument to hold the targeted variable at target.

Due to the small initial effect of changes in the money stock on the price level, the substantial long-run effect of money on prices, and the long lags between changes in the money stock and the response of prices, instrument instability may hinder efforts to set an intermediate price level target from quarter to quarter. This problem can be countered most easily by lengthening the period over which the price level is controlled so that the price level is targeted to achieve a growth rate of, say, 3 percent over four quarters, but its quarter-to-quarter growth rate is not constrained further. An alternative solution is to attempt to adjust the monetary instrument today to keep forecasted future levels of prices at target. This approach accepts some failure to keep the current price level at target while maintaining the overall framework of price level targeting. However, it works best when the price level can be fairly well predicted, which may not be the case. A final solution is to use a variable that is more controllable, such as the money stock or an interest rate, instead of adopting an intermediate price level target.

Inaccurate Macroeconomic Models

Another issue in any policymaking activity is the recognition that the policymaker works with a model of the economy and our macroeconomic models are imperfect. Hence policy decisions that appear correct based on a particular macroeconomic model may turn out badly because the model used to formulate the policy is only an approximation of reality, and perhaps a poor one at that. Following policy advice, however nicely derived, from an inappropriate or incorrect theoretical model is potentially dangerous, since the advice may lead to exactly the wrong policy action. This gives policymakers another reason to move slowly, since gradual moves will not lead to catastrophes and can be reversed if a problem occurs. In fact, policy actions are influenced somewhat by theory but are also influenced by the years of experience most policymakers have.

Conflicting Goals

In this chapter, we have seen how monetary policymakers can have conflicting goals. We have seen how price level goals and output goals cause conflict when a change in aggregate supply occurs, since the policy action that achieves the price level target exacerbates the failure to achieve the output target, and vice versa. Other goals can also cause conflict, and indeed Tinbergen's results suggest that conflict is inevitable whenever there are more goals than independent instruments.

The conflict among some of the Fed's goals is caused by changes in the identities of policymakers over time. For example, administrations change, the control of Congress may someday change, and presidents may appoint new members to the Board of Governors, particularly the chairpersonship. When these changes occur, the new personnel often want to change the previous policies. Under the present institutional arrangements, there is little to prevent new monetary policymakers from changing monetary policy, making long-term commitment to a monetary policy very questionable.

Conflict among Policymakers

Not only can a single policymaker have internal conflicts over goals, but two policymakers—specifically the monetary policymaker and the fiscal policymaker—can choose conflicting goals. The monetary policymaker (the Fed) controls the money supply and can adjust it in the pursuit of various macroeconomic goals. The fiscal policymaker (Congress) controls government spending and tax collections and can adjust them as it pursues its macroeconomic goals. In many countries these two policymakers are under the control of the ruling government, but in the United States (as well as Germany and Switzerland) the monetary authority is largely independent of the fiscal policymaker. This has both benefits and costs, but one cost is that the monetary and fiscal policymakers may disagree over the goals of policy. For example, the fiscal authority might have an output target and the monetary authority a price level target. If aggregate supply increases, the monetary authority will want to raise aggregate demand, but the fiscal policymaker will want to reduce it. The net effect is unclear, but neither policymaker is likely to achieve its target.

CONCLUSION

In this chapter, we saw the importance of having enough independent instruments to accomplish the policy goals or final targets. We also looked at the choice of intermediate targets, from historical choices such as the money stock or interest rates to recent proposals for commodity price or nominal GDP targets. Then we discussed the Fed's operating procedures over the last two decades and mentioned some practical problems in making monetary policy. In the next chapter, we use the framework provided here to study monetary policy in more detail. In particular, we turn to the best choice of policy in a particular situation or with a specific goal in mind. We also see that monetary policymaking has important strategic considerations, which leads us into a discussion of monetary policy as a game.

KEY TERMS

monetary policy actions

instruments

targets

intermediate target

operating procedure

price stability

countercyclical policy

operating target

procyclical policy

implementation lag

information lag

recognition lag

legislative lag

effectiveness lag

instrument instability

QUESTIONS AND PROBLEMS

1. In the long-run model, aggregate supply increases. If the Fed's final target is a price level target, should it increase, decrease, or keep constant the money stock? Why?

Continued on p. 706

Continued from p. 705

2. In the long-run model, a negative aggregate demand shock occurs. If the final target of the Fed is a price level target, should it increase, decrease, or keep constant the money stock? Why?

3. In the long-run model, a negative aggregate supply shock and a positive aggregate demand shock occur. If the Fed's final target is a price level target, should it increase, decrease, or keep constant the money stock? Why?

4. In the long-run model, a negative aggregate demand shock and a negative aggregate supply shock occur. If the Fed's final target is a price level target, should it increase, decrease, or keep constant the money stock? Why?

5. What are the possible goals of monetary policy? Which are important to you, and why? What other goals can you think that you would want the Fed to pursue?

6. If the Fed has an intermediate price level target, what must it do when velocity increases? What if it has an intermediate money target? How and why would the responses differ?

7. In a short-run model with upward-sloping aggregate supply, oil prices have increased by a large amount, causing a negative supply shock. What do you predict will happen to the economy? If the president of the United States asks you for a list of policy options, what will you say? In particular, what if the president wants to restore output to its original level? What if the president wants to combat inflation?

8. In a short-run model with upward-sloping aggregate supply, both the price level and output have declined. What could have been the cause? If the policymaker has a final target for both the price level and output, what action should it take?

9. The president of the United States sees an economy with low output levels and wants to stimulate output without causing inflation. The president asks you for advice. How do you reply?

10. If the implementation and effectiveness lags together are a year or more, how might this change your thoughts on using policy to achieve intermediate price level targets or nominal GDP targets?

11. Assume the following short-run model with upward-sloping aggregate supply. The economy starts in equilibrium with aggregate demand and supply intersecting at point A, with a price level of P_A and output Y_A. The final target level of price and output is represented by point T, with a price level equal to P_A but output above Y_A. If aggregate supply increases, what monetary policy action would you recommend? Illustrate your answer graphically.

12. Assume the following short-run model with upward-sloping aggregate supply. The economy starts in equilibrium with aggregate demand and supply intersecting at point A, with a price level of P_A and output Y_A. The target level of price and output is represented by point T, with a price level above P_A and output equal to Y_A. If aggregate demand decreases, what monetary policy action would you recommend? Illustrate your answer graphically.

13. Assume the economy is best represented by the long-run model, but the Fed thinks the aggregate supply curve is upward sloping. How can the Fed's policy decisions be adversely influenced by its use of the wrong model? Be specific and use graphical analysis.

14. Assume the economy is best represented by a model with upward-sloping aggregate supply, but the Fed thinks the aggregate supply curve is vertical. How can the Fed's policy decisions be adversely influenced by its use of the wrong model? Be specific and use graphical analysis.

SELECTIONS FOR FURTHER READING

Allen, S. D., and D. L. McCrickard. "The Influence of Elections on Federal Reserve Behavior." *Economics Letters,* 37 (September 1991), 51–55.

Ball, L., and S. G. Cecchetti. "Wage Indexation and Discretionary Monetary Policy." *American Economic Review,* 81 (December 1991), 1310–1319.

Barth, J., R. Sickles, and P. Wiest. "Assessing the Impact of Varying Economic Conditions on Federal Reserve Behavior." *Journal of Macroeconomics,* 4 (Winter 1982), 47–70.

Bradley, M. D., and D. W. Jansen. "Understanding Nominal GDP Targeting." Federal Reserve Bank of St. Louis *Review,* 71 (November 1989), 31–40.

Cecchetti, S. G. "Testing Short-run Neutrality." *Journal of Monetary Economics,* 17 (May 1986), 409–423.

Chou, N. T. "An Alternative Monetary Policy Target: The New Benchmark Divisia Monetary Index." *Applied Economics,* 23 (November 1991), 1699–1705.

Falk, B., and P. F. Orazem. "The Role of Systematic Fed Errors in Explaining the Money Supply Announcements Puzzle: A Note." *Journal of Money, Credit, and Banking,* 21 (August 1989), 401–406.

Karamouzis, N., and R. E. Lombra. "Federal Reserve Policy Making: An Overview and Analysis of the Policy Process, *Carnegie-Rochester Series on Public Policy,* (July 1989).

Luckett, D. G., and G. T. Potts. "Monetary Policy and Partisan Politics: A Note." *Journal of Money, Credit, and Banking,* 12 (August 1980), 540–546.

Mankiw, N. G., and J. A. Miron. "Should the Fed Smooth Interest Rates? The Case of Seasonal Monetary Policy." *Carnegie-Rochester Conference Series on Public Policy,* (Spring 1991), 41–69.

Marquis, M. H., and S. R. Cunningham. "Financial Innovation, Price Smoothing, and Monetary Policy." *Economic Inquiry,* 28 (October 1990), 831–850.

Witte, W. E. "Expectations, Monetary Policy Rules, and Macroeconomic Stability: Analysis of an Open Economy with Flexible Exchange Rates." *Journal of International Economics,* 11 (August 1981), 379–394.

20

Monetary Policy: Rules, Discretion, and Games

A problem every nation faces at one time or another is periods of recession. In the United States, for instance, dramatic rises in oil prices in the mid- and late 1970s led to periods of decline in real output. Between 1982 and 1990, the U.S. economy had one of the longest periods of sustained growth in real output, only to see real output fall again during the 1991 recession. Are these periods of recession unavoidable, or can unilateral actions by the Fed keep the economy from such declines?

Another problem nations frequently confront is periods of inflation. During the late 1970s and early 1980s, the U.S. inflation rate exceeded 10 percent. Can the Fed take unilateral actions that cure inflation, or is it beyond its ability to do anything at all about inflation? If there are policies the Fed can take to counter recessions or rises in the price level, should it actively pursue them?

In this chapter, we explore these issues and look at alternative views on the role of monetary policy in the economy. Some economists believe the Fed should actively pursue policies designed to stabilize the economy in the short run, whereas others think such active policies do more harm than good. This debate is heightened by another source of disagreement: Monetary policy can be implemented by either rules or discretion, and some economists have strong views on which approach is better. We will use the game theory apparatus developed in Chapter 5 to shed light on some of the reasons for this divergence of opinion.

SHOULD THE FED PURSUE AN ACTIVE OR PASSIVE MONETARY POLICY?

Imagine that short-run aggregate supply has drastically declined due to a dramatic rise in the price of oil brought on by increased tensions in the Middle East. Real GDP declines by 5 percent, and unemployment soars to nearly 12 percent. Should the Fed sit back and do nothing, or should it increase the money supply in an attempt to bring down interest rates, thus spurring investment, consumption, and aggregate demand? Monetary activists—those in favor of **active monetary policy**—argue that the Fed should not sit idly by in such times of economic upheaval and would favor such actions by the Fed. In contrast, some economists prefer a **passive monetary policy,** believing the Fed should do nothing in response to such shocks to the economy. In this section, we explore the reasons economists hold these different views and the implications of these views for the overall performance of the economy.

The Case for Active Monetary Policy

The U.S. economy is subject to periodic shifts in aggregate demand and supply that change the price level and real output. For instance, it experienced two major oil shocks in the past two decades: one in 1973 as a result of the Six-Day War in the Middle East and one in 1979 following the overthrow of the Shah of Iran. These oil shocks caused a temporary decline in aggregate supply, which ultimately led to temporary increases in the price level and declines in real GDP during the 1973–1975 and 1979–1982 periods (see Box 20.1 on p. 710). The U.S. economy also experiences temporary shocks to aggregate demand from time to time. One notable rise in aggregate demand was brought on by increased spending on the Vietnam War and by President Johnson's Great Society programs during the 1965–1968 period. This led to a rise in the price level, which at the time seemed unacceptable.

What should an activist Fed do in response to such changes in aggregate demand or aggregate supply? In discussing the case for activist monetary policy, we first look at what the Fed can do in the long run and then examine the effects of activist policy in the short run. We will see that the case for activist Fed policies changes as we move from the long run to the short run.

Activist Policies in the Long Run.
We saw in Chapter 16 that long-run real output is determined by the natural rate of output—the output the economy can produce with its given stock of productive resources, such as capital and labor. Consequently the long-run aggregate supply curve is vertical, meaning that Fed policies do not affect the economy's long-run real output. However, activist policies by the Fed can influence the long-run price level. To illustrate this, we first look at how activist policies can stabilize the price level when decreases in aggregate demand occur. Then we examine how activist policies can keep the price level from rising in the wake of declines in aggregate supply.

A Decrease in Aggregate Demand.
Suppose the economy is initially in long-run equilibrium at point A in Figure 20.1. Aggregate demand is given by AD, the price level is P_A, and real output is at its natural rate of Y_0. If there is an unanticipated decline in aggregate demand from AD to AD_1, the long-run equilibrium will move from point A to point B. Thus, if

The initial equilibrium is at point A. If aggregate demand declines to AD_1, the long-run equilibrium will move to point B if the Fed does nothing (passive policy), and thus the price level will fall to P_B. However, if the Fed increases the money supply by the correct amount, aggregate demand will return to AD, and the long-run equilibrium will be restored at point A. This illustrates that activist policy may be used to stabilize the long-run price level at P_A.

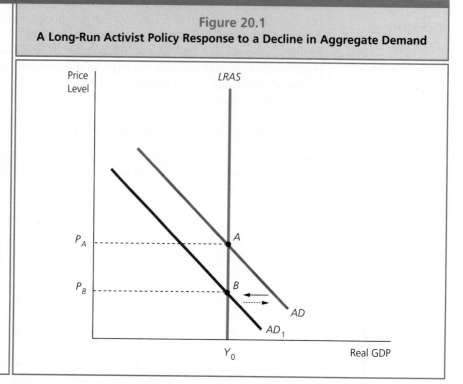

Figure 20.1
A Long-Run Activist Policy Response to a Decline in Aggregate Demand

the Fed pursues a passive monetary policy, the long-run effect of the negative shock to aggregate demand will be for real output to remain at Y_0, but the price level will fall from P_A to P_B.

The argument goes that the decline in the price level is costly to firms and consumers. In particular, firms must expend resources changing price tags, only to sell the same real output as they did before the decline in the price level. Furthermore, in the short run other costs are associated with a decline in the price level that are not captured in this long-run picture. For instance, consumers and firms might face financial strains as their debt obligations remain unchanged while incomes, the value of inventories, and the value of assets like real estate fall due to the decline in the price level. These short-run costs to consumers and firms can likewise be eliminated if the Fed pursues an activist policy.

In particular, suppose the Fed increases the money supply when it learns that aggregate demand has declined to AD_1 in Figure 20.1. This increase in the money supply shifts aggregate demand back to AD, restoring the long-run equilibrium at point A. At point A, the price level is at its initial level, and thus consumers and firms do not suffer the consequences of changes in

The Data Bank

Box 20.1

*The Path of the Price Level
and Output over Time*

Two goals of the Fed are a stable price level and consistent output growth. When the Fed makes policy decisions, it considers the effects of its decisions on these two variables as well as the effects on other policy targets. The accompanying figure plots both the path of the price level and real GDP (part a) and the path of the inflation rate and real GDP (part b) during the 1972–1992 period. We can use this information in conjunction with our knowledge of historical events to help identify periods in recent U.S. history when the economy was subject to changes in aggregate demand or supply.

For example, in the fall of 1973 OPEC raised the price of oil nearly fourfold. Economists

widely identified this as causing a reduction in aggregate supply. In the figure, we see that 1973 did mark the beginning of a two-year decline in real GDP, accompanied by a rising price level and higher inflation, especially in 1975. This is the sort of effect predicted when the aggregate supply curve shifts to the left.

From 1975 to 1979, we see a fairly steady increase in real GDP each year. We also see continual increases in the price level and a rising rate of inflation. This is evidence that while the economy was growing and aggregate supply was increasing, aggregate demand was also shifting to the right, and at a fast enough pace

Continued on p. 712

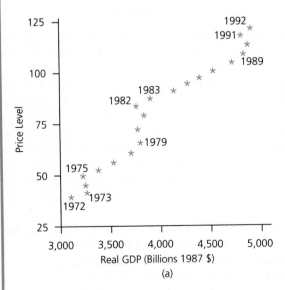

(a)

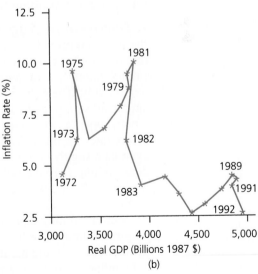

(b)

Continued from p. 711
to cause a continuing rise in the price level. Then, in 1979 came oil price hikes in connection with the fall of the shah of Iran and the taking of U.S. hostages by Iran. The resulting shift in aggregate supply caused the recession in 1980. Note that the inflation rate continued to increase even during the recession year, 1980, and rose again in 1981.

In 1982 we had another recession, but this one differed from the recessions in 1974–1975 and 1980. Now real GDP fell, but the inflation rate also dropped dramatically. This marked the beginning of the great reduction in inflation engineered by Paul Volcker (then chair of the Fed's Board of Governors) and supported by President Reagan. By slowing the growth of aggregate

demand, the Fed caused a reduction in output and in the rate of growth of prices. This can be contrasted with a recession due to aggregate supply, in which output would fall and the inflation rate would rise.

Finally, what about our most recent recession in 1991? This recession was also marked by a reduction in both the inflation rate and output, and can be identified with a reduction in aggregate demand. What factors contributed to this fall in aggregate demand? Two factors that stand out are the increases in taxes during 1990, as President Bush violated his "no new taxes" pledge, and the reduction in military spending with the end of the Cold War and the winding down of the Gulf War expenditures.

the price level. Thus, we see that activist policies can stabilize the price level, which eliminates price fluctuations due to changes in aggregate demand. Passive policy, on the other hand, results in fluctuations in the price level, meaning firms and consumers are continually strained by changes in the price level resulting from shifts in aggregate demand.

A Decrease in Aggregate Supply.

Can activist policies stabilize the long-run price level when a change in aggregate supply occurs? To see that the answer is yes, look at Figure 20.2. The economy begins in equilibrium at point A, with aggregate demand and supply given by AD and $LRAS$, respectively. The equilibrium price and output levels are P_A and Y_0. Suppose aggregate supply decreases, perhaps due to falling productivity, a declining labor supply, an increase in the price of imported oil, or increased regulation or tax rates on business or labor. Regardless of the cause, the reduction in aggregate supply is represented by the shift from $LRAS$ to $LRAS_1$. If the Fed does nothing (passive policy), the long-run equilibrium changes from point A to point B. In this case, the price level rises from P_A to P_B and output falls to Y_1.

Activist policy can affect the long-run equilibrium price level but not long-run output. The long-run decline in output in Figure 20.2 was caused by a reduction in the natural rate of output, and the Fed's instruments allow it to influence only aggregate demand. However, the Fed's influence on aggregate demand enables the Fed to stabilize the price level by pursuing an activist policy. In particular, if the economy moves to point B, prices in the economy rise, and firms must adjust their prices accordingly. If the Fed

Figure 20.2
A Long-Run Activist Policy Response to a Decline in Aggregate Supply

The initial equilibrium is at point A. If long-run aggregate supply declines to $LRAS_1$ and the Fed does nothing (passive policy), long-run equilibrium moves to point B. At B, output is lower (Y_1) and the price level is higher (P_B) than at A. Since the Fed cannot affect the natural rate of output, even an activist Fed cannot change this lower output level in the long run. However, if the Fed decreases the money supply by the correct amount, aggregate demand will fall to AD_1, resulting in an equilibrium at point C. Thus, the Fed can use activist monetary policy to stabilize the long-run price level at P_A, but it cannot affect long-run output.

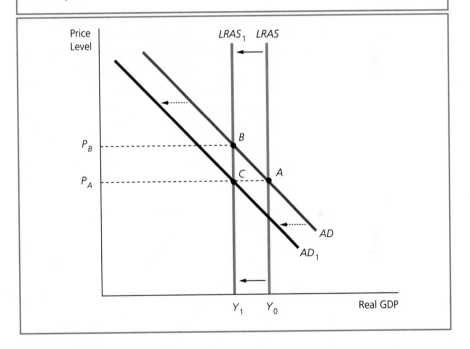

decreases the money supply, aggregate demand will fall from AD to AD_1, resulting in a new long-run equilibrium at point C. At C the price level is the same as at A, and thus firms do not need to change their prices.

The case for activist policy in the long run is thus very simple: By reducing the money supply when prices rise or increasing it when prices fall, the Fed can stabilize the price level. This means consumers and firms are not subject to the price variability that result from long-run fluctuations in aggregate demand or supply.

Activist Policies in the Short Run.   Since the short-run aggregate supply curve is not vertical, in the short run monetary policy will affect not only the price level but real output as well. To illustrate the case for activist policy in the short run, we next look at how activist policies can stabilize the economy in the wake of declining aggregate demand or short-run aggregate supply.

A Decrease in Aggregate Demand.

Figure 20.3 illustrates a reduction in aggregate demand. The economy begins in equilibrium at point A, where aggregate demand AD intersects short-run aggregate supply $SRAS$. The price level and real output are P_A and Y_A, respectively. Suppose aggregate demand decreases to AD_1. If the Fed does nothing, the new short-run equilibrium will be at point B, with a lower price level, P_B, and lower real

---

Figure 20.3
An Activist Policy to Stabilize the Economy in the Short Run in Response to a Decline in Aggregate Demand

The initial equilibrium is at point A. If aggregate demand declines to AD_1, the short-run equilibrium will move to point B if the Fed does nothing (passive policy), and thus the price level and real output will fall to P_B and Y_B, respectively. However, if the Fed increases the money supply by the correct amount, aggregate demand will return to AD, and the short-run equilibrium will be restored at point A. This illustrates that activist policy may be used to stabilize the short-run price level and short-run real output when a change occurs only in aggregate demand.

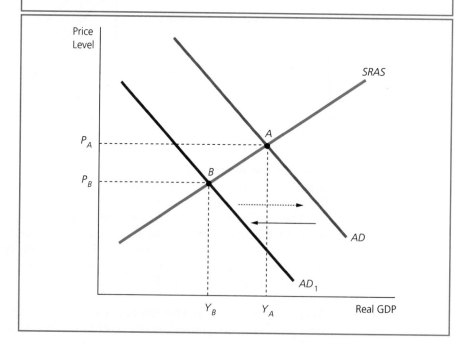

output, Y_B. The decline in aggregate demand leads to lower real output, and as a consequence fewer workers are needed to produce the economy's output. Some workers will be laid off, resulting in a rise in the unemployment rate.

Can activist policy eliminate the adverse effects of the decline in aggregate demand? In principle, yes. If the Fed responds to the decline in aggregate demand by increasing the money supply, aggregate demand will shift back to *AD*. This activist policy restores the initial equilibrium and returns both the price level and output to their initial values. Thus, we see that an activist policy of increasing the money supply when aggregate demand falls not only stabilizes short-run prices but also keeps short-run output from declining. Advocates of activist monetary policy naturally argue that the Fed should not sit back and watch output fall and unemployment rise when a simple injection of money into the economy can completely offset the adverse effects of falling aggregate demand.

A Decrease in Aggregate Supply.

Figure 20.4 shows a decrease in short-run aggregate supply. We will see that this creates somewhat of a dilemma for the Fed, since it finds itself having to choose between two evils.

In Figure 20.4, aggregate demand and supply start at *AD* and *SRAS*, so the initial short-run equilibrium is at point *A;* the initial price level is P_A, and output is at Y_A. A negative shock to supply shifts aggregate supply to $SRAS_1$, which moves the short-run equilibrium to point *B* if the Fed decides to do nothing. Thus, passive policy will result in a higher price level (P_B) and a lower real output level (Y_B) in the short run.

Can activist policy completely restore the economy to the initial equilibrium? The answer is no. To see this, notice that by increasing the money supply, an activist Fed could shift aggregate demand to AD_2, resulting in a short-run equilibrium at point *C*. This equilibrium has the same output as at point *A*, but a higher price level. Alternatively, the Fed could decrease the money supply, which would shift aggregate demand from *AD* to AD_1. This movement from point *B* to point *D* would return price to its original level (P_A) but result in an even more adverse effect on output, which would fall to Y_D.

Thus, when facing a decline in short-run aggregate supply, an activist Fed has the difficult choice between either moving the economy from point *B* to point *C* or moving it from point *B* to point *D*. The first choice keeps output from declining, but the expansionary monetary policy is inflationary. The second choice keeps the price level stable, but the contractionary monetary policy lowers real output more than doing nothing does. One thing is clear, however: Through appropriate increases or decreases in the money supply, activist policy allows the Fed to choose any equilibrium between point *D* and point *C* on the new short-run aggregate supply curve, $SRAS_1$. Which point it chooses depends on the strength of the Fed's preferences for keeping output constant or keeping inflation in check. The dilemma illustrated in Figure 20.4 is precisely the one the Fed faced in 1973, when OPEC

The initial equilibrium is at point A. If short-run aggregate supply declines to $SRAS_1$ and the Fed does nothing (passive policy), short run equilibrium moves to point B. At point B, output is lower (Y_B) and the price level is higher (P_B) than at point A. Since the Fed cannot affect aggregate supply, an activist Fed faces a difficult choice: It can either increase the money supply to shift aggregate demand to AD_2 to move the economy to a new short-run equilibrium at point C or reduce the money supply to move the economy to point D. Point C corresponds with the initial level of output (Y_A) but a higher price level (P_C); point D has a lower level of output (Y_D) but the initial price level (P_A). Whether the Fed chooses to stabilize real output (point C) or the price level (point D) is likely to be a tough political issue.

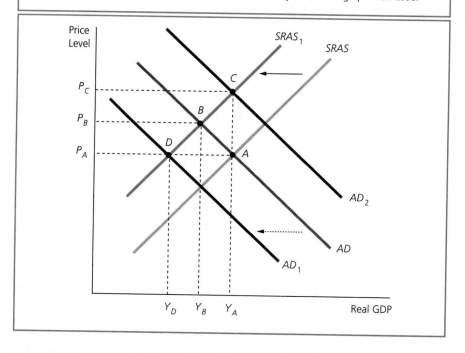

first hiked the price of oil by 200 percent. The Fed and other central banks around the globe faced a choice of fighting either the rise in prices or the decline in real output. The problem, as we first saw in Chapter 19, is that the Fed's instruments do not permit it to simultaneously solve both problems.

Proponents of activist policies point out that such policies at least allow the Fed to tackle either rising prices or lower real output when aggregate supply declines, whereas passive policies do not. But even among those who favor activist policies, debate sometimes arises about whether the better policy is to meet such supply shocks with increases or decreases in the money supply. Activists most concerned with jobs tend to focus on real output; those most concerned about inflation tend to emphasize the price level. Thus, in addition to the disagreements among economists that stem from the focus on short or long run models, there are disagreements that occur because the Fed's tools force it to choose between two evils. Box 20.2 looks at the extent to which these decisions vary depending on the party that controls the White House.

The Case for Passive Monetary Policy

The preceding analysis provides a very strong case for active monetary policy. We see that it can reduce, or in some instances entirely eliminate, the adverse effects of shocks to aggregate demand or short-run aggregate supply. Given this argument, you might wonder how anyone can dispute the merits of activist policy. But as we will see next, there are strong reasons the Fed should be, at the very least, extremely cautious in using monetary policy to eliminate the adverse effects of temporary shocks to the economy. We now discuss each of these arguments against activist policy.

It Takes Time for Monetary Policy to Have Effects.
We saw in Chapter 18 that real GDP is very slow to increase in response to a rise in the money supply. If an oil shock lasts only a few years, as did that of 1979, by the time the economy feels the full impact of the increase in the money supply called for by monetary activists, supply will already be back to normal. In this instance, activist policy actually increases the length of time it takes the economy to reach long-run equilibrium.

To see this, consider Figure 20.5 on p. 720, where the economy is initially at point A. A supply shock decreases short-run aggregate supply from $SRAS_0$ to $SRAS_1$, moving the economy to point B. The short-run effect of the negative supply shock is to reduce the level of real output and increase the price level. If the reduction in aggregate supply is only temporary, long-run aggregate supply does not shift. In this case, if the Fed does nothing, the economy will return to point A in, say, two years, when the oil shock ends and supply returns to $SRAS_0$.

If the Fed pursues an activist monetary policy today, it shifts aggregate demand to AD_1. But due to lags in the effect of changes in the money supply, as we saw in Chapter 18, the full impact of this increase in the money supply on aggregate demand will only be felt in two years, when aggregate supply is already back to $SRAS_0$. This means that in two years, the economy will be at point C—above the natural rate. Point C is not a long-run equilibrium, however, and over the next few years output will fall until the new long-run equilibrium is reached at point D—at a higher price level but the natural rate of output, Y_0.

Now think about what we just saw. If the Fed is passive (does nothing), the economy will be in long-run equilibrium at point A in two years, with a

Inside Money

Box 20.2

Inflation and Politics

Conventional wisdom has it that Republicans oppose inflation, whereas Democrats are willing to accept inflation in their greater concern about unemployment. However, as the accompanying table indicates, the U.S. experience with inflation during the various presidential administrations is quite diverse, and periods of high inflation cannot be identified with any one party. As we learned in Chapter 13, one reason is that the Fed is largely independent of the political process, and newly elected presidents inherit the Fed chair selected by the previous administration. Consequently, sometimes monetary policy during a Republican presidency is set by a Fed chair selected by a Democrat, and vice versa.

Nonetheless, notice in the table that the highest average inflation rate over a four-year administration, 8.2 percent, did occur during the administration of Jimmy Carter, a Democrat, and by the end of his term in office the inflation rate was hovering at 10 percent per year. But the greatest *increase* in the inflation rate occurred during 1973 through 1976, a period in which Nixon and then, after his resignation, Ford held office. In fact, the run-up in the inflation rate during the 1969–1976 period totaled 4.2 percent, the largest increase in the inflation rate during any one administration. The greatest increase in inflation during a Democrat's four-

Continued on p. 719

Years	Incumbent [Party]	Average Inflation Rate During Term in Office	Change from Previous Administration
1949–1952	Truman [D]	1.8%	NA
1953–1956	Eisenhower [R]	2.4	+.6
1957–1960	Eisenhower [R]	2.5	+.1
1961–1964	Kennedy/Johnson [D]	1.5	−1.0
1965–1968	Johnson [D]	3.5	+2.0
1969–1972	Nixon [R]	5.1	+1.6
1973–1976	Nixon/Ford [R]	7.7	+2.6
1977–1980	Carter [D]	8.2	+.5
1981–1984	Reagan [R]	6.2	−2.0
1985–1988	Reagan [R]	3.3	−2.9
1989–1992	Bush [R]	3.9	+.6
1993–1996	Clinton [D]	?	?

Continued from p. 718
year term was 2 percent—Johnson during 1965 through 1968. There were no eight-year Democratic administrations, although if we count the Kennedy/Johnson and Johnson administrations together, we have a mere 1 percent increase over the second Eisenhower administration.

If conventional wisdom has any truth, it must be from the decade of the 1980s. Ronald Reagan was president during the largest decrease in the inflation rate in the post–World War II United States. During his first term, inflation declined by 2 percent and dropped by another 2.9 percent during his second term. The average inflation rate for his second term, 3.3 percent, was the lowest for a four-year term since the Kennedy/Johnson administration of 1961 through 1964.

price level of P_A and real output of Y_0. If Fed policy is active, output will be below the natural rate (at point B) for the first two years, since it takes time for the Fed's policy to work. And once the policy does take effect, it will be too late. The activist policy only moves the economy to point C two years from now, which is above the natural rate. Consequently, prices will rise further and output will decline for an additional two years until the economy ultimately returns to long-run equilibrium at point D, where the price level is P_D and real output is Y_0. Thus, according to advocates of passive monetary policy, activist monetary policy can actually lengthen the time it takes the economy to reach the natural rate of output (Y_0) and result in higher inflation in the process.

Policy Actions That Are Too Large Are Dangerous.

The second argument for passive monetary policy is that the Fed can do more harm than good if it does not inject the proper amount of money into the economy. On paper (in our case, Figures 20.1 through 20.4), it is easy to see that the right dose of activist policy by the Fed can fix the economy's problem. But in reality, the precise location of the aggregate demand and supply curves is not known, nor is it known exactly how much the money supply must be increased to generate the cure. Thus, some economists argue, even a well-intentioned Fed is as likely to provide too much money as too little. The wrong monetary injection can harm the economy, much as the wrong dose of insulin can harm a diabetic. Those who favor passive monetary policy view the best policy as a hands-off one that will allow the economy to ultimately return to its long-run equilibrium through the natural self-correcting movements in short-run aggregate supply.

Activist Policy Can Be Addictive.

Opponents of activist monetary policy also argue that it may be difficult for the Fed to withdraw any money supply increase once the temporary shock is over. To see this argument, again consider Figure 20.5. The economy is initially at point A, but the temporary oil shock shifts short-run aggregate supply from $SRAS_0$ to

Figure 20.5
Potential Dangers of Activist Policy

The initial equilibrium is at point A. A temporary reduction in aggregate supply to $SRAS_1$ changes the equilibrium to point B. If the Fed does nothing, the equilibrium will return to point A in the long run, when the supply shock is over and short-run aggregate supply shifts back to $SRAS_0$—say, in two years. If the Fed pursues an activist policy in an attempt to shift aggregate demand to AD_1, the result could backfire. In particular, if it takes two years for increases in the money supply to take effect, the economy will already be back at point A when the full effects of the monetary policy are felt. Due to the lagged effect of monetary policy, this means the Fed's activist policy actually moves the economy to point C in two years. Since point C is not a long-run equilibrium, it will take two additional years for prices to adjust and for the economy to reach the final equilibrium under activist policy at point D. Thus, activist policy may actually increase the time it takes to get to long-run equilibrium (here from two years to four) and result in a higher price level (P_D) than passive policy would create (P_A).

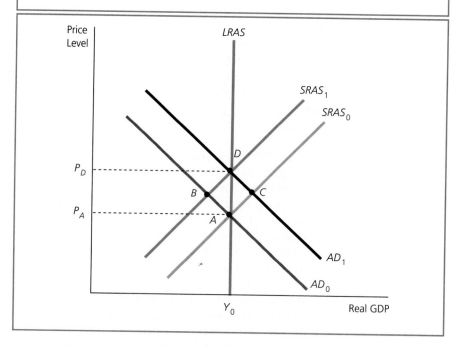

$SRAS_1$, resulting in a short-run equilibrium at point B. (The long run aggregate supply curve is not affected, since the oil price shock is temporary). Suppose the Fed increases the money supply in the correct dose, which (ignoring lagged effects) increases aggregate demand from AD_0 to AD_1 and thus moves the economy to a new equilibrium at point D. When the supply shock is over, aggregate supply will shift back to $SRAS_0$, resulting in another short-run equilibrium at point C—unless the Fed decreases the money supply. If the Fed removes the injection of money used to treat the economy, aggregate demand shifts back to AD_0, which returns us to point A—the long-run equilibrium. But if it does not, the short-run equilibrium is at point C—where prices are higher than at point A and rise further in the long run until we ultimately reach long-run equilibrium at point D. Notice that by failing to reduce the money supply and ending the policy treatment, the Fed actually generates a temporary rise in real output—at the expense of workers who are being paid lower real wages due to rising prices. In the long run, wages will rise and the economy will return to point D. Those opposed to activist policies fear the Fed may be less willing to reduce the money supply once the supply shock is over than it was to increase it in the first place. If the Fed does not reduce the money supply, the policy will lead to a period of rapidly rising prices until the economy ultimately returns to its natural rate of output and long-run equilibrium at point D with a higher price level. Later in this chapter, we will see that some economists believe the only way to eliminate this temptation is to take away the Fed's discretion in making monetary policy.

Even the Fed Makes Mistakes.   The final argument against activist policy is that it puts too much power in the hands of a few people who are prone to make mistakes or other errors in judgment. Milton Friedman, for instance, does not think the Fed should be given the power to doctor the economy but instead should be forced to adopt the passive policy of increasing the growth of money by 3 percent per year, regardless of any shocks to demand or supply. Friedman wrote,

> *Any system which gives so much power and so much discretion to a few men that . . . can have such far reaching effects is a bad system. It is a bad system to believers in freedom just because it gives a few men such power without any effective check by the body politic—this is the key political argument against an "independent" central bank. But it is a bad system even to those who set security [of the banking system] higher than freedom. Mistakes . . . cannot be avoided in a system which disperses responsibility yet gives a few men great power, and which thereby makes important policy actions highly dependent on accidents of personality.*[1]

So Who's Right?

The arguments for and against activist monetary policy clearly have merit. While economists differ in their views on this issue, most believe the Fed should merely let nature take its course when small or short-term shocks to the economy occur. There is much greater disagreement about whether the Fed should pursue activist policy for large or long-term shocks. One major

---

[1] Milton Friedman, *Capitalism and Freedom* (Chicago: University of Chicago Press, 1962), p. 50.

source of the disagreement concerns precisely what constitutes a "long-term" or "large" shock. Since there are Nobel laureates on both sides of this issue— Milton Friedman opposes activist policy, whereas James Tobin favors it—we'll let you form your own judgment about who is right.

Summary **Exercise 20.1**

Suppose a permanent increase in aggregate demand occurs. (a) What will be the short-run and long-run effects on the price level and real output if the Fed pursues a passive monetary policy? (b) On paper, is there an activist monetary policy that would keep the economy at the natural rate of output without causing any rise in the price level? (c) What are the potential dangers of your prescribed activist policy? In answering these questions, use graphs where appropriate.

Answer: (a) The accompanying figure illustrates the increase in aggregate demand. The initial equilibrium is at point *T*. The increase in aggregate demand from *AD* to AD_1 moves the short-run equilibrium to point *A*. Under a passive policy, this is the new short-run equilibrium, with a price level of P_A and output Y_A. In the long run wages will rise, shifting short-run aggregate supply to $SRAS_1$, and the new long-run equilibrium is at point *B*. Thus, the long-run effect of a passive policy is a price level of P_B and output of Y_0. (b) The Fed can take actions to counter the increase in the price level and real output associated with the move from point *T* to point *A*. To do so, the activist Fed reduces the money supply and hence aggregate demand, returning equilibrium to point *T*. There is no change in output or the price level from their original levels, and no further long-run adjustments occur. Point *T* can thus be restored as both the long-run and short-run equilibrium under an activist policy. (c) Some dangers of the activist policy are that the Fed can make a mistake, overshooting or undershooting its target for aggregate

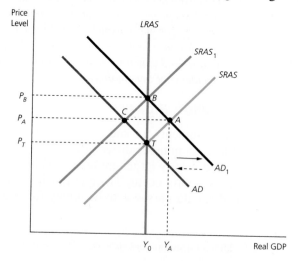

demand. Also, the Fed may be unable to respond quickly enough in reducing the money supply, or the economy may not respond quickly enough to the reduction in the money supply, so that by the time the reduction in aggregate demand occurs, the short-run aggregate supply curve has already shifted to $SRAS_1$. In this case, the policy can lead to a short-run equilibrium at a point like C, with higher prices and lower output than at T or A.

SHOULD MONETARY POLICY BE GUIDED BY RULES OR BY DISCRETION?

There is also considerable debate about whether Fed policies, be they activist or passive, should be determined at the Fed's own discretion or by a monetary policy rule. A **monetary policy rule** is a formula by which the money supply is set each period. It might be a passive rule—such as Milton Freidman's 3 percent growth rule, which says the money supply should grow 3 percent each year—or an activist rule such as the rule that monetary growth must decline by 7 percent if inflation ever reaches 10 percent. Many monetary policy rules are possible, but their key feature is that they carve into stone the policy actions of the Fed and thus preclude it from changing its policy at whim.

In contrast, **discretionary monetary policy** gives the Fed the flexibility to respond however it sees fit, with no constraint to follow some preexisting rule. With discretionary policy, the Fed might cut the money supply this month to counter inflation but do nothing two years from now when inflation is equally high. Without a rule, the Fed can alter its policies from year to year, or even from day to day, in any way it likes. This does not mean it will intentionally pursue bad policies. It means that whatever policies the Fed pursues, well intentioned or not, it is not bound to pursue the same policies in the future.

You might wonder whether it matters if the Fed's policies are carved in stone, particularly if the policies are activist policies designed to help the economy. If the Fed is interested in changing the money supply solely to maintain high output, low unemployment, and a low rate of inflation, will it be equally capable of achieving this activist goal under rules and under discretion? There are two views on this issue. One is that rules allow the Fed to function better than discretion does; the other is that the best policy is discretionary policy. We examine each view next.

The Case for Discretionary Monetary Policy

The main argument for discretionary policy is that it allows the Fed flexibility: The Fed can always choose to follow the dictates of a rule if doing so is the best way to increase real GDP, reduce unemployment, or lower inflation, but it still has the right and the ability to abandon the rule at its discretion. In contrast, monetary rules are a straightjacket that hinder the

Fed's functioning in its role as the central bank. Monetary policy rules, the argument goes, sacrifice the Fed's freedom of action without any offsetting benefit. Since the Fed can, at its discretion, always choose to use a rule to guide its policies, this flexibility subsumes rules as a special case of discretion. We examine a few additional arguments for discretion at the end of this section when we discuss the discretion today's Fed enjoys.

The Case for Monetary Policy Rules

The argument in favor of monetary policy rules is that in the absence of such rules, the Fed cannot credibly pursue monetary policies that will benefit the economy. We examine this through a simple example that illustrates the pitfalls of discretionary policy and the benefits of a monetary policy rule.

An Example of Fed Impotence Caused by Discretion.

Suppose the economy is in equilibrium at point *A* in Figure 20.6 and the Fed has the discretion to pursue whatever monetary policy it chooses. Despite its discretionary power, however, the Fed's goal is to achieve high output, low unemployment, and a low rate of inflation. One day the Fed makes the following announcement to labor unions:

> *Over the past three years the price level has been rising at 10 percent per year, and you have demanded 10 percent nominal wage hikes just to keep up with the higher cost of living. We must do something to stop this inflation, and here's what we'll do. We at the Fed will reduce the money supply by 7 percent if you will lower your nominal wage demands by 7 percent. Your reduced wage demands, coupled with our 7 percent reduction in the money supply, will lower the price level by 7 percent. With prices 7 percent lower, you will not need higher nominal wages anyway. In fact, if you go along with us, we'll immediately end up with a lower price level, at no cost to real GDP, employment, or your real wages!*

Let us use our aggregate demand and supply apparatus to evaluate the Fed's announcement. Starting at point *A*, if the Fed reduces the money supply by 7 percent and the labor union simultaneously reduces its wage demands by 7 percent, two things happen. First, the short-run aggregate supply curve shifts to the right to $SRAS_1$, due to the reduction in wages. Second, the reduction in the money supply shifts aggregate demand to the left of AD_1. As a result, the economy immediately moves from point *A* to point *D*, a new long-run equilibrium. At *D* real GDP is the same as at *A*, but the price level is 7 percent lower; the changes suggested by the Fed have indeed resulted in the same level of output and a lower price level. In fact, since the same level of output is produced at *D* as at *A*, it is also the case that the same number of workers are employed, and at the same real wage, as at *A*. Thus, the Fed's announcement is indeed correct: If workers and the Fed simulta-

Figure 20.6
Fed Impotence Caused by Discretion

Here the economy begins at point *A*. If workers take a 7 percent wage cut, short-run aggregate supply shifts to $SRAS_1$, with equilibrium at point *B*. If the Fed cuts the money supply by 7 percent, aggregate demand shifts leftward to AD_1, and equilibrium is at point *C*. Finally, if workers take a 7 percent pay cut *and* the Fed cuts the money supply by 7 percent, the equilibrium is at point *D*. Point *D* implies the same real output and real wage as at point *A*, but the price level is 7 percent lower than at *A*. While workers are no worse off at point *D* than they are at point *A*, they will be unwilling to accept wage cuts because they fear the Fed will renege on its promise to cut the money supply to move the economy to point *B*. Thus, the economy will remain at point *A* because neither workers nor the Fed find it in their interest to unilaterally take actions to lower the price level.

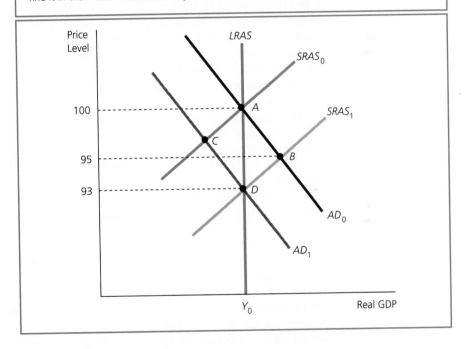

neously reduce wages and the money supply, the price level will fall with no adverse effects on real GDP, real wages, or employment.

Based on this reasoning, you might be tempted to conclude that the union would gladly sign a collective bargaining agreement with 7 percent nominal wage cuts. But if the union is smart, it will not sign such an agreement. Let us see why.

By signing an agreement with lower wages, the union has effectively locked itself into supplying labor at this nominal wage for the life of the contract—say, three years. This means that for the next three years, the short-run aggregate supply curve in Figure 20.6 is $SRAS_1$. Once the contract is signed, look what would happen if the Fed reneged on its promise to reduce the money supply. Aggregate demand would remain at AD_0, and the short-run equilibrium would move to point B. At B, real output and total employment in the economy are greater than they would otherwise be if the Fed cut the money supply as promised. This will most certainly tempt the Fed to renege on its promise, and who could blame it? Doing so will lead to higher real GDP and employment, and the economy will flourish for three years. Thus, we see the Fed has every incentive to renege on its promise to lower the money supply once the union contract is signed.

How do the union members fare if the Fed reneges? At point B in Figure 20.6, the nominal wage of union members is 7 percent lower than at point A, but prices are only 5 percent lower. Union workers are worse off, because their real wages will be lower over the next three years than they are at either point A or point D. In fact, it is this lower real wage that generates the increase in output from A to B. The stimulating effect on the economy comes out of the hides of workers if their unions sign such contracts. For this reason, smart union leaders will not fall victim to such ploys by a Fed that can pursue discretionary monetary policy. We stay at point A.

Proponents of monetary rules argue that the economy can move from point A to point D only if the Fed's hands are tied in a way that precludes it from reneging on its promises. For example, suppose the Fed's monetary policy was written in stone (or in the Constitution): "Thou shalt not inflate the money supply any more or any less than 3 percent per year." In this case, the Fed has no discretion whatsoever and must follow a very simple monetary policy rule. Since the inflation rate was 10 percent before the rule, we can think of it as resulting in a 7 percent decline in the money supply, compared to the situation at point A in Figure 20.6, or a shift in aggregate demand from AD_0 to AD_1. In this case, if the union did not agree to the 7 percent wage cuts, the short-run equilibrium would be at point C: Real output would decline, plants would close, and many union workers would be laid off or dismissed. Point C is not desirable from the union's perspective. In contrast, if the union accepted the wage cuts, short-run aggregate supply would shift to the right to $SRAS_1$, resulting in an immediate move to a new long-run equilibrium at point D and a higher employment rate than at point C. By taking away the Fed's discretion to inflate the money supply at whatever rate it chooses, the union would now have an incentive to agree to the wage cuts, allowing the economy to immediately move to point D. Taking away the Fed's discretion, according to the proponents of rules, enhances the stability of the economy.

Monetary Policy as a Game.   We can see the argument for rules more clearly if we use the tools of game theory first developed in Chapter 5 and view two key players as the monetary policymaker (the Fed) and the labor union. The Fed controls the money supply, while the wage negotiator sets the nominal wage paid by firms to workers. The resulting decision process is called a **monetary policy game.**

To simplify the analysis, suppose the Fed has but two possible actions: to lower monetary growth or to leave it constant. The union can either accept wage cuts or demand their current wages. These possible actions and the resulting payoffs for the union and the Fed are summarized in the payoff matrix in Table 20.1. The numerical values of the payoffs are hypothetical, but their relative magnitudes are consistent with the Fed's and the union's preferences (objectives) discussed earlier.

To see this, note that the Fed wants a low price level, but it also wants high output. The union wants high real wages for its workers, but not at the expense of excessive unemployment. The payoffs in each cell of the matrix, labeled a, b, c, and d, are consistent with union and Fed preferences for points *A, B, C,* and *D* in Figure 20.6. For instance, if no wage cuts or changes in the money supply occur, equilibrium in Figure 20.6 stays at point *A.* This

---

Table 20.1
A Monetary Policy Game

The Fed has two possible actions: to lower monetary growth or to leave it constant. The union can either accept wage cuts or demand their current wages. The first entry in each cell corresponds with the union's payoff, while the second entry is the Fed's payoff. The payoffs in each cell of the matrix, labeled *a, b, c,* and *d,* correspond with union and Fed preferences for points *A, B, C,* and *D* in Figure 20.6. For instance, if there are no wage cuts or changes in the money supply, equilibrium in Figure 20.6 stays at point *A.* This equilibrium corresponds with cell *a* of the payoff matrix, where the union gets a payoff of 5 and the Fed gets 2.

The equilibrium to the game is found as follows. If the union does not cut wages, the best policy for the Fed is to not reduce the money supply, since the payoff it gets by not reducing it (2) exceeds the payoff it gets by reducing it (1). If the union does cut wages, reducing the money supply in this case results in a payoff of only 3 for the Fed, while it gets a payoff of 4 if it does not decrease the money supply. The union will reason that it is not really in the Fed's interest to reduce the money supply. Therefore, the union earns 3 by cutting wages but 5 if it does not. Thus, the equilibrium for this game is cell *a;* neither the wage nor the money supply is cut.

		Fed	
	Action	No reduction in Money supply	Reduce money supply
Union	No wage cuts	*a* 5, 2	*c* 3, 1
	Wage cuts	*b* 3, 4	*d* 5, 3

equilibrium corresponds with cell *a* of the payoff matrix, where the union gets a payoff of 5 and the Fed gets 2. Cell *d* gives the same payoff of 5 to the union (since real wages and employment are identical at points *A* and *D*) but a higher payoff of 3 to the Fed (point *D* has a lower price level but the same output as point *A,* and thus the Fed prefers *D* to *A*). This is why the Fed's payoff is higher in cell *d* than in cell *a,* whereas the payoffs to the union are identical in cells *a* and *d.* Similar reasoning may be used to justify the relative payoffs in cells *b* and *c* (see the summary exercise at the end of this section).

Let us take as given the payoffs in Table 20.1 and consider the equilibrium outcome with discretionary monetary policy. If the union does not cut wages, the best policy for the Fed is not to reduce the money supply, since the payoff it gets by not reducing it (2) exceeds the payoff it gets by reducing it (1). If the union does cut wages, it is still not in the Fed's interest to reduce the money supply. Lowering the money supply in this case results in a payoff of only 3 for the Fed, whereas it gets a payoff of 4 if it does not reduce it. Thus, the Fed's decision not to reduce the money supply is a **dominant strategy;** regardless of the union's action, the Fed never does better by reducing the money supply. We conclude, as will the union, that the Fed will not lower the money supply. Given this fact, the union earns 3 by cutting wages but 5 if it does not. Thus, the equilibrium for this game is cell *a.* The union does not cut wages, and the Fed does not reduce the money supply—the same conclusion we reached earlier.

Now suppose the Fed does not have the discretion to change its policy; it is committed to reducing the money supply (a rule carved in stone). In this case, the Fed has no choice; it must reduce the money supply. Consequently, the first column of the payoff matrix in Table 20.1 is irrelevant. In effect, this policy rule results in the payoff matrix in Table 20.2. This matrix is identical to that in Table 20.1, except that now the Fed is forced to reduce the money supply. The only player who has the discretion to make a choice is the union.

Given the monetary policy rule, the union now has a strict incentive to cut wages, since the payoff it earns from doing so (5) is higher than that if it does not (3). This simple monetary policy rule results in an equilibrium in cell *d* of the matrix, which corresponds to point *D* in Figure 20.6. Cell *d,* the equilibrium with a monetary policy rule, gives the union the same payoff as in cell *a,* but the Fed receives a higher payoff in cell *d* than in cell *a.* This illustrates that by removing the Fed's discretion, the Fed's welfare (its ability to effectively function as the central bank) is improved at no cost to other players in the economy.

The basic lesson from our graphical and game theory analysis is very simple. If the Fed has the discretionary power to do something different tomorrow than it promised to do today, the union and other players in the economy will not take promises by the Fed seriously and will be unwilling to cooperate with its policies. This reduces the Fed's ability to achieve its

Table 20.2		
The Payoff Matrix When a Rule Commits		
the Fed to Reduce Money Growth		

When a rule forces the Fed to reduce the money supply, the only player having the discretion to make a choice is the union. In this case, the union has a strict incentive to cut wages, since the payoff it earns from doing so (5) is higher than that if it does not (3). The equilibrium under a rule to reduce the money supply is cell *d* of the matrix, which corresponds to point *D* in Figure 20.6. The end result is that both wages and the money supply are cut, increasing the Fed's welfare (its ability to effectively function as the central bank) at no cost to the union.

		Fed
	Action	Reduce money supply
Union	No wage cuts	*c* 3, 1
	Wage cuts	*d* 5, 3

goals. In contrast, if the Fed's policies are rule based, unions and other players in the economy will not have to fear the impact of changes in Fed policies and therefore are more likely to take actions that make the Fed more effective.

Why Does the Fed Have Discretion?

In this section, we have looked at the benefits of rules over discretion. Given the theoretical advantages of rules over discretion, you might be surprised to learn that the Fed has much discretion in its policymaking, subject to oversight only by Congress. We conclude our discussion of the rules versus discretion debate by examining a few reasons frequently given for the Fed's discretion.

Commitment Through Reputation Effects. The problem with monetary discretion is similar to that of political discretion: Politicians can say one thing to get elected but have the discretion to do something else once in office.[2] Similarly, the Fed can promise to cut the money supply if unions agree to wage cuts but renege on this promise once these cuts are in

---

[2] During the 1988 campaign, Bush announced, "Read my lips. No new taxes." He broke his promise in 1990 when he signed a massive tax bill into law. Clinton said he would balance the budget without raising taxes on the middle class and in one of the televised debates promised a middle-class tax cut. These promises were broken when he submitted his budget plan in 1993.

place. By breaking such a promise, the Fed can generate higher real output today, but the cost to the Fed is lost future credibility. If the Fed takes a long-run view, the benefits it can derive today by breaking a promise will be more than offset by the stream of lost future opportunities to influence behavior. Some argue that this **reputation effect** allows the Fed to credibly commit to honor its promises, even though it has the discretion to break them. If the Fed promises to cut the money supply by 7 percent, the union will take this promise at face value. Furthermore, the Fed will honor its promise because doing otherwise would ruin its reputation. This lost reputation would translate into many future years in which the Fed is unable to affect the action of the union, a pain no less severe than that suffered by the little boy who cried wolf.

For the reputation effect to make discretionary policy credible, the Fed must take the long-run view: It must value the future gains that arise from keeping a promise more than the current benefit of reneging on it. As we discussed in Chapter 13, the Fed is largely independent, making it more likely to take a long-run view of things than elected politicians. Modern politicians begin their campaigns as soon as they are elected, which makes for very shortsighted policies. Indeed, the Federal Reserve Act of 1913 intentionally set up the Fed as an independent arm of government. Since members of the Fed are not elected officials, they are more likely to take a longer-term view of policy instead of focusing on the short term, such as stimulating the economy just prior to an election. As a consequence, the Fed's reputation actually allows it to mimic policies that arise under a rule.

Rules Cannot Be Carved in Stone.   A related argument is that any monetary policy rule can itself be revoked; thus, a rule is no different than discretion. If the Fed announces today that it is adopting Friedman's passive money growth rule, nothing precludes it from adopting a different rule tomorrow. Since frequent changes in rules are merely disguised versions of discretionary monetary policy, the Fed cannot itself carve rules into stone.

Much thought has gone into legislated rules or constitutional provisions for constraining the Fed so that its discretion is limited or eliminated. While a congressional mandate to follow a policy rule will constrain the Fed, congressional mandates themselves can be revoked. Constitutional provisions are constraining and difficult to change, but even constitutions can be amended, just as prohibition was repealed. Thus, we see that in the final analysis, the only thing that will make the Fed's policies credible is its reputation.

The Fed Does Use Rules.   Finally, the Fed does use monetary rules to help guide its decision making. These rules are seldom announced, and when they are the Fed is very careful to follow them to preserve its reputation. These announcements are usually rather informal; the Fed chair might make a statement like ''Over the next two years, our goal is to reduce the growth rate of money to 3 percent.'' As Box 20.3 points out, sometimes

International Banking

Box 20.3

International Policy Coordination

The text has highlighted some of the game theory aspects of domestic monetary policy, but a host of international issues are easily analyzed as policy games. One of the most interesting issues is the variety of plans, agreements, and promises by the developed nations of the world to manage exchange rates. It seems agreements are always being negotiated at well-publicized summits for various nations, usually the United States, Japan, Germany, France, and the United Kingdom among them, to take actions that will stabilize the U.S. dollar. In September 1985, for example, the large industrial countries met at the Plaza Hotel in New York, and there was born the so-called Plaza Agreement, in which these five nations agreed to take actions to reduce the value of the dollar. This accord was well timed, because the dollar had already been declining in value for some time and continued to do so after the announced agreement, making the Plaza Agreement a success.

Next came the Baker-Miyazawa Agreement, negotiated by James Baker and Japan's finance minister, Kiichi Miyazawa, in November 1986. This agreement said the governments of Japan and the United States would now try to stabilize the dollar instead of trying to lower its value. When this agreement was reached, the yen/dollar exchange rate was just under 150 yen per dollar.

The Baker-Miyazawa Agreement did not accomplish its objective, since the dollar continued to fall in value. Other nations from the Plaza Agreement argued the dollar had fallen far enough and the depreciation of the dollar was hurting their exports and helping U.S. exports. A new meeting was called in February 1987, at which the five countries from the Plaza Agree-

ment were joined by Canada and Italy in a statement that the dollar's value should be stabilized at its current value and not allowed to depreciate further. This was the so-called Louvre Accord, and the yen/dollar exchange rate was about 130 yen per dollar.

In the summer of 1993, the yen per dollar rate hovered at 100 yen per dollar. All this talk of agreements to stabilize the dollar came to naught. It appears that, all rhetoric aside, nations are often unwilling to sacrifice domestic goals for the more esoteric pursuit of exchange rate stability.

Why do nations even care about the yen per dollar exchange rate or any other exchange rate with the dollar? Basically the problem is that exchange rates can have important effects on net exports and hence on aggregate demand and the domestic economy. Recall from Chapter 17 that an increase in the exchange rate (in foreign currency per U.S. dollar) means the demand for U.S. exports will decline and U.S. demand for imports will increase. This reduces net exports, lowers aggregate demand, and hence can decrease output and raise the unemployment rate. The converse is also true: A decline in the exchange rate can increase net exports and aggregate demand and stimulate the domestic economy.

During the 1980s, up until sometime in 1985, the U.S. dollar was appreciating. During this time, U.S. exports were hurt and U.S. imports of foreign goods and services soared to new heights. But in the second half of the 1980s, the U.S. dollar depreciated, which helped U.S. exports and reduced U.S. demand for im-

Continued on p. 732

Continued from p. 731
ports. U.S. net exports increased (although they were still negative), and this stimulated aggregate demand.

This example points out that countries around the world have an interest in the exchange rate between their currencies and other currencies. Particularly in a large country such as the United States, there is concern for what happens when the exchange rate appreci-ates and, especially, depreciates. When the U.S. currency depreciates and U.S. imports decline, nations in Europe and elsewhere see their net exports drop and the resultant slowdown in their economic growth and increase in unemployment. This is why they care about the value of the U.S. dollar and why so much time and effort have gone into various agreements and accords that attempted to coordinate policies to affect the value of the dollar—however futile.

these announcements take the form of political agreements made by cabinet members of different nations. In the next section, we will see how passive and active rules affect economic activity.

Summary Exercise 20.2

Use Figure 20.6 and the objectives of the Fed and the union to justify the relative magnitudes of the payoffs in Table 20.1.

Answer: The initial equilibrium in Figure 20.6 is at point *A,* and if the Fed does not reduce the money supply and workers do not cut wages, this will also be the final equilibrium. The price level is 100, and output is at the natural rate given by long-run aggregate supply. In constructing our payoff matrix in Table 20.1, we have assumed workers rank this outcome a 5 and the Fed ranks it a 2. What happens if the Fed reduces the money supply but workers do not cut wages? Here the reduction in the money supply shifts *AD* to the left to AD_1 in Figure 20.6. The equilibrium is at point *C,* with a price level below 100 but a reduction in output (and employment) below the natural rate. The Fed likes the lower price level but not the unemployment, and ranks this outcome a 1. Workers also like the lower price level, since it increases their real wage, but they don't like the unemployment, and rank this outcome a 3. Thus, both workers and the Fed prefer the equilibrium at point *A* to that at point *C.*

If the Fed does not cut the money supply but workers do cut wages, the wage cut increases short-run aggregate supply to $SRAS_1$, and equilibrium is at point *B.* Here the price level has fallen and output has risen relative to the initial equilibrium at point *A.* The Fed likes this outcome a lot and ranks it a 4. Workers have taken a wage cut, and although prices will fall, they won't fall enough to keep real wages constant. Thus, workers don't like point *B* as much as point *A,* since their real wage is lower at *B,* and hence they rank this outcome a 3.

Finally, if workers cut their wages and the Fed cuts the money supply, aggregate demand shifts to AD_1 and aggregate supply shifts to $SRAS_1$, so equilibrium is at point D. Here the real wage has not changed, because the fall in wages is matched by a reduction in prices. Workers like this equilibrium as much as that at point A, since employment and the real wage are the same. The Fed prefers point D, since the price level is lower, and ranks this outcome a 3.

PASSIVE VERSUS ACTIVE RULES

Monetary policy rules can be active or passive. **Active rules** are designed to manipulate the economy, whereas **passive rules** are immune to fluctuations in economic activity. To illustrate these rules, we now consider two very simple ones. The first is to keep the money supply constant, which is reminiscent of Milton Friedman's money growth rule. This is a *passive* rule. The second, called a **price stabilization rule,** is to change the money supply in response to changes in aggregate supply or demand to keep the price level constant. This is an *active* rule, since the money supply changes in response to changes in the economy. The idea of a price stabilization rule is to keep the price level (and hence inflation) in check.

A Change in Aggregate Demand

In Figure 20.7 the economy begins in equilibrium at point T, at a price level of P_T and a target output of Y_0. This initial equilibrium is a point of both short-run equilibrium, where aggregate demand, AD, intersects short-run aggregate supply, $SRAS$, and long-run equilibrium, where AD intersects long-run aggregate supply, $LRAS$.

Now suppose aggregate demand decreases to AD_1. In this case, the decrease in aggregate demand moves the economy from the initial equilibrium at point T to short-run equilibrium at point A, where output has fallen to Y_A and the price level has declined to P_A. Without further policy actions, wages will eventually adjust to the fall in the price level, shifting $SRAS$ rightward to $SRAS_1$. In the long run the equilibrium will occur at point B, with output at Y_0 but the price level declining even further, to P_B.

A Passive Rule: Keeping the Money Supply Constant.   We now examine what happens to the short-run and long-run equilibria if the Fed adopts the simplest possible rule: keeping the money supply constant. In the face of a decline in aggregate demand from AD to AD_1, the Fed, following a fixed money rule, will keep the money supply constant, leaving aggregate demand at AD_1. Both the price level and output will fall in the short run, although long-run adjustments in wages and hence short-run ag-

The initial equilibrium is at point *T*. When aggregate demand declines to AD_1, equilibrium moves from point *T* to point *A* in the short run. Under a passive money rule of keeping the money supply constant, long-run equilibrium is eventually restored at point *B*. Under an active rule of keeping the price level constant, the Fed can increase the money supply in response to the decline in aggregate demand, which causes aggregate demand to shift from AD_1 back to *AD*. This restores both the price level and real output to their initial levels of P_T and Y_0 in both the short and long run.

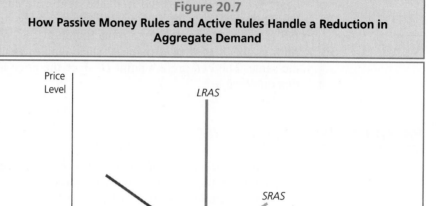

Figure 20.7

How Passive Money Rules and Active Rules Handle a Reduction in Aggregate Demand

gregate supply will restore output to the long-run full employment level at point *B*. However, notice that the price level falls in the long run to P_B.

An Active Rule: Stabilizing the Price Level.

With a price stabilization rule, the Fed wants to keep the price level at the initial level, P_T, which is in essence its final target. It will respond to the decline in aggregate demand by increasing the money supply to raise aggregate demand back to *AD*, restoring the initial equilibrium at point *T* in Figure 20.7 and the initial price level, P_T. Notice that by pursuing this price stabilization rule, the Fed will also restore output to the initial level, Y_0. It will do so by stimulating aggregate demand when the price level falls. With a price stabilization rule, a decline in aggregate demand triggers an increase in the money supply, and hence a rise in aggregate demand, to counteract the decline in the price level, and this restores both price and output to their initial levels.

The remarkable feature of this example is that a single instrument—the money supply—appears to allow the Fed to achieve two goals (or targets): real output and the price level. In reality, however, the "output target" is really being achieved not by the Fed but as a consequence of the natural functioning of the economy, at least in the long run. In other words, output Y_0 will be achieved in the long run even if the Fed does nothing. To see this, look again at Figure 20.7 and notice that after a change in aggregate demand, the economy will, in the long run, return to equilibrium at Y_0 even if the Fed does nothing. We have labeled this equilibrium point *B,* where output is Y_0 but the price level is lower than the target value of P_T. Thus, the "output target" is achieved in the long run not by monetary policy but by the natural functions of the economy. Monetary policy merely speeds up this adjustment to the long-run level of output by offsetting changes in aggregate demand, but it cannot achieve an arbitrarily selected level of output, as we explained in the previous chapter. It does, however, stabilize the price level at P_T in both the short and long run.

A Change in Aggregate Supply

Beginning at point *T* in Figure 20.8, where the price level is at its target value, P_T, and output is at Y_0, we now ask how the economy fares when a decrease in aggregate supply occurs and the Fed follows one of these two rules. Consider a decrease in short-run and long-run aggregate supply to $SRAS_1$ and $LRAS_1$, respectively. In this case, the short-run equilibrium moves from point *T* to point *A;* the price level rises to P_A, and output falls to Y_A. How do passive and active rules affect this outcome? We first consider Friedman's passive money growth rule.

A Passive Rule: Keeping the Money Supply Constant.
If the Fed keeps the money supply constant, aggregate demand does not change in response to the decline in aggregate supply. After the shift in short-run aggregate supply, the short-run equilibrium is at point *A*. With no change in the money supply, over time the short-run aggregate supply curve will gradually adjust as wages rise in response to the increase in the price level. Eventually short-run aggregate supply will shift further, to $SRAS_2$, and the long-run equilibrium will be at point *B,* with a price level of P_B and output at the new natural rate, Y_1.

An Active Rule: Stabilizing the Price Level.
If the Fed has adopted a price stabilization rule, then, after the shifts from *SRAS* to $SRAS_1$ and *LRAS* to $LRAS_1$, it reduces the money supply. This reduces aggregate demand to AD_1, which returns the price level back to P_T. Notice that by doing so, the Fed actually moves the economy from where it would be under passive policy (point *A*) to a point with even lower output (point *C*). But the price stabilization policy keeps the price level at P_T, which was the Fed's intent. Thus, the rule of stabilizing the price level forces the Fed to take actions that reduce output more in the short run than would have occurred under a passive rule.

Figure 20.8

How Passive Money Rules and Activist Price Stabilization Rules Handle a Reduction in Aggregate Supply

---

This graph shows the effect of an active versus a passive policy choice following a decline in aggregate supply. The initial equilibrium is at point T, and the decline in aggregate supply shifts long-run aggregate supply from $LRAS$ to $LRAS_1$ and short-run aggregate supply from $SRAS$ to $SRAS_1$. After short-run aggregate supply shifts to $SRAS_2$ the long-run equilibrium is at point B. Under an active price stabilization rule, the Fed reduces the money supply, and hence lowers aggregate demand to AD_1, to reduce the price level. In this case, the new equilibrium is at point C. Notice that the long-run effects of both rules on real output are identical: Output falls to the natural rate of Y_1. But the price stabilization rule results in a lower price level and moves the economy to long-run equilibrium much more rapidly.

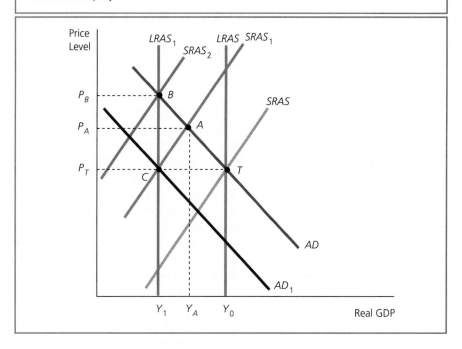

Political considerations make this rule very difficult to follow, since the Fed contributes to an already painful situation by reducing aggregate demand. Notice, however, that the Fed is merely speeding up a process that will occur anyway, since in the long run output must end up at the level dictated by the new long-run aggregate supply curve (Y_1). The problem is that many people are little concerned about the long run when they face losing their jobs. Most would rather lose them in the future—in the long run—instead of today.

The Pros and Cons of Activist Rules

The preceding examples highlight some features of the active versus passive policy debate. One feature is that passive rules usually appear inferior to active rules. Especially for shifts in aggregate demand, active rules can restore both output and the price level to their initial levels. Passive rules, however, rely on the movements of short-run aggregate supply to eventually restore output to the natural rate, and even this will not restore the price level to target. For decreases in aggregate supply the results are not so clear-cut, since in the short run the active price stabilization rule results in even lower output than the passive rule does. Even here, however, the long-run results favor the active policy, since output is at the natural rate under both rules, and the price level is at the target level only under the price stabilization rule.

There is often a tension between short-run and long-run policy goals, and this is reflected in the active versus passive rules debate. In our analysis of a decline in aggregate supply, we saw that the price stabilization rule achieved the long-run output very quickly, at a cost of reducing output in the short run. The passive policy allowed output to fall to the new natural rate more gradually as the short-run aggregate supply curve shifted. Thus, the passive policy rule does not immediately achieve the lower long-run level of output. Moreover, since passive policy rules rely on adjustments of short-run aggregate supply to achieve the natural rate of output, proponents of such policy tend to believe short-run aggregate supply responds fairly quickly to changes in the price level. They think wages and other input prices adjust to keep up with price level changes so that aggregate supply shifts to restore long-run equilibrium over a time span that might be a year or so instead of a decade or more. Proponents of active policy rules tend to place less trust in the speed of adjustment of short-run aggregate supply.

Even when the active rule looks favorable in some overall sense, usually some type of shift in aggregate demand or supply occurs for which the passive rule looks as good or better. Thus, there are few active rules that are always preferred to a passive rule.

Finally, although we examined only a single widely used and representative model, macroeconomics actually has many competing models. These models are often closely related and differ in subtle ways with respect to the determination of aggregate demand or supply, but these differences can alter the assessment about how well a certain activist policy works. Thus, it is somewhat unfortunate that different models have different implications for active policy rules such as price stabilization.

Summary
Exercise 20.3   Consider a temporary increase in short-run aggregate supply that leaves long-run aggregate supply unchanged. What happens to the economy if the Fed

adopts Friedman's passive rule? What if it follows an active price stabilization rule?

Answer: The figure shows a temporary increase in short-run aggregate supply. The initial equilibrium is at *T,* with a price level of P_T and output of Y_0. The short-run equilibrium after the shift in aggregate supply to $SRAS_1$ is at point *A,* with a price level of P_A and output of Y_A. Under a passive rule, the Fed does not change the money supply and the short run equilibrium is at point *A.* Comparing point *A* with point *T,* we see that the price level is lower in the short run and output is higher. In the long run, however, the short-run aggregate supply curve shifts back to *SRAS,* restoring equilibrium to point *T.*

In contrast, an activist Fed intent on stabilizing prices will react to the decrease in the price level at point *A* by increasing the money supply, raising aggregate demand to AD_1. Under a price stabilization rule, the short-run equilibrium is at point *B,* where the price level remains at P_T but output is higher (Y_B). In the long run, short-run aggregate supply shifts back to *SRAS,* meaning the Fed must decrease the money supply to return aggregate demand to *AD* to keep the price level constant at point *T.* Under a price stabilization rule, long-run output will return Y_0 (the same long-run level as under a passive rule), but the price level will remain at P_T in both the short and long run.

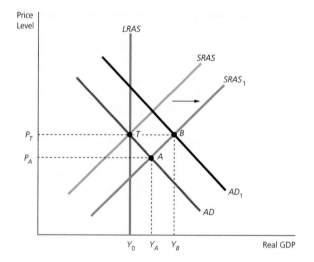

ANTICIPATED VERSUS UNANTICIPATED CHANGES IN THE MONEY SUPPLY

In concluding our discussion of monetary policy, it is useful to point out the difference between anticipated and unanticipated changes in the money supply. Anticipated changes in the money supply are changes that people in the economy fully expect to occur; unanticipated changes are those that differ from what people expected. We will see that this distinction is related to our game theory treatment of monetary policy presented earlier in this chapter, to our discussion of rational expectations in Chapter 12, and to the shapes of short- and long-run aggregate supply curves.

Unanticipated Increases in the Money Supply

Suppose the economy is initially in equilibrium at point A in Figure 20.9, and a union is on the verge of signing a labor contract. Union members

Figure 20.9
Unanticipated Changes in the Money Supply

The initial equilibrium is at point A. If workers expect the money supply to remain constant, their inflationary expectations will be zero and they will be willing to sign a contract paying wages of, say, $10 per hour. This gives rise to the upward-sloping short-run aggregate supply curve labeled $SRAS_0(\pi^e = 0)$, which is relevant with inflationary expectations of zero. In this case, if the money supply actually rises by more than workers expect, such as by 10 percent, this unanticipated increase will move the economy to point B. This is because workers were fooled into working at $10 per hour due to their failure to anticipate the higher price level caused by the unexpected increase in the money supply. Only in the long run will the economy move to point C.

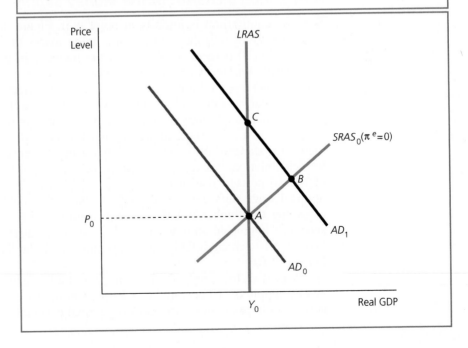

expect the Fed to keep the money supply constant and thus expect the price level to remain at P_0 over the life of their contract (say, one year). Consequently the union expects the inflation rate to be zero over the contract's life, which induces members to accept a wage of, say, $10 per hour. Once this contract is signed, the short-run aggregate supply curve is given by $SRAS_0(\pi^e = 0)$ in Figure 20.10, which indicates it was signed when inflationary expectations were zero.

Suppose that immediately after the contract is signed, an unanticipated increase in the money supply of 10 percent occurs. Since union members are locked into the contract, their wages will remain at $10 per hour. Consequently the unanticipated increase in the money supply results in an increase in aggregate demand to AD_1, creating a new short-run equilibrium at point B. The price level is higher, but worker wages remain at $10 per hour, since workers did not anticipate the higher money supply or prices. They have been induced to produce more output because they did not fully anticipate the increase in the money supply and the corresponding effect on the price level. Only in the long run (after the contract expires) will workers receive higher wages, ultimately leading to a long-run equilibrium at point C. When changes in the money supply are unanticipated, it is appropriate to use an upward-sloping short-run aggregate supply curve to evaluate the short-run effects of monetary policy. In the long run, a vertical aggregate supply curve is appropriate.

Anticipated Increases in the Money Supply

Suppose equilibrium is initially at point A in Figure 20.10. Now suppose that prior to signing the contract, the union learns the money supply will increase by 10 percent. In this case, the increase in the money supply is anticipated. Furthermore, having rational expectations, workers recognize that this increase in the money supply will raise prices by 10 percent over the next year, which increases their inflationary expectations to 10 percent. These higher inflationary expectations mean workers will not be willing to sign a contract for $10 per hour; they must receive $11 per hour to maintain their same standard of living. The higher wage demanded by workers is due to their inflationary expectations of 10 percent, thanks to their anticipation of the 10 percent rise in the money supply. The rise in their negotiated nominal wage shifts aggregate supply to the left, which is just another way of saying that higher inflationary expectations lead to a reduction in the short-run aggregate supply curve: The short-run aggregate supply curve, given the 10 percent inflationary expectations, will be $SRAS_1(\pi^e = 10\%)$ in Figure 20.10.

What does this imply about the impact of a Fed action that increases the money supply by 10 percent? If a 10 percent increase in the money supply is fully anticipated and workers form rational expectations of inflation, they

Figure 20.10

Anticipated Changes in the Money Supply

The initial equilibrium is at point A. If workers expect the money supply to increase by 10 percent, they will ultimately expect prices to rise by 10 percent as well. Given inflationary expectations of 10 percent, they will require wages of $11 per hour before they will sign a labor contract. This gives rise to the short-run aggregate supply curve labeled $SRAS_1 (\pi^e = 10\%)$. In this case, a 10 percent increase in the money supply results in an immediate movement from point A to point C, with no change in real output. Since the increase in the money supply was fully anticipated, workers were not fooled into signing contracts at a low nominal wage.

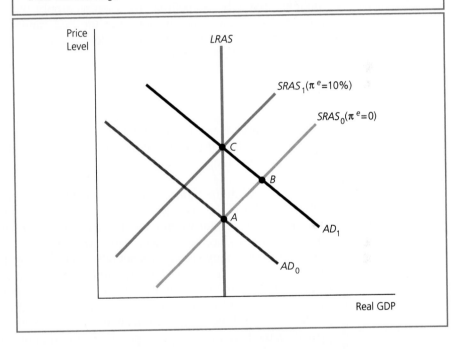

will only sign contracts that give rise to the short-run aggregate supply curve, $SRAS_1 (\pi^e = 10\%)$. In this case, when the 10 percent increase in the money supply shifts aggregate demand to AD_1, we immediately move from point A to point C; there is no temporary rise in output. This is in contrast to the case where the increase in the money supply is not anticipated; in that case the economy moves at first to point B and moves to point C only in the long run, after workers learn they have been surprised. Stated differently, when monetary policy is fully anticipated and workers form rational expectations, it is appropriate to use a vertical aggregate supply curve to analyze both the short-run and long-run effects of monetary policy.

Relevance for Monetary Policy

The moral of this story is that the only way the Fed can influence short-run output in the economy is either through (1) unanticipated changes in the money supply or (2) the failure of workers to form proper expectations of future prices based on what they know about monetary policy. If workers form rational expectations of inflation based on all relevant information as described in Chapter 12, the only way the Fed can have any impact on real output is to surprise them by increasing the money supply by more or less than they expect it to change. Furthermore, it is unlikely that the Fed would be able to continually inflate the money supply without workers eventually anticipating higher inflation. This is not to say that people can predict Fed policies perfectly. Sometimes the money supply will grow by more than expected and sometimes by less, but the Fed cannot systematically cause people's expectations to err on one side or the other. Eventually people will learn what the Fed is up to.

Summary
Exercise 20.4

Suppose workers expect the money supply to increase by 4 percent, but it actually rises by 10 percent. What impact, if any, will this have on short-run output? On long-run output?

Answer: With the money supply expected to grow at 4 percent, workers rationally expect the price level to rise by 4 percent as well. Thus, they will take this into account when they sign their wage agreements and negotiate 4 percent higher nominal wages. However, once they sign such a contract and learn the money supply has actually increased by 10 percent, they will be surprised. In fact, they will be unpleasantly surprised, since their real wages will decline in the short run. This lower real wage will induce firms to increase output in the short run, and the rise in output will be due purely to the fact that 6 percent of the increase in the money supply was unanticipated. In the long run, worker expectations of inflation will adjust, ultimately returning the real wage to its initial level. This rise in real wages will reduce output back to its natural rate in the long run.

CONCLUSION

In this chapter, we examined how the Fed can use monetary policy to influence economic activity. While in theory the Fed can stabilize the economy by using rules (or, if it has a good reputation, by using its discretion), there is considerable debate about whether the Fed should be allowed to pursue such activist policies. Those who argue most strongly for continued Fed independence and discretionary policymaking are often those who are happiest with the way the Fed has been conducting monetary policy. Those who think the Fed has done a poor job recently in pursuing monetary policy argue for various changes in the Fed's independence, either from executive and legislative influence or from the ability to pursue discretionary policy. What we can conclude, however, is that recent research on policymaking has found strong reasons to think that policymaking by rules is not automatically dominated by discretionary policymaking, even when the discretion is benevolent. Monetary policy does not eliminate the long-term consequences of changes in aggregate demand on real output; it can only speed up the journey to long-run equilibrium.

KEY TERMS

active monetary policy

passive monetary policy

monetary policy rule

discretionary monetary policy

monetary policy game

dominant strategy

reputation effect

active rule

passive rule

price stabilization rule

QUESTIONS AND PROBLEMS

1. Consider again the policy game in Table 20.1. If you multiply all payoffs by 2, does the solution change? If you add or subtract 10 from each payoff, does the solution change? What is the essential feature of the payoff matrix?

2. Suppose the Fed has two possible actions: to lower monetary growth, or to leave it constant. The Union can either accept wage cuts, or not. These possible actions, and resulting payoffs for the Union and the Fed, are summarized in the payoff matrix table. Given this payoff matrix, what outcome would you expect if the Fed has discretion?

3. Would your answer to problem 2 change if the Fed is guided by a rule that forces it to reduce the money supply? Explain.

4. How does the consideration of monetary policy games contribute to the debate over whether the Fed should follow a policy rule or act with discretion?

5. In Chapter 19 we discussed lags in implementing policy, and in this chapter we looked at related problems in following

Fed

	Action	No Reduction in Money Supply	Reduce Money Supply
Union	No Wage Cuts	a 5, 2	c 3, 3
	Wage Cuts	b 3, 4	d 5, 5

policy rules. How does the existence of lags influence the policy debate over active versus passive policy rules?

6. You are the monetary policymaker, and you have an output target of the long-run aggregate supply curve. The price level and output both increase, but you are unsure as to whether the long-run model or the short-run model more accurately describes the economy. What could cause both the price level and output to increase in the long-run model? In the short-run model?

7. You are the monetary policymaker, and you have an output target of the long-run aggregate supply curve. The price level has increased, and output has decreased. You are unsure whether the long-run model or the short-run model more accurately describes the economy. What could cause the price level to increase and output to decrease in the long-run model? In the short-run model?

8. Milton Friedman once considered—and rejected—a price stabilization rule for monetary policy. Instead he advocated a fixed money growth rule. His arguments were based on lags in policymaking and other problems in trying to control the price level. What arguments favor a fixed money rule. What arguments favor a price stabilization rule? Which do you prefer, and why?

9. In Chapter 19, we learned that some economists recommend a policy rule of stabilizing nominal GDP. This would mean keeping not the price level but the product of the price level and real output constant. The Fed would change the money supply

as needed to keep nominal GDP at this target level. Consider aggregate demand shocks, both positive and negative. What would the Fed, following a nominal GDP rule, have to do in response to these shocks? How would this action differ from following a price stabilization rule?

10. What do you see as potential conflicting goals between fiscal policymakers—the executive and legislative branches of the government—and the monetary policymaker? How are these conflicts resolved in practice?

11. To commit to following a rule, the Fed must give up its discretion. Is there a way for the Fed to do this in its current institutional setup?

12. Give an example of a situation in which the ability to commit to a rule describing how you will act in a given situation allows you to achieve an outcome preferable to the outcome you would get under discretion. How is your commitment to the rule enforced? Is your commitment to the rule credible?

13. George Bush once said, "Read my lips. No new taxes." Was this promise credible? What mechanism was available to ensure that this promise was kept? When it was broken, what were the effects?

14. William McChesney Martin, a former chair of the Board of Governors of the Federal Reserve System, said "The Federal Reserve's job is to take away the punch bowl just as the party gets going." Explain this remark. Does this statement indicate the Fed was following a passive or an active policy under Martin? Why?

SELECTIONS FOR FURTHER READING

Ahmed, S. "Wage Stickiness and the Non-Neutrality of Money: A Cross-Industry Analysis." *Journal of Monetary Economics,* 20 (July 1987), 25–50.

Culbertson, W. P., Jr., and F. Koray. "Interest Rates, the Forward Premium, and Unanticipated Money." *Southern Economic Journal,* 53 (October 1986), 393–399.

Loewy, M. B. "Reaganomics and Reputation Revisited." *Economic Inquiry,* 26 (April 1988), 253–263.

Skaggs, N. T., and C. L. Wasserkrug. "Banking Sector Influence on the Relationship of Congress to the Federal Reserve System." *Public Choice,* 41 (1983), 295–306.

Waller, C. J. "Monetary Policy Games and Central Bank Politics." *Journal of Money, Credit, and Banking,* 21 (November 1989), 422–431.

Waller, C. J. "Administering the Window: A Game-Theoretic Model of Discount-Window Borrowing." *Journal of Monetary Economics,* 25 (March 1990), 273–287.

Government Spending and Finance: The Deficit Problem

p to this point, we have focused on monetary policy. We would be remiss not to spend some time discussing fiscal actions of the government, especially given the recent concern over high federal budget deficits and growth in U.S. government debt. The **federal debt** is the total amount the federal government owes its creditors. By the end of 1993, the U.S. federal debt held by the public equaled $3.3 trillion, an almost incomprehensible amount. One way to get a handle on this number is to note that it amounts to about 50 percent of GDP. Another way is to calculate how much federal debt exists for each man, woman, and child in the United States. At the end of 1992, the per capita federal debt was about $12,900, or $51,600 for every family of four.

When the federal government runs a **budget deficit,** it spends more in a given year than it collects in taxes for that year. Much as you must increase your borrowing if your income is less than your expenditures, the federal deficit indicates the amount of funds the government must borrow. During 1992, the federal deficit was $290 billion. This represents an excess of federal spending over federal tax collection of about $1,140 per person, or $4,560 for a family of four. Moreover, this deficit represented nearly 10 percent of the outstanding federal debt, indicating that the debt is increasing at a rapid rate.

Why do we care about the deficit or about the size of the outstanding debt? Why has the size of the deficit grown in recent years? Can it be allowed to continue to grow? In this chapter, we answer these questions. In addition, we explore in more detail the government budget constraint introduced in Chapter 16, which ultimately links monetary and fiscal policy. Finally, we discuss the recent controversy over how the budget deficit affects interest rates and other aspects of the economy. The debate is between a traditional view, which holds that tax and bond financing of government expenditures have different effects on the economy, and the so-called Ricardian equivalence view, in which tax financing and bond financing have identical effects on the economy. In the Ricardian view, the important issue is government spending rather than how that spending is financed.

AN HISTORICAL LOOK AT GOVERNMENT SPENDING AND ITS FINANCE

It is helpful to examine the recent U.S. history of fiscal policy before delving into theoretical issues. In doing so, we note that fiscal policy is conducted on three levels in the United States: at the federal, the state, and local levels. All of these levels of governments can both tax and spend. The media often focus on the federal government, which is the largest of the three levels and the level with the ongoing deficits and growing debt. Indeed, as a rule of thumb, state and local governments run surpluses rather than deficits, because most have constitutional provisions that prohibit deficits. We begin by looking at the federal government budget and then examine state and local budgets.

The Federal Government Budget

The federal government budget consists of government tax receipts and government expenditures. Government tax receipts include the personal income tax, business taxes, and social security taxes. Taxes have remained steady at about 19 to 20 percent of GDP over the last two decades and at 18 to 19 percent of GDP since 1950, as the second column of Table 21.1 shows.

Government expenditures include purchases of goods and services, government transfer payments, and interest payments on the outstanding federal debt. Transfers are payments made by the government for which no good or service is received, such as social security payments, unemployment benefits, and income maintenance programs (sometimes called *welfare programs*). Transfers include transfers from the federal government to individuals, transfers to state and local governments, and subsidies to various entities. Column 3 of Table 21.1 shows they have made up a growing share of federal expenditures, from 5 percent of GDP in the 1950s to 7 percent in the 1960s, peaking to 13.4 percent in 1975 and staying roughly at that level from 1975 to the present. The large increase in transfers can be explained in part by the growth of the social security system and the various income maintenance programs begun during the "War on Poverty" in the mid-1960s.

Federal government purchases of goods and services have gone in the opposite direction from transfer payments. Purchases by the federal government include such goods as military supplies and federal highways and services such as those federal employees provide. These purchases were about 7 percent of GDP in 1950, rising to 11 percent by 1955, holding steady at 10 or 11 percent until 1970, declining with the end of the Vietnam War to about 8 percent of GDP in 1975, and remaining at about that level until the present. These figures are summarized in the fourth column of Table 21.1.

Together transfer payments and purchases of goods and services are called **primary spending,** since these spending categories are the main reason the government is involved in the economy (to promote the general

Table 21.1
Federal Government Budget Items as a Fraction of GDP, Selected Years
(data from fourth quarter of year)

Year	Taxes	Transfers	Purchases of Goods and Services	Interest on the Debt	Surplus (+) or Deficit (−)
1950	14.8%	4.9%	7.2%	1.4%	+ 1.2%
1955	17.0	4.4	11.0	1.6	− 0.0
1960	18.7	6.5	11.2	1.3	− 0.2
1965	17.6	6.6	10.1	1.2	− 0.3
1970	18.9	9.8	9.7	1.4	− 2.1
1975	19.0	13.4	8.1	1.5	− 3.9
1980	20.4	13.0	7.7	1.9	− 2.2
1985	19.5	12.3	8.5	3.1	− 4.5
1990	20.0	12.1	7.7	3.2	− 2.9
1993	19.9	13.6	7.0	2.8	− 3.5

SOURCES: U.S. Department of the Treasury, *Treasury Bulletin*, various issues; U.S. Department of the Treasury, *Monthly Statement of the Treasury*, various issues; *Federal Reserve Bulletin*, various issues; U.S. Department of Commerce, Bureau of Economic Analysis, *Survey of Current Business*, various issues; Citibase electronic database.

welfare, provide for the common defense, etc.). However, in addition to primary spending, another type of spending has grown considerably in recent years: interest payments on the outstanding federal debt (the amount of government bonds outstanding). When the federal government runs a deficit, it sells government bonds to raise the funds it needs to cover the deficit. These bonds promise to pay principal and interest according to some stated schedule. While the principal can be paid by selling new bonds (called *rolling over the debt*), the interest payments still appear as an expense in the current budget. Thus, the government must include the interest it pays on the outstanding stock of government bonds as part of its expenditures. Notice that this year's interest payments are not part of this year's primary spending.

Interest on the debt was a small item even in 1950, a mere five years after the end of World War II, during which the United States ran up a government debt that exceeded the size of GDP. In 1950, interest on the debt amounted to 1 percent of GDP and stayed there until 1975. By 1980 interest on the debt was 2 percent of GDP, reflecting the increased debt incurred during the severe recession of 1974–1975. By 1985 interest on the debt was 3 percent of GDP, and it was 3.2 percent of GDP in 1990. The increase in interest payments in the 1980s was due to the increased debt incurred during the deep recession of 1981–1982 and the deficits that persisted throughout the 1980s despite a strong recovery from the recession. These interest payments are shown in the fifth column of Table 21.1.

The last column of Table 21.1 includes data on the federal budget surplus (+) or deficit (−). In 1950 the federal budget was in surplus by an amount equaling 1 percent of GDP, meaning the federal government collected more in taxes than it spent. The budget was roughly in balance in 1960 and 1965, but by 1970 it grew to 2 percent of GDP. The deficit rose to 4 percent of GDP during the recession of 1975, falling below 3 percent in 1980, but then rising to almost 5 percent during 1985 before subsiding to 3 percent by 1990. Thus, the federal deficit as a fraction of GDP has shown an unsteady but upward trend from 1960 onward.

Figure 21.1 presents a clear view of the trend in the components of the federal budget. It shows the ratio to GDP of tax collections, transfers, government purchases, and interest payments from 1947 to 1992. In this graph we can detect a slight upward trend of tax collections as a fraction of GDP from the mid-1950s, although the trend is slight. More evident is the larger upward trend in transfers from the mid-1950s to the mid-1970s and the relative steadiness in transfers since then. The trend in government purchases

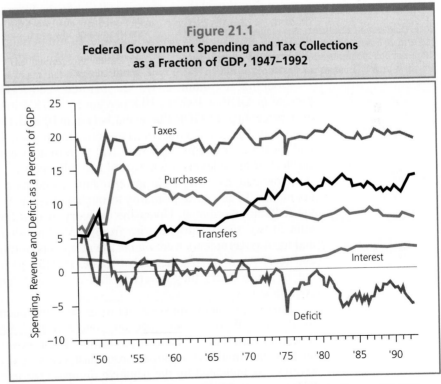

Figure 21.1
**Federal Government Spending and Tax Collections
as a Fraction of GDP, 1947–1992**

SOURCES: U.S. Department of Commerce, Bureau of Economic Analysis, *Survey of Current Business,* various issues; Citibase electronic database.

is also evident. These declined slowly from the mid-1950s until the late 1970s, when they recovered somewhat and then remained fairly steady until the end of the 1980s. Finally, interest payments on the debt were a fairly low component of expenditures, but began increasing fairly rapidly in 1980, with some leveling off beginning after 1985.

Altogether Figure 21.1 depicts a fairly constant ratio of tax collections to GDP, but with large changes in government purchases of goods and services and government transfer payments from the mid-1950s to the mid- or late 1970s, after which these spending categories held fairly constant. Interest payments on the debt began increasing in the mid-1970s and have shown a continuing upward trend. Later we will see that interest payments on the debt are an important indicator of whether the government can borrow to sustain a continual deficit over the long term.

We now turn to state and local government budgets. Then we look at how the aggregate government budget may be obtained by adding up the budget categories of the federal, state, and local governments.

State and Local Budgets

State and local governments are smaller than the federal government in terms of both of the taxes they collect and most spending categories. Also, state and local governments as a whole seldom run deficits of any size, since the majority are required by law to balance their budgets. Table 21.2 reports data on state and local government budgets.

Looking at column 2, we see that state and local taxes rose from 6.3 percent of GDP in 1950 to 10.8 percent by 1975. From 1975 to 1992, taxes as a percentage of GDP fluctuated between 10 and 11 percent, hitting 11.1 percent in 1992. Tax collections are not the only source of revenue to state and local governments, however, and government purchases of goods and services at these levels often exceed tax collections.

How can state and local governments spend more than they receive in tax monies? They do so primarily through grants and transfer payments from the federal government. Under the category of transfers in Table 21.2 (column 3), we see negative entries from 1955 through 1985, indicating state and local governments were *on net* the recipients of transfer payments. State and local governments themselves made transfer payments to individuals, but in those years they received that much and more from the federal government.

Interest payments on state and local debt are much different than those for the federal government, because state and local governments are sometimes net recipients of interest payments. These governments earn interest on their accumulated surpluses from past years, and this provides current revenue, as indicated by the negative numbers for interest payments in the fifth column of Table 21.2.

Table 21.2

State and Local Government Budget Items as a Fraction of GDP, Selected Years (data from fourth quarter of year)

Year	Taxes	Transfers	Purchases of Goods and Services	Interest on the Debt	Surplus $(+)$ or Deficit $(-)$
1950	6.3%	0.0%	6.5%	0.0%	-0.3%
1955	6.9	-0.2	7.3	0.0	-0.2
1960	8.4	-0.5	9.0	0.0	-0.0
1965	8.7	-0.8	9.5	-0.1	-0.1
1970	10.5	-0.7	11.4	-0.2	-0.0
1975	10.8	-1.3	12.0	-0.3	$+0.3$
1980	10.1	-1.1	11.0	-0.8	$+0.9$
1985	10.6	-0.3	10.8	-1.1	$+1.4$
1990	10.8	0.2	11.2	-1.1	$+0.5$
1993	11.0	0.7	11.2	-0.9	$+0.0$

SOURCES: U.S. Department of Commerce, Bureau of Economic Analysis, *Survey of Current Business,* various issues; Citibase electronic database, and *Economic Report of the President,* U.S. Government Printing Office, 1994.

It is clear that the big item in state and local spending is government purchases. These grew from 6.5 percent of GDP in 1950 to a high of 12.0 percent in 1975, after which they fluctuated between 10.7 and 11.4 percent, ending at 11.2 percent in 1993.

Figure 21.2 plots state and local government spending, taxes, transfers, net interest payments, and the surplus or deficit as a percentage of GDP from 1947 through 1992. Here the close relationship between taxes and government purchases is clear, as are the upward trend in these two variables through the early 1970s and their fairly constant value from the late 1970s onward. Notice that transfers and interest payments were both negative for most of this period, reflecting that they were actually providing net revenue to state and local governments over this time. Also, there were large budget surpluses beginning in the early 1970s and lasting until the beginning of the 1990s.

The Aggregate Government Budget

To obtain the aggregate government budget, we merely add together the federal, state, and local budget categories. This gives us a more accurate assessment of the overall size of government involvement in the economy.

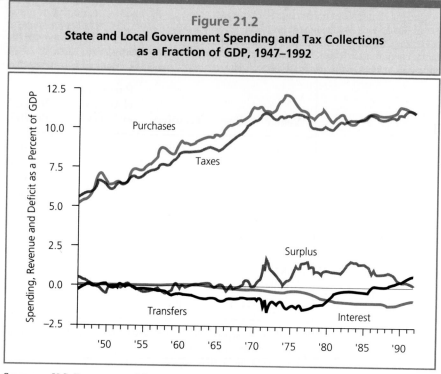

Figure 21.2
State and Local Government Spending and Tax Collections as a Fraction of GDP, 1947–1992

SOURCES: U.S. Department of Commerce, Bureau of Economic Analysis, *Survey of Current Business,* various issues; Citibase electronic database.

It also gives us budget numbers that are consistent with what we mean by government spending or taxes in our theoretical models, which do not distinguish among levels of government.

Table 21.3 presents the size of the various budget categories for the total government as a fraction of GDP. Notice we can still pick out many of the trends found from looking at Tables 21.1 and 21.2. We see that taxes as a percentage of GDP still rose, from 25.2 percent in 1950 to 30.5 percent in 1980. They declined somewhat in 1985, rose to 31 percent in 1990, and stayed at that level in 1993. However, it is generally clear that the various levels of government collected taxes of between 30 and 31 percent of U.S. GDP during the 1980s and so far in the 1990s.

We can also see the steep rise in aggregate transfer payments that we noticed in Table 21.1. Transfers rose from 5 percent of GDP in 1950 to 12.3 percent in 1980, dipped slightly in 1985, and rose again to 12.8 percent in 1990 and 14.3 percent in 1992. Thus, combining the state and local figures with the federal data reinforces the idea that transfer payments have been an ever rising component of aggregate government spending.

Table 21.3

Aggregate Government Budget Items as a Fraction of GDP, Selected Years (data from fourth quarter of year)

Year	Taxes	Transfers	Purchases of Goods and Services	Interest on the Debt	Surplus (+) or Deficit (−)
1950	25.2%	5.0%	13.7%	1.5%	+5.1%
1955	25.2	4.2	18.2	1.2	+1.6
1960	27.1	5.9	20.2	1.3	−0.2
1965	26.3	5.8	19.7	1.1	−0.4
1970	29.4	9.1	21.2	1.2	−2.1
1975	29.7	12.1	20.1	1.2	−3.6
1980	30.5	11.7	18.7	1.2	−1.3
1985	30.1	11.9	19.1	2.2	−3.1
1990	30.8	12.3	18.9	2.3	−2.5
1993	30.9	14.2	18.2	2.1	−3.5

SOURCES: U.S. Department of Commerce, Bureau of Economic Analysis, *Survey of Current Business,* various issues; Citibase electronic database.

The trend in aggregate government purchases is an interesting one. At the federal level, we saw a general tendency for government purchases to decline as a fraction of GDP. At the state and local levels, we saw a tendency for these purchases to rise. In Table 21.3 we see that aggregate government purchases were 18.2 percent of GDP in 1955 and 18.8 percent in 1992. In the intervening years, the percentage reached 20.2 percent in 1960 and 21.2 percent in 1970. However, the overall tendency is remarkably flat, especially after seeing the clear trends in the federal and the state and local data. This indicates a shifting of government purchases from the federal to state and local governments over the past three decades.

Aggregate spending for interest on the debt still showed an upward trend, but that trend is much flatter than what we saw looking only at the federal data, because the state and local governments were net recipients of interest payments. Finally, the surplus or deficit numbers also show the upward trend from the federal data, but the deficit numbers are somewhat smaller due to the state and local budget surpluses from 1970 onward.

Figure 21.3 plots the components of the aggregate government budget from 1947 through 1992. An upward trend in taxes is evident, as is the relatively flat trend in aggregate government purchases. The upward trend in transfers is visible, as is the slight upward trend in net interest payments

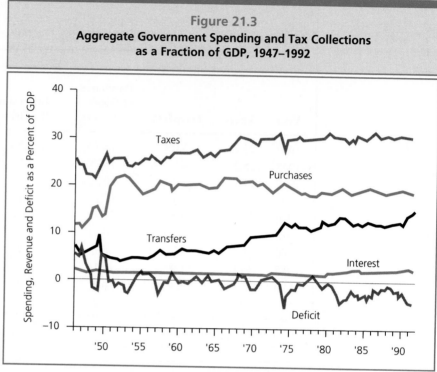

Figure 21.3
Aggregate Government Spending and Tax Collections as a Fraction of GDP, 1947–1992

SOURCES: U.S. Department of Commerce, Bureau of Economic Analysis, *Survey of Current Business,* various issues; Citibase electronic database.

on the debt. Finally, we see the deficit grew during 1975, largely due to the 1974–1975 recession. Since 1979 the aggregate budget deficit has worsened.

THE FEDERAL DEBT

The federal budget deficit tells us by how much government tax receipts fell short of government spending in a given year. In contrast, the federal debt indicates the cumulative effect of all past deficits that were financed by borrowing. How has the federal debt changed over the years? Is it a greater fraction of GDP today than it was when your parents were kids?

Figure 21.4 plots the total federal debt and the debt held by the public, both as a percentage of GDP. The total federal debt is the number often focused on by the news media and was $4,429 billion in September 1993. However, the total (or gross) federal debt includes the debt held by the public and the federal debt held by various government agencies. For instance, the Federal Reserve System owns federal debt—Treasury bills, notes, and bonds—that it has acquired via open market purchases. In September 1993,

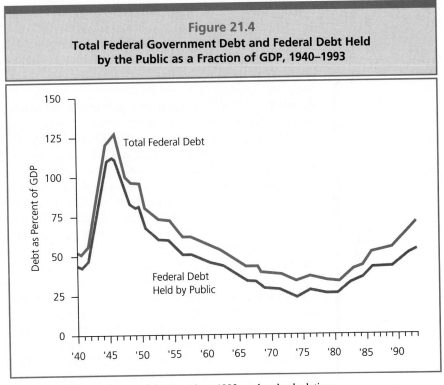

Figure 21.4

Total Federal Government Debt and Federal Debt Held by the Public as a Fraction of GDP, 1940–1993

SOURCES: *Economic Report of the President,* 1993; authors' calculations.

the Fed held $330 billion of the federal debt. Even larger amounts are held by agencies and trusts of the federal government, such as the Highway Trust Fund or the various Social Security Trust Funds. These holdings amounted to $1,122 billion in March 1993. Thus, the federal debt held by the public in March 1993 was not $4,429 billion but $2,995 billion.

Figure 21.4 shows the large increase in the debt during World War II, with debt held by the public peaking at more than 113 percent of GDP in 1946. From 1947 to 1974 the debt to GDP ratio declined fairly steadily, reaching a low of 24.5 percent in 1974. The recession of 1974–1975 caused an upward movement, which mostly ceased by 1979, when the debt held by the public was 26.3 percent of GDP. Then there began the present period of ongoing deficits and increases in the debt to GDP ratio, so that by 1992 the ratio of debt held by the public to GDP was 51.1 percent. The total debt was 68.2 percent of GDP in 1992.

Summary Exercise 21.1

(a) Some economists claim the large federal government deficits of the 1980s are to be blamed on an expansion of transfer payments. Others say these deficits were due to large military expenditures, which would show up in government purchases of goods and services. Still others blame the so-called Reagan tax cuts of the early 1980s. Based on the data, how do you assess these claims? (b) How do the federal budget deficit and the federal debt differ? How are they related?

Answer: (a) It is difficult to reach firm conclusions, but we can note the following relevant facts. Transfer payments did rise dramatically as a fraction of GDP, from less than 5 percent to 13 percent by 1975. However, transfers have remained about 13 percent of GDP since then, falling to 12 percent by 1990. Thus, it is difficult to blame an *increase* in transfers for the deficits of the 1980s. Government purchases as a fraction of GDP have been about 8 percent since 1975, but rose to 9 percent in 1985 before returning to 8 percent in 1990. Thus, there was a small rise in government purchases of about 1 percent of GDP in the first half of the 1980s. Finally, taxes have remained remarkably steady at about 19 to 20 percent of GDP from 1970 onward. They were 20 percent GDP in 1980, fell to 19 percent in 1985, and rose again to 20 percent in 1990. Thus, the picture that emerges from our rough look at the data is that a small but temporary tax decrease, coupled with a small but temporary increase in government purchases, contributed to larger deficits in the 1980s, but these factors alone cannot account for all of the increase. Something else must have changed as well, and we will see exactly what that was later in this chapter. (b) The federal deficit is the amount the government spends in a given year in excess of its tax receipts. The federal debt is the total amount the federal government owes to its creditors. The debt is thus the accumulation of borrowing used to finance budget deficits over time.

THE DEFICIT AND THE GROWING DEBT: ARE THEY BAD FOR THE ECONOMY?

Why is there concern over the ongoing deficits and the growing debt? What is the problem with continually running deficits and borrowing to pay for them? There are three areas of concern. The first is a fear that the large deficits will lead the government to attempt to finance them not with bond sales but through money creation. This causes inflation. The second is a concern that the deficits will place a burden on future generations; that is, deficits add to the debt, and interest payments on the debt will require higher taxes on future generations. The third is a fear of crowding out, the reduction in investment caused by government deficits. This reduction in investment causes the nation to end up with a smaller capital stock than it would have otherwise and hence have a slower growth rate than otherwise. We will look at each concern next.

Deficits Will Lead to Inflation

Many fear the government, facing large deficits and an ever growing debt (with an ever growing interest payment coming due), will be either tempted or forced to use money creation to help finance the deficits. This is perhaps best seen in terms of the government budget constraint, which we introduced in Chapter 16. The government budget constraint says government spending must be paid for by (1) taxes, (2) borrowing (selling government bonds), or (3) printing money. When the government has a deficit, it has chosen not to finance all of its spending with taxes. In this case, the usual procedure in the United States is to raise the necessary funds by selling government bonds. The fear that deficits will lead to inflation is a fear that the government will use the third choice, printing money. This process is called **monetizing the deficit.** Box 21.1 discusses how Mexico used money creation to help finance government spending in the 1980s.

We learned in Chapter 13 that the Federal Reserve System, or the Fed, is in charge of the U.S. money supply. It directly controls both the quantity of currency in circulation (that is, the number of Federal Reserve notes or dollar bills) and the quantity of reserves held by banks. The sum of currency in circulation and reserves is called the *monetary base,* and in Chapters 13 and 14 we saw how the Fed can control the monetary base and how changes in the monetary base cause changes in the money stock. Thus, the Fed is the entity that has the power to increase the money supply to the amount required to monetize the deficit.

To monetize the deficit, the Fed would engage in an open market purchase equal in dollar amount to U.S. Treasury borrowing. For example, suppose the deficit is $250 billion. The U.S. Treasury sells bonds for this amount. If the Fed then buys this same dollar amount of bonds, the debt in the hands of the public has not changed. What has changed is that the open market purchase has increased the monetary base by $250 billion.

To put this required increase in the monetary base into perspective, consider that the monetary base in February 1993 was $401 billion. Monetizing a $250 billion deficit—that is, increasing the monetary base by $250 billion—would cause a 62 percent increase in the monetary base and an equal percentage increase in the money supply. As we learned in Chapter 18, in the long run this will lead to a 62 percent increase in the price level, although the entire increase may take months or even years to occur (due to lags in the effects of monetary policy that we saw in Chapter 18 and discussed in Chapter 19). Monetizing the deficit is clearly inflationary until the economy moves to a new long-run equilibrium with a higher price level. Moreover, if the government decided to pursue this policy year in and year out, we would see continual increases in the money supply and the price level—in other words, continuing inflation. In fact, using money to finance current government spending is exactly what caused the hyperinflation in Serbia discussed in Box 19.1 in Chapter 19.

International Banking
Box 21.1

The Government Budget Constraint in Action: The Case of Mexico

The government budget constraint applies to all countries, not just to the United States. Here we look at Mexico, a country that relied heavily on money creation to finance its government deficits over much of the 1980s. Part a of the accompanying graph shows the government deficit, changes in bond holdings by the public, and changes in the monetary base for Mexico from 1968 through 1988. We stop in 1988 because the Mexican government reformed its fiscal policies in the late 1980s, ending its reliance on monetizing the deficit.

Notice that the Mexican government financed its deficits with nearly equal increases in borrowing (bond sales) and in the monetary base. The large increases in the monetary base should have led to large increases in the money supply and hence to high rates of inflation. Part b of the graph shows changes in the monetary base and the inflation rate in Mexico from 1968 to 1988. Notice that these two series moved fairly closely together and that the changes in the monetary base were as high as 80 or 90 percent per year. The inflation rate followed this pattern, with rates of 100 percent and even 130 percent per year over this period.

The example of Mexico should provide a cautionary note for anyone tempted to use money creation to finance the deficit. While this can be done, it comes at a price: a high and volatile inflation rate.

_____

Source for data: International Monetary Fund, *International Financial Statistics,* various issues.

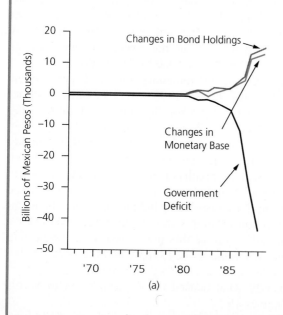

(a)

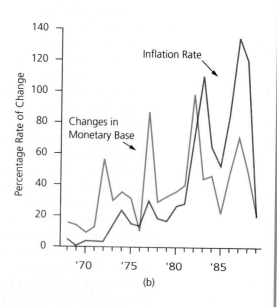

(b)

If monetizing the deficit leads to inflation, why are governments tempted to use this means of financing spending? The answer is that money can be created at very low cost to the government, yet individuals are willing to trade goods and services for this money. For example, the U.S. government can mint a quarter for approximately 4 cents and trade that quarter for 25 cents' worth of goods and services, thus making a profit of 21 cents on each quarter it mints. This profit from creating money, called **seigniorage,** is a source of revenue to the government. Seigniorage in itself is not a bad thing, and a government earns seigniorage in a growing economy even if it merely increases the money supply at a rate that keeps the price level constant. Since an increase in income occurs in a growing economy, this leads to a rise in money demand. The government can increase the money supply to accommodate the rise in demand while keeping the price level constant. However, the great profits that can be made by printing money can tempt a government that has difficulty paying for its spending to try to print money at a faster rate than the rate of economic growth, and this would cause inflation.

In the United States, the Federal Reserve Bank is a separate institution from the Treasury, yet the seigniorage earned by the Fed is still revenue to the government. When the Fed increases the monetary base, it earns seigniorage; in the United States, this occurs as the Fed buys U.S. government bonds. This reduces the amount of U.S. government debt in the hands of the public relative to what it would otherwise be. The U.S. Treasury then makes interest payments to the Fed, just as it would to a private owner of U.S. government bonds. This can be a substantial amount, since the Fed owns more than $300 billion in government bonds that it has acquired in open market purchases. However, most of these interest payments end up back in the hands of the U.S. Treasury. The Fed uses some of its interest income for its operating expenses and remits the rest to the Treasury.

How much seigniorage does the U.S. government collect? When we measure seigniorage, we measure the change in the monetary base. This is shown in Figure 21.5 along with the federal government deficit. In recent years, changes in the monetary base have averaged $27 billion out of a total federal deficit of about $200 billion and total federal spending of $1,400 billion. Thus, seignorage is a small share of the deficit and a still smaller share of federal spending.

The fact that seigniorage is a small component of government receipts in the United States should not be regarded as a bad thing, however. To increase seigniorage, the Fed would have to increase the growth rate of the monetary base, and this would lead to a rise in the inflation rate. Small countries (like Serbia) that cannot easily borrow funds in the capital market rely heavily on seigniorage to finance deficits and therefore tend to have high inflation rates. Nations with better access to capital markets (like the U.S.) or, more generally, nations interested in stable price levels and low inflation rates, will not turn to seigniorage as a major source of funding government spending. Still, there is the danger that any country with a large

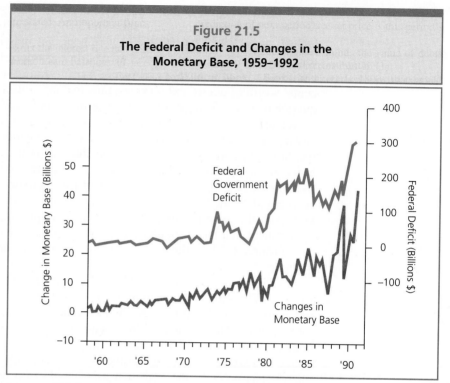

Figure 21.5
The Federal Deficit and Changes in the Monetary Base, 1959–1992

Sources: U.S. Department of Commerce, Bureau of Economic Analysis, *Survey of Current Business,* various issues; Citibase electronic database; authors' calculations.

outstanding debt may decide to pay off part of the debt by printing new money, thus causing hyperinflation. The U.S. government currently relies very little on money creation to satisfy its budget constraint, as shown in Box 21.2 on p. 762.

A Burden on Future Generations?

Some argue that the federal debt is a burden on future generations because they will have to pay higher taxes to at least make the interest payments on the debt. A graph like Figure 21.6 is often used when making this argument, since it shows that the federal government debt per person is growing rapidly. At the end of 1993, the debt per person was over $12,000. (This is the debt held by the public, not the total debt, which includes debt held by other branches of the federal government.) The argument is that every child born today is inheriting this level of indebtedness due to the actions of past generations.

The problem with this argument is that it looks at only half of what future generations will inherit. When existing holders of government bonds die, they pass these bonds on to their heirs. Future generations thus inherit

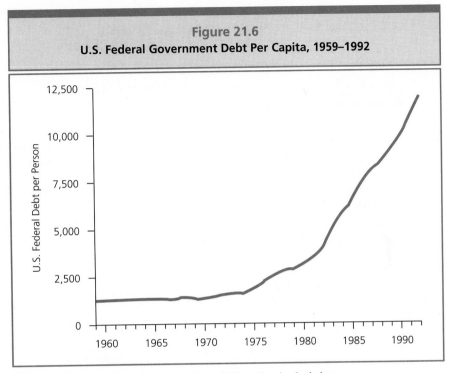

Figure 21.6
U.S. Federal Government Debt Per Capita, 1959–1992

SOURCES: *Economic Report of the President,* 1993; authors' calculations.

not only a liability of $12,000 per person but assets worth $12,000 as well. A simple example will illustrate this.

Dad borrows $12,000 from Mom. Since this loan is between family members, Dad's liability of $12,000 is Mom's asset. Unfortunately, Mom and Dad are killed in a car wreck, and their newborn daughter inherits their estate. Is she worse off having inherited Dad's $12,000 debt? Of course not; she has also inherited Mom's $12,000 asset. After Mom and Dad are gone, she is neither richer nor poorer than before due to Dad's debt to Mom.

The debt per capita figures for the United States can be thought of as debt within a very large family, all U.S. citizens. To the extent that debt is owed from one American to another, when this generation of Americans die off, a new generation of Americans will inherit not only the debt but also the bonds that represent the asset side of the debt. Just like the daughter in our example, this will not affect the overall wealth future generations inherit. Of course, the distribution of wealth may change, because taxes on some will pay for interest payments to others, but in the aggregate the effect on overall wealth may be small.

Note, however, that while the federal debt is largely owed to Americans, roughly 20 percent of it is held by non-U.S. bondholders. This debt owed to non-U.S. residents—about $2,200 per person—is a different matter. Passing this debt on to future generations of Americans will reduce their wealth in

The Data Bank

Box 21.2

The Government Budget Constraint in Action: The United States

The government budget constraint says that government spending must be financed by either taxation, bond sales, or money creation. What is the U.S. experience with this constraint? The accompanying figure graphs the government deficit, changes in bond holdings by the public, and changes in the monetary base for the United States from 1971 to 1993. Increases in bond holdings by the public represent bond sales in excess of redemptions and are one way for the government to finance its deficit. Changes in the monetary base is the other way. If the Fed wants to monetize the deficit, it must buy bonds equal to the deficit, and this open market purchase will increase the monetary base.

Notice that in the United States, the government deficit and changes in bond holdings

by the public are practically mirror images of each other. This indicates the U.S. government has for the most part chosen to finance its deficits with bond sales. Changes in the monetary base are a small part of deficit finance. For this reason, the large U.S. deficits have not led to high U.S. rates of inflation like those we saw for Mexico in Box 21.1

Sources: U.S. Department of Commerce, Bureau of Economic Analyis, *Survey of Current Business,* various issues; Board of Governors of the Federal Reserve System, *Aggregate Reserves of Depository Institutions,* various issues; *Federal Reserve Bulletin,* various issues; U.S. Department of the Treasury, *Treasury Bulletin,* various issues; *Federal Reserve Bulletin,* various issues; Citibase electronic database.

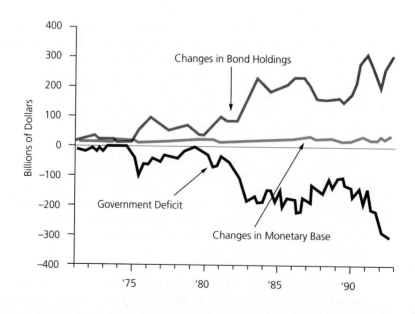

much the same way that your wealth would decline if your parents left you with a $2,200 debt you had to pay to the bank. The main point, however, is that the burden of the debt on future generations is largely balanced by the government bonds they will inherit.

More generally, whenever the government or any individual borrows, the important question is whether the borrowed funds are invested wisely or foolishly. If the government borrowing finances the purchase of capital goods that yield a high return to society, borrowing to finance this purchase is a very sensible action. If the government splurges funds on consumption spending—spending that does not yield a high return to society in the future—borrowing to finance this purchase may not be so sensible. This is like the difference between a household borrowing $100,000 to finance the purchase of a house, which might seem very reasonable, and a household borrowing $100,000 to finance a large party. In our hypothetical example, the daughter might not be happy paying off the $100,000 borrowed to finance a party, but she might think it reasonable to pay off the $100,000 borrowed to finance the house that she also inherits upon the death of her parents.

Crowding Out

Finally, large deficits are viewed as undesirable because they lead to crowding out. Crowding out occurs when an increase in government spending financed by borrowing raises interest rates and reduces investment and consumption. We first discussed crowding out in Chapter 16 in connection with bond-financed increases in government spending. Increased government borrowing raises the demand for loanable funds, driving up the interest rate and reducing investment and consumption spending. Thus, increases in government spending financed by borrowing lead to a reduction in investment spending and can cause the nation's capital stock to grow at a slower rate.

We also discussed an open economy version of crowding out in Chapter 17. In a large open economy such as the United States, an increase in government borrowing raises the demand for loanable funds, but this demand can be met by both the domestic and foreign supply of funds. Due to the possibility of borrowing funds from overseas, the interest rate does not rise as much as it would in a closed economy for any given increase in government borrowing. However, the rise in the interest rate does encourage an inflow of investment funds and hence a higher demand for the U.S. dollar, causing the dollar to appreciate and net export demand to decline. Thus, we saw that in the open economy, an increase in government borrowing results in a decrease in investment and consumption, due to the higher interest rate, and a decrease in net exports, due to the appreciation of the dollar. In an open economy, the crowding out of investment is less severe than in a closed economy, though this is balanced by crowding out of net exports and foreign ownership of U.S. bonds and equities.

Crowding out of private investment is the bane of fiscal policy. Debt financed expansionary fiscal policy reduces investment, which makes the nation's future capital stock smaller than it would be otherwise and thus reduces the future level of real GDP below where it would be otherwise. This feature forces the fiscal authority to make tradeoffs between future output and current output. The fiscal authority can increase aggregate demand and output today only at the cost of reducing the capital stock and output in the future.

Need this crowding-out effect occur? It seems that as long as investment responds to changes in the real interest rate, we will not be able to avoid the fall in private investment that results from an increase in the government deficit. However, even though the government spending may crowd out private investment, total investment may still increase. The government can buy capital, a process called **public investment.** If the government spending is for public investment, the total of private plus public investment may actually grow even though private investment declines.

Public investment occurs when the government purchases capital goods such as roads and buildings or when it invests in human capital—that is, in education and job training—that improves the quality of the labor force. In these cases the expansionary fiscal policy will still crowd out private investment, but total investment may not be affected because public investment is increased. As long as the government investment is as productive as private investment, there will be no reduction in the future capital stock and no reduction in future output. It is important that the government capital spending be productive, however, and many view this as a legitimate concern. Building expensive facilities for government workers, roads that go nowhere, or other nonproductive capital expenditures will not increase the *productive* capital stock and hence will not make up for the decrease in private investment. It is important that the government purchases be for productive capital, and cynical observers of government spending behavior might be skeptical of the government's ability to put the desire for productive capital for the common good over more specialized interests.

*Summary
Exercise 21.2*

List the ways the federal government engages in productive investment.

Answer: Answers can vary, but building interstate highways and the public transportation infrastructure are certainly potentially productive investment opportunities. Human capital investment—education and training of the work force—can also be productive. Investing in security, whether in capital for the FBI or for the national defense, can also be productive in a world that needs security forces to protect against crime and attack from abroad. These items are not productive in the sense of creating additional output, but they may be productive in defending the existing capital stock from plunder from within or without.

All of the above items, and others you may think of, are possible means by which the federal government can pursue investment opportunities. Whether or not that spending is productive depends on the situation and whether the capital good under consideration is useful and efficient in achieving the goal of additional output for society. Even if spending on highways can be productive, it may not be efficient to spend scarce government funds on a highway that goes nowhere. It may not be efficient to spend those funds on a private jet to fly generals around the country. And it may not be efficient to spend them to educate a large group of basket weavers.

RICARDIAN EQUIVALENCE AND FISCAL POLICY

The so-called Ricardian approach to fiscal policy argues that the choice between tax and bond financing of government spending is irrelevant to the rest of the economy.[1] Changes in government spending can affect the economy, but tax collection and deficit financing of government spending have equivalent effects.

The Ricardian view is summarized in the **Ricardian equivalence** proposition, which says that an increase in government spending might have an effect on the economy as the government consumes more of its output, but this increase has the same effect whether it is paid for now via a direct tax increase or paid for later by borrowing, which is repaid by a future tax increase. Any way of paying for the government spending will have the same present value, and hence taxpayers will pay the same present value of taxes whether taxes are raised today or postponed until the future by government borrowing.

Consider an example. This year the government runs a $250 billion deficit. It can finance this spending by collecting $250 billion in taxes now, or it can borrow $250 billion for one year and raise taxes the next year to retire the $250 billion in debt. If the interest rate is 10 percent, the $250 billion borrowed this year will grow to $275 billion next year. Thus, taxpayers face the choice of paying $250 billion now or $275 billion in one year. To make this choice, a taxpayer will compute the present value of both choices. But the present value of $275 billion one year from now, at 10 percent interest per year, is calculated as $275 billion/(1 + .1) = $250 billion. Thus, the present values of both options are the same, and the taxpayer is indifferent between the two. Both will have the same effect on the economy.

There are two special requirements for Ricardian equivalence to hold. First, the government and taxpayers must have to pay the same interest rate to borrow. If the government gets a lower rate, perhaps because it has less default risk than an individual taxpayer, taxpayers will prefer bond-financed government spending. For example, suppose the government can borrow at

---

[1] The Ricardian approach is named after David Ricardo, a classical economist of the eighteenth and early nineteenth centuries. Ricardo's views on fiscal policy have been developed much more formally in a series of articles by Robert Barro. See, for instance, Robert J. Barro, "On the Determination of the Public Debt," *Journal of Political Economy,* 87 (October 1979), 940–971.

10 percent interest, but taxpayers must pay 11 percent. Then the government can borrow $100 today and pay back $110 next year, whereas an individual would have to pay back $111. If the government seeks to finance $100 in spending today, it can borrow at 10 percent interest and charge taxpayers $110 in one year. But the present value of $110 to taxpayers is $110/(1 + .11) = $99. Thus, the present value of bond financing to taxpayers is below the present value of tax financing. In effect, taxpayers can benefit by taking advantage of the government's ability to borrow at low interest rates.

An extreme form of the preceding analysis holds in the case of taxpayers who find themselves unable to borrow at all. There are situations in which a borrower without collateral cannot find anyone willing to lend, even if the borrower reasonably expects a future income large enough to repay the loan. One good example of this is college students, who expect (or at least hope) to get high-paying jobs after graduation. These students are often unable to borrow large sums to finance their educations except through a government-guaranteed loan program. (One reason is that the bankruptcy laws would allow a heavily indebted student to declare bankruptcy before taking a job and quite likely get relief from his or her debts.) Taxpayers in this position who cannot borrow would find themselves reducing their already meager standard of living to pay any current tax increase. Such a taxpayer would prefer government bond financing, which would postpone the higher taxes until after the taxpayer had gotten the expected high-paying job.

The second requirement for Ricardian equivalence is that individuals must care about the future generation. Suppose the present value of a tax bill is the same whether paid today or in 50 years. But 50 years from now the identities of the taxpayers will change, since the older generation will have passed away and the younger generation inherits a large tax bill. Today's taxpayers can postpone paying a tax bill by having it come due in the next generation. If taxpayers care about the next generation, then they will not engage in such behavior, or if they do, they will want to accumulate a large enough sum to bequeath to their heirs an amount equal to the tax bill that will come due.

Is the Ricardian Equivalence Idea Correct?

As a theoretical proposition, Ricardian equivalence seems to require a lot of foresight and rationality on the part of taxpayers. Taxpayers must be able to calculate the present value not only of their future tax bills but the future tax bills of their heirs. Ricardian equivalence also requires that the government be unable to borrow at better rates than taxpayers and that taxpayers not be in a situation of being unable to borrow.

Many look at Ricardian equivalence as making assumptions that are much too strong to be true, and therefore they would reject the idea out of hand. Yet the predictions of Ricardian equivalence get strong support in the historical record. For example, Ricardian equivalence suggests that an increase in government spending financed by taxes will have the same effect on the economy as an increase in bond sales, whereas the traditional view is that bond financing is more stimulative but also causes interest rates to increase and crowds out private investment. Which view does the evidence favor?

One way to answer this question is to look at the behavior of interest rates during periods of high government deficit spending. Paul Evans did just that for four periods of high government spending in the United States: the Civil War, World War I, World War II, and the 1980s.[2] Figure 21.7 plots the first three periods. Part a shows the behavior of the interest rate on railroad bonds along with the deficit to GDP ratio. During the Civil War the deficit jumped from virtually 0 percent of GDP to 18 percent, but interest rates remained stable at about 7 percent. During Word War I (part b), the deficit increased from roughly 0 percent of GDP in 1917 to more than 20 percent in 1919. Still, interest rates remained stable at about 5 percent. Finally, during World War II (part c), the deficit increased to almost 30 percent of GDP, although the interest rate on AAA bonds remained below 4 percent. The evidence from these three periods does seem to support the Ricardian view; interest rates were unaffected by the large deficits during these periods.

Evans reports other evidence from the post–World War II United States, including the early 1980s, and he concludes there is no evidence of deficits causing a rise in the interest rate. His view, and the view of many others who have studied the historical data, is that the Ricardian equivalence idea, however hard to believe on the surface, is very difficult to refute from looking at the data.

The Impact of the Ricardian Equivalence Idea on Our Macroeconomic Model

The key point in the Ricardian view is that the method of financing the deficit is irrelevant to the effect of fiscal policy. Thus, any increase in government spending, whether financed by tax increases or by borrowing, has the same effect on the economy. The traditional view is that spending financed by borrowing results in a greater increase in aggregate demand than does tax-financed government spending. This is illustrated in Figure 21.8. The increase in spending raises aggregate demand to AD_1, but the rise in taxes reduces consumption, resulting in a leftward shift in aggregate demand to AD_2. The traditional argument is that if borrowing were used to pay for the spending, aggregate demand would fall below AD_2 due to crowding out (interest rates would rise, thus further reducing consumption and investment).

According to the Ricardian view, this traditional view is incorrect. Bond issues result in higher future taxes, whose present value is equal to the deficit

[2] Paul Evans, ''Do Large Deficits Produce High Interest Rates?'', *American Economic Review, 75* (March 1985), 68–87.

Figure 21.7
Interest Rates and the Deficit to GDP Ratio During the U.S. Civil War, World War I, and World War II

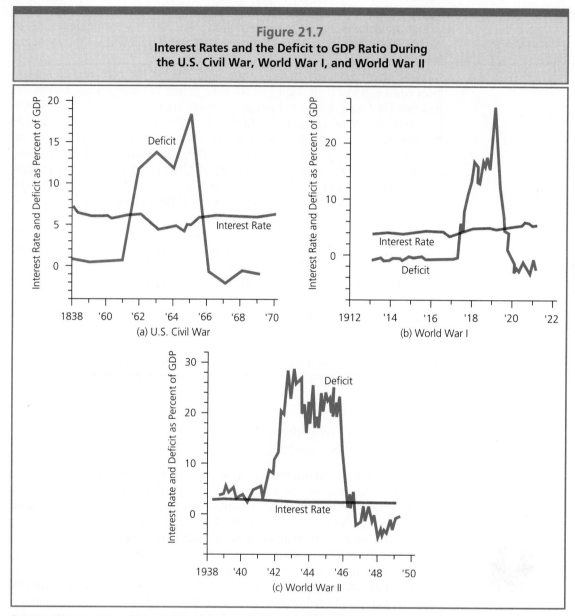

(a) U.S. Civil War

(b) World War I

(c) World War II

SOURCE: From *American Economic Review*, Vol. 75, No. 1. Copyright © 1985. Used with permission.

This figure shows the effect of an increase in government spending that is financed by taxes. The increase in government spending shifts aggregate demand to the right, but the increase in taxes reduces consumption and shifts aggregate demand to the left. The net effect is traditionally assumed to be positive, as shown here. Ricardian equivalence argues that the exact same shift would occur under bond-financed government spending.

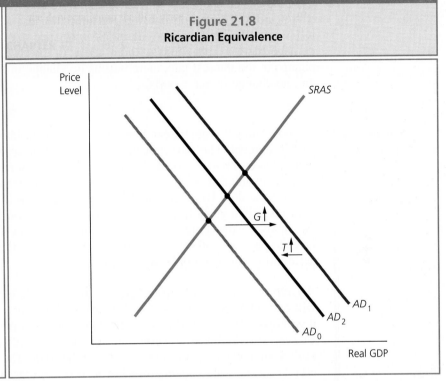

Figure 21.8
Ricardian Equivalence

itself. Hence, the increase in government spending raises aggregate demand, but the future taxes reduce aggregate demand just as much as if the government raised taxes today to pay for the increase in spending. Consumption demand is reduced today as households save to accumulate the funds they need to pay the future taxes. In this case, then, there is no difference between the two types of financing; regardless of whether taxes are raised or funds are borrowed, the effect of an increase in government spending is to ultimately shift aggregate demand from AD_0 to AD_2 in Figure 21.8.

Why doesn't government borrowing increase the demand for loanable funds and thus drive up the interest rate? Ricardians argue that the supply of loanable funds will also rise in response to an increase in government borrowing. This will happen because households, realizing their taxes are going to increase in the future, will begin saving now. This increased saving will result in an increased supply of loanable funds, which will counter the rise in interest rates due to the increase in demand.

Proponents of Ricardian equivalence argue that it applies equally well to an open economy, such as the model we developed in Chapter 17. The traditional view is that government borrowing leads to crowding out in net exports as well as investment and consumption. The Ricardian view is that, as in the closed economy, the increased future taxes call forth an increase in saving today. This results in lower consumption, just as if taxes had increased today, and the increased saving helps to finance the increased government demand for loanable funds without a rise in the interest rate. But with no change in the interest rate, there will be no change in the value of the dollar and no change in net exports.

Summary
Exercise 21.3

Suppose the government can borrow at 10 percent interest, but you have to pay 20 percent. The government requires $100 of tax from you, which you would have to borrow to be able to pay. You can borrow this $100 and pay 20 percent interest each year for two years. Alternatively, the government can borrow it at 10 percent and have you ''pay back'' the loan by raising your taxes two years from now. (a) How much would it cost you to borrow the funds versus letting the government borrow the funds and raise your taxes to pay the loan two years from now? (b) Does this example satisfy the assumptions underlying Ricardian equivalence?

Answer:　(a) If you borrow $100 at 20 percent interest, in two years you will owe $100 \times (1.20)^2 = 144. If the government borrows at 10 percent, it will owe $100 \times (1.10)^2 = 121, which you will then pay in taxes. Thus, you will save $23 if the government can borrow the funds for you and simply raise your taxes in the future to pay for the loan. The government will, in effect, act as your banker, offering a lower-interest loan than you could obtain from a private source. (b) No, since the example assumes the interest rate on government borrowing (10 percent) is lower than that for private borrowing (20 percent).

CAN THE FEDERAL DEFICIT CONTINUE TO GROW?

With ongoing federal deficits during the 1980s and 1990s, an important question is the extent to which these deficits can continue indefinitely. Can the government continue to satisfy its budget constraint by borrowing to pay for ongoing deficits? We will see in this section that the answer depends on the magnitude of the real interest rate relative to the rate of growth in real output. First, however, we need to emphasize the distinction between the primary deficit and the total deficit.

The Primary versus the Total Budget Deficit

The **primary deficit** is the amount the federal government spends on transfer payments and purchases over and above its current tax collections. This primary deficit does not include interest payments, which reflect spending today to pay the interest on the accumulation of past deficits (the federal debt). The **total deficit** is the difference between all government spending (both primary spending and interest payments) and tax collections. Since the U.S. government has an outstanding debt and thus makes interest payments, the total deficit exceeds the primary deficit. Furthermore, even if the government spends the same amount this year on new purchases and transfer payments that it raises in taxes, there will still be a total budget deficit. This is because the government must pay interest on the accumulation of past deficits—the national debt.

The Impact of Growing Deficits: An Illustrative Example

Can the government borrow to finance its primary deficit each year, and if so, can it do so forever? The answer depends in part on the growth rate of the economy. We can easily see this with a simple example. Consider a government whose primary spending on goods, services, and transfers equals $10 per year and whose tax collections are $5 per year, giving rise to a primary deficit of $5 each year. For simplicity, assume the government raises no revenue from seigniorage, so it must borrow to finance the deficits. To simplify our computations, let us suppose the real interest rate is 10 percent, there is no inflation, and the economy starts with no outstanding government bonds in year 1.

Given our assumptions, column 2 of Table 21.4 shows that the government runs a $5 primary deficit in each year, beginning in year 1. This deficit is simply tax collections minus government purchases and transfers. The economy starts with no outstanding debt, so in year 1 we begin with outstanding debt of zero (column 3). Since the outstanding debt is zero, the government owes no interest in year 1, which accounts for the zero in column 4 for that year. Thus, the total deficit in year 1—the sum of the primary deficit and interest payments on the outstanding debt—is $5 in column 5. Since the total government deficit is $5 at the end of year 1, it must borrow $5 to pay for its programs. Let's assume it does so by issuing bonds.

What happens in year 2? Again there is a primary deficit of $5 (column 2). There is outstanding debt of $5 (column 3), and the interest due on these bonds is 10 percent of $5, or $.50, which is entered in column 4. The total deficit in year 2 is the primary deficit in year 2 plus interest on the debt, or $5 + $.50 = $5.50. Now the government needs $5.50 to finance its programs and interest payments, and finances this amount by issuing bonds worth $5.50. The national debt thus rises by $5.50.

In year 3 the primary deficit is again $5, but now the outstanding debt is $10.50 ($5 from year 1 plus $5.50 from year 2). Interest is 10 percent of this amount, or $1.05, so the total deficit to be financed with new bonds is $5 + $1.05 = $6.05. Year 4 begins with a primary deficit of $5 and interest due on $16.55 in outstanding bonds, or $1.66. The deficit is $6.66, which is financed with another bond issue.

Table 21.4
A Hypothetical Ongoing Budget Deficit Financed by Borrowing

(1) Year	(2) Primary Deficit	(3) Outstanding Debt (bonds issued in previous years)	(4) Interest Payments on Outstanding Debt	(5) Total Deficit (2) + (4)	(6) GDP (0% growth)	(7) GDP (10% growth)
1	$5	$ 0.00	$ 0.00	$ 5.00	$100	$ 100.00
2	5	5.00	0.50	5.50	100	110.00
3	5	10.50	1.05	6.05	100	121.00
4	5	16.55	1.66	6.66	100	133.10
5	5	23.22	2.32	7.32	100	146.41
10	5	67.90	6.79	11.79	100	235.79
15	5	139.87	13.99	18.99	100	379.75
20	5	255.80	25.58	30.58	100	611.59
25	5	442.49	44.25	49.25	100	984.97
30	5	743.15	74.32	79.32	100	1,586.30

As you can see, the ongoing primary deficit of $5 and the growing interest payments on the outstanding debt cause a continual increase in the size of the outstanding debt and in the interest payments due on it. By year 10, the outstanding debt will rise to $67.90, with interest due of $6.79. By this time, the interest on the debt will exceed the primary deficit. By year 20, the outstanding debt is $255.80 and the interest payments are $25.58, more than five times the primary deficit. By year 30, the outstanding debt is $743.15, with interest payments of $74.32, or almost 15 times the size of the primary deficit. This example makes it clear that a relatively modest ongoing primary deficit financed (along with any interest due) with continual new bond issues will result in a stock of outstanding debt and interest due on that debt that eventually dwarfs the primary deficit itself.

Can this situation continue? The answer depends on how rapidly the economy is growing. The last two columns of Table 21.4 show what happens to GDP over time under two different scenarios. The first scenario (column 6) is no GDP growth, so GDP in every year is $100. In this case, we see that in year 30 the interest on the debt is $74.32, three-fourths of GDP. This is clearly unsustainable, since interest on the debt will in a few more years exceed the level of GDP, and there will be no conceivable way to repay the debt. In fact, long before interest on the debt is three-fourths of GDP, people will become very reluctant to lend to the government. Since the government cannot actually capture all of GDP, it cannot afford interest payments even approaching 100 percent of GDP.

Column 7 of Table 21.4 shows what happens when GDP grows at 10 percent per year; that is, GDP is $100 in year 1, ($100)(1.1) = $110 in year 2, ($100)(1.1)^2 = $121 in year 3, and so on. Notice that this growth rate leads to very large values of GDP in a few years. By year 10 GDP is $235.79, by year 20 it is $611.59, and by year 30 it is $1,586.30.

How does GDP growth affect the significance of the growing total budget deficit shown in column 5? Notice that the total deficit is growing at 10 percent a year. When GDP also grows at 10 percent per year as in column 7, the ratio of the total deficit to GDP remains constant. Thus, in year 1 the total deficit is $5 and GDP is $100, so the ratio is 5 percent. In year 5 the total deficit is $7.32 and GDP is $146.41, so the ratio is again 5 percent. In year 30 the total deficit is $79.32 and GDP is $1,586.30, so the ratio is yet again 5 percent. As long as the total deficit is a constant fraction of GDP, it is possible for the government to continue with this fiscal policy forever. The government's debt itself grows to a multiple of GDP, but it will eventually stabilize in this example at a bit less than twice GDP. In fact, by year 30 the debt is 46 percent of GDP and grows only to 49 percent of GDP in another 30 years. Is the U.S. debt a problem? This is the topic of Box 21.3.

The Bottom Line for the United States

The general conclusion from our example is that it is possible for the U.S. government to run ongoing deficits—even ongoing primary deficits—as long as the economy grows at a rate that at least equals the real interest rate on government debt. But if the economy grows at a slower rate than the real interest rate on government debt, ongoing primary deficits are not sustainable.

To draw conclusions for the United States, we need to know several things. First, is the United States in fact running primary budget deficits? Second, what is the real interest rate in the United States, and what is the rate of growth of real GDP? With this information, we can say something about the prospects for sustaining the present U.S. fiscal policy.

We begin with a graph of the primary and total federal deficits from 1947 to 1992 in Figure 21.9. Several things are clear in this picture. First, the U.S. primary budget deficit was much lower than the total deficit, and was actually in surplus in the late 1980s and early 1990s. Two episodes of large primary budget deficits occurred, one during the recession of 1974 to 1975 and a longer episode beginning with the recession of 1982 and persisting until 1987. These primary deficits built up the size of the debt and led to increases in the interest due on it. It is these interest payments that account for the growing discrepancy between the primary and total federal budget deficits.

Figure 21.10 provides information on the growth rate of real GDP in the United States relative to the real interest rate, calculated as the interest

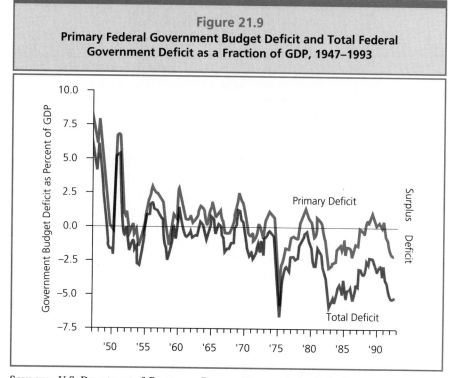

Figure 21.9
Primary Federal Government Budget Deficit and Total Federal Government Deficit as a Fraction of GDP, 1947–1993

SOURCES: U.S. Department of Commerce, Bureau of Economic Analysis, *Survey of Current Business,* various issues; Citibase electronic database.

rate on five-year government bonds minus the inflation rate. The inflation rate was measured by the percentage change in the GDP deflator. It is evident that the relationship between the rate of GDP growth and the real interest rate changed dramatically in the 1980s. Before that time real GDP growth exceeded the real interest rate, but in the 1980s the real interest rate exceeded real GDP growth. For the entire 1953–1990 period, the average rate of GDP growth exceeded the average real interest rate, but this trend may not persist into the next century. If real GDP growth continues to be lower than the real interest rate, as it has been since 1980, the government will be unable to continue running up primary deficits and paying for them by borrowing. However, the decline in real interest rates in the 1992–1994 period might lead us to expect a return to average real interest rates below the growth rate of real GDP.

Summary Exercise 21.4 How does the analysis in Table 21.4 change if the economy is growing at a rate higher than the real interest rate? To be specific, assume GDP grows at 20 percent per year instead of 10 percent or 0 percent as in Table 21.4. What

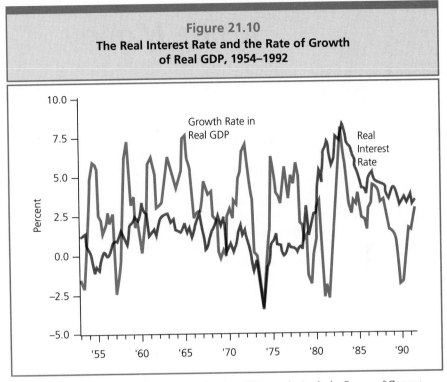

Figure 21.10

The Real Interest Rate and the Rate of Growth of Real GDP, 1954–1992

SOURCES: U.S. Department of Commerce, Bureau of Economic Analysis, *Survey of Current Business,* various issues; U.S. Department of Labor, Bureau of Labor Statistics, *The Consumer Price Index,* various issues; Citibase electronic database.

happens to the deficit as a fraction of GDP? Does the debt grow relative to GDP?

Answer: In this case, GDP grows from $100 in year 1 to $120 in year 2, $144 in year 3, $172.80 in year 4, and $207.36 in year 5. By year 10 GDP is $515.98, and in year 15 it is $1,283.92. This rapid growth in GDP causes the ratio of the deficit to GDP to decline. In year 1 the ratio is $5/$100 = 20%, but by year 5 it is $7.32/$207.36 = 3.5%, and by year 15 it has fallen to $18.98/$1,283.92 = 1.5%.

The debt to GDP ratio is $5/$120 = 4.2% in year 1, rising to $10.50/$120 = 8.8% in year 2 and $16.55/$172.80 = 9.6% in year 3. By year 5, the debt to GDP ratio is $23.22/$207.36 = 11.2%. This ratio hovers in the low teens for quite awhile—in year 10 it is 13 percent, in year 15 it is 10.9 percent—before it starts to decline toward zero. By year 30, the debt to GDP ratio is 3.8 percent and falling.

The conclusion is that economic growth will eventually reduce both the deficit to GDP ratio and, over a longer term, the debt to GDP ratio. However,

Inside Money

Box 21.3

Is Debt a Problem?

In 1992, the federal debt exceeded $3 trillion—slightly less than half of the U.S. gross domestic product. This means it would take half of the value of all U.S. goods and services produced in 1992 to pay back the amount the U.S. government owes to the public. You might be surprised to learn that mortgage debt in 1993 was a larger amount—$4 trillion, or two-thirds the value of 1992 GDP. Mortgage debt is borrowing used by people in the United States to buy real estate and houses.

Many people in the United States have mortgage debt that exceeds their current incomes. For instance, a family with income of $60,000 per year and a $180,000 mortgage has debt that is three times their income. This is of no concern to banks or individuals, since their ability to repay mortgages depends on the size of their current incomes relative to their mortgage payments. Given current interest rates, such a family can easily afford the monthly payments on a $180,000 mortgage. Moreover, in return for the mortgage, the family receives an asset (the house), which is worth more than $180,000 if the lender required a down payment. By focusing on debt, one looks only at the liability side of a balance sheet; the asset side includes the value of what the borrowed funds were used to purchase. In the case of mortgage debt, the asset is tangible real estate that could be liquidated for an amount in excess of the debt.

Similar reasoning applies to the federal debt, although it is complicated by two aspects of government spending. First, as we saw in Table 21.1, a large fraction of government spending is on transfer and interest payments, and these payments do not result in tangible assets owned by the government. Second, while the government does own many tangible assets, these assets are difficult to value. They range from buildings and monuments in Washington, D.C., and throughout the United States to mineral rights and land (the federal government owns half of the land in Alaska) to fighter jets and aircraft carriers. Some might argue that the United States even owns the moon, since we are the only nation to have set foot there. Of course, these government assets are much more difficult to value than residential property in the suburbs; what price could the government fetch for things like the Washington Monument? While the answer is far from clear, the point is that the federal government, like private individuals, owns tangible assets that at least partially offset the liability side of the balance sheet. And, like mortgage debt, the magnitude of the federal debt is not in and of itself a problem. The problem is that when the total deficit grows faster than real income in the economy each year, a time will eventually come when the economy will not produce enough income in a given year to pay interest on the accumulated debt.

these effects will not be quick, even when the economy grows at a much higher rate than the real interest rate.

CONCLUSION

In this chapter, we examined the causes and effects of large budget deficits and saw why it is inflationary to use monetary policy to pay for ongoing deficits. Ricardian equivalence argues that taxes and borrowing have identical effects on the economy, since people recognize that higher borrowing today ultimately means higher taxes tomorrow to pay back the debt, whereas those holding the traditional view believe borrowing has a more adverse effect on the economy.

We also looked at conditions under which ongoing deficits are sustainable by borrowing. If the growth in the U.S. economy exceeds the real interest rate on government borrowing over the foreseeable future, and if the primary deficit remains constant, the current U.S. budget deficit problem will present no long-term problems for the United States. However, if real interest rates continue to exceed the rate of economic growth, the United States will not be able to continue borrowing to meet its deficits. In this case, politicians and the Fed have but three choices, none of which is pleasant: raise taxes, cut spending, or print money—or some combination of all three.

KEY TERMS

federal debt

budget deficit

primary spending

monetizing the deficit

seigniorage

public investment

Ricardian equivalence

primary deficit

total deficit

QUESTIONS AND PROBLEMS

1. Suppose the fiscal and monetary authorities cooperate and decide they want to lower the interest rate. Can they do so? Use the macroeconomic model from Chapter 16 to answer this question.

2. Suppose the fiscal authority wants to keep the interest rate constant. If an increase in aggregate demand occurs, what should the fiscal policymaker do?

3. During the 1980s the real interest rate increased, output increased, and the inflation rate fell, but not to zero. Some blame this on a combination of tight monetary policy with a low rate of money growth and loose fiscal policy with a large deficit. Will lower money growth and an increase in government spending cause these effects in our theoretical model from Chapter 16?

4. Without including the recession of 1990–1991, the last three recessions were the severe recession from the first quarter of 1974 to the first quarter of 1975 (15 months), the recession of the second and third quarters of 1980 (6 months), and the severe recession from the fourth quarter of 1981 to the fourth quarter of 1982 (12 months). If the information and recognition lags are three months and the effectiveness lag only one month, how quickly must the legislature act to ensure that fiscal policy will be enacted and implemented before the end of each of these recessions? (You might also want to see how long it takes the average bill, or even the average fiscal policy bill, to pass through Congress. You could even look for examples of fiscal policy bills introduced during the recessions for more insight on this issue.)

5. In the United States seigniorage is collected by the Federal Reserve System, which issues newly minted base money in exchange for government bonds in open market operations. Does seigniorage have to be collected in this way? What if the government conducted open market operations in military hardware? It could directly pay suppliers with newly minted base money. Would this approach have any substantial differences from the present system of conducting open market operations only in government bonds?

6. In 1990 GDP was about $5,400 billion, the deficit about $180 billion, and the monetary base about $310 billion. Sometimes people talk about "printing money to pay off the debt." Let's just consider printing money to pay the deficit in 1990.

The deficit was $180 billion, so the government could have printed $180 billion in base money, making the monetary base $310 + $180 = $490 billion instead of $310 billion. This would have effectively paid for the entire deficit in 1990. However, what would have happened to the money supply? The monetary base would have increased by more than 50 percent. What would have happened to the price level? To inflation? Why do you think economists warn about the dangers of such an approach?

7. The federal government began running a primary budget surplus in 1990, but the recession of 1990–1991 may have eliminated that surplus. If the government emerges from the recession with a balanced primary budget but with the intention of always borrowing to pay the interest on the outstanding debt, will this be a sustainable policy? Why or why not?

8. Explain the Ricardian view of the choice between bond finance and tax finance. Why are taxpayers supposed to regard these two methods of financing spending as equivalent? Do you find these arguments convincing? Why or why not?

9. "The Ricardian view is that deficits are not important, so questions about the sustainability of government deficits or the government budget constraint are also not important." How do you respond to this statement?

10. Describe the potential for fiscal policy to influence aggregate supply. How does this help solve the instrument shortage problem policymakers face?

SELECTIONS FOR FURTHER READING

Ahking, F. W. "The Relationship between Government Deficits, Money Growth, and Inflation." *Journal of Macroeconomics,* 7 (Fall 1985), 447–467.

Allen, S. D. "The Effect of Federal Deficits and Debt on the Tax-Adjusted, Short-Term, Real Interest Rate." *Economics Letters,* 34 (October 1990), 169–173.

Borna, S., and K. G. Mantripragada. "Morality of Public Deficits: A Historical Perspective." *Public Budgeting and Finance,* 9 (Spring 1989), 33–46.

Finn, T. J. "The Feasibility of the Projected Federal Debt." *Public Finance Quarterly,* 18 (July 1990), 360–368.

Finn, T. J. "A Note on the Real Federal Deficit." *Eastern Economic Journal,* 14 (July–September 1988), 263–270.

Kulkarni, K. "Monetary Approach to Balance of Payments and Exchange Rate Determination: Recent Experience of Eight Countries." *Indian Economic Journal,* 37 (January–March 1990), 99–108.

McMillin, W. D., and T. R. Beard. "Do Budget Deficits Matter? Some Pre–World War II Evidence." *Journal of Economics and Business,* 40 (November 1988), 295–308.

Melvin, M., D. Schlagenhauf, and A. Talu. "The U.S. Budget Deficit and the Foreign Exchange Value of the Dollar." *Review of Economics and Statistics,* 71 (August 1989), 500–505.

Rockoff, H. "The Origins of the Federal Budget." *Journal of Economic History,* 45 (June 1985), 377–382.

Tran, D. T., and B. L. Sawhney. "Government Deficits, Capital Flows, and Interest Rates." *Applied Economics,* 20 (June 1988), 753–765.

Waller, C. J. "Deficit Financing and the Role of the Central Bank—A Game Theoretic Approach." *Atlantic Economic Journal,* 15 (July 1987), 25–32.

Glossary

Active monetary policy. When the Fed increases the money supply in an attempt to bring down interest rates, thus spurring investment and aggregate demand. (20)

Active rule. A monetary policy rule that prescribes changes in the money supply in response to changes in the economy. (20)

Adaptive expectations hypothesis. Views expectations as evolving relatively slowly over time, and being revised in light of past experience. (12)

Adjustment credit. Loans made to depository institutions to allow them to more gradually adjust their reserves and loan portfolios in response to changes in deposits. (13)

Adverse selection. In the loan market, the situation that occurs as the interest rate rises and honest borrowers decide not to borrow. The bank is left with an adverse pool of borrowers—those who know they are more likely to default. (5)

After-tax interest rate. The interest rate minus the amount of the interest payment that is due in income taxes. Calculated as the interest rate minus the interest rate times the tax rate. (3)

Aggregate demand curve. A relation between the price level and the aggregate quantity of goods and services demanded, holding other things such as interest rates and the money supply constant. (16)

Anticipated inflation. The amount of inflation that is expected (or anticipated). (3)

Appreciation. When the dollar appreciates, a dollar buys more units of foreign currency than before. (11)

Arbitragers. Buyers and sellers who try to take advantage of temporary profit opportunities caused by discrepancies between prices in various markets. (11)

Asymmetric information. A situation where parties engaged in a transaction have different information. For example, in the loan market, when borrowers have better information about their ability to repay a loan than does the bank. (5)

Balance of payments. An accounting summary of the value of payments between households, firms, and government in one country and the rest of the world. (17)

Balance of trade. The difference between merchandise exports and merchandise imports. (17)

Balance on services. That part of the balance of payments accounts that consists of exports and imports of services, including such things as military expenditures, tourism, transportation services, and investment income such as dividends, interest income, and royalties. (17)

Bank charter. Approval from a regulatory agency to form a bank, granted by the comptroller of the currency (for a national bank) or state banking commission (for a state bank). (7)

Bank panic. A period during which banks throughout the banking system face an increased desire for currency by depositors, which manifests itself as a widespread withdrawal of deposits from the banking system. (6)

Banker's acceptance. A short-term loan usually used by a firm to finance exchange of goods. The firm has been promised payment for a shipment and has a bill of exchange promising payment. The firm with the bill borrows with the bill of exchange as collateral. The bill of exchange is stamped as ''accepted'' by the bank. The accepting bank guarantees payment. (2)

Banking holding companies. Corporations that own one or more banks. (7)

Banknote. A written document issued by a bank and promising to pay the bearer on demand. (1)

Barter. The exchange of goods and services directly for other goods and services, without the use of money. (1)

Bearer bond. A bond that can be redeemed by whoever has it in his or her possession. It is payable ''to the bearer''. (2)

Best fit line. The line drawn through the points on the scattergram that is chosen by a statistical procedure to fit the best straight line to the scatter of points. (18)

Board of Governors. Consists of seven members appointed by the U.S. president and confirmed by the U.S. Senate. Responsible for monetary policy and regulation of the banking industry by the Federal Reserve System. (13)

Borrowed reserves. Reserves that banks borrow from the Fed and other depository institutions, without collateral. (13)

Bretton Woods. Under this fixed exchange rate system, the United States agreed to peg the U.S. dollar to a given amount of gold, and other nations pegged their currency to the U.S. dollar. (11)

Brokerage firms. Firms which link buyers and sellers of financial assets. (2)

Budget deficit. The result of the federal government spending more in a given year than it collects in taxes for that year. (21)

Call option. Gives a buyer the right to buy a financial asset at a specified price up to a specified expiration date. (9)

Call premium. The additional yield purchasers of callable bonds must receive in order to be willing to be exposed to call risk. (9)

Call risk. The risk that a bond will be called. (9)

Callable bonds. Bonds that the issuer may call, or redeem, after a specified period. (2)

Cambridge constant. The reciprocal of velocity. (15)

Cambridge theory of money demand. Asserts that people have two motives for holding money: (a) to make transactions, and (b) to store wealth. (15)

Capital account. That portion of the balance of payments that keeps track of investment by U.S. firms, households, and governments overseas, and investments by foreigners in the U.S. (17)

Capital gain. The increase in the value of an asset over and above the cost of obtaining that asset. (9)

Capital market instrument. A money market instrument with a maturity of more than one year. (2)

Central bank. A bank for the government and a bank for banks that oversees monetary policy. (13)

Certificates of Deposits (CD's). A debt instrument sold by banks and other depository institutions which is essentially a time deposit, paying the depositor a specified amount of interest during a specified term to maturity, and represented by a certificate. (2)

Change in demand. A shift in the entire demand curve caused by a change in income, tastes, expectations, or other determinants of demand. (4)

Change in quantity demanded. A movement along a given demand curve. (4)

Change in quantity supplied. A movement along a given supply curve. (4)

Change in supply. A shift in the entire supply curve. (4)

Classical view of money demand. Considers income to be the primary determinant of money demand. (15)

Closed economy model. A model that does not consider the impact of international trade on the economy. (16)

Collateral. Property or assets pledged as a security against default on a loan. (5)

Collusion. The act of two or more firms conspiring to act in concert in their pricing or output decisions in order to make both firms better off. (5)

Commercial banks. A depository institution which is relatively unrestricted in its ability to make loans, and which is legally able to accept demand deposits. (2)

Commercial loans. Bank loans to businesses. (2)

Commercial paper. An unsecured promise to pay back a specified (i.e. face) amount at a designated time in the future. The maturity at issue is no more than 270 days. Commercial paper is usually sold at a discount from the face amount. (2)

Commodity money. A physical commodity that is used as money even though it has alternative non-monetary uses. (1)

Complements. Goods or services that tend to be used jointly and thus have the property that when the price of one increases the demand for the other decreases. (4)

Complete crowding out. Describes a situation in which crowding out is complete, so that the increase in government spending causes a reduction in the sum of investment and consumption spending of an equal but opposite magnitude. (16)

Complete currency multiplier. Indicates how much currency holdings will change due to a change in the monetary base. (14)

Complete deposit multiplier. Indicates the multiple by which a given increase in the monetary base will increase total banking system deposits. (14)

Complete money multiplier. Determines the factor by which the money stock (currency plus deposits) changes due to a change in the monetary base. (14)

Comptroller of the Currency. An office of the Treasury which regulates the formation of national banks and is in charge of examining banks from time-to-time to verify their financial health. (7)

Consumer loans. Loans obtained by individuals for intermediate-term purchases such as automobile purchases, as well as merchandise purchased with credit cards. (2)

Consumption goods. Goods and services demanded by households. (16)

Corporate bond. A debt instrument issued by a corporation that states it will make specified interest payments (typically twice each year) and a principal amount or "face value" (usually $1000) at maturity (say 30 years from the date of issue). (2)

Corporate stock. An equity instrument that represents ownership of a share of the assets and earnings of a corporation. (2)

Countercyclical policy. Policy actions aimed at counteracting business cycle influences on the economy. (19)

Coupon rate. The percentage of the face value of a

bond that will be paid each year as an interest payment. (8)

Covered interest arbitrage. An arbitrage possibility that occurs when two countries have interest rates, a spot exchange rate, and a forward exchange rate that allow an arbitrager to profit. (11)

Credit unions. A depository instituion that operates as a cooperative, accepting deposits from and lending to only a closed group such as employees of a specific company, members of a specific labor union, or even members of a specific church. Unlike savings and loans, credit unions typically do not make mortgage loans. (2)

Crowding out in the open economy. In the open economy, an increase government spending financed by borrowing causes an increase in the interest rate which not only reduces consumption and investment, but also net exports counteracting the increase in government spending. It is most severe when exchange rates are flexible. (17)

Crowding out. Describes the effect of increases in government purchases on other private spending. Government borrowing raises interest rates and hence reduces investment and consumption spending. (16)

Currency. Coins and paper money. (1)

Current account. That portion of the balance of payments that consists of the merchandise account, the services account, and the balance of unilateral transfers. (17)

Current yield. The ratio of the annual coupon payment to the price paid for the bond. (8)

Debenture. A bond that is not backed by any specific collateral, but is instead backed by ''the full faith and credit'' of the selling firm or institution. (2)

Debt instrument. A written promise by a borrower to pay the owner of the instrument a specified amount (or amounts) in the future. (8)

Debt market. A market where lenders provide funds to borrowers for some specified period of time. (2)

Default risk premium. The difference between the interest rate charged on safe loans, loans considered default-free, and the interest rate charged on loans that have a higher default risk. (9)

Default risk. The risk that a borrower will not fully repay the principle and interest on a loan. (9)

Demand curve. The relationship between the price of a good or service and its quantity demanded. (4)

Demand deposits. Deposits in depository institutions, which can be withdrawn by depositors upon demand, i.e. whenever they choose. Demand deposits are transferable by check. (1)

Demand for net exports. The demand for exports minus the demand for imports. (17)

Depository Institution Deregulation and Monetary Control Act of 1980 (DIDMCA). Legislation designed to solve problems created in part by disintermediation. (7)

Depository institutions. Institutions which accept deposits from individuals and use the funds to participate in the debt market (i.e., to make loans). (2)

Depreciation. Depreciation of the U.S. dollar means the dollar buys fewer units of foreign currency than before. (11)

Derived demand. An individual bank's demand for deposits (and indeed the demand for any input into the production process) is called a derived demand because it is derived from the demand for loans that banks try to satisfy. (6)

Desired currency to deposit ratio. The amount of currency the public wishes to hold as a fraction of demand deposits. (14)

Desired excess reserve ratio. The amount of excess reserves banks wish to hold as a fraction of demand deposits. (14)

Determinants of demand. Variables that determine the position of the demand curve; changes in them shift the curve. (4)

Determinants of supply. Variables that determine the position of the supply curve; changes in them shift the curve. (4)

Direct finance. Finance that occurs when savers lend funds directly to borrowers. (1)

Dirty float. Situation where the exchange rate is determined by supply and demand, but the government influences supply and demand by buying and selling currency. (11)

Discount rate. The interest rate charged by the Fed on its loans to depository institutions. (13)

Discount window. Banks and other depository institutions can ''go to the window'' to borrow from the Fed. Presentation of assets as collateral is not required; banks merely promise to repay the loan in the future. (13)

Discount yield. Measure of yield frequently used in the case of Treasury Bills, but which understates the actual yield to maturity. (8)

Discretionary monetary policy. A situation where the Fed has the flexibility to respond however its sees fit, without any constraint to follow some preexisting rule. (20)

Disintermediation. Describes the phenomenon of depositors withdrawing funds from financial intermediaries in favor of direct finance. (7)

Diversification. Spreading your investment dollars over two or more different assets. Often done to reduce risk. (9)

Dividend yield. The ratio of the annual dividends per share to the price of the stock. (8)

Dividends. Earnings paid to shareholders. (8)

Dominant strategy. Situation in game theory where one player has an action or strategy that is best, regardless of what the other players do. (20)

Double coincidence of wants. A situation that occurs in a barter transactions between two individuals. The first individual has a good or service that the second individual wants, and the second individual has a good or service that the first individual wants. (1)

Dual banking. The system of banking in which banks can obtain either a state or a national charter. (7)

Economic growth. An increase in the economy's ability to produce real output of goods and services. (3)

Economies of scale. A technological condition that occurs when the average cost curve decreases as the amount of loans increases. (5)

Effectiveness lags increase. The time between when a policy action is made and when they result in changes in the economy. (19)

Efficient markets hypothesis. States that the current price of an asset, such as a share of stock, reflects all available information about the value of the asset. (12)

Elastic currency. A money supply which can be easily converted from demand deposits into currency. (13)

Elasticity. A measure of how responsive one variable is to a change in another variable. For instance, the elasticity of supply of deposits is the percentage change in the quantity supplied of deposits divided by the percentage change in the interest rate paid on deposits. (6)

Endogenous money supply. Upward sloping money supply curve that results when the determinants of the money supply—most notably the currency to deposit ratio and the desired excess reserve ratio—are endogenous and depend on economic variables like interest rates. (14)

Equation of exchange. MV = PY; links aggregate spending in an economy and the stock of money. (3, 15)

Equilibrium. Situation where there is no tendency for the price to change any further. (4)

Equity instruments. Shares of common stock; represent the ownership of a share of a firm. (8)

Equity market. A market where ownership shares of companies are bought and sold. (2)

Eurobonds. Bonds that are denominated in a currency other than that of the country of origin. (2)

Eurodollars. U.S. dollar deposits in banks (both overseas branches of U.S. banks and foreign banks) located in a foreign country. (2)

European Monetary System (EMS). An exchange rate system started by some nations of the European Economic Community in 1979. Presently the exchange rates between member countries are pegged to narrow bands, with an eventual goal of moving to a common currency. During the 1992-1993 period the bands were loosened and Great Britain stopped maintaining the pound sterling within the agreed-upon bands. (11)

Ex-ante real interest rate. See Real interest rate.

Ex-post real interest rate. The nominal interest rate minus the actual inflation rate. (3)

Excess reserves. Reserves in excess of required reserves. (13)

Exchange rate. The number of dollars you have to give up for each unit of the foreign currency. (11)

Exogenous money supply. Vertical money supply curve that results when changes in interest rates do not alter the currency to deposit ratio or the desired excess reserve ratios of banks. (14)

Expectations hypothesis. The hypothesis that longer-term interest rates are an average of the shorter term interest rates expected to prevail during the life of the longer-term asset. (10)

Expected value (mean). The sum of the outcomes weighted by their probabilities. (9)

Exports. Goods and services produced in the U.S. and sold to the rest of the world. (17)

Extended credit. Represents long term lending to troubled depository institutions. (13)

Face value. The amount paid when a financial instrument, like a Treasury Bill, matures. (8)

Federal debt. The total amount the federal government owes its creditors. (21)

Federal Deposit Insurance Corporation (FDIC). Established in 1934 to insure depositors against loss due to bank failure. (7)

Federal deposit insurance. Insurance issued by the FDIC that guarantees the full payment (up to $100,000) to owners of certain deposit accounts at member banks. (6)

Federal funds rate. Rate at which banks can borrow funds from another bank to obtain funds on a short-term (overnight) basis. (6)

Federal funds. Short-term (usually overnight) loans of reserve deposits between banks. (2)

Federal Open Market Committee. The policy-making arm of the Federal Reserve System. (13)

Federal Reserve Act of 1913. Established the Federal Reserve System. (7)

Federal reserve notes. U.S. paper money, also called dollar bills. (1)

Federal Reserve System (Fed). Established as the central bank for the United States by the Federal Reserve Act of 1913. (13)

Fee-based financial services. Financial services, like insurance and ATM services, for which prices are stated in dollars or other currency units. (4)

Fiat money. Paper money, money that does not represent a claim to any physical commodity. Fiat money is money which has a face value (or value as money) that exceeds its value as a commodity. Examples include U.S. Federal Reserve Notes. (1)

Financial Institutions Reform, Recovery, and Enforcement Act of 1989 (FIRREA). This act was directed at the problems facing the savings and loan industry during the late 1980's. It abolished the Federal Saving and Loan Insurance Corporation (FSLIC) and the Federal Home Loan Bank Board (FHLBB), which had regulated the savings and loan industry. (7)

Financial intermediary. A financial institution that accepts funds from savers, transforms them, and lends them to borrowers. (1)

Financial market. An institution or arrangement that facilitates the purchase and sale of financial instruments such as corporate stocks and bonds, government bonds, and more exotic things such as options and futures contracts. (2)

Financial service markets. Markets in which individuals and firms purchase services that enhance the workings of debt and equity markets. (2)

Fiscal policy. Government spending or tax policy. (16)

Fisher equation. The equation that sets the nominal interest rate equal to the real interest rate plus the expected inflation rate. (3)

Fixed exchange rates. Exchange rates in which a country or group of countries pledge to keep the exchange rate within a narrow band of a target level. (11)

Flexible (floating) exchange rates. The exchange rate is determined strictly by the intersection of private supply and demand, without any government intervention. (11)

Foreign exchange market. The market where different currencies are bought and sold. (11)

Forward exchange rate. An exchange rate and quantity of currency contracted for today, but the actual exchange takes place at a specific future date. (11)

Fractional reserve banking. A banking system in which bank reserves equal only a fraction of outstanding demand deposits. (1)

Free banking system. A system, begun in Michigan (1837) and New York (1838), to make entry into the banking industry less difficult by simplifying the process of obtaining a state charter and to make bank notes more safe: anyone could open a bank and issue notes so long as that person provided the requisite collateral. (13)

Frictional unemployment. Unemployment which occurs as people seek their first jobs, as people quit one job to seek another, or as people are displaced from jobs due to technical change and must seek another job. (16)

Full bodied money. A commodity money in which the commodity itself circulates as money. (1)

Future value. The value at some future date, given the prevailing interest rate, of a present amount. (3, 8)

Futures contract. A deal made now to take place at a specified future date, at a price and quantity specified today. (9)

Futures markets. Markets where futures contracts are traded. (9)

Garn-St. Germain Act of 1982. Legislation designed to make depository institutions more competitive with money market mutual funds.

Glass-Steagall Act (1933). Also known as the Banking Act of 1933, this legislation made fundamental changes in the structure of the banking industry. Among other things, it created the Federal Deposit Insurance Corporation or FDIC. (7)

Gold certificates. Paper claims that are redeemable for a specified amount of gold. (1)

Gold standard. International fixed exchange rate system in which currencies are pegged to specified amounts of gold. (11)

Government budget constraint. The restriction that the government cannot purchase goods and services without having a source of funds to pay for these purchases. (16)

Government purchases. Goods and services demanded by government. (16)

Government securities. Long-term debt instruments issued by the U.S. Treasury, and include such instruments as U.S. Treasury Bonds and Notes. (2)

Greenbacks. Fiat currency used during the Civil War that was not backed by gold or otherwise redeemable. (13)

Growth stock. The stock of a company that reinvests profits back into the firm in order to generate growth in earnings. (8)

Hedgers. Those who go to the forward market to buy or sell currency now in order to protect (hedge) against fluctuations in exchange rates. (11)

High powered money. Currency in the hands of the public plus commercial bank reserves, also called the monetary base. (14)

Human capital. The skills and training an individual acquires that makes her a productive employee or entrepreneur. (15)

Hyperinflation. An extended period in which inflation exceeds 100 percent per year. (15)

Illiquid. The description of a bank that lacks enough liquid assets to meet the immediate demands of its creditors and depositors. (6)

Imperfect information. In the loan market, when banks do not know for certain which borrowers will and will not repay loans, but only that some borrowers are more likely to repay than others. (5)

Implementation lags. The time between when a policy action is needed and the time when the action occurs. (19)

Import. A good or service made overseas but purchased by a U.S. resident. (17)

Income effect. The fact that a higher return on assets leaves a person with more income (or more wealth), which normally leads to the purchase of more assets. (16)

Income stock. The stocks of companies that have a low level of retained earnings and thus pay most of their earnings to shareholders, as dividends. (8)

Income. A flow of earnings over some given time interval (say, a week, month, or year). (1)

Independent monetary policy. A policy conducted through open market operations with the goal of changing the money supply without changing taxes or spending. (16)

Indirect finance. Finance that involves a middleman, a third party linking the borrower and lender. (1)

Inflation premium. The part of the nominal interest rate that is over and above the real interest rate. This compensates for the decline in purchasing power due to inflation. (3)

Inflation rate. The rate of change in the price level, stated as a percentage change on an annual basis. (3)

Inflation risk. Risk that the actual inflation rate will differ from that expected by borrowers and lenders. (9)

Inflation. A persistent, general rise in the average price of all goods. (3)

Inflationary expectations. Expectations or educated estimates of the inflation rate. (3)

Information lags. Lags in the availability of information about the state of the economy. (19)

Insolvent. The description of a bank with total liabilities that exceed the value of its assets. (6)

Instrument. In terms of monetary policy, variables the policymaker can control. (19)

Instrument instability. Arises when a change in the instrument affects the targeted variable over a number of future periods, leading to ever-widening swings in the instrument in order to stabilize the targeted variable. (19)

Insurance companies. Financial institutions that help protect individuals against certain risks, such as risks to health, disability, and life. (2)

Interest elasticity of demand for loans. The percentage change in the quantity demanded of loans divided by the percentage change in the interest rate. (5)

Interest Rate Adjustment Act (1961). Extended the Glass-Steagall interest rate limits to thrifts. (7)

Interest rate ceiling. A specified amount above which the interest rate is not permitted to rise. (4)

Interest rate floor. A feature of many financial instruments that prevent the interest rate from falling below some specified amount. (4)

Interest rate risk. The risk of a change in the overall level of interest rates, and the resulting change in bond prices. (9)

Intermediate target. This target is a value for a variable that the policy maker tries to achieve not because it is desirable in its own right, but because it helps achieve the final target. (19)

Intermediate-term assets. Assets in the debt market which mature between one and ten years from the date of issue. (2)

International Lending Supervisory Act of 1983. Legislation which addressed the issue of bank capitalization, and authorized the Federal Reserve System, the FDIC, and the Comptroller of the Currency to set and enforce minimum capital requirements. (7)

Inventory approach to money demand. Pioneered by William Baumol and James Tobin in the 1950s. Provides a microeconomic justification for including interest rates as a determinant of money demand. (15)

Investment bank. A firm that administers, promotes, and distributes new securities. (7)

Investment goods. Goods and services demanded by businesses for use as capital inputs into production. (16)

Junk bonds. Bonds that have a relatively high risk of default. (2)

Keynesians. Followers of John Maynard Keynes who view the economy as unstable and in need of government intervention and control. They tend to argue that the interest elasticity of money demand is—or can be—high. (15)

L monetary aggregate. M3 + short-term Treasury securities + commercial paper + savings bonds + banker's acceptances. (2)

Law of demand. A law of economics which states that as the price of a good or service rises, consumers will purchase less of it. (4)

Law of diminishing marginal returns. Economic principal which states that as the amount of one input increases and all other inputs remain constant, the marginal product of the input eventually begins to decline. (6)

Law of large numbers. Implies that if individual withdrawal decisions are independent and the number of depositors gets larger, the average fraction of deposits withdrawn by all depositors gets closer and closer to the probability that one depositor withdraws his deposits. (6)

Law of supply. More goods or services are provided when the price is high than when it is low. (4)

Legal reserves. Vault cash and reserve deposits at Federal Reserve banks. (14)

Legislative lags. Lags in the enactment of the appropriate legislation needed for a policy action to occur. (19)

Limited branching. Restrictions that limit the ability of banks to open offices within the state's boundary. (7)

Liquidity premium. The additional interest rate lenders must receive to compensate them for liquidity risk. (9)

Liquidity risk. Risk due to the possibility that it will be necessary to liquidate a bond or other debt instrument prior to maturity, with some probability that the price received in such a situation will be less than favorable. (9)

Liquidity. The relative ease with which an asset may be converted into the medium of exchange without substantially losing value. (1, 4)

Loanable funds. Funds supplied by lenders and demanded by borrowers. The prices of these financial services are stated as an interest rate. (4)

Location advantage. The competitive advantage that accrues to a firm when customers value the convenience of utilizing a firm located in close proximity to where they live. (5)

Long-run aggregate supply curve (LRAS). Characterizes the supply side of the macroeconomy in the long-run, i.e. summarizes the total quantity of goods and services that an economy will produce at various price levels, after allowing the prices of inputs and price expectations to adjust to any changes in the price level. (16)

Long-term assets. Assets in the debt market which mature more than ten years from the date of issue. (2)

M1 money aggregate. Currency + demand deposits + traveler's checks + other checkable deposits. (2)

M2 money aggregate. M1 + savings deposits + small time deposits + money market deposit accounts + money market mutual shares (not owned by institutions) + overnight repurchase agreements + overnight Eurodollars. (2)

M3 money aggregate. M2 + large denomination time deposits + money market mutual shares (institutional) + term repurchase agreements + term Eurodollars. (2)

Margin requirement. Requirement that a buyer of a security cannot borrow more than a specified percentage of its purchase price. (13)

Marginal cost. The change in total cost caused by a one-dollar change in the amount of loans. (5)

Marginal product. The change in total product (or total output) that results from a one-unit change in the usage of a variable input, holding the quantities of other inputs constant. (6)

Marginal resource cost of deposits. The change in a bank's cost of deposits arising from a one dollar change in its deposits. (6)

Marginal revenue product of deposits. The marginal product of deposits multiplied by the marginal revenue of a loan; indicates the additional revenue earned by a bank if it attracts another $1 in deposits. (6)

Marginal revenue. The change in total revenue caused by a one dollar increase in the amount of loans. (5)

Markov expectations hypothesis. Asserts that individuals expect the future to be like the most recent past. (12)

McFadden Act (1927). Legislation introduced to allow states to write laws regulating branch banking within their boundaries, and gave states the power to impose these rules on national banks and banks chartered in other states. (7)

Medium of exchange. Whatever is commonly accepted as payment for goods and services, or to repay debts. The distinguishing feature of money. (1)

Merchandise account. A part of the current account that consists of exports and imports of goods, where exports are a positive entry and imports a negative entry. (17)

Merchandise trade balance. The difference between merchandise exports and merchandise imports. (17)

Modern quantity theory of money demand. Model of money demand developed by Milton Friedman that builds on the simple quantity theory by emphasizing the unique property of money as the medium of exchange. (15)

Monetary aggregates. Ways of adding up the quantity of different assets in the economy into a measure of the money stock. (2)

Monetary base. Currency in the hands of the public plus commercial bank reserves, also called high powered money. (14)

Monetary economy. An economy in which money is

used in most transactions, such as buying or selling goods and services. (1)

Monetary policy actions. Government actions directed at the money supply. (19)

Monetary policy game. A situation where strategic interactions between the Fed and the private sector (e.g., a union) make the payoffs resulting from their actions interdependent. (20)

Monetary policy rule. A rule that dictates what the Fed does to the money supply in various situations. (20)

Monetizing the deficit. Paying for government spending by printing money. (21)

Money market mutual funds. Mutual funds that sell shares of the fund to savers and invests in short term, safe assets such as Treasury Bills, large bank certificates of deposit, commercial paper, and banker's acceptances. (2)

Money market. The financial market in which the most liquid, short-term debt obligations are traded. Typically this term refers to the market for financial instruments that mature in one year or less. (2)

Money stock. The total amount of money in the economy. (2)

Money supply curve. The amount of money that suppliers are willing and able to supply at various interest rates. (14)

Money supply equation. A relation that indicates how much money is created in the economy for a given monetary base:
$$M^S = [(1 + c^d)/(rr + e^d + c^d)] \times MB. \quad (14)$$

Money. Anything that is widely and generally accepted as a medium of exchange. (1)

Monopoly. The market structure in which there is only one seller for the entire market. (5)

Moral hazard. A situation created by ex post asymmetric information that induces one party to take an action that is undesirable from the other party's perspective. For instance, insurance reduces the incentive for individuals to guard themselves against risk. (6)

Moral suasion. The Fed's ability to persuade depository institutions and other financial institutions to behave in what it regards as the public's best interest. (13)

Mortgage. A debt instrument used to finance the purchase of homes and other forms of real estate when the underlying real estate serves as collateral for the loan. (2)

Moving average. A moving average is an average of the current and a given number of lagged values of a variable. Each time we add another observation we delete the observation furthest in the past when we calculate the moving average. (18)

Multiple deposit expansion. The process whereby depository institutions create money in the form of checkable deposits that are a multiple of the monetary base. (14)

Municipal bonds. Bonds issued by state and local governments to obtain long-term funds for such things as highways and schools. (2)

Mutual savings banks. A depository institution designed to promote mortgage lending, much like savings and loans, but owned cooperatively by members with a common interest, such as employees of a company, union members, or members of a church. (2)

National Banking Act of 1863. Created a new banking system with charters issued by the federal government. (7)

National Banks. Banks with charters issued by the Comptroller of the Currency. (7)

Natural rate of employment. The level of employment that occurs when there is only frictional unemployment. (16)

Natural rate of output. The level of output that corresponds to the long-run supply curve, i.e. the amount of goods that can be produced with available technology and the full employment of an economy's capital and labor resources. (16)

Net exports. The net foreign demand for U.S. goods and services, calculated as exports minus imports. (17)

Net income on investments. The net flow of investment income such as dividends, interest income, and royalties. (17)

Nominal interest rate. The interest rate stated in the loan contract. (3)

Nominal output. The current dollar value of the final goods and services produced in the economy in one year. (3)

Nominal Wage Rigidity. Nominal wages that are slow to adjust to changes in demand or supply of labor. (16)

Non-depository financial institutions. Financial institutions that do not accept deposits, but that serve various functions ranging from financial intermediation to selling insurance against risk. (2)

Official settlements balance. That part of the balance of payments that measures the change in official U.S. reserves. (17)

Oligopoly. The market structure in which a few firms compete for customers with each other. (5)

Open economy model. A model of an economy that is open to international trade. (17)

Open market purchase. The purchase of U.S. government securities by the Fed. (13)

Open market sale. The sale of U.S. government securities by the Fed. (13)

Operating procedure. A combination of intermediate targets and procedures for using the policy instruments to achieve the intermediate targets. (19)

Operating target. An immediate target of policy, a target for a variable that the Fed can definitely control on a daily or weekly basis, such as a category of reserves or a short run interest rate. (19)

Option contract. An instrument that gives the owner a right—but not an obligation—to sell or buy an item at a prespecified price within a prespecified period of time. (9)

Option markets. Markets were options are traded. (9)

Partial crowding out. Describes a situation in which crowding out is not complete, so the increase in government spending is greater than the resulting reduction in investment and consumption spending. (16)

Passive monetary policy. Situation where the Fed does not increase the money supply in an attempt to bring down interest rates in times of economic upheaval. (20)

Passive rule. A monetary policy rule that does not depend on the state of the economy, such as keeping growth in the money supply constant. (20)

Pension funds. Funds that gather regular contributions from employees, usually by payroll deduction, to provide retirement income to employees covered by the pension plan. (2)

Perpetuity. A loan that never matures; it consists of an infinite number of periodic interest payments, but no final payment of face value or principal. (3)

Physical capital. Economists' terminology for man-made inputs into the production process. (16)

Policy instruments. Variables that the policy maker can control. (19)

Policy targets. Variable that the policy maker tries to influence. (19)

Portfolio approach to Money Demand. (Also called the asset approach.) Developed in the 1950s by James Tobin. Provides an alternative justification for Keynes' view that interest rates affect money demand. (15)

Precautionary motive. The desire to hold money to meet unexpected expenditure requirements—for emergencies or the proverbial rainy day. (15)

Preferred habitat hypothesis. Combines key features of both the expectations hypothesis and the segmented markets hypothesis. It says that while investors do have a preference for loanable funds of a given term, they are willing to substitute away from their preferred term—if they are compensated for doing so. (10)

Present value. The value in the present (today) of funds available at some future date. (3, 8)

Price level. A measure of the average prices of goods and services in the economy. (3)

Price stability. Measured by the stability of the inflation rate, and by the amount by which inflation exceeds a target level. (19)

Price stabilization rule. A money policy rule that prescribes changes to the money supply in response to changes in aggregated supply or demand to keep the price level constant. (20)

Primary deficit. The amount the federal government spends on transfer payments and purchases over and above its current tax collections. Does not include interest payments on the debt. (21)

Primary market. The market where new issues of financial assets are bought and sold. (2)

Primary spending. Transfer payments and purchases of goods and services. Does not include interest payments on the debt. (21)

Procyclical policy. A policy that stimulates the economy during an expansion and restrains an economy during a recession. (19)

Public investment. Government investment. Occurs when the government purchases physical capital. (21)

Purchasing power parity. Theory which states that the equilibrium exchange rate makes the dollar cost of foreign and domestic goods identical. (11)

Pure competition. The market structure in which a large number of well-informed firms sell an identical product to a large number of well-informed buyers. No individual seller or buyer thinks that they can influence the market price. (5)

Purely competitive deposit market. Situation where individual banks are small relative to the entire market for deposits, and must pay the market rate on deposits. (6)

Put option. Gives a buyer the option to sell a financial asset at a specified price, up to the expiration date of the option. (9)

Rational expectations hypothesis. Views expectations as formed from all relevant information that is available, and revised not only in light of past experiences but also in light of new information or changes in the structure of the economy, including changes in the behavior of policy makers. (12)

Real bills doctrine. The view that loans made by the banking system that are ultimately used to fund the production of goods and services are not inflationary. (13)

Real interest rate. The nominal interest rate (the interest rate stated in the loan contact) minus the expected rate of inflation. (3)

Real money balances. The nominal money stock divided by the price level. It provides a measure of the purchasing power of money. (15)

Real output. The physical quantity of goods and services produced in the economy in one year. (3)

Recognition lags. Lags in the recognition of the monetary policy maker that a policy action is needed, based on the information available to it. (19)

Registered bond. A bond that is registered to the owner. (2)

Regulation Q. Restricted the maximum interest rate that banks could pay on savings and time deposits. (7)

Representative full bodied money. Paper money that represents a claim to a specific quantity of some commodity. (1)

Repurchase Agreement (''RP''). An agreement between two parties in which one agrees to sell a security today and then buy it back at a specific future date and for a specific price. (2)

Reputation effect. Allows the Fed to credibly commit to promises even when it has discretion. This is because the immediate gains from breaking a promise are more than offset by the stream of lost future opportunities. (20)

Required reserve ratio. The fraction of deposits banks are required to hold as reserves. (14)

Required reserves. Reserves banks must hold to satisfy requirements set by the Fed. (14)

Reserve ratio. The fraction of deposits banks keep in reserve. (6)

Ricardian equivalence. The key proposition of the Ricardian view, which says that any way of paying for government spending will have the same present value, and hence taxpayers will pay the same present value of taxes whether they are raised today or postponed to the future by government borrowing. (21)

Ricardian view. The view that borrowing and tax financing of government spending are essentially equivalent in their macroeconomic effects. (16)

Risk averse. Preferring a sure thing to an uncertain prospect with an identical expected value. (9)

Risk loving. Preferring the risky prospect to the sure thing, even though both have an identical expected value. (9)

Risk neutral. Differentiating between risky prospects only on the basis of their expected value. (9)

Risk. A situation in which individuals can list the possible outcomes and the corresponding probabilities of these outcomes. (9)

Savings and Loan Associations (S&L's). A depository institution originally designed as a mutual association of depositors designed to convert funds from savings accounts into mortgage loans. (2)

Scatter diagram. A graph which plots values of one variable on the vertical axis and values of another variable on the horizontal axis. (18)

Seasonal credit. Loans made to depository institutions facing strong seasonal variations in deposits and loans, such as banks in agricultural areas. (13)

Secondary market. The market where existing financial assets are bought and sold. (2)

Segmented markets hypothesis. The hypothesis that bonds with different maturities are not substitutable for one another; their yields are determined independently of one another. (10)

Seignorage. The profit from creating money and a source of revenue to the government. (21)

Semi-strong form market efficiency. Asserts that no publicly available information will help predict future asset prices or returns better than the last known value of the asset. (12)

Short-run aggregate supply (SRAS). Characterizes the supply side of the macroeconomy in the short-run, i.e. summarizes the total quantity of goods and services that an economy will produce at various price levels, holding constant such things as the prices of inputs, taxes, the stock of physical capital available to firms, and the level of technology. (16)

Short-run macroeconomic equilibrium. The determination of the equilibrium interest rate, price level, and level of real GDP corresponding to the intersection of aggregate demand and short run aggregate supply. (16)

Short-term assets. Assets in the debt market which mature in one year or less from the date of issue. (2)

Shortage. Situation where quantity demanded exceeds quantity supplied. (4)

Simple deposit multiplier. The multiple by which deposits increase in response to any increase in reserves. (14)

Simple quantity theory of money demand. Views transactions as the primary motive for holding money. (15)

Specie. Gold. (1)

Speculative motive. The part of Keynes' theory of money demand that implies that money demand depends on interest rates because of the effects of capital gains and losses on bonds. (15)

Speculators. Those who buy and sell in the forward market, not to hedge a position but to intentionally take a risky (or open) position in the market. (11)

Speed of adjustment. Determines how quickly expectations adjust to past errors in expectations. (12)

Spot rate. The current exchange rate, the rate at which you can exchange a foreign currency for U.S. dollars at this instant. (11)

Standard of deferred payment. The function that money performs when it is used as the standard for calculating payments deferred to a later date. (1)

State banking commissions. Control the formation of state banks, and examine state banks that are not members of the Federal Reserve or the FDIC. Regulations establish by these commissions vary from state to state. (7)

State banks. Banks chartered by the appropriate agency in the various states. (7)

Statewide branching. Practice that allows banks to freely open branches throughout the state. (7)

Statistical discrepancy. Measures the amount by which the balance of payments accounts do not really balance. (17)

Store of value. A means of storing today's purchasing power for use tomorrow. An important function of money. (1)

Strike price. Prespecified price of an option contact. (9)

Strong form market efficiency. Asserts that no current information, either publicly available or not, can improve on using the most recently known value of an asset price to predict the future value of the asset price. (12)

Subordinated bond. A bond whose claim on the assets of the issuer—the borrower—is subordinate to a claim by another bond. (2)

Substitutes. Goods or services that are related in the sense that when the price of one increases, the demand for the other increases because people substitute toward the one that is relatively cheaper. (4)

Substitution effect. As the return on an asset increases, people will substitute away from other assets and towards the one with the relatively higher returns. (16)

Supply curve. A schedule showing the relationship between the price of a good or service and its quantity supplied. (4)

Surplus. Situation where the quantity supplied exceeds quantity demanded. (4)

Symmetric information. In the loan market, when borrowers and banks have the same information about whether a loan will be repaid. (5)

Target. In terms of monetary policy, a goal or variable that the policymaker cannot directly control. (19)

Tax risk. The risk of changes in the tax treatment of interest income. (9)

Technical analysis. Charting or plotting historical data on asset prices. (12)

Term premium. The compensation required to induce investors to purchase an asset with a different term to maturity than their preferred one. (10)

Term structure of interest rates. The relationship between the yields of otherwise identical financial assets and their term to maturity. (10)

Token coins. Coins such as U.S. pennies, nickels, dimes, and quarters, which resemble commodity money coins but which are fiat money. The face value of these coins exceeds their value as a commodity. (1)

Total deficit. The difference between all government spending (both primary spending and interest payments) and tax collections. (21)

Total product. The total level of output produced with a given quantity of an input. (6)

Transaction motive. The desire to hold money because it is useful in making purchases. (15)

Transactions costs. The costs borne in making a transaction, such as a trade for goods, services, or assets. (1)

Transfer payments. Funds given to private individuals without a quid pro quo exchange. (16)

Treasury bills (T-bills). Short-term debt instruments used by the U.S. government to obtain funds. T-bills are sold at a discount from face value, pay no explicit interest payments, and have maturities of 3, 6, or 12 months. (2)

Triangluar arbitrage. Taking advantage of discrepancies between the spot exchange rate between two currencies and the exchange rate that can be obtained by trading one of the two currencies first for a third currency, and then trading that third currency for the other of the two currencies. (11)

Unanticipated inflation. The amount of inflation that is different from the expected (or anticipated) inflation rate. (3)

Uncertainty. A situation in which individuals cannot form probabilities over outcomes, either because they cannot list the possible outcomes or because they cannot estimate the probabilities to assign to the various outcomes. (9)

Underground economy. That part of the economy that is unrecorded in official measurements of economic activity because it consists of illegal activities and unrecorded cash transactions. (14)

Unified banking. System where banks serve both as commercial banks and investment banks. (7)

Uniform reserve requirements. Identical reserve requirements for commercial banks, savings and loans, and credit unions. (7)

Unilateral transfers. In the balance of payments accounts, the transfers of funds or goods for which no payment is expected in return. (17)

Unit banking. Restricting a bank to have only one office or to service a single location. (7)

Unit of account. A measure in which prices or values of goods and services are stated. An important function of money. (1)

Usury laws. Laws that restrict the interest rate that can be charged on loans and credit card balances. (7)

Value marginal product of deposits. The marginal product of deposits multiplied by the market interest rate on loans; indicates the additional revenue a purely competitive bank gets from an additional $1 of deposits. (6)

Variance. A probability—weighted sum of the squared deviations of potential outcomes from their mean. (9)

Velocity. The number of times the average unit of money changes hands in one year. (3)

Wage rigidity. Nominal wage stickiness or slow adjustment, due to formal and informal contracts. (16)

Weak form market efficiency. Claims that the best prediction of next period's asset price is this period's price. (12)

Wealth. The value of assets minus the value of debts owned by an individual or institution. (1)

Wildcat bank. Banks in the early 1800s that would purposely issue excessive notes and locate in remote places (near the ''wildcats'') to make redemption difficult. (13)

Yield curve. The relationship between interest rates on otherwise—identical financial assets and their term to maturity. (10)

Yield to maturity. The interest rate at which the amount used to purchase a financial asset, like a bond, would have to be invested in order to grow to the face value paid at maturity. (8)

Solutions

CHAPTER 1

3. **(a).** Bricks are durable to an extent, but may crack. Disadvantages include lack of divisibility and lack of portability. Bricks are not rare enough to make large transactions feasible with a portable amount of bricks.

   (b). Wine is durable to some extent, but bottles may crack and aging changes the value of a wine. Disadvantages include lack of divisibility (uncorking bottles exposes wine to oxygen and diminishes the value) and lack of portability.

   (c). Corn is durable if not exposed to the elements and is divisible. Corn is not rare enough to make large transactions feasible with a portable amount of corn.

   (d). Pearls are quite durable and portable but are not divisible.

   (e). Platinum is durable, divisible, and portable. It has no obvious disadvantages.

   (f). Uranium is divisible and durable (although it actually decays over time). Uranium is not portable, because the shielding required to protect users from the radiation would be too heavy to carry around easily.

5. In answering Question 4, the quarters would be most liquid. In London, England, the English pound is most liquid, followed by shares of IBM stock, then by either the used car or used computer. Next would come the roll of U.S. quarters, and last the house in Llano, Texas.

7. There would not be enough reserves on hand at the bank to satisfy the demand of depositors for their funds.

9. The bank will keep 10% ($100) in reserve and issue loans of $900. Liabilities will remain the same ($1,000).

11. Many depositors place their funds in the bank, and the bank then lends to a borrower. Banks investigate the credit-worthiness of a loan applicant and monitor the borrower to see that the loan will be repaid. If depositors were to each lend individually to the borrower, then each depositor might want to investigate and monitor the borrower. Banks economize on these costs, doing them once; otherwise of many depositors would duplicate each other's efforts.

13. Both are of equal value—one dollar. Whether you get a lot or a little gold, it will still be worth one dollar. This is easily confused with the *value of one dollar,* that is what can bought with one dollar. For example, if the price of a cup of coffee was one dollar, it wouldn't matter if you paid for it with a dollar bill or a speck of gold dust worth one dollar.

15. Accounts do not have to be kept in the same units as the medium of exchange. In fact, there are recent examples of countries using dollars as the unit of account and the local currency as the medium of exchange. This occurred in Israel in the early 1980s and in Bolivia throughout the 1980s. These were periods of high inflation in these countries. In order not to have to post changes in prices so often, prices would be posted in U.S. dollars but buyers would pay in shekels (in Israel) or in pesos (in Bolivia).

CHAPTER 2

1. Supermarkets purchase from wholesalers and sell to final consumers. They are middle-men. Financial intermediaries rent funds from depositors and lend these funds to borrowers, functioning as middlemen. They are more than just middlemen, though. Financial

intermediaries turn short term deposits into longer term loans. They also transform the term to maturity of assets.

3. Being able to buy and sell stock in the secondary market makes these assets more liquid, thus making them more attractive to investors. Their value is increased and the firm benefits by receiving a higher price for any new issues of stock.

5. The dollar bill is most liquid, followed by the U.S. Treasury Bill and the share of IBM stock. The municipal bond issued by a small town in Alaska is least liquid since there will be few traders buying and selling this bond.

7. A banker's acceptance is guaranteed to be honored, whereas an ordinary bank draft, or check, is not backed by any financial institution. For example, when you write a check to a store, the store is "taking your word for it" that you have enough money to cover the check.

9. The money market is the market for short term loans. For example, large credit-worthy firms can issue commercial paper.

11. **(a).** During the 30 years of the adjustable rate mortgage, the interest rate may vary. The percent you will pay each year will be that year's interest rate index plus 2%. However, it will not change by more than 3% from year to year and will never be below 7% or above 15%.

(b). 9% + 2% = 11%. This would be the maximum amount the rate could increase because this is an annual change of 3%(11%–8%), and that's the amount specified by the per year cap.

13. M1 contains only those financial instruments that serve as media of exchange.

15. Credit cards themselves are not money and are not exchanged for goods and services. A credit card is instead an identification card indicating that you have a line of credit at a financial institution. This line of credit is potential purchasing power. When you purchase something with your credit card, you are taking out an instant loan that you promise to repay when billed by your credit card company. When you make this payment, you are required to pay with money. Usually you will write a check making payment from your checking account balance.

CHAPTER 3

1. No. The inflation rate is a measure of the increase in the prices of all items in the economy, not just money and banking textbooks. An increase in the price of textbooks might just be a change in the price of these texts relative to the prices of all other goods.

3. The rate of money growth is 2.5%, calculated as (172.1–167.9)/167.9. The equation of exchange in growth rates form is $g_m + g_v = \pi + g_Y$. If $g_v = 0$ and $g_m = 2.5\%$, then in order to have $\pi = 0\%$, we would need $g_Y = 2.5\%$.

6. **(a).** $PV = \dfrac{\$10,000}{(1 + i)^5}$

    1. $10,000

    2. $7835.26

    3. $6209.21

(b). The higher the interest rate, the lower the present value of the future amount.

8. False: After the first year you will have (1.05) × $100 = $105. After the second year you will have (1.05) × $105 = $110.25.

10. False: The real rate of return equals the nominal interest rate minus the expected inflation rate. In this problem, r = 4% − 5% = −1%.

12. **(a).** $i_\tau = (1 - .28) \times .09 = .065 = 6.5\%$
   (b). $r = .09 - .06 = .03 = 3\%$
   (c). $r_\tau = (1 - .28) \times .09 - .06 = .005 = .5\%$

13. **(a).** The increased money growth rate is expected to increase the inflation rate, so expected inflation increases.
   (b). The increased expected inflation rate leads to a higher inflation premium on loans.
   (c). The higher inflation premium on loans leads to a higher nominal interest rate.

CHAPTER 4

1. Prices of fee-based financial services are quoted in dollars, while prices of interest-rate based financial services are expressed as percentages. It is possible to convert interest-rate-based into a fee-based price, and vice versa. For instance, suppose a bank charges 5 percent interest on a $10,000 loan. Then effectively, the bank could instead quote a price in dollars, indicating that it sells $10,000 loans for $500 (plus principal, of course). Similarly, insurance companies could quote prices of insurance policies as a percentage of the coverage. For instance, an insurance company that charges $500 to insure a $10,000 car could say that the price of a policy is 5 percent of the amount insured.

3. The reduction in automobile liability insurance claims reduces the cost to insurance companies of providing automobile liability insurance. Other things equal, this shifts the supply of auto insurance to the right. This increase in supply lowers the equilibrium price of automobile liability insurance and leads to a greater equilibrium quantity of automobile liability insurance.

9. **(a).** Your supply and demand graphs should show that the law increases the demand for personal loans. Other things equal, this raises the nominal interest rate on personal loans, and also raises the equilibrium quantity of personal loans.

10. **(d).** Since incomes decline during recessions, the supply of loanable funds in the form of savings deposits will likely decline. Your supply and demand graph should show that, other things equal, this tends to raise the equilibrium interest rate on savings deposits and reduce the equilibrium quantity of savings deposits.

13. **(a).** Higher expected returns on stocks would likely decrease the supply of loanable funds in the mortgage market, as potential lenders shift away from mortgages and into stocks. As a result of the decrease in supply of loanable funds in the mortgage market, mortgage interest rates would rise and the equilibrium quantity of mortgages would fall.

15. The statement is incorrect. While an increase in the demand for mortgages does tend to raise the mortgage interest rate, a higher mortgage interest rate does not increase the supply of mortgages; it increases the quantity supplied. There is no shift in supply caused by a shift in demand, but rather a movement along a given supply curve. Consequently, there is no self-correcting mechanism that tends to stabilize interest rates at their initial level.

16. **(a).** At a 33 percent marginal tax rate, a borrower holding a 12 percent mortgage would pay an effective after-tax interest rate of 8.04 percent.
   (b). For a 10 percent consumer loan, the after-tax interest rate would be 6.70 percent.

CHAPTER 5

1. Demanders of loanable funds include households, business, and government. Suppliers of loanable funds are savers.

2. In perfect competition, a bank cannot charge more on loans than the market interest rate. Attempts to do so will result in no loans being made.

3. **(a).** The higher interest rate on deposits will raise bank costs. Average and marginal cost curves will shift upward.

   (b). A greater frequency of default increases the cost of lending, shifting the average and marginal cost curves upward.

   (c). An increase in wages to loan processors increases administrative costs, shifting average and marginal cost curves upward.

4. See Figure 5.4 for an illustration.

   (a). The market interest rate rises.

   (b). The higher market interest rate signals a shift upward in the perfectly elastic demand curve facing an individual bank.

   (c). The higher market interest rate leads a perfectly competitive firm to make more loans, since $i = MC$ at a higher dollar amount of loans.

   (d). The higher interest rate on loans will lead to greater profits in the short run. In the long run, more suppliers enter the market until economic profits become zero again.

7. A bank may have market power for various reasons such as:
   - Economies of scale—larger banks can provide loans at lower average cost than smaller banks;
   - Location—borrowers value the convenience of utilizing a bank that is located close to them;
   - Regulation—the chartering and regulation of commercial banks may serve to limit competition and give banks location advantages.

8. False: By raising interest rates, a bank may lose some customers. However, if this bank has location advantage, some borrowers will still choose to use this bank since it is more convenient than others.

11. **(a).** 0

    (b). 25

12. **(a).** -5

    (b). 5

13. If the banks don't compete repeatedly, the equilibrium profits of both banks are zero. This is the only interest rate at which each bank is happy with the interest rate it is charging after seeing what the other bank is doing.

14. If Bank One charges 15% interest, Bank Two can charge 8% and earn $25. Next period and forever after Bank Two will earn $0. The present value of this is $25. Alternatively, Bank Two can charge 15% along with bank one and earn $5 per period ever after. The present value of this depends on the interest rate, but is $5 $\times$ (1 + r)/r. If r < .25, Bank Two will agree to collude at the 15% interest rate. Thus:

    (a). will collude; **(b).** will collude; **(c).** will not collude **(d).** will not collude.

16. With symmetric information, banks know which borrowers have a better probability of paying back the loan and which ones are more likely to default. The banks will then charge a higher interest rate to borrowers who are more likely to default. Therefore, we would not expect a single interest rate.

17. Since this bank is ignoring the probabilities of repaying the loan, this is a case of asymmetric information. The bank offering to issue a credit card to anyone, regardless of credit history, is likely to have more defaults than a bank that is more selective, so the interest rate on credit card loans will have to be higher to cover these losses.

18. To mitigate the situation identified in Question 17, as bank president you might:
    - Use credit reports, which will allow the bank to charge different rates to different borrowers;

- Build a reputation for being tough on borrowers who default on loans;
- Require collateral and down payments, creating incentives to repay loans.

CHAPTER 6

1. The demand for deposits is called a derived demand because it is derived from the demand for loans that the banks try to satisfy. Banks demand deposits because they need them to create loans.

2. Since Tenth National is a small bank in a large city, it probably operates in an environment of pure competition. As such, it must pay the market interest rate on deposits, which is determined by the intersection of the market supply and demand of deposits. Likewise, the bank must charge the market interest rate on loans.

4. (a). This means that a one dollar increase in deposits will increase the amount of loans issued by twenty cents.
   (c). To maximize profits, Town Bank should attract deposits up to the point where the value marginal product of deposits equals the interest rate paid on deposits. Here, the value marginal product of deposits is 2 percent, which is less than the 5 percent paid on deposits. Thus, Town Bank is not maximizing profits.

9. (a). Bertha Bank needs deposits as an input in issuing loans. Even though it is the only bank in town, to attract deposits it must offer depositors an incentive to deposit funds at the bank. While it might attract some depositors even if it did not pay interest on deposits, it would be unlikely to attract the amount needed to issue the profit-maximizing amount of loans.

10. If a bank with market power in the deposit market wants to attract more deposits, it must raise the deposit rate not only on new deposits, but also on the deposits it already has. This increases the cost of deposits more than just the amount paid on the last dollar of deposits.

11. (c). The value marginal product of deposits increases.

14. The law of large numbers says that when individual withdrawal decisions are independent and the number of depositors increases, a bank can accurately determine how much it can lend out and still cover the withdrawals of its many depositors. In fact, the bank knows that total withdrawals as a fraction of total deposits will be very close to the probability that any single depositor withdraws his or her funds from the bank. A bank can thus hold the fraction of deposits that equals this probability and be reasonably confident that it can cover withdrawals.

17. Those who leave deposits in the bank when it pays a low interest rate are likely to be the ones who usually keep a low balance in their account.

20. (b). Yes, because the privileges are effectively a form of insurance. This reduces Suzie's incentive to keep track of her balance when she writes checks, thus increasing the likelihood of a bounced check due to a form of moral hazard.

CHAPTER 7

1. A dual banking system is a system of banking in which banks can obtain either a state or national charter. The National Banking Act of 1863 created national banks and attempted to eliminate state banks by taxing bank notes issued by state banks. State banks survived through the innovation of demand deposits. As a consequence we have a dual banking system today.

3. State banks have the option of joining both, although state banks that join the Federal Reserve System are required to join FDIC.

5. **(a).** A national bank is required to join the FDIC, so the increased premium will not have an impact on a national bank's decision to obtain FDIC coverage.

   (b). State banks can opt out of FDIC coverage. This increase in cost of FDIC coverage might cause some state banks not to renew their FDIC insurance.

   (c). Since banks that obtain state charters can opt out of FDIC to avoid the higher premiums, the relative number of new banks that would open as state banks would likely increase.

7. The large number of individual banks in the U.S. is due primarily to branching restrictions that prevent banks from opening offices (branching) in different geographic regions.

9. A bank holding company is a corporation that owns one or more banks. Bank holding companies provide a means by which branching restriction can be at least partially circumvented. Bank holding companies also provide a mechanism for banks to diversify risks by "pooling" their assets with other institutions owned by the bank holding company. For these reasons, individual bank profits are stabilized to some degree and therefore individual banks are likely to benefit from being owned by a bank holding company.

11. If bank holding companies were illegal, banks would be more adversely affected by swings in local economies. This would likely increase the number of bank failures.

15. The primary means of decreasing the likelihood of bank failures are (1) regulating entry into the banking industry by screening bank charter applicants, and (2) requiring bank examinations to verify financial status of individual banks.

CHAPTER 8

1. **(a).** $PV = \dfrac{20,000}{(1.01)^5} = \$19,029.31$

   (b). $PV = \dfrac{20,000}{(1.05)^5} = \$15,670.52$

   (c). $PV = \dfrac{20,000}{(1.1)^5} = \$12,418.43$

3. You would save money by paying $20.00 for a 2 year subscription.

5. $P_{TB} = \dfrac{\$10,000}{1.085} = \$9,216.59.$

   Discount yield $= \dfrac{\$10,000 - \$9,216.59}{\$10,000} \times \dfrac{360}{365} = .077$, or 7.7 percent.

   Yield to maturity = 8.5 percent.

7. **(a).** $P_{CB} = \dfrac{\$1,000 + \$80}{1 + .06} = \$1,018.87.$

   Current yield $= \dfrac{\$80}{\$1,018.87} = .079$, or 7.9 percent.

   Yield to maturity = 6 percent.

9. Since the discount yield understates the actual yield to maturity on a Treasury bill, it follows that the yield to maturity on the Treasury bill exceeds 5 percent. Since the bank account pays only 5 percent, you would earn a higher return by purchasing the Treasury bill.

11. People buy stock because they expect *future* payments. These future payments might be in the form of dividends (as is likely for growth stocks) or in the form of payments due to a takeover or the liquidation of the firm's assets.

13. (a). $P_{GS} = \$2 \times \left(\dfrac{1 + .04}{.05 - .04}\right) = \$208.$

    (b). $P_{GS} = \$2 \times \left(\dfrac{1 + .04}{.06 - .04}\right) = \$104.$

15. When a stock or bond is purchased in the primary market, the issuing corporation or the government would receive funds.

CHAPTER 9

1. Risk is the concept in which the probabilities of outcomes is known. Uncertainty describes a situation in which probabilities of outcomes are unknown.

3. (a). Your graph should show that the supply of loanable funds decreases (shifts left). The firm must pay a higher nominal interest rate.
   (b). Your graph should show that the supply of loanable funds increases. The firm can pay a lower nominal interest rate.
   (c). Your graph should show that the supply of loanable funds decreases and the demand for loanable funds increases. The firm must pay a higher nominal interest rate.
   (d). Your graph should show that the supply of loanable funds decreases, causing the nominal interest rate to increase.

5. (a). The greater risk of default should lower the price of XYZ bonds.
   (b). The greater risk of default should raise the interest rate the XYZ must pay to borrow additional loanable funds.
   (c). The higher interest rate due to the greater default risk is, in effect, the increased default risk premium paid by XYZ.

7. (a). Price = PV = [$1,000,000 + (.1)($1,000,000)]/(1 + .10) = $1,000,000.
   (b). The default risk premium equals the difference between the interest rate on BUS's bond and the interest rate on an identical default free bond. Since investors believe BUS will not default, the default risk premium is zero.

9. Investors pay a lower price for callable bonds to compensate for the risk they face that the bond may be called in if the interest rate falls, thus they won't receive the entire amount of anticipated coupon payments.

11. False: Futures contracts can eliminate the uncertainty about future commodity prices. Since suppliers and demanders of a specific commodity both face this uncertainty, futures contracts can allow both parties to reduce their uncertainty, a benefit to both parties.

13. False: It is true that risk neutral investors differentiate between risky prospects only on the basis of expected value. However, bonds with identical characteristics such as face values, coupon payments, and maturities do not all have the same expected value. If a bond is risky relative to other bonds, its expected value will be lower and thus its price will also be lower.

CHAPTER 10

1. The date (e.g., March 17, 1995) and the broad type of financial instrument (by risk and liquidity—e.g., U.S. Treasury issues) are held constant along a yield curve. The yield and the term to maturity vary.

3. **One year bond issued January 1, 1996:** $(1 + .05) \times (1 + i) = 1 + .06)^2$. Solving for i, we have that $i = [(1.06)^2]/(1.05) - 1 = .0701$ or 7.01%.

   Two year bond issued January 1, 1996: $(1 + .05) \times (1 + i)^2 = (1 + .07)^3$. Solving for i, we have that $(1 + i)^2 = [(1.07)^3]/(1.05)$, or $i = \{[(1.07)^3]/(1.05)\}^{.5} - 1 = .0801$ or 8.01%.

   One year bond issued January 1, 1997: $(1 + .06)^2 \times (1 + i) = (1 + .07)^3$. Solving for i, we have that $(1 + i) = [(1.07)^3]/(1.06)^2$, or $i = \{[(1.07)^3]/[(1.06)^2]\} - 1 = .0903$ or 9.03%.

4. An upward sloping yield curve implies market expectations of higher short term interest rates in the future, while a downward sloping yield curve implies market expectations of lower short term interest rates in the future.

7. The term structure may be increasing, decreasing, or flat, depending on the desire of market participants for bonds with a one year maturity or bonds with a two years maturity.

9. To look at the term structure of interest rates, you should compare bonds that differ only in term to maturity. Corporate and government bonds differ in risk and in tax treatment, and hence should not be used to make inferences about the term structure.

11. **(a).** The expectations hypothesis suggests that two year bonds should yield $(1.05) \times (1.04) = (1 + i)^2$, or $i = .045 = 4.5\%$. However, investors require a 4% premium, or $4.5\% + 4\% = 8.5\%$, in order to invest in a two year bond.

    (b). The yield curve would be upward sloping.

13. **(a).** Next year's short-term rate would be expected to increase to compensate for inflation. Remember from Chapter 3 that the nominal interest rate equals the real interest rate plus the expected inflation rate.

    (b). Current one year interest rates would not be affected because inflation is expected to remain stable for this year.

    (c). Current two-year rates would increase.

CHAPTER 11

1. Long-term movements in exchange rates are caused by long-term changes in relative real incomes, price levels, tariffs, and interest rates across countries. Short-run changes in exchange rates are primarily due to changes in expectations of future exchange rates, which affect current exchange rates through the interest rate parity condition.

3. The dollar cost of the tulips falls to $326.67. The dollar has appreciated against the guilder. The guilder price of the car rises to 37,500 guilders. The guilder has depreciated against the dollar.

7. **(a).** The supply of dollars increases, while the demand for dollars falls. Therefore the exchange rate, expressed as lire per dollar, falls.

   (b). The supply of dollars falls, while the demand for dollars increases. Therefore the exchange rate, expressed as lire per dollar, rises.

9. Foreigners would purchase fewer debt obligations denominated in U.S. dollars, which in turn would decrease their demand for dollars. This would cause the dollar to depreciate relative to the yen.

11. **(a).** Possibilities include a steady rise in the U.S. price level relative to that in Britain, rising incomes in the U.S. relative to those in Britain, and a fall in tariffs on British imports relative to those imposed by the U.S. on British goods.

13. One possibility is for the Mexican central bank to intervene by buying pesos with their reserves of Western currencies, but this couldn't be sustained very long since these reserves would eventually be drained. An alternative is for the Mexican central bank to

reduce monetary growth, which is the probable cause of the rising price level that caused the depreciation in the first place.

CHAPTER 12

2. **(a).** Markov expectations.
   (b). Adaptive expectations (with zero speed of adjustment).
   (c). Rational expectations.
3. **(a).** 10 percent.
   (b). 10 percent.
   (c). Notice that if last year's forecast error was 6 percent, then last year's expectation of inflation must have been 4 percent. Therefore, this year's adaptive expectation of inflation is 7 percent.
5. The primary advantage of Markov expectation formation is that it requires minimal information and is relatively easy to form. However, Markov expectations may be subject to systematic forecast errors during periods of change.
9. Your completed table for the first five periods should look like this:

Period (t)	Actual Inflation Rate (π_t)	Expected Inflation Rate (π^e_t)	Forecast Error ($\pi_t - \pi^e_t$)
1	1%	1%	0%
2	2	1	1
3	3	2	1
4	4	3	1
5	5	4	1

Notice that expectations are not correct in periods 2-5, due to the changing inflationary environment.

11. Your completed table for the first four periods should look like this:

Period (t)	Money Growth Rate (g_{Mt})	Output Growth Rate (g_{Yt})	Actual Inflation Rate (π_t)	Rational Expectation of Inflation (π^{RE}_t)	Forecast Error ($\pi^e_t - \pi_t$)
1	2%	0%	1%	1%	0%
2	3	0	2	2	0
3	4	0	3	3	0
4	5	0	4	4	0

Notice that in these four periods, the banker's expectations are always correct. The reason is that in this problem there are no random variations in the actual inflation rate that are not accounted for in the simple quantity theory. In this problem velocity is not subject to the random variations that usually give rise nonsystematic forecast errors even in the presence of rational expectations.

12. Your completed table for the first five periods should look like this:

Period (t)	Actual Inflation Rate (π_t)	Adaptive Expectation Inflation Rate (π^e_t) when $\lambda = .2$	Adaptive Expectation Inflation Rate (π^e_t) when $\lambda = .8$
1	0%	0%	0%
2	5	0	0
3	5	1	4
4	5	1.8	4.8
5	5	2.44	4.96

Notice that the higher speed of adjustment leads to more rapid convergence to the higher permanent inflation rate that started in period 2.

14. The relevant variables are determinants of the supply and demand for short-term loanable funds presented in Chapter 4. These include inflationary expectations, taxes, interest on alternative sources and uses of funds, risk, wealth, liquidity, and the magnitude of government budget deficits.

CHAPTER 13

1. The seven members of the Board of Governors of the Federal Reserve System are appointed by the U.S. president and confirmed by the Senate. Their duties include setting reserve requirements, the discount rate, implementing selective credit controls. They also serve as voting members of the FOMC. Since they serve 14 year terms and a new one is appointed every two years, a two-team president can appoint up to 4 board members during his or her 8 years as president, assuming no resignations.

3. The FOMC has 12 voting members. The permanent voting members of the FOMC are the seven members of the Board of Governors. The presidents of five of the twelve regional Federal Reserve Banks also vote, but on a rotating basis. This committee directs open market operations though FOMC meetings, which occur eight times per year.

6. The Fed can purchase more U.S. government securities though open market operations, but doing so requires the Fed to "print money" to pay for them. According to the simple quantity theory, this increase in the money supply would tend to be inflationary.

7. The primary case for central bank independence is that it results in monetary policy guided by long-term economic goals rather than short-term political ones. As Box 13-4 illustrates, countries with independent central banks generally have lower inflation rates than those with less independent central banks.

11. The primary objective of the national banking system was to eliminate state banks by taxing state bank notes out of existence. In fact, state banks innovated by creating demand deposits, and as a result state banks and national banks now coexist.

16. DIDMCA gave the Fed authority to set reserve requirements at all federally insured depository institutions.

17. Banks prefer a lower reserve requirement, since it ultimately allows them to profit by issuing a greater number of loans. In contrast, the U.S. government indirectly benefits from higher reserve requirements. The higher the required reserve ratio, the more government bonds the Fed can purchase in open market operations to generate a given increase in the money supply. Since the Fed earns interest on its U.S. government securities and remits the proceeds to the Treasury, a government concerned solely with its revenue would therefore benefit from higher reserve requirements.

18. Both lead to the same initial change in banking system reserves, but infusions of reserves through the discount window are temporary and therefore not as expansive in the long-run.

19. The bank's assets are $50,000 in bonds, $10,000 in gold reserves, and $40,000 in loans. The bank has liabilities of $50,000 in bank notes and net worth of $50,000.

    (a). Net worth falls to zero, but the bank is still solvent. The bank has sufficient assets to meet the liabilities of noteholders.

    (b). Net worth falls to $10,000, and the bank is still solvent. The bank has sufficient assets to meet the liabilities of noteholders.

    (c). Net worth falls to $-$ $40,000, and the bank is insolvent. The bank does not have sufficient assets to meet the liabilities of noteholders.

    (d). Yes.

CHAPTER 14

1. Total deposits increase by $833,333.33; total loans increase by $733,333.33; total banking system reserves increase by $100,000.

3. Total deposits increase by $1,666,666.66.

5. Total banking system deposits will increase by $100/c^d$, while the money supply (currency plus deposits) will increase by $100 \times (1 + c^d)/c^d$. Notice that the lower the currency-to-deposit ratio, the greater the increase in deposits and the money supply.

7. This would, in effect, reduce the currency-to-deposit ratio, which would lead to an increase in the U.S. money supply.

9. This answer depends on where the $1 million comes from. For instance, if the eccentric millionaire withdraws $1,000,000 cash from her bank that is over and above her normal currency holdings, banking system reserves are effectively reduced until 2014. In effect, putting money in a time capsule is, in this case, like an open market sale, which drains the banking system of reserves and decreases the money supply. In contrast, if the $1 million is part of her normal currency holdings and she does not alter future holdings, it has no effect on the money supply. In this case, it doesn't matter whether she keeps money in her pocket, under her mattress, or in a time capsule.

11. More cash transactions translates into a greater currency to deposit multiplier. Thus, an increase in drug trafficking would likely decrease bank deposits, loans, and the money supply.

13. Since the opportunity cost of holding excess reserves increased, the excess reserve ratio would fall and the money supply would likely increase.

15. To increase the monetary base, the Fed purchases government securities, which in turn increases its interest income. Other things equal, the Fed is likely to prefer this method of increasing the money supply since decreasing the reserve ratio does not generate income.

17. The rise in loan rates will reduce the excess reserve ratio, while the rise in deposit rates reduces the currency-to-deposit ratio. These two factors tend to increase banking system deposits, loans, and the money supply.

19. Consumers and businesses would likely increase their desired currency-to-deposit ratios to avoid the tax on deposits. This would tend to decrease bank deposits, loans, and the money supply.

CHAPTER 15

1. The simple quantity theory of money demand is (in nominal terms)

$$M^d = \frac{P \times Y}{V}.$$

This theory of money demand views velocity as constant and stresses that people will want to hold more money if either the price level increases or the quantity of goods purchased increases. Under the simple quantity theory, the primary motive for holding money is to make transactions.

3. The portfolio approach is based on the idea that people choose their mix of money and other assets based on the average return and portfolio risk. Those who are very risk averse might choose to hold only money, while those who are risk neutral may choose to hold only stocks. Tobin argued that, because of income and substitution effects, an increase in returns on stocks and bonds will tend to reduce money holding. The portfolio approach thus implies that money demand depends on interest rates, and that money is an important component in a portfolio only because it is a safe asset—not because it is useful as the medium of exchange.

5. The modern quantity theory describes the determinants of money demand, the factors that determine how much money households and businesses will demand. This theory views money demand as similar to the demand for any durable good. Money is valued because it provides a stream of purchasing power services. The factors that influence individual and business demand for real money balances fall into three broad categories:

- Individual wealth and the scale of business activities;
- Factors that influence the opportunity cost of holding money;
- Tastes and preferences.

7. Increases in the required reserve ratio, excess reserve ratio, currency-to-deposit ratio, or the price level shift the real money supply curve to the left. Increases in the monetary base shift the real money supply curve to the right.

9. An increase in bank fees increases average money holdings, since it makes it more costly to convert other assets into money during the inventory period.

11. A transaction tax on securities market purchases or sales would reduce the return on nonmonetary assets, and therefore increase the demand for money balances.

13. Other things equal, an increase in income would increase the demand for real money balances, and increase the equilibrium interest rate. The Fed could counter this increase by increasing the monetary base, which would increase the supply of real money balances and reduce the interest rate.

CHAPTER 16

4. Government demand is exogenous. None of the factors listed in Question 4 would shift government demand for goods and services.

6. (a). An increase in the interest rate (due to factors other than changes in the price level) will result in a reduction in consumption and investment demand, and hence a reduction in aggregate demand.

(b). A decrease in the money supply results in a higher interest rate, and hence reduces consumption and investment demand as indicated in part (a). In addition, a decrease in the money supply represents a decrease in household wealth, and reduces consumption demand. For all these reasons a decrease in the money supply shifts aggregate demand to the left.

(c). An increase in household taxes reduces household demand for consumption of goods and services, shifting aggregate demand to the left.

(d). An investment tax credit increases investment demand, shifting aggregate demand to the right.

10. A decrease in government purchases directly lowers aggregate demand.

(a). Reducing taxes that affect only consumption will increase consumption demand and at least in part counter the decline in aggregate demand caused by the cut in government purchases. In the short run, the price level and real GDP decline. In the long run, the price level declines and real GDP remains at its original level, since long run aggregate supply has not shifted.

(b). Reducing in taxes that affect only aggregate supply will cause aggregate supply to increase or shift to the right. Since aggregate demand is shifting to the left, the long run impact is to increase real GDP and reduce the price level. In the short run the effects are similar, although there is a possibility that real GDP may decline, depending on the magnitudes of the leftward shift in AD and the rightward shift in SRAS.

(c). If the taxes affect both aggregate demand and aggregate supply, then the answer is a mixture of the answers to (a) and (b) above. In particular, in the short run the price level will decline and real GDP may rise or fall. In the long run, real GDP will rise and the price level will decline.

12. The reduction in government purchases shifts aggregate demand to the left. The reduction in the money supply leads both to a higher interest rate (which reduces investment and consumption demand) and a lower level of wealth (which reduces consumption demand). The final effect is to magnify the reduction in aggregate demand. The price level and real GDP will decline.

14. If crowding out is complete then an increase in government spending financed by bond sales is ineffective at increasing aggregate demand. Monetarists often argue this position, and suggest that fiscal policy should not be used in this way. (Changing tax rates is another matter entirely!) If crowding out is partial, then fiscal policy can be used to increase aggregate demand. Keynesians argue this position to suggest that fiscal policy be used to counter business cycle movements, especially recessions.

CHAPTER 17

1. (a). The U.S. resident's purchase shows up as an import of $1,000, a negative entry in the current account. The Frenchman's purchase of stock shows up as a capital inflow of $1,000, a positive entry in the capital account.

(b). With these two transactions, there is a current account balance of −$1,000 and a capital account balance of +$1,000. The balance of payments is zero. There is, however, a balance of trade deficit of $1,000.

3. **(a).** An increase in the U.S. price level makes foreign goods more attractive to U.S. consumers, increasing the demand for imports.

(b). An increase in the foreign price level makes foreign goods less attractive to U.S. consumers, decreasing the demand for imports.

(c). A decrease in the exchange rate (in foreign currency per dollar) makes foreign goods more costly to U.S. consumers, decreasing the demand for imports.

5. **(a).** An increase in U.S. interest rates will decrease consumer demand for both U.S. goods and imported goods, and hence raise net exports. However, an increase in foreign interest rates will decrease foreign consumer demand for both their goods and U.S. exports, and hence lower U.S. net exports. The final result is uncertain: U.S. net exports may rise, fall, or remain the same.

(b). If U.S. wealth increases, consumption demand and the demand for imports will increase, so net exports will decline. However, if foreign wealth increases, then their demand for our products will increase. This increases U.S. exports and U.S. net exports. The net effect is uncertain.

7. **(a).** An increase in the exchange rate (in foreign currency per U.S. dollar) causes net exports to decrease, decreasing aggregate demand and decreasing the price level and real GDP in the short run.

(b). A decrease in the foreign interest rate causes an increase in foreign demand for U.S. products, increasing U.S. net exports and hence aggregate demand. The price level and real GDP will increase in the short run.

(c). An increase in the U.S. tariff on household goods will reduce U.S. import demand, increasing U.S. net exports and aggregate demand. The price level and real GDP will increase in the short run.

(d). A technological improvement will increase aggregate supply, resulting in an increase in real GDP and a fall in the price level.

(e). A tariff on imported raw materials will increase the cost of production, shifting aggregate supply to the left. Real GDP will fall and the price level will rise.

9. Tariffs are taxes on imports. If the tariff is on an imported raw material, then the tariff increases the cost of an input into the production process. Anything that causes the prices of inputs to rise will shift aggregate supply to the left.

11. The increase in government purchases increases aggregate demand. The increase in borrowing leads to a higher U.S. interest rate and hence to partial crowding out. In addition, in the open economy the increase in the U.S. interest rate leads foreign investors to purchase U.S. assets. To do this, they must first obtain U.S. dollars, which drives up the exchange rate (in foreign currency per U.S. dollar). This reduces net exports and partially counters the increase in aggregate demand from the increases in government spending. If the crowding out is only partial, the effect will be that the exchange rate is higher, the interest rate is higher, the price level is higher, and real GDP is higher.

13. The government might try tariffs on consumer goods, subsidies for exports, increasing the U.S. interest rate, or any policy that would result in a decrease in the exchange rate (measured as units of foreign currency per dollar).

CHAPTER 18

2. In Chapter 16 we saw that long run aggregate supply was vertical while short run aggregate supply was upward sloping. In the long run an increase in the money supply

will increase the price level but not change real GDP. Nominal GDP will rise because the price level increases. These predictions accord well with the long run evidence presented in this chapter. In the short run an increase in the money supply is predicted to increase both the price level and real GDP, and hence increase nominal GDP. These predictions also match the evidence presented in this chapter.

4. Increased money growth would make short run aggregate supply relatively flat, with only a small upward slope.

6. The difference between M2 growth and CPI growth means that there is not a one-to-one relationship between money growth and inflation in the short run, especially over time periods of one year or less.

8. When nominal interest rates increase, the demand for real money balances declines. Thus increases in the inflation rate that lead to increases in the nominal interest rate will cause a reduction in real money balances.

10. Based on our theoretical model of Chapter 16, if the Fed raised M2 growth we would predict an increase in both real GDP and the inflation rate in the short run. In the long run we predict an equal increase in the inflation rate with no change in real GDP. Our empirical evidence in this chapter is basically in accord with this, and in addition points out that in the short run the effect on real GDP is stronger than the effect on inflation.

CHAPTER 19

1. Since aggregate supply shifts right, the only way to restore the price level to its target value is to increase aggregate demand. This requires an increase in the money stock.

3. Aggregate supply shifts left and aggregate demand shifts right. The price level will increase. In order to restore price level to its target value, aggregate demand must shift left, below the original position of aggregate demand. Hence the Fed should act to decrease money stock.

6. An increase in velocity causes an increase in aggregate demand, which tends to raise the price level. To counter this, the Fed should reduce the money stock to reduce aggregate demand and maintain the price level at target. However, with an intermediate money target the Fed would keep the money supply at target and not respond to the change in the price level.

8. A decline in both the price level and output requires a reduction in aggregate demand. This could be caused by a change in any of the determinants of aggregate demand discussed in Chapters 16 and 17. As long as aggregate supply has not shifted, the Fed could respond by increasing the money supply so as to restore aggregate demand to its original position and hence restore the price level and output to their original values.

13. If the economy adjusts quickly to always be on long run aggregate supply but the Fed does not recognize this, then the Fed may change the money supply in order to shift aggregate demand in an attempt to achieve an output target. This will be in vain, though, and would result in a higher price level if aggregate supply is vertical.

CHAPTER 20

1. The solution does not change. All that matters are the relative payoffs in the cells of the matrix.

3. The solution is the same regardless of whether or not the Fed has discretion. The reason is the Fed prefers reducing the money supply, regardless of what the union does. In other words, reducing the money supply is a dominant strategy for the Fed. This illustrates that a Fed with known preferences for lower monetary growth (and inflation) can move the economy to cell d of the matrix even in the absence of rules.

5. Lags focus the debate on the length of the lags. Proponents of passive monetary policies argue that the lagged effects of activist policies are sufficiently long that, by the time they affect the economy, they do more harm than good. Proponents of active policies argue that lags are sufficiently short to enable active policies to foster stabilization.

7. Long run decreases in real output are due solely to declines in long-run aggregate supply. Therefore, if the long run model is correct, the rise in the price level and decline in real output must be the result of a decline in long-run aggregate supply, which also raises the price level. In this case, the decline in real output is permanent. In contrast, a short-term negative shock to the short-run aggregate supply curve would also result in a rise in the price level, but would reduce real output only temporarily.

9. A policy maker following a nominal GDP target would reduce the money supply when aggregate demand rises and increase the money supply when aggregate demand falls. With aggregate demand shocks, the policy is the same as under a price stabilization rule.

11. The executive and legislative branches typically are more concerned with short term goals, whereas the Fed typically is concerned with longer-term goals. In practice, Congress and the President exert pressure on the Fed to worry about movements in the short-run equilibrium, but since the Fed is largely independent and members are appointed for longer terms and not subject to re-election, it doesn't always give in to these political pressures.

13. Putting the alarm clock across the room forces you to get out of bed to turn it off. In contrast, leaving the alarm next to your bed gives you the discretion to get out of bed in the morning or not. If you have an early morning exam, you might be better off eliminating your discretion in the morning by placing the alarm across the room prior to going to sleep. This commits you to get out of bed when the alarm rings. Of course, you could always stay in bed and listen to it chime.

15. An active Fed will increase the money supply when aggregate demand falls but reduce the money supply when the economy gets back on track. In this sense, the job of an active Fed is to slow down an expanding economy and speed up a slowing one.

CHAPTER 21

1. The fiscal authority could reduce their demand for loanable funds. The monetary authority could reduce the money supply.

3. A decline in the money supply will increase the nominal interest rate in our money demand-money supply model. In increase in government spending financed by bond issues will also increase the interest rate, as we can see in the loanable funds market when there is an increase in government demand for loanable funds to finance the deficit. Thus the nominal interest rate will increase with tight money and/or loose fiscal policy. The increase in the interest rate will also tend to reduce aggregate demand but the increased government spending will tend to raise aggregate demand. The net effect is indeterminant. If the slower money growth slows inflation while increasing the nominal interest rate, then the real interest rate could rise.

5. Open market operations in military hardware would not be any different from the current system of conducting open market operations only in government bonds.

6. An increase of the monetary base by 50% would increase the money supply by a similar amount, causing a huge increase in the price level and an unprecedented inflation rate for the U.S. Concern over the effect of such an action leads to economists warning about the danger of turning to printing money to finance the government deficit.

8. Point out the Ricardian idea that the present value of taxes to finance a given amount of government spending will be the same whether those taxes are levied today or over some future period.

10. Tax rates can influence aggregate supply. The instrument shortage problem discussed in the text is caused by the fact that fiscal and monetary policy both influence the economy via aggregate demand. However, to the extent that fiscal policy can affect aggregate supply, this has the potential for mitigating the instrument shortage problem.

Index

Accounting profits, 134
Active monetary policy, 709
  aggregate demand decrease, and, 709–711, 714–715
  aggregate supply decrease, and, 712–713, 715–717
  disadvantages of, 717–721
  long-run price level, and, 709
  in short run, 713–714
Active rules, 733–737
Actual reserves, effect of deposits on, 449, 453
Adaptive expectations approach, 372–379
  criticism of, 391–392
Adaptive inflationary expectations, 374–378, 382–383, 385
Adjustable-rate mortgages, 47–49
  interest rate floor, 124
Adjustment credit, 436
Adverse selection, 156–158, 229
  lenience on defaulters, 159
Aftertax interest rate, 85, 107, 109, 291–292
Aggregate demand
  alternative ways to derive, 544–545
  changes in, 543–544, 553–554, 626, 638, 643, 733
  components of, 530, 531
  consumption demand, 530–534
  decrease, and active monetary policy, 709–711, 714–715
  deficit financed government purchasing, effect on, 567, 568–569, 611–612
  defined, 527
  determinants of, 530, 545, 603–604, 626
  financing government purchases through money creation, effect on, 570–573, 614–615
  government purchases, 538–540
  income, dependence on, 541–543
  income tax increase, effect on, 563–564
  increases in, 559
  instruments, and, 671
  investment demand, 534–538
  IS-LM model of, 526, 544, 579–585
  net exports, 590

in open economy, 601–603
  quantity theory of money, and, 626–627
  recession of 1990-1991, and, 571–572
  shift by Federal Reserve System, 672–673
  short-run macroeconomic equilibrium, and, 552
  targets, and, 671
  tariff-financed government purchases, 608–610
Aggregate demand,
  expectations, and, 370
Aggregate demand curve, 527–528, 541–542
  changes, effect of, 543–544
  defined, 527
  for open economy, 601–602
  slope of, 528–530
Aggregate government budget, 751–754
Aggregate price level, 527, 528
Aggregate quantity demanded, 527, 528, 529
Aggregate supply
  change in, 735
  decrease, and active monetary policy, 712–713
  income tax increase, effect on, 564–565
  instruments, and, 671
  recession of 1990-1991, and, 571–572
  targets, and, 671
  tariff-financed government purchases, 610–611
Aggregate supply,
  expectations, and, 370
Aggregate supply curve, 638
  VAT, effect on, 562
Agriculture, seasonal activity in, 412
Akerlof, George, 156n
Alternative investments, return on, 118–120
Alternative sources of funds, interest on, 105–106
Alternative use of funds, interest on, effect on supply of loanable funds, 111
American Stock Exchange, 45–47
Amount of money supplied, 475
Angell, Norman, 10
Annual rate of interest, 73

Anticipated inflation, 82
Appreciation, 333
  interest rate parity, and, 346–347
Arbitrage, 354–356
  covered interest arbitrage, 355–356
  triangular, 354–355
Arbitrageurs, 354
ARM, *see* Adjustable-rate mortgages
Asset approach to money demand, 502
Assets
  considered as money, 3
  open market purchase, effect of, 427, 455
  open market sale, effect of, 429
  safe, 503
  on T-account, 447
  valuation of, 257–262
Asymmetric information, 154–158
  collateral, 160
  credit reports, 158–159
  down payments, 160–161
  reputation, 159–160
  status of loan portfolio, 204
ATM, *see* Automatic teller machines
Auction, of U.S. treasury bonds, 32
Automatic teller machines (ATM), 3
  branching restrictions, and, 214, 222
  service provided by commercial banks, 34
Automobile loans, 51
  term of, 453
Average cost curve, economies of scale, 140–143
Average money holdings, cost of holding money and, 499–501

Bailout, S&L, 209
Balance of payments, 587–588
  capital account, 590–591
  current account, 588–590
  recent accounts, 591–593
  statistical discrepancy, 591–592
Balance of trade, and financing government purchases through money creation, 614–615
Balance on services, 589
Balance sheet
  adjustment of loan and reserve holdings, 450–451

Balance sheet *(continued)*
  deposit, effect of, 448–449, 452
  open market purchase, effect of, 456–459
  withdrawal, effect of, 454–455
Bank certificates of deposit, *see* Certificates of deposit
Bank charters, 202, 203
  economic implications of, 220–222
Banker's acceptances, 44–45
  valuation of, 239–244
Bank failures
  free banking system, 410–411
  insurance for depositors against, 207
  probability of, 481–482
  See also Federal Deposit Insurance Corporation
Bank fees, cost of holding money and, 499–501
Bank holding companies, 212–214
  branching restrictions, effect on, 223
Bank Holding Company Act of 1956, 214, 231
Bank Holding Company Act of 1970, 214, 231
Banking Act of 1933, *see* Glass-Steagall Act
Banking Act of 1935, 416–417
Banking industry
  entry into, limitations on, 220–222
  evolution of, 14–22, 201–202
  International Lending Supervisory Act of 1983, 205
  law of diminishing marginal returns, 168
  regulatory legislation, 211
Banking regulation
  adverse selection, and, 229
  capitalization, 204–205
  economic impact of, 220–229
  free banking system, 409–410
  history of, 201–202
  International Lending Supervisory Act of 1983, 205
  legislation, chronology of, 231–232
  moral hazard, and, 229
  overlapping responsibilities, 205–206
  overview of, 211
  status of loan portfolio, 204
  supervision and examination, 202–206
Banking system
  creation of money by, 458–459
  determinants of money supply, 477–479

  elasticity of, *see* Elasticity of banking system
  infusion of new reserves into, 455–459
  open market purchases, and, 463–464
  See also Federal Reserve System
Banking system reserves, increasing, 415
Bank loans
  pure competition, 131
  substitute for loan by individual bank, 132
Bank note, 16–18
Banknotes
  versus checkable deposits, 407–408
  issued by First Bank of the United States, 408
  safety of, 409–410
  state, 412
Bank of North America, 407
Bank panic, 190–193, 482
  elastic currency, and, 414
  FDIC and, 208–209
  suspension of payments, 413
Bank runs
  due to seasonal business activity, 412–413
  fear of inconvertibility, and, 408
Banks
  benefits obtained by depositors from, 24–27
  branching restrictions, 212–214
  capitalization, 204–205
  charter, 202, 203
  collusive agreements, 151
  cost of administration, 134–135
  default risk premium, 276–279
  deposits, *see* Deposits
  differences in withdrawal rates, effect on, 189–190
  examination of, *see* Banking regulation
  financial intermediaries, 22–27
  fractional reserve banking, 18–22
  gold reserves banks, 408
  with imperfect information, 153–163
  with market power, 139–147, 176–184
  membership in Federal Reserve System, 206–207
  monopoly bank, 140–141
  oligopoly, 147–153
  private, 407
  state, *see* State banks
  state-chartered, 201, 202
  supervision of, *see* Banking regulation
  total bank reserves, 465–466

  total stock of money, effect on, 471
  trading in foreign exchange markets, 338
Bank withdrawals, 15
  bank panic, 190–193
  differences in rates, among households, 189–190
  law of large numbers, and, 185–190
  recession, effect on, 190
Barro, Robert J., 765n
Barter, 8
  efficiency of, 5
  intermediate exchanges, 5n
Baumol, William, 498
Bearer bond, 48
Best fit line, 628–629
  regression results, 663–664
Board of Governors of Federal Reserve System, 414–415, 416–417, 419–420
  reserve requirements set by, 431
Bond market analysis, 251–252
  loanable funds approach, 252–253
  supply and demand approach, 253–255
Bond prices, decline during free banking era, 411
Bonds
  bearer bond, 48
  callable, 286, 288–289
  capital gains on, 288–289
  coupon bonds, *see* Coupon bond
  default risk premium, 276–279
  liquidity risk, 282–285
  long-term, 39
  open market operations, 428–430
  price analysis, 252–255
  price of, 411
  relationship between interest rate and price, 279–282
  as store of value, 7
  tax rate on interest income, effect on investors in, 112–113
  types of, 48
  underwritten by banks, 216
Borrowed reserves, 434
Borrowed reserves targeting, 696
Borrower
  credit history of, 158–159
  default risk premium, 276–279
  monitoring of, 27
  sensitivity to interest rate changes, 132
  unanticipated inflation, effect of, 84
Borrowing
  Eurodollars, 44

from Federal Reserve System, 207
government purchases financed by, 567–570, 611–614
recession, effect on, 120–122
Branching restrictions
bank holding companies, and, 212–214
on banks, 212–214
economic implications of, 222–223
Bretton Woods system of foreign exchange, 363–364
Broker
defined, 34
in direct finance, 23
Brokerage firms, 41
Brokerage services
financial service, 34
Budget deficit, 614–617, 619, 746
crowding out caused by, 763–764
growth, impact of, 771–773
inflation, leading to, 757–760
and real interest rate, 652
Budgeting, 6
Bureau of Labor Statistics (BLS), measurement of CPI, 62
Business projects, profitability, effect on demand for loanable funds, 109, 121

Callable bonds, 48, 286
capital gains and, 288–289
Calling in loans, 412–413
Call loans, 412
Call option, 300
Call premium, 286–288
Call risk, 285–290
defined, 286
Cambridge *k,* 496, 655
Cambridge theory of money demand, 493–495
modified, 496–498, 654
Cantillon, Richard, 509
Capital account, 588, 590–591
Capital gains, 288–289
Capitalization, of banks, 204–205
Capital stock, short-run aggregate supply, 546
Carter, Jimmy, restriction of unsecured consumer credit by, 436
Cash-in-advance models, 504n
CBOT, *see* Chicago Board of Trade
CD, *see* Certificates of deposit
Ceiling, on adjustable-rate mortgages, 47
Central bank, defined, 407

Central banking in United States, history of
before 1791, 407–408
Banking Act of 1935, 416–417
Depository Institutions Deregulation and Monetary Control Act of 1980, 417–418
Federal Reserve Act of 1913, 414–416
Federal Reserve-Treasury Accord (1951), 417
Great Depression, 416
national banking system, 411–413
Central bank intervention, 357–359
Certificates of deposit (CD)
money market mutual funds investment in, 37
regulating withdrawal rates with, 190
Change in demand, 93
Change in net export demand, 595–596
Change in quantity demanded, 93
Change in quantity supplied, 96
Change in supply, 97
Check, 15–16
Checkable deposits
banknotes, compared with, 407–408
fees on, 480–481
Checking accounts
cost of, 489
no-fee, 189–190
Chicago Board of Trade (CBOT), futures contracts traded on, 297
Chicago Mercantile Exchange (CME), futures contracts traded on, 297
Churning, and open market operations, 432–433
Classical view of money demand, 490
Cambridge theory, 493–495
simple quantity theory, 490–492
Closed economy model, 526, 586
crowding out in, 607
Ricardian equivalence, and, 767–770
CME, *see* Chicago Mercantile Exchange
Coinage, debasement of, 8n
Coins, 9, 11
Collateral, 160
for mortgage, 47
Collusion, 151
COMEX, *see* Commodities Exchange
Commercial bank reserves, 466
Commercial banks, 35
Depository Institutions Deregulation and Monetary Control Act of 1980, 417–418

financial services provided by, 33–34
investment banking, engaging in, 215–216
sale of U.S. savings bonds through, 32
share of mortgage market, 49
Commercial loans, 51
Commercial paper, 42–43
interest rates, historical data, 87
Commodities Exchange (COMEX), futures contracts traded on, 297
Commodity money, 9–11
Commodity price target, 687–689
Compensating differential, 323n
Competition, repeated interaction, 151–153
Complements, 94–95
Complete crowding out, 569
Complete currency multiplier, 469
Complete deposit multiplier, 467–468
Complete money multiplier, 470–473, 479
Comptroller of currency
International Lending Supervisory Act of 1983, 205
responsibilities of, 205, 207
supervision and examination of banks, 204–206
Consumer credit, interest rates on, 116
Consumer goods, tariffs on, 610
Consumer loans, 51
default risk premium, 276
interest rates on, 116
Consumer price index (CPI), 62
Consumption
deficit financed government purchasing, effect on, 567–569, 611–612
financing government purchases through money creation, effect on, 614–615
income tax increase, effect on, 564
Consumption demand, 530–534
open economy macroeconomics, 601–602
short-run macroeconomic equilibrium, and, 552
Consumption demand curve, 532–533
Consumption demand function, 530
Consumption goods, 527
Consumption purchases, 615
Consumption taxes, 562–563
Corporate bonds, 47
alternative investments, effect of return on, 118–120
default risk, 276

Corporate bonds (continued)
  default risk premium, 277–279
  expectations, and, 370
  interest rates, historical data, 87
  ratings of, 276
Corporate stock, 45–47
Cost, marginal resource, 181–184
Cost curve, 134–136
  average, 140–143
  banks with market power, 144–146
  marginal resource cost curve, 182–183
Costs of administration, of banks, 134–135
Costs of holding money, 498
Countercyclical policy, 669
Counterfeiting, in free banking system, 410
Coupon bond, 75
  valuation of, 247–249
Coupon rate, 75, 244
Covered interest arbitrage, 355–356
CPI, see Consumer price index
Credit card loans, reserve requirement
  for, 436
Credit card services, owned by bank
  holding companies, 212
Credit check, transactions costs of, 26–27
Credit report, bank strategy for countering
  asymmetric information, 158–159
Credit unions, 36
  depository institutions, 35
  financial intermediaries, 23
  National Credit Union Administration,
    209n
  National Credit Union Shareholders In-
    surance Fund, 209n
Crimes, collusion, 151
Crowding out, 568–570
  budget deficit cause of, 763–764
  in closed economy, 607
  deficit financed government purchas-
    ing, 611–614
  in open economy, 607, 611–614
Currency
  in bank panics, 413
  defined, 3
  desired currency to deposit ratio, 465
  Federal Reserve System as keeper of,
    423, 424–425
  hedgers, 352–353
  holding money in form of, cost of, 480
  supplier of, 206
Currency holdings
  monetary base, relationship with, 469–
    470, See also Public holdings of
    currency

money creation, effect of, 466–467
Currency substitution, 505
Currency to deposit ratio, 467, 469, 479–
  480, 482, 515
  determinant of money supply, 479
  influence of income on, 481
Current account, 588–590
Current account balance, 590, 595
  deficit financed government purchas-
    ing, effect on, 612
Current account deficit, 617–619
Current yield, 245–247

Dealer, defined, 34
Debasement of coinage, 8n
Debenture, 48
Debt, see Federal debt
Debt instruments
  default-free, 275, 276–277
  defined, 239
  government securities, 51
  interest bearing, valuation of, 244–249
  liquidity risk, 282–285
  sold on discount basis, valuation of,
    240–244
  valuation of, 238–251
Debt markets, 33
Default, 47
Defaulter on loan, bank treatment of,
  159–160
Default-free debt instruments, 275
  default risk premium, 276–277
Default risk, 269, 275–282
Default risk on loans, 158–161
Default risk premium, 276–279
Deferred payment, standard of, 7–8
Deficit financing of government purchases, 567–570, 611–614
Demand
  for bank loans, 132
  change in, 93
  derived, 166–167
  determinants of, 93, 105, 242–243,
    243n
  for fee-based financial services, 93–
    96
  increase, impact of, 100, 101–102
  law of, 93
  loanable funds, 104–109
  for loans, 177
  reduction in, by honest borrowers, 158
  See also Aggregate demand
Demand, law of, 528

Demand curve, 93, 99, 117–118
  adverse selection, 156–158
  aggregate demand curve, see Aggre-
    gate demand curve
  banks with market power, 139–140,
    143–144, 146–147
  for bonds, 253
  for loanable funds, 104–105
  loans offered by individual bank, 137–
    138
  in microeconomics, defined, 527
  net export demand curve, 594–596, see
    Net Export demand curve
  purely competitive banking market,
    132
  shift in entire, 105
Demand deposits, 15–16, 202
  bank panics and, 191
  Glass-Steagall Act, and, 216
  introduction of, 412
Demand for deposits
  banks with market power, 176–184
  purely competitive banks, 171–176
Demand for net exports, 593–601
Demand loans, 453
Deposit insurance
  economic effect of, 228–229
  See also Federal deposit insurance
Deposit market
  market power in, 181–184
  purely competitive, 171, 177–180
Depositors
  benefits obtained from banks, 24–27
  insurance against bank failures, 207
  sorting of, 189–190
Depository Institution Deregulation and
  Monetary Control Act of 1980 (DI-
  DMCA), 123–124, 130, 207, 225,
  226–227, 231, 417–418
  disintermediation, and, 219
  reserve requirements, and, 431
Deposits
  account options as sorting method, 190
  balance sheet, effect on, 448–449, 452
  bank panic, 190–193
  branching restrictions, effect of, 222
  costs/benefits, 181–183
  demand deposits, 412
  determination of amount of deposits
    needed to generate loans, 173–176
  increase, effect on reserves, 453
  individual banks, 447
  insurance on, 207–210
  interest on, 32

liabilities, effect on, 449
of loan money, effect of, 458–459
marginal resource cost of deposits, 181–184
marginal revenue product of deposits, 178–180, 181, 183
market supply, effect on deposits to individual bank, 171–172
market supply of, 222
open market purchases, and, 455, 463–464
purely competitive banks, demand for deposits by, 171–176
required reserves held as, 447–448
on T-account, 447–448
total product, 167–168
uncertainty and, 185–197
value marginal product of, 173–176
Depreciation, 333, 344, 346–347
Derived demand, 166–167
Desired currency to deposit ratio, 471
Determinants
of aggregate demand, 530
of demand, 93, 105, 242–243, 243n
of supply, 97, 110–114, 122
Determinants of money supply, 474–476
banking system, 477–479
Federal Reserve, 476–477
public, 479–482
Diminishing marginal returns, law of, 168
Directors of Federal Reserve banks, 422
Dirty float, 357
Discount bonds, valuation of, 239–244
Discount rate, 434, 669
Discount window, 207, 434
Discount yield, 239–240
Discretionary monetary policy, 723–726, 726–729, 729–730
Dishonest borrowers, 154–156
Disintermediation, 218
District Federal Reserve banks, establishment of, 414–415
Diversification, 294–297
Dividends, 45
valuation, and, 257
Dividend yield, 259
Divisibility, of money, 13
Dollar price, 104
Domestic price level, 594–596
Domestic wealth, 597
Donaldson, Sam, 570
Double coincidence of wants, 5
Down payment, bank strategy for countering asymmetric information, 160–161

Dual banking, 201–202
Duopoly banks, 148–153
Durability, of money, 13
Durable goods, demand for, 506

Earnings, 259–260, 260–262
Economic activity
evidence of short-run effect of money growth on, 632–637
long-run relationship with money, 625–628
short-run relationship with money, 638–642
U.S. evidence of effect of money growth on, 628–632
Economic downturns, Federal Reserve System actions to increase money supply, 476
Economic efficiency, goal of banking regulation, 211
Economic expansion, Federal Reserve System actions to reduce money supply, 476
Economic growth, 61, 65, 560
as macroeconomic goal, 668
Economic output, and spending, 615–616
Economies of scale, 140–143
Effective aftertax interest rate, 85, 107, 109
Effectiveness lag, 701–702
Efficient markets, 393
hypothesis, 393–395
rational expectations, and, 395–396
semistrong-form market efficiency, 398–399
strong-form market efficiency, 399
weak-form market efficiency, 396
Efficient markets hypothesis, 393–395
Elastic currency, 414
Elasticity of banking system, 413, 414
Elasticity of demand, 132–133
Electronic banking, 214. See also Automatic teller machines
Electronic funds transfer (EFT), open market purchase using, 427
Endogenous money supply, 483
equilibrium with, 515–518
Endogenous money supply curve, 484–485
Equation of exchange, 69–71, 490–492, 626–627
in growth rate form, 630

money stock, and, 627
Equilibrium, 99, 510–512
aggregate demand, 541–542
in bond market, 254–255
changes in, 100–103, 553–556
endogenous money supply, 515–518
exogenous money supply, 512–515
IS-LM, 582–583
long-run equilibrium, see Long-run equilibrium
in monetary market, 519–520
short-run macroeconomic equilibrium, 550–556
See also Market equilibrium
Equilibrium interest rate
deficit financed government purchasing, effect on, 568
purely competitive banking market, 132
short-run macroeconomic equilibrium, 550–551
Equilibrium nominal interest rate, 552
Equilibrium price level, 550–552
Equilibrium quantity of real money balances, 516–517
Equity markets, 33
Eurobonds, 52
Eurodollars, 44
European Community
floating exchange rate system, and, 364
free trade in, 212
European Monetary System (EMS), 364
Evans, Paul, 767
Ex ante real interest rate, 82, 290–291
Excess reserve ratio, 482, 515
exogenous, 483
Excess reserves, 166, 433, 447–448
in calculation of total reserves, 465
complete deposit multiplier, 468–469
deposit from outside banking system, effect of, 457
deposits, effect of, 449, 453
desired excess reserve ratio, 465
fixed fraction of deposits held in, 483
loans from, 449–450
money creation, effect of, 466–467
negative, 463
open market purchases, and, 463–464
unexpected withdrawals, and, 479
Excess reserves to deposits ratio, 477–478
Exchange rates
arbitrage, 354–356

Exchange rates *(continued)*
  arbitrageurs, 354
  Bretton Woods system, 363–364
  central bank intervention, 357–359
  changes in, 596–597
  defined, 331
  expectations of future exchange rates,
    348–350
  financing government purchases
    through money creation, effect on,
    614–615
  fixed, 359–362
  flexible (floating), 357
  floating, 364
  fluctuation of, 335–336
  foreign exchange rate system, history
    of, 362–368
  forward exchange rate, 351–357
  gold standard, 362–363
  interest rate parity, 346–348
  interest rates, and, 340–342
  interpretation of, 331–335
  net exports and, 598
  price levels, and, 340
  purchasing power parity, 342–344
  short-run, determination, 344–351
  spot rate, 351–357
  tariffs, and, 340–342
  trade barriers, and, 340–342
Exogenous money supply, 483, 512–515
Exogenous money supply curve, 483–484
Expansion of loans, 458–459
Expectations
  changes in, effect of, 369
  consumption demand, 530
  financial markets, role in, 369–370
  net export demand, and, 599
  velocity, and, 509
Expectations formation, 370–371
  adaptive expectations, 372–379
  Markov expectations, 371–372
  rational expectations, 379–390
Expectations hypothesis, 311–319
Expectations of future exchange rates,
  348–350
Expected interest rate, interest rate, corre-
  lation between, 650–651
Expected real interest rate, 370
Expected return
  interest rate parity, and, 346–348
  risk-adjusted, 393, 396
Expected value, 271–272, 278
Expenditures, budgeting, 6
Export demand, and exchange rate, 596
Exports, 586, 587–588, 594

Ex post real interest rate, 82, 290–291
Extended credit, 436

Face value, 47, 75, 239
Fannie Mae, *see* Federal National Mort-
  gage Association
FDIC, *see* Federal Deposit Insurance
  Corporation
Federal Advisory Council, 415
Federal budget, 747–750
Federal budget deficits, 109, 122–123
Federal budget surplus, 749
Federal charter, constitutionality of, 408
Federal debt, 746, 754–755
  effect on future generations, 760–763
  held by non-U.S. bondholders, 762–
    763
  refinancing of, 51
Federal deposit insurance, 193–195
Federal Deposit Insurance Corporation
  (FDIC), 193, 207–210
  Federal Deposit Insurance Corporation
    Improvement Act, 210
  Financial Institutions Reform, Recov-
    ery, and Enforcement Act of 1989,
    210
  International Lending Supervisory Act
    of 1983, 205
  responsibilities of, 206, 207
  S&L crisis, and, 209–210
  supervision and examination of banks,
    204–206
Federal Deposit Insurance Corporation
  Improvement Act (FDICIA), 210,
  232
Federal Financial Institutions Examina-
  tion Council, report by, 211
Federal funds, 45
Federal funds rate, 45
  historical data, 87
  operating targets, and, 694
Federal Home Loan Mortgage Corpora-
  tion (FHLMC, or Freddie Mac), 49
Federal Housing Administration (FHA),
  49
Federal National Mortgage Association
  (FNMA, or Fannie Mae), 49
Federal Open Market Committee
  (FOMC), 417, 422–423, 694
Federal Reserve Act, 206, 231, 414–416
Federal Reserve banks
  Banking Act of 1935, 420
  ownership of, 421
  regional banks, 422

  required reserves held in, 447–448
  structure of, 420–422
Federal Reserve Board, *see* Board of
  Governors of Federal Reserve System
Federal Reserve districts, 421
Federal Reserve notes, 3, 12, 18, 206,
  427
Federal Reserve System, 206–207
  alteration of money supply, 673–
    678
  Banking Act of 1935, 416–417
  bank notes issued by, 18
  bank panics, deal with, 192–193
  business cycle, and, 668–669
  central bank intervention, and, 358–
    359
  changes in monetary base by, 476
  changes in required reserve ratio by,
    476–477
  Depository Institutions Deregulation
    and Monetary Control Act of 1980,
    417–418
  determinants of money supply, 476–
    477
  discount rate, 434–435
  discretionary policy *versus* rules, 729–
    732
  establishment of, 413–414
  Federal Reserve Act of 1913, 414–416
  Federal Reserve-Treasury Accord
    (1951), 417
  fixed exchange rates, and, 360–362
  Great Depression, and, 416
  history of, 414–415
  independence of, 439–440
  instruments of, 671
  intermediate targets, and, 679
  International Lending Supervisory Act
    of 1983, 205
  monetary policy, and expectations, 370
  money aggregates defined, 54–56
  moral suasion, use of, 437
  open market operations, analysis of,
    466–467
  open market purchase, and, 455–457
  operating procedures, 692–697
  policy instruments, 669–671
  political manipulation of, 439–440
  real bills doctrine, 415
  required purchase of of stock by mem-
    ber banks, 414
  roles of, 423–425
  shortage of policy instruments, 673
  structural reforms of, 1935, 417

supervision and examination of banks, 202–206

total stock of money, effect on, 471

U.S. official reserve assets, 590

uses of funds supplied by, 466

Federal Reserve-Treasury Accord (1951), 417

Fee-based financial services, 92, 93–96, 96–98, 98–103

Fees
on checkable deposits, 480–481
See also Bank fees

FHA, *see* Federal Housing Administration

FHLMA, *see* Federal Home Loan Mortgage Corporation

Fiat money, 11–12

Financial asset, *see* Financial instruments

Financial Institutions Reform, Recovery, and Enforcement Act of 1989 (FIRREA), 210, 232

Financial instruments, 41

Financial intermediary, 22, 23, 24

Financial markets, 31–33
efficient markets hypothesis, and, 394–395
expectations, role of, 369–370
Federal Reserve System as guardian of, 423, 424–425
New York Stock Exchange (NYSE), 31–32
strong-form market efficiency, 399
weak-form market efficiency in, 396

Financial market stability, 668

Financial service markets, 33–34

Fire and casualty insurance companies, 40

FIRREA, *see* Financial Institutions Reform, Recovery, and Enforcement Act of 1989

First Bank of the United States, 408–409

First-time borrower, credit history of, 159

Fiscal policy, 561–573
in open economy, 608–614

Fisher, Irving, 490–492, 650

Fisher effect, 118

Fisher equation, 81, 289–290, 369, 370, 650, 652

Fixed costs, 135

Fixed exchange rates, 359–362
Bretton Woods system, 363–364
deficit financed government purchasing, and, 613–614
gold standard, 362–363

multilateral government action, 359–360
in open economy, 607–608
unilateral government action, 359

Fixed money rule, 733

Fixed-payment loan, 74–75

Fixed-rate mortgages, 47–49

Flexible exchange rates, 357
deficit financed government purchasing, and, 613–614
government purchases financed by, 614–615
in open economy, 607–608

Floating exchange rates, and European Community, 364

Floor
on adjustable-rate mortgages, 47
interest rate, 124–125

FNMA, *see* Federal National Mortgage Association

FOMC, *see* Federal Open Market Committee

Foreign banks, Eurodollars, 44

Foreign demand for U.S. assets, 614–615

Foreign exchange, 335–351, 359

Foreign exchange markets
central bank intervention, 357–359
defined, 330
reason for, 330–331

Foreign exchange rate systems
Bretton Woods system, 363–364
gold standard, 362–363
history of, 362–368

Foreign exchange term premium, 356

Foreign inputs, 605

Foreign investment in U.S., in 1990, 586

Foreign ownership of banks, First Bank of the United States, 408

Foreign price level, 596

Foreign real interest rate, 597

Foreign wealth, 597

Forward exchange rate, 351–357
covered interest arbitrage, 355–356
defined, 352

Forward market, 352–356

Fractional reserve banking, 18–22, 168–169
bank panics and, 191

Fractional reserve banking system, banknotes and, 408

Fraud, in free banking system, 410

Freddie Mac, *see* Federal Home Loan Mortgage Corporation

Free banking system, 409–410

Free entry and exit, 131

Frictional unemployment, 560

Friedman, Milton, 506–508, 643, 702, 721, 722, 723

Full-bodied money, 9

Full employment, 560

Funds
alternative sources of, 105–106
alternative use of, 111
cost of, 134

Future exchange rates, expectations of, 348–350

Future interest rates, and expectations hypothesis, 316–317

Futures contract, 297, 298–299

Futures markets, risk minimization, 294, 297–299

Future value (FV), 75–78, 237–238

Game theory, 148–151

Garn-St. Germain Act of 1982, 219, 232

GDP, *see* Gross domestic product

German hyperinflation of 1930's, 570

Ginnie Mae, *see* Government National Mortgage Association

Glass-Steagall Act (Banking Act of 1933), 207, 214–215, 216–219, 225, 231

GNMA, *see* Government National Mortgage Association

Gold, 9, 15

Gold certificates, 10

Gold depository, Federal Reserve System as, 423, 425

Gold reserves banks, 408

Goods, 492, 508

Goods and services
aggregate government purchases of, 753
federal government purchases of, 429, 747
state and local government purchases of, 751

Government bonds
default risk premium, 276–279
deficit financing using, 757
held by non-U.S. bondholders, effect of, 760–762
inheritance, effect of, 760–762
interest on, effect of deficit on, 122–123
liquidity risk, and, 283–284

Government borrowing, in 1980's, 652

Government budget constraint, 561–573
deficit, and, 757

Government budget constraint *(continued)*
   open market purchase, and, 575
   United States experience with, 761
Government budget deficits, demand for
      loanable funds, effect on, 109
Government budgets
   aggregate, 751–754
   federal, 747–750
   state and local, 750–751
Government guaranteed loan program,
      766
Government-issued debt, default on, 275–
      276
Government National Mortgage Associa-
      tion (GNMA, or Ginnie Mae), 49
Government purchases, 527, 538–540,
      615
   deficit financed, 567–570, 611–614
   money creation, financed by, 570–573,
      614–615
   open economy macroeconomics, 601,
      608–614
   tariff-financed, 608–611
   tax-financed, 562–567, 608–611
Government securities, 51
Government spending, 539–540
   Ricardian equivalence, and, 765
Great Depression
   Banking Act of 1935, 416–417
   Federal Reserve System, and, 416
   output growth during, 630
Greenbacks, 411
Greenspan, Alan, 420
Gross domestic product (GDP), 63–64,
      331
   federal debt as percentage of, 754–755
   growth in, United Kingdom, 636–637,
      649
   interest payments on debt as percent-
      age of, 748–749, 751, 753
   in 1990, 586
   nominal, *see* Nominal gross domestic
      product
   purchases of goods and services as
      percentage of, 747, 749, 751, 753
   tax collections as percentage of, 750,
      751, 752
Gross domestic product (GDP) deflator,
      64
Growth rate of economy, and long-term
      budget deficit, 771–775
Growth stock, valuation of, 259, 260–262

Hedgers, 352–353
High-powered money, 466

Hoarding, 7
Holding companies, *see* Bank holding
      companies
Honest borrowers, 154–156
Household interest payments, 107–109
   See also Mortgage
Households
   consumption demand, 530–534
   withdrawal rates of, 189–190
Humphrey, David B., 143
Hyperinflation, 508, 760
   German hyperinflation of 1930's, 570

Illegal activity, cash used for, 482
Illiquid, defined, 190
IMF, *see* International Monetary Fund
IMM, *see* International Monetary Market
Immediate target, 693
Imperfect information, 153
Implementation lag, 700–701
Implicit interest, zero coupon bond, 75
Implicit price deflator, 65
Import demand, and exchange rate, 596–
      597
Imported inputs, 603, 605
   tariffs on, 610–611
Imports, 587–588, 594
Income
   aggregate demand, and, 541–543
   consumption demand, and, 530–532
   currency to deposit ratio, influence of,
      481
   demand for fee-based financial serv-
      ices, effect on, 95
   money, and, 643–645
   real, *see* Real income
   velocity, determinant of, 509
Income effect, 503, 528
Income equality, 566–567
Income maintenance programs, 747
Income stock, valuation of, 259–260
Income taxes, 563–566, 608
Independent monetary policy, 573
Indexation, 564, 570
Indexing, to CPI, 62
Indirect finance, 23–27
Individual bank, supply of deposits to,
      172
Individuals, money demand by, 507
Inflation, 627
   adaptive inflationary expectations,
      374–378, 382–383, 385
   anticipated, 82
   causes of, 67–71
   deficit leading to, 757–760

defined, 61, 65
effect on future value, 80–85
expected inflation, 534
Markov inflationary expectation, 372–
      373
monetizing deficit, and, 757–759
money growth, relation to, 658–660
output growth, relation to, 658–660
politics, and, 718–719
printing money to pay interest on debt,
      275n
P-star, and, 699–700
rational inflationary expectations, 381–
      390
relevant theory to explain, 381
seigniorage, and, 759
unanticipated, 82–85
United Kingdom, 636–637, 649
velocity, and, 658–659
Inflationary expectations, 71, 107, 111–
      112, 369
   adaptive, 374–378, 382–383, 385
   money demand and, 508
   mortgage interest rate and, 117–118
Inflation premium, 81–82, 83, 289–291
Inflation rate, 65
   expected inflation rate, 650
   money growth, relationship to, 627
   money growth rate, relation to, 650–
      651
   in 1980's, 651–652
   nominal interest rate, relationship be-
      tween, 650–651
Inflation risk, 289–291
Information lag, 700
Inheritance, and Ricardian equivalence,
      765–770
Input prices, supply curve, effect on, 97–
      98
Inputs, 97
   tariffs on, 610–611
Insider information
   semistrong-form market efficiency, 398
   strong-form market efficiency, 399
Insider trading, 398–399
Insolvent bank, 191, 193–195
Instrument instability, 703–704
Insurance, deposit, *see* Deposit insurance;
      Federal deposit insurance
Insurance claims, predictability of, 39, 40
Insurance companies, 39–40
Insurance market, equilibrium changes in,
      100–103
Interaction, repeated, oligopoly banks,
      151–153

Interdependence, of oligopolistic banks, 148–151
Interest
on alternative sources of funds, 105–106
on alternative use of funds, 111
defined, 73
implicit, 75
present value analysis, 78–79
reason for, 73
Interest-bearing loans, 457
Interest costs, cost of holding money and, 499–501
Interest elasticity of demand for loans, 132
Interest income
capital gains and, 288–289
marginal product of deposits, and, 178
tax rate on, effect on supply of loanable funds, 112
Interest payments
on aggregate debt, 753
on federal debt, 747, 748–749, 760
on state and local debt, 750
Interest rate(s), 104
adverse selection, effect on, 156–158
aftertax, 85
annual, 73
asymmetric information and, 154–156
banks with market power and, 139
bonds, 279–282
on borrowed reserves, 479
calculation of, 73
Cambridge *k,* and, 655
charged by banks with market power, 139–147
on checkable deposits, 480
on consumer credit, 116
covered interest arbitrage, 355–356
default risk premiums and, 279–282
deficit financed government purchasing, effect on, 567–568, 612
defined, 73
dependent on borrower's income, 154
on deposits, 171–172, 222
determinant of Cambridge theory of money demand, 654
disintermediation, and, 218
economic changes, effect on, 251–257
expected interest rate, correlation between, 650–651
financing government purchases through money creation, effect on, 570–573, 614–615
historical data, 86–88

honesty of borrowers and, 154–156
intermediate target, 680, 682–686
Keynes view of money demand, 495, 501, 509
on loans, 134–138
long-run exchange rate demand or supply factor, 342
marginal resource cost of deposits, and, 181–184
market, 172
market determined, 131
market interest rates on loans, 478–479
maturity, and, *see* Term structure of interest rates
monetary policy effect on, 514–515
money growth, effect of, 652
nominal, 82, 104, 107, 110
past trends in, 86–88
portfolio approach to money demand and, 503
and price of bonds, 279–282
and profit maximization, 143–147
quantity of loans issued, effect on, 139
real, *see* Expected real interest rate; Real interest rate
real money balances, and, 513
reserve requirements, and, 227
Ricardian equivalence, and, 765–766, 767
risk, as factor in, 269
term structure, 86
term structure of, *see* Term structure of interest rates
variation over time, 86–88
velocity and, 497, 655–657
war, and, 292, 293
See also Prime interest rate
Interest Rate Adjustment Act of 1961, 216–218, 231
Interest rate ceilings, 123–124
on deposits, 216–218
Interest rate floor, 124–125
Interest rate parity, 346–348
Interest rate restrictions
Glass-Steagall Act, and, 216–219
usury laws, 123–124, 224–225
Interest rate risk, 285–290
Interest rate stability, 669
Interest rate targeting, 696–697
Intermediate target, 667–689, 689–692
International Lending Supervisory Act of 1983, 205, 232
International Monetary Fund (IMF), special drawing rights, 591

International Monetary Market (IMM), futures contracts traded on, 297
International policy coordination, 731–732
International trade
balance of payments, 587–593
balance of trade, 614–615
demand for net exports, 593–601
loanable funds, effect on, 617–618
macroeconomic equilibrium, effect on, 601–607
open economy model, 586
International transactions, 44–45
Interstate banking, restrictions on, 214
Intertemporal substitution effect, 529n
Inventory, 7
Inventory approach to money demand, 498–502
Investment
budget deficit, and, 615–617
deficit financed government purchasing, effect on, 568–569
financing government purchases through money creation, effect on, 614–615
income tax increase, effect on, 564
liquidity of, 114
Investment banking, and Glass-Steagall Act, 215–216
Investment demand, 534–538
open economy macroeconomics, 601–602
short-run macroeconomic equilibrium, and, 552
Investment goods, 527
Investment purchases, 615
IS curve, 579–580
IS-LM equilibrium, 582–583
IS-LM model of aggregate demand, 544, 579–585
Issuer, creditworthiness, 275, 282

Junk bond, 48

Keynes, John Maynard, 495, 503
Keynesian view, 567
Keynesian view of money demand, 518–520
Keynes view of money demand, 495–496, 498–502, 502–504
Keynsians, 518, 570

L, money aggregate, 55
Labor, taxation on, 549
Lags, 700–702

Law of demand, 93
Law of diminishing marginal returns, 168
Law of large numbers, 185–190
Law of one price, 343–344
Law of supply, 97
Legal reserves, 447–448
    effect of loans on, 451
    held by rural banks, 412
Lenders
    unanticipated inflation, effect of, 84
    wealth of, effect on supply of loanable
        funds, 114
Lending long, 24–25
Letter of credit, banker's acceptances, 44
Liabilities
    deposits, effect of, 449
    open market purchase, effect of, 427,
        455
    open market sale, effect of, 429
    on T-account, 447
Life insurance
    owned by bank holding companies,
        212
    set up by banks, 216
Life insurance companies, 39–40
    financial intermediaries, 23
Limited branching, 212
Lines of credit, banks with other banks or
    Federal Reserve System, 25–26
Liquidation, of bank, 131
Liquidity
    of banking industry, 211
    borrowing short and lending long, 25–
        26
    defined, 3–4
    effect of secondary market on financial
        asset on, 32
    effect on supply of loanable funds, 114
    illiquid, defined, 190
    of investment, 114
    of money, 7
    of wealth, 507
Liquidity risk, 282–285
    defined, 282
    interest rate risk, and, 285
Liquid reserves, real bills doctrine, 415
Litigation, for loan default, 161
LM curve, 580–582
Loan(s)
    borrowing short and lending long, 24–
        25
    branching restrictions, effect of, 222
    calling in, 412–413, 453
    complete deposit multiplier, 469
    cost of issuing, 134

credit card loans, 436
default, effect of, 204
demand loans, 453
deposit into bank, effect of, 458–459
deposits as input in production of,
    166–171
discount window, 434
effect on available supply of money,
    19–22
elasticity of demand, 132–133
from excess reserves, 449–450, 457–
    458
expansion of, 458–459
fixed-payment, 74–75
government guaranteed loan program,
    766
interest on, 73
interest rate effect on quantity issued,
    139
liquidity of, 114
marginal product of deposits, and, 178
market interest rates on, 478–479
monopoly bank, 140–141
open market purchases, and, 463–464
optimal quantity of, determination of,
    136–137
perceived real cost of repayment, 107
quantity, determination of, 137–138
real bills doctrine, 415
simple, 73–74
simple deposit multiplier, 459–462
status of loan portfolio, 204
student loans, 766
on T-account, 447–448
technology for producing, 168–170
usury laws, and, 123–124, 224–225
value marginal product of deposits,
    173–176
See also Bank loans
Loanable funds
    bond price analysis, and, 252–253
    change in inflationary expectations,
        impact of, 107, 111–112
    default risk premium, 276–279
    deficit financed government purchas-
        ing, effect on, 568, 611–612
    defined, 104
    demand for, 104–109
    equilibrium in market for, 115–116, 617
    funding investment with, 534
    income tax increase, effect on, 564n
    interest rate ceiling and, 123–124
    interest rate floor and, 124–125
    international financial capital move-
        ments, 590

    liquidity, and, 284–285
    in 1980's, 652
    in open economy, 617–618
    quantity demanded, effects on, 105
    recession, effect on, 120–122
    reserve requirements, and, 226–228
    supply and demand, 284–285
    supply of, 110–115, 122
    usury laws, effect on, 225
Loanable funds model
    applications of, 116–125
    monetary policy analysis using, 520–
        522
Loan decision, 134–138, 143–147, 153–
    154
Loan portfolio of bank, 204
    branching restrictions, effect on, 222–
        223
Loan revenues, formula for, 134
Loan technology, 168–170
Local governments
    budget deficits, effect on demand for
        loanable funds, 109
    budgets, 750–751
Location advantages, market power and,
    141–143
Locke, John, 509
Long-run aggregate supply (LRAS)
    income tax increase, effect on, 557–
        559, 564, 566
    in open economy, 604–606
Long-run aggregate supply curve, 557–
    559, 605
Long-run equilibrium, 556–560
    monetary policy, and, 709–713
    VAT, effect on, 563
Long-run output, and active monetary
    policy, 712–713
Long-run price level, and active mone-
    tary policy, 709
Long-term bonds, held by life insurance
    companies, 39
Long-term debt, 33
    municipal bonds, 51–52
Loss, financial service markets as insur-
    ance against, 34
Lump-sum head tax, 562n

M1, money aggregate, 55
    velocity, and, 71, 627, 656–657
M2, money aggregate, 55
    percentage growth rate of, 658
    real GDP, and, 654
    velocity, and, 71, 627, 656–657
M3, money aggregate, 55

McFadden Act of 1927, 212, 231
Macroeconomic goals, 668
Macroeconomic model, 526–527
  aggregate demand, 527–546
  fiscal policy, 561–573
  government budget constraint, 561–573
  inaccurate, 704
  IS-LM model of aggregate demand, 579–585
  long-run equilibrium, 556–560
  monetary policy, 573–575
  short-run aggregate supply, 546–550, 675–678
  short-run macroeconomic equilibrium, 550–556
  vertical long-run aggregate supply, 556–560, 674–675
Macroeconomics
  demand for net exports, 593–601
  open economy, *see* Open economy macroeconomics
  policy issues, 420
Management fees, mutual funds, 37
Margin, on adjustable-rate mortgages, 47
Marginal cost, 136, 137–138
  of issuing loans, 154, 157, 222
Marginal cost curve, 157
Marginal interest rate, 85
Marginal product, 167–168
  deposits, 167–168, 178–180
  See also Value marginal product
Marginal resource cost curve, 182–183
Marginal resource cost of deposits (MRC), 181–184
Marginal returns, diminishing, 167–168
Marginal revenue, 137–138, 145, 146–147, 179–180
  of issuing loans, 154, 158
Marginal revenue product of deposits (MRP), 178–180, 181, 183
Marginal tax rate, 107, 109, 112
Margin requirement, 436
Market, 31
  See also Financial markets
Market demand, 132
  interest rate on deposits and, 171
Market-determined exchange rate, central bank intervention, 357–359
Market determined interest rate, 131
Market equilibrium
  deposits, 171–172
  fee-based financial services, 98–103
  initial, in government bonds, 122–123
  loanable funds, 115–116, 617

Market interest rate
  deposits, 172
  valuation of coupon bonds, and, 247–249
  valuation of debt instruments sold on discount basis, 240–244
Market power
  banks with, 139–147, 176–184
  in both loan and deposit markets, 177–180, 181–184
  small banks, 131–132
Market price, determination of, 99–100
Market risk, 269
Market supply
  branching restrictions, effect on, 222
  effect on deposits to individual bank, 171–172
Markov expectations hypothesis, 371–373
  criticism of, 391–392
Markov inflationary expectation, 372–373
Marshall, Alfred, 626
Mean, 271–272
Medium of exchange, 3, 5, 6
Merchandise account, 588–589
Merchandise trade balance, 589
Mergers, of troubled banking institutions, 219
Mexico
  money creation to finance government spending in, 758
  money demand in, 494
MMDA, *see* Money market deposit accounts
Modeling
  IS-LM model of aggregate demand, 579–585
  open economy model, *see* Open economy model
  See also Macroeconomic model
Modem, location advantages and, 143
Modern quantity theory of money demand, 506–509
Monetarians, 518
Monetary base, 466–467, 482
  changes in, 669
  complete deposit multiplier, 467–468
  complete money multiplier, 470–473
  currency holdings, relationship with, 469–470
  effect of changes in, 471–473
  Federal Reserve System influence on money supply through, 476

increase by Federal Reserve System, 757
  money stock, relationship with, 470–473
  recent movements in, 475
  seigniorage, and, 759
  total banking system deposits, relationship with, 467–468
Monetary economy, 6
Monetary multiplier, recent movements in, 475–476
Monetary policy, 573–575
  active, *see* Active monetary policy
  conflict among policymakers, 704–705
  definitions, 666–668
  discretionary, 723–726
  effect on interest rates, 514–515
  Federal Reserve System operating procedures, 692–697
  inaccurate macroeconomic models, 704
  instrument instability, 703–704
  instruments of, 669–671
  international policy coordination, 731–732
  lags, 700–702
  loanable funds model for analysis of, 520–522
  in open economy, 607, 619–621
  passive, *see* Passive monetary policy
  problems, 697–705
  P-star, 698–700
  quantitative impact of, 519
  in short run, 713–714
  in Yugoslavia, 677–678
Monetary policy actions, 422, 667
Monetary policy game, 726–729
Monetary policymaking
  discount window policy, 433–436
  discretion in setting, 439–440
  Federal Reserve System as policymaker, 423, 425
  independence of Federal Reserve System, 439–440
  moral suasion, 436–437
  open market operations, 413, 422, 427–431
  reserve requirements, 431–433
  selective credit controls, 436
Monetary policy rules, 723, 724–726
  active rules, 733–737
  monetary policy game, 726–729
  passive rules, 733–737
  price stabilization rule, 733

Monetary policy rules *(continued)*
use by Federal Reserve System, 729–732
Monetary supply, effect of increase in, 520
Monetizing the deficit, 757
Money
available supply of, 19–22
bank note, 18
commodity money, 9–11
costs of holding, 498
creation by commercial banking system, 458–459
defined, 3, 4, 7, 8, 9, 10–12, 12–13
demand, *see* Money demand
income, and, 643–645
intermediate exchange as, 5n
long-run relationship with economic activity, 625–628
long-run theoretical relationship with economic activity, 625–626
as medium of exchange, *see* Medium of exchange
multiple deposit expansion, 458–459
policy targets, and, 673–678
short-run relationship with economic activity, 638–642
short-run theoretical relationship with economic activity, 638
time value of, 75–79, 236–238
velocity of, 68–71
Money aggregates, 54–56
Money base, determinant of money supply, 475
Money creation
calculation of, 471–473
currency holdings, effect on, 466–467
for deficit financing, 757
excess reserves, effect on, 466–467
expectations, and, 370
general model of, 465–474
government purchases, financing, 570–573, 614–615
in Mexico, 758
profits in, 759
seigniorage, 759
Money demand
asset approach to, 502
Cambridge theory, 493–495
classical view of, 490–495
in growing economy, 759
historical perspective on, 509–510
inventory approach to, 492–502
Keynesian view, 495–506, 518–520
main variables of, 510

in Mexico, 494
modern quantity theory, 506–509
modified Cambridge theory, 496–498, 654
monetarist view, 518–520
money target, and, 694
overlap in theories of, 509
portfolio approach to, 502–504
simple quantity theory, 490–492
in United States, 511–512
velocity, and, 490–491, 493
Money demand and supply framework, 520–522
Money growth
evidence of short-run effect on economic activity, 632–637
inflation, relation to, 658–660
inflation rate, relationship to, 627
international evidence of effect on economic activity, 632–637
nominal income growth, relationship to, 627, 645–646
output growth, relation to, 658–660
reconciling short-run and long-run results, 643–648
United Kingdom, 636–637, 649
U.S. evidence of effect on economic activity, 628–632
Money growth rate
interest rate, effect on, 652
relation to inflation rate and expected inflation rate, 650–651
Money growth rule, 733
Money holdings, costs of, 498–502
Money market deposit accounts (MMDA), 219
Money market instruments, 41–45
Money market mutual funds, 37, 41, 218
Money multiplier
altered by Fed, 477
changes in, 669
Money stock
calculation of, 471
changes in, 627, 638
complete money multiplier, 470–473
definitions, 54–56, 465, 475
deposits, effect of, 453
desired currency to deposit ratio, 465
determinant of aggregate demand, 626
growth in, 67–68, 475–476
growth rate of, 70, 627, 628–632
inflation rate, evidence of relationship to, 640, 646–647
inflation rate, international evidence of relationship to, 633–634

inflation rate, U.S. evidence of relationship to, 629–630
intermediate targets, and, 684
monetary base, relationship with, 470–473
nominal GDP, evidence of relationship to, 639–640
nominal GDP, international evidence of relationship to, 632–633
nominal GDP, U.S. evidence of relationship to, 628–629
output rate, evidence of relationship to, 640, 647
output rate, international evidence of relationship to, 634
output rate, U.S. evidence of relationship to, 630–631
Money supply, 512
aggregate demand, and, 626
alteration by Federal Reserve System, 673–678
anticipated and unanticipated changes in, 738–739, 740–741
changes in, 626, 669
constant, 733–734, 735
currency to deposit ratio, effect of, 479–480
decrease in, 480
decrease in response to aggregate supply decline, 713
defined, 474
determinants of, *see* Determinants of money supply
endogenous, 483
exogenous, 483
increase in response to aggregate demand decline, 711
intermediate target, 680, 681, 684, 686–687
reserve requirements, effect of, 431–433
unanticipated increases in, 739–740
United States, central bank intervention, and, 358–359
Money supply curve, 482–484
Money supply equation, 474
Money supply process, 474
Monopoly bank, 140–141
Moody's rating system, 276, 277
Moral hazard, 193–195, 229
Moral suasion, 436–437, 670
Mortgage, 47–51
adjustable-rate, *see* Adjustable-rate mortgages
down payment and, 160

as fixed-payment loan, 75
future value analysis, 76–77
interest payments, tax deductibility of, 107–109
interest rates, historical data, 87
term of, 453
Mortgage debt held by institutions, 49–51
Mortgage funds, demand for, 107
Mortgage interest rate, and inflationary expectations, 117–118
MRC, *see* Marginal resource cost of deposits
MRP, *see* Marginal revenue product of deposits
Multilateral government action to fix exchange rates, 359–360
Multiple deposit expansion, 458–459
Municipal bonds, 51–52
    interest rates, historical data, 87
    tax policy and, 123
    tax rate on interest income, effect on investors in, 112–113
    tax risk, and, 291–292
Mutual funds, 37–39
    money market, 218
    set up by banks, 216
Mutual savings banks, 35–36

NASD, *see* National Association of Securities Dealers
NASDAQ, *see* National Association of Securities Dealers Automatic Quotation System
National Association of Securities Dealers (NASD), 32
    newspaper quotations of stock prices by, 32
National Association of Securities Dealers Automatic Quotation System, 32
National Banking Act of 1863, 201–202, 231
National banking system, 411–413
National banks, 202
    branching restrictions, 212
National Credit Union Administration (NCUA), 209n
National Credit Union Shareholders Insurance Fund (NCUSIF), 209n
National currency, result of Civil War, 412
National debt, *see* Federal debt
Natural rate of employment, 560
Natural rate of output, 559, 560
NCUA, *see* National Credit Union Administration

NCUSIF, *see* National Credit Union Shareholders Insurance Fund
Negative excess reserves, 463
Negotiable certificates of deposit, 43
Net export demand, 529–530, 595–596, 601–602
Net export demand curve, 594–596
    foreign price level, and, 596
Net exports, 527, 540, 590, 592–593, 615–617
    deficit financed government purchasing, effect on, 612
    demand for, 593–601
    exchange rate and, 598
    financing government purchases through money creation, effect on, 614–615
Net income on investments, 589
New classical economists, 559
New Keynsians, 559
New York Bond Exchange, 47
New York Futures Exchange (NYFE), futures contracts traded on, 297
New York Stock Exchange (NYSE), 31–32, 45–47
No-fee checking account, 189–190
Nominal gross domestic product (GDP) intermediate target, 680
    money growth, relationship to, 627, 645–646
    money stock, and, 627
    money stock, evidence of relationship to, 639–640
    money stock, international evidence of relationship to, 632–633
    money stock, U.S. evidence of relationship to, 628–629
Nominal gross domestic product (GDP) target, 689–692
Nominal income growth, relationship to money growth, 627, 645–646
Nominal interest rate, 82, 104, 107, 110
    deficit financed government purchasing, effect on, 568
    inflation rate, relationship between, 650–651
    in 1980's, 651–652
    opportunity cost of holding money balances, and, 655
    targets, and, 681, 682–684
Nominal money supply, 570
Nominal output, defined, 62–63
Nominal wage rigidity, 548
Nominal wages
    adjustment in, 557–559

short-run aggregate supply, 546, 549
    VAT, effect on, 562
Nonbank banks, 212
Nonborrowed reserves targeting, 695–696
Nondepository institutions, 36–37
Non-interest-bearing reserves, 457
Nontariff barriers, 599
North America Free Trade Agreement (NAFTA), impact on output and employment, 600
NYFE, *see* New York Futures Exchange

Office of Management and Budget (OMB), and Board of Governors of Federal Reserve System, 420
Official settlements balance, 593
Oligopoly banks, 147–153
Oligopoly interdependence, 148–151
OMB, *see* Office of Management and Budget
One price, law of, 343–344
Open economy macroeconomics, 586–587
    aggregate demand, 601–603
    balance of payments, 587–593
    demand for net exports, 593–601
    equilibrium, 601–607
    exchange rates, 607–608
    fiscal policy, 608–614
    loanable funds, 617–618
    monetary policy, 619–621
    open market operations, 619–621
Open economy model, 586
    Ricardian equivalence, and, 768–770
Open Market Investment Committee, 415, 417
Open market operations, 413, 422, 427–431, 432–433, 466–467, 669
    independent monetary policy through, 573–575
    in open economy, 619–621
Open market purchases, 427–429, 514
    bank loans, effect on, 467
    compared with open market sales, 462–463
    complete currency multiplier, 469–470
    Federal Reserve System, and, 455–457
    in open economy, 620–621
Open market sales, 429–431, 462–465
Operating procedures, 668
    federal funds rate targeting, 694–695
    interest rate targeting, 696–697
Operating regimes, 668
Operating target, 693

Opportunity costs, 134
of holding money, 489, 508, 655
Optimal money holdings, 501
Option contract, 299
Options markets, risk minimization, 294, 299–301
Output
and aggregate demand, 626, 638
long-run, 712–713
nominal value of, 64
Output growth, 627
inflation, relation to, 658–660
money growth, relation to, 658–660
money stock, evidence of relationship to, 640, 647
money stock, international evidence of relationship to, 634
money stock, U.S. evidence of relationship to, 630–631
Output level target, 674–678
Over-the-counter (OTC) market, 32

Paper money, 10–12
Partial crowding out, 568
deficit financed government purchasing, 612–613
Passive monetary policy, 709, 717, 717–721
Passive rules, 733–737
constant money supply, 733–734, 735
Payroll deduction, 32, 40
Penalty for early withdrawal, certificate of deposit, 43
Pension funds, 40, 124
Pensions, financial intermediaries, 23–24
Perfect competition, 131
Permanent income, 509
Persian Gulf War, and exchange rates, 350
Personal bank lines of credit, 51
Petty, Sir William, 509
Phillip IV (France), 8
Physical capital, 527, 534, 538
Physical capital stock, and short-run aggregate supply, 550
Policy goals, 667
Policy instruments, 667, 673, 693
Policy regimes, 668
Policy target, see Targets
Politics
and Board of Governors of Federal Reserve System, 420
inflation, and, 718–719
Portability of money, 12

Portfolio approach to money demand, 502–504
Possible outcomes, in calculating expected value, 271–272
PPI, see Producer price index
PPP, see Purchasing power parity
Precautionary motive, 495
Preferences, long-run exchange rate demand or supply factor, 340–342
Preferred-habitat hypothesis, 322–327
defined, 322
yield curves, and, 324–327
Present value (PV), 77, 237–238, 277, 281
of financing government spending, 765
Present value analysis, 78–79
Price expectations, and nominal wage rigidity, 548–549
Price level(s), 62, 64, 65, 68
aggregate demand, and, 626, 638
consumption demand, 530
decline in, 711
long-run, 709
long-run exchange rate demand or supply factor, 340
long-run exchange rate determination, and, 336
percentage growth rate of, 658
purchasing power parity, and, 343
short-run aggregate supply, 546
stabilization of, 734–735, 735–736
stabilization through active monetary policy, 709–711
wages, effect of, 546–548
Price level constant, 546
Price level effect, 534
Price level target, 674, 675–678
Price of variable inputs (other than labor), short-run aggregate supply, 546, 549
Prices
bonds, and interest rates, 279–282
of complements, 94–95
converting from one currency to another, 331–335
of corporate bond, 47, 277–282
default risk premiums and, 279–282
of goods, and money demand, 492
input, 97–98
intermediate target, 680
quotation of, 6
of substitutes, 94
tracking of, 62
unit of account, 6
Price stability, 668

Price stabilization rule, 733, 734–735, 735–736
Price takers, 130, 132
Primary deficit, 770–771
Primary market, 32, 255
Primary market transaction, issuance of stock, 45
Primary spending, 747
Prime interest rate
charged by banks, historical data, 87
recessions and, 120–122
Prime lending market, 120
Principal, 73, 75
Private banks, 407
Probability
expectations, and, 369
expected value, and, 271–272
as factor in uncertainty and risk, 270–271
law of large numbers, 185–190
Procyclical policy, 694–695
Producer price index (PPI), 62
Productivity, of deposits, 167
Profitability of business projects, effect on demand for loanable funds, 109, 121
Profit curve, 136
Profit maximization
banks with market power, 143–147, 176–177
bank with market power in both loan and deposit markets, 183–184
level of deposits, 175
purely competitive banks, 134, 137, 175
Profits
accounting versus economic, 134
from collusion, 151–153
and oligopoly banks, 148–151
P-star, 698–700
Public, determinants of money supply, 479–482
Public holdings of currency, 465
calculation of, 470
complete currency multiplier, 469–470
open market purchases, effect on, 467
supplied by Federal Reserve System, 466
Public investment, 764
Purchasing power, loans and, 82
Purchasing power parity (PPP), 342–344
Pure competition among banks, 130–139
Purely competitive banks, 130–139
demand for deposits by, 171–176

Purely competitive deposit market, 171, 177–180
Put option, 300
PV, *see* Present value

Quantity equation, 544, 657, 681
Quantity theory of money, 70, 626–627
Quotas, 599

Radford, R.A., 14
Rational expectations, and efficient markets, 395–396
Rational expectations hypothesis, 379–390, 391–392
Rational inflationary expectations, 381–390
Real balance effect, 529n
Real bills doctrine, 415
Real domestic interest rate, 597
Real estate investment returns, effect on other investments, 118–120
Real gross domestic product (GDP), 64, 65, 552
  financing government purchases through money creation, effect on, 572–573
  growth in, 630–631
  income tax increase, effect on, 566–567
  long-run aggregate supply curve, and, 558–559
  M2 money holdings, and, 654
  percentage growth rate of, 658
  P-star, and, 698–699
  real money balances, and, 654–655
  targets, and, 681, 682
  VAT, effect on, 562–563
Real income
  Cambridge *k,* and, 655
  determinant of Cambridge theory of money demand, 654
  long-run exchange rate demand or supply factor, 338–339
  long-run exchange rate determination, and, 336
  real money demand, and, 493–495, 498, 509
Real interest rate, 80–85, 289
  as constant, 650
  consumption demand, 530, 533
  deficit financed government purchasing, effect on, 568
  ex ante, 82, 290–291
  expected, 370
  ex post, 82, 290–291

financing government purchases through money creation, effect on, 570–573
  formula for, 81
  investment demand, and, 534–537
  long-term budget deficit, and, 771–775
  negative, significance of, 81
  in 1980's, 651–652
  short-run macroeconomic equilibrium, and, 551
Real interest rate effect, 529
Real money balances, 492, 496, 529n
  for business operations, 508
  Cambridge *k,* and, 655
  equilibrium quantity of, 516–517
  interest rate, and, 513
  real GDP, and, 654–655
  tastes, and, 508–509
Real money supply, determinants of, 514–515
Real money supply curve, 512–513, 515–516
Real output, 63, 65
  aggregate demand, and, 638
  changes in, 627, 643
  growth of, 627
  growth rate in, 70
  long-term budget deficit, and, 771–775
Real spending, and net export demand curve, 594
Recessions
  bank withdrawal rate, effect on, 190
  prime interest rate and, 120–122
  real money balances, and, 654
Recognition lag, 700
Registered bond, 48
Regulation Q, economic effect of, 216–219, 225–226
Regulator of banks, Federal Reserve System as, 423, 424
Repeated interaction, oligopoly banks, 151–153
Representative full-bodied money, 10
Repurchase agreements (repo), 44
Reputation, bank strategy for countering asymmetric information, 159–160
Reputation effect, 730
Required reserve ratio, 169, 448, 459–461, 465, 467, 482, 669–670
  complete money multiplier, 471
  determinant of money supply, 475, 477
  Federal Reserve System influence on money supply through, 476–477
Required reserves, 166, 429–431, 447–448, 453, 465

Reserve city banks, 412–413
Reserve deposits, 447–448
Reserve requirements, 226–228, 431–433, 477
  change in money supply, effect on, 431–433
Reserves
  actual, 449, 453
  borrowed, *see* Borrowed reserves
  borrowing, to offset decrease in deposits, 453
  change in, from within banking system, 448–455
  deposit from outside banking system, effect of, 455–459
  deposits, effect of, 449, 452–453
  excess, 166
  infusions and contractions of, 455–465
  open market purchases, and, 455–458, 463–464
  required, 166
  required reserve ratio, 459–461
  simple deposit multiplier, 459–462
  on T-account, 447–448
Reserves of foreign exchange, 359
Retirement income, pension funds, 40
Revenue curve, 134–136
  banks with market power, 144–146
Revenues
  loan formula for, 134
  state and local sources of, 750
Revolving credit, 51
Ricardian equivalence, 765–770
Ricardian view, 567
Ricardo, David, 765n
Risk
  attitudes toward, 273–274
  call risk, 285–290
  compensation for through interest rate, 154
  default risk, *see* Default risk
  defined, 270
  degrees of, 269
  effect on supply of loanable funds, 114
  elimination of, 294
  expected value, 271–272
  inflation risk, 289–291
  interest rate risk, 285–290
  liquidity risk, 282–285
  market risk, 269
  risk-adjusted expected return, 393, 396
  speculators, 353–354
  standard deviation, 273
  tax risk, 291–294
  valuing risky financial assets, 274–275

Risk (continued)
  variance, 272–273
  See also Uncertainty
Risk-adjusted expected return, 393, 396
Risk minimization, 294–303
  as bank function, 26
  diversification, 294, 295–297
  futures markets, 294, 297–299
  by insurance, 39
  options markets, 294, 299–300
Rolling over debt, 748

Safe asset, portfolio approach and, 503
Saving, and budget deficit, 615–617
Savings, considered as money, 3
Savings account
  sorting depositors by options in, 189–190
  as store of value, 7
Savings and loan associations (S&L), 23, 35
Savings and loan crisis, and changes in FDIC, 209–210
Savings bonds, see U.S. savings bonds
Say, J.B., 509
Scatter diagram, 628–629
SDR, see Special drawing rights
Seasonal credit, 436
Seasonal variations in business activity, bank response to, 412
Secondary market, 32–33, 255
  bond trading, 47
  government securities, 51
  municipal bonds, 51–52
  stock trading, 45–47
  U.S. treasury bills, 43
Second Bank of the United States, 409
Securities, and investment banking, 215–216
Securities dealer, and open market operations, 427–429
Segmented-markets hypothesis, 319–322
  defined, 319
  yield curves, and, 321–322
Seigniorage, 759
Selective credit controls, 436, 669–670
Semistrong-form market efficiency, 398–399
Senior, Nassau, 509
Serbia, money creation in, 570
Shareholder, 45
Shortage, 99
Short-run aggregate supply (SRAS), 546
  changes in, 546–548, 555–556

determinants of, 549–550
  income tax increase, effect on, 564–565
  in open economy, 603–604
  slope of, 546–549
  targets, and, 675–678
  VAT, effect on, 562–563
Short-run aggregate supply curve, 546–549, 643
Short-run macroeconomic equilibrium, 550–556
Short-term debt, 33
  U.S. treasury bills, 43
Short-term funds, 41, 120
Short-term loans, 45, 453
Silver, 9, 15
Simple deposit multiplier, 459–462, 464, 465
Simple loan, 73–74
Simple money multiplier, 465
Simple quantity theory, 388
Simple quantity theory of money demand, 490–492
S&L, see Savings and loan associations
S&L crisis, see Savings and loan crisis
Small banks, quantity of loans, 169
Small towns, single bank in, 140–141
Smith, Adam, 626
Social security payments, 747
Social security tax, 608
Sorting of depositors, 189–190
Special drawing rights (SDRs), 591
Specie, 15, 18–19
Speculative motive, 495
Speculators, 353–354
Speed of adjustment, 374, 376–378
Spending, and economic output, 615–616
Spot rate, 351–357
SRAS, see Short-run aggregate supply
Stabilization of business cycle, 668–669
Standard and Poor's, bond rating by, 276, 277
Standard deviation, 273
Standard of deferred payment, 7–8
State and local government budgets, 750–751
State banking commissions, responsibilities of, 205, 206–207
State banknotes, 412
State banks, 202
  branching restrictions, 212
  FDIC insurance, 207–208
  Federal Reserve System, and, 206
State-chartered banks, 201, 202
State governments

budget deficits, effect on demand for loanable funds, 109
  supervision and examination of banks, 204–206
Statewide branching, 212
Statistical discrepancy, 588
  balance of payments accounts, 591–592
Stock prices
  economic changes, effect on, 262–265
  newspaper quotes of, 32
Stocks
  purchased on margin, 436
  as store of value, 7
Strike price, 299
Subordinated bond, 48
Substitutes
  prices of, 94
  See also Alternative sources of funds
Substitution effect, 503, 528
Supply
  change in, 97
  decrease, impact of, 100–102
  determinants, 110–114
  determinants of, 97
  of fee-based financial services, 96–98
  law of, 97
  loanable funds, 110–115
  See also Aggregate supply; Long-run aggregate supply; Supply and demand
Supply and demand
  bond price analysis, and, 253–255
  currency, gold standard and, 362–363
  fee-based financial services, 92–103
  influence on market price, 98–100
  long-run exchange rate determination, and, 336–338
  for money, 370
Supply and demand analysis, demand for fee-based financial services, 93–96
Supply curve, 96, 99, 117–118
  aggregate supply curve, See Aggregate supply curve
  bank with market power in both loan and deposit markets, 183–184
  for bonds, 254
  determinants of demand, effect of, 93
  determinants of supply, effect of, 97
  input prices, effect of, 97–98
  for loanable funds, 110
  money supply curve, see Money supply curve
  purely competitive banking market, 132

real money supply curve, 512–513, 515–516

short-run aggregate supply curve, 546–549, 643

technology, effect of, 98

Surplus, 99

Suspension of payments, 413

Symmetric information, 153–154

Systematic forecasting errors, and rational expectations, 383–385

T-account, 15, 447–448

Targets, 667, 668–669

aggregate demand and supply, and, 671

effect of monetary policy on, 710–711

inflation rate, and, 681, 682

money, and, 673–678

nominal interest rate, and, 681, 682–684

policy instruments, link to, 693

Tariffs, 597–599

long-run exchange rate demand or supply factor, 340–342

short-run aggregate supply in open economy, 603–604

tariff-financed government purchases, 608–611

Tastes

consumption demand, 530, 534

demand for fee-based financial services, effect on, 95–96

net export demand, and, 599

real money balances, and, 508–509

Taxation

aftertax interest rate, 85

consumer credit interest, 116

consumption demand, 530, 534

consumption taxes, 562–563

government purchases financed through, 562–567, 608–611

household interest payments, deductibility of, 107–109

income from investment in physical capital, 538

income taxes, 563–566

interest income, effect of tax rate on supply of loanable funds, 112

interest rates on municipal bonds, and tax policy, 123

investment demand, and, 535–536, 538

on labor, 549

lump-sum head tax, 562n

to pay for interest payments on federal debt, 760

Ricardian equivalence, and, 765–770

short-run aggregate supply, 546, 549

tax deductible payments, 85

Tax Reform Act of 1982, 116

tax risk, 291–294

value-added tax (VAT), 562

See also Federal income taxation

Tax collections

aggregate budgets, component of, 752

federal budget, component of, 749

ratio to GDP, 750–751

state and local budgets, component of, 750

Tax Reform Act of 1982, interest rates on consumer credit and, 116

Tax risk, 291–294

T-bill, *see* U.S. treasury bills

Technical analysis, 396

Technology

short-run aggregate supply, 546, 550

supply curve, effect on, 98

Term

coupon bond, 75

of mortgage, 47

Term structure of interest rates, 86

defined, 306

expectations, and, 370

expectations hypothesis, 311–319

preferred-habitat hypothesis, 322–327

segmented-markets hypothesis, 319–322

yield curve, 306–309

Thorton, Henry, 509

Tinbergen, Jan, 671, 672, 673

Tobin, James, 498, 502, 508, 722

Total banking system deposits, 467–470

Total banking system reserves, effect of deposits on, 449

Total cost, in determination of optimal quantity of loans, 136–137

Total deficit, 771

Total money stock, calculation of, 465, 471

Total money supply, 479–480

Total output, 615

Total product, 167–168

Total reserves, calculation of, 465–466

Total revenue, in determination of optimal quantity of loans, 136–137

Total spending, increase in, money demand and, 490–492

Trade, *see* International trade

Trade barriers, long-run exchange rate demand or supply factor, 340–342

Transactions costs, 5–6

by financial intermediaries, 26–27

purely competitive bank loans, 131

secondary market, effect on, 32–33

Transactions motive, 495, 501, 504

Transfer payments

aggregate, 752

federal, 747

state and local, 751

Traveler's checks, 18

Treasury bills, *see* U.S. treasury bills

Treasury bonds, *see* U.S. treasury bonds

Triangular arbitrage, 354–355

Twin deficits, 614–619

Unanticipated inflation, 82–85

Unbacked money, 11

Uncertainty, defined, 269–270

Underground economy, 482

Uniform reserve requirements, 207

economic effect of, 226–228

Unilateral government action to fix exchange rates, 359

Unilateral transfer, 589–590

U.S. official reserve assets, 590

U.S. treasury

bond auction by, 32

Federal Reserve-Treasury Accord (1951), 417

seasonal demand for currency, and, 413

U.S. official reserve assets, 590

U.S. treasury bills (T-bill), 43–44

default risk of, 275

interest rates, historical data, 87

money market mutual funds investment in, 37

term to maturity, 306

valuation of, 239–244

U.S. savings bonds, 32, 124

U.S. treasury bonds, 32, 43–44, 275

Unit of account, 6–7

Unsecured consumer loans, reserve requirement for, 436

Usury laws, 123–124, 224–225

VA, *see* Veterans Administration

Valuation

assets, 257–262

banker's acceptances, 239–244

coupon bonds, 247–249

debt instruments, 238–251

equity instruments, 257–262

growth stock, 259, 260–262

Valuation *(continued)*
  income stock, 259, 260
  time value of money, 75–79, 236–238
Value-added tax (VAT), 562
Value marginal product (VMP), of deposits, 173–176
Variable costs, 135
Variance, 272–273
VAT, *see* Value-added tax
Vault cash, required reserves held as, 447
Velocity
  changes in, 643
  as constant, 658
  determinant of income, 509
  and economic growth, 68–71
  expectations, and, 509
  growth rate of, 70, 627
  inflation, and, 658–659
  interest rates and, 497, 655–657
  of M1 and M2, 71, 656–657
  modified Cambridge theory and, 496
  money demand and, 490–491, 493
  quantity theory of money, and, 626–627
  significance of, 68–69

Vertical long-run aggregate supply, 556–560, 625–626, 638
  output level target, 674–675
  price level target, 674
Veterans Administration (VA), 40
VMP, *see* Value marginal product
Volcker, Paul, 420

Wages
  effect on price level, 546–548
  nominal, *see* Nominal wages
  nominal wage rigidity, 548
Wall Street Journal
  futures contract listing in, 297, 298–299
  futures options listing in, 300, 301–302
War, and interest rates, 292, 293
Weak-form market efficiency, 396
Wealth
  consumption demand, 530, 533
  effect on supply of loanable funds, 114
  financing government purchases
    through money creation, effect on, 570–573

individual, and money demand, 507
Wealth effect, 503, 529
William the Conqueror, 8
Withdrawal
  from bank, *see* Bank withdrawals
  effect on balance sheet, 454–455
  unexpected, 479

Yen, exchange rate of, 333
Yield curve, 306–309
  defined, 306
  expectations hypothesis, and, 317
  preferred-habitat hypothesis, and, 324–327
  segmented-markets hypothesis, and, 321–322
Yield to maturity, 240, 245–247, 253
  default risk, and, 279–282
Yoder, Edwin, 570
Yugoslavia, monetary policy in, 677–678

Zero coupon bond, 75
Zero coupon instruments, 44